ACCA

Applied Skills

Audit and Assurance (AA)

Study Text

British library cataloguing-in-publication data

A catalogue record for this book is available from the British Library.

Published by:
Kaplan Publishing UK
Unit 2 The Business Centre
Molly Millars Lane
Wokingham
Berkshire
RG41 2QZ

ISBN 978-1-78740-864-7

© Kaplan Financial Limited, 2021

Acknowledgements

These materials are reviewed by the ACCA examining team. The objective of the review is to ensure that the material properly covers the syllabus and study guide outcomes, used by the examining team in setting the exams, in the appropriate breadth and depth. The review does not ensure that every eventuality, combination or application of examinable topics is addressed by the ACCA Approved Content. Nor does the review comprise a detailed technical check of the content as the Approved Content Provider has its own quality assurance processes in place in this respect.

This product includes content from the International Auditing and Assurance Standards Board (IAASB) and the International Ethics Standards Board for Accountants (IESBA), published by the International Federation of Accountants (IFAC) in 2020 and is used with permission of IFAC.

This product contains material that is ©Financial Reporting Council Ltd (FRC). Adapted and reproduced with the kind permission of the Financial Reporting Council. All rights reserved. For further information, please visit www.frc.org.uk or call +44 (0)20 7492 2300.

Kaplan Publishing are constantly finding new ways to make a difference to your studies and our exciting online resources really do offer something different to students looking for exam success.

This book comes with free MyKaplan online resources so that you can study anytime, anywhere. **This free online resource is not sold separately and is included in the price of the book.**

Having purchased this book, you have access to the following online study materials:

CONTENT	ACCA (including FBT, FMA, FFA)		FIA (excluding FBT, FMA, FFA)	
	Text	Kit	Text	Kit
Electronic version of the book	✓	✓	✓	✓
Check Your Understanding Test with instant answers	✓			
Material updates	✓	✓	✓	✓
Latest official ACCA exam questions*		✓		
Extra question assistance using the signpost icon**		✓		
Timed questions with an online tutor debrief using clock icon***		✓		
Interim assessment including questions and answers	✓		✓	
Technical answers	✓	✓	✓	✓

* Excludes BT, MA, FA, FBT, FMA, FFA; for all other papers includes a selection of questions, as released by ACCA
** For ACCA SBL, SBR, AFM, APM, ATX, AAA only
*** Excludes BT, MA, FA, LW, FBT, FMA and FFA

How to access your online resources

Kaplan Financial students will already have a MyKaplan account and these extra resources will be available to you online. You do not need to register again, as this process was completed when you enrolled. If you are having problems accessing online materials, please ask your course administrator.

If you are not studying with Kaplan and did not purchase your book via a Kaplan website, to unlock your extra online resources please go to www.mykaplan.co.uk/addabook (even if you have set up an account and registered books previously). You will then need to enter the ISBN number (on the title page and back cover) and the unique pass key number contained in the scratch panel below to gain access. You will also be required to enter additional information during this process to set up or confirm your account details.

If you purchased through the Kaplan Publishing website you will automatically receive an e-mail invitation to MyKaplan. Please register your details using this email to gain access to your content. If you do not receive the e-mail or book content, please contact Kaplan Publishing.

Your Code and Information

This code can only be used once for the registration of one book online. This registration and your online content will expire when the final sittings for the examinations covered by this book have taken place. Please allow one hour from the time you submit your book details for us to process your request.

Please scratch the film to access your unique code.

Please be aware that this code is case-sensitive and you will need to include the dashes within the pass... the ISBN.

Contents

Introduction

This document references IFRS® Standards and IAS® Standards, which are authored by the International Accounting Standards Board (the Board), and published in the 2020 IFRS Standards Red Book.

How to use the materials

These Kaplan Publishing learning materials have been carefully designed to make your learning experience as easy as possible and to give you the best chances of success in your examinations.

The product range contains a number of features to help you in the study process. They include:

(1) Detailed study guide and syllabus objectives

(2) Description of the examination

(3) Study skills and revision guidance

(4) Study text

(5) Question practice

The sections on the study guide, the syllabus objectives, the examination and study skills should all be read before you commence your studies. They are designed to familiarise you with the nature and content of the examination and give you tips on how best to approach your learning.

The **Study text** comprises the main learning materials and gives guidance as to the importance of topics and where other related resources can be found. Each chapter includes

- The **learning objectives** contained in each chapter, which have been carefully mapped to the examining body's own syllabus learning objectives or outcomes. You should use these to check you have a clear understanding of all the topics on which you might be assessed in the examination.

- The **chapter diagram** provides a visual reference for the content in the chapter, giving an overview of the topics and how they link together.

- The **content** for each topic area commences with a brief explanation or definition to put the topic into context before covering the topic in detail. You should follow your studying of the content with a review of the illustration/s. These are worked examples which will help you to understand better how to apply the content for the topic.

- **Test your understanding** sections provide an opportunity to assess your understanding of the key topics by applying what you have learned to short questions. Answers can be found at the back of each chapter.

- **Summary diagrams** complete each chapter to show the important links between topics and the overall content of the syllabus. These diagrams should be used to check that you have covered and understood the core topics before moving on.

- **Question practice** is provided at the back of each text.

KAPLAN PUBLISHING

Quality and accuracy are of the utmost importance to us so if you spot an error in any of our products, please send an email to mykaplanreporting@kaplan.com with full details, or follow the link to the feedback form in MyKaplan.

Our Quality Coordinator will work with our technical team to verify the error and take action to ensure it is corrected in future editions.

Icon Explanations

 Supplementary reading – These sections will help to provide a deeper understanding of core areas. The supplementary reading is **NOT** optional reading. It is vital to provide you with the breadth of knowledge you will need to address the wide range of topics within your syllabus that could feature in an exam question. **Reference to this text is vital when self-studying**.

 Definition – Key definitions that you will need to learn from the core content.

 Key point – Identifies topics that are key to success and are often examined.

 New – Identifies topics that are brand new in exams that build on from earlier exams.

 Test your understanding – Exercises for you to complete to ensure that you have understood the topics just learned.

 Illustration – Worked examples help you understand the core content better.

 Tricky topic – When reviewing these areas care should be taken and all illustrations and Test your understanding exercises should be completed to ensure that the topic is understood.

 Tutorial note – Included to explain some of the technical points in more detail.

 Footsteps – Helpful tutor tips.

 Links to other syllabus areas – This symbol refers to areas of interaction with other parts of your syllabus, either in terms of other ACCA papers that you have studied, or may go on to study, or even further professional qualifications that you may decide to pursue on completion of ACCA.

Online subscribers

Our online resources are designed to increase the flexibility of your learning materials and provide you with immediate feedback on how your studies are progressing.

If you are subscribed to our online resources you will find:

(1) Online reference material: reproduces your Study Text online, giving you anytime, anywhere access.

(2) Online testing: provides you with additional online objective testing so you can practice what you have learned further.

(3) Online performance management: immediate access to your online testing results. Review your performance by key topics and chart your achievement through the course relative to your peer group.

Syllabus for September 2021 to June 2022

Syllabus background

The aim of ACCA Audit and Assurance is to develop knowledge and understanding of the process of carrying out the assurance engagement and its application in the context of the professional regulatory framework.

Objectives of the syllabus

- Explain the concept of audit and assurance and the functions of audit, corporate governance, including ethics and professional conduct.

- Demonstrate how the auditor obtains and accepts audit engagements, obtains an understanding of the entity and its environment, assesses the risk of material misstatement (whether arising from fraud or other irregularities) and plans an audit of financial statements.

- Describe and evaluate internal controls, techniques and audit tests, including IT systems to identify and communicate control risks and their potential consequences, making appropriate recommendations. Describe the scope, role and function of internal audit.

- Identify and describe the work and evidence obtained by the auditor and others required to meet the objectives of audit engagements and the application of the International Standards on Auditing (ISAs).

- Explain how consideration of subsequent events and the going concern principle can inform the conclusions from audit work and are reflected in different types of auditor's report, written representations and the final review and report.

- Demonstrate employability and technology skills.

Core areas of the syllabus

- Audit framework and regulation.
- Planning and risk assessment.
- Internal control.
- Audit evidence.
- Review and reporting.
- Employability and technology skills.

ACCA Performance Objectives

In order to become a member of the ACCA, as a trainee accountant you will need to demonstrate that you have achieved nine performance objectives. Performance objectives are indicators of effective performance and set the minimum standard of work that trainees are expected to achieve and demonstrate in the workplace. They are divided into key areas of knowledge which are closely linked to the exam syllabus.

There are five Essential performance objectives and a choice of fifteen Technical performance objectives which are divided into five areas.

The performance objectives which link to this exam are:

(1) Ethics and professionalism (Essential)

(2) Governance risk and control (Essential)

(3) Prepare for and plan the audit and assurance process (Technical)

(4) Collect and evaluate evidence for an audit or assurance engagement (Technical)

(5) Review and report on the findings of an audit or assurance engagement (Technical)

The following link provides an in depth insight into all of the performance objectives:

https://www.accaglobal.com/content/dam/ACCA_Global/Students/per/PER-Performance-objectives-achieve.pdf

Progression

There are two elements of progression that we can measure: first how quickly students move through individual topics within a subject; and second how quickly they move from one course to the next. We know that there is an optimum for both, but it can vary from subject to subject and from student to student. However, using data and our experience of student performance over many years, we can make some generalisations.

A fixed period of study set out at the start of a course with key milestones is important. This can be within a subject, for example 'I will finish this topic by 30 June', or for overall achievement, such as 'I want to be qualified by the end of next year'.

Your qualification is cumulative, as earlier papers provide a foundation for your subsequent studies, so do not allow there to be too big a gap between one subject and another. We know that exams encourage techniques that lead to some degree of short term retention, the result being that you will simply forget much of what you have already learned unless it is refreshed (look up Ebbinghaus Forgetting Curve for more details on this). This makes it more difficult as you move from one subject to another: not only will you have to learn the new subject, you will also have to relearn all the underpinning knowledge as well. This is very inefficient and slows down your overall progression which makes it more likely you may not succeed at all.

In addition, delaying your studies slows your path to qualification which can have negative impacts on your career, postponing the opportunity to apply for higher level positions and therefore higher pay.

You can use the following diagram showing the whole structure of your qualification to help you keep track of your progress.

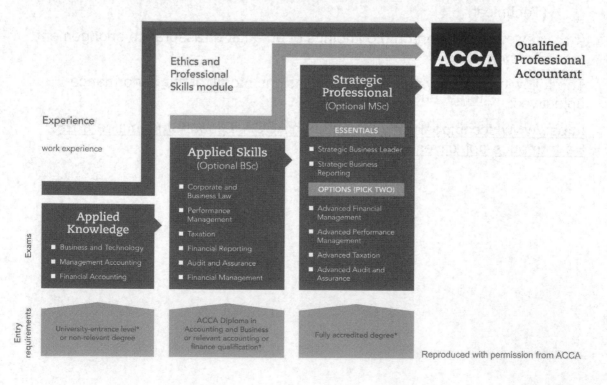

Reproduced with permission from ACCA

Syllabus objectives and chapter references

We have reproduced the ACCA's syllabus below, showing where the objectives are explored within this book. Within the chapters, we have broken down the extensive information found in the syllabus into easily digestible and relevant sections, called Content Objectives. These correspond to the objectives at the beginning of each chapter.

Syllabus learning objective	Chapter reference

A AUDIT FRAMEWORK AND REGULATION

1 The concept of audit and other assurance engagements

(a)	Identify and describe the objective and general principles of external audit engagements. [2]	1
(b)	Explain the nature and development of audit and other assurance engagements. [1]	1
(c)	Discuss the concepts of accountability, stewardship and agency. [2]	1
(d)	Define and provide the objectives of an assurance engagement. [1]	1
(e)	Explain the five elements of an assurance engagement. [2]	1
(f)	Describe the types of assurance engagement. [2]	1
(g)	Explain the level of assurance provided by an external audit and other review engagements and the concept of true and fair presentation. [1]	1

2 External audits

(a)	Describe the regulatory environment within which external audits take place. [1]	2
(b)	Discuss the reasons and mechanisms for the regulation of auditors. [1]	2
(c)	Explain the statutory regulations governing the appointment, rights, removal and resignation of auditors. [1]	2
(d)	Explain the regulations governing the rights and duties of auditors. [1]	2
(e)	Describe the limitations of external audits. [1]	1
(f)	Explain the development and status of International Standards on Auditing (ISAs). [1]	2
(g)	Explain the relationship between International Standards on Auditing and national standards. [1]	2

KAPLAN PUBLISHING

Syllabus learning objective		Chapter reference
(c)	Explain the process by which an auditor obtains an audit engagement. [2]	4
(d)	Discuss the importance and purpose of engagement letters and their contents. [1]	4
(e)	Explain the overall objectives and importance of quality control procedures in conducting an audit. [2]	6
(f)	Explain the quality control procedures that should be in place over engagement performance, monitoring quality and compliance with ethical requirements. [2]	6
2	**Objective and general principles**	
(a)	Identify the overall objectives of the auditor and the need to conduct an audit in accordance with ISAs. [2]	1 & 6
(b)	Explain the need to plan and perform audit engagements with an attitude of professional scepticism, and to exercise professional judgment. [2]	5
3	**Assessing audit risks**	
(a)	Explain the components of audit risk. [1]	5
(b)	Describe the audit risks in the financial statements and explain the auditor's response to each risk. [2]	5
(c)	Define and explain the concepts of materiality and performance materiality. [2]	5
(d)	Explain and calculate materiality levels from financial information. [2]	5
4	**Understanding the entity, its environment and the applicable financial reporting framework**	
(a)	Explain how auditors obtain an initial understanding of the entity, its environment and the applicable financial reporting framework. [2]	5
(b)	Describe and explain the nature and purpose of analytical procedures in planning. [2]	5
(c)	Compute and interpret key ratios used in analytical procedures. [2]	5
5	**Fraud, laws and regulations**	
(a)	Discuss the effect of fraud and misstatements on the audit strategy and extent of audit work. [2]	6
(b)	Discuss the responsibilities of internal and external auditors for the prevention and detection of fraud and error. [2]	6

Syllabus learning objective		Chapter reference

2 The use and evaluation of systems of internal control by auditors

(a) Explain how auditors record systems of internal control including the use of narrative notes, flowcharts and questionnaires. [2] — 8

(b) Evaluate internal control components, including deficiencies and significant deficiencies in internal control. [2] — 8

(c) Discuss the limitations of internal control components. [2] — 8

3 Tests of controls

(a) Describe computer systems controls including general IT controls and information processing controls. [2] — 8

(b) Describe control objectives, control procedures, control activities, direct controls, indirect controls and tests of control in relation to: — 8

   (i) The sales system

   (ii) The purchases system

   (iii) The payroll system

   (iv) The inventory system

   (v) The bank and cash system

   (vi) Non-current assets.

4 Communication on internal control

(a) Discuss the requirements and methods of how reporting significant deficiencies in internal control are provided to management and those charged with governance. [2] — 8

(b) Explain, in a format suitable for inclusion in a report to management, significant deficiencies within a system of internal control and provide control recommendations for overcoming these deficiencies to management. [2] — 8

(c) Discuss the need for auditors to communicate with those charged with governance. [2] — 8 & 12

5   Internal audit and governance, and the differences between external audit and internal audit

    (a)   Discuss the factors to be taken into account when assessing the need for internal audit. [2]   9

    (b)   Discuss the elements of best practice in the structure and operations of internal audit. [2]   9

    (c)   Compare and contrast the role of external and internal audit. [2]   9

6   The scope of the internal audit function, outsourcing and internal audit assignments

    (a)   Discuss the scope of internal audit and the limitations of the internal audit function. [2]   9

    (b)   Explain outsourcing and the associated advantages and disadvantages of outsourcing the internal audit function. [1]   9

    (c)   Discuss the nature and purpose of internal audit assignments including value for money, IT, financial, regulatory compliance, fraud investigations and customer experience. [2]   9

    (d)   Discuss the nature and purpose of operational internal audit assignments. [2]   9

    (e)   Describe the format and content of internal audit review reports and make appropriate recommendations to management and those charged with governance. [2]   9

D   AUDIT EVIDENCE

1   Assertions and audit evidence

    (a)   Explain the assertions contained in the financial statements about: [2]   7

        (i)   Classes of transactions and events and related disclosures

        (ii) Account balances and related disclosures at the period end.

    (b)   Describe audit procedures to obtain audit evidence, including inspection, observation, external confirmation, recalculation, re-performance, analytical procedures and enquiry. [2]   7

    (c)   Discuss the quality and quantity of audit evidence. [2]   7

    (d)   Discuss the relevance and reliability of audit evidence. [2]   7

KAPLAN PUBLISHING

2 **Audit procedures**

   (a) Discuss substantive procedures for obtaining audit evidence. [2]   7

   (b) Discuss and provide examples of how analytical procedures are used as substantive procedures. [2]   7

   (c) Discuss the problems associated with the audit and review of accounting estimates. [2]   10

   (d) Describe why smaller entities may have different control environments and describe the types of evidence likely to be available in smaller entities. [1]   10

   (e) Discuss the difference between tests of control and substantive procedures. [2]   7

3 **Audit sampling and other means of testing**

   (a) Define audit sampling and explain the need for sampling. [1]   7

   (b) Identify and discuss the differences between statistical and non-statistical sampling. [2]   7

   (c) Discuss and provide relevant examples of, the application of the basic principles of statistical sampling and other selective testing procedures. [2]   7

   (d) Discuss the results of statistical sampling, including consideration of whether additional testing is required. [2]   7

4 **The audit of specific items**

For each of the account balances stated in this sub-capability:

Explain the audit objectives and the audit procedures to obtain sufficient, appropriate evidence in relation to:

   (a) Receivables: [2]   10

      (i)   direct confirmation of accounts receivable

      (ii) other evidence in relation to receivables and prepayments

      (iii) other evidence in relation to current assets

      (iv) completeness and occurrence of revenue.

   (b) Inventory: [2]   10

      (i)   inventory counting procedures in relation to year-end and continuous inventory systems

      (ii) cut-off testing

      (iii) auditor's attendance at inventory counting

(iv) direct confirmation of inventory held by third parties

(v) valuation

(vi) other evidence in relation to inventory.

(c) Payables and accruals: [2]   10

  (i) supplier statement reconciliations and direct confirmation of accounts payable

  (ii) obtain evidence in relation to payables and accruals

  (iii) other evidence in relation to current liabilities

  (iv) purchases and other expenses, including payroll.

(d) Bank and cash: [2]   10

  (i) bank confirmation reports used in obtaining evidence in relation to bank and cash

  (ii) other evidence in relation to bank

  (iii) other evidence in relation to cash.

(e) Tangible and intangible non-current assets: [2]   10

  (i) evidence in relation to non-current assets

  (ii) depreciation

  (iii) profit/loss on disposal.

(f) Non-current liabilities, provisions and contingencies: [2] 10

  (i) evidence in relation to non-current liabilities

  (ii) provisions and contingencies.

(g) Share capital, reserves and directors' emoluments: [2] 10

  (i) evidence in relation to share capital, reserves and directors' emoluments.

5 Automated tools and techniques

(a) Explain the use of automated tools and techniques in the context of an audit, including the use of audit software, test data and other data analytics tools. [1] 7

(b) Discuss and provide relevant examples of the use of automated tools and techniques including test data, audit software and other data analytics tools. [2] 7

3   Written representations

(a)   Explain the purpose of and procedure for obtaining written representations. [2]   11

(b)   Discuss the quality and reliability of written representations as audit evidence. [2]   11

(c)   Discuss the circumstances where written representations are necessary and the matters on which representations are commonly obtained. [2]   11

4   Audit finalisation and the final review

(a)   Discuss the importance of the overall review in ensuring that sufficient, appropriate evidence has been obtained. [2]   11

(b)   Describe procedures an auditor should perform in conducting their overall review of financial statements. [2]   11

(c)   Explain the significance of uncorrected misstatements. [1]   11

(d)   Evaluate the effect of dealing with uncorrected misstatements. [2]   11

5   The Independent Auditor's Report

(a)   Identify and describe the basic elements contained in the independent auditor's report. [1]   12

(b)   Explain unmodified audit opinions in the auditor's report. [2]   12

(c)   Explain the circumstances in which a modified audit opinion may be issued in the auditor's report. [2]   12

(d)   Explain the impact on the auditor's report when a modified opinion is issued. [2]   12

(e)   Describe the format and content of key audit matters, emphasis of matter and other matter paragraphs. [2]   12

F   Employability and technology skills

1   Use computer technology to efficiently access and manipulate relevant information.

2   Work on relevant response options, using available functions and technology, as requirements, using the appropriate tools

3   Navigate windows and computer screens to create and amend responses to exam requirements, using the appropriate tools.

4   Present data and information effectively, using the appropriate tools.

The superscript numbers in square brackets indicate the intellectual depth at which the subject area could be assessed within the examination. Level 1 (knowledge and comprehension) broadly equates with the Knowledge module, Level 2 (application and analysis) with the Skills module and Level 3 (synthesis and evaluation) to the Professional level. However, lower level skills can continue to be assessed as you progress through each module and level.

References to ISA paragraph numbers within the study text are for copyright purposes only. Students are not required to learn this level of detail.

For a list of examinable documents, see the ACCA website:

accaglobal.com/audit-and-assurance

The Examination

Examination format

The syllabus is assessed by computer-based examination (CBE).

The CBE will contain 100 marks of exam content that needs to be completed within 3 hours. Prior to the start of the exam candidates are given an extra 10 minutes to read the exam instructions.

All questions are compulsory. The exam will contain both computational and discursive elements.

Some questions will adopt a scenario/case study approach.

The pass mark is 50%.

All questions follow a dating convention whereby the 'current date' is set at 1 July 20X5. This information will be stated in the question where relevant. Year-end dates of the entity being audited will then be flexed appropriately around this. For example in a planning question the entity could have a year end of 31 August 20X5. In an audit evidence/reporting question the year end could be 31 March 20X5. The application of this consistent dating convention allows candidates to be able to quickly determine where they are in the audit process.

Section A

Section A of the exam comprises three 10 mark case-based questions. Each case has five objective test questions worth 2 marks each.

There are no dependencies between the individual questions. Therefore, if you get one question wrong, it will not affect your ability to get the others correct.

OT questions in section A will be of varying styles as follows:

- Multiple choice – where you are required to choose one answer from a list of options provided by clicking on the appropriate 'radio button'.

- Multiple response – where you are required to select more than one response from the options provided by clicking on the appropriate tick boxes. The question will specify how many answers need to be selected, but the system won't stop you from selecting more answers than this.

- Fill in the blank – where you are required to type an answer into a box (usually numerical, but may be text). Any specific rounding requirements will be displayed.

- Drag and drop – where you are required to drag an answer and drop it into place. Some questions could involve matching more than one answer to a response area and some questions may have more answer choices than response areas, which means not all available answer choices need to be used.

- Drop down list – where you are required to select one answer from a drop down list. Some questions may contain more than one drop down list and an answer has to be selected from each one.

- Hot spot – where you are required to select one point on an image as your answer. When the cursor is hovered over the image, it will display as an 'X'. To answer, place the X on the appropriate point on the diagram.

- Hot area – these are similar to hot spot questions, but instead of selecting a specific point, you are required to select one or more areas in an image.

Section B

Section B of the exam comprises one 30 mark question and two 20 mark questions.

This section of the exam will predominantly examine one or more aspects of audit and assurance from planning and risk assessment, internal control or audit evidence, although topics from other syllabus areas may also be included.

Examination tips

Be sure you understand how to use the software before you start the exam. If in doubt, ask the assessment centre staff to explain it to you.

Questions are displayed on the screen and answers are entered using keyboard and mouse.

We recommend that 10 minutes should be spent reviewing the format and content of the requirements so that you understand what you need to do. Pay particular attention to section B, where questions will be based on longer scenarios than the 2 mark OT cases in section A.

Read each question carefully.

- Divide the time you spend on questions in proportion to the marks on offer.

- One suggestion for this examination is to allocate 1.8 minutes to each mark available (180 minutes/100 marks), so a 20 mark question should be completed in approximately 36 minutes.

Section A

You should begin by reading the OT questions that relate to the case, so that when you read through the information for the first time, you know what it is that you are required to do.

Once you have read through the information, you should first answer any of the OT questions that can be quickly answered. You should then attempt the other OT questions utilising the remaining time for that case.

If you don't know the answer, eliminate those options you know are incorrect and see if the answer becomes more obvious. After you have eliminated the options that you know to be wrong, if you are still unsure, guess.

Answer every question.

Each OT question is worth two marks. Therefore you have 18 minutes (1.8 minutes per mark) to answer the five OT questions relating to each case. It is likely that all of the cases will take the same length of time to answer, although some of the OT questions within a case may be quicker than other OT questions within that same case.

Work steadily. Rushing leads to careless mistakes and the OT questions are designed to include answers which result from careless mistakes.

Section A questions can be found at the end of each chapter.

Section B

The constructed response questions in section B will require a written response rather than being OT questions. Therefore, different techniques need to be used to score well.

Unless you know exactly how to answer the question, spend some time planning your answer. Stick to the question and tailor your answer to what you are asked. Pay particular attention to the verbs in the question e.g. 'Describe', 'State', 'Explain'.

If you get completely stuck with a question leave it and return to it later.

If you do not understand what a question is asking, state your assumptions. Even if you do not answer in precisely the way the examining team hoped, you may be given some credit, provided that your assumptions are reasonable.

When answering the constructed response questions, be concise. DO NOT write an essay.

Make sure that each point is clearly identifiable by leaving a line space between each of your points.

Some questions ask you to present your answer in the form of a report or letter. Use the correct format as there are easy marks to gain here for presentation.

Guidance on exam technique for the constructed response questions is given in the relevant chapters of the study text.

Section B style questions can be found in most chapters and also in Chapter 15.

All sections

Don't skip parts of the syllabus. The AA syllabus has 18 different questions so the examination can cover a very broad selection of the syllabus each sitting.

Spend time learning definitions.

Practice plenty of questions to improve your ability to apply the techniques.

Spend the last few minutes reading through your answers and making any additions or corrections.

Don't panic if you realise you've answered a question incorrectly. Try to remain calm, continue to apply examination technique and answer all questions required within the time available.

ACCA support

For additional support with your studies please also refer to the ACCA Global website.

Study skills and revision guidance

This section aims to give guidance on how to study for your ACCA exams and to give ideas on how to improve your existing study techniques.

Preparing to study

Set your objectives

Before starting to study decide what you want to achieve i.e. the type of pass you wish to obtain. This will decide the level of commitment and time you need to dedicate to your studies.

Devise a study plan

Determine which times of the week you will study.

Split these times into sessions of at least one hour for study of new material. Any shorter periods could be used for revision or practice.

Put the times you plan to study onto a study plan for the weeks from now until the exam and set yourself targets for each period of study. In your sessions make sure you cover the course, course assignments and revision.

If you are studying for more than one exam at a time, try to vary your subjects as this can help you to keep interested and see subjects as part of wider knowledge.

When working through your course, compare your progress with your plan and, if necessary, re-plan your work (perhaps including extra sessions) or, if you are ahead, do some extra revision/practice questions.

Effective studying

Active reading

You are not expected to learn the text by rote, rather, you must understand what you are reading and be able to use it to pass the exam and develop good practice. A good technique to use is SQ3Rs – Survey, Question, Read, Recall, Review:

(1) **Survey the chapter** – look at the headings and read the introduction, summary and objectives, to get an overview of what the chapter deals with.

(2) **Question** – whilst undertaking the survey, ask yourself the questions that you hope the chapter will answer for you.

(3) **Read** through the chapter thoroughly, answering the questions and making sure you can meet the objectives. Attempt the exercises and activities in the text, and work through all the examples.

(4) **Recall** – at the end of each section and at the end of the chapter, try to recall the main ideas of the section/chapter without referring to the text. This is best done after a short break of a couple of minutes after the reading stage.

(5) **Review** – check that your recall notes are correct.

You may also find it helpful to re-read the chapter to try to see the topic(s) it deals with as a whole.

Note-taking

Taking notes is a useful way of learning, but do not simply copy out the text. The notes must:

- be in your own words
- be concise
- cover the key points
- be well-organised
- be modified as you study further chapters in this text or in related ones.

Trying to summarise a chapter without referring to the text can be a useful way of determining which areas you know and which you don't.

Summarise the key points of a chapter.

Three ways of taking notes:

(1) **Make linear notes** – a list of headings, divided up with subheadings listing the key points. If you use linear notes, you can use different colours to highlight key points and keep topic areas together. Use plenty of space to make your notes easy to use.

(2) **Try a diagrammatic form** – the most common of which is a mind-map. To make a mind-map, put the main heading in the centre of the paper and put a circle around it. Then draw short lines radiating from this to the main subheadings, which again have circles around them. Then continue the process from the sub-headings to sub-sub-headings, advantages, disadvantages, etc.

(3) **Highlighting and underlining** – you may find it useful to underline or highlight key points in your study text – but do be selective. You may also wish to make notes in the margins.

KAPLAN PUBLISHING

Revision

The best approach to revision is to revise the course as you work through it. Also try to leave four to six weeks before the exam for final revision. Make sure you cover the whole syllabus and pay special attention to those areas where your knowledge is weak. Here are some recommendations:

Read through the text and your notes again and condense your notes into key phrases. It may help to put key revision points onto index cards to look at when you have a few minutes to spare.

Review any assignments you have completed and look at where you lost marks – put more work into those areas where you were weak.

Practise exam standard questions under timed conditions. If you are short of time, list the points that you would cover in your answer and then read the model answer, but do try to complete at least a few questions under exam conditions.

Also practise producing answer plans and comparing them to the model answer.

If you are stuck on a topic find somebody (a tutor) to explain it to you.

Read good newspapers and professional journals, especially ACCA's **Student Accountant**, this can give you an advantage in the exam.

Ensure you **know the structure of the exam** – how many questions and of what type you will be expected to answer.

During your revision attempt all the different styles of questions you may be asked.

Further reading

You can find further reading and technical articles under the student section of ACCA's website.

Technical update

This text has been updated to reflect Examinable Documents September 2021 to June 2022 issued by ACCA.

Introduction to assurance

Chapter learning objectives

This chapter covers syllabus areas:

- A1 – The concept of audit and other assurance engagements
- A2e – Limitations of external audits

Detailed syllabus objectives are provided in the introduction section of the text book.

PER

One of the PER performance objectives (PO4) is governance risk and control. You contribute to effective governance in your area. You evaluate, monitor and implement risk management procedures, complying with the spirit and the letter of policies, laws and regulations. Working through this chapter should help you understand how to demonstrate that objective.

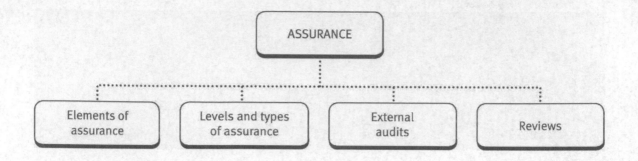

1 What is assurance?

An assurance engagement is: 'An engagement in which a practitioner obtains sufficient appropriate evidence in order to express a conclusion designed to enhance the degree of confidence of the intended users other than the responsible party about the outcome of the evaluation or measurement of a subject matter against criteria.'

[International Framework for Assurance Engagements, 7]

Giving assurance means offering an opinion about specific information so the users of that information are able to make **confident decisions** knowing that the **risk** of the information being 'incorrect' is **reduced**.

Elements of an assurance engagement

There are **five elements of an assurance engagement**:

1 **Three party involvement**

Practitioner – the reviewer of the subject matter who provides the assurance.

Intended users – the people using the subject matter to make economic decisions.

Responsible party – the party responsible for preparing the subject matter.

2 **Appropriate subject matter**

The information subject to examination by the practitioner.

3 **Suitable criteria**

The criteria against which the subject matter is evaluated, i.e. standards, guidance, laws and regulations.

4 **Sufficient appropriate evidence**

Sufficient appropriate evidence is needed to provide a basis for the opinion/conclusion.

5 **Written assurance report** in an appropriate form

The output of the assurance engagement expressing a conclusion/opinion about the subject matter.

[International Framework for Assurance Engagements, 20]

	Element	In relation to an audit	In relation to a forecast
1	Three party involvement		
	Practitioner	Auditor	Assurance provider
	Intended user	Shareholders	Directors / provider of finance
	Responsible party	Directors	Directors
2	Appropriate subject matter	Financial statements	Forecast
3	Suitable criteria	Financial reporting framework	Appropriate assumptions and financial reporting framework
4	Sufficient appropriate evidence	Obtained by performing audit procedures such as tests of controls, tests of detail and analytical procedures	Obtained by performing examination procedures such as inspection of documents, enquiries and analytical procedures
5	Written assurance report in an appropriate form	Independent auditor's report providing an opinion as to whether the financial statements give a true and fair view	Independent assurance report providing a conclusion on whether anything has come to the practitioner's attention to suggest the assumptions are not a reasonable basis for the forecast, and an opinion on whether the forecast has been prepared on the basis of those assumptions

Illustration 1 – Buying a house

Consider someone who is buying a house. There is a risk that the buyer pays a large sum of money to purchase a structurally unsafe property which needs further expenditure to make it habitable. To reduce this risk, it is normal for house buyers (the users) to pay a property surveyor (the practitioner) to perform a structural assessment of the house (the subject matter). The surveyor communicates any structural deficiencies identified (measured against building regulations/best practice and other criteria) in a written report to the house buyer. With this information, the potential buyer can make a decision whether or not to buy the house with the confidence that they know its structural condition. In this example, the responsible party is the current house owner, and the evidence would be obtained through visual inspection of the property.

Assurance engagements

Examples of assurance engagements include:

- Audit of financial statements

- Review of financial statements

- Systems reliability reports

- Verification of social and environmental information

- Review of internal controls

- Value for money audit in public sector organisations.

General principles the assurance provider must follow when performing such engagements include:

- Comply with ethical requirements.

- Apply professional scepticism and judgment.

- Perform acceptance and continuance procedures to ensure only work of acceptable risk is accepted.

- Agree the terms of engagement.

- Comply with quality control requirements.

- Plan and perform the engagement effectively.

- Obtain sufficient and appropriate evidence.

- Consider the effect of subsequent events on the subject matter.

- Form a conclusion expressing either reasonable or limited assurance as appropriate.

- Document the evidence to provide a record of the basis for the assurance report.

KAPLAN PUBLISHING

Types of assurance engagement

Two types of assurance engagement are permitted:

Reasonable assurance engagements	Limited assurance engagements
The practitioner:	The practitioner:
Gathers **sufficient appropriate evidence** to be able to draw **reasonable conclusions.**	Gathers **sufficient appropriate evidence** to be able to draw **limited conclusions.**
Performs very thorough procedures to obtain sufficient appropriate evidence including tests of controls and substantive procedures.	Performs significantly fewer procedures, mainly enquiries and analytical procedures.
Concludes that the subject matter **conforms in all material respects** with identified suitable criteria.	Concludes that the subject matter, with respect to identified suitable criteria, is **plausible in the circumstances.**
Gives a **positively** worded assurance **opinion.**	Gives a **negatively** worded assurance **conclusion.**
Gives a **high level** of assurance (confidence).	Gives a **moderate or lower level** of assurance than that of an audit.
In our opinion, the financial statements give a true and fair view of (or *present fairly, in all material respects*) the financial position of Murray Company as at December 31, 20X4, and of its financial performance and its cash flows for the year then ended in accordance with International Financial Reporting Standards.	**Nothing has come to our attention** that causes us to believe that the financial statements of Murray Company as of 31 December, 20X4 are not prepared, in all material respects, in accordance with an applicable financial reporting framework.

The confidence inspired by a reasonable assurance report is designed to be greater than that inspired by a limited assurance report. Therefore:

- There are more regulations/standards governing a reasonable assurance assignment.

- The procedures carried out in a reasonable assurance assignment will be more thorough.

- The evidence gathered will need to be of a higher quality.

2 External audit engagements

An external audit is an example of a **reasonable assurance** engagement.

Purpose of an external audit engagement

ISA 200 *Overall Objectives of the Independent Auditor and the Conduct of an Audit in Accordance with International Standards on Auditing* states the purpose of an external audit engagement is to **'enhance the degree of confidence of intended users in the financial statements.'**

This is achieved by the auditor expressing an opinion on whether the financial statements:

- Give a true and fair view (or present fairly in all material respects).

- Are prepared, in all material respects, in accordance with an applicable financial reporting framework.

[ISA 200, 3]

 The financial reporting framework to be applied will vary from country to country. In Audit & Assurance, it is assumed that International Financial Reporting Standards are the basis for preparing the financial statements.

 The accounting standards examinable for Audit & Assurance are those from Financial Accounting at the Applied Knowledge level.

True and fair

- **True:** factually correct information which conforms with accounting standards and relevant legislation, and agrees with the underlying records.

- **Fair:** clear, impartial and unbiased information which reflects the commercial substance of the transactions of the entity.

Objectives of the auditor

The objectives of an **auditor** are to:

- Obtain reasonable assurance about whether the financial statements as a whole are free from material misstatement, whether due to fraud or error.

- Express an opinion on whether the financial statements are prepared, in all material respects, in accordance with an applicable financial reporting framework.

- Report on the financial statements, and communicate as required by ISAs, in accordance with the auditor's findings.

[ISA 200, 11]

Need for external audit

- Shareholders provide the finance for a company and may or may not be involved in the day to day running of the company.

- Directors manage the company on behalf of the shareholders in order to achieve the objectives of that company (normally the maximisation of shareholder wealth).

- The directors must prepare financial statements to provide information on performance and financial position to the shareholders.

- The directors have various incentives to manipulate the financial statements and show a different level of performance.

- Hence the need for an independent review of the financial statements to ensure they give a true and fair view – the external audit.

In most developed countries, publicly quoted companies and large companies are required by law to produce annual financial statements and have them audited by an external auditor.

Companies that are not required to have a statutory audit may choose to have an external audit because the company's shareholders or other influential stakeholders want one, and because of the benefits of an audit.

Benefits of an audit

- Higher quality information which is more reliable, improving the reputation of the market.

- Independent scrutiny and verification may be valuable to management.

- Reduces the risk of management bias and fraud and error by acting as a deterrent. An audit may also detect bias, fraud and error.

- Enhances the credibility of the financial statements, e.g. for tax authorities or lenders.

- Deficiencies in the internal control system may be highlighted by the auditor.

Expectation gap

Some users incorrectly believe that an audit provides absolute assurance – that the audit opinion is a guarantee the financial statements are 'correct'. This and other misconceptions about the role of an auditor are referred to as the **'expectation gap'**.

Examples of the expectation gap

- A belief that the auditor tests **all** transactions and balances – tests are performed on a sample basis.

- A belief that the auditor will detect **all** fraud – the auditor is required to provide reasonable assurance that the financial statements are free from **material** misstatement, which may be caused by fraud.

- A belief that the auditor is responsible for **preparing** the financial statements – this is the responsibility of management.

Limitations of an audit

- **F**inancial statements include subjective estimates and other judgmental matters.

- **I**nternal controls may be relied on which have their own inherent limitations.

- **R**epresentations from management may have to be relied upon as the only source of evidence in some areas.

- **E**vidence is often persuasive not conclusive.

- **D**o not test all transactions and balances, only a sample are tested.

 The auditor provides reasonable assurance which is not absolute assurance. The **limitations of an audit** mean that it is not possible to provide a 100% guarantee of accuracy.

Limitations of an audit
• Nature of financial reporting – financial statement amounts are affected by management judgment and therefore subject to bias.
• Nature of audit procedures – information provided by the client may be incomplete or falsified documents may be provided.
• Timeliness of financial reporting – the relevance of information diminishes over time and the auditor cannot investigate every matter exhaustively.
[ISA 200, A48 – A50]

3 Review engagements

A review engagement is an example of a **limited assurance** engagement.

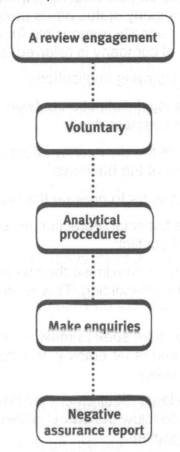

A review engagement

Voluntary

Analytical procedures

Make enquiries

Negative assurance report

Purpose and objective of a review engagement

A company which is not legally required to have an audit may choose to have a review of its financial statements instead. The review will still provide some assurance to users but is likely to cost less and be less disruptive than an audit.

The procedures will mainly focus on analytical procedures and enquiries of management. In particular, no tests of controls will be performed.

As only limited assurance is being expressed, the work does not need to be as in depth as for an audit.

The **objective of a review of financial statements** is to enable an auditor to state whether, on the basis of the procedures, which do not provide all the evidence required in an audit, anything has come to their attention that causes them to believe that the financial statements are not prepared in accordance with the applicable financial reporting framework.

Test your understanding 1

List and explain the elements of an assurance engagement.

(5 marks)

Test your understanding 2

Explain the term 'limited assurance' in the context of an examination of a company's cash flow forecast and explain how this differs from the assurance provided by an external audit.

(5 marks)

Test your understanding 3

Your firm has been approached to perform the external audit of Perth Co. Perth Co has grown over the last two years and has now reached the audit threshold. As this is the first year the company has required an audit, the directors are unsure about the purpose of the audit. They have been informed that an audit need not be as inconvenient or intrusive as they expect it to be as there are additional benefits that may arise from having an audit. The directors have indicated that they expect your firm to detect every fraud and error in the accounting records so that when they need to apply for finance to help them grow further, they can use the audited financial statements to support the loan application and this should make it easier to obtain the loan.

1   What level of assurance will be provided by the independent auditor's report?

   A   Absolute

   B   Reasonable

   C   Moderate

   D   Limited

2   Which of the following is NOT one of the five elements of an assurance engagement?

   A   Subject matter

   B   Suitable criteria

   C   Assurance file

   D   Written report

3 Which of the following is NOT a benefit of an audit?

A Increased credibility of the financial statements

B Deficiencies in controls may be identified during testing

C Fraud may be detected during the audit

D Sampling is used

4 Which of the following statements is false?

A The auditor will express an opinion as to whether the financial statements give a true and fair view

B The auditor must obtain sufficient and appropriate evidence to be able to form an audit opinion

C If the financial statements are found to contain material misstatements a negative audit opinion will be given

D An audit may not detect all fraud and error in the financial statements

5 Which of the following are examples of the expectation gap?

(i) The independent auditor's report confirms the financial statements are accurate.

(ii) An unmodified opinion means the company is a going concern.

(iii) The auditor tests all transactions.

(iv) The auditor can be sued for negligence if they issue an inappropriate opinion.

A (i), (ii) and (iii)

B (i), (ii) and (iv)

C (i) and (ii) only

D (ii) and (iii) only

4 Chapter summary

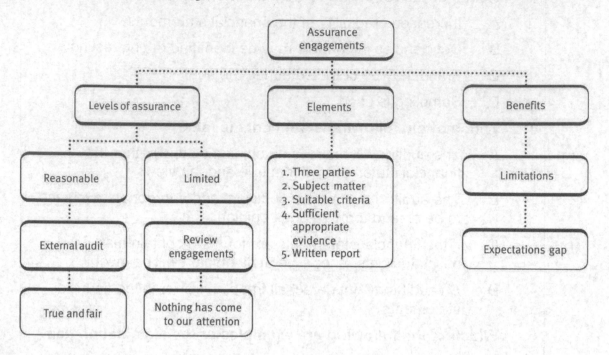

Test your understanding answers

Test your understanding 1

1 An assurance engagement will involve three separate parties:

    (i) Intended user – the person who requires the assurance report.

    (ii) Responsible party – the person or organisation responsible for preparing the subject matter to be reviewed.

    (iii) Practitioner (i.e. an accountant) – the professional, who will review the subject matter and provide the assurance.

2 A suitable subject matter. This is the information that the responsible party has prepared and which requires verification.

3 Suitable criteria. The subject matter is compared to the criteria in order for it to be assessed and an opinion/conclusion provided.

4 Sufficient and appropriate evidence has to be obtained by the practitioner in order to give the required level of assurance.

5 An assurance report contains the opinion/conclusion that is given by the practitioner to the intended user.

Test your understanding 2

Limited assurance in the context of a cash flow forecast	Assurance provided by an external audit
Limited assurance is a moderate level of assurance.	An audit provides reasonable assurance, which is a high level.
The objective of a limited assurance engagement in the context of a cash flow forecast is to obtain sufficient appropriate evidence that the forecast is plausible in the circumstances i.e. prepared on the basis of reasonable assumptions.	The objective of an audit is to obtain sufficient appropriate evidence that the financial statements conform in all material respects with the relevant financial reporting framework.

A limited assurance report provides a negative conclusion. The practitioner will state that nothing has come to their attention which indicates that the assumptions used to prepare the cash flow forecast are not reasonable. The assurance is therefore given on the absence of any indication to the contrary.	An auditor's report provides a positive opinion as to whether or not the financial statements give a true and fair view. A positive opinion means the auditor is confident about the statement they are making, i.e. confident that the financial statements give a true and fair view or confident that they do not give a true and fair view.
With limited assurance, limited procedures are performed. In the context of a forecast, procedures will be limited as the transactions and events haven't occurred yet.	More evidence will need to be obtained to provide reasonable assurance, and a wider range of procedures performed, including tests of controls.
A forecast relates to the future, which is inherently uncertain, and therefore it would not be possible to obtain assurance that it is free from material misstatement.	Financial statements relate to the past, and so the auditor should be able to obtain sufficient and appropriate evidence.
Less reliance can therefore be placed on the forecast than the financial statements.	

Test your understanding 3

1	B	Reasonable assurance is given in an independent auditor's report.
2	C	Assurance file.
3	D	Sampling provides a limitation of the audit process, not a benefit.
4	C	A negative conclusion is used for limited assurance engagements.
5	A	The auditor cannot confirm the accuracy of the financial statements as they contain estimates and judgments of management. The company may not be a going concern and the financial statements may correctly reflect this resulting in an unmodified audit opinion. The auditor does not test all transactions.

KAPLAN PUBLISHING

Rules and regulation

Chapter learning objectives

This chapter covers syllabus areas:

- A2 – External audits

Detailed syllabus objectives are provided in the introduction section of the text book.

PER

One of the PER performance objectives (PO4) is governance risk and control. You contribute to effective governance in your area. You evaluate, monitor and implement risk management procedures, complying with the spirit and the letter of policies, laws and regulations. Working through this chapter should help you understand how to demonstrate that objective.

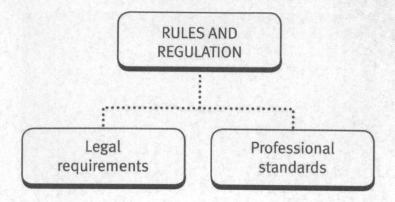

1 The need for regulation

The role of the auditor has come under increased scrutiny over the last 30 years due to an increase in high profile audit failures. The most high profile case, and the catalyst for regulatory change, was the collapse of Enron and its auditor Arthur Andersen.

In order to try and regain trust in the auditing profession, national and international standard setters and regulators have tried to introduce three initiatives:

- **Harmonisation** of auditing procedures, so that users of audit services are confident in the nature of audits being conducted around the world.

- Focus on **audit quality,** so that the expectations of users are met.

- Adherence to a strict **ethical code** of conduct, to try and improve the perception of auditors as independent, unbiased service providers.

In order to achieve this, practitioners have to follow regulatory guidance:

- **National corporate law (e.g. The Companies Act 2006 in the UK and The Sarbanes Oxley Act in the US).**

- **Auditing Standards** (the basis of this text is International Standards on Auditing).

- **Code of Ethics.** Covered in the chapter 'Ethics and acceptance'.

2 Legal requirements for audits and auditors

 In this section, the law referred to in most cases is UK law and the Companies Act 2006. Different countries may have different requirements but generally the same principles will apply across the world. Some of the knowledge learned in Corporate and Business Law will be relevant here.

National law includes:

- Which companies are required to have an audit

- Who can and cannot carry out an audit

- Auditor appointment, resignation and removal

- The rights and duties of an auditor.

Who needs an audit and why?

In most countries, companies are required by law to have an audit.

Small or owner-managed companies are often exempt. This is because there is less value in an audit for these companies.

Note that these exemptions often do not apply to companies in certain regulated sectors, e.g. financial services companies or companies listed on a stock exchange.

Reasons for exempting small companies from audit
• The owners and managers of the company are often the same people.
• The advice and value which accountants can add to a small company is more likely to concern other services, such as accounting and tax.
• The impact of misstatements in the financial statements of small companies is unlikely to be material to the wider economy.
• The audit fee and disruption of an audit are seen as too great a cost for any benefits the audit might bring.

Who may act as auditor?

To be **eligible** to act as **auditor,** a person must be:

- A member of a Recognised Supervisory Body (RSB), e.g. ACCA, and allowed by the rules of that body to be an auditor **or**

- Someone directly authorised by the state.

Conducting audit work	
Individuals who are authorised to conduct audit work may be:	To be eligible to offer audit services, a firm must be:
• Sole practitioners	• Controlled by members of a suitably authorised supervisory body or
• Partners in a partnership	
• Members of a limited liability partnership	• A firm directly authorised by the state.
• Directors of an audit company.	

Note: In some countries only individuals can be authorised to act as auditor and need to be directly authorised by the state.

Who may not act as auditor?

Excluded by law: The law in most countries excludes those who manage or work for the company, and those who have business or personal connections with them from auditing that company.

Excluded by the Code of Ethics: Auditors must also comply with a Code of Ethics. The Code of Ethics requires the auditor to consider any factors that would prevent them acting as auditor, such as independence, competence or issues regarding confidentiality. This is considered in more detail in the chapter 'Ethics and acceptance.

Who appoints the auditor?

Members (shareholders) – of the company appoint the auditor by voting them in.

Directors – can appoint the first auditor or to fill a 'casual vacancy'. This requires the members' approval at a members' meeting. In some countries the auditor may be appointed by the directors as a matter of course.

Secretary of State – if no auditor is appointed by the members or directors.

Auditors of public companies are appointed from one AGM to the next one.

Auditors of private companies are appointed until they are removed.

Removing the auditor

Arrangements for removing the auditor have to be structured in such a way that:

- the auditor has sufficiently secure tenure of office, to maintain independence of management.

- the auditor can be removed if there are doubts about their continuing ability to carry out their duties effectively.

Removal of the auditor can usually be achieved by a simple majority at a general meeting of the company. There are some safeguards, such as a specified notice period, to prevent the resolution to remove the auditor being suggested at short notice in order to influence the outcome of the vote.

The auditor can circulate representations stating why they should not be removed if applicable.

A statement of circumstances must be sent to the company and the regulatory authority to set out issues surrounding the cessation of office.

Resigning as auditor

In practice, if the auditor and management find it difficult to work together, the auditor will usually resign.

On resignation, the auditor issues written notice of the resignation and a statement of circumstances to the members and regulatory authority.

KAPLAN PUBLISHING

Notifying ACCA

If an auditor resigns or is removed from office before the end of their term of office, they must notify the ACCA.

The auditor's responsibilities on removal/resignation

The following is taken from UK law, but provides an example of the typical responsibilities of the auditor.

- Deposit at the company's registered office:
  - A statement of the circumstances connected with the removal/resignation, or
  - A statement that there are no such circumstances.
- Deal promptly with requests for clearance from new auditors.

The auditor's rights

During appointment as auditor

- Access to the company's books and records at any reasonable time.
- To receive information and explanations necessary for the audit.
- To receive notice of and attend any general meeting of members of the company.
- To be heard at such meetings on matters of concern to the auditor.
- To receive copies of any written resolutions of the company.

On resignation

- To request a General Meeting of the company to explain the circumstances of the resignation.
- To require the company to circulate the notice of circumstances relating to the resignation.

The auditor's duties

The external auditor's primary duty is to audit the financial statements and provide an opinion on whether the financial statements give a true and fair view (or are fairly presented in all material respects).

They may have additional reporting responsibilities required by local national law, such as confirming that the financial statements are properly prepared in accordance with those laws.

3 International regulation

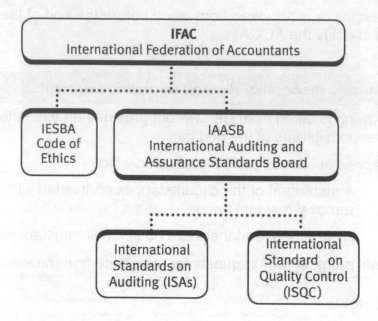

The International Federation of Accountants (IFAC)

The International Federation of Accountants (IFAC) is the global organisation for the accountancy profession.

IFAC promotes international regulation of the accountancy profession. By ensuring minimum requirements for accountancy qualifications, post qualification experience and guidance on accounting and assurance for accountants around the world, there will be greater public confidence in the profession as a whole.

International Standards on Auditing (ISAs)

One of the subsidiary boards of IFAC is the International Audit and Assurance Standards Board (IAASB). It is the IAASB's responsibility to develop and promote International Standards on Auditing (ISAs).

There are currently 37 ISAs and one International Standard of Quality Control, although not all are examinable for this syllabus. A list of examinable documents is available on the ACCA website. You do not need to learn the names or numbers of the ISAs but you do need to know and be able to apply the key principles and requirements of the standards.

Main features of ISAs

- ISAs are professional guidance that the auditor must follow to ensure each audit is performed consistently and to a required standard of quality.

- ISAs are not legal requirements. If a country has a law in place which is inconsistent with the requirements of the ISAs, local law should be followed.

- ISAs are written in the context of an audit of the financial statements but can be applied to the audit of other historical financial information.

- ISAs must be applied in all but exceptional cases. Where the auditor deems it necessary to depart from an ISA to achieve the overall aim of the audit, this departure must be justified.

- ISAs contain basic principles and requirements followed by application and other explanatory material to aid the auditor on how to follow the requirements.

Development of ISAs

For an ISA to be issued, a lengthy process of discussion and debate occurs to ensure the members affected by the guidance have had an input.

An exposure draft (ED) is issued for public comment and these comments may result in revisions to the ED.

Approval of two thirds of IAASB members is required for the ISA to come into force.

The relationship between international and national standards and regulation

IFAC is simply a grouping of accountancy bodies, therefore it has no legal standing in individual countries. Countries therefore need to have their own arrangements in place for:

- Regulating the audit profession
- Implementing auditing standards.

National standard setters

- May develop their own auditing standards and ethical standards
- May adopt and implement ISAs, possibly after modifying them to suit national needs.

In the event of a conflict between the two sets of guidance, local regulations will apply.

UK as an example

In the UK, the Financial Reporting Council (FRC) is currently the national regulator responsible for overseeing the accountancy profession.

The Audit and Actuarial Regulation Division within the FRC is responsible for the development of auditing standards and guidance in the UK, monitoring of auditors of public interest entities, and oversight and regulation of Recognised Supervisory Bodies (such as ACCA).

The Audit and Assurance team within the Audit Division take the ISAs as issued by the IAASB and modify them for UK use.

The Audit and Assurance team has also developed its own ethical standard which must be followed. The safeguards within the ethical standard are either the same as those required by the International Ethics Standards Board for Accountants (IESBA) International Code of Ethics for Professional Accountants, or more comprehensive. For example, partner rotation rules in the UK are more stringent than those required by the IESBA.

The Audit Quality Review (AQR) team monitors the quality of work performed by audit firms that perform audits of public interest entities in the UK. The AQR performs inspections of audit files to ensure firms are following the requirements of the ethical standard, auditing standards and quality control standard. Inspection reports are available to view on the FRC website.

The accountancy profession in the UK is therefore primarily self-regulated with little government involvement in the regulation of accountancy firms.

At the time of writing, the FRC is currently in transition to a new regulatory authority, The Audit, Reporting and Governance Authority (ARGA). This action is being taken in response to a number of high profile accounting irregularities over recent years, such as Carillion and Patisserie Valerie. The UK government ordered a review of the regulatory system which recommended the introduction of a new regulator. The FRC was criticised for being too close to those that it is supposed to regulate creating a conflict of interest resulting in an ineffective regulatory system. It is expected that ARGA will be more proactive in taking action against firms who fail to uphold the reputation of the profession.

4 The role of professional bodies

Professional bodies (such as the ACCA and ICAEW) promote quality within the profession through provision of:

- Rigorous qualifications to acquire the knowledge and skills needed to provide a competent service

- Support to members to demonstrate high professional and ethical values

- Technical expertise to governments on accounting and business matters. This input may help shape the introduction of new laws and regulations affecting the profession.

To obtain membership to a professional body, a person must:

- Successfully complete the exams provided by that body

- Be able to demonstrate appropriate practical experience (usually a minimum of three years)

- Complete an ethical assessment.

To maintain membership, a member must demonstrate continuing professional development (CPD) to ensure knowledge and skills are kept up to date. In addition, members must comply with a code of ethics and conduct to ensure they act in a professional manner at all times.

If a member is found not to have complied with the rules of the professional body, disciplinary action will be taken which may involve fines, reprimands, suspension from membership for a limited time, or withdrawal of membership. Most disciplinary matters will be dealt with internally by the relevant professional body. However, if the behaviour of the person or the firm is considered very serious, the matter can be referred to the national regulator and action can be taken at a higher level. This will generally be the case for significant public interest issues.

By having such rigorous membership requirements and disciplinary proceedings, the public can be assured that professional accountants are performing work of a high standard which increases trust in the profession as a whole.

Test your understanding 1

(a) **Explain FOUR rights that enable auditors to carry out their duties.** (4 marks)

(b) **State the circumstances in which a person is not eligible to act as an auditor.** (3 marks)

(c) **Describe the steps required to remove an auditor from an engagement.** (3 marks)

(Total: 10 marks)

Test your understanding 2

You have been asked to conduct a training workshop for your firm's new trainees which will cover the rules and regulations surrounding the auditing profession. You have prepared a short test for the trainees to take at the end of the workshop to assess whether they have understood the content covered.

1 **Which of the following statements is FALSE?**

A   Auditing standards are laws which must be followed during all audits

B   Auditing standards should be followed during all audits unless there are exceptional circumstances which would mean the audit objective would not be met

C   Auditing standards are professional regulations

D   Auditing standards may be different in different countries, even those using ISAs

2   **Which of the following are reasons for the audit profession issuing auditing standards?**

(i)   To ensure consistency of audits across different firms.

(ii)   To provide bureaucracy for auditors.

(iii) To ensure quality in the standard of audits performed.

A   All of them

B   (i) and (ii) only

C   (i) and (iii) only

D   (ii) and (iii) only

3   **Which of the following people may act as auditor for a company?**

A   The company's previous finance director who left the company five years ago to join the audit firm

B   A director of the company being audited who holds a valid audit certificate

C   An employee of the company being audited who holds a valid audit certificate

D   The wife of the finance director who works for a reputable audit firm

4   **In most jurisdictions, the auditors of a company will be appointed by which party?**

A   Directors

B   Audit committee

C   Government

D   Shareholders

5   **Which of the following statements is TRUE?**

A   The shareholders of most companies will also be the directors

B   The directors are the stewards of the company responsible for looking after the company on behalf of the owners

C   Directors will always have a vested interest in the company doing well because they own shares in the company they work for

D   Auditors are allowed to be business partners of the company directors

KAPLAN PUBLISHING

Test your understanding 3

You have recently started a training contract at an accountancy firm, Nauru & Co, to become a chartered certified accountant. You will be working in the audit and assurance department where your mother is an audit engagement partner.

Nauru & Co has several audit clients, although not as many as in the past due to the audit threshold being increased significantly over the last 15 years. Current regulations require all public interest entities and companies with revenue of $10 million and at least 50 employees to be audited.

Nauru & Co has recently won the tender for the audit of Vanuatu Co. Your mother will be the engagement partner for this client. You have confirmed that you are independent of management and those charged with governance of Vanuatu Co.

Malta Co has approached your firm for advice on whether they require an audit. Malta Co has 75 employees and revenue of $8 million. Malta Co is a financial institution providing banking and insurance services. Malta Co has three shareholders who are all directors of the company.

1 **Which of the following must you complete to become a chartered certified accountant?**

(i) Three years of exams.

(ii) Practical experience of a minimum of three years.

(iii) An ethics assessment.

A All of them

B (i) and (ii) only

C (i) and (iii) only

D (ii) and (iii) only

2 **Which of the following statements is TRUE in respect of the audit of Vanuatu Co?**

A You will be able to be a member of the audit team as you are independent of the client

B You will be able to be a member of the audit team as you are a new employee of the firm and have not had time to build up any relationships which will impact your independence

C You will not be able to be a member of the audit team as your mother is the engagement partner

D You will not be able to be a member of the audit team as you have no audit experience and therefore are not competent to perform audit work

3 **Which of the following statements is TRUE in respect of Malta Co?**

A Malta Co requires an audit as the number of employees is over 50

B Malta Co requires an audit because it is a financial services company

C Malta Co does not require an audit as revenue is below $10 million

D Malta Co does not require an audit as all shareholders are directors

4 **Which TWO of the following will ensure the quality of work performed by accountancy firms such as Nauru & Co is at a high standard?**

A The firm must establish its own quality control policies and procedures

B The firm will be subject to quality reviews by the courts

C The firm will be subject to quality reviews by the IAASB

D The threat of legal action by ACCA will encourage a high level of quality

E The firm will be subject to quality reviews by ACCA

5 **Which of the following is NOT a right of the auditor during appointment?**

A To speak at general meetings of the shareholders about audit matters

B To have access to the company's books and records

C To receive copies of the written resolutions of the company

D To receive notice of, and attend, board meetings of the directors

5   Chapter summary

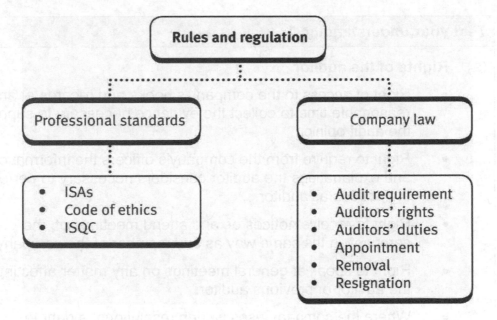

Test your understanding answers

Test your understanding 1

(a) **Rights of the auditor**

- Right of access to the company's books and records at any reasonable time to collect the evidence necessary to support the audit opinion.

- Right to require from the company's officers the information and explanations the auditor considers necessary to perform their duties as auditor.

- Right to receive notices of, and attend meetings of, the company in the same way as any member of the company.

- Right to speak at general meetings on any matter affecting the auditor or previous auditor.

- Where the company uses written resolutions, a right to receive a copy of those resolutions.

(b) **Auditor eligibility**

A person is not eligible to act as an auditor in the following circumstances:

- They are not a member of a recognised supervisory body (RSB) or not allowed to practise under the rules of an RSB.

- They are an officer or employee of the company.

- They are a business partner or employee of such a person.

(c) **Steps required to remove an auditor from an engagement**

- A decision must be made by the shareholders at a general meeting usually with a majority vote being required.

- Advance notice must be given to the company and the auditors prior to any general meeting.

- Auditors have the right to attend and speak at the general meeting or have representations read out on their behalf.

Test your understanding 2

1	A	Auditing standards are professional guidance, not law.
2	C	By issuing standards, audits should be performed more consistently which should improve quality.
3	A	An auditor cannot be an employee or director of the company or someone with a close personal relationship with someone that could influence the audit. An ex-employee or director can be involved with the audit once a cooling-off period has passed.
4	D	Shareholders.
5	B	Whilst directors may be shareholders of the company they work for, large public companies will have a significant number of shareholders who are not involved in the operations of the company. Auditors are not allowed to be business partners of the directors of a company they audit.

Test your understanding 3

1	D	To become a chartered certified accountant an individual must pass the required exams, demonstrate practical experience of a minimum of three years and complete an ethical assessment. The exams do not need to take three years. In some cases, individuals may take less time, in others they may take more time.
2	C	You will not be able to be on the audit team as your mother is the engagement partner and this creates an ethical threat. Your mother may be more lenient when reviewing your work which will impact on the quality of the engagement.
		All new auditors have to start somewhere. Competence is addressed by the firm providing adequate training and supervision of audit team members. All work will be reviewed to ensure it has been performed competently.
3	B	Malta Co requires an audit because it is a financial services company and therefore a public interest entity. Malta Co would not require an audit if it was not a public interest entity as the audit threshold has not been met. The audit threshold requires a company to meet both conditions, revenue of at least $10 million AND more than 50 employees.

4	A, E	All professional accountancy firms must comply with professional regulations including quality control standards. These standards require firms to implement quality control policies and procedures to ensure reports issued are appropriate. The firm must monitor its own policies and procedures to ensure they are relevant, adequate and working effectively. ACCA will periodically perform quality reviews of firms to ensure compliance with professional standards. Quality reviews are not undertaken by the IAASB as this is the body responsible for developing new ethical and auditing standards to be used by firms. The auditor's work is not subject to legal investigation or review unless a claim is brought against a firm for breach of contract or negligence.
5	D	The auditor only has a right to attend general meetings of the shareholders, not the meetings of the directors.

3

Corporate governance

Chapter learning objectives

This chapter covers syllabus areas:

- A3 – Corporate governance

Detailed syllabus objectives are provided in the introduction section of the text book.

PER

One of the PER performance objectives (PO4) is governance risk and control. You contribute to effective governance in your area. You evaluate, monitor and implement risk management procedures, complying with the spirit and the letter of policies, laws and regulations. Working through this chapter should help you understand how to demonstrate that objective.

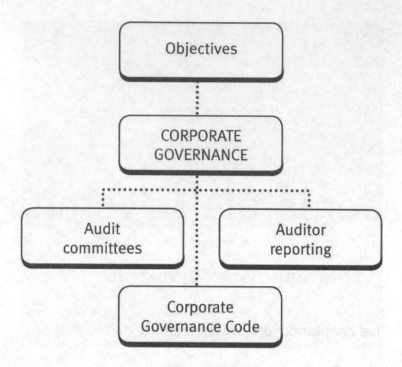

 This chapter further develops the principles of corporate governance covered in Business Technology (previously Accountant in Business) at the Applied Knowledge level.

1 Objectives and importance of corporate governance

Corporate governance is the means by which a company is operated and controlled.

The aim of corporate governance is to ensure that companies are run well in the interests of their shareholders, employees, and other key stakeholders such as the wider community.

The aim is to try and prevent company directors from abusing their power which may adversely affect these stakeholder groups. For example, the directors may pay themselves large salaries and bonuses whilst claiming they have no money to pay a dividend to shareholders. Similarly, they may be making large numbers of staff redundant but awarding themselves a pay rise.

In response to major scandals (e.g. Enron), regulators sought to change the rules surrounding the governance of companies, particularly publicly owned ones.

In the US the Sarbanes Oxley Act (2002) introduced a set of rigorous corporate governance laws. The UK Corporate Governance Code introduced a set of best practice corporate governance initiatives into the UK.

Advantages of a company following good corporate governance principles:

- Greater transparency
- Greater accountability
- Efficiency of operations
- Better able to respond to risks
- Less likely to be mismanaged.

High profile corporate failures

Carillion

In 2018, construction company Carillion was placed into liquidation after building up debts of £1.5 billion. The company was a major contractor for the UK government with contracts to build hospitals and schools, as well as facilities management and ongoing maintenance. It was the second largest construction company in the UK and employed more than 43,000 people. The company took on too many projects and failed to realistically price the contracts resulting in huge cost overruns and losses being made. In December 2017 the major banks refused to lend more money to Carillion and in 2018 the company went into liquidation.

The collapse of the company caused significant problems, not just for the shareholders, but for the significant number of employees who lost their jobs, the government contracts that were in progress that would not be completed, and for the suppliers who would not be paid.

One of the issues highlighted by Carillion was that of executive pay. Executive directors were earning significant amounts of money despite running the company into the ground. In 2016, the former chief executive director earned more than £2 million. The Institute of Directors has said that the collapse of Carillion is due to a lack of effective governance. Directors' remuneration allowed them to benefit despite the collapse of the company as there were no claw back conditions. The company could only request claw back from directors if there was gross misconduct or misstatement of financial results. The directors also received payoffs despite being responsible for the collapse.

The collapse of Carillion has also returned focus to the big accounting firms and their part in allowing companies to fail by not having raised the alarm much earlier.

Enron

In the year 2000 Enron, a US based energy company, employed 22,000 people and reported revenues of $101 billion. In late 2001 they filed for bankruptcy protection. After a lengthy investigation it was revealed that Enron's financial statements were sustained substantially by systematic, and creatively planned, accounting fraud.

In the wake of the fraud case the shares of Enron fell from over $90 each to just a few cents each, a number of directors were prosecuted and jailed and their auditors, Arthur Andersen, were accused of obstruction of justice and forced to stop auditing public companies. This ruling against Arthur Andersen was overturned at a later date but the damage was done and the firm ceased trading soon after.

This was just one of a number of high profile frauds to occur at that time.

The Enron scandal is an example of the abuse of the trust placed in the management of publicly traded companies by investors. This abuse of trust usually takes one of two forms:

- Direct extraction from the company of excessive benefits by management, e.g. large salaries, pension entitlements, share options, use of company assets (jets, apartments etc.)

- Manipulation of the share price by misrepresenting the company's profitability, usually so that shares in the company can be sold or options 'cashed in'.

In response, regulators sought to change the rules surrounding the governance of companies, particularly publicly owned ones. In the US the Sarbanes Oxley Act (2002) introduced a set of rigorous corporate governance laws and at the same time the Combined Code (now called the UK Corporate Governance Code) introduced a set of best practice corporate governance initiatives into the UK.

2 The Corporate Governance Code

The Organisation for Economic Co-operation and Development (OECD) has produced a set of six principles of corporate governance to guide policy makers when setting regulations for their own country.

The six OECD principles are:

- Ensuring the basis of an effective corporate governance framework

- The rights and equitable treatment of shareholders and key ownership functions

- Institutional investors, stock markets, and other intermediaries

- The role of stakeholders in corporate governance

- Disclosure and transparency

- The responsibilities of the board.

The UK Corporate Governance Code reflects the OECD principles.

The UK Corporate Governance Code is particularly important for publicly traded companies because large amounts of money are invested in them, either by 'small' shareholders, or from pension schemes and other financial institutions. The wealth of these companies significantly affects the health of the economies where their shares are traded.

The code is split into five parts:

- Board leadership and company purpose
- Division of responsibilities
- Composition, succession and evaluation
- Audit, risk and internal control
- Remuneration.

The Code does not set out a rigid set of rules; instead it offers flexibility through the application of principles and 'comply or explain' provisions and supporting guidance.

The main requirements provisions of the Code are given below.

Board leadership and company purpose

Principles

- A successful company is led by an effective board whose role is to promote long-term sustainable success thereby generating value for shareholders.

- The board should establish the company's purpose, values and strategy. The directors should lead by example and promote the desired culture.

- The board should ensure that the necessary resources are in place for the company to meet its objectives. The board should establish a framework of effective controls to enable risk to be assessed and managed.

- The board should ensure effective engagement with, and encourage participation from shareholders and stakeholders.

- The board should ensure that workforce policies and practices are consistent with the company's values. The workforce should be able to raise matters of concern.

Main provisions

- The board should describe in the annual report how opportunities and risks to the future success of the business have been considered and addressed.

- The board should assess and monitor culture. Where behaviour throughout the business is not consistent with the purpose, values or strategy, the board should ensure management has taken corrective action.

- In addition to formal general meetings, the chair should seek regular engagement with major shareholders. The board as a whole should understand the views of the shareholders.

- When 20% or more of votes have been cast against the board recommendation for a resolution, the company should explain what actions it intends to take to understand the reasons behind the result.

- The board should understand the views of the company's other key stakeholders and describe how their interests have been considered in board discussions. For engagement with the workforce, the company should use a director appointed from the workforce, a workforce advisory panel or a designated non-executive director (NED).

- The workforce should be able to raise concerns in confidence and anonymously ('whistleblowing').

- The board should take action to manage conflicts of interest.

- Directors' concerns about the operation of the board or management of the company that cannot be resolved should be minuted. On resignation, a NED should provide a written statement to the chair for circulation to the board if they have any concerns.

Board roles

The chair's role

- Leads the board of directors.

- Enables flow of information and discussion at board meetings.

- Ensures satisfactory channels of communication with the external auditors.

- Ensures effective operation of board sub-committees.

- The chair should be independent to enhance effectiveness.

The chief executive's role

- Ensures the effective operation of the company.

- Head of the executive directors.

Executive directors

The executive directors have responsibility for running the company on a day to day basis.

Non-executive directors (NEDs)

The NEDs monitor the executive directors and contribute to the overall strategy and direction of the organisation. They are usually employed on a part-time basis and do not take part in the routine executive management of the company.

NEDs will:

- participate at board meetings.

- bring experience, insight and contacts to assist the board.

- sit on sub-committees as independent, knowledgeable parties.

Advantages of participation by NEDs

- Oversight of the whole board.

- As they are independent they act as a 'corporate conscience'.

- They bring external expertise to the company.

Disadvantages

- It may be difficult to find the right NEDs who have the relevant skills and experience required by the company.

- They, and the sub-committees, may not be sufficiently well-informed or have time to fulfil the role competently.

- They are subject to the accusation that they are staffed by an 'old boys' network and may fail to report significant problems and approve unjustified pay rises.

- The cost. NEDs are normally remunerated and their fees can be quite expensive.

Division of responsibilities

Principles

- The chair leads the board and is responsible for its overall effectiveness.

- The chair should ensure effective contribution of all board members.

- The chair should ensure that directors receive clear, accurate and timely information.

- The board should be balanced so that no individual or small group of individuals can dominate board decisions.

- NEDs should have sufficient time to meet their board responsibilities and should hold management to account.

- The board should ensure it has the policies, processes, information, time and resources it needs to function effectively and efficiently.

Main provisions

- The chair should be independent on appointment.

- The chair and chief executive roles should not be taken by the same individual. The chief executive should not become the chair of the same company.

- At least half the board, excluding the chair should be independent NEDs.

- The board should identify the independent NEDs in the annual report. Independence would be deemed to be affected if a director:

  - is, or has been, an employee of the company or group within the last five years

  - has, or has had within the last three years, a material business relationship with the company either directly, or as a partner, shareholder, director or senior employee of a body that has such a relationship with the company

  - has received or receives remuneration from the company in addition to a director's fee, participates in the company's share option or a performance-related pay scheme, or is a member of the company's pension scheme

  - has close family ties with any of the company's advisers, directors or senior employees

  - holds cross-directorships or has significant links with other directors through involvement in other companies or bodies

  - represents a significant shareholder

  - has served on the board for more than nine years from the date of their first appointment.

- One of the independent NEDs should be appointed as a senior independent director to provide a sounding board for the chair.

- The NEDs and the senior independent director should meet without the chair present at least annually to appraise the chair's performance.

- NEDs appoint and remove executive directors and scrutinise performance against agreed performance objectives.

- The responsibilities of the chair, chief executive, senior independent director, board and committees should be set out in writing and publicly available.

- The annual report should set out the number of meetings of the board and its committees and the attendance of each director.

- New appointments to the board should take into account other demands on the director's time. Full time executive directors should not take on more than one NED role in a FTSE 100 company or other significant appointment. Appointments should not be made without prior approval of the board.

Composition, succession and evaluation

Principles

- Appointments to the board should be subject to a formal, rigorous and transparent procedure.

- An effective succession plan should be maintained for board and senior management.

- Appointments and succession should be based on merit and objective criteria and should promote diversity.

- The board and its committees should have a combination of skills, experience and knowledge.

- Annual evaluation of the board should consider its composition, diversity and how effectively members work together to achieve objectives.

Main provisions

- A nomination committee should be established to appoint board members.

- A majority of the committee members should be independent NEDs.

- The chair should not be a member of the committee when the committee is dealing with the appointment of their successor.

- All directors should be subject to annual re-election.

- The chair should not remain in post for more than nine years from the date of their first appointment. This period can be extended for a limited time to facilitate effective succession planning.

- Open advertising and/or an external search consultancy should be used for the appointment of the chair and NEDs.

- There should be a formal and rigorous annual evaluation of the performance of the board, its committees, the chair and the individual directors.

- The chair should consider having a regular external board evaluation at least every three years for FTSE 350 companies, and the external evaluator should be identified in the annual report.

- The annual report should describe the work of the nomination committee including the process used in making appointments, how the board evaluation has been conducted, the policy on diversity and inclusion and the gender balance of those in senior management.

Nomination committee

The role of the nomination committee is to decide on appointments of board directors and senior management. This is to ensure the best person for the job is recruited. The majority of this committee should be independent NEDs.

Advantages

- Reduces the risk of 'jobs for the boys'. Executive directors might appoint other directors with whom they are friends or used to work with but do not have the skills required.

- Reduces the risk of improperly affecting board decisions. Executives might appoint people to the board they know will vote in favour of the same decisions as them and can therefore influence board decisions which may not be in the best interests of the company.

Audit, risk and internal control including audit committees

Principles

- The board should establish formal and transparent policies and procedures to ensure the independence and effectiveness of internal and external audit functions and satisfy itself on the integrity of financial and narrative statements.

- The board should present a fair, balanced and understandable assessment of the company's position and prospects.

- The board should establish procedures to manage risk, oversee the internal control framework, and determine the nature and extent of the principal risks the company is willing to take in order to achieve its long-term strategic objectives.

Main provisions

- The board should establish an audit committee of independent NEDs, with a minimum membership of three, or in the case of smaller companies, two.

- The chair of the board should not be a member of the audit committee.

- At least one member must have recent and relevant financial experience.

- The committee as a whole must have competence relevant to the sector in which the company operates.

- The main roles and responsibilities of the audit committee include:

    - Monitoring the integrity of the financial statements.

    - Providing advice on whether the annual report and accounts are fair, balanced and understandable.

- Reviewing the company's internal financial controls and risk management systems.

- Monitoring and reviewing the effectiveness of the internal audit function.

- If there is no internal audit function in place, they should consider annually whether there is a need for one and make a recommendation to the board.

- Making recommendations in relation to the appointment and removal of the external auditor and their remuneration.

- Reviewing and monitoring the external auditor's independence and objectivity and the effectiveness of the audit process.

- Developing and implementing policy on the engagement of the external auditor to supply non-audit services.

- The annual report should describe the work of the audit committee including:

  - Significant issues considered relating to the financial statements.

  - How it has assessed the independence and effectiveness of the external audit process.

  - Where there is no internal audit function, an explanation for the absence and how internal assurance is achieved.

  - An explanation of how auditor independence and objectivity are safeguarded, if the external auditor provides non-audit services.

- The directors should explain in the annual report their responsibility for preparing the annual report and accounts.

- The board should carry out a robust assessment of the company's emerging and principal risks.

- The board should confirm in the annual report that it has completed this assessment, including a description of its principal risks, what procedures are in place to identify emerging risks, and an explanation of how these are being managed or mitigated.

- The board should monitor the company's risk management and internal control systems and, at least annually, carry out a review of their effectiveness and report on that review in the annual report. The monitoring and review should cover all material controls, including financial, operational and compliance controls.

- The board should state whether it considers it appropriate to adopt the going concern basis of accounting in preparing the financial statements, and identify any material uncertainties to the company's ability to continue to do so over a period of at least 12 months from the date of approval of the financial statements.

- The board should explain in the annual report how it has assessed the prospects of the company, over what period it has done so and why it considers that period to be appropriate.

- The board should state whether it has a reasonable expectation that the company will be able to continue in operation and meet its liabilities as they fall due over the period of their assessment.

Audit committees

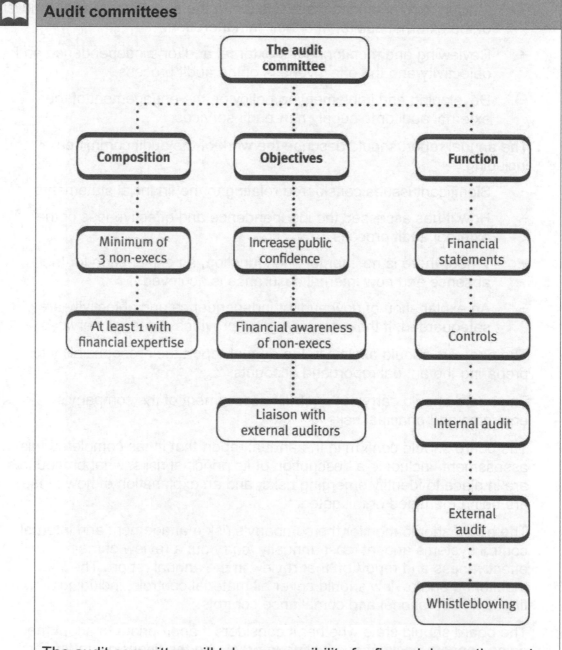

The audit committee will take responsibility for financial reporting and internal control matters. The audit committee is able to view a company's affairs in a detached and independent way and liaise effectively between the main board of directors and the internal and external auditors.

The objectives of the audit committee

- Increasing public confidence in the credibility and objectivity of published financial information (including unaudited interim statements).

- Assisting directors (particularly executive directors) in meeting their responsibilities in respect of financial reporting.

- Strengthening the independent position of a company's external auditor by providing an additional channel of communication.

Benefits of an audit committee

- Improved credibility of the financial statements through an impartial review of the financial statements and discussion of significant issues with the external auditors.

- Increased public confidence in the audit opinion as the audit committee will monitor the independence of the external auditors.

- Stronger control environment as the audit committee help to create a culture of compliance and control.

- The skills, knowledge and experience (and independence) of the audit committee members can be an invaluable resource for a business.

- It may be easier and cheaper to arrange finance, as the presence of an audit committee can give a perception of good corporate governance.

- It will be less of a burden to meet listing requirements if an audit committee (which is usually a listing requirement) is already established.

- The internal audit function will report to the audit committee increasing their independence and adding weight to their recommendations.

Problems

- Difficulties recruiting the right non-executive directors who have relevant skills, experience and sufficient time to become effective members of the committee.

- The cost. Non-executive directors are normally remunerated and their fees can be quite expensive.

FRC Guidance on audit committees

This guidance is designed to assist company boards when implementing the Corporate Governance Code.

- Companies with a premium listing are required to comply with the Code or explain why they have not done so.

- Audit committee arrangements should be proportionate to the task and will vary according to size and complexity of the company.

- There should be a frank, open working relationship and a high level of mutual respect between audit committee chair and board chair, the chief executive and the finance director.

- Management must ensure the audit committee is kept properly informed. All directors must cooperate with the audit committee.

- The core functions of audit committees are oversight, assessment and review. It is not the duty of the audit committee to carry out functions that belong to others. For example, they should make sure there is a proper system in place for monitoring of internal controls but should not do the monitoring themselves.

- The board should review the audit committee's effectiveness annually.

The audit committee should:

- Receive induction and training for new members and continuing training as required.

- Hold as many meetings as the roles and responsibilities require and it is recommended that no fewer than three meetings are held.

- Meet the external and internal auditors without management at least annually to discuss any issues arising from the audit.

- Report to the board on how it has discharged its responsibilities.

- Ensure the interests of the shareholders are properly protected in relation to financial reporting and internal control.

- Review and report to the board on the significant financial reporting issues and judgments in connection with the preparation of the financial statements.

- Consider the appropriateness of significant accounting policies, significant estimates and judgments.

- Receive reports from management on the effectiveness of systems and the conclusions of any testing carried out by internal and external auditors.

- Review the systems established by management to identify, assess, manage and monitor financial risks.

- Monitor and review the effectiveness of the company's internal audit function. Where there is no internal audit function the audit committee should consider annually the need for one and make a recommendation to the board.

- Review whistleblowing arrangements for staff of the company to raise concerns in confidence.

Annual report

A separate section of the annual report should describe the work of the committee. Specifically:

- A summary of the role of the audit committee.

- The names and qualifications of all members of the audit committee.

- The number of audit committee meetings.

- The significant issues that the committee considered in relation to the financial statements and how these issues were addressed.

- An explanation of how it has assessed the effectiveness of the external audit process and the approach taken to the appointment or reappointment of the external auditor.

- If the external auditor provides non-audit services, how auditor objectivity and independence is safeguarded.

- Where there is a disagreement between the audit committee and the board which cannot be resolved, the audit committee should have the right to report the issue to shareholders as part of its report within the annual report.

- The audit committee chair should be present at the AGM to answer questions.

External audit matters

The audit committee is responsible for making a recommendation on the appointment, reappointment and removal of the external auditors.

FTSE 350 companies should put the audit out to tender at least once every ten years to enable the audit committee to compare the quality and effectiveness of the services provided by the incumbent auditor with those of other firms.

The audit committee should:

- Annually assess and report to the board on the qualification, expertise and resources, and independence of the external auditors and the effectiveness of the audit process.

- Investigate reasons for the resignation of the external auditor and consider whether any action is required.

- Assess the independence and objectivity of the external auditor annually.

- Set and apply a formal policy for non-audit services that are pre-approved, require approval or are not allowed.

- Agree a policy for employment of former employees of the external auditor taking into account the Ethical Standards, paying particular attention to people who were part of the audit team. The audit committee should consider whether there has been any impairment of the auditor's independence and objectivity in respect of the audit.

- Monitor the external audit firm's compliance with ethical standards relating to partner rotation and fee levels.

Internal audit

Internal audit has an important role to play in assisting the board, and audit committee, fulfil their corporate governance responsibilities.

Internal audit will work closely with the audit committee. The audit committee will:

- Ensure that the internal auditor has direct access to the board chair and to the audit committee and is accountable to the audit committee.

- Review and assess the annual internal audit work plan.

- Receive periodic reports on the results of internal audit work.

- Review and monitor management's responsiveness to the internal auditor's findings and recommendations.

- Meet with the head of internal audit at least once a year without the presence of management.

- Monitor and assess the effectiveness of internal audit in the overall context of the company's risk management system.

The roles and functions of internal audit are covered in the chapter 'Internal audit'.

Risk management in practice

The main aim of risk management is to protect the business from unforeseen circumstances that could negatively impact the profitability of the company and stop it achieving its strategic goals.

The board must monitor the company's risk assessment and internal control systems annually. A risk committee may be established to perform this role. The risk committee will be responsible for advising the board on the company's risk appetite, reviewing and approving the risk management strategy and advising the board on risk exposures.

Companies face many risks, for example:

- The risk that products become technologically obsolete.
- The risk of losing key staff.
- The risk of a catastrophic failure of IT systems.
- The risk of changes in government policy.
- The risk of fire or natural disaster.

Companies need mechanisms in place to identify and then assess those risks. In so doing, companies can rank risks in terms of their relative importance by scoring them with regard to their likelihood and potential impact. This could take the form of a 'risk map'.

A risk map enables the company to assess the likelihood or probability of a risk occurring and the likely impact to the company.

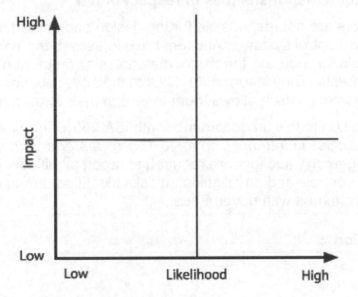

Once identified and assessed, the company must decide on appropriate ways to manage those risks.

Risk management can involve:

- Transferring the risk to another party e.g. by buying insurance or outsourcing part of the business.
- Avoiding the risk by ceasing the risky activity.
- Reducing the risk by implementing effective systems and controls.
- Accepting the risk and bearing the cost and consequence if the risk happens. This may be likely for risks which are deemed low in terms of probability or impact to the company.

A risk that ranked as highly likely to occur and high potential impact to the business would be prioritised as requiring immediate action. A risk that was considered both low likelihood and low impact might be ignored or insured against.

Internal controls and risk management

One way of minimising risk is to incorporate internal controls into a company's systems and procedures.

Director's responsibilities in respect of risk

It is the director's responsibility to implement internal controls and monitor their application and effectiveness.

The risks considered by management are numerous. They come from both external (environmental) and internal (operational) sources.

The main aim of risk management is to protect the business from unforeseen circumstances that could negatively impact the profitability of the company and stop it achieving its strategic goals.

Auditor's responsibilities in respect of risk

Auditors are not responsible for the design and implementation of their clients' control systems. Auditors have to assess the effectiveness of controls for reducing the risk of material misstatement of the financial statements. They incorporate this into their overall audit risk assessment, which allows them to design their further audit procedures.

In addition to this, in accordance with ISA 265 *Communicating Deficiencies in Internal Control to Those Charged With Governance and Management*, auditors are required to report significant deficiencies in client controls and any significant risks identified during the audit to those charged with governance.

Remuneration

Principles

- Remuneration should be designed to promote the long-term sustainable success of the company. Executive remuneration should be aligned to the company purpose, values and long-term strategy.

- The board should establish formal and transparent procedures for developing the policy for executive directors' remuneration.

- No director should be involved in setting his own pay.

- Directors should exercise independent judgment and discretion when authorising remuneration, taking account of company and individual performance, and wider circumstances.

Main provisions

- A remuneration committee comprising a minimum of three independent NEDs should be established.

- The chair of the board cannot chair the remuneration committee and can only be a member of the committee if they were independent on appointment.

- The remuneration committee should determine the policy for executive director remuneration and set remuneration for the chair, executive directors and senior management.

- The committee should review workforce remuneration and related policies taking these into account when setting the policy for executive director remuneration.

- NED remuneration should be determined by the board. It should reflect time commitment and responsibilities of the role and should not include share options or other performance related elements.

- Remuneration schemes should promote long-term shareholdings by executive directors. Shares awards should be released for sale on a phased basis and be subject to a total vesting and holding period of five years or more.

- Remuneration schemes should include provisions that enable a company to recover or withhold sums or share awards and specify the circumstances in which it would be appropriate to do so.

- Only basic salary should be pensionable and pension contribution rates should be aligned with those available to the workforce.

- Notice or contract periods should be one year or less. If it is necessary to offer longer periods to new directors the period should reduce to one year or less after the initial period.

- When determining the executive director remuneration policy and practices the committee should ensure remuneration arrangements are transparent, easy to understand, predictable, proportionate, and aligned to culture. The risks from excessive rewards should be identified and mitigated and the range of possible values of rewards should be identified and explained at the time of approving the policy.

- The work of the remuneration committee should be described in the annual report.

Remuneration committee

The role of the remuneration committee is to set the remuneration packages for the chair, executive directors and senior management. This is to ensure that they are paid fairly, but not excessively.

> **Advantages**
>
> - Decisions are based on agreement of several people, reducing the risk of bribes from directors in return for a higher package.
>
> - No director is involved in setting his own pay which could lead to excessive amounts being paid.
>
> - Long-term performance related elements will be included to avoid the risk that directors are rewarded for poor performance or rewarded for taking decisions which may have a positive outcome in the short-term but would not be good for long-term success of the company.

3 Relevance of corporate governance to external auditors

If a company complies with corporate governance best practice, the control environment of the company is likely to be stronger. There will be a greater focus on financial reporting and internal controls which should reduce control risk and inherent risk which together reduce the risk of material misstatements in the financial statements. In some jurisdictions, external auditors are required to report on whether companies are compliant with corporate governance principles.

There is significantly more communication between audit committees and external auditors in the current environment. If the company, including the audit committee, demonstrates good corporate governance, this should result in the company taking more responsibility for its actions, the independence of the auditor being greater, and the overall quality of the audit being higher.

Auditor reporting responsibilities

ISA (UK) 700 requires the auditor to report by exception in the auditors' reports of companies disclosing compliance with the UK Corporate Governance Code where the annual report includes:

- A statement given by the directors that they consider the annual report and accounts taken as a whole is fair, balanced and understandable and provides the information necessary for shareholders to assess the entity's performance, business model and strategy, that is inconsistent with the knowledge acquired by the auditor in the course of performing the audit.

- A section describing the work of the audit committee that does not appropriately address matters communicated by the auditor to the audit committee.

- An explanation, as to why the annual report does not include such a statement or section that is materially inconsistent with the knowledge acquired by the auditor in the course of performing the audit.

- Other information that, in the auditor's judgment, contains a material inconsistency.

Other countries may have different reporting requirements in accordance with local legislation and regulations.

Test your understanding 1

The directors of Murray Co are interested in being able to report that they comply with best practice corporate governance principles and have asked for your thoughts.

The finance director has provided you with the following information:

The board consists of the chief executive officer, finance director, HR director, production director and sales director. In addition, there are two non-executive directors who were appointed last year by the chief executive as they are his aunt and uncle. Previously they ran their own small cafe and used a firm of accountants for all financial matters due to their own lack of expertise in that area.

The contracts signed by the non-executive directors state that they are in place until they decide to leave or unless they are found guilty of misconduct. They receive an annual fee and a number of share options in Murray Co as their remuneration.

Since appointment, the two non-executives have formed an audit committee consisting of themselves and the human resources director as it was felt that the finance director would not be an independent member of the committee.

They have also formed a remuneration committee with the finance director and are currently in the process of proposing and approving the salaries for all of the directors for the coming year.

Required:

(a) **Explain whether Murray Co is required to comply with a code of corporate governance.**

(b) **Explain the strengths of Murray Co's current governance arrangements.**

(c) **Identify and explain the weaknesses in Murray Co's current governance arrangements and for each weakness recommend an action the company should take to remedy the weakness.**

Test your understanding 2

You are the audit manager of Tela & Co, a medium sized firm of accountants. Your firm has just been asked for assistance from Jumper & Co, a firm of accountants in an adjacent country. This country has just implemented the internationally recognised codes on corporate governance and Jumper & Co has a number of clients where the codes are not being followed. One example of this, from SGCC, a listed company, is shown below. As your country already has appropriate corporate governance codes in place, Jumper & Co have asked for your advice regarding the changes necessary in SGCC to achieve appropriate compliance with corporate governance codes.

Extract from financial statements regarding corporate governance:

Jiang Sheppard is the chief executive officer and board chair of SGCC. He appoints and maintains a board of five executive and two non-executive directors. While the board sets performance targets for the senior managers in the company, no formal targets are set for the board and no review of board policies is carried out. Board salaries are therefore set and paid by Jiang Sheppard based on his assessment of all the board members, including himself, and not their actual performance.

Internal controls in the company are monitored by the senior accountant, although a detailed review is assumed to be carried out by the external auditors. SGCC does not have an audit committee or an internal audit department.

Annual financial statements are produced, providing detailed information on past performance.

Required:

(i) Explain SIX corporate governance deficiencies in SGCC, and

(ii) Recommend the changes necessary to overcome each deficiency.
(12 marks)

Test your understanding 3

Cocklebiddy Co, a listed company, is currently reviewing its corporate governance practices to ensure they are compliant with regulations. The following is a description of the corporate governance policies they have in place:

- A remuneration committee comprising 3 non-executive directors.

- An audit committee comprising the finance director, the chief executive and 2 non-executive directors.

- Separate people taking on the roles of chair and chief executive.

1 **Which of the following best defines Corporate Governance?**

    A   Corporate governance refers to the importance a company attaches to systems and controls.

    B   Corporate governance is the means by which a company is operated and controlled.

    C   Corporate governance is the extent to which a company is audited, both internally and externally.

    D   Corporate governance is an appraisal activity as a service to the entity.

2 **In terms of the structure of the audit committee of Cocklebiddy Co, which of the following actions should be taken to become compliant with corporate governance regulations?**

    A   A minimum of one non-executive director should be recruited

    B   A minimum of one non-executive director should be recruited and the finance director should be removed

    C   A minimum of one non-executive director should be recruited and the finance director and chief executive should be removed

    D   No action necessary

3   Which TWO of the following are functions of audit committees?

(i)   Planning the annual external audit.

(ii)   Reviewing the effectiveness of internal financial controls.

(iii)   Reviewing and monitoring the external auditor's independence.

(iv)   Processing year-end journal adjustments to the financial statements.

A   (i) and (iv)

B   (i) and (iii)

C   (ii) and (iv)

D   (ii) and (iii)

4   Cocklebiddy Co does not currently have an internal audit function. Which of the following summarises the requirements of corporate governance regulations in respect of internal audit?

A   The audit committee must review the need for an internal audit function on an annual basis

B   The audit committee must establish an internal audit committee as soon as possible

C   There must either be an audit committee or internal audit function in place but there is no requirement to have both

D   The finance director must review the need for an internal audit function and should make a request to the audit committee if it is decided that an internal audit function would be beneficial

5   Which of the following is the main purpose of the remuneration committee?

A   To ensure that the costs of the company are kept under control

B   To ensure no director is involved in setting his own pay and the pay that is set is at an appropriate level

C   To ensure decision making power for the company is not concentrated in the hands of one individual

D   To ensure executives' pay is not performance related to reduce the risk of manipulation

4 Chapter summary

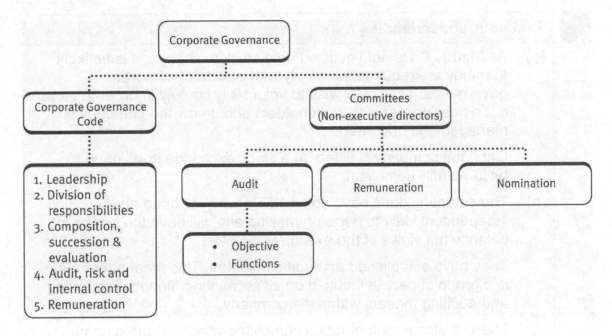

Test your understanding answers

Test your understanding 1

(a) As Murray Co is not yet listed on a stock exchange, it is unlikely that they are required to comply with a code of corporate governance. They may wish to voluntarily comply in order to send out a positive signal to stakeholders about how the company is managed and governed.

Once the company is listed on a stock exchange it will need to become fully compliant.

(b) The company does have some NEDs who will bring an independent view to decision making and will have the power to balance the views of the executive directors.

They have established an audit committee. This means that there is a group of people focused on all accounting, financial reporting and auditing matters within the company.

There is also a remuneration committee which will bring some independence and fairness into the decisions on salaries and rewards of the directors.

(c)

Weakness	Recommendation
There are not enough non-executive directors. Corporate governance principles require the board to be balanced, and currently the executive directors outweigh the NEDs. This means that the executives could ensure all of their proposals are passed at board meetings which reduces the effectiveness of the NEDs.	At least three more NEDs need to be recruited to ensure a balanced board.

There does not appear to be a chair. Corporate governance principles require that there is an independent chair to run the board and a chief executive in charge of running the company. This is to ensure there is not too much power in the hands of one person and so these two roles cannot be fulfilled by the same person.	An independent person should be appointed as chair.
The current NEDs do not appear to be independent. Independent NEDs will be more likely to challenge the decisions of the executive directors. As the two current NEDs are related to the CEO, it is unlikely they would challenge any decisions making them ineffective.	The two NEDS need to be replaced by independent people.
The NEDs appear to have a continuous contract. In order to make sure they work in the company's best interests, all directors should be subject to re-election at regular intervals. This does not appear to be the case here.	All directors should be subject to re-election on an annual basis.
The NEDs have share options as part of their remuneration. Corporate governance principles make it clear that in order to maintain their independence, NEDs should be paid a flat fee for their services based on the time commitment and responsibilities of the role. It should not be related to company performance.	All new NED contracts should have remuneration based on time commitment and responsibilities of the role.

An executive director sits on the audit committee. The sub-committees must be independent to ensure effectiveness, and so it is required that only NEDs sit on the audit committee.	The HR director should be removed from the audit committee and one of the newly appointed independent NEDs should take their place.
Nobody on the audit committee has financial experience. In order to provide valuable input into the accounting and auditing process, at least one member of the audit committee should have financial experience.	When recruiting the new NEDs, the company should look for at least one person with a financial background to sit on the audit committee.
An executive director sits on the remuneration committee. It is a requirement of corporate governance principles that no director should be involved in setting their own remuneration as this could lead to excessive pay being awarded.	The finance director should be removed from the remuneration committee and one of the newly appointed NEDs should take their place. The remuneration committee should set the salaries for the executives, senior management and chair. The board should determine the remuneration of the NEDs.

Test your understanding 2

Why the corporate governance code is not met and why this may cause problems	Recommendation
Jiang Sheppard is chief executive and chair of the company. Jiang Sheppard has too much power over the key decisions of the company.	An independent person should be appointed as chair.
The board ratio is 5:2 in favour of the executive directors. Executive directors can dominate board decisions which may not be in the best interests of the shareholders.	Three more NEDs should be appointed to balance the board.

Jiang Sheppard appoints all directors to the board. Jiang Sheppard may appoint directors who will support his voting at board decisions. There may be no clear and transparent process for determining appointments.	A nomination committee comprising a majority independent NEDs should be established to appoint directors and ensure there is no bias.
Jiang Sheppard sets the pay of the directors as well as setting his own pay. Jiang Sheppard may pay directors more if they agree to back his decisions. He may pay himself more than he deserves.	A remuneration committee comprising independent NEDs should be established to set the pay of the executive directors. The committee should make sure the pay promotes long-term, sustainable success.
The board's performance is not reviewed. If performance is not reviewed there is no accountability for poor performance. The board may not be as effective as it could be at maximising shareholder wealth.	Performance targets should be set and performance against these targets monitored on a regular basis. Directors should be required to explain any under-performance.
It is believed that the external auditor monitors the internal controls. The external auditor will only look at controls relevant to the audit but this cannot be relied upon to determine the effectiveness of the internal control systems across the company.	The audit committee should consider the need for an internal audit function. If the audit committee considers an internal audit function is not required they should describe in the annual report how internal assurance is achieved.
There is no audit committee. Corporate governance codes require an audit committee to be established to take responsibility for the oversight of financial reporting and audit matters.	An audit committee should be established comprising independent NEDs and they will be the main point of contact for internal auditors and external auditors.

Test your understanding 3		
1	B	Corporate governance refers to the means by which a company is operated and controlled.
2	C	The audit committee should comprise 3 independent non-executive directors. The chief executive and finance director should not be members of the audit committee. In addition, it should be confirmed that the NEDs currently sitting on the audit committee are independent.
3	D	Reviewing the effectiveness of internal financial controls and reviewing and monitoring the external auditor's independence.
4	A	There is no requirement for a company to have an internal audit function. The audit committee should review the need for one on an annual basis if the company does not have one.
5	B	Remuneration should be sufficient to attract, retain and motivate but should not be excessive. Directors should not be involved in setting their own pay. Performance related remuneration is encouraged but should promote the long-term sustainable success of the company.

Ethics and acceptance

Chapter learning objectives

This chapter covers syllabus areas:

- A4 – Professional ethics and ACCA's Code of Ethics and Conduct

- B1 – Obtaining, accepting and continuing audit engagements

Detailed syllabus objectives are provided in the introduction section of the text book.

PER

One of the PER performance objectives (PO1) is ethics and professionalism. The fundamental principles of ethical behaviour mean you should always act in the wider public interest. You need to take into account all relevant information and use professional judgment, your personal values and scepticism to evaluate data and make decisions. You should identify right from wrong and escalate anything of concern. You also need to make sure that your skills, knowledge and behaviour are up-to-date and allow you to be effective in your role. Working through this chapter should help you understand how to demonstrate that objective.

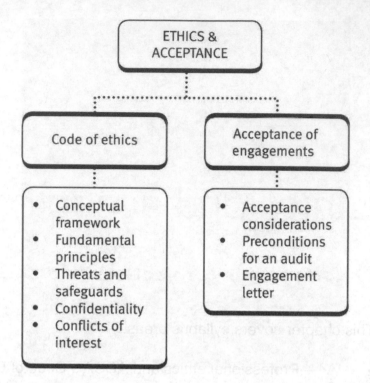

 This chapter further develops the ethical principles covered in Business Technology (previously Accountant in Business) at the Applied Knowledge level.

1   The need for professional ethics

 Practitioners need to **behave, and be seen to behave,** in an ethical, professional manner. This means taking active steps to act in an ethical manner in every professional situation.

Professional accountants have a responsibility to act in the public interest. The purpose of assurance engagements is to increase the confidence of the intended users; therefore the users need to trust the professional who is providing the assurance.

In order to be trusted the assurance provider needs to be independent of their client.

 Independence can be defined as having 'freedom from situations and relationships where objectivity would be perceived to be impaired by a reasonable and informed third party.'

 ### Reasonable and informed third party

The reasonable and informed third party does not need to be an accountant, but has enough relevant knowledge and experience to understand and evaluate the appropriateness of the accountant's conclusions in an impartial manner.

2 The IESBA and ACCA codes and the conceptual framework

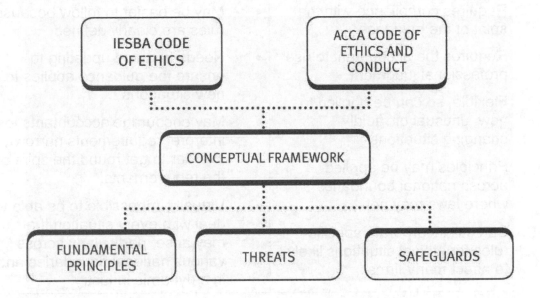

IFAC, through the IESBA, has issued a code of ethics, as has the ACCA. The ACCA Code of Ethics and Conduct is covered in this chapter. However, both of these Codes have the same roots and are, to all intents and purposes identical.

Both follow a conceptual framework which identifies:

- Fundamental principles of ethical behaviour

- Potential threats to compliance with these fundamental principles

- Possible safeguards which can be implemented to eliminate the threats identified, or reduce them to an acceptable level.

Ethical guidance can take either a principles-based approach or rules-based approach.

A conceptual framework relies on a principles-based approach.

Both IESBA and ACCA adopt a principles-based approach.

Principles-based approach	Rules-based approach
• Requires compliance with the spirit of the guidance. • Requires the accountant to use professional judgment. • Flexible, so can be applied to new, unusual or rapidly changing situations. • Principles may be applied across national boundaries where laws may not. • Can still incorporate specific rules for ethical situations likely to affect many firms.	• May be easier to follow because rules are clearly defined. • Needs frequent updating to ensure the guidance applies to new situations. • May encourage accountants to interpret requirements narrowly in order to get round the spirit of the requirements. • Virtually impossible to be able to deal with every situation that may arise, particularly across various national boundaries and in a dynamic industry.

Consequences

Practitioners should apply the spirit of the code in everyday practice. Professional bodies such as the ACCA have the right to discipline members who fail to comply with the code of ethics through a process of disciplinary hearings which can result in:

- Fines
- Suspension of membership
- Withdrawal of membership.

3 The fundamental principles

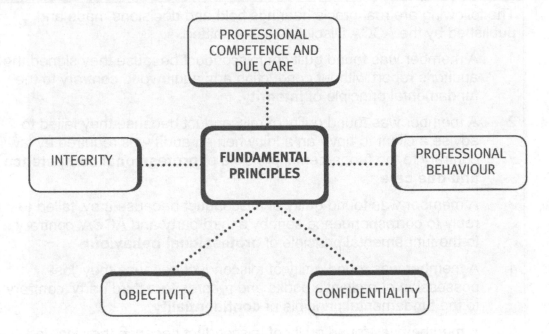

The fundamental principles establish the standard of behaviour expected of a professional accountant.

- **Objectivity:** A professional accountant must <u>not allow bias</u>, <u>conflicts</u> of interest or <u>undue influence of others</u> to compromise professional or business judgments.

- **Professional behaviour:** A professional accountant must <u>comply with relevant laws and regulations</u> and <u>avoid</u> any <u>conduct that might discredit the profession</u>.

- **Professional competence and due care**: A professional accountant must <u>attain</u> and <u>maintain</u> professional <u>knowledge and skill</u> at the level required to ensure that a client or employer receives <u>competent professional services</u> based on current developments in practice, legislation and techniques.

  A professional accountant must <u>act diligently</u> and in accordance with applicable technical and professional standards.

- **Integrity:** A professional accountant must be <u>straightforward</u> and <u>honest</u> in all professional and business relationships.

- **Confidentiality:** A professional accountant must respect the confidentiality of information acquired as a result of professional and business relationships.
  They should <u>not disclose</u> any such information to third parties <u>without</u> proper and specific <u>authority</u>, <u>unless there is a legal or professional right or duty to disclose</u>. Such confidential information <u>should not be used for the personal advantage</u> of members or third parties.

[ACCA Code of Ethics and Conduct, Section 110.1 A1]

Illustration 1 – Fundamentals principles

The following are real précis hearings held and decisions made and published by the ACCA Disciplinary Committee.

1   A member was found guilty of misconduct because they signed the auditor's report without conducting any audit work, contrary to the fundamental principle of **integrity**.

2   A member was found guilty of misconduct because they failed to advise a client to have an audit when an audit was required by law, contrary to the fundamental principle of **professional competence and due care**.

3   A member was found guilty of misconduct because they 'failed to reply to correspondence sent by a third party and ACCA' contrary to the fundamental principle of **professional behaviour**.

4   A member was found guilty of misconduct because they 'lost possession of a client's books and records to a third party' contrary to the fundamental principle of **confidentiality**.

5   A member was found guilty of misconduct because they 'carried out an audit of a company' in which they owned shares 'without implementing appropriate safeguards' contrary to the fundamental principle of **objectivity**.

As a result, a combination of the following sanctions were ordered by the ACCA Disciplinary Committee in each case:

- Suspension of membership
- Exclusion from ACCA
- A fine
- Ordered to pay costs
- Publication of the results of the decision and the member's name on the ACCA website
- Publication of the results of the decision and the member's name in the local press.

4 Threats and safeguards

Firms must establish procedures to:

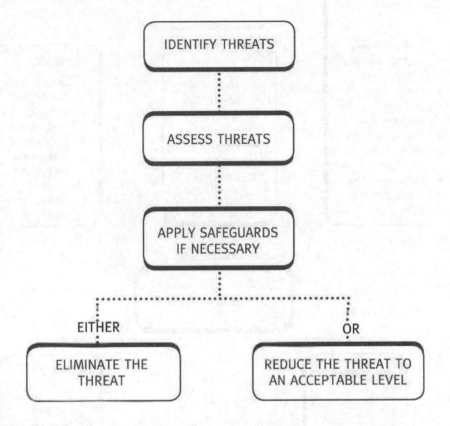

A **safeguard** is an action or measure that eliminates a threat, or reduces it to an acceptable level.

Identifying threats

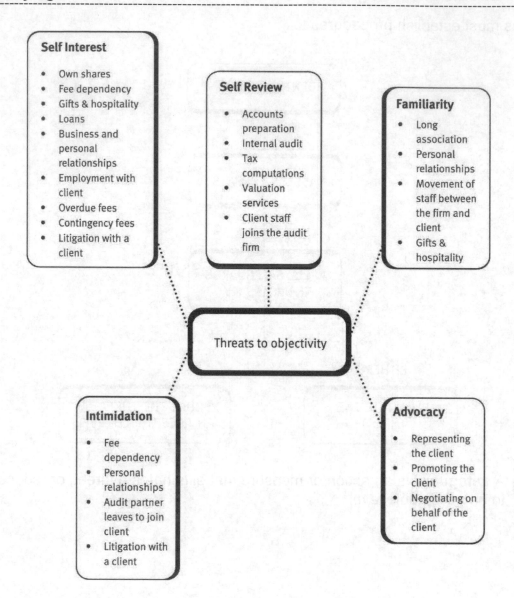

Self Interest

- Own shares
- Fee dependency
- Gifts & hospitality
- Loans
- Business and personal relationships
- Employment with client
- Overdue fees
- Contingency fees
- Litigation with a client

Self Review

- Accounts preparation
- Internal audit
- Tax computations
- Valuation services
- Client staff joins the audit firm

Familiarity

- Long association
- Personal relationships
- Movement of staff between the firm and client
- Gifts & hospitality

Threats to objectivity

Intimidation

- Fee dependency
- Personal relationships
- Audit partner leaves to join client
- Litigation with a client

Advocacy

- Representing the client
- Promoting the client
- Negotiating on behalf of the client

Self-interest threats

Where the auditor has a financial or other interest that will inappropriately influence their judgment or behaviour.

Threat	Safeguards
Fee dependency	*Non-listed clients*
Threats can be created if fees represent a large proportion of one partner or one office of the firm. [410.3 A4]	If fees from an audit client represent a large proportion of the firm's total fees, the firm should implement safeguards such as:
Over-dependence could lead the auditor to ignore adjustments required in the financial statements for fear of losing the client.	• Increasing the client base to reduce dependency
Factors relevant when evaluating the threat include:	• Having an appropriate reviewer who did not take part in the audit review the work performed.
• Operating structure of the firm	[410.3 A6]
• Whether the firm is well established or new	*Listed clients*
• The significance of the client to the firm	• A firm's independence is threatened, and should be reviewed, if total fees from a listed audit client exceed 15% of the firm's total fees for two consecutive years.
[410.3 A2]	• The firm should disclose the issue to those charged with governance at the client.
	• An engagement quality control review should be performed by a person not a member of the audit firm expressing the opinion, or by the professional regulatory body. This can be performed as either a pre-issuance review, before the 2nd year audit opinion is issued or a post-issuance review on the 2nd year audit before the 3rd year audit opinion is issued.
	[R410.4]

Threat	Safeguards
Gifts and hospitality Acceptance of goods, services or hospitality from an audit client can create self-interest, intimidation and familiarity threats as the auditor may feel indebted to the client.	Gifts and hospitality may not be accepted unless the value is trivial and inconsequential. [R420.3] Gifts and hospitality which are trivial and inconsequential but which are intended to improperly influence the behaviour of the recipient should not be accepted. [420.3 A2]
Owning shares/financial interests The auditor will want to maximise return from the investment and overlook audit adjustments which would affect the value of their investment.	A direct, or material indirect, financial interest in the audit client must not be held by: • the firm or a network firm • an audit team member or the immediate family of a team member • a partner working in the office connected with the audit engagement partner • any partner providing non-audit services to the audit client. [R510.4] An immediate family member may hold a financial interest such as pension or share options but must dispose of it as soon as practicable when the family member has the right to do so, e.g. when there is a right to exercise the option. [R510.5] Financial interests received indirectly e.g. by inheritance or gifted, must be disposed of immediately. [R510.9]
Loans and guarantees A loan or guarantee from (or deposit with) an assurance client that is a bank or similar institution will not create a threat to independence provided that: • it is on commercial terms, and • made in the normal course of business.	Loans and guarantees between an audit client and the firm, the audit team member, or their immediate family, that are not in the normal course of business or not on commercial terms are not permitted. [R511.5] Loans to audit clients are not permitted unless immaterial to the firm or individual, and the client. [R511.4]

Threat	Safeguards
Overdue fees A self-interest threat may be created if a significant amount of fees is not paid before the auditor's report for the following year is issued. [410.7 A1]	• Obtain partial or full payment for the fees. • Having an appropriate reviewer who did not take part in the audit review the work performed. [410.7 A2] When fees remain overdue for a significant amount of time, the firm should consider whether the overdue fees constitute a loan, and whether it is appropriate to seek reappointment or continue with the engagement. [R410.8]
Business relationships If audit firms (or members) enter into business relationships with clients (e.g. joint ventures, marketing arrangements), this leads to self-interest because the auditor would have an interest in the successful operation of the client. The purchase of goods and services from an assurance client would not normally give rise to a threat to independence, provided the transaction is in the normal course of business and on commercial terms. [520.6 A1]	A firm, network firm or audit team member should not have a close business relationship with an audit client unless any financial interest is immaterial and the business relationship is insignificant to the client, the firm or the audit team member. [R520.4] If the purchase of goods and services by an audit team member represents a material amount, that person should be removed from the audit team or they should reduce the magnitude of the transactions. [520.6 A2]
Potential employment with an audit client If a member of the engagement team has reason to believe they may become an employee of the client they will not wish to do anything to affect their potential future employment.	The firm must establish policies and procedures which require individuals to notify the firm of the possibility of employment with the client. [R524.5] Remove the individual from the assurance engagement. [524.5 A2] Perform an independent review of any significant judgments made by that individual. [524.5 A3]

Contingent fees	Fees based on a particular outcome, e.g. level of profits of the company, are not permitted for audit engagements. [R410.10]
The auditor would have incentive to ensure a particular outcome is achieved in order to maximise the audit fee. E.g. overlook audit adjustments that would reduce profit if the fee is calculated based on profit.	Contingent fees are not permitted for non-assurance services provided to an audit client if: • The fee is material to the firm. • The outcome of the non-assurance service is dependent on a future judgment related to the audit of a material amount of the financial statements. [R410.11]
Compensation and evaluation policies	**Key audit partners**
A self-interest threat is created when a member of the audit team is evaluated on, or compensated for, selling non-assurance services to that audit client. The significance of the threat will depend on: • The proportion of the individual's compensation or performance evaluation that is based on the sale of such services. • The role of the individual on the audit team. • Whether promotion decisions are influenced by the sale of such services. [411.3 A1]	A key audit partner shall not be evaluated on or compensated based on their success in selling non-assurance services to their audit client. [R411.4] **Audit team members** The firm shall: • Revise the compensation plan or evaluation process for that individual. • Remove that individual from the audit team. • Have an appropriate reviewer review the work of the member of the audit team. [411.3 A2 – A3]

Actual or threatened litigation	It may be possible to continue other assurance engagements, depending on the significance of the threat by:
Litigation could represent a breakdown of trust in the relationship between auditor and client. This may affect the impartiality of the auditor, and lead to a reluctance of management to disclose relevant information to the auditor. [430.3 A1] The significance of the threat depends on the materiality of the litigation and whether the litigation relates to a prior assurance engagement. [430.3 A2]	• Discussing the matter with the client. [430.3 A1] • If the litigation involves an individual, removing that individual from the engagement team. [430.3 A3] • Having an appropriate reviewer review the work done. [430.3 A4] If adequate safeguards cannot be implemented the firm must withdraw from or decline the engagement.

Familiarity threats

When the auditor becomes too sympathetic or too trusting of a client and loses professional scepticism, or where the relationship between the auditor and client goes beyond professional boundaries.

Threat	Safeguards
Long association of senior personnel Using the same senior personnel in an engagement team over a long period may cause the auditor to become too trusting/less sceptical of the client resulting in material misstatements going undetected. A self-interest threat may also be created as a result of the individual's concern about losing a longstanding client. [540.3. A2]	*All clients* • Rotate individuals off the audit team. • Change the role of the individual or the nature of the tasks they perform. • Have an appropriate reviewed review the work performed. • Perform regular independent internal or external quality reviews of the engagement. [540.3 A5 – A6] *Listed clients* • The engagement partner, EQCR or any other key audit partner must not act for a period of more than seven cumulative years ('time-on' period). • After the time-on period, the individual must serve a cooling-off period. [R540.5]

Threat	Safeguards
In relation to the individual the firm should consider: • The length and closeness of the individual's relationship with the client. • The length of time on the audit team. • The extent of direction, supervision and review of work of the individual. • The extent to which the individual has had the ability to influence the outcome of the audit. [540.3 A3 (a)] In relation to the audit client, the firm should consider: • Structural changes in the client's organisation. • Whether the client's management team has changed. • Whether the complexity of the subject matter has changed. [540.3 A3 (b)]	The cooling-off periods are as follows: • 5 years for an engagement partner. • 3 years for an EQCR. • 2 years for a key audit partner. [R540.11 – 13] In exceptional circumstances, a key audit partner may be permitted to serve a one year extension if continuity is important to maintain audit quality. [R540.7] If an audit client becomes a public interest entity, the length of time served as a key audit partner before the client became a public interest entity is taken into account. [R540.8] If a key audit partner was a key audit partner on that engagement at a different firm, the length of time served at the prior firm should be taken into account. [R540.18] An independent regulatory body may provide an audit firm with an exemption from partner rotation if the firm does not have sufficient people with the necessary knowledge and experience to enable partner rotation. [R540.9] During the cooling-off period, the individual shall not: • Be an engagement team member • Consult with the engagement team or client • Be responsible for, or provide, other professional services to the audit client. [R540.20]

Threat	Safeguards
Family and personal relationships A familiarity threat (and self-interest or intimidation threat) may occur when a member of the engagement team has a family or personal relationship with someone at the client who is able to exert significant influence over the financial statements (or subject matter of another assurance engagement). [521.4 A1]	*Audit team members* • Remove the individual from the engagement team. [521.4 A3] • Structure the engagement team so that the individual does not deal with matters that are the responsibility of the family member. [521.4 A4] *Other employees and partners of the firm* A firm should have policies and procedures in place to provide guidance when a partner (or employee) of the firm has a family or personal relationship with someone at the client who is able to exert significant influence over the subject matter, even when the individual is not a member of the engagement team. [R521.8] The firm should structure the individual's responsibilities to reduce any potential influence over the audit engagement and have an appropriate reviewer review the audit work performed. [521.8 A2]
Recruitment services Familiarity, self-interest or intimidation threats may arise if the firm is involved in recruiting senior personnel for the client. The firm may also be considered to be assuming management responsibilities. Reviewing qualifications and interviewing applicants to advise on financial competence is allowed. [609.3 A2]	Recruitment services may be provided to an audit client provided the client makes all management decisions including determining the suitability of the candidate, selecting a suitable candidate, determining employment terms and negotiating remuneration. [R609.4] The firm cannot provide recruitment services in respect of directors or senior management who would be in a position to exert significant influence over the financial statements. [R609.7]

Threat	Safeguards
Employment with an audit client A self-interest, familiarity or intimidation threat may arise where an employee or partner of the firm becomes a director or employee of an audit client (in a position to exert significant influence over the financial statements or other subject matter). [524.3 A1] The firm should ensure no significant connection remains between the individual and the firm, such as entitlement to benefits or payments from the firm, or participation in the firm's business and professional activities. [R524.4] The firm should consider: • The position taken at the client. • The involvement the person will have with the audit team. • The length of time since the individual was a member of the audit team. • The former position of the individual within the audit team. [524.4 A3]	• Modify the audit plan • Assign individuals to the audit team who have sufficient experience in relation to the individual who has joined the client. • Have an appropriate reviewer review the work of the former audit team member. [524.4 A4] *Partners joining listed clients as a director or employee in a position to exert influence over the financial statements* Independence is compromised unless, subsequent to the partner ceasing to be a key audit partner or senior partner, the client had issued audited financial statements covering a period of not less than 12 months, and the partner was not a member of the audit team with respect to the audit of those financial statements. [R524.6] If a senior or managing partner of the firm joins a listed audit client, independence is compromised unless twelve months have passed since the individual was the senior or managing partner. [R524.7]

Self-review threats

Where non-audit work is provided to an audit client and is then subject to audit, the auditor will be unlikely to admit to errors in their own work, or may not identify the errors in their own work.

Threat	Safeguards
Accounting and bookkeeping services Preparing accounting records or financial statements for an audit client might create a self-review threat. [601.1] Accounting and bookkeeping services include: • Preparing accounting records and financial statements • Recording transactions • Payroll services [601.3 A1] Discussing accounting treatments and proposing adjusting journal entries are a normal part of the audit process and do not create threats as long as the client is responsible for making decisions in the preparation of the financial statements. [601.3 A3]	*Non-listed clients* • A firm shall only provide a non-listed audit client with accounting and bookkeeping services which are routine or mechanical in nature. [R601.5] Services which are routine and mechanical in nature and therefore require little or no professional judgment include: • Preparing payroll calculations based on client-originated data. • Recording recurring transactions which are easily determinable. • Calculating depreciation when the client determines the accounting policy, useful life and residual value. • Posting transactions coded by the client to the ledger. • Posting client approved entries to the trial balance. • Preparing financial statements based on information in the client-approved trial balance. [601.4 A1] • Professionals who are not audit team members must be used to perform the service. • An appropriate reviewer who was not involved in providing the service should review the audit work or service performed. [601.5 A1]

Threat	Safeguards
	Listed clients
	A firm cannot provide a listed audit client with accounting and bookkeeping services. [R601.6]
	A firm can provide accounting services for divisions or related entities of a listed client if separate teams are used and divisions or related entities are collectively immaterial to the financial statements subject to audit. [R601.7]
Internal audit services	The audit firm must be satisfied that management takes full responsibility for the internal audit activities and internal controls. [R605.4]
In addition to the self-review threat, the auditor needs to be careful not to assume management responsibilities.	Professionals who are not audit team members must be used to perform the service. [605.4 A5]
The firm should consider: • The materiality of the related financial statement amounts. • The risk of misstatement of the assertions related to the financial statement amounts. • The degree of reliance that the audit team will place on the internal audit service. [605.4 A4]	A firm cannot provide internal audit services for a listed audit client, where the service relates to internal controls over financial reporting, financial accounting systems, or in relation to amounts or disclosures that are material to the financial statements. [R605.5]

Tax services

Providing tax services to an audit client might create a self-review and advocacy threat. [604.1]

Tax services include [604.3 A1]

- Tax return preparation
- Tax calculations for preparing accounting entries
- Tax planning and advisory services
- Tax services involving valuations
- Assistance in the resolution of tax disputes

The firm should consider [604.3 A2]

- The characteristics of the engagement.
- The level of tax expertise of the client's employees.
- The complexity of the tax regime.

Tax return preparation Completion of tax returns does **not** usually create a threat. [604.4 A1]	No safeguards required.
Tax calculations	*Non-listed clients* – use professionals who are not audit team members to perform the service, and an appropriate reviewer who was not involved in providing the service to review the audit work or service performed. [604.5 A5] *Listed clients* – The firm must not prepare tax calculations of current or deferred tax where the figures are material to the financial statements. Where the figures are immaterial, the safeguards for non-listed clients should be applied. [R604.6]
Tax planning and advisory services In addition to the considerations in 604.3 A2, the firm should consider: • The degree of subjectivity involved. • Whether the tax treatment is supported by a private ruling and cleared by the tax authority. [604.7 A3]	A firm shall not provide tax planning and advisory services to an audit client when the effectiveness of the tax advice depends on a particular accounting treatment. [R604.8] When providing such services, the firm should use professionals who are not audit team members to perform the service.

	An appropriate reviewer who was not involved in providing the service should review the audit work or service performed. [604.7 A4]
Tax services involving valuations If the valuation performed for tax purposes is not subject to external review and the effect is material to the financial statements, in addition to the considerations in 604.3 A2, the firm should consider: • The extent to which the valuation methodology is supported by tax law. • The degree of subjectivity. • The reliability of the underlying data. [604.9 A3]	When providing such services, the firm should: • Use professionals who are not audit team members to perform the service. • Have an appropriate reviewer who was not involved in providing the service to review the audit work or service performed. • Obtain pre-clearance from the tax authorities. [604.9 A4]
Assistance in the resolution of tax disputes In addition to the considerations in 604.3 A2, the firm should consider: • The extent to which the outcome of the dispute will have a material effect on the financial statements. • Whether the advice provided is the subject of the tax dispute. • The extent to which the matter is supported by tax law, regulation or established practice. • Whether the proceedings are conducted in public. [604.10 A3]	When providing such services, the firm should: • Use professionals who are not audit team members to perform the service. • Have an appropriate reviewer who was not involved in providing the service to review the audit work or service performed. [604.10 A4] A firm shall not act as an advocate for the audit client before a public tribunal or court in the resolution of a tax matter if the amounts are material to the financial statements. [R604.11] The firm is allowed to have a continuing advisory role e.g. • Responding to specific requests for information. • Providing factual accounts or testimony about the work performed. • Assisting the client in analysing the tax issues.

IT services

IT services may create a self-review threat and also be considered to be assuming management responsibilities.

The firm should consider:

- The nature of the service.
- The nature of IT systems and the extent to which they impact or interact with the client's accounting records or financial statements.
- The degree of reliance that the audit team will place on the IT systems.

[606.4 A1]

The firm can provide IT services which involve:

- Design or implementation of IT systems unrelated to internal controls or financial reporting.
- Implementation of off-the-shelf accounting software that was not developed by the audit firm and does not require significant customisation.
- Evaluating and making recommendations on a system designed or operated by another service provider or by the entity.

[606.3 A2]

All clients

When providing such services, the firm should use professionals who are not audit team members to perform the service. [606.4 A2]

The audit firm must be satisfied that management takes full responsibility for the IT controls and systems. [R606.4]

Listed clients

A firm shall not provide IT systems services to a listed client that form a significant part of the internal controls over financial reporting or generate information that is significant to the financial statements. [R606.5]

Valuation services

Providing valuation services to an audit client might create a self-review and advocacy threat. [603.1]

The firm should consider:

- The use and purpose of the valuation report, including whether the report will be made public.

- The extent of the client's involvement in determining matters of judgment.

- Whether the valuation will have a material effect on the financial statements.

- The degree of dependence on future events that might create significant volatility in the amounts involved.

- The degree of subjectivity.

[603.3 A3]

Some valuations will not involve significant subjectivity e.g. if the underlying assumptions are established by law or when techniques are widely accepted. [603.4 A1]

All clients

- Use professionals who are not audit team members to perform the service.

- Have an appropriate reviewer who was not involved in providing the service review the audit work or service performed.

[603.3 A4]

Non-listed clients

Valuation services shall not be provided to audit clients if the valuation involves a significant degree of subjectivity and the valuation will have a material effect on the financial statements. [R603.4]

Listed clients

Valuation services that are material to the financial statements (regardless of subjectivity) should not be provided to listed audit clients. [R603.5]

Corporate finance services	Where services can be provided:
Self-review and advocacy threats may be created if a firm:	• Use professionals who are not audit team members to perform the service.
• Assists an audit client in developing corporate strategies.	• Have an appropriate reviewer who was not involved in providing the service review the audit work or service performed.
• Identifies possible targets for the audit client to acquire.	[610.3 A3]
• Advises on disposal transactions.	*Prohibited services*
• Assists in raising finance.	• Corporate finance services that involve promoting, dealing in, or underwriting the audit client's shares. [R610.4]
• Provides structuring advice.	
[610.3 A1]	• Corporate finance services where
Factors affecting the existence and significance of any threat include:	– the effectiveness of the advice depends on a particular accounting treatment or presentation in the financial statements
• The degree of subjectivity involved.	
• Whether the outcome will have a material impact on the financial statements.	– the audit team has reasonable doubt as to the appropriateness of the accounting treatment, and
• Whether the effectiveness of the corporate finance advice depends on a particular accounting treatment.	– the outcome will have a material effect of the financial statements.
[610.3 A2]	[R610.5]

Legal services Providing legal services to an audit client might create a self-review and advocacy threat. [608.1] Legal services can only be provided by legally trained, or authorised, personnel. [608.3 A3] The firm should consider: • The materiality of the matter in relation to the financial statements. • The complexity of the legal matter and the degree of judgment necessary. [608.4 A2]	Where services are provided, the firm should: • Use professionals who are not audit team members to perform the service. • Have an appropriate reviewer who was not involved in providing the service review the audit work or service performed. [608.4 A3] A partner or employee of the firm must not act as general counsel for an audit client. [R608.5] A firm shall not act in an advocacy role for an audit client when the amounts involved are material to the financial statements. [R608.6]
Temporary personnel assignments The loan of personnel may create a self-review, advocacy and familiarity threat. [525.2] Staff may be loaned to the client provided: • The loan period is short. • The person does not assume management responsibilities. • The client is responsible for directing and supervising the person. [R525.4]	• Additional review of the work performed by the loaned personnel. • Not including the loaned personnel on the audit team. • Not giving the loaned personnel audit responsibility for any function that they performed during the loaned assignment. [525.3 A1]
Serving as a director or officer of an audit client A self-review and self-interest threat will be created if an individual from the audit firm serves as a director or officer of an audit client. [523.2]	A partner or employee shall not serve as a director or officer of an audit client. [R523.3] A partner or employee shall not serve as company secretary for an audit client unless permitted by local legislation, management makes all relevant decisions, and the duties performed are routine and administrative in nature. [R523.4]

Client staff joins audit firm (recent service with an audit client)	The audit team should not include individuals who during the period covered by the auditor's report have served as a director or employee of the audit client. [R522.3]
A self-interest, self-review, or familiarity threat may arise where an audit team member has recently served as a director or employee of the audit client. [522.2] When service with the audit client was prior to the period covered by the auditor's report, the significance of the threat will depend on: • The position the individual held with the client. • The length of time since the individual left the client. • The role of the audit team member. [522.4 A2]	When service with the audit client was prior to the period covered by the auditor's report, an appropriate reviewer should review the work performed by the audit team member. [522.4 A3]

Advocacy threats

Promoting the position of a client or representing them in some way would mean the audit firm is seen to be 'taking sides' with the client.

Examples include:

• Representing the client in court or in any dispute where the matter is material to the financial statements.

• Negotiating on the client's behalf for finance.

• Loan of personnel from an audit firm to an audit client.

• Providing valuation services to an audit client.

• Providing tax services to an audit client.

Intimidation threats

Actual or perceived pressures from the client, or attempts to exercise undue influence over the assurance provider, create an intimidation threat.

Examples include:

• Fee dependency

• Gifts and hospitality

• Family and personal relationships

• Recruitment services

• Employment with an audit client

• Litigation between the audit firm and client.

5 Confidentiality

External auditors are in a unique position of having a legal right of access to all information about their clients. The client must be able to trust the auditor not to disclose anything about its business to third parties as it could be detrimental to its operations.

Confidential information may be obtained from:

- The firm or employing organisation
- Business relationships i.e. current clients and previous clients
- Prospective clients and employers.

 Members of an assurance team should not disclose any information to anyone outside of the engagement team, whether or not they work for the same firm.

Circumstances in which disclosure is permitted or required

Information should only be disclosed with proper and specific authority, or when there is a legal or professional right or duty to disclose.

Disclosure of confidential information should only be made in the following circumstances:

(a) **Disclosure is required by law**

- Production of documents or other provision of evidence in the course of legal proceedings.
- Disclosure to the appropriate public authorities of infringements of the law that come to light.

(b) **Disclosure is permitted by law and is authorised by the client or the employer.**

(c) **There is a professional duty or right to disclose, when not prohibited by law**

- To comply with the quality review of ACCA or another professional body.
- To respond to an inquiry or investigation by ACCA or a regulatory body.
- To protect the professional interests of a professional accountant in legal proceedings.
- To comply with technical standards and ethics requirements.

Factors to be considered before disclosing confidential information include:

- Whether harm could be caused by the disclosure
- Whether all relevant information is known and substantiated
- Whether the information is to be communicated to appropriate recipients.

[ACCA Code of Ethics and Conduct, Section 114]

Disclosure of confidential information: specific examples

Permitted or required by law

Where there is a statutory right or duty to disclose, the professional accountant will do so without obtaining permission of the client. The most common offences members are likely to encounter in their professional work are in relation to:

- Fraud or theft including fraudulent financial reporting, falsification or alteration of accounting records or other documents and misappropriation of assets

- Tax evasion

- Money laundering

- Drug trafficking or terrorism

- Insider dealing, market abuse, and bribery

- Offences under company law

Public interest

An auditor may disclose information if they consider it to be in the public interest. There is no official definition of 'public interest'. The auditor must employ a combination of judgment and legal advice. A good rule of thumb is that if a member of the public could incur physical or financial damage that the auditor could knowingly have prevented, it is likely that the auditor has failed in their public duty.

In determining the need to disclose matters in the public interest the auditor should consider:

- The relative size of the amounts involved and the extent of the likely financial damage

- Whether members of the public are likely to be affected

- The likelihood of repetition

- The reasons for the client's unwillingness to make the disclosures

- The gravity of the matter

- Relevant legislation, accounting standards and auditing standards

- Legal advice obtained.

The auditor will be protected from the risk of liability provided that disclosure is made in the public interest, disclosure is made to an appropriate body or person, and there is no malice motivating the disclosure.

[ACCA Code of Ethics and Conduct, Section B1]

Conflicts of interest

A conflict of interest arises when the same audit firm is appointed for two companies that interact with each other, for example:

- Companies which compete in the same market

- Companies which trade with each other.

A conflict of interest may create a threat to the fundamental principles of objectivity and confidentiality.

It may be perceived that the auditor cannot provide objective services and advice to a company where it also audits a competitor.

Professional accountants should always act in the best interests of the client. However, where conflicts of interest exist, the firm's work should be arranged to **avoid the interests of one being adversely affected** by those of another and to prevent a breach of **confidentiality**.

In order to ensure this, the firm must **disclose** the nature of the conflict to the relevant parties and **obtain consent to act**.

The following additional safeguards should be implemented:

- Separate engagement teams (with different engagement partners and team members) who are provided with clear guidance on maintaining confidentiality.

- Review of the key judgments and conclusions by an independent person of appropriate seniority.

Measures which should be taken to reduce the threat of disclosure include:

- Procedures to limit access to client files

- Physical separation of confidential information including separate practice areas

- Signed confidentiality agreements by the engagement team members

- Specific training and communication.

If adequate safeguards cannot be implemented (i.e. where the acceptance/ continuance of an engagement would, despite safeguards, materially prejudice the interests of any clients), or if consent is refused, the firm must end or decline to perform professional services that would result in the conflict of interest.

[ACCA Code of Ethics and Conduct, Section 310]

Test your understanding 1

Murray case study: Ethical issues

You are an audit manager in Wimble & Co, a large audit firm which specialises in providing audit and accountancy services to manufacturing companies. Murray Co has asked your firm to accept appointment as external auditor. Murray Co manufactures sports equipment. Your firm also audits Barker Co, another manufacturer of sports equipment, and therefore your firm is confident it has the experience to carry out the audit.

You have been asked to take on the role of audit manager for Murray Co, should your firm accept the engagement. You own a small number of shares in Murray Co, as you used to be an employee of the company. Don Henman, who has been the engagement partner for Barker Co for twelve years, will take the role of engagement partner for Murray Co. The audit senior will be Tim Andrews, as his sister is the financial controller at Murray Co and therefore he knows the business well.

Your firm recently purchased some bibs, footballs and other equipment from Murray Co for the firm's annual football tournament. Murray Co has offered to provide this equipment free of charge to the firm if they accept the role as auditor.

Murray Co would also like your firm to provide taxation and accounting services. Specifically, the company would like you to prepare the financial statements and represent the company in a dispute with the taxation authorities.

The fees for last year's audit of Barker Co have not yet been paid, and you have been asked by Don Henman to look into the matter.

Required:

(a) **Describe the steps Wimble & Co should take to manage the conflict of interest arising from performing the audit of Murray Co and Barker Co.**

(4 marks)

(b) **Explain SIX ethical threats which may affect the independence of Wimble & Co in respect of the audit of Murray Co or Barker Co, and for each threat identify ways in which the threat might be reduced.**

Prepare your answer using two columns headed Ethical threat and Possible safeguard respectively

(12 marks)

6   Accepting/continuing an audit engagement

An audit firm should only take on clients and work of an appropriate level of risk. For this reason, the firm will perform 'client screening'. The firm will consider the following matters before accepting a new engagement or client:

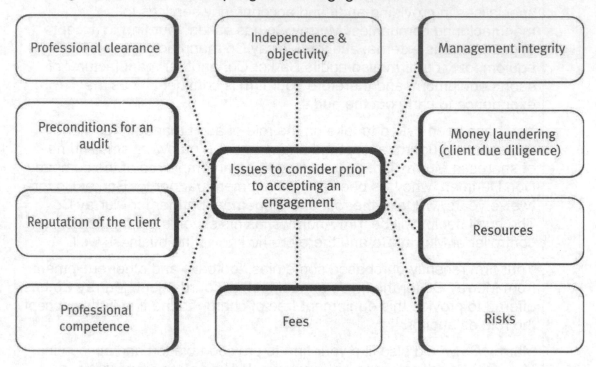

Professional clearance

If offered an audit role, the prospective audit firm must:

- Ask the client for permission to contact the existing auditor (and refuse the engagement if the client refuses).

- Contact the outgoing auditor, asking for all information relevant to the decision whether or not to accept appointment (e.g. overdue fees, disagreements with management, breaches of laws & regulations).

- If a reply is not received, the prospective auditor should try and contact the outgoing auditor by other means e.g. by telephone.

- If a reply is still not received, the prospective auditor may still choose to accept but must proceed with care.

- If a reply is received, consider the outgoing firm's response and assess if there are any ethical or professional reasons why they should not accept appointment.

- The existing auditor must ask the client for permission to respond to the prospective auditor.

- If the client refuses permission, the existing auditor should notify the prospective auditor of this fact.

Independence and objectivity

If the assurance provider is aware, prior to accepting an engagement, that the threats to objectivity cannot be managed to an acceptable level, the engagement should not be accepted.

Management integrity

A lack of integrity may indicate risks such as:

- Aggressive interpretation of accounting standards including window dressing of financial statements, management bias and inappropriate judgements.

- Weak control environment and possible override of controls.

- Intimidation of auditors.

- Criminal activities such as money laundering, fraud and breach of laws and regulations.

- Aggressive tax avoidance/evasion.

- Unreliable management representations.

Money laundering (client due diligence)

The firm must comply with money laundering regulations which require client due diligence to be carried out. If there is any suspicion of money laundering, or actual money laundering committed by the prospective client, the firm cannot accept the engagement.

Resources

The firm should consider whether there are adequate resources available at the time the engagement is likely to take place to perform the work properly. If there is insufficient time to conduct the work with the resources available the quality of the work could be affected.

Risks

Any risks identified with the prospective client (e.g. poor performance, poor controls, unusual transactions) should be considered. These risks can increase the level of engagement risk, i.e. the risk of issuing an inappropriate report.

Fees

The firm should consider the acceptability of the fee. The fee should be commensurate with the level of risk.

In addition, the creditworthiness of the prospective client should be considered as non-payment of fees can create a self-interest threat.

Professional competence

An engagement should only be accepted if the audit firm has the necessary skill and experience to perform the work competently.

Reputation of the client

The audit firm should consider the reputation of the client and whether its own reputation could be damaged by association.

If there are any reasons why the firm believes they may not be able to issue an appropriate report, they should not accept the engagement.

Preconditions for an audit

ISA 210 *Agreeing the Terms of Audit Engagements* and the Code of Ethics and Conduct provides guidance to the professional accountant when accepting new work.

Before accepting (or continuing with) an engagement, the auditor must establish whether the preconditions for an audit are present and that there is a common understanding between the auditor and management and, where appropriate, those charged with governance. [ISA 210, 3]

The preconditions for an audit are that management acknowledges and understands its responsibility for:

* Preparation of the financial statements in accordance with the applicable financial reporting framework.

* Internal control necessary for the financial statements to give a true and fair view.

* Providing the auditor with access to all relevant information and explanations.

[ISA 210, 6b]

If the client imposes a limitation on the scope of the auditor's work to the extent that the auditor believes it likely that a disclaimer of opinion will ultimately be issued, then the auditor shall not accept the engagement, unless required to do so by law. [ISA 210, 7]

Continuance

Once the engagement is complete, the audit firm must revisit the acceptance considerations again to ensure it is appropriate to continue for the following year. If any significant issues have arisen during the year, such as disagreements with management or doubts over management integrity, the firm may consider resigning.

7 Engagement letters

Purpose

The engagement letter specifies the nature of the contract between the firm and client. The letter will be **sent before the audit commences**.

Its purpose is to:

- Minimise the risk of any misunderstanding between the practitioner and client
- Confirm acceptance of the engagement
- Set out the terms and conditions of the engagement.

Changes to the engagement letter

The engagement letter should be **reviewed every year** to ensure that it is up to date but does not need to be reissued every year unless there are changes to the terms of the engagement.

ISA 210 requires the auditor to consider whether there is a need to remind the entity of the existing terms of the audit engagement for recurring audits. Some firms choose to send a new letter every year to emphasise its importance to clients.

The auditor should issue a new engagement letter if the scope or context of the assignment changes after initial appointment, or if there is a need to remind the client of the existing terms.

Reasons for changes would include:

- Changes to statutory duties due to new legislation
- Changes to professional duties, for example, due to new or updated ISAs
- Recent changes in senior management
- A significant change in ownership.

[ISA 210, A30]

The contents of the engagement letter

The auditor will agree the terms of the audit engagement with management or those charged with governance, as appropriate.
[ISA 210, 9]

The terms are recorded in a written audit engagement letter and should include:

- The objective and scope of the audit of the financial statements
- The responsibilities of the auditor
- The responsibilities of management

- Identification of the applicable financial reporting framework for the preparation of the financial statements

- Reference to the expected form and content of any reports to be issued by the auditor.

[ISA 210, 10]

In addition the following items will be included:

- Reference to professional standards, regulations and legislation applicable to the audit

- Limitations of an audit

- Expectation that management will provide written representations

- Basis on which the fees are calculated

- Agreement of management to notify the auditor of subsequent events after the auditor's report is signed

- Agreement of management to provide draft financial statements in time to allow the audit to be completed by the deadline

- Form (and timing) of any other communication during the audit.

[ISA 210, A24]

Other matters that the engagement letter may cover include:

- Arrangements concerning the involvement of internal auditors and other staff of the entity

- Limitations to the auditor's liability

- Any obligations to provide audit working papers to other parties.

[ISA 210, A26]

The content of the engagement letter should be agreed with the client before any engagement related work commences.

The client's acknowledgement of the terms of the letter should be formally documented in the form of a director's signature.

Illustration 2 – Murray Co engagement letter

Wimble & Co
14 The Grove
Kingston
KI4 6AP

25 November 20X4

To the Board of Directors of Murray Co.

This letter and the attached terms of business dated 25 November 20X4 set out the basis on which we are to provide services as auditors and your and our respective responsibilities.

The objective and scope of the audit: You have requested that we audit the financial statements of Murray Co, which comprise the statement of financial position as at December 31, and the statement of profit or loss, statement of changes in equity and statement of cash flows for the year then ended, and a summary of significant accounting policies and other explanatory information.

We are pleased to confirm our acceptance and our understanding of this audit engagement by means of this letter. Our audit will be conducted with the objective of our expressing an opinion on the financial statements.

The responsibilities of the auditor: We will conduct our audit in accordance with International Standards on Auditing (ISAs). Those standards require that we comply with ethical requirements and plan and perform the audit to obtain reasonable assurance about whether the financial statements are free from material misstatement. An audit involves performing procedures to obtain audit evidence about the amounts and disclosures in the financial statements. The procedures selected depend on the auditor's judgment, including the assessment of the risks of material misstatement of the financial statements, whether due to fraud or error. An audit also includes evaluating the appropriateness of accounting policies used and the reasonableness of accounting estimates made by management, as well as evaluating the overall presentation of the financial statements.

Because of the inherent limitations of an audit, together with the inherent limitations of internal control, there is an unavoidable risk that some material misstatements may not be detected, even though the audit is properly planned and performed in accordance with ISAs.

In making our risk assessments, we consider internal control relevant to Murray Co's preparation of the financial statements in order to design audit procedures that are appropriate in the circumstances, but not for the purpose of expressing an opinion on the effectiveness of Murray Co's internal control. However, we will communicate to you in writing concerning any significant deficiencies in internal control relevant to the audit of the financial statements that we have identified during the audit.

The responsibilities of management: Our audit will be conducted on the basis that management acknowledge and understand that they have responsibility:

(a) For the preparation and fair presentation of the financial statements in accordance with International Financial Reporting Standards.

(b) For such internal control as management determines is necessary to enable the preparation of financial statements that are free from material misstatement, whether due to fraud or error.

(c) To provide us with:

(i) Access to all information of which management is aware that is relevant to the preparation of the financial statements such as records, documentation and other matters.

(ii) Additional information that we may request from management for the purpose of the audit.

(iii) Unrestricted access to persons within the entity from whom we determine it necessary to obtain audit evidence.

As part of our audit process, we will request from management written confirmation concerning representations made to us in connection with the audit. We look forward to full cooperation from your staff during our audit.

Report: We will report to the members of Murray Co as a body, whether in our opinion the financial statements present fairly in all material respects, the financial position of Murray Co as at December 31, and its financial performance and its cash flows for the year then ended in accordance with International Financial Reporting Standards. The form and content of our report may need to be amended in the light of our audit findings.

Fees: Our fees, which will be billed as work progresses, are based on the time required by the individuals assigned to the engagement plus out-of-pocket expenses. Individual hourly rates vary according to the degree of responsibility involved and the experience and skill required.

Limitation of liability: To the fullest extent permitted by law, we will not be responsible for any losses, where you or others supply incorrect or incomplete information, or fail to supply any appropriate information or where you fail to act on our advice or respond promptly to communications from us.

Our work is not, unless there is a legal or regulatory requirement, to be made available to third parties without our written permission and we will accept no responsibility to third parties for any aspect of our professional services or work that is made available to them.

Confirmation of your agreement: Please sign and return the attached copy of this letter to indicate your acknowledgement of, and agreement with, the arrangements for our audit of the financial statements including our respective responsibilities.

If this letter and the attached terms of business are not in accordance with your understanding of our terms of appointment, please let us know.

Wimble & Co

Wimble & Co

Acknowledged and agreed on behalf of Murray Co by (signed)

....

Date

Further explanation of engagement letter contents

To the Board of Directors of Murray Co...

- Although the auditor's report is issued to the shareholders, the engagement letter is addressed to and signed by the directors of a company.

The responsibilities of the auditor... The responsibilities of management...

- It is important to set out the directors' and auditor's responsibilities for clarity and to reduce any expectation gap.

- The responsibilities of the auditor include the scope of the audit, i.e. the process by which the auditor will form their opinion. The same description of the scope of an audit is included in the auditor's report.

We will report to the members of Murray Co as a body...

- It is important to define who the intended users of the report are, i.e. who can place reliance on it.

Confirmation of your agreement...

- Both the client and the auditor must sign and retain a copy of the engagement letter for reference and to support the contract agreed.

Test your understanding 2

Explain each of the FIVE fundamental principles of ACCA's Code of Ethics and Conduct.

(5 marks)

Test your understanding 3

You are a manager in the audit department of Whilling and Abel. A potential new client, Truckers Co, a haulage company, has approached your firm to perform the external audit in addition to some other non-audit services for the year-ending 30 September 20X5. Your audit firm was recommended to Truckers Co by an existing client, O&P, a shipping company who is also a major customer of Truckers Co.

You have been chosen to lead the engagement as you have experience of auditing haulage companies as you also manage the audit of O&P.

Whilst arranging the initial meeting with the directors of Truckers Co you discover that you studied accountancy with the finance director at university.

Truckers Co has not made a profit for the last two years. The directors explain that this is largely due to escalating costs in the industry including fuel price rises. They are confident they have now controlled their costs for the current year. They have also been approached to tender for a large profitable contract which would improve the company's financial performance going forward. They would like you to assist them with the preparation of this tender and present with them on the day.

The prior year financial statements are being audited by another audit firm. The finance director tells you that the current auditors have identified material misstatements but the board of directors are refusing to make these adjustments. If adjusted, it would turn the break-even position into a loss.

The current auditors have replied to your professional clearance letter and have informed you that they are still owed fees relating to the prior year.

You calculate that the potential fees from Truckers Co would amount to approximately 14% of your firm's total fee income.

Required:

(a) **Identify and explain THREE threats to objectivity if Whilling and Abel accept Truckers Co as a new audit client. For each threat, recommend how the threat can be managed.**

Prepare your answer using two columns headed Ethical threat and Possible safeguard respectively.

(6 marks)

(b) **Explain the matters, other than ethical threats, that should be considered by Whilling and Abel prior to accepting the engagement.** **(4 marks)**

(Total: 10 marks)

Test your understanding 4

You are holding a training course for your firm's new recruits covering the topic of ethics. The training will focus on the fundamental principles of ethical behaviour which accountants must follow. You have compiled the following quiz for the end of the session to test their understanding of the course content.

1 **Which of these is NOT a fundamental ethical principle?**

   A   Integrity

   B   Independence

   C   Objectivity

   D   Professional competence and due care

2 **Which of these statements provides the best explanation of integrity?**

   A   Members should act diligently and in accordance with applicable technical and professional standards

   B   Members should not bring the profession into disrepute

   C   Members should not use client information for personal advantage

   D   Members should be straightforward and honest in all professional and business relationships

3 **A member was found guilty of ethical misconduct by failing to respond to the professional clearance requests from another audit firm. This is a breach of which fundamental principle?**

   A   Integrity

   B   Independence

   C   Professional behaviour

   D   Professional competence and due care

4 **Which of the following statements best describes the conceptual framework approach to ethics?**

   A   A set of rules which must be followed in all circumstances

   B   A set of principles which the auditor applies based on professional judgment

   C   The conceptual framework is set out in company law

   D   A set of principles which the auditor applies at their discretion

5   **Why do auditors need to be independent?**

A   To ensure users of the auditor's report can place reliance on it and have faith it is not biased

B   To ensure the financial statements give a true and fair view

C   To provide more regulation for auditors to increase the perception of quality

D   The law requires it

Test your understanding 5

You are the audit manager responsible for the audit of Broome Co, a listed company. You have been informed by one of the audit juniors that the finance director has offered to take the audit team to a World Cup Final at the expense of the client as a thank you for an efficient audit.

The finance director has requested that you attend a social event where the company will outline a new rights issue of ordinary shares to shareholders. The finance director believes that the presence of the external auditor will add credibility to the rights issue and increase the chance of raising the required finance.

1   **Which of the following is NOT a threat to objectivity?**

A   Independence

B   Self-review

C   Advocacy

D   Intimidation

2   **Which ethical threat would be created if the audit manager attends the social event where the client will outline a new rights issue to shareholders?**

A   Familiarity

B   Advocacy

C   Self-review

D   Self-interest

3   **Which of the following is likely to be the most significant threat created by the offer of tickets to the World Cup Final?**

A   Intimidation

B   Advocacy

C   Self-review

D   Self-interest

4　What is the restriction, if any, on the level of fee income that can be received from recurring work from Broome Co before a situation of dependency is presumed to exist?

A　5%

B　10%

C　15%

D　No restriction

5　For clients where the level of fees must be monitored, what safeguard can the firm apply to reduce the threat to an acceptable level?

(i)　Rotation of audit team members on an annual basis.

(ii)　Discussion of the matter with the audit committee.

(iii)　Assign an engagement quality control review partner.

A　(i) and (ii) only

B　(i) and (iii) only

C　(ii) and (III) only

D　(i), (ii) and (iii)

8 Chapter summary

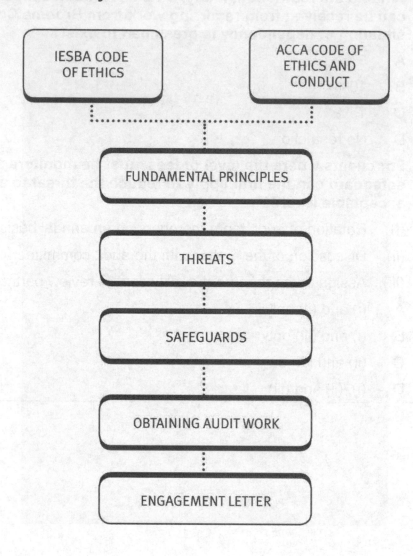

Test your understanding answers

Test your understanding 1

(a) **Conflict of interest**

Wimble & Co must inform both clients of the conflict and obtain their consent to act.

Separate teams and engagement partners must be used for each audit.

Procedures should be in place to prevent access to information e.g. using teams from different offices.

The audit teams should sign confidentiality agreements.

An independent review partner should be assigned to ensure the safeguards have been effective.

(b) **Threats and safeguards**

Ethical threat	Possible safeguard
Financial interest The audit manager owns shares in Murray Co. This creates a **self-interest threat:** the audit manager may be reluctant to identify misstatements or modify the audit opinion for fear of damaging the value of their shareholding.	The audit manager must dispose of the shares immediately.
Previous employment with the client The audit manager used to work for Murray Co. This creates a **self-review threat**.	The audit manager should not be assigned to the audit of Murray Co if they would be audited accounting records they had prepared whilst employed at the client.

If employment with the client was recent, the audit manager may be auditing work for which they were responsible when working for Murray Co. They may not identify errors in their own work, or if they are identified, they may not be brought to the client's attention.

In addition, a familiarity threat may arise as the audit manager is likely to have friendships with previous colleagues which could result in the audit manager not applying sufficient professional scepticism and trusting the client too much.

Gifts and hospitality Murray Co has offered free equipment to the auditor. Accepting gifts or hospitality from an audit client may create **self-interest** and familiarity threats. The auditor may feel indebted to the client or the offer may be seen to be a bribe from the client for a clean audit opinion.	The firm should evaluate the gift offered and unless trivial and inconsequential, the audit team must not accept the equipment. If the offer of free equipment is considered to be an inducement to accept the engagement, the offer should be declined, even if considered trivial and inconsequential.
Long association The engagement partner for Barker Co has been in place for twelve years. **Familiarity** and **self-interest** threats are created by using the same senior personnel on an assurance engagement for a long period of time. The audit partner may be too trusting of the client and may lack professional scepticism.	• Rotate the senior personnel. • Independent review of the senior personnel's work. • Independent quality control review of the engagement.

Personal relationship The audit senior's sister is the financial controller at Murray Co and is therefore in a position to exert significant influence over the financial statements. Family and personal relationships between a member of an assurance team and a director of the client, or an employee of the client in a position to exert significant influence over the subject matter, may create **familiarity, self-interest or intimidation threats**. The audit senior may be too trusting of his sister and not apply sufficient professional scepticism.	Tim Andrews should not be on the audit team for Murray Co.
Representing the client Murray Co would like the audit firm to represent the company in a dispute with the taxation authorities. This would create **advocacy** and **self-review** threats as the audit firm would be seen to be taking sides with their client.	Firms must not represent audit clients in such disputes. The request should be politely declined.
Overdue fees The fee for last year's audit of Barker Co has not yet been paid. Overdue fees create a **self-interest threat** where they remain unpaid for some time. The auditor may be reluctant to raise issues with the client in case they refuse to pay. In addition, overdue fees could be perceived to be a loan. An audit firm must not enter into any loan arrangement with a client.	Request payment from the client. Do not perform any more work for the client until the outstanding fees have been paid. The auditor's report must not be issued until payment has been received.

Provision of other services

Murray Co would like the audit firm to prepare the financial statements.

Preparing the financial statements and then auditing them creates a significant self-review threat. If the auditor reviews work they were responsible for, they may not identify errors they have made.

- The firm must only perform work of a routine or mechanical nature.

- Use staff who are not part of the audit team to prepare the financial statements.

- Arrange an independent partner or senior staff member to review the work performed.

Tutorial note: If an audit client is a listed or other public interest entity, the firm must not provide any accounting or bookkeeping services.

Test your understanding 2

Fundamental principles

Integrity. A professional accountant should be honest and straightforward in performing professional services.

Objectivity. A professional accountant should be fair and not allow personal bias, conflict of interest or influence of others to override objectivity.

Professional competence and due care. When performing professional services, a professional accountant should show competence and due care by acting diligently when performing their work and keeping up-to-date with developments in practice, legislation and techniques.

Confidentiality. A professional accountant should respect the confidentiality of information acquired during the course of providing professional services and should not use or disclose such information without obtaining client permission.

Professional behaviour. A professional accountant should act in a manner consistent with the good reputation of the profession and refrain from any conduct which might discredit the profession.

Test your understanding 3

(a) **Threats and safeguards**

Ethical threat	Possible safeguard
The audit manager knows one of the directors socially. This creates a familiarity threat. The auditor may be too trusting of the client or too sympathetic to the client's needs.	A different audit manager should be assigned to the audit of Truckers Co.
You are the audit manager of one of Trucker Co's major customers. This creates a conflict of interest where it may be difficult to act objectively for both clients. In addition, there is a risk that confidential information may be passed between the clients.	A different audit manager should be assigned to the audit of Truckers Co. Different teams should be used for the audit of Truckers Co and O&P and the audit team members should sign confidentiality agreements.
The audit manager has been asked to present at the tender for a contract. This would create an advocacy threat as the audit firm would be promoting the client.	The auditor should politely decline the invitation to present at the tender explaining their reasons.
The audit firm will provide non-audit services in addition to the external audit. This represents a self-review threat. The audit firm may ignore or overlook their own errors when auditing the financial statements.	The audit firm should ensure separate teams work on each engagement. An independent partner review of the files for each engagement should be arranged.
Total fees received from Trucker Co will represent 14% of the audit firm's total income. Fee dependence creates a self-interest threat. The firm may not wish to raise issues with the client for fear of losing them.	Whilling & Abel should to attempt to reduce dependency by increasing its client base. An independent review of the audit work should be arranged to ensure objectivity is not impaired. **Tutorial note:** If the client is a listed company, fee dependency is presumed when fees exceed 15% for two consecutive years.

(b) **Acceptance considerations**

Professional clearance

In addition, Truckers Co have not paid the current audit firm for the prior year audit. The firm should consider whether it is advisable to accept the client they could also be at risk of irrecoverable debts in the future.

Disagreements with the current auditors

The directors are refusing to make adjustments proposed by the current auditors which is cause for concern as Whilling and Abel may encounter the same problems in future.

Financial difficulties

Truckers Co has been loss-making for two years the most recent financial statements show a break even position which would be adjusted to a loss if management agreed to make the adjustments proposed by the auditors. Truckers Co may be in financial difficulties which may mean the company ceases to trade.

Integrity of management

The issues mentioned with regard to the current auditors suggest there may be a lack of management integrity. This increases the risk of difficulties with the audit which may mean the audit is too high a level of risk to accept.

Preconditions for an audit

The audit firm must only accept audits where management has confirmed the preconditions are in place, such as confirming responsibility for the preparation of the financial statements. If the preconditions are not present, the firm must not accept the engagement.

Money laundering client due diligence

The audit firm must comply with money laundering regulations and perform client due diligence. If the information gathered suggests a risk of money laundering, the firm must not proceed with the engagement.

Competence

The audit firm must ensure it is competent to perform the work otherwise audit risk will be too high.

Resources

The firm must assess whether they have sufficient resources available at the required time to perform the engagement.

Test your understanding 4

1	B	Whilst independence is an important characteristic for an auditor, it is not one of the fundamental principles.
2	D	Integrity means straightforward and honest.
3	C	Professional behaviour incorporates professional courtesy e.g. responding promptly to requests from other auditors.
4	B	The conceptual framework approach requires the auditor to assess each situation individually and act in a manner that would be seen as appropriate for a professional accountant. Principles rather than rules are used as principles can apply across national boundaries. The Code of ethics is professional guidance but not a legal requirement.
5	A	Independence means freedom from bias and influence.

Test your understanding 5

1	A	The threats to objectivity are self-interest, self-review, familiarity, advocacy and intimidation.
2	B	The audit manager may be seen to be promoting the company and encouraging the shareholders to subscribe to the rights issue.
3	D	Self-interest. The auditor may feel they owe the client something in return if they accept such an expensive gift. The offer of gifts and hospitality may also create a threat to intimidation if the client uses the offer to attempt to influence the outcome of the audit. As the offer in this case is a thank you for performing an efficient audit, and there is no implication of undue pressure, the most significant threat arising is self-interest.
4	C	15%.
5	C	Independence matters should be discussed with the audit committee and an engagement quality review partner should be assigned. Rotation of the audit team would not provide a safeguard for this self-interest threat.

Risk

Chapter learning objectives

This chapter covers syllabus areas:

- B2b – Explain the need to plan and perform audit engagements with an attitude of professional scepticism and to exercise professional judgment

- B3 – Assessing audit risks

- B4 – Understanding the entity, its environment and the applicable financial reporting framework

Detailed syllabus objectives are provided in the introduction section of the text book.

PER

One of the PER performance objectives (PO18) is to is to prepare for and plan the audit process. You plan and control the engagement process, including the initial investigation. You also plan and monitor the audit programme – legally and ethically. Working through this chapter should help you understand how to demonstrate that objective.

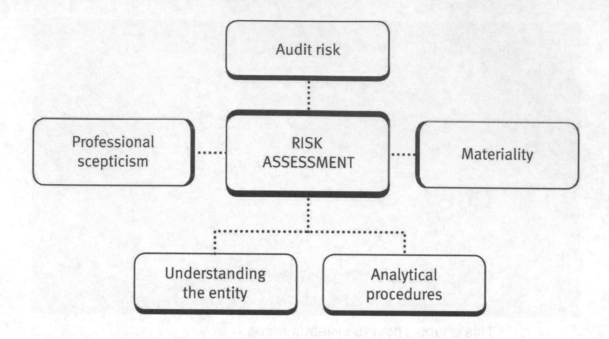

1 Audit risk

One of the main requirements of the auditor is to:

'...obtain sufficient appropriate evidence to reduce audit risk to an acceptably low level...'

[ISA 200 *Overall Objectives of the Independent Auditor and the Conduct of an Audit in Accordance with ISAs*, 17]

 Audit risk is the risk that the auditor expresses an inappropriate opinion when the financial statements are materially misstated.
[ISA 200, 13c]

This means that they give an unmodified audit opinion when the financial statements are materially misstated.

If this were to happen, the auditor could be sued by the intended users, disciplinary action could be taken by the relevant professional body and the firm could damage its reputation.

To avoid these potentially damaging consequences, the auditor will plan and perform the audit in such a way that audit risk is reduced to an acceptably low level.

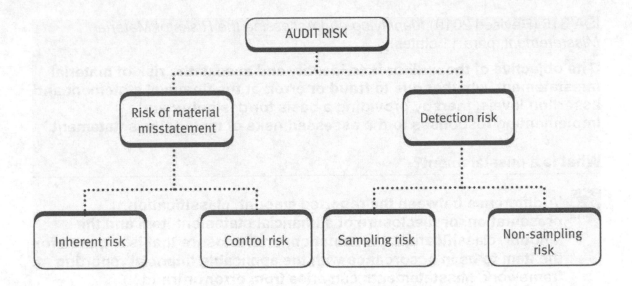

Another way of showing this interaction is:

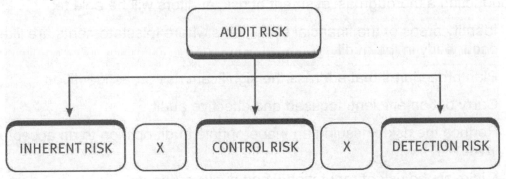

Audit risk comprises the risk of material misstatement and detection risk.

 Tutorial note

The auditor can only influence detection risk, as inherent risk and control risk are influenced by the client. In order to reduce audit risk to an acceptable level, the auditor must reduce detection risk, for example, by assigning more experienced people to the audit team, performing a wider range of procedures and testing larger sample sizes.

Risk of material misstatement

 Risk of material misstatement is **the risk that the financial statements are materially misstated prior to the audit**. [ISA 200, 13n]

This will be due to fraud or errors occurring during the year when transactions have been processed or when the financial statements have been prepared.

ISA 315 (Revised 2019) *Identifying and Assessing the Risks of Material Misstatement,* para 11 states*:*

'The objective of the auditor is to identify and assess the risk of material misstatement, whether due to fraud or error, at the financial statement and assertion levels, thereby providing a basis for designing and implementing responses to the assessed risks of material misstatement.'

What is a misstatement?

 'A difference between the reported amount, classification, presentation, or disclosure of a financial statement item and the amount, classification, presentation, or disclosure that is required for the item to be in accordance with the applicable financial reporting framework. Misstatements can arise from error or fraud.'

[ISA 450 *Evaluation of Misstatements Identified During The Audit*, 4a]

In conducting a thorough assessment of risk, auditors will be able to:

- Identify areas of the financial statements where misstatements are likely to occur early in the audit.

- Plan procedures that address the significant risk areas identified.

- Carry out an efficient, focused and effective audit.

- Reduce the risk of issuing an inappropriate audit opinion to an acceptable level.

- Minimise the risk of reputational and punitive damage.

 Categories of misstatement

There are three categories of misstatements:

(i) Factual misstatements: a misstatement about which there is no doubt.

(ii) Judgmental misstatements: a difference in an accounting estimate that the auditor considers unreasonable, or the selection or application of accounting policies that the auditor considers inappropriate.

(iii) Projected misstatements: a projected misstatement is the auditor's best estimate of the total misstatement in a population through the projection of misstatements identified in a sample.

[ISA 450, A6]

KAPLAN PUBLISHING

The risk of material misstatement comprises inherent risk and control risk.

Inherent risk

 Inherent risk is 'the susceptibility of an assertion about a class of transaction, account balance or disclosure to misstatement that could be material, before consideration of any related controls'. [ISA 200, 13ni]

- Complex accounting treatment is an example of an inherent risk. For example, where an accounting standard provides guidance on a specific accounting treatment, this might not be understood by the client resulting in material misstatement.

- Inherent risk can arise due to the nature of the industry, entity or the nature of the balance itself. For example, inventory is inherently risky if it quickly becomes obsolete as it may not be valued appropriately at the lower of cost and net realisable value (NRV) as required by IAS®2 *Inventories*.

Inherent risk factors may be qualitative or quantitative. Qualitative inherent risk factors include:

- Complexity
- Subjectivity
- Change
- Uncertainty
- Susceptibility to misstatement due to management bias.

[ISA 315 (Revised 2019), A7]

 Examples of inherent risks

Property, plant and equipment will be:

- overstated if expenditure on repairs is treated as capital expenditure.

- overstated if asset lives have been extended for depreciation purposes without any justification for the increase.

- overstated if assets ordered but not delivered by the reporting date are included in the financial statements.

- understated if capital expenditure has been incorrectly expensed.

Provision liabilities will be:

- overstated if there is no obligation created at the reporting date.

- overstated if it is not probable that payment will need to be made.

- understated if an inappropriate estimate of the provision is made.

Intangible assets will be:

- overstated if research costs have been capitalised rather than expensed.

- overstated if amortisation has not been charged on development projects which are now generating benefits for the company.

- overstated if an impairment charge has not been made for intangible assets which are impaired.

- understated if development costs have been expensed rather than capitalised.

Revenue will be overstated if it has been recognised before the performance obligations within the contract have been fulfilled.

Control risk

 Control risk is '**the risk that a misstatement that could occur and that could be material, will not be prevented, or detected and corrected on a timely basis by the entity's controls**'. [ISA 200, 13nii]

The client should have controls in place, such as authorisation, segregation of duties, reconciliations, physical controls etc. to prevent and detect misstatements occurring when transactions are initiated, processed and recorded.

If effective controls are in place, the control system will either prevent the misstatements from occurring, or will detect misstatements that have occurred and the client can take action to correct them.

If controls are not effective, control risk will increase and there will be a greater risk of misstatements occurring in the financial statements.

Controls are covered in more detail in the chapter 'Systems and controls'.

Detection risk

 Detection risk is '**the risk that the procedures performed by the auditor to reduce audit risk to an acceptably low level will not detect a misstatement that exists and that could be material**'. [ISA 200, 13e]

Detection risk comprises **sampling risk** and **non-sampling risk**:

- **Sampling risk** is the risk that the auditor's conclusion based on a sample is different from the conclusion that would be reached if the whole population was tested, i.e. the sample was not representative of the population from which it was chosen. [ISA 530 *Audit Sampling*, 5c]

- **Non-sampling risk** is the risk that the auditor's conclusion is inappropriate for any other reason, e.g. the application of inappropriate procedures or the failure to recognise a misstatement. [ISA 530, 5d]

The auditor must amend the audit approach in response to risk assessment to ensure they detect the material misstatements in the financial statements.

This can be achieved by:

- Emphasising the need for professional scepticism.

- Assigning more experienced staff to complex or risky areas of the engagement.

- Changing the nature, timing and extent of direction and supervision of members of the engagement team and the review of work performed.

- Incorporating additional elements of unpredictability in the selection of further audit procedures.

- Changing the overall audit strategy, e.g.

    - The auditor's determination of performance materiality.

    - The auditor's plans to test the operating effectiveness of controls.

    - The nature, timing and extent of substantive procedures.

[ISA 330 *The Auditor's Response to Assessed Risks*, A1]

Professional scepticism

 Professional scepticism is: **'An attitude that includes a questioning mind, being alert to conditions which may indicate possible misstatement due to fraud or error, and a critical assessment of audit evidence**.' [ISA 200, 13l]

This requires the audit team to have a good knowledge of how the client's activities are likely to affect its financial statements. The audit team should discuss these matters in a planning meeting before deciding on the detailed approach and audit work to be used.

Professional scepticism is necessary for the critical assessment of audit evidence gathered when performing the risk assessment procedures, and assists the auditor in remaining alert to audit evidence that is not biased towards corroborating the existence of risks or that may be contradictory to the existence of risks.

Professional scepticism is an attitude that is applied by the auditor when making professional judgments that then provides the basis for the auditor's actions. The auditor applies professional judgment in determining when the auditor has audit evidence that provides an appropriate basis for risk assessment. [ISA 315 (Revised 2019), A12]

How to apply professional scepticism

Professional scepticism requires the auditor to **be alert to:**

- Audit **evidence that contradicts other** audit **evidence.**

- Information that brings into question **the reliability of documents and responses to enquiries** to be used as audit evidence.

- Conditions that may indicate **possible fraud**.

- Circumstances that suggest **the need for audit procedures in addition to those required by ISAs.**

[ISA 200, A20]

Exercising professional scepticism

Example 1

A customer of a client is having financial difficulties and has not paid any invoices for 6 months when the client's credit terms are 10 days. The auditor has asked the FD about the outstanding debt and whether it should be written off. The FD has informed the auditor that they believe the debt will be paid as they have never experienced irrecoverable debts with this customer in the past, as a result, no expense has been recognised.

To exercise professional scepticism, the auditor should seek alternative, corroborative evidence to support the FD's claim as they may not want to make allowance for the debt as this will reduce profit. The auditor could review bank statements post year-end to identify if payment has been made or could review any correspondence between the customer and the client indicating when payment might be made. These procedures provide more reliable evidence than an enquiry with management who may tell the auditor what they think the auditor wants to hear to avoid an adjustment to the financial statements. Obtaining a written representation from management is only marginally more reliable than an enquiry. Client generated evidence is always the least reliable form of evidence and the auditor should always look for better quality evidence where possible due to the risk of management bias.

Example 2

An audit client is being sued by an ex-employee for unfair dismissal. The FD tells the auditor that the company's lawyer believes it is probable that the employee's claim will not succeed, as a result, no provision has been recognised.

To exercise professional scepticism, the auditor should review correspondence received from the lawyer confirming this position. More reliable evidence would be obtained if the auditor obtained a direct, external confirmation from the lawyer confirming the position as this evidence would not have been obtained via the client.

2 Materiality

What is materiality?

'Misstatements, including omissions, are considered to be material if they, individually or in the aggregate, could reasonably be expected to influence the economic decisions of users taken on the basis of the financial statements.'

[ISA 320 *Materiality in Planning and Performing an Audit*, 2]

International Accounting Standards Board definition of materiality
The following definition of materiality is given in IAS 1 *Presentation of Financial Statements*, effective from 1 January 2020: 'Information is material if omitting, misstating or obscuring it could reasonably be expected to influence the decisions that the primary users of general purpose financial statements make on the basis of those financial statements, which provide financial information about a specific reporting entity.'

What is the significance of materiality?

If the financial statements contain material misstatement they cannot be deemed to show a true and fair view.

As a result, the focus of an audit is identifying the significant risks of material misstatement in the financial statements and then designing procedures aimed at identifying and quantifying them.

How is materiality determined?

The determination of materiality is a **matter of professional judgment**. The auditor must consider:

- Whether the misstatement would affect the economic decision of the users

- Both the size and nature of misstatements

- The information needs of the users as a group.

Materiality is a subjective matter and should be considered in light of the client's circumstances.

Material by size

ISA 320 recognises the need to establish a financial threshold to guide audit planning and procedures. For this reason the following benchmarks may be used as a starting point:

- ½ – 1% revenue
- 5 – 10% profit before tax
- 1 – 2% total assets.

The above are common benchmarks but different audit firms may use different benchmarks or different thresholds for each client.

 Tutorial note

In the exam, use the lowest end of the range for assessing whether a misstatement is material. If the misstatement is greater than ½% revenue/ 5% of profit before tax /1% total assets, assume it is material.

Material by nature

Materiality is not only looked at from a financial perspective. Some items may be material by nature. Examples include:

- Misstatements that affect compliance with regulatory requirements.
- Misstatements that affect compliance with debt covenants.
- Misstatements that, when adjusted, would turn a reported profit into a loss for the year.
- Misstatements that, when adjusted, would turn a reported net-asset position into a net-liability position.
- Transactions with directors, e.g. salary and benefits, personal use of assets, etc.
- Disclosures in the financial statements relating to possible future legal claims or going concern issues, for example, could influence users' decisions and may be purely narrative. In this case a numerical calculation is not relevant.

Illustration 1 – Murray Co materiality

Financial statement extracts	20X4	20X3
	$000	$000
Revenue	21,960	19,580
Total assets	9,697	7,288
Profit before tax	1,048	248

Materiality	Lower	Upper
Revenue	½%	1%
	110	220
Profit before tax	5%	10%
	52	105
Total assets	1%	2%
	97	194

Materiality is not normally based on revenue, except in circumstances when It would not be meaningful to base materiality on profit, e.g. because the entity being audited is a not-for-profit entity or where there is a small profit (or a loss) as this will result in over-auditing of the financial statements (as was the case for Murray Co in the prior year).

More than $105,000 profit is material to the statement of profit or loss, therefore preliminary materiality is likely to be set lower than this amount. Less than $52,000 is not material to profit (or to the statement of financial position) so preliminary materiality should not be less than this amount.

A suitable preliminary materiality level is most likely to be one that lies within the overlap of the ranges calculated for profit and total assets. $97,000 (1% of total assets) represents 9% profit. As this is at the lower end of the assets range, this would be a relatively prudent measure of materiality (resulting in a higher level of audit work).

$105,000 (10% of profit) represents 1.1% of total assets. Preliminary materiality could be set at this end of the range if this was a recurring audit. However, as this is the first year auditing this client, preliminary materiality is likely to be lower.

The financial statements are draft and therefore more errors may be expected than if they were actual figures. Consequently, sample sizes for audit testing should be increased (i.e. preliminary materiality should be set at a relatively lower level).

Taking all of these factors into consideration, a suitable range for **preliminary materiality** is **$97,000 – $105,000**.

Performance materiality

It is unlikely, in practice, that auditors will be able to design tests that identify individual material misstatements. It is much more common that misstatements are material in aggregate (i.e. in combination).

For this reason, ISA 320 introduces the concept of **performance materiality**.

 Performance materiality is 'The amount set by the auditor at less than materiality for the financial statements as a whole to reduce to an appropriately low level the probability that the aggregate of uncorrected and undetected misstatements exceeds materiality for the financial statements as a whole.' [ISA 320, 9]

- The auditor sets **performance materiality** at a value **lower than overall materiality**, and uses this lower threshold when designing and performing audit procedures.

- This **reduces** the **risk** that the auditor will fail to identify misstatements that are material when added together.

3 Risk assessment procedures

The auditor should perform the following risk assessment procedures:

- **Enquiries** with management, of appropriate individuals within the internal audit function (if there is one), and others (with relevant information) within the client entity (e.g. about external and internal changes the company has experienced)

- **Analytical procedures**

- **Observation** (e.g. of control procedures)

- **Inspection** (e.g. of key strategic documents and procedural manuals).

[ISA 315 (Revised 2019), 14]

Understanding the entity, its environment, the applicable financial reporting framework and its system of internal control

The auditor is required to obtain an understanding of:

- Aspects of the entity and its environment:

  - The complexity of the entity's organisational structure. A more complex structure increases the risk of material misstatement.

  - Ownership and governance. This includes consideration of the level of distinction between the owners, management and those charged with governance.

  - The business model including the extent to which the business model integrates the use of IT. This includes consideration of whether the entity has multiple legacy IT systems which are not well integrated and therefore increase the risk of material misstatement, and whether the IT systems are outsourced to a third party service provider.

  - Industry, regulatory and other external factors.

    The measures used, internally and externally, to assess the entity's financial performance.

- The applicable financial reporting framework, and whether the entity's accounting policies are appropriate and consistent with the applicable financial reporting framework.

- The components of the entity's system of internal control and control deficiencies. (Covered in more detail in the chapter 'Systems and controls')

[ISA 315 (Revised 2019), 19, 20, A56]

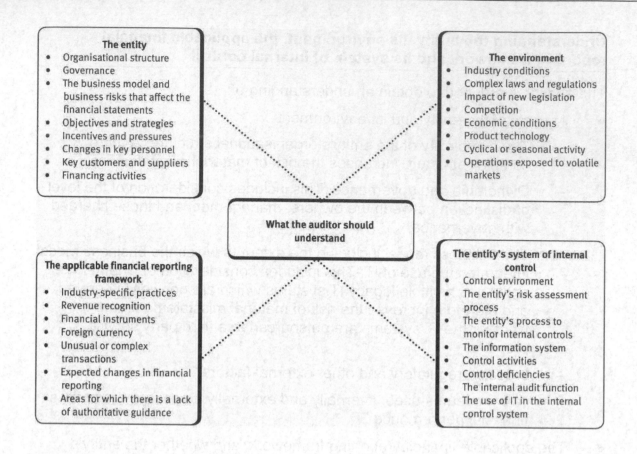

The entity
- Organisational structure
- Governance
- The business model and business risks that affect the financial statements
- Objectives and strategies
- Incentives and pressures
- Changes in key personnel
- Key customers and suppliers
- Financing activities

The environment
- Industry conditions
- Complex laws and regulations
- Impact of new legislation
- Competition
- Economic conditions
- Product technology
- Cyclical or seasonal activity
- Operations exposed to volatile markets

What the auditor should understand

The applicable financial reporting framework
- Industry-specific practices
- Revenue recognition
- Financial instruments
- Foreign currency
- Unusual or complex transactions
- Expected changes in financial reporting
- Areas for which there is a lack of authoritative guidance

The entity's system of internal control
- Control environment
- The entity's risk assessment process
- The entity's process to monitor internal controls
- The information system
- Control activities
- Control deficiencies
- The internal audit function
- The use of IT in the internal control system

The auditor will use this understanding to assess the identified risks of material misstatement (inherent and control risks) at the financial statement level and the assertion levels to design further audit procedures in response to these risks. [ISA 315 (Revised 2019), 13]

The information used to obtain this understanding can come from a wide range of sources:

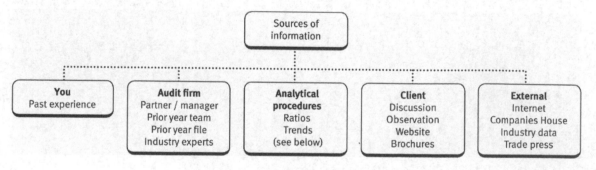

Sources of information

You
Past experience

Audit firm
Partner / manager
Prior year team
Prior year file
Industry experts

Analytical procedures
Ratios
Trends
(see below)

Client
Discussion
Observation
Website
Brochures

External
Internet
Companies House
Industry data
Trade press

Analytical procedures

 'Evaluations of financial information through analysis of plausible relationships among both financial and non-financial data and investigation of identified fluctuations, inconsistent relationships or amounts that differ from expected values by a significant amount.'
[ISA 520 *Analytical Procedures*, 4]

Analytical procedures are fundamental to the auditing process.

The auditor is **required to perform analytical procedures as risk assessment procedures in accordance with ISA 315 (Revised 2019)** in order to:

- Help identify inconsistencies, **unusual transactions or events, and amounts, ratios, and trends** that might have audit implications. [A27]

- Help identify **risks of material misstatement due to fraud**. [A27]

- Identify and assess aspects of the entity of which the auditor was unaware. [A28]

Analytical procedures include **comparisons** of the entity's financial information with, for example:

- Comparable information for **prior periods.**

- **Anticipated results** of the entity, such as budgets or forecasts, or expectations of the auditor, such as an estimation of depreciation.

- Similar **industry information,** such as a comparison of the entity's ratio of sales to accounts receivable with industry averages or with other entities of comparable size in the same industry.

[ISA 520, A1]

When performing analytical procedures, the auditor will also consider **relationships**, for example between:

- Related figures such as revenue and receivables, purchases and payables; and

- Financial and non-financial information such as payroll costs and number of employees.

[ISA 520, A2]

Data analytics may be used to perform analytical procedures for example using software to extract data from the client's information system to perform a comparison of actual recorded amounts to budgeted amounts.
[ISA 315 (Revised 2019), A31]

Analytical procedures during the audit

Analytical procedures can be used at all stages of an audit.

Preliminary analytical procedures

ISA 315 (Revised 2019) requires the auditor to perform analytical procedures as a risk assessment procedure in order to help the auditor to obtain an understanding of the entity and assess the risk of material misstatement.

Substantive analytical procedures

ISA 500 *Audit Evidence* allows the auditor to use analytical procedures as a substantive procedure to help detect misstatement.

Final analytical procedures

In addition, ISA 520 *Analytical Procedures* requires the auditor to use analytical procedures at the completion stage of the audit when forming an overall conclusion as to whether the financial statements are consistent with the auditor's understanding of the entity.

Automated tools and techniques, including audit software and data analytic tools, are increasingly being used to perform this analysis. This is covered in more detail in the chapter 'Evidence'.

Key ratios

Profitability ratios

Gross margin: gross profit/sales revenue × 100%

Operating margin: operating profit/sales revenue × 100%

Auditors would expect the relationships between costs and revenues to stay relatively stable. Things that can affect these ratios include: changes in sales prices, bulk purchase discounts, economies of scale, new marketing initiatives, changing energy costs, wage inflation.

Therefore, any unusual fluctuation in the profitability ratios could mean the figures are materially misstated. For example, if the gross margin improves, this could be caused by any or all of the following:

- Overstated revenue because of inappropriate revenue recognition or cut-off issues.

- Understated cost of sales because of incomplete recording of purchases.

- Understated cost of sales because of overvaluation of closing inventory.

Efficiency ratios

These ratios show how efficient the business is at converting assets into cash or how long it takes to pay suppliers.

Receivables collection period: receivables/revenue × 365

Payables payment period: payables/purchases × 365

Inventory holding period: inventory/cost of sales × 365

Asset turnover: revenue/total assets

Any changes can indicate significant issues, such as:

- Overvaluation of receivables if sufficient allowance is not made.

- Overvaluation of inventory if damaged or obsolete inventory has not been written down.

- Inadequate disclosure of going concern issues if the company has poor cash flow and is unable to pay its suppliers.

Liquidity ratios

Current ratio: current assets/current liabilities

Quick ratio: (current assets-inventory)/current liabilities

These ratios indicate the ability of a company to meet its short-term debts. As a result, these are key indicators when assessing going concern. If there are indicators of going concern uncertainties, the financial statements must include disclosure and the auditor must evaluate the adequacy of the disclosures.

Investor ratios

Gearing: borrowings/(share capital + reserves)

Return on capital employed (ROCE): profit before interest and tax/(share capital + reserves + borrowings)

Gearing is a measure of external debt finance to internal equity finance. ROCE indicates the returns those investments generate.

Any change in gearing or ROCE could indicate a change in the financing structure of the business or it could indicate changes in overall performance of the business. These ratios are important for identifying potentially material changes to the statement of financial position (new/repaid loans or share issues) and for obtaining an overall picture of the annual performance of the business.

4   Exam focus – Audit risk questions

Audit risk identification and explanation

Audit risk is regularly examined and it is important to answer the question from an auditor's perspective rather than the perspective of the client.

The auditor is trying to detect material misstatements in the financial statements to avoid issuing the wrong opinion. The auditor is not looking to identify risks which affect the profitability of the client, they are not business consultants.

A common mistake that students make in exams is to explain business risks rather than audit risks. Business risks are not examinable in this syllabus. Therefore take care to ensure your answer is relevant to the requirement.

For example:

Identification of risk from the scenario	Audit risk explanation	NOT Audit risk (business risk)
Customers are struggling to pay debts.	Receivables may be overstated if irrecoverable debts are not written off.	Irrecoverable debts may arise reducing the profits of the company.
The client operates in a fast paced industry.	Inventory may be overstated if the inventory is obsolete and net realisable value is lower than cost.	Inventory may have to be written off reducing the profits of the company.
Revenue is falling due to recession. The cash flow forecast shows negative cash flows for the next 12 months.	If other factors are present, this could mean the company is unable to continue to trade for the foreseeable future and going concern disclosures may be required. There is a risk that adequate disclosure is not made.	Falling revenue will result in reduced profits and possible going concern issues.

In the exam, make sure you explain the risk by stating the area of the financial statements which is at risk of material misstatement. A risk of material misstatement will affect either a balance in the financial statements, a disclosure in the notes to the financial statements or the basis of preparation.

This can be achieved in several ways:

- State the financial statement assertion affected, e.g. cut-off, valuation, completeness, etc.

- State the specific area of the financial statements affected. For example, where a receivable balance is overvalued and potentially irrecoverable, an appropriate explanation would be 'trade receivables are overstated' or 'the allowance for receivables is understated'. No marks will be awarded for stating 'assets are overstated' or 'profit is overstated'.

- State the risk to the balance e.g. overstated or understated. Misstated is only awarded if it is clear that the balance could be either over or understated.
- State the component of audit risk affected, e.g. inherent, control or detection risk.

Auditor responses to risks

Once the risks are identified, you must suggest a **relevant** audit response to the risk identified.

The response must specifically deal with the risk. You should not suggest audit responses that address the balance generally.

Audit risk	Relevant response	Irrelevant response	Explanation
Customers are struggling to pay debts. Receivables may be overstated if irrecoverable debts are not written off.	Inspect after date cash receipts from customers to see if paid post year-end proving the debt is appropriately valued.	Obtain the receivables listing and cast it to verify arithmetical accuracy.	The risk identified is overvaluation. Obtaining the listing does not provide evidence that the debts are appropriately valued.
	Review the aged receivables listing for old debts which may not be recoverable and discuss the need for an allowance to be made with management.	Obtain external confirmation from customers to confirm existence.	External confirmation is providing evidence of existence but not valuation.
		The company should improve its credit control procedures.	This is a client response not an auditor response.
The client operates in a fast paced industry. Inventory may be overstated if obsolete items are not written off.	Obtain the aged inventory listing and review for old items. Discuss with management the need for these to be written down in the financial statements.	The company should discount the inventory in order to sell it.	This is a client response not an auditor response.

		Attend the inventory count to confirm existence of the inventory.	As written, the response of attending the inventory count is confirming existence, not valuation. This should be reworded to say attend the inventory count and look out for old or obsolete items that should be written down in the financial statements.
Revenue is falling due to recession. The cash flow forecast shows negative cash flows for the next 12 months. Going concern disclosures may not be adequate if the company has trading difficulties.	Assess the client's ability to continue as a going concern by examining the forecasts prepared by management and assess the reasonableness of the assumptions used in the forecasts.	Perform an analysis of past performance and assess the profitability of the company. Calculate liquidity ratios.	Analysing past performance does not help indicate how the company will perform in the future. Profitability is not the best indicator of going concern as profits can be distorted by accounting policies. A company can be profitable but not have sufficient cash available to pay its suppliers and employees. Calculation of ratios can help identify indicators of going concern problems but further procedures would need to be performed to obtain evidence of the company's ability to continue to trade.

Test your understanding 1

Murray case study: Audit risks

Your firm Wimble & Co has recently accepted appointment as auditor of Murray Co (a manufacturer of sports equipment).

Having sold your shares in Murray Co, you have been assigned as audit manager and you have started planning the audit (although you were an employee of Murray Co, this was many years ago and you did not have any involvement in the preparation of the financial statements). You have held a meeting with the client and have ascertained the following:

Murray Co manufactures sports equipment. Most items of equipment, such as tennis rackets, hockey sticks and goals, take less than one day to manufacture. Murray Co's largest revenue generating product, ergometers (rowing machines), takes up to one week to manufacture. Murray Co refurbished the assembly line for the ergometers during the year. Murray Co uses a third party warehouse provider to store the manufactured ergometers and approximately one quarter of the other equipment.

Historically, Murray Co has only sold to retailers. For the first time this year, Murray Co has made sales directly to consumers, via a new website. The website is directly linked to the finance system, recording sales automatically. Website customers pay on ordering. The website development costs have been capitalised. This initiative was implemented to respond to market demands, as retailer sales have fallen dramatically in the last two years. Some of Murray Co's retail customers are struggling to pay their outstanding balances. Several of the sales team were made redundant last month as a result of the falling retailer sales.

Murray Co is planning to list on the stock exchange next year.

Required:

Using the information provided, describe SIX audit risks and explain the auditor's response to each risk in planning the audit of Murray Co.

Note: Prepare your answer using two columns headed Audit risk and Auditor's response respectively.

(12 marks)

Test your understanding 2

Murray case study: Analytical procedures

Draft Statement of financial position as at 31 December 20X4

	20X4 $000	20X3 $000
Non-current assets		
Property plant and equipment	5,350	4,900
Website development	150	0
	5,500	4,900
Current assets		
Inventory	2,109	1,300
Trade receivables	2,040	1,050
Cash and cash equivalents	48	38
	4,197	2,388
	9,697	7,288
Equity		
Share capital (50c shares)	2,100	2,100
Retained earnings	2,959	2,156
	5,059	4,256
Non-current liabilities		
Long term loan	2,800	1,500
Current liabilities		
Provisions	240	195
Trade and other payables	1,400	1,205
Accruals	18	12
Bank overdraft	180	120
	1,838	1,532
	9,697	7,288

Draft Statement of profit or loss for the year ended 31 December 20X4

	20X4	20X3
	$000	$000
Revenue	21,960	19,580
Cost of sales	(18,560)	(17,080)
Gross profit	3,400	2,500
Operating expenses	(2,012)	(2,012)
Operating profit	1,388	488
Finance cost	(340)	(240)
Profit before tax	1,048	248
Taxation	(245)	(24)
Profit for the period	803	224

Required:

Using the financial information provided, and the information from TYU 1, perform analytical procedures on the draft financial statements of Murray Co describe the audit risks that should be considered when planning the audit of Murray Co.

(10 marks)

Test your understanding 3

It is 1 July 20X5. You are an audit senior at JPR Edwards & Co and you are currently planning the audit of Hook Co for the year ending 30 September 20X5. Your firm was recently appointed as auditor after a successful tender to provide audit and tax services. JPR Edward & Co were asked to tender after the lead partner, Neisha Selvaratalm, met Hook Co's CEO, Taylor Tucker, at a charity cricket match. Hook Co was unhappy with the previous auditors as it was felt the audit did not add much value to the company.

Hook Co manufactures electrical goods such as MP3 players, smartphones and personal computers for larger companies with established brands. Its key client, which represents 70% of its revenue, was the market leader in smartphones and MP3 players last year with 60% market share.

Hook Co uses a number of suppliers to source components for its products. Most suppliers are based in the UK, however microchips are imported from a number of overseas suppliers. Hook Co's products are assembled and packaged in one factory in the UK before being distributed to customers across the UK. The work-in-progress balance is expected to be material at the year end.

During the year, Hook Co started developing smartphone applications. $1 million has been spent on an application called 'snore-o-meter' which allows users to record the sounds they make while they are asleep. There was a technical difficulty in production which meant the launch of 'snore-o-meter' has been delayed from June to October 20X5.

To fund the expansion into smartphone applications Hook Co is seeking a listing on the London Stock Exchange in the fourth quarter of the year.

Required:

Using the information provided, describe FIVE audit risks and explain the auditor's response to each risk in planning the audit of Hook Co.

Note: Prepare your answer using two columns headed Audit risk and Auditor's response respectively.

(10 marks)

Test your understanding 4

Define materiality and explain how the level of materiality is assessed.

(5 marks)

Test your understanding 5

You have received the latest management accounts from your client, Esperence Co, to help with your risk assessment for the forthcoming audit. The management accounts show actual results for the year to date, January to October inclusive. In October, Esperence Co received a claim from a customer as a result of a defective product.

1   **Which of the following is an example of an audit risk for Esperence Co?**

 A The client is being sued by a customer for a defective product and if the claim is successful, the compensation awarded is likely to be significant

 B The client is being sued by a customer for a defective product. The publicity of the case could damage the company's reputation

 C The client will have to spend a significant amount of money on improving its quality control procedures to avoid the same defects occurring again

 D Provisions may be understated if the probable payment resulting from the court case is not recognised as a liability in the financial statements

2   **Which of the following is the correct formula for calculating the payables payment period using the management accounts of Esperence Co?**

 A Payables/Cost of sales × 304

 B Payables/Cost of sales × 365

 C Payables/Revenue × 304

 D Payables/Revenue × 365

3   **Which of the following is not an analytical procedure?**

 A Calculation of gross profit margin and comparison with prior year

 B Recalculation of a depreciation charge

 C Comparison of revenue month by month

 D Comparison of expenditure for current year with prior year

4   **Which of the following is not a ratio?**

 A Gross profit margin

 B Acid test

 C Inventory turnover

 D Revenue growth

5   **You have used the management accounts to calculate the gross profit margin and found it to be higher than the prior year figure. Which of the following would provide a possible explanation?**

A   Sales prices have been reduced to increase sales volumes

B   Prices charged by suppliers have increased but the company has not increased sales prices to customers to cover the increased costs

C   Closing inventory has been overvalued

D   Administration expenses have decreased

Test your understanding 6

You are the audit manager responsible for planning the audit of Fremantle Co. The draft financial statements show profit before tax of $3m and total assets of $50m. You have held a planning meeting with the client and have performed preliminary analytical procedures on the draft financial statements. You are currently assessing preliminary materiality for the audit and performing further risk assessment procedures.

1   **Which of the following statements is false in relation to materiality?**

A   Materiality can be assessed by size or nature

B   A balance which is omitted from the financial statements cannot be material

C   Materiality is a matter of professional judgment for the auditor

D   There is an inverse relationship between risk and materiality. If audit risk is high, the materiality level set by the audit will be lower

2   **Which of the following procedures is NOT required to be performed in accordance with ISA 315 (Revised 2019)** *Identifying and Assessing the Risks of Material Misstatement*?

A   Inspection

B   Observation

C   External confirmation

D   Enquiry

3 **Based on the above draft figures, what would be an appropriate level at which to set preliminary materiality?**

A $150,000 for the statement of profit and loss and $500,000 for the statement of financial position

B $500,000 for the statement of profit and loss and $150,000 for the statement of financial position

C $1,500 for the statement of profit and loss and $50,000 for the statement of financial position

D $50,000 for the statement of profit and loss and $1,500 for the statement of financial position

4 **Performance materiality should be used by the auditor when performing substantive testing during the audit. Which of the following best describes performance materiality?**

A The maximum amount of misstatement the auditor is willing to accept

B The amount at which the auditor deems the misstatement to be trivial

C An amount which could influence the economic decisions of the users taken on the basis of the financial statements

D An amount set below materiality for the financial statements as a whole to reduce, to an acceptably low level, the risk that misstatements could be material in aggregate

5 **Professional scepticism must be applied by the auditor during the audit. Which of the following is NOT an application of professional scepticism?**

A A critical evaluation of the evidence

B An open and questioning mind

C The auditor should not believe anything the client tells them

D The auditor must be alert to fraud and error

5 Chapter summary

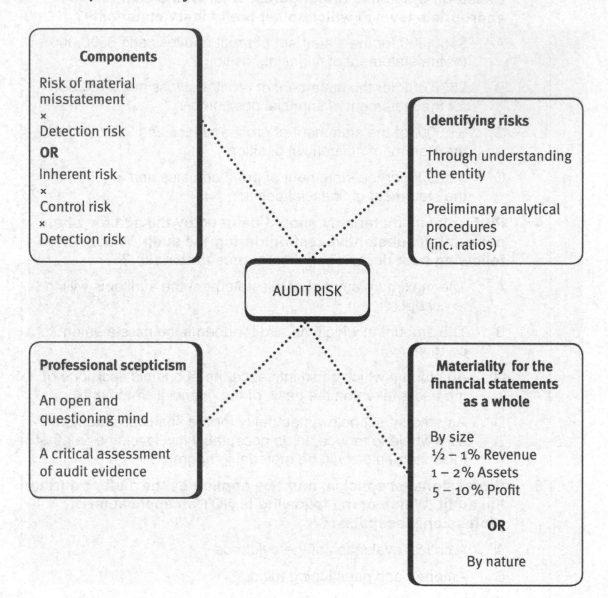

Components

Risk of material misstatement
×
Detection risk

OR

Inherent risk
×
Control risk
×
Detection risk

Identifying risks

Through understanding the entity

Preliminary analytical procedures (inc. ratios)

AUDIT RISK

Professional scepticism

An open and questioning mind

A critical assessment of audit evidence

Materiality for the financial statements as a whole

By size
½ – 1% Revenue
1 – 2% Assets
5 – 10% Profit

OR

By nature

Test your understanding answers

 Test your understanding 1

Audit risks	Auditor's response
Murray Co is a new audit client. There is a lack of cumulative audit knowledge and experience. Detection risk is increased. Opening balances may be misstated as Wimble & Co did not perform the audit last year.	More time and resource will need to be devoted to obtaining an understanding of Murray Co at the start of the audit. More substantive procedures will need to be planned and performed, and larger samples tested in order to lower detection risk. Opening balances will need to be agreed to the prior year signed financial statements. The previous auditor could be contacted to obtain relevant working papers.
Inventory is stored at a third party warehouse. It may be difficult to obtain sufficient appropriate evidence over the quantity and condition of inventory held. There is increased detection risk over completeness, existence and valuation of inventory.	Additional procedures should be performed to ensure that inventory quantities and condition have been confirmed for both third party and company owned locations, e.g. • Attend the inventory count at the third party warehouses (if one is to be performed) to review the controls in operation. • Inspect any reports produced by the auditors of third party warehouses in relation to the adequacy of controls over inventory. • Obtain external confirmation from the third party regarding the quantity and condition of the inventory.

Ergometers take up to one week to manufacture. There is likely to be a material work in progress (WIP) inventory balance at the year-end. Determining the value and quantity of WIP is complex. There is a risk of misstatement of WIP inventory.	The percentage of completion basis should be discussed with the client and assessed for reasonableness. The WIP calculation should be agreed to supporting documentation such as purchase invoices for materials and timesheets and payroll records for labour. The overhead calculation should be recalculated and reviewed for any non-production overheads.
Murray Co refurbished the assembly line for the ergometers during the year. Expenditure incurred may have been incorrectly capitalised or incorrectly expensed as repairs. There is a risk that that non-current assets are over or understated.	Review a breakdown of the costs and agree to invoices to assess the nature of the expenditure. Agree capital expenditure to inclusion within the asset register, and agree repairs to expenses in the statement of profit or loss.
There is a new website directly linked to the finance system which records sales automatically. There is increased risk over completeness of income if the system fails to record all sales made on the website. There is a risk that revenue is understated.	Extended controls testing to be performed over the sales cycle. Use test data to confirm that sales entered into the website are automatically transferred to the finance system. Detailed testing to be performed over the completeness of income by tracing orders through to GDNs, sales invoices and into the sales day book.
The website development costs have been capitalised. In order to be capitalised, it must meet all of the criteria under IAS ® 38 *Intangible Assets*. Research costs should be expensed rather than capitalised. There is a risk that intangible assets are overstated.	A breakdown of the development expenditure should be reviewed and tested in detail to ensure that only projects which meet the capitalisation criteria are included as an intangible asset, with the balance being expensed.

Retailer sales have fallen dramatically in the last two years. If retailer sales continue to fall and direct consumer sales do not compensate for the loss of retailer revenue, Murray Co may not be able to continue to operate for the foreseeable future. There is a risk that disclosures of material uncertainties relating to going concern may be inadequate.	Perform a detailed going concern review, including: Obtain and review the company's cash flow forecast and evaluate the reasonableness of the assumptions used to understand if management will have sufficient cash. Review the post year-end order book from retailers and post year-end direct consumer sales to assess if the revenue figures in the cash flow are reasonable.
Several of the sales team were made redundant last month as a result of the falling retailer sales. Under IAS 37 *Provisions, Contingent Liabilities and Contingent Assets*, a redundancy provision will be required for any staff not yet paid at the year-end. There is a risk of understated liabilities.	Discuss with management the progress of the redundancy programme. Review post year-end bank statements for any redundancy payments made and agree to the year-end provision.
Some retail customers are struggling to pay their outstanding balances to Murray Co. The balances may be irrecoverable debts that should be written off. There is a risk of overstatement of receivables and understatement of the irrecoverable debt allowance and expense.	Extended post year-end cash receipts testing to assess valuation. Review of the aged receivables ledger to identify long outstanding debts. The allowance for receivables should be discussed with management if it is considered inadequate.
Murray Co is planning to list on the stock exchange next year. There is an increased risk of manipulation of the financial statements. There is a risk of overstatement of assets and profits, and understatement of expenses and liabilities.	Increase the level of professional scepticism and be alert to the risks identified in order to achieve a successful listing. Plan and perform procedures to ensure accounting estimates and judgmental areas are reasonable.

Test your understanding 2

Audit risks identified using analytical procedures

Revenue has increased by 12%.	Retailer sales at Murray Co have fallen dramatically in the last two years. The increase in revenue is not consistent with this. Although Murray Co has started selling directly to consumers for the first time this year, it is unlikely that these sales will have compensated for the loss in retailer sales at this early stage. In addition, revenue may be deliberately overstated by Murray Co in order to increase the chances of a successful listing. There is a risk that revenue is overstated.
Gross margin has increased from 12.8% (2,500/19,580) to 15.5% (3,400/21,960).	The margins for direct consumer sales are likely to be higher than retailer sales, which may explain this increase. However, the increase could also be caused by overstatement of revenue, as explained above, or understatement of cost of sales due to incomplete recording of costs or overvaluation of closing inventory.
Operating expenses has no movement.	This is unusual given the increase in revenue and cost of sales. There is a risk that the prior year figure has been incorrectly presented in the current year column.
Operating margin has increased from 2.5% (488/19,580) to 6.3% (1,388/21,960).	Operating margin has increased at a greater rate than gross margin. Given that this is the first year of direct consumer sales, the operating margin would not be expected to increase significantly, as the level of operating expenses would normally be higher at this early stage. This indicates potential overstatement of revenue and understatement of operating expenses.
The inventory holding period has increased from 28 days (1,300/17,080 × 365) to 41 days (2,109/18,560 × 365).	As sales have increased, this could be because of an increase in demand and therefore the need to hold more inventory. However, as retailer sales at Murray Co have fallen dramatically, there is a risk that some of the inventory is bespoke, and may therefore be obsolete. There is a risk that inventory is overstated.

The trade receivables collection period has increased from 20 days (1,050/19,580 × 365) to 34 days (2,040/21,960 × 365).	Given that website customers pay on ordering, the collection period would be expected to fall. However, some of Murray Co's retail customers are struggling to pay their outstanding balances. Trade receivables may be overstated, and the allowance for doubtful debts understated.
The trade payables payment period has increased from 26 days (1,205/17,080 × 365) to 28 days (1,400/18,560 × 365).	An increase in the payables payment period could be caused by understatement of cost of sales. The increase in gross profit margin also highlighted this as a potential risk.
Current ratio has improved from 1.6:1 to 2.3:1. Quick ratio has improved from 0.71: 1 to 1.14:1.	Murray Co appears to be managing its working capital effectively. However, given the plans to list on the stock exchange next year, this may be indicative of manipulation of the financial statements in order to increase the chances of a successful listing. In addition, Murray Co has increased its long and short-term finance during the year.

 Test your understanding 3

Audit risks and effect on audit approach

Risk and explanation	Effect on audit approach
Hook Co is a new audit client. There is a lack of cumulative audit knowledge and experience. Detection risk is increased. Opening balances may be misstated as JPR Edwards & Co did not perform the audit last year.	More time and resource will need to be devoted to obtaining an understanding of Hook Co at the start of the audit. More substantive procedures will need to be planned and performed, and larger samples tested in order to lower detection risk. Opening balances will need to be agreed to the prior year signed financial statements. The previous auditor could be contacted to obtain relevant working papers.

Hook Co is expected to have a material work-in-progress balance at the year end. The calculation and valuation of work in progress is subjective. There is a risk of overstatement of inventory.	Appropriate time should be allocated to attending the inventory count and understanding the inventory valuation process for work in progress. The basis for assessing the percentage of completion of WIP should be discussed with management to ensure it is reasonable. Purchase invoices should be inspected to verify cost; payroll records and job cards should be inspected to verify the labour element of WIP and finished goods. Overheads included in WIP and finished goods should be recalculated and reviewed to ensure only production overheads are included.
Hook Co manufactures electrical goods for the entertainment market. This is a rapidly changing market and goods can become obsolete quickly which may result in the NRV falling below cost. There is a risk of overstatement of inventory.	The aged inventory listing should be reviewed for old or obsolete items and compared with the allowance made to write the inventory down to NRV, to ensure the allowance is adequate. If the allowance does not appear adequate, it should be discussed with management.
Hook Co's key client represents 70% of its revenue. Hook Co may be over reliant on this client which could threaten its going concern status if this key client was lost. There is a risk that disclosures of material uncertainties relating to going concern are inadequate.	Procedures should be designed at the planning stage to allow the auditor to assess the going concern risk faced by Hook Co. Contracts and other correspondence from the key customer should be reviewed to identify any specific risks that the client may be lost. Analytical procedures should be designed to assess the impact on Hook Co's financial position if the contract is not renewed.

Hook Co spent $1m on developing a new product. There is a risk that Hook Co has capitalised development expenditure which should have been expensed through the statement of profit or loss as research costs. If the application does not meet the criteria required to classify as development costs they should be expensed to the statement of profit or loss in the year they were incurred. There is a risk of overstatement of intangible assets.	Enquiries should be made as to how Hook Co identifies whether the criteria for capitalisation have been met in accordance with the relevant accounting standard. Where amounts have been capitalised, further procedures should be performed to assess whether the criteria of IAS 38 have been met e.g. review budgets to ensure resources have been allocated to the development, review project plans to ensure the development is expected to be completed, and review forecasts to ensure the product is expected to generate a profit.
Hook Co is aiming to list on the London Stock Exchange this year. The directors may have greater incentive to 'window dress' the accounts to show a more favourable position in order to increase the proceeds generated. Assets and profits may be overstated and liabilities understated to make the company appear a more attractive investment.	Increased professional scepticism is required when performing the audit. Procedures should be planned to ensure areas of judgment and estimates exercised by the directors are reasonable and can be justified. Special consideration should be given to sales cut-off testing.

Test your understanding 4

Materiality is defined as follows:

'Misstatements, including omissions, are considered to be material if they, individually or in aggregate, could reasonably be expected to influence the economic decisions of users taken on the basis of the financial statements.' [ISA 320 *Materiality in Planning and Performing an Audit*, 2]

In assessing the level of materiality there are a number of areas that should be considered. Firstly the auditor must consider both the amount (quantity) and the nature (quality) of any misstatements, or a combination of both. The quantity of the misstatement refers to the relative size of it and the quality refers to an amount that might be low in value but due to its prominence could influence the user's decision, for example, directors' transactions.

The assessment of what is material is ultimately a matter of the auditors' professional judgment, and it is affected by the auditor's perception of the financial information needs of users of the financial statements.

Materiality is often calculated using benchmarks such as 5% of profit before tax or 1% of assets. These values are useful as a starting point for assessing materiality.

In assessing materiality, the auditor must consider that a number of errors each with a low value may, when aggregated, amount to a material misstatement.

In calculating materiality the auditor should also consider setting the performance materiality level. This is the amount set by the auditor, below materiality for the financial statements as a whole, and is used for particular transactions, account balances and disclosures.

Test your understanding 5

1	D	Options A, B and C are business risks. An audit risk must be described in terms of a risk of material misstatement (i.e. the impact on the financial statements) or a detection risk (why the auditor may not detect the misstatement).
2	A	Payables/Cost of sales × 304. There are 304 days in the period January to October.
3	B	Recalculation is not an analytical procedure. An analytical procedure evaluates relationships between data.
4	D	Revenue growth is a trend rather than a ratio. Acid test is another name for the quick ratio.
5	C	If closing inventory is overvalued, a larger figure will be deducted from cost of sales and, therefore, cost of sales will be lower and gross profit will be higher. A and B would both cause gross profit margin to fall. D would have no impact as administrative expenses do not affect gross profit.

Test your understanding 6

1	B	The financial statements can be materially misstated by the omission of a balance or disclosure.
2	C	External confirmation is not listed in ISA 315 (Revised 2019) as a risk assessment procedure. It is usually used as a substantive procedure.
3	A	Using 5% of PBT and 1% of total assets an appropriate level of materiality would be $150,000 for the statement of profit or loss and $500,000 for the statement of financial position.
4	D	A and B both refer to tolerable misstatement. C is a description of materiality for the financial statements as a whole.
5	C	Professional scepticism involves being alert to possible frauds and errors but does not require complete mistrust of the client.

Planning

Chapter learning objectives

This chapter covers syllabus areas:

- B1e – Objectives and importance of quality control procedures in conducting an audit

- B1f – Quality control procedures over engagement performance, monitoring quality and compliance with ethical requirements

- B2 – Planning and risk assessment: objective and general principles

- B5 – Fraud, laws and regulations

- B6 – Audit planning and documentation

Detailed syllabus objectives are provided in the introduction section of the text book.

PER

One of the PER performance objectives (PO18) is to prepare for and plan the audit process. You plan and control the engagement process, including the initial investigation. You also plan and monitor the audit programme – legally and ethically. Working through this chapter should help you understand how to demonstrate that objective.

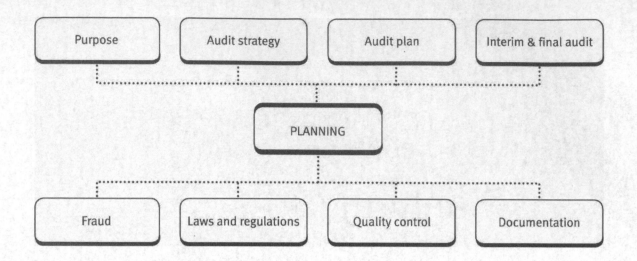

1 Purpose of planning

'The objective of the auditor is to plan the audit so that it will be performed in an effective manner.'
[ISA 300 *Planning an Audit of Financial Statements*, 4]

Audits are potentially complex, risky and expensive processes. Although firms have internal manuals and standardised procedures, it is vital that engagements are planned.

Benefits of planning

Planning enables the auditor to:

- Devote appropriate attention to important areas of the audit.

- Identify and resolve potential problems on a timely basis.

- Organise and manage the audit so that it is performed in an effective and efficient manner.

- Select team members with appropriate capabilities and competencies.

- Direct and supervise the team and review their work.

- Effectively coordinate the work of others, such as experts and internal audit.

[ISA 300, 2]

 Planning ensures that the risk of performing a poor quality audit (and ultimately giving an inappropriate audit opinion) is reduced to an acceptable level.

Conducting the audit in accordance with ISAs:

In order to achieve the overall objectives of the auditor, the audit must be conducted in accordance with ISAs. This will:

- Ensure that the auditor is fulfilling all of their responsibilities.

- Allow a user to have as much confidence in one auditor's opinion as another's and therefore to rely on one audited set of financial statements to the same extent that they rely on another.

- Ensure that the quality of audits internationally, is maintained to a high standard (thereby upholding the reputation of the profession).

- Provide a measure to assess the standard of an auditor's work (necessary when determining their suitability as an authorised practitioner).

Professional scepticism and professional judgment

Auditors are also required to perform audits with an attitude of professional scepticism. Professional scepticism was explained in the previous chapter. Having an enquiring mind in itself is not sufficient to comply with a risk based method of auditing, the auditor must also use professional judgment.

 Professional judgment is the application of relevant training, knowledge and experience in making informed decisions about the courses of action that are appropriate in the circumstances of the audit engagement. [ISA 200, 13k]

Therefore the use of a risk based approach requires skill, knowledge, experience and an inquisitive, open mind.

 Although risk assessment is a fundamental element of the planning process, risks can be uncovered at any stage of the audit, and procedures must be adapted in light of revelations that indicate further risks of material misstatement. It is the responsibility of the most senior reviewer (usually the engagement partner) to confirm that the risk of material misstatement has been reduced to an acceptable level.

The planning process

Planning consists of a number of elements. They can be summarised as:

- Preliminary engagement activities:

  - Performing procedures regarding the continuance of the client engagement.

  - Evaluating compliance with ethical requirements.

  - Ensuring there are no misunderstandings with the client as to the terms of the engagement.

  [ISA 300, 6]

  The preliminary engagement activities were covered in the chapter Ethics and acceptance.

- Planning activities:
    - Developing the audit strategy
    - Developing an audit plan.

[ISA 300, 7]

The audit strategy and the audit plan must be documented in the audit working papers. Any updates to them must also be documented.

2 The audit strategy

The audit strategy sets the scope, timing and direction of the audit.

The diagram below summarises some of the matters the auditor may consider in establishing the strategy.

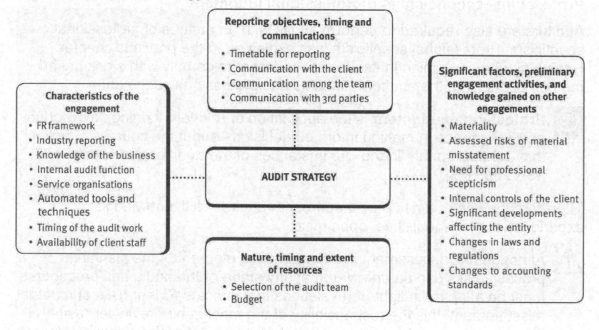

[ISA 300, Appendix]

The audit strategy allows the auditor to determine:

- The resources to deploy for specific audit areas (e.g. experience level, external experts).

- The amount of resources to allocate (i.e. number of team members).

- When these resources are to be deployed.

- How the resources are managed, directed and supervised, including the timings of meetings, debriefs and reviews.

[ISA 300, A8]

3 The audit plan

Once the audit strategy has been established, the next stage is to develop a specific, detailed plan to address how the various matters identified in the overall strategy will be applied.

The strategy sets the overall approach to the audit and the plan fills in the operational details of how the strategy is to be achieved.

The audit plan should include specific descriptions of:

- The nature, timing and extent of risk assessment procedures.

- The nature, timing and extent of further audit procedures, including:

  - **What** audit procedures are to be carried out

  - **Who** should do them

  - **How** much work should be done (sample sizes, etc.)

  - **When** the work should be done (interim vs. final)

- Any other procedures necessary to conform to ISAs.

[ISA 300, 9]

The relationship between the audit strategy and the audit plan

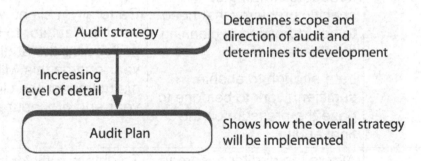

Audit strategy — Determines scope and direction of audit and determines its development

Increasing level of detail

Audit Plan — Shows how the overall strategy will be implemented

4 Interim and final audit

The auditor must consider the timing of audit procedures such as whether to carry out an interim audit and a final audit, or just a final audit.

For an interim audit to be justified, the client normally needs to be of a sufficient size because this may increase costs. However, an interim audit should improve risk assessment and make final procedures more efficient.

 It is important to note that the interim audit and final audit are two stages of the same audit. One set of financial statements are audited. One auditor's report will be issued. The audit work however is being performed in two stages – some work before the year-end and some work after the year-end.

	Interim audit	Final audit
Timing	Completed part way through a client's accounting year (i.e. before the year-end). Early enough not to interfere with year-end procedures at the client and to give adequate warning of specific problems that need to be addressed in planning the final audit. Late enough to enable sufficient work to be done to ease the pressure on the final audit.	Takes place after the year-end at a time agreed with the client which enables them to file their financial statements with the relevant authorities by the required deadline. Generally a client would not want the auditor to be performing the audit at the year-end as this will cause disruption for the client's year-end procedures.
Purpose	Allows the auditor to spread out their procedures and enables more effective planning for the final stage of the audit. Useful when there is increased detection risk due to a tight reporting deadline.	To obtain sufficient appropriate evidence in respect of the financial statements to enable the auditor's report to be issued. The auditor's report will be issued once the final audit is complete and this signifies the end of the audit.

| Work performed | • Documenting systems
 • Evaluating controls.

 Additional activities that can be performed include:

 • Testing of specific and complete material transactions, e.g. purchasing new non-current assets.

 • Testing of transactions such as sales, purchases and payroll for the year to date.

 • Assessing risks that will affect work conducted at the final audit.

 • Attending perpetual inventory counts. | • Audit of statement of financial position balances which will only be known at the year-end.

 • Transaction testing for transactions that have occurred since the interim audit took place.

 • Testing of year-end journals, which may include adjustments to the transactions tested at the interim audit.

 • Obtaining evidence that the controls tested at the interim audit have continued to operate during the period since the interim audit took place.

 • Completion activities such as going concern and subsequent events reviews, overall review of the financial statements and communication of misstatements with management and those charged with governance. |

Impact of interim audit work on the final audit

- If the controls tested at the interim stage provided evidence that control risk is low, fewer substantive procedures can be performed.

- If substantive procedures have been performed at the interim stage, fewer procedures will be required at the final audit in general. This will mean the final audit will require less time to perform.

- The auditor's report can be signed closer to the year-end resulting in more timely reporting to shareholders.

- If the interim audit identified areas of increased risk, for example, controls were found not to be working effectively, increased substantive procedures will be required at the final audit.

5 Fraud and error

Misstatement in the financial statements can arise from either fraud or error. The distinguishing factor is whether the underlying action that resulted in the misstatement was intentional or unintentional. [ISA 240, 2]

Fraud

 Fraud is **an intentional act by one or more individuals among management, those charged with governance, employees or third parties, involving the use of deception to obtain an unjust or illegal advantage**.
[ISA 240 *the Auditor's Responsibilities Relating to Fraud in an Audit of Financial Statements*, 11a]

Fraud can be split into two types:

- Fraudulent financial reporting – deliberately misstating the financial statements to make the company's performance or position look better/worse than it actually is.

- Misappropriation – theft of a company's assets such as cash or inventory.

[ISA 240, 3]

Error

An error can be defined as an unintentional misstatement in financial statements, including the omission of amounts or disclosures, such as the following:

- A mistake in gathering and processing data from which financial statements are prepared.

- An incorrect accounting estimate arising from oversight or a misinterpretation of facts.

- A mistake in the application of accounting principles relating to measurement, recognition, classification, presentation or disclosure.

[ISA 450 *Evaluation of Misstatements Identified During the Audit*, A1]

Directors' responsibilities in respect of fraud

The primary responsibility for the prevention and detection of fraud rests with those charged with governance and the management of an entity. This is achieved by:

- Implementing an **effective system of internal control,** reducing opportunities for fraud to take place and increasing the likelihood of detection (and punishment).

- Creating a **culture** of honesty, ethical behaviour, and active oversight by those charged with governance.

The directors should be aware of the potential for fraud and this should feature as an element of their risk assessment and corporate governance procedures.

The audit committee should review these procedures to ensure that they are in place and working effectively.

This will normally be achieved in conjunction with the internal auditors.

[ISA 240, 4]

Internal auditors

Internal auditors can help management fulfil their responsibilities in respect of fraud and error. Typical functions the internal auditor can perform include:

- Testing the effectiveness of the internal controls at preventing and detecting fraud and error and provide recommendations for improvements to the controls.

- Performing fraud investigations to:

  - identify how the fraud was committed

  - identify the extent of the fraud

  - provide recommendations on how to prevent the fraud from happening again.

- Performing surprise asset counts to identify misappropriation.

The presence of an internal audit department may act as a deterrent to fraud in itself as there is a greater chance of being discovered.

External auditor's responsibilities in respect of fraud

The auditor's role is two-fold:

- Assess the risk of material misstatement due to fraud, and

- Respond to the assessed risks.

Assessing the risk of fraud

The auditor should:

- Obtain reasonable assurance that the financial statements are free from material misstatement, whether caused by fraud or error. [ISA 240, 5]

- Apply professional scepticism and remain alert to the possibility that fraud could take place. [ISA 240, 8]

  This means that the auditor must recognise the possibility that a material misstatement due to fraud could occur, regardless of the auditor's prior experience of the client's integrity and honesty.

- Consider the potential for management override of controls and recognise that audit procedures that are effective for detecting error may not be effective for detecting fraud. [ISA 240, 8]

This can be achieved by performing the following procedures:

- Discuss the susceptibility of the client's financial statements to material misstatement due to fraud with the engagement team. [ISA 240, 15]

  This discussion should include consideration of:

  – Incentives to commit fraud such as profit related bonuses or applications for finance.

  – Opportunities to commit fraud such as ineffective internal controls.

  – Management's attitude e.g. disputes with the auditor over auditing matters or failure to remedy known deficiencies.

  [ISA 240, Appendix 1]

- Enquire of management about their processes for identifying and responding to the risk of fraud. [ISA 240, 17]

- Enquire of management, internal auditors and those charged with governance if they are aware of any actual or suspected fraudulent activity. [ISA 240, 18 - 21]

- Consideration of relationships identified during analytical procedures. [ISA 240, 22]

Responding to the assessed risks

The following procedures must be performed:

- Review journal entries made to identify manipulation of figures recorded or unauthorised journal adjustments:

  – Enquire of those involved in financial reporting about unusual activity relating to adjustments.

  – Select journal entries and adjustments made at the end of the reporting period.

  – Consider the need to test journal entries throughout the period. [ISA 240, 32a]

- Review management estimates for evidence of bias:

  – Evaluate the reasonableness of judgments and whether they indicate any bias on behalf of management.

  – Perform a retrospective review of management judgments reflected in the prior year. [ISA 240, 32b]

- Review transactions outside the normal course of business, or transactions which appear unusual and assess whether they are indicative of fraudulent financial reporting. [ISA 240, 32c]

- Obtain written representation from management and those charged with governance that they:

  - acknowledge their responsibility for internal controls to prevent and detect fraud.

  - have disclosed to the auditor the results of management's fraud risk assessment.

  - have disclosed to the auditor any known or suspected frauds.

  - have disclosed to the auditor any allegations of fraud affecting the entity's financial statements.
    [ISA 240, 39]

There is an unavoidable risk that some material misstatements may not be detected even if properly planned in accordance with ISAs as fraud is likely to be concealed. [ISA 240, 5]

The ability to detect fraud depends on the skill of the perpetrator, collusion, relative size of amounts manipulated, and the seniority of the people involved. [ISA 240, 6]

Reporting of fraud and error

- If the auditor identifies a fraud they must communicate the matter on a timely basis to the appropriate level of management (i.e. those with the primary responsibility for prevention and detection of fraud). [ISA 240, 40]

- If the suspected fraud involves management the auditor must communicate the matter to those charged with governance. [ISA 240, 41]

- If the auditor has doubts about the integrity of those charged with governance they should seek legal advice regarding an appropriate course of action. [ISA 240, A65]

- In addition to these responsibilities, the auditor must also consider whether they have a responsibility to report the occurrence of a suspicion to a party outside the entity. Whilst the auditor does have an ethical duty to maintain confidentiality, it is likely that any legal responsibility will take precedence. In these circumstances it is advisable to seek legal advice. [ISA 240, 43]

- If the fraud has a material impact on the financial statements the audit opinion will be modified. When the opinion is modified, the auditor will explain why it has been modified and this will make the shareholders aware of the fraud.

6 Laws and regulations

Guidance relating to laws and regulations in an audit of financial statements is provided in ISA 250 (Revised) *Consideration of Laws and Regulations in an Audit of Financial Statements.*

 Non-compliance – Acts of omission or commission, either intentional or unintentional, committed by the entity, which are contrary to the prevailing laws or regulations. Non-compliance does not include personal misconduct unrelated to the business activities of the entity.
[ISA 250, 12]

Responsibilities are considered from the perspective of both auditors and management.

Responsibilities of management

It is the responsibility of management, with the oversight of those charged with governance, to ensure that the entity's operations are conducted in accordance with relevant laws and regulations, including those that determine the reported amounts and disclosures in the financial statements. [ISA 250, 3]

Responsibilities of the auditor

The auditor must perform audit procedures to help identify non-compliance with laws and regulations that may have a material impact on the financial statements.

The auditor must obtain sufficient, appropriate evidence regarding compliance with laws and regulations generally recognised to have a **direct effect** on the determination of material amounts and disclosures in the financial statements (e.g. completeness of a tax provision in accordance with tax law, or the presentation of the financial statements in accordance with the applicable financial reporting framework). [ISA 250, 6a]

The auditor must perform audit procedures to help identify non-compliance with **other laws and regulations** that may have a material impact on the financial statements (e.g. data protection, environmental legislation, public health and safety). Non-compliance in respect of such matters could affect the company's ability to continue as a going concern or could result in the need for material liabilities to be recognised or disclosed. [ISA 250, 6b]

Audit procedures to identify instances of non-compliance

- **Obtaining a general understanding** of the legal and regulatory framework applicable to the entity and the industry, and of how the entity is complying with that framework. [ISA 250, 13]

- **Enquiring of management and those charged with governance** as to whether the entity is in compliance with such laws and regulations. [ISA 250, 15a]

- **Inspecting correspondence** with relevant licensing or regulatory authorities. [ISA 250, 15b]

- **Remaining alert** to the possibility that other audit procedures applied may bring instances of non-compliance to the auditor's attention. [ISA 250, 16]

- **Obtaining written representation** from the directors that they have disclosed to the auditors all those events of which they are aware which involve possible non-compliance, together with the actual or contingent consequences which may arise from such non-compliance. [ISA 250, 17]

Investigations of possible non-compliance

When the auditor becomes aware of information concerning a possible instance of **non-compliance** with laws or regulations, they should:

- Understand the **nature of the act and circumstances** in which it has occurred.

- Obtain further information to **evaluate the possible effect** on the financial statements.

[ISA 250, 19]

Audit procedures when non-compliance is identified

- Enquire of management of the penalties to be imposed.

- Inspect correspondence with the regulatory authority to identify the consequences.

- Inspect board minutes for management's discussion on actions to be taken regarding the non-compliance.

- Enquire of the company's legal department as to the possible impact of the non-compliance.

Reporting non-compliance

- The auditor must report non-compliance to management and those charged with governance, unless prohibited by law or regulation. [ISA 250, 23]

- If the auditor believes the non-compliance is intentional and material, the matter should be reported to those charged with governance. [ISA 250, 24]

- If the auditor suspects management or those charged with governance are involved in the non-compliance, the matter should be reported to the audit committee or supervisory board. [ISA 250, 25]

- If the non-compliance has a material effect on the financial statements, a qualified or adverse opinion should be issued. [ISA 250, 26]

- The auditor should also consider whether they have any legal or ethical responsibility to report non-compliance to third parties (e.g. to a regulatory authority). [ISA 250, 29]

NOCLAR: Auditor responsibilities in addition to ISA 250

The IESBA *Code of Ethics for Professional Accountants* sets out new ethical requirements in relation to an entity's compliance with laws and regulations.

The ethical standard, *Responding to Non-compliance with Laws and Regulations* (NOCLAR), provides guidance to accountants as to the actions that should be taken if they become aware of an illegal act committed by a client or employer.

The additional requirements have been introduced to address concerns that the duty of confidentiality was acting as a barrier to the disclosure of potential NOCLAR to public authorities in the appropriate circumstances. Auditors were resigning from client relationships without NOCLAR issues being appropriately addressed.

NOCLAR sets out responsibilities in relation to:

- Responding to identified or suspected non-compliance

- Communicating identified or suspected non-compliance with other auditors

- Documenting identified or suspected non-compliance.

The aim is to generate an earlier response by management or those charged with governance, and timelier intervention from public authorities on reports of potential NOCLAR, thereby mitigating adverse consequences for stakeholders and the general public.

7 Quality control

ISA 220 *Quality Control for an Audit of Financial Statements* requires the firm to establish a system of quality control to ensure the firm complies with professional standards and issues reports that are appropriate in the circumstances. [ISA 220, 6]

Policies and procedures should be established which address:

- Leadership responsibilities for quality within the firm
- Relevant ethical requirements
- Acceptance and continuance of client relationships and specific engagements
- Human resources
- Engagement performance
- Monitoring.

[ISA 220, A1]

The Audit and Assurance syllabus requires an understanding of the relevant ethical requirements, engagement performance and monitoring.

Relevant ethical requirements

The firm should ensure compliance with the requirements of the ACCA Code of Ethics and Conduct covered in Chapter 4.

The engagement partner must:

- Identify circumstances which threaten independence.
- Determine whether they create a threat to independence.
- Take appropriate action to eliminate the threats or reduce them to an acceptable level.

[ISA 200, 11]

Engagement performance

Engagement performance comprises direction, supervision and review of the engagement.

Direction involves informing team members of:

- Their responsibilities
- Objectives of the work to be performed
- The nature of the business

- Risks

- Problems that may arise

- The detailed approach to the performance of the engagement.

[ISA 220, A14]

Supervision includes:

- Tracking the progress of the audit to ensure the timetable can be met

- Considering the competence of the team

- Addressing significant matters arising and modifying the planned approach accordingly

- Identifying matters for consultation. Consultation may be required where the firm lacks appropriate internal expertise.

[ISA 220, A16]

Review responsibilities include consideration of whether:

- The work has been performed in accordance with professional standards

- Appropriate consultations have taken place

- The work performed supports the conclusions reached

- The evidence obtained is sufficient and appropriate to support the auditor's report.

- The objectives of the engagement procedures have been achieved.

[ISA 220, A18]

The engagement partner should perform a review of critical areas of judgment, significant risks and other areas of importance throughout the audit. The extent and timing of the partner's reviews should be documented. [ISA 220, A19]

Engagement Quality Control Review

Listed entities and other high risk clients should be subject to an engagement quality control review (EQCR). [ISA 220, 19]

This is also referred to as a pre-issuance review or 'Hot' review.

High risk clients include those which are in the public interest, those with unusual circumstances and risks, and those where laws or regulations require an EQCR.

An EQCR includes:

- Discussion of significant matters with the engagement partner.

- Review of the financial statements and proposed auditor's report.

- Review of selected audit documentation relating to significant judgments and conclusions reached. This includes:

    - Significant risks and responses to those risks

    - Judgments with respect to materiality and significant risks

    - Significance of uncorrected misstatements

    - Matters to be communicated to management and those charged with governance, and where applicable, other parties such as regulatory bodies.

- Evaluation of conclusions reached in forming the audit opinion.

[ISA 220, 20]

For listed entity audits, the EQCR should also consider:

- Independence of the engagement team.

- Whether appropriate consultation has taken place on contentious matters or differences of opinion.

- Whether documentation reflects the work performed in relation to significant judgments.

[ISA 220, 21]

Eligibility criteria

The engagement quality control reviewer:

- Should have the technical qualifications to perform the role, including the necessary experience and authority, and

- Should be objective. To be objective the reviewer should not be selected by the engagement partner and should not participate in the engagement.

[ISA 220, 7c]

Note: An engagement quality control reviewer may also be referred to as an independent review partner.

Monitoring

Quality control policies alone do not ensure good quality work. Firms should carry out post-issuance or 'cold' reviews to ensure that quality control procedures are adequate, relevant and operating effectively. [ISA 220, 23]

	Post-issuance (cold) review
Purpose	To assess whether the firm's policies and procedures were implemented during an engagement and to identify any deficiencies therein.
When	After the auditor's report has been signed.
Which files	A selection of completed audit files.
Conducted by	A dedicated compliance or quality department/a qualified external consultant/an independent partner.
Matters considered	Working papers should demonstrate that: • Sufficient appropriate evidence has been obtained. • All matters were resolved before issuing the auditor's report. All working papers should be: • On file • Completed • Signed as completed • Evidence as reviewed.
Outcomes	A report of the results will be provided to the partners of the firm highlighting deficiencies that require corrective action. Recommendations will be made including: • Communication of findings • Additional quality control reviews • Training • Changes to the firm's policies and procedures • Disciplinary action.

Other aspects of quality control

Leadership

The engagement partner takes responsibility for the overall quality of the engagement. [ISA 220, 8]

The engagement partner should emphasise the importance of:

- Performing work that complies with professional standards.
- Complying with the firm's quality control policies and procedures.
- Issuing auditor's reports that are appropriate in the circumstances.
- The engagement team's ability to raise concerns without fear of reprisal.

[ISA 220, A3a]

Acceptance and continuance of client relationships

The firm should ensure only clients and work of an acceptable level of risk are accepted. This requires consideration of:

- Integrity of management
- Competence of the engagement team
- Compliance with ethical requirements
- Significant matters that have arisen during the current or previous audit
  engagement and their implications for continuing the relationship.

[ISA 220, A8]

Human resources

The engagement partner should ensure that the engagement team collectively have the competence and capabilities to perform the audit in accordance with professional standards. This includes knowledge of professional standards, knowledge of relevant industries in which the client operates, the ability to apply judgment and an understanding of the firm's quality control policies and procedures. [ISA 220, A11]

8 Audit documentation

Purposes of audit documentation

ISA 230 *Audit Documentation* requires auditors to prepare and retain written documentation that:

- Provides evidence of the auditor's basis for their report.

- Provides evidence that the audit was planned and performed in accordance with ISAs and applicable legal and regulatory requirements.

[ISA 230, 2]

In addition, audit documentation:

- Assists the engagement team to plan and perform the audit.

- Assists members of the engagement team responsible for supervision to direct, supervise and review the audit work.

- Enables the engagement team to be accountable for its work.

- Retains a record of matters of continuing significance to future audits.

- Enables the quality control reviews to be performed.

- Enables the external quality inspections to be performed.

[ISA 230, 3]

Form and content of audit documentation

Documentation should be sufficient to enable an experienced auditor, with no previous connection to the audit, to understand:

- The nature, timing and extent of audit procedures performed.

- The results of the procedures performed and the evidence obtained.

- The significant matters arising during the course of the audit and the conclusions reached thereon, and significant professional judgments made in reaching those conclusions.

[ISA 230, 8]

Retention of working papers

Documentation is retained in an audit file, which should be completed in a timely fashion after the date of the auditor's report (normally not more than 60 days after) and retained for the period required by national regulatory requirements (this is normally five years from the date of the auditor's report).

[ISA 230, A21, A23]

Illustration 1 – Wimble & Co working paper

Client:	*Murray Co*	Reference:	*RA1*
Period end:	*31/12/X4*	Prepared by:	*Rob Cash*
Subject	*Risk Assessment*	Date prepared:	*Dec 1 20X4*

Objective: To identify the risks of material misstatement in the financial statements of Murray Co for the year-ended 31 December 20X4, in order to provide a basis for designing and performing audit procedures that respond to the assessed risks.

Work performed: Discussion among the engagement team of the

susceptibility of the financial statements to material misstatement. RA1/1of the financial statements to material misstatement: **RA1/1**

A summary of the understanding of the entity and its environment obtained, detailing the key elements including internal control components, sources of information and risk assessment procedures performed: **RA/2**

Analytical procedures performed: **RA/3**

Results: The identified and assessed risks of material misstatement: **RA/4**

Conclusions: The overall responses to address the risks of material misstatement: **RA/5**

Reviewed by: *An Audit Manager*

Date reviewed: *December 5 20X4*

Wimble & Co working paper

Features of Wimble & Co working paper

Name of client: identifies the client being audited.

Period-end date: identifies the period to which the audit work relates.

Subject: identifies the topic of the working paper such as the area of the financial statements being audited, or the overall purpose of the work.

Working paper reference: provides a clear reference to identify the working paper. RA1 is the first working paper in the risk assessment section.

Preparer: identifies the name of the audit team member who prepared the working paper to enable any queries to be directed to the relevant person.

Date prepared: the date the audit work was performed, the end of the time period to which issues were considered.

Objective: this explains the relevance of the work being performed (in relation to financial statement assertions where appropriate).

Work performed: the work done cross-referenced to supporting working papers, including details of the sources of information, and items selected for testing (where relevant).

Results of work performed: any significant issues identified, exceptions or other significant observations including whether further audit work is necessary.

Conclusions: key points (including whether the area is true and fair where relevant).

Reviewer: the name of the audit team member who reviewed the work. This provides evidence of the review as required by ISA 220.

Date of review: this must be before the audit opinion is signed.

Types of audit documentation

Audit documentation includes:

- Planning documentation
  - overall audit strategy
  - audit plan
- Audit programmes
- Summary of significant matters
- Written representation from management
- Checklists
- Correspondence
- Copies of client records.

Example contents of a permanent audit file

For large audits, much of the knowledge of the business information may be kept on a **permanent file** and the audit plan may contain a summary or simply cross reference to the permanent file. Typical information on a permanent file includes:

- Names of management, those charged with governance, shareholders
- Systems information
- Background to the industry and the client's business
- Title deeds
- Directors' service agreements
- Copies of contract and agreements.

Example contents of a current audit file

The audit work for a specific period is kept on a **current file.**

Typically, there are at least three sections:

- Planning
- Performance
- Completion.

Planning

The main element of this section is likely to be the Audit Planning Memorandum.

This document is the written audit plan and will be read by all members of the audit team before work starts. Its contents are likely to include:

- Background information about the client, including recent performance

- Changes since last year's audit (for recurring clients)

- Key accounting policies

- Important laws and regulations affecting the company

- Trial balance (or draft financial statements)

- Preliminary analytical procedures

- Key audit risks

- Overall audit strategy

- Materiality assessment

- Timetable of procedures

- Deadlines

- Staffing and a budget (hours to be worked × charge out rates)

- Locations to be visited.

Performance

Working papers are likely to consist of:

- Lead schedule – showing total figures, which agree to the financial statements.

- Back-up schedules – breakdowns of totals into relevant sub-totals.

- Audit work programme detailing:
    - The objectives being tested
    - Work completed
    - How samples were selected
    - Conclusions drawn
    - Who did the work
    - Date the work was completed
    - By whom it was reviewed.

Completion

The completion (also known as review) stage of an audit has a number of standard components:

- Going concern review
- Subsequent events review
- Final analytical procedures
- Accounting standards (disclosure) checklist
- Written representation from management
- Summary of adjustments made since trial balance produced
- Summary of unadjusted misstatements
- Draft final financial statements
- Draft report to those charged with governance and management letter.

Security of working papers

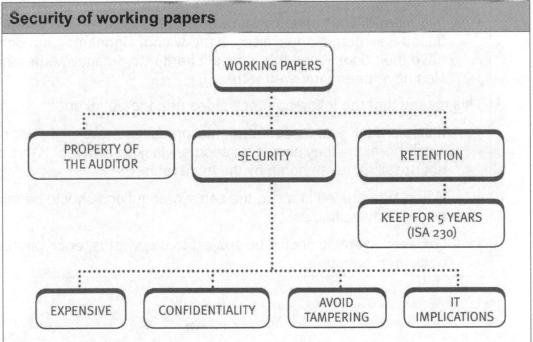

Who owns the working papers?

The auditor owns the audit working papers. This is important because:

- Access to the working papers is controlled by the auditor, not the client, which is an element in preserving the auditor's independence.
- In some circumstances care may need to be taken when copies of client generated schedules are incorporated into the file.

Security

Working papers must be kept secure.

- By its nature, audit evidence will comprise confidential, sensitive information. If the files are lost or stolen, the auditor's duty of confidentiality will be compromised.

- Audits are expensive. If the files are lost or stolen, the evidence they contain will need to be recreated, so the work will need to be done again. The auditors may be able to recover the costs from their insurers, but otherwise it will simply represent a loss to the firm.

- There have been cases of unscrupulous clients altering auditors' working papers to conceal frauds.

The implications of IT-based audit systems are also far reaching.

- By their nature, laptops are susceptible to theft, even though the thief may have no interest in the contents of the audit file. Nevertheless, all the problems associated with re-performing the audit and breaches of confidentiality remain.

- It is more difficult to be certain who created or amended computer based files than manual files – handwriting, signatures and dates have their uses – and this makes it harder to detect whether the files have been tampered with.

This means that the following precautions need to be taken.

- If files are left unattended at clients' premises – overnight or during lunch breaks – they should be securely locked away, or if this is not possible, taken home by the audit team.

- When files are left in a car, the same precautions should be taken as with any valuables.

- IT-based systems should be subject to passwords, encryption and back up procedures.

KAPLAN PUBLISHING

Test your understanding 1

It is 1 July 20X5. You have recently been assigned as audit senior for the audit of Rock Co for the year-ending 31 August 20X5. Your firm has audited this company for a number of years but this is the first year you will have worked on this audit.

Rock Co is a company listed on a stock exchange. Rock Co is engaged in the wholesale import, manufacture and distribution of basic cosmetics and toiletries for sale to a wide range of stores, under a variety of different brand names.

Required:

(a) **Describe the procedures you will perform in order to obtain an understanding of Rock Co.**

(10 marks)

(b) You are now nearing the completion of the audit of Rock Co. You have been asked to perform a review of the audit file before it is passed to the audit manager and the audit engagement partner for their review. You have been asked to concentrate on the proper completion of the audit working papers. Some of the audit working papers have been produced electronically but all of them have been printed out for you.

Required:

Describe the types of audit working papers you should expect to see in the audit file and the features of those working papers that show that they have been properly completed.

(10 marks)

(Total: 20 marks)

Test your understanding 2

You are the audit manager responsible for planning the audit of Rottnest Co. During the planning of the audit you have identified an increased risk of material misstatement due to fraud. The audit strategy and audit plan reflect this increased risk.

1 **Which of the following statements regarding fraud is TRUE?**

   A   The auditor may not detect all material fraud in the financial statements but this won't necessarily mean the auditor has been negligent due to the nature of fraud and the likelihood of concealment

   B   The auditor must detect all material fraud in the financial statements

   C   The auditor must detect every fraud in the financial statements

   D   The auditor is not responsible for detecting fraud as this is management's responsibility

2 **If material misstatement as a result of fraud is detected during the audit, and is not corrected by management, how will this be communicated to the shareholders?**

   A   The auditor must send a letter to the shareholders informing them of the fraud

   B   The auditor must speak at the annual general meeting and specifically inform them

   C   The auditor will report it to the police and the police will notify the shareholders

   D   Through the auditor's report as the opinion will be modified

3 **Which of the following procedures must the auditor perform to respond to the risk of fraud?**

   (i)   The auditor must obtain written representation from management confirming they have disclosed all known and suspected frauds to the auditor.

   (ii)   The auditor must incorporate an unpredictable element into the design of their audit procedures.

   (iii) The auditor must test year-end journal entries and estimates which may be used to manipulate the financial statements.

   A   (i) and (ii) only

   B   (i) and (iii) only

   C   (ii) and (iii) only

   D   (i), (ii) and (iii)

4   Which of the following statements is TRUE in respect of the audit plan?

A   The audit plan sets out the scope, direction and framework for the audit

B   The audit plan contains the detailed audit procedures designed to obtain sufficient appropriate evidence including the objective of each procedure and the sample size to be tested

C   The plan includes preliminary engagement activities such as materiality and risk assessment

D   The audit plan is developed before the audit strategy

5   Which matters will NOT be included in the audit strategy?

A   Risk assessment and materiality

B   Communications with the client

C   Specific audit procedures to respond to the risks assessed

D   The need for professional scepticism

Test your understanding 3

Your firm has recently been appointed auditor of Albany Co, a large company with sophisticated computer systems. The planning is due to commence shortly. It has been agreed with the client that an interim and final audit will be performed.

1   Which of the following is NOT a benefit of planning the audit?

A   It ensures the audit is performed efficiently and effectively

B   It helps identify the resources to be allocated

C   It ensures the financial statements will be correct

D   It minimises the risk of issuing an inappropriate audit opinion

2   Which of the following is NOT part of the planning stage of the audit?

A   Preliminary materiality assessment

B   Risk assessment

C   Developing the audit strategy

D   Final analytical procedures

3   **Which of the following is the most appropriate time to perform an interim audit?**

A   After the year-end before the auditor's report is signed

B   Before the year-end

C   At the same time as the final audit

D   After the auditor's report has been signed

4   **Which of the following will NOT be performed at the interim audit?**

A   Obtaining written representation from management

B   Tests of controls

C   Transaction testing for transactions that have occurred to date

D   Performing risk assessment procedures

5   **What are the main reasons for performing an interim audit?**

(i)   To increase fee income for the firm.

(ii)   To reduce time pressure at the final audit.

(iii) To assess the level of control risk and determine the amount of substantive testing required at the final audit.

A   (i) and (ii) only

B   (i) and (iii) only

C   (ii) and (iii) only

D   (i), (ii) and (iii)

Test your understanding 4

You are an engagement partner within Mosaic Co. Your firm has an established reputation for performing high quality audits. Your firm has a quality control procedures document which is updated regularly. The procedures document is published in the employee handbook which each employee receives a copy of on joining the firm. The procedures are also available on your firm's intranet site so staff are able to access it at any time. The firm's procedures have been designed to ensure compliance with ISA 220 *Quality Control for an Audit of Financial Statements*.

1   At the start of an audit, all audit team members are required to attend a planning meeting where they are informed of the nature of the client, the risks identified to date and any other issues of which they should be aware when performing the audit.

This is an example of which element of quality control?

A   Direction

B   Consultation

C   Review

D   Supervision

2   **Which of the following is NOT an element of a quality control system?**

A   Human resources

B   Engagement performance

C   Engagement quality control review

D   Monitoring

3   **Which of the following are primary reasons why a firm should perform audits to a high standard of quality?**

(i)   To maintain confidence in the audit profession.

(ii)   To ensure auditor's reports issued are appropriate.

(iii)   To avoid punishment.

(iv)   To ensure clients receive a competent and professional service.

A   (i) and (ii)

B   (i), (iii) and (iv)

C   (iii) and (iv)

D   (i), (ii) and (iv)

4   Which of the following should NOT perform an Engagement Quality Control Review?

A   External consultant

B   Engagement partner of the client subject to review

C   Engagement partner of the audit firm not involved with the client subject to review

D   Senior manager or director of the audit firm not involved with the client subject to review

5   Which of the following statements regarding quality control is FALSE?

A   Where deficiencies in quality control procedures are identified the firm should take action such as providing additional training or increasing the frequency of quality control reviews.

B   The firm only needs to act on quality control deficiencies identified by an external quality control review such as that performed by the ACCA.

C   The firm should monitor its quality control procedures and policies on a regular basis to ensure they are working effectively.

D   Every person within the audit firm has a responsibility to ensure quality control is adhered to.

9 Chapter summary

Purpose
- Enables an efficient & effective audit
- Resolve matters in a timely way
- Selection of team

Audit strategy
- Characteristics
- Significant factors & preliminary engagement activities
- Reporting objectives
- Resources

Audit plan
- Procedures to be performed
- Team member assigned
- Sample sizes
- Timing of the work

Interim audit
- Work performed before year end
- Reduces pressure on final audit
- Controls testing & substantive procedures

Planning

Laws & regulations
- Responsibilities
- Procedures to identify non-compliance
- Procedures to assess impact of non-compliance
- Reporting

Documentation
- Experienced auditor test
- Permanent file
- Current file
- Custody and retention

Quality control
- Direction
- Supervision
- Review
- Engagement QC review
- Monitoring

Fraud
- Responsibilities
- Risk assessment
- Responding to fraud risk
- Reporting

Test your understanding answers

Test your understanding 1

(a) **Procedures to obtain an understanding of Rock Co**

- Review prior year working papers, and speak with the audit manager responsible for the prior year audit, to obtain an understanding of the client and to establish any matters that require attention in the current year.

- Enquire of Rock Co's management if there have been any significant changes to the business or issues arising during the year such as major customers or suppliers being lost or won.

- Enquire how management responds to the risk of fraud within the company and whether any frauds have been identified during the year.

- Enquire of management whether there has been any change in the financing of the company during the year e.g. new loans taken out or new share capital issued.

- Review press reports / perform an internet search to identify any media coverage relating to the client.

- Review industry journals for information about the performance of the industry which can be used to compare with the client's performance and help identify unusual trends.

- Review management accounts, financial information provided to the stock exchange or draft financial statements that may be available to establish trends in the business.

- Perform analytical procedures to establish areas that indicate potential material misstatement and require attention during the audit.

- Review systems documentation (either generated by Rock Co or held by the firm) to identify changes in controls.

- Perform a walkthrough test to confirm understanding of how the internal controls operate.

- Review stock exchange requirements to identify any changes during the year.

- Review industry journals / correspondence with regulatory bodies to obtain an understanding of the legal and regulatory framework the company operates within.

(b) **Types and features of audit working papers**

Types of audit working papers include:

- Systems documentation (flowcharts, systems manuals, narrative notes, checklists and questionnaires, etc.)
- Constitutional documents
- Agreements with banks and other providers of finance
- Details of other advisors used by the entity such as lawyers
- Regulatory documentation relating to the stock exchange listing
- Audit planning documentation
- Audit work programs
- Working papers showing the work performed
- External confirmations from third parties such as the bank and customers confirming balances at the year-end
- Lead schedules showing summaries of work performed and conclusions on individual account areas and the amounts to be included in the financial statements
- Trial balance, management accounts and financial statements
- Schedule of unadjusted differences
- Schedule of review points
- Report to management
- Written representation letter.

Features of audit working papers

- All working papers should show the name of the preparer and the date prepared, and the name of the reviewer and the date reviewed, by means of signatures and dates. These may be electronic in the case of electronic working papers.
- Audit planning documentation should include the risk assessment cross-referenced to the audit program, and the audit program should cross-reference to the audit working papers.
- Working papers showing the work performed should be cross-referenced to the audit program and the lead schedule on that particular section of the audit file, and should describe the nature of the work performed, the evidence obtained, and the conclusions reached.

- Each section of the audit file should have a lead schedule cross-referenced to the relevant working papers.

- The trial balance should be cross-referenced to the relevant sections of the audit file where the audit work is documented, and to the financial statements.

- The schedule of unadjusted differences should be cross-referenced to the sections of the file to which they relate.

- A schedule of review points should be 'cleared' to show that all outstanding matters have been dealt with.

Test your understanding 2

1	A	The auditor should plan and perform the audit to have a reasonable expectation of detecting material fraud and error. However, if a fraud is very well concealed, even a very thorough audit may not detect it.
2	D	Material misstatements are brought to the attention of the shareholders by modifying the audit opinion.
3	D	All three procedures must be performed to respond to the risk of fraud.
4	B	Options A and C describe aspects of the audit strategy The audit strategy is developed before the audit plan.
5	C	Specific procedures are included in the audit plan.

Test your understanding 3

1	C	Financial statements cannot be verified as being correct due to the inclusion of estimates and judgments.
2	D	'Final' analytical procedures are performed at the completion stage of the audit.
3	B	The interim audit helps to develop the audit strategy. It should take place before the year-end to avoid interfering with the client's year-end procedures but should not be so early that it is of little use.
4	A	Written representations are obtained at the end of the audit, just before the auditor's report is signed.
5	C	An interim audit may result in increased fees for the firm if a greater amount of work is performed, however, this is not a reason for performing an Interim audit. The interim audit is a means of spreading the workload over a longer period to avoid time pressure.

Test your understanding 4

1	A	Briefing of the audit teams forms part of the direction of the audit.
2	C	Engagement quality control review is part of engagement performance and monitoring.
3	D	Quality is important for upholding the reputation of the profession and the firm in order to maintain investor confidence. Avoiding punishment is not the primary reason for ensuring a quality audit is performed.
4	B	An EQCR should be performed by someone independent of the engagement and someone of suitable authority such as a senior manager, director or partner.
5	B	The firm should perform its own quality control reviews and take action as necessary to ensure quality control procedures are followed.

Evidence

Chapter learning objectives

This chapter covers syllabus areas:

- C1a – The need to obtain an understanding of internal control relevant to the audit

- D1 – Assertions and audit evidence

- D2 – Audit procedures

- D3 – Audit sampling and other means of testing

- D5 – Automated tools and techniques

- D6 – The work of others

Detailed syllabus objectives are provided in the introduction section of the text book.

PER

One of the PER performance objectives (PO19) is to collect and evaluate evidence for an audit. Carry out an internal or external audit from collecting evidence, through to forming an opinion. You demonstrate professional scepticism and make sure judgments are based on sufficient valid evidence. Working through this chapter should help you understand how to demonstrate that objective.

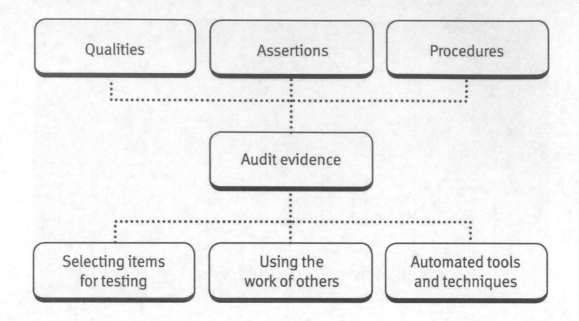

1 Audit evidence

 ISA 500 *Audit Evidence* states the objective of the auditor, in terms of gathering evidence, is:

'to design and perform audit procedures in such a way to enable the auditor to obtain sufficient appropriate audit evidence to be able to draw reasonable conclusions on which to base the auditor's opinion.' [ISA 500, 4]

- **Sufficiency** relates to the **quantity** of evidence.

- **Appropriateness** relates to the **quality** or relevance and reliability of evidence.

[ISA 500, 5b, 5e]

Sufficient evidence

The auditor needs to gather 'enough' evidence to form a conclusion. This is a matter of professional judgment. When determining whether there is enough evidence the auditor must consider:

- The risk of material misstatement

- The materiality of the item

- The nature of accounting and internal control systems

- The results of controls tests

- The auditor's knowledge and experience of the business

- The size of a population being tested

- The size of the sample selected to test

- The reliability of the evidence obtained.

Sufficient evidence

Consider the audit of a bank balance:

The auditor will confirm year-end bank balances directly with the bank. This is a good source of evidence but on its own is not sufficient to give assurance regarding the completeness and final valuation of bank and cash amounts. The key reason is timing differences. The client may have received cash amounts or cheques before the end of the year, or may have paid out cheques before the end of the year, that have not yet cleared the bank account. For this reason the auditor should also review and reperform the client's year-end bank reconciliation. In combination these two pieces of evidence will be sufficient to give assurance over the bank balances.

Appropriate evidence

Appropriateness of evidence breaks down into two important concepts:

* Reliability
* Relevance.

Reliability

The auditor should always attempt to obtain evidence from the most trustworthy and dependable source possible.

* Evidence obtained from an independent external source is more reliable than client generated evidence.

* Evidence obtained directly by the auditor is more reliable than evidence obtained indirectly.

* Client generated evidence is the least reliable source of evidence. If the client is manipulating the financial statement figures they may produce fictitious evidence to support the figures. Client generated evidence is more reliable if effective controls are in place. This doesn't mean the auditor should not rely on client generated evidence. It simply means that where more reliable evidence is available, the auditor should obtain it.

* In addition, written evidence is more reliable than oral evidence as oral representations can be withdrawn or challenged. Original documents are more reliable than copies or documents transformed into electronic form as it may be difficult to see if these have been tampered with.

[ISA 500, A31]

Broadly speaking, the more reliable the evidence the less of it the auditor will need. However, if evidence is unreliable it will never be appropriate for the audit, no matter how much is gathered. [ISA 500, A4]

Relevance

Relevance means the evidence relates to the financial statement assertions being tested. [ISA 500, A27]

For example, when attending an inventory count, the auditor will:

- Select a sample of items from physical inventory and trace them to inventory records to confirm the **completeness** of accounting records

- Select a sample of items from inventory records and trace them to physical inventories to confirm the **existence** of inventory assets.

Whilst the procedures are similar in nature, their purpose (and relevance) is to test different **assertions** regarding inventory balances.

2 Financial statements assertions

The objective of audit testing is to assist the auditor to reach a conclusion as to whether the financial statements are free from material misstatement.

The auditor will perform a range of tests on the significant classes of transactions and account balances. These tests focus on the **financial statements assertions**.

 Assertions: 'Representations, explicit or otherwise, with respect to the recognition, measurement, presentation and disclosure of information in the financial statements which are inherent in management representing that the financial statements are prepared in accordance with the applicable financial reporting framework.

Assertions are used by the auditor to consider the different types of potential misstatements that may occur when identifying, assessing and responding to the risks of material misstatement.'

[ISA 315 (Revised 2019), 12a]

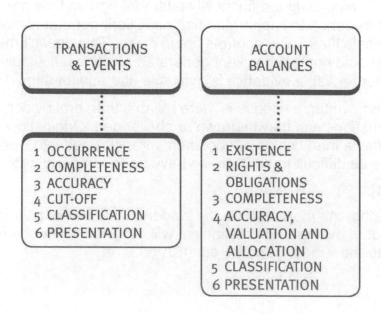

Assertions about classes of transactions and events, and related disclosures, for the period under audit

Occurrence – the transactions and events recorded and disclosed have occurred and pertain to the entity.

Completeness – all transactions and events that should have been recorded have been recorded, and all related disclosures that should have been included have been included.

Accuracy – amounts and other data have been recorded appropriately and related disclosures have been appropriately measured and described.

Cut-off – transactions and events have been recorded in the correct accounting period.

Classification – transactions and events have been recorded in the proper accounts.

Presentation – transactions and events are appropriately aggregated or disaggregated and clearly described, and related disclosures are relevant and understandable in the context of the applicable financial reporting framework.

[ISA 315 (Revised 2019), A190a]

Assertions about account balances and related disclosures at the period end

Existence – assets, liabilities and equity interests exist.

Rights and obligations – the entity holds or controls the rights to assets and liabilities are the obligations of the entity.

Completeness – all assets, liabilities and equity interests that should have been recorded have been recorded, and all related disclosures that should have been included have been included.

Accuracy, valuation and allocation – assets, liabilities and equity interests have been included in the financial statements at appropriate amounts and any resulting valuation or allocation adjustments have been appropriately recorded, and related disclosures have been appropriately measured and described.

Classification – assets, liabilities and equity interests have been recorded in the proper accounts.

Presentation – account balances are appropriately aggregated or disaggregated and clearly described, and related disclosures are relevant and understandable in the context of the applicable financial reporting framework.

[ISA 315 (Revised 2019), A190b]

Inventory misstatements

There are many ways inventory could be materially misstated:

- Items might not be counted and therefore not be included in the balance. This would mean the inventory balance was not **complete**.

- Items delivered after the year-end could be included in this accounting period. This would mean the inventory did not **exist** at the year-end date.

- Damaged or obsolete inventory might not be **valued** appropriately at the lower of cost and net realisable value.

- Purchase costs might not be recorded accurately. This would also affect **valuation**.

- Inventory stored at the client's site may belong to a 3rd party. The client would not have the **right** to include this inventory in their financial statements.

Addressing disclosures in the audit of financial statements

Disclosures are an important part of the financial statements and seen as a way for communicating further information to users. Poor quality disclosures may obscure understanding of important matters.

Concerns have been raised about whether auditors are giving sufficient attention to disclosures during the audit. The IAASB believes that where the term financial statements is used in the ISAs it should be clarified that this is intended to include all disclosures subject to audit.

Recent changes to ISAs include:

- Emphasis on the importance of giving appropriate attention to addressing disclosures.

- Focus on matters relating to disclosures to be discussed with those charged with governance, particularly at the planning stage.

- Emphasis on the need to agree with management their responsibility to make available information relevant to disclosures, early in the audit process.

3   Sources of audit evidence

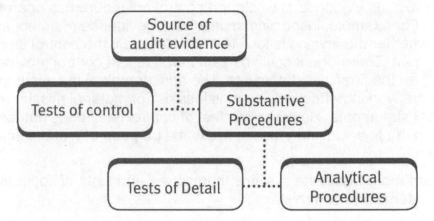

Auditors can obtain assurance from:

 Tests of control: Audit procedures '**designed to evaluate the operating effectiveness of controls in preventing, or detecting and correcting material misstatement**'.

Substantive procedures: Audit procedures '**designed to detect material misstatements at the assertion level**'.

[ISA 330, 4]

Tests of controls

In order to design further audit procedures the auditor must assess the risk of material misstatement in the financial statements.

 Remember: Audit risk = Inherent risk × Control risk × Detection risk

Internal controls are a vital component of this risk model, they are the mechanisms that clients design in an attempt to prevent, detect and correct misstatement. This is not only necessary for good financial reporting, it is necessary to safeguard the assets of the shareholders and is a requirement of corporate governance.

 The stronger the control system, the lower the control risk. This reduces the risk of material misstatement in the financial statements.

In order to be able to rely on controls the auditor will need to:

- Ascertain how the system operates

- Document the system in audit working papers

- Assess the design and operating effectiveness of the control system

- Test the operation of the system

- Determine the impact on the audit approach for specific classes of transactions, account balances and disclosures.

The focus of a test of control is not the monetary amount of a transaction. A test of control provides evidence of whether a control procedure has operated effectively. For example, inspecting an invoice for evidence of authorisation. It is irrelevant whether the invoice is for $100 or $1000 as it the control being tested, not the amount. Therefore, it could be said that a test of control provides indirect evidence over the financial statements. The auditor makes the assumption that if controls are working effectively there is less risk of material misstatement in the financial statements. However, the test of control itself does not test the figure within the financial statements, this is the purpose of a substantive procedure.

We will learn more about the systems themselves and tests of controls in the chapter 'Systems and controls'.

Substantive procedures

Substantive procedures consist of:

- **Tests of detail:** to verify individual transactions and balances.

- **Substantive analytical procedures** (as seen in the chapter 'Risk'): involve analysing relationships between information to identify unusual fluctuations which may indicate possible misstatement.

Tests of detail v analytical procedures

A test of detail looks at the supporting evidence for an individual transaction such as inspection of a purchase invoice to verify the amount/date/classification of a specific purchase. If there are 5000 purchase invoices recorded during the accounting period, this one test of detail has only provided evidence for one of those transactions.

An analytical procedure would be used to assess the reasonableness of the purchases figure in total. For example, calculating the percentage change in purchases from last year and comparing this with the percentage change in revenue to see if they move in line with each other as expected.

The analytical procedure is not looking at the detail of any of the individual purchases but at the total figure. It is possible that there are a number of misstatements within the purchases population which would only be discovered by testing the detail as they may cancel each other out. An analytical procedure would not detect these misstatements.

Because of this, analytical procedures should only be used as the main source of substantive evidence where the internal controls have been found to be reliable, as there is less chance of misstatements being present as the control system would have detected and corrected them.

In some circumstances the auditor may rely solely on substantive testing:

- The auditor may choose to rely solely on substantive testing where it is considered to be a more efficient or more effective way of obtaining audit evidence, e.g. for smaller organisations.

- The auditor may have to rely solely on substantive testing where the client's internal control system cannot be relied on.

The auditor must always carry out substantive procedures on material items. [ISA 330 *The Auditor's Response to Assessed Risks*, 18].

The auditor is required to carry out the following substantive procedures:

- Agreeing the financial statements to the underlying accounting records.

- Examination of material journals and other adjustments made in preparing the financial statements.

[ISA 330, 20]

4 Types of audit procedure

The auditor can adopt the following procedures to obtain audit evidence:

- Inspection of records, documents or physical assets.

- Observation of processes and procedures, e.g. inventory counts.

- External confirmation obtained in the form of a direct written response to the auditor from a third party.

- Recalculation to confirm the numerical accuracy of documents or records.

- Reperformance by the auditor of procedures or controls.

- Analytical procedures.

- Enquiry of knowledgeable parties.

[ISA 500, A14 – A22]

In the chapter 'Procedures' we will look in detail at how these procedures are applied to specific items in the financial statements.

Explanation of audit procedures

Inspection of documents and records: examining records or documents, in paper or electronic form.

- May give evidence of rights and obligations, e.g. title deeds.

- May give evidence that a control is operating, e.g. invoices stamped as paid or authorised for payment by an appropriate signature.

- May give evidence about cut-off, e.g. the dates on invoices, despatch notes, etc.

- Confirms sales values and purchases costs.

Inspection of tangible assets: physical examination of an asset.

- To obtain evidence of existence of that asset.

- May give evidence of valuation, e.g. evidence of damage indicating impairment of inventory or non-current assets.

Observation: looking at a process or procedure being performed by others.

- May provide evidence that a control is being operated, e.g. segregation of duties or a cheque signatory.

- Only provides evidence that the control was operating properly at the time of the observation. The auditor's presence may have had an influence on the operation of the control.

- Observation of a one-off event, e.g. an inventory count, may give good evidence that the procedure was carried out effectively.

Enquiry: seeking information from knowledgeable persons, both financial and non-financial, within the entity or outside.

Whilst a major source of evidence, the results of enquiries will usually need to be corroborated in some way through other audit procedures. This is because responses generated by the audit client are considered to be of a low quality due to their inherent bias.

The answers to enquiries may be corroborative evidence. In particular, they may be used to corroborate the results of analytical procedures.

Written representations from management are part of overall enquiries. These involve obtaining written statements from management to confirm oral enquiries. These are considered further in the chapter 'Completion and review'.

External confirmation: obtaining a direct response (usually written) from an external, third party.

- Examples include:
  - – Circularisation of receivables
  - – Circularisation of payables where supplier statements are not available
  - – Confirmation of bank balances in a bank letter
  - – Confirmation of actual/potential penalties from legal advisers
  - – Confirmation of inventories held by third parties.
- May provide good evidence of existence of balances, e.g. receivables confirmation.
- May not provide reliable evidence of valuation, e.g. customers may confirm receivable amounts but, ultimately, be unable to pay in the future.

Recalculation: manually or electronically checking the arithmetical accuracy of documents, records, or the client's calculations, e.g. recalculation of the translation of a foreign currency transaction.

Reperformance: the auditor's independent execution of procedures or controls that were originally performed as part of the entity's internal control system, e.g. reperformance of a bank reconciliation.

Analytical procedures: analysis of plausible relationships between data. See below.

 Analytical procedures as substantive tests

We have already seen analytical procedures used as a risk assessment procedure at the planning stage (preliminary analytical procedures). Later in the text we will see them performed at the completion stage of the audit. Here we consider their use as substantive procedures, i.e. procedures designed to detect material misstatement.

Analytical procedures are used to identify trends and understand relationships between sets of data. This in itself will not detect misstatement but will identify possible areas of misstatement. As such, analytical procedures cannot be used in isolation and should be coupled with other, corroborative, forms of testing, such as enquiry of management.

When performing analytical procedures, the auditor does not simply look at current figures in comparison to last year, they may consider other points of comparison, such as budgets and industry data.

Other techniques are also available, including:

- Ratio analysis

- Trend analysis

- Proof in total, for example: an auditor might create an expectation of payroll costs for the year by taking last year's cost and inflating for pay rises and changes in staff numbers.

Analytical procedures are useful for assessing several assertions at once as the auditor is effectively auditing a whole account balance or class of transaction to see if it is reasonable.

They can be used to corroborate other audit evidence obtained, such as statements by management about changes in cost structures.

By using analytical procedures the auditor may identify unusual items that can then be further investigated to ensure that a misstatement doesn't exist in the balance.

However, in order to use analytical procedures effectively, the auditor needs to be able to create an expectation. It would be difficult to do this if operations changed significantly from the prior year. If the changes were planned, the auditor could use forecasts as a point of comparison, although these are inherently unreliable due to the number of estimates involved. In this situation it would be pointless comparing with past results as the business would be too different to be able to conduct effective comparison.

It would also be difficult to use analytical procedures if a business had experienced a number of significant one-off events in the year as these would distort the figures making comparison to both prior year and budget meaningless.

The suitability of analytical procedures as substantive tests

To use analytical procedures, the auditor must:

1   Develop an expectation

2   Define the difference or threshold of variation which is considered acceptable

3   Calculate the difference between the recorded amount and expected amount

4   Investigate the differences which are greater than the acceptable level of variation established in step 2.

KAPLAN PUBLISHING

The suitability of this approach depends on four factors:

- The assertion(s) under scrutiny
- The reliability of the data
- Whether the expectation developed by the auditor is sufficiently precise to identify a misstatement that may be material either individually or in aggregate
- Whether the difference between the recorded amount and expected amount is acceptable.

Assertions under scrutiny

Analytical procedures should be suitable for the assertion being tested. They are clearly unsuitable for testing the existence of inventories. They are, however, suitable for assessing the value of inventory in terms of the need for allowances against old inventories, identified using the inventory holding period ratio.

Analytical procedures are more suitable for testing balances which are likely to be predictable over time meaning relationships between data can be analysed to identify usual fluctuations e.g. the relationship between payroll cost and the number of employees.

Reliability of data

The source of the information will affect reliability as discussed earlier in the chapter. Reliability of comparable information is also an important factor. If controls over financial data are weak, the data is likely to contain misstatement and is therefore not suitable as a basis for assessment.

Expectation developed by the auditor

The auditor's ability to develop an expectation will depend on the availability of reliable information.

The auditor will be able to develop a more precise expectation if disaggregated information is obtained and analysed. For example, when performing analytical procedures over revenue, it may be more meaningful if sales by month/customer/product/region are analysed rather than the revenue figure as a whole.

The difference between recorded amount and expected amount

The amount of acceptable variation between the expected figure and the actual figure will impact whether analytical procedures provide sufficient appropriate evidence. If the level of variation from actual is higher than the level of variation the auditor is willing to accept, further procedures will be necessary to ensure the balance in the financial statements is not materially misstated.

5 Relying on the work of others

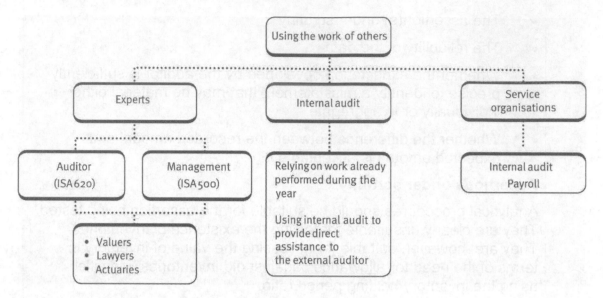

There are two types of expert an auditor may use:

1   Management's expert – an employee of the client or someone engaged by the audit client who has expertise that is used to assist in the preparation of the financial statements.

2   Auditor's expert – an employee of the audit firm or someone engaged by the audit firm to provide sufficient appropriate evidence.

Relying on the work of a management's expert

ISA 500 *Audit Evidence* provides guidance on what the auditor should consider before relying on the work of a management's expert.

The auditor must:

*   Evaluate the competence, capabilities and objectivity of that expert.

*   Obtain an understanding of the work of that expert.

*   Evaluate the appropriateness of that expert's work as audit evidence for the relevant assertion.

[ISA 500, 8]

 Relying on the work of a management's expert

The auditor should ensure the expert management has chosen to use is competent to perform the work requested by the client. If the expert does not have relevant qualifications or experience, the work may not be reliable.

The auditor should assess whether the expert management has chosen is objective. If the expert is a close relative of a director at the client company, the expert may produce a report containing information provided by the client rather than being the result of work they have performed.

Relying on the work of an auditor's expert

ISA 620 *Using the Work of an Auditor's Expert* provides guidance to auditors.

If the auditor lacks the required technical knowledge to gather sufficient appropriate evidence to form an opinion, they may have to rely on the work of an expert.

Examples of such circumstances include:

- The valuation of complex financial instruments, land and buildings, works of art, jewellery and intangible assets.

- Actuarial calculations associated with insurance contracts or employee benefit plans.

- The estimation of oil and gas reserves.

- The interpretation of contracts, laws and regulations.

- The analysis of complex or unusual tax compliance issues.

[ISA 620, A1]

The auditor must determine if the expert's work is adequate for the auditor's purposes. [ISA 620, 5b]

To fulfil this responsibility the auditor must **evaluate whether the expert has the necessary competence, capability and objectivity for the purpose of the audit**. [ISA 620, 9]

Evaluating competence [ISA 620, A15]

Information regarding the competence, capability and objectivity on an expert may come from a variety of sources, including:

- Personal experience of working with the expert

- Discussions with the expert

- Discussions with other auditors

- Knowledge of the expert's qualifications, memberships of professional bodies and licences.

- Published papers or books written by the expert.

- The audit firm's quality control procedures.

Evaluating objectivity [ISA 620, A20]

Assessing the objectivity of the expert is particularly difficult, as they may not be bound by a similar code of ethics as the auditor and, as such, may be unaware of the ethical requirements and threats with which auditors are familiar.

It may therefore be relevant to:

- Make enquiries of the client about known interests or relationships with the chosen expert.

- Discuss applicable safeguards with the expert.

- Discuss financial, business and personal interests in the client with the expert.

- Obtain written representation from the expert.

Agreeing the work [ISA 620, 11]

Once the auditor has considered the above matters they must then obtain written agreement from the expert of the following:

- The nature, scope and objectives of the expert's work.

- The roles and responsibilities of the auditor and the expert.

- The nature, timing and extent of communication between the two parties.

- The need for the expert to observe confidentiality.

Evaluating the work [ISA 620, 12]

Once the expert's work is complete the auditor must scrutinise it and evaluate whether it is appropriate for audit purposes.

In particular, the auditor should consider:

- The reasonableness of the findings and consistency with other evidence.

- The significant assumptions made.

- The use and accuracy of source data.

Reference to the work of an expert

The auditor cannot devolve responsibility for forming an audit opinion, they must use their professional judgment to assess whether the evidence produced by the expert is sufficient and appropriate to support the audit opinion.

The use of an auditor's expert is not mentioned in an unmodified auditor's opinion unless required by law or regulation. Reference to the work of an expert may be included in a modified opinion if it is relevant to the understanding of the modification. This does not diminish the auditor's responsibility for the opinion. [ISA 620, 14 & 15]

Relying on internal audit

ISA 610 *Using the Work of Internal Auditors* provides guidance.

An internal audit department forms part of the client's system of internal control. If this is an effective element of the control system it may reduce control risk, and therefore reduce the need for the auditor to perform detailed substantive testing.

Additionally, external auditors may be able to co-operate with a client's internal audit department and place reliance on their procedures in place of performing their own.

Before relying on the work of internal audit, the external auditor must assess the effectiveness of the internal audit function and assess whether the work produced by the internal auditor is adequate for the purpose of the audit.

Evaluating the internal audit function [ISA 610, 15]

- The extent to which the internal audit function's **organisational status** and relevant policies and procedures support the **objectivity** of the internal auditors.

- The **competence** of the internal audit function.

- Whether the internal audit function applies a systematic and disciplined **approach**.

Evaluating objectivity [ISA 610, A7]

- Whether the internal audit function reports to those charged with governance or has direct access to those charged with governance.

- Whether the internal audit function is free from operational responsibility.

- Whether those charged with governance are responsible for employment decisions such as remuneration.

- Whether any constraints are placed on the internal function by management or those charged with governance.

- Whether the internal auditors are members of a professional body which requires compliance with ethical requirements.

Evaluating competence [ISA 610, A8]

- Whether the resources of the internal audit function are appropriate and adequate for the size of the organisation and nature of its operations.

- Whether there are established policies for hiring, training and assigning internal auditors to internal audit engagements.

- Whether internal auditors have adequate technical training and proficiency, including relevant professional qualifications and experience.

- Whether the internal auditors have the required knowledge of the entity's financial reporting and the applicable financial reporting framework and possess the necessary skills to perform work related to the financial statements.

- Whether the internal auditors are members of a professional body which requires continued professional development.

Evaluating the systematic and disciplined approach [ISA 610, A11]

- Existence, adequacy and use of internal audit procedures and guidance.

- Application of quality control standards such as those in ISQC 1.

If the external auditor considers it appropriate to use the work of the internal auditors they then have to determine the areas and extent to which the work of the internal audit function can be used (by considering the nature and scope of work) and incorporate this into their planning to assess the impact on the nature, timing and extent of further audit procedures. [ISA 610, 17]

Evaluating the internal audit work [ISA 610, 23]

- The work was properly planned, performed, supervised, reviewed and documented.

- Sufficient appropriate evidence has been obtained.

- The conclusions reached are appropriate in the circumstances.

- The reports prepared are consistent with the work performed.

To evaluate the work adequately, the external auditor must reperform some of the procedures that the internal auditor has performed to ensure they reach the same conclusion. [ISA 610, 24]

The extent of the work to be performed on the internal auditor's work will depend on the amount of judgment involved and the risk of material misstatement in that area. [ISA 610, 24]

When reviewing and reperforming some of the work of the internal auditor, the external auditor must consider whether their initial expectation of using the work of the internal auditor is still valid. [ISA 610, 25]

Note that the auditor is not required to rely on the work of internal audit. In some jurisdictions, the external auditor may be prohibited or restricted from using the work of the internal auditor by law.

Responsibility for the auditor's opinion cannot be devolved and no reference should be made in the auditor's report regarding the use of others during the audit.

Using the internal audit to provide direct assistance

External auditors can consider whether the internal auditor can provide direct assistance with gathering audit evidence under the supervision and review of the external auditor. ISA 610 provides guidance to aim to reduce the risk that the external auditor over uses the internal auditor.

The following considerations will be made:

- Direct assistance cannot be provided where laws and regulations prohibit such assistance, e.g. in the UK. [ISA 610, 26]

- The competence and objectivity of the internal auditor. Where threats to objectivity are present, the significance of them and whether they can be managed to an acceptable level must be considered. [ISA 610, 27]

- The external auditor must not assign work to the internal auditor which involves significant judgment, a high risk of material misstatement or with which the internal auditor has been involved. [ISA 610, 30]

- The planned work must be communicated with those charged with governance so agreement can be made that the use of the internal auditor is not excessive. [ISA 610, 31]

Where it is agreed that the internal auditor can provide direct assistance:

- Management must agree in writing that the internal auditor can provide such assistance and that they will not intervene in that work. [ISA 610, 33a]

- The internal auditors must provide written confirmation that they will keep the external auditors information confidential. [ISA 610, 33b]

- The external auditor will provide direction, supervision and review of the internal auditor's work. [ISA 610, 34]

- During the direction, supervision and review of the work, the external auditor should remain alert to the risk that the internal auditor is not objective or competent. [ISA 610, 35]

Documentation [ISA 610, 37]

The auditor should document:

- The evaluation of the internal auditor's objectivity and competence.

- The basis for the decision regarding the nature and extent of the work performed by the internal auditor.

- The name of the reviewer and the extent of the review of the internal auditor's work.

- The written agreement of management mentioned above.

- The working papers produced by the internal auditor.

Use of service organisations

Many companies use service organisations to perform business functions such as:

- Payroll processing

- Receivables collection

- Pension management.

If a company uses a service organisation, audit evidence will need to be obtained from the service organisation instead of, or in addition to, the client. This needs to be considered when planning the audit.

ISA 402 *Audit Considerations Relating to an Entity Using a Service Organisation* provides guidance to auditors.

Planning the audit

The auditor will need to:

- Obtain an understanding of the service organisation sufficient to identify and assess the risks of material misstatement.

- Design and perform audit procedures responsive to those risks.

[ISA 402, 1]

This requires the auditor to obtain an understanding of the service provided:

- Nature of the services and their effect on internal controls.

- Nature and materiality of the transactions to the entity.

- Level of interaction between the activities of the service organisation and the entity.

- Nature of the relationship between the service organisation and the entity including contractual terms.

[ISA 402, 9]

The auditor should determine the effect the use of a service organisation will have on their assessment of risk. The following issues should be considered:

- Reputation of the service organisation.

- Existence of external supervision.

- Extent of controls operated by service provider.

- Experience of errors and omissions.

- Degree of monitoring by the user.

Sources of information about the service organisation

- Obtaining a type 1 or type 2 report from the service organisation's auditor.

  A Type 1 report provides a description of the design of the controls at the service organisation prepared by the management of the service organisation. It includes a report by the service auditor providing an opinion on the description of the system and the suitability of the controls. [ISA 402, 8b]

  A Type 2 report is a report on the description, design and operating effectiveness of controls at the service organisation. It contains a report prepared by management of the service organisation. It includes a report by the service auditor providing an opinion on the description of the system, the suitability of the controls, the effectiveness of the controls and a description of the tests of controls performed by the auditor. [para 8c]

  If the auditor intends to use a report from a service auditor they should consider:

  - The competence and independence of the service organisation auditor.

  - The standards under which the report was issued.

- Contacting the service organisation through the client.

- Visiting the service organisation.

- Using another auditor to perform procedures that will provide the necessary information about controls at the service organisation.

[ISA 402, 12]

Responding to assessed risks

The auditor should determine whether sufficient appropriate evidence is available from the client and if not, perform further procedures or use another auditor to perform procedures on their behalf. [ISA 402, 15]

If controls are expected to operate effectively:

- Obtain a type 2 report if available and consider:
  - Whether the date covered by the report is appropriate for the audit.
  - Whether the client has any complementary controls in place.
  - The time elapsed since the tests of controls were performed.
  - Whether the tests of controls performed by the auditor are relevant to the financial statement assertions.

    [ISA 402, 17]

- Perform tests of controls at the service organisation.

- Use another auditor to perform tests of controls.

[ISA 402, 16]

The auditor should enquire of the client whether the service organisation has reported any frauds to them or whether they are aware of any frauds. [ISA 402, 19]

Impact on the auditor's report

If sufficient appropriate evidence has not been obtained, a qualified or disclaimer of opinion will be issued. [ISA 402, 20]

The use of a service organisation auditor is not mentioned in the auditor's report unless required by law or regulation. Reference to the work of a service organisation auditor may be included in a report containing a modified opinion if it is relevant to the understanding of the modification. This does not diminish the auditor's responsibility for the opinion. [ISA 402, 21]

Benefits to the audit

- Independence: because the service organisation is external to the client, the audit evidence derived from it is regarded as being more reliable than evidence generated internally by the client.

- Competence: because the service organisation is a specialist, it may be more competent in executing its role than the client's internal department resulting in fewer errors.

- Possible reliance on the service organisation's auditors: it may be possible for the audit firm to confirm information directly with the service organisation's auditors.

Drawbacks

The main disadvantage of outsourced services from the auditor's point of view concerns access to records and information.

The auditor has a legal right to access the client's records and to receive answers and explanations that they consider necessary for the audit. They do not have such rights over records and information held by a third party such as a service organisation.

If access to records and other information is denied by the service organisation, this may impose a limitation on the scope of the auditor's work. If sufficient appropriate evidence is not obtained, this will result in a modified audit opinion.

6 Selecting items for testing

The auditor has three options for selecting items to test:

1 Select all items to test (100% testing) [ISA 500, A54]

This approach may be taken where the population is very small and it is easy for the auditor to test all items. Alternatively, if it is an area over which the auditor requires greater audit confidence, for example an area that is material by nature or is considered to be of significant risk, the auditor may decide to test all items within the population.

2   Selecting specific items for testing [ISA 500, A55]

Items with specific characteristics may be chosen for testing such as:

- High value items within a population

- All items over a certain amount

- Items to obtain information.

Although less than 100% of the population is being tested, this does not constitute sampling. As explained below, sampling requires all items in the population to have a chance of selection. In the categories above, only the items with the specific characteristics have a chance of selection.

3   Sampling [ISA 500, A57]

The definition of sampling, as described in ISA 530 *Audit Sampling* is:

 'The application of audit procedures to less than 100% of items within a population of audit relevance such that all sampling units have a chance of selection in order to provide the auditor with a reasonable basis on which to draw conclusions about the entire population.' [ISA 530, 5a]

The need for sampling

It will usually be impossible to test every item in an accounting population because of the costs involved.

It is also important to remember that auditors give reasonable not absolute assurance and therefore do not certify that the financial statements are 100% accurate.

Selecting an appropriate sample

When sampling, the auditor must choose a representative sample.

- If a sample is representative, the same conclusion will be drawn from that sample as would have been drawn had the whole population been tested.

- For a sample to be representative, it must have the same characteristics as the other items in the population from which it was chosen.
  [ISA 530, A12]

- In order to reduce sampling risk and ensure the sample is representative, the auditor can increase the size of the sample selected or use stratification.

Stratification [ISA 530, Appendix 1]

Stratification is used in conjunction with sampling. Stratification is the process of breaking down a population into smaller subpopulations. Each subpopulation is a group of items (sampling units) which have similar characteristics.

The objective of stratification is to enable the auditor to reduce the variability of items within the subpopulation and therefore allow sample sizes to be reduced without increasing sampling risk.

For example the auditor may stratify the population of revenue into three subpopulations: revenue from Product A, revenue from Product B and revenue from Product C. The auditor may select a sample of revenue from Product A. The results of the testing of that sample can be extrapolated across the whole subpopulation of revenue from Product A. A sample may be selected of revenue from Product B and again, the results of that testing can be extrapolated across that subpopulation. Revenue from Product C may not be tested if it is considered immaterial.

Statistical and non-statistical sampling

 Statistical sampling means any approach to sampling that uses:

- Random selection of samples, and
- Probability theory to evaluate sample results.

Any approach that does not have both these characteristics is considered to be non-statistical sampling. [ISA 530, 5g]

The approach taken is a matter of auditor judgment. [ISA 530, A9]

Statistical sampling methods [ISA 530, Appendix 4]

- **Random selection** – this can be achieved through the use of random number generators or tables.

- **Systematic selection** – where a constant sampling interval is used (e.g. every 50th balance) and the first item is selected randomly.

- **Monetary unit selection** – selecting items based upon monetary values (usually focusing on higher value items).

Non-statistical sampling methods

- **Haphazard selection** – auditor does not follow a structured technique but avoids bias or predictability.

- **Block selection** – this involves selecting a block of contiguous items from the population (i.e. next to each other). To reduce sampling risk, many blocks should be selected as valid references cannot be made beyond the period or block examined.

When non-statistical methods (haphazard and block) are used, the auditor uses judgment to select the items to be tested. Whilst this lends itself to auditor bias it does support the risk based approach, where the auditor focuses on those areas most susceptible to material misstatement.

Designing a sample [ISA 530, A5, A6]

When designing a sample the auditor has to consider:

- The purpose of the procedure
- The combination of procedures being performed
- The nature of evidence sought
- Possible misstatement conditions.

Illustration 1 – Murray Co sampling

Sampling

Murray Co deals with large retail customers, and therefore has a low number of large receivables balances on the receivables ledger. Given the low number of customers with a balance on Murray Co's receivables ledger, all balances would probably be selected for testing. However, for illustrative purposes the following shows how a sample of balances would be selected using systematic and Monetary Unit Sampling.

Credit and zero balances on the receivables ledger have been removed. The number of items to be sampled has been determined as six. The customer list has been alphabetised.

Systematic Sampling

There are 19 customers with balances in the receivables ledger. The sampling interval is calculated by taking the total number of balances and dividing it by the sample size. The sampling interval (to the nearest whole number) is therefore three. The first item is chosen randomly, in this case item 10. Every third item after that is then also selected for testing until six items have been chosen.

$000 Customer Ref	Customer Name	Balance $	Item number	Sampling Item
A001	Anfield United Shop	176	1	
B002	The Beautiful Game	84	2	
B003	Beckham's	42	3	(5)
C001	Cheryl & Coleen Co	12	4	
D001	Dream Team	45	5	
E001	Escot Supermarket	235	6	(6)
G001	Golf is Us	211	7	
G002	Green Green Grass	61	8	
H001	HHA Sports	59	9	
J001	Jilberts	21	10	(1)
J002	James Smit Partnership	256	11	
J003	Jockeys	419	12	
O001	The Oval	92	13	(2)
P001	Pole Vaulters	76	14	
S001	Stayrose Supermarket	97	15	
T001	Trainers and More	93	16	(3)
W001	Wanderers	89	17	
W003	Walk Hike Run	4	18	
W004	Winners	31	19	(4)

KAPLAN PUBLISHING

Monetary Unit Sampling

Monetary Unit Sampling can utilise either the random or systematic selection method. This example illustrates the systematic selection method.

The cumulative balance is calculated.

The sampling interval is calculated by taking the total value on the ledger of $2,103,000 (to the nearest $000) and dividing by the sample size of 6. The sampling interval is therefore $351,000.

The first item is chosen randomly (a number between 1 and 2,103,000), in this case 233. Each item after that is selected by adding the sampling interval to the last value, until six items have been selected.

$000

Customer Ref	Customer Name	Balance $	Cumulative	Sampling Item
A001	Anfield United Shop	176	176	
B002	The Beautiful Game	84	260	(1) $233
B003	Beckham's	42	302	
C001	Cheryl & Coleen Co	12	314	
D001	Dream Team	45	359	
E001	Escot Supermarket	235	594	(2) $584
G001	Golf is Us	211	805	
G002	Green Green Grass	61	866	
H001	HHA Sports	59	925	
J001	Jilberts	21	946	(3) $935
J002	James Smit Partnership	256	1,202	
J003	Jockeys	419	1,621	(4) $1,286
O001	The Oval	92	1,713	(5) $1,637
P001	Pole Vaulters	76	1,789	
S001	Stayrose Supermarket	97	1,886	
T001	Trainers and More	93	1,979	
W001	Wanderers	89	2,068	(6) $1,988
W003	Walk Hike Run	4	2,072	
W004	Winners	31	2,103	

Evaluating deviations and misstatements in a sample

Deviations

Any issues identified during a test of control are called **deviations**.

The auditor will:

- Determine a level of deviation they are willing to accept – tolerable deviation rate.

- Test the sample stated in the audit plan.

- Extend the sample if deviations are identified.

- Compare the actual deviation rate to the tolerable deviation rate.

- Increase the level of substantive testing over the balance if the actual deviation rate exceeds the tolerable deviation rate.

- Communicate the control deficiency causing the deviation with management and those charged with governance.
  Communication of control deficiencies is covered in more detail in the chapter 'Systems and controls'.

Evaluating deviations in a sample

The auditor tests a sample of 100 purchase orders for evidence of authorisation and identifies 10 have not been authorised. This gives an initial deviation rate of 10%.

The auditor will extend the testing to obtain more evidence about the deviation rate. A further 20 invoices are tested and no further deviations are identified, the deviation rate is now 8.3% (20 / 120 × 100).

The tolerable deviation rate has been set at 5%. Therefore, the actual deviation rate is higher than the deviation rate the auditor is willing to accept. Increased substantive testing will be required over purchases as reliance cannot be placed on the controls.

Misstatements

Misstatements are differences between the amounts actually recorded and what should have been recorded. Misstatements are identified when performing substantive tests of detail.

The auditor will:

- Determine a level of misstatement they are willing to accept – tolerable misstatement.

- Test the sample stated in the audit plan.

- Consider the nature and cause of the misstatement. If the misstatement is an anomaly (isolated), no further procedures are required as the misstatement is not representative of further misstatements.

- Project the misstatement found in the sample across the population as a whole, if the misstatement is not isolated.

- Compare the total projected misstatement to tolerable misstatement.

  - If the total projected misstatement in the sample is less than tolerable misstatement, the auditor may be reasonably confident that the risk of material misstatement in the whole population is low and no further testing will be required.

  - If the total projected misstatement in the sample exceeds tolerable misstatement, the auditor will extend the sample in order to determine the total misstatement in the population.

- Communicate the misstatement with management and ask them to correct it. Communication of misstatements is covered in more detail in the chapter 'Completion and review'.

 Evaluating misstatements in a sample

A sample of $50,000 has been tested out of a population of $800,000. Misstatements of $2,000 were found. Tolerable misstatement has been set at $10,000.

The auditor needs to consider whether the misstatement is an anomaly and therefore isolated, or whether the misstatement is likely to be representative of further misstatements in the population.

If the misstatement is an anomaly, no further procedures will be necessary.

If the misstatement is representative of further misstatements, the auditor will extrapolate the effect of the misstatement across the population to assess whether the projected misstatement is greater than tolerable misstatement.

Here, the auditor might expect that there are misstatements of $32,000 ($2,000/$50,000 × $800,000) in the population.

As the projected misstatement of $32,000 exceeds tolerable misstatement of $10,000, further audit testing will be required.

7 Automated tools and techniques

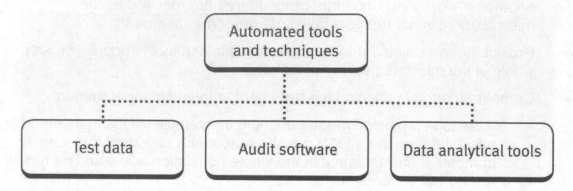

Test data

Test data involves the auditor submitting 'dummy' data into the client's system to ensure that the system correctly processes it and that it prevents or detects and corrects misstatements. The objective of this is to test the operation of application controls within the system.

To be successful test data should include both data with errors built into it and data without errors. Examples of errors include:

- Codes that do not exist, e.g. customer, supplier and employee.

- Transactions above predetermined limits, e.g. salaries above contracted amounts, credit above limits agreed with customer.

- Invoices with arithmetical errors.

- Submitting data with incorrect batch control totals.

Data may be processed during a normal operational cycle ('live' test data) or during a special run at a point in time outside the normal operational cycle ('dead' test data). Both have advantages and disadvantages, for example:

- Live tests could interfere with the operation of the system or corrupt master files/standing data.

- Dead testing avoids this issue but only gives assurance that the system works when not operating live. This may not be reflective of the strains the system is put under in normal conditions.

Advantages of test data

- Enables the auditor to test programmed controls which wouldn't otherwise be able to be tested.

- Once designed, costs incurred will be minimal unless the programmed controls are changed requiring the test data to be redesigned.

Disadvantages of test data

- Risk of corrupting the client's systems.

- Requires time to be spent on the client's system if used in a live environment which may not be convenient for the client.

Audit software

Audit software is used to interrogate a client's system. It can be either packaged, off-the-shelf software or it can be purpose written to work on a client's system. The main advantage of these programs is that they can be used to scrutinise large volumes of data, which it would be inefficient to do manually. The programs can then present the results so that they can be investigated further.

Specific procedures they can perform include:

- Extracting samples according to specified criteria, such as:

  - random

  - over a certain amount e.g. individually material balances or expenses

  - below a certain amount e.g. debit balances on a payables ledger or credit balances on a receivables ledger

  - at certain dates e.g. receivables or inventory over a certain age

- Calculating ratios and select indicators that fail to meet certain predefined criteria (i.e. benchmarking)

- Casting ledgers and schedules

- Recalculation of amounts such as depreciation

- Preparing reports (budget vs actual)

- Stratification of data (such as invoices by customer or age)

- Identifying changes to standing data e.g. employee or supplier bank details

- Produce letters to send out to customers and suppliers.

These procedures can simplify the auditor's task by selecting samples for testing, identifying risk areas and by performing certain substantive procedures. The software does not, however, replace the need for the auditor's own procedures.

Advantages of audit software

- Calculations and casting of reports will be quicker.

- More transactions can be tested as compared with manual testing.

- The computer files are tested rather than printouts.

- Can be cost effective once set up.

Disadvantages of audit software

- Bespoke software (specific to one client) can be expensive to set up.

- Training of audit staff will be required incurring additional cost.

- The audit software may slow down or corrupt the client's systems.

- If errors are made in the design of the software, issues may go undetected by the auditor.

Computer-assisted audit techniques (CAATs)

General advantages of CAATs

- Enables the auditor to test more items more quickly.

- The auditor is able to test the system rather than printouts.

- The results of CAATs can be compared with other tests to increase audit confidence.

- Audit tests can be performed more cost effectively.

Disadvantages of CAATs

- CAATs can be expensive and time consuming to set up.

- Client permission and cooperation may be difficult to obtain.

- Potential incompatibility with the client's computer system.

- The audit team may not have sufficient IT skills and knowledge to create the complex data extracts and programming required.

- The audit team may not have the knowledge or training needed to understand the results of the CAATs.

- Data may be corrupted or lost during the application of CAATs.

Other types of computer-assisted audit techniques

Integrated test facilities – this involves the creation of dummy ledgers and records to which test data can be sent. This enables more frequent and efficient test data procedures to be performed live and the information can simply be ignored by the client when printing out their internal records.

Embedded audit software – this requires a purpose written audit program to be embedded into the client's accounting system. The program will be designed to perform certain tasks (similar to audit software) with the advantage that it can be turned on and off at the auditor's wish throughout the accounting year. This allows the auditor to gather information on certain transactions (perhaps material ones) for later testing, and can identify peculiarities that require attention.

Data analytical tools

 Data analytics (DA) is the science and art of discovering and analysing patterns, deviations and inconsistencies, and extracting other useful information in the data of underlying or related subject matter of an audit through analysis, modelling, visualisation for the purpose of planning and performing the audit.

Big data refers to data sets that are large or complex.

Big data technology allows the auditor to perform procedures on very large or complete sets of data rather than samples.

Features of data analytics

- DA can be used throughout the audit to help identify risks, test the controls, and as part of substantive procedures. The results still need to be evaluated using the professional skills and judgment of the auditor in order to analyse the results and draw conclusions.

- DA can incorporate a wider range of data. For example data can be extracted and analysed from social media, public sector data, industry data and economic data.

Benefits of data analytics

- The quality of the audit can be enhanced by the use of DA. DA enables the auditor to obtain a greater understanding of the entity and its environment. Professional scepticism and professional judgment are improved when the auditor has a better understanding. In addition, DA allows the auditor to manipulate 100% of the data in a population quickly, reducing sampling risk.

- Results can be visualised graphically which may increase the user-friendliness of the reports.

- Audit procedures can be performed more quickly and to a higher standard. This provides more time to analyse and interpret the results rather than gathering the information for analysis.

- Audit procedures can be carried out on a continuous basis rather than focused on the year end.

- Reporting to the client and users will be more timely as the work may be completed within weeks rather than months after the year-end.

- The use of DA may result in more frequent interaction between the auditor and client over the course of the year.

- A reduction in billable hours as audit efficiency increases. Although this is good news for the client, it will mean lower fees for the auditor.

Limitations of data analytics

There are still limitations to the audit and therefore auditors need to be careful not to place too much confidence into the use of DA which could have a negative impact on audit quality.

- As with analytical procedures in general, the quality of DA depends on the reliability of the underlying data used. The data may not be complete, well-controlled or from a reliable source.

- Financial statements still contain a significant amount of estimates.

- DA will not replace the need for auditors to use professional scepticism and professional judgment.

Because of these limitations, the auditor is still only able to give reasonable assurance even though 100% of a population may be tested.

Automated tools and techniques during the audit

Risk assessment

- DA may be used to analyse the number of journals posted manually and automatically by the system; the number of people processing journals and the time of day the journals are posted. This can help with the auditor's assessment of risk due to fraud if:

  - The number of manual versus automatic journals increases significantly.

  - The number of people processing journals increases.

  - Journals are posted outside of normal working hours.

- DA may be used to perform ratio analysis at the risk assessment stage to help identify risks of material misstatement.

- The information system of a client can be accessed directly or by download to enable the auditor to obtain an understanding of how transactions flow through the system.

Substantive procedures

- Drones may be used to perform inspections of inventory where the auditor is unable to attend or physical access is restricted.

- DA can be used to perform substantive analytical procedures such as ratio analysis or trend analysis in respect of sales and purchases.

- DA may be used to identify if ledgers with zero balances are due to a number of offsetting transactions indicating that the ledger balance may be significant.

The Growing Use of Data Analytics in an Audit

What it means for the profession

- Larger accountancy firms are developing their own data analytic platforms. This requires significant investment in computer hardware and software, training of staff and quality control.

- Small firms are unlikely to have the resources available to develop their own software as the cost is likely to be too prohibitive. However, external computer software companies have developed audit systems that work with popular accounting systems such as Sage, Xero and Intuit which many clients of small accountancy firms may be using.

- Medium sized firms may also find the level of investment too restrictive and may therefore be unable to compete with the larger audit firms for listed company audits. However, these firms may find that listed companies require systems and controls assurance work which their auditors would not be allowed to perform under ethical standards.

Developments within the profession

Currently, ISAs take a systems-based approach to audit, which seeks to obtain audit evidence by placing reliance on internal controls rather than on carrying out extensive substantive tests of detail. The development of DA represents a significant progression away from traditional auditing methods. Therefore, as they become more widely used, ISAs will need to be updated to reflect this innovation in auditing techniques.

The IAASB has a responsibility to develop standards that reflect the current environment and facilitate a high quality audit. Auditors, audit oversight authorities and standard setters need to work together to explore how developments in technology can support enhanced audit quality.

Auditors and businesses operate in an environment with larger volumes of transactions, greater complexity and greater regulation as a result of corporate failures. Technological change means information systems are capable of capturing, analysing and communicating significantly more data than previously. As a result, stakeholders are expecting the auditor to perform an audit that includes greater use of technology including DA.

Challenges that impact the use of Data Analytics

Data acquisition and retention – The entity's data will need to be transferred to the auditor raising concerns over data security and privacy as well as creating storage problems for such large data sets.

Conceptual challenges – Auditors will be asking questions they have never asked in the past and the client may be hesitant to provide all of the information requested.

Legal and regulatory challenges – Regulations may prohibit data leaving the jurisdiction the entity is located. This may pose a problem if the IT facilities of the client are located in a different country.

Resource availability – Data scientists may form part of a centralised department which supports all engagement teams within the firm. The resources are likely to be limited which will put a strain on resources.

How regulators and audit oversight authorities maintain oversight – These bodies have little experience themselves of inspecting audits using DA.

Investment in retraining and reskilling auditors – Changing the auditor's mind-set from traditional audit methods will require time and investment.

The use of DA and developments in auditing standards will impact:

Risk assessment – DA may improve the risk assessment process.

Quality control – Audit firms will need to consider how specialist teams are supervised and how they interact with the audit teams they support. Firms will need to consider the integrity of the DA software to ensure it does what it is supposed to.

Group audits – DA may help by enabling better analytical procedures to be performed in respect of components that are not significant components. Also, the audit procedures may be more centralised enabling the group auditor to perform more procedures rather than relying on the work of a component auditor.

Estimates and fair values – Due to large volumes of data that feed into the models used to develop accounting estimates, DA may be valuable in addressing audit risks associated with these data sources.

Smaller audit firms – Smaller firms may not be able to make the required investment to develop DA tools. Audits of public sector entities may prove challenging as home-grown systems are more prevalent and data capture may be more difficult.

Education – Auditors and accountants will need to be re-skilled to realise the potential of DA. Training and qualifications will need to reflect the increased use of DA for new entrants to the profession.

Ethics – Due to auditors having access to large volumes of client data, there may be a need to update the Code of Ethics to enhance the requirements for confidentiality.

Other auditing standards – There is also likely to be a need to revise other auditing standards such as ISA 240 (Fraud), ISA 320 (Materiality), ISA 330 (Responses to risks), ISA 500 (Audit Evidence), ISA 520 (Analytical Procedures) and ISA 530 (Audit Sampling).

FRC Audit Quality Thematic Review – The Use of Data Analytics in the Audit of Financial Statements

With the increasing use of data analytics, the FRC has performed a review to identify what is working well with a view of sharing information to promote continuous improvement in audit quality. The Audit Quality Review (AQR) team assessed the use of DA in the six largest audit firms.

Current use of data analytics

- Analyse all transactions in a population, stratify the population and identify outliers for further examination.

- Reperform calculations

- Match transactions as they pass through the system

- Assist in segregation of duties testing

- Compare client data with externally obtained data

- Perform sensitivity analysis.

Impact on audit quality

Audit quality is a driver for the implementation of DA. DA can:

- Deepen the auditor's understanding of the entity.

- Facilitate testing of the highest risk areas through stratification.

- Enhance the use of professional scepticism.

- Improve consistency on group audits

- Enable the auditor to test entire datasets.

- Improve audit efficiency.

- Increase the possibility of identifying fraud.

- Provide a channel for enhanced communication with audit committees.

Good practices observed during the AQR

- Focused roll out of a DA tool.

- Clear positioning within the audit methodology.

- Testing or trial running the DA tool.

- Using specialist staff and clearly defined roles between the specialists and the core engagement team.

- Central running of DA for group audits.

- Clearly documenting the DA tool using flowcharts.

Summary of key findings

- The introduction of mandatory retendering in the UK has provided incentive for firms to develop DA tools as this acts as a key differentiator.

- UK firms are at the forefront of developing DA tools.

- The pace of change is not as fast as expected by audit committees and investors.

- Whilst some firms are investing heavily in DA tools, they are not monitoring their use by audit teams or effectiveness at providing appropriate evidence.

- Some audit teams have over-emphasised their use to audit committees. In some cases DA have been used to provide insight to the audit committee rather than to generate audit evidence. In another case, a firm described a DA tool as launched in a report but was described to the Audit Quality Review team as being in pilot stage.

- All firms used DA to assist with journal entry testing, however, most firms are not using DA tools routinely in other audit areas.

- For complex entities it can take two years to achieve the full benefits of a DA approach.

- The main barrier to effective use relates to difficulties obtaining entity data and audit teams often lack expertise to extract the data required.

- The use of DA techniques was higher at firms where the audit methodology clearly defines the purpose of the DA.

- In the audits tested, insufficient evidence audit evidence was retained on file.

  - Criteria input into the DA tool was not retained.

  - Screenshots omitted important information.

  - Evidence produced by specialists was omitted.

  - Firm's archiving tools were not able to archive DA evidence.

  - It may not be technically, practically or legally possible for the audit firm to retain audit evidence for the file retention period required by auditing standards.

Exploring the Growing Use of Technology in the Audit, with a Focus on Data Analytics

In September 2016, IAASB issued a request for input from accounting firms, regulatory bodies, standard setters, academics and public sector organisations to obtain information about the current use and future direction of the use of data analytics.

The key messages from the Feedback Statement published in January 2018 are:

- ISAs are not 'broken' and should remain principles-based. There should be no rush to change requirements in ISAs at present.

- ISAs should be updated in a way that reflects current technology but remains technologically neutral to provide the ability to accommodate future changes in technology. ISA 500 *Audit Evidence* and ISA 230 *Audit Documentation* were highlighted as priorities for revision.

- Non-authoritative, practical guidance with real-life examples of the use of DA is needed. This process has already commenced.

- The use of DA does not reduce the need to exercise professional scepticism and judgment. Both are integral to understanding the benefits and limitations of using DA in the audit.

Areas of concern

Regulators and oversight authorities are most concerned with data acquisition, auditor skills and compliance with ISAs.

- Audit clients may be reluctant to give access to live systems and this may cast doubt on the reliability of the data being analysed.

- Currently auditors tend to have insufficient understanding of IT to design effective procedures using DA.

- Audit evidence generated from DA must demonstrate that the requirements of the ISAs have been met, particularly the documentation requirements.

Accounting firms are also concerned about retraining and re-skilling not only auditors, but also regulators and audit committees who will need to understand the DA performed as part of assessing the work of the auditor. There is also concern that these authorities have little experience themselves of inspecting audits involving the use of DA.

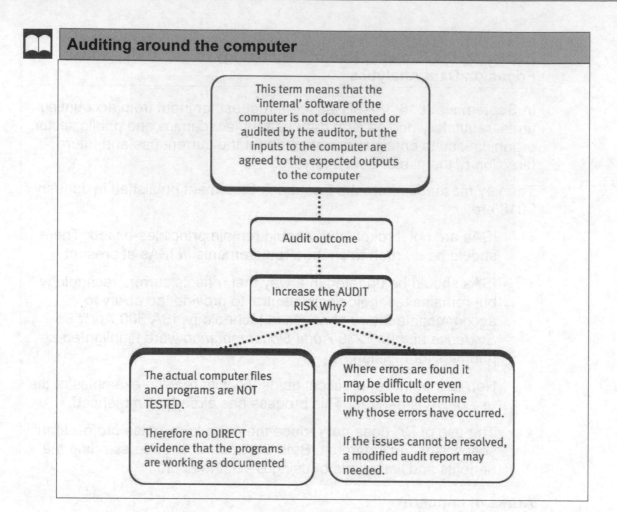

Auditing around the computer

This term means that the 'internal' software of the computer is not documented or audited by the auditor, but the inputs to the computer are agreed to the expected outputs to the computer

Audit outcome

Increase the AUDIT RISK Why?

The actual computer files and programs are NOT TESTED.

Therefore no DIRECT evidence that the programs are working as documented

Where errors are found it may be difficult or even impossible to determine why those errors have occurred.

If the issues cannot be resolved, a modified audit report may needed.

Test your understanding 1

List FOUR factors that influence the reliability of audit evidence.

(4 marks)

Test your understanding 2

List and explain FOUR methods of selecting a sample of items to test from a population in accordance with ISA 530 *Audit Sampling*.

(4 marks)

Test your understanding 3

List and explain FOUR factors that will influence the auditor's judgment regarding the sufficiency of the evidence obtained.

(4 marks)

Test your understanding 4

You are assigned to the audit of Lamp Co. You are currently reviewing the audit work performed to date.

Tolerable deviation rate is 5%.

Tolerable misstatement is $3,000.

Tests of controls over revenue

During controls testing, the audit team tested a sample of 50 sales invoices for evidence of a second person checking the prices charged on the invoice to the company's approved price list, the goods invoiced to the goods despatched note and an arithmetical check of the invoice total. In four cases the checks had not been performed.

The sample was chosen by selecting every 37th invoice in the population.

Substantive procedures over purchases

During substantive testing, the audit team tested a sample of 50 purchase invoices listed in the purchase day book and traced the amounts back to the physical invoices for accuracy. Two invoices were recorded inaccurately, resulting in a total misstatement within the sample of $198.

The total of the sample tested was $2,500. The total purchases figure included in the statement of profit or loss is $43,000.

The sample was chosen by the auditor selecting 50 invoices from anywhere in the purchase day book, trying to avoid bias.

1   In respect of the tests of controls over revenue, which TWO of the following are appropriate responses?

(i)   Pick alternative items to test in place of those just tested and ignore the deviations.

(ii)   Extend the sample size.

(iii)   Perform increased substantive testing.

(iv)   Extrapolate the deviation across the population.

A   (i) and (ii)

B   (ii) and (iii)

C   (i) and (iv)

D   (iii) and (iv)

2   **In respect of the substantive testing performed over purchases, what action should the auditor now take?**

   A   Inform the client of the misstatement and ask them to correct it

   B   Calculate the materiality of the misstatement in relation to the financial statements

   C   Extend the sample

   D   Compare the misstatement with the tolerable deviation rate

3   **Select the sampling method used in each of the procedures stated.**

Test of controls over revenue	Haphazard	Random	Systematic
Substantive procedure over purchases	Haphazard	Random	Systematic

4   **Which of the following statements is TRUE?**

   A   Sampling refers to where less than 100% of the items in a population are tested and have an equal chance of selection

   B   Deviations must be extrapolated to determine the effect on the population

   C   Block sampling is where the auditor tests all items in a population

   D   Monetary unit sampling is a statistical method of sampling

5   **Select whether the following statements are TRUE or FALSE.**

Statistical sampling methods are more reliable than non-statistical methods	TRUE	FALSE
The auditor must always use stratification to ensure a representative sample is tested	TRUE	FALSE
More than one sampling method may be used to test one population	TRUE	FALSE
A deviation occurs when a result differs from expectation during a substantive procedure	TRUE	FALSE

KAPLAN PUBLISHING

Test your understanding 5

You are planning the audit of Wyndham Co. The company sells diamonds and other precious stones. You have decided to use the work of an auditor's expert to provide sufficient appropriate evidence over the valuation of inventory.

1   **Before appointing an auditor's expert, what factors must the auditor consider?**

(i)   Competence

(ii)   Capability

(iii)   Objectivity

(iv)   Reliability of the source data

A   (i), (ii) and (iii)

B   (ii), (iii) and (iv)

C   (i) (iii) and (iv) only

D   (i), (ii), (iii) and (iv)

2   **How can the auditor assess the competence of an auditor's expert?**

(i)   Obtain copies of professional certificates and make enquiries of the expert's experience.

(ii)   Ask for confirmation from the expert of their independence.

(iii)   Inspect the register of members of the relevant professional body for the name of the expert.

A   (i) and (ii) only

B   (ii) and (iii) only

C   (i) and (iii) only

D   (i), (ii) and (iii)

3   **What must be agreed with the auditor's expert in writing before the work is performed?**

(i)   Responsibilities of each party

(ii)   Inherent limitations of the audit

(iii)   Deadline for the work

(iv)   Scope and objectives

A   (i), (ii), (iii) and (iv)

B   (i), (iii) and (iv) only

C   (iii) and (ii) only

D   (i), (ii) and (iv) only

4   **Which of the following statements is TRUE in respect of the expert's work?**

   A   The auditor can rely on the expert's work and does not need to review it

   B   The auditor may choose not to review the expert's work if it is an area in which the auditor has knowledge or experience

   C   The auditor must review the assumptions and source data used by the expert to ensure they were reasonable and reliable

   D   The auditor will engage a second expert to review the work of the first to ensure sufficient appropriate evidence has been obtained

5   **Which of the following statements best describes a management's expert?**

   A   A management's expert is an employee of the company

   B   A management's expert is someone appointed by the company to provide evidence for the auditor

   C   A management's expert is someone recommended by the auditor which management appoints to provide evidence for the audit

   D   A management's expert is someone appointed by the company to provide evidence for management which may be relied upon by the auditor

8   Chapter summary

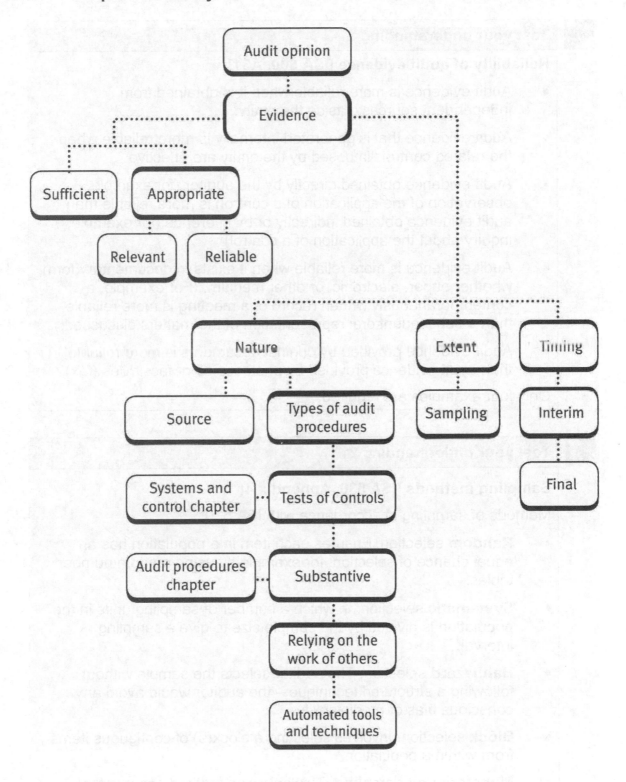

Test your understanding answers

Test your understanding 1

Reliability of audit evidence [ISA 500, A31]

- Audit evidence is more reliable when it is obtained from independent sources outside the entity.

- Audit evidence that is generated internally is more reliable when the related controls imposed by the entity are effective.

- Audit evidence obtained directly by the auditor (for example, observation of the application of a control) is more reliable than audit evidence obtained indirectly or by inference (for example, inquiry about the application of a control).

- Audit evidence is more reliable when it exists in documentary form, whether paper, electronic, or other medium. (For example, a contemporaneously written record of a meeting is more reliable than a subsequent oral representation of the matters discussed.)

- Audit evidence provided by original documents is more reliable than audit evidence provided by photocopies or facsimiles (fax).

Only four examples are required.

Test your understanding 2

Sampling methods [ISA 530, Appendix 4]

Methods of sampling in accordance with ISA 530:

- **Random** selection. Ensures each item in a population has an equal chance of selection, for example by using random number tables.

- **Systematic** selection. In which a number of sampling units in the population is divided by the sample size to give a sampling interval.

- **Haphazard** selection. The auditor selects the sample without following a structured technique – the auditor would avoid any conscious bias or predictability.

- **Block** selection. Involves selecting a block(s) of contiguous items from within a population.

- **Monetary unit sampling.** This selection method ensures that each individual $1 in the population has an equal chance of being selected.

Note: Only four sampling methods were required.

Test your understanding 3

Sufficiency of evidence

- Assessment of risk at the financial statement level and/or the individual transaction level. As risk increases then more evidence is required.

- The materiality of the item. More evidence will normally be collected on material items whereas immaterial items may simply be reviewed to ensure they appear materially correct.

- The nature of the accounting and internal control systems. The auditor will place more reliance on good accounting and internal control systems limiting the amount of audit evidence required.

- The auditor's knowledge and experience of the business. Where the auditor has good knowledge of the business and trusts the integrity of staff then less evidence will be required.

- The findings of audit procedures. Where findings from related audit procedures are satisfactory (e.g. tests of controls) then less substantive evidence will be collected.

- The source and reliability of the information. Where evidence is obtained from reliable sources (e.g. written evidence) then less evidence is required than if the source was unreliable (e.g. verbal evidence).

Test your understanding 4

1	B	Extend the sample size and perform more substantive tests. The auditor should never disregard deviations or misstatements identified during testing. It is not appropriate to extrapolate a deviation rate across a population.
2	C	The misstatement must be extrapolated across the population. 198 / 2,500 × 43,000 = $3,406. This exceeds tolerable misstatement of $3,000 therefore the auditor must perform further audit procedures by extending the sample.
3	Systematic Haphazard	Tests of control over revenue have used systematic sampling. This is when a constant sampling interval is used e.g. every 37th item. Substantive procedures over purchases have used haphazard sampling. This is when the auditor selects the sample without a pattern and tries to avoid bias.
4	D	Sampling is when each item in a population has a chance of selection. They do not need to have an equal chance. Deviations are not extrapolated as the deviation rate will be the same across the population. Block sampling is where items next to each other in the population are tested.
5	False False True False	Statistical sampling methods are not necessarily more reliable than non-statistical methods. The auditor must use professional judgment to choose whichever is appropriate in the circumstances. Stratification should be used when a population is not homogenous. If the population is homogenous, stratification will not be necessary. More than one sampling method may be used to test the same population. If the population has been stratified, the auditor may use different sampling methods for each sub-population. A deviation occurs when a result differs from expectation when the auditor performs tests of controls.

KAPLAN PUBLISHING

Test your understanding 5		
1	A	Reliability of source data is evaluated after the expert has performed the work.
2	C	An independence confirmation from the expert would confirm objectivity but not competence.
3	B	Inherent limitations of an audit would not be communicated to the expert. This would be included in an audit engagement letter.
4	C	The auditor cannot just rely on the expert's work. They must review it to ensure it provides sufficient appropriate evidence and therefore must consider the assumptions and source data. If the auditor already had knowledge and experience in this area there would be no need to use an auditor's expert. If the auditor has evaluated the competence, capability and objectivity of the expert before using them, there should be no need to appoint a second expert to the review the first expert's work.
5	D	A management's expert is appointed by management to produce evidence to be used by management. If the evidence is reliable and relevant to the external audit, the auditor may choose to rely on that work.

Systems and controls

Chapter learning objectives

This chapter covers syllabus areas:

- C1 – Internal control systems

- C2 – The use and evaluation of internal control systems by auditors

- C3 – Tests of controls

- C4 – Communication on internal control

Detailed syllabus objectives are provided in the introduction section of the text book.

PER

One of the PER performance objectives (PO19) is to collect and evaluate evidence for an audit. Carry out an internal or external audit from collecting evidence, through to forming an opinion. You demonstrate professional scepticism and make sure judgments are based on sufficient valid evidence. Working through this chapter should help you understand how to demonstrate that objective.

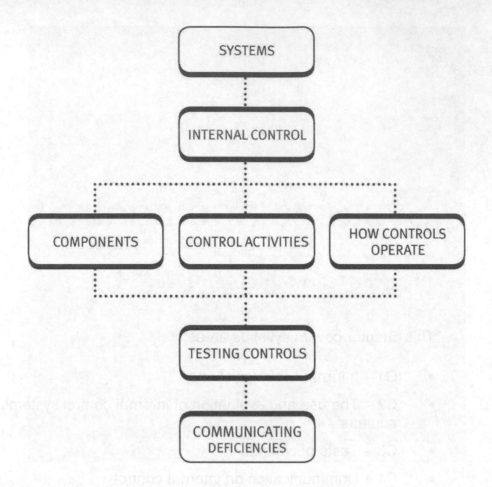

The basics of an internal control system were covered in Business Technology (previously Accountant in Business) at the Applied Knowledge level. This chapter develops this area further and looks at how the internal control system of a client influences the audit approach taken and the audit evidence gathered.

1 Effect of controls on the audit

This chapter considers the basic components of an internal control system, and how the auditor fulfils their objectives for assessing control risk.

As we saw in Chapter 5, control risk is one of the factors affecting the risk of material misstatement. If a client's system of internal control is designed appropriately, implemented and working effectively, there will be less risk of material misstatement in the financial statements as the controls will have either prevented the misstatements from occurring in the first place, or will have detected the misstatements and prompted action for them to be corrected. The auditor will use this assessment of control risk to determine the impact on the audit strategy and audit plan.

Impact of tests of controls on the audit strategy and plan

The extent of substantive testing to be carried out will depend on the results of the auditor's assessment of control risk.

If control risk is low

- The auditor can **place more reliance on internal controls** and evidence generated internally within the entity.

- This increases the appropriateness of interim audit testing and allows the auditor to **reduce the quantity of detailed substantive procedures** performed at the final audit stage.

- The audit strategy and plan will be updated to reflect that fewer substantive procedures will be required or smaller sample sizes can be tested at the final audit stage.

If control risk is high

The auditor will:

- Increase the volume of procedures conducted at and after the year-end. [ISA 330, A2]

- Increase the level of substantive procedures, in particular, tests of detail. [ISA 330, A2]

- Increase the locations included in the audit scope. [ISA 330, A2]

- Place less reliance on analytical procedures as the information produced by the client's systems is not reliable.

- Place less reliance on written representations from management if the control environment is weak.

- Obtain more evidence from external sources e.g. external confirmations from customers and suppliers.

- Update the audit strategy and plan to reflect the additional testing required at the final audit stage.

Limitations of internal controls

The auditor can never eliminate the need for substantive procedures entirely because there are inherent limitations to the reliance that can be placed on internal controls due to:

- Human error – mistakes made by those responsible for performing controls.

- Ineffective controls – controls which do not work as intended.

- Collusion of staff – staff work together (collude) to bypass the control of segregation of duties.

- The abuse of power by those with ultimate controlling responsibility (management override) – management may falsify accounting records or post unauthorised journals to present a different result in the financial statements.

- Use of management judgment on the nature and extent of controls it chooses to implement.

[ISA 315 (Revised 2019), Appendix 3, 22 - 24]

As a result of these limitations, the auditor must always perform substantive testing on material balances in the financial statements. [ISA 330, 18]

Examples of control limitations

Human error

Warehouse staff are required to check the quantity of the goods received to the authorised purchase order however an error may be made when counting.

Ineffective controls

The sales manager is required to authorise the mileage claims of sales representatives within their department. The authorisation process should include a check that the mileage claimed is reasonable however the department manager performs no checks and simply signs off the claim as authorised.

Collusion

Within the payroll department, a payroll clerk processes timesheets and overtime claims and the payroll manager authorises the payroll for payment, however the clerk and manager are related and collude to enable the clerk to increase the overtime paid to herself which she shares with the manager.

Management override

During the preparation of the financial statements, the finance director falsifies the accounting records by posting a journal to increase revenue to show a desired level of profit required to meet a loan covenant.

Use of management judgment

Last year's report to management contained several recommendations for improvements to the client's controls which exposed the company to fraud and error. During the current year audit the audit manager identified that no action had been taken in response to the recommendations. When the matter was discussed with the finance director, the audit manager was told that the cost of implementing the controls outweighed the benefits and therefore the company would not be acting on the recommendations.

2 Components of an internal control system

ISA 315 (Revised 2019), states that the auditor needs to understand an entity's internal controls. To assist this process it identifies five components of an internal control system:

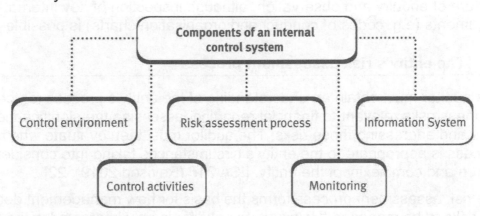

[ISA 315 (Revised 2019),12m]

(i) The control environment

The control environment includes the **governance and management** function of an organisation.

It focuses largely on the **attitude, awareness and actions** of those responsible for designing, implementing and monitoring internal controls.

The control environment sets the tone of an organisation and provides the foundation for the other components of the internal control system.

[ISA 315 (Revised 2019), Appendix 3, 4]

Elements of the control environment:

- How management's responsibilities are carried out, demonstrating management's commitment to integrity and ethical values.

- How those charged with governance demonstrate independence from management and exercise oversight of the internal control system.

- How the entity assigns authority and responsibility in pursuit of its objectives.

- How the entity attracts, develops and retains competent people including recruitment policies, training policies and performance appraisals.

- How the entity holds individuals accountable for their responsibilities e.g. performance measures and disciplinary policies.

[ISA 315 (Revised 2019), Appendix 3, 6]

When assessing the control environment, the auditor may consider how management has responded to the findings and recommendations of the internal audit function regarding identified control deficiencies.

The auditor must also assess whether any controls implemented as a result of those recommendations have been subsequently evaluated by the internal audit function. [ISA 315 (Revised 2019), Appendix 4, 7]

Evidence regarding the control environment is usually obtained through a mixture of enquiry and observation, although inspection of key internal documents (e.g. codes of conduct and organisation charts) is possible.

(ii) The entity's risk assessment process

The auditor must obtain an understanding of the entity's process for identifying business risks relevant to financial reporting, assessing the significance of those risks and addressing those risks. The auditor must then evaluate whether the process is appropriate to the entity's circumstances taking into consideration the nature and complexity of the entity. [ISA 315 (Revised 2019), 22]

The risk assessment process forms the basis for how management determines the risks to be managed. However, the auditor is only interested in the business risks relevant to the preparation of the financial statements.
[ISA 315 (Revised 2019), Appendix 3, 7, 8]

Business risks relevant to financial reporting are threats to the achievement of ongoing business objectives and can lead to misstatement in the financial statements.

Examples include:

- New information systems and technology

- Rapid growth

- New accounting requirements/principles

- Maintaining the integrity of data and information processing

- Risks to the entity's business strategy if the entity's IT strategy does not effectively support the business strategy

- Interruptions in the IT environment when the entity does not make necessary updates to the IT environment or such updates are not timely.

[ISA 315 (Revised 2019), Appendix 3, 9]

If the client has robust procedures for assessing the business risks it faces, the risk of misstatement overall will be lower.

If the auditor identifies instances where management failed to identify risks of material misstatement, they should obtain an understanding of why the entity's process failed to identify the risks and consider the implications for the audit.
[ISA 315 (Revised 2019), 23]

(iii) The entity's process to monitor the system of internal control

This is the client's continual process of evaluating the effectiveness of controls over time and taking necessary remedial action.

Monitoring can be either ongoing or performed on a separate evaluation basis (or a combination of both).

[ISA 315 (Revised 2019), Appendix 3, 10]

Monitoring of internal controls is often the key role of the internal audit function.

(iv) The information system and communication

The information system relevant to financial reporting consists of all of the activities and policies relevant to financial reporting and communication. It includes the procedures within both computerised and manual systems.

The information system includes all of the procedures and records which are designed to:

- Initiate, record, process and report transactions.
- Maintain accountability for assets, liabilities and equity.
- Resolve incorrect processing of transactions.
- Process and account for system overrides.
- Transfer information to the general/nominal ledger.
- Capture information relevant to financial reporting for other events and conditions.
- Ensure information required to be disclosed is appropriately reported.

[ISA 315 (Revised 2019), Appendix 3, 15]

(v) Control activities

Control activities are the policies (statements of what should or should not be done) and procedures (actions to implement policies) to achieve the control objectives of management and those charged with governance.

Examples of specific control activities include those relating to:

- Authorisation to confirm the validity of a transaction.
- Reconciliations to address the completeness or accuracy of transactions.
- Verifications to address the completeness, accuracy or validity of transactions.
- Physical or logical controls to prevent theft of assets or data.
- Segregation of duties to reduce opportunity for any person to commit and conceal fraud in the normal course of their duties.

[ISA 315 (Revised 2019), Appendix 3, 20]

Examples of control activities

Authorisation

- A manager signing off an employee's timesheet to confirm that the hours stated have been worked and can be paid. This should ensure the employee is not claiming for hours not worked.

- A manager signing a purchase order to confirm the order can be placed with the supplier. This should ensure that the goods are for a valid business use and the items are needed.

Reconciliation

- Preparation of a bank reconciliation to ensure cash transactions have been recorded completely and accurately.

- Reconciliation of supplier statements with the payables ledger to ensure completeness and accuracy of payables.

Verification

- Managers should compare actual spend against budgeted spend to detect unusual fluctuations. If actual spend is significantly higher than budget, the department may have spent more than it should or it could indicate an error when processing the transactions.

- Batch totals used when inputting data to ensure items are not omitted.

Physical or logical controls

- Restrictions on access to assets such as keeping cash in a safe to prevent theft.

- Password restrictions to prevent unauthorised access to computer files.

Segregation of duties

- Warehouse staff should not be responsible for the inventory count as this would not detect if goods were being stolen by staff throughout the year.

- Employees who authorise transactions should not be the ones who originate the transaction.

Controls may be **direct or indirect**. A direct control addresses the risk of material misstatement at the assertion level. Indirect controls support the direct controls. [ISA 315 (Revised 2019), A5]

For example, a manager's review of the payroll total each month to ensure the amount to be paid is in line with expectation is an indirect control as it does not specifically address an assertion. Agreeing the amounts on the payroll list to individual payslips would address the assertion of accuracy and is therefore a direct control.

IT controls

The level of risk arising from the IT environment will vary from client to client depending on the nature and extent to which the entity uses technology. More complex IT systems may involve the use of emerging technologies such as blockchain, or may involve the client changing the source code of the program. Less sophisticated systems may simply be a user interface in which the client enters data which the system processes.

Regardless of the scale of complexity, the auditor must always identify the IT application and other aspects of the entity's IT environment that are subject to risks arising from the use of IT and identify the related risks arising from the use of IT and the general controls in place to address those risks.
[ISA 315 (Revised 2019), 26]

IT controls are normally divided into **general** controls and **information processing** controls. An effective IT system should include both.

General controls

General IT controls support the continued proper operation of the IT environment, including effective functioning of the information processing controls and the integrity of information in the information system. [ISA 315 (Revised 2019), 12d]

E.g. controls over:

- Access – Preventing unauthorised access to applications, databases, operating system, networks.

- Program changes or other changes to the IT environment – Segregation of duties, system development, data conversion.

- Process to manage IT operations – job scheduling, job monitoring, backup and recovery, intrusion detection.

[ISA 315 (Revised 2019, Appendix 6, 2]

Information processing controls

Information processing controls relate to the processing of information in IT applications or manual processes that directly address risks to the integrity of information. [ISA 315 (Revised 2019), 12d]

These controls may be automated (embedded in IT applications) or manual (e.g. input or output controls). [ISA 315 (Revised 2019), A6]

Examples include:

- Batch total checks (e.g. when entering invoices onto the system the system may give a batch total i.e. the number of invoices actually entered. The clerk entering the invoices can then double check that the correct number of invoices has been entered and none have been missed or entered twice).

- Sequence checks (to ensure the number sequence is complete and no items are missing).

- Matching master files to transaction records (e.g. matching prices on sales invoices to the company's price list to ensure the prices being applied are correct).

- Arithmetic checks (to verify arithmetical accuracy).

- Range checks (to ensure that data entered is within a reasonable range).

- Existence checks (e.g. to check employees exist).

- Authorisation of transaction entries (to ensure the transaction is valid and should be processed).

- Exception reporting (the system may generate an exception report when something which isn't usual has occurred e.g. changes to bank details of employees which wouldn't be expected to change often).

3 Ascertaining the systems

Procedures used to obtain evidence regarding the design and implementation of controls include:

- Enquiries of relevant personnel.

- Observing the application of controls.

- Tracing a transaction through the system to understand what happens (a walkthrough test).

- Inspecting documents, such as internal procedure manuals.

It should also be noted that enquiry alone is not sufficient to understand the nature and extent of controls.

The auditor can also use existing knowledge of the client and the operation of the systems. However, they cannot simply rely on their knowledge from the prior year audit as changes may have occurred. Systems knowledge must be updated and the systems tested once more if it relates to an area of significant risk. For controls which do not address a significant risk, the auditor must test the controls at least once every third audit. [ISA 330, A37]

4 Documenting client's systems

The auditor must document the client's control systems before evaluating whether the system is adequate and working effectively.

Possible ways of documenting systems include:

- **Narrative notes** – a written description of a system.

- **Flowcharts** – a diagrammatical representation of the system.

- **Questionnaires** – a prepared list of questions in relation to the client's control system. There are two types of questionnaire that can be used:

  Internal Control Questionnaire (ICQ) – a list of controls is given to the client and they are asked whether or not those controls are in place.

  Internal Control Evaluation Questionnaire (ICEQ) – the client is asked to describe the controls they have in place for a given control objective.

- **Organisation chart** – a diagram showing reporting lines, roles and responsibilities.

 Tutorial note

A control objective identifies the risk that the entity needs to manage i.e. the reason for a control procedure or activity being required.

For example, a risk within a purchasing system is that purchases could be made for personal use and paid by the company. Therefore the control objective is to ensure goods cannot be purchased for personal use.

Most companies would have a control procedure in place to prevent this risk from occurring such as authorisation of purchase orders by a responsible official.

ICQ wording	ICEQ wording
Does a supervisor authorise all weekly timesheets?	How does the company ensure that only hours worked are recorded on timesheets?
Does the company perform a regular credit check on all customers?	How does the company try to minimise the risk of irrecoverable debts?
Does a manager or director authorise purchase orders before an order is placed?	How does the company ensure goods are only purchased for a valid business use?
Is a bank reconciliation performed regularly?	How does the company ensure discrepancies in the cash book are identified and resolved?
Is a regular inventory count performed?	How does the company ensure its inventory system is up to date and discrepancies in the inventory records are identified and corrected?
Is a regular reconciliation performed between the physical non-current assets and the non-current asset register?	How does the company ensure the non-current asset register is up to date and accurate?

The method adopted is a matter of auditor judgment.

Documentation Method	Advantages	Disadvantages
Narrative notes	• Simple to record • Facilitates understanding by all audit staff	• May be time consuming and cumbersome if the system is complex • May be more difficult to identify missing controls
Flow charts	• Easy to view the whole system in one diagram • Easy to spot missing controls due to the use of standard symbols	• May be difficult to amend as the whole diagram may need to be re-drawn • There is still a need for narrative notes to accompany the flow chart increasing the time involved to document the system fully
Internal control questionnaires (ICQs)	• Quick to prepare as a standard questionnaire can be used for all clients • Can ensure all common controls are present	• Controls may be overstated as the client knows the answer the auditor is looking for is 'yes' • Unusual controls are unlikely to be included on a standard questionnaire and may not be identified • May contain a number of irrelevant controls
Internal control evaluations (ICEs)	• The client has to respond with the control they have in place rather than a yes/no answer which should mean controls are less likely to be overstated • Quick to prepare	• The client may still overstate controls as they may say a control is in place for the control objective even if it is not • The checklist may contain control objectives not relevant to the client • Unusual risks and therefore objectives may not be identified

5 Testing the system

Tests of controls are performed only on those controls that the auditor has determined are suitably designed to prevent, or detect and correct a material misstatement in a relevant assertion. [ISA 330, A20]

Controls will only be worth testing if they are designed appropriately in the first place (i.e. they are capable of preventing or detecting and correcting misstatements) and implemented (i.e. the controls exist and the entity is using them). When a control is not designed or implemented effectively, there is no benefit in testing it. [ISA 315 (Revised 2019), A175, A176, A179]

Typical methods of controls testing include:

- Observation of control activities, e.g. observing the inventory count to ensure it is conducted effectively and in accordance with the count instructions.

- Inspection of documents recording performance of the control, e.g. inspecting an order for evidence of authorisation.

- Using test data to ensure the programmed controls are working effectively. See the 'Evidence' chapter).

Designing valid tests of controls

To design a test of control, the auditor must first identify the controls they want to test.

A control is an activity applied in addition to the normal processing of the system to ensure that the system has operated as it should.

Just because errors have not been made does not mean that controls have worked effectively. The person performing the processing may not have made any errors. There may have been no controls in place. A control is an additional activity to ensure the person has not made any errors.

For example, if the client claims to perform bank reconciliations, the auditor should look at the file containing the reconciliations to verify that they are done, and then reperform the reconciliation to ensure it has been done properly, to test the effectiveness of the control. Simply performing the reconciliation and finding that it reconciles does not prove that the client has done the reconciliation themselves. Therefore, reperformance of the reconciliation on its own is not a valid test of control.

Similarly, if the auditor performs a sequence check on a set of documents and finds the sequence is complete, it does not mean the client has performed a sequence check. It may just mean that no documents have gone missing. The auditor must look for evidence that the client has performed a sequence check to confirm no documents have gone missing.

6 Communicating control deficiencies

ISA 265 *Communicating Deficiencies in Internal Control to Those Charged with Governance and Management* requires the auditor to:

- Communicate any deficiencies that are of sufficient importance to merit management's attention to management. [ISA 265, 10]

- Communicate significant deficiencies to those charged with governance. [ISA 265, 9]

Deficiencies occur when:

- A control is designed, implemented or operated in such a way that it is unable to prevent, or detect and correct misstatements in the financial statements on a timely basis, or

- A control necessary to prevent, or detect and correct, misstatements in the financial statements on a timely basis is missing.

[ISA 265, 6a]

Significant deficiencies are those which merit the attention of those charged with governance. [ISA 265, 6b]

The external auditor should consider the following when determining if a deficiency in internal controls is significant:

- The likelihood of the deficiencies leading to material misstatements in the financial statements in the future.

- The susceptibility to loss or fraud of the related asset or liability.

- The subjectivity and complexity of determining estimated amounts.

- The financial statement amounts exposed to the deficiencies.

- The volume of activity that has occurred or could occur in the account balance or class of transactions exposed to the deficiency or deficiencies.

- The importance of the controls to the financial reporting process.

- The cause and frequency of the exceptions detected as a result of the deficiencies in the controls.

- The interaction of the deficiency with other deficiencies in internal control.

[ISA 265, A6]

The auditor will communicate the deficiencies in a management letter or report to management. It is usually sent at the end of the audit process.

 In the exam you may be required to prepare extracts for inclusion in a report to management. This requires you to identify and explain the deficiencies within the control system described in a scenario. You will have to suggest a recommendation to overcome each deficiency.

Deficiency	A clear description of what is wrong.
Consequence	What could happen if the deficiency is not corrected?
	Focus on what matters to the client – the risk of a reduction in revenue, extra costs, stolen assets, errors in the accounts.
Recommendation	This must deal with the specific deficiency you have identified. It must also provide greater benefits than the cost of implementation.
	Try to specify exactly how the recommended control should operate, for example, suggest who should carry out the control procedure, and how frequently it should be performed.

 When the auditor reports deficiencies, it should be made clear that:

- The report is not a comprehensive list of deficiencies, but only those that have come to light during normal audit procedures.

- The report is for the sole use of the company.

- No disclosure should be made to a third party without the written agreement of the auditor.

- No responsibility is assumed to any other parties.

If you are asked for a covering letter in the exam, you should include the above matters within it.

e.g Management letter extract

Deficiency	**Consequence**	**Recommendation**
Purchase invoices were missing from the sequentially numbered invoice file.	There is a possibility that purchases and liabilities are not completely recorded. This could result in late payment of invoices which could cause damage to the company's relationship with the supplier resulting in removal of credit terms or discounts.	All invoices should be sequentially filed on receipt by the accounts department. Regular sequence checks should be performed to ensure completeness. Any missing items should be investigated and copies requested if necessary.

7 Sales system

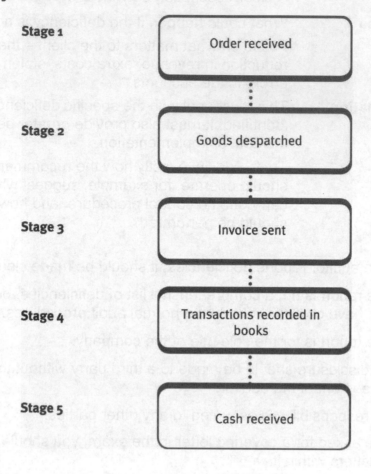

Stage 1	Order received
Stage 2	Goods despatched
Stage 3	Invoice sent
Stage 4	Transactions recorded in books
Stage 5	Cash received

Objectives

The objectives of controls in the sales system are to ensure that:

Stage	Objective
Ordering	• Goods are only supplied to customers who pay promptly and in full. • All orders are processed.
Despatch	• Orders are despatched promptly and in full to the correct customer. • All orders are despatched.
Invoicing	• All goods despatched are invoiced. • Invoices are raised accurately.

Recording	• Only valid sales are recorded.
	• All sales and related receivables are recorded and in the correct accounts.
	• Revenue is recorded in the period to which it relates.
	• Sales are recorded accurately and related receivables are recorded at an appropriate value.
Cash received	• Cash received is allocated against the correct customer and invoices to minimise disputes.
	• Overdue debts are followed up on a timely basis.
	• Irrecoverable debts are identified and written off appropriately.

Test your understanding 1

Murray case study: Sales cycle

Ordering

For all new customers, a sales manager completes a credit application which is checked with a credit agency and a credit limit is entered into the sales system by the credit controller. Credit checks are not reperformed unless a customer requests an increase to their credit limit. If an increase is requested, a new check will be performed and the credit limit revised.

The orders are entered into the sales system by a sales assistant. After the order has been accepted, the sales assistant checks that the goods are available and that the order will not take the customer over their credit limit.

Goods despatch

When the warehouse receives the order, a goods despatch note (GDN) is generated and a member of the warehouse team packs the goods using the GDN. A second member of the team double checks the details on the GDN to the goods packed, signing the GDN to evidence the check.

Four copies of the GDN are produced. One copy is sent with the goods and retained by the customer. A second is sent with the goods, signed by the customer and returned to Murray Co to confirm receipt of the goods which is filed in the warehouse. A third copy is sent to the sales team who update the system and the fourth copy is sent to the accounts department.

Invoicing

Sales invoices are raised by the accounts department using the GDNs. Sales invoices are not sequentially numbered, and no review is performed to ensure all goods have been invoiced.

Sales invoices are prepared using the approved company price list, which is updated quarterly. Payment terms are stated on the sales invoice and all customers have 10 days to pay their invoice.

Discounts must be requested by a sales manager and authorised by the sales director to allow the accounts team to raise an invoice.

Recording transaction

The receivables ledger is reviewed for credit balances by the senior accountant on a monthly basis and the receivables ledger is reconciled with the receivables ledger control account when the sales ledger manager has time. Monthly customer statements are sent to customers.

Cash receipt

Receipts are counted by the office assistant, recorded by the cashier in the cash book, and the sales ledger clerk is notified of the receipt. The sales ledger clerk agrees the amount received to the amount invoiced and marks the invoice as paid.

The credit controller reviews the aged receivables analysis on a fortnightly basis to assess the level of slow moving debts and an allowance is made for any debts which are considered doubtful. Debts which are more than six months overdue are chased up.

Required:

In respect of the sales system of Murray Co:

(a)   (i)   **Identify and explain FIVE DIRECT CONTROLS which the auditor may seek to place reliance on; and**

     (ii)   **Describe a TEST OF CONTROL the auditor should perform to assess if each of these controls is operating effectively.**

     Note: Prepare your answer using two columns headed Direct control and Test of control respectively.   **(10 marks)**

(b)   **Identify and explain FIVE DEFICIENCIES and provide a recommendation to address each of these deficiencies.**

     Note: Prepare your answer using two columns headed Control deficiencies and Control recommendation respectively. **(10 marks)**

     (Total: 20 marks)

Illustration 1: Murray Co goods despatch note

The key document in the sales cycle is the goods despatch note:

Murray Co

"Supplying Equipment to the Sporting Nation"

Goods Despatch Note

Ref: AB123456MC

www.murraysports.com

Murray Company

1 Murray Mound,
Wimbledon, London
WN1 2LN

Destination

Customer Ref: W004

Customer Name: Winners Co

Customer Address: 2 Edinburgh St,

Dunblaine, Scotland DL2 2ES

Order Number:

ZY987654WS

Line	Product Number	Description	Quantity	Quantity Quality and quantity of goods checked and agreed
001	4378493729	Tennis racket	24	*Yes*
002	3257845743	Tennis balls (packs of 6)	6	*Yes*
003	4357849574	Tennis court net	3	*Yes*
004	3473895789	Tennis scoreboard	3	*Yes*
005	4574895743	Winner's trophy	1	*Yes*
006	3457435437	Runner-up trophy	1	*Yes*
007	4830998543	Participant's medal	24	*Yes*

Signed:

A Warehouse Packer

8 Purchase system

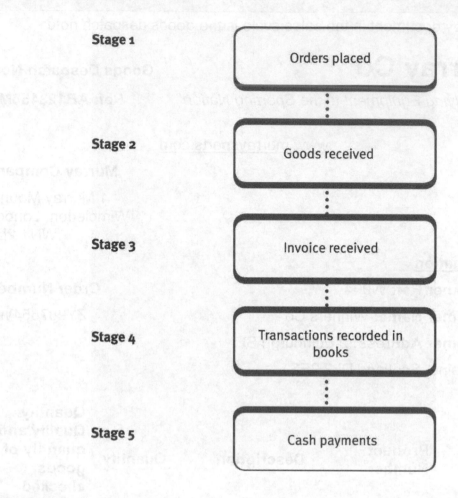

Stage 1 — Orders placed

Stage 2 — Goods received

Stage 3 — Invoice received

Stage 4 — Transactions recorded in books

Stage 5 — Cash payments

Objectives

The objectives of controls in the purchases system are to ensure that:

Stage	Objective
Ordering	• All purchases are made with suppliers who have been checked for quality, reliability and pricing.
	• Purchases are only made for a valid business use.
	• Orders are placed taking consideration of delivery lead times to avoid disruption to the business.
Goods received	• Only goods ordered by the company are accepted.
	• Goods received are recorded promptly.
Invoice received	• Invoices received relate to goods actually received.
	• Invoices received relate to the company.
	• Invoices received are correct in terms of quantities, prices, discounts.

Recording	• All purchases and related payables are recorded.
	• Purchases are recorded accurately and related payables are recorded at an appropriate value.
	• Purchases are recorded in the period to which they relate.
	• Purchases and payables are recorded in the correct accounts.
Cash payments	• Payments are only made for goods received.
	• Payments are only made once.
	• All payments are made on time.

Test your understanding 2

Murray case study: Purchases cycle

Ordering

Goods or services are obtained by placing a purchase requisition with the centralised purchasing department. Requisitions are sequentially pre-numbered and a weekly sequence check is performed. All requisitions must be authorised by an appropriate manager.

On receipt of a purchase requisition, a purchase officer agrees the manager's signature to the signatory list held on file and checks inventory levels where appropriate. Orders are placed with suppliers using sequentially pre-numbered purchase orders.

Orders can only be placed with suppliers from the approved supplier list. Suppliers can only be added to the approved suppliers list by the procurement team once the terms of the contract have been agreed, and references obtained. Written confirmation is requested for all orders placed, and the purchase officer agrees the quoted price against the agreed price list and ensures any bulk discounts to which Murray Co is entitled, have been honoured.

Goods receipt

Goods are received into the central warehouse. Goods are inspected for condition and quantity by a warehouse operative, and agreed to the purchase order before the supplier's delivery note is signed to accept the goods.

A sequentially pre-numbered goods received note (GRN) is prepared by the warehouse team manager, and grid-stamped. The grid stamp is signed by the warehouse operative to confirm that the goods have been inspected for condition and quantity and agreed to the purchase order.

The warehouse manager updates the inventory system on a daily basis from the prepared GRNs. The warehouse manager checks the sequence of purchase orders received on a weekly basis and informs the purchasing department of any missing orders so that they can be followed up.

Invoicing

On receipt of an invoice by the head office accounts team, the invoice is matched to and filed with the relevant GRN, using the purchase order number marked on the invoice (if there is no purchase order number marked on the invoice, this must be obtained from the supplier). The invoice number is noted on the GRN grid stamp. The invoice is also checked to the original purchase order to ensure the agreed prices and discounts have been honoured.

A monthly check of GRNs is made by the purchase ledger manager, to identify any GRNs for which no invoice has been received.

Recording transaction

The purchase ledger clerk enters invoices into the system in batches. A batch control sheet is used, which details the number of invoices and the total value. These details are checked to the system batch report.

Each invoice is stamped as 'recorded' once the details have been entered onto the system. The purchase ledger manager inspects the file of invoices on a monthly basis to ensure that all invoices have been recorded.

Suppliers are required to submit monthly supplier statements, which are reconciled to the supplier's ledger account by the purchase ledger manager. The purchase ledger is reconciled to the purchase ledger control account on a monthly basis by the purchase ledger manager, and reviewed by the company accountant.

Cash payment

The list of payments is sent to the company accountant, who agrees the details of each payment to the relevant invoice and signs each invoice to authorise payment and evidence the check. The list of payments is signed by the accountant once all invoices have been checked, and sent to the cashier's office for payment.

If any individual payment is for more than $25,000 or total payments are for more than $250,000 a second signatory is required. These payments must also be checked and signed by either the financial controller, or finance director.

Payments are made by the cashier's office by bank transfer. Invoices are stamped as 'paid', and returned to the purchase ledger team who record the payment and file the invoices (separately from invoices not yet paid).

The purchase ledger manager checks GRNs on a monthly basis to ensure that invoices have been received and paid on a timely basis.

Required:

In respect of the purchases system for Murray Co:

(i) **Identify and explain TEN DIRECT CONTROLS which the auditor may seek to place reliance on; and**

(ii) **Describe a TEST OF CONTROL the auditor should perform to assess if each of these controls is operating effectively.**

Note: Prepare your answer using two columns headed Direct control and Test of control respectively.

(20 marks)

Illustration 2: Murray Co goods received note

The key document in the purchases cycle is the goods received note:

Murray Co

Goods Received Note: A2012/123478

Purchase Order number: MC/34324832809/RC

Date of receipt: 31st August 20X4

Time of receipt: 12:48pm

Description	Quantity ordered	Quantity received	Quality of goods checked
Vectran	75kg	75kg	Yes

Sign to confirm quantity and quality of goods checked:

Warehouse Operative

Invoice number:

Problems with fraud

Fraud is specifically designed to mislead people. Consider the following example:

- A company only deals with suppliers on a list authorised by the finance director (FD).

- Payments to suppliers are made after the purchases clerk identifies the monthly payments to be made and prepares the cheques.

- The cheques are signed by the FD, who confirms the amounts paid and supplier names to supporting documentation.

- The cheques are countersigned by the managing director, who does not check the details but has a good knowledge of who the suppliers are.

- This appears like a sensible combination of authorisation controls and segregation of duties. The auditor would place reliance on the control system and reduce substantive testing of purchases.

However, now consider the implication if one of the suppliers is actually controlled by the FD. The supplier regularly overcharges the company and the purchases clerk is being bribed by the FD in return for their silence.

It is for this reason that the auditor must always perform some substantive procedures and must always maintain an attitude of professional scepticism.

Non-current assets

Expenditure on non-current assets should be controlled in a similar way to other purchases. However, because of the significant amounts involved, additional controls should be in place.

Control objectives

- Assets are only purchased if there is a business need.
- Assets are purchased at an appropriate price.
- The company can afford the capital expenditure proposed.
- Capital expenditure is appropriately treated in the accounting records.
- Capital expenditure is completely and accurately recorded in the accounting records.
- Assets are covered by adequate insurance to prevent loss to the company.
- Documents relating to assets are safeguarded from theft or damage.

Control	Test of control
Requisitions for capital expenditure should be made by an appropriate person.	Inspect the requisition for the signature of the person requisitioning the assets.
	Ensure this is a person of suitable authority by agreeing the name to a list of people authorised to make such requisitions.
Authorisation for purchases of non-current assets should be at a more senior level.	Inspect the purchase order for signature of appropriate senior person(s).
Several quotations should be obtained before purchase in order to obtain the best price.	Inspect the purchase requisition for the quotations to ensure they have been obtained.

An annual capital expenditure budget for each department should be prepared and authorisation should only be given for purchases which have been budgeted.	Inspect the annual budget to ensure it has been prepared. Inspect board minutes to confirm the budget has been approved by the board. Inspect orders for capital expenditure items to ensure they have been authorised by a responsible official.
Regular review of revenue expenditure should be performed to ensure items of a capital nature have not been expensed in error.	Inspect management accounts/revenue expenditure lists for evidence of review. Enquire of management how discrepancies are dealt with.
A regular reconciliation of the asset register to the physical assets held should be performed.	Inspect the reconciliation of the asset register and evidence of approval by a senior person to ensure the reconciliation has been performed correctly.
An asset register should be maintained which includes cost, depreciation, location, responsible employee, insurance details, etc.	Inspect the asset register to ensure details expected to be recorded have been recorded to ensure good control is maintained over assets.
Adequate insurance cover should be purchased.	Inspect insurance policies to ensure they are in place. Review the policies to ascertain the level of cover in place and compare this with the value of assets to ensure it is sufficient.
Documentation such as title deeds, vehicle registration documents, insurance policies, etc. should be stored in a secure, fire-proof location.	Inspect the storage facilities for important documentation to ensure it is appropriately secure and adequate backups have been maintained in case of a fire or flood.

9 Payroll system

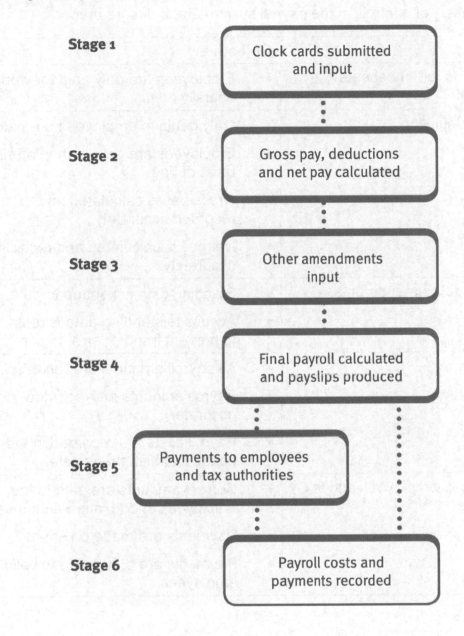

Stage 1 — Clock cards submitted and input

Stage 2 — Gross pay, deductions and net pay calculated

Stage 3 — Other amendments input

Stage 4 — Final payroll calculated and payslips produced

Stage 5 — Payments to employees and tax authorities

Stage 6 — Payroll costs and payments recorded

Objectives

The objectives of controls in the payroll system are to ensure that:

Stage	Objective
Clock cards (or timesheets) submitted.	• Employees are only paid for work actually done.
Payroll calculation	• Only genuine employees are paid. • Employees are paid at the correct rates of pay. • Gross pay is calculated and recorded accurately. • Net pay is calculated and recorded accurately.
Standing data amendments	• Standing data is kept up to date. • Access to standing data is restricted to prevent fraud or error occurring.
Recording	• All payroll amounts are recorded. • Payroll amounts are recorded accurately. • Payroll costs are recorded in the period to which they relate.
Payments to employees and tax authorities	• Correct amounts are paid to the employees and taxation authorities. • Payments are made on time. • Payments are only made to valid employees.

Test your understanding 3

Murray case study: Payroll cycle

Clock cards submitted and input

Murray Co employs a total of 300 people, 200 of these being workers who are paid weekly in cash. Weekly paid workers are required to record their times of arrival and departure at the factory using a clock card which is inserted in a time recording clock. Use of the time recording clock is supervised by the relevant factory manager.

On a weekly basis the cards are collected and passed to the works office where the clerk totals up the hours worked on each card and lists the total hours worked (a 'hash' total). The cards and the total hour's list are then passed to the wages clerk who enters the hours worked into the payroll system and agrees the total entered.

Gross pay, deductions and net pay calculated

The payroll system calculates the gross and net pay and a payroll report is generated by the payroll manager. The payroll manager recalculates a sample of employee wages and compares his figures to the amounts calculated by the payroll system. He passes the payroll report to the wages clerk who creates a payment list detailing the payments to be made to the monthly paid employees and the taxation authority.

The payroll report and payment list are passed to the company accountant. The company accountant reviews the payment list for any unusual amounts and compares each employee's net pay on the payroll report to the payment list. He also compares the totals with the previous week as a reasonableness check. Once all of these procedures are complete, the company accountant signs both documents and raises a cheque requisition for the weekly paid workers. The signed payroll report is returned to the payroll clerk who generates the payslips from the payroll system. The payslips, cheque requisition and signed payment list are then passed to the cashier's department for processing.

Payments to employees and tax authorities

Employees are paid in cash at the employees' request. The cashier draws a cheque for the net amount of the payroll which is then signed by two directors. The cheque is given to a secure cash transit company who draw the money from the bank and deliver it under guard to the cashier. The cashier then puts the money into pay envelopes along with a pay slip for weekly paid workers.

The sealed envelopes and relevant clock cards are then used for pay-outs. Each worker obtains their money once they have identified themselves and signed their clock card. Unclaimed wages are held for three weeks before being banked.

Monthly paid workers and the tax authorities are paid by bank transfer on the last day of each month, as per the payment list authorised by the company accountant.

Payroll costs and payments recorded

A copy of the payroll list is sent to the head office accounts team who record the payroll expense and payments made. Any unclaimed wages are notified by the wages office to the head office team on an anomalies list completed once all of the clock cards have been returned. The head office accounts team check the bank statements to ensure that this money has been banked.

Standing data and other amendments

Leaver and joiner forms must be completed and authorised by the employee's immediate manager and the finance director at least one month before the amendment is required to the payroll. Other amendments to standing data, e.g. pay rises and hourly rates, are completed on a specific form for this purpose, and authorised in the same way. A monthly report of amendments to standing data is sent to the finance director for review and authorisation. Standing data files are sent to departmental managers on a quarterly basis for review.

Required:

In respect of the payroll system for Murray Co:

(i) Identify and explain TEN DIRECT CONTROLS which the auditor may seek to place reliance on; and

(ii) Describe a TEST OF CONTROL the auditor should perform to assess if each of these controls is operating effectively.

Note: Prepare your answer using two columns headed Direct control and Test of control respectively.

(20 marks)

10 Inventory system

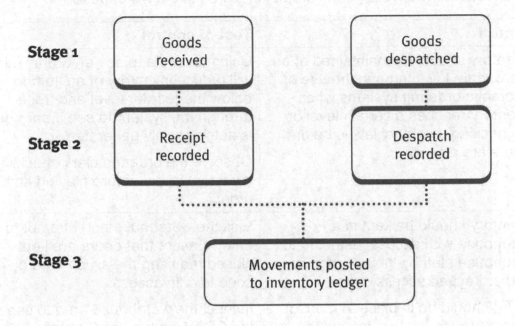

Objectives

The objectives of controls in the inventory system are to ensure that:

- Inventory levels meet the needs of production (raw materials and components) and customer demand (finished goods).
- Inventory levels are not excessive, preventing obsolescence and unnecessary storage costs.
- Inventory is safeguarded from theft, loss or damage.
- Inventory received and despatched is recorded on a timely basis.
- All inventory is recorded.
- Inventory should be recorded at the appropriate value.
- Only inventory owned by the company is recorded.

The following controls over inventory relate to the period after purchase and before sale i.e. when the goods are being stored in the warehouse.

Control	Test of control
Inventory should be maintained at an appropriate level through the use of automatic ordering systems when inventory reaches a certain level or by checking inventory levels before orders are placed.	Using test data, place an order which will reduce inventory of an item to below the reorder level and trace through the system to see if an order is automatically generated. Observe the ordering clerk checking inventory levels before placing an order.
Inventory should be kept in a warehouse with access restricted to warehouse staff by the use of swipe card or keypad access. CCTV should be in place to monitor people around the entrance to the warehouse to ensure people do not follow other people into the warehouse without the need for a code/swipe card.	Visit the warehouse and attempt to enter. Ensure that doors are kept closed requiring the swipe card or code to gain access. Inspect the warehouse area to see the CCTV in place and visit the location of the camera feed to ensure the cameras are monitored.
Inventory should be kept in appropriate conditions e.g. temperature controlled environment for perishable items.	Visit the warehouse and inspect the conditions of storage. Inspect evidence of monitoring the conditions on a regular basis such as temperature logs.
Fire/smoke/heat detectors and sprinkler systems should be in place to reduce the risk of damage caused by fire.	Inspect the warehouse to see the detectors and sprinkler systems are in place. Inspect certificates confirming they have been checked and tested on a regular basis.
Inventory should be insured in case of theft or damage.	Inspect insurance policies to ensure they cover inventory, that adequate cover is in place by comparing against inventory value, and that the policy has not lapsed.
Inventory movements should be recorded in the system promptly using the GRNs and GDNs. The GRNs and GDNs should be stamped to confirm they have been input and the system is up to date.	Inspect the GRNs and GDNs to see they have been stamped as entered into the system. Compare the date on the stamp to the date on the GRN/GDN to ensure they have been entered promptly.

Inventory counts should take place on a regular basis so that physical inventory quantities can be reconciled with the accounting system on a regular basis to ensure the records are accurate and up to date.	Obtain inventory counting instructions and review to ensure the count will be appropriately organised and controlled. Attend the inventory count to ensure the count is carried out in accordance with the instructions and perform test counts to ensure the client's counts are carried out accurately.
Inventory should be reviewed during the count for damage or obsolescence and valued separately from the other inventory by making an allowance to write the inventory down to net realisable value.	During the count, review the inventory to ensure damaged or obsolete items are separately identified.

See the 'Procedures' chapter for detailed controls over inventory counts.

11 Bank and cash system

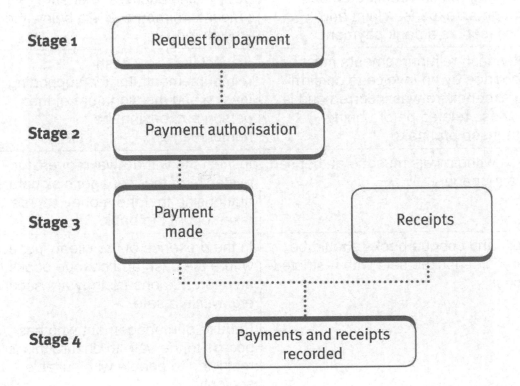

KAPLAN PUBLISHING

Objectives

The objectives of controls in the cash cycle are to ensure that:

- Petty cash levels are kept to a minimum, preventing theft.

- Payments can only be made for legitimate business expenditure.

- Cash can only be withdrawn for business purposes.

- Cash is safeguarded to prevent theft.

- Receipts are banked on a timely basis to prevent theft.

- Cash movements are recorded on a timely basis.

The following controls over cash relate to the period after receipt from a customer and before being used to pay for expenses. In addition, there should be adequate controls over access to cash and bank records.

Control	Test of control
An imprest system of petty cash should be used for items of expenditure less than $x. All other reimbursements should be made through an expense claim and processed as a bank payment.	In the presence of the client, count the petty cash to ascertain that the level is at the limit set. Inspect the petty cash vouchers to ensure amounts reimbursed are below the limit stated.
Petty cash reimbursements must be supported by an invoice to confirm the expenditure was incurred and is business related before being authorised and paid.	Inspect the petty cash reimbursements for the supporting invoice and the signature of the person authorising the reimbursement.
Cash withdrawals must be authorised by a manager.	Inspect the withdrawal request for evidence of the manager's signature authorising that the money can be taken out of the bank.
Cash and cheque books should be stored in a locked safe with restricted access.	In the presence of the client, inspect where the cash and cheque books are stored to ensure they are secure, e.g. within a safe. Enquire of management who has access to the safe to ensure this is restricted to people with suitable seniority.

Controls over bank transfers and online banking should be in place, e.g. secure passwords and PINs.	Enquire of management who has access to the online banking system. Inspect transactions in the banking system for the username of the person initiating and authorising transactions to ensure this corroborates what has been said. Assess whether the person authorising the transactions is of suitable seniority.
Cash and cheques received should be banked frequently.	Inspect the paying in books or bank statements to identify how frequently deposits are paid in to ensure this is adequate.
Bank reconciliations should be prepared on a regular basis (e.g. weekly) and reviewed by a responsible official to confirm it has been reconciled properly.	Inspect the file of bank reconciliations to ensure they are performed regularly. Inspect the reconciliation for a manager's signature as evidence it has been reviewed and approved. Reperform the reconciliation to ensure it has been carried out effectively.

Exam question approach

The exam is likely to include one, or both, of the following requirements:

- Identify and explain the **control deficiencies** from the scenario and provide **recommendations** to overcome the deficiencies.

- Identify and explain the **direct controls** from the scenario and describe **tests of controls** the auditor would perform to obtain evidence that the control is working effectively.

Control deficiencies

Identification of the deficiencies is usually quite straightforward. You should look for information which indicates:

- Controls are missing e.g. Sales orders are not sequentially numbered.

- Controls are not effective e.g. Bank reconciliations are supposed to be performed but often don't get done due to lack of time.

Work with the information provided. Do not assume that because something isn't mentioned it isn't happening.

Explanation of the deficiency requires you to explain the implication for the company or a risk of misstatement in the accounting records. It is not an explanation if you only say this should not be done or this should be done. You must explain what the control would achieve if it was in place and working effectively. The explanation needs to be sufficiently detailed. If you only explain the deficiency in part you will not earn the explanation marks.

Recommendation

For the recommendation, suggest the control procedure which needs to be implemented. This also needs to be sufficiently detailed. Try and recommend which person within the company should perform the control and how frequently. Sometimes a control requires more than one element to be effective, therefore make sure you suggest everything that needs to happen to make the control effective.

	Control deficiency	**Recommendation**
Poor answer	Sales orders are not sequentially numbered. *Deficiency is not explained. Why does it matter if the sales orders are not sequentially numbered?*	Orders should be sequentially numbered. *Recommendation is not sufficiently detailed. How does the client know the sequence is complete?*
Better answer	Sales orders are not sequentially numbered. Orders will be difficult to trace and orders may not be fulfilled. *Deficiency is still not fully explained. What are the consequences to the company if they have unfulfilled orders?*	Orders should be sequentially numbered. A sequence check should be performed and any breaks in the sequence investigated and resolved. *Recommendation is now sufficiently detailed.*
Good answer	Sales orders are not sequentially numbered. Sales orders may not be completely recorded resulting in unfulfilled orders. Orders received but not recorded will be difficult to trace. Customers will be dissatisfied if orders are not fulfilled resulting in complaints and loss of future revenue.	Orders should be sequentially numbered. A sequence check should be performed and any breaks in the sequence investigated and resolved. *Recommendation is sufficiently detailed.*

	Control deficiency	Recommendation
Poor answer	Bank reconciliations are supposed to be performed but often don't get done due to lack of time. *Deficiency is not explained. Why does it matter if the bank reconciliation does not get performed?*	Bank reconciliations should be performed. *Recommendation is not sufficiently detailed. Who should perform the bank reconciliation? How often should it be performed? How does management know it has actually been done?*
Better answer	Bank reconciliations are supposed to be performed but often don't get done due to lack of time. Errors could occur. *Deficiency is still not fully explained. Errors in what?*	Bank reconciliations should be performed weekly. *Recommendation is slightly better but is still not sufficiently detailed.*
Good answer	Bank reconciliations are supposed to be performed but often don't get done due to lack of time. Errors could occur. The cash book may be incorrect resulting in misstatement of the bank and cash figure in the financial statements.	Bank reconciliations should be performed on a weekly basis by someone independent of maintaining the cash book and the reconciliation should be reviewed by a responsible official. *Recommendation is now sufficiently detailed.*

Direct controls

Direct controls are control procedures which are properly designed, in place and working effectively at addressing the risk of material misstatement at the assertion level.

Read the scenario and look for mention of controls such as reconciliations being performed, authorisation of transactions, segregation of duties, restricted access to valuable items, etc.

A control is an activity that is performed **in addition** to the normal processing of the system, to ensure that the system has operated as it should. For example, raising a sales invoice is part of a normal sales system, it is not a control. A control would be someone performing a check to confirm the sales invoice had been raised accurately, or someone performing a check to confirm completeness of sales invoices in relation to GDNs. A control to confirm accuracy of invoices might be a sales manager agreeing the price on the invoice to the company's authorised price list and recalculating the invoices to confirm accuracy before they are sent to the customer. A control to confirm completeness of sales invoices might be that sales invoices are matched to GDNs and every week a sales manager performs a review of sales invoices to identify any unmatched invoices which are then investigated.

Make sure that there is nothing mentioned which would make the control ineffective. For example, duties may be segregated between two individuals who are related. This increases the risk of collusion which negates the control. Reconciliations might be performed infrequently and not reviewed by anyone. Therefore the control is ineffective as it is not being performed all of the time, and no-one is checking that it has been performed correctly.

Tests of controls

A test of control is an audit procedure which will provide evidence as to whether the control procedure is in place and working effectively.

The focus of a test of control is the control procedure. If a direct control identified is segregation of duties between calculating payroll and making the payroll payment, the auditor will need to obtain evidence that these duties are segregated e.g. by observing the procedures and inspecting procedures documents and organisation charts to ensure different people are responsible for each task.

Tests of controls are not substantive procedures. Therefore, when testing the control, the auditor does not need to test the balance which will go into the financial statements.

	Direct control	Test of control
Poor answer	GDNs are matched to sales invoices. *There is no explanation of the control objective.*	Agree the amount recorded on the sales invoice and GDN to the sales day book. *This is a substantive procedure, not a test of control. The objective of the test of control is to confirm the control is in place, i.e. that the GDNs are matched to the sales invoices.*
Better answer	GDNs are matched to sales invoices. This reduces the risk of errors. *The control explanation is too vague. Reduces the risk of errors in what?*	Inspect the GDNs and sales invoices. *The test of control does not explain the objective of the test. What are we inspecting the GDNs and invoices for?*
Good answer	GDNs are matched to sales invoices by a finance clerk and signed to confirm the matching has been performed. This ensures the customer is invoiced for the correct goods which will reduce the risk of disputes and ensure sales are recorded accurately.	Inspect a sample of GDNs and related invoices to confirm the details match and inspect for evidence of the finance clerk's signature confirming the matching has been performed.

Test your understanding 4

Rhapsody Co supplies a wide range of garden and agricultural products to trade and domestic customers. The company has 11 divisions, with each division specialising in the sale of specific products, for example, seeds, garden furniture, and agricultural fertilizers. The company has an internal audit department which provides reports to the audit committee on each division on a rotational basis.

Products in the seed division are offered for sale to domestic customers via an Internet site. Customers review the product list on the Internet and place orders for packets of seeds using specific product codes, along with their credit card details, onto Rhapsody Co's secure server. Order quantities are normally between one and three packets for each type of seed. Order details are transferred manually onto the company's internal inventory control and sales system and a two part packing list is printed in the seed warehouse. Each order and packing list is given a random alphabetical code based on the name of the employee inputting the order, the date and the products being ordered.

In the seed warehouse, the packets of seeds for each order are taken from specific bins and despatched to the customer with one copy of the packing list. The second copy of the packing list is sent to the accounts department where the inventory and sales computer is updated to show that the order has been despatched. The customer's credit card is then charged by the inventory control and sales computer. Irrecoverable receivables in Rhapsody Co are currently 3% of the total sales.

The computer system checks that for each charge made to a customer's credit card account, the order details are on file to prove that the charge was made correctly.

Required:

In respect of sales in the seeds division of Rhapsody Co:

(i)   **Explain FOUR deficiencies in the sales system, and**

(ii)   **For each deficiency provide a recommendation to overcome that deficiency.**

Note: Prepare your answer using two columns headed Control deficiency and Control recommendation respectively.

(8 marks)

Test your understanding 5

Whilst performing tests of controls, many control deviations were found. The auditor has therefore concluded that reliance cannot be placed on the internal controls.

Required:

Explain THREE actions that the auditor may now take in response to this problem.

(3 marks)

Test your understanding 6

(a) **Define 'tests of control' and explain the importance of tests of control in the audit of a company.**

(2 marks)

(b) You are an audit senior working at a medium sized firm of auditors. One of your clients, Numero Uno, is an exclusive hotel situated in the centre of Big City. As part of your audit procedures, you are assessing the controls surrounding payroll. You have read last year's audit file and have obtained the following information:

The hotel employs both full and part time staff. Due to the nature of the business most of the work is done in shifts. All staff are paid on a monthly basis.

New members of staff are given an electronic photo identification card on the day they join by the personnel department. This card is used to 'clock in' and 'clock out' at the start and end of the shift to record the hours worked.

At the end of each week the information recorded on the system is sent automatically to the payroll department and also to the head of each of the three main operating divisions: Rooms, Food & Beverage and Corporate Events. Each head of division must reply to the payroll department by email to authorise the hours worked by their staff.

The payroll clerk collates all the authorised information and inputs the hours worked into a standardised computerised payroll package. This system is password protected using an alphanumerical password that is only known to the payroll clerk and the finance manager.

Once the hours have been entered, the calculations of gross pay and taxation are calculated automatically along with any other statutory deductions. Once calculated, a payroll report is produced and printed. The finance manager reviews the report and compares the data to last month to identify and follow up any unusual variances. When he is satisfied with the information, he authorises the payroll run by signing the payroll report and the payroll clerk submits the data.

Payslips are sent to the home address of each employee and payment is made by bank transfer.

Required:

In respect of the payroll system for Numero Uno:

(i)   Identify and explain FOUR DIRECT CONTROLS which the auditor may seek to place reliance on; and

(ii) Describe a TEST OF CONTROL the auditor should perform to assess if each of these controls is operating effectively.

Note: Prepare your answer using two columns headed Direct control and Test of control respectively.

(8 marks)

(Total: 10 marks)

Test your understanding 7

You are testing the controls over the payroll system of Bunbury Co. You have confirmed that the following controls have operated throughout the year:

- Sample check of payroll calculations by a payroll manager.

- Review of the payroll listing once prepared before details are entered into the banking system.

- Segregation of duties between calculation of monthly payroll and responsibility for changes to standing data.

- Each department manager receives a list of employees in their department for them to sign to confirm those employees should be paid.

1   **Which of the following is the main reason for the control of segregation of duties between calculation of payroll and responsibility for changes to standing data?**

    A   Changes to standing data must be performed by a manager whereas payroll calculations can be performed by a payroll clerk

    B   If one person was responsible for both they would be more likely to make errors due to a high workload

    C   If one person was responsible for both they could increase their salary and make fraudulent payments to themselves

    D   Each individual role within an organisation must be carried out by different people

2   **Which of the following procedures would provide the most reliable evidence that the first control, payroll calculations are checked by a payroll manager, is working effectively?**

    A   Enquiry with the payroll clerk performing the payroll calculation

    B   Enquiry with the payroll manager performing the check

    C   Recalculation of the payroll amounts by the auditor

    D   Inspection of the payroll report for evidence that a sample of payroll amounts are checked

3   **Which of the following is NOT a test of control?**

    A   Inspection of employee contracts to confirm the salary the employee should be paid

    B   Inspection of payroll reports for evidence of authorisation by the manager

    C   Inspection of the list of employees for each department for evidence of the department manager's review

    D   Observation of the payroll function to confirm segregation of duties is in place

4   **Which of the following is a control objective relevant to the control that each department manager reviews the list of employees?**

    A   To ensure payroll is accurately calculated

    B   To ensure only valid employees are paid

    C   To ensure employees are paid for the correct hours

    D   To ensure employees are paid at the correct salary

5   **Which of the following could be used by Bunbury Co to monitor the effectiveness of the company's controls?**

A   Internal audit assignments

B   Performing bank reconciliations

C   Authorisation of payments

D   Segregation of duties

Test your understanding 8

You are performing the risk assessment for the audit of Kununurra Co, a client your firm has audited for the past two years. From your review of last year's audit file you have found that no significant control deficiencies were identified. The systems are documented on the permanent audit file in the form of flow charts and narrative notes.

1   **Which of the following best describes the requirement of the auditor in respect of the controls documentation?**

A   The auditor must document the systems this year as they may have changed since last year

B   The auditor may enquire whether the systems have changed since last year, and if not, no further work is necessary

C   The auditor must perform procedures to ensure the systems work as documented on file e.g. by performing walkthrough tests

D   No work is necessary on systems documentation unless the client informs the auditor that changes have occurred

2   **Which of the following best describes the auditor's approach in respect of reliance on internal controls?**

A   Tests of controls must be performed over material areas of the financial statements

B   Tests of controls must be performed each year over areas of significant risk where the auditor is hoping to place reliance on controls

C   Tests of controls are not necessary this year as no deficiencies were identified last year

D   Tests of controls must be performed over all areas irrespective of whether the auditor is planning to place reliance on those controls

3   **Which of the following questions would NOT be included in an internal control evaluation questionnaire?**

   A   How does the company ensure sales are only made to creditworthy customers?

   B   How does the company ensure that purchases are only made for a valid business use?

   C   How does the company ensure that all purchases are recorded?

   D   Is access to the warehouse restricted to authorised personnel only?

4   **Internal controls should be monitored on an ongoing basis to ensure they are adequate, relevant and working effectively. Which of the following will NOT monitor the internal controls of a company?**

   A   External auditor

   B   Management

   C   Consultancy firm hired by management

   D   Internal auditor

5   **Match the description to the appropriate method of documenting a control system.**

A diagram depicting the controls in place at each stage of a process	ICQ/ICE	Flowchart	Narrative notes
A disadvantage of this method may be that controls are overstated	ICQ/ICE	Flowchart	Narrative notes
An advantage of this method is that they are easy to prepare in advance and therefore efficient	ICQ/ICE	Flowchart	Narrative notes
For larger systems this method may be time consuming and it may be difficult to identify missing controls	ICQ/ICE	Flowchart	Narrative notes

12 Chapter summary

SYSTEMS AND CONTROLS
- Revenue
- Purchases
- Payroll
- Inventory
- Cash and bank
- Non-current assets

UNDERSTAND THE COMPONENTS OF THE CONTROL SYSTEM
- Control environment
- Risk assessment process
- Information systems
- Control activities
- Monitoring

CONTROL ACTIVITIES
- Authorisation
- Reconciliations
- Verifications
- Physical or logical controls
- Segregation of duties

DOCUMENT THE SYSTEMS
- Narrative notes
- Flowcharts
- ICQs
- Organisation charts

TEST THE SYSTEMS
- Tests of controls
- Test data

COMMUNICATE DEFICIENCIES
- All deficiencies to management
- Significant deficiencies to TCWG

Test your understanding answers

Test your understanding 1

(a) **Direct controls and tests of control**

Direct control	Test of control
Credit checks are performed and credit limits set: sales are only made to customers that are likely to make a full and prompt payment, reducing the risk of irrecoverable debts. Irrecoverable debts will reduce profit and cash inflows and if not written off will result in overstatement of receivables.	Inspect a sample of customer files to ensure a credit check has been performed. Inspect the customer's account within the system to ensure credit limits have been put in place.
A second member of warehouse team checks the goods packed, signing the GDN to evidence the check: segregation of duties. Segregation of duties reduces the risk of theft and fraud which results in loss for the company and potential misstatements in the accounting records.	Visit a warehouse and observe the goods despatch process to assess whether all goods are double checked against the GDN prior to signing and sending out. Inspect the GDN for evidence of the signature to confirm the physical goods have been checked to the GDN and the GDN has been checked against the order prior to despatch.
Customers sign the GDN and return it to Murray Co: this helps to minimise disputes as proof of delivery and acceptance of goods is obtained. Disputes with customers may result in overstatement of receivables and also a loss of customer goodwill.	Inspect a sample of GDNs retained by the warehouse to ensure they are signed by customers to confirm receipt of goods and to confirm they are retained in the warehouse in case of disputes.

The invoice is raised from the GDN: this ensures the invoice relates to the actual quantity of goods despatched rather than the order which may be different.	Inspect the GDNs for evidence of being matched to invoices. Agree the details on both to ensure the control has been effective.
This reduces the risk of customers being invoiced incorrectly which would result in misstatement of revenue and receivables. This could also cause customer dissatisfaction and a loss of customer goodwill.	
Sales invoices are prepared using the company price list: this ensures customers are invoiced correctly.	Inspect the price list for approval by the directors.
Incorrect invoicing will result in misstatement of revenue and receivables. This could also cause customer dissatisfaction and a loss of customer goodwill.	Obtain a copy of the current price list and, for a sample of invoices, agree that the correct prices have been used.
	Agree the prices in the system to the approved price list.
	Enquire of management who has authority to amend standing data such as prices in the system to ensure only persons of suitable authority have access.
	Try to input a change to the prices in the system using a user ID of a clerk to ensure that the system does not allow access to this standing data.
Discounts must be requested by a sales manager and authorised by the sales director: segregation of duties and authorisation.	With the client's permission, attempt to process an invoice with a sales discount without authorisation from the sales director. The system should reject the invoice.
This reduces the risk of fraud and unauthorised discounts which will result in loss of revenue for the company and possible misstatement within the accounting records.	Inspect sales orders with discounts given for evidence of the sales director's signature authorising the discount.

Review of the receivables ledger for credit balances: identifies possible overpayments or errors within the receivables ledger. Errors in the accounting records can be promptly corrected.	Inspect the receivables ledger for evidence of monthly review for credit balances such as a manager's signature.
Monthly customer statements sent to customers: reminds customers of the invoices they need to pay and enables them to identify errors in invoices which can be notified to Murray Co. This can reduce the risk of irrecoverable debts. Irrecoverable debts will reduce profit and cash inflows and if not written off will result in overstatement of receivables.	For a sample of customers, inspect copies of monthly statements sent out to confirm statements are in fact issued.
Receipts are counted by the office assistant, recorded by the cashier, and the sales ledger clerk agrees the amount received to the amount invoiced: segregation of duties. Segregation of duties reduces the risk of fraud which could cause misstatement in the accounting records and loss for the company.	Observe the cash receipt process to assess the adequacy of segregation of duties.

(b)   **Control deficiencies and recommendations**

Control deficiency	Recommendation
Credit checks are only reperformed if a customer requests an increase to their credit limit. A customer's credit rating may have deteriorated but Murray Co will not know and continue to give the same level of credit which increases the risk of irrecoverable debts, affecting profit and cash flow. Irrecoverable debts may result in possible overstatement of receivables.	Credit checks should be performed annually to ensure the credit limit originally given to the customer is still appropriate. If the credit status has changed, the credit limit should be revised.

Credit limits are checked after the order has been accepted. The customer may not have sufficient credit which may result in irrecoverable debts and a reduction to profit. Irrecoverable debts may result in overstatement of receivables.	Credit limits should be checked before the order is confirmed to ensure the customer has sufficient credit.
Sales invoices are not sequentially numbered. Goods may not have been invoiced which will result in lost revenue and profit for the company. The company will not be able to identify if any invoices are missing resulting in understatement of revenue.	Sales invoices should be sequentially numbered and a sequence check should be performed by the accounts department on a daily/weekly basis. Any breaks in the sequence should be investigated.
No review is performed to ensure all goods have been invoiced. Goods may not have been invoiced which will result in understatement of revenue.	A review should be performed to ensure that every GDN has a matching invoice to ensure all goods have been invoiced.
The receivables ledger is only reconciled when the sales manager has time. Errors may exist within the receivables accounting records which will not be identified and resolved on a timely basis.	The receivables ledger should be reconciled to the control account on a monthly basis. The reconciliations should be reviewed by a different, responsible official to ensure the reconciliation has been performed properly.
The credit controller only follows up on balances which are six months overdue. This increases the risk of irrecoverable debts which will reduce profit and cash inflows. Irrecoverable debts may result in overstatement of receivables.	Credit control procedures should be followed to ensure full and prompt payment by customers, e.g. a telephone call to the customer followed by a letter.

Test your understanding 2

Ordering

Control	Test of control
Centralised purchasing department: ensures that purchasing is cost effective and only necessary goods and services are procured, reducing the risk of loss to the company and unnecessary cash outflow. Over-ordering of goods could lead to a build-up of inventory levels which could result in overstatement of inventory.	Inspect the organisation chart to verify that a centralised purchasing department is in place. Enquire of the purchasing director whether all purchases must go through the department, or if some purchases are made within individual departments, to assess the effectiveness of the control. Inspect a sample of purchase orders to ensure they have been generated by the central purchasing department.
Requisitions are authorised and manager's signature agreed: ensures only necessary goods and services are procured, reducing the risk unnecessary cash outflow. Unnecessary goods could lead to a build-up of inventory levels which could result in overstatement of inventory.	Inspect a sample of requisitions for the signature of an appropriate manager.
Inventory levels are checked prior to ordering: ensures only necessary goods and services are procured, reducing the risk of inventory becoming obsolete which could lead to overstatement of inventory and loss for the company.	Inspect a sample of requisitions for evidence of inventory levels being checked first, such as a signature. Observe the ordering process to see the ordering clerk checking inventory levels first.

Sequentially pre-numbered purchase orders and a weekly check by warehouse manager: ensures that all goods and services ordered are received so any missing purchase orders can be followed up. This reduces the risk of production delays which will result in dissatisfied customers and a loss of customer goodwill. Missing purchase orders will result in an incomplete audit trail and may affect the auditor's ability to obtain sufficient and appropriate evidence over purchases.	Review the purchase orders for evidence of the warehouse manager's weekly sequence check such as a signature to confirm it has been performed.
Approved supplier list: gives assurance about the quality of goods and services and reliability of the suppliers. Poor quality supplies will affect the quality of the product sold resulting in complaints from customers and damage to the company's reputation reducing future sales. If product quality is affected, there is a risk of overstatement of inventory and understatement of refund liabilities.	For a sample of purchase orders placed, agree the supplier name to the approved supplier list. Attempt to place an order with an unapproved supplier. The system should not allow it to proceed.
Prices are agreed to the price list and discounts checked: ensures that the correct prices are being charged by the supplier and discounts are being obtained. This ensures accuracy of purchases and payables and reduces the risk of loss to the company and unnecessary cash outflow.	Inspect a sample of purchase orders for evidence of prices having been agreed to the price list such as a signature of the person checking. Select a sample of orders and agree to the authorised price list to test the effectiveness of the control.

Goods receipt

Control	Test of control
Goods received into the central warehouse. Having one, secure delivery area prevents goods received being lost or stolen reducing the risk of loss to the company and misstatement of inventory balances.	Visit a warehouse and inspect the delivery area for security of goods e.g. locked area, security guard, CCTV.
Goods are inspected for condition and quantity and agreed to the purchase order. This prevents Murray Co from paying for unnecessary, or poor quality goods which would result in loss for the company and unnecessary cash outflow. Damaged goods received and not returned to the supplier may result in overstatement of inventory.	Observe the goods receipt process to ensure goods are inspected for condition and quantity before the supplier's delivery note is signed. Inspect the delivery note for a signature confirming the goods have been checked on arrival.
Sequentially pre-numbered goods received note (GRN) prepared by the warehouse team manager and a sequence check performed by the purchase ledger manager. This ensures that all goods received are recorded which will ensure completeness of inventory balances.	Inspect evidence of the sequence check being performed such as a signature of the warehouse manager.
Grid stamp: a grid stamp is a grid that can be ink-stamped onto any document, with boxes for recording different information such as confirmation the goods have been inspected for condition and agreed to the purchase order. This prevents Murray Co from paying for unnecessary or poor quality goods reducing the risk of loss to the company and unnecessary cash outflow. This reduces the risk of inappropriate valuation of inventory.	Inspect a sample of GRNs to ensure they are grid-stamped and signed by the warehouse operative to confirm the goods have been inspected and agreed to the PO.

Inventory system updated on a daily basis by the warehouse manager: prevents unnecessary goods being ordered and ensures accuracy of inventory balances. This reduces the risk of not being able to fulfil customer orders which could result in dissatisfied customers and a loss of customer goodwill.	Inspect a sample of GRNs for the previous day to ensure the inventory system has been updated for them.

Invoicing

Control	Test of control
The invoice is matched to the GRN: by matching the invoice to the GRN and not the original order it ensures that only goods that have been received are paid for, reducing the risk of loss to the company and unnecessary cash outflow and ensuring accuracy of purchases and payables.	Inspect a sample of invoices and ensure they are filed with the relevant GRN, and the invoice number is written on the GRN.
Using the purchase order number marked on the invoice: when placing an order, the supplier will be given the purchase order number. This allows the purchase to be matched to the relevant GRN and requisition and the company can efficiently trace the relevant documentation in case of queries.	Inspect a sample of invoices for the PO number and that it is matched to the relating GRN and requisition.
The invoice number is noted on the GRN grid stamp, and a monthly check of GRNs with no invoice: this prevents goods received being invoiced twice which would cause loss to the company and overstatement of purchases and payables.	Review the GRN for the grid stamp. Inspect evidence of signature to confirm the monthly check has been carried out by the purchase ledger manager.

Recording transaction

Control	Test of control
Batch controls: the system will notify the clerk inputting the data of how many invoices have been input. This will be checked to the physical number of invoices and will highlight if too many or too few invoices have been entered. This ensures accuracy of the purchases and payables figures in the accounting records enabling invoices to be paid on time reducing the risk of disputes with suppliers.	Inspect a sample of batch control sheets for evidence of completion and agreement to the batch system report.
Invoice stamped as 'recorded' and checks to ensure all invoices recorded: Prevents under or overstatement of trade payables reducing the risk of disputes with or late payments to suppliers.	Select a sample of invoices recorded on the system and inspect them to ensure they are marked as 'recorded'.
Supplier statement reconciliations: enables errors in the recording of purchases, payments and liabilities to be identified and corrected. This reduces the risk of disputes with suppliers and ensures accuracy of the accounting system relating to purchases and payables.	For a sample of suppliers, inspect the monthly supplier statements received for evidence of the reconciliation being performed. Reperform the reconciliation to confirm it has been reconciled correctly to test the effectiveness of the control.
Control account reconciliation: ensures that credits and payments recorded in individual supplier ledgers have also been recorded in the accounts (and vice versa). Segregation of duties monitors performance of controls and ensures accuracy of the accounting system in relation to purchases and payables.	Inspect the control account reconciliations for evidence of performance and review on a monthly basis. Reperform the reconciliation to ensure it has been carried out effectively.

Cash payment

Control	Test of control
The company accountant checks and authorises payments: payments should only be authorised by a senior member of the finance department to prevent error or fraud which could result in loss for the company and misstatements in the accounting records.	For a sample of payments made, inspect the payment list for evidence of the company accountant's review and authorisation.
Individual payments of more than $25,000 or total payments of more than $250,000 require a second signatory: a second signatory prevents fraud on unusual transactions which could result in loss for the company and misstatements in the accounting records. The additional check by the financial controller or finance director further enhances this control.	Inspect a sample of invoices > $25,000 for evidence of a second signatory and agree that the signature is of someone with authority to authorise such amounts. Inspect the invoices for the additional signature of the financial controller or finance director.
Payments are made by the cashier's office and recorded by the purchase ledger team: segregation of duties prevents fraud which could result in loss for the company and misstatements in the accounting records.	Observe the process of payments from the cashier's office to ensure segregation of duties is in place.
*Invoices are stamped as 'paid' and filed separately from invoices not yet paid: this prevents invoices being paid twice which could result in loss for the company and unnecessary cash outflow.	Inspect the file of paid invoices and ensure they are kept separate from invoices not yet paid. Inspect them stamped as 'Paid'.
*GRNs are checked on a monthly basis: to ensure that suppliers are paid on a timely basis, which ensures that early settlement discounts available are obtained, and supplier goodwill is maintained.	Review evidence of the purchase ledger manager's monthly invoice review such as a signature.

KAPLAN PUBLISHING

Test your understanding 3

Clock cards submitted and input

Control	Test of control
Clock card to record time and supervision of clock card use: ensures that only genuine employees are paid for work done. This reduces the risk of unnecessary additional expense for the company which reduces profit and ensures occurrence of payroll costs.	Observe the use and supervision of clocking in and out procedures to ensure that employees are not able to clock in for other people.
Hash total and agreement of the total: segregation of duties by performing and checking the procedure reduces the risk of human error and therefore the risk of incorrect payments being made which will affect accuracy of payroll costs.	Observe the process of the works office clerk totalling the hours and passing the list to the wages clerk to confirm segregation of duties is in place. Inspect a sample of payroll sheets for the wages clerk's signature as evidence they have checked the total hours list.

Payroll calculation and payment list created

Control	Test of control
Payroll is calculated automatically by the payroll system and the payroll manager recalculates a sample of wages: Calculation by the system is less vulnerable to error and a sample check by the payroll manager ensures accuracy of payroll costs and minimises the risk of incorrect payments being made.	Review a sample of the calculations performed by the payroll manager.
Payroll is calculated by the payroll department. The company accountant raises the cheque requisition and authorises the payment list. The cashier's department makes the relevant payments: segregation of duties prevents fraud and error which could result in loss for the company and misstatement of payroll costs.	Inspect the monthly payment list and payroll report for the company accountant's signature. For a sample of cheques raised for wages, inspect the cheque requisition to ensure it has been completed by the company accountant.

Review of payroll by the company accountant: ensures that any anomalies can be identified and resolved. Payroll is a significant cost for most companies. It is important that a responsible individual, independent of preparation of payroll, undertakes this role to ensure accuracy, completeness and occurrence of payroll costs. This reduces the risk of payments to ghost employees or incorrect amounts being paid which would cause unnecessary expense and reduce profit.	Inspect the payroll report and payment list for the signature of the company accountant confirming the reports have been checked to each other and a review has been performed.

Payments to employees and tax authorities

 Tutorial note

The payment of wages in cash is not a deficiency provided adequate controls are implemented over the payment process.

Control	Test of control
Payroll cheque is signed by two directors: this is likely to be a large amount of money and therefore requires authorisation by two senior personnel to prevent fraud and error which could result in loss to the company and misstatement of payroll costs.	Inspect the bank mandate to ensure it requires the signature of two directors for large cheques.
Cash is delivered by a secure transit company, under guard: due to the amount of cash likely to be needed to pay the weekly paid workers, it would not be appropriate for Murray Co staff to go to the bank to get the money themselves as this would threaten their personal safety and could be liable to theft. This could result in misstatement of cash balances.	Observe the cash being delivered by the security firm. Inspect invoices for services of the security firm to ensure the service is provided weekly.

Payroll costs and payments recorded

Control	Test of control
Workers must identify themselves and sign their clock cards before receiving their money: ensures occurrence of payroll cost as only genuine employees are paid.	Observe payment of weekly wages to confirm identification is checked. Inspect a sample of clock cards to ensure they have been signed by the worker.
The head office accounts team record the payroll expense and payments and the wages office notifies the team of unclaimed wages: segregation of duties prevents fraud and error which could result in loss for the company and misstatement of payroll costs.	Inspect the list of unclaimed wages to see it has been prepared. Enquire of the wages office and the head office team that this notification occurs on a weekly basis to corroborate that the control works effectively.
Bank statements are checked for deposit of unclaimed wages: prevents misappropriation which would result in loss for the company and misstatement of bank balances.	Inspect the list of unclaimed wages and bank statements for evidence that the unclaimed amounts are checked as being been banked.

Standing data and other amendments

Control	Test of control
Completion and authorisation of standing data forms: ensures that only genuine employees are paid and at authorised rates of pay (occurrence and accuracy of payroll). This reduces the risk of payments being made to ghost employees or incorrect amounts being paid which would cause unnecessary expense and reduce profit.	Select a sample of employees with pay rises or other amendments from human resources records and inspect the system details to ensure that the relevant payroll form has been completed and authorised on a timely basis.

Use of specific forms, such as for starters and leavers: prevents errors in processing information. This reduces the risk of incorrect payments being made which would result in employee dissatisfaction or payments being made to people no longer working for the company which would result in loss to the company (occurrence and accuracy of payroll).	Select a sample of leavers and joiners from human resources records and trace the changes to the system to ensure that payroll forms have been completed and authorised on a timely basis.
Monthly review of standing data amendments and quarterly review of standing data files: ensures that any unauthorised amendments to standing data are identified and resolved. This reduces the risk of payments being made to ghost employees or incorrect amounts being paid which would cause unnecessary expense and reduce profit (occurrence and accuracy of payroll).	Select a sample of amendments made to standing data and trace to the monthly report authorised by the finance director, and the relevant amendment form. Inspect the standing data files sent to departmental managers for evidence of review. For any anomalies identified by departmental managers, enquire of and corroborate the reasons for the anomaly and what action was taken to resolve the issue.

Test your understanding 4

Deficiency and effect

Recording of orders

Orders placed on the website are transferred manually into the inventory and sales system. Manual transfer may result in errors in the accounting system.

Customers will be sent incorrect goods resulting in increased customer complaints and a loss of customer goodwill.

Recommendation

The computer system should be upgraded so that order details are transferred directly between the two computer systems. This will remove manual transfer of details, limiting the possibility of human error.

Control over orders and packing lists

Each order/packing list is given a random alphabetical code. This type of code makes it difficult to check completeness of orders.

Packing lists can be lost resulting in goods not being despatched to the customer which will result in a loss of customer goodwill. The order may be sent but the customer's credit card may not be charged which would result in understatement of revenue.

Orders/packing lists should be controlled with a numeric sequence.

At the end of each day, a sequence check should be performed and any gaps in the sequence should be investigated.

Obtaining payment

The customer's credit card is charged after despatch of goods to the customer, meaning that goods are already sent to the customer before payment is authorised.

Rhapsody Co will not be paid for the goods despatched where the credit company rejects the payment request. Given that customers are unlikely to return seeds, Rhapsody Co will automatically incur an irrecoverable debt which reduces profit and cash inflow and leads to a potential overstatement of receivables.

Authorisation to charge the customer's credit card should be obtained prior to despatch of goods and the card should be charged on despatch to ensure Rhapsody Co is paid for all goods sent to customers.

Completeness of orders

There is no overall check that all orders recorded on the inventory and sales system have actually been invoiced and the customer's credit card charged.

Orders despatched may not have been invoiced resulting in understatement of revenue and profit. If the credit card has not been charged the company will experience a reduction in cash flow.

An exception report of orders not invoiced should be generated each week. Orders where there is no corresponding invoice should be investigated.

Test your understanding 5

The auditor can increase the amount of controls testing in that audit area. This may indicate that the control deficiency was not as bad as initially thought.

The problem can be raised with management and those charged with governance so that corrective action can be taken.

The auditor can perform additional substantive procedures on the audit area. If controls have not worked effectively there is a greater risk of misstatement. Substantive procedures will be used to quantify the misstatement.

If the matter is not resolved, then the auditor will also need to consider the implications for the auditor's report.

Test your understanding 6

(a) **Tests of control**

A test of control tests the operating effectiveness of controls in preventing, detecting or correcting material misstatements.

It is important for the external auditor to test controls to ensure their initial understanding obtained when assessing the control environment and internal controls is appropriate.

This will allow the auditor to identify and assess the risks of material misstatements in the financial statements and determine the amount of reliance that can be placed on the internal control system.

The auditor is then able to design substantive audit procedures to reduce detection risk, and therefore audit risk, to an acceptable level.

(b) **Direct controls and tests of control**

Direct control (i)	Test of control (ii)
All staff are assigned a unique ID card by the personnel department to record hours worked. Segregation of duties between allocating the cards and processing payroll will reduce the risk of fraud such as the creation of 'ghost' employees by the payroll department.	Ask a sample of employees to confirm who provided them with their unique ID card on joining the business. Inspect the ID cards for existence. Agree the employee details to HR records.

Hours worked are authorised by divisional heads. There is a reduced risk that hours are overstated as the divisional head is more likely to identify errors or anomalies. This reduces the risk of incorrect payments being made which will cause misstatement of payroll costs.	Inspect the emails sent each month by the head of division authorising the hours worked.
The payroll system is password protected with an alphanumerical password known only to the payroll clerk and finance manager. The password is difficult to guess and therefore will limit the risk of unauthorised access which could lead to payroll data being manipulated and payroll costs being misstated. This reduces the risk of fraud and loss to the company.	The auditor should use test data and enter a 'dummy' password into the payroll system to ensure that access is not granted.
Payroll calculations are automatically calculated by the standardised payroll software. Calculation by the system is less vulnerable to error. This ensures accuracy of payroll costs and minimises the risk of incorrect payments being made which could result in dissatisfied employees.	The auditor should recalculate a sample of employee's monthly pay from across the year and compare to the calculations on the payroll report for those months.
The finance manager reviews the payroll report and compares to last month before the final payroll is processed. The comparison of data to the prior month should highlight any errors before the payroll is processed. This reduces the risk of incorrect payments being made to employees which could result in misstatement of payroll and dissatisfied employees.	For a sample of months, inspect the payroll reports for evidence of the finance manager's signature confirming that the review has been performed.
Payslips are sent to the home address of each employee. This should reduce the risk that payslips are misplaced or manipulated. It would also reduce the risk of a confidentiality breach.	Ask a sample of employees to confirm they receive their monthly payslips via post to their home address. Observe the process of sending payslips to employees.

Test your understanding 7		
1	C	Segregation of duties helps to prevent fraud.
2	D	Enquiry is not the most reliable form of evidence as the clerk or the manager could say what they think the auditor wants to hear. Recalculation of payroll by the auditor is a substantive test and does not confirm the manager has performed the necessary checks.
3	A	Inspection of employee contracts to confirm salary details is a substantive procedure.
4	B	The department manager would identify if any fictitious employees or employees who had left the company were included on the list and could notify the payroll department before any invalid payments were made.
5	A	Internal audit can monitor the effectiveness of controls by regularly testing them. B, C and D are all examples of control activities that would be tested for effectiveness.

Test your understanding 8

1	C	The auditor must ensure the systems documentation held on file is still correct. This can be achieved through a combination of enquiry and walkthrough tests but enquiry alone is not sufficient appropriate evidence.
2	B	Tests of controls must be performed when the auditor is planning to place reliance on controls over areas of significant risk. If the auditor has decided that substantive testing is more efficient for a specific balance, it is not necessary to test the controls over that area. Reliance can be placed on the results of tests of controls performed in previous years to some extent, however, the auditor must perform tests of controls over some areas. For areas where controls are not tested this year, the auditor must ensure they are tested within a three-year cycle.
3	D	An internal control evaluation questionnaire asks the client to respond with the control in place that addresses a risk. Restricted access as given in answer D is a control. This question would be included in an internal control questionnaire rather than an internal control evaluation questionnaire.
4	A	The external auditor should not monitor the controls, as this requires ongoing involvement in the company on a regular basis. Whilst the external auditor may test the controls and identify deficiencies, this does not constitute monitoring. Management is ultimately responsible for the internal controls including assessing whether they are effective and whether any improvements are required. They may utilise an external consultant or internal audit function to help them fulfil this responsibility.
5		**Flowchart** – a diagram depicting controls in place at each stage **ICQ/ICE** – a disadvantage of this method may be that controls are overstated **ICQ/ICE** – An advantage of this method is that they are easy to prepare in advance and therefore efficient **Narrative notes** – For larger systems this method may be time consuming and it may be difficult to identify missing controls

Internal audit

Chapter learning objectives

This chapter covers syllabus areas:

- C5 – Internal audit and governance, and the differences between external audit and internal audit

- C6 – The scope of the internal audit function, outsourcing and internal audit assignments

Detailed syllabus objectives are provided in the introduction section of the text book.

PER

One of the PER performance objectives (PO19) is to collect and evaluate evidence for an audit. Carry out an internal or external audit from collecting evidence, through to forming an opinion. You demonstrate professional scepticism and make sure judgments are based on sufficient valid evidence. Working through this chapter should help you understand how to demonstrate that objective.

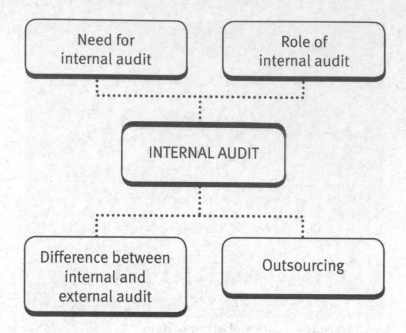

1 The need for internal audit

 Internal audit is an independent, objective assurance and consulting activity designed to add value and improve an organisation's operations.

A company must create a strong system of internal control in order to fulfil its responsibilities.

However, it is not sufficient to simply have mechanisms in place to manage a business, the effectiveness of those mechanisms must be regularly evaluated. All systems need some form of monitoring and feedback. This is the role of internal audit.

Having an internal audit department is generally considered to be best practice, but is not required by law. This allows flexibility in the way internal audit is established to suit the needs of a business.

In small, or owner managed businesses there is unlikely to be a need for internal audit because the owners are able to exercise more direct control over operations, and are accountable to fewer stakeholders.

The need for internal audit (IA) therefore will depend on:

- Scale and diversity of activities. In a larger, diversified organisation there is a risk that controls don't work as effectively because of the delegation of responsibility down the organisation. Internal audit can report back to the audit committee if controls are not as effective as they should be.

- Complexity of operations. The more complex the organisation is, the greater the benefit obtained from having an IA function as there is greater risk of things going wrong. With larger organisations the consequences of poor controls/risk management/corporate governance practices are likely to be greater.

- Number of employees. The greater the number of employees the greater the risk of fraud.

- Cost/benefit considerations. It will be worthwhile establishing an IA function if the benefits outweigh the costs. For example a company might be losing money as a result of fraud, not using the most cost effective or reliable suppliers, or incurring fines for non-compliance with laws and regulations. If these costs outweigh the cost of employing an IA function it will be beneficial to the company to establish a department.

- The desire of senior management to have assurance and advice on risk and control. The directors may wish to have the comfort that there is ongoing monitoring of the organisation to help them discharge their responsibilities.

- The current control environment and whether there is a history of fraud or control deficiencies. If so it will be beneficial for the company to establish an internal audit function to prevent and detect fraud.

2 The difference between internal and external auditors

	External audit	Internal audit
Objective	Express an opinion on the truth and fairness of the financial statements in a written report.	Improve the company's operations by reviewing the efficiency and effectiveness of internal controls.
Reporting	Reports to shareholders.	Reports to management or those charged with governance.
Availability of report	Publicly available.	Not publicly available. Usually only seen by management or those charged with governance.
Scope of work	Verifying the truth and fairness of the financial statements.	Wide in scope and dependent on management's requirements.
Appointment and removal	By the shareholders of the company.	By the audit committee or board of directors.
Relationship with company	Must be independent of the company.	May be employees (which limits independence) or an outsourced function (which enhances independence).

3 The role of the internal audit function

The role of internal audit can vary depending on the requirements of the business.

Key activities of the internal audit function

- Assessing whether the company is demonstrating best practice in corporate governance.

- Evaluating the company's risk identification and management processes.

- Testing the effectiveness of internal controls.

- Assessing the reliability of financial and operating information.

- Assessing the economy, efficiency and effectiveness of operating activities (value for money).

- Assessing compliance with laws and regulations.

- Providing recommendations on the prevention and detection of fraud.

Most of these activities can be seen as helping management comply with corporate governance requirements.

Additional roles

In addition to the above, internal audit will carry out ad hoc assignments, as required by management. For example:

- Fraud investigations – this may involve detecting fraud, identifying the perpetrator of a fraud and quantifying the loss to the company as a result of a fraud.

- IT systems reviews – performing a review of the computer environment and controls.

- Mystery shopper visits – for retail and service companies the internal audit staff can pose as customers to ensure that customer service is at the required level.

- Contract audits – making sure that where material or long term contracts are entered into by the organisation, the contract is written to protect the organisation appropriately and contractual terms are being adhered to by the supplier in line with the service level agreement.

- Asset verification – such as performing cash counts and physical inspection of non-current assets to verify existence.

- Providing direct assistance to the external auditor – internal audit staff can help the external auditor with their procedures under their supervision, in accordance with ISA 610. This is covered in the 'Evidence' chapter.

Qualities of an effective internal audit function

- Sufficiently resourced, both financially and in terms of qualified, experienced staff.

- Well organised, so that it has well developed work practices.

- Independent and objective to provide an unbiased view of the organisation's operations.

- The chief internal auditor should be appointed by the audit committee to reduce management bias.

- The department should have no operational responsibilities to reduce the threat of self-review.

- The audit committee should set the plan of work.

- There should be no limitation on the scope of their work i.e. full access to every part of the organisation.

Limitations of internal audit

- Internal auditors may be employees of the company they are reporting on and therefore may not wish to raise issues in case they lose their job.

- In smaller organisations in particular, internal audit may be managed as part of the finance function. They will therefore have to report on the effectiveness of financial systems of which they form a part and may be reluctant to say their department (and manager) has deficiencies.

- If the internal audit staff have worked in the organisation for a long time, possibly in different departments, there may be a familiarity threat as they will be auditing the work of long standing colleagues and friends.

It is therefore difficult for internal audit to remain truly objective. However, acceptable levels of independence can be achieved through one, or more, of the following strategies:

- Reporting channels separate from the management of the main financial reporting function.

- Reviews of internal audit work by managers independent of the function under scrutiny.

- Outsourcing the internal audit function to a professional third party.

4 Outsourcing the internal audit function

In common with other areas of a company's operations, the directors may consider that outsourcing the internal audit function represents better value than an in-house department.

Outsourcing is where the company uses an external company to perform its internal audit service instead of employing its own staff.

Advantages

- Professional firms follow an ethical code of conduct and should therefore be independent of the client.

- Professional firms should have qualified, competent staff who receive regular development and have a broader range of expertise.

- An outsourcing firm will have specialist skills readily available therefore outsourcing can be used to overcome a skills shortage.

- Professional firms can be employed on a flexible basis, i.e. on an individual engagement basis rather than full time employment which may prove more cost effective.

- Employment costs of permanent staff are avoided.

- The risk of staff turnover is passed to the outsourcing firm.

- Professional firms are responsible for their activities and hold insurance.

- There is likely to be greater focus on cost and efficiency of the internal audit work as this will affect profitability of the assignment.

- The company will obtain access to new market place technologies without the associated costs, e.g. data analytic tools and audit software.

- Management time in administering an in-house department will be reduced.

Disadvantages

- Professional firms lack the intimate knowledge and understanding of the organisation that employees have.

- The decision may be based on cost with the effectiveness of the function being reduced.

- Engagements with professional firms are constrained by contractual terms. Flexibility and availability may not be as high as with an in-house function.

- Fees charged by professional firms may be high.

- An ethical threat may arise if the service is provided by the external audit firm. E.g. the ACCA Code of Ethics and Conduct prohibits external auditors of a listed company from providing internal audit services for the same client where the service relates to financial reporting systems.

- Pressure on the independence of the outsourced function, for example, if management threaten not to renew the contract.

- Lack of control over the quality of service.

5 Internal audit assignments

Internal auditors perform many different types of assignment. Common examples include:

- Value for money assignments
- Operational audits
- The audit of IT systems
- Financial audit.

Value for money

Value for money (VFM) is concerned with obtaining the best possible combination of services for the least resources. It is often referred to as a review of the three Es:

- **Economy** – obtaining the best quality of resources for the minimum cost.
- **Efficiency** – obtaining the maximum departmental/organisational outputs with the minimum use of resources.
- **Effectiveness** – achievement of goals and targets (departmental/organisational etc.).

Comparisons of value for money achieved by different organisations (or branches of the same organisation) are often made using performance indicators that provide a measure of economy, efficiency or effectiveness. This is particularly common in the not-for-profit sector (i.e. public services and charities), but it can apply to any company.

For example, a company chooses the cheapest supplier for the materials it needs. The supplier has a lead time for delivery of 6 weeks. If the company needs a supplier that can deliver at short notice on a regular basis this will not be effective.

If a company sources lower quality materials at a price 10% cheaper than its current supplier but uses 50% more as a result of the lower quality, this is not efficient.

Value for money: hospital

Examples of value for money indicators for a hospital might include:

- Economy – cost of medical supplies per annum.
- Efficiency – number of patients treated per year, utilisation rate of beds/operating theatre.
- Effectiveness – recovery rates, number of deaths.

Operational audits

An operational audit is a systematic review of the efficiency and effectiveness of operations within the organisation. The focus of the audit is on the processes which take place within the organisation to identify if they can be streamlined and performed more efficiently. The more efficient a process is, the more profitable the organisation should be.

For example, during an operational audit the internal auditor may find that orders are manually entered into a sales system to record an order. A copy of the order is passed to the despatch department who manually enter the details into the despatch system. A copy of the goods despatch note is sent to the finance department for invoicing and the details are manually entered into the invoice.

In addition to the risk of error that arises each time the details are manually entered, this is a time consuming and inefficient process.

The internal auditor may recommend that an integrated system is introduced to remove the need for the data to be entered by each department. If the order system links to the despatch system and the despatch system links to the finance system, no manual entry will be required after the order has been entered in the first instance.

The audit of IT systems

The external auditor considers IT systems from the perspective of whether they provide a reliable basis for the preparation of financial statements, and whether there are internal controls which are effective in reducing the risk of misstatement.

Internal audit will also consider this, however, its role is much wider in scope and will also consider whether:

- the company is getting value for money from its IT system.
- the procurement process for the IT system was effective.
- the ongoing management/maintenance of the system is appropriate.

Whilst this is an ongoing role, project auditing can be used to look at whether the objectives of a specific project, such as implementing new IT systems, were achieved.

Financial audit

The main aim of a financial reporting system is to create accurate, complete and timely information which can be used for decision making and business planning. This information is also needed to satisfy the requirements of actual and potential investors and trading partners.

Typical examples of financial information include:

- Financial statements

- Monthly management accounts

- Forecasts and projections.

The main aim of internal financial audits is to ensure that the information produced is reliable and produced in an efficient and timely manner. If not, executive decisions may be based on unreliable information.

The other aim of a financial audit is to assess the financial health of a business. More importantly it is about ensuring there are mechanisms in place for the early identification of financial risk, such as:

- Adverse currency fluctuations

- Adverse interest rate fluctuations

- Cost price inflation.

In both cases the focus of internal audit will be on the processes and controls that underpin the creation of the various financial reports to ensure they are as effective as possible for assisting decision making and the risk management processes of the company.

6   Reporting

Unlike an independent external auditor's report, the internal audit report does not have a formal reporting structure. It is likely that the format is agreed with the audit committee or board of directors prior to commencing the assignment.

These reports will generally be for internal use only. The external auditors may inspect them if they are intending to place reliance on the work of internal audit.

A typical report will include:

- Terms of reference – the requirements of the assignment.

- Executive summary – the key risks and recommendations that are described more fully in the body of the report.

- Body of the report – a detailed description of the work performed and the results of that work.

- Appendix – containing any additional information that doesn't belong in the body of the report but which is relevant to the assignment.

 In the exam you may be asked to take the role of an internal auditor performing an audit assignment to test controls or identify improvements in efficiency that can be made.

The internal audit report can be set out in the same way as the report to management that has been seen in the 'Systems and controls' chapter, describing the deficiencies identified, consequences of those deficiencies and recommendations for improvement.

Test your understanding 1

Murray Co's internal audit function

The internal audit function at Murray Co consists of a head of internal audit, two senior internal audit managers, four internal audit managers, seven internal auditors and an internal audit assistant. The head of internal audit has been in post for twelve years, and the other members of the team have varying lengths of service from two to fifteen years.

The head of internal audit is responsible for recruiting staff into the internal audit team. The head of internal audit was appointed by the audit committee.

The head of internal audit reports to the audit committee and agrees the scope of work for the internal audit function with the audit committee.

The internal audit staff have no operational responsibility. Where the staff have previously transferred from another department within Murray Co, the head of internal audit ensures that another member of the team carries out the audit of that system.

Murray Co's internal audit function follows the International Standards for the Professional Practice of Internal Auditing issued by the Global Institute of Internal Auditors.

Barker Co's internal audit function

The internal audit function at Barker Co consists of a chief internal auditor, one senior internal audit manager, one audit manager, one auditor and an audit assistant. The chief internal auditor has been in post for ten years, and the other members of the team have varying lengths of service from five to nine years.

The finance director is responsible for recruiting all staff into the internal audit function. The chief internal auditor reports to the finance director and agrees the scope of work for the internal audit function with him.

The internal audit team spend 50% of their time carrying out internal audit assignments and 50% of their time working in the finance department. Due to the limited number of staff in the team, this has resulted in the internal auditors reviewing their own work.

Barker Co's internal audit team follow a variety of standards, in accordance with their own professional training.

Required:

Compare and contrast the effectiveness of Murray Co and Barker Co's internal audit functions.

(6 marks)

Test your understanding 2

You are the senior manager in the internal audit department of Octball Co, a limited liability company. You report to the chief internal auditor and have a staff of six junior auditors to supervise, although the budget allows for up to ten junior staff.

In a recent meeting with the chief internal auditor, the difficulty of staff recruitment and retention was discussed. Over the past year, five junior internal audit staff have left the company, but only two have been recruited. Recruitment problems identified include the location of Octball Co's head office in a small town over 150 kilometres from the nearest major city and extensive foreign travel, often to cold climates.

Together with the chief internal auditor you believe that outsourcing the internal audit department may be a way of alleviating the staffing problems. You would monitor the new outsourced department in a part-time role taking on additional responsibilities in other departments, and the chief internal auditor would accept the post of finance director (FD) on the board, replacing the retiring FD.

Two firms have been identified as being able to provide the internal audit service:

- The NFA Partnership (NFA), a large local firm specialising in the provision of accountancy and internal audit services. NFA does not audit financial statements or report to members.

- T&M, Octball Co's external auditors, who have offices in 75 countries and employ in excess of 65,000 staff.

Required:

(a) **Discuss the advantages and disadvantages of appointing NFA as internal auditors for Octball Co.**

(8 marks)

(b) **Discuss the matters T&M need to consider before they could accept appointment as internal auditors for Octball Co.**

(7 marks)

(c) **Assume that an outsourcing company has been chosen to provide internal audit services. Describe the control activities that Octball Co should apply to ensure that the internal audit service is being maintained to a high standard.**

(5 marks)

(Total: 20 marks)

Test your understanding 3

You are an audit senior working at Monkey, Mia & Co. You have been seconded to your firm's internal audit department to broaden your experience. You have been assigned to an internal audit assignment to test the effectiveness of the computer systems at a large company. Your firm won the contract to provide internal audit services to the company after the company took the decision to outsource its internal audit function and make the existing internal audit staff redundant.

1   **With which of the following should the internal auditor not be involved?**

    A   Identifying deficiencies in internal controls

    B   Providing recommendations to management on how to overcome the deficiencies identified

    C   Implementing the new controls recommended

    D   Evaluating the effectiveness of the new controls implemented

2   **Which TWO of the following statements are TRUE?**

    (i)   Internal auditors always report directly to shareholders.

    (ii)   The format of the independent external auditor's report is determined by management.

    (iii)   The internal auditor's work may be determined by management.

    (iv)   All external audits must be planned and performed in accordance with International Auditing Standards and other regulatory requirements.

    A   (i) and (iv)

    B   (i) and (iii)

    C   (ii) and (iii)

    D   (iii) and (iv)

3   **Which of the following is NOT part of the role of internal audit?**

    A   Risk identification and monitoring

    B   Expression of opinion to the shareholders on whether the annual financial statements give a true and fair view

    C   Fraud investigations

    D   Assessing compliance with laws and regulations

4 **Which of the following is NOT a valid reason to outsource the internal audit function?**

A   The external audit will be more efficient as the external audit staff will have a good understanding of the company if they are also involved with the internal audit work

B   Outsourcing may be more cost effective as compared with employing staff and providing training and other employment benefits

C   A professional firm is likely to be more experienced and able to provide better recommendations for improvements

D   Greater independence of an external service provider

5 **Identify whether the following statements are true or false.**

	True	False
Internal audit reports must be produced in a standardised format as set out by the financial reporting framework	True	False
Internal audit reports are issued to shareholders	True	False
There is no legal requirement for companies to have an internal audit department	True	False
The presence of an internal audit function may act as a deterrent for fraud	True	False

7 Chapter summary

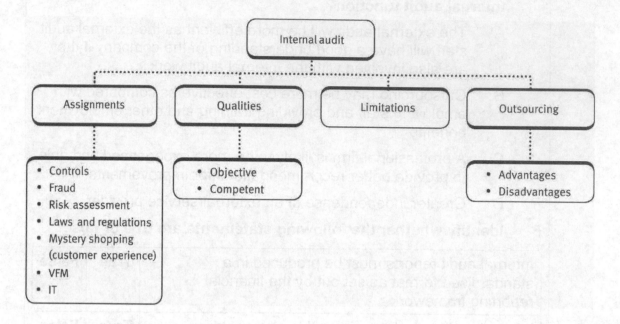

Test your understanding answers

 Test your understanding 1

Reporting system

The chief internal auditor at Barker Co reports into the finance director. This limits the effectiveness of the internal audit reports as the finance director will also be responsible for some of the financial systems that the internal audit function is reporting on. Similarly, the chief internal auditor may soften or limit criticism in reports to avoid confrontation with the finance director.

To ensure independence, the chief internal auditor should report into the audit committee, as at Murray Co.

Recruitment of staff

All of the internal audit team at Barker Co are recruited by the finance director. The finance director may appoint personnel who are less likely to criticise his work. To ensure independence, the head of internal audit should be appointed by the audit committee, and they should then recruit and appoint the rest of the team, as at Murray Co.

Scope of work

The scope of work of internal audit at Barker Co is decided by the finance director in discussion with the chief internal auditor. This means that the finance director may try and influence the chief internal auditor regarding the areas that the internal audit department is auditing, possibly directing attention away from any contentious areas that the director does not want auditing.

To ensure independence, the scope of work of the internal audit department should be decided by the chief internal auditor, perhaps with the assistance of an audit committee, as at Murray Co.

Audit work

The internal audit team at Barker Co review their own work. This limits independence as the auditor may overlook or fail to identify errors or deficiencies in those areas. This is a self-review threat.

If possible, the internal audit team should not have operational responsibility. However, if this is not possible, the internal audit work should be arranged as at Murray Co, so that no member of the team reviews areas where they have operational responsibility.

Lengths of service of internal audit staff

The internal audit team staff of both companies have been employed for a long time. This may limit their effectiveness as they will be very familiar with the systems being reviewed and therefore may not be sufficiently objective to identify errors in those systems.

However, there are sufficient staff at Murray Co to ensure that the team can be rotated into different areas of internal audit work, and their work can be independently reviewed. Due to the small number of staff in the internal audit team, Barker Co may not be able to achieve this.

Given the extent of limitations, it may be appropriate for Barker Co to outsource its internal audit function.

Variation of standards

Staff at Barker Co follow the auditing standards with which they are familiar. Standards of internal audit are not uniform across the profession. This could lead to inconsistency in the way each internal audit assignment is performed. This can lead to manipulation of internal audit aims and measurement. Barker Co should follow an agreed, recognised set of professional internal audit standards, such as those followed by Murray Co.

Test your understanding 2

(a) **Benefits of outsourcing to NFA**

Expertise available

NFA will be able to provide the necessary expertise for internal audit work. They may be able to provide a broader range of expertise as they serve many different clients, therefore staff may be available for specialist work that Octball Co could not afford to employ.

Obtain skills as and when required

If internal audit is only required for specific functions or particular jobs each year then the expertise can be purchased as required. Taking this approach will minimise in-house costs.

Independence

As an independent firm which does not perform the audit of the financial statements, it is likely that they can provide a high level of service with appropriate objectivity. In particular, there will be no self-review threats.

Audit techniques – training

Outsourcing will remove the need for training internal staff. The outsourcing firm will be responsible for training its staff and keeping them up-to-date with new auditing techniques and processes.

Continuity of service – staffing

As provision of internal audit services is NFA's main activity, they should also be able to budget for client requirements. As a larger internal auditing firm, they may be able to offer staff better career progression which should assist staff retention.

Problems with outsourcing to NFA

Fee pressure

NFA may experience some fee pressure, but only in respect of maintaining cost effectiveness of the internal audit department. The relationship needs to be managed carefully to ensure that NFA does not decrease the quality of its work due to insufficient fees.

Knowledge

NFA will not have any prior knowledge of Octball Co. This is a disadvantage as it will mean the partnership will need time to ascertain the accounting systems and controls in Octball Co before commencing work. However, provision of an independent view may identify control deficiencies that the current internal audit department have missed.

Location

NFA may not be able to provide this service to Octball Co as they are a local firm and therefore the issue of travel and working away from home would remain.

(b) **Matters to be considered by T&M**

Independence

T&M need to ensure that independence can be maintained in a number of areas:

– Independence regarding recommending systems or preparing working papers and subsequent checking of those systems or working papers. While the internal audit department may need to carry out these functions, T&M must ensure that separate staff are used to provide the internal and external audit functions.

– Staff from T&M will be expected to follow the ethical guidance of ACCA which means that steps will be taken to avoid conflicts of interest or other independence issues such as close personal relationships building up with staff in Octball Co. Any real or perceived threats to independence will lower the overall trust that can be placed on the internal audit reports produced by T&M.

Skills

T&M must ensure that they have staff with the necessary skills and sufficient time to undertake the internal audit work in Octball Co. As a firm of auditors, T&M will automatically provide training for its staff as part of the in-house compliance with association regulations (e.g. compulsory CPD). T&M will need to ensure that staff providing the internal audit function to Octball Co are aware of relevant guidance for internal auditors.

Fee pressure

There may be fee pressure on T&M, either to maintain the cost effectiveness of the internal audit department, or to maintain the competitiveness of the audit fee itself in order to keep the internal audit work.

Knowledge

As the external auditor, T&M will already have knowledge of Octball Co. This will assist in establishing the internal audit department as systems documentation will already be available and the audit firm will already be aware of potential deficiencies in the control systems.

(c) **Controls to maintain the standard of the internal audit department**

  – If T&M are appointed, the internal and external audits should be performed by different departments within the firm.

  – Performance measures such as cost, areas reviewed, etc. should be set and reviewed. Explanations should be obtained for any significant variances.

  – Appropriate audit methodology should be used, including clear documentation of audit work carried out, adequate review, and appropriate conclusions drawn.

  – Working papers should be reviewed, ensuring adherence to International Standards on Auditing where appropriate and any in-house standards on auditing.

  – The work plan for internal audit should be agreed prior to the work commencing and this should be followed by the outsourcing company.

Test your understanding 3

1	C	Internal auditors should not implement new controls as this would create a self-review threat when the controls are tested at a later date.
2	D	Internal audit work may be determined by management or the audit committee if there is one. External audits must be conducted in accordance with ISAs.
3	B	An audit opinion presented to the shareholders must be expressed by an independent external auditor.
4	A	Ethical guidance issued to external auditors requires separate teams to provide internal and external services. Therefore the internal audit staff assigned will not have existing knowledge gained from the external audit.

5

Internal audit reports must be produced in a standardised format as set out by the financial reporting framework	True	**False**
Internal audit reports are issued to shareholders	True	**False**
There is no legal requirement for companies to have an internal audit department	**True**	False
The presence of an internal audit function may act as a deterrent for fraud	**True**	False

Procedures

Chapter learning objectives

This chapter covers syllabus areas:

- D2 – Audit procedures
- D4 – The audit of specific items
- D7 – Not-for-profit organisations

Detailed syllabus objectives are provided in the introduction section of the text book.

PER

One of the PER performance objectives (PO19) is to collect and evaluate evidence for an audit. Carry out an internal or external audit from collecting evidence, through to forming an opinion. You demonstrate professional scepticism and make sure judgments are based on sufficient valid evidence. Working through this chapter should help you understand how to demonstrate that objective.

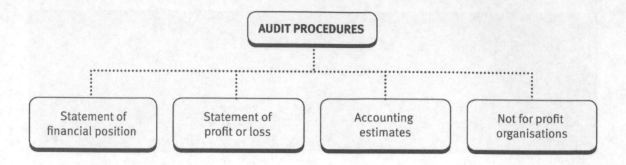

1 Exam focus

We dealt with the principles of audit evidence in an earlier chapter. This chapter deals with the **application** of those principles.

 Audit procedures must be designed to respond to the specific risks of material misstatement identified for each individual client. In the exam, you should make your answers specific to the scenario. It is highly likely the scenario focuses on a specific risk such as valuation of inventory, recoverability of receivables, etc. Therefore audit procedures must focus on these features rather than general audit procedures over the balance in question.

 Remember that the auditor's role is to obtain sufficient appropriate evidence that the financial statements are prepared in all material respects with the relevant financial reporting framework. For this reason, you will need to have a good understanding of the accounting standards.

Writing good audit procedures

An audit procedure should be a clear instruction of how the audit evidence is to be gathered.

It should contain an ACTION applied to a SOURCE to achieve an OBJECTIVE.

In other words, it should describe what needs to be done, how it should be done and why it should be done.

 Read the procedure back and consider whether a person with no audit experience will understand it.

Example: Audit objective − Test the existence of non-current assets

Good answer	Bad answer
Select a sample of assets from the non-current asset register and physically inspect them to verify existence.	Check a sample of assets.
Explanation	
The good procedure above clearly states: • from where the sample should be chosen – the non-current asset register • how they should be checked – physically inspect • the objective of the test – existence	The badly worded procedure is not sufficiently described: • From which population should the sample be selected? • How should the auditor 'check' existence? • What are the assets being checked for?

Example: Audit objective − Test the valuation of trade receivables

Good answer	Bad answer
Inspect post year end bank statements to identify if payment has been received post year end. If so, agree the amount to the receivables ledger at the year end.	Perform a receivables circularisation for a sample of customers to confirm the balances are in existence at the year end.
Explanation	
The good answer is a well explained procedure which tests the assertion of valuation in relation to receivables.	The bad answer tests the assertion of existence, not valuation. It is a well written procedure, but not relevant for the stated audit objective.

This chapter is a starting point to help you familiarise yourself with the basic auditing techniques, to allow you to apply them to questions. It is not an exhaustive summary of all audit procedures.

Each section starts with:

Key assertions – these are the assertions most likely to be at risk, however, the auditor must obtain assurance over all relevant assertions.

Sources of evidence – these are the documents that are likely to provide the best evidence over the balance being tested.

 There are several ways to design audit procedures:

- Identify the financial statement assertion to be tested.

  E.g. to test accuracy of a sale the auditor will need to agree the amount on the sales invoice matches the amount recorded in the sales day book.

- Identify the sources of evidence available.

  E.g. when testing payroll, evidence can come from payslips issued to employees. The auditor can agree amounts recorded on the payslip to the amounts recorded in the payroll payment list.

- Identify the types of procedure the auditor can use from ISA 500.

  E.g. analytical procedures. When testing receivables, the auditor may calculate the receivables collection period and compare it with the prior year to identify any unusual variation.

2 Directional testing

The concept of directional testing derives from the principle of double-entry bookkeeping, i.e. for every debit there should be a corresponding credit. Therefore any misstatement of a debit entry will also result in a misstatement of a credit entry.

The auditor primarily tests debit entries (assets and expenses) for overstatement and credit entries (liabilities and income) for understatement, indirectly testing the corresponding entries at the same time, e.g. directly testing payables for understatement also indirectly tests expenses/cost of sales for understatement.

Testing for understatement

A balance will be understated if:

- Items that should be included are not included i.e. the balance is not complete, or

- An item which has been included is recorded at an amount lower than it should be i.e. an error has been made.

Testing for understatement tests the assertions of completeness and accuracy & valuation.

To test for understatement the auditor must select the sample from outside of the accounting system and trace the transaction through to the accounting system.

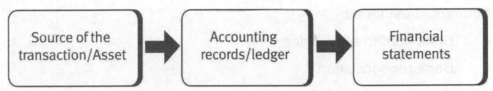

For example, select a sample of goods despatch notes and trace to the related sales invoice and into the sales day book to confirm completeness.

Testing for overstatement

A balance will be overstated if:

- Items are included that should not be included, or

- An item which has been included is recorded at an amount higher than it should be i.e. an error has been made.

Testing for overstatement tests the assertions of existence, rights and obligations, occurrence and accuracy & valuation.

To test for overstatement the auditor must select the sample from the accounting system and trace the transaction through to the supporting documentation.

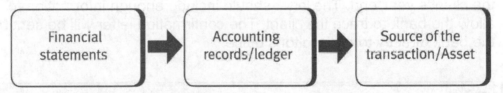

For example, from the sales day book, select a sample of sales invoices and trace to the actual sales invoice and related goods despatch note to confirm occurrence.

3 Bank and cash

The key assertions for bank and cash are existence and valuation.

Sources of evidence:

- Bank confirmation letter
- Bank reconciliation
- Cash book
- Bank statements

The bank and cash included in the financial statements must exist and be included at the appropriate amount. The cash book figure is the balance which should be included in the financial statements. This may differ to the bank statement balance due to timing differences. Therefore the bank reconciliation must be reviewed to ensure the differences can be explained.

The bank confirmation letter provides direct confirmation of bank balances from the bank. It is third party, independent, written evidence and therefore very reliable.

The client must give permission to the bank to release this information to the auditor, as they too have a duty of confidentiality to their clients.

The confirmation request should be sent a minimum of two weeks before the client's year-end. The letter should include enough information to allow the bank to trace the client. The confirmation letter will be sent by the bank directly to the auditor's office.

Test your understanding 1 – Bank and cash

Murray Co

Bank reconciliation as at 31 December 20X4	$
Balance per cash book	(180,345.22)
Add Unpresented cheques	2,223.46
Less Outstanding lodgements	(1,600.34)
Difference	1.34
Balance per bank statement	(179,720.76)

Required:

Describe substantive procedures the auditor should perform to obtain sufficient and appropriate audit evidence in relation to Murray Co's year-end bank balances.

Illustration 1 – Murray Co Bank confirmation letter

Wimble & Co
14 The Grove
Kingston
KI4 6AP

Manager (Audit Confirmations)
National Bank Anytown Branch
High Street, Anytown, AT1 1 HS

14 December 20X4

Dear Sir,

Re: Murray Co

In accordance with the agreed practice for provision of information to auditors, please forward information on our mutual client as detailed below on behalf of the bank, its branches and subsidiaries. This request and your response will not create any contractual or other duty with us.

Company name: Murray Co

Main account number: 01789311

Sort code: 04-83-12

Information required

- Standard   x
- Trade finance   x
- Derivative and commodity trading
- Custodian arrangements
- Other information (see attached)

Audit confirmation date: 31/12/X4

The Authority to Disclose Information signed by your customer is already held by you. This is dated 30/11/X4. Please advise us if this Authority is insufficient for you to provide full disclosure of the information requested.

The contact name is: Don Henman (Audit engagement partner)

Telephone: 01234 123456

Yours faithfully,

Wimble & Co

Wimble & Co

Cash counts

Where cash in hand is material, or when fraud is suspected, a cash count should be arranged to verify existence.

The auditor should make sure that all cash balances are counted at the same time to avoid manipulation of the balances between different sites.

The auditor should always be accompanied by a member of the client staff to avoid any allegations from the client of theft by the auditor.

The details of the cash counts should be recorded, such as the locations counted, the amount counted at each location, the client staff present, the auditor performing the tests and the date performed.

Non-current liabilities

The key assertion for liabilities is completeness and valuation.

Sources of evidence:

- Loan agreement
- Cash book
- Bank statements
- Bank confirmation letter

The loan balances must be complete and valued appropriately in the financial statements. Allocation must be assessed as the client should show how much of the loan is due to be paid within one year (included as a current liability) and how much of the loan is due to be paid outside of one year (included as a non-current liability).

The bank confirmation letter will provide details of loans held, the amounts outstanding, accrued interest and any security provided in relation to those loans.

Third party evidence will be available in the form of the bank confirmation letter and the original loan agreement.

Procedures include:

- Obtain a breakdown of all loans outstanding at the year-end, cast to verify arithmetical accuracy and agree the total to the financial statements: **completeness**.

- Agree the balance(s) outstanding to the bank confirmation letter: **accuracy & valuation, rights & obligations**.

- Inspect the bank confirmation letters for any loans listed that have not been included in the financial statements: **completeness**.

- Inspect the bank confirmation letter for details of any security over assets and agree the details to the disclosure in the financial statements: **presentation**.

- Inspect financial statements for disclosures of interest rates, and the split of the loan between current and non-current: **allocation, classification, presentation**.

- Recalculate the split between current and non-current liabilities: **allocation, classification, and presentation**.

- Inspect the loan agreement for restrictive covenants (terms) and determine the effect of any loan covenant breaches: **allocation, classification, presentation.** [If loan covenants have been breached the loan may become repayable immediately and should therefore be included as a current liability].

- Inspect the cash book for loan repayments made: **existence, accuracy & valuation**.

- For the related finance cost in the statement of profit or loss, recalculate the interest charge and any interest accrual in accordance with terms within the loan agreement, to ensure mathematical accuracy: **accuracy** of finance costs in the statement of profit or loss, **completeness** of accruals.

4 Non-current assets

 The key assertions for non-current assets are existence, valuation, completeness and rights and obligations.

Sources of evidence:

- Non-current asset register

- Purchase invoices (additions)

- Sales invoices / capital disposal forms (disposals)

- Bank statements and cash book

- Physical assets

- Ownership documents including title deeds and registration documents

- Depreciation policy and rates

- Capital expenditure budgets / capital replacement plans

Non-current assets must exist, be completely recorded, be valued appropriately and must be owned or controlled by the entity.

The auditor needs to obtain sufficient appropriate evidence over:

- Existing assets i.e. assets purchased in previous periods

- Additions

- Disposals

- Revaluations

- Depreciation

- Related disclosures (the property, plant and equipment note, depreciation policies, useful economic lives, revaluations).

Test your understanding 2 – Non-current assets

Murray Co

Non-current assets: Property, plant and equipment note

	Land & buildings $000	Fixtures, fittings & equipment $000	Motor vehicles $000	Total $000
Cost at 1 January 20X4	3,000	2,525	375	5,900
Additions	–	1,050	75	1,125
Disposals	–	(300)	–	(300)
Cost at 31 December 20X4	3,000	3,275	450	6,725
Accumulated depreciation at 1 January 20X4	386	489	125	1,000
Charge for the year	97	338	56	491
Disposals	–	(116)	–	(116)
Accumulated depreciation at 31 December 20X4	483	711	181	1,375
Carrying value at 31 December 20X4	2,517	2,564	269	5,350
Carrying value at 31 December 20X3	2,614	2,036	250	4,900

Required:

Describe substantive procedures the auditor should perform to obtain sufficient and appropriate audit evidence in relation to Murray Co's year-end non-current assets.

Illustration 2 – Depreciation proof-in-total

The depreciation charge for fixtures and fittings for the year-ended 31 December 20X4 included in the draft financial statements of Murray Co is $338,000 (to the nearest $000).

Murray Co's depreciation policy is to depreciate fixtures and fittings using the straight line method. The useful economic life for fixtures and fittings is ten years.

Exercise:

Create an expectation of the fixtures and fittings depreciation charge for the year-ended 31 December 20X4.

Solution

The total cost of fixtures and fittings in the draft financial statements of Murray Co is $3,275,000 (to the nearest $000).

We can set an expectation for total depreciation for fixtures and fittings for the year-ended 31 December 20X4 as $3,275,000/10 = $328,000 (to the nearest $000).

The difference of $10,000 is 3% more than our expectation. If this is within an acceptable level of variation (as determined by the judgment of the auditor) the auditor will conclude that depreciation is not materially misstated.

Intangible non-current assets

Development costs

The key assertion for development costs is existence.

Sources of evidence:

- Breakdown of expenditure during the year

- Purchase invoices

- Bank statements and cash book

- Timesheets

- Development expenditure/project plans

- Project test/trial results

- Cash flow forecasts

- Licence agreement

- Third party valuation report e.g. for brand names and trademarks

- Amortisation policy and rates

Development costs should only be capitalised as an intangible asset if the recognition criteria of IAS 38 *Intangible Assets* have been met. The audit procedures suggested below focus on obtaining evidence that the treatment of the relevant item complies with these requirements.

Procedures include:

- Obtain a breakdown of capitalised costs, cast for mathematical accuracy and agree to the amount included in the financial statements **valuation**.

- For a sample of costs included in the breakdown, agree the amount to invoices or timesheets: **valuation**.

- Inspect board minutes for any discussions relating to the intended sale or use of the asset: **existence**.

- Discuss details of the project with the project manager or management to evaluate compliance with IAS 38 criteria: **existence**.

- Inspect project plans and other documentation to evaluate compliance with IAS 38 criteria: **existence**.

- Inspect budgets to confirm financial feasibility: **existence**.

- Inspect the financial statement disclosure in the draft financial statements to ensure compliance with IAS 38: **presentation**.

Other intangible assets

- Inspect purchase documentation for the company name and the cost of the purchased intangible assets: **existence, rights and obligations and valuation**.

- Inspect specialist valuation report and agree to the amount included in the general ledger and the financial statements: **valuation**.

Amortisation

- Inspect the budgets/forecasts for the next few years to ascertain the period over which economic benefits are expected to be generated and compare with the amortisation policy, to assess reasonableness of the amortisation period: **valuation**.

- Recalculate the amortisation charge to verify arithmetical accuracy: **accuracy, valuation**.

- For intangibles such as licences, inspect the licence agreement to confirm the amortisation period corresponds to the licence period: **valuation**.

5 Inventory

 The key assertions for inventory are existence, valuation, completeness and rights and obligations.

Sources of evidence:

- Aged inventory listing
- Inventory assets
- Inventory count sheets
- Purchase invoices
- Goods received notes
- Sales invoices
- Goods despatch notes
- Client calculations of overhead allocation, absorption and apportionment and percentage of completion for work-in-progress

Inventory assets must exist, be completely recorded, be valued appropriately and must be owned or controlled by the entity.

When auditing inventory there are two main factors to consider

- Quantity of inventory – determined by the inventory count
- Valuation of the individual inventory items – usually assessed at the final audit

ISA 501 *Audit Evidence – specific considerations for selected items* requires the auditor to:

- Attend the physical inventory count (unless impracticable), if inventory is material to the financial statements, and
- Perform procedures on the final inventory records to determine whether they accurately reflect the count results.

Attendance at the inventory count is required to:

- Evaluate management's instructions and procedures for the inventory count.
- Observe the performance of the count.
- Inspect the inventory.
- Perform test counts.

[ISA 501, 4]

 The inventory count is the responsibility of the client. The auditor does not perform the count.

Test your understanding 3 – Inventory

Murray Co's inventory count instructions are as follows:

1   A finance manager must supervise the inventory count.

2   No goods are to be received or despatched during the inventory count.

3   Each team will consist of two members of staff from the finance department. One person must count the items. The second person will record the count on sequentially numbered count sheets.

4   The teams will be allocated a team number and will be provided with a map of the warehouse. Each area of the warehouse is marked on the map with the number of the team that is to count inventory in that area. The warehouse manager will be in attendance to ensure each team is clear about which area they are counting, before it is counted.

5   Once a section is counted it must be tagged to confirm it has been counted. Yellow tags are to be used by the first counting team to confirm the count has been performed.

6   Once the first count is complete, a second count will take place, with each team counting an area that they were not responsible for on the first count (according to the warehouse map). Any discrepancies should be notified to the finance director immediately. Green tags are to be used to confirm the count has been checked by a second team.

7   Sequentially numbered count sheets will contain the product description from the inventory system but no system quantities.

8   Any items of inventory in the warehouse that are not listed on the count sheets should be recorded on a blank, sequentially numbered count sheet.

9   Inventory count sheets must be recorded in ink. If a mistake is made, it should be crossed out neatly and the correct information written next to it.

10   Any damaged or obsolete items will be moved to a designated area. After the count, an assessment of the goods will be made by the finance manager with advice from a sales manager and the warehouse manager, to determine the allowance appropriate for the condition of the items.

11   After the count, the finance manager should review the warehouse to ensure all sections have been tagged with both yellow and green tags to confirm the count is complete.

12 The count sheets must be signed by each team member responsible for completing the sheets and returned to the finance manager who will perform a sequence check to confirm all count sheets have been returned.

13 The finance manager will compare the inventory count sheets to the inventory records and any adjustments will be updated by another finance manager not involved in the count.

Required:

(a) **Describe the procedures that should be performed by the auditor before attending the inventory count of Murray Co.**

(b) **Describe the audit procedures that should be performed whilst in attendance at the inventory count of Murray Co.**

(c) **Describe the substantive procedures that should be performed during the final audit of Murray Co.**

Continuous/perpetual inventory systems

A continuous or perpetual inventory system is one which keeps a real time track of inventory. As a sale is made, the inventory system is updated to reflect the reduction in quantity. As purchases are received, the system is updated to reflect the increase in quantity. This enables the business to know its inventory balance at any point in time.

Over time, the inventory levels stated in the perpetual inventory system may gradually diverge from actual inventory levels, due to unrecorded transactions or theft, so periodically, a count should be performed to compare system balances to actual quantities and the system can be updated accordingly.

Where the client uses a continuous inventory system, lines of inventory are counted periodically (say monthly) throughout the year so that by the end of the year all lines have been counted.

Where the client uses this type of system the auditor should:

- Attend at least one count to ensure adequate controls are applied during the counts (in the same way as for a year-end count).

- Inspect the number and value of adjustments made as a result of the count. If significant adjustments are required after each count, this would indicate that the system figures for inventory cannot be relied upon at the year-end and a full count will be required.

- If the system balance for inventory is deemed reliable as a result of these procedures, further procedures to verify valuation and rights will still be required.

The auditor will still need to perform the audit procedures usually performed at the final audit such as:

- Inspect GRNs and GDNs around the year-end to confirm correct cut-off. Goods received before the year-end should be traced through to inclusion in the inventory listing whilst goods received after the year-end should not be included. Similarly, goods despatched before the year-end should not be included within inventory whereas goods despatched post year-end should be included in the year-end inventory balance.

- Review purchase invoices and post year-end sales invoices to ascertain if net realisable value (NRV) is above cost or if an adjustment is required.

- Compare the inventory holding period with prior year to identify slow-moving inventory which needs to be written down to the lower of cost and net realisable value.

- Inspect purchase invoices for the name of the client to confirm rights and obligations.

Advantages and disadvantages of perpetual counts

Advantages

- Reduces time constraints for the auditor, and enables them to attend counts relating to lines at greater risk of material misstatement.

- Slow-moving and damaged inventory is identified and adjusted for in the client's records on a continuous basis meaning the year-end valuation should be more accurate.

Disadvantages

- The auditor will need to obtain sufficient appropriate evidence that the system operates effectively at all times, not just at the time of the count.

- Additional procedures will be necessary to ensure that the amount included for inventory in the financial statements is appropriate, particularly with regard to cut-off and year-end allowances.

Third party inventory stored at the client

If the client stores inventory on behalf of a third party, they should have procedures in place to ensure this inventory is not included in their own records. During the inventory count the inventory belonging to a third party must be separately identifiable, and preferably moved to different location, to minimise the risk of it being counted as part of the client's inventory which would overstate the inventory balance in the financial statements.

Inventory held by third parties

Some companies will not have space to store all of their inventory and may use a third party storage facility. The inventory held at the third party still needs to be counted and included in the client's inventory records. The auditor will need to obtain sufficient appropriate audit evidence that the inventory actually exists and belongs to the client.

Procedures include:

- Where a third party holds inventory on behalf of the client, obtain external confirmation from the third party of the quantity and condition of the goods to confirm **rights and valuation**.

- If inventory held by the third party is material, the auditor should attend the inventory count to verify **existence** of the inventory.

- The auditor can also obtain a report from the third party's auditors confirming the reliability of the internal controls at the third party.

Standard costs

Standard costs are often used by manufacturing companies where it would be too time-consuming to collect actual cost information for each individual unit produced. The company establishes an expected cost of producing one item based on a normal level of activity. This is used to value the inventory.

Any difference between actual cost and standard cost is taken to a variance account in the statement of profit or loss. A large variance on the variance account would indicate that the standard costs are not a close approximation of the actual costs and therefore the inventory valuation will not be reliable.

Standard costs are more likely to be reliable if they are updated on a regular basis. How frequently the standard costs should be updated will depend on how often the cost of components used in the manufacturing process changes.

Audit procedures must be performed to assess the reasonableness of the standard costs as a means of valuing inventory, including:

- Obtain the breakdown of the standard cost calculation and agree a sample of costs to invoices.

- Enquire of management the basis for the standard costs and how often they are updated to reflect current costs.

- Inspect the variance account and assess the level of variance for reasonableness. Discuss with management any significant variances arising.

Inventory count: cut-off procedures

The inventory count(s) will be affected by goods despatched and goods received.

During the count, inventory movements should preferably stop to enable the count to be conducted without being affected by deliveries.

For some organisations this won't be possible as they may operate production and deliveries 24 hours a day.

In these types of organisations the client should move the items requiring despatch to a different location to that being counted prior to the count taking place. Any deliveries of goods should be made to a different location while the count is ongoing to enable the count to be conducted without movement of items.

A separate count can then be performed on the items delivered during the count and these can be added to the warehouse items counted.

By having such controls in place, the completeness and existence of inventory at the count date can be verified as well as the cut-off assertion for purchases and sales.

6 Receivables

The focus of testing for receivables is valuation and existence.

Sources of evidence:

- Aged receivables listing
- Sales invoices
- Goods despatch notes
- Receivables circularisation letters
- Post year end bank statements
- Policy for allowance for doubtful receivables

The receivables balance included in the financial statements must exist and be included at the appropriate amount.

Receivables will be overstated if irrecoverable receivables have not been written off or doubtful receivables have not been written down. Audit procedures will therefore obtain evidence regarding the recoverability of amounts outstanding at the year end.

Third party evidence will be obtained in the form of a receivables circularisation letter which will confirm existence of amounts outstanding at the year end.

Receivables circularisations

The auditor will send a circularisation letter to a sample of customers asking them to confirm the balance owed to the client at the year end. This is considered to be a reliable source of evidence for certain financial statement assertions, such as existence, because it is documentary evidence sent directly to the auditor from an external source. They will not be reliable evidence for the valuation assertion as the customer only confirms the transaction price and does not have to state any intention to pay the invoice.

Circularisation letters can be positive or negative.

A positive receivables circularisation requires customers to respond to the auditor's request for information. The auditor can include the balance per the client's ledger and ask the customer to reply stating whether or not the balance is correct. Alternatively, the auditor can ask the customer to respond by stating the balance they believe they owe the client, but the auditor does not provide the balance per the client's ledger to the customer.

A **negative receivables circularisation** requests customers to respond only if they disagree with the balance provided by the auditor. This is only suitable if the risk of material misstatement is low as the customer may confirm an incorrect balance if it is in their favour.

Steps in undertaking a positive receivables circularisation

- Obtain consent from the client to perform the circularisation.

- Obtain a list of trade receivables at the year end, cast this and agree it to the receivables ledger control account total.

- Select a sample from the receivables list ensuring that a number of nil, old, credit and large balances are selected.

- Circularisation letters should be prepared on the client's letterhead paper, requesting a confirmation of the year-end receivables balance, and for replies to be sent directly to the auditor's office using a pre-paid envelope.

- An appropriate member of client staff, such as the finance director, should be requested to sign all the letters prior to them being sent out by a member of the audit team.

- Where no response is received, follow this up with another letter or a phone call and where necessary alternative procedures should be performed such as after date cash testing and inspection of sales invoices and GDNs relating to the receivable.

- When replies are received, they should be reconciled to the client's receivables records, and any differences such as cash or goods in transit should be investigated further.

ISA 505 External Confirmations

ISA 505 External Confirmations requires the auditor to maintain control over external confirmation requests when using external confirmations as a source of audit evidence.

This can be achieved by the auditor:

- Preparing the confirmation letters and determining the information to be requested and the information that should be included in the request.

- Selecting the sample of external parties from which to obtain confirmation.

- Sending the requests to the confirming party.

[ISA 505, 7]

Illustration 3 – Murray Co positive confirmation letter

Customer Co

Customer's address

7 January 20X5

Dear Sirs

As part of their normal audit procedures we have been requested by our auditors, Wimble & Co, to ask you to confirm the balance on your account with us at 31 December 20X4, our year-end.

The balance on your account, as shown by our records, is shown below. After comparing this with your records will you please be kind enough to sign the confirmation and return a copy to the auditor in the prepaid envelope enclosed. If the balance is not in agreement with your records, will you please note the items making up the difference in the space provided.

Please note that this request is made for audit purposes only and has no further significance.

Your kind co-operation in this matter will be greatly appreciated.

Yours faithfully

Chief Accountant

Murray Co

Wimble & Co address

Dear Sirs

We confirm that, except as noted below *, a balance of $XX was owing by us to Murray & Co at 31 December 20X4.

(space for customer's signature)

* Details of differences

"7 January 20X5": The confirmation letter should be **sent as soon as possible after the year-end,** to increase the chance of an accurate and timely response.

"As part of their normal audit procedures, we have been requested by our auditors to confirm the balance on your account with us at 31 December 20X4... please be kind enough to sign the confirmation and return a copy to the auditor...": It is the **client** who **writes to their customers** requesting the information but the **response** must be sent directly to the auditors to reduce the risk of the client interfering with any response.

"...in the prepaid envelope enclosed": Making it as easy as possible to respond increases the chance that sufficient customers will confirm balances for it to be a valid audit test.

"If the balance is not in agreement with your records, will you please note the items making up the difference in the space provided": Requesting the customer to complete the reconciliation increases the reliance the auditor can place on this evidence (although the auditor will review the reconciliation and investigate any unreconciled differences or disagreements).

Test your understanding 4 – Receivables

Murray Co

Aged receivables analysis at 31 December 20X4 ($000)

Ref	Customer Name	Total	Current	30–60 days	60–90 days	90–120 days	120 days
A001	Anfield United Shop	**176**	95	76	5	0	0
B001	Bibs and Balls	**0**	0	(24)	0	24	0
B002	The Beautiful Game	**84**	62	0	20	0	2
B003	Beckham's	**42**	32	10	0	0	0
C001	Cheryl & Coleen Co	**12**	12	0	0	0	0
D001	Dream Team	**45**	0	31	14	0	0
E001	Escot Supermarket	**235**	97	65	0	0	73
G001	Golf is Us	**211**	0	0	0	100	111
G002	Green Grass	**61**	50	11	0	0	0
H001	HHA Sports	**59**	40	0	19	0	0
J001	Jilberts	**21**	11	10	0	0	0
J002	James Smit Partnership	**256**	73	102	34	45	2
J003	Jockeys	**419**	278	120	21	0	0
O001	The Oval	**92**	48	44	0	0	0
P001	Pole Vaulters	**76**	0	0	76	0	0
P002	Polo	**0**	0	0	0	0	0
S001	Stayrose Supermarket	**97**	24	23	23	27	0
T001	Trainers and More	**93**	73	20	0	0	0
T002	Tike Co	**(54)**	0	0	0	0	(54)
W001	Wanderers	**89**	60	29	0	0	0
W002	Whistlers	**(9)**	645	(654)	0	0	0
W003	Walk Hike Run	**4**	0	0	0	0	4
W004	Winners	**31**	21	10	0	0	0
Total		**2,040**	**1,621**	**(127)**	**212**	**196**	**138**

> **Required:**
>
> (a) Identify, with reasons, FOUR trade receivables balances from the aged receivables analysis that should be selected for further testing.
>
> (b) Describe substantive procedures the auditor should perform to obtain sufficient and appropriate audit evidence in relation to Murray Co's trade receivables.

Prepayments

Prepayments are services or goods which a company has paid for in advance. Therefore the client should include the value of any prepayments as a receivable in the financial statements.

- Inspect bank statements to ensure payment has been made before the year-end: **existence**.

- Inspect invoices to ensure payment relates to goods or services not yet received: **existence**.

- Recalculate the amount prepaid to confirm mathematical accuracy: **valuation**.

- Compare prepayments with the prior year to identify any missing items or any new prepayments which require further testing: **existence, valuation, and completeness. (Analytical procedure)**.

7 Payables and accruals

 The focus of testing for liabilities is completeness.

Sources of evidence:

- Aged payables listing

- Purchase invoices

- Goods received notes

- Post year end bank statements

- Supplier statements

- Supplier circularisations (where supplier statements are not available)

The payables balance included in the financial statements must be complete.

Payables will be understated if all liabilities in relation to purchases made have not been recorded.

Third party evidence will be obtained in the form of supplier statements and supplier circularisation letters.

Trade payables

Procedures include:

- Obtain a list of trade payables, cast to verify arithmetical accuracy and agree to the general ledger and the financial statements: **completeness, classification, presentation**.

- Reconcile the total of the individual payables accounts with the control account: **completeness**.

- Obtain supplier statements and reconcile these to the payables balances. Investigate any reconciling items: **existence, completeness, obligations and valuation**.
  Note: Supplier statement reconciliations provide the most reliable evidence in respect of payables as they provide external confirmation of the balance.

- Inspect after date payments, if they relate to the current year then follow through to the payables ledger or accruals listing: **completeness**.

- Inspect invoices received after the year-end in respect of goods delivered before the year-end and trace through to the accruals listing: **completeness**.

- Enquire of management their process for identifying goods received but not invoiced and ensure that it is reasonable: **completeness**.

- Select a sample of goods received notes immediately before the year-end and follow through to inclusion in the year-end payables balance: **completeness of payables** and **cut-off of purchases**.

- Select a sample of payable balances and perform a trade payables' circularisation, follow up any non-replies and any reconciling items between the balance confirmed and the ledger balance: **completeness** and **existence**.

- Inspect the trade payables ledger for any debit balances, for any significant amounts discuss with management and consider reclassification as current assets: **valuation** of payables and **completeness of receivables, classification**.

- Compare the list of trade payables and accruals against the prior year list to identify any significant omissions: **completeness. (Analytical procedure)**

- Calculate the trade payables payment period and compare to prior year, investigate any significant differences: **completeness** and **valuation**. **(Analytical procedure)**

Accruals

Procedures include:

- Obtain the list of accruals from the client, cast it to confirm mathematical accuracy and agree to the general ledger and the financial statements: **completeness, classification**.

- Recalculate a sample of accrued costs by reference to contracts and payment schedules (e.g. loan interest): **valuation (accuracy** of purchases and other expenses).

- Inspect invoices received post year-end to confirm the actual amount and assess whether the accrual is reasonable: **valuation**.

- Compare the accruals this year to last year to identify any missing items or unusual fluctuation in amount and discuss this with management: **completeness and valuation. (Analytical procedure)**

Test your understanding 5 – Payables

Murray Co's trade payables balance at 31 December 20X4 is $1,400,000 (to the nearest $000). The total balance has already been agreed to the payables ledger which shows that trade payables consists of fifteen suppliers.

A junior member of the audit team, Rob Cash, has been testing five of these balances by reconciling supplier statements to the balances on the payables ledger. He is unable to reconcile a material balance, relating to Racket Co, which supplies Vectran material to Murray Co, for stringing tennis rackets. He has asked for your assistance on the audit work which should be carried out on the differences.

The balance of Racket Co on Murray Co's purchase ledger is shown below:

Payables ledger Supplier: Racket Co

Date	Type	Reference	Status	Dr ($)	Cr ($)	Balance ($)
10.10	Invoice	6004	Paid 1		21,300	
18.10	Invoice	6042	Paid 1		15,250	
23.10	Invoice	6057	Paid 1		26,340	
04.11	Invoice	6080	Paid 2		35,720	
15.11	Invoice	6107	Paid 2		16,320	
26.11	Invoice	6154	Paid 2		9,240	
30.11	Payment	Cheque	Alloc 1	61,630		
	Discount		Alloc 1	1,260		
14.12	Invoice	6285			21,560	
21.12	Invoice	6328			38,240	
31.12	Payment	Cheque	Alloc 2	60,050		
	Discount		Alloc 2	1,230		
31.12	**Balance**					**59,800**

Racket Co have sent the following supplier statement:

Date	Type	Reference	Status	Dr ($)	Cr ($)	Balance ($)
07.10	Invoice	6004		21,300		
16.10	Invoice	6042		15,250		
22.10	Invoice	6057		26,340		
02.11	Invoice	6080		37,520		
13.11	Invoice	6107		16,320		
22.11	Invoice	6154		9,240		
10.12	Receipt	Cheque			61,630	
04.12	Invoice	6210		47,350		
12.12	Invoice	6285		21,560		
18.12	Invoice	6328		38,240		
28.12	Invoice	6355		62,980		
31.12	**Balance**					**234,470**

Racket Co's terms of trade with Murray Co allow a 2% cash discount on invoices where Racket Co receives a cheque from the customer by the end of the month following the date of the invoice (i.e. a 2% discount will be given on November invoices paid by 31 December).

On Murray Co's payables ledger, under 'Status' the cash and discount marked 'Alloc 1' relate to the invoices marked 'Paid 1' (similarly for 'Alloc 2' and 'Paid 2').

Murray Co's goods received department checks the goods when they arrive and issues a goods received note (GRN). A copy of the GRN and the supplier's advice note is sent to the purchases accounting department.

Required:

(a) **Prepare a statement reconciling the balance on Murray Co's payables ledger to the balance on Racket Co's supplier's statement.**

(b) **Describe the audit work you will carry out on each of the reconciling items you have determined in your answer to part (a) above, in order to determine the balance which should be included in the financial statements.**

8 Provisions and contingencies

 IAS 37 *Provisions, Contingent Liabilities and Contingent Assets* requires an entity to recognise a provision if:

- a present obligation has arisen as a result of a past event
- payment is probable ('more likely than not'), and
- the amount can be estimated reliably.

If payment is only possible, a contingent liability must be disclosed in the notes to the financial statements.

A contingent asset can only be recognised if it is virtually certain to be received. If it is probable that an inflow of economic benefits will result, a disclosure should be made in the financial statements. If it is only possible, it should be ignored.

Provisions and contingent liabilities

Audit testing will focus on whether an obligation exists, whether payment is probable or possible, and whether the provision is valued appropriately.

Completeness is a key assertion as the company may understate liabilities to improve its financial position.

Contingent assets

Audit testing will focus on whether payment is virtually certain or probable, and whether the receivable is valued appropriately.

Existence is a key assertion as the company may overstate contingent assets to improve its financial position.

Examples of contingent assets include:

- Amounts due to be received from an insurance claim
- Amounts due to be received in respect of a legal claim
- Amounts due to be received from a liquidator in respect of an investment or bankrupt receivable.

Provisions and contingent liabilities

Procedures include:

- Obtain a breakdown of the provisions, cast it and agree the figure to the financial statements: **accuracy** and **presentation**.
- Enquire with the directors, or inspect relevant supporting documentation, to confirm that a present obligation exists at the year-end: **rights and obligations**.
- Inspect relevant board minutes to ascertain whether payment is probable: **existence**.

- Recalculate the liability and agree components of the calculation to supporting documentation: **completeness**.

- Inspect post year-end bank statements to identify whether any payments have been made, compare actual payments to the amounts provided to assess whether the provision is reasonable: **valuation**.

- Inspect the financial statement disclosure of the provisions and contingent liabilities to ensure compliance with IAS 37: **presentation**.

- Obtain a written representation from management that they believe the provisions and contingent liabilities are treated appropriately in the financial statements, are valued appropriately and are complete: **valuation** and **completeness**.

Illustration 4 – Murray Co provisions

The statement of financial position shows that Murray Co has $240,000 provisions for the year ended 31 December 20X4. The majority of the balance relates to provisions for warranties ($200,000). $40,000 of the provision relates to a claim made by an ex-employee of Murray Co who is claiming for unfair dismissal.

The audit plan includes the following audit procedures in relation to these provisions:

Warranty provision procedures

- Obtain a breakdown of the warranty provision and recalculate to verify arithmetical accuracy.

- Enquire of management the basis used for the provision and assess whether this is reasonable.

- Compare previous year actual warranty costs with the amount provided for to assess whether management's process is reasonable.

- Compare warranty claims post year-end to the warranty provision at the year-end to assess whether the provision is adequate.

- Review product returns and complaints to assess whether there is a need for a higher provision than in previous years.

- Calculate warranty costs/revenue and compare with prior year to assess whether the level of provision is consistent with the prior year. Discuss any change in proportion with management.

Legal provision procedures

- Enquire with the directors when the employee was dismissed to confirm that a present obligation exists at the year-end.

- Inspect correspondence between the employee and Murray to verify that the employee was dismissed before the year-end.

- Inspect relevant board minutes to ascertain whether it is probable that the payment will be made to the employee.

- Obtain confirmation from Murray's lawyer about the likely outcome and probability of payment.

- Inspect correspondence received from the lawyer regarding the legal provision to assess whether a provision should be recognised and if so, whether the amount of the provision is adequate.

- Obtain a breakdown of the costs to be provided and recalculate to ensure completeness.

- Agree the components of the calculation to supporting documentation, e.g. fee estimate from Murray Co's lawyer, claim received from the ex-employee.

- Inspect post year-end bank statements to identify whether any payments have been made and compare actual payments to the amounts provided to assess whether the provision is reasonable.

Procedures relevant to both provisions

- Obtain a written representation from management to confirm the adequacy and reasonableness of the provisions.

- Inspect the financial statement disclosure to ensure compliance with IAS 37 *Provisions, Contingent Liabilities and Contingent Assets*.

Contingent assets

Procedures include:

- Review correspondence from third parties (lawyer, insurance company, insolvency practitioner) regarding the value likely to be received and probability of payment. Agree the figure into the disclosure note relating to the contingent asset: **existence, accuracy & valuation and presentation**.

- Review correspondence from third parties (court, insurance company, insolvency practitioner) confirming the amount awarded to the client. Agree the figure to other receivables and other income within the financial statements: **accuracy & valuation, existence, rights & obligations, and presentation**.

- Review post year end bank statements and cash book to confirm the amount received: **accuracy & valuation, existence, rights & obligations, and presentation**.

> **ISA 501 *Audit Evidence – special considerations for selected items***
>
> ISA 501 requires the auditor to design and perform audit procedures in order to identify litigation and claims involving the entity which may give rise to a risk of material misstatement. Procedures include enquiring of management, reviewing meeting minutes and reviewing legal expense accounts. [ISA 501, 9]

9 Accounting estimates

There are many accounting estimates in the financial statements, e.g. allowances for receivables, depreciation of property, plant and equipment, provisions, etc.

Accounting estimates are inherently risky because they relate to the future and therefore documentary evidence may be limited. This makes it difficult for the auditor to obtain sufficient appropriate evidence regarding the balance.

Inherent risk is increased because management judgment is needed to determine accounting estimates. As a result, estimates may be used to manipulate the financial statements and show a desired result.

Professional scepticism is essential for the auditor to ensure the accounting estimates are reasonable and are not being used to introduce bias into the financial statements.

ISA 540 (Revised) *Auditing Accounting Estimates and Related Disclosures* requires the auditor to obtain an understanding necessary to allow the auditor to identify and assess the risks of material misstatement relating to accounting estimates. [13]

This involves obtaining an understanding of:

- The entity's environment including the requirements of the financial reporting framework and regulatory factors relevant to accounting estimates. [13b, c]

- The entity's internal controls related to accounting estimates including the control activities, the need for specialised skills, and the governance in place over the financial reporting process relevant to estimates, and how management reviews the outcome of previous accounting estimates and responds to the results of the review. [13e, f, j]

The auditor must separately assess inherent risk and control risk when assessing the risk of material misstatement relating to accounting estimates. When assessing inherent risk the auditor should consider:

- The degree to which the estimate is subject to estimation uncertainty.

- The degree of complexity and subjectivity involved in the method, assumptions and data used to make the estimate.

- The degree of complexity and subjectivity used in the selection of management's point estimate. [16]

When responding to the risk of material misstatement in the accounting estimates, the auditor must perform the following procedures:

- Obtain evidence from subsequent events.

- Test how management made the estimate.

- Develop an auditor's point estimate or range. [18]

10 Share capital, reserves and director's remuneration

 Each of these areas are material by nature.

Share capital

 Sources of evidence:

- Share register

- Share certificates

- Bank statements and cash book

- Board minutes

- Registrar of companies (e.g. Companies House)

Procedures include:

- Agree authorised share capital and nominal value disclosures to underlying shareholding agreements/statutory constitution documents.

- Inspect cash book for evidence of cash receipts from share issues and ensure amounts not yet received are correctly disclosed as share capital called-up not paid in the financial statements.

- Inspect board minutes to verify the amount of share capital issued during the year.

Dividends

 Sources of evidence:

- Board minutes

- Bank statements and cash book

- Dividend warrant

Procedures include:

- Inspect board minutes to agree dividends declared before the year-end.

- Inspect bank statements to agree dividends paid before the year-end.

- Inspect dividend warrants to agree dividend payment.

Directors' emoluments

 Sources of evidence:

- Directors' service contracts
- Board minutes
- Bank statements and cash book
- Payroll records
- Written representation from management

Procedures include:

- Obtain and cast a schedule of directors' remuneration split between wages, bonuses, benefits, pension contributions and other remuneration, and agree to the financial statement disclosures.

- Inspect payroll records and agree the figures disclosed for wages, bonuses, and pension contributions.

- Inspect bank statements to verify the amounts actually paid to directors.

- Inspect board minutes for discussion and approval of directors' bonus announcements or other additional remuneration.

- Obtain a written representation from directors that they have disclosed all directors' remuneration to the auditor.

Reserves

- Agree opening reserves to prior year closing reserves and reconcile movements.

- Agree movements in reserves to supporting documentation (e.g. revaluation reserve movements to the independent valuer's report).

11 Statement of profit or loss

 Due to the volume of transactions processed during the year, most companies will have controls in place over revenue, purchases and payroll. The auditor will therefore seek to place reliance on internal controls over these areas.

Substantive procedures will still need to be performed as these areas will be material to the financial statements and the auditor is likely to perform **substantive analytical procedures** as an efficient way of obtaining substantive audit evidence where controls are working effectively.

Some specific tests of detail will be performed when testing the statement of profit or loss items. In addition, some evidence will be obtained over revenue and purchases indirectly through the direct tests performed on the corresponding receivables and payables in the statement of financial position (directional testing).

Payroll

 The focus of testing for payroll is completeness, accuracy and occurrence.

Sources of evidence:

- Payroll control account
- Payroll payment listing
- Payslips
- Contracts of employment
- Hourly rates of pay
- Timesheets
- Bank statements and cash book
- Starters and leavers forms

Payroll will be understated if all employees who should have been paid have not been paid.

Payroll will be overstated if fictitious employees, or employees who no longer work for the entity, are paid.

Payroll will be misstated if errors are made in the payroll calculations.

Procedures include:

- Agree the total wages and salaries expense per the payroll control account to the general ledger and the financial statements: **completeness and presentation**.

- Cast the monthly payroll listings to verify the accuracy of the payroll expense: **accuracy**.

- Recalculate the gross and net pay for a sample of employees and agree to the payroll records: **accuracy**.

- Recalculate statutory deductions to confirm whether correct deductions for this year have been included within the payroll expense: **accuracy**.

- Select a sample of joiners and leavers, agree their start/leaving date to supporting documentation, recalculate that their first/last pay packet was accurately calculated and recorded: **completeness, occurrence, accuracy**.

- For salaries, agree the total net pay per the payroll records to the bank transfer listing of payments and to the cashbook: **occurrence**.

- For cash wages, agree that the total cash withdrawn for wage payments equates to the weekly wages paid plus any surplus cash subsequently banked: **completeness, occurrence**.

- Agree the year-end tax liability to the payroll records and subsequent payment to the post year-end cash book: **occurrence**.

- For a sample of individuals, agree the amount per the payroll listing to the personnel records, and timesheets if applicable: **accuracy**.

Analytical procedures

- Perform a proof in total of total wages and salaries incorporating joiners and leavers and any pay increase awarded during the year. Compare this to the actual wages and salaries in the financial statements and investigate any significant differences: **completeness, accuracy**.

- Compare the payroll figure for this year to last year to identify any unusual fluctuations and discuss them with management: **completeness, accuracy.**

Illustration 5 – Murray Co payroll proof in total

Total payroll for the year-ending 31 December 20X3 was $1,220,000 (to the nearest $000). At this time Murray Co had 34 employees.

Total payroll for the year-ending 31 December 20X4 is $1,312,000 (to the nearest $000). Murray Co now has 37 employees.

All employees received a 5% pay rise on 31 March 20X4.

Exercise:

Create an expectation of the total payroll cost for year-ended 31 December 20X4.

Solution

The average salary per employee in 20X3 was $35,882 ($1,220,000/34).

All employees received a 5% pay rise in March. The average value of this pay rise is therefore $1,346 per employee in 20X4 (5% × 9/12 × $35,882).The average salary for 20X4 is $37,228 ($35,882 + $1,346), therefore the **expectation for total payroll for the year-ending 31 December 20X4 is $1,377,000** (37 × $37,228) to the nearest $000.

The **difference** ($65,000) is **less than 5%** more than our expectation. If this is within an acceptable level of variation (as determined by the judgment of the auditor) the auditor will conclude that the payroll cost is not materially misstated.

Revenue

 The focus of testing for revenue is completeness, cut-off, occurrence and accuracy.

Sources of evidence:

- Revenue control account
- Sales day book
- Sales invoices
- Customer contracts
- Goods despatch notes
- Sales orders

Revenue will be understated if all sales transactions are not recorded.

Revenue will be overstated if fictitious sales, or sales which have been returned, are recorded.

Revenue will be misstated if errors are made in the sales invoice calculations.

Procedures include:

- Inspect a sample of GDNs before and after the year-end and ensure they have been recorded in the sales day book in the correct period: **cut-off.** In most cases, the despatch of goods indicates that the seller has fulfilled its performance obligations and therefore the sale can be recorded.

- Recalculate discounts and sales tax applied for a sample of large sales invoices: **accuracy**.

- Select a sample of customer orders and agree these to the despatch notes and sales invoices through to inclusion in the sales day book: **completeness**.

- Inspect credit notes issued after the year-end, trace to GDN and invoice and ensure the sale has been reversed: **occurrence.**

Analytical procedures

- Compare revenue against prior year and investigate any significant fluctuations: **cut-off, occurrence, accuracy and completeness.**

- Compare revenue with budget/forecast and investigate any significant fluctuations: **cut-off, occurrence, accuracy and completeness.**

- Calculate the gross profit margin and compare to prior year. Investigate any significant differences: **cut-off, occurrence, accuracy and completeness.**

Purchases and other expenses

 The focus of testing for purchases is completeness, cut-off, occurrence, accuracy and classification.

Sources of evidence:

- Purchase control account
- Purchase day book
- Purchase invoices
- Supplier contracts
- Goods received notes
- Purchase orders

Purchases will be understated if all purchase transactions are not recorded, including around the year-end.

Purchases will be overstated if goods purchased through the business for personal use are recorded, or purchases which have been returned, are recorded.

Purchases will be misstated if errors are made when recording purchase invoices or if purchases have been misclassified.

Procedures include:

- Inspect GRNs before and after the year-end and ensure they have been recorded in the purchase day book in the correct period: **cut-off**. In most cases, the company takes ownership for goods when they are received and therefore the purchase expense (and corresponding liability) should be recorded.

- Recalculate discounts and sales tax applied for a sample of purchase invoices: **accuracy**.

- Select a sample of purchase orders and agree these to the GRNs and purchase invoices through to inclusion in the purchase day book: **completeness**.

- Inspect purchase invoices for a sample of purchases/expenses in the purchase day book for the amount, name of the client and description of the goods: **accuracy, occurrence and classification**.

Analytical procedures

- Compare expenses for each category year on year and investigate any significant fluctuations: **cut-off, accuracy, completeness, classification and occurrence.**

- Compare expenses against budget and investigate any significant fluctuations: **cut-off, accuracy, completeness, classification and occurrence.**

- Calculate gross profit margin and compare with prior year to identify any possible misstatement of purchases. Discuss any significant movement with management: **cut-off, accuracy, completeness, and occurrence.**

- Calculate operating profit margin and compare with prior year. Investigate any significant fluctuations: **cut-off, accuracy, completeness, classification and occurrence.**

12 Audits of smaller entities

The characteristics of smaller entities can lead to both advantages and disadvantages:

- **Lower risk** – Smaller entities may be engaged in relatively simple activities which reduces risk.

- **Direct control by owner managers** – This can be a strength because they know what is going on and have the ability to exercise real control. However, they are also in a strong position to manipulate the figures or put personal transactions through the business.

- **Simpler systems** – Smaller entities are less likely to have sophisticated IT systems, but pure, manual systems are becoming increasingly rare. This is good news in that many of the bookkeeping errors associated with smaller entities may now be less prevalent. However, a system is only as good as the person operating it.

Evidence implications

- The normal rules concerning the relationship between risk and the quality and quantity of evidence apply, irrespective of the size of the entity.

- The quantity of evidence may be less than for a larger organisation due to fewer transactions occurring.

- It may be more efficient to carry out a full substantive audit in a smaller organisation.

Problems

- **Management override** – Smaller entities will have a key director or manager who will have significant power and authority. This could mean controls are lacking in the first place or they are easy to override.

- **No segregation of duties** – Smaller entities tend to have a limited number of accounts clerks who process information. To overcome this, the directors should authorise and review all work performed.

- **Less formal approach** – Smaller entities tend to have simple systems and fewer controls due to reliance on trust and lack of complexity. Therefore, less reliance can be placed on internal controls.

13 Audits of Not-For-Profit Organisations

Not-for-profit (NFP) organisations include charities and public sector entities. Below are some important features of a NFP.

- Profit maximisation is not its main objective. Objectives will be either social or philanthropic.

- There are no shareholders.

- They will not distribute dividends.

Financial statements

NFP organisations, such as charities which are not established as charitable companies, will need to prepare:

- A **statement of financial activities** showing income and expenditure similar to a statement of profit or loss. As the organisation does not exist to make a profit, any additional income over expenditure is known as a surplus and any expenditure in excess of income is a deficit.

- A **balance sheet** showing assets and liabilities, the same as a statement of financial position.

- A **cash flow statement**.

- **Notes to the financial statements**.

Audit risks

Control risk

Some NFP entities, particularly small charities, may have less effective internal control systems due to:

- being controlled by trustees who usually only work on a part-time basis, and are volunteers. They may not devote sufficient time to adequately oversee the strategic direction of the organisation.

- a lack of segregation of duties, as the organisation may not employ many staff in order to keep overheads down.

- the use of volunteers, who are likely to be unqualified and have little awareness of the importance of controls.

- the use of less formalised systems and controls.

Income

With many charities, much of the income received is by way of donation. Some of these transactions will not be accompanied by invoices, orders or despatch notes. For cash donations in particular there is a greater risk of theft.

NFPs may apply for grant income which will only be provided if certain criteria are met, otherwise the money may have to be repaid. It is also likely that if the organisation does not comply with the terms and conditions of the grant, the grant will be repayable. There is a risk that grant income which has to be repaid has not been provided for within current liabilities.

Restricted funds

Some donations are given with clauses stating the money must be used for a particular purpose. For example, money may be donated to a hospital to purchase a specific piece of equipment, or to be used by a specific department. These restricted funds must be shown separately in the balance sheet and the auditor must review donations to ensure that restricted funds are shown as such.

Going concern

Assessing the going concern status of a NFP entity may also be more difficult, particularly for charities who are reliant on voluntary donations. Many issues, such as economic factors, could impact on its ability to generate income in the short-term. Trends can also have an effect. For example, charities raising money for medical research such as cancer and heart disease are seeing higher numbers of donations, whereas charities such as animal protection are seeing a decline in income.

Complexity of regulations

NFPs may have complex internal and external regulations governing its activities, reporting requirements and taxation system. This means the audit team will need to have knowledge of these regulations, and experience of auditing this type of specialised entity, in order to be able to perform the audit with sufficient competence and due care.

Audit testing

Sufficient appropriate evidence will still need to be obtained through either a mixture of tests of controls and substantive procedures, or substantive procedures only if the controls are ineffective or not in place.

Procedures will still involve enquiries, inspection, analytical procedures, etc.

Other planning activities

In addition to the specific audit risks that need to be considered at the risk assessment stage, the same planning activities are required as for the audit of a company. Differences that will require consideration are:

- The materiality assessment may be lower to compensate for the higher risk, therefore more testing may be required.

- The choice of audit team should include staff with experience of this type of entity and knowledge of the regulations and financial reporting requirements.

Reporting

If sufficient appropriate evidence is not obtained with respect to the above matters, as well as the usual risks of material misstatement faced by any organisation, the auditor will have to modify the audit opinion.

Other reporting responsibilities

Quite often, the scope of the external audit of a NFP is much larger than that for a company.

In addition to the financial statement audit, the following may also be required:

- Value for money audit – assessing whether the organisation is getting the most from the money spent. These are discussed in more detail in the chapter 'Internal audit'.

- Regularity audit – ensuring the expenditure of the organisation is in accordance with the regulations/legislation governing it.

- Audit of performance indicators – auditing the targets of the organisation that have to be reported to stakeholders such as waiting times in an A&E department.

Illustration 6 – Not-for-profit organisation

The Thames Pool Trust (TPT) is a not-for-profit organisation. TPT owns a large area of park space. Within the park is an open-air pool which locals can pay to use. TPT does not employ any staff directly. Day-to-day operations are run by a local organisation, EmCA, under a management agreement, and TPT receives a share of EmCA's operating surplus.

To raise funds to pursue its charitable objective, TPT stages six summer picnic concerts each year. Each event has an audience capacity of 1,200 with a ticket price of $40, and is entirely staffed by volunteers.

Income and expenditure account

	Notes	20X5	20X4
Income:		$000	$000
Share of operating surplus from EmCA	1	49	38
Summer concerts	2	268	275
Total income		317	313
Expenditure:			
Operation of pool	3	(27)	(57)
Summer concerts	4	(242)	(203)
Surplus for year		48	53

Statement of financial position

	Notes	20X5	20X4
		$000	$000
Non-current assets	5	38	55
Current assets:			
Amount due from EmCA		89	102
Cash at bank		877	805
		966	907
Total assets		1,004	962
Funds		1,000	952
Non-current liabilities		4	10
		1,004	962

Notes:

1   Under the management agreement, EmCA submits monthly reports of pool attendance and pool fees received, as well as expense reports. A monthly statement shows TPT's share of EmCA's operating surplus.

2   Income includes ticket sales and the sale of food and drink.

3   Included within pool operation costs are audit fees of $4,000 (20X4: $4,000) and depreciation of $17,000 (20X4: $36,000). The remainder of the costs relate to sundry support costs.

4   Summer concert expenditure includes fees to the bands and the cost of food and drink.

5   The non-current assets note indicates that depreciation expense is the only movement during the year and that the majority of assets are already fully depreciated.

Audit strategy

Audit risk assessment

The greatest risks of material misstatement are:

- Understatement (completeness) of concert income – decreased by $7,000 (2.5%).

- Overstatement of concert expenses – increased by $39,000 (19.2%).

There may be detection risk if adequate accounting records are not maintained for all income and expenditure. For example, if bands are paid cash in hand on the day of the concert there may not be any audit trail for this expense.

Control implications

Controls should be in place to ensure the completeness of income, for example:

- Pre-numbered tickets for each concert

- Recording issues of concert tickets for sale

- Requiring the return of unsold concert tickets

- Reconciling ticket income against the number of tickets sold

- Only allowing admission by ticket. Tickets should be checked at the gate and once scanned/checked, cannot be used again to gain entry. If ticket sales were allowed on the gate, volunteers may pocket the cash.

- Purchase of items within the concert such as food and drink must be by credit or debit card. No cash should be accepted, to reduce the risk of theft by the volunteers.

- Reconciling pool income recorded to the number of visitors on a daily basis.

- Reconciling pool income recorded to the cash/credit card receipts on a daily basis.

Audit plan

Due to the audit risks identified, the audit approach will be substantive.

Share of operating surplus from EmCA and amounts due from EmCA

- Obtain a breakdown by month of the operating surplus from EmCA, cast and agree to the financial statements.

- Agree the monthly surplus amounts to the breakdown to confirm accuracy.

- Using the monthly reports of pool attendance and fees, calculate the expected income for the pool and compare to the amount included in the financial statements.

- Obtain direct confirmation from EmCA of the amount due.

- Agree after-date cash receipts to the amounts due at the year end.

Income from and expenditure on the summer concerts

- Obtain ticket sale data and multiply by the ticket price to confirm the amount of income recorded.

- Compare income for the current year to the prior year and investigate any significant differences e.g. enquire with management why concert income is 2.5% lower this year and consider whether the explanation is reasonable.

- Perform a reasonable test comparing recorded ticket income with maximum revenue (1,200 × $40 × 6) = $288,000.

- Agree the cost of beverages to purchase invoices to confirm accuracy of recording.

- Calculate mark-up on cost to confirm the completeness of income.

- Compare costs by category to the prior year and investigate any significant differences.

- Inspect invoices to confirm the fees paid to the bands, if available.

- Agree amounts paid to bands to the cash book and bank statements.

Pool operating costs

- Obtain a breakdown of operating costs, cast and agree to the financial statements.

- Agree a sample of costs to invoice, cash book and bank statements.

- Perform analytical procedures by comparing the costs to prior year and investigate any significant differences.

Non-current assets

- Obtain the non-current asset register, cast and agree the total to the financial statements.

- Trace a sample of assets from the NCA register to the physical assets to confirm existence.

- Trace a sample of physical assets through to inclusion in the NCA register to confirm completeness.

- Recalculate the depreciation expense to confirm arithmetical accuracy.

Cash at bank

- Obtain a bank confirmation letter confirming the bank balances at the year end.

- Obtain and cast the bank reconciliation and agree the balance per the cash book to the cash book and financial statements.

- Trace reconciling items on the bank reconciliation to the post year end bank statements and pre-year-end cash book.

The procedures above are typical audit procedures that would be used in the audit of a profit making entity. Audits of NFPs are not different to those of a profit making company, however, the audit risks are different due to the nature of the entity.

In addition to the financial statement audit, a value for money audit may be performed to assess whether TPT is getting value for money from the services provided by EMCA. A VFM audit may identify that TFT could obtain a more cost effective service by using another provider or by managing its own activities instead of outsourcing.

Test your understanding 6

(a)   List and explain FOUR assertions that relate to the recording of classes of transactions.

(4 marks)

(b)   List FOUR assertions relevant to the audit of tangible non-current assets and state one audit procedure which provides appropriate evidence for each assertion.

(4 marks)

(Total: 8 marks)

Test your understanding 7

You are an audit senior working at a medium sized firm of auditors. One of your clients is an exclusive hotel, Numero Uno, situated in the centre of Big City.

Numero Uno prides itself on delivering a first class dining experience and is renowned for its standards of service and cooking. Its inventory therefore consists of the very best foods and beverages from around the world.

Food products held in inventory are mostly fresh as the head chef will only work with the very best ingredients. Food inventory is stored in the kitchens and managed by the head chef himself.

The majority of beverages held at the hotel are expensive wines that have been sourced from exclusive vineyards. The hotel also stocks a wide range of spirits and mixers. All beverages are stored either in the hotel cellar or behind the bar. The cellar can only be accessed by the duty manager who holds the key. As part of your audit procedures you will attend the year-end inventory count of the hotel's beverages.

Required:

(a)   Describe the audit procedures an auditor would conduct before and whilst attending the inventory count of the beverages in the hotel.

(7 marks)

(b)   Identify and explain THREE financial statement assertions that are most relevant to inventory.

(3 marks)

(c)   Apart from attending the inventory count, describe the substantive procedures an auditor would carry out to confirm the valuation of the wine and spirits held in inventory at the year-end.

(5 marks)

(Total: 15 marks)

 Test your understanding 8

(a)   Describe the steps an auditor should take when conducting a trade receivables confirmation (circularisation) test.

(4 marks)

(b)   Explain why a direct confirmation test may not provide sufficient appropriate audit evidence on its own.

(3 marks)

You are the audit manager in charge of the audit of Builders Mate, a limited liability company with a year ended 31 March. Builders Mate has been an audit client for three years. Builders Mate sells small tools, plant and equipment exclusively to the building trade. It has 12 warehouse style shops located throughout the country. Builders Mate does not manufacture any products.

The audit fieldwork is due to commence in 3 weeks' time and you are preparing the audit work programme for the trade receivables section of the audit. Extracts from the client's trial balance show the following information.

	$
Trade receivables control account	124,500
General trade receivables allowance	(2,490)
Specific trade receivables allowance	0

From your review of last year's audit file you have determined that last year there were 2 specific allowances of $5,000 and $2,000 as well as a 3% general allowance.

Initial conversations with the client indicate that there are no specific allowances to be made this year, however, the general allowance will be reduced from 3% to 2%.

You are aware that two of Builders Mate's major customers went into administration during the year and they are likely to be liquidated in the near future. Both of these customers owed material amounts at the yearend.

Required:

(c) **Describe substantive procedures the auditor should perform on the year-end trade receivables of Builders Mate.**

(9 marks)

(d) **Describe how audit software could facilitate the audit of trade receivables.**

(4 marks)

(Total: 20 marks)

 Test your understanding 9

You are auditing the revenue section of the financial statements of Ningaloo Co. Internal controls have been evaluated as effective. Substantive procedures have not yet been performed. During the risk assessment you identified that a performance related bonus has been introduced for salesmen who reach a target sales figure each quarter.

1   **Which of the following statements is correct?**

A   As controls are working effectively within Ningaloo Co the audit plan does not need to contain any substantive procedures as full reliance can be placed on the control system

B   The auditor will perform the same level of substantive procedures as were performed in the prior year

C   The level of substantive procedures may be reduced as a result of the controls being found to work effectively

D   The level of substantive procedures should increase if controls are found to be working effectively

2   'Select a sample of goods despatch notes from just before and just after the year-end and trace to the sales day book'. Which financial statement assertion is addressed by this audit procedure?

   A   Occurrence

   B   Completeness

   C   Cut-off

   D   Accuracy

3   Which of the following statements is correct with regard to directional testing?

   A   A procedure that directly tests receivables for overstatement will indirectly test revenue for understatement

   B   A procedure that directly tests receivables for overstatement will indirectly test revenue for overstatement

   C   To test revenue for overstatement the auditor must choose a sample from outside of the accounting system, such as GDNS, and trace them into the accounting system

   D   To test revenue for understatement the auditor must choose a sample from within the accounting system and trace it to the GDN

4   Which of the following is an analytical procedure that can be used to test revenue?

   A   Comparison of revenue in the current year to revenue in the prior year

   B   Review of credit notes issued post year-end

   C   Inspection of a sample of goods despatch notes and sales invoices

   D   Recalculation of the sales day book

5   Sales managers have recorded fictitious sales in order to earn a larger bonus. Which of the following assertions is affected by this?

   A   Existence

   B   Completeness

   C   Accuracy

   D   Occurrence

Test your understanding 10

You are performing procedures over the non-current assets balance for your client Leveque Co. The balance consists of motor vehicles, fixtures and fittings and land and buildings. Motor vehicles are replaced on a three-year cycle. Fixtures and fittings are replaced as and when required. The company uses the following depreciation rates:

- Land and buildings – no depreciation is charged due to values increasing

- Fixtures and fittings – 10% straight line

- Motor vehicles – 20% straight line.

1 **Which of the following best describes the audit risk resulting from the depreciation policy used for land and buildings?**

    A   Land and buildings may not exist

    B   Land and buildings may not be completely recorded

    C   Land and buildings may be understated

    D   Land and buildings may be overstated

2 **Which of the following procedures provides the most reliable evidence to assess whether 10% straight line is an appropriate rate for fixtures and fittings?**

    A   Enquire of the client whether the rate is appropriate and how they chose that rate

    B   Contact the supplier of the fixtures to ask how long the fixtures should last

    C   Review disposals of fixtures and fittings to identify how long the assets had been used by Leveque Co and whether any significant profit or loss on disposal arose

    D   Compare the rate with other audit clients of your firm

3 **Which of the following statements is true in respect of Leveque's motor vehicles?**

    A   The depreciation rate is unreasonable as the company only uses the assets for three years therefore depreciation should be charged over three years

    B   Motor vehicles have a useful life of longer than five years therefore depreciation should be charged over a longer period

    C   The depreciation rate is reasonable

    D   The depreciation charge for motor vehicles is unlikely to be material therefore the rate used does not matter

4   **The audit plan includes a procedure to trace a sample of assets included in the non-current asset register to the physical asset. Which assertion is being tested?**

   A   Existence

   B   Completeness

   C   Valuation

   D   Rights and obligations

5   **Which of the following procedures provides the most reliable evidence when confirming rights and obligations for a non-current asset?**

   A   Physical inspection of the assets

   B   Inspection of the fixtures and fittings invoice

   C   Inspection of a valuation report for land and buildings

   D   Written representation from management confirming ownership

Test your understanding 11

You are assigned to the audit team of Carnarvon Co performing testing over non-current assets.

1   **Which of the following is NOT an audit procedure from ISA 500 *Audit Evidence*?**

   A   Inspection

   B   Enquiry

   C   Check

   D   Recalculate

2   **Which of the following audit procedures would confirm the existence of property, plant and equipment?**

   A   Recalculate the depreciation charge using the company's accounting policy

   B   Physically inspect a sample of assets listed in the non-current asset register

   C   Reconcile the schedule of property, plant and equipment with the general ledger

   D   Review the repairs and maintenance expense account in the statement of profit or loss for items of a capital nature

3   **Which of the following is NOT a financial statement assertion relevant to your testing of non-current assets?**

A   Occurrence

B   Completeness

C   Rights and obligations

D   Existence

4   **Which of the following issues would result in a misstatement in the non-current assets balance?**

(i)   An error in recording the cost of the asset.

(ii)   A misclassification between fixtures & fittings and motor vehicles.

(iii)   The depreciation charge has been correctly credited to accumulated depreciation but debited to the irrecoverable debt expense account.

(iv)   A purchase invoice not being recorded in the asset register.

A   (ii) and (iv)

B   (i) and (iii)

C   (ii) and (iii)

D   (i) and (iv)

5   **When testing the assertion of rights and obligations over land and buildings, which of the following would provide the most reliable evidence?**

A   Inspection of the insurance policy

B   Physical inspection of the land and buildings

C   Inspection of the title deeds

D   Inspection of the non-current asset register

14 Chapter summary

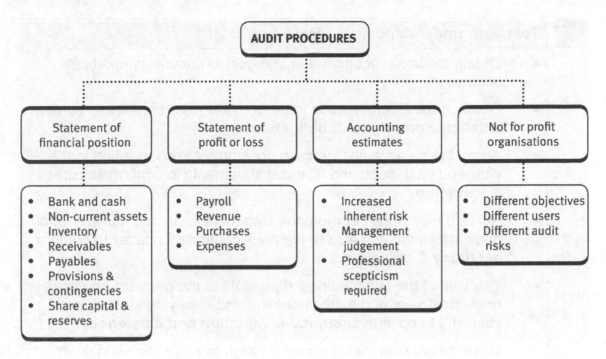

AUDIT PROCEDURES

Statement of financial position
- Bank and cash
- Non-current assets
- Inventory
- Receivables
- Payables
- Provisions & contingencies
- Share capital & reserves

Statement of profit or loss
- Payroll
- Revenue
- Purchases
- Expenses

Accounting estimates
- Increased inherent risk
- Management judgement
- Professional scepticism required

Not for profit organisations
- Different objectives
- Different users
- Different audit risks

Test your understanding answers

Test your understanding 1 – Bank and cash

- Obtain the bank reconciliation and cast to ensure arithmetical accuracy.

- Obtain a bank confirmation letter from Murray's bankers to confirm **existence and rights & obligations**.

- Agree the balance per the cash book on the reconciliation to the year-end cash book and financial statements to confirm **accuracy & valuation**.

- Agree the balance per the bank statement to an original year-end bank statement and also to the bank confirmation letter to confirm **accuracy & valuation**.

- Trace all of the outstanding lodgements to the pre year-end cash book, post year-end bank statement and to paying-in-book pre year-end to confirm **accuracy & valuation and existence**.

- Trace all unpresented cheques through to a pre year-end cash book and post year-end statement. For any unusual amounts or significant delays obtain explanations from management to confirm **accuracy & valuation and completeness**.

- Examine any old unpresented cheques to assess if they need to be written back into the purchase ledger to confirm **accuracy & valuation and completeness**.

- Inspect the bank confirmation letter for details of any security provided by the company or any legal right of set-off as this may require disclosure to confirm appropriate **presentation**.

- Review the cash book and bank statements for any unusual items or large transfers around the year-end, as this could be evidence of window dressing. This verifies **completeness, existence**.

- Count the petty cash in the cash tin at the year-end and agree the total to the balance included in the financial statements to confirm **accuracy & valuation, and existence**.

Test your understanding 2 – Non-current assets

- Obtain the non-current asset register, cast and agree the totals to the financial statements: **completeness, classification, presentation**.

- Select a sample of assets from the non-current asset register and physically inspect them: **existence**.

- Select a sample of assets visible at the Murray's premises and inspect the asset register to ensure they are included: **completeness**.

- Inspect assets for condition and usage to identify signs of impairment: **valuation**.

- For revalued assets, inspect the independent valuation report and agree the amount stated to the amount included in the general ledger and the financial statements: **valuation**; and ensure that all assets in the same class have been revalued.

- Obtain a list of additions and for a sample, agree the cost to supplier invoice: **valuation**.

- Select a sample from the list of additions and review the description on the invoice to confirm that they relate to capital expenditure items rather than repairs and maintenance: **existence**.

- Inspect a breakdown of repairs and maintenance expenditure for the year to identify items of a capital nature: **completeness.**

- For a sample of assets included in the non-current asset register, inspect supplier invoices (for equipment), title deeds (for property), and registration documents (for motor vehicles) to ensure they are in the name of the client: **rights and obligations**.

Disposals

- Obtain a breakdown of disposals, cast the list and agree all assets have been removed from the non-current asset register: **existence**.

- Select a sample of disposals and agree sale proceeds to supporting documentation such as sundry sales invoices: **accuracy of profit on disposal**.

- Recalculate the profit/loss on disposal and agree to the statement of profit or loss: **accuracy of profit on disposal**.

Depreciation

- Inspect the capital expenditure budgets for the next few years to assess the appropriateness of the useful economic lives in light of plans to replace assets: **valuation**.

- Review profits and losses on disposal of assets disposed of in the year to assess the reasonableness of the depreciation policies (if depreciation policies are reasonable, there should not be a significant profit or loss): **valuation**.

- Compare depreciation rates to companies with the same type of assets to assess reasonableness: **valuation**.

- Recalculate the depreciation charge for a sample of assets to verify arithmetical accuracy: **accuracy, valuation**.

- Recalculate the depreciation charge for revalued assets to ensure the charge is based on the new carrying value: **accuracy, valuation**.

- Perform a proof in total calculation for the depreciation charged for each category of assets, discuss with management if significant fluctuations arise: **completeness, valuation**. **(Analytical procedure)**

- Inspect the financial statement disclosure of the depreciation charges and policies in the draft financial statements and compare to the prior year to ensure consistency: **presentation**.

Test your understanding 3 – Inventory

(a) **Before the inventory count**

- Contact the client to obtain a copy of the inventory count instructions to understand how the count will be conducted and assess the effectiveness of the count process.

- Review working papers obtained from the previous auditor (in subsequent years inspect prior year working papers) to understand the inventory count process and identify any issues that should be taken into account this year.

- Contact the client to obtain details of date, time and locations of the inventory count(s).

- Obtain a list of locations where inventory is stored and select which locations will be attended by the audit firm if not all locations can be visited. Priority should be given to locations with a high value of inventory or locations with poor controls.

- Consider the need for using an expert to assist in valuing the inventory being counted.

- Ascertain whether any inventory is held by third parties, and if possible, make arrangements to visit the third party site.

- Request a direct confirmation of inventory balances held at the year-end from any third party warehouse providers regarding quantities and condition of inventory owned by the client.

(b) **During the count**

Tests of controls

- Observe the count to ensure that the inventory count instructions are being followed. For example:

  - No movements of inventory occur during the count.

  - Teams of two people perform the count.

  - Sections of inventory are tagged as counted to prevent double counting.

  - Damaged/obsolete items have been separately identified so they can be valued appropriately.

- Inspect the count sheets to ensure they have been completed in pen rather than pencil.

- Inspect the count sheets to ensure they show the description of the goods but do not show the quantities expected to be counted.

- Re-perform the sequence check on the count sheets to ensure none are missing.

- Enquire of the counting staff which department they work in to ensure they are not warehouse staff.

Substantive procedures

- Select a sample of items from the inventory count sheets and physically inspect the items in the warehouse: **existence**.

- Select a sample of physical items from the warehouse and trace to the inventory count sheets to ensure that they are recorded accurately: **completeness**.

- Enquire of management whether goods held on behalf of third parties are segregated and recorded separately: **rights and obligations**.

- Inspect the inventory being counted for evidence of damage or obsolescence that may affect the net realisable value: **valuation**.

- Record details of the last deliveries prior to the year-end. This information will be used in the final audit to ensure that no further amendments have been made: **completeness & existence**.

- Obtain copies of the inventory count sheets at the end of the inventory count, ready for checking against the final inventory listing at the final audit: **completeness** and **existence**.

- Attend the inventory count at the third party warehouses: **completeness and existence**.

(c) **At the final audit**

- Trace the items counted during the inventory count to the final inventory list to ensure it is the same as the one used at the year-end and to ensure that any errors identified during counting procedures have been rectified: **completeness, presentation**.

- Cast the list (showing inventory categorised between finished goods, WIP and raw materials) to ensure arithmetical accuracy and agree totals to financial statement disclosures: **completeness, classification**.

- Trace goods received immediately prior to the year-end to year-end payables and inventory balances: **completeness & existence**.

- Trace goods despatched immediately prior to year-end to the general ledger to ensure the items are not included in inventory and revenue (and receivables where relevant): **completeness & existence**.

- Inspect purchase invoices for the name of the client: **rights and obligations**.

- Inspect purchase invoices for a sample of inventory items to agree the cost of the items: **valuation**.

- Inspect post year-end sales invoices for a sample of inventory items to determine if the net realisable value is reasonable. This will also assist in determining if inventory is held at the lower of cost and net realisable value: **valuation**.

- Recalculate work-in-progress and finished goods valuations using payroll records for labour costs and utility bills for overhead absorption: **valuation**.

- Inspect the ageing of inventory items to identify old/slow-moving amounts that may require an allowance, and discuss these with management: **valuation**.

- Calculate the inventory holding period and compare this to prior year to identify slow-moving inventory which requires an allowance to bring the value down to the lower of cost and NRV: **valuation. (Analytical procedure)**

- Calculate the gross profit margin and compare this to prior year, investigate any significant differences that may highlight an error in cost of sales and closing inventory: **valuation. (Analytical procedure)**

Test your understanding 4 – Receivables

(a) **Jockeys:** the outstanding balance is over 20% of the total receivables balance at the year-end and is therefore material.

Golf is Us: this large and old balance may require write-off or a specific allowance to be made if the recoverability of the amount is in doubt (similarly for Escot supermarket).

Tike & Co: the large and old credit balance on the listing suggests that an error may have been made. A payment from another customer may have been misallocated to this account or the customer may have overpaid an invoice, or paid an invoice twice in error. It may be appropriate to reclassify this balance, along with the balance for Whistlers, as a trade payable.

Whistlers: although the amount is small, the credit balance appears to be due to a difference between a recent large payment and the outstanding balance. This error may indicate other potential errors, and requires further investigation.

There are other balances that could be identified and justified for similar reasons to the above.

(b) **Receivables procedures**

- Obtain the aged receivables listing, cast it and agree the total to the financial statements: **accuracy and presentation**.

- Agree the receivables ledger control account with the receivables ledger list of balances: **completeness** and **existence**.

- Select a sample of year-end receivable balances and agree back to valid supporting documentation of GDN and sales order: **existence**.

- Inspect after date cash receipts and follow through to pre year-end receivable balances: **valuation, rights and obligations** and **existence**.

- Select a sample of goods despatch notes (GDN) before and just after the year-end and follow through to the sales invoice to ensure they are recorded in the correct accounting period: **completeness** and **existence** (**cut-off** of revenue).

- Perform a positive receivables circularisation of a representative sample of Murray Co's year-end balances, for any non-replies, with Murray Co's permission, send a reminder letter to follow-up: **existence** and **rights and obligations**.

- Inspect the aged receivables report to identify any slow-moving balances (such as Bibs and Balls, Golf is Us, James Smit Partnership) and discuss these with the credit control manager to assess whether an allowance or write-down is necessary: **valuation** and **allocation**.

- Discuss any significant balances with management (such as Escot, Jockeys, Golf is Us, James Smit Partnership, Stayrose Supermarket) to identify any issues regarding payment: **valuation**.

- Inspect customer correspondence in respect of any slow-moving/aged balances to assess whether there are any invoices in dispute: **valuation**.

- Inspect board minutes of Murray Co to assess whether there are any material disputed receivables that may require write-off: **valuation**.

- Inspect the receivables ledger for any credit balances (such as Whistler and Tike) and discuss with management whether these should be reclassified as payables: **existence of receivables** and **completeness of payables, classification**.

- Inspect a sample of post year-end credit notes to identify any that relate to pre year-end transactions to ensure that they have not been included in receivables: **existence** (**occurrence** of revenue).

- Calculate the average receivables collection period and compare this to prior year, investigate any significant differences: **completeness** and **valuation. (Analytical procedure)**

Test your understanding 5 – Payables

Many companies send out monthly statements of account as part of their credit control procedures. It is likely that audit clients will receive a number of these statements from suppliers at the year-end. These can be reconciled to the payables control account to ensure the accounting records are correct. This is known as a supplier statement reconciliation and is an important source of audit evidence.

There are two main reasons why there may be a variance:

- **Timing differences,** e.g. invoices sent by the supplier but not yet received by the customer; payments sent by the customer but not yet received by the supplier; returns and credit notes not yet appearing on the supplier's statement; or

- **Errors.**

(a) **Reconciliation of payables ledger balance to balance on supplier's statement:**

		$	$
Balance per payables ledger:			**59,800**
Differences:			
(i)	31.11: Discount not allowed by supplier	1,260	
(ii)	04.11: Transposition error, invoice 6080	1,800	
(iii)	04.12: Invoice 6210 not on payables ledger	47,350	
(iv)	28.12: Invoice 6355 not on payables ledger	62,980	
(v)	31.12: Cash in transit	60,050	
(vi)	Discount not allowed	1,230	
			174,670
Balance per supplier's statement:			**234,470**

(b) **Audit work**

(i) The date of the cash payment for the October invoices suggests that Racket Co will not have received the cheque for $61,630 until after the 30 November and so Murray Co may not be entitled to the 2% cash discount. The entry in Murray Co's ledger suggest the cheque was posted on 30 November however this is not conclusive evidence that the cheque was actually sent to Racket Co on this date.

- The auditor should enquire with Murray Co's payables ledger controller about this item, and inspect correspondence with Racket Co to establish entitlement to the discount.

- If Murray Co is obliged to pay the 2% disallowed discount, this should be added to the payables ledger balance.

- If Racket Co will allow the discount, there is no need to make any adjustments to the payables ledger balance.

(ii) The apparent transposition error on invoice 6080 should be checked by inspecting the invoice.

- If the invoice shows $37,520, then an additional payable of $1,800 should be included at the year-end to correct this error.

- No adjustment will be necessary if Murray Co's figure is correct.

(iii) It appears that invoice 6210 for $47,350 has not been included on Murray Co's payables ledger.

- The auditor should enquire with the warehouse manager whether these goods have been received.

- The GRNs around the expected delivery date should be inspected to identify the relevant GRN.

- Correspondence with Racket Co should be reviewed for discussions relating to a dispute regarding these goods (if relevant).

- If the goods have been received, the purchase invoices file should be inspected to identify if there is a related purchase invoice.

- If there is a purchase invoice, the auditor should enquire with the purchases department why the invoice has not been posted to the payables ledger. This may be because of a dispute (e.g. an incorrect price, the wrong quantity or a fault with the goods).

- If the goods relating to this invoice are in inventory (or have been sold) a purchase accrual should be made for this item (note that the actual quantity of goods received should be accrued for) and correspondence relating to this invoice with Racket Co should be inspected to assess what payment has been agreed.

- If the goods have not been received, no adjustment needs to be made (but a copy of correspondence disputing the delivery/invoice should be placed on file as evidence).

(iv) The appropriate treatment of invoice 6355 depends on whether or not Murray Co received the goods before the year-end.

- The auditor should inspect the GRN for the date to determine if the goods were received before the year-end.

- If the date is before the year-end, Murray Co should be asked to include a purchase accrual at the year-end for this invoice.

(v) The cheque on 31 December appears to be cash in transit.

- The auditor should inspect Murray Co's bank statement to confirm that the cheque was cleared by the bank after the year-end.

- If the cheque cleared within one week of the year-end (with most other cheques issued immediately before the year-end) then this is valid cash in transit.

- If most cheques issued immediately before the year-end take more than a week to clear, this indicates window-dressing of the financial statements (i.e. the cheques were actually sent out after the year-end), in which case the amounts should be credited back to trade payables and debited back to cash.

(iv) If, as appears likely, the cheque for $60,050 is not received by Racket Co until sometime after the year-end, then the discount of $1,230 may be disallowed. If this discount is disallowed, it should be added to payables at the year-end (see (i) above).

Test your understanding 6

(a) **Assertions: classes of transactions**

- **Occurrence**: The transactions and events that have been recorded and disclosed have actually occurred and pertain to the entity.

- **Completeness**: All transactions and events that should have been recorded have been recorded.

- **Accuracy**: The amounts and other data relating to recorded transactions and events have been recorded appropriately.

- **Cut-off**: Transactions and events have been recorded in the correct accounting period.

- **Classification**: Transactions and events have been recorded in the proper accounts.

- **Presentation**: Transactions and events are appropriately aggregated or disaggregated and clearly described, and related disclosures are relevant and understandable in the context of the applicable financial reporting framework.

Note: Only four assertions required.

(b) **Tangible non-current assets: assertions and procedures**

- **Completeness:** Agree a sample of assets physically verified on the premises back to the asset register to ensure that all non-current assets are recorded.

- **Existence:** Physically inspect a sample of assets included in the non-current asset register to verify existence.

- **Accuracy, valuation and allocation:** Recalculate the depreciation charge to ensure arithmetical accuracy.

- **Rights and obligations**: Inspect an appropriate document of ownership for example, a purchase invoice, for the client's name to confirm the entity owns or controls the asset.

- **Classification/Presentation:** Inspect the non-current asset disclosure note in the financial statements and agree the figures to the non-current asset register to ensure assets are properly disclosed under the correct headings as required by IAS 16 *Property, Plant and Equipment.*

Test your understanding 7

(a) **Before the count**

- Inspect prior year working papers to understand the inventory count process and identify any issues that should be taken into account this year.

- Contact Numero Uno (client) to obtain inventory count instructions for this year to understand how the count will be conducted and assess the effectiveness of the count process.

- Ascertain whether any inventory is held by third parties. Determine how to gather sufficient appropriate evidence e.g. by visiting the premises or requesting an external confirmation.

- Consider the need for using an expert to assist in valuing the inventory being counted. There may be some specialty wines and spirits that require expert valuation.

During the count

- Observe the count to ensure that the instructions are being followed.

- Inspect the bottles being counted for evidence of damage or obsolescence that may affect the net realisable value and hence overall valuation of inventory.

- Select a sample of beverages from the inventory count sheets and physically inspect the items in the cellar or bar to confirm they exist.

- Select a sample of physical beverages from the cellar or bar and trace to the inventory count sheets to ensure that they are recorded accurately and therefore that the records are complete.

- Record cut-off information by obtaining details of the last deliveries prior to the year-end. This information will be used in final audit to ensure that no further amendments have been made which could result in overstatement or understatement of inventory.

(b) **Inventory assertions**

Identify	Explain
Existence	The inventory recorded actually exists.
Rights and obligations	The company owns or controls the asset and therefore has the right to record the inventories in its financial statements.
Completeness	All inventory balances have been recorded.
Accuracy, valuation and allocation	Inventories are valued appropriately (i.e. at lower of cost and net realisable value).
Cut-off	Inventory movements around the year-end are recorded in the correct period.
Presentation	Inventory is disclosed properly in the financial statements as raw materials, work in progress and finished goods.

(c) **Substantive procedures**

– Trace the items counted during the inventory count to the final inventory listing to ensure the quantities are the same and any errors identified during counting procedures have been rectified.

– Inspect purchases invoices for a sample of beverages to agree cost, ensuring that the description of goods on the invoice matches the beverage.

– For beverages sold to customers after the year-end, inspect a sample of restaurant bills/invoices back to the final inventory records ensuring that the sales value exceeds the cost. Where sales value is less than cost, ensure that the beverage is stated at the realisable value.

– For high value items such as champagne, vintage wine and exotic spirits, use an expert valuer to review the net realisable value of a sample of items to ensure the value is reasonable.

– Inventory noted during the count as obsolete or damaged should be traced to the inventory records to ensure the valuation has been adjusted to take this into account. The expert valuer may provide assistance with these valuations.

Test your understanding 8

(a) **Trade receivables circularisation**

– Obtain client approval to perform a direct confirmation of trade receivables.

– Obtain the list of receivables balances, and cast it.

– Select a suitable sample from the list of receivables balances using an appropriate sampling technique.

– Prepare the confirmation letters ensuring the contact details are correct and return details clearly state that the reply should be made direct to the auditor. A business reply envelope, addressed to the auditor, could be included for this purpose.

– Ask the client to print the letters on client-headed paper and sign them. The letters should then be returned to the auditor.

– The auditor should send the letters, including any follow-up requests. This process should be controlled by the auditor to ensure the integrity of the test.

– Reconcile replies received to the audit client's receivables accounting records.

– Perform alternative audit procedures on balances where no response to the confirmation letter is received.

(b) **Sufficiency of the evidence from a direct confirmation test**

– There is often a low response rate from trade receivables meaning that other audit procedures will be required for these balances.

– The type of confirmation letter, whether a positive or negative confirmation request, will influence the sufficiency of evidence gathered. Negative confirmations provide less persuasive audit evidence than positive confirmations and it is unlikely that a negative confirmation will provide sufficient evidence on its own.

– The reliability of the responses to the confirmation requests may be in doubt, for example if there is a risk of fraud being perpetrated.

– Mistakes and errors may be present in the accounting records of the trade receivables confirming the balance outstanding.

– Customers may agree with balances containing errors in their favour.

(c) Substantive procedures for trade receivables

- Obtain the receivables listing, cast it to verify arithmetical accuracy and agree the total to the financial statements.

- Confirm the trade receivables control account balance matches the sum of the individual trade receivables ledger accounts to confirm completeness.

- For a sample GDNs around the year-end, trace to the sales invoice and ledger accounts to ensure that the transactions have been recorded in the correct accounting period.

- Select a sample of individual trade receivables and perform a direct confirmation test using a positive confirmation letter.

- Inspect the cash book and bank statements for cash received post year-end.

- Recalculate the general allowance based on the 2% figure to ensure arithmetical accuracy.

- Discuss with management why the general allowance has reduced from 3% to 2% and assess the reasonableness of the explanations provided and the reason for not making specific allowances for the two customers in administration who owe material amounts at the year-end.

- Inspect the aged receivables analysis to identify aged debts that may require a specific allowance. Discuss with management any such balances and ensure specific allowances are made if appropriate.

- Confirm that the specific allowances made in the prior year were either written-off or the cash was recovered in the current accounting period.

(d) Audit software

- Audit software can be used to prepare an aged receivables analysis and to identify potential irrecoverable debts using a range of criteria set by the auditor.

- Audit software can be used to quickly identify credit balances or negative balances within the receivables ledger.

- Audit software will be more efficient and accurate at casting the receivables ledger and recalculating figures such as the general allowance.

- It could also select a sample for testing and prepare direct confirmation letters.

Test your understanding 9		
1	C	Substantive procedures must be performed on all material balances, even if controls are working effectively. This is due to the inherent limitations of controls. However, the level may be reduced if controls are found to be effective.
2	C	Selecting transactions around the year-end tests the assertion of cut-off.
3	B	If the receivable was overstated the related sale would also be overstated. To test for overstatement the auditor must choose a sample from within the accounting system and trace it back to supporting documentation.
4	A	B, C and D are all substantive tests of detail as they focus attention on individual sales transactions. Comparison of sales in the current year to the prior year is an analytical procedure as it is focused on identifying unusual trends or fluctuations which may indicate misstatement.
5	D	Occurrence. The transaction will not have occurred if it is fictitious. Existence is not relevant to the statement of profit or loss.

Test your understanding 10

1	D	Depreciation affects the valuation assertion therefore options A and B are incorrect. If depreciation has not been charged, the assets will be overvalued therefore option C is incorrect.
2	C	Enquiry on its own is not the most reliable form of evidence and should be corroborated with other procedures. The auditor would not contact the supplier and this would not provide evidence of the useful life of the fixtures to Leveque Co. Comparison with other clients is only useful if those clients are in the same type of industry and using the same type of assets in the same manner as Leveque Co.
3	A	The depreciation rate should match the usage of the asset by the company, therefore the rate should be based on 3 years not 5 years. As no figures are given for the motor vehicles it cannot be said that depreciation will be immaterial.
4	A	Testing from the ledger to the source addresses the assertion of existence.
5	B	Physical inspection verifies existence. A valuation certificate verifies the valuation of the land and buildings. Neither of these procedures confirms the assets are owned or controlled by Leveque Co. Written confirmation is not a reliable form of evidence for the assertion of rights and obligations as better procedures can be performed. The purchase invoice for fixtures and fittings should contain the name of the client which would help verify rights and obligations.

Test your understanding 11

1	C	Check is not a valid procedure. Every procedure 'checks' something. The auditor can check through inspection, enquiry, observation, etc.
2	B	Option A tests the accuracy of a depreciation charge. Options C and D test the completeness of PPE. Option B confirms existence.
3	A	Occurrence is an assertion relevant to the statement of profit or loss, not the statement of financial position.
4	D	A misclassification between motor vehicles and fixtures & fittings will not affect the overall non-current assets balance. The depreciation charge has been correctly credited to accumulated depreciation therefore the asset's carrying value will be correctly calculated. The mis-posting to irrecoverable debt expense will mean the classification of the expense in the statement of profit or loss is incorrect. An error recording the cost of the asset will mean the asset is misstated. If the purchase invoice relating to the asset is not recorded, assets will be understated.
5	C	The other procedures do not confirm the client owns or controls the assets. The title deeds in the client's name will confirm ownership.

Completion and review

Chapter learning objectives

This chapter covers syllabus areas:

- E1 – Subsequent events
- E2 – Going concern
- E3 – Written representations
- E4 – Audit finalisation and the final review

Detailed syllabus objectives are provided in the introduction section of the text book.

PER

One of the PER performance objectives (PO20) is to review and report on the findings of an audit. You complete an audit, preparing the formal documentation and reporting any control deficiencies to management. You report back to managers in a formal audit report. Working through this chapter should help you understand how to demonstrate that objective.

1 Introduction

After the auditor has completed the substantive testing there are still many procedures that need to be performed before they can sign the auditor's report. These include:

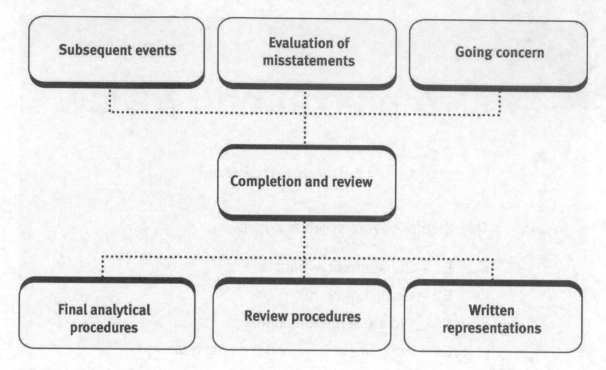

2 Subsequent events

 A subsequent event is: **An event occurring between the date of the financial statements and the date of the auditor's report, and facts that become known to the auditor after the date of the auditor's report**. [ISA 560 *Subsequent Events*, 5e].

ISA 560 *Subsequent Events,* para 4, requires the auditor to:

*   Obtain sufficient appropriate audit evidence about whether events occurring between the date of the financial statements and the date of the auditor's report, that require adjustment or disclosure are appropriately reflected in accordance with the applicable financial reporting framework.

*   Respond appropriately to facts that become known to the auditor after the date of the auditor's report.

IAS 10 *Events After the Reporting Period* identifies two types of event after the reporting period:

*   Adjusting

*   Non-adjusting.

Illustration 1 – Adjusting and non-adjusting events

Adjusting events

These are events that provide additional evidence relating to conditions existing at the reporting date. Such events provide new information about the items included in the financial statements and hence the financial statements should be adjusted to reflect the new information.

Examples of **adjusting** events include:

- Allowances for damaged inventory and doubtful receivables.

- Amounts received or receivable in respect of insurance claims which were being negotiated at the reporting date.

- The determination of the purchase or sale price of non-current assets purchased or sold before the year-end.

- Agreement of a tax liability.

- Discovery of errors/fraud revealing that the financial statements are incorrect.

Non-adjusting events

These are events concerning conditions which arose after the reporting date. If material, disclosure is required in the notes to the financial statements indicating what effect the events may have. Such events, therefore, will not have any effect on items in the statements of financial position or statement of profit or loss for the period.

Examples of **non-adjusting** events include:

- Issue of new share or loan capital.

- Major changes in the composition of the group (for example, mergers, acquisitions or reconstructions).

- Losses of non-current assets or inventory as a result of fires or floods.

- Strikes, government action such as nationalisation.

- Purchases/sales of significant non-current assets.

(IAS 10 *Events After the Reporting Period*)

Auditor responsibilities

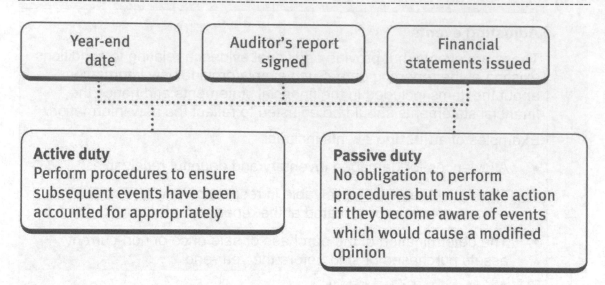

Year-end date → **Auditor's report signed** → **Financial statements issued**

Active duty
Perform procedures to ensure subsequent events have been accounted for appropriately

Passive duty
No obligation to perform procedures but must take action if they become aware of events which would cause a modified opinion

Between the date of the financial statements and the date of the auditor's report

- The auditor should perform procedures to identify events that might require adjustment or disclosure in the financial statements.
  [ISA 560, 6]

- If material adjusting events are not adjusted for, or material non-adjusting events are not disclosed, the auditor will ask management to make the necessary amendments to the financial statements.

- If the identified adjustments or disclosures necessary are not made then the auditor should consider the impact on the auditor's report and whether a modification to the opinion is necessary.

Subsequent events procedures

- Enquiring of management if they are aware of any events, adjusting or non-adjusting, that have not yet been included or disclosed in the financial statements.

- Enquiring into management procedures/systems for the identification of events after the reporting period.

- Reading minutes of members' and directors' meetings.

- Reviewing accounting records including budgets, forecasts, cash flows, management accounts and interim information.

[ISA 560, 7]

- Obtaining a written representation from management confirming that they have informed the auditor of all subsequent events and accounted for them appropriately in the financial statements. [ISA 560, 9]

- Inspection of correspondence with legal advisors. [ISA 560, A8]

- Reviewing the progress of known risk areas and contingencies. [ISA 560, A9]

- Considering relevant information which has come to the auditor's attention, from sources outside the entity, including public knowledge, competitors, suppliers and customers.

- Inspecting after date receipts from receivables.

- Inspecting the cash book after the year-end for payments/receipts that were not accrued for at the year-end.

- Inspecting the sales price of inventories after the year-end.

Between the date of the auditor's report and the date the financial statements are issued

- The auditor is under no obligation to perform audit procedures after the auditor's report has been issued, however, if they become aware of a fact which would cause them to amend the auditor's report, they must take action. [ISA 560, 10]

- This will normally be in the form of asking the client to amend the financial statements, auditing the amendments and reissuing the auditor's report.

- If management do not amend the financial statements and the auditor's report has not yet been issued to the client, the auditor can still modify the opinion. [ISA 560, 13a]

- If the auditor's report has been provided to the client, the auditor shall notify management and those charged with governance not to issue the financial statements before the amendments are made.

  If the client issues the financial statements despite being requested not to by the auditor, the auditor shall take action to prevent reliance on the auditor's report. [ISA 560, 13b]

  Legal advice should be sought in this situation as the course of action to prevent reliance on the auditor's report depends on the auditor's legal rights and obligations. [ISA 560, A16]

After the financial statements are issued

- The auditor is under no obligation to perform audit procedures after the financial statements have been issued, however, if they become aware of a fact which would have caused them to amend the auditor's report, they must take action.

- The auditor should discuss the matter with management and consider if the financial statements require amendment. [ISA 560, 14]

- The auditor should perform audit procedures on the amendments to ensure they have been put through correctly. [ISA 560, 15a]

- The auditor should review the steps taken by management to ensure anyone who is in receipt of the previously issued financial statements is informed. [ISA 560, 15b]

- Issue a new auditor's report including an emphasis of matter or other matter paragraph to draw attention to the fact that the financial statements and auditor's report have been reissued. [ISA 560, 16]

- If management refuses to recall and amend the financial statements, the auditor shall take action to prevent reliance on the auditor's report. [ISA 560, 17]

Test your understanding 1

Murray case study: Subsequent events review for the year-ended 31 December 20X4

1   On 2 January 20X5, Golf is Us, a major customer of Murray Co, was placed into administration owing $211,000.

2   On 3 January 20X5, the sales director left the company. The sales director is suing Murray Co for constructive dismissal. If successful, the claim amounts to $280,000.

3   On 5 February 20X5 there was a fire at the premises of the third party warehouse provider, which destroyed all inventory held there. Approximately one half of Murray Co's inventory was stored in these premises. The total value of inventory stored at the premises was $1,054,000.

4   The financial statements include a $40,000 provision for an unfair dismissal case brought by an ex-employee of Murray Co. On 7 February 20X5 a letter was received from the claimant's solicitors stating that they would be willing to settle out-of-court for $25,000. It is likely the company will agree to this.

Financial statement extracts	31 Dec 20X4	31 Dec 20X3
	$000	$000
Revenue	21,960	19,580
Total assets	9,697	7,288
Profit before tax	1,048	248

Required:

For each of the events above discuss whether the financial statements require amendment in order to avoid a modified audit opinion.

3 Going concern

 The going concern concept

Going concern is the assumption that the entity will continue in business for the foreseeable future.

- The period that management (and therefore the auditor) is required to consider is the period required by the applicable financial reporting framework or by law or regulation if longer.

  Generally the period is a minimum of twelve months from the year-end. In some jurisdictions the period is a minimum of twelve months from the date the financial statements are approved (e.g. the UK).
  [ISA 570, 13]

- Consideration of the foreseeable future involves making a judgment about future events, which are inherently uncertain.

  Uncertainty increases with time and judgments can only be made on the basis of information available at any point. Subsequent events can overturn that judgment.
  [ISA 570, 5]

The going concern concept – significance

Whether or not a company can be classed as a going concern affects how its financial statements are prepared.

Financial statements are prepared using the going concern basis of accounting, unless:

- management either intends to liquidate the entity or to cease trading, or

- has no realistic alternative but to do so.

(ISA 570, 2)

Where the assumption is made that the company will cease trading, the financial statements are prepared using the **break-up or liquidation basis** under which:

- The basis of preparation and the reason why the entity is not regarded as a going concern are disclosed.

- Assets are recorded at likely sale values.

- Inventory and receivables may need to be written down as inventory may be sold for a lower price or may be scrapped, and receivables may not pay if they know the company is ceasing to trade.

- Additional liabilities may arise (redundancy costs for staff, the costs of closing down facilities, etc.).

Responsibilities for going concern

Director's responsibilities in respect of going concern

- It is the directors' responsibility to assess the company's ability to continue as a going concern when they are preparing the financial statements. [ISA 570, 4]

- In order to do this the directors should prepare forecasts to help assess whether they are likely to be able to continue trading for the next 12 months as a minimum.

- If they are aware of any material uncertainties which may affect this assessment, the directors should disclose these in the financial statements.

- When the directors are performing their assessment they should take into account a number of relevant factors such as:

    - Current and expected profitability

    - Debt repayment

    - Sources (and potential sources) of financing.

Auditor's responsibilities in respect of going concern

ISA 570 *Going Concern*, para 9, states that the auditor shall:

- Obtain sufficient appropriate evidence regarding the appropriateness of management's use of the going concern basis of accounting in the preparation of the financial statements.

- Conclude on whether a material uncertainty exists about the entity's ability to continue as a going concern.

- Report in accordance with ISA 570.

Indicators of going concern problems

Typical indicators and explanations of going concern problems include the following:

- Net current liabilities (or net liabilities overall): indicates an inability to meet debts as they fall due.

- Borrowing facilities not agreed or close to expiry of current agreement: lack of access to cash may make it difficult for a company to manage its operating cycle.

- Defaulted loan agreements: loans normally become repayable on default, the company may find it difficult to repay loan.

- Unplanned sales of non-current assets: indicates an inability to generate cash from other means and as non-current assets generate income, sale of assets will cause a decline in income and therefore profit.

- Missing tax payments: results in fines and penalties, companies normally prioritise tax payments indicating a lack of working capital.

- Failure to pay the staff: indicates a significant lack of working capital.

- Negative cash flow: indicates overtrading.

- Inability to obtain credit from suppliers: suggests failure to pay suppliers on time and working capital problems.

- Major technology changes: inability or insufficient funds to keep up with changes in technology will result in loss of custom and obsolescence of inventory.

- Legal claims: successful legal claims may result in significant cash payments that can only be settled with liquidation.

- Loss of key staff: may result in an inability to trade.

- Over-reliance on a small number of products, staff, suppliers or customers: loss may result in an inability to trade.

- Customers ceasing to trade or having cash flow difficulties: likely to become an irrecoverable debt and therefore payment won't be received.

- Emergence of a successful competitor: will impact revenue if customers switch.

- Uninsured/under-insured catastrophes: the company may not have enough cash to survive.

- Changes in laws and regulations: the cost of compliance may be more than the company can afford.

[ISA 570, A3]

Audit procedures

Audit procedures to assess management's evaluation of going concern

- Evaluate management's assessment of going concern. [ISA 570, 12]

- Assess the same period that management has used in its assessment and if this is less than 12 months, ask management to extend its assessment. [ISA 570, 13]

- Consider whether management's assessment includes all relevant information. [ISA 570, 14]

Audit procedures to perform where there is doubt over going concern

- Analyse and discuss cash flow, profit and other relevant forecasts with management. This should include assessment of the reasonableness of the assumptions used to prepare the forecasts.

- Analyse and discuss the entity's latest available interim financial statements.

- Review the terms of debentures and loan agreements and determine whether any have been breached.

- Read minutes of meetings for reference to financing difficulties.

- Enquire of the entity's lawyer regarding the existence of litigation and claims and the reasonableness of management's assessments of their outcome and the estimate of their financial implications.

- Confirm the existence, legality and enforceability of arrangements to provide or maintain financial support with related and third parties and assess the financial ability of such parties to provide additional funds.

- Review events after the year-end to identify those that either mitigate or otherwise affect the entity's ability to continue as a going concern.

[ISA 570, A16]

- Review correspondence with customers for evidence of any disputes that might impact recoverability of debts and affect future sales.

- Review correspondence with suppliers for evidence of issues regarding payments that might impact the company's ability to obtain supplies or credit.

- Review correspondence with the bank for indication that a bank loan or overdraft may be recalled.

- Obtain written representation from management regarding its plans for the future and how it plans to address the going concern issues.
  [ISA 570, 16e]

 Tutorial note

Audit procedures should focus on cash flows rather than profits. A company can continue to trade as long as it can pay its debts when they fall due. Therefore identify procedures to obtain evidence about the amount of cash that is likely to be received and the amount of cash that it likely to be paid out and consider whether there is any indication of cash flow difficulties.

Going concern disclosures required by the directors in the financial statements

1   Where there is any **material uncertainty over the future of a company**, the directors should include disclosure in the financial statements.
A material uncertainty exists when the magnitude of its potential impact and likelihood of occurrence is such that disclosure of the nature and implications of the uncertainty is necessary for the fair presentation of the financial statements and for the financial statements not to be misleading. [ISA 570, 18]

The disclosure should explain:

– the principal events or conditions that cast significant doubt on the entity's ability to continue as a going concern and management's plans to deal with them

– that the company may be unable to realise its assets and discharge its liabilities in the normal course of business.

[ISA 570, 19]

2   Where the directors have been **unable to assess going concern in the usual way** (e.g. for less than one year beyond the date on which they sign the financial statements), this fact should be disclosed.

3   Where the **financial statements are prepared on a basis other than the going concern basis**, the basis used should be disclosed.

Reporting implications

The auditor should modify the audit opinion if the directors have not made adequate disclosure of any material uncertainty related to going concern or if the directors have not prepared the financial statements on the appropriate basis.

The auditor should issue an unmodified opinion with additional communication if the directors have appropriately disclosed going concern uncertainties or prepared the financial statements on the break-up basis.

Reporting implications in relation to going concern are covered in more detail in the Reporting chapter.

Examination of a cash flow forecast

One way of assessing the client's ability to continue as a going concern is to examine the **reasonableness of the assumptions** used to prepare the cash flow forecast.

The following procedures are typical of those that would be performed in the examination of a cash flow forecast:

- Agree the opening balance of the cash forecast to the cash book, to ensure accuracy.

- Consider how reasonable company forecasts have been in the past by comparing past forecasts with actual outcomes. If forecasts have been reasonable in the past, this would make it more likely that the current forecast is reliable.

- Determine the assumptions that have been made in the preparation of the cash flow forecast. For example, if the company is operating in a poor economic climate, you would not expect cash flows from sales and realisation of receivables to increase, but either to decrease or remain stable. If costs are rising you would expect payments to increase in the cash flow forecast.

- Agree the timing of receipts from realisation of receivables and payments to suppliers with credit periods and previous trade receivables and payables payment periods.

- Examine the company's detailed budgets for the forecast period and discuss any specific plans with the directors.

- Examine the assessment of the non-current assets required to meet production needs. Agree cash outflows for non-current assets to supplier quotations.

- For acquisitions of buildings, agree the timing and amount of cash outflows to the expected completion date and consideration in the sale and purchase agreement.

- Consider the adequacy of the increased working capital and the working capital cash flows included in the forecast.

- If relevant, compare actual performance in the most recent management accounts to the forecast figures.

- Recalculate the cash flow forecast balances to verify arithmetical accuracy.

- Inspect board minutes for any other relevant issues which should be included within the forecast.

Test your understanding 2

Murray case study: Going concern review for the year-ended 31 December 20X4

On 2 January 20X5, Golf is Us, a major customer of Murray Co, was placed into administration owing $211,000.

On 3 January 20X5, the sales director left the company and has yet to be replaced. The sales director is suing Murray Co for constructive dismissal.

On 5 January 20X5 there was a fire at the premises of the third party warehouse provider, which destroyed all inventory held there. Approximately one half of Murray Co's inventory was stored in these premises.

The assembly line for ergometers (rowing machines) was refurbished during the year at a cost of $1 million. The additional $1.5 million loan facility provided to Murray Co during the year is secured, in part, on the refurbished assembly line. The assembly line broke down during January and six weeks later is still not working.

The company is seeking new funding through an initial public offering of shares in the company (i.e. listing on the stock exchange). In the event that the initial public offering does not proceed, this will require Murray Co's existing banking arrangements to be renegotiated and additional funding to be raised from either existing or new investors.

The financial statements of Murray Co show an overdraft at 31 December 20X4 of $180,000 (20X3: $120,000). The overdraft limit is $250,000. The cash flow forecast shows negative monthly cash flows for the next twelve months. As a result of cash shortages in February 20X5, a number of suppliers were paid late.

Required:

Using the information provided, explain the potential indicators that Murray Co is not a going concern.

4 Overall review of the financial statements

Before forming an opinion on the financial statements and deciding on the wording of the auditor's report, the auditor should conduct **an overall review**.

The auditor should perform the following procedures:

1 Review the financial statements to ensure:

   – Compliance with accounting standards and local legislation disclosure requirements. This is sometimes performed using a disclosure checklist.

   – Accounting policies are sufficiently disclosed and to ensure that they are in accordance with the accounting treatment adopted in the financial statements.

   – They adequately reflect the information and explanations previously obtained and conclusions reached during the course of the audit.

2 Perform analytical procedures to corroborate conclusions formed during the audit and assist when forming an overall conclusion as to whether the financial statements are consistent with the auditor's understanding of the entity. [ISA 520, 6]

3 Review the aggregate of the uncorrected misstatements to assess whether a material misstatement arises. If so, discuss the potential adjustment with management.

The purpose of review procedures

Review forms part of the engagement performance quality control procedures covered in the Planning chapter.

As part of the overall review, the auditor should assess whether:

- The audit work was performed in accordance with professional standards.

- Significant matters have been raised for further consideration and appropriate consultations have taken place.

- There is a need to revise the nature, timing and extent of the work performed.

- The audit evidence gathered by the team is sufficient and appropriate to support the audit opinion.

[ISA 220, A18]

The auditor should ensure that initial assessments made at the start of the audit are still valid in light of the information gathered during the audit and that the audit plan has been flexed to meet any new circumstances.

5 Evaluation of misstatements

The auditor must consider the effect of misstatements on both the audit procedures performed and ultimately, if uncorrected, on the financial statements as a whole. Guidance on how this is performed is given in ISA 450 *Evaluation of Misstatements Identified During the Audit.*

The auditor must:

- Accumulate a record of all identified misstatements, unless they are clearly trivial. [ISA 450, 5]

- Consider if the existence of such misstatements indicates that others may exist, which, when aggregated with other misstatements, could be considered material. [ISA 450, 6a]

- If so, consider if the audit strategy and plan need to be revised. [ISA 450, 6]

- Communicate all accumulated misstatements to an appropriate level of **management** on a timely basis and request that **all** misstatements are corrected. [ISA 450, 8]

- If management refuses to correct some or all of the misstatements the auditor should consider their reasons for refusal and take these into account when considering if the financial statements are free from material misstatement. [ISA 450, 9]

Evaluation of uncorrected misstatements

If management has failed to correct all of the misstatements, the auditor should:

- Reassess materiality to determine whether it is still appropriate in the circumstances as the level of risk may be deemed higher as a result of management's refusal. [ISA 450, 10]

- Determine whether the uncorrected misstatements, either individually or in aggregate, are material to the financial statements as a whole, considering both the size and nature of the misstatements and the effect of misstatements related to prior periods (e.g. on corresponding figures, comparatives and opening balances). If an individual misstatement is considered material it cannot be offset by other misstatements. [ISA 450, 11]

- Communicate the uncorrected misstatements to **those charged with governance** and explain the effect this will have on the audit opinion. [ISA 450, 12]

- Request a written representation from management and those charged with governance that they believe the effects of uncorrected misstatements are immaterial. [ISA 450, 14]

Evaluation of misstatements

You are at the completion stage of the audit of Murray Co. The profit before tax for the year is $1,048,000 and total assets are $9,697,000. The following matters have not been corrected by management and have been left for your attention:

1   An irrecoverable debt of $211,000 has not been written off.

2   An adjustment to a provision relating to the unfair dismissal of an ex-employee of $15,000 has not been made.

3   Website development costs of $50,000 were incorrectly capitalised.

4   Work in progress was overvalued by $45,000.

All of these misstatements must be communicated to management and requested to be adjusted in accordance with ISA 450.

The irrecoverable debt must be written off to avoid a modified opinion as it is individually material. A material misstatement cannot be off-set by other misstatements.

Even if management agree to write-off the irrecoverable debt, the other uncorrected misstatements are material in aggregate even though they are not material individually.

The adjustments required are:

- Provision: DR Provision (SFP), CR Provision expense (P&L) – $15,000

- Website development costs: DR Expenses (P&L), CR Website development costs (SFP) – $50,000

- Work in progress: DR Closing inventory (P&L), CR Inventory (SFP) – $45,000.

The overall adjustment required to the P&L is $80,000. This represents 7.6% of PBT and is material.

The misstatements will need to be adjusted to avoid a modified opinion.

6 Written representations

 A written representation is: **A written statement by management provided to the auditor to confirm certain matters or to support other audit evidence.** [ISA 580 *Written Representations*, 7].

Purpose of written representations

ISA 580 *Written Representations* requires the auditor to obtain written representations from management:

- That they have fulfilled their responsibility for the preparation of the financial statements. [ISA 580, 6a]

- To support other audit evidence relevant to the financial statements or specific assertions if deemed necessary by the auditor or required by specific ISAs. [ISA 580, 6b]

- That they have provided the auditor with all relevant information. [ISA 580, 11a]

- That all transactions have been recorded and reflected in the financial statements. [ISA 580, 11b]

A representation to support other audit evidence may be appropriate where more reliable forms of evidence are not available, particularly in relation to matters requiring management judgment or knowledge restricted to management. Examples include:

- Whether the selection and application of accounting policies are appropriate.

- Whether the following matters have been measured, presented and disclosed in accordance with the relevant financial reporting framework:

  - Plans or intentions that may affect the carrying value or classification of assets and liabilities.

  - Liabilities, both contingent and actual.

  - Title to, or control over, assets.

  - Aspects of laws, regulations and contractual agreements that may affect the financial statements, including non-compliance.

[ISA 580, A10]

- That the directors have communicated all deficiencies in internal control to the auditor. [ISA 580, A11]

- Specific assertions about classes of transactions, accounts balances and disclosures requiring management judgment. [ISA 580, A13]

Note that written representations cannot be a substitute for more reliable evidence that should be available and do not constitute sufficient appropriate evidence on their own, about any of the matters with which they deal. [ISA 580, 4]

Written representations should only be sought to support other audit evidence.

Process for obtaining a written representation

In practice, the auditor will draft the wording of the written representation letter but it must be printed on client headed paper, addressed to the auditor and signed by the client.

The letter must be signed by an appropriate senior member of client management, with appropriate responsibilities for the financial statements and knowledge of the matters concerned. This would normally be the chief executive and chief financial officer.

The date of the written representation letter should be the same as the date the financial statements are authorised. It must be obtained and signed before the auditor's report is finalised.

Reliability of written representations

Written representations are client generated, and may be subject to bias. It is therefore, potentially, an unreliable form of audit evidence.

The auditor must consider the reliability of written representations in terms of:

- Concerns about the competence, integrity, ethical values or diligence of management. [ISA 580, 16]

- Inconsistencies with other forms of evidence. [ISA 580, 17]

Steps if written representations are inconsistent with other evidence

- Consider the reliability of representations in general.

- Reconsider the initial risk assessment.

- Consider the need to perform further audit procedures.

[ISA 580, A23]

 Tutorial note

In the exam, when obtaining a written representation as a substantive procedure, you must include an explanation of **what** the written representation is for. For example, 'Obtain a written representation from management confirming the completeness of directors' remuneration including the bonus'.

If there are concerns about the competence, integrity, ethical values or diligence of management:

- The auditor must consider whether the engagement can be conducted effectively.

- If they conclude that it cannot then they should withdraw from the engagement, where permitted by laws and regulations.

- If they are not permitted to withdraw they should consider the impact on the auditor's report. It is likely that this would lead to a disclaimer of opinion.

[ISA 580, A24]

Steps if management refuse to provide written representations

Although possibly unreliable, written representations are a necessary and important source of evidence.

If management refuse to provide requested written representations, the auditor should:

- Discuss the matter with management to understand why they are refusing.

- Re-evaluate the integrity of management and consider the effect that this may have on the reliability of other representations (oral or written) and audit evidence in general.

- Consider the implication for the auditor's report.

[ISA 580, 19]

Audit reporting implications

The auditor should issue a disclaimer of opinion if:

- The auditor concludes there is sufficient doubt about the integrity of management which means the written representations are not reliable, or

- Management does not provide the written representations required in relation to confirming their responsibility to prepare the financial statements and to provide the auditor with information, and confirming completeness of transactions.

[ISA 580, 20]

Illustration 2 – Murray Co-written representation letter

Murray Co

1 Murray Mound, Wimbledon

London WN1 2LN

Wimble & Co

2 Court Lane, Wimbledon

London WN1 2LN

1 July 20X5

Dear Wimble & Co,

This written representation is provided in connection with your audit of the financial statements of Murray Company for the year-ended December 31, 20X4 for the purpose of expressing an opinion as to whether the financial statements give a true and fair view in accordance with International Financial Reporting Standards.

We confirm that:

Financial Statements

- We have fulfilled our responsibilities, as set out in the terms of the audit engagement dated 25 November 20X4, for the preparation of the financial statements in accordance with International Financial Reporting Standards; in particular the financial statements give a true and fair view in accordance therewith.

- Significant assumptions used by us in making accounting estimates, including those measured at fair value, are reasonable. (ISA 540)

- All events subsequent to the date of the financial statements and for which International Financial Reporting Standards require adjustment or disclosure have been adjusted or disclosed. (ISA 560)

- The effects of uncorrected misstatements are immaterial, both individually and in the aggregate, to the financial statements as a whole. A list of the uncorrected misstatements is attached. (ISA 450)

- The basis and amount of the warranty provision are reasonable. (specific matter)

Information provided

- We have provided you with:

  - Access to all information of which we are aware that is relevant to the preparation of the financial statements, such as records, documentation and other matters.

  - Additional information that you have requested from us for the purpose of the audit.

  - Unrestricted access to persons within the entity from whom you determined it necessary to obtain audit evidence.

- All transactions have been recorded in the accounting records and are reflected in the financial statements.

- We have disclosed to you the results of our assessment of the risk that the financial statements may be materially misstated as a result of fraud. (ISA 240)

- We have disclosed to you all information in relation to fraud or suspected fraud that we are aware of and that affects the entity and involves:

  - Management

  - Employees who have significant roles in internal control; or

  - Others where the fraud could have a material effect on the financial statements. (ISA 240)

- We have disclosed to you all information in relation to allegations of fraud, or suspected fraud, affecting the entity's financial statements communicated by employees, former employees, analysts, regulators or others. (ISA 240)

- We have disclosed to you all known instances of non-compliance or suspected non-compliance with laws and regulations whose effects should be considered when preparing financial statements. (ISA 250)

- We have disclosed to you all information in relation to settlement of the unfair dismissal, including our intentions thereon. (specific matter)

- We have disclosed to you all information in relation to the constructive dismissal brought by the previous Sales Director, including our intention thereon. (specific matter)

Ed Perry

Edward Perry

Finance Director, Murray Co

Maria Williams

Maria Williams

Managing Director, Murray Co

Test your understanding 3

Smithson Co provides scientific services to a wide range of clients. Typical assignments range from testing food for illegal additives to providing forensic analysis on items used to commit crimes to assist law enforcement officers.

The audit is nearly complete. As audit senior you have reported to the engagement partner that Smithson Co is having some financial difficulties. Income has fallen due to the adverse effect of two high-profile court cases, following which a number of clients withdrew their contracts with Smithson Co. A senior employee then left Smithson Co, stating lack of investment in new analysis machines was increasing the risk of incorrect information being provided by the company. A cash flow forecast prepared internally shows Smithson Co requiring significant additional cash within the next 12 months to maintain even the current level of services.

Required:

(a) **Define 'going concern' and discuss the auditor's and directors' responsibilities in respect of going concern.**

(5 marks)

(b) **State the audit procedures that may be carried out to try to determine whether or not Smithson Co is a going concern.**

(10 marks)

(c) **Explain the audit procedures and actions the auditor may take where the auditor has decided that Smithson Co is unlikely to be a going concern.**

(5 marks)

(Total: 20 marks)

Test your understanding 4

Potterton Co is a listed company that manufactures body lotions under the 'ReallyCool' brand. The company's year-end is 31 March 20X5, and today's date is 1 July 20X5. Profit before taxation is $4 million.

The audit is nearing completion, but two issues remain outstanding:

1   On 27 May 20X5 a legal claim was made against the company on behalf of a teenager who suffered severe burns after using 'ReallyCool ExtraZingy Lotion' in July 20X4. Potterton Co is considering an out-of-court settlement of $100,000 per year for the remaining life of the claimant. However, no adjustment or disclosure has been made in the financial statements.

2   At a board meeting on 30 April 20X5, the directors of Potterton Co proposed a dividend of $2 million. It is highly likely that the shareholders will approve the dividend at the annual general meeting on 3 September 20X5. The directors have recorded the dividend in the draft statement of changes in equity for the year-ended 31 March 20X5.

Required:

(a)   **Explain whether the two outstanding issues are adjusting or non-adjusting events, in accordance with IAS 10 *Events after the Reporting Period*.**

(8 marks)

(b)   **Describe appropriate audit procedures in order to reach a conclusion on the two outstanding issues.**

(5 marks)

(c)   **Explain the likely impact on the audit opinion if the directors refuse to make any further adjustments or disclosures in the financial statements of Potterton Co.**

(4 marks)

(Total: 17 marks)

Test your understanding 5

(a)   List SIX items that could be included in a written
         representation.

(3 marks)

(b)   List THREE reasons why auditors obtain written
         representations.

(3 marks)

(Total: 6 marks)

Test your understanding 6

The audit of Leonora Co is nearly complete and you are performing your
procedures in respect of going concern. During the audit you have
identified several indicators that the company may not be able to
continue as a going concern.

1   **In relation to responsibilities for going concern, which of the
       following is TRUE?**

A   The auditor chooses the basis of preparation for the financial
       statements.

B   The client should make adequate disclosure of going concern
       uncertainties and the auditor should assess the adequacy of
       them.

C   The auditor will make disclosure of going concern
       uncertainties in the financial statements.

D   The auditor will notify the shareholders immediately of any
       going concern issues identified during the audit.

2	State whether each of the following statements are true or false in respect of assessing the going concern status of Leonora Co.		
A	The auditor should prepare forecasts to assess whether Leonora Co are likely to be able to continue trading	True	False
B	The directors of Leonora Co should prepare forecasts for a period of at least 12 months to assess whether the company is likely to be able to continue trading	True	False
C	If the directors of Leonora Co prepare forecasts for a period of less than 12 months, the auditor should ask them to extend their assessment period	True	False
D	If the directors of Leonora Co prepare forecasts for a period of less than 12 months, the auditor should extend the assessment period by preparing a forecast for the additional 6 months	True	False

3 **Which of the following is correct in respect of going concern?**

    A   All companies must prepare financial statements using the going concern basis of accounting.

    B   If there are material uncertainties regarding going concern, the financial statements must be prepared on the break up basis.

    C   Going concern means the company is no longer profitable.

    D   The directors of the company must disclose material uncertainties regarding going concern in the notes to the financial statements.

4 **Which of the following are indicators of going concern problems?**

    (i)   Declining revenues.

    (ii)   Significant outstanding receivables.

    (iii)   Loan repayments due to be made.

    (iv)   Declining current and quick ratios.

    A   (i), (ii) and (iii) only

    B   (ii), (iii) and (iv) only

    C   (i), (ii), (iii) and (iv)

    D   (iii) only

5   **Which of the following procedures is NOT appropriate for obtaining evidence as to whether the going concern basis of accounting is appropriate?**

A   Obtain external confirmation from a customer regarding their outstanding balance.

B   Examine cash flow forecasts.

C   Discuss with management their plans for the future.

D   Inspect correspondence with the bank regarding loan or overdraft facilities.

Test your understanding 7

It is 1 July 20X5. You are currently performing subsequent events procedures for the audit of Kookynie Co. From a review of the board minutes you identify that a customer is suing the company for an injury they suffered on the client's premises on 5 April 20X5. The client's year-end is 31 March 20X5. The directors are proposing to amend the financial statements to include a provision for the amount of compensation they expect to have to pay to the customer. Legal advice received indicates that the claim is possible to succeed.

1   **Which of the following statements is TRUE with regard to subsequent events?**

A   The auditor must perform audit procedures to identify events occurring after the date of the financial statements up to the date the auditor's report is signed that could have an effect on the financial statements

B   The auditor does not need to consider any events which occur after the date of the financial statements as it is outside of the reporting period

C   The auditor has no responsibility after the auditor's report has been signed, even if they become aware of events occurring which means the opinion is now incorrect

D   The auditor only needs to consider subsequent events communicated to them by the directors

2 **Which of the following statements is FALSE in respect of subsequent events?**

A The auditor must ensure the client has complied with IAS 10 *Events After the Reporting Period* when performing the audit of subsequent events

B The auditor must comply with IAS 10 *Events After the Reporting Period* when performing the audit of subsequent events

C The auditor must comply with ISA 560 *Subsequent Events* when performing the audit of subsequent events

D Events after the reporting period may be adjusting or non-adjusting

3 **Which of the following is TRUE in respect of adjusting events?**

A Adjusting events are those events which occur before the auditor's report has been signed

B Adjusting events are those which occur after the year-end date

C Adjusting events are those which occur after the year-end date and provide evidence of a condition existing at the year-end date

D Adjusting events require disclosure in the notes to the financial statements

4 **In respect of the customer's claim, which of the following statements is TRUE?**

A If the claim is probable rather than possible, a provision should be recognised in the financial statements dated 31 March 20X5

B The injury was caused after the year-end therefore was not a condition in existence at the year-end

C The injury was caused after the year-end therefore has no impact on the financial statements being audited

D The claim is an adjusting event and the financial statements should reflect the claim

5   **Which of following procedures would NOT be appropriate in respect of Kookynie Co's subsequent events review?**

A   Inspect correspondence from the lawyers regarding the likely outcome of the case and the estimate of compensation if the claim is successful

B   Discuss with management the details of the accident giving rise to the claim

C   Obtain written representation from management that all known subsequent events have been disclosed to the auditor and reflected in the financial statements.

D   Telephone the lawyer to discuss further details of the case of which the client may not be aware

---

Test your understanding 8

You are completing the audit of Balladonia Co and you are waiting for the client to sign and return the written representation letter. The directors have expressed concern about signing the letter. They have stated that the auditor has been provided with all of the information required and therefore do not understand why the written representation is necessary.

1   **State whether each of the following statements is true or false in respect of written representations.**

A	As you have received all other information during the audit, the decision by management not to provide the written representation letter is not an issue that would affect the auditor's report	True	False
B	A written representation is an important piece of evidence which the auditor must obtain	True	False
C	A written representation does not need to be obtained if the wording would be the same as last year's written representation	True	False
D	Failure by management to provide a written representation letter may cast doubt over management integrity	True	False

2   **Which of the following statements is FALSE?**

A   Written representations include confirmation that management has fulfilled its responsibilities in respect of the financial statements and has provided the auditor with all records and information during the audit.

B   Written representations should only be relied on where there is limited other evidence available such as matters of judgment or matters confined to management.

C   The auditor would obtain a written representation regarding the reasonableness of a depreciation charge as this is an accounting estimate.

D   Failure to obtain a written representation is likely to result in a disclaimer of opinion.

3   **Which of the following would be the auditor's first course of action after being informed that management is unwilling to provide the written representation?**

A   Discuss the matter with management and try to resolve the issue

B   Discuss the matter with those charged with governance and try to resolve the issue

C   Discuss the matter with the shareholders and try to resolve the issue

D   Modify the audit opinion

4   **Written representation is required from management to confirm they believe the effects of any uncorrected misstatements are immaterial. Which of the following best describes a misstatement?**

A   An error in the financial statements

B   A fraud which has a material effect on the financial statements

C   An omission of a balance from the financial statements

D   A difference between what has been reported in the financial statements and what should have been reported in the financial statements

5   **During the audit of Balladonia Co you discovered
    misstatements totalling $20,000. Profit before tax is $570,000.
    Which of the following describes the most appropriate course
    of action?**

A   Ignore the misstatements if they are deemed immaterial

B   Modify the audit opinion as a result of misstatement

C   Request the client to correct the misstatements

D   Include an Emphasis of Matter paragraph in the auditor's
    report to highlight that misstatements are present in the
    financial statements

7 Chapter summary

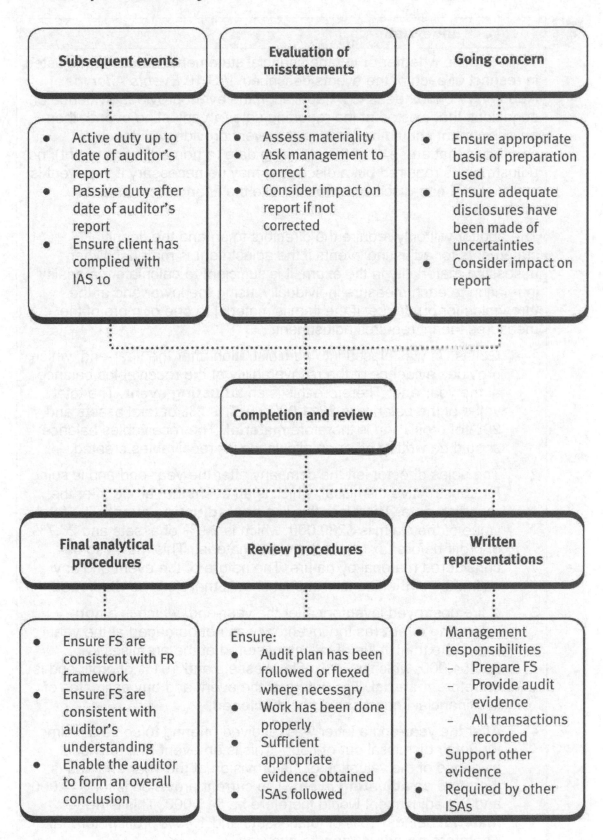

Subsequent events

- Active duty up to date of auditor's report
- Passive duty after date of auditor's report
- Ensure client has complied with IAS 10

Evaluation of misstatements

- Assess materiality
- Ask management to correct
- Consider impact on report if not corrected

Going concern

- Ensure appropriate basis of preparation used
- Ensure adequate disclosures have been made of uncertainties
- Consider impact on report

Completion and review

Final analytical procedures

- Ensure FS are consistent with FR framework
- Ensure FS are consistent with auditor's understanding
- Enable the auditor to form an overall conclusion

Review procedures

Ensure:
- Audit plan has been followed or flexed where necessary
- Work has been done properly
- Sufficient appropriate evidence obtained
- ISAs followed

Written representations

- Management responsibilities
  - Prepare FS
  - Provide audit evidence
  - All transactions recorded
- Support other evidence
- Required by other ISAs

Test your understanding answers

Test your understanding 1

To determine whether or not the financial statements should be adjusted in respect of each of the events described, IAS 10 *Events After the Reporting Period* needs to be applied. If the event provides evidence of conditions that existed at the reporting date (an adjusting event), then an adjustment should be made. If the event provides evidence of conditions that arose after the reporting date (a non-adjusting event), no adjustment is required but a disclosure may be necessary if the event is material and non-disclosure would make the financial statements misleading.

The auditor will only require the directors to amend the financial statements for adjusting events if the adjustment is material. When assessing materiality in the exam, it is sufficient to calculate materiality in relation to each measure individually, using the lower end of the thresholds for prudence. If the item is material to one or more of the measures then it requires adjustment.

1   Golf is Us was placed into administration after the year-end, which provides evidence of the recoverability of the receivables balance at the year-end. Therefore this is an **adjusting event.** The total value of the balance is $211,000 which is 2% of total assets and 20% of profit, and is therefore **material.** The receivables balance should be written off or an allowance for receivables created.

2   The sales director left the company after the year-end and is suing for constructive dismissal, which is an event that arose after the reporting date. Therefore this is a **non-adjusting event.** The total value of the claim is $280,000, which is 2.9% of assets and 26.7% of profit before tax and is therefore material. This may also be considered material by nature. The nature of the event and any estimates of the financial impact should therefore be **disclosed**.

3   A fire destroyed inventory after the year-end, which is a **non-adjusting event** (as the inventory was not damaged at the year-end). The total value of inventory stored at the premises is $1,054,000, which is 11% of total assets and 101% of profit and is therefore **material.** The nature of the event and any estimates of the financial impact should be **disclosed**.

4   After the year-end a letter was received offering to settle a claim for unfair dismissal out-of-court. This is an event that provides evidence of the valuation of the provision at the year-end and is therefore an **adjusting event.** The current provision is for $40,000 and the adjustment would therefore be $15,000. This is **not material** being 0.15% of total assets and 1.43% profit before tax. Therefore **no adjustment** is necessary.

Test your understanding 2

Going concern indicators at Murray Co:

Indicator	Explanation
A major customer has been placed into administration	Unless the customer can be replaced, this will result in significant loss of future revenues. The debt outstanding is unlikely to be paid resulting in a negative impact on cash flow.
The sales director left the company and has yet to be replaced.	Loss of a key director will impact on the company's revenue. As Murray Co has already lost a major customer, without an experienced sales director to generate new business, the company will face significantly reduced revenue and cash flows.
The sales director is suing Murray Co for constructive dismissal.	Murray Co will need to pay expensive legal costs in order to defend this litigation, squeezing cash flows even further. In addition, this may damage its reputation and make it difficult to recruit a suitable replacement or other key staff. Any compensation awarded to the sales director will mean further outflow of cash.
Murray Co is seeking new funding through an initial public offering of shares in the company.	If Murray Co does not obtain new funding through a listing, alternative finance will need to be obtained in order to continue to operate. This may not be easy to obtain given the other problems.
Murray Co is operating close to its overdraft limit.	Murray Co is heavily dependent on a short-term source of finance that is repayable on demand. It may be difficult to obtain further sources of finance if the overdraft limit is reached.

The cash flow forecast shows negative monthly cash flows for the next twelve months.	If the company continues to have cash outflows then the overdraft will increase further and there may be no cash available to pay debts as they fall due.
A number of suppliers have been paid late.	If suppliers are paid late they may refuse to supply Murray Co with goods/components or impose cash on delivery terms which will disrupt production, and delay sales to customers. This may cause them to lose customers altogether.
The loan facility is secured, in part, on the refurbished assembly line which has broken down.	The bank may withdraw the loan facility if the asset on which it is secured is significantly impaired. Murray Co does not have sufficient cash to repay the loan. Unless Murray Co can negotiate with the bank or raise alternative finance (or sell non-current assets), they will have no realistic alternative but to liquidate.
The assembly line broke down during January, and six weeks later is still not working.	If Murray Co cannot meet customer orders due to manufacturing problems. Refunds may have to be given and customer goodwill may be lost. Future revenues may fall which will put further pressure on cash flows.
A fire at the premises of the third party warehouse provider destroyed approximately one half of Murray Co's inventory.	Murray Co may not be able to meet customer orders if it does not have sufficient inventory. If the company is not covered by insurance, profit and cash flow will be significantly impacted.

Test your understanding 3

(a) **Going concern**

Going concern means that the entity will continue in operational existence for the foreseeable future without the intention or the necessity of liquidation or otherwise ceasing trade. It is one of the accounting principles given in IAS 1 *Presentation of Financial Statements*.

The auditor's responsibilities are:

- To consider the appropriateness of management's use of the going concern basis of accounting when preparing the financial statements.

- To conclude on whether a material uncertainty exists about the entity's ability to continue as a going concern.

- To report to the members in accordance with ISA 570 *Going Concern*.

The directors are responsible for:

- Preparing the financial statements on an appropriate basis, be that the going concern or the breakup basis.

- Disclosing material uncertainties relating to going concern in the financial statements.

(b) **Audit procedures regarding going concern**

- Obtain a copy of the cash flow forecast and assess the reasonableness of the assumptions used in the forecast.

- Discuss with the directors their view of whether Smithson Co can continue as a going concern. Ask for their reasons and try and determine whether these are reasonable.

- Enquire of the directors whether they have considered any other forms of finance for Smithson Co to make up the cash shortfall identified in the cash flow forecast.

- Obtain a copy of any interim financial statements of Smithson Co to determine the level of sales/income after the year-end and whether this matches the cash flow forecast.

- Enquire about the possible lack of capital investment within Smithson Co identified by the employee leaving. Review the purchase policy with the directors.

– Consider the extent to which Smithson Co rely on the senior employee who recently left the company. Ask the HR department whether the employee will be replaced soon.

– Obtain a solicitor's letter and review to identify any legal claims against Smithson Co related to below standard services being provided to clients. Where possible, consider the financial impact on Smithson Co and whether insurance is available to mitigate any claims.

– Review Smithson Co's order book to try and determine the value of future orders compared to previous years.

– Review the bank letter to determine the extent of any bank loans and whether repayments due in the next 12 months can be made without further borrowing.

– Review other events after the end of the financial year and determine whether these have an impact on Smithson Co.

– Obtain a written representation confirming the directors' opinion that Smithson Co is a going concern.

(c) **Audit procedures and actions if Smithson Co is not considered to be a going concern**

– Discuss the situation again with directors. Consider whether additional disclosures are required in the financial statements or whether the financial statements should be prepared on the break-up basis.

– Explain to the directors that if additional disclosure or restatement of the financial statements is not made then the auditor will have to modify the audit opinion.

– Consider implications for the auditor's report. Where the directors provide adequate disclosure of the going concern situation of Smithson Co, then a section should be included in the auditor's report headed 'Material Uncertainty Related to Going Concern' to draw attention to the going concern disclosures.

– Where the directors do not make adequate disclosure of the going concern situation then modify the audit opinion due to material misstatement due to inadequate disclosure.

– The modification will be an 'except for' qualification or an adverse opinion depending on whether the issue is material or material and pervasive.

– The 'Basis for Opinion' section will be amended to 'Basis for Adverse Opinion' or 'Basis for Qualified Opinion' to explain the reason for the modified opinion.

Test your understanding 4

(a) **Analysis of events**

Legal claim

The legal claim is an adjusting event because it provides evidence of a condition existing at the end of the reporting period. As at 31 March 20X5, the claimant had purchased and used the product, and the damage to the claimant's skin had already occurred.

The legal claim is material, because, if the claimant lived for, say, another 40 years, the company would owe $4 million. This is 100% of the current year profit before tax.

Therefore profit should be reduced and liabilities increased by the expected value of the claim.

Proposed dividend

The proposed dividend is a non-adjusting event because the condition arose after the end of the reporting period. No liability for the dividend can exist until the shareholders approve the dividend.

The proposed dividend is material because it constitutes 50% ($2m/$4m × 100) of the company's profit before tax, as well as being material by nature.

Therefore the dividend should not be recognised in the financial statements for the year-ended 31 March 20X5. However, the proposed dividend should be disclosed in a note to the financial statements.

(b) **Audit procedures**

Legal claim

– Review legal correspondence in order to understand the likely outcome of the legal claim.

– Review customer correspondence/legal files in order to identify other similar claims which could give rise to additional liabilities.

– Discuss with the production director the likely cause of the burns (e.g. allergy in user or inadequate printed instructions on product use) to determine the likelihood of any claim being successful in court.

– Review trade/consumer press to identify whether the claim might damage the reputation of the Reallycool brand which could impact future revenues or even create a going concern threat.

– Propose adjustment of the financial statements to the directors.

Proposed dividend

– Inspect board minutes in order to confirm the amount of the proposed dividend.

– Propose an adjustment to the financial statements to remove the dividend from being recognised in the statement of changes in equity but ensure that the dividend proposal is disclosed within the notes.

(c) **Impact on audit opinion**

– The auditor must modify the audit opinion if the directors refuse to make the relevant adjustments in the financial statements requested by the auditors.

– Both the legal claim (which should have been recognised) and the proposed dividend (which should have been disclosed rather than recognised) are materially misstated.

– The auditor must express a qualified ('except for') opinion if they conclude that the misstatements are material, but not pervasive, to the financial statements.

– The auditor must express an adverse opinion if they conclude that misstatements are both material and pervasive to the financial statements.

– Given the size of the amounts involved, an adverse opinion may be appropriate in these circumstances.

Tutorial note: If the requirement asked for implications for the auditor's report, the following points should also be included in the answer:

– The 'Basis for Opinion' section will be amended to 'Basis for Adverse' or 'Basis for Qualified Opinion' to explain the reason for the modified opinion.

– As Potterton Co is listed, the Key Audit Matters section will reference the 'Basis for Adverse/Qualified Opinion' section.

Test your understanding 5

(a) Items to be included in a written representation letter

- All books, records and relevant information have been made available to the auditors.

- Financial statements have been prepared in accordance with an applicable financial reporting framework.

- All transactions have been recorded and reflected in the financial statements.

- The effects of uncorrected misstatements are immaterial to the financial statements.

- Any instances of non-compliance with laws and regulations have been disclosed to the auditor.

- The directors believe the company can continue to trade as a going concern.

- The directors have no plans that will materially alter the carrying value or classification of assets or liabilities in the financial statements.

- No plans to abandon any product lines that will result in any excess or obsolete inventory.

- All subsequent events have been disclosed to the auditor and reflected appropriately in the financial statements.

- No irregularities involving management or employees that could have a material effect on the financial statements.

(b) Reasons why the auditor obtains written representations

- Formal confirmation by management of their responsibilities.

- To support other evidence relevant to the financial statements if determined necessary by the auditor, e.g. matters requiring management judgment.

- Required by ISA 580 and other ISAs.

Test your understanding 6

1	B	The directors (client) must make the disclosures in the financial statements. The auditor will audit them.
2	A – False	The auditor should review the forecasts prepared by the directors. The auditor should not prepare them.
	B – True	The directors (client) should prepare the forecasts to assist with their assessment of going concern in order to determine the appropriate basis on which to prepare the financial statements.
	C – True	The directors are required to consider at least a 12 month period for their going concern assessment. The auditor must ask them to extend their assessment if they fail to consider at least 12 months.
	D – False	The auditor should not extend the assessment or prepare forecasts for the client.
3	D	The financial statements should be prepared on the break up basis if the company is not a going concern. If there are material uncertainties regarding going concern, these must be disclosed by the directors. A company may be profitable but not have the cash to pay its debts when they fall due.
4	C	All are indicators of going concern problems.
5	A	Obtaining external confirmation from a customer may confirm the balance owed but does not provide evidence that the money will be received.

KAPLAN PUBLISHING

Test your understanding 7

1	A	The auditor has an active duty up to the date the auditor's report is signed. If they become aware of events after this date that would cause them to modify their opinion they must take action.
2	B	IAS 10 *Events After the Reporting Period* refers to the accounting treatment the client should comply with. The auditor must comply with ISA 560 *Subsequent Events*.
3	C	Adjusting events provide evidence of conditions existing at the year-end (IAS 10, 3a).
4	B	As the injury was suffered after the year-end it is a non-adjusting event. Therefore a provision is not required at 31 March 20X5. If it is material, disclosure should be made.
5	D	The auditor has no right to contact the lawyer in this manner. A lawyer confirmation letter may be sent with client permission. It would not be professional for the lawyer to discuss details of the case that are not known to the client with the auditor.

Test your understanding 8

1	A – False	A written representation is required by ISA 580. Without it the auditor does not have sufficient appropriate evidence to form a conclusion and must therefore modify the auditor's report.
	B – True	A written representation contains written confirmation from the directors that they have fulfilled their responsibilities in relation to the financial statements and providing the auditor with all of the information required. As such, it is an important piece of evidence
	C – False	The written representation must be dated just before the date of the auditor's report. Even if the wording is the same, a written representation must be obtained each year.
	D – True	The engagement letter states that written representations will be required. Failure to provide one casts doubt over management integrity as it may indicate that information is being concealed from the auditor.
2	C	Sufficient other evidence is available to assess the reasonableness of depreciation.
3	A	The first course of action would be to try and resolve the issue with management. If that failed the auditor could discuss the matter with those charged with governance. The shareholders would not be involved in this issue. The audit opinion would be modified if the issue could not be resolved with management or those charged with governance.
4	D	Errors, frauds and omissions are all types of misstatement. Therefore the best description of a misstatement is answer D.
5	C	Even if misstatements are immaterial they should not be ignored altogether. The client will be asked to correct them. There is no need to modify the audit opinion if they remain uncorrected provided the refusal to correct does not indicate the presence of other misstatements. An Emphasis of Matter paragraph is not appropriate in this situation. There is no need to communicate immaterial matters to the users of the financial statements.

Reporting

Chapter learning objectives

This chapter covers syllabus areas:

- E5 – The Independent Auditor's Report
- C4c – Communicating with those charged with governance

Detailed syllabus objectives are provided in the introduction section of the text book.

PER

One of the PER performance objectives (PO20) is to review and report on the findings of an audit. You complete an audit, preparing the formal documentation and reporting any control deficiencies to management. You report back to managers in a formal audit report. Working through this chapter should help you understand how to demonstrate that objective.

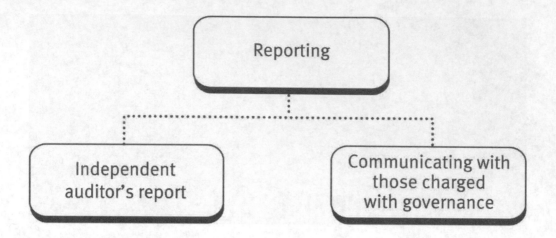

1 The independent auditor's report

When the audit work is complete, the auditor will prepare the auditor's report containing an opinion on the financial statements.

The objectives of the auditor are:

- To form an opinion on the financial statements based on an evaluation of the conclusions drawn from the audit evidence obtained, and

- To express clearly that opinion through a written report.

[ISA 700 *Forming an Opinion and Reporting on Financial Statements*, 6]

The auditor forms an opinion on whether the financial statements are prepared, in all material respects, in accordance with the applicable financial reporting framework.

Below is an illustration of and auditor's report and this chapter goes through each section in turn.

 Illustration 1 – Auditor's report

INDEPENDENT AUDITOR'S REPORT

To the Shareholders of Murray Company

Report on the Audit of the Financial Statements [sub-title is not included if there is no separate Report on Other Legal and Regulatory Requirements]

Opinion

We have audited the financial statements of the Murray Company (the Company), which comprise the statement of financial position as at 31 December, 20X4, and the statement of comprehensive income, statement of changes in equity and statement of cash flows for the year then ended, and notes to the financial statements, including a summary of significant accounting policies.

In our opinion, the accompanying financial statements present fairly, in all material respects, (or give a true and fair view of) the financial position of the Company as at December 31, 20X4, and its performance and its cash flows for the year then ended in accordance with International Financial Reporting Standards.

Basis for Opinion

We conducted our audit in accordance with International Standards on Auditing (ISAs). Our responsibilities under those standards are further described in the Auditor's Responsibilities for the Audit of the Financial Statements section of our report. We are independent of the Company in accordance with the ethical requirements that are relevant to our audit of the financial statements in [jurisdiction], and we have fulfilled our other ethical responsibilities in accordance with these requirements. We believe that the audit evidence we have obtained is sufficient and appropriate to provide a basis for our opinion.

Key audit matters [listed companies only]

Key audit matters are those matters that, in our professional judgment, were of most significance in our audit of the financial statements of the current period. These matters were addressed in the context of our audit of the financial statements as a whole, and in forming our opinion thereon, and we do not provide a separate opinion on these matters.

[Description of each key audit matter in accordance with ISA 701]

[Additional communications – only included if required]

Other information

Management is responsible for the other information. The other information comprises the Chair's statement, but does not include the financial statements and the auditor's report thereon.

Our opinion on the financial statements does not cover the other information and we do not express any form of assurance conclusion thereon.

In connection with our audit of the financial statements, our responsibility is to read the other information and, in doing so, consider whether the other information is materially inconsistent with the financial statements or our knowledge obtained in the audit or otherwise appears to be materially misstated. If, based on the work we have performed, we conclude that there is a material misstatement of this information, we are required to report that fact. We have nothing to report in this regard.

Responsibilities of Management and Those Charged With Governance for the Financial Statements

Management is responsible for the preparation and fair presentation of these financial statements in accordance with International Financial Reporting Standards, and for such internal control as management determines is necessary to enable the preparation of financial statements that are free from material misstatement, whether due to fraud or error.

In preparing the financial statements, management is responsible for assessing the Company's ability to continue as a going concern, disclosing as applicable, matters related to going concern and using the going concern basis of accounting unless management either intends to liquidate the Company or to cease operations, or has no realistic alternative but to do so.

Those charged with governance are responsible for overseeing the Company's financial reporting process.

Auditor's Responsibilities for the Audit of the Financial Statements

Our objectives are to obtain reasonable assurance about whether the financial statements as a whole are free from material misstatement, whether due to fraud or error, and to issue an auditor's report that includes our opinion. Reasonable assurance is a high level of assurance, but is not a guarantee that an audit conducted in accordance with ISAs will always detect a material misstatement when it exists. Misstatements can arise from fraud or error and are considered material if, individually or in the aggregate, they could reasonably be expected to influence the economic decisions of users taken on the basis of these financial statements.

As part of an audit in accordance with ISAs, we exercise professional judgment and maintain professional scepticism throughout the audit. We also:

- Identify and assess the risks of material misstatement of the financial statements, whether due to fraud or error, design and perform audit procedures responsive to those risks, and obtain audit evidence that is sufficient and appropriate to provide a basis for our opinion. The risk of not detecting a material misstatement resulting from fraud is higher than for one resulting from error, as fraud may involve collusion, forgery, intentional omissions, misrepresentations, or the override of internal control.

- Obtain an understanding of internal control relevant to the audit in order to design audit procedures that are appropriate in the circumstances, but not for the purpose of expressing an opinion on the effectiveness of the Company's internal control.

- Evaluate the appropriateness of accounting policies used and the reasonableness of accounting estimates and related disclosures made by management.
- Conclude on the appropriateness of management's use of the going concern basis of accounting and, based on the audit evidence obtained, whether a material uncertainty exists related to events or conditions that may cast significant doubt on the Company's ability to continue as a going concern. If we conclude that a material uncertainty exists, we are required to draw attention in our auditor's report to the related disclosures in the financial statements or, if such disclosures are inadequate, to modify our opinion. Our conclusions are based on the audit evidence obtained up to the date of our auditor's report. However, future events or conditions may cause the Company to cease to continue as a going concern.
- Evaluate the overall presentation, structure and content of the financial statements, including the disclosures, and whether the financial statements represent the underlying transactions and events in a manner that achieves fair presentation.

We communicate with those charged with governance regarding, among other matters, the planned scope and timing of the audit and significant findings, including any significant deficiencies in internal control that we identify during our audit.

We also provide those charged with governance with a statement that we have complied with relevant ethical requirements regarding independence, and to communicate with them all relationships and other matters that may reasonably be thought to bear on our independence, and where applicable, related safeguards.

From the matters communicated with those charged with governance, we determine those matters that were of most significance in the audit of the financial statements of the current period and are therefore the key audit matters. We describe these matters in our auditor's report unless law or regulation precludes public disclosure about the matter or when, in extremely rare circumstances, we determine that a matter should not be communicated in our report because the adverse consequences of doing so would reasonably be expected to outweigh the public interest benefits of such communication.

[Report on Other Legal and Regulatory Requirements – as required by local law, regulation or national auditing standards]

[Other matter – only included if required]

Wimble & Co

Wimble & Co, London

1 July 20X5

[ISA 700, Appendix]

2 Title and addressee

The title clearly identifies the report as an Independent Auditor's Report.

The addressee identifies the intended user of the report and shows to whom the auditor owes a duty of care.

3 Auditor's opinion

The auditor's opinion provides the auditor's conclusion as to whether the financial statements give a true and fair view.

The audit opinion can be **unmodified or modified**.

Nature of issue	Not material	Material but Not Pervasive	Material & Pervasive
Misstatement	Unmodified opinion True and fair view*	Modified Qualified Opinion Except for ...	Modified Adverse Opinion FS do not give a true and fair view*
Inability to obtain sufficient appropriate audit evidence	Unmodified opinion True and fair view*	Modified Qualified Opinion Except for ...	Modified Disclaimer of Opinion Do not express an opinion

* ISA 700 allows the wording 'true and fair view' or 'fairly presents'.

Unmodified opinion

The auditor will give an unmodified opinion when they conclude that the financial statements are prepared, in all material respects, in accordance with the applicable financial reporting framework. [ISA 700, 16]

This will mean:

- The financial statements adequately disclose the significant accounting policies.

- The accounting policies selected are consistently applied and appropriate.

- Accounting estimates made by management are reasonable.

- Information is relevant, reliable, comparable and understandable.

- The financial statements provide adequate disclosures to enable the users to understand the effects of material transactions and events.

- The terminology used is appropriate.

[ISA 700, 13]

Modified opinion

The auditor will need to modify the opinion when they conclude that:

- Based on the evidence obtained, **the financial statements** as a whole **are not free from material misstatement**. This is where the client has not complied with the applicable financial reporting framework.

- They have been **unable to obtain sufficient appropriate evidence** to be able to conclude that the financial statements as a whole are free from material misstatement. This is evidence the auditor would expect to exist to support the figures in the financial statements.

[ISA 705 *Modifications to the Opinion in the Independent Auditor's Report*, 6]

The nature of the modification depends on whether the auditor considers the matter to be **material but not pervasive**, or **material and pervasive**, to the financial statements.

Pervasive

A matter is considered '**pervasive**' if, in the auditor's judgment:

- The effects are not confined to specific elements, accounts or items of the financial statements

- If so confined, represent or could represent a substantial proportion of the financial statements, or

- In relation to disclosures, are fundamental to users' understanding of the financial statements.

[ISA 705, 5a]

In brief, a pervasive matter must be fundamental to the financial statements, therefore rendering them unreliable as a whole.

Qualified opinion

- If the misstatement or lack of sufficient appropriate evidence is **material but not pervasive**, a **qualified opinion** will be issued. [ISA 705, 7]

- This means the matter is material to the area of the financial statements affected but does not affect the remainder of the financial statements.

- Although significant to users' decision making, a material matter can be isolated while the remainder of the financial statements may be relied upon.

- The opinion will state that '**Except for**' this matter, the financial statements give a true and fair view.

Illustration 2 – Murray Co Qualified opinion due to misstatement

Qualified Opinion

We have audited the financial statements of Murray Company (the Company), which comprise the statement of financial position as at 31 December, 20X4, and the statement of comprehensive income, statement of changes in equity and statement of cash flows for the year then ended, and notes to the financial statements, including a summary of significant accounting policies.

In our opinion, **except for the effects of the matter described in the Basis for Qualified Opinion section of our report, the accompanying financial statements give a true and fair view**.................. *(remainder* of wording as per an unmodified opinion).

Basis for Qualified Opinion

No allowance has been provided in the financial statements for a receivable for which recoverability is in doubt, which, in our opinion, is not in accordance with International Financial Reporting Standards. The allowance for the year ended 31 December 20X4 should be $211,000 based on the value of the receivable in current assets and the likely recoverability of the amount. Accordingly, current assets should be reduced by an allowance of $211,000 and the profit for the year and accumulated profit should be decreased by the same amount.

We conducted our audit in accordance with International Standards on Auditing (ISAs). Our responsibilities under those standards are further described in the Auditor's Responsibilities for the Audit of the Financial Statements section of our report. We are independent of the Company in accordance with the ethical requirements that are relevant to our audit of the financial statements in [jurisdiction], and we have fulfilled our other ethical responsibilities in accordance with these requirements. **We believe that the audit evidence we have obtained is sufficient and appropriate to provide a basis for our qualified opinion.**

Illustration 3 – Murray Co Qualified opinion due to inability to obtain sufficient and appropriate evidence

Qualified Opinion

We have audited the financial statements of the Murray Company (the Company), which comprise the statement of financial position as at 31 December, 20X4, and the statement of comprehensive income, statement of changes in equity and statement of cash flows for the year then ended, and notes to the financial statements, including a summary of significant accounting policies.

In our opinion, **except for the possible effects of the matter described in the Basis for Qualified Opinion section of our report, the accompanying financial statements give a true and fair view**...............(remainder of wording as per an unmodified opinion).

Basis for Qualified Opinion

As described in note 8 to the financial statements, Murray Company is the defendant in a lawsuit alleging constructive dismissal. The Company has filed a counter action, and preliminary hearings and discovery proceedings on both actions are in progress. The liability has been disclosed as contingent In accordance IAS 37 *Provisions, Contingent Liabilities and Contingent Assets*. We have been unable to obtain a response to our request for information from the solicitors representing Murray Company in the case. We were unable to confirm or verify by alternative means the likely success of the lawsuit and therefore unable to determine whether disclosure of a contingent liability is appropriate, or whether a provision for the value of the claim of $280,000 should be included in the statement of financial position as at 31 December 20X4 and an associated expense included in the statement of profit or loss for the year ended 31 December 20X4. Consequently, we were unable to determine whether any adjustments to these amounts were necessary.

We conducted our audit in accordance with International Standards on Auditing (ISAs). Our responsibilities under those standards are further described in the Auditor's Responsibilities for the Audit of the Financial Statements section of our report. We are independent of the Company in accordance with the ethical requirements that are relevant to our audit of the financial statements in [jurisdiction], and we have fulfilled our other ethical responsibilities in accordance with these requirements. **We believe that the audit evidence we have obtained is sufficient and appropriate to provide a basis for our qualified opinion.**

Adverse opinion

An **adverse opinion** is issued when a misstatement is considered **material and pervasive**. [ISA 705, 8]

This will mean the financial statements **do not give a true and fair view**.

Examples include:

- Preparation of the financial statements on the wrong basis.

- Non-consolidation of a material subsidiary.

- Material misstatement of a balance which represents a substantial proportion of the assets or profits e.g. would change a profit to a loss.

Illustration 4 – Murray Co Adverse opinion

Adverse Opinion

We have audited the financial statements of the Murray Company (the Company), which comprise the statement of financial position as at 31 December, 20X4, and the statement of comprehensive income, statement of changes in equity and statement of cash flows for the year then ended, and notes to the financial statements, including a summary of significant accounting policies.

In our opinion, **because of the significance of the matter discussed in the Basis for Adverse Opinion section of our report, the accompanying financial statements do not give a true and fair view**.......... (remainder of wording as per an unmodified opinion).

Basis for Adverse Opinion

As explained in note 12 to the financial statements, the financial statements have been prepared on the going concern basis. However, in our opinion, due to the number and significance of the material uncertainties, Murray Co is not a going concern in accordance with IAS 1 *Presentation of Financial Statements* and therefore the financial statements should not be prepared on the going concern basis.... [explanation of the various effects on the amounts presented in the financial statements].

We conducted our audit in accordance with International Standards on Auditing (ISAs). Our responsibilities under those standards are further described in the Auditor's Responsibilities for the Audit of the Financial Statements section of our report. We are independent of the Company in accordance with the ethical requirements that are relevant to our audit of the financial statements in [jurisdiction], and we have fulfilled our other ethical responsibilities in accordance with these requirements. **We believe that the audit evidence we have obtained is sufficient and appropriate to provide a basis for our adverse opinion.**

Disclaimer of opinion

A **disclaimer of opinion** is issued when the auditor has not obtained sufficient appropriate evidence and the effects of any possible misstatements could be **pervasive**. [ISA 705, 9]

The auditor **does not express an opinion** on the financial statements in this situation.

Examples include:

- Failure by the client to keep adequate accounting records.

- Refusal by the directors to provide written representation.

- Failure by the client to provide evidence over a single balance which represents a substantial proportion of the assets or profits or over multiple balances in the financial statements.

Illustration 5 – Murray Co Disclaimer of opinion

Disclaimer of Opinion

We were engaged to audit the financial statements of Murray Company (the Company), which comprise the statement of financial position as at 31 December, 20X4, and the statement of comprehensive income, statement of changes in equity and statement of cash flows for the year then ended, and notes to the financial statements, including a summary of significant accounting policies.

We do not express an opinion on the accompanying financial statements. Because of the significance of the matter described in the Basis for Disclaimer of Opinion section of our report, **we have not been able to obtain sufficient appropriate evidence to provide a basis for an audit opinion on these financial statements**.

Basis for Disclaimer of Opinion

Due to a fire at a third party warehouse provider's premises, the records relating to inventory held there were destroyed. We were unable to confirm or verify by alternative means closing inventory of $1,054,000 deducted from cost of sales included in the statement of profit or loss for the year ended 31 December 20X4, and the inventory balance of $1,054,000 included in the statement of financial position as at 31 December 20X4.

As a result, we were unable to determine whether any adjustments to the financial statements might have been necessary in respect of recorded or unrecorded inventory or cost of sales, and the associated elements of the statement of changes in equity and statement of cash flows.

Responsibilities of Management and Those Charged With Governance for the Financial Statements

[Wording as per ISA 700]

> *Auditor's Responsibilities for the Audit of the Financial Statements*
>
> Our responsibility is to conduct an audit of the financial statements in accordance with International Standards on Auditing and to issue an auditor's report. However, because of the matter described in the Basis for Disclaimer of Opinion section of our report, we were not able to obtain sufficient appropriate evidence to provide a basis for an audit opinion on these financial statements.
>
> We are independent of the Company in accordance with ethical requirements that are relevant to our audit of the financial statements in [jurisdiction], and we have fulfilled our other ethical responsibilities in accordance with these requirements.

Impact of a disclaimer of opinion

Where a disclaimer of opinion is being issued:

- The statement that sufficient appropriate evidence to provide a basis for the auditor's opinion has been obtained is not included.

- The statement that the financial statements have been audited is changed to 'we were engaged to audit the financial statements'.

[ISA 705, 19]

- The statements regarding the audit being conducted in accordance with ISAs, and independence and other ethical responsibilities, are positioned within the Auditor Responsibilities section rather than the Basis for Disclaimer of Opinion section. [ISA 705, A25]

- The Key Audit Matters section is not included in the report as to do so would suggest the financial statements are more credible in relation to those matters which would be inconsistent with the disclaimer of opinion on the financial statements as a whole. [ISA 705, 29]

Management imposed limitation of scope

If management impose a limitation of scope after the audit has been accepted the auditor must:

- Request that management remove the limitation. [ISA 705, 11]

- If management refuse, communicate with those charged with governance. [ISA 705, 12]

- Perform alternative audit procedures if possible. [ISA 705, 12]

- Issue a qualified audit opinion if the matter is considered material but not pervasive. [ISA 705, 13a]

- Withdraw from the audit if the matter is pervasive. If withdrawal is not possible before issuing the auditor's report, a disclaimer of opinion should be issued. [ISA 705, 13b]

4 Basis for Opinion section

Within a report containing an unmodified or modified opinion

The basis for opinion section refers to the professional standards the auditor has followed in order to be able to form an opinion on the financial statements, to provide confidence to users that the report can be relied upon.

Within a report containing a modified opinion

When the auditor modifies the opinion, the basis for opinion section will explain the reason why the opinion is modified e.g. which balances are misstated, which disclosures are missing or inadequate, which balances the auditor was unable to obtain sufficient appropriate evidence over and why. [ISA 705, 20b]

The title of the section must reflect the type of opinion being issued. Therefore the auditor must amend the heading 'Basis for Opinion' to 'Basis for Qualified Opinion', 'Basis for Adverse Opinion' or 'Basis for Disclaimer of Opinion', as appropriate. [ISA 705, 20a]

Where a qualified or adverse opinion is being issued, the auditor must amend the statement '...the audit evidence is sufficient and appropriate to provide a basis for the auditor's qualified/adverse opinion ' [ISA 705, 25]

If possible, a quantification of the financial effect of the modification will be included. [ISA 705, 21]

If the material misstatement relates to narrative disclosures, an explanation of how the disclosures are misstated should be included, or in the case of omitted disclosures, the disclosure should be included if the information is readily available. [ISA 705, 22]

Nature of issue	Not material	Material but Not Pervasive	Material & Pervasive
Misstatement	Unmodified opinion True and fair view Basis for opinion	Modified Qualified Opinion Except for ... Basis for qualified opinion	Modified Adverse Opinion FS do not give a true and fair view Basis for adverse opinion
Inability to obtain sufficient appropriate audit evidence	Unmodified opinion True and fair view Basis for opinion	Modified Qualified Opinion Except for ... Basis for qualified opinion	Modified Disclaimer of Opinion Do not express an opinion Basis for disclaimer of opinion

5 Key Audit Matters section

ISA 701 *Communicating Key Audit Matters in the Independent Auditor's Report* requires auditors of **listed companies** to determine key audit matters and to communicate those matters in the auditor's report. [ISA 701, 5]

 Key audit matters are those that in the auditor's professional judgment were of most significance in the audit and are selected from matters communicated to those charged with governance.
[ISA 701, 8]

The auditor of a non-listed entity may voluntarily, or at the request of management or those charged with governance, include key audit matters in the auditor's report.

The purpose of including these matters is to assist users in understanding the entity, and to provide a basis for the users to engage with management and those charged with governance about matters relating to the entity and the financial statements. [ISA 701, 3]

Each key audit matter should describe why the matter was considered to be significant and how it was addressed in the audit.

Key audit matters include:

- Areas of higher assessed risk of material misstatement, or significant risks identified in accordance with ISA 315 (Revised 2019) *Identifying and Assessing the Risks of Material Misstatement*.

- Significant auditor judgments relating to areas in the financial statements that involved significant management judgment, including accounting estimates that have been identified as having high estimation uncertainty.

- The effect on the audit of significant events or transactions that occurred during the period.

[ISA 701, 9]

Specific examples include:

- Significant fraud risk

- Goodwill

- Valuation of financial instruments

- Fair values

- Effects of new accounting standards

- Revenue recognition

- Material provisions such as a restructuring provision

- Implementation of a new IT system, or significant changes to an existing system.

Illustration 6 – Key Audit Matter

Integrated website and finance systems	How our audit addressed the Key Audit Matter
During the year the company introduced a new website which enables customers to order online. The website is integrated with the finance system. There is a risk of material misstatement in relation to completeness of revenue.	• Obtaining an understanding of the new system and the controls management implemented to ensure the system works effectively. • Testing controls over the new website and finance system. • Performing substantive tests of detail over completeness of income.

Note that a matter giving rise to a qualified or adverse opinion, or a material uncertainty related to going concern are by their nature key audit matters. However, they would not be described in this section of the report. Instead, a reference to the Basis for qualified or adverse opinion or the going concern section would be included. [ISA 701, 15]

If there are no key audit matters to communicate, the auditor shall:

- Discuss this with the engagement quality control reviewer, if one has been appointed.

- Communicate this conclusion to those charged with governance. [ISA 701, 17b]

- Explain in the key audit matters section of the auditor's report that there are no matters to report. [ISA 701, 16]

6   Additional communications

In certain circumstances auditors are required to make additional communications in the auditor's report even though the financial statements show a true and fair view. Issues requiring communication include:

- **Material Uncertainty Related to Going Concern** (ISA 570 *Going Concern*)

- **Emphasis of Matter paragraph** (ISA 706 *Emphasis of Matter Paragraphs and Other Matter Paragraphs in an Auditor's Report*)

- **Other Matter paragraph** (ISA 706)

It is important to note that these **do not impact the wording of the opinion** and do not constitute either a qualified, adverse or disclaimer of opinion.

Material Uncertainty Related to Going Concern

This section is included when there is a material uncertainty regarding the going concern status which the directors have adequately disclosed in the financial statements. The auditor uses this section to draw the attention of the user to the client's disclosure note. [ISA 570, 22]

Illustration 7 – Material Uncertainty Related to Going Concern

We draw attention to Note 6 in the financial statements, concerning the uncertainty of Murray Company's future funding. The Company is seeking new funding through an initial public offering of shares. In the event that the initial public offering does not proceed, this will require the Company's existing banking arrangements to be renegotiated and additional funding to be raised from either existing or new investors. This condition indicates the existence of a material uncertainty which may cast significant doubt on the Company's ability to continue as a going concern. The financial statements do not include any adjustments that would result if the Company was unable to continue as a going concern. Our opinion is not modified in respect of this matter.

Emphasis of Matter paragraph

An Emphasis of Matter paragraph is used to refer to **a matter that has been appropriately presented or disclosed in the financial statements** by the directors. The auditor's judgment is that these matters are **of such fundamental importance to the users' understanding** of the financial statements that the auditor should emphasise the disclosure. [ISA 706, 7a]

Examples of such fundamental matters include:

- An uncertainty relating to the future outcome of exceptional litigation or regulatory action.

- A significant subsequent event occurs between the date of the financial statements and the date of the auditor's report.

- Early application of a new accounting standard.

- Major catastrophes that have had a significant effect on the entity's financial position.

[ISA 706, A5]

In addition, an Emphasis of Matter paragraph will be used where:

- The financial statements have been prepared on a basis other than the going concern basis.

- The corresponding figures have been restated.

- The financial statements have been recalled and reissued or when the auditor provides an amended auditor's report.

Illustration 8 – Emphasis of Matter Paragraph

We draw attention to Note 12 of the financial statements, which describes the effects of a fire at the premises of a third party warehouse provider. Our opinion is not modified in respect of this matter.

Position in the auditor's report

An Emphasis of matter paragraph is usually included after the Basis for Opinion section. When a Key Audit Matters section is presented in the auditor's report, an Emphasis of Matter paragraph may be presented either directly before or after the Key Audit Matters section, based on the auditor's judgment as to the relative significance of the information included in the Emphasis of Matter paragraph.

The heading of the paragraph can be amended to provide further context, for example, Emphasis of Matter – Subsequent event. [ISA 706, A16]

 Tutorial notes

An Emphasis of Matter paragraph is not used to draw attention to immaterial misstatements. The fact that they are immaterial means they do not warrant the attention of the shareholders.

An Emphasis of Matter paragraph can only be used when adequate disclosure has been made of the matters mentioned above. The auditor can only emphasise something that is already included.

Where adequate disclosure has not been made the opinion will need to be modified and an Emphasis of Matter paragraph should NOT be used.

An Emphasis of Matter should not be used to highlight an issue already included in the Key Audit Matters section. The auditor must use judgment to determine which section they consider is the most appropriate to highlight the issue.

Other Matter paragraph

An Other Matter paragraph is included in the auditor's report if the auditor considers it necessary to communicate to the users regarding **matters other than those presented or disclosed in the financial statements** that, in the auditor's judgment, are **relevant to understanding the audit, the auditor's responsibilities, or the auditor's report**.
[ISA 706, 7b]

Examples of its use include:

- To communicate that the auditor's report is intended solely for the intended users, and should not be distributed to or used by other parties. [ISA 706, A14]

- When law, regulation or generally accepted practice requires or permits the auditor to provide further explanation of their responsibilities. [ISA 706, A11]

- To explain why the auditor has not resigned, when a pervasive inability to obtain sufficient appropriate evidence is imposed by management (e.g. denying the auditor access to books and records) but the auditor is unable to withdraw from the engagement due to legal restrictions. [ISA 706, A10]

- To communicate audit planning and scoping matters where laws or regulations require. [ISA 706, A9]

- Where an entity prepares one set of accounts in accordance with a general purpose framework and another set in accordance with a different one (e.g. one according to UK and one according to International standards) and engages the auditor to report on both sets. [ISA 706, A13]

Illustration 9 – Other Matter Paragraph

The financial statements of Murray Co for the year ended December 31, 20X3, were audited by another auditor who expressed an unmodified opinion on those statements on May 31, 20X4.

Position in the auditor's report

When an Other Matter paragraph is included to draw the users' attention to a matter relating to other reporting responsibilities addressed in the auditor's report, the paragraph may be included in the Report on Other Legal and Regulatory Requirements section.

When relevant to all auditor's responsibilities or users' understanding of the auditor's report, the Other Matter paragraph may be included as a separate section following the Report on the Other Legal and Regulatory Requirements.

The heading may be amended to provide further context, for example, Other Matter – Scope of the audit.
[ISA 706, A16]

 Tutorial note

An Other Matter paragraph does not include confidential information or information required to be provided by management. [ISA 706, A15]

7 Other Information section

 Other information refers to financial or non-financial information, other than the financial statements and auditor's report thereon, included in the entity's annual report.
[ISA 720 (Revised) *The Auditor's Responsibilities Relating to Other Information*, 12c]

Examples of other information include:

- Chair's report

- Operating and financial review

- Social and environmental reports

- Corporate governance statements.

If the auditor obtains the final version of the other information before the date of the auditor's report, they must read it to identify any material inconsistencies with the financial statements or the auditor's knowledge obtained during the audit. [ISA 720, 3]

If the auditor identifies a material inconsistency they should:

- Perform procedures to evaluate the inconsistency. The auditor should consider whether it is the financial statements or the other information that requires amendment. [ISA 720, 16]

- Discuss the matter with management and ask them to make the correction. [ISA 720, 17]

- If management refuse to make the correction, communicate the matter to those charged with governance. [ISA 720, 17b]

- If the matter remains uncorrected the auditor must describe the material misstatement in the Other Information section of the auditor's report. [ISA 720, 18a]

- Alternatively, the auditor should withdraw from the engagement if possible under applicable law or regulation as the issue casts doubt over management integrity. [ISA 720, 18b]

The Other Information section within the auditor's report:

- Identifies the other information obtained by the auditor prior to the date of the auditor's report.

- States that the auditor has not audited the other information and accordingly does not express an opinion or conclusion on that information.

- Includes a description of the auditor's responsibilities with respect to the other information.

- States either that the auditor has nothing to report or provides a description of the material misstatement if applicable.

[ISA 720, 22]

Purpose

The auditor must not be knowingly associated with information which is misleading. [ISA 720, 4]

Misstatement of other information exists when the other information is incorrectly stated or otherwise misleading (including because it omits or obscures information necessary for a proper understanding of a matter). [ISA 720, 12b]

Material misstatements or inconsistencies in the other information may undermine the credibility of the financial statements and the auditor's report. [ISA 720, 3]

Tutorial notes

The auditor must retain a copy of the final version of the other information on the audit file. [ISA 720, 25b]

If the auditor issues a disclaimer of opinion on the financial statements, the Other Information section should not be included in the auditor's report as to do so may overshadow the disclaimer of opinion. [ISA 720, A58]

8 Responsibilities of management and auditors

The responsibilities of management and auditors are included to help minimise the expectation gap.

The section on management responsibilities clarifies that management is responsible for preparing the financial statements and for the internal controls.

The section on auditor's responsibilities clarifies that the auditor is responsible for expressing reasonable assurance as to whether the financial statements give a true and fair view and express that opinion in the auditor's report. The section also describes the auditor's responsibilities in respect of risk assessment, internal controls, going concern and accounting policies.

9 Report on Other Legal and Regulatory Requirements

This section highlights any additional reporting responsibilities, if applicable. This may include responsibilities in some jurisdictions to report on the adequacy of accounting records, internal controls over financial reporting, or other information published with the financial statements such as the Strategic Report in the UK.

10 Signature, auditor's address and date

The signature identifies the audit firm responsible for the auditor's report and opinion. If the company is a listed company, the report would include the name of the engagement partner.

The auditor's address identifies the specific office of the engagement partner responsible for the report in case of any queries.

The date identifies the date up to which the audit work has been performed. Any information that comes to light after this date will not have been considered by the auditor when forming their opinion. The report must be signed and dated after the date the directors approved the financial statements. Often, the financial statements are approved and the auditor's report signed on the same day.

Going concern reporting implications

Situation	Impact on audit opinion	Impact on auditor's report
No material uncertainty exists regarding going concern.	Unmodified – Financial statements give a true and fair view.	No impact
Material uncertainty exists and is adequately disclosed by management.	Unmodified – Financial statements give a true and fair view.	Additional communication: 'Material Uncertainty Related to Going Concern'.
Material uncertainty exists which is not adequately disclosed or is omitted.	Modified – qualified or adverse.	Basis for qualified/adverse opinion will explain the going concern issues management has failed to disclose adequately.
Company is not a going concern and has prepared the financial statements on the break up basis appropriately and made adequate disclosure of this fact.	Unmodified – Financial statements give a true and fair view.	Additional communication: Emphasis of matter paragraph.
Company is not a going concern and has prepared the financial statements using the going concern basis of accounting.	Modified – adverse opinion.	Basis for adverse opinion will explain the incorrect basis of accounting has been used and quantify the effect of this on the financial statements.
The period assessed by management is less than twelve months from the statement of financial position date and management is unwilling to extend the assessment.	Modified – qualified or disclaimer due to an inability to obtain sufficient appropriate audit evidence regarding the use of the going concern basis of accounting.	Basis for qualified/disclaimer opinion explaining that sufficient appropriate evidence was not obtained to form a conclusion on whether the going concern basis of preparation is appropriate.

Exam question approach

The exam will regularly feature a requirement asking for the implications for the auditor's report if issues identified during the audit are not resolved. The following approach should be taken to answer this type of requirement.

Explain the implications for the auditor's report

1   Materiality assessment – if the issue is not material it won't affect the auditor's report. Calculate the percentage of assets and profit the issue represents and state whether this is material or not material.

2   Identify the type of issue

–   Material misstatement – non-compliance with an accounting standard.

–   Inability to obtain sufficient appropriate evidence – evidence the auditor would expect to obtain hasn't been obtained.

–   Material uncertainty – significant events where the outcome will only be known in the future.

–   Inconsistency with the other published information – contradiction between the financial statements and the other information which is not subject to audit e.g. chair's statement, corporate social responsibility (CSR) report, etc.

–   A matter that is of importance to the scope of the audit, the auditor's assessment of materiality, assessment of risk of material misstatement or other key audit matter that the auditor should specifically refer to in their report.

3   Comment on the issue

–   Which accounting standard has not been complied with and why?

–   Which piece of evidence has not been obtained and why?

–   What event/outcome is uncertain?

–   What is the contradiction in the unaudited information?

–   Explain why the auditor focused specifically on the key audit matters described in greater detail in the auditor's report e.g. involved a high degree of management judgment, required complex accounting treatment creating significant risk of material misstatement.

4 State whether the issue is material but not pervasive or material and pervasive. If it is isolated or relatively small in impact it will be material but not pervasive. If it makes the financial statements as a whole unreliable it will be material and pervasive.

5 Conclude on the opinion

 – Unmodified if there are no material misstatements and sufficient appropriate evidence has been obtained, or

 – Modified if there is material misstatement or the auditor has been unable to obtain sufficient appropriate evidence.

6 State the name of opinion and the key wording of that opinion

 – Unmodified – 'The financial statements give a true and fair view'

 – Qualified – 'Except for the matter described in the basis for opinion, the financial statements give a true and fair view'

 – Adverse – 'The financial statements do not give a true and fair view'

 – Disclaimer – 'The auditor does not express an opinion'

Tutorial Note: Do not list every possible opinion. Select the one which is most appropriate for the situation.

7 State any other reporting implications

 – Basis for modified opinion if the opinion is modified

 – Material Uncertainty Related to Going concern section

 – Emphasis of Matter paragraph

 – Other Matter paragraph

 – An inconsistency needs to be described in the Other Information section

 – Requires inclusion in the Key Audit Matters section for a listed entity.

11 Communicating with those charged with governance

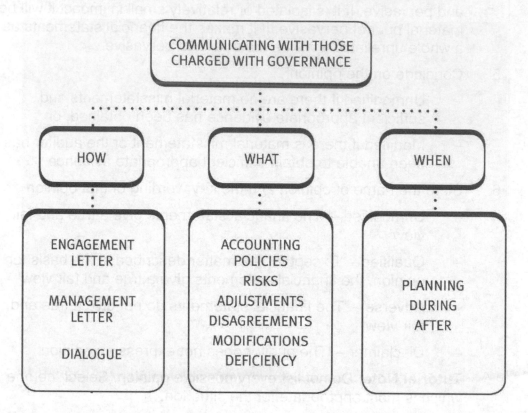

ISA 260 *Communication with Those Charged with Governance* and ISA 265 *Communicating Deficiencies in Internal Control to Those Charged with Governance and Management*, require the external auditor to engage in communications with management.

The main forms of formal communication between the auditors and management are: the engagement letter (see 'Ethics and Acceptance' chapter); and another written communication, usually sent at the end of the audit, which is often referred to as 'the management letter.'

In addition, the auditor will communicate with those charged with governance throughout the audit as required.

Reasons for communicating with those charged with governance

- To communicate responsibilities of the auditor and an overview of the scope and timing of the audit.

- To obtain information relevant to the audit.

- To report matters from the audit on a timely basis.

- To promote effective two-way communication.

[ISA 260, 9]

Matters to be communicated

- The auditor's responsibilities in relation to the financial statements audit. [ISA 260, 14]

- The planned scope and timing of the audit including, for example:

  - How the auditor plans to address the risks of material misstatement

  - The application of materiality in the context of an audit

  - Preliminary views about matters which may be key audit matters

  - The auditor's approach to the entity's system of internal control

  - The extent to which the auditor is planning to use the work of internal audit and the arrangements for so doing

  - Business risks that may result in material misstatements

  - Communications with regulators.

[ISA 260, 15, A13, A14]

- Significant findings from the audit, such as:

  The auditor's views about qualitative aspects of the entity's accounting practices/policies

  - Significant difficulties encountered during the audit

  - Significant matters arising during the audit that were discussed with management

  - Written representations the auditor is requesting

  - Circumstances that affect the form and content of the auditor's report, if any. This includes any expected modifications to the opinion, key audit matters and material uncertainty related to going concern

  - Other matters that, in the auditor's opinion, are significant to the oversight of the reporting process.

[ISA 260, 16 & A24]

- Matters of auditor independence including:

  - A statement that the firm has complied with ethical requirements,

  - Professional fees for audit and non-audit services charged during the period

  - Safeguards applied to eliminate or reduce threats to independence.

[ISA 260, 17]

Ultimately what constitutes a matter requiring the attention of those charged with governance is a matter of professional judgment. Typical examples include:

- Delays in obtaining information for the audit.

- An unreasonably brief time within which to complete the audit.

- Expected limitations on the audit, either imposed by management or other circumstances.

- The potential effect on the financial statements of any material risks and exposures, such as pending litigation, that are required to be disclosed in the financial statements.

- A summary of identified misstatements, whether corrected or not by the entity and a request that they are adjusted.

- Material uncertainties related to events and conditions that may cast significant doubt on the entity's ability to continue as a going concern.

- Any other matters agreed upon in the terms of the audit engagement.

 Timing of communication with those charged with governance

Stage of audit	Communication required
Planning	Significant risks identified by the auditor
	How the auditor plans to address the risks
	Auditor's approach to internal control relevant to the audit
	Application of materiality in the context of an audit
During the audit	If any situation occurs and it would not be appropriate to delay communication until the audit is concluded
Conclusion of the audit	Major findings from the audit work.
	Delays caused by management

The auditor must take care not to compromise the effectiveness of the audit by communicating too much information about the planned scope and timing of the audit to such an extent that procedures become too predictable.

Test your understanding 1

Murray case study: Auditor's report

As a result of the going concern review undertaken at the completion stage, the audit engagement partner has decided that there is a material uncertainty regarding the going concern status of Murray Co. The partner has requested that the directors make adequate disclosure in the final version of the financial statements for the year ended 31 December 20X4.

Required:

Describe the impact on the auditor's report for the year ended 31 December 20X4 if:

(i)   The directors include disclosure regarding the material uncertainty over going concern, which in the partner's view is adequate.

(3 marks)

(ii)   The directors refuse to include any disclosure on the matter.

(3 marks)

(Total: 6 marks)

Test your understanding 2

ISA 260 *Communication with Those Charged with Governance* deals with the auditor's responsibility to communicate with those charged with governance in relation to an audit of financial statements.

Required:

(i)   Describe TWO specific responsibilities of those charged with governance.

(2 marks)

(ii)   Explain FOUR examples of matters that might be communicated to them by the auditor.

(4 marks)

(Total: 6 marks)

Test your understanding 3

Henry

(a) Aragon Co operates a perpetual inventory system. No year-end count is performed. You have reviewed the level of adjustments made each month after each perpetual count and concluded that due to the significance of the adjustments, the inventory system is not reliable. You have requested that a full year-end count is performed but management has refused saying it would be too disruptive. The inventory balance is $4 million. Sales revenue is $50 million and profit for the year is $15 million.

(b) Boleyn Co has not made allowance for an irrecoverable debt of $50,000 in respect of a customer declared bankrupt just after the year-end. Profit for the year is $500,000.

(c) Seymour Co is being sued by a competitor for the theft of intellectual property. The amount of the claim is material and the case could go either way. The claim is not mentioned anywhere in the financial statements.

(d) Howard Co is a cash retailer. There is no system to confirm the accuracy of cash sales.

(e) Cleves Co has neglected to include a statement of profit or loss in its financial statements.

(f) Parr Co is involved in a major court case that would bankrupt the company if lost. The directors assess and disclose the case as a contingent liability in the accounts. The auditor agrees with the treatment and disclosure.

Required:

For each of the above situations describe the implications for the independent auditor's report.

(18 marks)

Test your understanding 4

You are the audit manager of Brakes Co, a listed client. Brakes Co is a global manufacturer of braking systems for use in domestic and commercial motor vehicles. $250,000 was raised through a new share issue in the year. Draft profit before tax is $9m and total assets are $37m. The audit is nearly complete and you are undertaking an overall review of the audit evidence on file.

(a) **Explain the importance of the overall review of evidence obtained.**

(3 marks)

(b) During your review you notice that the section of the file relating to share capital and reserves is incomplete.

Required:

Describe audit procedures that should be performed in respect of Brake's share capital and reserves.

(4 marks)

(c) The following matters arising during the audit of Brakes Co have been noted on file for your attention:

(i) A customer of Brakes Co had to withdraw one of their family car models this year due to concerns over the safety of the braking system. The customer has lodged a legal claim against Brakes Co for $10 million for the negligent supply of faulty braking systems. The company's lawyers believe that there is an 80% chance that Brakes Co will lose the case but the directors believe that their quality control procedures have always been robust and that the braking systems will be proven to have been safe. They have however decided to disclose the matter in the financial statements as a contingent liability.

(5 marks)

(ii) Brakes Co also produces and sells brake fluid. Another customer has recently returned a small batch of brake fluid because the fluid appeared to be contaminated with oil. Brakes Co issued the customer with a credit note for the full value of $137,500 and correctly accounted for this in the draft financial statements. As the brake fluid was returned before the year-end, Brakes Co has included it in the year-end inventory listing at cost of $125,000. Brakes Co may be able to re-filter and re-sell the brake fluid at the original selling price, but filtering will cost a further $62,500.

(4 marks)

(iii) Four months ago, Brakes Co began renting some additional warehouse space from a third party storage provider, Wheels Co. At the year end, raw materials with a value of $3.2 million belonging to Brakes Co were stored at Wheels Co's premises. The directors of Brakes Co did not make you aware of the new third party storage facility. Consequently, no audit procedures were performed to verify the raw materials.

(4 marks)

Required:

Discuss each of these issues and describe the impact on the independent auditor's report if the above issues remain unresolved.

Note: The mark allocation is shown against each of the three issues above.

(13 marks)

(Total: 20 marks)

 Test your understanding 5

You are about to issue the auditor's report for Exmouth Co, a listed client. Half way through the year the company suffered a major computer systems failure which destroyed the accounting records for the year to date. Backups had not been kept and so the company has had to reconstruct the figures for the first six months.

1   **Which opinions are most appropriate for Exmouth Co?**

A   Qualified or adverse

B   Unmodified or adverse

C   Unmodified or disclaimer

D   Qualified or disclaimer

2   **What is the purpose of the Basis for Opinion paragraph in an auditor's report which contains an unmodified opinion?**

A   To state the opinion on the financial statements

B   To confirm the audit has been conducted in accordance with ISAs and ethical requirements

C   To highlight a material uncertainty related to going concern which has been adequately disclosed

D   To highlight management's responsibilities to the users of the financial statements

3 **Which of the following shows the correct order of the elements to be included in the auditor's report of Exmouth Co?**

A Opinion, date, auditor's address, signature

B Title, opinion, signature, key audit matters

C Addressee, opinion, auditor's responsibilities, date

D Responsibilities of management, basis for opinion, date, addressee

4 **Which of the following describes the wording of a disclaimer of opinion?**

A The financial statements give a true and fair view

B The financial statements do not give a true and fair view

C The auditor does not express an opinion on the financial statements

D Except for the matter described, the financial statements give a true and fair view

5 **Which of the following statements is correct in relation to the auditor's report of Exmouth Co?**

A The Key Audit Matters section should be used to describe the matter giving rise to the modified opinion, in this case that the auditor has been unable to obtain sufficient appropriate evidence

B If a disclaimer of opinion is to be issued, the Key Audit Matters section should not be included in the auditor's report as to do so may suggest other aspects of the financial statements are reliable

C An Emphasis of Matter paragraph should be included to draw attention to the inability to obtain sufficient appropriate evidence

D The auditor will conclude that the financial statements do not give a true and fair view

Test your understanding 6

You are about to issue the auditor's report for two listed clients, Kalgoorlie Co and Cundeelee Co. The financial statements show the following:

	Kalgoorlie	Cundeelee
	$000	$000
Profit before tax	10	245
Total assets	2,300	6,500
Uncorrected misstatements:		
Overstatement of receivables due to an irrecoverable debt not being written off	15	
Overstatement of inventory due to failure to value at lower of cost and NRV		85

1   **Which of the following is the most appropriate opinion for Kalgoorlie Co?**

    A   Adverse

    B   Disclaimer

    C   Qualified

    D   Unmodified

2   **Which of the following is the most appropriate opinion for Cundeelee Co?**

    A   Adverse

    B   Disclaimer

    C   Qualified

    D   Unmodified

3   **If the misstatement of inventory had been $10,000 instead of $85,000, which is the most appropriate opinion for Cundeelee Co?**

    A   Adverse opinion

    B   Unmodified opinion with emphasis of matter

    C   Qualified opinion

    D   Unmodified opinion

4 **You have also identified a material uncertainty related to going concern during your audit of Kalgoorlie Co. This has been adequately disclosed by management. How will this impact the auditor's report?**

A The report should include a section titled 'Emphasis of Matter' which will refer to the management's disclosure note

B The report should include a section titled 'Material Uncertainty Related to Going Concern' which will refer to the management's disclosure note

C The report should include a section titled 'Going concern issues' which will refer to the management's disclosure note

D As management has adequately disclosed the uncertainty related to going concern, the auditor does not need to refer to the matter as the financial statements include the appropriate information

5 Included within the financial statements of Cundeelee Co is a provision for a legal case of which the outcome is uncertain at this date. Adequate disclosure of the matter has been included by management. The case represents a significant uncertainty and you have included an emphasis of matter in the auditor's report to refer to the client's disclosure of the uncertainty.

What other implications will there be for the auditor's report, if any, in respect of this matter?

A The opinion should be modified as a result of the significant uncertainty

B No further reporting implications

C The Key Audit Matters section should describe the uncertainty

D The Basis for Opinion section should describe the uncertainty

12   Chapter summary

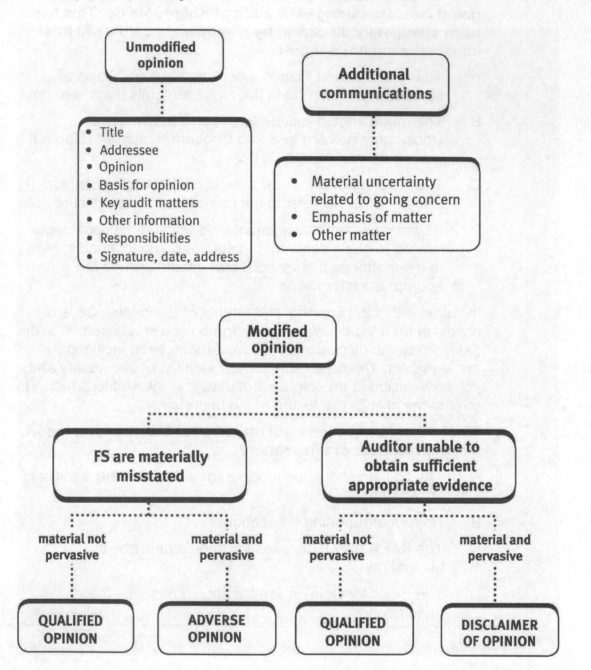

Test your understanding answers

 Test your understanding 1

(i)   If the directors make adequate disclosures regarding the material uncertainty over the going concern status of Murray Co, the financial statements will show a true and fair view.

As there is no material misstatement, or lack of sufficient appropriate evidence on this matter, the audit opinion can remain unmodified.

Additional communication will be required in the form of a Material Uncertainty Related to Going Concern paragraph. This will draw the shareholder's attention to the disclosure note.

The paragraph will state that our opinion is not modified in this respect.

The paragraph will be inserted below the basis for opinion paragraph.

(ii)   If the directors refuse to make any disclosures, then in the auditor's opinion, the financial statements are materially misstated.

The audit opinion will need to be modified due to this material misstatement.

The type of opinion given depends on whether the auditor considers the misstatement to be material and pervasive or material but not pervasive.

If it is pervasive, an adverse opinion will be given. The opinion will state 'In our opinion the financial statements do not give a true and fair view/are not fairly presented'.

If it is not considered pervasive, a qualified opinion will be given. The opinion will state 'Except for the matter described in the basis for qualified opinion paragraph below, in our opinion the financial statements show a true and fair view/are fairly presented'.

The basis for opinion paragraph will need to change to a basis for qualified/adverse opinion and will explain the reason for the modified opinion.

Test your understanding 2

(i) Those charged with governance are responsible for overseeing:

– The strategic direction of the entity

– Obligations related to the accountability of the entity. This includes overseeing the financial reporting process

– Promotion of good corporate governance

– Risk assessment processes

– The establishment and monitoring of internal controls

– Compliance with applicable law and regulations

– Implementation of controls to prevent and detect fraud and errors.

(ii) General audit matters that might be communicated to those charged with governance are:

1 The auditor's responsibilities in relation to financial statement audit. This includes:

– A statement that the auditor is responsible for forming and expressing an opinion on the financial statements.

– That the auditor's work is carried out in accordance with ISAs and in accordance with local laws and regulations.

2 Planned scope and timing of the audit. This includes:

– The audit approach to assessing the risk of serious misstatement, whether arising from fraud or error.

– The audit approach to the internal control system and whether reliance will be placed on it.

– The timing of interim and final audits, including reporting deadlines.

3 Significant findings from the audit. This includes:

– Significant difficulties encountered during the audit, including delays in obtaining information from management.

– Significant deficiencies in internal control and recommendations for improvement.

– Audit adjustments, whether or not recorded by the entity, that have, or could have, a material effect on the entity's financial statements. For example, the bankruptcy of a material receivable shortly after the year-end that should result in an adjusting entry.

4   A statement on independence issues affecting the audit. This includes:

  –   That the audit firm has ensured that all members of the audit team have complied with ethical requirements.

  –   That appropriate safeguards are in place where a potential threat to independence has been identified.

Test your understanding 3

(a) **Aragon**

  –   Inventory is material as it represents 8% of sales revenue and 27% of profit.

  –   There is a lack of sufficient appropriate audit evidence over inventory. The auditor cannot form a conclusion as to whether inventory is materially misstated or free from material misstatement.

  –   The audit opinion will be modified.

  –   A qualified opinion using the 'except for' wording will be issued as the matter is material but not pervasive.

  –   The basis for opinion section will be amended to basis for qualified opinion.

  –   The basis for qualified opinion section will explain the reason for the qualified opinion and quantify the effect of the issue on the financial statements.

(b) **Boleyn**

  –   The balance is material as it represents 10% of profit.

  –   An irrecoverable debt has not been written off. The financial statements will be materially misstated due to overstatement of receivables.

  –   The audit opinion will be modified.

  –   A qualified opinion using the 'except for' wording will be issued as the matter is material but not pervasive.

  –   The basis for opinion section will be amended to basis for qualified opinion.

  –   The basis for qualified opinion section will explain the reason for the qualified opinion and quantify the effect of the issue on the financial statements.

(c) **Seymour**

- The claim is material and represents an uncertainty that should be communicated to the users of the financial statements.

- As the claim could go either way, a contingent liability should be disclosed. Failure to do this will mean the financial statements are materially misstated.

- The audit opinion will be modified.

- A qualified opinion using the 'except for' wording will be issued as the matter is material but not pervasive.

- The basis for opinion section will be amended to basis for qualified opinion.

- The basis for qualified opinion section will explain the reason for the qualified opinion and quantify the effect of the issue on the financial statements.

(d) **Howard**

- There is no system to confirm cash sales therefore the auditor cannot form a conclusion as to whether revenue is materially misstated or free from material misstatement.

- The auditor is unable to obtain sufficient appropriate evidence for a significant class of transactions in the financial statements.

- The issue is material and pervasive.

- The audit opinion will be modified.

- A disclaimer of opinion will be issued stating that the auditor does not express an opinion on the financial statements.

- The basis for opinion section will be amended to a basis for disclaimer of opinion.

- The basis for disclaimer of opinion section will explain the reason for the disclaimer and quantify the effect of the issue on the financial statements.

- The statement referring to the audit being conducted in accordance with ISAs and ethical requirements will be moved from the basis for opinion section and included in the Auditor responsibilities section.

- The statement within the auditor's report that sufficient appropriate evidence has been obtained will be removed.

- The statement that the financial statements have been audited will be changed to the auditor was engaged to audit the financial statements.

(e) **Cleves**

- The financial statements do not contain a statement of profit or loss which is one of the primary financial statements and must be presented.

- The financial statements are misstated and the effect is pervasive.

- The audit opinion will be modified.

- An adverse opinion will be issued stating that the financial statements do not give a true and fair view.

- The basis for opinion section will be amended to a basis for adverse opinion.

- The basis for adverse opinion section will explain the reason for the adverse opinion and quantify the effect of the issue on the financial statements.

(f) **Parr**

- The claim is material and represents an uncertainty that should be communicated to the users of the financial statements.

- The directors have correctly disclosed the matter in the financial statements.

- The audit opinion will be unmodified as the financial statements give a true and fair view.

- Additional communication will be required to highlight the disclosure made by the client to the user.

- This could be achieved by including an emphasis of matter paragraph. The emphasis of matter paragraph will refer to the client's disclosure of the court case to make the users aware of it.

- Alternatively, the auditor may consider the issue a material uncertainty related to going concern and refer to the court case by including a going concern section in the report instead of an emphasis of matter.

- The choice of how the auditor should refer to the matter in the auditor's report is a matter of professional judgment.

Test your understanding 4

(a) Overall review of evidence is important as it enables the auditor to ensure:

- sufficient appropriate evidence has been obtained.

- the evidence supports the conclusions reached, and is appropriately documented.

- work has been performed in accordance with professional standards.

Review of the audit work is also important for the appraisal and development of staff.

(b) Audit procedures: Share capital

- Agree authorised share capital and nominal value disclosures to underlying shareholding agreements/statutory constitution documents.

- Inspect the cash book for evidence of cash receipts from share issues and ensure amounts not yet received are correctly disclosed as share capital called-up not paid in the financial statements.

- Inspect board minutes to verify the issue of share capital during the year.

Audit procedures: Reserves

- Agree opening reserves to prior-year closing reserves and reconcile movements.

- Agree movements in reserves to supporting documentation (e.g. agree revaluation reserve movements to an independent valuer's report).

(c) Impact on auditor's report:

(i) Faulty brake systems

The amount of $10m is 111% ($10m/$9m) of profit before tax and is therefore material.

The $10m provision would turn a profit of $9m into a loss of $1m and is also therefore pervasive.

It is probable that Brakes Co will lose the legal case and therefore the claim of $10m should be provided for in the financial statements in accordance with IAS 37 *Provisions, Contingent Liabilities and Contingent Assets*.

The audit opinion will be modified as the financial statements are materially misstated.

An adverse opinion will be issued stating that the financial statements do not give a true and fair view.

The basis for opinion section will be amended to a basis for adverse opinion.

The basis for adverse opinion section will explain the reason for the adverse opinion and quantify the effect of the issue on the financial statements.

The Key Audit Matters section will reference the 'Basis for Adverse Opinion'.

(ii) Contaminated brake fluid

Inventory should be valued at the lower of cost and net **realisable value** (IAS 2 *Inventories*, 9).

The contaminated brake fluid cost $125,000. If sold at the original price charged of $137,500, the net realisable value will be $75,000 ($137,500 less $62,500 re-filtering costs). Inventory is therefore overstated by $50,000.

$50,000 is not material at 0.6% of profit ($50,000/$9m) and 0.1% of total assets ($50,000/$37m).

The misstatement should be brought to the attention of management and they should be asked to correct it. However, as the misstatement is not material, the audit opinion will not be modified in respect of this matter and no reference to the misstatement will be required in the auditor's report.

(iii) Inventory held at third party premises

The auditor has not obtained sufficient appropriate evidence over the inventory held at third party premises.

The inventory is material to the statement of profit or loss at 36% of profit ($3.2m/$9m) and the statement of financial position at 8.6% of total assets ($3.2m/$37m).

If alternative sources of evidence cannot be obtained, it will be necessary to modify the audit opinion due to an inability to obtain sufficient appropriate evidence.

A qualified opinion using the 'except for' wording will be necessary.

The basis for opinion section will be amended to a basis for qualified opinion.

The basis for qualified opinion section will explain the reason for the qualified opinion and quantify the effect of the issue on the financial statements.

The Key Audit Matters section will reference the 'Basis for Qualified Opinion'.

Test your understanding 5

1	D	Qualified or disclaimer. Six months of accounting records have been lost meaning sufficient appropriate evidence will not be available. Whether the matter is deemed material but not pervasive or material and pervasive will depend on the auditor's assessment of the reconstruction of figures for the first six months.
2	B	A 'basis for opinion' paragraph confirms the audit has been conducted in accordance with ISAs and ethical requirements.
3	C	Addressee, opinion, auditor's responsibilities, date.
4	C	A disclaimer of opinion is where the auditor does not express an opinion.
5	B	ISA 705 states that where a disclaimer of opinion is issued, the Key Audit Matters section should not be included in the auditor's report.

Test your understanding 6

1	A	Whilst the misstatement represents less than 1% of total assets, it represents 150% of PBT and would turn the profit to a loss which is pervasive. Therefore an adverse opinion would be appropriate.
2	C	The misstatement represents 35% of PBT and 1.3% of total assets. This is material but not pervasive. A qualified opinion is appropriate.
3	D	The misstatement would represent 4.1% of PBT and 0.15% of total assets. This is not material. An unmodified opinion would be appropriate.
4	B	A section titled 'Material Uncertainty Related to Going Concern' will be included in the auditor's report.
5	B	No further reporting implications. The Key Audit Matters section should not describe matters already described in an Emphasis of Matter paragraph. The Basis for Opinion section would only describe matters giving rise to a modified opinion. As management has included the provision and disclosure of the legal case in the financial statements there is no reason to modify the audit opinion.

Summary of key ISAs

Chapter learning objectives

This section is designed to help you with the key requirements of the International Auditing Standards.

200 series: General principles and responsibilities

ISA 200 *Overall Objectives of the Independent Auditor and the Conduct of an Audit in Accordance with International Standards on Auditing*

Objectives of the auditor [11]:

- To obtain reasonable assurance about whether the financial statements as a whole are free from material misstatement, whether due to fraud or error.

- To express an opinion on whether the financial statements are prepared, in all material respects, in accordance with an applicable financial reporting framework.

- To report on the financial statements, and communicate as required by the ISAs, in accordance with the auditor's findings.

Responsibilities of management [A2]:

- Preparation of the financial statements in accordance with the applicable financial reporting framework, including their fair presentation.

- Internal control necessary to enable preparation of financial statements that are free from material misstatement, whether due to fraud or error.

- To provide the auditor with:

  - Access to all information relevant to the preparation of the financial statements

  - Unrestricted access to persons within the entity from whom the auditor determines it necessary to obtain evidence.

Risk:

- Audit: the risk of issuing an inappropriate opinion. [13c]

- Inherent: the susceptibility of an assertion about a class of transaction (e.g. revenue) or account balance (e.g. receivables) or disclosure to material misstatement before the consideration of any related internal controls. [13ni]

- Control: the risk that material misstatement could occur in an assertion about a class of transactions, account balance or disclosure and will not be prevented, or detected and corrected by the entity's controls. [13nii]

- Detection: the risk that audit procedures do not detect material misstatements. [13e]

An auditor must perform the audit with professional scepticism: an attitude that includes a questioning mind, being alert to conditions which indicate possible misstatement due to error or fraud, and a critical assessment of audit evidence. [13l]

Inherent limitations of audit [A47]:

Audit evidence is persuasive rather than conclusive because of:

- The nature of financial reporting
- The nature of audit procedures
- The need to conduct audit a within reasonable time and at reasonable cost.

ISA 210 *Agreeing the Terms of Audit Engagements*

The auditor should establish whether the preconditions for an audit are present [6]:

- Determine whether an acceptable financial reporting framework is to be applied in the preparation of the financial statements; and
- Obtain agreement of management that it acknowledges and understands its responsibilities.

Contents of engagement letter [10]:

- Objective and scope of the audit.
- Responsibilities of the auditor.
- Responsibilities of management.
- Identification of the applicable financial reporting framework.
- Expected form and content of any reports to be issued.

ISA 220 *Quality Control for an Audit of Financial Statements*

The firm should have a system of quality control to ensure [2]:

- Compliance with professional standards, and
- Reports issued are appropriate in the circumstances.

The engagement partner takes responsibility for the overall quality of the engagement including the direction, supervision and performance of the engagement. [8 & 15]

An engagement quality control reviewer must be assigned for listed entities and high risk engagements focusing on significant matters and areas involving significant judgment. [19 & 20]

The firm's quality control processes must be monitored to ensure they are relevant, adequate and operating effectively. [23]

ISA 230 *Audit Documentation*

Objective of documentation [2]:

- Evidence of the basis for the independent auditor's report

- Evidence that audit planned and performed in accordance with ISAs and legal/regulatory requirements.

Audit documentation should enable an experienced independent auditor with no previous connection to the audit to understand [8]:

- Nature, timing & extent of audit procedures performed:

- Results of audit procedures performed.

- Significant conclusions and professional judgments made in reaching those conclusions.

ISA 240 *The Auditor's Responsibilities Relating to Fraud in an Audit of Financial Statements*

Objectives of the auditor [11]:

- Identify risks of material misstatement due to fraud.

- Obtain sufficient appropriate evidence regarding assessed risks.

- Respond appropriately to fraud or suspected fraud identified.

Definition [12a]: An intentional act involving use of deception to obtain unjust/illegal advantage.

Two types of fraud [3]:

- Fraudulent financial reporting.

- Misappropriation of assets.

Audit procedures must be performed to: [33]:

- Test the appropriateness of journal entries.

- Review accounting estimates for bias.

- Identify significant transactions outside the normal course of business.

ISA 250 (Revised) *Consideration of Laws and Regulations in an Audit of Financial Statements*

Auditor's objectives [11]:

- Obtain sufficient appropriate evidence regarding compliance with provisions of laws/regulations that may materially affect FS.

- Perform audit procedures to identify instances of non-compliance that may materially affect FS.

- Respond appropriately to identified or suspected non-compliance during the audit.

ISA 260 (Revised) *Communication With Those Charged With Governance*

Those charged with governance [10a]:

- Those with responsibility for overseeing the strategic direction of the entity.

Matters to be communicated:

- Auditor's responsibility in relation to the FS audit [14]

- Planned scope and timing of audit [15]

- Significant findings from audit [16]

- Auditor's independence (listed companies). [17]

ISA 265 *Communicating Deficiencies in Internal Control to Those Charged With Governance and Management*

Reporting responsibilities:

- Significant deficiencies, to those charged with governance [9]

- Significant deficiencies and other deficiencies, to an appropriate level of management. [10]

What makes deficiencies significant [A6]:

- Likelihood of material misstatement in the FS.

- Susceptibility to loss or fraud of the related asset.

- Volume of activity in the related account balance.

- Interaction of the deficiency with other deficiencies.

300 & 400 series: Assessment and response to assessed risks

ISA 300 *Planning an Audit of Financial Statements*

Benefits of planning [2]:

- Helps the auditor to devote appropriate attention to important areas of the audit.

- Helps identify and resolve potential problems on a timely basis.

- Assists in the selection of a suitable audit team.

- Helps the direction and supervision of the audit team.

- Assists the auditor to perform an efficient and effective audit.

Content of audit strategy [8]:

- Characteristics of the engagement

- Reporting objectives (e.g. reporting timetable)

- Factors significant in directing the team's efforts

- Results of preliminary engagement activities

- Nature, timing and extent of resources.

Content of audit plan [9]:

Nature, timing and extent of:

- Planned risk assessment procedures.

- Planned further audit procedures at the assertion level.

- Other planned procedures required to comply with ISAs.

ISA 315 (Revised 2019) *Identifying and Assessing the Risks of Material Misstatement*

Understanding the entity and its environment, and the applicable financial reporting framework [19]:

- Organisational structure, ownership and governance, business model

- Industry, regulatory and other external factors:

- Measures used internally and externally to assess financial performance

- The applicable financial reporting framework and accounting policies

- How inherent risk factors affect susceptibility of assertions to misstatement and the extent to which they do so.

Understanding the components of the entity's system of internal control:

- Control environment [21]

- Entity's risk assessment process [22]

- The entity's process to monitor the system of internal control [24]

- Information system and communication [25]

- Control activities. [26]

Assertions [A190]:

- Transactions and events and related disclosures: Occurrence; completeness; accuracy; cut-off; classification; presentation.

- Account balances and related disclosures: Existence; rights & obligations; completeness; accuracy, valuation & allocation; classification; presentation.

ISA 320 *Materiality in Planning and Performing an Audit*

Materiality: Misstatements, including omissions, are considered to be material if they, individually or in the aggregate, could reasonably be expected to influence the economic decisions of users taken on the basis of the financial statements. [2]

Performance materiality: an amount set at less than materiality for the FS as a whole, to reduce to an appropriately low level the probability that the aggregate of uncorrected and undetected misstatements exceeds materiality for the FS as a whole. [9]

ISA 330 *The Auditor's Responses to Assessed Risks*

The auditor shall design and perform audit procedures whose nature, timing and extent are based on and are responsive to the assessed risks of material misstatement at the assertion level. [6]

Substantive procedures: to detect material misstatements at assertion level, comprising tests of details and substantive analytical procedures. [4a]

Test of controls: to evaluate the operating effectiveness of controls in preventing, or detecting and correcting material misstatements at the assertion level. [4b]

If the auditor intends to rely on controls over an area of significant risk, the auditor shall test those controls in the current period. [15]

ISA 402 *Audit Considerations Relating to an Entity Using a Service Organisation*

The auditor of the user entity must obtain an understanding of the services provided by the service organisation and their effect on the user entity's system of internal control, sufficient to provide an appropriate basis for the identification and assessment of the risks of material misstatement and perform audit procedures responsive to those risks. [7]

An understanding of the services provided by the service organisation may be obtained from the client. [9]

If sufficient understanding is not obtained from the client, the auditor should perform one or more of the following procedures [12]:

- Obtaining a type 1 or type 2 report

- Contacting the service organisation

- Visiting the service organisation and performing procedures that will provide the necessary information about the relevant controls at the service organisation

- Using another auditor to perform procedures and provide information about the controls.

ISA 450 *Evaluation of Misstatements Identified During the Audit*

A misstatement is: A difference between the amount, classification, presentation, or disclosure of a reported financial statement item and the amount, classification, presentation, or disclosure that is required for the item to be in accordance with the applicable financial reporting framework. Misstatements can arise from error or fraud. [4a]

Requirements:

- Accumulate misstatements identified during the audit. [5]

- Determine whether the audit strategy and audit plan needs to be revised. [6]

- Communicate all misstatements accumulated with the appropriate level of management on a timely basis. [8]

- Determine whether uncorrected misstatements are material. [11]

- Request a written representation that uncorrected misstatements are not material. A summary of the uncorrected misstatements shall be included in the written representation. [14]

500 series: Evidence

ISA 500 *Audit Evidence*

Characteristics:

- Sufficiency: measure of quantity, affected by quality of evidence and risk of material misstatement. [5e]

- Appropriateness: measure of quality, linked to relevance and reliability. [5b]

Relevance: linked to FS assertions. [A27]

Reliability [A31]:

- Independent evidence is more reliable than client generated.

- Internally generated evidence is more reliable when related internal controls are effective.

- Evidence obtained directly by the auditor is more reliable than evidence obtained indirectly.

- Documentary evidence is more reliable than oral.

- Original documents are more reliable than copies or documents transformed into electronic form.

Procedures:

- Inspection [A14]

- Observation [A17]

- External confirmation [A18]

- Recalculation [A19]

- Reperformance [A20]

- Analytical procedures [A21]

- Enquiry. [A22]

ISA 501 *Audit Evidence – Specific Considerations for Selected Items*

The auditor should obtain sufficient appropriate evidence regarding [3]:

- Existence and condition of inventory.

- Completeness of litigation and claims involving the entity.

- Presentation and disclosure of segment information.

ISA 505 *External Confirmations*

External confirmations provide more persuasive evidence as the evidence is obtained directly by the auditor from an independent source. This is important where there is a higher assessment of audit risk. [3]

Definitions:

External confirmation – audit evidence obtained by the auditor directly from a third party in paper form or by electronic or other medium. [6a]

Positive confirmation request – a request for the third party to confirm whether they agree or disagree with the information in the request, or provide the requested information. [6b]

Negative confirmation request – a request for the third party to respond directly to the auditor only if they disagree with the information provided in the request. [6c]

ISA 520 *Analytical Procedures*

Definition: Evaluation of financial information through analysis of plausible relationships among both financial and non-financial data. [4]

May be used as a substantive procedure. [5]

Must be used at the completion stage when forming an overall conclusion to ensure the financial statements are consistent with the auditor's understanding of the entity. [6]

ISA 530 *Audit Sampling*

Definitions:

- Audit sampling: The application of audit procedures to less than 100% of items within a population to provide the auditor with a reasonable basis to draw conclusions on entire population. [5a]

- Sampling risk: The risk the auditor's conclusion based on the sample may be different from the conclusion if the entire population were subjected to the same audit procedure. [5c]

- Non-sampling risk: The risk the auditor reaches an erroneous conclusion for any reason not related to sampling risk. [5d]

- Statistical sampling: random selection of the sample and the use of probability theory to evaluate results. [5g]

- Tolerable misstatement: A monetary amount set by the auditor in respect of which the auditor seeks to obtain an appropriate level of assurance that the monetary amount set by the auditor is not exceeded by the actual misstatement in the population. [5i]

KAPLAN PUBLISHING

Factors affecting sample sizes for substantive procedures [Appendix 3]:

- The higher the assessed risk of material misstatement, the larger the sample size.

- The more the auditor is relying on other procedures, the smaller the sample size.

- The greater the level of assurance the auditor requires, the larger the sample size.

- The lower the tolerable misstatement, the larger the sample size.

- The greater the amount of misstatement the auditor expects to find, the larger the sample size.

- When a population can be appropriately stratified, the aggregate of the sample sizes will be less than the sample size if one sample had been tested from the whole population.

- For large populations, the size of the population has little effect on the sample size.

ISA 540 (Revised) *Auditing Accounting Estimates and Related Disclosures*

Obtain sufficient and appropriate evidence about whether accounting estimates and related disclosures are reasonable in the context of the financial reporting framework. [11]

Audit procedures required will vary in relation to the estimation uncertainty. [3]

Professional scepticism should be increased in relation to the assessed level of inherent risk, and where accounting estimates are subject to a greater degree of estimation uncertainty. [8]

The auditor is required to:

- Separately assess inherent risk and control risk to assess the risk of material misstatement. [16]

- Respond to the risk of material misstatement by [18]:

    - Reviewing events after the reporting period

    - Testing how management made the estimate

    - Developing an independent estimate

- Request written representation from management about whether the methods, significant assumptions and data using in making the estimates are appropriate. [37]

ISA 560 *Subsequent Events*

Obtain sufficient appropriate evidence about whether events occurring between the date of the financial statements and the date of the auditor's report that require adjustment of or disclosure in the financial statements are appropriately reflected in those financial statements. [4]

Between the date of the financial statements and the date of the auditor's report, perform procedures to identify events that require adjustment or disclosure in the financial statements. [6]

No obligation to perform audit procedures after the date of the auditor's report. If a fact becomes known that would cause the auditor to amend the auditor's report, discuss the matter with management and determine whether the financial statements need amendment. [10]

If amendment is required and management do not amend the financial statements and then issue the financial statements, the auditor must take action to prevent reliance on the auditor's report. [13b]

ISA 570 (Revised) *Going Concern*

Auditor must [9]:

- Obtain sufficient appropriate evidence regarding the appropriateness of management's use of the going concern basis of accounting.

- Conclude whether a material uncertainty exists about the entity's ability to continue as a going concern.

- Report in accordance with ISA 570.

ISA 580 *Written Representations*

Definition: A written statement by management provided to the auditor to confirm certain matters or to support other audit evidence. [7]

Contents:

- Management responsibility for preparation of FS. [10]

- Completeness of information provided to the auditor. [11a]

- All transactions recorded in FS. [11b]

- Plans that may affect the carrying value of the assets. [A10]

- As required by other ISAs e.g. ISA 240, 250, 450, 560, 570, 580. [Appendix 1]

600 series: Using the work of others

ISA 610 *Using the Work of Internal Auditors*

Evaluating the internal audit function [15]:

- The extent to which the internal audit function's organisational status and relevant policies and procedures support the objectivity of the internal auditors.
- The level of competence of the internal audit function.
- Whether the internal audit function applies a systematic and disciplined approach, including quality control.

Evaluating the internal audit work [23]:

- The work was properly planned, performed, supervised, reviewed and documented.
- Sufficient appropriate evidence has been obtained.
- The conclusions reached are appropriate in the circumstances.
- The reports prepared are consistent with the work performed.

Using internal audit to provide direct assistance

The external auditor may use the internal audit function to provide direct assistance with the external audit under the supervision and review of the external auditor.

- Direct assistance cannot be provided in countries where national law prohibits such assistance. [26]
- Internal auditor must be objective and competent. [27]
- External auditor must not assign work which is judgmental, a high risk of material misstatement or with which the internal auditor has been involved. [30]
- External auditor must not use the internal auditor excessively. [31]
- Management must agree not to intervene with the work. [33a]
- Internal auditor must observe confidentiality. [33b]

ISA 620 *Using the Work of an Auditor's Expert*

The auditor must:

- Evaluate the competence, capability and objectivity of the expert. [9]
- Obtain an understanding of the field of expertise. [10]
- Agree in writing the work to be performed. [11]
- Evaluate the adequacy of the expert's work for audit purposes. [12]

700 series: Audit conclusions and reporting

ISA 700 (Revised) *Forming an Opinion and Reporting on Financial Statements*

Content of an independent auditor's report:

- Title: [21]
    - reference to independent auditor
- Addressee: [22]
    - shareholders/members
- Auditor's Opinion: [23]
    - Identifies the entity, subject matter and reporting date [24]
    - FS give true and fair view in accordance with the applicable FR framework [25b]
- Basis for Opinion: [28]
    - Audit conducted in accordance with ISAs and ethical requirements
    - States whether the auditor believes that the audit evidence obtained is sufficient and appropriate for forming an opinion
- Going Concern: [29]
    - Reference to any going concern disclosures made by management
- Key Audit Matters (listed companies) [30]
- Other Information [32]
- Responsibilities of Management for the Financial Statements: [34]
    - Preparation of FS
    - Internal controls
    - Assessing the entity's ability to continue as a going concern
- Auditor's Responsibilities for the Audit of the Financial Statements: [38]
    - The objectives of the auditor are to obtain reasonable assurance about the FS and issue an auditor's report containing an opinion
- Name of Engagement Partner (listed entities) [46]
- Signature of the Auditor [47]
- Auditor's address [48]
- Date of the Auditor's Report [49]

ISA 701 *Communicating Key Audit Matters in the Independent Auditor's Report*

Key audit matters (KAM) are those that in the auditor's professional judgment were of most significance in the audit and are selected from matters communicated with those charged with governance. [8]

KAM include: [9]

- Areas of higher assessed risk of material misstatement

- Significant auditor judgments relating to areas of significant management judgment

- Significant events of transactions that occurred during the period.

The description of each KAM will address: [13]

- Why it is considered a key audit matter

- How the matter was addressed in the audit.

ISA 705 (Revised) *Modifications to the Audit Opinion in the Independent Auditor's Report*

Definitions:

- Modified opinion: qualified, adverse or disclaimer of opinion [5b]

- Pervasive: not confined to specific elements or representing a substantial proportion of a single element [5a]

Modifications:

- FS as a whole not free from material misstatement [6a]

  - Material but not pervasive: qualified [7a]

  - Material and pervasive: adverse [8]

- Unable to obtain sufficient appropriate evidence [6b]

  - Material but not pervasive: qualified [7b]

  - Material and pervasive: disclaimer [9]

When the auditor modifies the opinion, the basis for opinion is amended to 'Basis for Qualified Opinion', 'Basis for Adverse Opinion' or 'Basis for Disclaimer of Opinion' as appropriate. [20a]

The 'Basis for...' section includes a description of the matter giving rise to the modification. [20b]

ISA 706 (Revised) *Emphasis of Matter Paragraphs and Other Matter Paragraphs in the Independent Auditor's Report*

Emphasis of matter

- Refers to matters appropriately presented or disclosed that are fundamental to the user's understanding of the FS. [7a]

Other matter

- Refers to matters relevant to the user's understanding of the audit, the auditor's responsibilities or the auditor's report. [7b]

ISA 720 (Revised) *The Auditor's Responsibilities Relating to Other Information in Documents Containing Audited Financial Statements*

Auditor responsibilities:

- Read other information to identify material inconsistencies with the FS or the auditor's knowledge which indicates material misstatement of the FS or the other information. [3]

- If an inconsistency is identified:

  - Perform procedures to conclude whether it is the financial statements or the other information that requires amendment. [16]

  - If other information is wrong, ask management to correct it. [17]

  - If the matter remains uncorrected, describe the inconsistency in the Other Information section of the auditor's report or withdraw from the engagement where withdrawal is possible. [18]

Financial reporting revision

Chapter learning objectives

This section is designed to help you with the key requirements of the accounting standards examinable for this exam.

This chapter outlines the main requirements of the accounting standards examined in Financial Accounting at the Applied Knowledge level which are examinable for Audit & Assurance.

IAS 1 Presentation of Financial Statements

This standard provides formats for the statement of profit or loss and other comprehensive income, statement of financial position, and statement of changes in equity.

Accounting policies should be selected so that the financial statements comply with all international standards and interpretations.

IAS 1 requires that other comprehensive income is presented in two categories, namely items that:

- will not be reclassified to profit or loss, and

- may be reclassified to profit or loss in future reporting periods.

IAS 2 Inventories

Inventories should be valued 'at the lower of cost and net realisable value' (IAS 2, para 9).

IAS 2 says that the cost of inventory includes:

- Purchase price including import duties, transport and handling costs

- Direct production costs e.g. direct labour

- Direct expenses and subcontracted work

- Production overheads (based on the normal levels of activity)

- Other overheads, if attributable to bringing the product or service to its present location and condition.

IAS 2 specifies that cost excludes:

- Abnormal waste

- Storage costs

- Indirect administrative overheads

- Selling costs.

Some entities can identify individual units of inventory (e.g. vehicles can be identified by a chassis number). Those that cannot should keep track of costs using either the first in, first out (FIFO) or the weighted average cost (AVCO) assumption.

Some entities may use standard costing for valuing inventory. Standard costs may be used for convenience if it is a close approximation to actual cost, and is regularly reviewed and revised.

IAS 7 Statement of Cash Flows

IAS 7 requires a statement of cash flow that shows cash flows generated from:

- Operating activities
- Investing activities
- Financing activities.

IAS 10 Events After the Reporting Period

Definitions

Events after the reporting period are **'those events, favourable and unfavourable, that occur between the statement of financial position date and the date when the financial statements are authorised for issue'** (IAS 10, para 3).

Adjusting events after the reporting period are those that 'provide evidence of conditions that existed at the reporting date' (IAS 10, para 3a).

Non-adjusting events after the reporting period are **'those that are indicative of conditions that arose after the reporting period'** (IAS 10, para 3b).

Accounting treatment

Adjusting events affect the amounts stated in the financial statements so they must be adjusted.

Non-adjusting events do not concern the position as at the reporting date so the financial statements are not adjusted. If the event is material then the nature and its financial effect must be disclosed.

IAS 16 Property, Plant and Equipment

Cost of an asset

IAS 16 states that property, plant and equipment is initially recognised at cost.

An asset's cost is its purchase price, less any trade discounts or rebates, plus any further costs directly attributable to bringing it into working condition for its intended use.

Subsequent expenditure on non-current assets is capitalised if it:

- Enhances the economic benefits of the asset e.g. adding a new wing to a building.

- Replaces part of an asset that has been separately depreciated and has been fully depreciated; e.g. a furnace that requires new linings periodically.

- Replaces economic benefits previously consumed, e.g. a major inspection of aircraft.

Depreciation

The aim of depreciation is to spread the cost of the asset over its life in the business.

- IAS 16 requires that the depreciation method and useful life of an asset should be reviewed at the end of each year and revised where necessary. This is not a change in accounting policy, but a change of accounting estimate.

- If an asset has parts with different lives, (e.g. a building with a flat roof), the component parts should be capitalised and depreciated separately.

Revaluation of property, plant and equipment

Revaluation of PPE is optional. If one asset is revalued, all assets in that class must be revalued.

Valuations should be kept up to date to ensure that the carrying amount does not differ materially from the fair value at each statement of financial position date.

Revaluation gains are credited to **other comprehensive income** unless the gain reverses a previous revaluation loss of the same asset previously recognised in the statement of profit or loss.

Revaluation losses are debited to the statement of profit or loss unless the loss relates to a previous revaluation surplus, in which case the decrease should be debited to other comprehensive income to the extent of any credit balance existing in the revaluation surplus relating to that asset.

Depreciation is charged on the revalued amount less residual value (if any) over the **remaining useful life** of the asset.

An entity may choose to make an annual transfer of excess depreciation from revaluation reserve to retained earnings. If this is done, it should be applied consistently each year.

IAS 27 Separate Financial Statements

This standard applies when an entity has interests in subsidiaries, joint ventures or associates and either elects to, or is required to, prepare separate **non-consolidated financial statements**.

If separate financial statements are produced, investments in subsidiaries, associates or joint ventures can be measured:

- at cost

- using the equity method

- in accordance with IFRS® 9 *Financial Instruments*.

IAS 28 Investments in associates and joint ventures

Joint ventures

A joint venture is a **'joint arrangement whereby the parties that have joint control of the arrangement have rights to the net assets of the arrangement'** (IAS 28, para 3). This will normally be established in the form of a separate entity to conduct the joint venture activities.

Associates

An associate is defined as an entity **'over which the investor has significant influence'** (IAS 28, para 3).

Significant influence is the **'power to participate in the financial and operating policy decisions of the investee but is not control or joint control over those policies'** (IAS 28, para 3).

It is normally assumed that significant influence exists if the holding company has a shareholding of 20% to 50%.

Equity accounting

In the consolidated financial statements of a group, an investment in an associate or joint venture is accounted for using the equity method.

The **consolidated statement of profit or loss** will show a single figure in respect of the associate or joint venture. This is calculated as the investor's share of the associate or joint venture's profit for the period.

In the **consolidated statement of financial position**, the 'investment in the associate/joint venture' is presented in non-current assets. It is calculated as the initial cost of the investment plus/(minus) the investor's share of the post-acquisition reserve increase/(decrease).

The associate or joint venture is outside the group. Therefore transactions and balances between group companies and the associate or joint venture are not eliminated from the consolidated financial statements.

IAS 37 Provisions, Contingent Liabilities and Contingent Assets

IAS 37 provides the following definitions:

- A provision is **'a liability of uncertain timing or amount'** (IAS 37, para 10).

- A contingent liability is a possible obligation arising from past events whose existence will only be confirmed by an uncertain future event outside of the entity's control.

- A contingent asset is a possible asset that arises from past events and whose existence will only be confirmed by an uncertain future event outside of the entity's control.

Provisions

Provisions should be recognised when:

- An entity has a present obligation (legal or constructive) as a result of a past event

- It is probable that an outflow of economic benefits will be required to settle the obligation, and

- A reliable estimate can be made of the amount of the obligation.

Measurement of provisions:

- The provision amount should be the best estimate of the expenditure required to settle the present obligation.

- Where the time value of money is material, the provision should be discounted to present value.

Restructuring provisions:

- Provisions can only be recognised where an entity has a constructive obligation to carry out the restructuring.

- A constructive obligation arises when there is a detailed formal plan which identifies:

    - The business concerned

    - The principal location, function and approximate number of employees being made redundant

    - The expenditures that will be incurred

    - When the plan will be implemented

    - There is a valid expectation that the plan will be carried out by either implementing the plan or announcing it to those affected.

Specific guidance:

- Future operating losses should not be recognised.

- Onerous contracts should be recognised for the present obligation under the contract.

Contingent liabilities should not be recognised. They should be disclosed unless the possibility of a transfer of economic benefits is remote.

Contingent assets should not be recognised. If the possibility of an inflow of economic benefits is probable they should be disclosed.

IAS 38 Intangible Assets

IAS 38 says that an intangible asset is **'an identifiable non-monetary asset without physical substance'** (IAS 38, para 8).

Initial recognition

IAS 38 states that an intangible asset is initially recognised at cost if all of the following criteria are met.

1   It is identifiable – it could be disposed of without disposing of the business at the same time.

2   It is controlled by the entity – the entity has the power to obtain economic benefits from it, for example patents and copyrights give legal rights to future economic benefits.

3   It will generate probable future economic benefits for the entity – this could be by a reduction in costs or increasing revenues.

4   The cost can be measured reliably.

If an intangible does not meet the recognition criteria, then it should be charged to the statement of profit or loss as expenditure is incurred.

Items that do not meet the criteria are internally generated goodwill, brands, mastheads, publishing titles, customer lists, research, advertising, start-up costs and training.

Subsequent treatment

Intangible assets should be amortised over their useful lives.

If it can be demonstrated that the useful life is indefinite, no amortisation should be charged but an annual impairment review must be carried out.

Intangible assets can be revalued but fair values must be determined with reference to an active market. Active markets have homogenous products, willing buyers and sellers at all times and published prices. In practical terms, most intangible assets are likely to be valued using the cost model.

Research and development

The recognition of internally generated intangible assets is split into a research phase and a development phase.

Costs incurred in the research phase must be charged to the statement of profit or loss as they are incurred.

IAS 38 says that costs incurred in the development phase should be recognised as an intangible asset if they meet the following criteria:

(a) The project is technically feasible

(b) The asset will be completed then used or sold

(c) The entity is able to use or sell the asset

(d) The asset will generate future economic benefits (either because of internal use or because there is a market for it)

(e) The entity has adequate technical, financial and other resources to complete the project

(f) The expenditure on the project can be reliably measured.

Amortisation of development costs will occur over the period that benefits are expected.

IFRS 3 Business Combinations

On acquisition of a subsidiary, the purchase consideration transferred and the identifiable net assets acquired are recorded at fair value.

Fair value is **'the price that would be received to sell an asset, or paid to transfer a liability, in an orderly transaction between market participants at the measurement date'** (IFRS 13, para 9).

Purchase consideration

Purchase consideration is measured at fair value. Note that:

- Deferred cash consideration should be discounted to present value using a rate at which the acquirer could obtain similar borrowing.

- The fair value of the acquirer's own shares is the market price at the acquisition date.

- Contingent consideration is included as part of the consideration at its fair value, even if payment is not probable.

Goodwill and the non-controlling interest

The non-controlling interest (NCI) at acquisition is measured at either:

- Fair value, or

- The NCI's proportionate share of the fair value of the subsidiary's identifiable net assets.

Gain on bargain purchase

If the net assets acquired exceed the fair value of consideration, then a gain on bargain purchase (negative goodwill) arises.

After checking that the calculations have been done correctly, the gain on bargain purchase is credited to profit or loss.

Other adjustments

Other consolidation adjustments need to be made in order to present the parent and its subsidiaries as a single economic entity. Transactions that require adjustments include:

- Interest on intragroup loans

- Intragroup management charges

- Intragroup sales, purchases and unrealised profit in inventory

- Intragroup transfer of non-current assets and unrealised profit on transfer

- Intragroup receivables, payables and loans.

IFRS 10 Consolidated Financial Statements

IFRS 10 states that consolidated financial statements must be prepared if one company controls another company.

Control, according to IFRS 10, consists of three components:

1 **Power** over the investee: this is normally exercised through the **majority of voting rights,** but could also arise through other contractual arrangements.

2 **Exposure** or rights to variable returns (positive and/or negative), and

3 The **ability to use power** to affect the investor's returns.

It is normally assumed that control exists when one company owns more than half of the ordinary shares in another company.

IFRS 15 Revenue from Contracts with Customers

Revenue recognition is a five step process.

1 **Identify the contract**

A contract is an agreement between two or more parties that creates rights and obligations.

2 **Identify the separate performance obligations within a contract**

Performance obligations are, essentially, promises made to a customer.

3 **Determine the transaction price**

The transaction price is the amount the entity expects to be entitled in exchange for satisfying all performance obligations. Amounts collected on behalf of third parties (such as sales tax) are excluded.

4 **Allocate the transaction price to the performance obligations in the contract**

The total transaction price should be allocated to each performance obligation in proportion to stand-alone selling prices.

5 **Recognise revenue when (or as) a performance obligation is satisfied.**

For each performance obligation an entity must determine whether it satisfies the performance obligation over time or at a point in time.

An entity satisfies a performance obligation over time if one of the following criteria is met:

(a) **'the customer simultaneously receives and consumes the benefits provided by the entity's performance as the entity performs**

(b) **the entity's performance creates or enhances an asset (for example, work in progress) that the customer controls as the asset is created or enhanced, or**

(c) **the entity's performance does not create an asset with an alternative use to the entity and the entity has an enforceable right to payment for performance completed to date'** (IFRS 15, para 35).

For a performance obligation satisfied over time, an entity recognises revenue based on progress towards satisfaction of that performance obligation.

If a performance obligation is not satisfied over time then it is satisfied at a point in time. The entity must determine the point in time at which a customer obtains control of the promised asset.

Questions and Answers

Test your understanding 1 – Confidentiality

Client confidentiality underpins the relationship between Chartered Certified Accountants in practice and their clients. It is a core element of ACCA's Code of Ethics and Conduct.

Required:

(a) **Explain the circumstances in which external auditors are permitted or required to disclose information relating to their clients to third parties without the knowledge or consent of the client.**

(4 marks)

(b) A waste disposal company has breached tax regulations, environmental regulations and health and safety regulations. The auditor has been approached by the tax authorities, the government body supervising the award of licences to such companies and a trade union representative. All of them have asked the auditor to provide them with information about the company. The auditor has also been approached by the police. They are investigating a suspected fraud perpetrated by the managing director of the company and they wish to ask the auditor certain questions about him.

Describe how the auditor should respond to these types of request.

(6 marks)

(Total: 10 marks)

Test your understanding 2 – Ethical threats

You are a manager in the audit firm of JT & Co and this is your first time you have worked on one of the firm's established clients, Pink Co. The main activity of Pink Co is providing investment advice to individuals regarding saving for retirement, purchase of shares and securities and investing in tax efficient savings schemes. Pink Co is a listed company regulated by the relevant financial services authority.

You have been asked to start the audit planning for Pink Co, by Mrs Goodall, a partner in JT & Co. Mrs Goodall has been the engagement partner for Pink Co, for the previous seven years and so has a sound knowledge of the client. Mrs Goodall has informed you that she would like her son Simon to be part of the audit team this year; Simon is currently studying for his first set of papers for his ACCA qualification. Mrs Goodall also informs you that the audit senior, received investment advice from Pink Co during the year and intends to do the same next year.

In an initial meeting with the finance director of Pink Co, you learn that the audit team will not be entertained on Pink Co's yacht this year as this could appear to be an attempt to influence the audit opinion. Instead, the audit team has been invited to a day at the horse races costing less than two fifths of the expense of using the yacht.

JT & Co has done some consulting work previously and the invoice is still outstanding.

Required:

Identify and explain FIVE threats to independence in relation to the audit of Pink Co by JT & Co. For each threat, recommend how the threat can be managed.

Prepare your answer using two columns headed Ethical threat and Possible safeguard respectively

(10 marks)

Test your understanding 3 – Analytical risk assessment

(a) With reference to ISA 520 *Analytical Procedures* explain:

(i) what is meant by the term 'analytical procedures'

(1 mark)

(ii) the different types of analytical procedures available to the auditor

(3 marks)

(iii) the situations in the audit when analytical procedures are used.

(3 marks)

It is 1 July 20X5. You are an audit senior in Quest & Co and you are planning the audit of Tribe Co for the year ending 31 July 20X5. Tribe Co sells bathrooms from 15 retail outlets. Sales are made to individuals, with income being in the form of cash and debit cards. All items purchased are delivered to the customer using Tribe Co's own delivery vans as most bathrooms are too big for individuals to transport in their own motor vehicles. The directors of Tribe Co indicate that the company has had a difficult year, but are pleased to present some acceptable results to the members.

The statement of profit or loss for the last two financial years are shown below:

Statement of profit or loss

	31 July 20X5	31 July 20X4
	$000	$000
Revenue	11,223	9,546
Cost of sales	(5,280)	(6,380)
	5,943	3,166
Operating expenses		
Administration	(1,853)	(1,980)
Selling and distribution	(1,472)	(1,034)
Interest payable	(152)	(158)
Investment income	218	–
Profit before tax	2,684	(6)

Statement of financial position extract

Cash and bank	380	(1,425)

Required:

(b)   **As part of your risk assessment procedures for Tribe Co, identify and provide a possible explanation for unusual changes in the statement of profit or loss.**

(8 marks)

(Total: 15 marks)

Test your understanding 4 – Audit risk

It is 1 July 20X5. You are an audit senior in Staple and Co and you are commencing the planning of the audit of Smoothbrush Paints Co (Smoothbrush) for the year ending 31 August 20X5. Smoothbrush is a paint manufacturer and has been trading for over 50 years. It operates from one central site which includes the production facility, warehouse and administration offices.

Smoothbrush sells all of its goods to large home improvement stores, with 60% being to one large chain store Homewares. The company has a one-year contract to be the sole supplier of paint to Homewares. It secured the contract through significantly reducing prices and offering a four-month credit period, the company's normal credit period is one month.

Goods in/purchases

In recent years, Smoothbrush has reduced the level of goods directly manufactured and instead started to import paint from South Asia. Approximately 60% is imported and 40% manufactured. Within the production facility is a large amount of old plant and equipment that is now redundant and has minimal scrap value. Purchase orders for overseas paint are made six months in advance and goods can be in transit for up to two months. Smoothbrush accounts for the inventory when it receives the goods.

To avoid the disruption of a year-end inventory count, Smoothbrush has this year introduced a continuous/perpetual inventory counting system. The warehouse has been divided into 12 areas and these are each to be counted once over the year. At the year-end it is proposed that the inventory will be based on the underlying records. Traditionally Smoothbrush has maintained an inventory allowance based on 1% of the inventory value, but management feels that as inventory is being reviewed more regularly it no longer needs this allowance.

Finance Director

In May 20X5 Smoothbrush had a dispute with its finance director (FD) who immediately left the company. The directors have temporarily asked the financial controller to take over the role while they recruit a permanent replacement. The former FD has notified Smoothbrush of intention to sue for unfair dismissal. The directors are not proposing to make any provision or disclosure for this, as they are confident the claim has no merit.

Required:

(a) Explain EIGHT audit risks identified at the planning stage of the audit of Smoothbrush Paints Co.   (8 marks)

(b) Discuss the importance of assessing risks at the planning stage of an audit.   (6 marks)

(c) Describe the substantive procedures the auditor should perform to obtain sufficient and appropriate audit evidence in relation to the valuation of Smoothbrush Paints Co's inventory.   (3 marks)

(d) Describe the substantive procedures the auditor should perform to obtain sufficient and appropriate audit evidence in relation to the completeness of Smoothbrush Paints Co's provisions or contingent liabilities.   (3 marks)

(Total: 20 marks)

Test your understanding 5 – Fraud

Fraud and error present risks to an entity. Both internal and external auditors are required to deal with risks to the entity. However, the responsibilities of internal and external auditors in relation to the risk of fraud and error differ.

Required:

(a) **Explain how the internal audit function helps an entity deal with the risk of fraud and error.**

(5 marks)

(b) **Explain the responsibilities of external auditors in respect of the risk of fraud and error in an audit of financial statements.**

(5 marks)

(c) Stone Holidays is an independent travel agency. It takes commission on holidays sold to customers through its chain of high street shops. Staff are partly paid on a commission basis. Well-established tour operators run the holidays that Stone Holidays sells. The networked reservations system through which holidays are booked, and the computerised accounting system, are both well-established systems used by many independent travel agencies.

Payments by customers, including deposits, are accepted in cash and by debit and credit card. Stone Holidays is legally required to pay an amount of money (based on its total sales for the year) into a central fund maintained to compensate customers if the agency should cease operations.

Describe the nature of the risks to which Stone Holidays is subject arising from fraud and error.

(5 marks)

(Total: 15 marks)

Test your understanding 6 – Quality control

You are the partner responsible for quality control within your firm. You are reviewing the findings from a recent post-issuance (cold) review performed by your firm's compliance department. The following issues were identified.

Client A

Some working papers had not been signed off by the team member who completed the work. Some working papers were not dated and some did not have a signature confirming they had been reviewed.

Client B

A mandatory procedure included in the audit plan which required a written representation letter to be obtained, had not been completed. A comment had been added by the audit manager stating that there were no issues requiring a written representation from management.

Client C

An audit test over purchases required a sample of 30 invoices to be tested. 27 had been tested and found to be recorded accurately and completely. Three invoices could not be found. No further invoices were identified for testing and a conclusion was drawn based on the 27 items tested.

Client D

The audit of a material provision was performed by the audit junior as the audit manager was too busy finishing off work for the previous audit client on which they had been working.

Client E

The planning section of the file has not been completed. The audit procedures performed were copied over from the previous year's file and the same approach and sample sizes have been used for this year's audit.

Required:

Describe the quality control issues arising from each of the findings.

(10 marks)

Test your understanding 7 – Controls

You are carrying out the audit of the purchases system of Spondon Furniture. The company has revenue of $10 million and all the shares are owned by Mr and Mrs Fisher, who are non-executive directors and are not involved in the day-to-day running of the company.

The bookkeeper maintains all the accounting records and prepares the annual financial statements.

The company uses a standard computerised accounting package.

You have determined that the purchases system operates as follows:

- When materials are required for production, the production manager sends a handwritten note to the buying manager. For orders of other items, the department manager or managing director sends handwritten notes to the buying manager. The buying manager finds a suitable supplier and raises a purchase order. The purchase order is signed by the managing director. Purchase orders are not issued for all goods and services received by the company.

- Materials for production are received by the goods received department, who issue a goods received note (GRN), and send a copy to the bookkeeper. There is no system for recording receipt of other goods and services.

- The bookkeeper receives the purchase invoice and matches it with the goods received note and purchase order (if available). The managing director authorises the invoice for posting to the ledger.

- The bookkeeper analyses the invoice into relevant nominal ledger account codes and then posts it.

- At the end of each month, the bookkeeper prepares a list of payables to be paid. This is approved by the managing director.

- The bookkeeper prepares the cheques and remittances and posts the cheques to the payables ledger and cashbook.

- The managing director signs the cheques and the bookkeeper sends the cheques and remittances to the payables.

Mr and Mrs Fisher are aware that there may be deficiencies in the above system and have asked for advice.

Identify and explain FIVE control deficiencies in Spondon's purchases system and suggest improvements to overcome the deficiencies. **(10 marks)**

Test your understanding 8 – Inventory count

DinZee Co assembles fridges, microwaves, washing machines and other similar domestic appliances from parts procured from a large number of suppliers. As part of the interim audit work two weeks prior to the company year-end, you are testing the procurement and purchases systems and attending the inventory count.

On the day of the inventory count, you attended depot nine at DinZee Co. You observed the following activities:

Pre-numbered count sheets were being issued to client staff carrying out the count. The count sheets showed the inventory ledger balances for checking against physical inventory.

All count staff were drawn from the inventory warehouse and were counting in teams of two.

Three counting teams were allocated to each area of the stores to count. The teams were allowed to decide which pair of staff counted which inventory within each area. Staff were warned that they had to remember which inventory had been counted.

Information was recorded on the count sheets in pencil so amendments could be made easily as required.

Any inventory not located on the pre-numbered inventory sheets was recorded on separate inventory sheets which were numbered by staff as they were used.

At the end of the count, all count sheets were collected and the numeric sequence of the sheets checked. The sheets were not signed.

Required:

(a) **Describe FOUR procedures that an auditor will normally perform prior to attending the client's premises on the day of the inventory count.** **(4 marks)**

(b) **Identify and explain SIX deficiencies in the control system for counting inventory, and state how each deficiency can be overcome.** **(12 marks)**

(c) **State the aim of a test of control and the aim of a substantive procedure and in respect of your attendance at DinZee Co's inventory count, state one test of control and one substantive procedure that you should perform.** **(4 marks)**

(Total: 20 marks)

Test your understanding 9 – Evidence and procedures

You are the auditor of BearsWorld, a company which manufactures and sells small cuddly toys by mail order. The company is managed by Azariah, although due to other business commitments Azariah only visits the office once a week. BearsWorld employs two assistants. One assistant maintains the payables ledger, orders inventory and pays suppliers. The other assistant receives customer orders and despatches cuddly toys. Azariah authorises important transactions such as wages and large orders.

At any time, about 100 different types of cuddly toys are available for sale. All sales are paid for at the time of ordering. Customers pay using credit cards and occasionally by sending cash. Revenue is over $5.2 million.

You are planning the audit of BearsWorld and are considering using some of the procedures for gathering audit evidence recommended by ISA 500 *Audit Evidence* as follows:

- Analytical procedures
- Inquiry
- Inspection
- Observation
- Recalculation.

Required:

For each of the above procedures in relation to the audit of Bearsworld:

(i)   Explain its use in gathering audit evidence.

(ii)   Describe one example how it could be used.

(iii)   Explain the benefits of each procedure.

(iv)   Explain the limitations of each procedure.

(20 marks)

Test your understanding 10 – Procedures

(i)   Describe FIVE types of procedures for obtaining audit evidence; and

(ii)   For each type of procedure, describe an example relevant to the audit of BANK balances.

   Note: The total marks will be split equally between each part.

(10 marks)

Test your understanding 11 – Audit risk NFP

(a) **Explain the term 'audit risk' and the three elements of risk that contribute to total audit risk.**

(4 marks)

The EuKaRe charity was established in 1960. The charity's aim is to provide support to children from disadvantaged backgrounds who wish to take part in sports such as tennis, badminton and football.

EuKaRe has a detailed constitution which explains how the charity's income can be spent. The constitution also notes that administration expenditure cannot exceed 10% of income in any year.

The charity's income is derived wholly from voluntary donations. Sources of donations include:

- Cash collected by volunteers asking the public for donations in shopping areas.

- Cheques sent to the charity's head office.

- Donations from generous individuals. Some of these donations have specific clauses attached to them indicating that the initial amount donated (capital) cannot be spent and that the income (interest) from the donation must be spent on specific activities, for example, provision of sports equipment.

The rules regarding the taxation of charities in the country EuKaRe is based are complicated, with only certain expenditure being allowable for taxation purposes and donations of capital being treated as income in some situations.

Required:

(b) **Describe SIX audit risks and explain the auditor's response to each risk in planning the audit of EuKaRe.**

(12 marks)

(c) **Explain why the control environment may be weak at the charity EuKaRe.**

(4 marks)

(Total: 20 marks)

Test your understanding 12 – NFP audit

Ajio is a charity whose constitution requires that it raises funds for educational projects. These projects seek to educate children and support teachers in certain countries. Charities in the country in which Ajio operates have recently become subject to new audit and accounting regulations. Charity income consists of cash collections at fundraising events, telephone appeals, and money left to the charity by deceased persons. The charity is small and the trustees do not consider that the charity can afford to employ a qualified accountant. The charity employs a part-time bookkeeper and relies on volunteers for fundraising. Your firm has been appointed as accountants and auditors to this charity. Accounts have been prepared in the past by a volunteer who is a recently retired Chartered Certified Accountant but these accounts have not been audited.

Required:

(a)   **Explain the audit risks associated with the audit of Ajio.**

(4 marks)

(b)   **Describe the audit procedures to be performed on income and expenditure from fund raising events.**

(6 marks)

Note: You are not required to deal with the detail of accounting for charities in either part of the question.

(Total: 10 marks)

Test your understanding 13 – Subsequent events

It is 1 July 20X5. You are working on the audit of Grains 4U Co (Grains), a manufacturer of breakfast cereals which has three factories, four warehouses and three distribution depots spread across North America. The audit for the year ended 31 March 20X5 is almost complete and the financial statements and auditor's report are due to be signed shortly. Profit before taxation is $7.9 million. The following events have occurred subsequent to the year-end and no amendments or disclosures have been made in the financial statements.

Event 1 – Fire

On 15 May 20X5, a fire occurred at the largest of the distribution depots. The fire resulted in extensive damage to 40% of the company's vehicles used for dispatching goods to customers, however, there have been no significant delays to customer deliveries. The company estimates the level of damage to the vehicles to be in excess of $650,000. Only a minimal level of inventory, approximately $25,000, was damaged. Grain's insurance company has started to investigate the fire to assess the likelihood and level of payment, however, there are concerns the fire was started deliberately, and if true, would invalidate any insurance cover.

Event 2 – Inventory

On 18 May 20X5, it was discovered that a large batch of Grain's new cereal brand 'Loopy Green Loops' held in inventory at the year end was defective, as the cereal contained too much green food colouring. To date no sales of this new cereal have been made. The cost of the defective batch of inventory is $915,000 and the defects cannot be corrected. However, the scrapped cereal can be utilised as a raw material for an alternative cereal brand at a value of $50,000.

Required:

For each of the two subsequent events described above:

(i) **Based on the information provided, explain whether the financial statements require amendment, and**

(ii) **Describe audit procedures which should now be performed in order to form a conclusion on any required amendment.**

Note: The marks will be split equally between each event.

(Total: 10 marks)

Test your understanding 14 – Written representations

(a) Explain the purpose of a written representation.

(3 marks)

(b) You are the manager in charge of the audit of Crighton-Ward, a public limited liability company which manufactures specialist cars and other motor vehicles for use in films. Audited revenue is $140 million with profit before tax of $7.5 million.

All audit work up to, but not including, obtaining a written representation has been completed. A review of the audit file has disclosed the following outstanding points:

Lion's Roar

The company is facing a potential legal claim from the Lion's Roar company in respect of a defective vehicle that was supplied for one of its films. Lion's Roar maintains that the vehicle built was not strong enough while the directors of Crighton-Ward argue that the specification was not sufficiently detailed. Dropping a vehicle 50 metres into a river and expecting it to continue to remain in working condition would be unusual, but this is what Lion's Roar expected.

Solicitors are unable to determine liability at the present time. A claim for $4 million being the cost of a replacement vehicle and lost production time has been received by Crighton-Ward from Lions' Roar. The directors' opinion is that the claim is not justified.

Depreciation

Depreciation of specialist production equipment has been included in the financial statements at the amount of 10% per annum using the reducing balance method. The treatment is consistent with prior accounting periods (which received an unmodified audit opinion) and other companies in the same industry. Sales of old equipment show negligible profit or loss on sale. The audit senior, who is new to the audit, feels that depreciation is being undercharged in the financial statements.

Required:

(b) Discuss whether or not a paragraph is required in the written representation for each of the above matters.

(4 marks)

(c) A suggested format for the written representation has been sent by the auditor to the directors of Crighton-Ward. The directors have stated that they will not sign the written representation this year on the grounds that they believe the additional evidence that it provides is not required by the auditor.

Required:

Discuss the actions the auditor may take as a result of the decision made by the directors not to sign the written representation.

(3 marks)

(Total: 10 marks)

Test your understanding 15 – Auditors' reports

It is 1 July 20X5. You are reviewing the working papers of several audit assignments recently carried out by your audit firm. Each of the audit engagements is nearing completion and the auditor's reports are due to be issued soon. In each case the year end of the company is 31 March 20X5. The following issues have been brought to your attention.

(a) **Eliud Co** (Profit before tax $150,000)

On 3 April 20X5 a letter was received informing the company that a customer, who owed the company $30,000 as at the year-end had been declared bankrupt on 31 March 20X5. At the time of the audit it was expected that unsecured creditors, such as Eliud Co, would receive nothing in respect of this debt. The directors refuse to change the financial statements to provide for the loss, on the grounds that the notification was not received by the statement of financial position date.

Total debts shown in the statement of financial position amounted to $700,000. **(5 marks)**

(b) **Brigid Co** (Profit before tax $500,000)

On 31 May 20X5 a customer sued the company for personal damages arising from a defect in one of its products. Shortly before the year-end the company made an out-of-court settlement with the customer of $10,000, although this agreement is not reflected in the financial statements. Further, the matter subsequently became known to the press and was extensively reported. The company's legal advisers have now informed you that further claims have been received following the publicity, although they are unable to place a figure on the potential liability arising. The company has referred to the claims in a note to the financial statements stating that no provision has been made because the claims are not expected to be material. **(5 marks)**

(c) Kenenisa Co (Profit before tax $250,000)

The audit work revealed that a trade investment stated in the statement of financial position at $500,000 has suffered a permanent fall in value of $300,000. The directors have refused to recognise an impairment charge in respect of the asset.

(5 marks)

(d) Mary Co (Profit before tax $100,000)

Mary Co is a construction company, currently building a warehouse on its own premises and using some of its own workforce. The labour cost has been included in the cost of the non-current asset in the statement of financial position at a value of $10,000. During the audit it was discovered that the direct labour cost records for the early part of the year have been accidentally destroyed.

(5 marks)

Required:

Discuss each of the issues and describe the impact on the auditor's reports, if any, should these issues remain unresolved.

(Total: 20 marks)

Test your understanding 16 – Corporate Governance 1

You are an audit manager of Satsuma & Co and have been assigned to the audit of Tangerine Tech Co (Tangerine), a company which is planning to list on a stock exchange within six months. The listing rules of the stock exchange require compliance with corporate governance principles, and the directors are unsure whether they are following best practice in relation to this. They have asked the audit engagement partner for their view on this matter.

Tangerine's board comprises six executive directors, a non-executive chair and three other non-executive directors (NEDs). The chair and one of the NEDs are former executive directors of Tangerine and on reaching retirement age were asked to take on non-executive roles. The company has established an audit committee, and all NEDs are members including the chair who chairs the committee. All four members of the audit committee were previously involved in sales or production related roles.

All of the directors have been members of the board for at least four years. As the chair does not have an executive role, he has sole responsibility for liaising with the shareholders and answering any of their questions. The company has not established an internal audit function to monitor internal controls.

Required:

Using the information above describe FIVE corporate governance weaknesses faced by Tangerine Tech Co and provide a recommendation to address each weakness to ensure compliance with corporate governance principles.

(10 marks)

Test your understanding 17 – Corporate Governance 2

1   **What is meant by corporate governance?**

(2 marks)

2   **Why are external auditors interested in corporate governance?**

(2 marks)

3   **Who should make up a typical audit committee?**

(1 mark)

4   **What is the audit committee's role?**

(5 marks)

5   **Why does a company need an audit committee if it has a good relationship with its external auditors?**

(2 marks)

6   **A company has identified one of its major risks as loss of key staff.**

Explain:

–   **What they should do as a result of this?**

–   **How they might reduce or even eliminate the risk?**

–   **Why the auditor is interested in this, given that it is not a direct financial risk?**

(3 marks)

(Total: 15 marks)

Test your understanding 18 – Internal audit

Flylo is an airline. The company owns some of its fleet of aircraft. Other aircraft are leased from third parties. Flylo has an internal audit function that has recently been expanded. Your firm is the external auditor of Flylo. Your firm has been asked to investigate the extent to which it may be able to rely on the work of internal audit in the following areas:

- Sales and ticketing

- Fleet acquisition and maintenance

- Trade payables and long-term debt financing (borrowings).

Required:

(a) **Explain why the work of the internal auditors, in the three areas noted above, is likely to be useful to you as the external auditor.**

(6 marks)

(b) **Explain the matters that should be considered by the external auditor when evaluating the internal audit function and whether reliance can be placed on its work.**

(4 marks)

(Total: 10 marks)

Test your understanding answers

Test your understanding 1 – Confidentiality

(a) **Disclosure of information without client consent**

The auditor must disclose information which is required by law, for example:

- Production of documents or other provision of evidence in the course of legal proceedings.

- Disclosure to the appropriate public authorities of infringements of the law that come to light e.g. money laundering.

The auditor must disclose information when there is a professional duty or right to disclose, when not prohibited by law:

- To comply with the quality review of ACCA or another professional body.

- To respond to an inquiry or investigation by ACCA or a regulatory body.

- To protect the professional interests of a professional accountant in legal proceedings.

- To comply with technical standards and ethics requirements.

Factors to be considered before disclosing confidential information include:

- Whether harm could be caused by the disclosure

- Whether all relevant information is known and substantiated

- Whether the information is to be communicated to appropriate recipients.

(b) **Response to requests**

- The auditor must not disclose information without the consent of the client or unless the necessary statutory documentation is provided by the person(s) requesting the information.

- Unless the auditor has reason to believe that there is a statutory duty not to inform the client that an approach has been made, the client should first be approached to see if consent can be obtained, and to see if the client is aware of the investigations. The auditor should ensure that the client is aware of the fact the voluntary disclosure may work in the client's favour. If the client refuses, the auditor should inform the client if the auditor has a statutory duty of disclosure.

- Legal advice should be sought in all of the cases described.

– Where the auditor is made aware of potential actions against the client that may have an effect on the financial statements, the auditor must consider the effect on the auditor's report. If the client is aware of the investigation, the auditor will be able to seek audit evidence to support any necessary provisions or disclosures in the financial statements.

– The auditor should consider whether the suspected fraud relating to the managing director relates to the company and affects the financial statements.

– The auditor will be in a very difficult situation if they become aware of an action that may materially affect the financial statements, but where the client is not, and where auditors are under a statutory duty not to inform the client. This situation will not be improved by the resignation of auditors as they may be obliged to make a statement on resignation. Legal advice is essential in such circumstances.

– Tax authorities normally have powers to ask clients to disclose information voluntarily. Such voluntary disclosure is often looked on favourably by the tax authorities and the courts. Tax authorities normally also have statutory powers to demand information from both clients and auditors.

– The power of the police to demand information is sometimes less clear and auditors and clients should take care to ensure that the appropriate authority to disclose is in place. Those sections of the police investigating serious frauds usually have more powers than the general police.

– It is unlikely that trade union representatives have any statutory powers to demand information.

Test your understanding 2 – Ethical threats

Threat	Managing the threat
Mrs Goodall has been the engagement partner for the last seven years. This creates a familiarity threat. Mrs Goodall may be too trusting of or too close to the client to be able to make objective decisions due to this long association.	Mrs Goodall should be rotated from the engagement team. It may be possible to allow Mrs Goodall to continue as engagement partner for one further year in order to safeguard audit quality. Audit committee approval must be obtained in order to allow this and an engagement quality control review should be arranged.

There may be the impression of lack of independence as Simon is related to the engagement partner. Simon could be tempted not to identify errors in case this prejudiced his mother's relationship with the client. In addition, if Mrs Goodall reviews Simon's work, she may not review it as thoroughly as the other audit staff due to their relationship.	To demonstrate complete independence, Simon should not be part of any audit or assurance team for which Mrs Goodall is partner.
As long as the audit senior paid a full fee to Pink Co for the investment advice (i.e. it is on normal commercial terms) there is no ethical threat as investment advice is in the normal course of business for Pink Co. However, if the audit senior received a discount on the services or preferential rates, as a benefit of being part of the audit team, this would create a self-interest threat. The audit senior may overlook issues identified during the audit because of the preferential treatment.	The audit team (and other employees of the firm) should be asked not to use the services of Pink Co, or other audit clients unless prior agreement has been obtained from the relevant engagement partner.
The audit team has been offered a day at the horse races at the end of the audit which creates a self-interest threat. Unless the value is trivial and inconsequential, hospitality is not allowed. The fact that the horse race day costs less than the yacht expense is irrelevant. The auditors may feel indebted to the client and therefore overlook issues identified during the audit.	The day out should not be accepted. The rationale for accepting hospitality in previous years should be investigated.
There are outstanding fees creating a self-interest threat. JT & Co may be reluctant to identify misstatements for fear of not getting paid. In addition, outstanding fees may be considered to be a loan. Loans to clients are not permitted.	Payment for work should be arranged before the audit is commenced, or a payment plan agreed.

Test your understanding 3 – Analytical risk assessment

(a) (i) Explanation of analytical procedures

'Analytical procedures' means the evaluation of financial and other information and the review of plausible relationships in that information. The review also includes identifying fluctuations and relationships that do not appear consistent with other relevant information or results.

(ii) Types of analytical procedures

Analytical procedures can be used as:

– Comparison of comparable information to prior periods to identify unusual changes or fluctuations in amounts.

– Comparison of actual or anticipated results of the entity with budgets and/or forecasts, or the expectations of the auditor in order to determine the potential accuracy of those results.

– Comparison to industry information either for the industry as a whole or by comparison to entities of similar size to the client to determine whether key ratios, such as gross profit margin and the receivables collection period, are reasonable.

(iii) Use of analytical procedures

Risk assessment procedures

Analytical procedures are used at the beginning of the audit to help the auditor obtain an understanding of the entity and assess the risk of material misstatement. Audit procedures can then be directed to these risky areas.

Analytical procedures as substantive procedures

Analytical procedures can be used as substantive procedures in determining the risk of material misstatement at the assertion level during work on the statement of profit or loss and statement of financial position.

Analytical procedures in the overall review at the end of the audit

Analytical procedures help the auditor at the end of the audit in forming an overall conclusion as to whether the financial statements as a whole are consistent with the auditor's understanding of the entity.

(b) **Profit before tax**

Overall, Tribe Co's result has changed from a loss to a profit. Given that revenue has only increased by 17% and that expenses, at least administration expenses, appear low, then there is the possibility that expenditure may be understated.

Revenue – increase 17%

According to the directors, Tribe Co has had a difficult year. Reasons for the increase in revenue must be ascertained as the change does not conform to the directors' comments. It is possible that the industry as a whole has been growing allowing Tribe Co to produce this good result. Alternatively, incorrect revenue recognition may have been applied.

Cost of sales – fall 17%

A fall in cost of sales is unusual given that revenue has increased significantly. This may have been caused by an incorrect inventory valuation and the use of different (cheaper) suppliers which may cause problems with faulty goods in the next year.

Gross profit (GP) – increase 88%

This is a significant increase with the GP% changing from 33% last year to 53% this year. Identifying reasons for this change will need to focus initially on the change in revenue and cost of sales.

Administration – fall 6%

A fall is unusual given that revenue is increasing and so an increase in administration to support those sales would be expected. Expenditure may be understated, or there has been a decrease in the number of administration staff.

Selling and distribution – increase 42%

This increase does not appear to be in line with the increase in revenue as selling and distribution would be expected to increase in line with revenue. There may be misallocation of expenses from administration or the age of Tribe Co's delivery vans is increasing resulting in additional service costs.

Investment income – new this year

This is expected given the cash surplus in the year, although the amount is still very high indicating possible errors in the amount or other income generating assets not disclosed on the statement of financial position extract.

> ### Interest payable – small fall
>
> Given that Tribe Co has a considerable cash surplus this year, continuing to pay interest is surprising. The amount may be overstated.
>
> Reasons for the lack of fall in interest payment e.g. loans that cannot be repaid early, must be determined. If the interest is associated with the overdraft that was in the SOFP last year, this may have only been paid off just before the year-end.

Test your understanding 4 – Audit risk

(a) **Audit risks**

Inventory valuation

Smoothbrush supplies 60% of its goods to Homewares at a significantly reduced selling price. Inventory may be overvalued if the net realisable value is lower than cost.

Receivables

Smoothbrush has extended its credit terms to Homewares from one month to four months. There is an increased risk as balances outstanding become older that they may be irrecoverable resulting in overstatement of receivables.

Plant and equipment

The production facility has a large amount of unused plant and equipment. This plant and equipment should be stated at the lower of its carrying value and recoverable amount, which may be at scrap value depending on its age and condition. Plant and equipment may be overvalued.

Cut-off

Smoothbrush imports goods from South Asia and the paint can be in transit for up to two months. The company accounts for goods when they receive them. Therefore at the year-end only goods that have been received into the warehouse should be included in the inventory balance and a respective payables balance recognised. Cut-off of purchases and inventory may not be accurate.

Inventory system

A new inventory system was introduced in the year. This could result in inventory balances being misstated if the records and new system have not been set up correctly.

Inventory allowance

Smoothbrush previously maintained an inventory allowance of 1%, however, this year it has decided to remove this. Unless all slow-moving/obsolete items are identified at the year-end and their value adjusted, there is a risk that the overall value of inventory may be overstated.

Legal action

The company's finance director (FD) has left and is intending to sue Smoothbrush for unfair dismissal. However, the company does not intend to make any provision or disclosure for any potential payment to the FD. Provisions or contingent liability disclosures may not be complete.

Lack of FD

Inherent risk is higher due to the changes in the finance department. The financial controller has been appointed as temporary FD and this lack of experience could result in increased risk of errors arising in the financial statement. In addition, the previous FD is not available to help with the audit.

Perpetual Inventory system

Inventory may be misstated if the perpetual inventory counts are not complete and accurate. The inventory counts should cover all of the inventory lines but if any of the warehouses are not counted then this will need to be done at the year-end. In addition, inventory adjustments arising from the counts must be verified and updated by an appropriate member of the finance team to ensure the records are accurate.

(b) **Importance of assessing risks**

– Assessing engagement risk at the planning stage will ensure that attention is focused early on the area's most likely to cause material misstatements.

– A thorough risk assessment will also help the auditor to fully understand the entity, which enables an effective audit to be performed. Any unusual transactions or balances would also be identified early, so that these could be addressed in a timely manner.

– As auditors adopt a risk based audit approach, these risks need to be assessed early in order for the audit strategy and detailed work programmes to be developed.

– Assessing risks early should also result in an efficient audit. The team will only focus their time and effort on key areas as opposed to balances or transactions that might be immaterial or unlikely to contain errors.

– Assessing risk early should ensure that the most appropriate team is selected with more experienced staff allocated to higher risk areas and high risk balances.

– A thorough risk analysis should ultimately reduce the risk of an inappropriate audit opinion being given. The audit would have focused on the main risk areas and hence any material misstatements should have been identified.

– It should enable the auditor to have a good understanding of the risks of fraud, money laundering, etc. Assessing risk should enable the auditor to assess whether the client is a going concern.

(c) **Substantive procedures to confirm valuation of inventory**

– Select a representative sample of goods in inventory at the year-end, agree the cost per the records to a recent purchase invoice and ensure that the cost is correctly stated in the inventory records.

– Select a sample of inventory from the inventory listing and review post year-end sales invoices to ascertain if NRV is above cost or if an adjustment is required.

– For a sample of manufactured items obtain cost sheets and agree:

– raw material costs to recent purchase invoices

– labour costs to time sheets or wage records

– overheads allocated are of a production nature.

– Review aged inventory reports and identify any slow-moving goods. Discuss with management why these items have not been written down.

– Compare the level/value of aged product lines to the total inventory value to assess whether the allowance for slow-moving goods of 1% should be reinstated.

– Review the inventory records to identify the level of adjustments made throughout the year for damaged/obsolete items. If significant, consider whether the year-end records require further adjustments and discuss with management whether any further write downs/allowance may be required.

– Follow up on any damaged/obsolete items noted by the auditor at the inventory counts attended, to ensure that the inventory records have been updated correctly.

– Calculate the average inventory holding period for the current year and compare to prior year. Discuss any significant variations with management.

– Compare the gross margin for current year with prior year. Fluctuations in gross margin could be due to inventory valuation issues. Discuss significant variations in the margin with management.

(d) **Substantive procedures to confirm completeness of provisions or contingent liabilities**

– Discuss with management the nature of the dispute between Smoothbrush and the former FD, to ensure that a full understanding of the issue is obtained and to assess whether an obligation exists.

– Review any correspondence with the former FD to assess if a reliable estimate of any potential payments can be made.

– Review correspondence with the company's lawyers to obtain their views as to the probability of the FD's claim being successful.

– Review board minutes and any company correspondence to assess whether there is any evidence to support the former FD's claims of unfair dismissal.

– Obtain a written representation from the directors of Smoothbrush confirming their view that the former FD's chances of a successful claim are remote, and hence no provision or contingent liability is required.

Test your understanding 5 – Fraud

(a) **Internal audit function: risk of fraud and error**

Internal audit can help management manage risks in relation to fraud and error, and exercise proper stewardship by:

– Commenting on the process used by management to identify and classify the specific fraud and error risks to which the entity is subject.

– Periodically auditing or reviewing systems or operations to determine whether the risks of fraud and error are being effectively managed.

– Where deficiencies which provide opportunity for fraud and error are identified, making recommendations for improvements.

– Monitoring the incidence of fraud and error and investigating serious cases.

In practice, the work of internal audit often focuses on the adequacy and effectiveness of internal control procedures for the prevention, detection and reporting of fraud and error. Routine internal controls (such as the controls over computer systems and the production of routine financial information) and non-routine controls (such as controls over year-end adjustments to the financial statements) are relevant.

It should be recognised however that many significant frauds bypass normal internal control systems and that in the case of management fraud in particular, much higher level controls (those relating to the high level governance of the entity) need to be reviewed by internal audit in order to establish the nature of the risks, and to manage them effectively.

(b) **External auditors: fraud and error in an audit of financial statements**

– External auditors are required by ISA 240 *The Auditor's Responsibilities Relating to Fraud in an Audit of Financial Statements* to consider the risks of material misstatements in the financial statements due to fraud. Their audit procedures will then be based on that risk assessment.

– Regardless of the risk assessment, auditors are required to be alert to the possibility of fraud throughout the audit and maintain an attitude of professional scepticism, notwithstanding the auditors' past experience of the honesty and integrity of management and those charged with governance.

- Members of the engagement team should discuss the susceptibility of the entity's financial statements to material misstatements due to fraud.

- Auditors should make enquiries of management regarding management's assessment of fraud risk, its process for dealing with risk, and its communications with those charged with governance and employees. They should enquire of those charged with governance about the oversight process.

- Auditors should also enquire of management and those charged with governance about any suspected or actual instance of fraud.

- Auditors should consider fraud risk factors, unusual or unexpected relationships, and assess the risk of misstatements due to fraud, identifying any significant risks. Auditors should evaluate the design of relevant internal controls, and determine whether they have been implemented.

- Auditors should determine an overall response to the assessed risk of material misstatements due to fraud and develop appropriate audit procedures, including testing certain journal entries, reviewing estimates for bias, and obtaining an understanding of the business rationale of significant transactions outside the normal course of business.

- Appropriate written representations should be obtained from management confirming they have informed the auditor of all known or suspected frauds.

- External auditors are only concerned with risks that might cause material error in the financial statements. External auditors might therefore pay less attention than internal auditors to small frauds (and errors), although they must always consider whether evidence of single instances of fraud (or error) are indicative of more systematic problems.

- It is accepted that because of the hidden nature of fraud, an audit properly conducted in accordance with ISAs might not detect a material misstatement in the financial statements arising from fraud. In practice, routine errors are much easier to detect than frauds.

- Where auditors encounter suspicions or actual instances of fraud (or error), they must consider the effect on the financial statements, which will usually involve further investigations.

- They should also consider the need to report to management and those charged with governance.

–   Where serious frauds (or errors) are encountered, auditors need also to consider the effect on the going concern status of the entity, and the possible need to report externally to third parties, either in the public interest or for regulatory reasons. Many entities in the financial services sector are subject to this type of regulatory reporting and many countries have legislation relating to the reporting of money laundering activities, for example.

(c)   **Nature of risks arising from fraud and error: Stone Holidays**

–   Stone Holidays is subject to all of the risks of error arising from the use of computer systems. If programmed controls do not operate properly, for example, the information produced may be incomplete or incorrect.

–   Inadequate controls also give rise to the risk of fraud by those who understand the system and are able to manipulate it in order to hide the misappropriation of assets, such as receipts from customers.

–   All networked systems are also subject to the risk of error because of the possibility of the loss or corruption of data in transit. They are also subject to the risk of fraud where the transmission of data is not securely encrypted.

–   All entities that employ staff who handle company assets (such as receipts from customers) are subject to the risk that staff may make mistakes (error) or that they may misappropriate those assets (fraud) and then seek to hide the error or fraud by falsifying the records.

–   Stone Holidays is subject to problems arising from the risk of fraud perpetrated by customers using stolen credit or debit cards or even cash. Whilst credit card companies may be liable for such frauds, attempts to use stolen cards can cause considerable inconvenience.

–   There is a risk of fraud perpetrated by senior management who might seek to lower the amount of money payable to the central fund (and the company's tax liability) by falsifying the company's sales figures, particularly if a large proportion of holidays are paid for in cash.

–   There is a risk that staff may seek to maximise the commission they are paid by entering false transactions into the computer system that are then reversed after the commission has been paid.

Test your understanding 6 – Quality control

Client A

Failure to sign off a working paper makes it difficult to identify the person responsible for the work in case of any query. If the working papers had been reviewed, the reviewer should have identified this issue and investigated who had performed the work and asked them to sign the working papers.

Completion dates of audit work are essential in order to identify the information that would have been available to the auditor at the time the procedures were completed. With the passage of time, more information can come to light which would change the conclusion. If the working papers had been reviewed, the reviewer should have identified this issue and asked the preparer to date the working papers.

Review of the working papers is an important quality control procedure. Every team member's work should be reviewed by someone more senior to ensure it has been performed properly and to the appropriate standard. If a review has not been performed there could be material misstatements that have not been detected during the audit which could result in an inappropriate auditor's report being issued.

Client B

The comment on the file stating that there are no matters requiring written representation would indicate that the audit manager does not understand the professional standards that should be followed during an audit, specifically the requirements of ISA 580 *Written Representations*.

Written representations are required by ISA 580. By not obtaining a written representation the audit firm does not have sufficient appropriate evidence to support the audit opinion.

Written representations should include matters such as management confirming they have prepared financial statements that give a true and fair view and that they have provided the auditor with all of the information required for the audit.

The audit partner should not have signed the auditor's report without the written representation being on file.

Client C

A sample of 30 was chosen for a purchases test yet only 27 were tested and a conclusion drawn from those items.

Sample sizes are chosen to ensure sufficient appropriate evidence has been obtained. As only 27 items were tested instead of 30, sufficient appropriate evidence has not been obtained in this instance.

The three missing invoices could be evidence of a wider control deficiency or a material fraud. Further investigation should have been performed to discover the reason for the missing invoices.

The issue may indicate a lack of supervision if the audit team member was unsure how to proceed after discovering the issue.

The issue would also indicate a lack of review as the matter was not identified during the review process.

Client D

Provisions are inherently risky as they are often determined by the judgment of management. As such they should be audited by someone with suitable experience and judgment.

An audit junior should not have performed this task. Tasks should be allocated to team members of appropriate experience and competence. Junior members of staff are usually allocated lower risk areas which require little experience and judgment. More senior members of the team should be assigned the riskier areas of the audit.

It is stated that the audit manager was too busy to perform the audit of the provision due to other client work. This may indicate that the workload of staff is not manageable. Audit quality could have been affected on both clients as work may be rushed to get it completed which may result in material misstatements going undetected.

Client E

Planning is an important and compulsory part of the audit process. ISA 300 *Planning an Audit of Financial Statements* requires the audit to be planned in order to ensure that the audit is performed in an efficient and effective manner and an appropriate audit approach is taken which addresses the risks of the audit.

The auditor should not simply copy last year's procedures and approach as this may not be appropriate for this year's circumstances.

By failing to plan the audit properly, ISA 300 has not been complied with and therefore the audit has not been performed in accordance with professional standards.

General points

The quality control issues identified raise doubts over the performance of several audits conducted by the firm.

If it is discovered that an inappropriate auditor's report was issued in any of these cases the firm could face action by the ACCA and by the client.

Any action taken against the firm could damage its reputation as well as result in a loss of clients and financial penalties.

The firm's policies and procedures should be communicated again to staff to remind them of the requirements and their importance.

Further training is recommended to ensure staff are aware of how to comply with the requirements.

Disciplinary action may be necessary in respect of staff who have been found to be deliberately disregarding company policy.

Test your understanding 7 – Controls

Deficiency (1 mark)	Recommendation (1 mark)
1 Hand written orders are not sequentially numbered. Orders could be placed for goods not required resulting in a build-up of inventory which could lead to overstatement of inventory balances and a reduction in profit. Alternatively, orders could be lost and not placed leading to potential stock outs. This will mean customer orders cannot be fulfilled leading to customer dissatisfaction.	Orders should be sequentially pre-numbered. A sequence check should be performed on a regular basis to ensure completeness. Orders should be authorised by a manager before being placed to ensure the goods are required.
2 Purchase orders are not issued for all goods and services. Goods/services could be purchased that are not legitimate (occurrence of purchases). This will increase costs for the company.	Purchase orders should be required for all goods. For services, a budget should be set and quotes obtained. Purchase orders should be authorised by someone other than the person requesting the goods to ensure they are for business use.

3	There is no system for recording receipt of other goods and services. Failure to record goods received could lead to over-ordering as inventory levels will be inaccurate. This will result in additional cost for the company and possible overstatement of inventory due to obsolescence.	A goods received note should be completed and used to update the inventory records on a daily basis.
4	Goods received are not checked against the purchase order. Goods could be received that have not been ordered. Incorrect quantities could be received. This will lead to production delays if the wrong goods have been received and delays in fulfilling customer orders leading to customer dissatisfaction.	Agree the GRN to the purchase order to ensure the correct goods are being delivered.
5	There is no review of the bookkeeper's work e.g. posting of invoices into the nominal ledger. Errors could go undetected resulting in misstatement of purchases and payables and incorrect payments to suppliers.	A review of the nominal ledger postings by a manager should be performed on a regular basis.
6	A list of payables is given to the managing director without supporting documentation. The managing director will not know if payables are valid or correct therefore could be paying incorrect amounts resulting in misstatement of payables and poor cash flow management.	The managing director should also review source documents before signing the list to ensure payments are for a valid business use.
7	There is a lack of segregation of duties as the managing director authorises invoices, approves payment and signs cheques. Fraud could occur and go undetected as the managing director could create a fictitious purchase invoice to support a payment to him or herself. This will cause loss for the company.	Segregate duties by sharing the responsibility with another manager.

Test your understanding 8 – Inventory count

(a) **Procedures prior to inventory count attendance**

- Review prior year working papers to identify any issues encountered which the auditor should be prepared for this year.

- Obtain inventory count instructions from the client to ascertain whether appropriate controls and procedures will be in place during the count.

- Enquire with management whether there have been any control issues relating to inventory during the year.

- Enquire of the client whether any inventory is held at third parties and assess whether attendance is required at those sites.

(b) **Deficiencies in counting inventory**

Deficiency	How to overcome deficiency
Inventory sheets stated the quantity of items expected to be found in the store. Count teams will focus on finding that number of items making undercounting of inventory more likely – teams may stop counting when 'correct' number of items found.	Count sheets should not state the quantity of items so as not to pre-judge how many units will be found.
Count staff were all drawn from the stores. Count staff are also responsible for the inventory. There could be a temptation to hide errors or missing inventory that they have removed from the store illegally resulting in misstatement of the inventory balance.	Count teams should include staff who are not responsible for inventory to provide independence in the count.
Count teams are allowed to decide which areas to count. There is a danger that teams will either omit inventory from the count or even count inventory twice due to lack of precise instructions on where to count. This will result in either under or overstatement of inventory.	Each team should be given a precise area of the store to count.

Count sheets were not signed by the staff carrying out the count. Lack of signature makes it difficult to raise queries regarding items counted because the actual staff carrying out the count are not known.	All count sheets should be signed to confirm who actually carried out the count of individual items.
Inventory is not marked to indicate it has been counted. As above, there is a danger that inventory will be either omitted or included twice in the count resulting in either under or overstatement of inventory.	Inventory should be marked in some way to show that it has been counted to avoid this error.
Recording information on the count sheets in pencil. Recording in pencil means that the count sheets could be amended after the count has taken place, not just during the count. The inventory balances will then be incorrectly recorded.	Count sheets should be completed in ink.
Count sheets for inventory not on the pre-numbered count sheets were only numbered when used. Additional inventory sheets could be lost as there is no control of the sheets actually being used. Sheets may not be numbered by the teams, again giving rise to the possibility of loss and understatement of inventory.	All inventory sheets, including those for 'extra' inventory, should be pre-numbered.

(c) **Tests of controls and substantive procedures**

The aim of a test of control is to evaluate the operating effectiveness of controls in preventing, or detecting and correcting material misstatements at the assertion level.

Example: Observe the count teams to ensure they are counting in accordance with the client's inventory count instructions.

The aim of a substantive procedure is to ensure that there are no material errors at the assertion level in the client's financial statements.

Example: Record the condition of items of inventory to ensure that the valuation is appropriate on the final inventory listing.

Test your understanding 9 – Evidence and procedures

Audit procedures

(i) **Analytical procedures** consist of evaluations of financial information made by a study of plausible relationships among both financial and non-financial data.

Inquiry means to seek relevant information from sources, both financial and non-financial, either inside or outside the company being audited. Evidence may be obtained orally or in writing.

Inspection is the examination of records, documents and tangible assets.

Observation involves looking at a process or procedure as it is being performed to ensure that the process actually works as documented.

Recalculation means the checking of the mathematical accuracy of documents or records.

(ii) **Analytical procedures**

Compare revenue year on year to try to identify whether income has been understated, possibly by cash being stolen prior to banking. There is no control over the opening of post so cash could be withdrawn by one assistant, and the deficit made up by a fraud on customers.

Inquiry

Obtain statements from suppliers to check the completeness of liabilities at the end of the year. As there is no control over purchases, invoices could have been misplaced resulting in lower purchases and trade payables figures.

Inspection

The assets of the company, namely cuddly toys in inventory at the end of the year, can be inspected to ensure the inventory exists and that the toys are saleable in their current condition.

Observation

Procedures such as the opening of the post and recording of customer orders can be observed to ensure that all orders are recorded in the sales day book and cash book.

Recalculation

Recalculating the cash book to confirm that the total amount of cash recorded is accurate and can be included in the revenue figure (cash receipts should equal revenue as there are no receivables).

(iii) **Analytical procedures**

This method of collecting evidence will be useful in BearsWorld because it will help to identify unusual changes in income and expenditure. As BearsWorld is a relatively small company, monitoring gross profit will show relatively small changes in sales margin or purchasing costs. Decisions by Azariah to amend margins can therefore be traced into the actual sales made.

Enquiry

Enquiry evidence will be very useful in the audit of BearsWorld, especially where this is derived from third parties. Third party evidence is generally more reliable than client originated evidence as there is a decreased likelihood of bias. Trade payables can therefore be verified using supplier statement reconciliations.
A review of any customer complaints file (if these letters are kept) will also help to identify any orders that have not been despatched.

Inspection

Inspection of documents within BearsWorld will be useful, particularly regarding checking whether expenses are bona fide. All purchase invoices, for example, should be addressed to BearsWorld and relate to purchases expected from that company, e.g. cuddly toys for resale, office expenses, etc.

Observation

Observation may be useful because it will show how the assistants perform their work and whether there are any obvious deficiencies in the processes of the company.

Recalculation

Recalculation evidence is very useful for checking additions on invoices, balancing of control accounts, etc. This means that the arithmetical accuracy of the books and records in BearsWorld can be confirmed.

(iv) **Analytical procedures**

The technique may be limited in its application because it will not detect errors or omissions made consistently year on year. If either assistant is defrauding the company (for example by removing cash) each year, then analytical procedures will not detect this. Analytical procedures will also not detect misstatements which cancel each other out, i.e. one misstatement may overstate the balance but another may understate the balance. The auditor would not detect these misstatements using analytical procedures.

Enquiry

External inquiry evidence will be less useful in the audit of sales and receivables because there are no receivables as goods are paid for prior to despatch. Internal evidence will be available from Azariah and the assistant, however the lack of segregation of duties means that this may not be so reliable.

Inspection

Inspection of documents can be time consuming. However, given the poor internal control system within BearsWorld, the auditor may have no choice but to use this method of gathering evidence.

The fact that an invoice is addressed to the company does not confirm completeness of recording so inspection of the cash book for unusual payments verified by checking the purchase invoice will also be required. Additional substantive testing would also be required due to poor controls.

Observation

Observation tests will be of limited usefulness because the assistants may act differently when an auditor is present. The same problem will apply to any observations carried out by Azariah.

Recalculation

The main weakness of recalculation checking is that calculations can only be carried out on figures that have been recorded. If there are any omissions then checks cannot be carried out.

Test your understanding 10 – Procedures

Inspection

Inspection involves examining records or documents, whether internal or external, in paper form, electronic form, or other media, or a physical examination of an asset.

Inspect the bank reconciliation for any outstanding lodgements and agree to the pre year-end cash book, post year-end bank statement and also to paying-in-book pre year-end.

Observation

Observation consists of looking at a process or procedure being performed by others.

Observe the process for the opening of mail and logging of any cheques received from customers to ensure adequate segregation of duties.

Analytical procedures

Analytical procedures consist of evaluations of financial information through analysis of plausible relationships among both financial and nonfinancial data. Analytical procedures also encompass such investigation as is necessary of identified fluctuations or relationships which are inconsistent with other relevant information or which differ from expected values by a significant amount.

Review the year-end bank balance against prior year to identify any significant fluctuations as these could be evidence of window dressing and discuss with management.

Inquiry

Inquiry consists of seeking information from knowledgeable persons, both financial and non-financial, within the entity or outside the entity.

Inquire of management as to whether the company has opened/closed any bank accounts during the period.

KAPLAN PUBLISHING

Recalculation

Recalculation consists of checking the mathematical accuracy of documents or records. Recalculation may be performed manually or electronically.

Recalculate the additions in the cash book to confirm accuracy of the amount.

External confirmation

An external confirmation represents audit evidence obtained by the auditor as a direct written response to the auditor from a third party, in paper form, electronic form or by other medium.

Obtain a standard bank confirmation from each bank the company has undertaken banking transactions with during the year.

Re-performance

Re-performance involves the auditor's independent execution of procedures or controls which were originally performed as part of the entity's internal control.

Re-perform the year-end bank reconciliation to ensure the process was undertaken accurately.

Test your understanding 11 – Audit risk NFP

(a) **Audit risk**

Audit risk is the risk that an auditor gives an inappropriate opinion on the financial statements being audited.

Inherent risk is the susceptibility of an assertion to a misstatement that could be material individually or when aggregated with misstatements, before considering any related controls.

Control risk is the risk that a material misstatement could occur in an assertion that could be material, individually or when aggregated with other misstatements, and will not be prevented or detected on a timely basis by the company's controls.

Detection risk is the risk that the auditors' procedures will not detect a misstatement that exists in an assertion that could be material, individually or when aggregated with other misstatements.

(b)

Audit risk	Auditor's response
Income is from voluntary donations only. It will be difficult to estimate future income. There is a risk that disclosure of going concern issues is not adequate in the financial statements.	Review forecasts and enquire with the trustees and management of the charity about their fundraising plans for the future. Obtain written representation from the trustees that they believe the charity can continue in existence for the foreseeable future.
Risk to completeness of income as cash donations may be stolen in the absence of any controls. No invoices will be raised and therefore there will be no evidence of the income received.	Assess what controls exist over cash donations (if any). Test the effectiveness of the controls in place. There may need to be a modified opinion due to lack of sufficient appropriate evidence.
There is a risk that the funds are not spent in accordance with the aims of the charity (regularity audit).	Inspect the constitution of the charity to understand its aims. Review a breakdown of expenditure to ensure it is in line with the constitution.
The taxation rules are quite complex for the charity resulting in a risk to the reasonableness of the tax accrual at the year-end.	Consult with a tax expert or audit staff with relevant knowledge to assess the tax rules and recalculate the tax charge and liability to ensure arithmetical accuracy.
According to the constitution of the charity, only 10% of expenditure can be on administration. There is a risk that administration costs are deliberately misstated to ensure this restriction is met.	Inspect the constitution of the charity to understand its aims. Review the breakdown of other types of expenditure to identify any admin costs incorrectly classified if the 10% limit has been exceeded.
Some donations are made for an intended purpose. There is a risk that these restricted funds are not disclosed as such in the financial statements.	Obtain supporting documentation for any donations and agree the expenditure to the terms of the donation. Any discrepancies should be reported to management.

(c) **Weak control environment**

Lack of segregation of duties

There is normally a limited number of staff working in the charity meaning that a full system of internal control including segregation of duties cannot be implemented.

Volunteer staff

Many staff are volunteers and so will only work at the charity on an occasional basis. Controls will be performed by different staff on different days making the system potentially unreliable.

Lack of qualified staff

As staff are mainly volunteers they may not have professional qualifications or experience to implement or maintain good control systems.

No internal audit department

Any control system will not be monitored effectively, mainly due to the lack of any internal audit department. The charity will not have the funds or experience to establish internal audit.

Attitude of the trustees

Where trustees are not professionally trained or have little time to devote to the charity, there may be a perception that controls are not important. The overall control environment may therefore be weak as other charity workers may not appreciate the importance of maintaining good controls.

Test your understanding 12 – NFP audit

(a) **Audit risks**

–   Charities can be viewed as inherently risky because they are often managed by non-professionals and are susceptible to fraud, although many charities and the volunteers that run them are people of the highest integrity who take a great deal of care over their work.

–   Charities are also at risk of being in violation of their constitutions, which is important where funds are raised from public or private donors who may object strongly if funds are not used in the manner expected. Other charities and regulatory bodies supervising charities may also object.

– Most small charities have a high level of control risk because formal internal controls are expensive and are not often in place. This means that donations may be susceptible to misappropriation. Charities have to rely on the trustworthiness of volunteers.

– Ajio is a new client and as a result detection risk is higher due to a lack of cumulative knowledge and experience.

(b) **Audit procedures: fundraising events**

– Attend a fundraising event and observe the procedures employed in collecting, counting, banking and recording the cash. This will help provide audit evidence that funds have not been misappropriated and that all income from such events has been recorded. Sealed boxes or tins that are opened in the presence of two volunteers are often used for these purposes.

– Perform cash counts at the events to provide evidence that cash has been counted correctly and that there is no collusion between volunteers to misappropriate funds.

– Examine bank paying-in slips, bank statements and bank reconciliations and ensure that these agree with records made at events. This also provides evidence as to the completeness of income.

– Examine the records of expenditure for fundraising events (hire of equipment, entertainers, purchase of refreshments, etc.) and ensure that these have been properly authorised (where appropriate) and that receipts have been obtained for all expenditure. This provides evidence as to the completeness and accuracy of expenditure.

– Review the income and expenditure of fundraising events against any budgets that have been prepared and investigate any significant discrepancies.

– Ensure that all necessary licences (such as public entertainment licences) have been obtained by the trustees for such events in order to ensure that no action is likely to be taken against the charity or volunteers.

– Obtain written representation from the trustees to the effect that there are no outstanding unrecorded liabilities for such events for completeness of expenditure and liabilities.

Test your understanding 13 – Subsequent events

Event 1 – Fire

This event occurred after the reporting period and is not an event which provides evidence of a condition at the year-end and hence this is a non-adjusting event.

As the company is insured, only uninsured losses suffered by Grains 4U Co (Grains) will need to be accounted for, which in the normal course of events is likely to be an immaterial amount. However, the insurance company is investigating, as there is a possibility the fire was started deliberately, and this will invalidate the insurance policy.

If this is the case, the total damaged assets of $675,000 (650 + 25) would be material as they represent 8.5% (675/7,900) of profit before tax.

Therefore as a material non-adjusting event, the assets should not be written down to their scrap value in the current year financial statements. However, the directors should include a disclosure note detailing the fire and the total value of assets which may be impacted due to the possibility of a lack of an insurance settlement.

Procedures

- Obtain a schedule showing the damaged property, plant and equipment and agree the carrying value to the non-current asset register to confirm the total value of affected assets.

- Obtain a breakdown of the inventory stored at the distribution centre on 15 May 20X5 and compare to earlier records or despatch documents to ascertain the likely level of inventory at the time of the fire.

- Review any correspondence from the insurance company confirming the amount of the claim, and the current status of their investigation into the fire and any likely payments to assess the extent of any uninsured amounts.

- Discuss with the directors whether they will disclose the effect of the fire in the financial statements.

Event 2 – Inventory

Grains has identified that inventory at the year-end with a cost of $915,000 is defective. This information was obtained after the year-end but provides further evidence of the net realisable value of inventory at the year-end and hence is an adjusting event.

The inventory of $915,000 must be written down to its net realisable value of $50,000.

The write down of $865,000 (915 – 50) is material as it represents 10.9% (865/7,900) of profit before tax.

Hence, the directors should amend the financial statements by writing down the inventory to $50,000.

Procedures

- Discuss the matter with the directors and enquire if they are prepared to write down the cost of the inventory to net realisable value.

- Review the board minutes to assess whether this event was the only case of defective inventory as there could potentially be other inventory which requires writing down.

- Obtain a schedule showing the defective inventory and agree to supporting production documentation that it was produced prior to 31 March, otherwise it will not require a write down at the year end.

- Discuss with management how they have assessed the scrap value of $50,000 and agree this amount to any supporting documentation to confirm the value.

Test your understanding 14 – Written representations

(a) Written representations are a form of audit evidence. They are written by the company's directors and sent to the auditor, just before the auditor's report is signed.

Written representations are required for two reasons:

- For the directors to acknowledge their collective responsibility for the preparation of the financial statements and to confirm that they have approved those statements.

- To confirm any matters which are material to the financial statements where representations are crucial to obtaining sufficient and appropriate audit evidence.

In the latter situation, other forms of audit evidence are normally limited because knowledge of the facts is confined to management and the matter is one of judgment or opinion.

Obtaining written representations does not mean that other evidence does not have to be obtained. Audit evidence will still be collected and the representation will support that evidence. Any contradiction between sources of evidence should be investigated.

(b) **Lion's Roar**

It is appropriate to include the claim in the written representation.

The amount of the claim is material being 50% of profit before taxation.

There is also a lack of definitive supporting evidence for the claim. The two main pieces of evidence available are the claim from Lion's Roar itself and the legal advice from Crighton Ward's solicitors. However, any claim amount cannot be accurately determined because the dispute has not been settled.

The directors have stated that they believe the claim not to be justified, which is one possible outcome of the dispute. However, in order to obtain sufficient evidence to show how the treatment of the potential claim was decided for the financial statements, the auditor must obtain this opinion in writing.

Depreciation

Including the point in the written representation is inappropriate because the auditor appears to have obtained sufficient evidence to confirm the accounting treatment.

The lack of profit or loss on sale confirms that the depreciation charge is appropriate. Large profits would indicate over-depreciation and large losses would indicate under-depreciation. The amount also meets industry standards which suggests that Crighton-Ward's accounting policy is acceptable.

(c) Lack of written representation

– Discuss the situation with the directors to try and resolve the issue that the directors have raised. Ascertain exact reasons why the directors will not sign the letter.

– Explain the need for the written representation again and note that the requirement to obtain a written representation letter was included in the engagement letter.

– Consider whether amendments can be made to the letter to incorporate the directors' concerns that will still provide the auditor with appropriate and sufficient audit evidence.

– Explain that if the auditor does not receive sufficient and appropriate audit evidence, then the audit opinion will have to be modified due to an inability to obtain sufficient appropriate evidence.

Test your understanding 15 – Auditor's report

(a) Eliud Co

The receivable of $30,000 represents 20% of profit and more than 4% of receivables therefore is material.

The bankruptcy of the customer provides evidence of a condition existing at the statement of financial position date. It should therefore be treated as an adjusting event in accordance with IAS 10 *Events After the Reporting Period*. The receivable should be written off in full in the financial statements at 31 March 20X5.

The company has overstated receivables and profit by $30,000.

Impact on the auditor's report

– The financial statements are materially misstated.

– The matter is material but not pervasive.

– A qualified opinion should be issued with the 'except for' wording.

– The 'Basis for Opinion' section will be amended to a 'Basis for Qualified Opinion' to explain the reason for the qualified opinion.

(b) Brigid Co

The amount of $10,000 represents only 2% of the stated profit before tax and therefore is not material.

The potential losses may be more significant than the figure of $10,000 since other claims are now pending. The auditor may conclude that the whole legal matter is potentially material.

There is uncertainty with regard to the outcome of the pending claims and the potential liability which may arise as a result of the product defect. The appropriate accounting treatment will depend on whether the chance of loss is probable, possible or remote. If it is probable a provision should be recognised. If it is possible a contingent liability should be disclosed. If it is remote the financial statements will not be affected. (IAS 37 *Provisions, Contingent Liabilities and Contingent Assets*).

Liabilities may be understated or contingent liabilities may not be adequately disclosed.

Impact on the auditor's report

– Management has chosen to ignore both the actual loss (which is not individually material) and the potential loss (which may be material). If the auditor does not believe that the management's view is acceptable, or does not think that the disclosure is adequate, the financial statements will be materially misstated.

– If the potential claims are still considered immaterial, the opinion will be unmodified stating that the financial statements give a true and fair view.

– If the potential claims are considered material, a qualified opinion with the 'except for' wording should be issued.

– If the auditor believes that the claims are likely to be successful and are likely to be substantial then an adverse opinion should be issued stating that the financial statements do not show a true and fair view.

– The 'Basis for Opinion' section will be amended to a 'Basis for Qualified Opinion' or 'Basis for Adverse Opinion' to explain the reason for the modified opinion.

(c) **Kenenisa Co**

The fall in value is material and pervasive as the adjustment would have the effect of turning a profit before tax of $250,000 into a loss of $50,000.

Investments should be written down if they are impaired. A fall in the value of one asset must not be offset against an increase in the value of another asset. Each asset has to be considered separately.

As the company admits that a permanent fall in value has taken place it should write the value of the assets down otherwise assets will be overstated.

Impact on the auditor's report

– The financial statements are materially misstated.

– The matter is material and pervasive.

– An adverse opinion should be issued stating that the financial statements do not show a true and fair view.

– The 'Basis for Opinion' section will be amended to a 'Basis for Adverse Opinion' to explain the reason for the adverse opinion.

(d) **Mary Co**

The $10,000 represents 10% of profit before tax, and so would appear to be material.

Since the accounting records were only destroyed for the early part of the year, the auditor would still be able to confirm the calculations for the later part of the year. In these particular circumstances the auditor may consider that the amount of any error (which is likely to be considerably less than $10,000) is not material.

The company must include the cost of its own labour and materials in the construction of the warehouse, since these have been used to create a capital asset.

Impact on the auditor's report

–   There is a lack of sufficient appropriate evidence to support the treatment of the $10,000 labour costs therefore the auditor does not know whether the costs are materially misstated.

–   Assuming that the extent of any potential misstatement is considered not material, an unmodified opinion will be issued stating that the financial statements give a true and fair view.

–   If the possible misstatement is considered material, a qualified opinion with the 'except for' wording will be required.

–   If modified, the 'Basis for Opinion' section will be amended to a 'Basis for Qualified Opinion' to explain the reason for the qualified opinion.

Tutorial note: If any of the companies were listed, the Key Audit Matters section would reference the Basis for Qualified Opinion.

 Test your understanding 16 – Corporate governance 1

The board comprises six executives and only three non-executive directors (NEDs), excluding the chair. There should be an appropriate balance of executives and NEDs, to ensure that the board makes the correct objective decisions, which are in the best interest of the stakeholders of the company, and no individual or group of individuals dominates the board's decision-making.	At least half of the board, excluding the chair, should be NEDs. Hence the board of Tangerine Tech Co (Tangerine) should consider recruiting and appointing additional independent NEDs to satisfy this requirement.
One of the NEDs and the chair are former executive directors of Tangerine who were asked to take on their existing roles following retirement. As former executive directors, they were previously employed by the company and so will not bring the required level of independence and objective judgment to the role as is necessary. The independence of the other NEDs cannot be assessed.	Independent non-executives with relevant experience and skills should be appointed to the board of Tangerine. A review should be under taken of the independence of all existing NEDs. Any who are not independent should ideally be replaced or supplemented by independent NEDs. The board chair must be independent on appointment therefore must be replaced.

The board chair, who is a NED, also has the role of audit committee chair. The chair of the board should not be a member of the audit committee as this will compromise the independence of the audit committee and give too much power to the board chair.	The board chair should cease to be a member of audit committee. One of the newly appointed independent NEDs should be appointed as audit committee chair.
All four members of the audit committee were previously involved in sales or production related roles. At least one member of the audit committee should have recent and relevant financial experience. None of the NEDs were former finance directors and so it is unlikely they possess the required financial experience.	The company should ensure when they recruit the new independent NEDs that at least one of them has the required recent and relevant financial experience.
All of the directors have been members of the board for at least four years. The shareholders should review on a regular basis that the composition of the board of directors is appropriate, and that there is an appropriate re-election process in place to ensure this can be achieved.	The directors should be subject to re-election annually by the shareholders. At the current year's annual general meeting it should be proposed that the directors are subject to re-election.
The chair has sole responsibility for liaising with the shareholders and answering any of their questions. However, this is a role which the board as a whole should undertake.	All members of the board should be involved in ensuring that satisfactory dialogue occurs with shareholders, for example, all should attend meetings with shareholders such as the annual general meeting. The board should state in the annual report the steps they have taken to ensure that the members of the board, and in particular the non-executive directors, develop an understanding of the views of major shareholders about the company.

Currently Tangerine has not established an internal audit function. The audit committee should consider the effectiveness of internal controls and internal audit could support this role. Where there is no internal audit function, the audit committee is required to consider annually the need for one.	Further consideration should be given to establishing an internal audit function. Having an internal audit function will help the audit committee to discharge their responsibility for monitoring internal controls. However, the costs of establishing an internal audit function should be considered against the benefits.

Test your understanding 17 – Corporate governance 2

1 **Corporate governance definition**

The term corporate governance refers to the means by which a company is directed and controlled in the interests of all stakeholders. It will include consideration of:

– Directors' responsibilities

– Composition of the board of directors

– Audit requirements (internal and external).

2 **External auditors and corporate governance**

If a company has good standards of corporate governance and is managed well in the interests of all stakeholders, the auditors are likely to conclude that control risk is lower and therefore audit risk is reduced. As a result of this they may be able to reduce the extent of the audit procedures they carry out.

The audit committee should take responsibility for ensuring the external auditor is independent and for monitoring and assessing the quality and effectiveness of the external audit.

The external auditor may have to report on whether the company is compliant with corporate governance requirements.

3 **Composition of the audit committee**

The audit committee should be made up of independent non-executive directors and include at least one person with recent and relevant financial experience.

4 **Role of the audit committee**

– Monitoring the integrity of the financial statements.

– Reviewing the company's internal financial controls.

– Monitoring and reviewing the effectiveness of the internal audit function.

- If no internal audit function is in place, they should consider annually whether there is a need for one and make a recommendation to the board. The reasons for there being no internal audit function should be explained in the annual report.

- Making recommendations in relation to the appointment and removal of the external auditor and their remuneration.

- Reviewing and monitoring the external auditor's independence and objectivity and the effectiveness of the audit process.

- Developing and implementing policy on the engagement of the external auditor to supply non-audit services.

5 Need for an audit committee

The existence of an audit committee will enhance the company's corporate governance profile by:

- Improving public confidence

- Providing further support to directors

- Strengthening the independence of the external auditor

- Improving internal controls.

6 Risk management

The risk committee should discuss the issue and assess its seriousness in relation to its likelihood and potential impact. They should then decide what action is appropriate in order to manage the risk.

This risk might be reduced by:

- Ensuring favourable employment packages for such individuals

- Ensuring training for other staff assists in case of succession issues

- Ensure key tasks are not carried out by just one person.

Loss of key staff may impact the control environment and increase control risk, particularly if duties are no longer segregated.

The auditor must consider the possible impact of all significant risks as any of these could ultimately have financial consequences or going concern issues, hence impacting the audit opinion.

Test your understanding 18 – Internal audit

(a) **Use of the work of the internal auditors by external auditors**

Sales and ticketing

- The sales function is likely to be integrated with the accounting and internal control system used to produce the revenue figure in the financial statements on which the external auditor reports and is therefore useful.

- The internal auditors' work on the ticketing system relates to an operational area which does not have a direct impact on the financial statements. Ticketing may have an indirect effect because it is likely to be integrated with the sales system and there is likely to be some crossover between the controls over ticketing and controls over sales generally. The work of the internal auditors is therefore likely to be of some use to the external auditor.

Fleet acquisition and maintenance

- The internal auditors' work on the fleet acquisition system is likely to be relevant to the external auditor because owned aircraft and leased aircraft will constitute a substantial element of statement of financial position assets and liabilities. The related depreciation and finance charges will be included in the statement of profit or loss.

- Much of the internal auditors' work is likely to relate to ensuring that company policy has been complied with. Company policy will relate to the authorisation for, and acquisition of, aircraft and ensuring the appropriate accounting treatment is being used. The external auditor will want to ensure that the company's policies are both appropriate and complied with.

- It is also possible that the internal auditors' work may involve some verification of the statement of profit and loss and statement of financial position figures. Given the likely materiality of the amounts involved, this work will also be of interest to the external auditor.

- It is possible that the internal auditors' work may also relate to the quality of aircraft, and other operational aspects of fleet management. These issues may also be relevant to the external auditor as they relate to compliance with laws and regulations.

– Maintenance expenditure in the statement of profit or loss may be material and the work of the internal auditors is therefore of interest to external auditors. The internal auditors' work is likely to relate to the authorisation and correct accounting for maintenance expenditure (capitalisation or expensing) which will affect the financial statements.

Trade payables and long term debt financing

– The extent of the external auditor's interest in the internal auditors' work on trade payables and long term financing will depend on the materiality of the amounts involved. Trade payables (for certain types of routine maintenance, and payables due to the service organisations, for example) may be material. Long term debt financing is very likely to be material as many airlines have substantial debt financing.

– Internal audit work on trade payables is likely to involve ensuring that routine internal controls are properly designed and are operating effectively. This will be relevant to the external auditor.

– There are substantial financial statement disclosures required for debt financing. The internal auditors' assistance with ensuring that disclosures are properly made, as well as with ensuring that any covenants have been complied with and that the accounting for the financing is appropriate, may also be helpful to the external auditor.

(b) **Evaluating the internal audit function**

– The firm will seek to ensure that there is an appropriate structure within the department itself, with appropriate reporting lines outside of the department, preferably reporting into the audit committee.

– The internal audit function has recently been expanded and there are likely to be changes in the way it is organised. The function should have operational independence within the organisation and formal terms of reference that encompass the recent changes made.

– The function should have a systematic and disciplined approach to its work including quality control procedures.

– Staff should be appropriately trained, experienced and qualified. The head of the internal audit department should preferably be professionally qualified.

References

The Board (2020) IAS 1 *Presentation of Financial Statements. London*: IFRS Foundation.

The Board (2020) IAS 2 *Inventories*. London: IFRS Foundation.

The Board (2020) IAS 7 *Statement of Cash Flows*. London: IFRS Foundation.

The Board (2020) IAS 10 *Events after the Reporting Period*. London: IFRS Foundation.

The Board (2020) IAS 16 *Property, Plant and Equipment*. London: IFRS Foundation.

The Board (2020) IAS 27 *Separate Financial Statements*. London: IFRS Foundation.

The Board (2020) IAS 28 *Investments in Associates and Joint Ventures*. London: IFRS Foundation.

The Board (2020) IAS 37 *Provisions, Contingent Liabilities and Contingent Assets*. London: IFRS Foundation.

The Board (2020) IAS 38 *Intangible Assets*. London: IFRS Foundation.

The Board (2020) IFRS 3 *Business Combinations*. London: IFRS Foundation.

The Board (2020) IFRS 10 *Consolidated Financial Statements*. London: IFRS Foundation.

The Board (2020) IFRS 15 *Revenue from Contracts with Customers*. London: IFRS Foundation.

Employability and technology skills

Chapter learning objectives

This chapter contains an overview of the employability and technology skills syllabus area. This is relevant for all ACCA Applied Skills (except LW) and Strategic Professional exams.

1 Purpose of chapter

This chapter explains the content included within the employability and technology skills syllabus area. A similar syllabus area is included in all Applied Skills (except LW) and Strategic Professional level syllabi.

ACCA exams utilise software and technology similar to those used in the modern workplace. By studying ACCA exams, candidates will be equipped with both technical syllabus knowledge and practical, applied software skills. The employability and technology skills syllabus area is included within the syllabus to acknowledge this acquired skillset.

2 Content of the employability and technology skills syllabus area

The employability and technology skills syllabus area is outlined in the syllabus and study guide. It consists of the following:

1   Use computer technology to efficiently access and manipulate relevant information.

2   Work on relevant response options, using available functions and technology, as would be required in the workplace.

3   Navigate windows and computer screens to create and amend responses to exam requirements, using the appropriate tools.

4   Present data and information effectively, using the appropriate tools.

By using a computer-based examination (CBE), the ACCA has enabled the use of word processing, spreadsheet, screen navigation and data processing functionalities to become part of their assessment range. This replicates the skills used in the modern workplace, whether in accounting practice, in industry or outside of accountancy altogether.

Whilst sitting an exam, candidates will be using the functionality of the CBE software in a variety of ways e.g. to prioritise information within the question data provided, to organise and present their answers in a manageable fashion, to use shortcuts and software functionality to increase efficiency. Skills garnered in the workplace can be used in the examination and vice versa.

This reflects that exams offered at Applied Skills and Strategic Professional are designed to be relevant and accessible to all students. The delivery mode and assessment types require students to demonstrate similar skills to those required in the modern workplace. Offering computer-based exams (CBE) at all levels gives students the opportunity to focus on the application of knowledge to scenarios, using a range of tools – spreadsheets, word processing and presentations. This not only allows students to demonstrate their technical and professional skills, but also their use of the technology relevant to the modern workplace. CBEs, therefore, offers the candidate an examination delivery method that allows them to demonstrate their knowledge and skills with the technology they are most familiar with, in the classroom or at work.

3 CBE support and the ACCA Exam Practice Platform

ACCA candidates can access the ACCA's Exam Practice Platform to practice attempting questions using the CBE software. It is imperative that candidates are familiar with the software before attempting the exam.

The link to the AA Exam Practice Platform access gateway can be found here:

https://bit.ly/39OE1Yz

This requires a MyACCA login to access the platform.

Support, access to other subjects, tutorial videos and CBE advice can be found here:

https://bit.ly/2IIBV6Y

4 Contents of the CBE and Exam Practice Platform

On entering the Exam Practice Platform, candidates will access their dashboard, as follows:

Candidates should click their appropriate subject in the right hand side menu. There they will be able to 'assign' content to their workspace. Candidates can assign a blank workspace or ACCA official resources (which include past exams presented using the CBE software for the candidates to attempt) to their workspace.

This will be added to the candidate's 'Self-Assigned Material' listing as below:

When working within the assignment the candidate will use response options to provide their answer.

The **Response Options** are where the candidate will attempt their answers.

Up to two types of response option will be provided for AA. Not every option will appear in each exam.

The response options are:

– the word processor, and

– the spreadsheet.

The candidate must determine which of the response options is the most suitable for their specific answer.

These replicate the functionality of widely used software packages. The ACCA has developed this software, for use during home question practice and under exam conditions, to replicate the practical skill sets and work-based behaviours adopted by various industries throughout the world. By studying the ACCA qualification, candidates will improve, not only on their technical knowledge and understanding, but also on skills applied on a daily basis within their work environments. Candidates should practise questions using the CBE platform to ensure they are familiar with the various functions available within their specific examination.

Word Processor

The word processor response option will appear as follows:

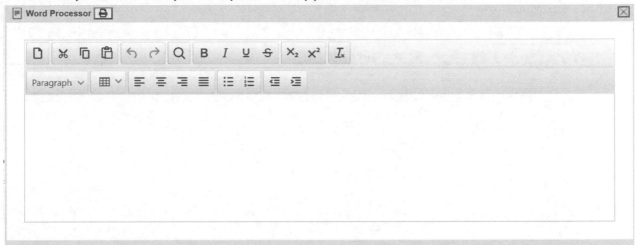

This resource has the following advantages and disadvantages:

Advantages	Disadvantages
It is easier to continue typing without entering new cells or becoming concerned about cell width	It cannot automatically perform calculations
Answers can be more easily split into paragraphs to make them more visually appealing and easier to mark	Numerical tables can be difficult to label and align
Bullet points can be used to present lists	
Text can be easily aligned and justified	
Superscript and subscript can be easily added to express terms such as 42, for example	

It is, therefore, best suited to discursive answers where candidates are asked, for example, to discuss, analyse or evaluate issues from a scenario or calculation.

The word processing software application could be used in the workplace within the writing of meeting agendas, meeting minutes, external letters, marketing output, briefings, audit reports, textbooks and instructional documentation.

Spreadsheet

The spreadsheet response option, when relevant, will appear as follows:

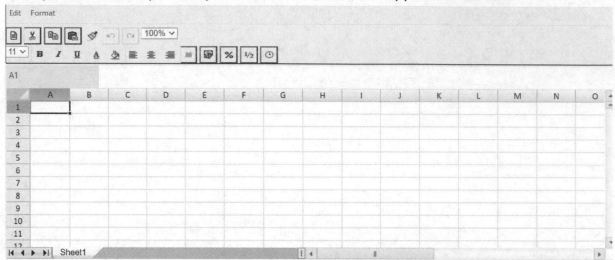

The spreadsheet software uses the same functionality as other commonly used spreadsheet software. Basic formulae functionality, such as SUM, power functions (e.g. SQRT) and the use of brackets are all reproduced within the ACCA software. Candidates are advised to practise questions using the software so that they are familiar with the functions available and how they can be utilised to the candidate's advantage through improved efficiency.

This resource has the following advantages and disadvantages:

Advantages	Disadvantages
This can quickly and easily perform calculations (e.g. using sums for totals or formulae for calculations)	Text will carry over beyond one cell and may go across and beyond the page width making answers difficult to follow (and mark)
Data within tables can be easily aligned	Bullet points are difficult to use
Shortcut icons can be used to quickly round figures, change numbers to percentages etc	
Tables can easily and quickly be copied when calculations need to be reperformed (e.g. for sensitivity analysis, tax calculations for more than one person, financial statements for more than one company etc)	
Column width can be adjusted to label length	

It is, therefore, best suited for performing calculations within the examination e.g. ratio calculations.

Spreadsheet software is ubiquitous in the modern workplace. It has the capacity to record, store and organise huge swathes of data and information relating to all aspects of a business. Examples of only a few of its possible practical applications include the preparation of management and financial accounts, operational controls and record-keeping e.g. expense claims, data analytics, project appraisals, sample size selection and tax computations.

5 Chapter summary

The CBE software will replicate the work that is performed by accountants in a typical workplace. It will be used across the syllabus to support a candidate's answer by providing suitable response options for different types of answers.

These response options will be most suitable in the following instances (when available):

– For discursive answers: it is best to use the word processing option

– For calculations: it is best to use the spreadsheet option.

Index

HISTOLOGY AND CELL BIOLOGY
An Introduction to Pathology

Abraham L. Kierszenbaum, MD, PhD
Professor and Chair
Department of Cell Biology and Anatomical Sciences
The Sophie Davis School of Biomedical Education/
The City University of New York Medical School
New York, New York

 Mosby

An Affiliate of Elsevier Science

Mosby, Inc.
An Affiliate of Elsevier Science
11830 Westline Industrial Drive
St. Louis, Missouri 63146

Printed in the United States of America

ISBN: 0–323–01639–1

Library of Congress Cataloging-in-Publication Data

Kierszenbaum, Abraham L.

Histology and cell biology: an introduction to pathology / Abraham L. Kierszenbaum

p.   cm.

Includes index.

ISBN 0–323–11639–1

1. Histology, Pathological.   2. Pathology, Cellular.   I. Title

RB25.K54 2002   616.07—dc21   2001051399

DEDICATION

This book is dedicated with appreciation and love to Laura L. Tres, my academic colleague, research partner, best friend, spouse, and mother of our two daughters Adriana and Silvia.

To the beloved memory of my mother and my father, who now would understand why.

PREFACE

This book is about a visual approach to learning histology within the context of cell biology, in preparation for studying pathology and clinical medicine. The visual approach emerged from over thirty years of experience teaching histology to medical students and from a need to communicate and reinforce relevant concepts to be mastered under increasing time constraints due to changes in the basic science curriculum in most medical schools. The focal point of the visual approach is to provide medical students with an integrated method leading to the understanding of pathologic abnormalities. The cell biology component, although not complete, provides the necessary ingredients for integration with histology. Pathology students may find this book useful for refreshing basic concepts of histology. Histology and pathology are visually oriented sciences and the visual cues included in this book can facilitate interpretation opportunities in clinical practice.

This book consists of six parts, each preceded by a learning objectives section. Part I brings together histology and cell biology within the context of basic tissues. Chapter 3, Cell Signaling, is an uncommon section in a histology book. It serves to unify the concept that the study of tissues and organs cannot be separated from physiology, biochemistry, and molecular biology. Parts II to VI present several organ systems grouped by their most relevant function for the purpose of integration. Students may find the grouping of organs useful for learning. In Part VI, Organ Systems: Reproductive System, the chapter headings depart from the traditional designation to emphasize prominent functions. All the information is presented in a clear, concise, and student-friendly manner using color graphics and photographs that are meant to be studied. In some cases the graphics reiterate the concise text; in others they add information complementing or extending the text. Students may find this visual approach convenient for reviewing complex concepts and integrate them when the time of the board examinations arrives. Teachers may find the visual approach useful for delivering a lecture using the same or a different presentation sequence.

There are many people who were involved in this project to be acknowledged and thanked. My thanks go to several classes of The Sophie Davis School of Biomedical Education/The City University of New York Medical School, who used the previous black and white printed versions of this book. They provided valuable feedback to make the message clearer and more consistent. The book is far better because of their insights from a student's perspective. My colleagues, who worked with me throughout the years, deserve much of the credit. Edward W. Gresik invested time and energy to make sure that the written words and graphics reflected the concepts that we wanted to deliver to our students. Ilia I. Glezer, Grace Migliorisi, and Wan-hua Amy Yu provided valuable visual material included in the book, as well as encouragement, suggestions, and comments. Laura L. Tres reviewed every single line of text and illustrations. She made sure, in her natural and effective way, that changes were introduced to dispel doubts and possible misinterpretations. My special appreciation goes to Charles A. Blake and his colleagues of the Department of Cell Biology and Neuroscience, University of South Carolina at Columbia, for providing valuable comments and suggestions. To the group of scholars of the 2000 Harvard-Macy Program for Physician Educators and to Gordon Harper, who examined the first laser color printed version of this book, my gratitude for their remarks and support. Finally, I thank Harcourt Health Sciences for making it possible that our students can finally have a color version of this book.

Abraham L. Kierszenbaum

HISTOLOGY AND CELL BIOLOGY
An Introduction to Pathology

Learning objectives

Part I, **Basic Tissues and Integrated Cell Biology**, includes the four classic tissues: **epithelium**, **connective tissue**, **muscle tissue**, and **nervous tissue**. Included in the connective tissue chapter is adipose tissue, cartilage, bone, and ossification. **Blood** and **hematopoiesis** have also been included as part of the connective tissue. The **nervous tissue** chapter includes basic aspects of the central and peripheral nervous tissue, in addition to the **sensory organs** for vision and hearing.

In Chapters 1, 2, and 3:

1. You will learn how epithelia can be classified and review aspects of cell biology related to the polarized nature of epithelial tissues and the participation of cell adhesion molecules and junctional complexes in stabilizing the cohesive nature of epithelia.

2. You will learn which components are present in the **cytoskeleton** and the **cell nucleus**.

3. You will learn how epithelial glands are classified and review aspects of the **plasma membrane** and **cytomembranes**, as well as **organelles** and **inclusions**.

4. A special chapter on **cell signaling** will consolidate your knowledge of how cells interact with each other via hormones and growth factors.

In Chapters 4 and 5:

1. You will learn the criteria for the classification of different types of connective tissue, including the specialized connective tissues.

2. You will learn how a resident cell type, the **fibroblast**, is responsible for the synthesis of collagen, elastic fibers, and extracellular matrix components.

3. You will learn how immigrant cells, such as **macrophages**, **lymphocytes**, **mast cells**, and **plasma cells**, contribute to the function of the connective tissue.

4. You will learn the structure and function of the adipose tissue, various types of cartilage, the organization of bone, and the mechanism of bone formation using mesenchyme or hyaline cartilage as templates.

In Chapter 6:

1. You will learn how to recognize blood cell types and the origin of red blood cells, leukocytes, and platelets in the bone marrow.

2. You will learn how selectins and integrins participate in the extravasation of inflammatory cells into the connective tissue by the mechanism of homing.

In Chapter 7:

1. You will learn how to differentiate three types of muscle, **skeletal**, **cardiac**, and **smooth muscle**, and apply the principles learned in the cytoskeleton section of Chapter 1, to understand functional principles.

2. You will learn basic aspects of muscular dystrophies.

In Chapters 8 and 9:

1. You will learn how neurons and glial cells interact with each other in the central nervous system and how nerves are structurally assembled in the peripheral nervous system.

2. You will learn the histologic details of two sensory organs, the **eye** and the **ear**, and apply the principles learned in the nervous tissue chapter to understand their structure and function.

1. EPITHELIUM

Classification

The epithelium is a tightly cohesive sheet of cells which covers or lines body surfaces (for example, skin, intestine, secretory ducts) and forms the functional units of secretory glands (for example, salivary glands, liver).

The traditional classification and nomenclature of different types of epithelia are based on the **two-dimensional shape of cells as observed under the light microscope**.

Epithelia are classified into three major categories on the basis of the number of cell layers and the shape of the cells at the outermost layer:

1. **Simple epithelia** (Figure 1–1) are formed by only one layer of cells and are subdivided into **simple squamous**, **simple cuboidal**, and **simple columnar**, according to the height and width of the cells. The specific name **endothelium** is used for the simple epithelium lining the blood and lymphatic vessels. **Mesothelium** is the simple epithelium lining all body cavities (peritoneum, pericardium, and pleura).

2. **Stratified epithelia** (Figure 1–2) are composed of two or more cell layers. Stratified epithelia are subclassified according to the shape of the cells at the superficial or outer layer into **stratified squamous**, **stratified cuboidal**, and **stratified columnar**. Stratified squamous is the epithelium most frequently found and can be subdivided into **moderately keratinized or highly keratinized** types. The cells of the outer layer of a moderately keratinized squamous epithelium **can display nuclei** (for example, esophagus and vagina). **Nuclei are absent in the outer layer of the highly keratinized stratified squamous epithelium** (for example, the epidermis of the skin).

The basal cells aligned along the basal lamina are mitotically active and replace the differentiating cells of the upper layers.

3. **Pseudostratified epithelia** (Figure 1–3) consist of basal and columnar cells resting on the basal lamina. However, only the columnar cells reach the luminal surface. Since the nuclei of the basal and columnar cells are seen at different levels, one has the impression of a stratified epithelial organization. Within this category are

1. The **pseudostratified columnar ciliated epithelium** of the trachea.

2. The **pseudostratified columnar epithelium with stereocilia** of the epididymis.

3. The **transitional epithelium** of the urinary passages, also referred to as **urothelium**. The urothelium also consists of basal and columnar or superficial cells. An important feature of this epithelium is that its height varies with distention and contraction of the organ (see Chapter 14, Urinary System).

Although this classification ignores specialized functional aspects of epithelia, the traditional classification is still useful from a descriptive point of view. We will use the morphologic classification of epithelia as an introduction to a more contemporary view of this basic tissue: its **polarity**.

Epithelia line surfaces and cavities and have three domains (Figure 1–4):

1. The **apical domain** is exposed to the lumen or external environment.

2. The **lateral domain** faces neighboring epithelial cells linked to each other by cell adhesion molecules and junctional complexes.

3. The **basal domain** is associated with a **basal lamina** that separates the epithelium from underlying connective tissue. The basal lamina is reinforced by components of the connective tissue. The whole structure is designated the **basement membrane**.

Epithelial cells are attached to each other by junctional complexes and adhesion molecules. Epithelial cells are specialized to fulfill important roles such as

Figure 1–1

Simple epithelium: All the cells are in contact with the basal lamina and the apical domain reaches the lumen

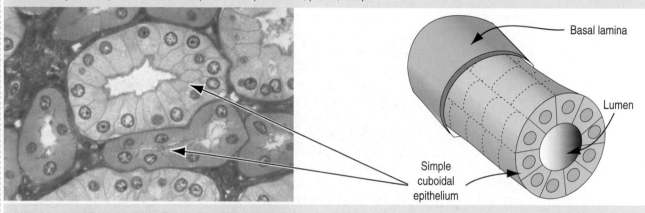

Red blood cells in the lumen

Flat nucleus of an endothelial cell

Basal lamina

Lumen

Simple squamous epithelium

Simple squamous epithelium (endothelium)

The inner lining of all blood vessels consists of a single layer of squamous endothelial cells. The thinness of the simple squamous epithelial cells reflects its primary function in rapid exchange of substances between blood and tissue.

A similar epithelium (called **mesothelium**) covers the peritoneum, pleura, and pericardium.

Basal lamina

Lumen

Simple cuboidal epithelium

Simple cuboidal epithelium (collecting tubule, kidney)

The inner lining of kidney tubules and thyroid follicles consists of a single layer of cuboidal cells. Cuboidal cells are highly polarized and participate in absorption, secretion (thyroid gland), and active ion transport (kidney).

Like the endothelium, a basal lamina attaches the cell to the subjacent connective tissue.

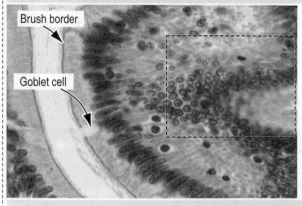

Brush border

Goblet cell

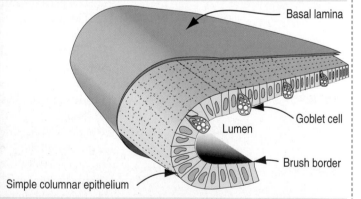

Basal lamina

Goblet cell

Lumen

Brush border

Simple columnar epithelium

Simple columnar epithelium (small intestine)

The small intestine is lined by columnar epithelial cells with the nucleus in the basal portion of the cell. The apical domain contains finger-like projections called **microvilli** forming a **brush border**.

Microvilli participate in the absorption of proteins, sugar, and lipids which are released at the basolateral domain into the blood circulation for transport to the liver.

Columnar cells are oriented in different directions. The **box** indicates clusters of nuclei observed in a transverse section of the columnar epithelium through its most basal region. A transverse section passing through the apical region will display cytoplasmic profiles without visible nuclei.

Main characteristics of epithelia

1. Epithelia derive from the ectoderm, mesoderm, and endoderm.
2. Epithelia line and cover all body surfaces, except the articular cartilage.
3. The basic functions of epithelia are: **protection** (skin), **absorption** (small and large intestine), **transport of material** at the surface (mediated by cilia), **secretion** (glands), **excretion** (tubules of the kidney), **gas exchange** (lung alveolus), and **gliding between surfaces** (mesothelium).
4. Most epithelial cells renew continuously by mitosis.
5. Epithelia lack a direct blood and lymphatic supply. Nutrients are delivered by diffusion.
6. Epithelial cells have almost no free intercellular substances (unlike connective tissue).
7. The cohesive nature of an epithelium is maintained by both **cell adhesion molecules** and **junctional complexes**.
8. Epithelia are anchored to a **basal lamina**. The basal lamina and connective tissue components cooperate to form the **basement membrane**.
9. Epithelia have structural and functional **polarity**.

Figure 1–2

Stratified epithelium: It is composed of two or more cell layers; named according to the shape of the cells at the upper layer

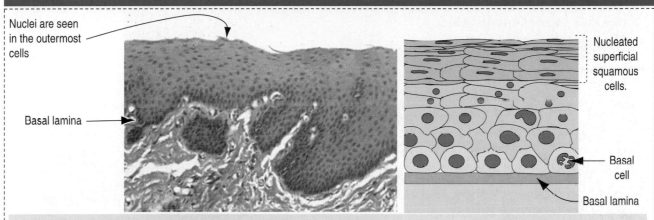

Nuclei are seen in the outermost cells

Basal lamina

Nucleated superficial squamous cells.

Basal cell

Basal lamina

Stratified squamous epithelium with moderate keratin (esophagus)
This epithelium consists of undifferentiated **basal cells** specialized for **mitotic division**. Stratified cells covering the basal layer are differentiating cells. Cells of the outer layer are highly differentiated: they increase their **keratin content** to protect the tissue from the mechanical action of ingested food. **The outermost cells retain their nuclei.**

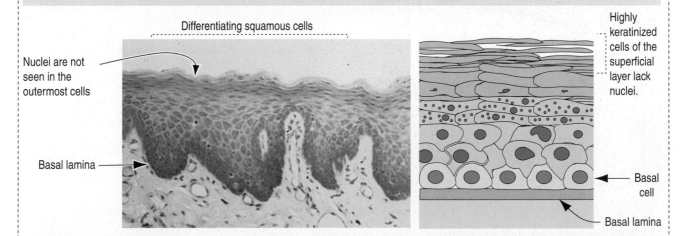

Differentiating squamous cells

Nuclei are not seen in the outermost cells

Basal lamina

Highly keratinized cells of the superficial layer lack nuclei.

Basal cell

Basal lamina

Stratified squamous epithelium with abundant keratin (epidermis)
This highly keratinized epithelium consists of undifferentiated **basal cells** specialized for **mitotic division**. Stratified cells covering the basal layer are differentiating cells. Cells of the outer layer contain abundant **keratin** to prevent water loss and penetration of chemical and physical insults. **The outermost cells lack nuclei.**

Figure 1–3

| Pseudostratified epithelium: All the cells are in contact with the basal lamina but not all of them reach the lumen |

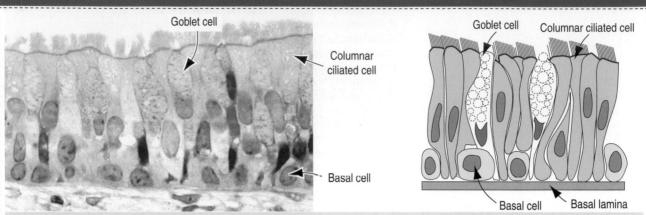

Pseudostratified columnar ciliated epithelium (trachea)
This epithelium consists of three major cell types: 1. **Columnar cells** with **cilia** on their apical domain. 2. **Basal cells** anchored to the basal lamina. 3. **Goblet cells**, a mucus-secreting epithelial cell. Both columnar ciliated and goblet cells attach to the basal lamina and reach the lumen. Basal cells do not reach the lumen.

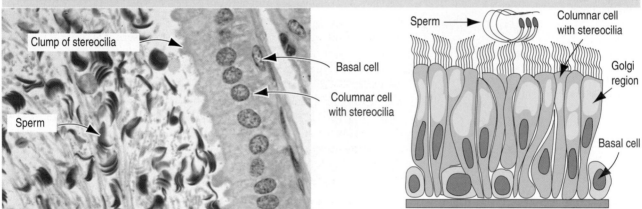

Pseudostratified columnar epithelium with stereocilia (epididymis)
The epididymal epithelium contains two major cell types. 1. Columnar cells with **stereocilia** and highly developed Golgi apparatus (called **principal cells**). 2. Basal cells attached to the basal lamina. Both basal and principal cells are associated with the basal lamina. Only principal cells reach the lumen. **Sperm** can be visualized in the lumen.

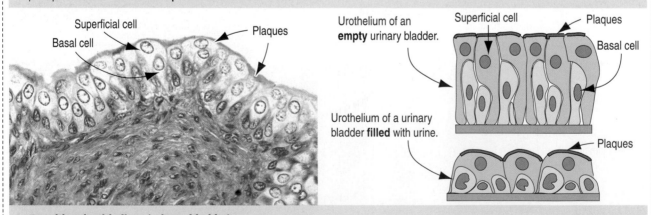

Transitional epithelium (urinary bladder)
The transitional epithelium, lining the urinary passages (also called **urothelium**), consists of two cell types: 1. **Columnar** or **superficial cells** extending from the basal lamina to the lumen. 2. **Basal cells** attached to the basal lamina. Essentially, the urothelium is a pseudostratified epithelium although it has the appearance of a stratified squamous epithelium. A characteristic of the urothelium is that superficial cells respond to tensional forces —caused by urine— by changing their geometry and surface configuration. **Plaques** of aggregated proteins are found on the apical plasma membrane of the superficial cells.

absorption and secretion or to act as a water or gas barrier. We will study several cell barriers and their functional significance.

Epithelial cell polarity

Epithelial cells have two major domains (Figure 1–4):

1. An **apical domain**.
2. A **basolateral domain**.

Each domain is defined by specific structural and functional characteristics. For example, the apical domain has structures important for the **protection** of the epithelial surface (such as **cilia** in the respiratory tract) or for the **absorption** of substances (such as **microvilli** in the intestinal epithelium).

Junctional complexes and **cell adhesion molecules** are present at the basolateral domain to anchor epithelial cells to each other and to the basement membrane.

The **apical domain** of some epithelial cells can display three types of differentiation:

1. **Cilia**.
2. **Microvilli**.
3. **Stereocilia**.

Cilia (sing., **cilium**; Figure 1–5) are motile cell projections originating from **basal bodies** anchored by **rootlets** to the apical portion of the cytoplasm. A basal body contains nine **triplet** microtubules in a **helicoid array** without a central microtubular component. By contrast, a cilium consists of an assembly called an **axoneme, formed by a central pair of microtubules surrounded by nine concentrically arranged microtubular pairs. This assembly is known as the 9 + 2 microtubular doublet arrangement.** The axoneme is also a component of the sperm tail, or **flagellum**.

The trachea and the oviduct are lined by **ciliated** epithelial cells. In these epithelia, ciliary activity is important for the local defense of the respiratory system and for the transport of the fertilized egg to the uterine cavity.

Microvilli (singular, **microvillus**; see Figure 1–5) are finger-like cell projections of the apical epithelial cell surface containing a core of cross-linked microfilaments (a polymer of G-actin monomers). At the cytoplasmic end of the microvillus, bundles of actin and other proteins extend into the **terminal web**, a filamentous network of cytoskeletal proteins running parallel to the apical domain of the epithelial cell.

Figure 1–4

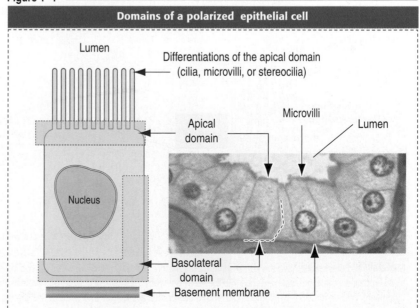

Domains of a polarized epithelial cell

Lumen

Differentiations of the apical domain (cilia, microvilli, or stereocilia)

Apical domain

Microvilli

Lumen

Nucleus

Basolateral domain

Basement membrane

Figure 1–5

Apical differentiations of epithelial cells

Cilium

A core of microtubule **triplets** in a helicoidal arrangement

A core of microtubule **doublets** in a 9 + 2 arrangement

Basal body

Rootlets
Centriole

Microtubule-organizing center

Cilium

Basal lamina

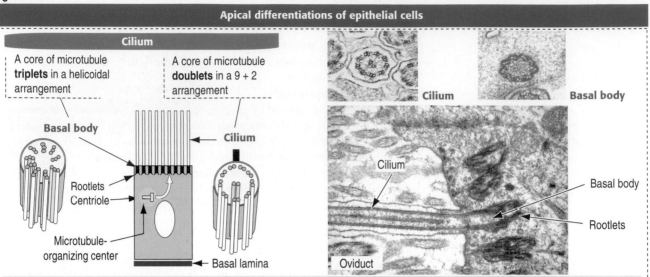

Cilium

Basal body

Cilium

Basal body

Rootlets

Oviduct

Cilia develop from **basal bodies** located in the apical domain of the cytoplasm. Basal bodies derive from **centrioles** with which they share a similar substructure: **nine peripheral microtubule triplets**. **Rootlets** anchor the basal body to the cytoplasm. Central microtubules are not present in basal bodies and centrioles. Centrioles, but not basal bodies, are surrounded by a dense material called the **microtubule-organizing center**. The cilium consists of a concentric array of nine microtubule doublets surrounding a central pair of microtubules (9 + 2 organization).

Microvillus

A core of actin-containing microfilaments

Microvillus

Terminal web

Basal lamina

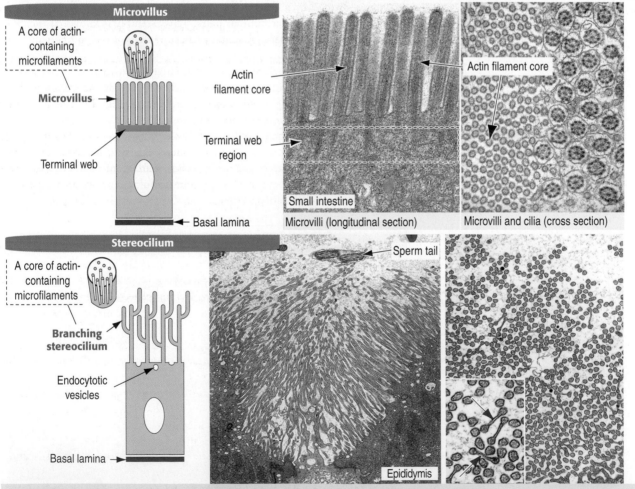

Actin filament core

Actin filament core

Terminal web region

Small intestine

Microvilli (longitudinal section)

Microvilli and cilia (cross section)

Stereocilium

A core of actin-containing microfilaments

Branching stereocilium

Endocytotic vesicles

Basal lamina

Sperm tail

Epididymis

Microvilli and **stereocilia** have the same substructure: A core of **actin microfilaments** and actin-associated proteins.
In the intestinal epithelium, actin extends into the **terminal web**, a network of cytoskeletal proteins in a collar-like arrangement at the apical domain of the cytoplasm. While microvilli have comparable length, **stereocilia are longer and branch** and the apical domain of the cell contains endocytotic vesicles.
Stereocilia are typical of the epididymal epithelium. The bridges connecting adjacent stereocilia (red arrows) are indicators of their branching.

Figure 1–6

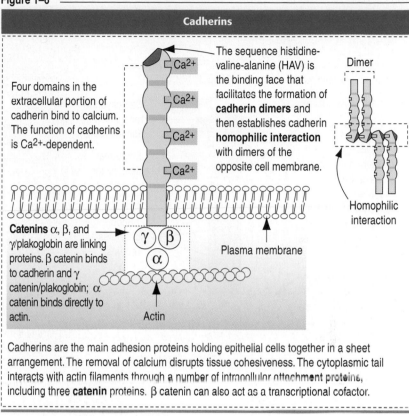

Cadherins

Four domains in the extracellular portion of cadherin bind to calcium. The function of cadherins is Ca²⁺-dependent.

The sequence histidine-valine-alanine (HAV) is the binding face that facilitates the formation of **cadherin dimers** and then establishes cadherin **homophilic interaction** with dimers of the opposite cell membrane.

Dimer

Homophilic interaction

Plasma membrane

Catenins α, β, and γ/plakoglobin are linking proteins. β catenin binds to cadherin and γ catenin/plakoglobin; α catenin binds directly to actin.

Actin

Cadherins are the main adhesion proteins holding epithelial cells together in a sheet arrangement. The removal of calcium disrupts tissue cohesiveness. The cytoplasmic tail interacts with actin filaments through a number of intracellular attachment proteins, including three **catenin** proteins. β catenin can also act as a transcriptional cofactor.

The intestinal epithelium and portions of the nephron in the kidney are lined by epithelial cells with microvilli, forming a **brush border**. In general, a brush border is indicative of the **absorptive** function of the cell.

Stereocilia (singular, **stereocilium**; see Figure 1–5) are long and **branching** finger-like projections of the apical epithelial cell surface. Like microvilli, stereocilia contain a core of cross-linked actin with other proteins. **Stereocilia do not have axonemes**. Stereocilia are typical of the epithelial lining of the epididymis and contribute to the process of sperm maturation occurring in this organ.

Cell adhesion molecules and cell junctions

A sheet of epithelial cells forming the lining of the small intestine results from the tight attachment of similar cells to each other and to the **basal lamina**, a component of the extracellular matrix. **Cell adhesion molecules** enable interepithelial cell contact, and this contact is stabilized by specialized **cell junctions**. A consequence of this arrangement is the apical and basolateral domain polarity of an epithelial sheet.

Although cell adhesion molecules and cell junctions are considered here within the framework of epithelia, you will learn that nonepithelial cells can also utilize cell adhesion molecules and junctions to establish contact with each other, enabling cell-cell communication. A typical example of nonepithelial cells connected by specialized junctions is the cardiac muscle (see Chapter 7, Muscle Tissue).

There are two major classes of cell adhesion molecules:

1. **Ca²⁺-dependent molecules**, including **cadherins** and **selectins**.

2. **Ca²⁺-independent molecules**, that comprise the **immunoglobulin superfamily** and **integrins**.

Many cells can use different cell adhesion molecules to mediate cell-cell attachment. Integrins are mainly involved in cell–extracellular matrix interactions. Cadherins and integrins establish a link between the internal cytoskeleton of a cell and the exterior of another cell (cadherins) or the extracellular matrix

Figure 1–7

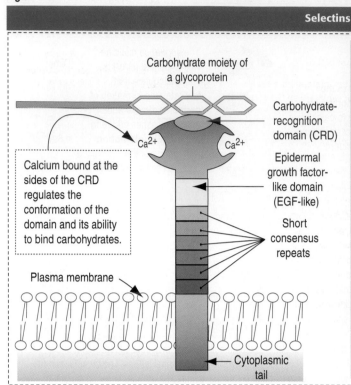

Selectins

Carbohydrate moiety of a glycoprotein

Carbohydrate-recognition domain (CRD)

Ca²⁺   Ca²⁺

Calcium bound at the sides of the CRD regulates the conformation of the domain and its ability to bind carbohydrates.

Epidermal growth factor-like domain (EGF-like)

Short consensus repeats

Plasma membrane

Cytoplasmic tail

Selectins have three extracellular domains: 1. A **carbohydrate-recognition domain** (CRD) specific for a particular sugar (galactose, mannose, *N*–acetylglucosamine, and others). 2. A domain homologous to a repeat found in epidermal growth factor (**EGF-like**). 3. A number of **consensus repeats** found in complement regulatory proteins.

There are three major types of selectins: 1. L-selectin, carried by lymphocytes and with binding affinity to sulfated carbohydrates. 2. E-selectin, expressed by activated endothelial cells. 3. P-selectin, expressed by platelets and activated endothelial cells.

Selectins, together with integrins and intercellular cell adhesion molecules (ICAMs), play a significant role in inflammation and in the periodic migration of lymphocytes from the circulation into lymphoid organs ("**homing**").

(integrins).

Cadherins (Figure 1–6) are a family of Ca²⁺-dependent molecules with a major role in cell adhesion and differentiation. A loss of cadherins is associated with the acquisition of invasive behavior by tumor cells (**metastasis**) as we will see in Chapter 4, Connective Tissue.

There are more than 40 different cadherins. **E-cadherin** is an epithelial cadherin found along the lateral cell surfaces and is responsible for the maintenance of most epithelial layers. The removal of calcium or the use of a blocking antibody to E-cadherin in epithelial cell cultures breaks down cell-cell attachment, and the formation of stabilizing junctions is disrupted. E-cadherin molecules form **dimers,** which bind to dimers of the **same class of cadherins in the opposite cell membrane** by a **homophilic interaction** mechanism in a parallel alignment fashion. This "like-to-like" binding requires the presence of calcium and results in a specialized "zipper-like" cell-cell adhesion pattern.

N-cadherin is found in the central nervous system, the lens of the eye, and in skeletal and cardiac muscle. **P-cadherin** is observed in placenta (trophoblast).

The cytoplasmic domain of cadherins is linked to **actin** through intermediate proteins called **catenins** (α, β and γ). Members of the cadherin family are also present **between cytoplasmic plaques** of the zonula and the macula adherens. β catenin plays a significant role in **colorectal carcinogenesis** (see Chapter 16, Lower Digestive Segment).

Selectins (Figure 1–7), like cadherins, are Ca²⁺-dependent cell adhesion molecules. Unlike cadherins, selectins bind to carbohydrates and, therefore, belong to the group of **lectins** (Lat. *lectum*, to select). Each selectin has a carbohydrate-recognition domain (CRD) with binding affinity to a **specific oligosaccharide** attached to a protein (glycoprotein) or a lipid (glycolipid). The molecular configuration of the CRD is controlled by calcium.

Selectins participate in the movement of **leukocytes** (Gr. *leukos*, white, *kytos*, cell) circulating in blood (neutrophils, monocytes, B and T cells) toward tissues by **extravasation**. Extravasation is the essence of "homing," a mechanism that

Figure 1–8

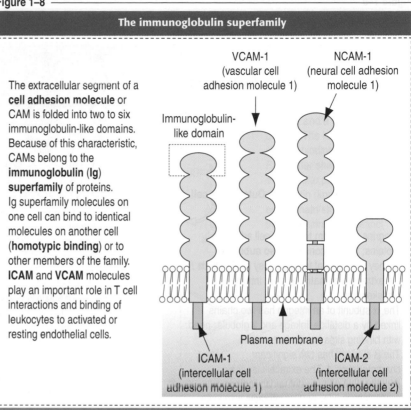

The immunoglobulin superfamily

The extracellular segment of a **cell adhesion molecule** or CAM is folded into two to six immunoglobulin-like domains. Because of this characteristic, CAMs belong to the **immunoglobulin (Ig) superfamily** of proteins. Ig superfamily molecules on one cell can bind to identical molecules on another cell (**homotypic binding**) or to other members of the family. **ICAM** and **VCAM** molecules play an important role in T cell interactions and binding of leukocytes to activated or resting endothelial cells.

Immunoglobulin-like domain

VCAM-1 (vascular cell adhesion molecule 1)

NCAM-1 (neural cell adhesion molecule 1)

Plasma membrane

ICAM-1 (intercellular cell adhesion molecule 1)

ICAM-2 (intercellular cell adhesion molecule 2)

enables leukocytes to escape from blood circulation and reach the sites of inflammation (see Figure 1–11). Homing also permits thymus-derived T cells to "home" in peripheral lymph nodes (see Chapter 10, Immune-Lymphatic System).

The three major classes of cell surface selectins are:

1. **P-selectin**, found in platelets and activated endothelial cells lining blood vessels.

2. **E-selectin**, found on activated endothelial cells.

3. **L-selectin**, found on leukocytes.

P-selectin is stored in cytoplasmic vesicles in endothelial cells. When endothelial cells are activated by inflammatory signaling, P-selectin appears on the cell surface. On their surface, leukocytes contain **sialyl Lewis-x antigen**, a specific oligosaccharide ligand for P-selectin. P-selectin binding to the antigen slows down streaming leukocytes in blood, and they begin to roll along the endothelial cell surfaces. P-selectins get additional help from members of the immunoglobulin (Ig) superfamily and integrins to stabilize leukocyte attachment, leading to extravasation (see Figure 1–11).

N-CAM (for **n**eural **c**ell **a**dhesion **m**olecule) belongs to the Ig superfamily and mediates both homophilic and heterophilic interactions. Unlike cadherins and selectins, members of the Ig superfamily are Ca^{2+}-independent cell adhesion molecules, and are encoded by a single gene. Members of the Ig superfamily are generated by the alternative messenger RNA (mRNA) splicing and have differences in glycosylation.

A conserved feature shared by all members of the Ig superfamily is an extracellular segment with one or more **folded domains characteristic of immunoglobulins** (Figure 1–8). Of particular interest is **CD4**, both a member of the Ig superfamily and the receptor for the **human immunodeficiency virus type 1 (HIV-1)** in a subclass of lymphocytes known as T cells or helper cells. We will discuss the significance of several members of the Ig superfamily in Chapter 10, Immune-Lymphatic System.

Figure 1–11

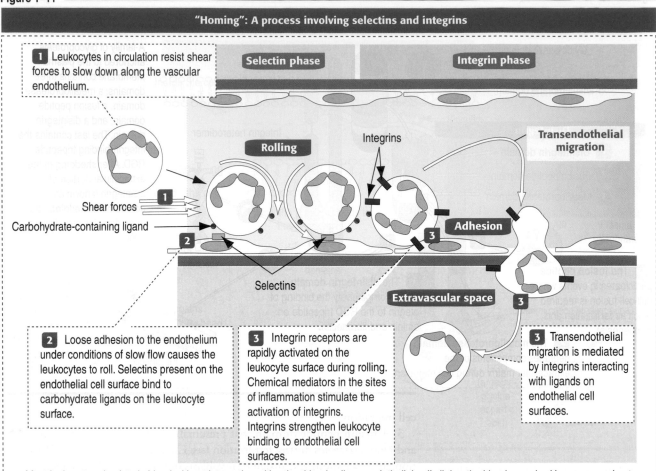

"Homing": A process involving selectins and integrins

Selectin phase **Integrin phase**

1 Leukocytes in circulation resist shear forces to slow down along the vascular endothelium.

Rolling

Integrins

Transendothelial migration

Shear forces
Carbohydrate-containing ligand

1

2

3

Adhesion

Selectins

Extravascular space

3

2 Loose adhesion to the endothelium under conditions of slow flow causes the leukocytes to roll. Selectins present on the endothelial cell surface bind to carbohydrate ligands on the leukocyte surface.

3 Integrin receptors are rapidly activated on the leukocyte surface during rolling. Chemical mediators in the sites of inflammation stimulate the activation of integrins. Integrins strengthen leukocyte binding to endothelial cell surfaces.

3 Transendothelial migration is mediated by integrins interacting with ligands on endothelial cell surfaces.

Most leukocytes circulate in blood without interacting with other blood cells or endothelial cells lining the blood vessels. However, a subset of **lymphocytes** participates in a continuous recirculation process through lymphoid tissues. This "homing" process involves many diverse adhesion molecules that help lymphocytes to home to various lymphoid compartments of the body.

The lymphocyte-endothelial cell interaction requires two types of cell adhesion proteins: **selectins** and **integrins**. **Neutrophils** use a similar mechanism to escape from blood vessels, primarily postcapillary venules, into inflammatory sites. The migration of leukocytes from the bloodstream to the tissue occurs in several steps as illustrated.

1. They determine **epithelial cell polarity** by separating the apical domain from the basolateral domain and preventing the free diffusion of lipids and proteins between them.

2. They prevent the free passage of substances across an epithelial cell layer (**paracellular pathway barrier**).

Cell membranes of two adjacent cells come together at regular intervals to seal the apical intercellular space. These areas of close contact continue around the entire surface of the cell like a belt, forming anastomosing strips of the four-span transmembrane protein **occludin**. Occludin interacts with four major proteins: **ZO-1, ZO-2, ZO-3**, and **AF-6. Claudins** (Lat. *claudere*, to close), a family of 16 transmembrane proteins forming linear fibrils in the occluding junctions, confer barrier properties on the paracellular pathway. A mutation in the gene encoding claudin 16 is the cause of a rare human **renal magnesium wasting syndrome** characterized by hypomagnesemia and seizures.

Occluding junctions can be visualized by **freeze-fracturing** as a network of **branching and anastomosing sealing strands**. We will discuss in Chapter 2, Epithelial Glands, the procedure of freeze-fracturing for the study of cell membranes.

Anchoring junctions are found below the occluding junctions, usually near the apical surface of an epithelium. There are three classes of **anchoring junctions**

Figure 1–12

Anchoring junctions

Occluding junctions
They define cell polarity and control the passage of substances between adjacent cells. Occluding junctions have a **beltlike** distribution like a ribbon internally bracing the cells.

Zonula adherens or belt desmosome
This anchorage junction has a **beltlike** distribution and is associated with **actin** filaments.

Macula adherens or spot desmosome
This anchorage junction has a **spotlike** distribution and is associated with **intermediate filaments**.

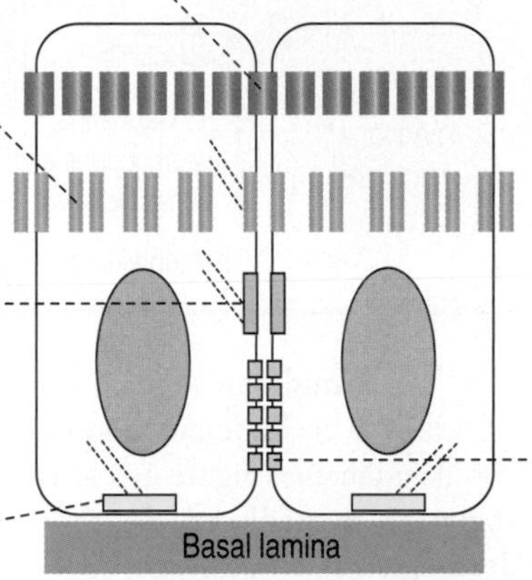

Hemidesmosome
Hemidesmosomes link the basal domain of an epithelial cell to the basal lamina. **Intermediate filaments** are associated with a **plaque**.

Note that occluding and gap junctions **are not** associated with cytoskeletal components.

Basal lamina

Gap or communicating junctions
They connect functionally two adjacent cells. A gap junction is formed by **connexons**, channel–like structures that enable the passage of small molecules (~ 1.2 kDa) between cells.

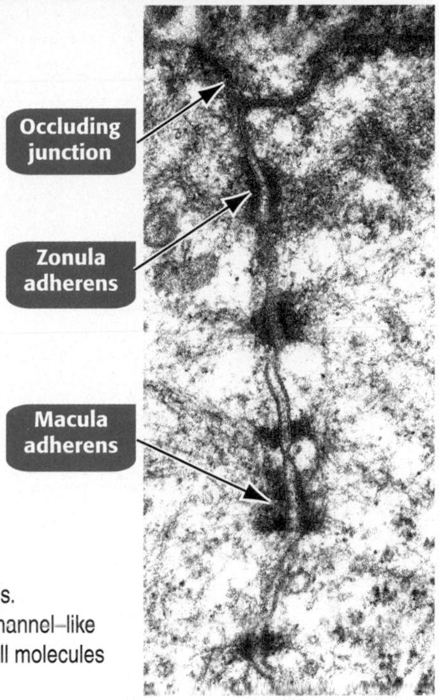

Occluding junction

Zonula adherens

Macula adherens

(see Figures 1–12, 1–14, 1–16 and 1–17):
1. The zonula adherens or belt desmosome.
2. The macula adherens or spot desmosome.

Figure 1–13

Occluding or tight junctions

Transcellular pathway

Paracellular pathway

Lumen

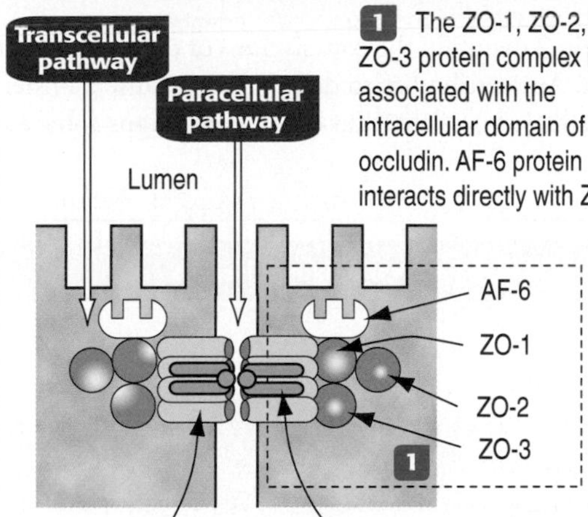

1 The ZO-1, ZO-2, and ZO-3 protein complex is associated with the intracellular domain of occludin. AF-6 protein interacts directly with ZO-1.

AF-6
ZO-1
ZO-2
ZO-3

Occludin is an integral membrane phosphoprotein. Interaction between occludin and claudin molecules on adjacent cells regulates the **paracellular pathway**.

Claudin is a transmembrane protein that creates the **paracellular diffusion barrier** for solutes, ions, and water.

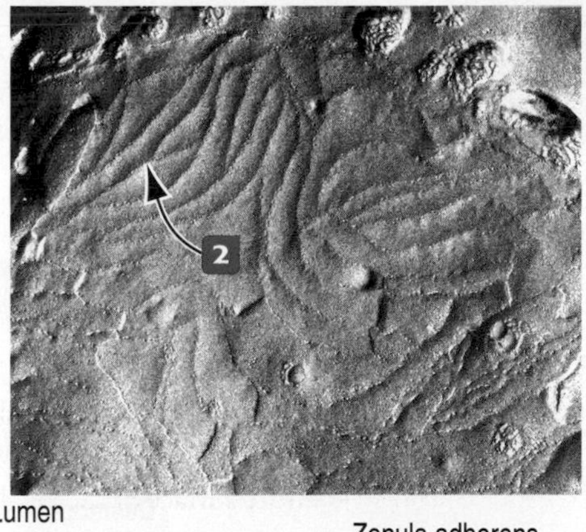

2 In **freeze-fracture preparations**, occluding junctions appear as branching and **interconnected sealing ridges** forming a network near the apical domain of the cell. The ridges represent the integral membrane protein occludin associated with the fractured protoplasmic face (PF).

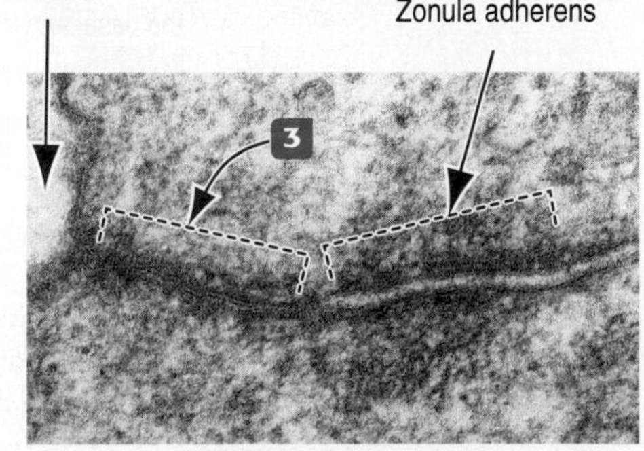

Lumen

Zonula adherens

3 In thin sections, the intercellular space is occluded by **occludin**, **claudin**, and **associated proteins**. The **zonula adherens** or belt desmosome is usually found below occluding or tight junctions.

Figure 1–14

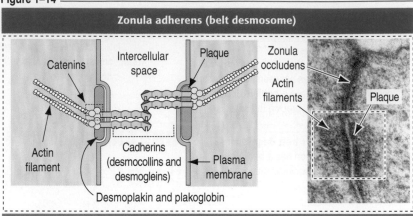

Zonula adherens (belt desmosome)

3. The **hemidesmosome**.

Like the occluding junctions, the **zonula adherens** is a **beltlike junction**. The zonula adherens (Figure 1–14) is associated with **actin microfilaments**. This association is mediated by the interaction of **cadherins** (**desmocollins** and **desmogleins**) with **catenins** (α, β, and γ). The main desmogleins expressed in the epidermis of the skin are desmoglein 1 and desmoglein 3 (Figure 1–15).

The **macula adherens** (also called **desmosome**), is a **spot-like** junction associated with **intermediate filaments** (also known as **tonofilaments**) extending from one spot to another on the lateral and basal cell surfaces of epithelial cells (Figure 1–16). Spot desmosomes provide strength and rigidity to an epithelial cell layer.

Contrasting with occluding junctions, adjacent cell membranes linked by zonula and macula adherens are separated by a relatively wide intercellular space. This space is occupied by the glycosylated portion of proteins of the **cadherin** family, **desmogleins** and **desmocollins**, anchored to **cytoplasmic plaques** containing **desmoplakin** and **plakoglobin**. The cytoplasmic plaques are attached to the cytosolic face of the plasma membrane. The interlocking of similar cadherins binds two cells together by Ca^{2+}-dependent homophilic interaction, as we have already seen.

Desmoglein 1 and **desmoglein 2** maintain the cohesiveness of the epidermis, a stratified squamous epithelium. Autoantibodies to desmoglein 1 cause a blistering disease (disruption of cell adhesion) of the skin called **pemphigus foliaceus** (see Figure 1–15).

Figure 1–15

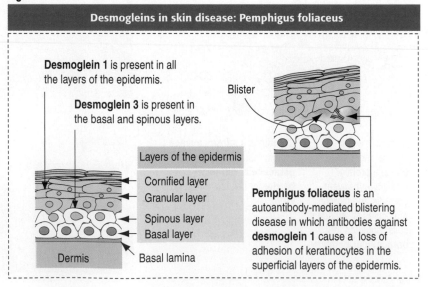

Desmogleins in skin disease: Pemphigus foliaceus

Figure 1–16

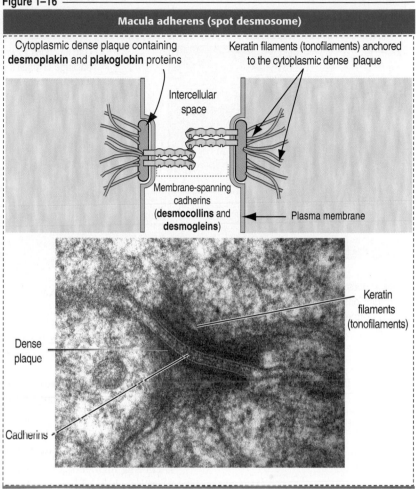

Macula adherens (spot desmosome)

Cytoplasmic dense plaque containing **desmoplakin** and **plakoglobin** proteins

Keratin filaments (tonofilaments) anchored to the cytoplasmic dense plaque

Intercellular space

Membrane-spanning cadherins (**desmocollins** and **desmogleins**)

Plasma membrane

Keratin filaments (tonofilaments)

Dense plaque

Cadherins

Hemidesmosomes are **asymmetrical** structures anchoring the basal domain of an epithelial cell to the underlying basal lamina (Figure 1–17).

Hemidesmosomes have a different organization when compared to a macula adherens or desmosome. A hemidesmosome consists of:

1. A **cytoplasmic plate** associated with intermediate filaments (also called **keratins** or **tonofilaments**).

Figure 1–17

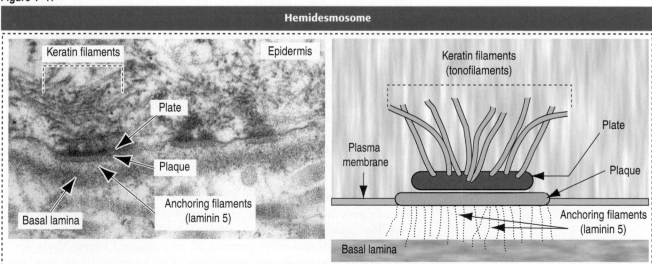

Hemidesmosome

Keratin filaments

Epidermis

Plate

Plaque

Anchoring filaments (laminin 5)

Basal lamina

Keratin filaments (tonofilaments)

Plasma membrane

Plate

Plaque

Anchoring filaments (laminin 5)

Basal lamina

Figure 1–18

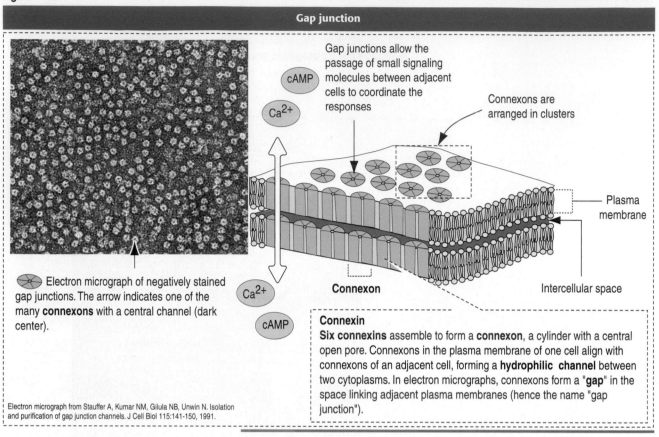

Gap junction

Electron micrograph of negatively stained gap junctions. The arrow indicates one of the many **connexons** with a central channel (dark center).

Electron micrograph from Stauffer A, Kumar NM, Gilula NB, Unwin N. Isolation and purification of gap junction channels. J Cell Biol 115:141-150, 1991.

Gap junctions allow the passage of small signaling molecules between adjacent cells to coordinate the responses

cAMP
Ca^{2+}
Ca^{2+}
cAMP

Connexons are arranged in clusters

Plasma membrane

Connexon

Intercellular space

Connexin
Six connexins assemble to form a **connexon**, a cylinder with a central open pore. Connexons in the plasma membrane of one cell align with connexons of an adjacent cell, forming a **hydrophilic channel** between two cytoplasms. In electron micrographs, connexons form a "**gap**" in the space linking adjacent plasma membranes (hence the name "gap junction").

2. A **membrane plaque** linking the hemidesmosome to the basal lamina by **anchoring filaments** (composed of **laminin 5**).

Although hemidesmosomes look like half-desmosomes, none of the biochemical components present in the desmosome is found in hemidesmosomes. Hemidesmosomes increase the overall stability of epithelial tissues by linking intermediate filaments of the cytoskeleton with components of the basal lamina. We will consider additional details of the hemidesmosomes and their role in autoimmune diseases of the skin when we discuss the structure of intermediate filaments in the cytoskeleton section.

Communicating junctions, or **gap junctions**, are formed by integral membrane proteins called **connexins**. **Six connexins associate to form a connexon**, a hollow cylindrical structure that spans the plasma membrane. The end-to-end alignment of connexons in adjacent cells provides a direct channel of communication (1.5 to 2.0 nm in diameter) between the cytosol of two adjacent cells (Figure 1–18). Connexons have a **clustering** tendency and can form patches of about 0.3 mm in diameter.

These junctions facilitate the movement of molecules as large as 1.2 nm in diameter (such as Ca^{2+} and cyclic adenosine monophosphate, [cAMP]) between cells. The connexon channels close when the concentration of Ca^{2+} is high. This junction is responsible for the chemical and electrical "**coupling**" between adjacent cells. A typical example is **cardiac muscle cells** connected by gap junctions to enable the transmission of electrical signals.

Clinical significance: Connexin mutations in human disease

Several diseases occur when genes encoding connexins are mutated. For example, mutations in **connexin 26**, highly expressed in cells of the cochlea, are associated with **deafness**. Mutations in **connexin 32** are found in **Charcot-Marie-Tooth neuropathies** resulting in progressive degeneration of peripheral nerves, charac-

Figure 1–19

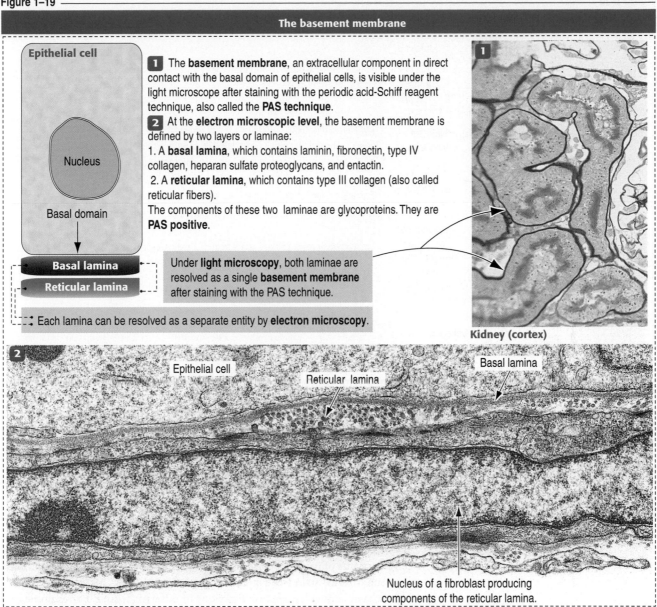

The basement membrane

Epithelial cell

Nucleus

Basal domain

1 The **basement membrane**, an extracellular component in direct contact with the basal domain of epithelial cells, is visible under the light microscope after staining with the periodic acid-Schiff reagent technique, also called the **PAS technique**.

2 At the **electron microscopic level**, the basement membrane is defined by two layers or laminae:

1. A **basal lamina**, which contains laminin, fibronectin, type IV collagen, heparan sulfate proteoglycans, and entactin.

2. A **reticular lamina**, which contains type III collagen (also called reticular fibers).

The components of these two laminae are glycoproteins. They are **PAS positive**.

Basal lamina

Reticular lamina

Under **light microscopy**, both laminae are resolved as a single **basement membrane** after staining with the PAS technique.

Each lamina can be resolved as a separate entity by **electron microscopy**.

Kidney (cortex)

Epithelial cell   Reticular lamina   Basal lamina

Nucleus of a fibroblast producing components of the reticular lamina.

The periodic acid-Schiff (PAS) reaction

PAS is a widely used histochemical technique to demonstrate 1,2-glycol or 1,2-aminoalcohol groups such as those present in glycogen, mucus, and glycoproteins.

Periodic acid, an oxidant, converts these groups to **aldehydes**. The **Schiff reagent**, a colorless fuchsin, reacts with the aldehydes to form a characteristic **red-purple (magenta)** product.

Some important PAS-positive structures are the **basement membrane**, **glycocalyx**, **mucus** produced by goblet cells, stored **glycoprotein hormones** in cells of the pituitary gland, and **collagens**.

terized by distal muscle weakness and atrophy, and impairment of deep tendon reflexes. Mutations in **connexin 50** are associated with **congenital cataracts**, leading to blindness.

Laminin, fibronectin, and the basement membrane

We have seen that integrins mediate cell-matrix interactions by their binding affinity to the RGD domain in laminin and fibronectin (see Figure 1–9). **Laminin** and **fibronectin** are distinct proteins of the extracellular matrix and are associated with collagens, proteoglycans, and other proteins to organize a **basement membrane**, the supporting sheet of most epithelia.

The basement membrane consists of two components (Figure 1–19):

1. The **basal lamina**, a sheetlike extracellular matrix in direct contact with epithelial cell surfaces. The basal lamina results from the self-assembly of laminin molecules with type IV collagen, entactin, and proteoglycans. 2. A **reticular lamina** —formed by collagen fibers— supports the basal lamina and is continuous with the connective tissue.

Both the basal and reticular laminae can be distinguished by electron micros-

Figure 1–20

Laminin and fibronectin

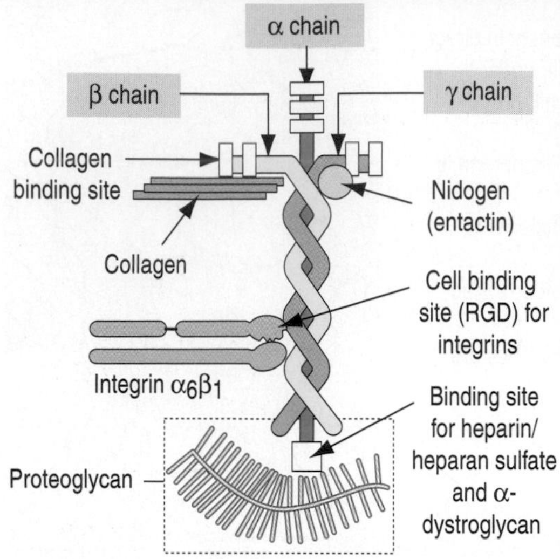

Laminin

Laminin is the major component of the basal lamina. It consists of three disulfide-linked polypeptide chains designated α, β, and γ chains. Variants for each chain give rise to several laminin isoforms with different structure and function.

Laminins have binding sites for cell surface receptors (**integrins**), **type IV collagen**, and other adhesion proteins (like **nidogen**, also known as **entactin**).

Laminin monomers self-associate to form a network that is part of the **basal lamina**.

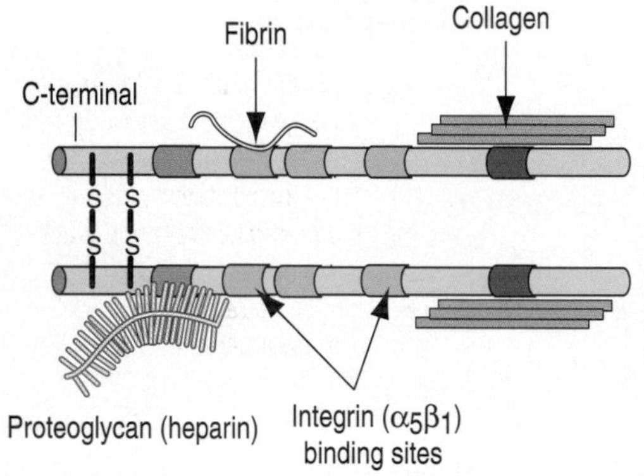

Fibronectin

Fibronectin is a glycoprotein formed by two identical chains joined by disulfide linkages close to the C-terminal.

There are two forms of fibronectin: 1. **Plasma fibronectin**, produced by **hepatocytes** and secreted into the bloodstream. 2. **Cellular fibronectin**, produced by **fibroblasts**, forms part of the extracellular matrix.

Fibronectin has two binding sites for **integrins**, **collagen**, **heparin**, and **fibrin**.

copy. Under the light microscope, the combined basal and reticular laminae receive the name of basement membrane, which can be recognized by the **periodic acid-Schiff** (**PAS**) stain (see Figure 1–19).

The basal lamina has specific functions in different tissues. For example, the double basal lamina of the renal corpuscle constitutes the most important element of the **glomerular filtration barrier** during the initial step in the formation of urine (see Chapter 14, Urinary System). In skeletal muscle, the basal lamina maintains the integrity of the tissue and its disruption gives rise to muscular dystrophies (see Chapter 7, Muscle Tissue). During the migration of primordial germinal cells, a basal laminal material guides the migrating cells toward the gonadal ridge in preparation for the development of the gonads. Thus, the basal lamina not only provides support to epithelia but also participates in other nonepithelial cell functions.

Laminin (Figure 1–20) is a cross-shaped protein consisting of three chains: the **α chain**, the **β chain**, and the **γ chain**. Laminin molecules can associate with each other to form a meshlike polymer. Laminin and **type IV collagen** are the major components of the basal lamina, and both are synthesized by epithelial cells resting on the lamina. Laminin has binding sites for **entactin** (also called nidogen), **proteoglycans** (in particular, heparan sulfate, also called **perlecan**), **α-dystroglycan** (see Chapter 7, Muscle Tissue), and **integrins**.

Fibronectin (see Figure 1–20) consists of two protein chains cross-linked by disulfide bonds. Fibronectin is the main adhesion molecule of the extracellular

Figure 1–21

Summary of cell junctions and cell adhesion molecules

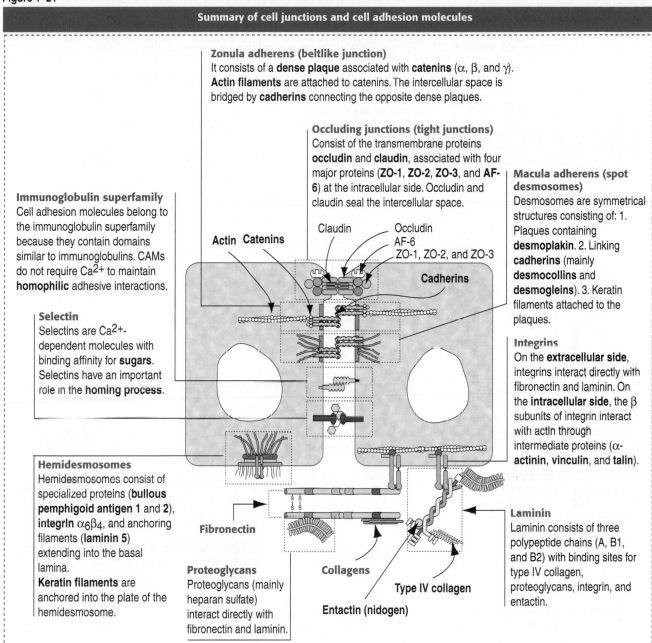

Zonula adherens (beltlike junction)
It consists of a **dense plaque** associated with **catenins** (α, β, and γ). **Actin filaments** are attached to catenins. The intercellular space is bridged by **cadherins** connecting the opposite dense plaques.

Occluding junctions (tight junctions)
Consist of the transmembrane proteins **occludin** and **claudin**, associated with four major proteins (**ZO-1, ZO-2, ZO-3**, and **AF-6**) at the intracellular side. Occludin and claudin seal the intercellular space.

Claudin
Occludin
AF-6
ZO-1, ZO-2, and ZO-3

Actin   Catenins

Cadherins

Macula adherens (spot desmosomes)
Desmosomes are symmetrical structures consisting of: 1. Plaques containing **desmoplakin**. 2. Linking **cadherins** (mainly **desmocollins** and **desmogleins**). 3. Keratin filaments attached to the plaques.

Immunoglobulin superfamily
Cell adhesion molecules belong to the immunoglobulin superfamily because they contain domains similar to immunoglobulins. CAMs do not require Ca^{2+} to maintain **homophilic** adhesive interactions.

Selectin
Selectins are Ca^{2+}-dependent molecules with binding affinity for **sugars**. Selectins have an important role in the **homing process**.

Integrins
On the **extracellular side**, integrins interact directly with fibronectin and laminin. On the **intracellular side**, the β subunits of integrin interact with actin through intermediate proteins (α-**actinin**, **vinculin**, and **talin**).

Hemidesmosomes
Hemidesmosomes consist of specialized proteins (**bullous pemphigoid antigen 1 and 2**), **integrin** $\alpha_6\beta_4$, and anchoring filaments (**laminin 5**) extending into the basal lamina.
Keratin filaments are anchored into the plate of the hemidesmosome.

Fibronectin

Laminin
Laminin consists of three polypeptide chains (A, B1, and B2) with binding sites for type IV collagen, proteoglycans, integrin, and entactin.

Proteoglycans
Proteoglycans (mainly heparan sulfate) interact directly with fibronectin and laminin.

Collagens

Type IV collagen

Entactin (nidogen)

matrix of the connective tissue and is produced by fibroblasts. Fibronectin has binding sites for **heparin** present in proteoglycans, several types of **collagens** (types I, II, III, and V), and **fibrin** (derived from fibrinogen during blood coagulation).

Fibronectin circulating in blood is synthesized in the liver by hepatocytes. It differs from fibronectin produced by fibroblasts in that it lacks one or two repeats (designated EDA and EDB for extra domain A and extra domain B) as a result of alternative mRNA splicing. Circulating fibronectin binds to fibrin, a component of the blood clot formed at the site of blood vessel damage. The RGD domain of immobilized fibronectin binds to integrin expressed on the surface of activated platelets, and the blood clot enlarges. We return to the topic of blood coagulation or hemostasis in Chapter 6, Blood and Hematopoiesis.

Cell-cell interactions

We will summarize the highlights of cell adhesion molecules and cell junctions.

Figure 1–22

Immunocytochemical localization of antigens

Two techniques are generally used: direct and indirect immunocytochemistry. Immunocytochemistry requires that cells under study are made permeable, usually with a detergent, so that antibody molecules (immunoglobulins) can enter a cell and bind to an antigen.

Direct immunofluorescence

The immunoglobulin molecule cannot enter into an intact cell.

After detergent treatment, the immunoglobulin molecule enters the cell and binds to the antigen.

Antigen

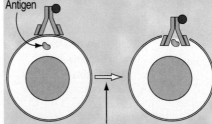

Detergent treatment makes the cell membrane permeable to the antibody.

Direct immunocytochemistry involves a specific antibody or some agent with specific binding affinity to an antigen tagged with a visible marker. Visible markers attached to the immunoglobulin molecule can be a fluorescent dye such as **fluorescein** (green fluorescence) or **rhodamine** (red fluorescence). When examined with a fluorescence microscope, only labeled components are visible as bright, fluorescent structures. Direct immunofluorescence involves a single incubation step and provides a simple detection system. Gold particles (electron-dense) attached to immunoglobulin molecules are convenient markers for immunocytochemistry at the electron microscopic level.

Indirect immunofluorescence

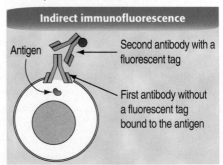

Second antibody with a fluorescent tag

First antibody without a fluorescent tag bound to the antigen

Antigen

Indirect immunocytochemistry involves a second antibody tagged with a visible marker. This second antibody binds to a nontagged first antibody specific for an antigen. The indirect method requires two separate incubations (one each for the first and second antibody) and is more specific for the identification of antigens.

An epithelium is a continuous sheet of polarized cells supported by a basement membrane. The polarized nature of an epithelium depends on the occluding or tight junctions that separate the polarized cells into apical and basolateral regions. Tight junctions control the paracellular pathway of solutes, ions, and water.

The cohesive nature of the epithelium depends on three factors: cell junctions, cell adhesive molecules in general, and the interaction of integrins with the extracellular matrix, produced to a large extent by fibroblasts. The basal lamina is essential for the differentiation of epithelial cells during embryogenesis.

Note in Figure 1–21 that:

1. The basal domain of epithelial cells interacts with the basal lamina through hemidesmosomes and integrins. Hemidesmosomes contain integrins.

2. Integrins interact directly with laminin and fibronectin, in particular the RGD domain to which integrins bind.

3. Collagens and proteoglycans do not interact directly with the basal domain of epithelial cells. Instead, this interaction is mediated by laminin and fibronectin, which contain specific binding sites for collagens, proteoglycans, and entactin.

4. The lateral domains of adjacent epithelial cells are cross-linked by occluding junctions, anchoring junctions (belt and spot desmosomes), and gap junctions (not shown in Figure 1–21).

5. Cadherins are part of belt and spot desmosomes. Selectins and members of the Ig superfamily are independent molecules.

Figure 1–23

Microfilaments form the core of intestinal microvilli

Brush border—formed by microvilli— at the apical domain of the intestinal columnar epithelial cells

Intestinal microvillus

Glycocalyx

Cap

Actin bundle

Actin filament rootlets

Terminal web

Glycocalyx

Cap

Actin cross-linking proteins

Myosin I

Villin

Calmodulin

Fimbrin

Membrane-linking proteins

F-actin

Terminal web

Spectrin isoform connecting fibrils

Intermediate filaments

The cytoskeleton

The cytoskeleton is a three-dimensional network of proteins distributed throughout the cytoplasm of eukaryotic cells.

The cytoskeleton has roles in:

1. **Cell movement** (crawling of blood cells along blood vessel walls; migration of fibroblasts during wound healing; movement of cells during embryonic development).

2. **Support and strength for the cell.**

3. **Phagocytosis.**

4. **Cytokinesis.**

5. **Cell-cell and cell–extracellular matrix adherence.**

6. **Changes in cell shape.**

The components of the cytoskeleton were originally identified by **electron microscopy.** These early studies described a system of cytoplasmic "cables" that fell

Figure 1–24

Role of actin-binding proteins in the assembly and disassembly of the actin filament

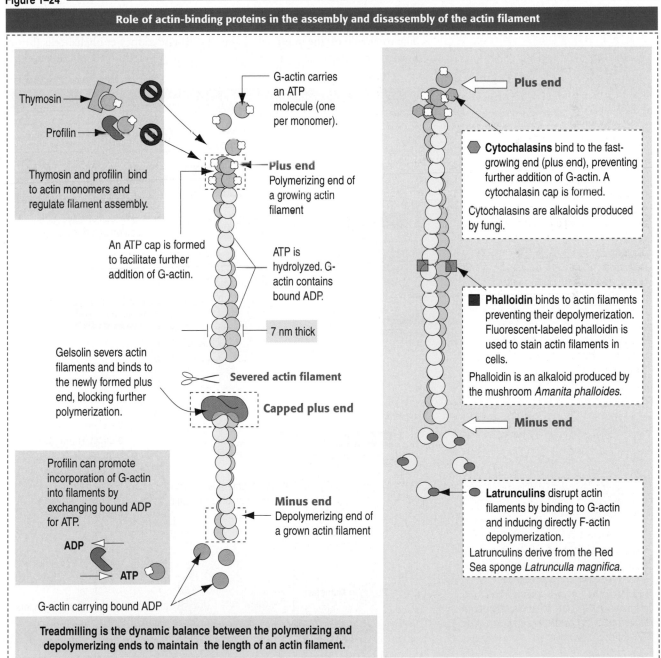

Thymosin

Profilin

Thymosin and profilin bind to actin monomers and regulate filament assembly.

G-actin carries an ATP molecule (one per monomer).

Plus end
Polymerizing end of a growing actin filament

An ATP cap is formed to facilitate further addition of G-actin.

ATP is hydrolyzed. G-actin contains bound ADP.

7 nm thick

Gelsolin severs actin filaments and binds to the newly formed plus end, blocking further polymerization.

Severed actin filament

Capped plus end

Profilin can promote incorporation of G-actin into filaments by exchanging bound ADP for ATP.

ADP

ATP

G-actin carrying bound ADP

Minus end
Depolymerizing end of a grown actin filament

Plus end

Cytochalasins bind to the fast-growing end (plus end), preventing further addition of G-actin. A cytochalasin cap is formed.

Cytochalasins are alkaloids produced by fungi.

Phalloidin binds to actin filaments preventing their depolymerization. Fluorescent-labeled phalloidin is used to stain actin filaments in cells.

Phalloidin is an alkaloid produced by the mushroom *Amanita phalloides*.

Minus end

Latrunculins disrupt actin filaments by binding to G-actin and inducing directly F-actin depolymerization.

Latrunculins derive from the Red Sea sponge *Latrunculla magnifica*.

Treadmilling is the dynamic balance between the polymerizing and depolymerizing ends to maintain the length of an actin filament.

into three size groups:

1. **Microfilaments** (7 nm thick).
2. **Intermediate filaments** (10 nm thick).
3. **Microtubules** (25 nm in diameter).

Biochemical studies, involving the extraction of cytoskeletal proteins from cells with detergents and salts, and in vitro translation of specific mRNA, showed that each class of filaments has a unique protein organization. Once cytoskeletal proteins were purified, they were used as antigens for the production of antibodies. Antibodies are used as tools for the localization of the various cytoskeletal proteins in the cell. Both the **immunocytochemical localization** of cytoskeletal proteins (Figure 1–22) and **cell treatment with various chemical agents** disrupting the normal organization of the cytoskeleton have been instrumental in understanding the organization and function of the cytoskeleton.

Microfilaments

The main component of microfilaments is **actin**. Actin filaments are composed of globular monomers (**G-actin**), which polymerize to form filaments (**F-actin**). The microvilli of the intestinal (Figure 1–23) and kidney epithelial cells (brush border) are typical examples of the organization of F-actin into microfilaments.

Figure 1–25

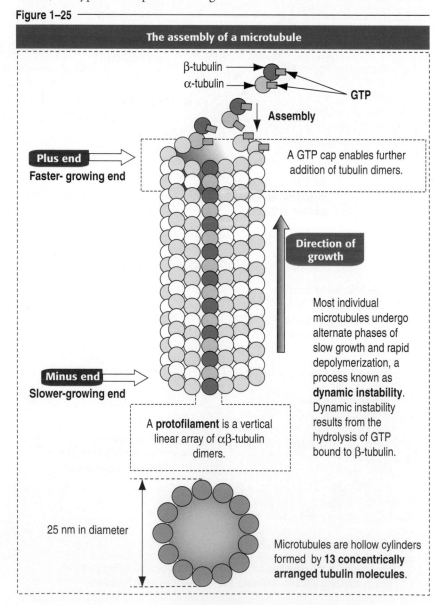

The assembly of a microtubule

β-tubulin
α-tubulin
GTP

Assembly

Plus end
Faster- growing end

A GTP cap enables further addition of tubulin dimers.

Direction of growth

Most individual microtubules undergo alternate phases of slow growth and rapid depolymerization, a process known as **dynamic instability**. Dynamic instability results from the hydrolysis of GTP bound to β-tubulin.

Minus end
Slower-growing end

A **protofilament** is a vertical linear array of αβ-tubulin dimers.

25 nm in diameter

Microtubules are hollow cylinders formed by **13 concentrically arranged tubulin molecules**.

Growth of actin filaments may occur at both ends; however, one end (the **plus end**) grows faster than the other end (the **minus end**). Actin monomers have a binding site for adenosine triphosphate (**ATP**) which is hydrolyzed to adenosine diphosphate (**ADP**) following polymerization. Therefore, **actin polymerization is ATP-dependent**.

Actin polymerization proceeds by a mechanism known as **treadmilling: G-actin monomers added on the plus end of the filament move, or treadmill, along the filament until it is lost by depolymerization at the minus end** (Figure 1–24).

The assembly of actin monomers into filaments and the organization of these filaments into thick bundles are controlled by various types of **actin-binding proteins**. For example, a bundle of parallel actin filaments, forming the core of the **microvillus**, is held together by actin-linking proteins, **villin** and **fimbrin**. Side arms of **myosin-I** and the Ca^{2+}-binding protein **calmodulin** anchor the bundle to the plasma membrane (see Figure 1–23).

Actin-binding proteins **thymosin**, **profilin**, and **gelsolin** participate in the assembly and disassembly of actin filaments.

Thymosin captures actin monomers and **prevents** their assembly into filaments.

Profilin (see Figure 1–24) has a dual role:

1. Like thymosin, profilin binds to actin monomers and blocks their incorporation into filaments.

2. Conversely, profilin can favor the assembly of monomeric G-actin into filaments by facilitating the exchange of bound ADP for ATP. Note that **only ATP-actin monomers** can be assembled into filaments.

Gelsolin (see Figure 1–24) has a dual role:

1. It is a **capping protein** and prevents the loss and addition of actin monomers.

2. It is a **severing protein**. In the presence of Ca^{2+}, gelsolin fragments actin filaments and remains bound to the plus end, forming a cap that prevents further filament growth.

Actin filaments predominate at the periphery of the cell, where they form a network beneath the plasma membrane, in association with actin-binding proteins.

Two examples are relevant: 1. The **intestinal microvilli** (see Figure 1–23). 2. The **plasma membrane of red blood cells** (discussed in Chapter 6, Blood and Hematopoiesis). The major actin-binding protein in red blood cells is **spectrin**, a

Figure 1–26

The mitotic apparatus

The mitotic apparatus consists of two components:
1. The **mitotic center**.
2. The **mitotic spindle**.
The three components of the mitotic center are the **microtubule organizing center** surrounding a pair of **centrioles**, and **radiating microtubules** (also called astral microtubules), anchoring the mitotic center to the plasma membrane.
The mitotic spindle consists of two major classes of microtubules originating in the mitotic center: the **kinetochore microtubules**, anchored to the **centromeres** of the metaphase chromosomes, and the **polar microtubules**, which overlap with each other in the center of the cell and are not attached to chromosomes.

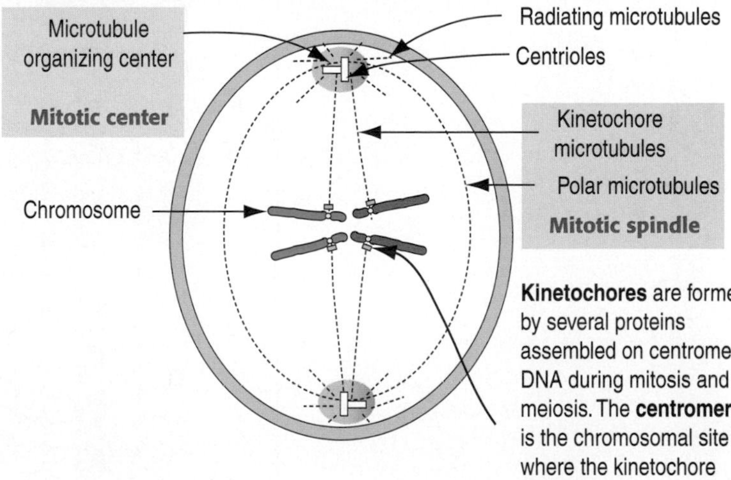

Kinetochores are formed by several proteins assembled on centromeric DNA during mitosis and meiosis. The **centromere** is the chromosomal site where the kinetochore assembles.

Figure 1–27

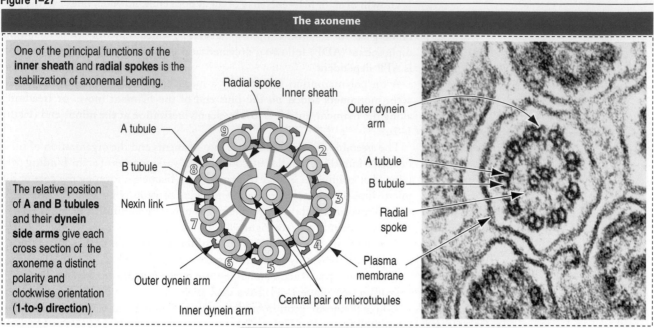

The axoneme

One of the principal functions of the **inner sheath** and **radial spokes** is the stabilization of axonemal bending.

The relative position of **A and B tubules** and their **dynein side arms** give each cross section of the axoneme a distinct polarity and clockwise orientation (**1-to-9 direction**).

Radial spoke — Inner sheath — A tubule — B tubule — Nexin link — Outer dynein arm — Inner dynein arm — Central pair of microtubules — Plasma membrane — Radial spoke — B tubule — A tubule — Outer dynein arm

tetramer consisting of two distinct polypeptide chains (α and β).

Microtubules

Microtubules are composed of **tubulin dimers** (Figure 1–25). Each tubulin dimer consists of two tightly-bound tubulin molecules: α and β-**tubulin**. Tubulin subunits are arranged in longitudinal rows called **protofilaments**. Thirteen

Figure 1–28

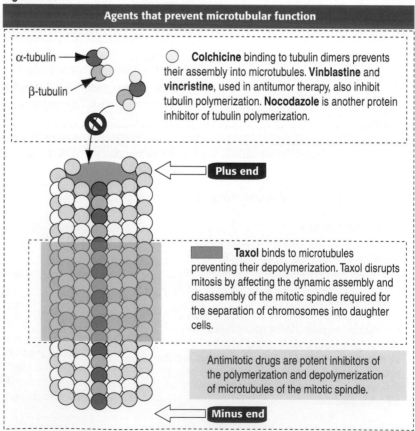

Agents that prevent microtubular function

α-tubulin

β-tubulin

Colchicine binding to tubulin dimers prevents their assembly into microtubules. **Vinblastine** and **vincristine**, used in antitumor therapy, also inhibit tubulin polymerization. **Nocodazole** is another protein inhibitor of tubulin polymerization.

Plus end

Taxol binds to microtubules preventing their depolymerization. Taxol disrupts mitosis by affecting the dynamic assembly and disassembly of the mitotic spindle required for the separation of chromosomes into daughter cells.

Antimitotic drugs are potent inhibitors of the polymerization and depolymerization of microtubules of the mitotic spindle.

Minus end

protofilaments associate side by side with each other to form a cylinder or **micro-tubule** with a hollow core. The diameter of a microtubule is 25 nm.

Like actin filaments, microtubules are structurally **polarized**. Microtubules have a **plus end** which, in the presence of a low **Ca²⁺ concentration** (less than 10 μM) and guanosine triphosphate (**GTP**), grows more rapidly than the **minus end** (see Figure 1–25).

However, unlike actin filaments, most individual microtubules appear to undergo **alternate phases of slow growth and rapid depolymerization**. This process, called **dynamic instability**, results in the continued and rapid turnover of microtubules occurring during **mitosis** and **meiosis**.

Microtubules with dynamic instability are usually observed in actively dividing and motile cells. However, cells like neurons contain long-lived microtubules stabilized by **microtubule-associated proteins** (**MAPs**). These MAPs

1. Protect microtubules from disassembling (for example, kinetochore proteins of the anaphase-promoting complex (APC; see Mitosis in the Cell Nucleus section).

2. Inhibit tubulin dissociation (such as **tau**, **MAP1**, and **MAP2** proteins).

3. Link adjacent microtubules and other cellular structures (for example, cytoplasmic dynein and kinesin bound to microtubules and transporting vesicles).

During **mitosis**, the polymerization of tubulin is coordinated by a **pericentriolar material**, an amorphous, electron-dense substance, part of the **mitotic center** (Figure 1–26). This material represents a **microtubule organizing center** or **centrosome** of the mitotic spindle and it is found around a pair of **centrioles**.

A **centriole** is a small cylinder (0.2 μm wide and 0.4 μm long), composed of **nine microtubule triplets**. During interphase, centrioles are oriented at right angles to each other. Before mitosis, centrioles replicate and form **two pairs**. During mitosis, each pair can be found at opposite poles of the cell, where they direct the formation of the **mitotic** or **meiotic spindle**. Spindle microtubules, which undergo extensive rounds of polymerization and depolymerization, attach to the centromeric region of metaphase chromosomes (see Figure 1–48).

Microtubules in cilia and flagella

Cilia and flagella are motile cytoplasmic extensions containing a core of microtubules called the **axoneme** (Figure 1–27). The axoneme consists of nine peripheral microtubule doublets surrounding a central pair of microtubules. This arrange-

Figure 1–29

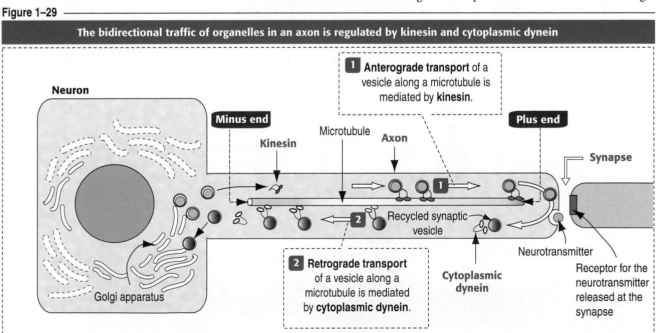

The bidirectional traffic of organelles in an axon is regulated by kinesin and cytoplasmic dynein

Neuron

Minus end

Kinesin

Microtubule

Axon

Plus end

Synapse

1 **Anterograde transport** of a vesicle along a microtubule is mediated by **kinesin**.

2 **Retrograde transport** of a vesicle along a microtubule is mediated by **cytoplasmic dynein**.

Recycled synaptic vesicle

Cytoplasmic dynein

Neurotransmitter

Receptor for the neurotransmitter released at the synapse

Golgi apparatus

ment is known as the **9 + 2** configuration.

Each peripheral doublet consists of a complete microtubule (called an **A tubule**, with **13 protofilaments**), sharing its wall with a second, partially completed microtubule (called a **B tubule**, with **10 to 11 protofilaments**). Extending inward from the A tubule are **radial spokes** that insert into an amorphous **inner sheath** surrounding the central microtubule pair. Adjacent peripheral doublets are linked by the protein **nexin**.

Projecting from the sides of the A tubule are sets of protein arms: the **inner** and **outer arms of dynein**, a microtubule-associated adenosine triphosphatase (ATPase). In the presence of ATP, the sliding of peripheral doublets relative to each other bends cilia and flagella. Sliding and bending of microtubules are the basic events of their motility.

Figure 1–30

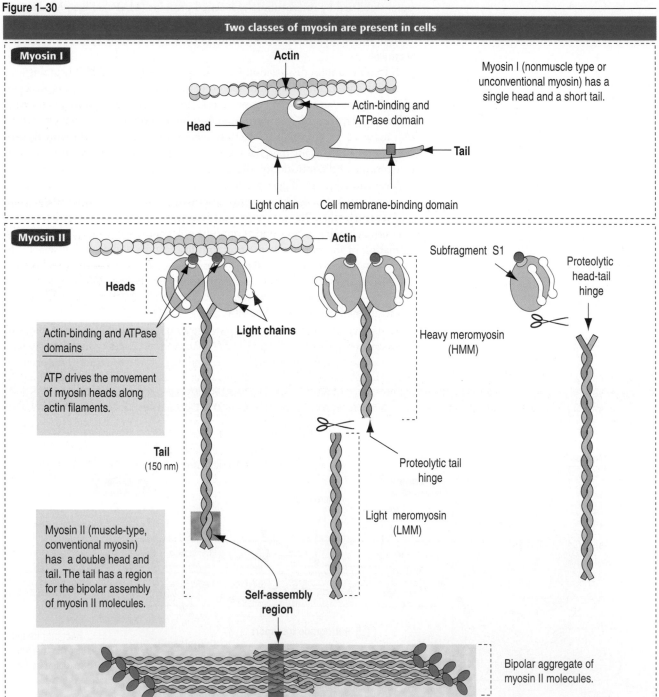

Two classes of myosin are present in cells

Myosin I

Actin

Actin-binding and ATPase domain

Head

Light chain — Cell membrane-binding domain

Tail

Myosin I (nonmuscle type or unconventional myosin) has a single head and a short tail.

Myosin II

Actin

Heads

Light chains

Subfragment S1

Proteolytic head-tail hinge

Actin-binding and ATPase domains

ATP drives the movement of myosin heads along actin filaments.

Heavy meromyosin (HMM)

Tail (150 nm)

Proteolytic tail hinge

Light meromyosin (LMM)

Myosin II (muscle-type, conventional myosin) has a double head and tail. The tail has a region for the bipolar assembly of myosin II molecules.

Self-assembly region

Bipolar aggregate of myosin II molecules.

Clinical significance: Microtubules, treatment of cancer, and sterility

Drugs affecting the polymerization and depolymerization of microtubules during mitosis are useful in both cell biology and in the treatment of cancer. For example, **colchicine, colcemid, vincristine,** and **vinblastine** bind to tubulin and inhibit microtubule polymerization, thus blocking mitosis. **Taxol** has an opposite effect: stabilizes microtubules instead of inhibiting their assembly. Stabilized microtubules also block cell division (Figure 1–28).

Kartagener's syndrome is an autosomal recessive disorder frequently associated with **bronchiectasis** (permanent dilation of bronchi and bronchioles) and **sterility** in males.

Kartagener's syndrome is the result of structural abnormalities in the axoneme (**defective or absent dynein**) that prevent mucociliary clearance in the airways (leading to persistent infections) and reduce sperm motility (leading to sterility).

Motor proteins

The transport of organelles along microtubules: Axonal transport

Axons are cytoplasmic extensions of neurons responsible for the conduction of neuronal impulses. Membrane-bound vesicles containing **neurotransmitters** produced in the cell body of the neuron travel to the terminal portion of the axon, where the content of the vesicle is released at the **synapse**.

Bundles of microtubules form tracks within the axon to carry these vesicles. Vesicles are transported by two motor proteins (Figure 1–29):

1. Kinesin.
2. Cytoplasmic dynein.

Kinesins and cytoplasmic dyneins participate in two types of intracellular transport movements:

1. **Saltatory movement**, defined by the continuous and random movement of

Figure 1–31

Comparison of motor proteins				
	Myosin I	**Myosin II**	**Kinesin**	**Cytoplasmic dynein**
Number of heads	One	Two	Two	Two
Tail binds to	Cell membrane	Myosin II	Vesicle	Vesicle
Head binds to	**Actin**	**Actin**	**Microtubule**	**Microtubule**
Direction of head motion toward the	Plus end	Plus end	Plus end	Minus end

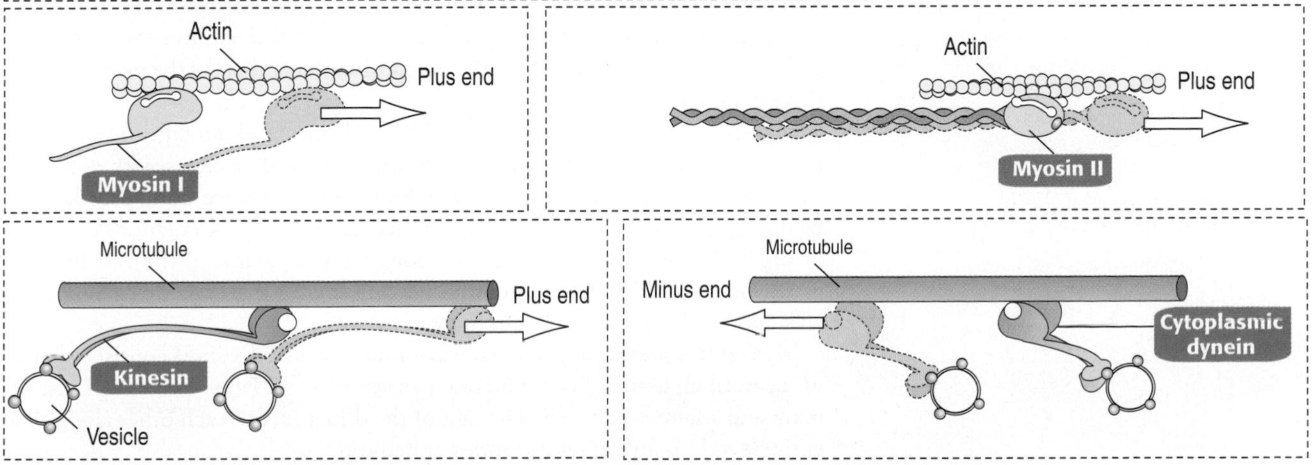

Figure 1–32

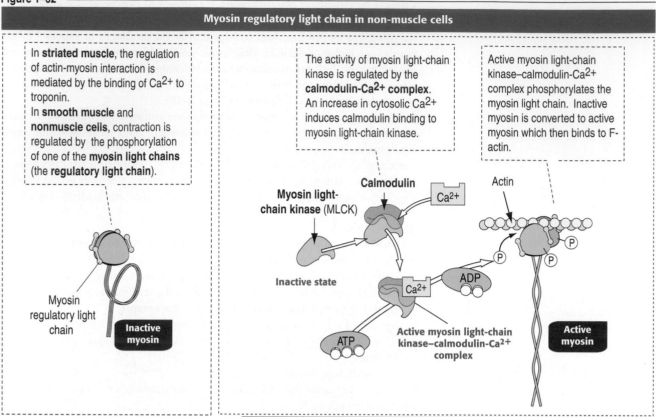

| Myosin regulatory light chain in non-muscle cells |

In **striated muscle**, the regulation of actin-myosin interaction is mediated by the binding of Ca^{2+} to troponin.
In **smooth muscle** and **nonmuscle cells**, contraction is regulated by the phosphorylation of one of the **myosin light chains** (the **regulatory light chain**).

Myosin regulatory light chain

Inactive myosin

The activity of myosin light-chain kinase is regulated by the **calmodulin-Ca^{2+} complex**. An increase in cytosolic Ca^{2+} induces calmodulin binding to myosin light-chain kinase.

Active myosin light-chain kinase–calmodulin-Ca^{2+} complex phosphorylates the myosin light chain. Inactive myosin is converted to active myosin which then binds to F-actin.

Myosin light-chain kinase (MLCK)

Calmodulin

Ca^{2+}

Actin

Inactive state

Ca^{2+}

ADP

ATP

Active myosin light-chain kinase–calmodulin-Ca^{2+} complex

Active myosin

mitochondria and vesicles.

2. **Axonal transport**, a more directed intracellular movement of membrane-bound structures. In both cases, movement is driven by motor proteins interacting with either microtubules or actin filaments.

Kinesins and cytoplasmic dyneins both have two ATP-binding heads and a tail. Energy derives from continuous ATP hydrolysis by ATPases present in the heads. The head domains interact with microtubules and the tail binds to specific receptor binding sites on the surface of vesicles and organelles.

Kinesin uses energy from ATP hydrolysis to move vesicles from the cell body of the neuron toward the end portion of the axon (**anterograde transport**). Cytoplasmic dynein also uses ATP as an energy source to move vesicles in the opposite direction (**retrograde transport**).

The myosin family associates with actin to form contractile structures

Members of the myosin family of proteins bind and hydrolyze ATP to provide energy for their movement along actin filaments from the minus end to the plus end. **Myosin I** and **myosin II** are the predominant members of the myosin family (Figure 1–30).

Myosin I is found in all cell types and has only one head domain and a tail. The head is associated with a single light chain. The head interacts with actin filaments and contains ATPase, which enables myosin I to move along the filaments by binding, detaching, and rebinding (molecular motor). The tail binds to vesicles or organelles. When myosin I moves along an actin filament, the vesicle or organelle is transported. Myosin I molecules are smaller than myosin II molecules, lack a long tail, and do not form dimers.

Myosin II is present in muscle and nonmuscle cells. Myosin II consists of a pair of identical molecules. Each molecule consists of an ATPase-containing head domain and a long rodlike tail. The tails of the dimer link to each other along their entire length to form a two-stranded coiled rod.

Figure 1–33

Fine structure of the major components of the cytoskeleton

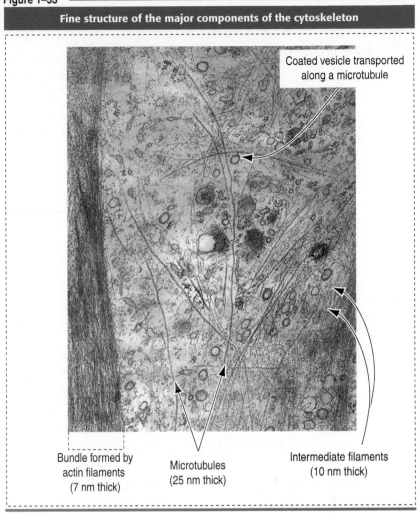

Coated vesicle transported along a microtubule

Bundle formed by actin filaments (7 nm thick)

Microtubules (25 nm thick)

Intermediate filaments (10 nm thick)

Heads and tails can be cleaved by enzymatic treatment into **light meromyosin** (**LMM**) and **heavy meromyosin** (**HMM**). LMM forms filaments but lacks ATPase activity, and does not bind to actin. HMM binds to actin, is capable of ATP hydrolysis and does not form filaments. HMM is responsible for generating force during muscle contraction. HMM can be cleaved further into two subfragments called **S1**. Each S1 fragment contains ATPase and binds actin. Figure 1–31 provides a summary of the structural and functional characteristics of motor proteins.

Actin-myosin contraction assemblies in nonmuscle cells

In nonmuscle cells, actin filaments interact with bipolar filaments of myosin II. Tropomyosin mediates actin-myosin II interaction.

A typical example of actin-myosin II contraction in nonmuscle cells is the process of **cytokinesis**, at the end of mitosis. A **contractile ring**, consisting of actin and myosin II, assembles under the plasma membrane. At telophase, the contractile ring constricts the center of the dividing cell to divide the cell into two daughter cells. The contractile process is regulated by **phosphorylation of one of the myosin light chains** (called the **regulatory light chain**) catalyzed by the enzyme **myosin light-chain kinase** (**MLCK**). The activity of MLCK is regulated by the Ca^{2+}-binding protein **calmodulin** (Figure 1–32).

Phosphorylation of the myosin light chain enables:

1. The assembly of myosin II into filaments.
2. Contractile activity.

Figure 1–34

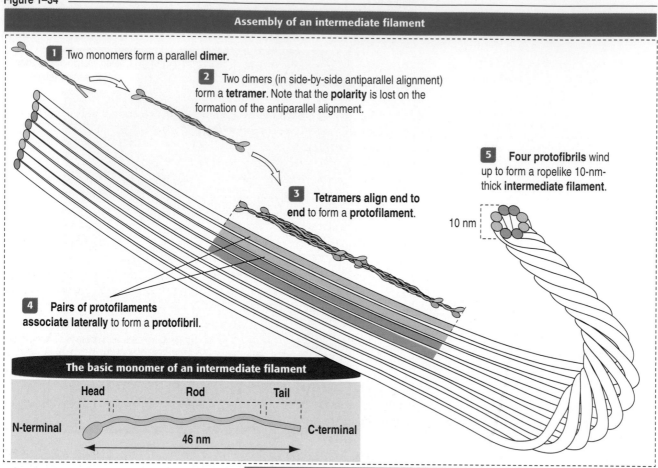

Assembly of an intermediate filament

1 Two monomers form a parallel **dimer**.

2 Two dimers (in side-by-side antiparallel alignment) form a **tetramer**. Note that the **polarity** is lost on the formation of the antiparallel alignment.

5 **Four protofibrils** wind up to form a ropelike 10-nm-thick **intermediate filament**.

10 nm

3 **Tetramers align end to end** to form a **protofilament**.

4 **Pairs of protofilaments associate laterally to form a protofibril.**

The basic monomer of an intermediate filament

Head | Rod | Tail

N-terminal | C-terminal

46 nm

Intermediate filaments

Intermediate filaments (Figure 1–33) represent a heterogeneous group of structures so named because their diameter (10 nm) is intermediate between that of microtubules (25 nm) and microfilaments (7 nm). Intermediate filaments are the most stable cytoskeletal structures.

Detergent and salt treatments extract microfilament and microtubule components and leave intermediate filaments insoluble. All intermediate filaments have a common monomer consisting of a central α-helical rod flanked by head and tail domains (Figure 1–34).

The structure of the intermediate filament does not fluctuate between assembly and disassembly states like microtubules and microfilaments. Unlike actin and tubulin, the assembly and disassembly of intermediate filament monomers are regulated by **phosphorylation**.

Intermediate filament protein monomers consists of three domains (see Figure 1–34): A central α-helical **rod domain** is flanked by a nonhelical N-terminal **head domain** and a C-terminal **tail domain**. The major **function** of intermediate filaments is **to provide mechanical support for the cell**.

Six types of intermediate filament proteins have been identified on the basis of sequence similarities in the rod domain. They are referred to as **types I** through **VI**. About 50 intermediate filament proteins have been reported so far.

Types I (acidic keratins) and II (neutral to basic keratins)
This class of proteins forms the intermediate filament cytoskeleton of **epithelial cells (cytokeratins)**. Equal amounts of acidic (40 to 60 kDa) and neutral-basic (50 to 70 kDa) cytokeratins **combine** to form this type of intermediate filament protein. **Types I and II intermediate filaments are associated with the cytoplasmic plaques of desmosomes and hemidesmosomes.**

In the **epidermis** of the skin, the basal cells express keratins K5 and K14. The upper differentiating cells express keratins K1 and K10. In some regions of the epidermis, such as in the palmoplantar region, keratin K9 is found. Mutations in K5 and K14 cause hereditary blistering skin diseases belonging to the clinical type **epidermolysis bullosa simplex** (see Clinical significance: Intermediate filaments and blistering diseases).

Type III

Vimentin (54 kDa) is generally found in cells of **mesenchymal origin**. In some cells, vimentin establishes a structural link between the plasma membrane and nuclear lamins.

Desmin (53 kDa) is a component of **skeletal muscle cells** and is localized to the Z disk of the **sarcomere** (see Chapter 7, Muscle Tissue). This intermediate filament protein keeps individual contractile elements of the sarcomeres attached to the Z disk and plays a role in coordinating muscle cell contraction. Desmin is also found in **smooth muscle cells**.

Glial fibrillary acidic protein (GFAP, 51 kDa) is observed in **astrocytes** and some Schwann cells (refer to Chapter 8, Nervous Tissue).

Peripherin (57 kDa) is a component of neurons of the peripheral nervous system and is coexpressed with neurofilament proteins (see Chapter 8, Nervous Tissue).

Type IV

Neurofilaments (NFs) are found in axons and dendrites of **neurons**. Three types of proteins can be found in a neurofilament: **NF-L** (60 to 70 kDa), **NF-M** (105 to 110 kDa), and **NF-H** (135 to 150 kDa), for low, middle, and high-molecular-weight neurofilaments, respectively.

α-internexin (66 kDa) is found predominantly in the central nervous system (particularly in the spinal cord and optic nerve).

Type V

Nuclear lamins A, B, and C (60 to 75 kDa) **differ from the other intermediate filament proteins in that they organize an orthogonal meshwork** in association with the inner membrane of the nuclear envelope. Lamins provide mechanical support for the nuclear envelope and bind chromatin.

Figure 1–35

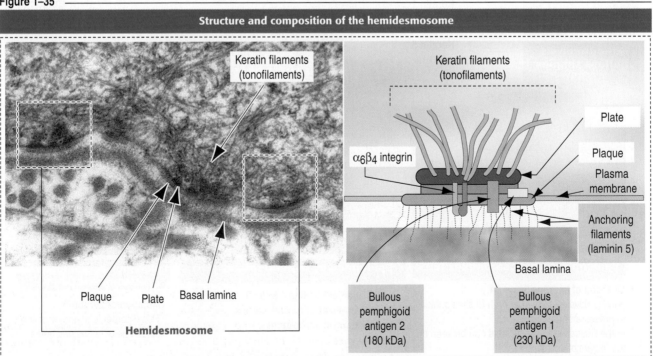

Structure and composition of the hemidesmosome

Keratin filaments (tonofilaments)

Plaque — Plate — Basal lamina

Hemidesmosome

Keratin filaments (tonofilaments)

Plate

Plaque

Plasma membrane

α6β4 integrin

Anchoring filaments (laminin 5)

Basal lamina

Bullous pemphigoid antigen 2 (180 kDa)

Bullous pemphigoid antigen 1 (230 kDa)

Figure 1–36

Pathogenesis of bullous pemphigoid, an autoimmune disease

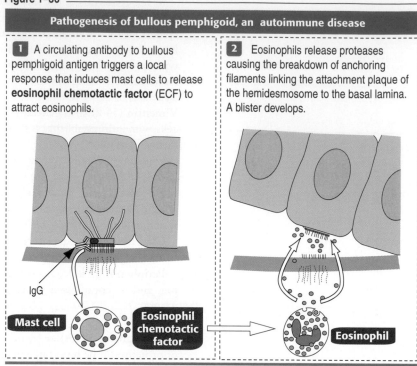

1 A circulating antibody to bullous pemphigoid antigen triggers a local response that induces mast cells to release **eosinophil chemotactic factor** (ECF) to attract eosinophils.

2 Eosinophils release proteases causing the breakdown of anchoring filaments linking the attachment plaque of the hemidesmosome to the basal lamina. A blister develops.

IgG

Mast cell

Eosinophil chemotactic factor

Eosinophil

During mitosis, the **phosphorylation** of lamin **serine residues** causes a transient disassembly of the meshwork, followed by a breakdown of the nuclear enve-

Figure 1–37

Examples of skin diseases caused by abnormal intermediate filament keratins

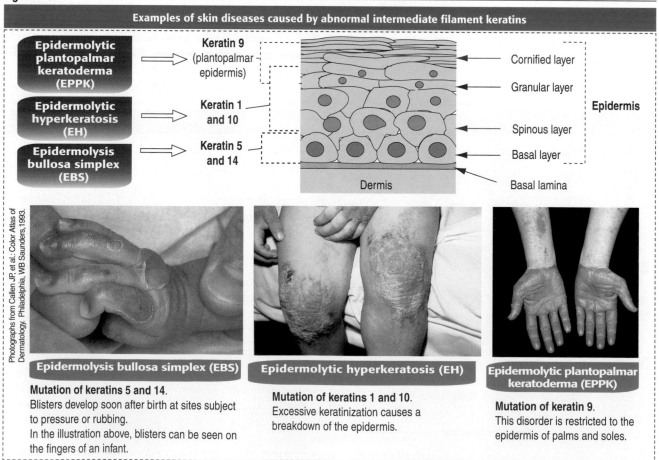

Epidermolytic plantopalmar keratoderma (EPPK) → Keratin 9 (plantopalmar epidermis)

Epidermolytic hyperkeratosis (EH) → Keratin 1 and 10

Epidermolysis bullosa simplex (EBS) → Keratin 5 and 14

Cornified layer

Granular layer

Epidermis

Spinous layer

Basal layer

Basal lamina

Dermis

Photographs from Callen, JP, et al.: Color Atlas of Dermatology. Philadelphia, WB Saunders, 1993.

Epidermolysis bullosa simplex (EBS)

Mutation of keratins 5 and 14.
Blisters develop soon after birth at sites subject to pressure or rubbing.
In the illustration above, blisters can be seen on the fingers of an infant.

Epidermolytic hyperkeratosis (EH)

Mutation of keratins 1 and 10.
Excessive keratinization causes a breakdown of the epidermis.

Epidermolytic plantopalmar keratoderma (EPPK)

Mutation of keratin 9.
This disorder is restricted to the epidermis of palms and soles.

lope into small fragments. At the end of mitosis, lamins are **dephosphorylated** and both the lamin meshwork and the nuclear envelope reorganize. See the cell nucleus section concerning the mechanism of phosphorylation and dephosphorylation of lamins during the cell cycle.

Type VI

Nestin (200 kDa) is a single type of intermediate filament protein expressed in stem cells of the central nervous system.

Hemidesmosomes and intermediate filaments

Hemidesmosomes are specialized integrin-mediated junctions observed in basal cells of the stratified squamous epithelium attaching to the basement membrane (Figure 1–35).

Inside the cell, a protein named **bullous pemphigoid antigen 1** —a protein without a transmembrane domain, homologous with desmoplakin, and localized to the intracellular portion of the hemidesmosomal plaque — links the β_4 integrin subunit to **intermediate filaments** (also called **tonofilaments**).

On the extracellular side, integrin $\alpha_6\beta_4$ associates with **laminin 5**, a protein present in specialized structures called **anchoring filaments**. Anchoring filaments link hemidesmosomes to the basal lamina. In addition to $\alpha_6\beta_4$ integrin, hemidesmosomes have another **transmembrane** component called **bullous pemphigoid antigen 2**, a protein sharing homology with members of the **collagen family**. Bullous pemphigoid antigens 1 and 2 were discovered in patients with bullous pemphigoid, an autoimmune disease.

Clinical significance: Intermediate filaments and blistering diseases

Bullous pemphigoid is an autoimmune blistering disease similar to **pemphigus vulgaris** (therefore called "pemphigoid").

Blisters or bullae develop at the epidermis-dermis junction when circulating immunoglobulin G (IgG) cross-reacts with bullous pemphigoid antigen 1 or 2. IgG-antigen complexes lead to the formation of complement complexes (C3, C5b, and C9), which damage the attachment of hemidesmosomes and perturb the synthesis of anchoring proteins by basal cells (Figure 1–36).

The production of local toxins causes the degranulation of mast cells and release of chemotactic factors attracting eosinophils. Enzymes released by eosinophils cause blisters or bullae.

Intermediate filaments strengthen the cellular cytoskeleton. The expression of mutant keratin genes results in the **abnormal assembly of keratin filaments**, which **weakens the mechanical strength of cells** and causes inherited skin diseases, as shown in Figure 1–37:

1. **Epidermolysis bullosa simplex** (EBS), characterized by skin blisters after minor trauma. EBS is determined by **keratin 5** and **14** mutant genes.

2. **Epidermolytic hyperkeratosis** (EH), in which patients have excessive keratinization of the epidermis due to mutations of **keratin 1** and **10** genes.

3. **Epidermolytic plantopalmar keratoderma** (EPPK), a skin disease producing fragmentation of the epidermis of palms and soles, caused by a mutation of the **keratin 9** gene.

The cell nucleus

The mammalian cell nucleus consists of three major components: 1. the **nuclear envelope**, 2. **chromatin**, and 3. the **nucleolus**.

The **nuclear envelope** consists of two concentric membranes separated by a perinuclear space. The **inner nuclear membrane** is associated with the **nuclear lamina, chromatin,** and **ribonucleoproteins**. The **outer nuclear membrane** is continuous with the membranes of the endoplasmic reticulum and can be associated with ribosomes.

The **nuclear pore complex** has a **tripartite structure**, composed of a **central**

Figure 1–38

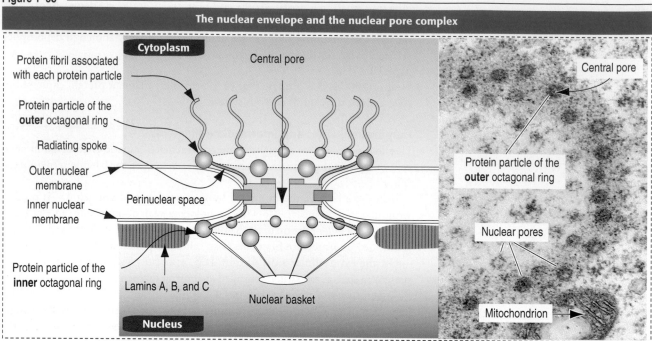

The nuclear envelope and the nuclear pore complex

Cytoplasm

Protein fibril associated with each protein particle

Protein particle of the **outer** octagonal ring

Radiating spoke

Outer nuclear membrane

Inner nuclear membrane

Protein particle of the **inner** octagonal ring

Central pore

Perinuclear space

Lamins A, B, and C

Nuclear basket

Nucleus

Central pore

Protein particle of the **outer** octagonal ring

Nuclear pores

Mitochondrion

cylindrical body placed between **inner** and **outer octagonal rings**, each consisting of eight protein particles. The central cylinder consists of a central plug and eight radiating **spokes** (Figure 1–38). The exact role of individual nuclear pore complex proteins in nucleocytoplasmic trafficking is not yet clear.

Figure 1–39

The transport of proteins into the nucleus

Nuclear localization sequence (Pro-Lys-Lys-Lys-Arg-Lys-Val)

Cargo protein

Cytoplasmic receptor (importin αβ complex).

1 A **cargo protein** with a nuclear localization sequence binds to the importin αβ complex.

2 The importin αβ complex bound to the nuclear localization signal of the cargo protein, moves across the **nuclear pore complex**.

3 Inside the nucleus, GTP bound to **Ran** (a small GTPase) induces the dissociation of the cargo protein by binding to importin β.
An **export cycle** involves RanGTP, which induces binding of a cargo protein to **exportin** for cytoplasmic transport (not shown).

4 The Ran-GTP–importin β complex is transported back to the cytoplasm, where Ran-GTP changes into Ran-GDP by Ran GTPase–activating protein (Ran GAP) and importin β is released.

Importin β

Cytoplasm

Nucleus

Ran GDP

Ran GTP

Ran GAP (Ran GTPase–activating protein)

Ran GTP

Figure 1–40

Structure of the chromatin fiber: The nucleosome

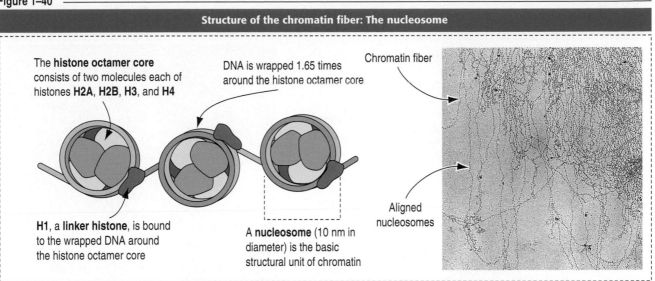

The **histone octamer core** consists of two molecules each of histones **H2A**, **H2B**, **H3**, and **H4**

DNA is wrapped 1.65 times around the histone octamer core

Chromatin fiber

Aligned nucleosomes

H1, a **linker histone**, is bound to the wrapped DNA around the histone octamer core

A **nucleosome** (10 nm in diameter) is the basic structural unit of chromatin

Figure 1–41

X chromosome inactivation

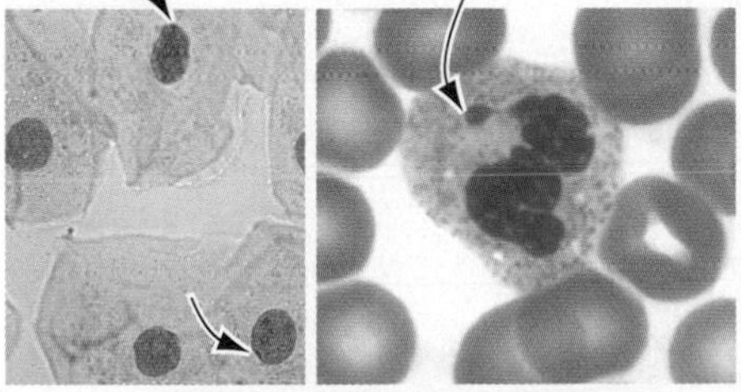

Barr body in scrapped cells of the oral epithelium

Drumstick in a neutrophil

Dosage compensation

The inactive chromosome X remains condensed during most of the interphase of the cell cycle.

It is visualized as a densely stained chromatin mass (**Barr body** or X chromatin) in a variable number of nuclei (about 30%-80%) of a normal female. A small **drumstick** is observed in 1%-10% of neutrophils in the female.

The inactivation of one of the X chromosomes is **random** (paternal or maternal X chromosome).

If a cell has more than two X chromosomes, the extra ones are inactivated and the maximum number of Barr bodies per nucleus will be one less than the total number of X chromosomes in the karyotype.

Nuclear pore complexes embedded in the nuclear envelope establish bidirectional communication gates for the trafficking of macromolecules between the cytoplasm and the nucleus. Small molecules (smaller than 40 to 60 kDa) can diffuse through the nuclear pore complex. However, proteins of any size, containing a **nuclear localization amino acid sequence** (Pro-Lys-Lys-Lys-Arg-Lys-Val), can be imported into the nucleus by an energy-dependent mechanism (requiring both ATP and GTP).

Protein nuclear import is mediated by the cytosolic protein complex **importin αβ** (Figure 1–39). The protein with the nuclear localization sequence binds to importin αβ and translocates through the nuclear pore complex. Inside the nucleus, **Ran-GTP** activates the dissociation of the cargo from importin α by binding to importin β. Then, the Ran-GTP–importin β complex is transported to the cytoplasm, where **RanGAP** (Ran-GTPase activating protein) causes hydrolysis of Ran-bound GTP to GDP. Importin β is released in the presence of Ran-GDP.

Chromatin is defined as particles or "beads" (called **nucleosomes**) on a double stranded DNA string (Figure 1–40). Each nucleosome consists of a **histone octamer core** and about two turns of DNA wound around the histone core. The histone octamer contains two molecules each of H2A, H2B, H3, and H4 histones. H1 histone cross-links the DNA molecule wrapped around the octamer.

Chromatin is packed in separate chromosomes that can be visualized during mitosis (or meiosis). During interphase (phases G_1, S, and G_2 of the cell cycle), individual chromosomes cannot be identified as such but are present in a diffuse or noncondensed state.

Diffuse chromatin, called **euchromatin** ("good chromatin"), is transcriptionally (RNA synthesis) active and represents about 10% of total chromatin. Euchromatin is the site of synthesis on **nonribosomal RNAs**, including **mRNA** and **transfer RNA (tRNA)** precursors. **All mature RNA species derive from precursors of larger molecular mass.** Condensed chromatin, called **heterochromatin** ("different chromatin"), is transcriptionally inactive and represents about 90% of total chromatin (Figure 1–41).

Dosage compensation: Inactivation of one of the X chromosomes

The random inactivation of one of the two X chromosomes in every **female somatic** cell is known as **dosage compensation**. **Both X chromosomes in the germinal cell line (oocytes) remain active.** The inactivation is random because either the paternal or the maternal X chromosome is inactivated. The choice remains nonrandom for all subsequent cell descendants. The transcriptional inacti-

Figure 1–42

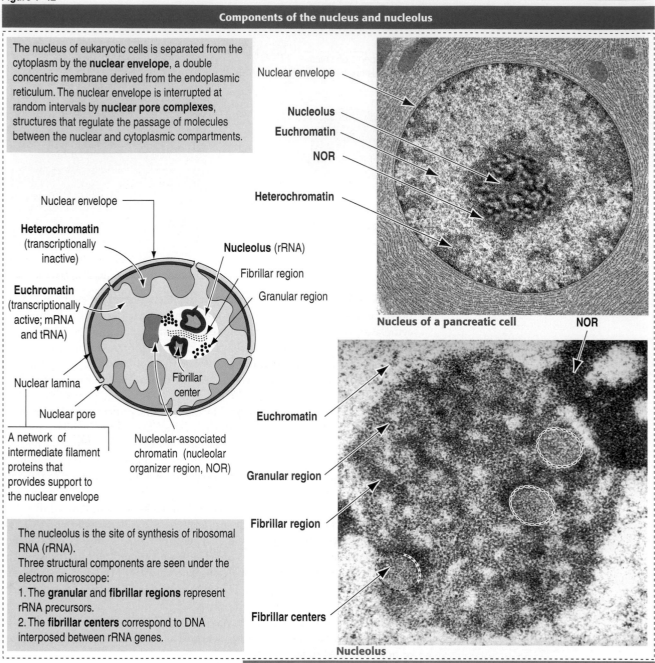

| Components of the nucleus and nucleolus |

The nucleus of eukaryotic cells is separated from the cytoplasm by the **nuclear envelope**, a double concentric membrane derived from the endoplasmic reticulum. The nuclear envelope is interrupted at random intervals by **nuclear pore complexes**, structures that regulate the passage of molecules between the nuclear and cytoplasmic compartments.

Nuclear envelope

Heterochromatin
(transcriptionally inactive)

Euchromatin
(transcriptionally active; mRNA and tRNA)

Nucleolus (rRNA)

Fibrillar region

Granular region

Nuclear lamina

Fibrillar center

Nuclear pore

A network of intermediate filament proteins that provides support to the nuclear envelope

Nucleolar-associated chromatin (nucleolar organizer region, NOR)

The nucleolus is the site of synthesis of ribosomal RNA (rRNA).
Three structural components are seen under the electron microscope:
1. The **granular** and **fibrillar regions** represent rRNA precursors.
2. The **fibrillar centers** correspond to DNA interposed between rRNA genes.

Nuclear envelope

Nucleolus
Euchromatin

NOR

Heterochromatin

Nucleus of a pancreatic cell   **NOR**

Euchromatin

Granular region

Fibrillar region

Fibrillar centers

Nucleolus

vation of one of the two X chromosomes is observed in the trophoblast on day 12 after fertilization and on day 16 in the embryo.

In humans, the inactivated X chromosome is recognized by the presence of the **Barr body**, a heterochromatin mass observed adjacent to the nuclear envelope or in the form of a **drumstick** in polymorphonuclear leukocytes (see Figure 1–41). If a cell has more than two X chromosomes, the extra chromosomes X are inactivated and more than one Barr body is visualized.

The nucleolus

The **nucleolus** is the site of synthesis of **ribosomal RNA (rRNA)**. The nucleolus is a large spherical intranuclear structure consisting of three major structural components (Figure 1–42):

1. A **fibrillar center** (corresponding to chromatin).

Figure 1–43

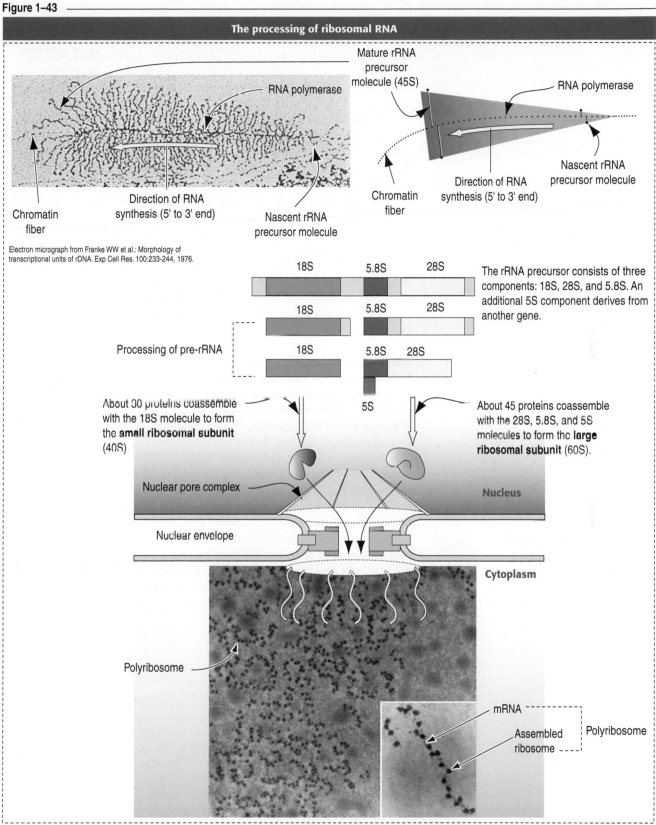

The processing of ribosomal RNA

Mature rRNA
precursor
molecule (45S)

RNA polymerase

RNA polymerase

Direction of RNA
synthesis (5' to 3' end)

Nascent rRNA
precursor molecule

Chromatin
fiber

Chromatin
fiber

Direction of RNA
synthesis (5' to 3' end)

Nascent rRNA
precursor molecule

Electron micrograph from Franke WW et al.: Morphology of
transcriptional units of rDNA. Exp Cell Res. 100:233-244, 1976.

18S   5.8S   28S

The rRNA precursor consists of three
components: 18S, 28S, and 5.8S. An
additional 5S component derives from
another gene.

18S   5.8S   28S

Processing of pre-rRNA

18S   5.8S   28S

About 30 proteins coassemble
with the 18S molecule to form
the **small ribosomal subunit**
(40S)

5S

About 45 proteins coassemble
with the 28S, 5.8S, and 5S
molecules to form the **large
ribosomal subunit** (60S).

Nuclear pore complex

Nucleus

Nuclear envelope

Cytoplasm

Polyribosome

mRNA

Assembled
ribosome

Polyribosome

2. Dense **fibrils** (corresponding to ribonucleoproteins).

3. **Granules** (representing precursors of rRNA-containing ribonucleoproteins).
The nucleolus dissociates during mitosis, then reappears at the beginning of

the G_1 phase. More than one nucleolar mass, each representing the product of a chromosome with a **nucleolar organizing region** (**NOR**), can be observed in the nucleus. However, in some cells with an extended interphase, like neurons, a single large nucleolus is organized by the fusion of several nucleolar masses.

The active process of rRNA synthesis can be visualized at the electron microscopic level (Figure 1–43) by spreading the contents of nuclei of cells with hundreds of nucleoli (for example, amphibian oocytes).

rRNA genes can be seen as repeating **gene units** along the chromatin axis, like "Christmas trees," pointing in the same direction and separated by nontranscribed **spacers**. The entire rRNA gene region is covered by more than 100 **RNA polymerase I** molecules synthesizing an equivalent number of **fibrils**, each with a terminal **granule**.

Each fibril represents an rRNA precursor (45S) ribonucleoprotein molecule oriented perpendicularly to the chromatin axis like the branches of the tree. The **45S rRNA** precursor is detached from chromatin axis and cleaved into **28S, 18S, and 5.8S rRNAs.**

The 18S rRNA and associated proteins form the **small ribosomal subunit.** Both the 28S and 5.8S, together with 5S rRNA made outside the nucleolus, and associated proteins form the **large ribosomal subunit.** Recall that the mRNA precursor is transcribed by RNA polymerase II and the tRNA precursor by RNA polymerase III.

Localization of nucleic acids

Cytochemistry and **autoradiography** (Figure 1–44) provide information about the cellular distribution and synthesis of nucleic acids, respectively. The **Feulgen reaction is specific for the localization of DNA.** Basic dyes, such as toluidine blue, stain both DNA and RNA. Pretreatment with deoxyribonuclease (DNAse) and ribonuclease (RNAse) defines the distribution sites of DNA and RNA by selective removal of one of the nucleic acids.

Autoradiography and **radiolabeled precursors** for one of the nucleic acids can determine the timing of their synthesis. In this technique, a radioactive precursor of DNA ([³H]thymidine) or RNA ([³H]uridine) is exposed to living cells. As a result of exposure to the radiolabel, any synthesized DNA or RNA will contain the precursor. The radioactivity is detected by coating the cells with a thin layer of a photographic emulsion. Silver-containing crystals of the emulsion are exposed to structures of the cell containing radioactive DNA or RNA. After development of the emulsion, silver grains indicate the location of the labeled structures. This approach has been used extensively for determining the duration of the several phases of the cell cycle.

The cell cycle

The cell cycle is defined as **the interval between two successive mitotic divisions resulting in the production of two daughter cells** (Figure 1–45). The cell cycle is traditionally divided into two major phases: 1. **interphase**, and 2. **mitosis** (also known as the **M phase**).

The most relevant event of interphase is the **S phase**, when the DNA in the nucleus is replicated. S phase is preceded by an interval or **gap** called the G_1 **phase.** The beginning of mitosis is preceded by the G_2 **phase**, a phase in which the cell makes sure that DNA replication is completed before starting the M phase. Essentially, G_1 and G_2 phases provide time for cell growth before and after DNA synthesis. Cell growth is required for doubling the cell mass in preparation for cell division.

Cells in G_1 can either make a commitment to DNA replication and enter the S phase or stop their progression into the following S phase. If a cell does not enter the S phase, it remains in a **resting state** known as G_0 (G zero), where it can remain for days, months, or years before reentering the cell cycle.

Figure 1–44

Feulgen reaction

1 **Hydrolysis with hydrochloric acid** forms aldehyde groups on deoxyribose (DNA sugar) but not ribose (RNA sugar).

2 DNA-containing chromatin stains purple because aldehyde groups reacting with the colorless **Schiff's reagent** yield a **purple product**.

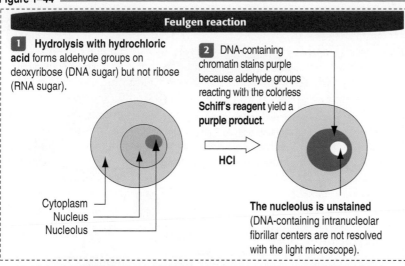

HCl

Cytoplasm
Nucleus
Nucleolus

The nucleolus is unstained (DNA-containing intranucleolar fibrillar centers are not resolved with the light microscope).

Basophilia

1 **Toluidine blue**, a basic dye, binds to the negatively charged phosphate groups on DNA and RNA. Therefore, chromatin (DNA), the nucleolus (RNA), and ribosomes attached to the endoplasmic reticulum (RNA) stain blue. These structures are **basophilic**.

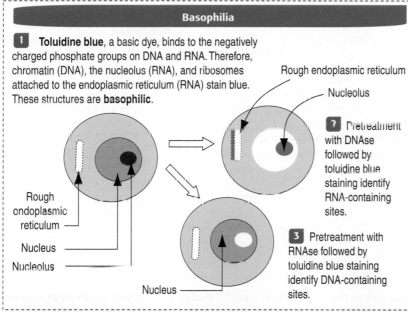

Rough endoplasmic reticulum

Nucleolus

? Pretreatment with DNAse followed by toluidine blue staining identify RNA-containing sites.

Rough endoplasmic reticulum
Nucleus
Nucleolus

Nucleus

3 Pretreatment with RNAse followed by toluidine blue staining identify DNA-containing sites.

Autoradiography

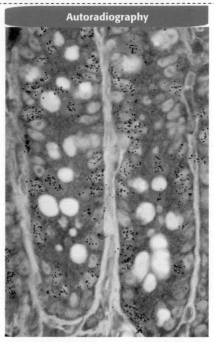

This autoradiogram illustrates the uptake of [^{3}H]thymidine by nuclei of intestinal epithelial cells (duodenum).

The radiolabeled precursor was injected into an experimental animal which was sacrificed 24 hours later.

Histologic sections were coated with a photographic emulsion and exposed in the dark for 48 hours. Development of the photographic emulsion followed by staining of the section reveals the localization of silver grain on some nuclei that were passing through the S phase (DNA synthesis) of their cell cycle.

Feulgen reaction

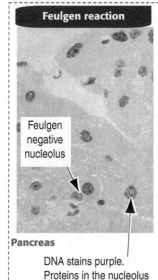

Feulgen negative nucleolus

Pancreas

DNA stains purple. Proteins in the nucleolus are stained green.

PAS reaction

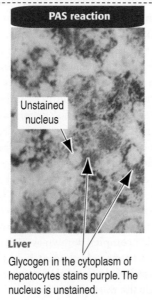

Unstained nucleus

Liver

Glycogen in the cytoplasm of hepatocytes stains purple. The nucleus is unstained.

Basophilia

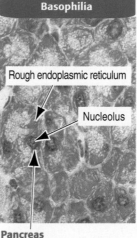

Rough endoplasmic reticulum

Nucleolus

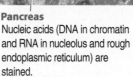

Pancreas
Nucleic acids (DNA in chromatin and RNA in nucleolus and rough endoplasmic reticulum) are stained.

Basophilia after RNAse

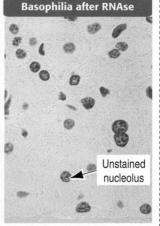

Unstained nucleolus

Pancreas
After RNAse treatment, only chromatin stains. Nucleoli and rough endoplasmic reticulum are not stained.

Figure 1–45

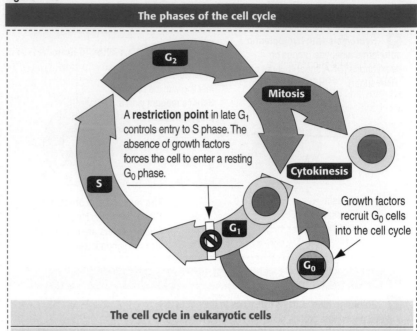

The phases of the cell cycle

G₂

Mitosis

A **restriction point** in late G₁ controls entry to S phase. The absence of growth factors forces the cell to enter a resting G₀ phase.

Cytokinesis

S

Growth factors recruit G₀ cells into the cell cycle

G₁

G₀

The cell cycle in eukaryotic cells

The cell cycle is divided into **four phases**: G₁ (gap 1), S, G₂ (gap 2), and mitosis. Mitosis is followed in most cases by cytokinesis. DNA replication occurs during the S phase and can be detected by **autoradiography** using [³H]thymidine as a precursor.

The **duration of the phases of the cell cycle** is variable. The mitotic phase is the shortest (about 1 hour for a total cycle time of 24 hours). The G₁ phase is the longest (about 11 hours). The S phase is completed within 8 hours, G₂ in about 4 hours.

Some cells stop cell division or divide occasionally to replace cells lost by injury or cell death. These cells leave the G₁ phase of the cell cycle and become quiescent by entering the so-called **G₀ phase**. Although G₀ cells are metabolically active, they have lost their proliferation potential unless appropriate extracellular signals enable their reentry to the cell cycle.

Control of the cell cycle by cyclins and cyclin-dependent protein kinases

Two type of proteins regulate the cell cycle: **cyclins** and **cyclin-dependent protein kinases**. Cyclins bind to **cyclin-dependent protein kinases** (identified first in yeast and designated **Cdc2** for **cell division cycle**), which then phosphorylate selected proteins. The cyclic assembly, activation, and disassembly of the cyclin-Cdc2 complex drive the cell cycle to completion.

Phosphorylation of Cdc2 is critical for its protein kinase activity. In its unphosphorylated state, Cdc2 —bound or unbound to cyclin— does not have kinase activity. When phosphorylation occurs, a conformational change of Cdc2 enables either interaction or activation of the already bound cyclin partner. This interaction exposes the **substrate binding surface** of the Cdc2-cyclin complex, resulting in a significant increase in the binding affinity of the complex for protein substrates. Figure 1–45 provides additional details on how the phosphorylation and dephosphorylation of specific amino acids regulate the activity of the cyclin B-Cdc2 complex during the cell cycle.

Two cyclin-Cdc2 complexes are important to remember (Figure 1–46):

1. A **G₁ cyclin-Cdc2 complex** (known as **start kinase**), which triggers cell entry into the S phase after passing **checkpoint 1**, just before the S phase.

2. A **mitotic cyclin B-Cdc2 complex** (known as **M-phase promoting factor, MPF**), formed gradually during the G₂ phase to activate distinct substrates to initiate mitosis, after forcing the cell to pass through **checkpoint 2**, just before

Figure 1–46

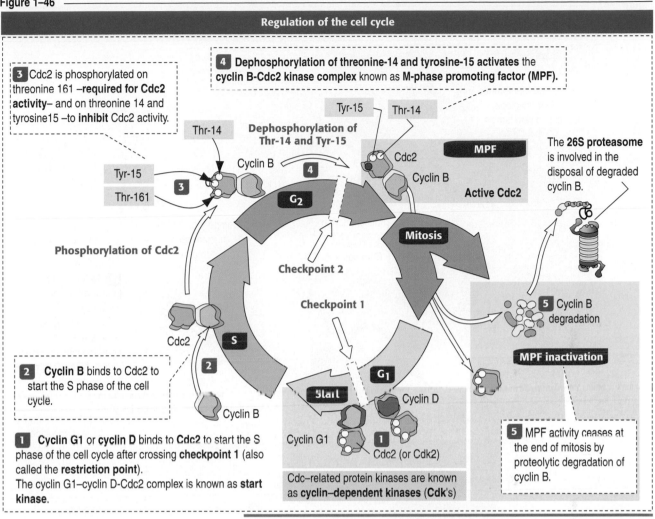

Regulation of the cell cycle

3 Cdc2 is phosphorylated on threonine 161 –**required for Cdc2 activity**– and on threonine 14 and tyrosine15 –to **inhibit** Cdc2 activity.

4 **Dephosphorylation of threonine-14 and tyrosine-15 activates** the **cyclin B-Cdc2 kinase complex** known as **M-phase promoting factor (MPF).**

Tyr-15 Thr-14

Thr-14

Dephosphorylation of Thr-14 and Tyr-15

Cyclin B

4

Cdc2

MPF

Tyr-15

Cyclin B

Active Cdc2

The **26S proteasome** is involved in the disposal of degraded cyclin B.

Thr-161

3

G₂

Mitosis

Phosphorylation of Cdc2

Checkpoint 2

Checkpoint 1

Cdc2

S

2

2 **Cyclin B** binds to Cdc2 to start the S phase of the cell cycle.

Cyclin B

5 Cyclin B degradation

MPF inactivation

Start

G₁

Cyclin G1

1

Cyclin D

1 **Cyclin G1** or **cyclin D** binds to **Cdc2** to start the S phase of the cell cycle after crossing **checkpoint 1** (also called the **restriction point**). The cyclin G1–cyclin D-Cdc2 complex is known as **start kinase.**

Cdc2 (or Cdk2)

Cdc–related protein kinases are known as **cyclin–dependent kinases (Cdk's)**

5 MPF activity ceases at the end of mitosis by proteolytic degradation of cyclin B.

mitosis.

Analysis of the dynamics of the cell cycle: Autoradiography and FACS

The various phases of the cell cycle can be studied by autoradiography. Cells in the S phase can be recognized by detecting the synthesis of DNA using [³H]thymidine as a radiolabeled precursor. Cells can be stained through the developed emulsion layer to determine the precise localization sites of the overlapping silver grains.

The time progression of cells through the different phases of the cell cycle can be estimated using both brief and prolonged [³H]thymidine pulses. The number of cells radiolabeled during interphase (generally about 30%), represent the **labeling index** of the S phase. The fraction of radiolabeled cells seen in mitosis (**mitotic index**) indicates that the radiolabeled precursor, which entered the cell during the S phase, progressed through the G_2 phase into M phase.

An alternative to autoradiography is the measurement of **DNA content (C value:** 1.5 pg per haploid cell) using a **fluorescence-activated cell sorter (FACS).** Cells are stained with a fluorescent dye, which binds to DNA. The amount of fluorescence detected by the FACS is equivalent to the amount of DNA in each cell (for example, 2C in G_1; 4C at the end of S phase; 4C during G_2).

Breakdown and reassembly of the nuclear envelope

The disassembly of the nuclear envelope occurs at the end of the mitotic and meiotic prophase. It involves the fragmentation of the nuclear envelope into

Figure 1–47

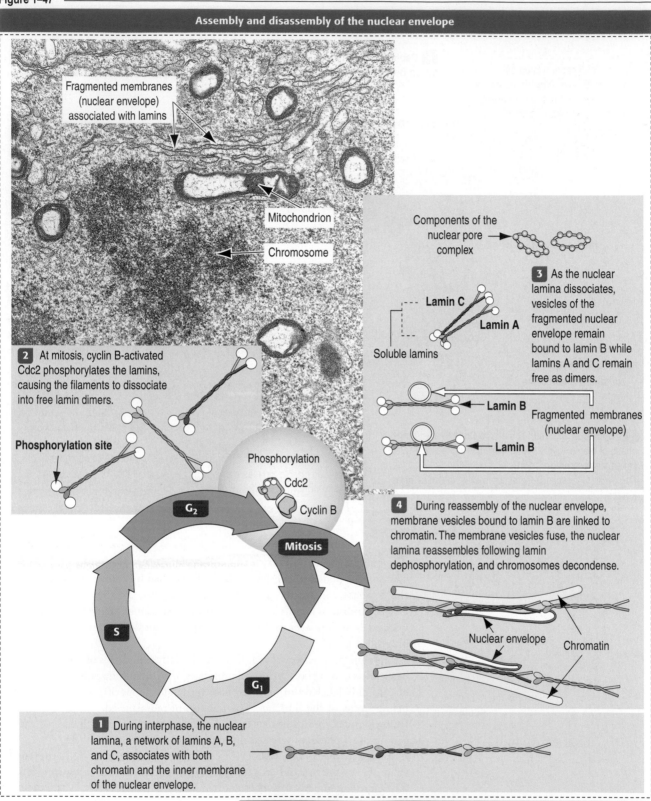

Assembly and disassembly of the nuclear envelope

Fragmented membranes (nuclear envelope) associated with lamins

Mitochondrion

Chromosome

Components of the nuclear pore complex

3 As the nuclear lamina dissociates, vesicles of the fragmented nuclear envelope remain bound to lamin B while lamins A and C remain free as dimers.

Lamin C

Lamin A

Soluble lamins

Lamin B

Lamin B

Fragmented membranes (nuclear envelope)

2 At mitosis, cyclin B-activated Cdc2 phosphorylates the lamins, causing the filaments to dissociate into free lamin dimers.

Phosphorylation site

Phosphorylation

Cdc2

Cyclin B

G$_2$

Mitosis

S

G$_1$

4 During reassembly of the nuclear envelope, membrane vesicles bound to lamin B are linked to chromatin. The membrane vesicles fuse, the nuclear lamina reassembles following lamin dephosphorylation, and chromosomes decondense.

Nuclear envelope

Chromatin

1 During interphase, the nuclear lamina, a network of lamins A, B, and C, associates with both chromatin and the inner membrane of the nuclear envelope.

vesicles, the dissociation of the nuclear pore complexes, and the depolymerization of the nuclear lamina (Figure 1–47).

The nuclear lamina is composed of fibrous proteins, **lamins**, which associate with each other to form a filamentous lamina. **Phosphorylation** of lamins — catalyzed by Cdc2 protein kinase— results in the disassembly of the nuclear lamina.

Lamin B remains associated with nuclear envelope fragmented vesicles. **Lamins A** and **C** dissociate from the nuclear envelope and remain as free soluble dimers in the cytosol.

The reassembly of the nuclear envelope starts with the binding of nuclear envelope vesicles to chromosomes mediated by **dephosphorylated** lamin B. The vesicles then fuse, the nuclear lamina and nuclear pore complexes reassemble, and chromosomes decondense.

Tumor suppressor genes

Tissues use two strategies to restrict cell proliferation:

1. By limiting mitogenic factors, such as platelet-derived growth factor (PDGF) and fibroblast growth factor (FGF), that **stimulate cell growth**.

2. By regulatory genes that actively **suppress proliferation**. These genes, called **suppressor genes**, control normal cell proliferation.

The **retinoblastoma model** provides important clues on how suppressor genes work (Figure 1–48). Each cell has duplicate copies of the **retinoblastoma (Rb) gene** as a safety backup. When the **two copies** of the **Rb** gene are mutated, an abnormal **Rb protein** induces cancerous growth of retinal cells.

When a single copy of the Rb gene pair is mutated, the remaining Rb gene copy functions normally and suppresses unregulated cell proliferation unless a second mutation occurs. In children with only a single intact Rb gene copy, all cells of the developing embryo grow normally. Late in gestation, during the development of the eye and its retina, retinal cells may lose the normal copy of the Rb gene and a retinoblastoma develops.

The Rb gene specifies a **nuclear protein** involved in regulating the activity of a group of proteins —**transcription factors**— involved in DNA synthesis and cell cycle progression. When Rb protein is **dephosphorylated**, it binds to transcription factors. Although the Rb protein–transcription factor complex can bind to target genes, the activity of the transcription factors is repressed.

However, when Rb protein is **phosphorylated** by the **cyclic–dependent kinase (Cdk4)–cyclin D** complex, it dissociates from the transcription factor complex, which then activates specific gene expression (Figure 1–49). Therefore, phosphorylated Rb protein switches transcription factors from suppression to activa-

Figure 1–48

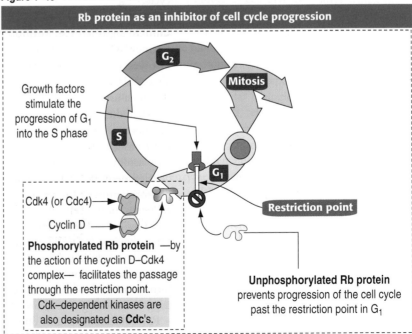

Rb protein as an inhibitor of cell cycle progression

G₂

Mitosis

Growth factors stimulate the progression of G₁ into the S phase

S

G₁

Restriction point

Cdk4 (or Cdc4)

Cyclin D

Phosphorylated Rb protein —by the action of the cyclin D–Cdk4 complex— facilitates the passage through the restriction point.

Cdk–dependent kinases are also designated as **Cdc's**.

Unphosphorylated Rb protein prevents progression of the cell cycle past the restriction point in G₁

Figure 1–50

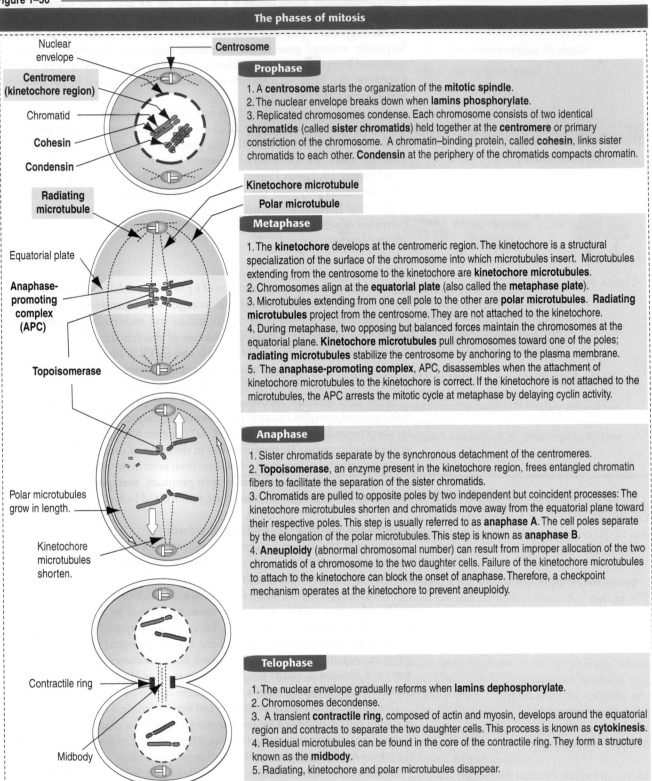

The phases of mitosis

Prophase

1. A **centrosome** starts the organization of the **mitotic spindle**.
2. The nuclear envelope breaks down when **lamins phosphorylate**.
3. Replicated chromosomes condense. Each chromosome consists of two identical **chromatids** (called **sister chromatids**) held together at the **centromere** or primary constriction of the chromosome. A chromatin–binding protein, called **cohesin**, links sister chromatids to each other. **Condensin** at the periphery of the chromatids compacts chromatin.

Metaphase

1. The **kinetochore** develops at the centromeric region. The kinetochore is a structural specialization of the surface of the chromosome into which microtubules insert. Microtubules extending from the centrosome to the kinetochore are **kinetochore microtubules**.
2. Chromosomes align at the **equatorial plate** (also called the **metaphase plate**).
3. Microtubules extending from one cell pole to the other are **polar microtubules**. **Radiating microtubules** project from the centrosome. They are not attached to the kinetochore.
4. During metaphase, two opposing but balanced forces maintain the chromosomes at the equatorial plane. **Kinetochore microtubules** pull chromosomes toward one of the poles; **radiating microtubules** stabilize the centrosome by anchoring to the plasma membrane.
5. The **anaphase-promoting complex**, APC, disassembles when the attachment of kinetochore microtubules to the kinetochore is correct. If the kinetochore is not attached to the microtubules, the APC arrests the mitotic cycle at metaphase by delaying cyclin activity.

Anaphase

1. Sister chromatids separate by the synchronous detachment of the centromeres.
2. **Topoisomerase**, an enzyme present in the kinetochore region, frees entangled chromatin fibers to facilitate the separation of the sister chromatids.
3. Chromatids are pulled to opposite poles by two independent but coincident processes: The kinetochore microtubules shorten and chromatids move away from the equatorial plane toward their respective poles. This step is usually referred to as **anaphase A**. The cell poles separate by the elongation of the polar microtubules. This step is known as **anaphase B**.
4. **Aneuploidy** (abnormal chromosomal number) can result from improper allocation of the two chromatids of a chromosome to the two daughter cells. Failure of the kinetochore microtubules to attach to the kinetochore can block the onset of anaphase. Therefore, a checkpoint mechanism operates at the kinetochore to prevent aneuploidy.

Telophase

1. The nuclear envelope gradually reforms when **lamins dephosphorylate**.
2. Chromosomes decondense.
3. A transient **contractile ring**, composed of actin and myosin, develops around the equatorial region and contracts to separate the two daughter cells. This process is known as **cytokinesis**.
4. Residual microtubules can be found in the core of the contractile ring. They form a structure known as the **midbody**.
5. Radiating, kinetochore and polar microtubules disappear.

1. Chemically cross-link DNA (alkylating agents).
2. Inhibit enzymes required for DNA synthesis (nucleotide analogues).
3. Affect microtubules of the mitotic spindle (taxol, vinblastine, see The cytoskeleton). These agents are usually administered in combination, during short periods or continuously, depending on the sensitivity of the type of tumor and

Figure 1–51

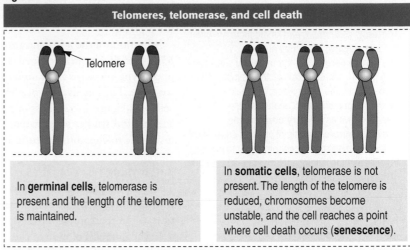

Telomeres, telomerase, and cell death

In **germinal cells**, telomerase is present and the length of the telomere is maintained.

In **somatic cells**, telomerase is not present. The length of the telomere is reduced, chromosomes become unstable, and the cell reaches a point where cell death occurs (**senescence**).

avoiding toxic effects on the highly sensitive organs such as the bone marrow, the intestinal epithelium, the kidneys, and the nervous system.

Resistance of tumors to chemotherapeutic agents may be:

1. **Intrinsic resistance** (tumors typically refractory to many agents —melanoma, liver cancer, renal cell carcinoma).

2. **Acquired resistance** (tumors becoming resistant to chemotherapy, after initial sensitivity).

One form of acquired resistance is caused by genes of the **multidrug-resistance (*mdr*) gene family** (Figure 1–52). These genes encode ATP dependent pumps involved in the transport of large organic compounds. We will see again the *mdr* gene family of proteins in Chapter 17, Digestive Glands, when we discuss the mechanism of bile secretion by hepatocytes.

The most studied gene involved in resistance to cancer chemotherapy is *mdr-1*. Repeated exposure to certain chemotherapeutic agents correlates with overexpression of *mdr-1* and increased export of antitumoral agents once they enter the tumor cell.

DNA damage induced by chemotherapy and radiotherapy triggers the activation of **p53**, a transcription factor tetramer that destroys terminally damaged cells through the activation of a cell death program, or **apoptosis**. The effects of

Figure 1–52

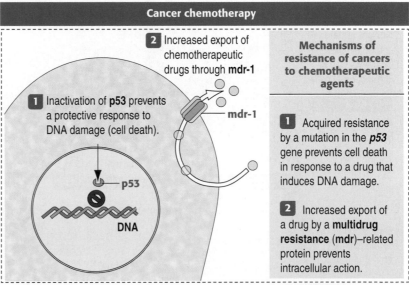

Cancer chemotherapy

2 Increased export of chemotherapeutic drugs through **mdr-1**

1 Inactivation of **p53** prevents a protective response to DNA damage (cell death).

mdr-1

p53

DNA

Mechanisms of resistance of cancers to chemotherapeutic agents

1 Acquired resistance by a mutation in the *p53* gene prevents cell death in response to a drug that induces DNA damage.

2 Increased export of a drug by a **multidrug resistance (mdr)**–related protein prevents intracellular action.

Centromere and kinetochore

The terms centromere and kinetochore are often used as synonyms but they are not.

The **centromere** is the chromosomal site associated with microtubules of the spindle. Centromeres can be recognized cytologically as a narrow chromatin region on metaphase chromosomes known as **primary constriction**.

The **kinetochore** consists of proteins assembled on the chromatin of the centromere. Both the centromere and the kinetochore mediate attachment of the microtubular spindle.

p53 are mediated by **p21**, an inhibitor of Cdk4. Activation of *p53* leads to arrest of the cell cycle at G₁, enabling cells to repair DNA damage before proceeding to the S phase.

Mutations of the *p53* gene are observed in 50% of human cancers. The loss of *p53* expression by an autosomal dominant mutation is responsible for a multicancer phenotype known as **Li-Fraumeni syndrome**. Therefore, *p53* **is a tumor suppressor gene**. The inactivation of *p53* expression is disrupted in drug-resistant cancer cells (see Figure 1–52). Loss of *p53* expression is observed in human cancer cells and clinical studies suggest that inactivation of *p53* expression correlates with resistance to chemotherapeutic agents.

Karyotyping

There are **22 pairs of autosomes** and **one pair of sex chromosomes (XX or XY) in the human**. Chromosomes can be classified according to the length and position of the centromere into seven groups, identified by the letters A to G.

In the notation of human cytogenetics, the total number of chromosomes (46) is followed by the total number of sex chromosomes (Figure 1–53). For example, a **normal male** is identified as **46,XY** (46 chromosomes, including the XY chromosomal pair) and the female as **46,XX** (46 chromosomes, including the XX chromosomal pair). **Extra autosomes are indicated by placing the number of the extra chromosomes after the sex chromosomes with a plus (+) sign.** For example, **47,XX+21** is the karyotype of a female with trisomy 21 (**Down syndrome**). A male with an extra X chromosome is symbolized as **47,XXY**. A plus or minus sign is placed following a chromosome symbol to indicate the increase or decrease in arm length. The letter **p** symbolizes the **short arm** and **q** the **long arm**. For example, **47,XY,+17p+** identifies a male with 47 chromosomes, including an additional chromosome 17, with an increase in the length of its short arm.

Figure 1–53

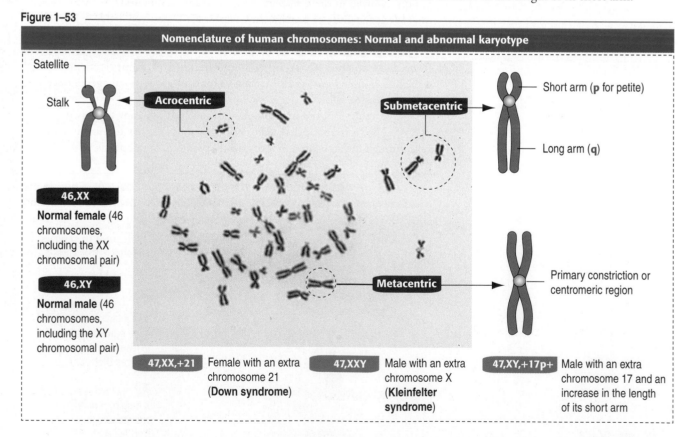

Nomenclature of human chromosomes: Normal and abnormal karyotype

Satellite

Stalk

Acrocentric

46,XX

Normal female (46 chromosomes, including the XX chromosomal pair)

46,XY

Normal male (46 chromosomes, including the XY chromosomal pair)

Submetacentric

Short arm (**p** for petite)

Long arm (**q**)

Metacentric

Primary constriction or centromeric region

47,XX,+21 Female with an extra chromosome 21 (**Down syndrome**)

47,XXY Male with an extra chromosome X (**Kleinfelter syndrome**)

47,XY,+17p+ Male with an extra chromosome 17 and an increase in the length of its short arm

2. EPITHELIAL GLANDS

Development of epithelial glands

Most glands develop as epithelial outgrowths into the underlying connective tissue (Figure 2–1). **Exocrine glands** remain connected to the surface of the epithelium by an excretory duct that transports the secretory product to the outside. **Endocrine glands lack an excretory duct**, and their product is released into the blood circulation.

Figure 2–1

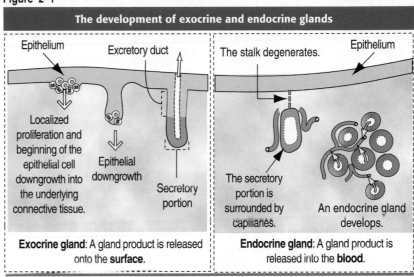

The development of exocrine and endocrine glands

Epithelium • Excretory duct

Localized proliferation and beginning of the epithelial cell downgrowth into the underlying connective tissue.

Epithelial downgrowth

Secretory portion

Exocrine gland: A gland product is released onto the **surface**.

The stalk degenerates. • Epithelium

The secretory portion is surrounded by capillaries.

An endocrine gland develops.

Endocrine gland: A gland product is released into the **blood**.

Typically, endocrine glands are surrounded by fenestrated capillaries and commonly store the secretions they synthesize and release after stimulation by chemical or electrical signals. Exocrine and endocrine glands can be found together (for example, in pancreas), as separate structures in endocrine organs (thyroid, parathyroid), or as single cells (enteroendocrine cells). Endocrine glands will be studied later in Chapter 18, Neuroendocrine System, and Chapter 19, Endocrine System.

Classification of epithelial glands

Glands are classified according to the type of **excretory duct** into **simple** and **compound** classes. The gland can be **simple** (Figure 2–2) when the excretory

Figure 2–2

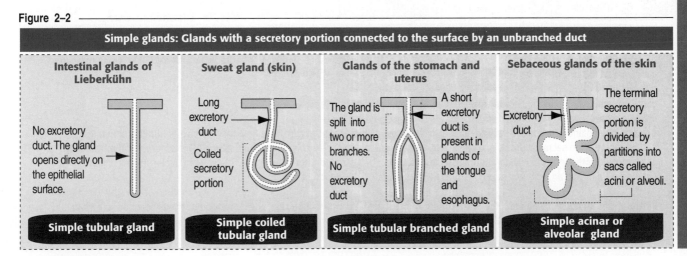

Simple glands: Glands with a secretory portion connected to the surface by an unbranched duct

Intestinal glands of Lieberkühn	Sweat gland (skin)	Glands of the stomach and uterus	Sebaceous glands of the skin
No excretory duct. The gland opens directly on the epithelial surface.	Long excretory duct / Coiled secretory portion	The gland is split into two or more branches. No excretory duct	A short excretory duct is present in glands of the tongue and esophagus.	Excretory duct / The terminal secretory portion is divided by partitions into sacs called acini or alveoli.
Simple tubular gland	**Simple coiled tubular gland**	**Simple tubular branched gland**	**Simple acinar or alveolar gland**

Figure 2–3

Compound glands: Glands with their secretory products draining into a branching duct

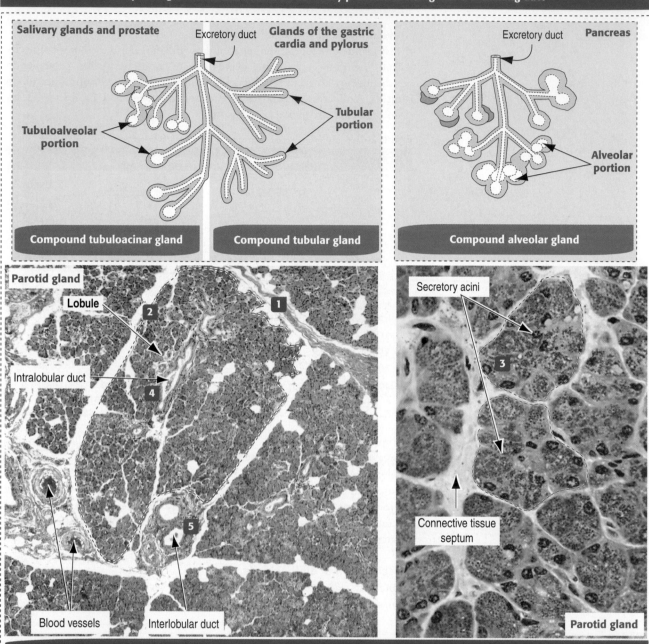

A **compound gland** is surrounded by a connective tissue capsule which sends partitions or **septa 1** inside the gland to organize large units called **lobes** (not shown).

Lobes are subdivided by connective tissue into small subunits called **lobules 2**.

A compound gland consists of a varying number of secretory units classified according to their morphology as **tubular, acinar 3**, or **tubuloacinar**. The secretion drains into an excretory duct located within the lobule (**intralobular duct 4**). Generally, the **intralobular excretory ducts** are formed by an **intercalated duct** followed by a **striated duct** (not shown). The striated duct—present only in salivary glands—drains into an excretory duct continuous with an **intralobular duct** (not shown).

Intralobular ducts combine with other **intralobular ducts** to form an **interlobular duct 5. Interlobular ducts** combine with other **interlobular ducts** to form an **intralobar duct** of larger diameter (not shown). **Intralobar ducts** converge to form a **lobar duct**. See Figure 2–4, and Chapter 17, Digestive Glands, for additional information.

Figure 2–4

Histologic overview of a compound salivary gland

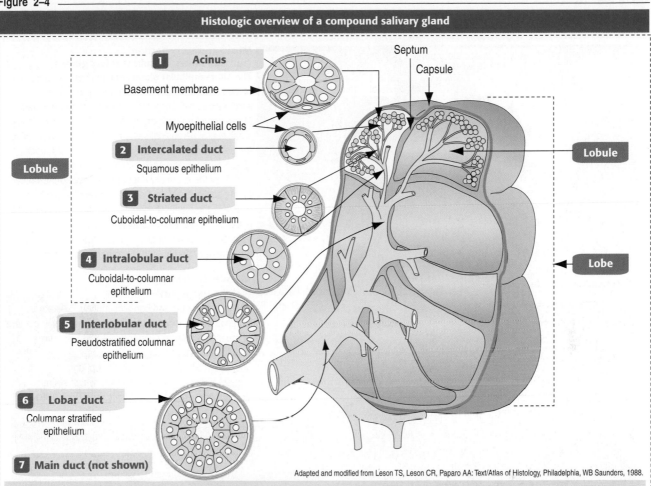

Adapted and modified from Leson TS, Leson CR, Paparo AA: Text/Atlas of Histology, Philadelphia, WB Saunders, 1988.

1 **Acinus**
Basement membrane
Myoepithelial cells
2 **Intercalated duct**
Squamous epithelium
3 **Striated duct**
Cuboidal-to-columnar epithelium
4 **Intralobular duct**
Cuboidal-to-columnar epithelium
5 **Interlobular duct**
Pseudostratified columnar epithelium
6 **Lobar duct**
Columnar stratified epithelium
7 **Main duct (not shown)**

Septum
Capsule
Lobule
Lobe
Lobule

All **compound exocrine glands** contain epithelial components (secretory acini and ducts) called **parenchyma**, and supporting connective tissue, including blood vessels and nerves, the **stroma**.

The gland is enclosed by a connective tissue **capsule** which branches inside the gland forming **septa** (sing. *septum*) that subdivide the parenchyma. In large compound glands, the parenchyma is anatomically subdivided into **lobes**. Adjacent lobes are separated by an **interlobar septum**. A lobe is formed by **lobules**, separated from each other by a thin **interlobular septum**.

Septa support the major branches of the **excretory duct**. **Interlobular ducts** extend along **interlobular septa**; **interlobar ducts** extend along **interlobar septa**. However, **intralobular ducts** lie within lobules and are surrounded by little connective tissue.

Intralobular ducts are lined by a **simple cuboidal-to-columnar epithelium**, whereas the epithelial lining of **interlobular ducts** is pseudostratified columnar. **Lobar ducts** are lined by a **columnar stratified epithelium**.

duct is **unbranched** or **compound** when the excretory duct is **branched** (Figure 2–3). Therefore, glands can be classified as **simple** and **compound according to the branching pattern of the excretory duct**.

The secretory portion can be unicellular or multicellular

An **exocrine gland** has two components: a **secretory portion** and an **excretory duct**. The **secretory portion** of a gland may be composed of one cell type (**unicellular**: for example, **goblet cells** in the respiratory epithelium and intestine) or many cells (**multicellular**).

According to the **shape** of the secretory portion (see Figures 2–2 and 2–3), glands can be **tubular**, **coiled**, or **alveolar** (Lat. *alveolus*, small hollow sac; pl. *alveoli*), also called **acinar** (Lat. *acinus*, grape; pl. *acini*).

Tubular glands are found in the large intestine. The sweat glands of the skin are typical coiled glands. The sebaceous gland of the skin is an example of an alveolar gland.

Figure 2–5

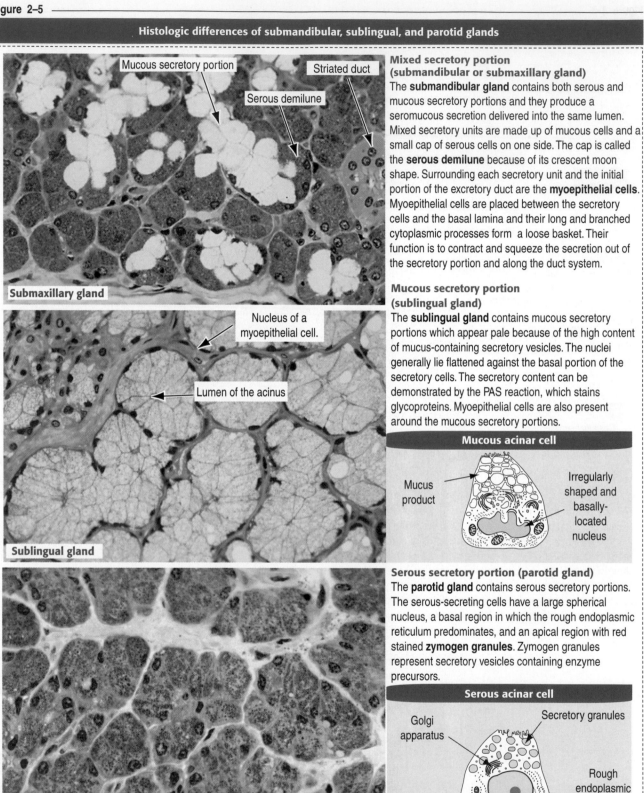

Histologic differences of submandibular, sublingual, and parotid glands

Mucous secretory portion

Striated duct

Serous demilune

Submaxillary gland

Nucleus of a myoepithelial cell.

Lumen of the acinus

Sublingual gland

Parotid gland

Mixed secretory portion (submandibular or submaxillary gland)
The **submandibular gland** contains both serous and mucous secretory portions and they produce a seromucous secretion delivered into the same lumen. Mixed secretory units are made up of mucous cells and a small cap of serous cells on one side. The cap is called the **serous demilune** because of its crescent moon shape. Surrounding each secretory unit and the initial portion of the excretory duct are the **myoepithelial cells**. Myoepithelial cells are placed between the secretory cells and the basal lamina and their long and branched cytoplasmic processes form a loose basket. Their function is to contract and squeeze the secretion out of the secretory portion and along the duct system.

Mucous secretory portion (sublingual gland)
The **sublingual gland** contains mucous secretory portions which appear pale because of the high content of mucus-containing secretory vesicles. The nuclei generally lie flattened against the basal portion of the secretory cells. The secretory content can be demonstrated by the PAS reaction, which stains glycoproteins. Myoepithelial cells are also present around the mucous secretory portions.

Mucous acinar cell

Mucus product

Irregularly shaped and basally-located nucleus

Serous secretory portion (parotid gland)
The **parotid gland** contains serous secretory portions. The serous-secreting cells have a large spherical nucleus, a basal region in which the rough endoplasmic reticulum predominates, and an apical region with red stained **zymogen granules**. Zymogen granules represent secretory vesicles containing enzyme precursors.

Serous acinar cell

Golgi apparatus

Secretory granules

Rough endoplasmic reticulum

The shape of the secretory portion
Glands can be classified as **simple tubular** or **simple alveolar** (or acinar) according to the **shape of the secretory portion**. In addition, tubular and alveolar secre-

Figure 2–6

Mechanisms of glandular secretion

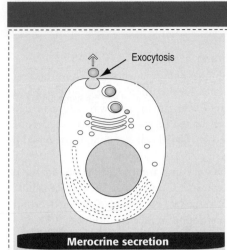

Exocytosis

Merocrine secretion

The secretory vesicle approaches the apical domain of an epithelial cell. The vesicular membrane fuses with the plasma membrane to release its contents into the extracellular space.

The fused plasma membrane can be taken back into the cell by **endocytosis** and recycled for further use by secretory vesicles.

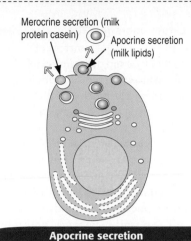

Merocrine secretion (milk protein casein)

Apocrine secretion (milk lipids)

Apocrine secretion

Some of the apical cytoplasm is pinched off with the contained secretions.

Mammary glands secrete milk lipids by apocrine secretion and the milk protein casein by merocrine secretion.

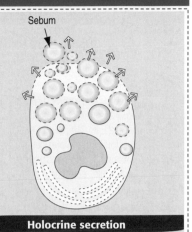

Sebum

Holocrine secretion

The cell produces and accumulates a secretory product in the cytoplasm –such as sebum in sebaceous glands– and then disintegrates to release the secretory material.

tory portions can coexist with branching excretory ducts; the gland is called **a compound tubulo-alveolar** (or acinar) gland (for example, the salivary glands). The mammary gland is an example of a compound alveolar gland.

A compound gland (Figure 2–4) is surrounded by a **capsule. Septa** or **trabeculae** extend from the capsule into the glandular tissue. Large septa divide the gland into a number of **lobes.** Branches from the septa separating adjacent lobes divide the lobes into smaller compartments called **lobules.**

During development, a main excretory duct gives rise to branches that lie either between (**interlobar**) or within lobes (**intralobar**). Small branches derived from each of these ducts generate small subdivisions that constitute the **lobule** of a gland. These branches can be found first between lobules (**interlobular**) and within lobules (**intralobular**). Additional details are presented in Chapter 17, Digestive Glands.

The type of secretion

Based on the type of secretion, exocrine glands can be classified as **mucous glands,** when their products are rich in **glycoproteins** and water; **serous glands,** with secretions enriched with **proteins** and water; and **mixed glands,** which contain both mucous and serous cells (Figure 2–5).

The mechanism of secretion

Exocrine glands can also be classified on the basis of **how the secretory product is released** (Figure 2–6).

In **merocrine secretion**, the product is released by **exocytosis**. Secretory granules are enclosed by a membrane that fuses with the apical plasma membrane during discharge or exocytosis. An example is the secretion of zymogen granules by the pancreas.

In **apocrine secretion**, the release of the secretory product involves **partial loss of the apical portion of the cell.** An example is the secretion of **lipids** by epithelial cells of the mammary gland. **Proteins** secreted by epithelial cells of the mammary gland follow the merocrine pathway (exocytosis).

In **holocrine secretion** (Gk. *holos*, all), the secretory product constitutes **the entire cell and its product**. An example is the sebaceous glands of the skin, which produce a secretion called **sebum**.

Cytomembranes: The plasma membrane

A review of major concepts of cytomembranes and organelles (lysosomes and mitochondria) and their clinical relevance is presented in this chapter. Epithelial glands are a convenient topic for this integration. We initiate the review by addressing the structural and biochemical characteristics of the plasma membrane. Additional information related to plasma membrane–mediated cell signaling is presented in Chapter 3, Cell Signaling.

The **plasma membrane** determines the structural and functional boundaries of a cell. Intracellular membranes, called **cytomembranes**, separate diverse cellular processes into compartments known as **organelles.** For example, the nucleus, mitochondria, and lysosomes are membrane-bound organelles; lipids and glycogen are not membrane-bound and are known as **inclusions**.

The plasma membrane consists of both **lipids** and **proteins**. The phospholipid bilayer is the fundamental structure of the membrane and forms a bilayer barrier between two aqueous compartments: the extracellular and intracellular compartments. Proteins are embedded within the phospholipid bilayer and carry out specific functions of the plasma membrane such as cell-cell recognition and selective transport of molecules.

The phospholipid bilayer

The four major phospholipids of plasma membranes are **phosphatidylcholine, phosphatidylethanolamine, phosphatidylserine**, and **sphingomyelin** (Figure 2–

Figure 2–7

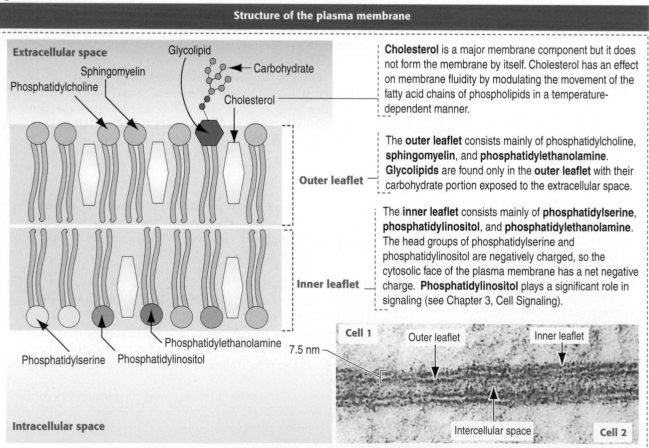

Structure of the plasma membrane

Cholesterol is a major membrane component but it does not form the membrane by itself. Cholesterol has an effect on membrane fluidity by modulating the movement of the fatty acid chains of phospholipids in a temperature-dependent manner.

The **outer leaflet** consists mainly of phosphatidylcholine, **sphingomyelin**, and **phosphatidylethanolamine**. **Glycolipids** are found only in the **outer leaflet** with their carbohydrate portion exposed to the extracellular space.

The **inner leaflet** consists mainly of **phosphatidylserine**, **phosphatidylinositol**, and **phosphatidylethanolamine**. The head groups of phosphatidylserine and phosphatidylinositol are negatively charged, so the cytosolic face of the plasma membrane has a net negative charge. **Phosphatidylinositol** plays a significant role in signaling (see Chapter 3, Cell Signaling).

The glycocalyx

The extracellular domain of a plasma membrane is generally glycosylated by the carbohydrate portions of glycolipids and transmembrane glycoproteins. The surface of the cell is, therefore, covered by a carbohydrate coat, known as the **glycocalyx**.

The glycocalyx protects the cell surface and facilitates cell-cell interactions. An appropriate example is the mechanism of **homing**, a process allowing leukocytes to leave blood vessels and mediate inflammatory responses. As you recall, the initial step in adhesion between endothelial cells and leukocytes is mediated by **selectins**, a family of transmembrane proteins which recognize specific sugars on the cell surface.

7). They represent more than half the lipid of most membranes. A fifth phospholipid, **phosphatidylinositol**, is localized to the inner leaflet of the plasma membrane.

In addition to phospholipids, the plasma membrane of animal cells contains **glycolipids** and **cholesterol**. Glycolipids, a minor membrane component, are found in the outer leaflet, with the carbohydrate moieties exposed on the cell surface.

Cholesterol, a major membrane constituent, is present in about the same amounts as are phospholipids. Cholesterol, a rigid ring structure, does not form a membrane but is inserted into the phospholipid bilayer to modulate membrane fluidity by restricting the movement of phospholipid fatty acid chains at high temperatures.

Cholesterol is not present in bacteria.

Two general aspects of the phospholipid bilayer are important to remember:

1. **The structure of phospholipids accounts for the function of membranes as barriers between two aqueous compartments.** The hydrophobic fatty acid chains in the interior of the phospholipid bilayer are responsible for the membranes being impermeable to water-soluble molecules.

2. **The phospholipid bilayer is a viscous fluid.** The long hydrocarbon chains of the fatty acids of most phospholipids are loosely packed and can move in the interior of the membrane. Therefore, phospholipids and proteins can diffuse laterally within the membrane to perform critical membrane functions.

Membrane proteins

Most plasma membranes consist of about 50% lipid and 50% protein (Figure 2–8). The carbohydrate component of glycolipids and glycoproteins represents 5 to 10% of the membrane mass.

According to the **fluid mosaic model** of the membrane structure, membranes are two-dimensional fluids in which proteins are inserted into lipid bilayers. It is difficult for membrane proteins and phospholipids to switch back and forth between the inner and outer leaflets of the membrane. However, because they exist in a fluid environment, both proteins and lipids are able to diffuse laterally through

Figure 2–8

Peripheral and integral proteins of the plasma membrane

Plasma membrane: Peripheral and integral proteins

Integral membrane proteins are inserted into the lipid bilayer.

Peripheral membrane proteins are linked indirectly to the plasma membrane by protein-protein interactions.

The extracellular portion of integral and peripheral membrane proteins are generally glycosylated. The intracellular portion of membrane proteins are bound to cytoskeletal components.

Most integral membrane proteins are transmembrane proteins spanning the membrane through α-helical regions.

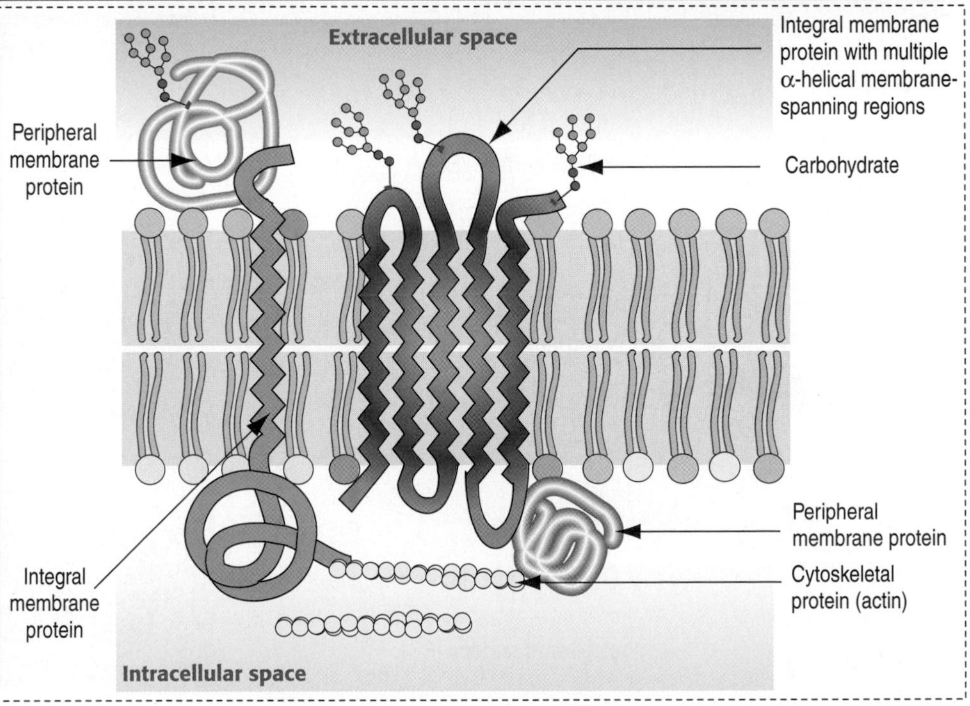

Peripheral membrane protein

Integral membrane protein

Extracellular space

Integral membrane protein with multiple α-helical membrane-spanning regions

Carbohydrate

Peripheral membrane protein

Cytoskeletal protein (actin)

Intracellular space

the plane of the membrane. However, not all proteins can diffuse freely; the mobility of membrane proteins is limited by their association with the cytoskeleton.

Restrictions in the mobility of membrane proteins are responsible for the polarized nature of epithelial cells, divided into distinct **apical** and **basolateral domains** that differ in protein composition and function. Occluding or tight junctions between adjacent epithelial cells (discussed earlier in Chapter 1, Epithelium) not only seal the space between cells but also serve as barriers to the diffusion of proteins and lipids between the apical and basolateral domains.

Two major classes of membrane-associated proteins are recognized: **peripheral proteins** and **integral membrane proteins**.

Peripheral membrane proteins are not inserted into the hydrophobic interior of the membrane but are, instead, indirectly associated with membranes through protein-protein ionic bond interactions which are disrupted by solutions of **high salt concentration** or **extreme pH**.

Portions of integral membrane proteins are inserted into the lipid bilayer. They can only be released by solubilization using **detergents**. Detergents are chemical agents that contain both hydrophobic and hydrophilic groups. The **hydrophobic domains** of the detergent penetrate the membrane lipids and bind to the membrane-inserted hydrophobic portion of the protein. The **hydrophilic domains** combine with the protein, forming aqueous-soluble detergent-protein complexes.

Many integral proteins are **transmembrane proteins**, spanning the lipid bilayer, with segments exposed on both sides of the membrane. Transmembrane proteins can be visualized by the **freeze-fracture technique**.

Difference between a surface and a face in freeze-fracturing

The **freeze-fracture technique** is valuable for the visualization of intramembranous proteins with the electron microscope. This technique provided the first evidence for the presence of transmembrane proteins in the plasma membrane and cytomembranes.

The following diagram indicates the nomenclature for the identification of surfaces and faces in electron micrographs of freeze-fracture preparations.

Figure 2–9

Freeze-fracturing: Difference between surface and face

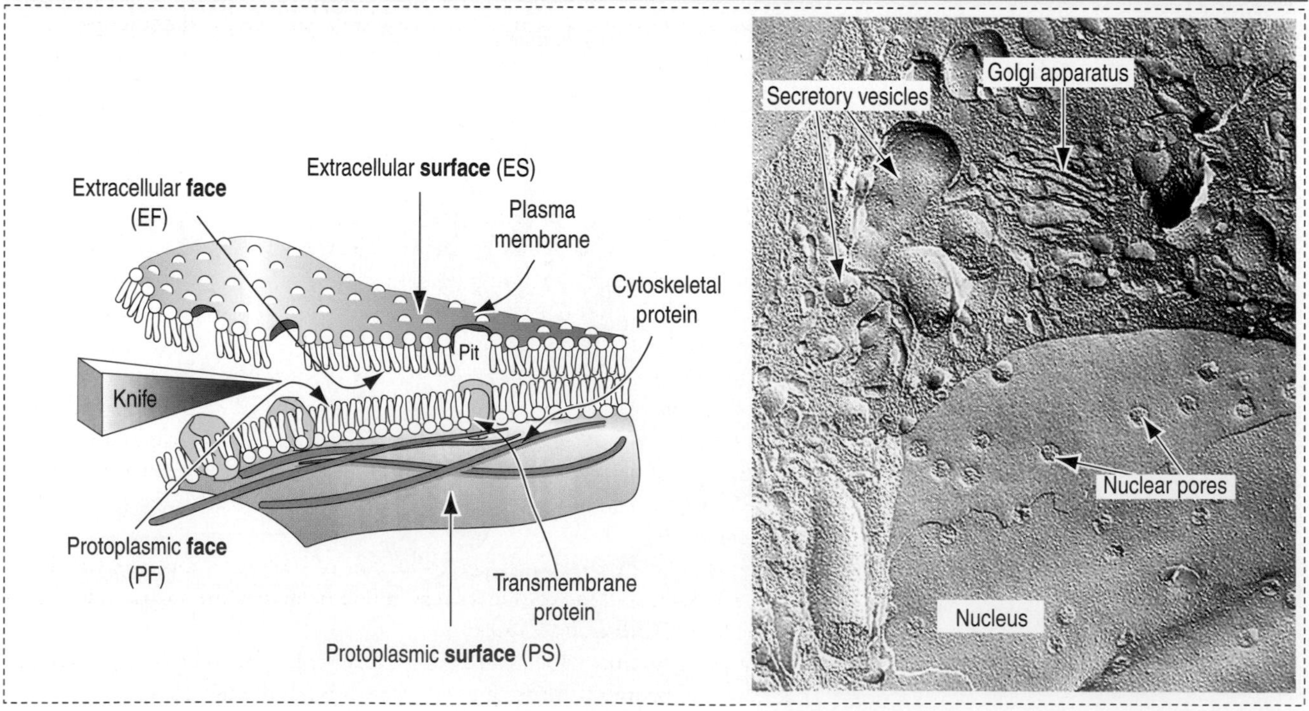

Figure 2–10

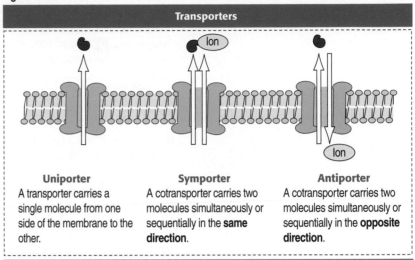

Transporters

Uniporter
A transporter carries a single molecule from one side of the membrane to the other.

Symporter
A cotransporter carries two molecules simultaneously or sequentially in the **same direction**.

Antiporter
A cotransporter carries two molecules simultaneously or sequentially in the **opposite direction**.

You should distinguish the difference between a **surface** and a **face** (Figure 2–9): Surface is a real physiologic component of a membrane. A face is artificially created by freeze-fracturing of the membrane through its hydrophobic core.

The **surface** of the plasma membrane exposed to the **extracellular space** is labeled **ES**, for **extracellular surface**. The surface of the plasma membrane exposed to the **cytoplasm** (also called protoplasm) is labeled **PS**, for **protoplasmic surface**.

The face of the membrane leaflet looking to the **extracellular space** (the exocytoplasmic leaflet in the illustration) is labeled **EF**, for **extracellular face**. Similarly, the face of the leaflet facing the **protoplasmic space** (identified as a protoplasmic leaflet) is **PF**, for **protoplasmic face**.

Now that we have an understanding of what surface and face represent, remember that **faces** are chemically **hydrophobic** and **surfaces** are chemically **hydrophilic**. One last point: Note that a transmembrane protein stays with the protoplasmic leaflet, leaving a complementary **pit** in the opposite exocytoplasmic leaflet. Why? Cytoskeletal components may be directly or indirectly attached to the tip of the protein exposed to the cytoplasmic side and will not let go.

The internal environment of the cell

Most biological molecules cannot diffuse through the phospholipid bilayer. Specific transport proteins, such as **carrier proteins** and **channel proteins**, mediate the selective passage of molecules across the membrane, thus allowing the cell to control its internal composition.

Molecules (such as **oxygen** and **carbon dioxide**) can cross the plasma membrane down their concentration gradient by dissolving first in the phospholipid bilayer and then in the aqueous environment at the cytosolic or extracellular side of the membrane. This mechanism, known as **passive diffusion**, does not involve membrane proteins. Lipid substances can also cross the bilayer.

Other biological molecules (such as **glucose, charged molecules**, and **small ions** —H^+, Na^+, K^+, and Cl^-) are unable to dissolve in the hydrophobic interior of the phospholipid bilayer. They require the help of specific **transport proteins** (Figure 2–10) and **channel proteins**, which facilitate the diffusion of most biological molecules.

Like passive diffusion, **facilitated diffusion** of biological molecules **is determined by concentration and electrical gradients across the membrane**. However, facilitated diffusion requires:

1. **Carrier proteins**, which can bind specific molecules to be transported, or
2. **Channel proteins**, forming open gates through the membrane.

Figure 2–11

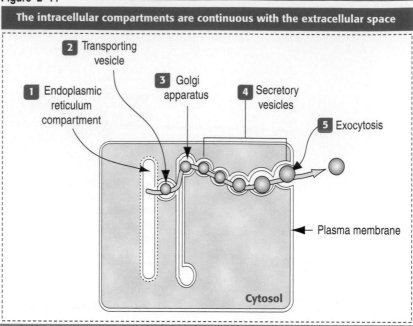

The intracellular compartments are continuous with the extracellular space

Carrier proteins transport sugars, amino acids and nucleosides. **Channel proteins are ion channels involved in the rapid transport of ions** (faster transport than carrier proteins), are **highly selective of molecular size and electrical charge**, and **are not continuously open.**

Some channels open in response to the binding of a signaling molecule and are called **ligand-gated channels.** Other channels open in response to changes in electric potential across the membrane and are called **voltage-gated channels.**

In general, the endoplasmic reticulum is an interconnected network of membrane-bound channels within the cytoplasm, part of the **cytomembrane** system and distinct from the **plasma membrane.**

The endoplasmic reticulum system, defined structurally by **cisternae** (flat sacs), **tubules,** and **vesicles,** divides the cytoplasm into two compartments:

1. The **luminal** or **endoplasmic compartment.**

2. The **cytoplasmic** or **cytosolic compartment.**

Products released into the luminal compartment of the rough endoplasmic reticulum are transported to the Golgi apparatus by a transporting vesicle and eventually to the exterior of the cell by exocytosis. One can visualize the sequence in which the lumen of the cytomembrane system is interconnected and remains as such in an imaginary stage; you can realize that the **luminal compartment of a secretory cell is continuous with the exterior of the cell** (Figure 2–11). The surrounding space is the cytosolic compartment in which soluble proteins, cytoskeletal components, and organelles are present.

Now, let's imagine that we can visualize the membrane of each component of the cytomembrane system as consisting of two leaflets (Figure 2–12): 1. the **exocytoplasmic leaflet** (facing the extracellular space) and the **protoplasmic leaflet** (facing the cytosolic compartment). Let us also imagine that exocytoplasmic and protoplasmic leaflets form a continuum. During the freeze-fracturing process, the knife fractures the membrane as it jumps from one fracture plane to the other across the hydrophobic core and splits the membrane into two leaflets. The knife cannot stay with a single membrane because cytomembrane-bound organelles occupy different levels and have random orientations within the cell.

This randomness will be apparent during the examination of the replica. The replica is generated by evaporating a very thin layer of a heavy metal (generally platinum with a thickness of 1.0 to 1.5 nm) at a 45° angle to produce a contrast-

Figure 2–12

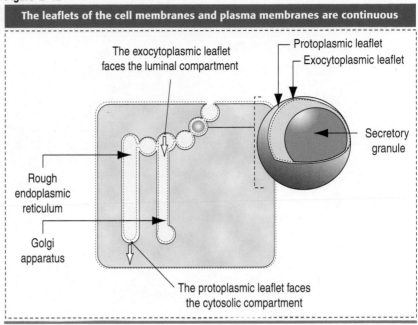

The leaflets of the cell membranes and plasma membranes are continuous

The exocytoplasmic leaflet faces the luminal compartment

Protoplasmic leaflet
Exocytoplasmic leaflet

Rough endoplasmic reticulum

Golgi apparatus

Secretory granule

The protoplasmic leaflet faces the cytosolic compartment

ing shadowing effect.

The platinum replica is then detached from the real specimen by floating it on a water surface, mounted on a metal grid, and examined under the electron microscope.

Keep in mind that the sample may contain a combination of exocytoplasmic and protoplasmic leaflets which, in turn, can expose surfaces and faces. Remember that membrane proteins tend to remain associated with the cytoplasmic (protoplasmic) leaflet and appear as particles on the PF (protoplasmic face). A shallow complementary pit is visualized in the EF (exocytoplasmic face).

The endoplasmic reticulum

The **rough endoplasmic reticulum** is recognized under the light microscope as a diffuse basophilic cytoplasmic structure called **ergastoplasm**.

The rough endoplasmic reticulum is involved in the synthesis of proteins, carried out by their attached **ribosomes** (Figure 2–13), and in the addition of oligosaccharides to many proteins. Most proteins exit the rough endoplasmic reticulum in vesicles transported to the **cis** portion of the Golgi apparatus (see Figures 2–16 and 2–17). Other proteins are retained by the rough endoplasmic reticulum to participate in the initial steps of protein synthesis (see Figure 2–15). The retained proteins contain the targeting sequence Lys-Asp-Glu-Leu (KDEL) at the C-terminal. A lack of the KDEL sequence marks proteins for transport to the Golgi apparatus.

The **smooth endoplasmic reticulum** lacks ribosomes and is generally in proximity to deposits of glycogen and lipids in the cytoplasm. The smooth endoplasmic reticulum has an important role in **detoxification reactions** required for the conversion of harmful lipid-soluble or water-insoluble substances into water-soluble compounds more convenient for discharge by the kidney.

The rough endoplasmic reticulum and protein synthesis and sorting

The role of the endoplasmic reticulum in protein synthesis and sorting was demonstrated by incubating pancreatic acinar cells in a medium containing radiolabeled amino acids and localizing radiolabeled proteins by autoradiography. The secretory pathway taken by secretory proteins includes the following sequence: rough endoplasmic reticulum, to Golgi apparatus, to secretory vesicles, to the

Figure 2–13

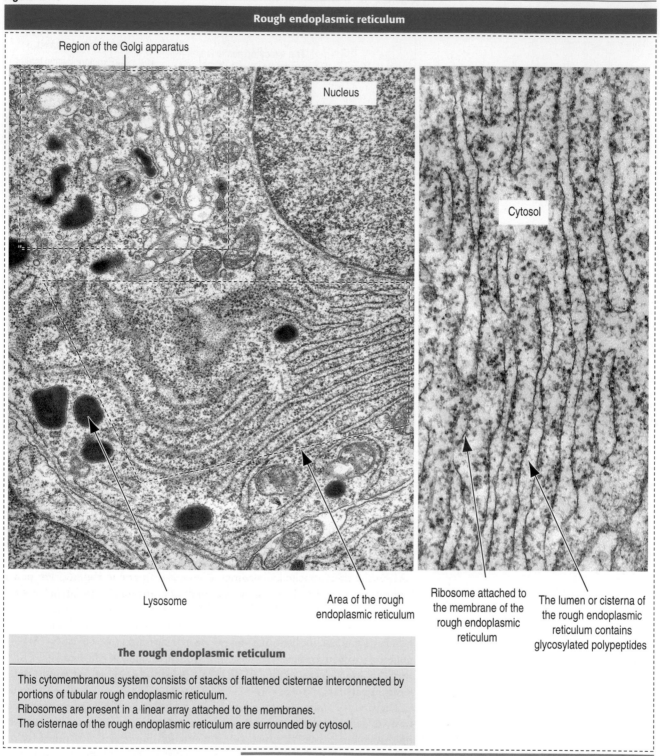

Rough endoplasmic reticulum

Region of the Golgi apparatus

Nucleus

Cytosol

Lysosome

Area of the rough endoplasmic reticulum

Ribosome attached to the membrane of the rough endoplasmic reticulum

The lumen or cisterna of the rough endoplasmic reticulum contains glycosylated polypeptides

The rough endoplasmic reticulum

This cytomembranous system consists of stacks of flattened cisternae interconnected by portions of tubular rough endoplasmic reticulum.

Ribosomes are present in a linear array attached to the membranes.

The cisternae of the rough endoplasmic reticulum are surrounded by cytosol.

extracellular space or lumen (Figure 2–14). Plasma membrane and lysosomal proteins also follow the sequence of rough endoplasmic reticulum to Golgi apparatus but are retained within the cell.

Proteins targeted to the nucleus, mitochondria, or peroxisomes are synthesized on free ribosomes and then released into the cytosol. In contrast, proteins for secretion or targeted to the endoplasmic reticulum, Golgi apparatus, lysosomes, or plasma membrane are synthesized by membrane-bound ribosomes and then transferred to the rough endoplasmic reticulum as protein synthesis progresses.

Figure 2–14

Protein synthesis, transport, and secretion by exocrine pancreatic cells

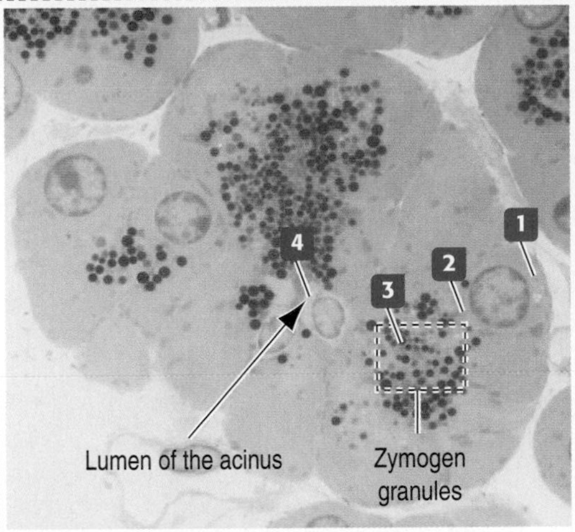

Lumen of the acinus

Zymogen granules

Pancreatic acinus (light microscopy)

Pancreatic acinar cells secrete newly synthesized proteins into the digestive tract.

When cells were labeled with a radioactive amino acid to trace the intracellular pathway of the secreted proteins, it was found by autoradiography that, after a 3-minute labeling, newly synthesized proteins were localized in the rough endoplasmic reticulum **1**.

Following further incubation with nonradioactive amino acids (chase), the proteins were found to translocate to the Golgi apparatus **2** and then, within secretory vesicles as zymogen granules **3** to the plasma membrane and the extracellular space **4**.

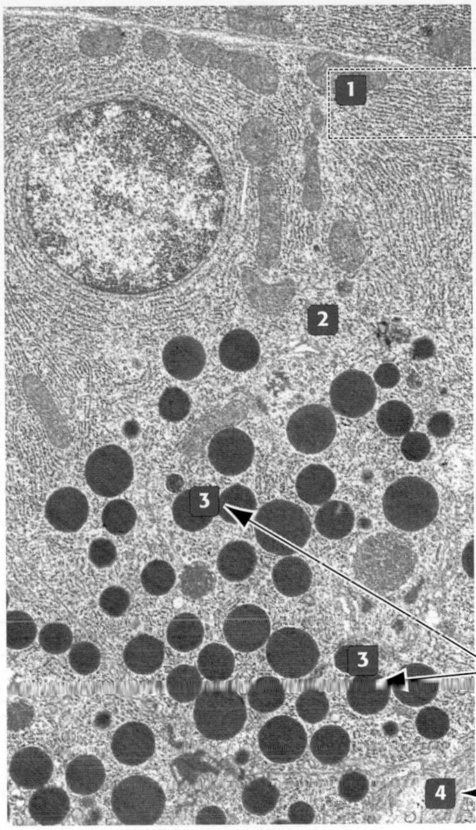

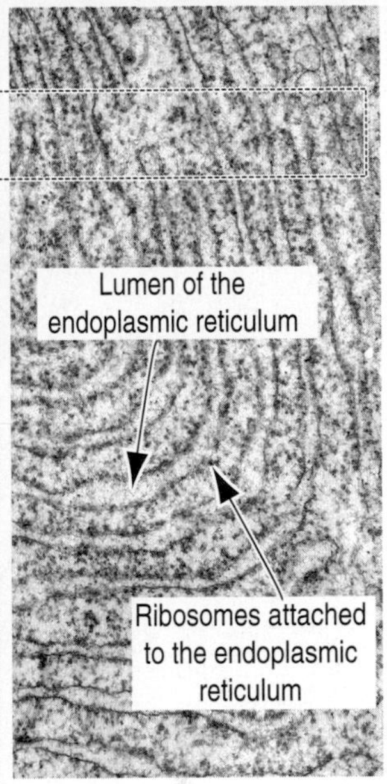

Lumen of the endoplasmic reticulum

Ribosomes attached to the endoplasmic reticulum

Zymogen granules within secretory vesicles

Lumen of the acinus

Pancreatic acinar cells (electron microscopy)

Ribosomes attach to the endoplasmic reticulum under the guidance of the amino acid sequence of the polypeptide chain being synthesized. Ribosomes synthesizing proteins for secretion are directed to the endoplasmic reticulum by a signal sequence at the growing end of the polypeptide chain. The mechanism by which secretory proteins are directed to the endoplasmic reticulum is explained by the **signal hypothesis** proposed by David Sabatini and Günter Blobel in 1971 (Figure 2–15).

The Golgi apparatus and the protein sorting pathways

The Golgi apparatus is a cellular organelle highly developed in secretory cells. Its main function is the **addition of oligosaccharides to proteins and lipids.**

The opposite site of the Golgi stack, the **trans** or **exit face**, known as the **trans-Golgi network**, gives rise to vesicles that exit the stack for various destinations. A **medial compartment** of stacks links the **cis** and **trans** compartments (Figures 2–16 and 2–17).

Functional differences between the cis, medial, and trans compartments of the Golgi apparatus are indicated by the presence of specific **glycosyltransferases** in each compartment. Glycosyltransferases are enzymes that transfer sugars to terminal portions of the oligosaccharide chains of glycoproteins and glycolipids.

Glycosyltransferases can be demonstrated by **cytochemical reactions**, by providing an enzyme substrate that gives rise to a visible product after enzymatic activity, or by **immunocytochemistry**, using specific antibodies.

The glycosylation pathway can be traced by **electron microscopic autoradiography** using [³H]fucose, a carbohydrate present only at the terminal portion of

Figure 2–15

Protein synthesis: The signal hypothesis

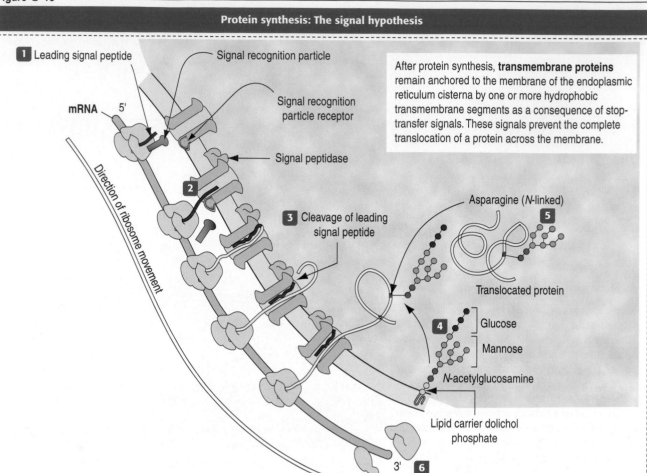

After protein synthesis, **transmembrane proteins** remain anchored to the membrane of the endoplasmic reticulum cisterna by one or more hydrophobic transmembrane segments as a consequence of stop-transfer signals. These signals prevent the complete translocation of a protein across the membrane.

1 The synthesis of a protein starts with a **leading signal peptide**. A **signal recognition particle** (SRP) binds to the ribosome and stops further growth of the protein. The complex is anchored to the cytoplasmic side of the endoplasmic reticulum cisterna where SRP binds to the **SRP receptor**. After binding, SRP is removed from the complex.

2 The protein reinitiates its growth and the leading peptide crosses the lipid bilayer into the lumen of the RER.

3 **Signal peptidase** removes the leading peptide and protein elongation continues.

4 A sugar chain linked to the **lipid carrier dolichol phosphate** is attached to the asparagine residue (N-glycosylation).

5 The synthesized protein is released. **Glucose** and one **mannose** are removed from the previously attached oligosaccharide.

6 Ribosome subunits disassemble at the 3'-end of the mRNA.

the oligosaccharide chain.

Secretory products can be released from the cell (**exocytosis**) by two mechanisms:

1. **By continuous exocytosis.**
2. **By selective exocytosis of stored secretory granules.**

Continuous exocytosis does not require a triggering signal (for example, the secretion of immunoglobulins by plasma cells). This mechanism is known as the **constitutive secretory pathway.** In the second mechanism, selective exocytosis, cell products are released under control of a chemical or electrical signal (for

Figure 2–16

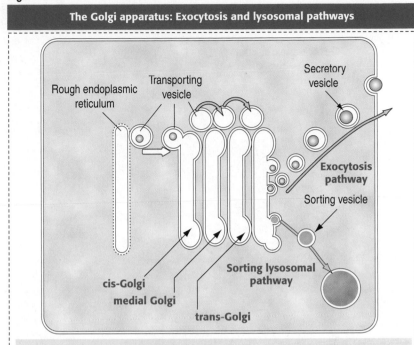

The Golgi apparatus: Exocytosis and lysosomal pathways

Rough endoplasmic reticulum

Transporting vesicle

Secretory vesicle

Exocytosis pathway

Sorting vesicle

cis-Golgi

medial Golgi

Sorting lysosomal pathway

trans-Golgi

The Golgi apparatus

First described in 1000 by Camillo Golgi (1843-1926) in neurons impregnated with osmium salts, this structure consists of orderly stacks of flattened disklike cisternae and associated vesicles.

The cisterna closest to the endoplasmic reticulum is the **cis face** whereas the cisterna closest to the apical domain of the cell is the **trans face**. The **medial region** is the site where most protein glycosylation occurs. The membranes of the Golgi apparatus are devoid of ribosomes.

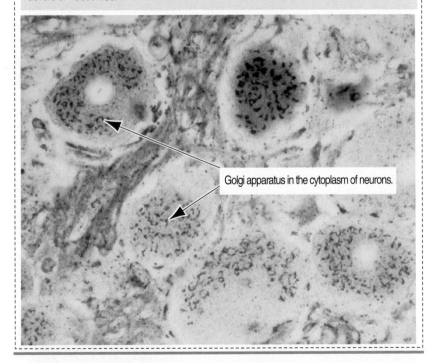

Golgi apparatus in the cytoplasm of neurons.

example, the secretion of hormones by cells of the anterior hypophysis). This mechanism is called the **regulated secretory pathway**.

Not all cell products are released by exocytosis. Some products remain within

Figure 2–17

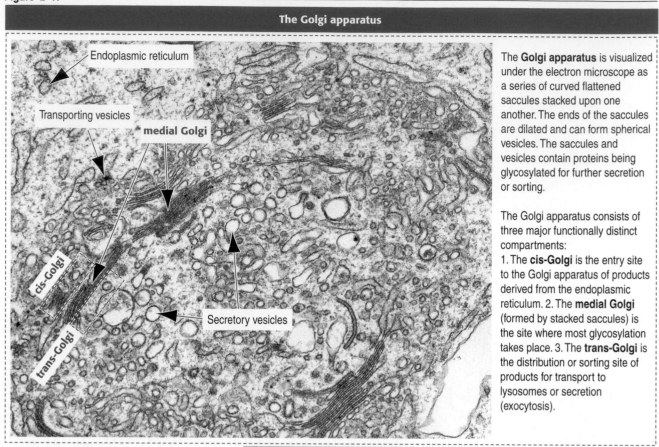

The Golgi apparatus

Endoplasmic reticulum

Transporting vesicles

medial Golgi

cis-Golgi

trans-Golgi

Secretory vesicles

The **Golgi apparatus** is visualized under the electron microscope as a series of curved flattened saccules stacked upon one another. The ends of the saccules are dilated and can form spherical vesicles. The saccules and vesicles contain proteins being glycosylated for further secretion or sorting.

The Golgi apparatus consists of three major functionally distinct compartments:
1. The **cis-Golgi** is the entry site to the Golgi apparatus of products derived from the endoplasmic reticulum. 2. The **medial Golgi** (formed by stacked saccules) is the site where most glycosylation takes place. 3. The **trans-Golgi** is the distribution or sorting site of products for transport to lysosomes or secretion (exocytosis).

the cell after being "sorted" by the Golgi apparatus.

Lysosomal hydrolases are synthesized in the rough endoplasmic reticulum, transported to the cis-Golgi and finally sorted to **lysosomes**. This sorting mechanism

Figure 2-18

The Golgi apparatus: Lysosomal sorting pathways

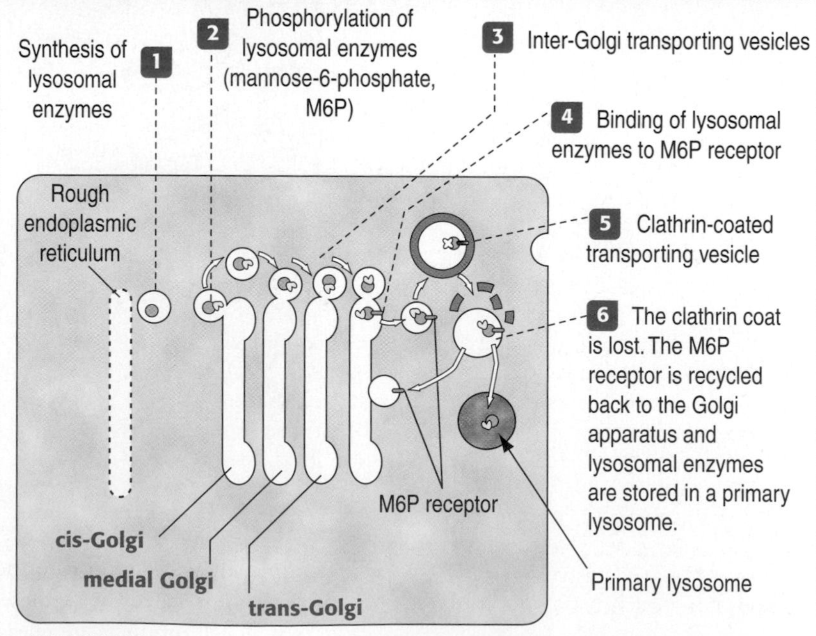

Synthesis of lysosomal enzymes **1**

2 Phosphorylation of lysosomal enzymes (mannose-6-phosphate, M6P)

3 Inter-Golgi transporting vesicles

4 Binding of lysosomal enzymes to M6P receptor

5 Clathrin-coated transporting vesicle

6 The clathrin coat is lost. The M6P receptor is recycled back to the Golgi apparatus and lysosomal enzymes are stored in a primary lysosome.

Rough endoplasmic reticulum

M6P receptor

cis-Golgi

medial Golgi

trans-Golgi

Primary lysosome

Figure 2–19

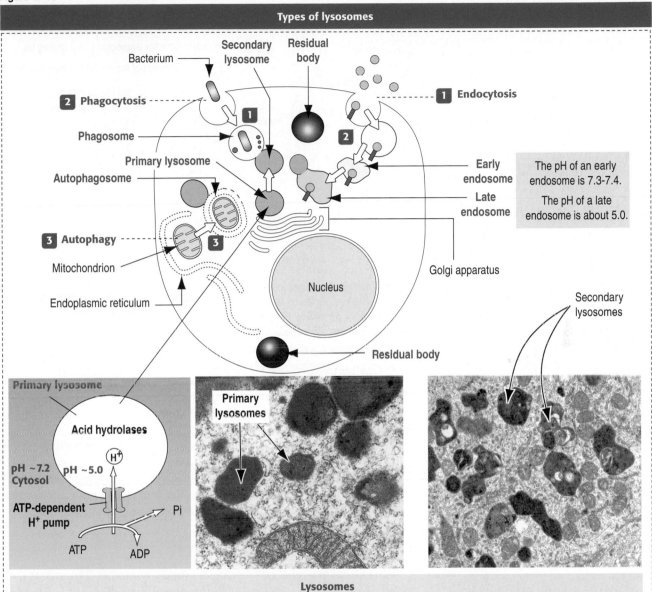

Types of lysosomes

Lysosomes

Lysosomes are organelles which contain about 40 types of hydrolytic enzymes active in an acidic environment (~ pH 5.0). Their function is to degrade proteins, nucleic acids, oligosaccharides, and phospholipids.

The surrounding membrane has three characteristics:

1. It separates hydrolytic enzymes from the cytosol.

2. It harbors transport proteins (**lysosomal glycoprotein A and B**) that translocate breakdown products from the lysosome into the cytosol (amino acids, sugars, and nucleotides).

3. It contains an **ATP-dependent H+ pump** to maintain an acidic intralysosomal environment.

There are **three major pathways for the intracellular degradation of materials** . **Extracellular particles** can be taken up by **phagocytosis** and **endocytosis**. **Aged intracellular components are degraded by autophagy**.

1 Endocytosis: The material that is endocytosed is delivered to an early endosome and then to a late endosome. The membrane of a late endosome contains the H+ pump, the early endosome does not. A primary lysosome fuses with the late endosome to begin its catalytic function. Endocytosis is characteristic of receptor-mediated endocytosis of polypeptide hormones and growth factors.

2 Phagocytosis: The material that is phagocytosed is enclosed within a phagosome which then fuses with a lysosome. Abundant phagosomes are observed in macrophages.

3 Autophagy: Autophagy starts with the endoplasmic reticulum enclosing an aged cell component to form an autophagosome which then fuses with a lysosome and its content is digested. Autophagy plays a significant role in tissue remodeling during differentiation. A **residual body** is a structure containing partially digested material.

Figure 2–20

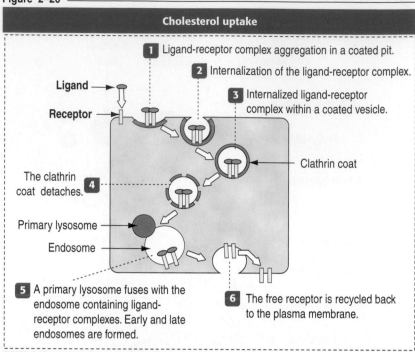

Cholesterol uptake

1 Ligand-receptor complex aggregation in a coated pit.

2 Internalization of the ligand-receptor complex.

3 Internalized ligand-receptor complex within a coated vesicle.

Ligand

Receptor

Clathrin coat

The clathrin coat detaches. **4**

Primary lysosome

Endosome

5 A primary lysosome fuses with the endosome containing ligand-receptor complexes. Early and late endosomes are formed.

6 The free receptor is recycled back to the plasma membrane.

involves two important steps (Figure 2–18):

1. The insertion of **mannose-6-phosphate** (**M6P**) into oligosaccharides attached to glycoproteins destined to lysosomes.

2. The presence of the **transmembrane M6P receptor protein** in the transporting vesicle.

By this mechanism, M6P-containing lysosomal enzymes are separated from other glycoproteins in vesicles with the M6P receptor. After being transported to a clathrin coated transporting vesicle, lysosomal enzymes dissociate from the M6P receptor and become surrounded by a membrane to form a **primary lysosome**. Membranes containing free M6P receptor are returned back to the Golgi apparatus for **recycling**.

Lysosomes

Two types of lysosomes are recognized: **primary lysosomes** (Figure 2–19), defined as the primary storage site of lysosomal hydrolases, and **secondary lysosomes**, regarded as lysosomes engaged in a catalytic process.

The plasma membrane can internalize extracellular particles and fluids using vesicles resulting from the invagination of the membrane by a process called **endocytosis**. The reverse process, called **exocytosis**, represents transport to the outside of products processed or synthesized by the cell.

Endocytosis involves two major types of vesicles:

1. **Phagocytic clathrin independent vesicles**, used to internalize particles (for example, virus or bacteria).

2. **Clathrin-coated vesicles**, to take in small macromolecules.

The internalization of fluids, known as **pinocytosis**, involves vesicles known as **caveolae** coated by a protein called **caveolin**.

Endocytosis has two important roles:

1. **To bring material into the cell**.

2. **To recycle the plasma membrane**.

Receptor-mediated endocytosis: The uptake of cholesterol

The internalization of a **ligand** (such as low-density lipoprotein [LDL] cholesterol, transferrin, polypeptide hormones, or growth factors) by a cell requires a

Figure 2–21

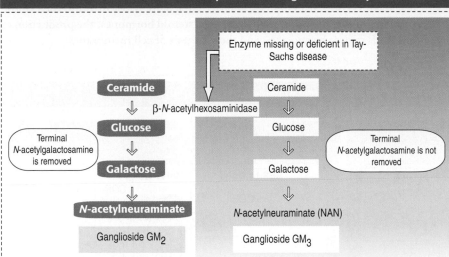

Lysosomal storage diseases: Tay-Sachs disease

Gangliosides are sphingolipids rich in carbohydrates predominant in the nervous system. Gangliosides are degraded inside lysosomes by removing their terminal sugars. In **Tay-Sachs disease**, the content of ganglioside M_2 (GM_2) in the brain is high because the removal of the terminal N-acetylgalactosamine is slow or it does not occur. **The missing lysosomal enzyme is β-N-acetylhexosaminidase**.
Neurons contain lipids within lysosomes. Retarded psychomotor development and weakness are early symptoms. Dementia, blindness and death usually occur within 3 years after birth. Amniocentesis to assay for β-N-acetylhexosaminidase activity during prenatal development can diagnose the inherited autosomal recessive disease.

Lysosomal storage disorders

The hydrolytic enzymes within lysosomes are involved in the breakdown of sphingolipids, glycoproteins, and mucopolysaccharides into soluble products. These molecular complexes can derive from the turnover of intracellular organelles or enter the cell by phagocytosis.

A number of genetic diseases lacking lysosomal enzymes result in the progressive accumulation within the cell of partially degraded insoluble products. This condition leads to clinical conditions known as **lysosomal storage disorders**.

These disorders include broad categories depending on the major accumulating insoluble product and the substrate for the defective lysosomal enzyme.
The **deficient breakdown of sphingolipids** is the cause of:
1. **Gaucher's disease**, characterized by defective activity of a **glucocerebrosidase**, resulting in the accumulation of glucocerebrosides in the spleen and central nervous system.
 2. **Niemann-Pick disease**, defined by a defective **sphingomyelinase**, leading to the accumulation of sphingomyelin and cholesterol in the spleen and central nervous system.
3. **Tay-Sachs disease**, characterized by a deficiency of **hexosaminidase**, resulting in the accumulation of gangliosides in the central nervous system.

The **diagnosis** of these three lysosomal storage disorders is based on the detection of enzymatic activity in leukocytes and cultured fibroblasts of the patients.

specific **membrane receptor** (Figure 2–20).

The **receptor-ligand complex** is internalized by a process called **receptor-mediated endocytosis**. This process involves the assembly of the protein **clathrin** on the cytoplasmic side of the plasma membrane which forms a coated crater called a **coated pit**. The function of clathrin is to concentrate receptor-ligand complexes in a small surface area of the plasma membrane. Receptors with their bound ligands move by lateral diffusion in the plane of the lipid bilayer. The coated pit invaginates to form a **coated vesicle**, which pinches off from the plasma membrane to transport receptor-ligand complexes to a specific intracellular pathway, usually an **endosome**.

LDL carries about 75% of the cholesterol and circulates in blood for about 2 to 3 days. Approximately 70% of LDL is cleared from blood by cells containing LDL receptors; the remainder is removed by a scavenger pathway using a receptor-independent mechanism.

After internalization, the clathrin coat of the coated vesicle is removed and the uncoated vesicle fuses with a larger vesicle, the endosome, with an internal low pH. In this acidic environment, LDL detaches from the receptor and is delivered to a **primary lysosome**, which changes into a **secondary lysosome**.

The LDL receptor is recycled back to the plasma membrane, the LDL particle is degraded by lysosomal enzymes, and free cholesterol is released into the cytosol. **Cholesterol is required for the synthesis of steroid hormones, the production of bile acids** in liver hepatocytes, and the **synthesis of cell membranes**.

Figure 2–22

Vesicular transport: Clathrin and coat proteins (COPI and COPII)

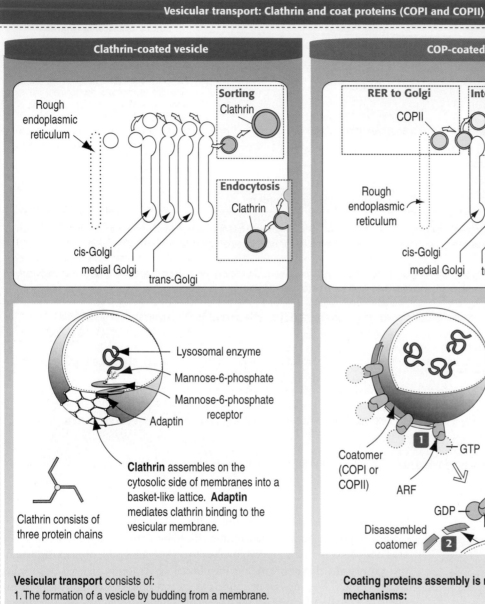

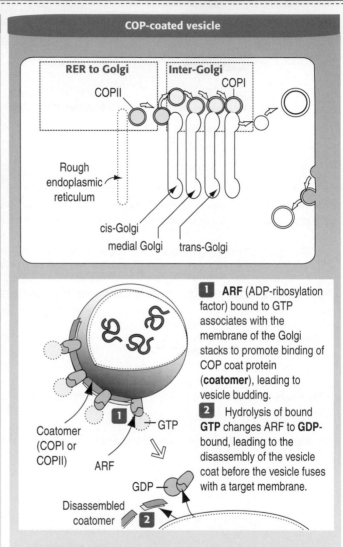

Vesicular transport consists of:
1. The formation of a vesicle by budding from a membrane.
2. The assembly of a protein coat on the cytosolic surface of transport vesicles.

There are **two types of coated vesicles**:
1. **Clathrin-coated**, found in endocytic **vesicles** and **vesicles sorted from the trans-Golgi to a lysosome**.
2. **COP-coated vesicles** (COP stands for coat protein), observed in transporting vesicles between stacks of the Golgi apparatus (**COPI-coated vesicles**) or from the rough endoplasmic reticulum to the Golgi apparatus (**COPII-coated vesicles**).

Coating proteins assembly is regulated by two different mechanisms:

1. Clathrin binding to a vesicle is mediated by **adaptins**.
2. COP binding to a vesicle is mediated by **GTP-bound ARF**. The nonbinding form of ARF is **GDP-bound**. ARF is a member of the **Ras protein family** (involved as oncogenes in cancer; see the MAP kinase pathway in Chapter 3, Cell Signaling).

Ras-related proteins (called **Rab proteins**) are also involved in vesicular transport.

Clinical significance: Familial hypercholesterolemia: Lysosomal storage disorders

The human disease **familial hypercholesterolemia** is characterized by an elevation of LDL cholesterol, the predominant cholesterol transport protein in the plasma. The primary defect is a **mutation in the gene encoding the LDL receptor**, required for the internalization of dietary cholesterol by most cells. High levels of LDL cholesterol in blood plasma lead to the formation of **atherosclerotic plaques** in the coronary vessels, a common cause of **myocardial infarction**.

Patients with familial hypercholesterolemia have three types of defective receptors:

1. LDL receptors incapable of binding LDL cholesterol.
2. LDL receptors that bind LDL cholesterol but at a reduced capacity.
3. LDL receptors that can bind LDL cholesterol normally but are incapable of internalization.

Lysosomal storage disorders or **diseases** are caused by the progressive accumulation of cell membrane components within cells because of a hereditary deficiency of enzymes required for their breakdown. An example is **Tay-Sachs disease** (Figure 2–21).

Vesicular transport

A continual process of **budding** and **fusion** of **transport vesicles** mobilizes products from the rough endoplasmic reticulum to the Golgi apparatus, between membranous stacks of the Golgi apparatus, and from the Golgi apparatus to other components of the cytomembrane system. We have seen that a vesicular transport pathway can internalize cholesterol by a receptor-mediated endocytosis mecha-

Figure 2–23

Vesicular fusion: Target membrane recognition and fusion

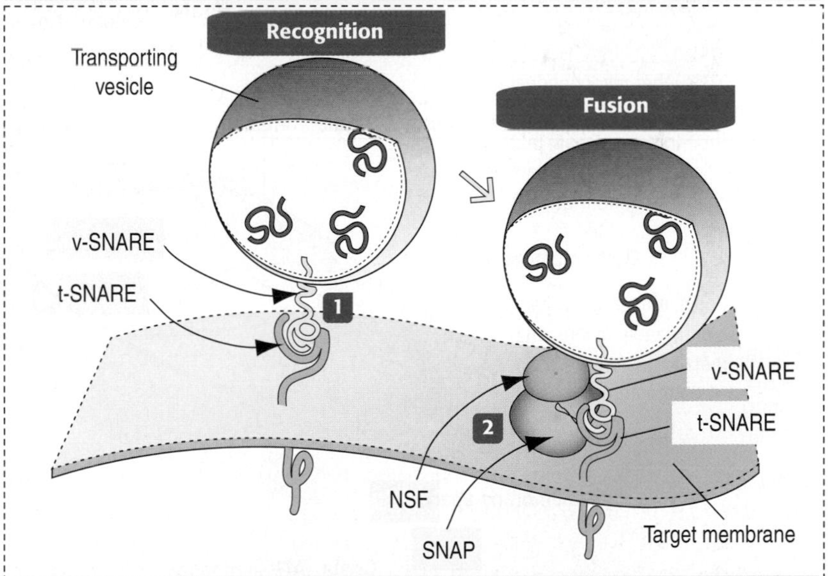

Recognition

Transporting vesicle

Fusion

v-SNARE

t-SNARE

1

v-SNARE

t-SNARE

2

NSF

SNAP

Target membrane

Vesicle fusion involves two steps:

1 The **recognition** of the appropriate target membrane by a receptor on the **vesicle** (**v-SNARE**) and a receptor on the **target membrane** (**t-SNARE**).

2 The **fusion** of the vesicle and target membranes. Fusion involves two proteins: (1) **NSF** (for *N*-ethylmaleimide-**s**ensitive **f**usion); (2) **SNAP**s (for **s**oluble **N**SF **a**ttachment **p**roteins). NSF and SNAP are recruited by SNAREs (for **SNAP** **re**ceptors) to induce fusion of vesicle and target membranes.

Figure 2–24

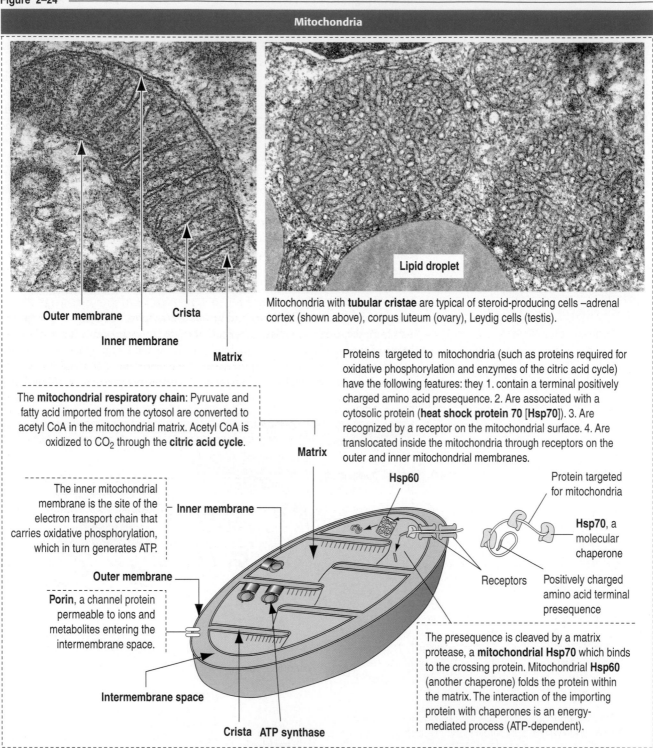

Mitochondria

Outer membrane

Crista

Inner membrane

Matrix

Lipid droplet

Mitochondria with **tubular cristae** are typical of steroid-producing cells –adrenal cortex (shown above), corpus luteum (ovary), Leydig cells (testis).

Proteins targeted to mitochondria (such as proteins required for oxidative phosphorylation and enzymes of the citric acid cycle) have the following features: they 1. contain a terminal positively charged amino acid presequence. 2. Are associated with a cytosolic protein (**heat shock protein 70 [Hsp70]**). 3. Are recognized by a receptor on the mitochondrial surface. 4. Are translocated inside the mitochondria through receptors on the outer and inner mitochondrial membranes.

The **mitochondrial respiratory chain**: Pyruvate and fatty acid imported from the cytosol are converted to acetyl CoA in the mitochondrial matrix. Acetyl CoA is oxidized to CO_2 through the **citric acid cycle**.

Matrix

Hsp60

Protein targeted for mitochondria

The inner mitochondrial membrane is the site of the electron transport chain that carries oxidative phosphorylation, which in turn generates ATP.

Inner membrane

Hsp70, a molecular chaperone

Outer membrane

Receptors

Positively charged amino acid terminal presequence

Porin, a channel protein permeable to ions and metabolites entering the intermembrane space.

Intermembrane space

Crista ATP synthase

The presequence is cleaved by a matrix protease, a **mitochondrial Hsp70** which binds to the crossing protein. Mitochondrial **Hsp60** (another chaperone) folds the protein within the matrix. The interaction of the importing protein with chaperones is an energy-mediated process (ATP-dependent).

nism involving inward budding of clathrin-coated pits and vesicles.

The vesicular transport mechanism involves two types of coated vesicles (Figure 2-22):

1. **Clathrin-coated vesicles**, transporting products from the Golgi apparatus to lysosomes, and endocytic vesicles, carrying products from the exterior of the cell to lysosomes (for example, cholesterol).

2. **COP-coated vesicles** (COP stands for <u>co</u>at <u>p</u>rotein), transporting products between stacks of the Golgi apparatus (**COPI-coated vesicles**), and from the rough

endoplasmic reticulum to the Golgi apparatus (**COPII-coated vesicles**).

Adaptins mediate the binding of clathrin to the vesicular membrane as well as select specific molecules to be trapped in a vesicle. For example, an adaptin binds to the cytosolic domain of the M6P receptor to guide lysosomal enzymes into clathrin-coated vesicles for lysosomal sorting.

A guanosine triphosphate (GTP)-binding protein called **ARF** (for <u>a</u>denosine diphosphate [ADP]-<u>r</u>ibosylation <u>f</u>actor), is required for the assembly of COPI and COPII molecules to form a protein coat called a **coatomer** on the cytosolic side of a transporting vesicle. When GTP is converted to guanosine diphosphate (GDP) by hydrolysis, the coatomer dissociates from the vesicle just before the vesicle fuses with a target membrane. ARF is related to **Ras proteins**, a group of oncogene proteins also regulated by the alternate binding of GTP and GDP (see the MAP kinase pathway in Chapter 3, Cell Signaling).

Vesicle fusion to a target membrane

The fusion of a transporting vesicle to a target membrane (Figure 2-23) requires:

1. The **recognition of the specific target membrane** (for example, a transporting vesicle containing lysosomal enzymes fuses with the membrane of a lysosome).

2. The **vesicle and target membranes fuse** to deliver the transported product.

Vesicle fusion is mediated by two interacting cytosolic proteins: **NSF** (for <u>N</u>-ethylmaleimide-<u>s</u>ensitive <u>f</u>usion) and **SNAPs** (for <u>s</u>oluble <u>N</u>SF <u>a</u>ttachment <u>p</u>roteins).

NSF and SNAP bind to specific membrane receptors called SNARE (for <u>SNAP</u> <u>re</u>ceptors). SNAREs are present on the transporting vesicle (v-SNARE) and target (t-SNARE) membranes and represent **docking proteins**. Following docking, the SNARE complex recruits NSF and SNAPs to produce the fusion of the vesicle and target membranes.

Mitochondria

The mitochondrion (*Gr. mito*, thread; *chondrion*, granule) is a highly compartmentalized organelle. It consists of outer and inner membranes separated by an intermembrane space (Figure 2–24). The inner membrane folds into partitions or cristae. Cristae project into the mitochondrial matrix.

The **outer mitochondrial membrane** contains **porin**, a membrane channel pro-

---

Figure 2–25

ATP synthase

ATP synthase is an enzyme complex that synthesizes ATP from ADP and inorganic phosphate. It is present on the inner mitochondrial membrane and cristae. The **F0 portion** forms a channel through which protons cross the membrane. The **F1 portion** uses the free energy derived from H^+ movement from the intermembrane space down the matrix to catalyze the synthesis of ATP. An electrochemical proton gradient is established when H^+ is transferred back to the intermembrane space.

Oxidative phosphorylation is the process by which the enzymatic oxidation of cell metabolites is converted into ATP (energy). This process consists of:

1. Electrons generated by biochemical reactions.

2. A membrane-bound **electron transport system**, which generates energy for the movement of H^+ into the intermembrane space.

3. **ATP synthase**, which uses the H^+ gradient to generate ATP during the H^+ flow from the intermembrane space to the mitochondrial matrix.

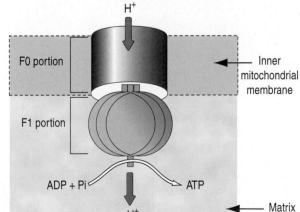

tein that enables the free diffusion of ions and metabolites into the intermembrane space.

The **inner mitochondrial membrane** contains **cardiolipin**, a phospholipid. **Cristae** contain:

1. **Adenosine triphosphate (ATP) synthase.**
2. Proteins of the **respiratory electron transfer chain.**
3. **Transport proteins** that regulate the flow of metabolites in and out of the mitochondrial matrix.

The **matrix** occupies the space between the inner mitochondrial membrane and cristae. Enzymes in the matrix metabolize **pyruvate. amino acids**, and **fatty acids** to produce **acetyl coenzyme A (CoA)**. Acetyl CoA is oxidized in the **citric acid Krebs cycle** to produce **carbon dioxide** and **reduced nicotinamide adenine dinucleotide (NADH)**. NADH is oxidized to produce electrons for transport along the respiratory chain.

Multiple copies of mitochondrial circular DNA, transfer RNAs, and ribosomes are present in the matrix. Although most mitochondrial proteins are encoded by genes in the cell nucleus, some are encoded by mitochondrial DNA, and DNA mutations can cause severe abnormalities. Mitochondrial DNA encodes 13 polypeptides that are subunits of proteins required for oxidative phosphorylation.

Enzyme proteins transported to the matrix must cross the outer and inner mitochondrial membranes. **Targeting polypeptide signals** and **chaperones (Hsp60** and **Hsp70)** enable proteins to reach the matrix (see Figure 2–24).

ATP synthase (Figure 2–25) synthesizes ATP from ADP plus inorganic phos-

Figure 2–26

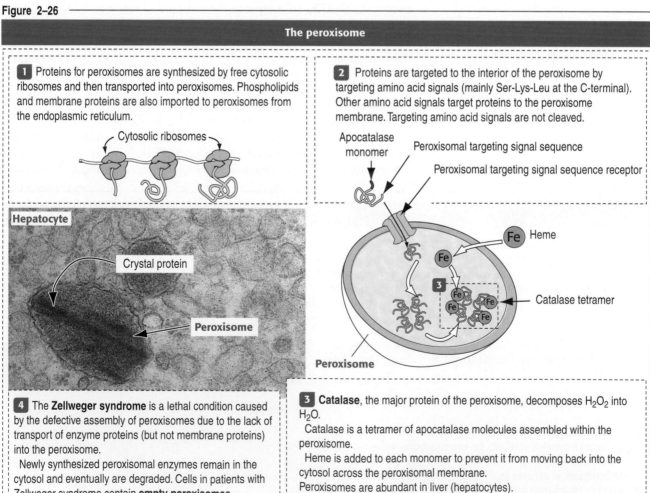

The peroxisome

1 Proteins for peroxisomes are synthesized by free cytosolic ribosomes and then transported into peroxisomes. Phospholipids and membrane proteins are also imported to peroxisomes from the endoplasmic reticulum.

Cytosolic ribosomes

2 Proteins are targeted to the interior of the peroxisome by targeting amino acid signals (mainly Ser-Lys-Leu at the C-terminal). Other amino acid signals target proteins to the peroxisome membrane. Targeting amino acid signals are not cleaved.

Apocatalase monomer

Peroxisomal targeting signal sequence

Peroxisomal targeting signal sequence receptor

Fe Heme

Fe

3

Fe Fe Fe Fe

Catalase tetramer

Peroxisome

Hepatocyte

Crystal protein

Peroxisome

4 The **Zellweger syndrome** is a lethal condition caused by the defective assembly of peroxisomes due to the lack of transport of enzyme proteins (but not membrane proteins) into the peroxisome.

Newly synthesized peroxisomal enzymes remain in the cytosol and eventually are degraded. Cells in patients with Zellweger syndrome contain **empty peroxisomes**.

3 **Catalase**, the major protein of the peroxisome, decomposes H_2O_2 into H_2O.

Catalase is a tetramer of apocatalase molecules assembled within the peroxisome.

Heme is added to each monomer to prevent it from moving back into the cytosol across the peroxisomal membrane.

Peroxisomes are abundant in liver (hepatocytes).

phate (Pi) to transport protons (H+) against their concentration gradient (from the intermembrane space to the matrix). ATP synthase is associated with the cristae and consists of three major components:

1. **F1**, directly involved in ATP synthesis.
2. **F0**.
3. A **stalk** linking F1 to F0 proteins. The **F0** complex provides the H+-transporting channel of ATP synthase.

Clinical significance: Mitochondrial inheritance

Mitochondria are transmitted by the mother (maternal inheritance). Both males and females can be affected by mitochondrial diseases, but males never transmit the disorder. **Males do not transmit mitochondria at fertilization.**

Myoclonic epilepsy with ragged red fibers (MERRF) is characterized by generalized muscle weakness, loss of coordination (**ataxia**), and multiple seizures. The major complications are respiratory and cardiac failure because the respiratory and cardiac muscles are affected.

Histologic preparations of muscle biopsies of individuals with MERRF display a peripheral red-stained material corresponding to **aggregates of abnormal mitochondria**, giving a ragged appearance to red muscle fibers. **MERRF is caused by a point mutation in a mitochondrial DNA gene encoding tRNA for lysine.** An abnormal tRNA causes a deficiency in the synthesis of two complexes of the oxidative phosphorylation chain (complexes I and IV). Consequently, neurons and muscle cells, highly dependent on mitochondrial oxidative phosphorylation, are the most affected.

Three maternally inherited mitochondrial diseases affect males more severely than females:

1. About 85% of individuals affected by **Leber's hereditary optic neuropathy (LHON)** are male. The disease is confined to the eye. Individuals suffer a sudden loss of vision in the second and third decades of life.
2. **Pearson marrow-pancreas syndrome** (anemia and mitochondrial myopathy observed in childhood).
3. **Male infertility**. Almost all the energy for sperm motility derives from mitochondria.

Peroxisomes

Peroxisomes are membrane-bound structures (Figure 2–26). They are assembled from proteins synthesized on free ribosomes and then imported into peroxisomes. Peroxisomes contain about 50 different enzymes. **Catalase**, a major peroxisomal enzyme, decomposes hydrogen peroxide into water or is utilized to oxidize other organic compounds (uric acid, amino acids, and fatty acids). The oxidation of fatty acids by mitochondria and peroxisomes provides metabolic energy.

Peroxisomes participate in the biosynthesis of lipids. For example, cholesterol and dolichol are synthesized in both peroxisomes and endoplasmic reticulum. In liver, peroxisomes are involved in the synthesis of **bile acids** (derived from cholesterol).

Peroxisomes contain enzymes involved in the synthesis of **plasmalogens**, phospholipids in which one of the hydrocarbon chains is linked to glycerol by an ether bond (instead of an ester bond). Plasmalogens are membrane components of heart and brain.

Clinical significance: Zellweger syndrome

The **Zellweger syndrome** (see Figure 2–26) is lethal within the first decade of life. Multiple peroxisomal enzymes fail to be imported into peroxisomes. The primary defect is a mutated gene encoding the receptor for the peroxisome-targeted proteins that does not recognize the signal Ser-Lys-Leu at the C-terminal of enzymes directed to peroxisomes.

3. CELL SIGNALING

Cells respond to extracellular signals produced by other cells or by themselves. This mechanism, called **cell signaling**, allows cell-cell communication and is necessary for the functional regulation and integration of multicellular organisms. Our discussion in this chapter provides the basis not only for understanding normal cell function but also as an introduction to the role of abnormal cell signaling in human disease.

Signaling molecules are either **secreted** or **expressed at the cell surface** of one cell. Signaling molecules can bind to receptors on the surface of another cell or the same cell.

Different types of signaling molecules transmit information in multicellular organisms, and their mechanisms of action on their target cells can be diverse. Some signaling molecules can act on the cell surface after binding to cell surface receptors; others can cross the plasma membrane and bind to intracellular receptors in the cytoplasm and nucleus.

When a signaling molecule binds to its receptor, it initiates a cascade of intracellular reactions to regulate critical functions such as **cell proliferation, differentiation, movement, metabolism,** and **behavior**. Because of their critical role in the control of normal cell growth and differentiation, signaling molecules have acquired significant relevance in cancer research.

Cell signaling mechanisms

Five major types of cell-cell signaling are considered (Figure 3–1):

1. **Endocrine cell signaling** involves a signaling molecule, called a **hormone**, secreted by an **endocrine cell and transported through the circulation to act on distant target cells**. An example is the steroid hormone testosterone produced in the testes, that stimulates the development and maintenance of the male reproductive tract.

2. **Paracrine cell signaling** is mediated by a signaling molecule acting **locally** to regulate the behavior of a **nearby cell**. An example is the action of **neurotransmitters** produced by nerve cells and released at a **synapse**. See also the side box.

3. **Autocrine cell signaling** is defined by **cells responding to signaling molecules that they themselves produce**. A classic example is the response of cells of the immune system to foreign antigens or growth factors that trigger their own proliferation and differentiation. Abnormal autocrine signaling leads to the unregulated growth of cancer cells.

4. **Neurotransmitter cell signaling**, a specific form of paracrine signaling.

5. **Neuroendocrine cell signaling**, a specific form of endocrine signaling.

Mechanisms of action of cell signaling molecules

Cell signaling molecules exert their action after binding to receptors expressed by their target cells. Target cells, in turn, can determine either a **negative** or **positive feedback** action to regulate the release of the targeting hormone (Figure 3–2).

Cell receptors can be expressed on the **cell surface** of the target cells. Some receptors are **intracellular proteins** in the **cytosol** or the **nucleus** of target cells. Intracellular receptors require that the signaling molecules **diffuse across the plasma membrane** (Figure 3–3).

Steroid hormones belong to this class of signaling molecules. Steroid hormones are synthesized from **cholesterol** and include **testosterone, estrogen, progesterone,** and **corticosteroids**.

Testosterone, estrogen, and progesterone are **sex steroids** and are produced by

Figure 3–1

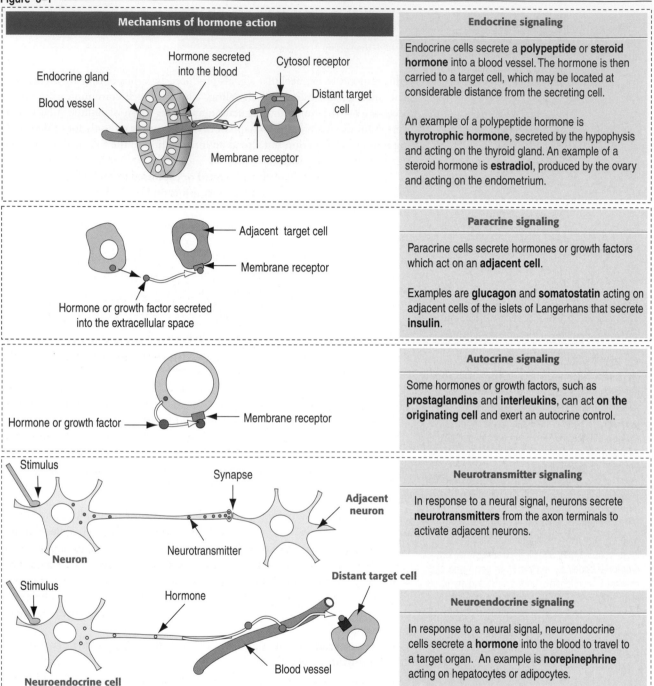

Mechanisms of hormone action

Endocrine signaling

Endocrine cells secrete a **polypeptide** or **steroid hormone** into a blood vessel. The hormone is then carried to a target cell, which may be located at considerable distance from the secreting cell.

An example of a polypeptide hormone is **thyrotrophic hormone**, secreted by the hypophysis and acting on the thyroid gland. An example of a steroid hormone is **estradiol**, produced by the ovary and acting on the endometrium.

Paracrine signaling

Paracrine cells secrete hormones or growth factors which act on an **adjacent cell**.

Examples are **glucagon** and **somatostatin** acting on adjacent cells of the islets of Langerhans that secrete **insulin**.

Autocrine signaling

Some hormones or growth factors, such as **prostaglandins** and **interleukins**, can act **on the originating cell** and exert an autocrine control.

Neurotransmitter signaling

In response to a neural signal, neurons secrete **neurotransmitters** from the axon terminals to activate adjacent neurons.

Neuroendocrine signaling

In response to a neural signal, neuroendocrine cells secrete a **hormone** into the blood to travel to a target organ. An example is **norepinephrine** acting on hepatocytes or adipocytes.

Highlights of steroid hormones

1. They derive from **cholesterol**.
2. They bind mainly to **intracellular receptors** in the cytosol and nucleus.
3. They circulate in blood **bound to a protein**.
4. They are **nonpolar** molecules.
5. Steroid hormones **are not stored in the producing endocrine cell**.
6. Steroid hormones **can be administered orally** and are readily absorbed in the gastrointestinal tract.

the gonads. Corticosteroids are produced by the cortex of the adrenal gland and include two major classes: **glucocorticoids**, which stimulate the production of glucose, and **mineralocorticoids**, which act on the kidney to regulate water and salt balance.

There are three signaling molecules that are structurally and functionally distinct from steroids but act on target cells by binding to intracellular receptors after entering the cell by diffusion across the plasma membrane. They include **thyroid hormone** (produced in the thyroid gland to regulate development and metabolism), **vitamin D$_3$** (regulates calcium metabolism and bone growth), and **retinoids** (synthesized from vitamin A to regulate development).

Steroid receptors are members of the **steroid receptor superfamily**. They act as

Figure 3–2

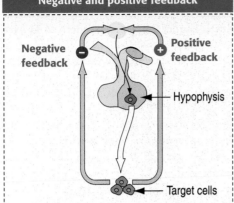

Mechanisms of hormone action: Negative and positive feedback

Negative feedback −
Positive feedback +

Hypophysis

Target cells

Feedback loops and cell signaling

Various feedback loops coordinate the secretion of hormones. For example, a **negative feedback loop** prevents the unregulated release of a hormone from the hypophysis into the blood circulation when the target cell or tissue may be nonresponsive.
A **positive feedback loop** (more rarely) occurs when the hypophysis senses a decrease in the blood levels of a hormone produced by the target cell or tissue. See Chapter 19, Endocrine System, for additional details.

Highlights of peptide hormones

1. They are synthesized as **precursor molecules** (prohormones).
2. They are stored in **membrane-bound secretory vesicles**.
3. They are generally **water soluble** (polar).
4. They circulate in blood as **unbound molecules**.
5. Peptide hormones **cannot be administered orally**.
6. They usually bind to **cell surface receptors**.

Figure 3–3

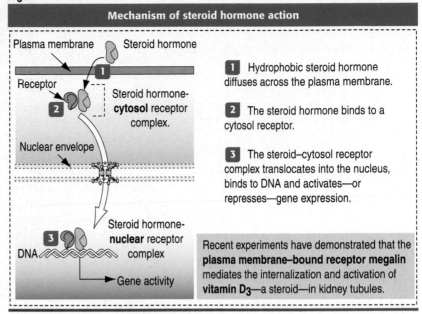

Mechanism of steroid hormone action

Plasma membrane — Steroid hormone

1

Receptor

2

Steroid hormone-**cytosol** receptor complex.

Nuclear envelope

3

Steroid hormone-**nuclear** receptor complex

DNA

Gene activity

1 Hydrophobic steroid hormone diffuses across the plasma membrane.

2 The steroid hormone binds to a cytosol receptor.

3 The steroid–cytosol receptor complex translocates into the nucleus, binds to DNA and activates—or represses—gene expression.

Recent experiments have demonstrated that the **plasma membrane–bound receptor megalin** mediates the internalization and activation of **vitamin D₃**—a steroid—in kidney tubules.

transcription factors through their DNA binding domains, which have transcription activation or repression functions. Steroid hormones and related molecules can therefore regulate gene expression.

In the **androgen insensitivity syndrome** (also known as the **testicular feminization syndrome [Tfm]**), there is a mutation in the gene expressing the **testosterone receptor** such that the receptor cannot bind the hormone, and hence the cells do not respond to the hormone. Although genetically male, the individual develops the secondary sexual characteristics of a female. We discuss the androgen insensitivity syndrome during our treatment of the male reproductive system.

Nitric oxide

Nitric oxide is a signaling molecule. It is a simple gas synthesized from the amino acid **arginine** by the enzyme **nitric oxide synthase**. It acts as a paracrine signaling molecule in the nervous, immune, and circulatory systems. Like steroid hormones, nitric oxide can diffuse across the plasma membrane of its target cells. Unlike steroids, nitric oxide does not bind to an intracellular receptor to regulate transcription. Instead, **it regulates the activity of intracellular target enzymes**.

The following are relevant characteristics of nitric oxide:

1. It is an unstable molecule with a limited half-life (seconds).
2. It has local effects.
3. A well-defined function of nitric oxide signaling is the **dilation of blood vessels**. For example, the release of the neurotransmitter acetylcholine from nerve cell endings in the blood vessel muscle cell wall stimulates the release of nitric oxide from endothelial cells.

Nitric oxide increases the activity of the second messenger cyclic guanosine monophosphate (cGMP; see later in this section) in smooth muscle cells, which then causes cell muscle relaxation and blood vessel dilation. **Nitroglycerin, a pharmacologic agent used in the treatment of heart disease, is converted to nitric oxide, which increases heart blood flow by dilation of the coronary blood vessels.**

Cell signaling molecules binding to cell surface receptors

A large variety of signaling molecules bind to cell surface receptors. Several groups are recognized:

Highlights of eicosanoids

1. They **derive from polyunsaturated fatty acids** with 18, 20, and 22 carbons.
2. **Arachidonic acid** is the main precursor.
3. This group includes **prostaglandins, leukotrienes, thromboxanes**, and **prostacyclin**.
4. They have primary **autocrine** and **paracrine** actions.
5. The **synthesis of eicosanoids is regulated by hormones**.
6. They usually bind to **cell surface receptors**.

Figure 3–4

G protein-coupled receptors

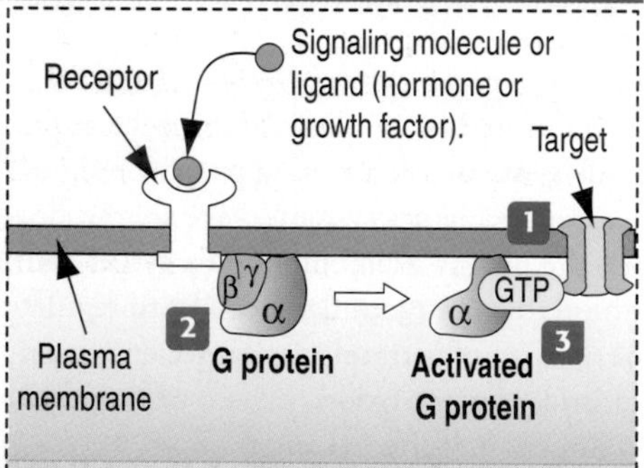

G protein

1 G protein transmits a cell surface signal to an adjacent **target molecule** (**adenylate cyclase** or **ion channel**).

2 G protein consists of three subunits (α, β, and γ). The α subunit regulates G protein activity. In the resting state, GDP is bound to the α subunit in a complex with β and γ subunits.

3 Hormone binding stimulates the release of GDP and its exchange for GTP. The activated GTP-bound α subunit dissociates from β and γ and interacts with a target to induce a response.

1. **Peptides**: This group includes **peptide hormones** (insulin, glucagon, and hormones secreted by the hypophysis), **neuropeptides**, secreted by neurons (**enkephalins** and **endorphins**, which decrease pain responses in the central nervous system), and **growth factors**, which control cell growth and differentiation (**nerve growth factor**, NGF; **epidermal growth factor**, EGF; **platelet-derived growth factor**, PDGF; and **cytokines**).

NGF is a member of a family of peptides called **neurotrophins** which regulate the development and viability of neurons. EGF stimulates cell proliferation and is essential during embryonic development and in the adult. PDGF is stored in blood platelets and released during clotting.

2. **Neurotransmitters**: These cell-signaling molecules are released by neurons and act on cell surface receptors present in neurons or other type of target cells (such as muscle cells). This group includes **acetylcholine, dopamine, epinephrine** (adrenaline), **serotonin, histamine, glutamate**, and **γ-aminobutyric acid** (GABA). The release of neurotransmitters from neurons is triggered by an **action potential**. Released neurotransmitters diffuse across the **synaptic cleft** and bind to surface receptors on the target cells.

There are differences that distinguish the **mechanism of action of neurotransmitters**. For example, **acetylcholine is a ligand-gated ion channel**. It induces a change in conformation of ion channels to control ion flow across the plasma membrane in target cells.

As we will see soon, neurotransmitter receptors can be associated to G proteins, a class of signaling molecules linking cell surface receptors to intracellular responses.

Some neurotransmitters have a **dual function**. For example, epinephrine (produced in the medulla of the adrenal gland) can act as a neurotransmitter and as a hormone to induce the breakdown of glycogen in muscle cells.

3. **Eicosanoids and leukotrienes**: These are lipid-containing cell-signaling molecules which, **in contrast to steroids, bind to cell surface receptors**.

Prostaglandins, prostacyclin, thromboxanes, and **leukotrienes** are members of this group of molecules. They stimulate blood platelet aggregation, inflammatory responses, and smooth muscle contraction.

Eicosanoids are synthesized from **arachidonic acid**. During the synthesis of prostaglandins, arachidonic acid is converted to **prostaglandin H$_2$** by the enzyme **prostaglandin synthase**. This enzyme is inhibited by **aspirin** and **anti-inflammatory drugs. Inhibition of prostaglandin synthase by aspirin reduces pain, inflammation, platelet aggregation, and blood clotting** (prevention of strokes).

Pathways of intracellular signaling by cell surface receptors

When a cell-signaling molecule binds to a specific receptor, it activates a series of **intracellular targets located downstream of the receptor**. Several molecules associated with receptors have been identified.

1. **G protein-coupled receptors** (guanine nucleotide–binding proteins): Members of a large family of **G proteins** (more than 1000 proteins) are present at the inner leaflet of the plasma membrane (Figure 3–4).

When a signaling molecule or **receptor ligand** binds to the extracellular portion of a cell surface receptor, its cytosolic domain undergoes a conformational change that enables binding of the receptor to a G protein. This contact activates the G protein which then dissociates from the receptor and triggers an intracellular signal to an enzyme or ion channel. We return to the G protein when we discuss the cyclic adenosine monophosphate (cAMP) pathway.

2. **Tyrosine kinases as receptor proteins** (Figure 3–5): These surface receptors are themselves enzymes that phosphorylate substrate proteins on **tyrosine** residues. **EGF, NGF, PDGF, insulin, and several growth factors are receptor protein tyrosine kinases**. Most of the receptor protein tyrosine kinases consist of single polypeptides, although the insulin receptor and other growth factors con-

Figure 3–5

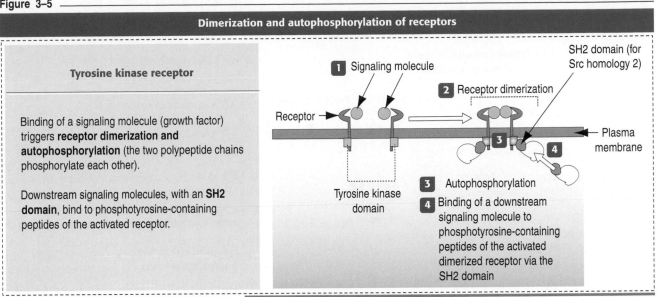

Dimerization and autophosphorylation of receptors

Tyrosine kinase receptor

Binding of a signaling molecule (growth factor) triggers **receptor dimerization and autophosphorylation** (the two polypeptide chains phosphorylate each other).

Downstream signaling molecules, with an **SH2 domain**, bind to phosphotyrosine-containing peptides of the activated receptor.

sist of a pair of polypeptide chains.

Binding of a ligand (a growth factor) to the extracellular domain of these receptors induces **receptor dimerization** which results in **receptor autophosphorylation** (the two polypeptide chains phosphorylate one another). The autophosphorylation of the receptors determines the binding of the tyrosine kinase domain to downstream signaling molecules. Downstream signaling molecules bind to phosphotyrosine residues through domains called **SH2 domains** (for Src homology 2). Src (for **sarcoma**) is a gene present in the tumor-producing Rous sarcoma virus and encodes a protein that functions as a protein tyrosine kinase.

3. **Cytokine receptors:** This family of receptors stimulate **intracellular protein-tyrosine kinases**, which **are not intrinsic components of the receptor.** A growth factor ligand induces the dimerization and cross-phosphorylation of the associated tyrosine kinases. Activated kinases phosphorylate the receptors, providing binding sites for downstream signaling molecules that contain the SH2 domain.

The cytokine receptors–associated tyrosine kinases belong to two families: the **Src family** and the **Janus kinase family** (**JAK**).

4. **Receptors linked to other enzymes** (**protein tyrosine phosphatases** and **protein serine and threonine kinases**): Some receptors associate with protein tyrosine phosphatases to remove phosphate groups from phosphotyrosine residues. Therefore, **they regulate the effect of protein tyrosine kinases by arresting signals initiated by protein tyrosine phosphorylation.**

Members of the **transforming growth factor-β** (**TGF-β**) family are protein kinases that phosphorylate serine and threonine residues (rather than tyrosine). TGF-β inhibits the proliferation of their target cells. Like tyrosine kinase and cytokine receptors, binding of ligand to the TGF-β receptor induces receptor dimerization and the cytosolic protein serine or threonine kinase domain cross-phosphorylates the polypeptide chains of the receptor.

Major pathways of intracellular cell signaling

Upon ligand binding, most cell surface receptors stimulate intracellular target enzymes to **transmit and amplify a signal.** An amplified signal can be propagated to the nucleus to regulate gene expression in response to an external cell stimulus.

The major intracellular signaling pathways include the cAMP and cGMP path-

Figure 3–6

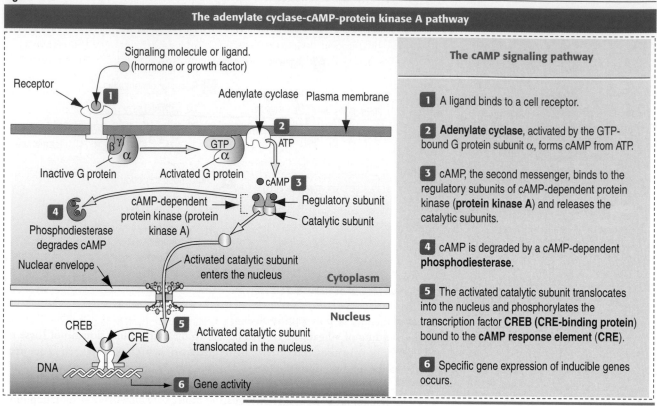

The adenylate cyclase-cAMP-protein kinase A pathway

The cAMP signaling pathway

1 A ligand binds to a cell receptor.

2 **Adenylate cyclase**, activated by the GTP-bound G protein subunit α, forms cAMP from ATP.

3 cAMP, the second messenger, binds to the regulatory subunits of cAMP-dependent protein kinase (**protein kinase A**) and releases the catalytic subunits.

4 cAMP is degraded by a cAMP-dependent **phosphodiesterase**.

5 The activated catalytic subunit translocates into the nucleus and phosphorylates the transcription factor **CREB (CRE-binding protein)** bound to the **cAMP response element (CRE)**.

6 Specific gene expression of inducible genes occurs.

ways, the phospholipase C–Ca²⁺ pathway, the NF-κB transcription factor pathway, the Ca²⁺-calmodulin pathway, the MAP kinase pathway, and the JAK-STAT pathway.

The cAMP pathway

The intracellular signaling pathway mediated by **cAMP** was discovered in 1958 by Earl Sutherland while studying the action of **epinephrine**, a hormone that breaks down glycogen into glucose before muscle contraction.

When epinephrine binds to its receptor, there is an increase in the intracellular concentration of cAMP. cAMP is formed from adenosine triphosphate (ATP) by the action of the enzyme **adenylate cyclase** and degraded to adenosine monophosphate (AMP) by the enzyme **cAMP phosphodiesterase**. This mechanism led to the concept of a **first messenger** (epinephrine) mediating a cell-signaling effect by a **second messenger**, cAMP. The epinephrine receptor is linked to adenylate cyclase by G protein, which stimulates cyclase activity upon epinephrine binding.

The intracellular signaling effects of cAMP (Figure 3–6) are mediated by the enzyme **cAMP-dependent protein kinase** (or **protein kinase A**). **In its inactive form, protein kinase A is a tetramer composed of two regulatory subunits** (to which cAMP binds) **and two catalytic subunits**. Binding of cAMP results in the **dissociation of the catalytic subunits.** Free catalytic subunits can phosphorylate **serine residues** on target proteins.

In the epinephrine-dependent regulation of glycogen metabolism, protein kinase A phosphorylates two enzymes:

1. **Phosphorylase kinase**, which in turn phosphorylates glycogen phosphorylase to break down glycogen into glucose-1-phosphate.

2. **Glycogen synthase**, which is involved in the synthesis of glycogen. Phosphorylation of glycogen synthase prevents the synthesis of glycogen.

Note that an elevation of cAMP results in two distinct events: the breakdown of glycogen and, at the same time, a blockage of further glycogen synthesis. Also note that the binding of epinephrine to a single receptor leads to a signal amplification mechanism during intracellular signaling mediated by many molecules of cAMP. cAMP signal amplification is further enhanced by the phosphorylation of many molecules of phosphorylase kinase and glycogen synthase by the catalytic subunits dissociated from protein kinase A. It is important to realize that protein phosphorylation can be rapidly reversed by **protein phosphatases present in the cytosol and as transmembrane proteins. These protein phosphatases can terminate responses initiated by the activation of kinases by removing phosphorylated residues.

cAMP also has an effect on the transcription of specific target genes that contain a regulatory sequence called the **cAMP response element** (**CRE**). Catalytic subunits of protein kinase A enter the nucleus after dissociation from the regulatory subunits. Within the nucleus, catalytic subunits phosphorylate a transcription factor called **CRE-binding protein** (**CREB**), which activates cAMP-inducible genes.

Finally, cAMP effects can be direct, independent of protein phosphorylation. An example is the direct regulation of **ion channels in the olfactory epithelium**. **Odorant receptors** in sensory neurons of the nose are linked to G protein, which stimulates adenylate cyclase to increase intracellular cAMP.

cAMP does not stimulate protein kinase A in sensory neurons but acts directly to open Na⁺ channels in the plasma membrane to initiate membrane depolarization and nerve impulses.

The cGMP pathway

cGMP is also a second messenger. It is produced from guanosine triphosphate (GTP) by guanylate cyclase and degraded to GMP by a phosphodiesterase. Guanylate cyclases are activated by nitric oxide and peptide signaling molecules.

The best characterized role of cGMP is in photoreceptor rod cells of the retina, where it converts light signals to nerve impulses. A detailed description of this cell signaling process can be found in Chapter 9; Sensory Organs: Vision and Hearing in the eye section.

The phospholipase C–Ca²⁺ pathway

Another second messenger involved in intracellular signaling derives from

Figure 3–7

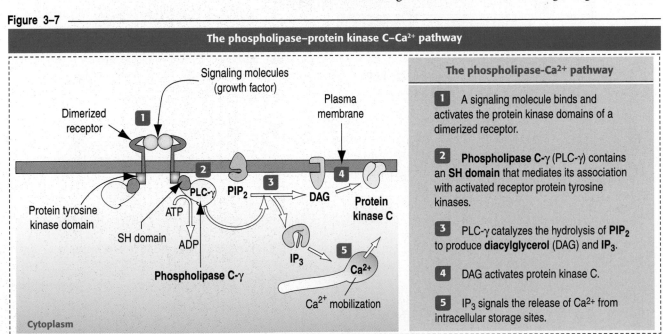

The phospholipase–protein kinase C–Ca²⁺ pathway

The phospholipase-Ca²⁺ pathway

1 A signaling molecule binds and activates the protein kinase domains of a dimerized receptor.

2 **Phospholipase C-γ** (PLC-γ) contains an **SH domain** that mediates its association with activated receptor protein tyrosine kinases.

3 PLC-γ catalyzes the hydrolysis of **PIP₂** to produce **diacylglycerol** (DAG) and **IP₃**.

4 DAG activates protein kinase C.

5 IP₃ signals the release of Ca²⁺ from intracellular storage sites.

Figure 3–8

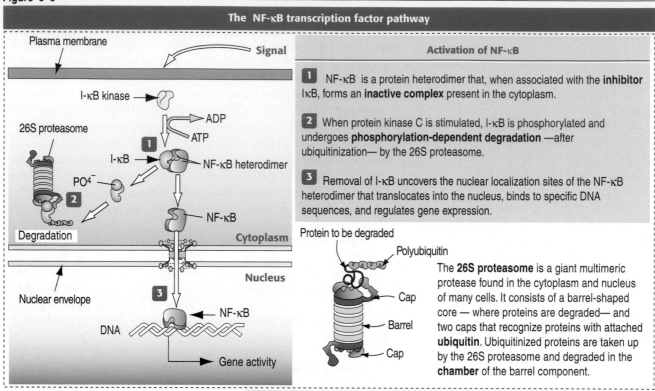

The NF-κB transcription factor pathway

Plasma membrane

Signal

I-κB kinase

ADP
ATP

1

26S proteasome

I-κB

NF-κB heterodimer

PO4⁻

2

Degradation

NF-κB

Cytoplasm

Nuclear envelope

Nucleus

3

DNA

NF-κB

Gene activity

Activation of NF-κB

1 NF-κB is a protein heterodimer that, when associated with the **inhibitor** IκB, forms an **inactive complex** present in the cytoplasm.

2 When protein kinase C is stimulated, I-κB is phosphorylated and undergoes **phosphorylation-dependent degradation** —after ubiquitinization— by the 26S proteasome.

3 Removal of I-κB uncovers the nuclear localization sites of the NF-κB heterodimer that translocates into the nucleus, binds to specific DNA sequences, and regulates gene expression.

Protein to be degraded

Polyubiquitin

Cap

Barrel

Cap

The **26S proteasome** is a giant multimeric protease found in the cytoplasm and nucleus of many cells. It consists of a barrel-shaped core — where proteins are degraded— and two caps that recognize proteins with attached **ubiquitin**. Ubiquitinized proteins are taken up by the 26S proteasome and degraded in the **chamber** of the barrel component.

the phospholipid **phosphatidylinositol 4,5-bisphosphate** (PIP₂) present in the inner leaflet of the plasma membrane (Figure 3–7).

The hydrolysis of PIP₂ by the enzyme **phospholipase C (PLC)** —stimulated by a number of hormones and growth factors— produces two second messen-

Figure 3–9

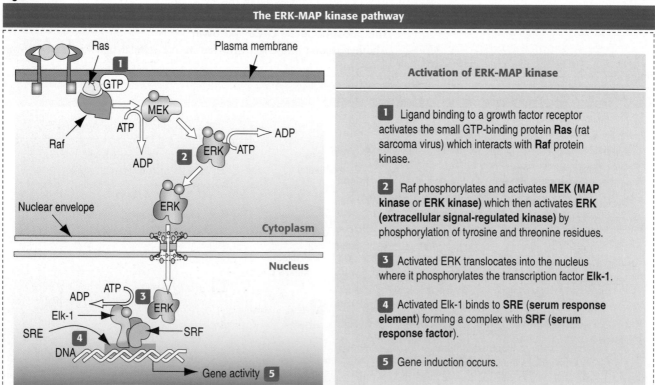

The ERK-MAP kinase pathway

Ras

Plasma membrane

1

GTP

MEK

ATP

ADP

Raf

ERK

ATP

2

ERK

Nuclear envelope

Cytoplasm

Nucleus

ADP

ATP

3

ERK

Elk-1

SRE

4

SRF

DNA

Gene activity **5**

Activation of ERK-MAP kinase

1 Ligand binding to a growth factor receptor activates the small GTP-binding protein **Ras** (rat sarcoma virus) which interacts with **Raf** protein kinase.

2 Raf phosphorylates and activates **MEK (MAP kinase or ERK kinase)** which then activates **ERK (extracellular signal-regulated kinase)** by phosphorylation of tyrosine and threonine residues.

3 Activated ERK translocates into the nucleus where it phosphorylates the transcription factor **Elk-1**.

4 Activated Elk-1 binds to **SRE (serum response element)** forming a complex with **SRF (serum response factor)**.

5 Gene induction occurs.

Transcription factor genes

Genes encoding proteins that turn on (activate) or turn off (repress) other genes are called **transcription factors**. Many transcription factors have **common DNA-binding domains** and can also activate or repress a single target gene as well as other genes (a **cascade effect**). Therefore, mutations affecting genes encoding transcription factor have **pleiotropic effects** (Gr. *pleion*, more; *trope*, a turning toward). Examples of transcription factor genes include **homeobox-containing genes**, **high mobility group (HMG)-box containing genes**, and **T-box family**.

The HMG domain of **Sox** proteins can bend DNA, and facilitate the interaction of enhancers with a distantly located promoter region of a target gene. Several *SOX* genes act in different developmental pathways. For example, **Sox9** protein is expressed in the gonadal ridges of both sexes but is upregulated in males and downregulated in females before gonadal differentiation. Sox9 also regulates **chondrogenesis** and the expression of **type II collagen** (see Chapter 4, Connective Tissue). Mutations of the *SOX9* gene cause skeletal defects (**campomelic dysplasia**), and **sex reversal** (XY females).

gers: **diacylglycerol** and **inositol 1,4,5-trisphosphate (IP$_3$)**.

These two messengers stimulate two downstream signaling pathway cascades: **protein kinase C** and **Ca^{2+} mobilization**.

Two forms of PLC exist: **PLC-β** and **PLC-γ**. PLC-β is activated by G protein. PLC-γ contains SH2 domains that enable association with receptor protein tyrosine kinases. Tyrosine phosphorylation increases PLC-γ activity, which in turn stimulates the breakdown of PIP$_2$.

Diacylglycerol, derived from PIP$_2$ hydrolysis, activates members of the **protein kinase C** family (**protein serine and threonine kinases**).

Phorbol esters are tumor growth promoting agents acting, like diacylglycerol, by stimulation of protein kinase C activities. Protein kinase C activates other intracellular targets such as protein kinases of the **MAP kinase pathway** to produce the phosphorylation of transcription factors leading to changes in gene expression and cell proliferation.

The NF-κB transcription factor pathway

NF-κB (for nuclear factor involved in the transcription of the κ light chain gene in B lymphocytes) is a transcription factor involved in immune responses in several cells and is stimulated by protein kinase C (Figure 3–8). In its **inactive state**, the NF-κB protein heterodimer is bound to the **inhibitory subunit I-κB** and the complex is retained in the cytoplasm. The phosphorylation of I-κB—triggered by I-κB kinase—leads to the destruction of I-κB by the 26S proteasome and the release of NF-κB. The free NF-κB heterodimer translocates into the nucleus to activate gene transcription in response to immunologic and inflammatory signaling.

The Ca^{2+}–calmodulin pathway

Although the second messenger diacylglycerol remains associated with the plasma membrane, the other second messenger IP$_3$, derived from PIP$_2$, is released into the cytosol to activate ion pumps and free Ca^{2+} from intracellular storage sites. High cytosolic Ca^{2+} concentrations (from a basal level of 0.1 μM to an increased 1.0 μM concentration after cytosolic release) activate several Ca^{2+}-dependent protein kinases and phosphatases.

Figure 3–10

The JAK-phosphorylated STAT dimer pathway

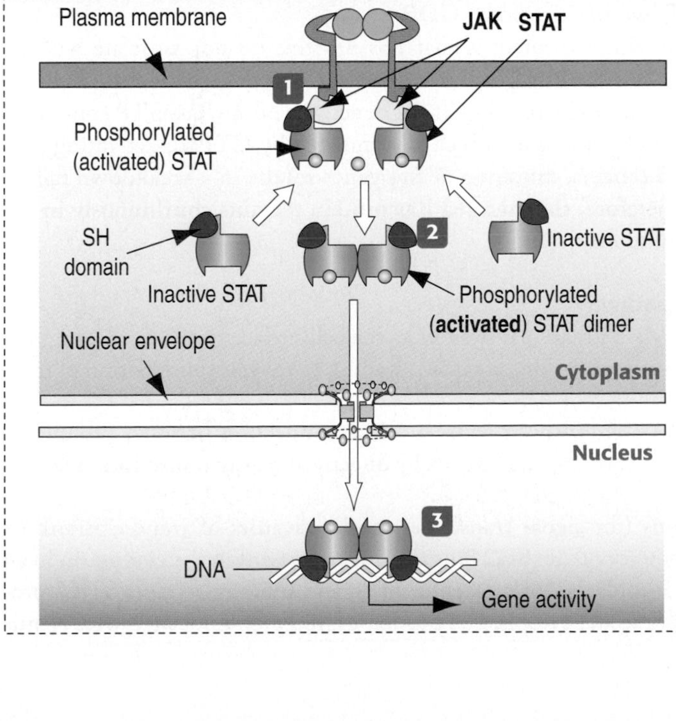

The JAK-STAT pathway

1 Ligand binding to a cytokine receptor leads to the attachment of the inactive transcription factor STAT to the receptor-associated **JAK protein tyrosine kinase** via their **SH2 domains**.

2 Phosphorylated **STAT dimerizes**.

3 The phosphorylated STAT dimer translocates to the nucleus where it activates transcription of target genes.

Calmodulin is a Ca^{2+}-dependent protein that is activated when the Ca^{2+} concentration increases to 0.5 µM. Ca^{2+}-calmodulin complexes bind to a number of cytosolic target proteins to regulate cell responses. Note that Ca^{2+} **is an important second messenger** and that its intracellular concentration can be increased not only by its release from intracellular storage sites but also by increasing the entry of Ca^{2+} into the cell from the extracellular space.

The MAP kinase pathway

This pathway involves evolutionarily conserved protein kinases (yeast to humans) with roles in cell growth and differentiation. **MAP kinases** (for <u>m</u>itogen-<u>a</u>ctivated <u>p</u>rotein <u>k</u>inases) are protein serine and threonine kinases activated by growth factors and other signaling molecules (Figure 3–9).

A well-characterized form of MAP kinase is the ERK family. Members of the **ERK** (for <u>e</u>xtracellular <u>s</u>ignal-<u>r</u>egulated <u>k</u>inase) family act **through either protein tyrosine kinase or G protein-associated receptors**. Both cAMP and Ca^{2+}-dependent pathways can stimulate or inhibit the ERK pathway in different cell types.

The activation of ERK is mediated by two protein kinases: **Raf**, a protein serine or threonine kinase, which, in turn, activates a second kinase called **MEK** (for <u>M</u>AP kinase or <u>E</u>RK <u>k</u>inase). Stimulation of a growth factor receptor leads to the activation of the GTP-binding protein **Ras** (for <u>rat sarcoma virus</u>), which interacts with Raf. Raf phosphorylates and activates MEK which then activates ERK by phosphorylation of serine and threonine residues. ERK then phosphorylates nuclear and cytosolic target proteins.

In the nucleus, activated ERK phosphorylates the transcription factors **Elk-1** and **serum response factor (SRF)**, which recognize the regulatory sequence called **serum response element (SRE)**.

In addition to ERK, mammalian cells contain two other MAP kinases called **JNK** and **p38 MAP kinases**. Cytokines and ultraviolet irradiation stimulate JNK and p38 MAP kinase activation mediated by small GTP-binding proteins different from Ras. These kinases are not activated by MEK but by a distinct dual kinase called **MKK** (for <u>M</u>AP <u>k</u>inase <u>k</u>inase).

A key element in the ERK pathway is the **Ras proteins**, a group of oncogenic proteins of tumor viruses that cause sarcomas in rats. Mutations in the Ras gene have been linked to human cancer. **Ras proteins are guanine nucleotide–binding protein with functional properties similar to the G protein α subunits** (activated by **GTP** and inactivated by **GDP**).

A difference with G protein is that Ras proteins do not associate with βγ subunits. Ras is activated by **guanine nucleotide exchange factors** to facilitate the release of GDP in exchange for GTP. The activity of the Ras-GTP complex is terminated by GTP hydrolysis, which is stimulated by **GTPase-activating proteins. In human cancers, mutation of Ras genes results in a breakdown failure of GTP and, therefore, the mutated Ras protein remains continuously in the active GTP-bound form.**

The JAK-STAT pathway

The preceding MAP kinase pathway links the cell surface to the nucleus signaling mediated by a protein kinase cascade leading to the phosphorylation of transcription factors.

The **JAK-STAT pathway** provides a close connection between protein-tyrosine kinases and transcription factors by directly affecting transcription factors (Figure 3–10).

STAT proteins (for <u>s</u>ignal <u>t</u>ransducers and <u>a</u>ctivators of <u>t</u>ranscription) are transcription factors with an SH2 domain and are present in the **cytoplasm** in an inactive state. Stimulation of a receptor by ligand binding recruits STAT proteins, which bind to the cytoplasmic portion of receptor-associated **JAK** (<u>J</u>anus kinase) **protein tyrosine kinase** through their SH2 domain and become phosphorylated. Phosphorylated STAT proteins then dimerize and translocate into the nucleus, where they activate the transcription of target genes.

Stem cells, a multipotent cell population

Cells in the body show an extreme range in ability to divide and grow. Some cells (for example, nerve cells and erythrocytes) reach a mature, differentiated state and usually do not divide. Such cells are referred to as **postmitotic cells**. Other cells, called **stem cells**, show continuous division throughout life (for example, epithelial cells lining the intestine and stem cells that give rise to the various blood cell types).

Many other cells are intermediate between these two extremes and remain quiescent most of the time but can be triggered to divide by appropriate signals. Liver cells are an example. If the liver is damaged, cell division can be triggered to compensate for the lost cells.

Stem cells have three properties: **self-renewal**, **proliferation**, and **differentiation**.

Figure 3–11

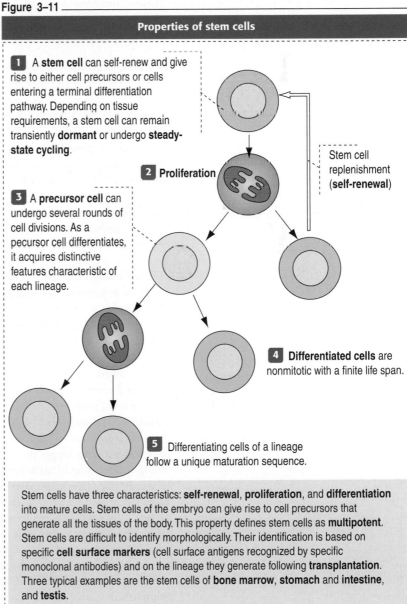

Properties of stem cells

1 A **stem cell** can self-renew and give rise to either cell precursors or cells entering a terminal differentiation pathway. Depending on tissue requirements, a stem cell can remain transiently **dormant** or undergo **steady-state cycling**.

2 Proliferation

Stem cell replenishment (**self-renewal**)

3 A **precursor cell** can undergo several rounds of cell divisions. As a pecursor cell differentiates, it acquires distinctive features characteristic of each lineage.

4 **Differentiated cells** are nonmitotic with a finite life span.

5 Differentiating cells of a lineage follow a unique maturation sequence.

Stem cells have three characteristics: **self-renewal**, **proliferation**, and **differentiation** into mature cells. Stem cells of the embryo can give rise to cell precursors that generate all the tissues of the body. This property defines stem cells as **multipotent**. Stem cells are difficult to identify morphologically. Their identification is based on specific **cell surface markers** (cell surface antigens recognized by specific monoclonal antibodies) and on the lineage they generate following **transplantation**. Three typical examples are the stem cells of **bone marrow**, **stomach** and **intestine**, and **testis**.

Stem cells have the potential to generate a large number of mature cells continuously throughout life. When stem cells divide by mitosis, some of the progeny differentiates into a specific cell type. Other progeny remains as stem cells (Figure 3–11). The intestinal epithelium, the epidermis of the skin, the hematopoietic system, and the seminiferous epithelium share this property. We discuss in detail the significance of stem cells in each of these tissues in the appropriate chapters. Following stress and injury, other tissues, such as liver, muscle, and the nervous system, can regenerate mature cells.

For example, it has been shown that bone marrow stem cells can produce muscle tissue as well as hematopoietic tissue in an appropriate host system (see Chapter 7, Muscle Tissue). Cultured stem cells of the central nervous system are capable of hematopoiesis in transplanted irradiated mouse recipients.

Recall that embryonic stem cells, forming the **inner cell mass** of the early embryo (the blastocyst), give rise to all the tissues and organs except the placenta. Embryonic stem cells provide an experimental source of medically useful differentiating tissues such as pancreatic islets for the treatment of diabetes, skin for the treatment of burns and wounds, regenerating cartilage for the treatment of arthritis, and endothelial cells for the repair of blood vessel, affected by arteriosclerosis. A potential complication is that embryonic stem cells injected into mature mice develop an embryonic tumor called a **teratoma**.

In vitro cell proliferation, senescence, and telomerase

Cell culture techniques have been a powerful tool for examining the factors that regulate cell growth and for comparing the properties of normal and cancer cells.

Many cells grow in tissue culture, but some are much easier to grow than others. Culture medium contains **salts**, **amino acids**, **vitamins**, and a source of energy such as **glucose**. In addition, most cells require a number of **hormones** or **growth factors** for sustained culture and cell division. These factors are usually provided by addition of **serum** to the culture medium.

For some cell types the components supplied by serum have been identified, and these cells can be grown in **serum-free, hormone and growth factor–supplemented medium**. Some of these factors are hormones, such as insulin. A number of growth factors have been identified, for example, EGF, fibroblast growth factor (FGF), and PDGF.

When normal cells are placed in culture in the presence of adequate nutrients and growth factors, they will grow until they cover the bottom of the culture dish, forming a monolayer. Further cell division then ceases. This is called **density-dependent inhibition of growth**. The cells become quiescent but can be triggered to enter the cell cycle and divide again by an additional dose of growth factor or by replating at a lower cell density.

Cells cultured from a tissue can be kept growing and dividing by regularly replating the cells at lower density once they become confluent. After about 50 cell divisions, however, the cells begin to stop dividing and the cultures become **senescent**. The number of divisions at which this occurs depends on the age of the individual from which the initial cells were taken. Cells from an embryo will thus keep growing longer than cells taken from an adult.

In our discussion of mitosis (see Figure 1–51), we called attention to the role of **telomerase**, an enzyme that maintains the ends of chromosomes, or **telomeres**. In normal cells, insufficient telomerase activity limits the number of mitotic divisions and forces the cell into **senescence**, defined as the finite capacity for cell division. **Telomere shortening and the limited life span of a cell are regarded as potent tumor suppressor mechanisms**. Most human tumors express **human telomerase reverse transcriptase (hTERT)**. The ectopic expression of hTERT in primary human cells confers endless growth in culture. The use of telomerase inhibitors in cancer patients is currently being pursued.

Occasionally cells that would normally stop growing become altered and ap-

Figure 3–12

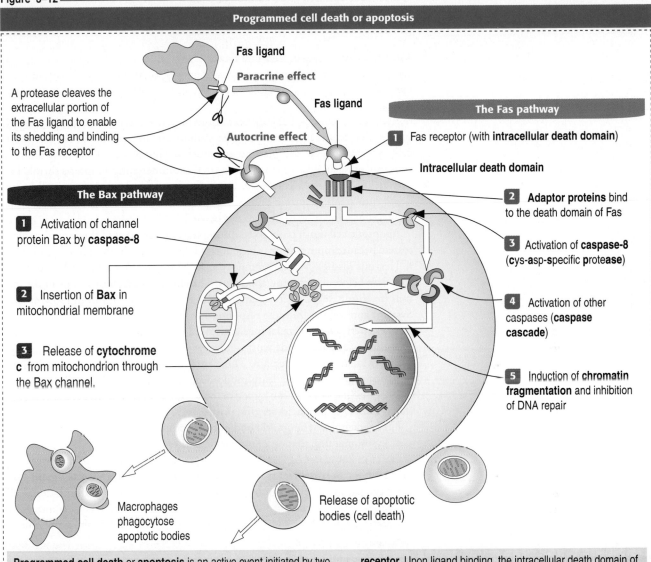

Programmed cell death or apoptosis

A protease cleaves the extracellular portion of the Fas ligand to enable its shedding and binding to the Fas receptor

Fas ligand

Paracrine effect

Fas ligand

Autocrine effect

The Fas pathway

1 Fas receptor (with **intracellular death domain**)

Intracellular death domain

2 **Adaptor proteins** bind to the death domain of Fas

3 Activation of **caspase-8** (**cys-asp-specific protease**)

4 Activation of other caspases (**caspase cascade**)

5 Induction of **chromatin fragmentation** and inhibition of DNA repair

The Bax pathway

1 Activation of channel protein Bax by **caspase-8**

2 Insertion of **Bax** in mitochondrial membrane

3 Release of **cytochrome c** from mitochondrion through the Bax channel.

Macrophages phagocytose apoptotic bodies

Release of apoptotic bodies (cell death)

Programmed cell death or **apoptosis** is an active event initiated by two interrelated pathways:
1. The **Fas pathway**.
2. The **Bax pathway**.
The end point of the two pathways is the activation of proteases –called **caspases** (because they cleave proteins at the cys-asp site)– to break down the cell into fragments (**apoptotic bodies**).

In the **Fas pathway**, a **Fas ligand** produced by adjacent cells (**paracrine effect**) or the cell programmed to die (**autocrine effect**), binds to the **Fas**

receptor. Upon ligand binding, the intracellular death domain of the Fas receptor enables the coupling of **adaptor proteins** which in turn activate **caspase-8**. Caspase-8 activates additional caspases to initiate cell breakdown.
In the **Bax pathway**, Bax protein –a channel protein– is inserted in the mitochondrial membrane to facilitate the leakage of **cytochrome c**, an activator of caspases.
Cell death occurs when chromatin is fragmented and structural components of the cells are packaged into apoptotic bodies. Macrophages capture apoptotic bodies.

pear to become **immortal**. Such cells are called a **cell line**. Cell lines are very useful experimentally and still show most of the phenotype and growth characteristics of the original cells.

An additional change known as **transformation** is associated with the potential for **malignant growth**. Transformed cells no longer show normal growth control and have many alterations, such as **anchorage-independent growth**. Normal cells can grow when anchored to a solid substrate.

Cells in culture can be transformed by **chemical carcinogens** or by **infection with certain viruses** (tumor viruses). Tumor viruses will also cause tumors in certain host animals, but in different species they may cause ordinary infections.

Cancer cells cultured from tumors also show the characteristics of transformation. We will discuss at the end of this chapter the role of retroviruses in carcinogenesis.

Apoptosis or programmed cell death

Under normal physiologic conditions, damaged or senescent cells commit suicide through a genetically regulated cell death program called **apoptosis** (Gr. *apo*, off; *ptosis*, fall).

Apoptosis (Figure 3–12) is different from **necrosis**. Necrosis is a nonphysiologic process that occurs in acute injury (for example, in an ischemic stroke). Necrotic cells lyse and release cytoplasmic and nuclear contents into the environment, thus triggering an inflammatory reaction. Cells undergoing apoptosis shrink, lose intercellular adhesion, condense, fragment the chromatin, and the cell breaks down into small apoptotic bodies. Apoptotic bodies are phagocytosed by macrophages and inflammation does not occur.

Apoptotic cell death is observed during the development of the central nervous system because more neurons are generated than survive in the adult (see Chapter 8, Nervous Tissue). Mature granulocytes in peripheral blood have a life span of 1 to 2 days before undergoing apoptosis. The clonal selection of T cells in the thymus (to eliminate selfreactive lymphocytes; see Chapter 10, Immune-Lymphatic System) and cellular immune responses involve apoptosis.

The genetic and molecular mechanisms of apoptosis emerged in the late 1980s in studies of the nematode worm *Caenorhabditis elegans*, in which 131 cells are precisely killed and 959 remain. There are four sequential steps in apoptosis:

1. Commitment to cell death induced by extracellular or intracellular factors.
2. Cell killing or execution by activation of intracellular proteases called **caspases** (for **c**ysteine **asp**artic acid-specific prote**ases**).
3. Phagocytosis of apoptotic bodies by macrophages.
4. Lysosomal degradation of apoptotic bodies.

Fas (also known as APO-1 or CD95) is a cell membrane protein that belongs to the **tumor necrosis factor (TNF) receptor family**. A ligand, **Fas ligand**, initiates programmed cell death by binding to the **Fas receptor** and initiates a cell-signaling cascade consisting of the sequential activation of **procaspases** into active **caspases**. Caspases cleave two DNA repair enzymes (**poly-ADP–ribose polymerase**

Figure 3–13

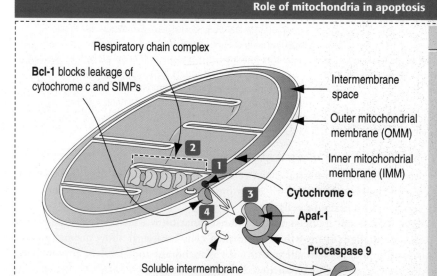

Role of mitochondria in apoptosis

Respiratory chain complex

Bcl-1 blocks leakage of cytochrome c and SIMPs

Intermembrane space

Outer mitochondrial membrane (OMM)

Inner mitochondrial membrane (IMM)

Cytochrome c

Apaf-1

Procaspase 9

Soluble intermembrane proteins (SIMPs)

Active caspase 9

Cytochrome c in apoptosis

1 Cytochrome c is located between the IMM and OMM and is an essential component of the mitochondrial respiratory chain.

2 Cytochrome c shuttles electrons between respiratory chain complexes III and IV. If cytochrome c is not present, electron flow stops and ATP synthesis does not occur.

3 During apoptosis, **cytochrome c is released across the OMM and interacts with apoptosis protease activating factor-1 (Apaf-1)**, which activates procaspase 9. Caspase 9 activates other caspases leading to the proteolytic destruction of the cell.

4 Bcl-2 blocks the release of cytochrome c and SIMPs.

Figure 3–14

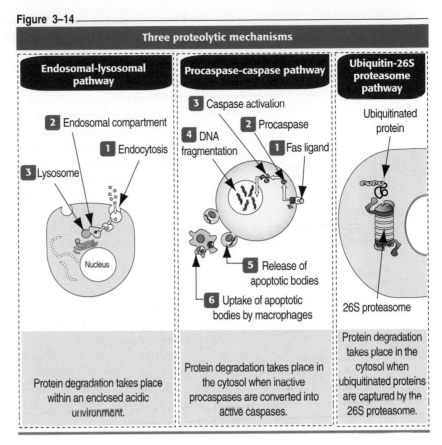

Three proteolytic mechanisms

Endosomal-lysosomal pathway

2 Endosomal compartment

1 Endocytosis

3 Lysosome

Nucleus

Protein degradation takes place within an enclosed acidic environment.

Procaspase-caspase pathway

3 Caspase activation

2 Procaspase

4 DNA fragmentation

1 Fas ligand

5 Release of apoptotic bodies

6 Uptake of apoptotic bodies by macrophages

Protein degradation takes place in the cytosol when inactive procaspases are converted into active caspases.

Ubiquitin-26S proteasome pathway

Ubiquitinated protein

26S proteasome

Protein degradation takes place in the cytosol when ubiquitinated proteins are captured by the 26S proteasome.

[**PARP**], and DNA protein kinase), and unrestricted fragmentation of chromatin occurs.

In addition, the protein **Bax** induces leakage of mitochondrial **cytochrome c** into the cytosol, which activates additional apoptotic proteases. The cell damaging effect of Bax is blocked by binding of the protein **bcl-2** to Bax (Figure 3–13).

Apoptosis is observed in graft rejection, a number of autoimmune diseases, neurodegeneration, heart disease, and cancer (lymphoproliferative disorders).

Products of genes involved in the regulation and execution of apoptosis are potential targets for diagnosis and therapeutic intervention in disease processes.

Three major cellular mechanisms are involved in proteolysis

In addition to the **procaspase-caspase pathway** activated by Fas ligand (see Figure 3–12), the intracellular degradation of residual or misfolded proteins (**proteolysis**) can occur by the classic **endosomal-lysosomal pathway** (see Figure 2–19) and the **ubiquitin-proteasome pathway** (Figure 3–14). We have seen that the endosomal-lysosomal mechanism operates within a membrane-bound acidic compartment. In contrast, the procaspase-caspase pathway and the ubiquitin/proteasome pathway carry out proteolysis in the cytosol.

The ubiquitin-proteasome pathway involves two successive regulated steps:

1. The attachment of a chain of ubiquitin molecules to a protein substrate by an enzymatic cascade.

2. The degradation of target proteins by the **26S proteasome**.

The 26S proteasome is a giant (~2000 kDa) multimeric protease present in the nucleus and cytoplasm. Structurally, the 26S proteasome consists of a barrel-shaped core capped by two structures that recognize ubiquitinated proteins. Protein degradation occurs within a chamber of the barrel-shaped core. Proteins degraded by the 26S proteasome include molecules involved in the regulation of the cell cycle (cyclins), transcription factors, and the processing of antigens involved in the activation of inflammatory and immune responses.

Proto-oncogenes and oncogenes

A proto-oncogene is a normal gene encoding a regulatory protein of the cell cycle, cell differentiation, or a cell-signaling pathway. Proto-oncogenic proteins mimic growth factors, hormone receptors, G proteins, intracellular enzymes, and transcription factors.

An **oncogene** is a **mutated proto-oncogene** which encodes an **oncoprotein** able to disrupt the normal cell cycle and to cause cancer.

Proto-oncogenes and oncogenes are designated by an **italicized three-letter** name. An oncogene present in a virus has the prefix **v**. A proto-oncogene present in a cell has the prefix **c**.

A protein encoded by a proto-oncogene or oncogene has the same three-letter designation as the proto-oncogene or oncogene. However, the letters are not italicized and the first letter is capitalized.

Anti-oncogenes are also called **tumor suppressor genes**. A loss of activity of a tumor suppressor gene product results in constitutive activation of cell growth.

Proto-oncogenes and oncogenes

Genes that cause cancer are called **oncogenes** (Gr., *onkos*, bulk, mass; *genos*, birth). Most oncogenes originate from **proto-oncogenes** (Gr., *prōtos*, first). Proto-oncogenes are involved in the **four basic regulatory mechanisms of cell growth** by expressing:

1. **Growth factors.**
2. **Growth factor receptors.**
3. **Signal transduction molecules.**
4. **Nuclear transcription factors.**

An oncogene results from the mutation of a proto-oncogene. Oncogenes express constantly active products leading to unregulated cell growth and differentiation. A cell becomes **transformed** when it changes from regulated to unregulated growth.

Although most animal viruses destroy the cells they infect, several types of viruses are able to establish a long-term infection, in which the cell is not killed. This stable virus–host cell interaction perpetuates the viral information in the cell, usually by direct insertion into cellular DNA.

The first oncogenes to be identified came from the study of **retroviruses**. All vertebrate animals, including humans, inherit genes related to retroviral genes and transmit them to their progeny. These are called **endogenous proviruses**, whereas those that infect a cell are called **exogenous proviruses**.

Cancer viruses isolated from every type of vertebrate animal induce a wide variety of tumors and belong to several virus types: **RNA-containing tumor viruses**, called **retroviruses**, and **DNA-containing tumor viruses**, including the **polyomaviruses**, the **papillomaviruses**, the **adenoviruses**, and the **herpesviruses**.

Retroviruses and polyomaviruses have received the most attention because they carry one or two genes that have specific cancer-inducing properties: so-called **viral oncogenes**. Retroviruses and polyomaviruses, like cellular genes, are subject to mutations. A group of such mutants of **Rous sarcoma virus** (RSV; species of origin: chicken) has proved useful for determining the role of the **viral** gene v-*src*. The *src*-like sequences in normal cells constitute a **cellular** gene called **c-*src***, a **proto-oncogene**.

The **viral** *src* derives directly from the **cellular** *src*. A precursor of RSV seems to have acquired a copy of c-*src* during infection of a chicken cell. The resulting RSV manipulated its picked up gene to transform subsequently infected cells.

c-src is harmless but its close relative v-src causes tumors and transform cells after RSV infection. A chicken fibroblast produces about 50 times more src RNA and protein than an uninfected fibroblast containing only the c-*src* gene. The c-*src* gene assumed great significance when it was recognized that many other retroviruses carry oncogenes, often different from v-*src*. Each of these genes is also derived from a distinct, normal cellular precursor.

The classification of genes as proto-oncogenes is based on the understanding that mutant forms of these genes participate in the development of cancer. However, proto-oncogenes serve different biochemical functions in the control of normal growth and development. They can also undergo a variety of mutations that convert them to dominant genes capable of inducing cancers in the absence of viruses.

Proto-oncogenes can indeed be mutated in their native chromosomal location. Recall a few aspects of the retrovirus cell cycle (Figure 3–15): In the initial stages of infection, the **viral RNA is copied into DNA** by the viral enzyme **reverse transcriptase**. Once synthesized, the viral DNA molecule is transported into the nucleus and inserted randomly as a **provirus** at any one of the available sites of host chromosomal DNA. Proviruses contain signals for the regulation of their own viral genes, but such signals can be transmitted to the proto-oncogene, coercing it to produce larger than normal amounts of RNA and a protein.

RSV-infected cells produce a 60 kDa protein. This protein was identified as

Some oncogenes and tumor suppressor proteins linked to human cancers

Chronic myelogenous leukemia: The *c-abl* proto-oncogene translocated from chromosome 9 to chromosome 22 (called the Philadelphia chromosome) encodes a fusion protein with constitutive active tyrosine kinase activity.

Burkitt's lymphoma: The **c-*myc*** proto-oncogene is translocated from chromosome 8 to chromosome 14. This translocation places c-*myc* under the control of an active immunoglobulin locus (immunoglobulin heavy-chain gene, Cm) and detached from its normal regulatory elements. Burkitt's lymphoma is endemic in some parts of Africa and affects mainly children or young adults. It generally involves the maxilla or mandible. It responds to chemotherapy.

p53: Inactivation of this **tumor suppressor protein**, a transcription factor expressed in response to DNA damage (Figure 1–52), is associated with 50%-60% of human cancers. Inactive p53 enables the progression of cells containing damaged DNA through the cell cycle.

Figure 3–15

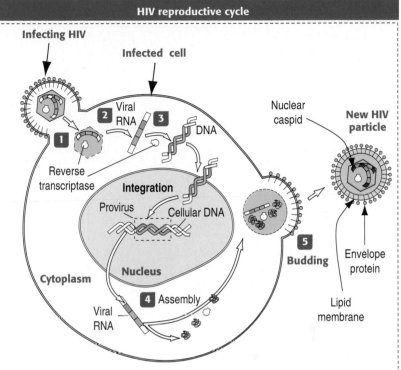

HIV reproductive cycle

1 The life cycle of a retrovirus begins when the virus binds and enters a cell and introduces its genetic material (RNA) and proteins into the cytoplasm.

2 The genome of a typical retrovirus includes three coding regions: **gag**, **pol**, and **env**, specifying, respectively, proteins of the viral core, the enzyme **reverse transcriptase**, and constituents of the viral coat.

3 In the cytoplasm, reverse transcriptase converts viral RNA into DNA which is then inserted into cellular DNA. This process is called **integration**.

4 The provirus DNA directs the synthesis of viral proteins and RNA.

5 The proteins enclose the RNA, forming viral particles that bud from the cell.

the product that the **v-*src* gene** uses to transform cells. It was designated **p60**$^{v\text{-}src}$. This protein can function as a **protein kinase** and, within a living cell, many proteins can be phosphorylated by **Src kinase** activity. The target for phosphorylation is **tyrosine** residues.

Cell transformation by the v-*src* oncogene causes a tenfold increase in total cellular phosphotyrosine in cellular target proteins restricted to the inner side of the **cell membrane**. Many other proteins encoded by proto-oncogenes or involved in control of cell growth function like the Src protein, such as protein kinases, are often specific for tyrosine.

4. CONNECTIVE TISSUE

Classification

The connective tissue provides the **supportive** and **connecting** framework (or **stroma**) for all the other tissues of the body. The connective tissue is formed by **cells** and the **extracellular matrix (ECM)**. The ECM represents a combination of **collagens, noncollagenous glycoproteins,** and **proteoglycans (ground substance)** surrounding cells of the connective tissue. The cells of the connective tissue have important roles in the **storage of metabolites, immune and inflammatory responses,** and **tissue repair after injury.**

Unlike epithelial cells, which are almost free of intercellular material, **connective tissue cells are widely separated by components of the ECM.** In addition, epithelial cells lack direct blood and lymphatic supply, whereas connective tissue is directly supplied by blood and lymphatic vessels and nerves.

Connective tissue can be classified into three major groups (Figure 4–1): **embryonic connective tissue, adult connective tissue,** and **special connective tissue.**

Embryonic connective tissue is a loose tissue formed during early embryonic development. This type of connective tissue, found primarily in the **umbilical cord,** consists predominantly of a **hydrophilic ECM** and therefore has a jelly-like consistency. Because of this consistency, it is also called **mucoid connective tissue** or **Wharton's jelly.**

Adult connective tissue has considerable structural diversity because **the proportion of cells to fibers and of ground substance varies from tissue to tissue.** This variable cell-to-ECM ratio is the basis for the subclassification of adult connective tissue into two types of connective tissue proper:

1. **Loose** (or **areolar**) **connective tissue.**
2. **Dense connective tissue.**

Loose connective tissue contains **more cells than collagen fibers** and is generally found in the **mucosa** and **submucosa** of various organs and surrounding blood vessels, nerves, and muscles. This type of connective tissue facilitates dissection as performed by anatomists, pathologists, and surgeons.

Dense connective tissue contains **more collagen fibers than cells.** When the collagen fibers are **preferentially oriented** —as in tendons, ligaments, and the cornea— the tissue is called **dense regular connective tissue.** When the collagen fibers are **randomly oriented** —as in the dermis of the skin— the tissue is called **dense irregular connective tissue.**

In addition, **reticular** and **elastic fibers** predominate in irregular connective tissue.

Reticular connective tissue contains **reticular fibers,** which form the **stroma** of organs of the lymphoid-immune system (for example, lymph nodes and spleen), the hematopoietic bone marrow, and the liver. This type of connective tissue provides a delicate meshwork to allow passage of cells and fluid.

Elastic connective tissue contains irregularly arranged **elastic fibers** in ligaments of the vertebral column or concentrically arranged **sheets** or **laminae** in the wall of the aorta. This type of connective tissue provides **elasticity.**

The **special connective tissue** comprises types of connective tissue with **special properties** not observed in the embryonic or adult connective tissue proper. There are four types of special connective tissue (Figure 4–2):

1. **Adipose tissue.**
2. Cartilage.
3. **Bone.**
4. Hematopoietic tissue (bone marrow).

Adipose tissue has more cells (called **adipose cells** or **adipocytes**) than col-

Figure 4–1

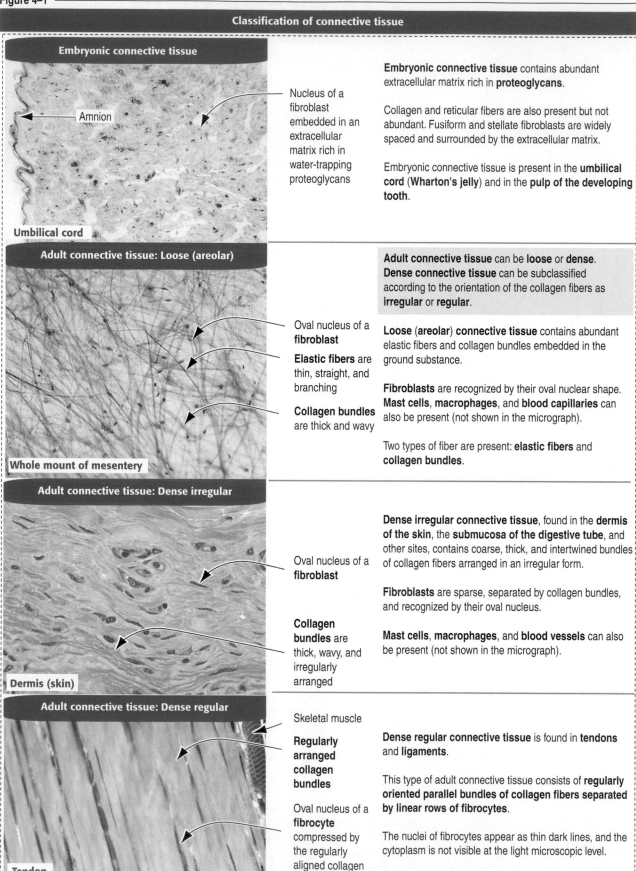

Classification of connective tissue

Embryonic connective tissue

Amnion

Nucleus of a fibroblast embedded in an extracellular matrix rich in water-trapping proteoglycans

Umbilical cord

Embryonic connective tissue contains abundant extracellular matrix rich in **proteoglycans**.

Collagen and reticular fibers are also present but not abundant. Fusiform and stellate fibroblasts are widely spaced and surrounded by the extracellular matrix.

Embryonic connective tissue is present in the **umbilical cord (Wharton's jelly)** and in the **pulp of the developing tooth**.

Adult connective tissue: Loose (areolar)

Oval nucleus of a **fibroblast**

Elastic fibers are thin, straight, and branching

Collagen bundles are thick and wavy

Whole mount of mesentery

Adult connective tissue can be **loose** or **dense**. **Dense connective tissue** can be subclassified according to the orientation of the collagen fibers as **irregular** or **regular**.

Loose (areolar) connective tissue contains abundant elastic fibers and collagen bundles embedded in the ground substance.

Fibroblasts are recognized by their oval nuclear shape. **Mast cells**, **macrophages**, and **blood capillaries** can also be present (not shown in the micrograph).

Two types of fiber are present: **elastic fibers** and **collagen bundles**.

Adult connective tissue: Dense irregular

Oval nucleus of a **fibroblast**

Collagen bundles are thick, wavy, and irregularly arranged

Dermis (skin)

Dense irregular connective tissue, found in the **dermis of the skin**, the **submucosa of the digestive tube**, and other sites, contains coarse, thick, and intertwined bundles of collagen fibers arranged in an irregular form.

Fibroblasts are sparse, separated by collagen bundles, and recognized by their oval nucleus.

Mast cells, **macrophages**, and **blood vessels** can also be present (not shown in the micrograph).

Adult connective tissue: Dense regular

Skeletal muscle

Regularly arranged collagen bundles

Oval nucleus of a **fibrocyte** compressed by the regularly aligned collagen bundles

Tendon

Dense regular connective tissue is found in **tendons** and **ligaments**.

This type of adult connective tissue consists of **regularly oriented parallel bundles of collagen fibers separated by linear rows of fibrocytes**.

The nuclei of fibrocytes appear as thin dark lines, and the cytoplasm is not visible at the light microscopic level.

Figure 4–2

Classification of connective tissue

Adult connective tissue: Reticular tissue

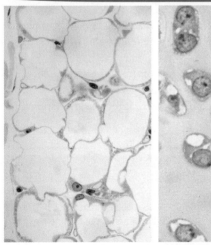

Lymphatic nodule

Reticular fibers (type III collagen) can be identified in the stroma of this lymphatic nodule after impregnation with **silver salts**. Reticular fibers are **argyrophilic**.

Reticular connective tissue is an adult-type connective tissue in which **reticular fibers** predominate. **Reticular connective tissue is characteristic of lymphatic tissues**.

Reticular fibers, synthesized by fibroblasts (also called **reticular cells**), are thin and branching structures.

Reticular fibers form a meshwork in which lymphoid cells are embedded.

Adult connective tissue: Elastic tissue

Artery

Elastic fibers are arranged in concentric and discontinuous sheets in the wall of this artery. In this section, elastic laminae appear as wavy pink bands.

Elastic connective tissue is an adult-type connective tissue in which **elastic fibers** predominate. **Elastic connective tissue is characteristic of the walls of large blood vessel** and **ligaments**.

Elastic fibers in the wall of a blood vessel, synthesized by **smooth muscle cells**, form **discontinuous lamellae or membranes** in a concentric arrangement around the lumen.

Special types of connective tissue

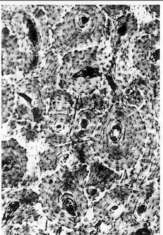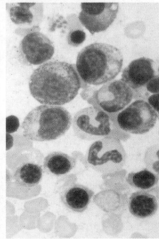

Adipose tissue   Cartilage   Bone   Hematopoietic tissue

lagen fibers and ground substance. This type of connective tissue is the most significant energy storage site of the body.

The **hematopoietic tissue** is found in the marrow of selected bones. This type of connective tissue is discussed later (see Chapter 6, Blood and Hematopoiesis).

Cartilage and **bone** are also regarded as **special connective tissue** but are traditionally placed in separate categories. Essentially, cartilage and bone are dense

Type I collagen
Present in **bone**, **tendon**, **dentin**, and **skin** as banded fibers with a transverse periodicity of 64 nm. This type of collagen provides tensile strength.

Type II collagen
Observed in **hyaline** and **elastic cartilage** as fibrils thinner than type I collagen.

Type III collagen
Present in the **reticular lamina of basement membranes**, as a component of reticular fibers. This is the first collagen type synthesized during wound healing and then is replaced by type I collagen.

Reticular fibers can be better recognized after impregnation with silver salts because reticular fibers are **argyrophilic** (silver-loving; Gk. *argyros*, silver). Reticular fibers –and collagens in general– are glycoproteins and can be recognized with the **PAS reaction** because of their carbohydrate content.

Silver impregnation is a valuable tool in pathology for the recognition of distortions in the distribution of reticular fibers in pathologic alterations of lymphoid organs.

Type IV collagen
Present in the **basal lamina**. This type of collagen does not form bundles. Single molecules of type IV collagen bind to one of the type IV collagen-binding sites of laminin.

Type V collagen
Observed in **amnion** and **chorion** in the fetus and in muscle and tendon sheaths. **This type of collagen does not form banded fibrils.**

Characteristics of collagens

Collagens contain at least one triple-helical domain.

In fibrillar collagen (types I, II, III, and V), the completely processed molecule contains only one triple helix which accounts for almost the entire length of the molecule.

In other collagens, such as type IV collagen or **FACIT** (for *fibril associated collagens with interrupted triple helices*; types IX, XII, and XIV collagens), several shorter triple-helical segments are separated by nontriple-helical domains.

Collagens form aggregates (fibrils, filaments, or bundles) either alone or with the ground substance.

connective tissues with specialized cells and ground substance. An important difference is that cartilage has a **noncalcified ECM**, whereas the ECM of bone is **calcified**. These two types of specialized connective tissue fulfill weight-bearing and mechanical functions that are discussed later (see Cartilage and Bone).

Cell components of the connective tissue
The four major cell components of the connective tissue are the **fibroblast**, the **macrophage**, the **mast cell**, and the **plasma cell**.

Under light microscopy, the **fibroblast** appears as a spindle-shaped cell with an elliptic nucleus. The cytoplasm is very thin and generally not resolved by the light microscope. Under **electron microscopy**, the fibroblast shows the typical features of a protein-secreting cell: a well-developed rough endoplasmic reticulum and a Golgi apparatus.

The fibroblast synthesizes and continuously secretes mature proteoglycans and glycoproteins and the precursor molecules of various types of collagens and elastin. Different types of collagen proteins and proteoglycans can be recognized as components of the **basement membrane**. As you remember, **type IV collagen** is found in the **basal lamina** and **type III collagen** appears in the **reticular lamina** as a component of **reticular fibers**. Heparan sulfate proteoglycans and the glycoprotein fibronectin are two additional products of the fibroblast that appear in the basement membrane. The protein collagen is a component of collagen and reticular fibers. However, elastic fibers do not contain collagen.

Synthesis, secretion, and assembly of collagen
The synthesis of collagen starts in the rough endoplasmic reticulum (RER) following the typical pathway of synthesis for export from the cell (Figure 4–3).

Preprocollagen is synthesized **with a signal peptide** and released as **procollagen** within the cisterna of the RER. **Procollagen** consists of three polypeptide α chains, **lacking** the signal peptide, assembled in a **triple helix**.

Hydroxyproline and **hydroxylysine** are typically observed in collagen. **Hydroxylation of proline and lysine residues occurs in the RER** and requires **ascorbic acid** (vitamin C) as a cofactor. Inadequate wound healing is characteristic of **scurvy**, caused by vitamin C deficiency.

Packaging and secretion of procollagen take place in the Golgi apparatus. Upon secretion of procollagen, the following three events occur in the extracellular space:

1. **Enzymatic (procollagen peptidase) removal of most of the nonhelical endings of procollagen** to give rise to soluble **tropocollagen molecules**.

2. **Self-aggregation of tropocollagen molecules** by a stepwise overlapping process to form **collagen fibrils**.

Types of collagen

The so-called **reticular cell** is a fibroblast that synthesizes reticular fibers, containing type III collagen. Reticular fibers form the stroma of bone marrow and lymphoid organs.

The osteoblast in bone, chondroblast in cartilage, and odontoblast in teeth also synthesize collagen. These cell types are fibroblast equivalents in their respective tissues. Therefore, the synthesis of collagen is not limited to the fibroblast in connective tissue. In fact, **epithelial cells synthesize type IV collagen.**

A fibroblast may simultaneously synthesize more than one type of collagen.

Smooth muscle cells, found in the wall of arteries, intestine, the respiratory tree, and uterus, **can synthesize types I and III collagen.**

Figure 4–3

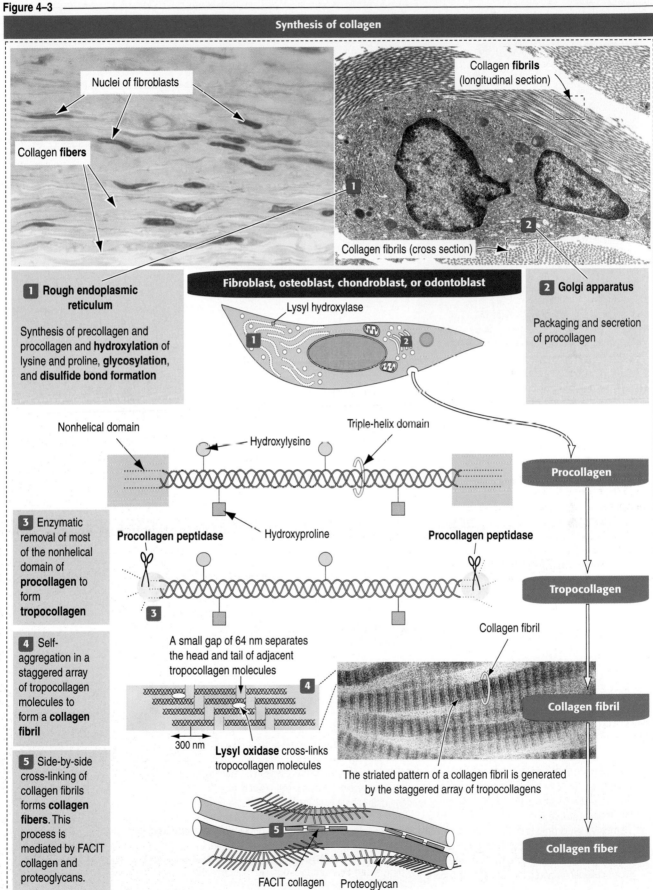

Synthesis of collagen

Nuclei of fibroblasts

Collagen **fibers**

Collagen **fibrils** (longitudinal section)

1

2

Collagen fibrils (cross section)

1 Rough endoplasmic reticulum

Synthesis of precollagen and procollagen and **hydroxylation** of lysine and proline, **glycosylation**, and **disulfide bond formation**

Fibroblast, osteoblast, chondroblast, or odontoblast

Lysyl hydroxylase

1

2

2 Golgi apparatus

Packaging and secretion of procollagen

Nonhelical domain

Hydroxylysine

Triple-helix domain

Procollagen

3 Enzymatic removal of most of the nonhelical domain of **procollagen** to form **tropocollagen**

Procollagen peptidase

Hydroxyproline

Procollagen peptidase

3

Tropocollagen

4 Self-aggregation in a staggered array of tropocollagen molecules to form a **collagen fibril**

A small gap of 64 nm separates the head and tail of adjacent tropocollagen molecules

4

Collagen fibril

300 nm

Lysyl oxidase cross-links tropocollagen molecules

The striated pattern of a collagen fibril is generated by the staggered array of tropocollagens

Collagen fibril

5 Side-by-side cross-linking of collagen fibrils forms **collagen fibers**. This process is mediated by FACIT collagen and proteoglycans.

5

FACIT collagen   Proteoglycan

Collagen fiber

Figure 4–4

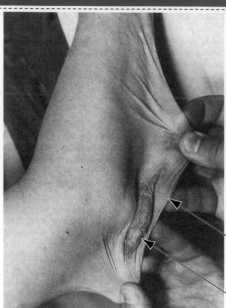

Pathology of collagen: Ehlers-Danlos syndrome

Ehlers-Danlos syndrome

An inherited defect in the **procollagen peptidase**–triggered removal of the nonhelical endings of procollagen results in the formation of defective collagen fibrils. Another form of the syndrome involves a mutation of the gene encoding the enzyme **lysyl hydroxylase**, required for the **post-translational modification of lysine into hydroxylysine**. **Lysyl oxidase** stabilizes the staggered array of tropocollagen molecules by catalyzing **the formation of aldol cross-links between hydroxylysine side chains**. Defective hydroxylation of lysine decreases the strength of the collagen molecule in Ehlers-Danlos syndrome.

This syndrome can be divided into several clinically distinct subtypes, most of them characterized by **joint dislocation** (hip and other large joints) and **hyperelasticity of the skin**.

Hyperelasticity and folds of the skin

Pseudotumor over the elbow

Steinmann B et al., The Ehlers-Danlos Syndrome. In ConnectiveTissue and its Heritable Disorders. New York, Wiley-Liss, 1993.

3. **Cross-linking of tropocollagen molecules,** leading to the formation of **collagen fibers. Lysyl oxidase** catalyzes cross-links between tropocollagens.

Groups of collagen fibers orient along the same axis to form **collagen bundles.** The formation of collagen bundles is guided by proteoglycans and other glycoproteins, including **FACIT collagens**, characterized by short triple-helical segments separated by domains lacking the triple helical arrangement.

Figure 4–5

Pathology of collagen: Molecular defects

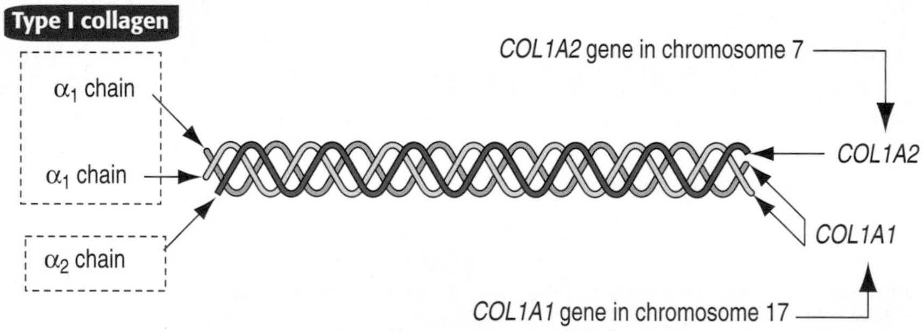

Type I collagen

α_1 chain

α_1 chain

α_2 chain

COL1A2 gene in chromosome 7

COL1A2

COL1A1

COL1A1 gene in chromosome 17

Clinical disorders associated with defects in collagen

A mutation in **COL1A1** and **COL1A2** genes, encoding the α_1 and α_2 chains of type I collagen, respectively, involves cleavage sites for the N-terminal region of the molecule and interferes with the conversion of procollagen to collagen. This leads to defective cross-linking and a consequent reduction in the tensile strength of tendons (rich in type I collagen). This mutation is observed in some clinical forms of **Ehlers-Danlos syndrome**.

Strickler syndrome is characterized by myopia, hypoplasia of the lower jaw, and arthritis associated with dysplasia of the epiphyses. Type II collagen is abundant in cartilage and vitreous humor (eye). The **COL2A1** gene is mutated.

Osteogenesis imperfecta type I is associated with bone fragility. **COL1A1** point mutations determine a reduction in the production of type I collagen required for normal ossification.

Clinical significance: Ehlers-Danlos syndrome

Ehlers-Danlos syndrome is clinically characterized by **hyperelasticity of the skin** (Figure 4–4) and **hypermobility of the joints**. The major defect resides in the connective tissue. Several clinical subtypes are observed. They are classified by the degree of severity and the mutations in the collagen genes. For example, the type IV form of Ehlers-Danlos syndrome —caused by a mutation in the *COL3A1* gene— is associated with severe vascular alterations leading to the development of varicose veins and spontaneous rupture of major arteries. A deficiency in the synthesis of type III collagen, prevalent in the wall of blood vessels, is the major defect. Ehlers-Danlos type VII displays congenital dislocation of the hips and marked joint hypermobility. Mutations in the *COL1A1* and *COL1A2* genes (Figure 4–5), encoding type I collagen, disrupt the cleavage site at the N-terminal of the molecule and affect the conversion of procollagen to collagen in some individuals.

Synthesis, secretion, and assembly of elastic fibers

Like collagen, the synthesis of elastic fibers involves both the RER and the Golgi apparatus (Figure 4–6).

Elastic fibers are synthesized by the **fibroblast** (in skin and tendons), the **chondroblast**, the **chondrocyte** (in elastic cartilage of the auricle of the ear, epiglottis, larynx, and auditory tubes), and **smooth muscle cells** (in large blood vessels like the aorta and in the respiratory tree).

Proelastin, the precursor of elastin, is secreted as **tropoelastin**. In the extracellular space, tropoelastin interacts with **fibrillin** to organize **immature elastic fibers**, which aggregate to form **mature elastic fibers**. Elastin contains two characteristic but uncommon amino acids: **desmosine** and **isodesmosine**. These amino acids are responsible for cross-linking mature elastic fibers and enable their stretching and recoil, like rubberbands. **Elastic fibers do not contain collagen.**

Under the light microscope, elastic fibers stain **black** or **dark blue** with **orcein**, a natural dye obtained from lichens.

Under the electron microscope, a cross section of an elastic fiber shows a dense core of elastin surrounded by microfibrils containing a number of **microfibril-associated glycoproteins (MAGPs)** and **fibrillin**. Fibrillin is a 35-kDa glycoprotein.

Clinical significance: Marfan syndrome

Marfan syndrome is an autosomal dominant disorder in which the elastic tissue is weakened. Defects are predominantly observed in three systems: the **ocular**, **skeletal**, and **cardiovascular** systems. The **ocular defects** include **myopia** and **detached lens** (ectopia lentis). The **skeletal defects** (Figure 4–7) include long and thin arms and legs (**dolichostenomelia**), hollow chest (**pectus excavatum**), scoliosis, and elongated fingers (**arachnodactyly**). Cardiovascular abnormalities are life-threatening. Patients with Marfan syndrome display **prolapse of the mitral valve** and **dilation of the ascending aorta**. Dilation of the aorta leads to dissecting aneurysm (Gk. *aneurysma*, widening) or rupture. Medical treatment, such as administration of β-adrenergic blockers to reduce the force of systolic contraction in order to diminish stress on the aorta and limited heavy exercise, increase the survival rate of patients with Marfan syndrome.

Defects observed in Marfan syndrome are caused by abnormalities in the connective tissue, which becomes too elastic, with poor recoiling. In the skeletal system, the periosteum, a relatively rigid layer covering the bone, is abnormally elastic and does not provide an oppositional force during bone development, resulting in skeletal defects.

A mutation of the **fibrillin 1 gene** on chromosome 15 is responsible for Marfan syndrome. Fibrillin is present in the aorta, suspensory ligaments of the lens (see Chapter 9, Sensory Organs), and the periosteum (see Bone).

Figure 4–6

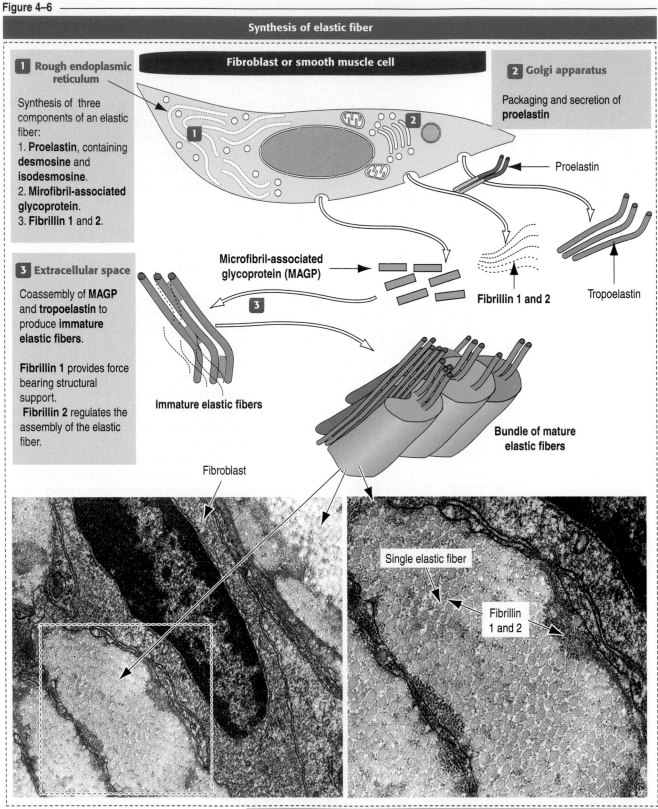

Synthesis of elastic fiber

Fibroblast or smooth muscle cell

1 Rough endoplasmic reticulum

Synthesis of three components of an elastic fiber:
1. **Proelastin**, containing **desmosine** and **isodesmosine**.
2. **Mirofibril-associated glycoprotein**.
3. **Fibrillin 1** and **2**.

2 Golgi apparatus

Packaging and secretion of **proelastin**

Proelastin

Tropoelastin

Microfibril-associated glycoprotein (MAGP)

Fibrillin 1 and 2

3 Extracellular space

Coassembly of **MAGP** and **tropoelastin** to produce **immature elastic fibers**.

Fibrillin 1 provides force bearing structural support.
Fibrillin 2 regulates the assembly of the elastic fiber.

Immature elastic fibers

Bundle of mature elastic fibers

Fibroblast

Single elastic fiber

Fibrillin 1 and 2

A homologous **fibrillin 2 gene** is present on chromosome 5. Mutations in the fibrillin 2 gene cause a disease called **congenital contractural arachnodactyly**. This disease affects the skeletal system, but ocular and cardiovascular defects are not observed.

More than 100 different fibrillin mutations have been observed. One muta-

Figure 4–7

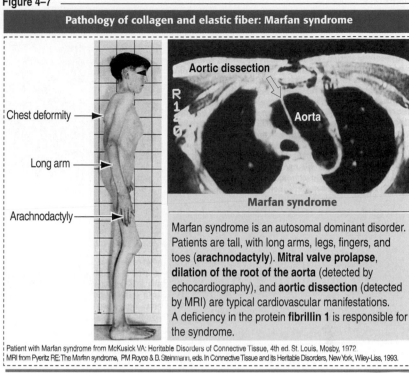

Pathology of collagen and elastic fiber: Marfan syndrome

Chest deformity

Long arm

Arachnodactyly

Aortic dissection

Aorta

Marfan syndrome

Marfan syndrome is an autosomal dominant disorder. Patients are tall, with long arms, legs, fingers, and toes (**arachnodactyly**). **Mitral valve prolapse**, **dilation of the root of the aorta** (detected by echocardiography), and **aortic dissection** (detected by MRI) are typical cardiovascular manifestations. A deficiency in the protein **fibrillin 1** is responsible for the syndrome.

Patient with Marfan syndrome from McKusick VA: Heritable Disorders of Connective Tissue, 4th ed. St. Louis, Mosby, 1972.
MRI from Pyeritz RE: The Marfan syndrome, PM Royce & B. Steinmann, eds. In Connective Tissue and its Heritable Disorders, New York, Wiley-Liss, 1993.

tion of the fibrillin 1 gene can decrease fibrillin synthesis and diminish the deposition of this glycoprotein in the ECM. Another mutation prevents the assembly of microfibrils or coassembly of defective fibrillin with normal fibrillin protein produced by a normal allele in the heterozygote.

The macrophage

Macrophages have **phagocytic** properties and derive from **monocytes**, cells formed in the bone marrow (Figure 4–8).

Monocytes circulate in blood and migrate into the connective tissue, where they differentiate into macrophages. Macrophages have specific names in certain organs; for example, they are called **Kupffer cells** in the liver, **osteoclasts** in bone, and **microglial cells** in the central nervous system. Macrophages migrate to the site of inflammation, attracted by certain mediators, particularly C5a (a member of the complement cascade; see Chapter 10, Immune-Lymphatic System).

Macrophages in the connective tissue have the following structural features:

1. They contain abundant **lysosomes** required for the breakdown of phagocytic materials.

2. Active macrophages have numerous **phagocytic vesicles** (or **phagosomes**) for the transient storage of ingested materials.

3. The nucleus has an irregular outline.

Macrophages of the connective tissue have **three major functions**:

1. **To turn over senescent fibers and ECM material.**

2. The **presentation of antigens to lymphocytes as part of inflammatory and immunologic responses** (see Chapter 10, Immune-Lymphatic System).

3. **Production of cytokines** (for example, **interleukin-1**, an activator of helper T cells, and **tumor necrosis factor-α**, an inflammatory mediator).

The mast cell

Like macrophages, **mast cells originate in the bone marrow** from precursor cells lacking cytoplasmic granules. When mast cell precursors migrate into the connective tissue or the lamina propria of mucosae, they proliferate and accumulate cytoplasmic granules. **Mast cells and basophils circulating in blood derive from**

Figure 4–8

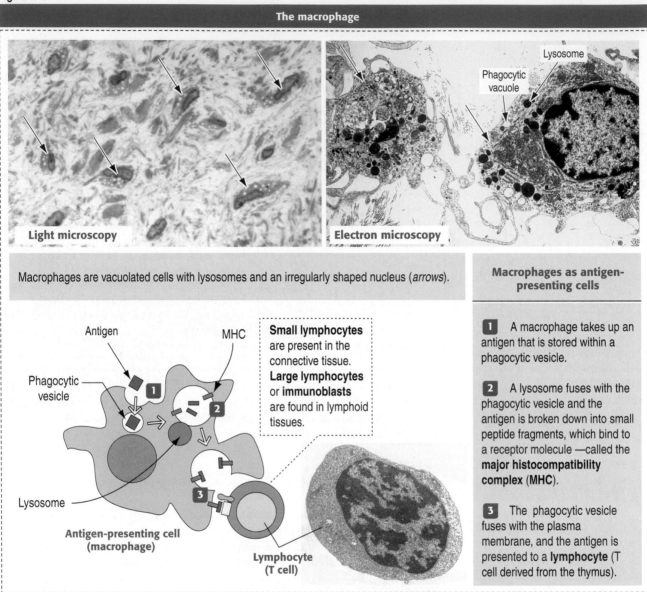

The macrophage

Light microscopy

Electron microscopy

Lysosome

Phagocytic
vacuole

Macrophages are vacuolated cells with lysosomes and an irregularly shaped nucleus (*arrows*).

**Macrophages as antigen-
presenting cells**

Antigen

MHC

Phagocytic
vesicle

Small lymphocytes
are present in the
connective tissue.
Large lymphocytes
or **immunoblasts**
are found in lymphoid
tissues.

Lysosome

**Antigen-presenting cell
(macrophage)**

Lymphocyte
(T cell)

1 A macrophage takes up an
antigen that is stored within a
phagocytic vesicle.

2 A lysosome fuses with the
phagocytic vesicle and the
antigen is broken down into small
peptide fragments, which bind to
a receptor molecule —called the
**major histocompatibility
complex (MHC)**.

3 The phagocytic vesicle
fuses with the plasma
membrane, and the antigen is
presented to a **lymphocyte** (T
cell derived from the thymus).

the same progenitor in the bone marrow.

The **mast cell** is the source of **vasoactive mediators** contained in **cytoplasmic granules** (Figure 4–9). These granules contain **histamine, heparin,** and **chemotactic mediators** to attract monocytes, neutrophils, and eosinophils circulating in blood to the site of mast cell activation. Leukotrienes are vasoactive products of mast cells. **Leukotrienes are not present in granules; instead, they are released from the cell membrane of the mast cells as metabolites of arachidonic acid.**

There are two populations of mast cells: **mucosal mast cells** (found predominantly in intestine and lung), and **connective tissue mast cells.**

Connective tissue mast cells differ from mucosal mast cells in the number and size of cytoplasmic granules, which tend to be more abundant in connective tissue mast cells. Although these two cell populations have the same cell precursor, the definitive structural and functional characteristics of mast cells depend on the site of differentiation (mucosa or connective tissue).

The plasma cell

The plasma cell, which derives from the differentiation of **B lymphocytes** (also called **B cells**), synthesizes and secretes a single class of immunoglobulin (Figure

4–10).

Immunoglobulins are glycoproteins, and therefore plasma cells have the three structural characteristics of cells active in protein synthesis and secretion:
1. A well-developed **rough endoplasmic reticulum.**

Figure 4–9

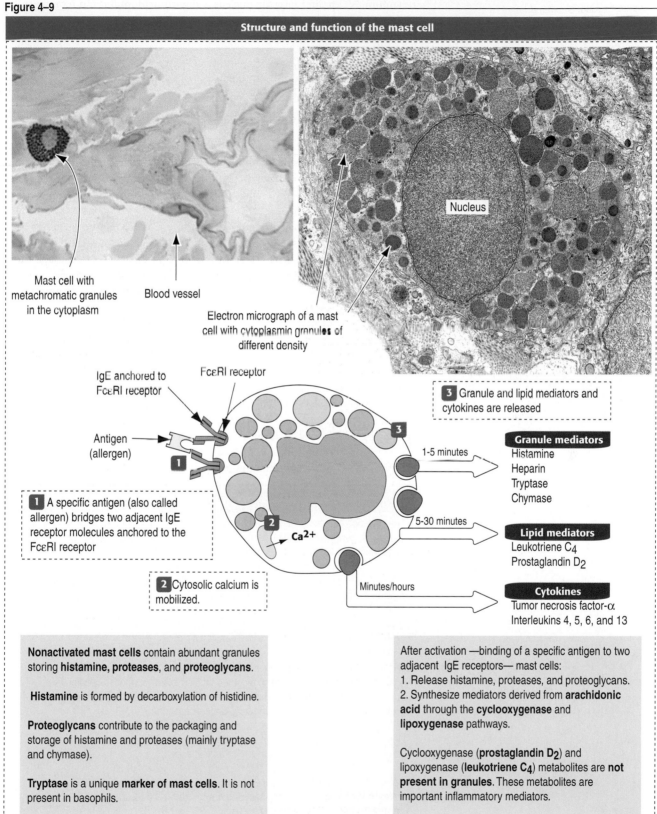

Structure and function of the mast cell

Mast cell with metachromatic granules in the cytoplasm

Blood vessel

Electron micrograph of a mast cell with cytoplasmic granules of different density

Nucleus

IgE anchored to FcεRI receptor

FcεRI receptor

Antigen (allergen)

1 A specific antigen (also called allergen) bridges two adjacent IgE receptor molecules anchored to the FcεRI receptor

2 Cytosolic calcium is mobilized.

Ca²⁺

3 Granule and lipid mediators and cytokines are released

1-5 minutes

Granule mediators
Histamine
Heparin
Tryptase
Chymase

5-30 minutes

Lipid mediators
Leukotriene C₄
Prostaglandin D₂

Minutes/hours

Cytokines
Tumor necrosis factor-α
Interleukins 4, 5, 6, and 13

Nonactivated mast cells contain abundant granules storing **histamine, proteases**, and **proteoglycans**.

Histamine is formed by decarboxylation of histidine.

Proteoglycans contribute to the packaging and storage of histamine and proteases (mainly tryptase and chymase).

Tryptase is a unique **marker of mast cells**. It is not present in basophils.

After activation —binding of a specific antigen to two adjacent IgE receptors— mast cells:
1. Release histamine, proteases, and proteoglycans.
2. Synthesize mediators derived from **arachidonic acid** through the **cyclooxygenase** and **lipoxygenase** pathways.

Cyclooxygenase (**prostaglandin D₂**) and lipoxygenase (**leukotriene C₄**) metabolites are **not present in granules**. These metabolites are important inflammatory mediators.

2. An extensive **Golgi apparatus**.

3. A prominent **nucleolus**.

At the light microscopic level, most of the cytoplasm of a plasma cell is **basophilic** because of the large amount of ribosomes associated with the endoplasmic reticulum. A clear area near the nucleus is slightly **acidophilic** and represents the Golgi apparatus. The nucleus has a characteristic cartwheel configuration created by the particular distribution of heterochromatin.

The extracellular matrix

The ECM is a combination of **collagens**, **noncollagenous glycoproteins**, and **proteoglycans** surrounding cells and fibers of the connective tissue.

Recall that the **basement membrane** contains several ECM components such as **laminin**, **fibronectin**, various types of **collagen**, and **heparan sulfate proteoglycan**. In addition, epithelial and non-epithelial cells have receptors for ECM constituents. An example is the family of **integrins** with binding affinity for laminin and fibronectin. Integrins interact with the cytoskeleton, strengthening cell interactions with the ECM by establishing focal contacts or modifying cell shape or adhesion.

Several noncollagenous glycoproteins of the ECM mediate interactions with cells and regulate the assembly of ECM components. Noncollagenous glycoproteins have a widespread distribution in several connective tissues, although cartilage and bone contain specific types of noncollagenous glycoproteins. We will study them later when we discuss the processes of **chondrogenesis** (formation of cartilage) and **osteogenesis** (bone formation).

Proteoglycan aggregates (Figure 4–11) are the major components of the ECM. Each proteoglycan consists of **glycosaminoglycans** (**GAGs**), proteins complexed with polysaccharides. GAGs are linear polymers of disaccharides with sulfate residues. GAGs control the biological functions of proteoglycans by establishing links with cell surface components, growth factors, and other ECM constituents.

Different types of GAGs are attached to a **core protein** to form a proteoglycan. The core protein, in turn, is linked to a **hyaluronan molecule** by a **linker protein**. The hyaluronan molecule is the axis of a **proteoglycan aggregate**. Proteoglycans are named according to the prevalent GAG (for example, **proteoglycan chondroitin sulfate**, **proteoglycan dermatan sulfate**, **proteoglycan heparan sulfate**).

Mast cells and allergic hypersensitivity reactions

The secretion of specific vasoactive mediators plays an important role in the regulation of vascular permeability and bronchial smooth muscle tone during **allergic hypersensitivity reactions** (for example, in **asthma**, **hay fever**, and **eczema**).

The surface of **mast cells** and **basophils** contains **immunoglobulin E** (IgE) **receptors**. **Antigens bind to two adjacent Ig E receptors** and the mast cell becomes **IgE-sensitized**. An IgE-sensitized mast cell releases Ca^{2+} from intracellular storage sites and the content of the cytoplasmic granules is rapidly discharged by a process known as **degranulation**.

The release of **histamine** during **asthma** (Gk. *asthma*, panting) causes dyspnea (Gk. *dyspnoia*, difficulty with breathing) triggered by the histamine-induced spasmodic **contraction of the smooth muscle surrounding the bronchioles** and **the hypersecretion of goblet cells and mucosal glands of bronchi**.

During **hay fever**, histamine increases **vascular permeability** leading to edema (excessive accumulation of fluid in intercellular spaces).

Mast cells in the connective tissue of skin release **leukotrienes** which induce increased vascular permeability associated with **urticaria** (Lat. *urtica*, stinging nettle), a transient swelling in the dermis of the skin.

Figure 4–10

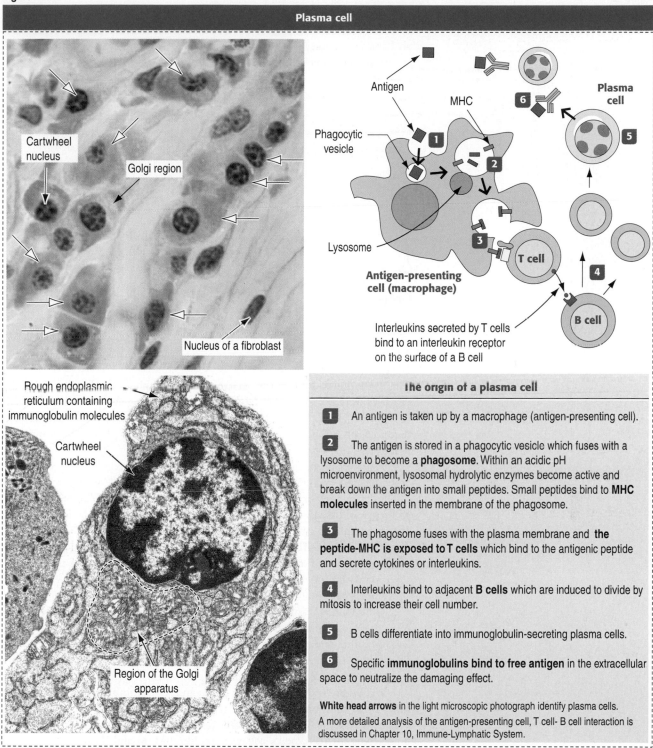

Plasma cell

Cartwheel nucleus

Golgi region

Nucleus of a fibroblast

Rough endoplasmic reticulum containing immunoglobulin molecules

Cartwheel nucleus

Region of the Golgi apparatus

Antigen

Phagocytic vesicle

MHC

Lysosome

Antigen-presenting cell (macrophage)

Plasma cell

T cell

B cell

Interleukins secreted by T cells bind to an interleukin receptor on the surface of a B cell

The origin of a plasma cell

1 An antigen is taken up by a macrophage (antigen-presenting cell).

2 The antigen is stored in a phagocytic vesicle which fuses with a lysosome to become a **phagosome**. Within an acidic pH microenvironment, lysosomal hydrolytic enzymes become active and break down the antigen into small peptides. Small peptides bind to **MHC molecules** inserted in the membrane of the phagosome.

3 The phagosome fuses with the plasma membrane and **the peptide-MHC is exposed to T cells** which bind to the antigenic peptide and secrete cytokines or interleukins.

4 Interleukins bind to adjacent **B cells** which are induced to divide by mitosis to increase their cell number.

5 B cells differentiate into immunoglobulin-secreting plasma cells.

6 Specific **immunoglobulins bind to free antigen** in the extracellular space to neutralize the damaging effect.

White head arrows in the light microscopic photograph identify plasma cells.

A more detailed analysis of the antigen-presenting cell, T cell- B cell interaction is discussed in Chapter 10, Immune-Lymphatic System.

Recall that the **embryonic connective tissue** of the umbilical cord (**Wharton's jelly**) is predominantly ECM material surrounding the two umbilical arteries and the single umbilical vein. Proteoglycans have extremely high charge density and, therefore, significant osmotic pressure. These attributes enable a connective tissue bed to resist compression because of the very high swelling capacity of these molecules. The umbilical blood vessels, crucial elements for fetal-maternal fluid, gas, and nutritional exchange, are surrounded by a proteoglycan-enriched type of connective tissue to provide resistance to compression.

Figure 4–11

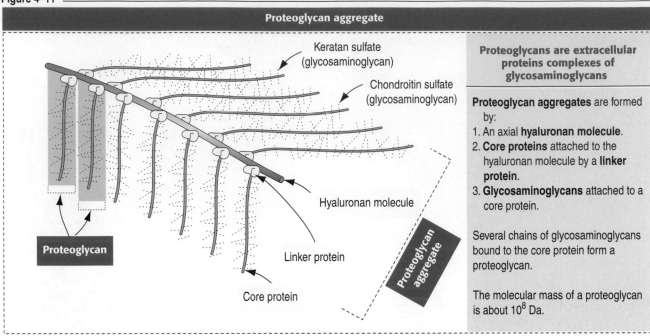

Proteoglycan aggregate

Keratan sulfate
(glycosaminoglycan)

Chondroitin sulfate
(glycosaminoglycan)

Hyaluronan molecule

Proteoglycan

Linker protein

Core protein

Proteoglycan aggregate

Proteoglycans are extracellular proteins complexes of glycosaminoglycans

Proteoglycan aggregates are formed by:
1. An axial **hyaluronan molecule**.
2. **Core proteins** attached to the hyaluronan molecule by a **linker protein**.
3. **Glycosaminoglycans** attached to a core protein.

Several chains of glycosaminoglycans bound to the core protein form a proteoglycan.

The molecular mass of a proteoglycan is about 10^8 Da.

Degradation of the ECM

The ECM can be degraded by **matrix metalloproteinases**, a family of zinc-dependent proteases **secreted as latent precursors (zymogens)** proteolytically activated in the ECM. The activity of matrix metalloproteinases in the extracellular space can be specifically inhibited by **tissue inhibitors of metalloproteinases (TIMPs)**.

The expression of matrix metalloproteinase genes is regulated by cytokines, growth factors and cell contact with the ECM.

The degradation of the ECM occurs normally during the development, growth, and repair of tissues. However, excessive degradation of the ECM is observed in several pathologic conditions such as rheumatoid arthritis, osteoarthritis, and diseases of the skin. Tumor invasion, metastasis, and tumor angiogenesis require the participation of matrix metalloproteinases whose expression increases in association with tumorigenesis.

Members of the family of matrix metalloproteinases include:

1. **Collagenases.** Collagenases 1, 2 and 3 can degrade types I, II, III, and V collagens. Collagenase 1 is synthesized by fibroblasts, chondrocytes (cartilage), keratinocytes (epidermis), monocytes and macrophages, hepatocytes (liver), and tumor cells. Collagenase 2 is stored in cytoplasmic granules of polymorphonuclear leukocytes and released in response to a stimulus. Collagenase 3 can degrade several collagens (types I, II, III, IV, IX, X, and XI), laminin and fibronectin, and other ECM components.

2. **Stromelysins (1, 2, and metalloelastase),** which degrade basement membrane components (type IV collagen and fibronectin) and elastin.

3. **Gelatinases A and B** can degrade type I collagen. Gelatinases are produced by alveolar macrophages.

4. **Membrane-type matrix metalloproteinases** are produced by tumor cells.

Matrix metalloproteinases are a target of therapeutic intervention to inhibit tumor invasion and metastasis.

Clinical significance: Molecular biology of tumor invasion

Invasion and **metastasis** are two important events of **carcinoma** (Gk. *karkinoma*, from *karkinos*, crab, cancer + *oma*, tumor), a tumor derived from epithelial tis-

Figure 4–12

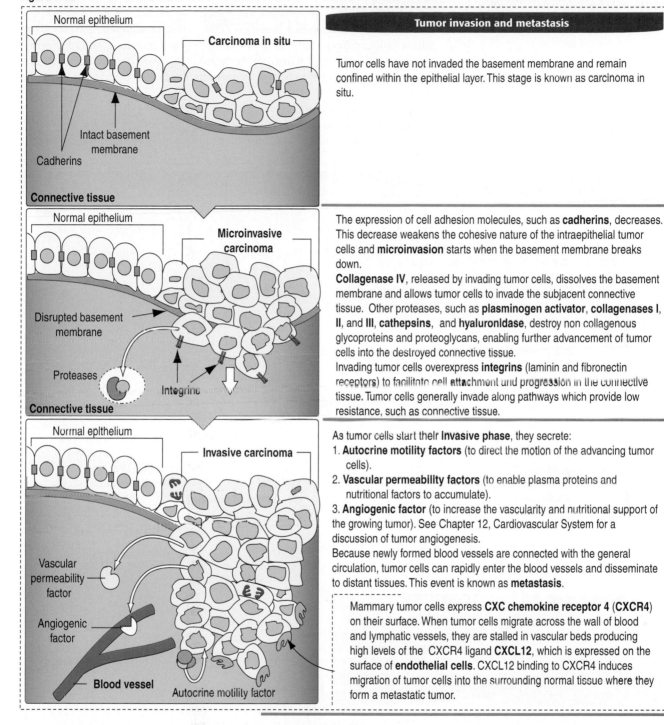

Normal epithelium

Carcinoma in situ

Intact basement membrane

Cadherins

Connective tissue

Tumor invasion and metastasis

Tumor cells have not invaded the basement membrane and remain confined within the epithelial layer. This stage is known as carcinoma in situ.

Normal epithelium

Microinvasive carcinoma

Disrupted basement membrane

Proteases

Integrine

Connective tissue

The expression of cell adhesion molecules, such as **cadherins**, decreases. This decrease weakens the cohesive nature of the intraepithelial tumor cells and **microinvasion** starts when the basement membrane breaks down.

Collagenase IV, released by invading tumor cells, dissolves the basement membrane and allows tumor cells to invade the subjacent connective tissue. Other proteases, such as **plasminogen activator**, **collagenases I, II,** and **III**, **cathepsins**, and **hyaluronidase**, destroy non collagenous glycoproteins and proteoglycans, enabling further advancement of tumor cells into the destroyed connective tissue.

Invading tumor cells overexpress **integrins** (laminin and fibronectin receptors) to facilitate cell attachment and progression in the connective tissue. Tumor cells generally invade along pathways which provide low resistance, such as connective tissue.

Normal epithelium

Invasive carcinoma

Vascular permeability factor

Angiogenic factor

Blood vessel

Autocrine motility factor

As tumor cells start their **invasive phase**, they secrete:
1. **Autocrine motility factors** (to direct the motion of the advancing tumor cells).
2. **Vascular permeability factors** (to enable plasma proteins and nutritional factors to accumulate).
3. **Angiogenic factor** (to increase the vascularity and nutritional support of the growing tumor). See Chapter 12, Cardiovascular System for a discussion of tumor angiogenesis.

Because newly formed blood vessels are connected with the general circulation, tumor cells can rapidly enter the blood vessels and disseminate to distant tissues. This event is known as **metastasis**.

Mammary tumor cells express **CXC chemokine receptor 4 (CXCR4)** on their surface. When tumor cells migrate across the wall of blood and lymphatic vessels, they are stalled in vascular beds producing high levels of the CXCR4 ligand **CXCL12**, which is expressed on the surface of **endothelial cells**. CXCL12 binding to CXCR4 induces migration of tumor cells into the surrounding normal tissue where they form a metastatic tumor.

sues. **Adenoma** is a structurally benign tumor of epithelial cell origin lacking invasive and metastatic properties. Malignant carcinomas may arise from benign adenomas. For example, a small benign adenoma or **polyp** of the colon can become an invasive carcinoma.

Sarcoma (Gk. *sarx*, flesh + *oma*) is a tumor derived from the connective tissues (muscle, bone, cartilage) and mesodermal cells. For example, fibrosarcoma derives from fibroblasts and osteosarcoma from bone.

Invasion is defined by the **breakdown of the basement membrane** by tumor cells and implies the transition from **precancer** to **cancer**. **Metastasis** is the spread of tumor cells throughout the body through blood and lymphatic vessels, generally leading to death. Figure 4–12 illustrates and describes the initial events of tumor cell invasion.

Many carcinomas produce members of the matrix metalloproteinase family to digest various types of collagen as we have seen in the preceding section. Normal tissues produce tissue inhibitors of metalloproteinases that are neutralized by carcinoma cells. Tumors that behave aggressively are capable of overpowering the protease inhibitors.

One critical event during metastasis is angiogenesis, the development of blood vessels. Blood vessels supply oxygen and nutrients required for tumor growth. Angiogenesis is stimulated by tumor cells, in particular the proliferation of capil-

Figure 4–13

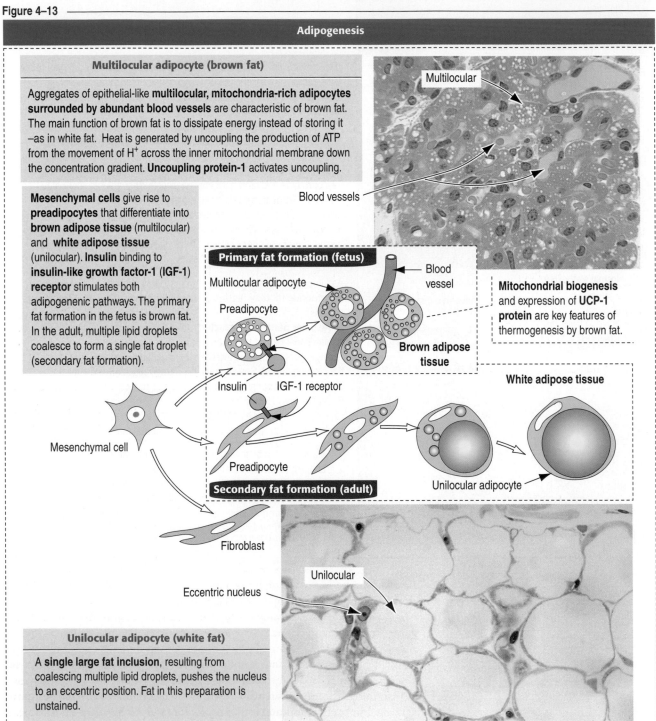

Adipogenesis

Multilocular adipocyte (brown fat)

Aggregates of epithelial-like **multilocular, mitochondria-rich adipocytes surrounded by abundant blood vessels** are characteristic of brown fat. The main function of brown fat is to dissipate energy instead of storing it –as in white fat. Heat is generated by uncoupling the production of ATP from the movement of H$^+$ across the inner mitochondrial membrane down the concentration gradient. **Uncoupling protein-1** activates uncoupling.

Mesenchymal cells give rise to **preadipocytes** that differentiate into **brown adipose tissue** (multilocular) and **white adipose tissue** (unilocular). **Insulin** binding to **insulin-like growth factor-1 (IGF-1) receptor** stimulates both adipogenenic pathways. The primary fat formation in the fetus is brown fat. In the adult, multiple lipid droplets coalesce to form a single fat droplet (secondary fat formation).

Multilocular

Blood vessels

Mitochondrial biogenesis and expression of **UCP-1 protein** are key features of thermogenesis by brown fat.

Primary fat formation (fetus)

Multilocular adipocyte

Blood vessel

Preadipocyte

Brown adipose tissue

Insulin   IGF-1 receptor

Mesenchymal cell

Preadipocyte

Secondary fat formation (adult)

White adipose tissue

Unilocular adipocyte

Fibroblast

Unilocular

Eccentric nucleus

Unilocular adipocyte (white fat)

A **single large fat inclusion**, resulting from coalescing multiple lipid droplets, pushes the nucleus to an eccentric position. Fat in this preparation is unstained.

Figure 4–14

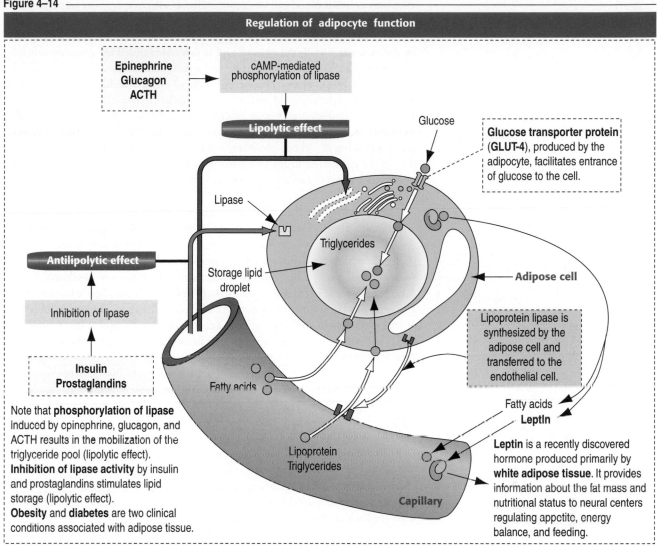

Regulation of adipocyte function

Epinephrine
Glucagon
ACTH

cAMP-mediated
phosphorylation of lipase

Lipolytic effect

Glucose

Glucose transporter protein (GLUT-4), produced by the adipocyte, facilitates entrance of glucose to the cell.

Lipase

Triglycerides

Antilipolytic effect

Storage lipid droplet

Adipose cell

Inhibition of lipase

Lipoprotein lipase is synthesized by the adipose cell and transferred to the endothelial cell.

**Insulin
Prostaglandins**

Fatty acids

Fatty acids
Leptin

Note that **phosphorylation of lipase** induced by epinephrine, glucagon, and ACTH results in the mobilization of the triglyceride pool (lipolytic effect).
Inhibition of lipase activity by insulin and prostaglandins stimulates lipid storage (lipolytic effect).
Obesity and **diabetes** are two clinical conditions associated with adipose tissue.

Lipoprotein
Triglycerides

Capillary

Leptin is a recently discovered hormone produced primarily by **white adipose tissue**. It provides information about the fat mass and nutritional status to neural centers regulating appetite, energy balance, and feeding.

Detection of fat in histologic sections

Fat is usually dissolved by solvents (xylene) used during paraffin embedding. Only the nucleus and a narrow cytoplasmic rim, surrounding a central empty space, can be visualized.

Fat that is fixed and stained with **osmium tetroxide** appears **brown**. This reagent is also used for the visualization of lipid-rich myelin in nerves (see Chapter 8, Nervous Tissue).

Alcoholic solutions of fat-soluble dyes (such as **Sudan III** or **Sudan black**) can also be used for the detection of fat in **frozen sections**.

lary endothelial cells forming new capillaries in the tumoral growth. In Chapter 12, Cardiovascular System, we discuss the mechanism of action and targets of **endostatin** and **angiostatin**, two new proteins that inhibit angiogenesis.

Adipose tissue or fat

There are two classes of adipose tissue:

1. **White fat**, the **major reserve of long-term energy**.
2. **Brown fat**, which serves primarily to **dissipate energy** instead of storing it.

Like fibroblasts, the primitive **preadipocyte** derives from a mesenchymal cell precursor that gives rise to **preadipocytes**. Preadipocytes can follow two cell differentiation pathways: one pathway results in the formation of white fat; the other generates brown fat. Adipogenesis occurs during both the prenatal and postnatal states of the individual and is reduced as age increases.

Under the influence of **insulin** —bound to **insulin-like growth factor-1** (IGF-1) **receptor**— preadipocytes synthesize **lipoprotein lipase** and begin to accumulate fat in small droplets. Small droplets fuse to form a single large lipid-storage droplet, a characteristic of mature **unilocular** (Lat. *unus*, single; *loculus*, small place) **adipocytes** (also called **adipose cell**) (Figure 4–13). The single lipid-storage droplet pushes the nucleus to an eccentric position and the adipocyte assumes a "signet-ring" appearance. **You should be able to distinguish adipocytes from capillaries in histologic sections: capillaries appear as single structures** that may contain blood cell elements, whereas adipocytes form aggregates.

Lipid droplets contain about 95% triglycerides rich in carotene, a lipid-soluble pigment that gives the so-called white fat a yellowish color. **Each lipid droplet is in direct contact with the cytosol and is not surrounded by a cytomembrane.** Therefore, lipid droplets can be classified as cell **inclusions.**

The **main function** of white fat is storage of energy. Unlike brown fat, white fat responds slightly to cold and acts as an **insulator.** The blood supply to white fat, mainly capillaries, is not as extensive as in brown fat. Adipose tissue also **insulates the body against heat loss, fills spaces, and cushions certain anatomic parts,** behaving as a shock-absorber in the soles of the feet, around the kidneys, and in the orbit around the eye. Most adipose tissues form at sites where loose connective tissue is present, such as the subcutaneous layer —or hypodermis— of the skin

The accumulation and release of lipids by mature adipocytes is regulated by three major hormones: **insulin, catecholamines,** and **prostaglandins** (Figure 4–14). Adipose tissue is innervated by the **sympathetic nervous system.**

Preadipocytes can differentiate into mature **multilocular** (Lat. *multus,* many; *loculus,* small place) **adipocytes** of **brown fat** in the **fetus** and **newborn. Brown fat** is found in the neck, shoulders, back, perirenal, and para-aortic regions of the body. Brown fat is mostly lost during childhood. Brown fat is supplied by **abundant blood vessels,** and **sympathetic adrenergic nerve fibers.** Lipochrome pigment and abundant **mitochondria,** rich in cytochromes, give this type of fat a brownish color.

As stated initially, the main function of brown fat is **to dissipate energy in the form of heat (thermogenesis)** in cold environments as a protective mechanism in the newborn. Thermogenesis by brown fat cells has two requirements (Figure 4–13):

1. **Mitochondrial biogenesis.**
2. The expression of **uncoupling protein-1 (UCP-1).**

UCP-1 dissipates the proton gradient established across the inner mitochondrial membrane when electrons pass along the respiratory chain. UCP-1 uncouples ATP production from the movement of protons down their concentration gradient and heat is generated.

Clinical significance: Obesity

Obesity is a disorder of energy balance. It occurs when energy intake exceeds energy expenditure. Protection against obesity without consideration of energy intake results in an increase in circulating levels of triglycerides, and excessive accumulation of fat in liver (**steatosis**). The metabolic activities of adipocytes have very significant clinical consequences. An increase in visceral adiposity is associated with a higher risk of insulin resistance (see Chapter 19, Endocrine System), **dyslipidemia** (alteration in blood fat levels) and cardiovascular disease.

One of the secreted products of adipocytes is **leptin**, a 16-kDa protein encoded by the *ob* gene. Leptin is released into the circulation and acts peripherally to regulate body weight. Leptin acts on hypothalamic targets involved in appetite and energy balance. Leptin-deficient mice (*ob/ob*) are obese and infertile. Both conditions are reversible with leptin administration.

The leptin receptor in hypothalamic target cells shares sequence homology with cytokine receptors. During inflammation, the release of the cytokines **interleukin-1** and **tumor necrosis factor-α** increases leptin in serum, an indication that leptin interacts with cytokines to influence responses to infection and inflammatory reactions. Infections, injury, and inflammation upregulate leptin gene expression and serum protein levels. As we discuss later, leptin has a role in bone formation.

Figure 4–15

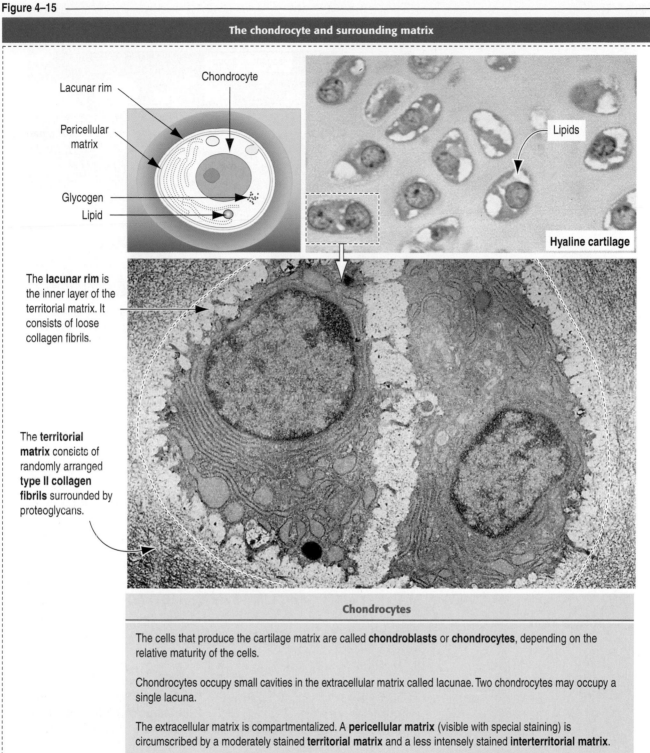

The chondrocyte and surrounding matrix

Lacunar rim

Chondrocyte

Pericellular matrix

Glycogen

Lipid

Lipids

Hyaline cartilage

The **lacunar rim** is the inner layer of the territorial matrix. It consists of loose collagen fibrils.

The **territorial matrix** consists of randomly arranged **type II collagen fibrils** surrounded by proteoglycans.

Chondrocytes

The cells that produce the cartilage matrix are called **chondroblasts** or **chondrocytes**, depending on the relative maturity of the cells.

Chondrocytes occupy small cavities in the extracellular matrix called lacunae. Two chondrocytes may occupy a single lacuna.

The extracellular matrix is compartmentalized. A **pericellular matrix** (visible with special staining) is circumscribed by a moderately stained **territorial matrix** and a less intensely stained **interterritorial matrix**.

Cartilage

Like the fibroblast and the adipocytes, the **chondroblast** derives from a mesenchymal cell. Chondroblasts contain lipids and glycogen, a well-developed RER (basophilic cytoplasm), and Golgi apparatus. The proliferation of chondroblasts results in growth of the cartilage.

Like the typical connective tissue, **the cartilage consists of cells and ECM surrounded by the perichondrium**. The perichondrium is formed by a layer of

Figure 4–16

Interstitial growth

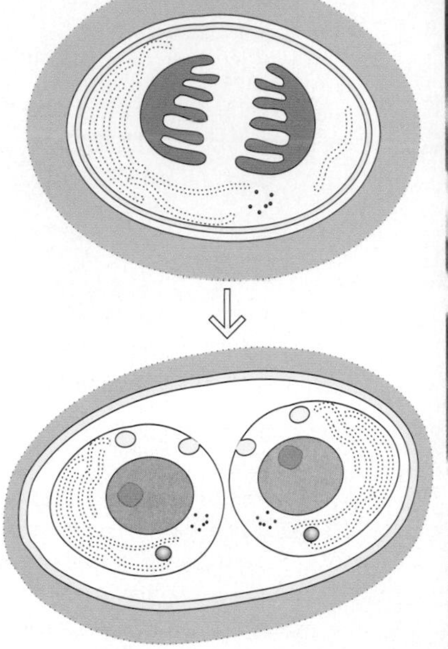

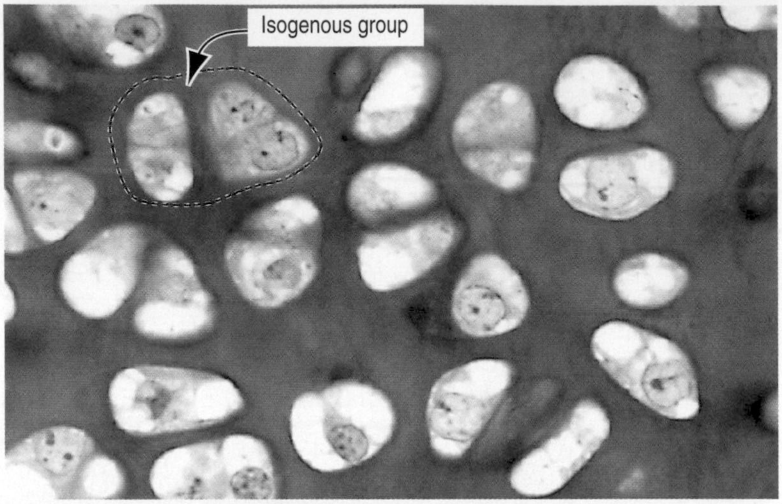

After cell division, daughter cells remain within the same space or lacuna forming an **isogenous group** (Gk. *isos*, equal; *genos*, family, kind)

Isogenous group

During embryogenesis, mesenchymal cells aggregate and differentiate into chondroblasts which form **centers of chondrogenesis**. A center of chondrogenesis consists of chondroblasts surrounded by extracellular matrix. Chondroblasts divide by mitosis and the daughter cells remain within the same space or lacuna forming an **isogenous cell group**. The isogenous group is surrounded by **territorial matrix**. A wider **interterritorial matrix** surrounds the territorial matrix.
This growth process, known as **interstitial growth** of the cartilage, is very active during **endochondral ossification** (see Chapter 5, Osteogenesis).

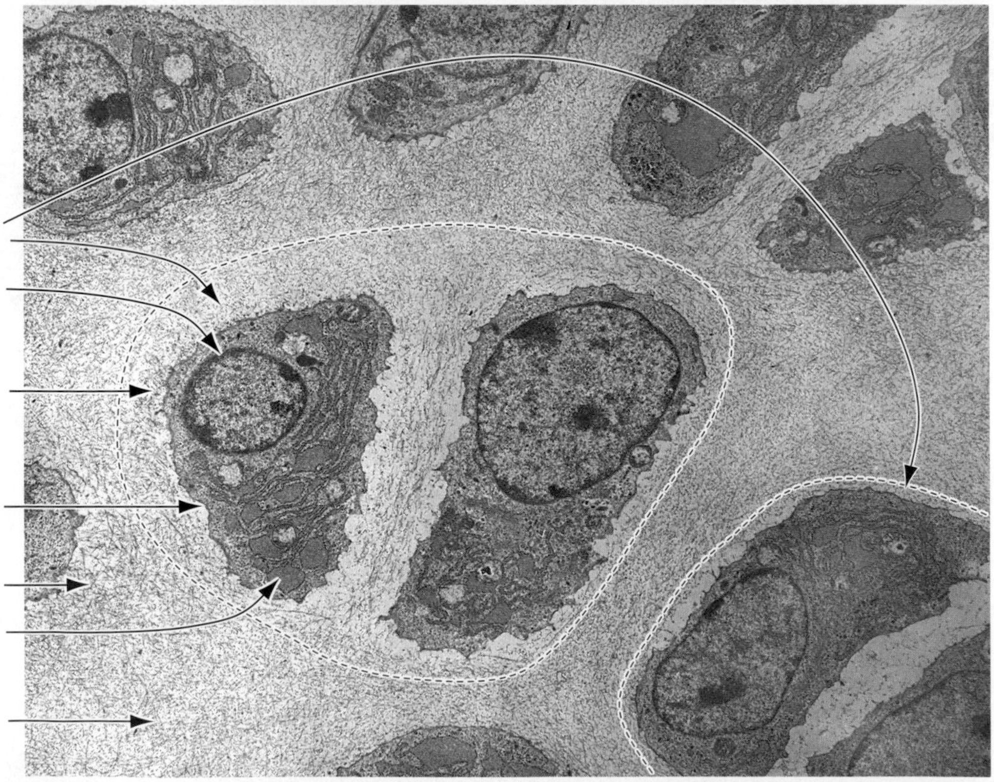

Isogenous groups
Nucleus
Territorial matrix
Lacunar rim
Type II collagen
Rough endoplasmic reticulum
Interterritorial matrix

undifferentiated cells that can differentiate into chondroblasts.

Unlike the typical connective tissue, the cartilage is **avascular** and cells receive nutrients by diffusion through the ECM. At all ages, chondrocytes have significant nutritional requirements. Although they rarely divide in the adult cartilage,

Figure 4-17

Appositional growth

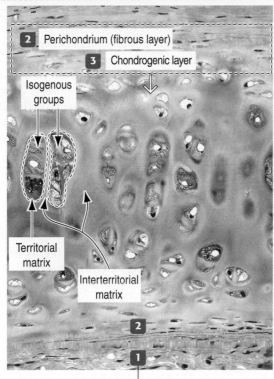

2 Perichondrium (fibrous layer)

3 Chondrogenic layer

Isogenous groups

Territorial matrix

Interterritorial matrix

2

1

Surrounding connective tissue

2 The **outermost cells** of the developing cartilage are spindle-shaped and clustered in a regular layer called **perichondrium**, a transitional zone between cartilage and the surrounding general connective tissue.

3 The **inner cells of the perichondrium**, the **chondrogenic layer**, differentiate into **chondroblasts** which synthesize and secrete **type II collagen** precursors and other extracellular matrix components.

4 By this mechanism, new layers of cells and extracellular matrix are added to the surface of the cartilage by the process of **appositional growth** and the overall size of the cartilage increases. This process increases the size of the initial **anlagen** (Ger. plan, outline) of the future skeleton.

A mutation in the gene expressing the **transcription factor Sox9** causes **campomelic dysplasia** in humans consisting in bowing and angulation of long bones, hypoplasia of the pelvic and scapular bones, abnormalities of the vertebral column, decrease in the number of ribs, and craniofacial abnormalities. **Sox9 controls the expression of type II collagen and the proteoglycan aggrecan**. Sox9-null chondrogenic cells remain in the perichondrium and do not differentiate into chondrocytes. Other members of the Sox family participate in chondrogenesis.

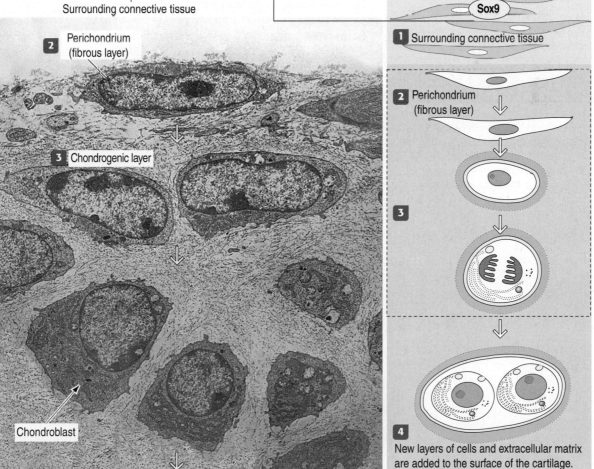

Perichondrium (fibrous layer)

Chondrogenic layer

Chondroblast

Sox9

1 Surrounding connective tissue

2 Perichondrium (fibrous layer)

3

4 New layers of cells and extracellular matrix are added to the surface of the cartilage.

they continuously synthesize molecules to replace a constantly turned-over ECM, in particular, proteoglycans (Figure 4–15).

Growth of cartilage (chondrogenesis)

Cartilage grows by two mechanisms (Figures 4–16 and 4–17):

1. By **interstitial growth** (from chondrocytes **within the cartilage**; Figure 4–16).

2. By **appositional growth** (from undifferentiated cells at **the surface of the cartilage** or **perichondrium**, Figure 4-17).

During chondrogenesis, chondroblasts produce and deposit **type II collagen** fibers and ECM (**hyaluronic acid and GAGs**, mainly chondroitin sulfate and keratan sulfate) until chondroblasts are separated and trapped within spaces in the matrix called **lacunae** (Lat. small lake). The cells are then called **chondrocytes**. The space between the chondrocyte and the wall of the lacuna seen in histologic preparations is an artifact of fixation.

The matrix in close contact with each chondrocytes forms a bluish (with hematoxylin and eosin), metachromatic, or PAS-positive basket-like structure called the **territorial matrix**.

Each cluster of chondrocytes (known as an **isogenous group**) enveloped by the territorial matrix is separated by a wide but pale **interterritorial matrix**.

Types of cartilage

There are three major types of cartilage (Figure 4–18):

1. **Hyaline cartilage**.
2. **Elastic cartilage**.
3. **Fibrocartilage**.

Hyaline cartilage is the most widespread cartilage in humans. Its name derives from the clear appearance of the matrix (Gk. *hyalos*, glass).

In the fetus, hyaline cartilage forms most of the skeleton before it is reabsorbed and replaced by bone by a process known as **endochondral ossification**.

In adults, hyaline cartilage persists as the nasal, laryngeal, tracheobronchial, and costal cartilage. **The articular surface of synovial joints** (knee, shoulder) **is hyaline cartilage and does not participate in endochondral ossification**. Articular surfaces are not lined by an epithelium.

The hyaline cartilage contains:

1. **Cells** (chondrocytes).
2. **Fibers** (**type II collagen** synthesized by chondrocytes).
3. **ECM** (also synthesized by chondrocytes).

Chondrocytes have the structural characteristics of a protein-secreting cell (well-developed RER and Golgi apparatus, and large nucleolus) and store lipids and glycogen in the cytoplasm. Chondrocytes are coated by a pericellular matrix, surrounded by the territorial and interterritorial matrices, respectively. A lacunar rim separates the cell from the territorial matrix.

The surface of hyaline cartilage is covered by the **perichondrium**, a fibrocellular layer that is continuous with the periosteal cover of the bone and that blends into the surrounding connective tissue. **Articular cartilage lacks a perichondrium**.

The perichondrium consists of two layers:

1. An **outer fibrous layer**, which contains bundles of type I collagen and elastin.

2. An **inner layer**, called the **chondrogenic layer**, formed by flat chondrocytes aligned tangentially to the margin of the cartilage.

The ECM contains hyaluronic acid, proteoglycans (rich in the GAGs chondroitin sulfate and keratan sulfate), and a high water content (70 to 80% of its weight). **Aggrecan** is a large proteoglycan characteristic of cartilage.

The **transcription factor Sox9** is required for expression of cartilage-specific ECM components such as type II collagen and the proteoglycan aggrecan. Sox9

Figure 4–18

Types of cartilage

Hyaline cartilage

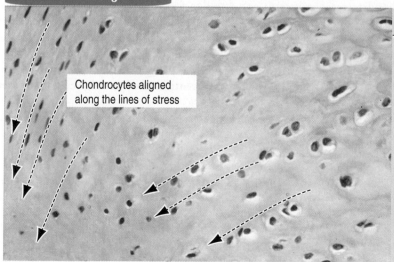

Hyaline cartilage has the following features:

1 It is **avascular**.

2 It is surrounded by **perichondrium** (except in articular cartilage). The perichondrium has an **outer fibrous layer**, an **inner chondrogenic layer**, and **blood vessels**.

3 It consists of chondrocytes surrounded by territorial and interterritorial matrices containing **type II collagen** interacting with proteoglycans.

4 It occurs in the **temporary skeleton of the embryo**, **articular cartilage**, and the **cartilage of the respiratory tract** (nose, larynx, trachea, and bronchi) and costal cartilages.

Elastic cartilage

Perichondrium

Chondrocytes

Elastic fibers

Elastic cartilage has the following features:

1 It is **avascular**.

2 It is surrounded by **perichondrium**.

3 It consists of chondrocytes surrounded by territorial and interterritorial matrices containing **type II collagen** interacting with proteoglycans and **elastic fibers**, which can be stained by **orcein** for light microscopy.

4 It occurs in the **external ear**, **epiglottis**, and **auditory tube**.

Fibrocartilage

Chondrocytes aligned along the lines of stress

Fibrocartilage has the following features:

1 It is generally **avascular**.

2 It **lacks a perichondrium**.

3 It consists of **chondrocytes** and **fibroblasts** surrounded by **type I collagen** and a less rigid extracellular matrix. Fibrocartilage is considered an intermediate tissue between hyaline cartilage and dense fibrous tissue.

4 It predominates in the **intervertebral disks**, **articular disks of the knee**, **mandible**, **sternoclavicular joints**, and **pubic symphysis**.

Figure 4–19

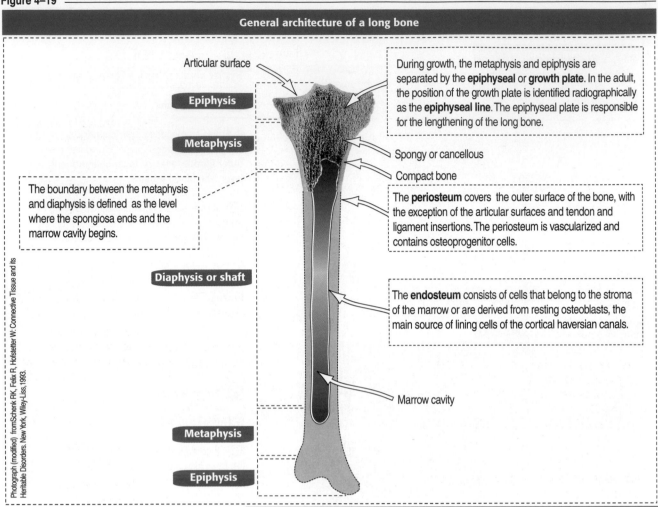

General architecture of a long bone

Articular surface

Epiphysis

Metaphysis

During growth, the metaphysis and epiphysis are separated by the **epiphyseal** or **growth plate**. In the adult, the position of the growth plate is identified radiographically as the **epiphyseal line**. The epiphyseal plate is responsible for the lengthening of the long bone.

Spongy or cancellous

Compact bone

The boundary between the metaphysis and diaphysis is defined as the level where the spongiosa ends and the marrow cavity begins.

The **periosteum** covers the outer surface of the bone, with the exception of the articular surfaces and tendon and ligament insertions. The periosteum is vascularized and contains osteoprogenitor cells.

Diaphysis or shaft

The **endosteum** consists of cells that belong to the stroma of the marrow or are derived from resting osteoblasts, the main source of lining cells of the cortical haversian canals.

Marrow cavity

Metaphysis

Epiphysis

activates the expression of collagen by the *Col2a1* gene. A lack of Sox9 expression prevents the chondrogenic layer to differentiate into chondrocytes. Mutations in the *Sox9* gene cause the rare and severe dwarfism **campomelic dysplasia** (Figure 4–17).

The structure of the **elastic cartilage** is similar to that of hyaline cartilage except that the ECM contains abundant **elastic fibers** synthesized by chondrocytes. Elastic cartilage is found in the auricle of the external ear, a major portion of the epiglottis, and some of the laryngeal cartilages. The specialized matrix of the cartilage has remarkable flexibility and the ability to regain its original shape after deformation.

Unlike hyaline cartilage, **fibrocartilage** is **opaque**, the matrix contains **type I collagen fibers**, the ECM has a **low concentration of proteoglycans** and **water**, and **it lacks a perichondrium**.

Fibrocartilage has great tensile strength and forms part of the intervertebral disk, pubic symphysis, and sites of insertion of tendon and ligament into bone.

The fibrocartilage is sometimes difficult to distinguish from dense regular connective tissue of some regions of tendons and ligaments. Fibrocartilage is distinguished by characteristic chondrocytes within lacunae, forming short columns (in contrast to flattened fibroblasts or fibrocytes lacking lacunae, surrounded by the dense connective tissue and ECM).

Bone

Bone is a rigid inflexible connective tissue in which the ECM has become im-

Figure 4–20

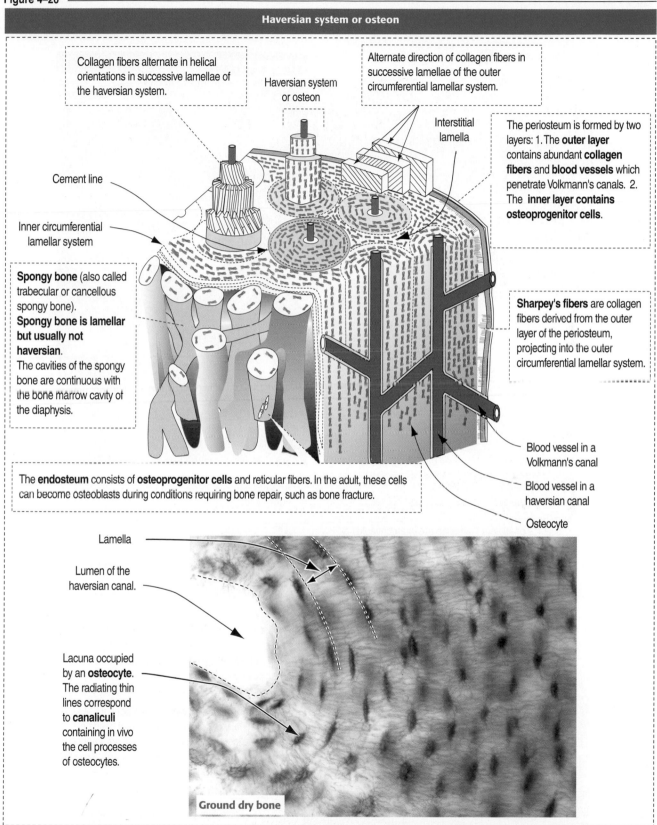

Haversian system or osteon

Collagen fibers alternate in helical orientations in successive lamellae of the haversian system.

Haversian system or osteon

Alternate direction of collagen fibers in successive lamellae of the outer circumferential lamellar system.

Interstitial lamella

The periosteum is formed by two layers: 1. The **outer layer** contains abundant **collagen fibers** and **blood vessels** which penetrate Volkmann's canals. 2. The **inner layer contains osteoprogenitor cells**.

Cement line

Inner circumferential lamellar system

Spongy bone (also called trabecular or cancellous spongy bone). **Spongy bone is lamellar but usually not haversian.** The cavities of the spongy bone are continuous with the bone marrow cavity of the diaphysis.

Sharpey's fibers are collagen fibers derived from the outer layer of the periosteum, projecting into the outer circumferential lamellar system.

The **endosteum** consists of **osteoprogenitor cells** and reticular fibers. In the adult, these cells can become osteoblasts during conditions requiring bone repair, such as bone fracture.

Blood vessel in a Volkmann's canal

Blood vessel in a haversian canal

Osteocyte

Lamella

Lumen of the haversian canal.

Lacuna occupied by an **osteocyte**. The radiating thin lines correspond to **canaliculi** containing in vivo the cell processes of osteocytes.

Ground dry bone

pregnated with salts of calcium and phosphate by a process called **mineralization**. Bone is highly vascularized and metabolically very active.

The functions of bone are:

Figure 4–21

Organization of compact bone: The osteon

2 Haversian canal of an osteon.　**3** Interstitial lamellae

Cement line

Lacuna occupied in vivo by an osteocyte and its cell processes.

Ground dry bone

Photographs from Schenk RK, Felix R, Hofstetter W: Connective tissue and its heritable disorders. New York, Wiley-Liss,1993.

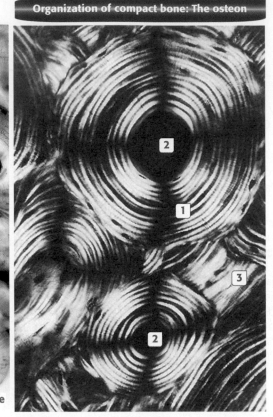

Organization of compact bone: The osteon

Polarized light photograph from: Schenk RK, Felix R, Hofstetter W: Connective tissue and its heritable disorders. New York, Wiley-Liss, 1993.

1 Concentric array of lamellar bone
Osteocytes are concentrically arranged between lamellae.
Osteocytes of adjacent lamellae are interconnected by cell processes lodged in canaliculi.
Cell processes are linked by **gap junctions**.
The metabolic and signaling transport along the cell processes is limited to a distance of about 100 μm.

Array of lamellar bone visualized by polarized light. Note:

1 The concentric array of the lamellae.

2 The variation in diameter of the osteons.

3 The banding distribution of interstitial lamellae.

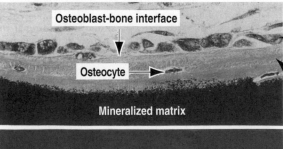

Osteoblast-bone interface

Osteocyte

Mineralized matrix

Osteoblasts are linearly arranged. In contrast to a true epithelium, the intercellular space is not sealed by tight junctions. However they are polarized cells since the bone matrix they produce is released along the osteoblast-bone interface.

Osteoid, a newly synthesized bone ECM, is gradually deposited in the form of bands or lamellae. Eventually, osteoblasts are trapped within the osteoid and become osteocytes when the matrix is calcified.

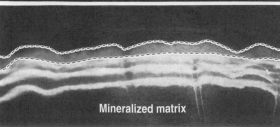

Mineralized matrix

Layer of osteoblasts.

Formation of lamellar bone. Lamellae are visualized after labeling with a fluorochrome. The mineralization front advances 1-2 μm/day.

Figure 4–22

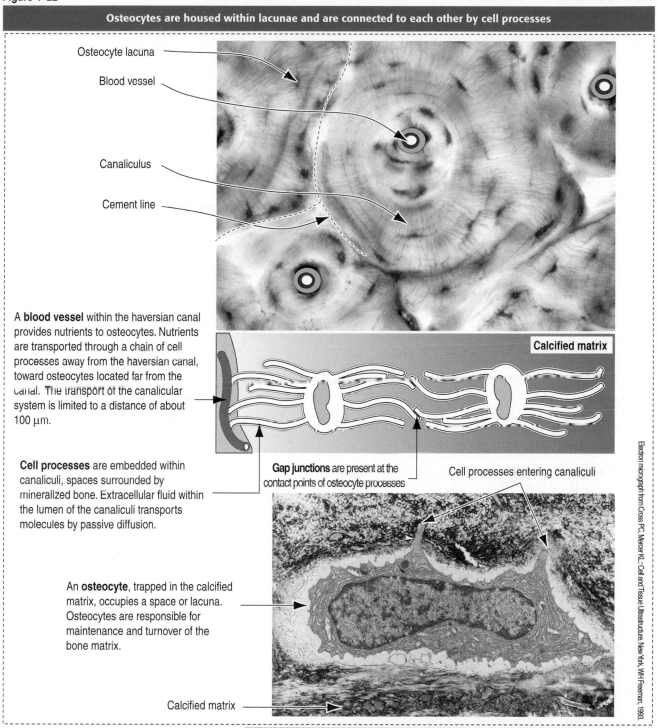

Osteocytes are housed within lacunae and are connected to each other by cell processes

Osteocyte lacuna

Blood vessel

Canaliculus

Cement line

Calcified matrix

A **blood vessel** within the haversian canal provides nutrients to osteocytes. Nutrients are transported through a chain of cell processes away from the haversian canal, toward osteocytes located far from the canal. The transport of the canalicular system is limited to a distance of about 100 μm.

Cell processes are embedded within canaliculi, spaces surrounded by mineralized bone. Extracellular fluid within the lumen of the canaliculi transports molecules by passive diffusion.

Gap junctions are present at the contact points of osteocyte processes

Cell processes entering canaliculi

An **osteocyte**, trapped in the calcified matrix, occupies a space or lacuna. Osteocytes are responsible for maintenance and turnover of the bone matrix.

Calcified matrix

Electron micrograph from Cross PC, Mercer KL: *Cell and Tissue Ultrastructure.* New York, WH Freeman, 1993.

1. Support and protection for the body and its organs.
2. A reservoir for calcium and phosphate ions.

Classification of bone

Based on its gross appearance (Figure 4–19), two forms of bone are distinguished:
1. **Compact bone.**
2. **Spongy or cancellous bone.**

Compact bone appears as a solid mass. Spongy bone consists of a network of **bony spicules** or **trabeculae** delimiting spaces occupied by the bone marrow.

Figure 4–23

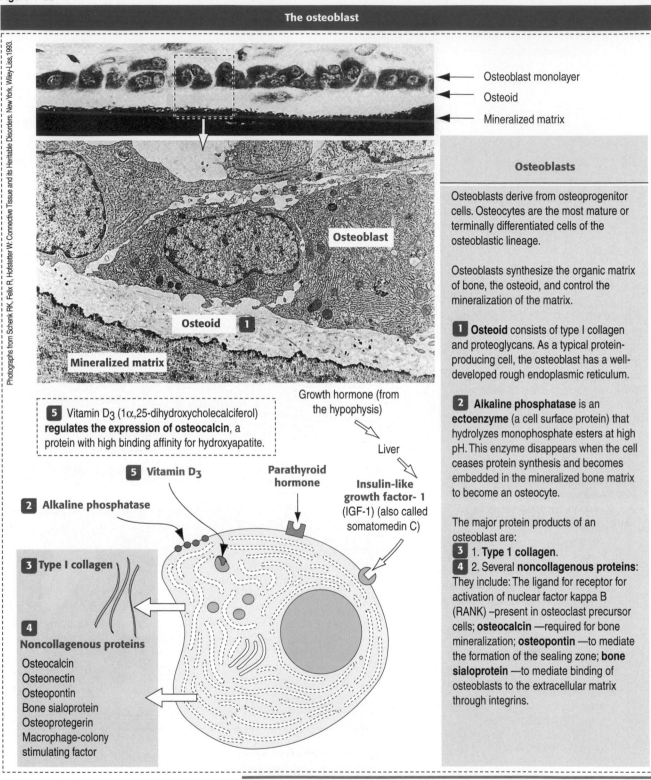

The osteoblast

Photographs from Schenk RK, Felix R, Hofstetter W: Connective Tissue and its Heritable Disorders. New York, Wiley-Liss,1993.

→ Osteoblast monolayer
→ Osteoid
→ Mineralized matrix

Osteoblast

Osteoid 1

Mineralized matrix

Growth hormone (from the hypophysis)

Liver

5 Vitamin D₃ (1α,25-dihydroxycholecalciferol) **regulates the expression of osteocalcin**, a protein with high binding affinity for hydroxyapatite.

Insulin-like growth factor- 1 (IGF-1) (also called somatomedin C)

5 **Vitamin D₃**

Parathyroid hormone

2 **Alkaline phosphatase**

3 **Type I collagen**

4

Noncollagenous proteins

Osteocalcin
Osteonectin
Osteopontin
Bone sialoprotein
Osteoprotegerin
Macrophage-colony stimulating factor

Osteoblasts

Osteoblasts derive from osteoprogenitor cells. Osteocytes are the most mature or terminally differentiated cells of the osteoblastic lineage.

Osteoblasts synthesize the organic matrix of bone, the osteoid, and control the mineralization of the matrix.

1 **Osteoid** consists of type I collagen and proteoglycans. As a typical protein-producing cell, the osteoblast has a well-developed rough endoplasmic reticulum.

2 **Alkaline phosphatase** is an **ectoenzyme** (a cell surface protein) that hydrolyzes monophosphate esters at high pH. This enzyme disappears when the cell ceases protein synthesis and becomes embedded in the mineralized bone matrix to become an osteocyte.

The major protein products of an osteoblast are:
3 1. **Type 1 collagen**.
4 2. Several **noncollagenous proteins**: They include: The ligand for receptor for activation of nuclear factor kappa B (RANK) –present in osteoclast precursor cells; **osteocalcin** —required for bone mineralization; **osteopontin** —to mediate the formation of the sealing zone; **bone sialoprotein** —to mediate binding of osteoblasts to the extracellular matrix through integrins.

In long bones, such as the femur, the shaft or **diaphysis** consists of compact bone forming a hollow cylinder with a central marrow space, called the **medullary** or **marrow cavity**.

The ends of the long bones, called **epiphyses**, consist of **spongy bone** covered by a thin layer of compact bone. In the growing individual, epiphyses are separated from the shaft or diaphysis by a cartilaginous **epiphyseal plate**, connected to the diaphysis by spongy bone. A tapering transitional region, called the **meta-physis,** connects the epiphysis and the diaphysis. **Both the epiphyseal plate and adjacent spongy bone represent the growth zone, responsible for the increase in length of the growing bone.**

The **articular surfaces**, at the ends of the long bones, are covered by **hyaline cartilage,** the **articular cartilage.** Except on the articular surfaces and at the insertion site of tendons and ligaments, most bones are surrounded by the **periosteum,** a layer of specialized connective tissue with **osteogenic potential.**

The **marrow cavity** of the diaphysis and the spaces within spongy bone are lined by **endosteum,** also with osteogenic potential.

Two types of bone are identified on the basis of the **microscopic organization of the ECM:**

1. **Lamellar bone,** typical of the mature or compact bone.

2. **Woven bone,** observed in the developing bone.

The **lamellar bone** consists of **lamellae,** largely composed of **bone matrix,** a mineralized substance deposited in layers or lamellae, and **osteocytes,** each occupying a cavity or **lacuna** with radiating and branching **canaliculi** that penetrate the lamellae of adjacent lacunae.

The lamellar bone displays four distinct patterns (Figure 4–20):

1. The **osteons** or **haversian systems,** formed by concentrically arranged lamellae around a longitudinal vascular channel.

2. The **interstitial lamellae,** observed between osteons and separated from them by a thin layer known as the **cement line.**

3. The **outer circumferential lamellae,** visualized at the external surface of the compact bone under the periosteum.

4. The **inner circumferential lamellae,** seen on the internal surface subjacent to the endosteum.

The **vascular channels** in compact bone have two orientations with respect to the lamellar structures:

1. The longitudinal capillaries and postcapillary venules, running in the center of the osteon within a space known as the **haversian canal** (Figures 4–20, 4–21 and 4–22).

2. The haversian canals are connected with one another by transverse or oblique canals known as **Volkmann's canals,** containing blood vessels from the marrow and some from the periosteum.

The periosteum and endosteum

During embryonic and postnatal growth, the **periosteum** consists of an **inner layer** of bone-forming cells (osteoblasts) in direct contact with the bone. The inner layer is the **osteogenic layer.** In the adult, the periosteum contains inactive connective tissue cells that retain their osteogenic potential in case of bone injury and repair.

The **outer layer** is rich in blood vessels, some of them entering Volkmann's canals, and thick anchoring collagen fibers, called **Sharpey's fibers,** that penetrate the outer circumferential lamellae deep in the bone (see Figure 4–20).

The **endosteum** consists of squamous cells and connective tissue fibers covering the spongy walls housing the bone marrow and extending into all the cavities of the bone, including the haversian canals.

The bone matrix

The **bone matrix** consists of **organic** (35%) and **inorganic** (65%) components. The organic bone matrix contains **type I collagen fibers** (90%); **proteoglycans,** enriched in **chondroitin sulfate, keratan sulfate,** and **hyaluronic acid;** and **noncollagenous proteins.**

Type I collagen is the predominant protein of the bone matrix. In mature lamellar bone, collagen fibers have a highly ordered arrangement with changing

Figure 4–24

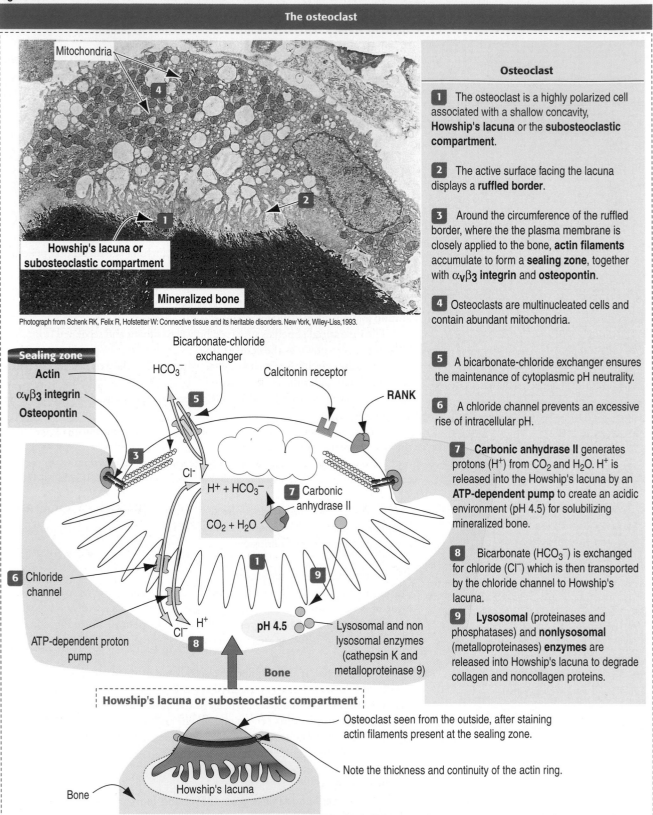

The osteoclast

Mitochondria

4

2

1

Howship's lacuna or subosteoclastic compartment

Mineralized bone

Photograph from Schenk RK, Felix R, Hofstetter W: Connective tissue and its heritable disorders. New York, Wiley-Liss,1993.

Sealing zone

Actin
$\alpha_V\beta_3$ integrin
Osteopontin

Bicarbonate-chloride exchanger

HCO_3^-

5

Calcitonin receptor

RANK

3

Cl^-

$H^+ + HCO_3^-$

7 Carbonic anhydrase II

$CO_2 + H_2O$

6 Chloride channel

1

9

Cl^-

pH 4.5

Lysosomal and non lysosomal enzymes (cathepsin K and metalloproteinase 9)

ATP-dependent proton pump

H^+

Cl^-

8

Bone

Howship's lacuna or subosteoclastic compartment

Osteoclast seen from the outside, after staining actin filaments present at the sealing zone.

Note the thickness and continuity of the actin ring.

Bone

Howship's lacuna

Osteoclast

1　The osteoclast is a highly polarized cell associated with a shallow concavity, **Howship's lacuna** or the **subosteoclastic compartment**.

2　The active surface facing the lacuna displays a **ruffled border**.

3　Around the circumference of the ruffled border, where the the plasma membrane is closely applied to the bone, **actin filaments** accumulate to form a **sealing zone**, together with $\alpha_V\beta_3$ **integrin** and **osteopontin**.

4　Osteoclasts are multinucleated cells and contain abundant mitochondria.

5　A bicarbonate-chloride exchanger ensures the maintenance of cytoplasmic pH neutrality.

6　A chloride channel prevents an excessive rise of intracellular pH.

7　**Carbonic anhydrase II** generates protons (H^+) from CO_2 and H_2O. H^+ is released into the Howship's lacuna by an **ATP-dependent pump** to create an acidic environment (pH 4.5) for solubilizing mineralized bone.

8　Bicarbonate (HCO_3^-) is exchanged for chloride (Cl^-) which is then transported by the chloride channel to Howship's lacuna.

9　**Lysosomal** (proteinases and phosphatases) and **nonlysosomal** (metalloproteinases) **enzymes** are released into Howship's lacuna to degrade collagen and noncollagen proteins.

orientations with respect to the axis of the haversian canal in successive concentric lamellae.

Noncollagenous matrix proteins include **osteocalcin**, **osteopontin**, and os-

Figure 4–25

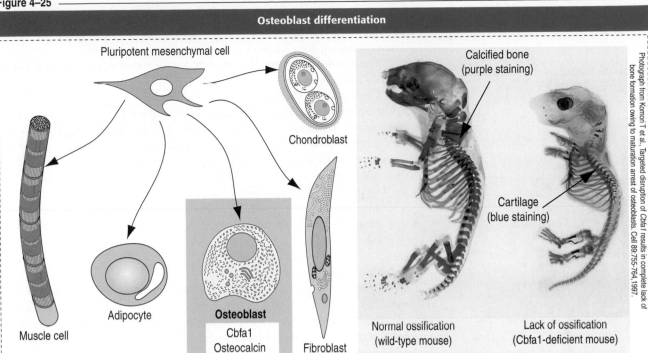

Osteoblast differentiation

Pluripotent mesenchymal cell

Chondroblast

Muscle cell

Adipocyte

Osteoblast

Cbfa1
Osteocalcin

Fibroblast

Calcified bone
(purple staining)

Cartilage
(blue staining)

Normal ossification
(wild-type mouse)

Lack of ossification
(Cbfa1-deficient mouse)

Photograph from Komori T et al., Targeted disruption of *Cbfa1* results in complete lack of bone formation owing to maturation arrest of osteoblasts. Cell 89:755-764, 1997.

Clinical significance: Transcriptional control of osteoblast differentiation

Bone formation depends on the synthesis and deposition of bone extracellular matrix by osteoblasts. **Bone remodeling** results from the coordinated function of osteoblasts and ostoclasts and is tightly regulated by autocrine, paracrine, and endocrine mechanisms (parathyroid hormone, calcitonin, and sex steroids). **Osteoporosis** is an estrogen-dependent bone remodeling disease in which the coordinated osteoblast-osteoclast function is disrupted and leads to a reduction in bone mass and high risk of bone fracture. **The main function of a differentiated osteoblast is the mineralization of the bone matrix or osteoid**.

Osteoblasts derive from a pluripotent mesenchymal cell that gives rise to muscle cells, adipocytes, fibroblasts, and chondroblasts. Two osteoblast specific genes control the differentiation of the osteoblast progeny: **Cbfa1** (for *co*re-*b*inding *fa*ctor family) –encoding a **transcription factor** that induces the differentiation of osteoblasts and controls the expression of osteocalcin– and **osteocalcin** –specific

secretory protein expressed only in terminally differentiated osteoblasts.

Cbfa1-deficient mice have a skeleton consisting of cartilage without any indication of osteoblast differentiation represented by bone formation and mineralization. In addition, because osteoblasts regulate the formation of osteoclasts, Cbfa1-deficient mice lack osteoclasts. Patients with **cleidocranial dysplasia** (hypoplastic clavicles and delayed ossification of sutures of certain skull bones) have a *Cbfa1* gene mutation.

Leptin, a peptide synthesized by **adipocytes** with binding affinity to its receptor localized in the **hypothalamus**, is also a regulator of bone formation through its action on osteoblasts by a hypothalamically controlled mechanism that is presently unknown. Patients with generalized **lipodystrophy** (absence of adipocytes and white fat) exhibit **osteosclerosis** (hardening of bone) and accelerated bone growth.

teonectin, synthesized by osteoblasts and with unique properties in the mineralization of bone.

Osteocalcin and osteopontin synthesis increases following stimulation with the active vitamin D metabolite, 1α,25-dihydroxycholecalciferol. Osteocalcin inhibits osteoblast function.

Osteonectin is not exclusively an osteoblast product and is present in tissues undergoing remodeling and morphogenesis.

Bone sialoprotein is also a bone matrix component.

Osteoprotegerin, RANKL, and **macrophage colony-stimulating factor** are products of osteoblasts required for regulating the differentiation of **osteoclasts** (see Figure 4–26).

The **inorganic component of the bone** is represented predominantly by deposits of **calcium phosphate** with the crystalline characteristics of **hydroxyapatite.** The crystals are distributed along the length of collagen fibers through an assembly process assisted by noncollagenous proteins.

Cellular components of bone

Actively growing bone contains cells of two different lineages:

1. The **osteoblast lineage**, which includes the **osteoprogenitor cells, osteoblasts,** and **osteocytes.**
2. The **monocyte-macrophage-osteoclast lineage.**

Osteoprogenitor cells are of **mesenchymal origin** and have the **properties of stem cells: the potential for proliferation** and **a capacity to differentiate.** Osteoprogenitor cells progress to osteoblasts by a regulatory mechanism involving growth and transcription factors and are present in the inner layer of the periosteum and the endosteum. Osteoblasts change into osteocytes when they are trapped within the mineralized matrix they produce.

Osteoprogenitor cells persist throughout postnatal life as **bone-lining cells;** they are reactivated in the adult during the repair of bone fractures and other injuries.

Osteoblasts and osteocytes

Osteoblasts are epithelial-like cells with cuboidal or columnar shapes, forming a **monolayer** covering all sites of active bone formation. Osteoblasts are highly polarized cells: they deposit **osteoid, the nonmineralized organic matrix of the bone,** along the osteoblast-bone interface. Osteoblasts initiate and control the subsequent mineralization of the osteoid.

In electron micrographs, osteoblasts display the typical features of cells actively engaged in protein synthesis, glycosylation, and secretion. Their specific products are **type I collagen, osteocalcin, osteopontin,** and **bone sialoprotein** (see Figure 4–23). Osteoblasts give a strong cytochemical reaction for **alkaline phosphatase** that disappears when the cells become embedded in the matrix as osteocytes. In addition, osteoblasts produce growth factors, in particular members of the **bone morphogenetic protein family,** with bone-inductive activities.

When bone formation is completed, osteoblasts flatten out and transform into osteocytes.

Osteocytes, the most mature or terminally differentiated cell of the osteoblast lineage, maintain the ECM of bone.

Osteocytes are highly branched cells with their body occupying small spaces between lamellae, called **lacunae.** Small channels, the **canaliculi,** course through the lamellae and interconnect neighboring lacunae. Adjacent cell processes — found within canaliculi— are connected by **gap junctions** (see Figure 4–22).

Nutrient materials diffuse from a neighboring blood vessel, within the haversian canal, through the canaliculi into the lacunae.

The life of an osteocyte depends on this nutrient diffusion process and the life of the bone matrix depends on the osteocyte. Osteocytes can remain alive for years provided vascularization is continuous.

In compact bone, 4 to 20 lamellae are concentrically arranged around the haversian canal; they contain a blood vessel, either a capillary or a postcapillary venule.

Clinical significance: Osteoblast differentiation

Osteoblasts derive from a pluripotent mesenchymal cell that is also the precursor of muscle cells, adipocytes, fibroblasts, and chondroblasts.

The differentiation of the osteoblast is controlled by growth and transcription factors. Several members of the **bone morphogenetic protein (BMP) family** and **transforming growth factor** β can regulate the embryonic development and differentiation of the osteoblast.

Two osteoblast-specific genes modulate the differentiation of the osteoblast progeny (see Figure 4–25): *Cbfa1* (for *c*ore-*b*inding *fa*ctor family) encodes a **transcription factor** that induces the differentiation of osteoblasts and controls

Figure 4–26

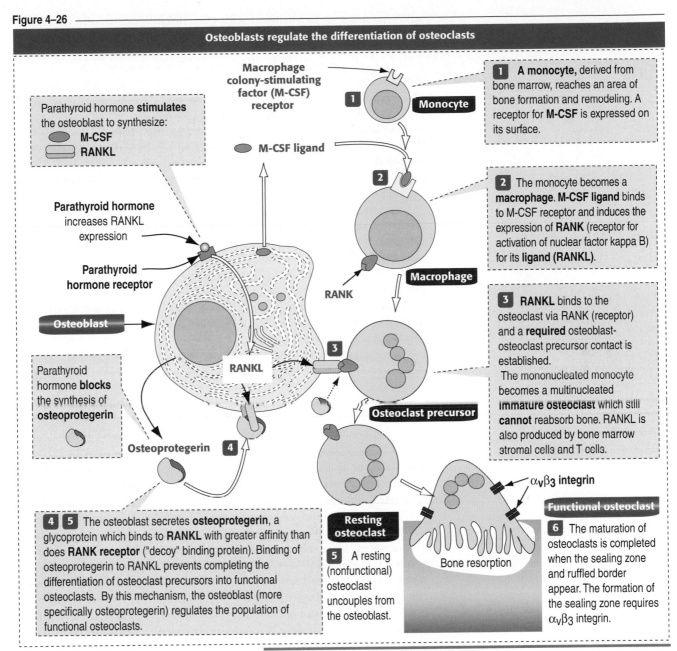

Osteoblasts regulate the differentiation of osteoclasts

Parathyroid hormone **stimulates** the osteoblast to synthesize:
- M-CSF
- RANKL

Macrophage colony-stimulating factor (M-CSF) receptor

M-CSF ligand

Parathyroid hormone increases RANKL expression

Parathyroid hormone receptor

Osteoblast

Parathyroid hormone **blocks** the synthesis of **osteoprotegerin**

RANKL

Osteoprotegerin

1 A monocyte, derived from bone marrow, reaches an area of bone formation and remodeling. A receptor for **M-CSF** is expressed on its surface.

Monocyte

2 The monocyte becomes a **macrophage**. **M-CSF ligand** binds to M-CSF receptor and induces the expression of **RANK** (receptor for activation of nuclear factor kappa B) for its **ligand (RANKL)**.

Macrophage

RANK

3 **RANKL** binds to the osteoclast via RANK (receptor) and a **required** osteoblast-osteoclast precursor contact is established.
The mononucleated monocyte becomes a multinucleated **immature osteoclast** which still **cannot** reabsorb bone. RANKL is also produced by bone marrow stromal cells and T cells.

Osteoclast precursor

$\alpha_V\beta_3$ **integrin**

Functional osteoclast

Resting osteoclast

Bone resorption

4 **5** The osteoblast secretes **osteoprotegerin**, a glycoprotein which binds to **RANKL** with greater affinity than does **RANK** receptor ("decoy" binding protein). Binding of osteoprotegerin to RANKL prevents completing the differentiation of osteoclast precursors into functional osteoclasts. By this mechanism, the osteoblast (more specifically osteoprotegerin) regulates the population of functional osteoclasts.

5 A resting (nonfunctional) osteoclast uncouples from the osteoblast.

6 The maturation of osteoclasts is completed when the sealing zone and ruffled border appear. The formation of the sealing zone requires $\alpha_V\beta_3$ integrin.

the expression of osteocalcin. Cbfa1 is the earliest and most specific indicator of osteogenesis and its expression is induced by **BMP7**, followed by the expression of osteocalcin and osteopontin. **Osteocalcin** is a specific secretory protein expressed only in terminally differentiated osteoblasts under the control of Cbfa1.

Cbfa1-deficient mice develop to term and have a skeleton consisting of cartilage. There is no indication of osteoblast differentiation or bone formation in these mice. In addition, Cbfa1-deficient mice lack osteoclasts. As we will discuss soon, osteoblasts regulate the formation of osteoclasts. Consistent with the skeletal observations in the Cbfa1-deficient mice is a condition in humans known as **cleidocranial dysplasia** (CCD). CCD is characterized by hypoplastic clavicles, delayed ossification of sutures of certain skull bones, and mutations in the *Cbfa1* gene.

Leptin, a peptide synthesized by **adipocytes** with binding affinity to its receptor in the **hypothalamus**, regulates bone formation by a central mechanism. Although details of the leptin-hypothalamic control mechanism are unknown, mice deficient in leptin or its receptor have a considerably higher bone mass than wild-type mice. In fact, patients with generalized **lipodystrophy** (absence of adipocytes and white fat) exhibit **osteoesclerosis** (increased bone hardening) and accelerated bone growth.

Osteoclasts

The **osteoclasts** do not belong to the osteoprogenitor cell lineage. Instead, osteoclasts derive from the **monocyte-macrophage progenitor cell lineage** in the bone marrow, which diverges into the **osteoclast progenitor pathway**.

The osteoclast precursor cells are **monocytes**, which reach the bone through the blood circulation and fuse into multinucleated cells with as many as 30 nuclei to form osteoclasts by a process regulated by osteoblasts and stromal cells of the bone marrow (see Figure 4–26).

After attachment to the target bone matrix, osteoclasts generate a secluded acidic environment required for bone resorption. Bone resorption involves first the dissolution of the inorganic components of the bone (bone demineralization) mediated by H^+-ATPase (adenosine triphosphatase) within an acidic environment, followed by enzymatic degradation of the organic component by a lysosomal protease, cathepsin K.

Osteoclasts play an essential role in bone remodeling and renewal. This process involves removal of bone matrix at several sites, followed by its replacement with new bone by osteoblasts.

The osteoclast is a large (up to 100 μm in diameter) and highly polarized cell that occupies a shallow concavity called **Howship's lacuna** or the **subosteoclastic compartment** (Figure 4–24).

The cell domain facing the lacuna has deep infoldings of the cell membrane, the **ruffled border**. When the cell is not active, the ruffled border disappears and the osteoclast enters into a resting phase. Around the circumference of the ruffled border —at the point where the cell membrane is closely applied to the bone just at the margins of the lacuna— **actin filaments** accumulate and participate, together with $\alpha_v\beta_3$ **integrin**, to form a **sealing zone**. The sealing zone seals off the bone resorption lacuna.

The cytoplasm of the osteoclast is **very rich in mitochondria**, the source of ATP to drive the H^+ pumps required for the **acidification of the subosteoclastic compartment** for the subsequent **activation of lysosomal** and **nonlysosomal enzymes**.

Osteoclasts are transiently active in response to a metabolic demand for the mobilization of calcium from bone into blood. Osteoclast activity is directly regulated by **calcitonin** (synthesized by neural crest derived parafollicular or **C cells** of the thyroid follicle), **vitamin D_3**, and regulatory molecules produced by osteoblasts and stromal cells of the bone marrow (see below).

Regulation of osteoclast differentiation

Macrophage colony-stimulating factor (M-CSF) is a secretory product of osteoblasts. M-CSF is required for the survival and proliferation of the osteoclast precursor, the monocyte-macrophage (Figure 4–26). Both **osteoblasts** and **stromal cells of the bone marrow** produce **activation nuclear factor kappa B (NF-κB) ligand (RANKL)** with binding affinity to the **RANK receptor**. We have seen in Chapter 3, Cell Signaling (Figure 3–8), that NF-κB is a critical transcription factor heterodimer activated in response to inflammatory or immunologic signaling.

The interaction of the RANK receptor on osteoclast precursor cells with RANKL exposed on the surface of osteoblasts determines cell-cell contact required for further maturation of the osteoclast precursor. Osteoblasts synthesize **osteoprotegerin**, a protein with high binding affinity for RANKL. Osteoprotegerin is a soluble "decoy" protein that binds to RANKL and prevents RANK-RANKL interaction. Consequently, **osteoprotegerin modulates the** osteoclastogenic process.

Two proteins are essential for osteoclastogenesis:

1. M-CSF induces macrophages to become **proliferating osteoclast precursors.**

2. RANKL stimulates M-CSF-induced cells to **differentiate** into functional osteoclasts.

RANK and RANKL are members of the **tumor necrosis factor** receptor and ligand superfamilies.

Parathyroid hormone stimulates the expression of osteoclastogenic RANKL. By this mechanism, the pool of RANKL increases relative to osteoprotegerin. An excess of parathyroid hormone enhances osteoclastogenesis (see Chapter 19, Endocrine System).

In the *op/op* mutant mouse, the lack of M-CSF results in **osteopetrosis** (Gk. *osteon*, bone; *petra*, stone; *osis*, condition), a family of diseases caused by **osteoclast dysfunction.** For comparison, **osteoesclerosis** is an increase in bone mass due an **increase in osteoblastic activity.** In humans, osteopetrosis is characterized by **high-density bone** due to **absent osteoclastic activity.** In long bones, this condition leads to the **occlusion of marrow spaces** and to **anemia.**

Clinical significance: Osteoporosis and osteomalacia

Osteoporosis (Gk. *osteon*, bone; *poros*, pore; *osis*, condition) is defined as the loss of bone mass leading to bone fragility and susceptibility to fractures.

The major factor in osteoporosis is the deficiency of the sex steroid **estrogen** that occurs in postmenopausal women. In this condition, the amount of reabsored old bone —due to an increase in the **number of osteoclasts** —exceeds the amount of formed new bone. This accelerated turnover state can be reversed by estrogen therapy and calcium and vitamin D supplementation. Osteoporosis and osteoporotic fractures are also observed in men.

Osteoporosis is asymptomatic until it produces skeletal deformity and bone fractures (typically in the spine, hip, and wrist). The **vertebral bones** are predominantly **trabecular bone** surrounded by a thin rim of compact bone. Therefore, they may be crushed or may wedge anteriorly, resulting in pain and in a reduction in height. Elderly persons with osteoporosis are unlikely to have a hip fracture unless they fall.

The diagnosis of osteoporosis is made radiologically or, preferentially, by measuring bone density by dual-energy x-ray absorptiometry (DEXA). DEXA measures photon absorption from an x-ray source to estimate the amount of bone mineral content.

Osteomalacia (Gk. *osteon*, bone; *malakia*, softness) is a disease characterized by a progressive softening and bending of the bones. Softening occurs because of a defect in the **mineralization of the osteoid** due to lack of vitamin D or renal tubular dysfunction (see Chapter 14, Urinary System). In the young, a defect in **mineralization of cartilage** in the growth plate (see Chapter 5, Osteogenesis), causes a defect called **rickets (juvenile osteomalacia).** Osteomalacia can result from a deficiency of vitamin D (for example, intestinal malabsorption) or heritable disorders of vitamin D activation (for example, **renal 1α-hydroxylase deficiency** in which **calciferol** is not converted to the active form of vitamin D, **calcitriol**; see vitamin D in Chapter 19, Endocrine System).

5. OSTEOGENESIS

Bone formation (osteogenesis or ossification)

Bone develops by replacement of a preexisting connective tissue. The two processes of bone formation or osteogenesis observed in the embryo are: (1) **intramembranous bone formation**, in which bone tissue is laid down directly in primitive connective tissue or **mesenchyme** (Figures 5–1 and 5–2), and (2) **endochondral bone formation**, in which bone tissue replaces a preexisting **hyaline cartilage**, the template or anlage of the future bone (Figures 5–3, 5–4 and 5–5).

The mechanism of bone matrix deposition during intramembranous and endochondral ossification is essentially the same: **A primary trabecular network or primary spongiosa is first laid down and then transformed into mature bone.** But there is a difference: **in endochondral ossification, cartilage is replaced by bone matrix.**

Intramembranous bone formation

Membrane bones such as the flat bones of the skull develop by intramembranous ossification. Intramembranous ossification occurs in the following sequence (Figure 5–1):

Figure 5–1

Intramembranous ossification

1 Mesenchymal cells aggregate without a cartilage intermediate. This process is controlled by **patterning signals** from polypeptides of the **Wnt, hedhehog, fibroblast growth factor**, and **transforming growth factor**–β families.

2 Mesenchymal cells differentiate into **osteoblasts**. A **bone blastema** is formed. Osteocytes within the core of the blastema are interconnected by cell processes forming a **functional syncytium**. Osteoblasts line the surface of the bone blastema.

3 **Bone matrix** (osteoid) is deposited by osteoblasts. Later, Ca²⁺, transported by blood vessels, is used in the **mineralization process** and **primary bone tissue** is formed. **Osteoclasts** initiate the modeling of the bone tissue.

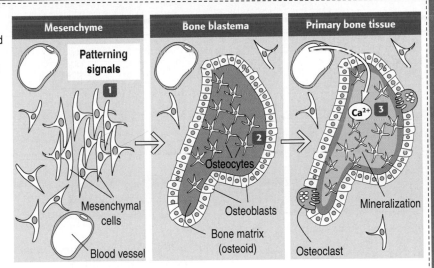

Organization of a primary ossification center

Multiple individual trabeculae enlarge by appositional growth and eventually fuse together as a primary ossification center organized during the first stage of intramembranous ossification.

Although **primary bone tissue** formation begins as an **interstitial** process, it soon becomes **appositional**.

Osteocytes become trapped within the calcified osteoid.

At the surface of the osteoid, osteoblasts continue the appositional deposit of matrix, mainly **type I collagen** and **noncollagenous proteins**.

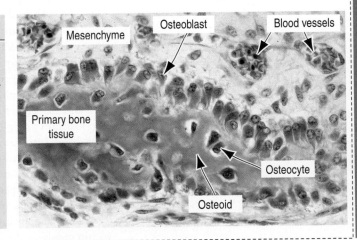

Figure 5–2

Intramembranous ossification

The continued deposition of bone on trabecular surfaces determines the occlusion of the intertrabecular spaces, and **compact bone is formed**. In other areas, the thickening of the trabeculae does not occur and the connective tissue in the intertrabecular space differentiates into **hematopoietic tissue**. The primary spongiosa persists as **cancellous bone**.

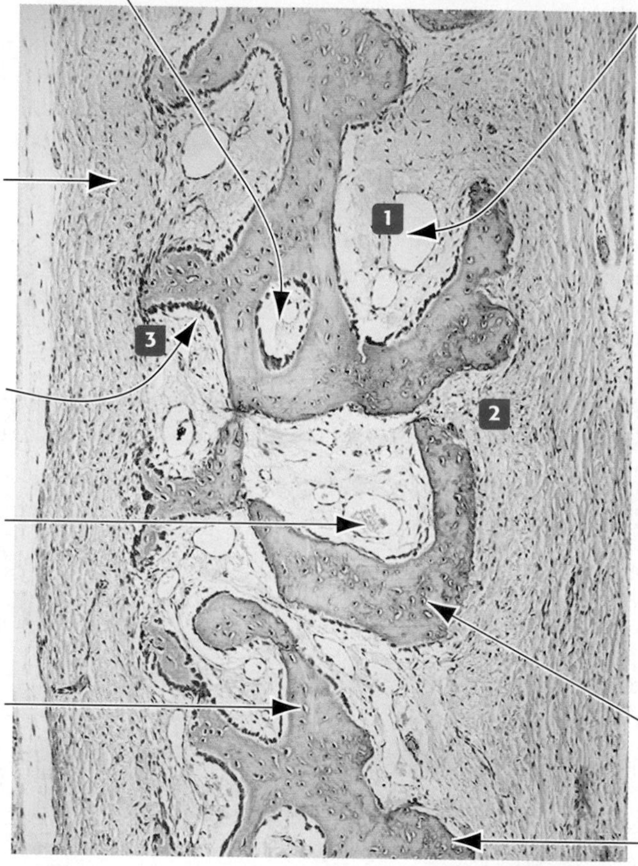

Blood vessel

The mesenchymal cells located near the periosteal surface condense to form the **periosteum**

Monolayer of osteoblasts

Blood vessel

Trabecula

Intramembranous ossification

The frontal and parietal bones and part of the occipital, temporal, mandible, and maxilla bones develop by intramembranous ossification.

Intramembranous ossification requires:

1 A **well-vascularized primitive connective tissue**.

2 Bone formation is **not preceded** by the formation of a **cartilage**.

3 An aggregate of mesenchymal cells differentiates **directly** into osteoid-producing osteoblasts.

Osteoblasts organize thin trabeculae of woven bone, forming an irregular network called **primary spongiosa**.

Acidophilic osteoid

1. The embryonic mesenchyme changes into a highly vascularized connective tissue. Fibroblast-like mesenchymal cells, embedded in a gelatinous extracellular matrix containing collagen fibers, aggregate.

2. Mesenchymal cells acquire the typical columnar form of **osteoblasts** and begin to secrete **bone matrix**. Numerous ossification centers develop and eventually fuse, forming a network of anastomosing **trabeculae** resembling a sponge, the so-called **spongy bone** or **primary spongiosa**.

3. Because collagen fibers in the newly formed trabeculae are **randomly** oriented, the early intramembranous bone is described as **woven bone** —in contrast with **lamellar bone** formed later during bone remodeling.

4. Calcium phosphate is deposited in the bone matrix, which is laid down by **apposition. Interstitial bone growth does not occur**.

5. Bone matrix mineralization leads to two new developments (Figure 5–2): the entrapment of osteoblasts as **osteocytes**, as trabeculae thicken, and the partial closing of the perivascular channels, which assume the new role of **hematopoiesis** by conversion of mesenchymal cells into blood-forming cells.

Osteocytes remain connected to each other by cytoplasmic processes enclosed within canaliculi, and new osteoblasts are generated from osteoprogenitor cells adjacent to the blood vessels.

The final developmental events include:

1. **The conversion of woven bone to lamellar bone.** In lamellar bone, the newly synthesized collagen fibers are aligned into **regular** bundles. Lamellae arranged in concentric rings around a central blood vessel occupying the haversian canal form **osteons** or **haversian systems.** Membrane bones remain as spongy bone in the center, the **diploe,** enclosed by an outer and an inner layer of compact bone.

2. The condensation of the external and internal connective tissue layers to form the **periosteum** and **endosteum,** respectively, containing fusiform cells with osteoprogenitor cell potential.

At birth, bone development is not complete, and the bones of the skull are separated by spaces (**fontanelles**) housing osteogenic tissue. The bones of a young child contain both woven and lamellar bony matrix.

Endochondral ossification

Endochondral ossification is the process by which **skeletal cartilage templates** are replaced by bone. As you recall, intramembranous ossification is the process by which a **skeletal mesenchymal template** is replaced by bone without passing through the cartilage stage. Bones of the extremities, vertebral column, and pelvis derive from a hyaline cartilage template.

As in intramembranous ossification, a **primary ossification center** is formed during endochondral ossification (see Figure 5–3). Unlike intramembranous ossification, this center of ossification derives from proliferated chondrocytes that have deposited an extracellular matrix containing type II collagen.

Shortly after, chondrocytes in the central region of the cartilage undergo maturation to hypertrophy and synthesize a matrix containing **type X collagen,** a marker for hypertrophic chondrocytes. **Angiogenic factors** secreted by hypertrophic chondrocytes (**vascular endothelial cell growth factor, VEGF**) induce the forma-

Figure 5–3

Endochondral ossification: Primary ossification center

2 Proliferation of chondrocytes followed by their hypertrophy at the midpoint of the shaft initiates the formation of the **primary ossification center.** Hypertrophic chondrocytes secrete **vascular endothelial cell growth factor** to induce sprouting of blood vessels from the perichondrium. Then, **calcification of the matrix** and **apoptosis of hypertrophic chondrocytes** occur.

Primary center of ossification

Shaft

1 Hyaline cartilage is the template of a long bone.

3 Osteoprogenitor cells of the perichondrium form the **periosteal collar.**

4 Blood vessels, forming the **periosteal bud,** branch in opposite directions.

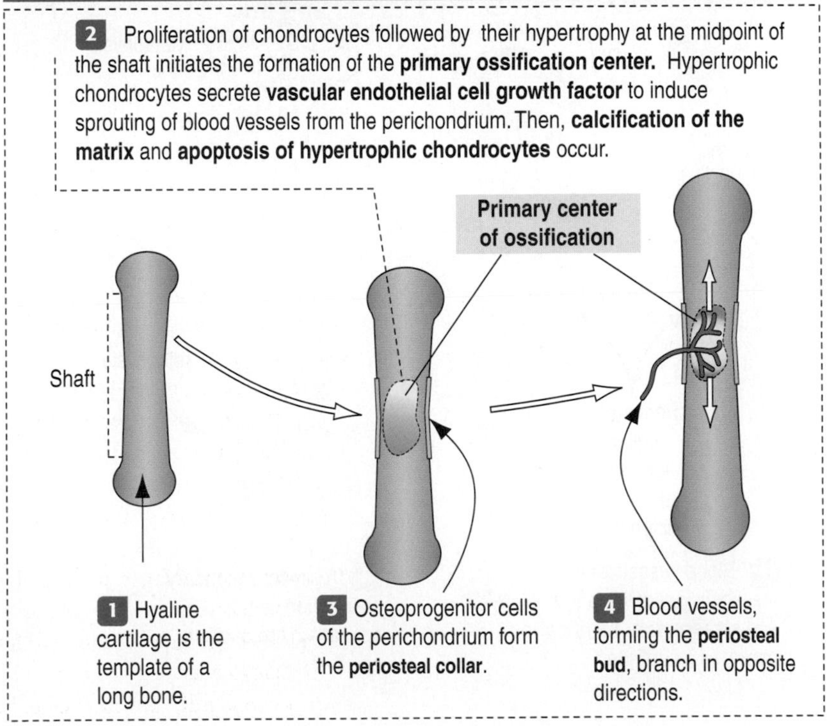

tion of blood vessels from the perichondrium. Osteoprogenitor and hematopoietic cells arrive with the newly formed blood vessels.

These events result in the formation of the primary ossification center. Hypertrophic chondrocytes undergo apoptosis as **calcification of the matrix** in the middle of the shaft of the cartilage template takes place.

At the same time, the inner perichondrial cells exhibit their osteogenic potential, and a thin **periosteal collar** of bone is formed around the midpoint of the shaft, the **diaphysis**. Consequently, the primary ossification center ends up located inside a tube of bone. **The periosteal collar formed under the periosteum by intramembranous ossification consists of woven bone.**

The following sequence of events defines the next steps of endochondral ossification (Figure 5–4):

1. **Blood vessels** invade the space formerly occupied by the hypertrophic chondrocytes, and they branch and project toward either end of the center of ossification. Blind capillary ends extend into the cavities formed within the calcified cartilage.

2. **Osteoprogenitor cells** and hematopoietic stem cells reach the core of the calcified cartilage through the perivascular connective tissue surrounding the invading blood vessels. Then, osteoprogenitor cells differentiate into **osteoblasts** that aggregate on the surfaces of the calcified cartilage and begin to deposit **bone**

Figure 5–4

Endochondral ossification: Secondary ossification centers

The **metaphysis** is the portion of the diaphysis nearest to the epiphyses. The **epiphyseal cartilagenous growth plate** between the metaphysis and the epiphysis will be eventually replaced by bone. The bone at this site is particularly dense and is recognized as an **epiphyseal line**. **Indian hedgehog (Ihh)**, a member of the hedgehog protein family, stimulates chondrocyte proliferation in the growth plate and prevents chondrocyte hypertrophy.

4 Blood vessels from the diaphysis and epiphysis intercommunicate.
5 All the epiphyseal cartilage is replaced by bone, except for the **articular surface**.

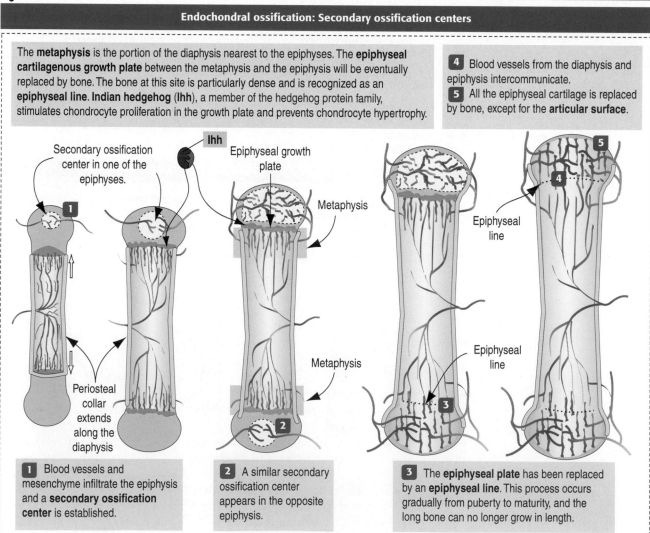

1 Blood vessels and mesenchyme infiltrate the epiphysis and a **secondary ossification center** is established.

2 A similar secondary ossification center appears in the opposite epiphysis.

3 The **epiphyseal plate** has been replaced by an **epiphyseal line**. This process occurs gradually from puberty to maturity, and the long bone can no longer grow in length.

Figure 5–5

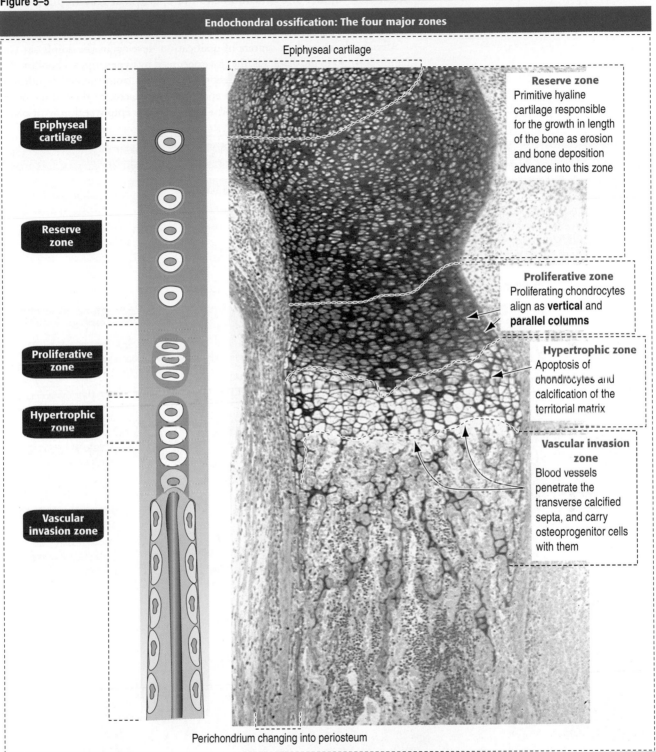

Endochondral ossification: The four major zones

Epiphyseal cartilage

Epiphyseal cartilage

Reserve zone

Proliferative zone

Hypertrophic zone

Vascular invasion zone

Reserve zone
Primitive hyaline cartilage responsible for the growth in length of the bone as erosion and bone deposition advance into this zone

Proliferative zone
Proliferating chondrocytes align as **vertical** and **parallel columns**

Hypertrophic zone
Apoptosis of chondrocytes and calcification of the territorial matrix

Vascular invasion zone
Blood vessels penetrate the transverse calcified septa, and carry osteoprogenitor cells with them

Perichondrium changing into periosteum

matrix (**osteoid**).

3. At this developmental step, a **primary center of ossification**—defined by both the **periosteal collar** (**intramembranous ossification type**) and the center of ossification in the interior of the cartilage template—is organized at the diaphysis. **Secondary centers of ossification** develop later in the **epiphyses**.

The **growth in length of the long bones** depends on the interstitial growth of the hyaline cartilage while the center of the cartilage is being replaced by bone at the equidistant zones of ossification.

Secondary centers of ossification and the epiphyseal growth plate

Up to this point, we have analyzed the development of **primary centers of ossification** in the **diaphysis** of long bones that occurs by the third month of fetal life.

After birth, **secondary centers of ossification** develop in the **epiphyses** (see Figure 5–4). As in the diaphysis, the space occupied by hypertrophic chondrocytes is invaded by blood vessels and osteoprogenitor cells from the perichondrium. Most of the hyaline cartilage of the epiphyses is replaced by the spongy bone, except for the **articular cartilage** and a thin disk, the **epiphyseal growth plate**,

Figure 5–6

Endochondral ossification: The zones of proliferation, hypertrophy, and vascular invasion

Proliferative zone

1 The proliferative zone contains **flattened chondrocytes in columns** or clusters parallel to the growth axis. Chondrocytes are separated by the territorial matrix. All the chondrocytes within a cluster share a common territorial matrix. A cluster of cells in this zone, with its territorial matrix, is the **chondron**, the functional unit of growth.

The names of the zones reflect the predominant activity. The limits between the zones are not precise.

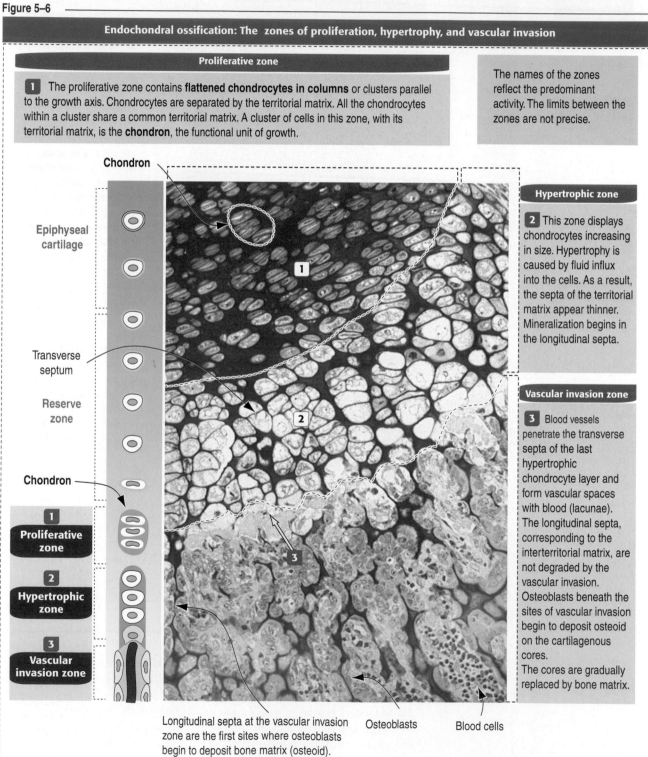

Chondron

Epiphyseal cartilage

Transverse septum

Reserve zone

Chondron

1 Proliferative zone

2 Hypertrophic zone

3 Vascular invasion zone

Hypertrophic zone

2 This zone displays chondrocytes increasing in size. Hypertrophy is caused by fluid influx into the cells. As a result, the septa of the territorial matrix appear thinner. Mineralization begins in the longitudinal septa.

Vascular invasion zone

3 Blood vessels penetrate the transverse septa of the last hypertrophic chondrocyte layer and form vascular spaces with blood (lacunae). The longitudinal septa, corresponding to the interterritorial matrix, are not degraded by the vascular invasion. Osteoblasts beneath the sites of vascular invasion begin to deposit osteoid on the cartilagenous cores. The cores are gradually replaced by bone matrix.

Longitudinal septa at the vascular invasion zone are the first sites where osteoblasts begin to deposit bone matrix (osteoid).

Osteoblasts

Blood cells

Figure 5–7

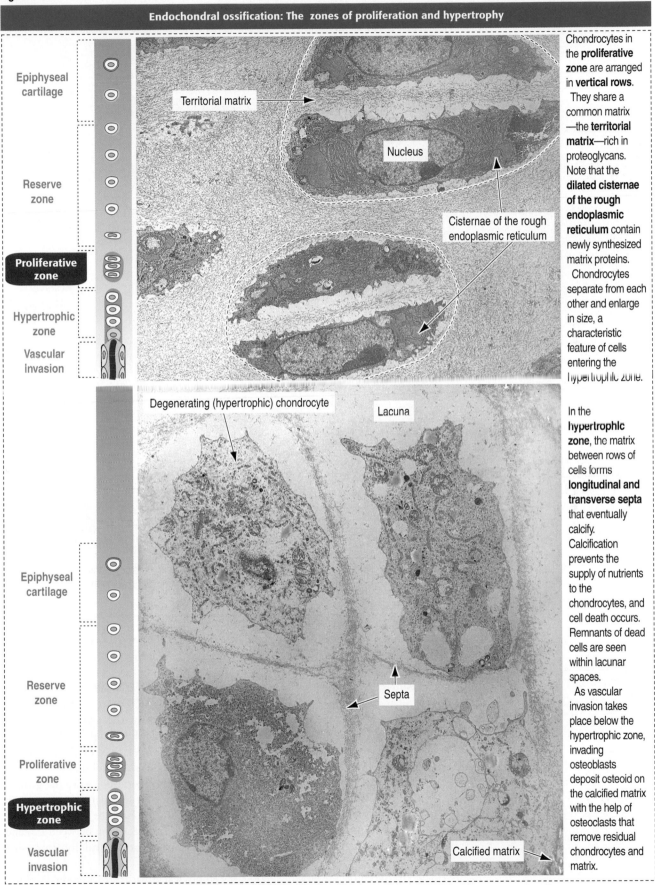

Endochondral ossification: The zones of proliferation and hypertrophy

Epiphyseal cartilage

Reserve zone

Proliferative zone

Hypertrophic zone

Vascular invasion

Territorial matrix

Nucleus

Cisternae of the rough endoplasmic reticulum

Chondrocytes in the **proliferative zone** are arranged in **vertical rows**. They share a common matrix —the **territorial matrix**—rich in proteoglycans. Note that the **dilated cisternae of the rough endoplasmic reticulum** contain newly synthesized matrix proteins. Chondrocytes separate from each other and enlarge in size, a characteristic feature of cells entering the hypertrophic zone.

Degenerating (hypertrophic) chondrocyte

Lacuna

Epiphyseal cartilage

Reserve zone

Proliferative zone

Hypertrophic zone

Vascular invasion

Septa

Calcified matrix

In the **hypertrophic zone**, the matrix between rows of cells forms **longitudinal and transverse septa** that eventually calcify. Calcification prevents the supply of nutrients to the chondrocytes, and cell death occurs. Remnants of dead cells are seen within lacunar spaces.

As vascular invasion takes place below the hypertrophic zone, invading osteoblasts deposit osteoid on the calcified matrix with the help of osteoclasts that remove residual chondrocytes and matrix.

Figure 5–8

Endochondral ossification: Zones of hypertrophy and vascular invasion

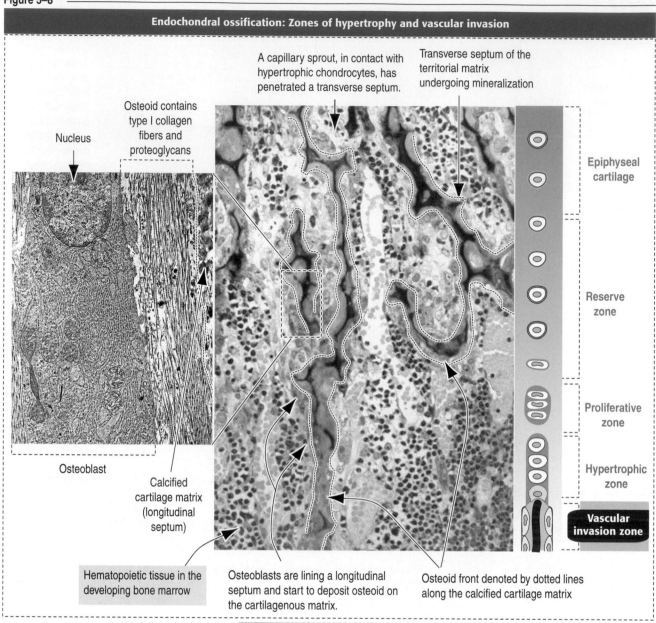

A capillary sprout, in contact with hypertrophic chondrocytes, has penetrated a transverse septum.

Transverse septum of the territorial matrix undergoing mineralization

Osteoid contains type I collagen fibers and proteoglycans

Nucleus

Osteoblast

Calcified cartilage matrix (longitudinal septum)

Hematopoietic tissue in the developing bone marrow

Osteoblasts are lining a longitudinal septum and start to deposit osteoid on the cartilagenous matrix.

Osteoid front denoted by dotted lines along the calcified cartilage matrix

Epiphyseal cartilage

Reserve zone

Proliferative zone

Hypertrophic zone

Vascular invasion zone

located between the epiphyses and the diaphysis. The epiphyseal growth plate is responsible for subsequent growth in length of the bone.

Clinical significance: The epiphyseal growth plate and dwarfism

Indian hedgehog (Ihh), a member of the hedgehog family of proteins secreted by chondrocytes, **regulates chondrocyte proliferation of the growth plate in a paracrine fashion and delays chondrocyte hypertrophy** (Figure 5–9). Ihh also regulates bone formation in the perichondrial collar. A lack of expression of Ihh protein in mutant mice results in dwarfism and lack of endochondral ossification. Essentially, **Ihh maintains the pool of proliferating chondrocytes in the growth plate by delaying their hypertrophy.** In addition, Ihh stimulates the expression of **parathyroid hormone–related peptide (PTH-RP) receptor** in perichondrial chondrocytes adjacent to the articular surface. A feedback loop between Ihh and PTH-RP regulates the balance between proliferating and hypertrophic chondrocytes.

At the end of the growing period, the epiphyseal growth plate is gradually elimi-

Figure 5–9

Growth plates and bone growth in length

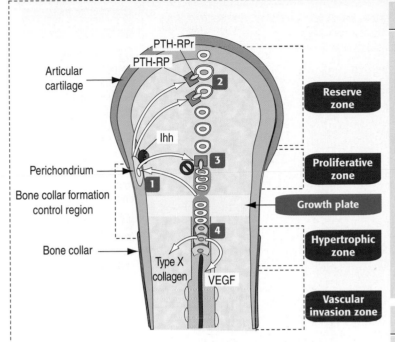

Articular cartilage

PTH-RPr
PTH-RP

2

Ihh

Perichondrium

1

3

Bone collar formation control region

Bone collar

4

Type X collagen

VEGF

Reserve zone

Proliferative zone

Growth plate

Hypertrophic zone

Vascular invasion zone

Note that PTH-RP has **opposite effects** to ensure the maintenance of the growth plate and longitudinal growth of long bones. Growth plate inactivation occurs at puberty when the height of the individual is determined. Growth plate inactivation is the direct result of an increase of **estrogen secretion** at puberty in both women and men.

Ihh is the vertebrate equivalent of a protein member of the fruit fly *Drosophila melanogaster* gene *hedgehog* involved in pattern determination of the limbs and trunks.

Growth of the epiphyseal growth plate cartilage

1 **Indian hedgehog (Ihh)** protein—secreted by chondrocytes of the proliferative zone—signals the synthesis and secretion of **parathyroid hormone–related protein (PTH-RP)** by cells of the chondrogenic layer of the perichondrium (epiphysis). Ihh has two functions: (1) regulation of the formation of the bone collar; (2) stimulation of PTH-RP secretion.
2 PHT-RP binds to its receptor (**PTH-RPr**) on the surface of chondrocytes of the reserve zone to **stimulate** their proliferation.
3 PTH-RP also binds to chondrocytes of the proliferative zone to **inhibit** their differentiation into hypertrophic chondrocytes.
4 Chondrocytes of the hypertrophic zone secrete **type X collagen**—a marker of differentiation—and **vascular endothelial growth factor** (**VEGF**)—an inducer of vascular invasion.

Clinical significance: Metaphyseal chondrodysplasia

Mutations of the genes encoding PTH-RP and PTH-RPr give rise to **Jansen's disease** or **metaphyseal chondrodysplasia**.
An excess of PTH-RP causes **hypercalcemia** and delay in maturation of proliferative chondrocytes into hypertrophic chondrocytes.
Circulating **parathyroid hormone cannot compensate for PTH-RP deficiencies** because the avascular nature of the cartilage makes parathyroid hormone circulating in blood relatively inaccessible to chondrocytes.

nated by a continuum established between the diaphysis and the epiphyses. No further growth in length of the bone is possible once the epiphyseal growth plate disappears at puberty.

Zones of endochondral ossification

As we have seen (see Figure 5–4), the deposition of bone in the center of the diaphysis is preceded by an erosion process in the hyaline cartilage template. This center of erosion, defined as the **primary ossification center**, extends in both directions of the template, in parallel with the formation of a bony collar.

The bony collar provides strength of the midsection of the diaphysis or shaft as the cartilage is weakened by the gradual removal of the cartilage before its replacement by bone.

The continuing process of cartilage erosion and bone deposition can be visualized histologically (see Figure 5–5). **Four major zones** can be distinguished, starting at the end of the cartilage and approaching the zone of erosion:

1. The **reserve zone** is a site composed of primitive hyaline cartilage and is responsible for the growth in length of the bone as the erosion and bone deposition process advances. Essentially, chondrocytes are "running" as osteoclast-mediated erosion "chases" the chondrocytes of the reserve zone (see Figures 5–6 and 5–10).

2. The **proliferative zone** is characterized by active proliferation of chondrocytes

Figure 5–10

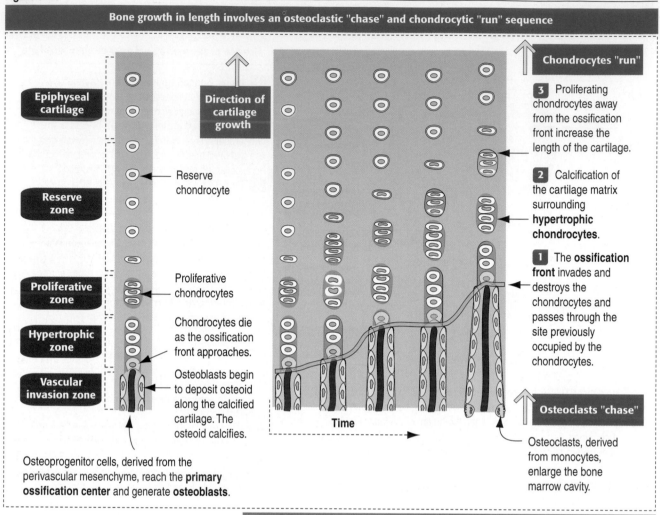

Bone growth in length involves an osteoclastic "chase" and chondrocytic "run" sequence

Epiphyseal cartilage

Direction of cartilage growth

Chondrocytes "run"

Reserve chondrocyte

Reserve zone

3 Proliferating chondrocytes away from the ossification front increase the length of the cartilage.

2 Calcification of the cartilage matrix surrounding **hypertrophic chondrocytes**.

Proliferative chondrocytes

Proliferative zone

Chondrocytes die as the ossification front approaches.

1 The **ossification front** invades and destroys the chondrocytes and passes through the site previously occupied by the chondrocytes.

Hypertrophic zone

Vascular invasion zone

Osteoblasts begin to deposit osteoid along the calcified cartilage. The osteoid calcifies.

Time

Osteoclasts "chase"

Osteoprogenitor cells, derived from the perivascular mesenchyme, reach the **primary ossification center** and generate **osteoblasts**.

Osteoclasts, derived from monocytes, enlarge the bone marrow cavity.

aligning as cellular **columns** parallel to the long axis of the cartilage template. This mitotically active zone represents the "running away" zone of the cartilage, a mechanism that eventually determines the elongation of the bone (see Figures 5–6 and 5-7). We have already seen how **Ihh** and **PTH-RP** modulate the population of hypertrophic chondrocytes as a mechanism to ensure active growth plates until puberty (Figure 5–9).

3. The **hypertrophic zone** is defined by both **chondrocyte apoptosis** and **calcification** of the territorial matrix surrounding the columns of previously proliferated chondrocytes (see Figures 5–6 and 5–7). The secretion of type X collagen is a marker of hypertrophic chondrocytes during the endochondral ossification process.

Chondrocytes in this zone are significantly enlarged (hypertrophic). As a result, the septa separating adjacent columns appear thinner due to a compression effect mediated by the hypertrophic chondrocytes. A provisional calcification begins in the **longitudinal septa. The** deepest layer, proximal to the vascular invasion zone, displays the blind end of capillary sprouts (Figure 5–8) derived from the developing bone marrow cavity occupied by hematopoietic cells (see Chapter 6, Blood and Hematopoiesis).

4. The **vascular invasion zone** is the site where blood vessels penetrate the transverse septa and carry migrating **osteoprogenitor cells** with them. Recall that hypertrophic chondrocytes secrete **VEGF** to stimulate angiogenesis in this zone (see Figure 5–9).

Osteoprogenitor cells give rise to osteoblasts that begin lining the surfaces of the exposed cores of calcified cartilage (stained blue—basophilic—in the light microscopy photograph in Figure 5–8) and initiate the deposition of **osteoid** (stained pink—acidophilic—in Figure 5–8). The osteoid contains abundant type I collagen fibers embedded in the extracellular matrix.

The cartilage struts are gradually replaced by bone. The deposit of osteoid denotes the beginning of osteogenesis and results in the formation of **bone spicules** and, later, in **trabeculae**. As a consequence, **cancellous bone** appears in the midsection of the template.

As the ossification process advances toward the adjacent proliferative zones (a "chase" effect), the bone marrow cavity increases in size owing to loss of cartilage and erosion of newly formed bone spicules by osteoclasts. Recall that the periosteal collar grows in length and thickness (by appositional growth) at the midsection of the shaft and compensates for the loss of endochondral bone while also strengthening the gradually eroding cartilage template.

The reserve zone persists by continuous cell division and is responsible for a continued growth in length by the epiphyseal growth plate, which remains between the diaphysis and epiphysis of the bone. The **epiphyseal growth plate** becomes reduced to an **epiphyseal line** from puberty to maturity, and the long bone no longer grows in length.

After endochondral ossification, the general organization of a long bone is remodeled by combined **reabsorption** mediated by **osteoclasts** in certain areas and the deposition of new bone in others. As a result, spongy bone is replaced by compact bone by a process in which osteoblasts produce overlapping layers of bone or lamellae on the surface of longitudinal cavities occupied by blood vessels. Consequently, a concentric arrangement of bone lamellae encircles a blood vessel entrapped within a canal to form a **primitive haversian system**.

Some variation exists in the literature concerning the classification of the zones of endochondral ossification. The reserve, proliferative, hypertrophic, and vascular invasion zones summarized earlier provide a simple way to guide you through the complexity of bone formation and the understanding of the mechanisms of bone repair.

Growth in width of the diaphysis

As the bone grows in length, new layers of bone are added to the outer portions of the diaphysis by appositional growth. As a result, the thickness of the diaphysis increases. Simultaneous erosion of the inner wall of the diaphysis results in enlargement of the marrow cavity.

New bone in the form of haversian systems is added beneath the periosteum by its osteogenic layer. The surface of the diaphysis has **longitudinal ridges** with **grooves** between them. The periosteum contains blood vessels.

The following sequence is observed (Figure 5–11):

1. The ridges and grooves are lined by osteoblasts that proliferate and deposit osteoid. As a result, the ridges grow toward one another and enclose a periosteal vessel within a tunnel. Adjacent longitudinal periosteal capillaries within the tunnels are connected by transverse blood vessels. The latter become part of **Volkmann's canals. Unlike haversian canals, Volkmann's canals are not surrounded by concentric lamellae.**

2. Osteoblasts lining the tunnel deposit new lamellae and convert the tunnel into a haversian system, a central blood vessel surrounded by lamellae.

3. Appositional growth continuously adds lamellae under the periosteum in the cortical region of the diaphysis, which become the **outer circumferential lamellae.** This modeling process occurs with the participation of osteoclasts that erode bone at the outer circumferential lamellae-osteon boundary. As a consequence, interstitial lamellae fill the spaces between the osteons and what remains of the outer circumferential lamellar system.

Figure 5–11

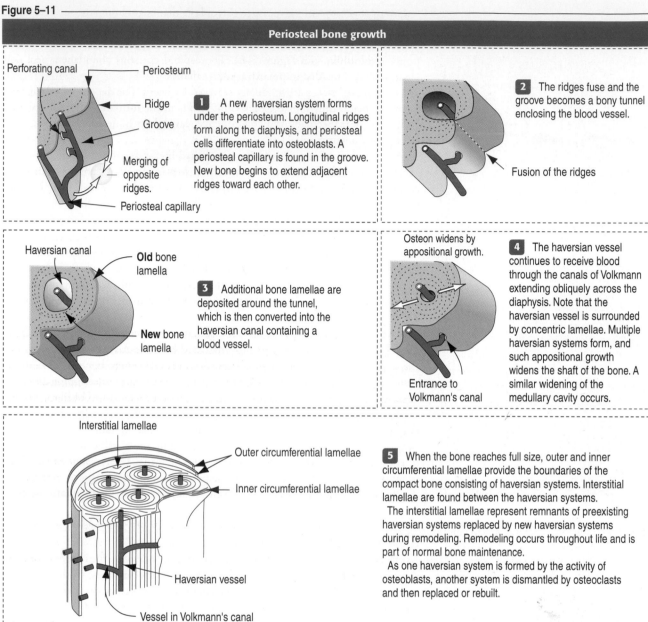

Periosteal bone growth

1 A new haversian system forms under the periosteum. Longitudinal ridges form along the diaphysis, and periosteal cells differentiate into osteoblasts. A periosteal capillary is found in the groove. New bone begins to extend adjacent ridges toward each other.

Perforating canal
Periosteum
Ridge
Groove
Merging of opposite ridges.
Periosteal capillary

2 The ridges fuse and the groove becomes a bony tunnel enclosing the blood vessel.

Fusion of the ridges

3 Additional bone lamellae are deposited around the tunnel, which is then converted into the haversian canal containing a blood vessel.

Haversian canal
Old bone lamella
New bone lamella

Osteon widens by appositional growth.

4 The haversian vessel continues to receive blood through the canals of Volkmann extending obliquely across the diaphysis. Note that the haversian vessel is surrounded by concentric lamellae. Multiple haversian systems form, and such appositional growth widens the shaft of the bone. A similar widening of the medullary cavity occurs.

Entrance to Volkmann's canal

Interstitial lamellae
Outer circumferential lamellae
Inner circumferential lamellae
Haversian vessel
Vessel in Volkmann's canal

5 When the bone reaches full size, outer and inner circumferential lamellae provide the boundaries of the compact bone consisting of haversian systems. Interstitial lamellae are found between the haversian systems.

The interstitial lamellae represent remnants of preexisting haversian systems replaced by new haversian systems during remodeling. Remodeling occurs throughout life and is part of normal bone maintenance.

As one haversian system is formed by the activity of osteoblasts, another system is dismantled by osteoclasts and then replaced or rebuilt.

4. Osteoblasts lining the inner surface develop the **inner circumferential lamellae** by a similar mechanism described for the outer circumferential lamellae, except that the blood vessels enclosed in the tunnels are not periosteal but, instead, branches of the nutrient artery formed originally from a periosteal bud, as described earlier.

Clinical significance: Osteopetrosis, rickets, and fibrodysplasia ossificans progressiva

Ossification includes **growth, modeling,** and **remodeling** (turnover) of the bone, processes mediated by osteoblasts and osteoclasts under the control of **parathyroid hormone** and **vitamin D_3**. A number of conditions can alter the skeleton by affecting cell-mediated bone remodeling or disturbing the mineralization of the extracellular matrix.

Osteopetrosis ("stonelike bone") includes a group of hereditary diseases characterized by **abnormal osteoclast function**. The bone is abnormally brittle and breaks like a soft stone. The marrow canal is not developed, and most of the bone

Figure 5–12

Ectopic ossification

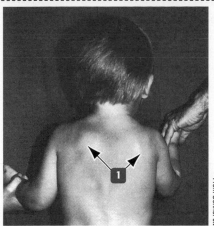

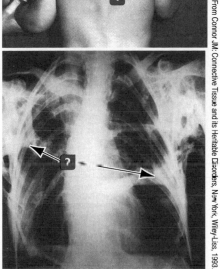

From Connor JM: Connective Tissue and its Heritable Disorders, New York, Wiley-Liss, 1993.

Fibrodysplasia ossificans progressiva

1 Ectopic ossification is observed as lumps in the muscles of the neck and back. Lumps are first noted in children 1–3 years old.

2 Ectopic bone is visualized in radiographs after the initial appearance of ossifying lumps. Bone matures and develops a normal trabecular architecture.

is woven because of absent remodeling.

We have already discussed a mutation in the *colony-stimulating factor-1* gene whose expression is required for the formation of osteoclasts (see Bone in Chapter 4, Connective Tissue). A clinical variant of osteopetrosis, also known as **marble bone disease**, or **Albers-Schönberg disease**, is caused by a deficiency in **carbonic anhydrase II**, required by osteoclasts to accumulate H$^+$ in the Howship's resorption lacunae and acidify the environment for the activation of secretory lysosomal enzymes.

Rickets and **osteomalacia** are a group of bone diseases characterized by a **defect in the mineralization of the bone matrix** (osteoid), most often caused by a **lack of vitamin D$_3$**. Rickets is observed in children and produces skeletal deformities. Osteomalacia is observed in adults and is caused by poor mineralization of the bone matrix.

Osteoporosis consists of an increase in the porosity of bone, resulting in a decrease in bone mass. Osteoporosis predisposes bone to fracture. **Senile** and **postmenopausal osteoporosis** are the most frequent forms. Postmenopausal osteoporosis is characterized by **estrogen deficiency**, which accelerates bone loss. Estrogen replacement protects against bone loss.

Fibrodysplasia ossificans progressiva (FOP) is an inherited disorder of the connective tissue. The main clinical features are **skeletal malformations** and the **ossification of soft tissues** (muscles of the neck and back; Figure 5–12). Ectopic bone formation also occurs in ligaments, fasciae, aponeuroses, tendons, and joint capsules. Aberrant bone formation in patients with FOP occurs when **lymphocytes** present in the sites of injury synthesize excess **bone morphogenetic protein-4**, a product that contributes to the development of the skeleton in the normal embryo.

Joints

Bones are interconnected by articulations, or joints, that permit movement. **Synarthroses** are the joints that permits little or no movement (cranial bones; ribs and the sternum). **Amphiarthroses** enable slight movement (intervertebral disks and bodies). **Diarthroses** permit free movement.

In a **diarthroidal joint**, a **capsule** links the ends of the bones. The capsule is lined by a **synovial membrane** that encloses the articular or synovial cavity. The **synovial cavity** contains a **fluid** necessary for reducing the friction between the hyaline cartilage covering the opposing articular surfaces.

The articular cartilage is almost typical hyaline cartilage; except that it **lacks a perichondrium** and has a unique collagen fiber organization in the form of overlapping arches. Collagen arcades sustain the mechanical stress on the joint surfaces.

The **joint capsule** consists of **two layers**: an outer layer of dense connective tissue with blood vessels and nerves, and an inner layer, called the **synovial membrane**. The inner surface of the synovial membrane is covered by one to two layers of **synovial cells** overlying the connective tissue (Figure 5–13). There are two classes of synovial cells: (1) **type A macrophage-like synovial cells**, and (2) **type B fibroblast-like synovial cells**. There is no basal lamina separating synovial cells from the connective tissue. The connective tissue contains a rich network of **fenestrated capillaries**.

Synovial fluid is a combined product of the synovial cells and the ultrafiltrate of the capillaries. The fluid is rich in **hyaluronic acid**, **glycoproteins**, and **leukocytes**.

Clinical significance: Rheumatoid arthritis

Rheumatoid arthritis is a common chronic inflammatory and destructive disease of the joints that starts with a proliferative process of the synovial membrane, leading to the erosion of the articular cartilage and destruction of the

Figure 5–13

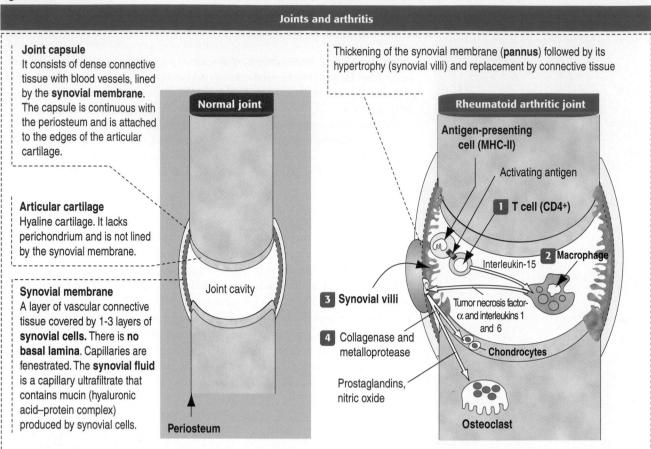

Joints and arthritis

Joint capsule
It consists of dense connective tissue with blood vessels, lined by the **synovial membrane**. The capsule is continuous with the periosteum and is attached to the edges of the articular cartilage.

Articular cartilage
Hyaline cartilage. It lacks perichondrium and is not lined by the synovial membrane.

Synovial membrane
A layer of vascular connective tissue covered by 1-3 layers of **synovial cells**. There is **no basal lamina**. Capillaries are fenestrated. The **synovial fluid** is a capillary ultrafiltrate that contains mucin (hyaluronic acid–protein complex) produced by synovial cells.

Normal joint

Joint cavity

Periosteum

Thickening of the synovial membrane (**pannus**) followed by its hypertrophy (synovial villi) and replacement by connective tissue

Rheumatoid arthritic joint

Antigen-presenting cell (MHC-II)

Activating antigen

1 **T cell (CD4+)**

2 Macrophage

Interleukin-15

3 **Synovial villi**

Tumor necrosis factor-α and interleukins 1 and 6

4 Collagenase and metalloprotease

Chondrocytes

Prostaglandins, nitric oxide

Osteoclast

Rheumatoid arthritis

Rheumatoid arthritis is a chronic inflammatory disease characterized by the presence of **1** activated CD4+ T cells, plasma cells, **2** macrophages, and **3** **synovial cells** changing the synovial membrane lining into villus-type inflammatory tissue called **pannus**. Within the pannus, cellular responses lead to release of **4** **metalloproteases** and other effector molecules.

The initial cause of rheumatoid arthritis is a peptide antigen presented to T cells (CD4+) which, in turn, release **interleukin-15** to activate synovial macrophages normally present in the synovial membrane. Synovial macrophages secrete **proinflammatory cytokines—tumor necrosis factor-α** and **interleukins 1 and 6**—to induce the proliferation of synovial cells, which then release **collagenase**, **extracellular matrix metalloproteases**, **prostaglandins**, and **nitric oxide** targeted to the destruction of the **articular cartilage** and subjacent **bone tissue**. Both the chronic destruction of the articular cartilage and the hypertrophy of the synovial membrane are characteristic features of rheumatoid arthritis.

subjacent bone.

The initial event is the activation of CD4+ T cells by an undetermined antigen. Activated CD4+ T cells stimulate the production of **tumor necrosis factor-α (TNF-α)**, **interleukin-2 (IL-2)** and **interleukin-6 (IL-6)**, and the secretion of **metalloproteinases** by monocytes, macrophages, and fibroblast-like synovial cells. Activated CD4+ T cells stimulate B cells to differentiate into **plasma cells** to produce immunoglobulins and **rheumatoid factor**.

TNF-α, IL-1 and IL-6 are key cytokines in driving inflammation in rheumatoid arthritis (Figure 5–14). TNF-α and IL-1 can be detected in synovial fluid of patients with rheumatoid arthritis. TNF-α and IL-1 stimulate fibroblast-like synovial cells, osteoclasts, and chondrocytes to release cartilage- and bone-destroying matrix metalloproteinases.

Figure 5–14

Synovial membrane in rheumatoid arthritis

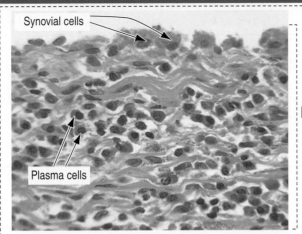

Synovial cells

Plasma cells

The **synovial membrane** normally consists of a lining of one or two cell layers of synovial cells and underlying loose connective tissue. The synovial-lining cells are designated **type A** (**macrophage-like synovial cells**) and **type B** (**fibroblast-like synovial cells**).

Synovial membrane in rheumatoid arthritis

In **rheumatoid arthritis**, the synovial membrane becomes thickened by the proliferation (hyperplasia) and enlargement (hypertrophy) of the synovial lining cells. A synovial membrane with abundant villi develops. T and B cells and plasma cells infiltrate the connective tissue of the synovial membrane. T cells and macrophages can be found in the synovial fluid.

Neutralization of proinflammatory effectors in the treatment of rheumatoid arthritis

Proinflammatory cytokine (tumor necrosis factor-α and interleukins 1 and 6)

Cytokine roooptor

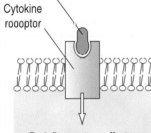

Proinflammatory effectors

Blockade of the cytokine receptor by **1** receptor antagonist or **2** antibody to cytokine receptor

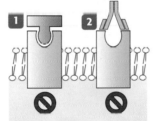

No proinflammatory effector

Soluble cytokine receptor

Blocking cytokine antibody

No proinflammatory effector

Anti-inflammatory cytokines prevent expression of proinflammatory effectors

Anti-inflammatory cytokine

No proinflammatory effector

Binding of tumor necrosis factor-α and interleukin 1 or 6 to their receptors triggers the production of inflammatory effector molecules by synovial cells. Proinflammatory effectors determine a progressive damage of the joint (cartilage and bone erosion).

Pro-inflammatory cytokines cannot bind to the cytokine receptor because receptor antagonists or a monoclonal antibody occupies binding sites for proinflammatory cytokines produced by synovial cells. No proinflammatory effector is produced by synovial cells.

Soluble cytokine receptor (etanercept) or a monoclonal antibody targeting a pro-inflammatory cytokine (infliximab) prevents cytokine binding to the cytokine receptor. No proinflammatory effector is produced by synovial cells.

Anti-inflammatory cytokines bind to the cytokine receptor and inhibit the expression of proinflammatory effectors.

The neutralization of proinflammatory cytokines by soluble receptors or monoclonal antibodies is currently used in the treatment of patients with rheumatoid arthritis. Figure 5–14 provides a summary of the major therapeutic strategies for suppressing inflammation and preventing joint damage.

6. BLOOD AND HEMATOPOIESIS

Blood

Blood is a specialized connective tissue consisting of **cells** and **plasma**. These components may be separated by centrifugation if blood is collected in the presence of anticoagulants. The sedimented erythrocytes (RBCs) constitute about 45% of blood volume. This percentage of erythrocyte volume is the **hematocrit**. Sitting on top of the erythrocyte layer is the **buffy coat** layer, which contains **leukocytes** (white blood cells) and **platelets**. The translucent supernatant fraction above the packed RBCs consists of plasma. Normal adult blood volume measures **5 to 6 L**.

Plasma

Plasma is the fluid component of blood (Figure 6–1). Plasma contains salts and organic compounds (including amino acids, lipids, vitamins, proteins, and hormones). In the absence of anticoagulants, the cellular elements of blood, together with plasma proteins (mostly **fibrinogen**), form a clot in the test tube. The fluid portion is called **serum**, which is essentially fibrinogen-free plasma.

Cellular elements of the blood
Red blood cells (erythrocytes)

RBCs, also called erythrocytes (Gk. *erythros*, red; *kytos*, cell), are non-nucleated, biconcave-shaped cells measuring **7.8 μm** in diameter (unfixed). RBCs lack organelles and consist only of a plasma membrane, its underlying cytoskeleton, hemoglobin, and glycolytic enzymes.

RBCs (average number: $4–5 \times 10^6/mm^3$) circulate for **120 days**. Senescent RBCs are removed by phagocytosis or destroyed by **hemolysis** in the spleen. RBCs are replaced in the circulation by **reticulocytes**, which complete their hemoglobin synthesis and maturation 1 to 2 days after entering the circulation. Reticulocytes account for 1% to 2% of circulating RBCs. RBCs transport oxygen and carbon dioxide and are confined to the circulatory system.

Figure 6–1

Blood: Plasma, serum, and cells

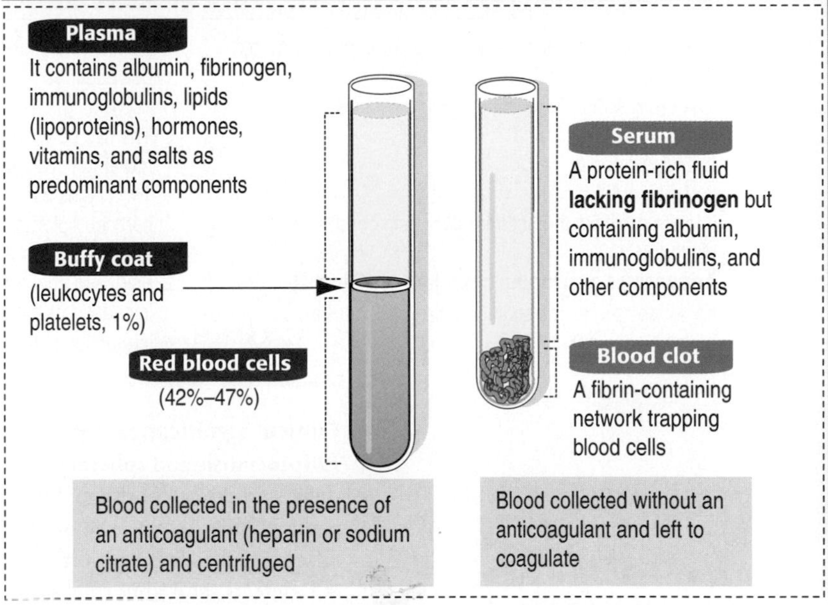

Plasma
It contains albumin, fibrinogen, immunoglobulins, lipids (lipoproteins), hormones, vitamins, and salts as predominant components

Buffy coat
(leukocytes and platelets, 1%)

Red blood cells
(42%–47%)

Serum
A protein-rich fluid **lacking fibrinogen** but containing albumin, immunoglobulins, and other components

Blood clot
A fibrin-containing network trapping blood cells

Blood collected in the presence of an anticoagulant (heparin or sodium citrate) and centrifuged

Blood collected without an anticoagulant and left to coagulate

Figure 6–2

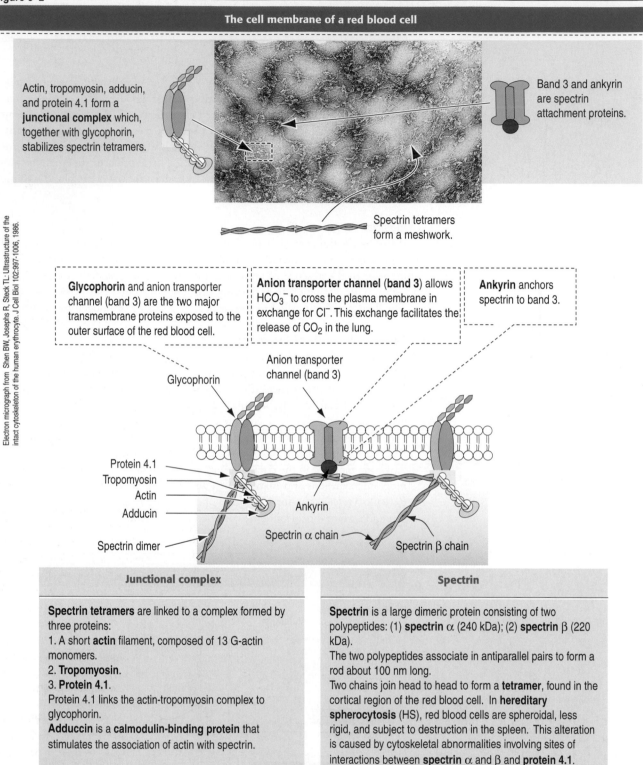

The cell membrane of a red blood cell

Actin, tropomyosin, adducin, and protein 4.1 form a **junctional complex** which, together with glycophorin, stabilizes spectrin tetramers.

Band 3 and ankyrin are spectrin attachment proteins.

Spectrin tetramers form a meshwork.

Electron micrograph from Shen BW, Josephs R, Steck TL: Ultrastructure of the intact cytoskeleton of the human erythrocyte. J Cell Biol 102:997-1006, 1986.

Glycophorin and anion transporter channel (band 3) are the two major transmembrane proteins exposed to the outer surface of the red blood cell.

Anion transporter channel (band 3) allows HCO_3^- to cross the plasma membrane in exchange for Cl^-. This exchange facilitates the release of CO_2 in the lung.

Ankyrin anchors spectrin to band 3.

Glycophorin

Anion transporter channel (band 3)

Protein 4.1
Tropomyosin
Actin
Adducin

Ankyrin

Spectrin dimer

Spectrin α chain

Spectrin β chain

Junctional complex	Spectrin
Spectrin tetramers are linked to a complex formed by three proteins: 1. A short **actin** filament, composed of 13 G-actin monomers. 2. **Tropomyosin**. 3. **Protein 4.1**. Protein 4.1 links the actin-tropomyosin complex to glycophorin. **Adduccin** is a **calmodulin-binding protein** that stimulates the association of actin with spectrin.	**Spectrin** is a large dimeric protein consisting of two polypeptides: (1) **spectrin** α (240 kDa); (2) **spectrin** β (220 kDa). The two polypeptides associate in antiparallel pairs to form a rod about 100 nm long. Two chains join head to head to form a **tetramer**, found in the cortical region of the red blood cell. In **hereditary spherocytosis** (HS), red blood cells are spheroidal, less rigid, and subject to destruction in the spleen. This alteration is caused by cytoskeletal abnormalities involving sites of interactions between **spectrin** α and β and **protein 4.1**.

Clinical significance: Cytoskeletal and hemoglobin abnormalities

Elliptocytosis and **spherocytosis** are alterations in the shape of RBCs caused by defects in the cytoskeleton. **Elliptocytosis**, an autosomal dominant disorder characterized by the presence of oval-shaped RBCs, is caused by defective self-association of spectrin subunits, abnormal binding of spectrin to ankyrin, protein 4.1 defects, and abnormal glycophorin (Figure 6–2). **Spherocytosis** is also an

Figure 6–3

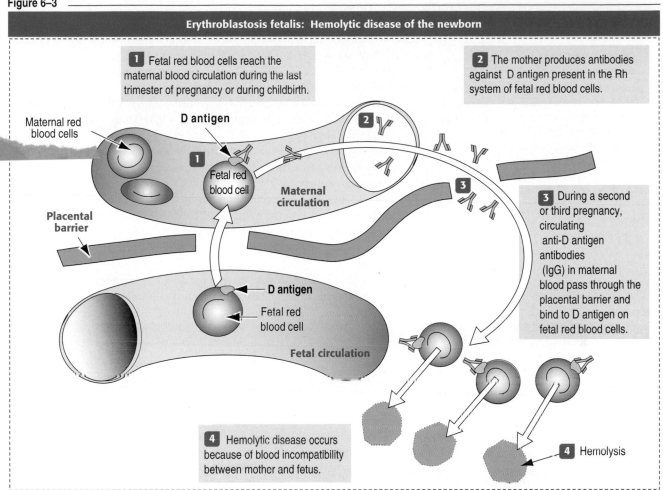

Erythroblastosis fetalis: Hemolytic disease of the newborn

1 Fetal red blood cells reach the maternal blood circulation during the last trimester of pregnancy or during childbirth.

2 The mother produces antibodies against D antigen present in the Rh system of fetal red blood cells.

Maternal red blood cells

D antigen

Fetal red blood cell

Maternal circulation

Placental barrier

3 During a second or third pregnancy, circulating anti-D antigen antibodies (IgG) in maternal blood pass through the placental barrier and bind to D antigen on fetal red blood cells.

D antigen

Fetal red blood cell

Fetal circulation

4 Hemolytic disease occurs because of blood incompatibility between mother and fetus.

4 Hemolysis

Hemolysis in erythroblastosis fetalis

The hemolytic process in erythroblastosis fetalis causes **hemolytic anemia** and **jaundice**. Hemolytic anemia causes hypoxic injury to the heart and liver leading to generalized edema (**hydrops fetalis**; Gk. *hydrops*, edema). Jaundice causes damage to the central nervous system (**kernicterus**; Ger. jaundice of brain nuclei). Hyperbilirubinemia is significant and unconjugated bilirubin is taken up by the brain tissue.

---

autosomal dominant condition involving a deficiency in **spectrin**. The common clinical features of elliptocytosis and spherocytosis are **anemia, jaundice**, and **splenomegaly** (enlargement of the spleen). **Splenectomy** is usually curative, since the spleen is the primary site responsible for the destruction of elliptocytes and spherocytes.

Hemoglobin genetic defects ($\alpha_2\beta S_2$) cause **sickle cell anemia** and **thalassemia** (Gk. *thalassa*, sea; observed in populations along the Greek and Italian coasts). **Sickle cell anemia** results from a point mutation in which **glutamic acid** is replaced by **valine** at the sixth position in the β-globin chain. Defective hemoglobin (Hb S) tetramers aggregate and polymerize in deoxygenated RBCs, changing the biconcave disk shape into a rigid and less deformable sickle-shaped cell. Hb S leads to severe **chronic hemolytic anemia** and **obstruction of postcapillary venules** (see Spleen in Chapter 10, Immune-Lymphatic System).

Thalassemia syndromes are heritable anemias characterized by defective synthesis of either the α or β chains of the normal hemoglobin tetramer ($\alpha_2\beta_2$). The specific thalassemia syndromes are designated by the affected globin chain: **α-thalassemia** and **β-thalassemia**. **Thalassemia** syndromes are defined by anemia caused by defective synthesis of the hemoglobin molecule and hemolysis.

Clinical significance: Erythroblastosis fetalis

Erythroblastosis fetalis is an antibody–induced hemolytic disease in the newborn that is caused by blood group incompatibility between mother and fetus (Figure 6–3). This incompatibility occurs when the fetus inherits RBC antigenic determinants that are foreign to the mother. ABO and Rh blood group antigens are of

Primary and specific (secondary) granules

Primary and specific (secondary) granules are membrane-bound lysosomes that contain enzymes. **Peroxidase is a marker enzyme of primary granules. The presence of alkaline phosphatase and a lack of peroxidase characterize the secondary granules.** Why are primary granules azurophilic with the Wright's blood stain method? Because primary granules contain sulfated glycoproteins which presumably account for this deep-blue (azure) staining.

particular interest.

Essentially, the mother becomes sensitized to blood group antigens on **red blood cells**, which can reach maternal circulation during the last trimester of pregnancy (when the cytotrophoblast is no longer present as a barrier, as we shall study in Chapter 23, Fertilization, Placentation, and Lactation) or during childbirth. Within the Rh system, **D antigen** is the major cause of Rh incompatibility. The initial exposure to the Rh antigen during the first pregnancy does not cause crythroblastosis fetalis because **IgMs** are produced and IgMs cannot cross the placenta because of their large size.

Subsequent exposure to D antigen during the second or third pregnancy leads to a strong **IgG** response (IgGs can cross the placenta).

Rh-negative mothers are given anti-D globulin soon after the delivery of an Rh-positive baby. Anti-D antibodies mask the antigenic sites on the fetal RBCs that may have leaked into the maternal circulation during childbirth. This prevents long-lasting sensitization to Rh antigens.

Leukocytes

Leukocytes ($2–4 \times 10^5/mm^3$) are categorized as either **granulocytes** (**containing primary and specific or secondary cytoplasmic granules**) or **agranulocytes** (con-

Figure 6–4

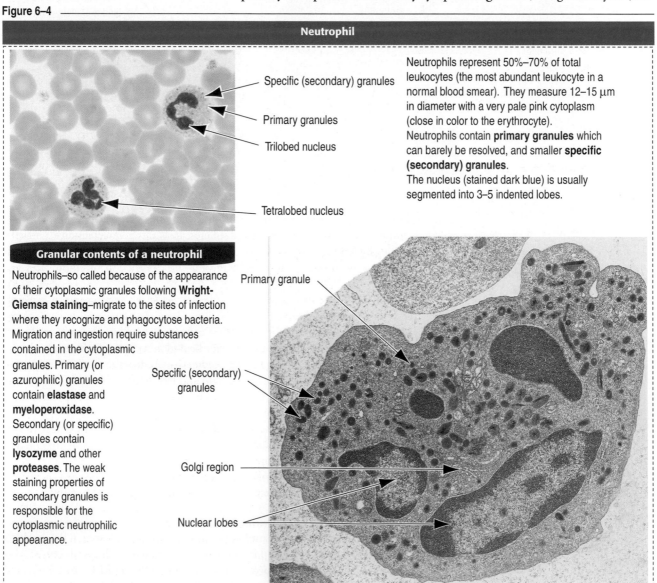

Neutrophil

Specific (secondary) granules
Primary granules
Trilobed nucleus

Tetralobed nucleus

Neutrophils represent 50%–70% of total leukocytes (the most abundant leukocyte in a normal blood smear). They measure 12–15 μm in diameter with a very pale pink cytoplasm (close in color to the erythrocyte).
Neutrophils contain **primary granules** which can barely be resolved, and smaller **specific (secondary) granules**.
The nucleus (stained dark blue) is usually segmented into 3–5 indented lobes.

Granular contents of a neutrophil

Neutrophils–so called because of the appearance of their cytoplasmic granules following **Wright-Giemsa staining**–migrate to the sites of infection where they recognize and phagocytose bacteria. Migration and ingestion require substances contained in the cytoplasmic granules. Primary (or azurophilic) granules contain **elastase** and **myeloperoxidase**. Secondary (or specific) granules contain **lysozyme** and other **proteases**. The weak staining properties of secondary granules is responsible for the cytoplasmic neutrophilic appearance.

Primary granule
Specific (secondary) granules
Golgi region
Nuclear lobes

Figure 6–5

Eosinophil

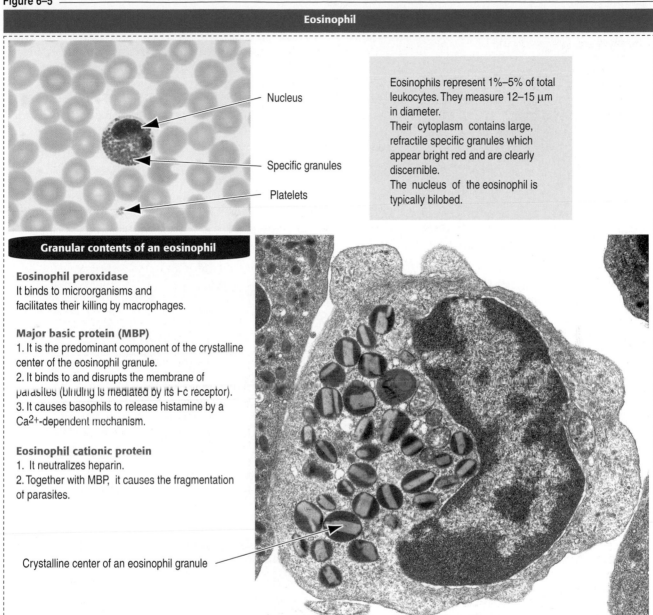

Nucleus

Specific granules

Platelets

Eosinophils represent 1%–5% of total leukocytes. They measure 12–15 μm in diameter.
Their cytoplasm contains large, refractile specific granules which appear bright red and are clearly discernible.
The nucleus of the eosinophil is typically bilobed.

Granular contents of an eosinophil

Eosinophil peroxidase
It binds to microorganisms and facilitates their killing by macrophages.

Major basic protein (MBP)
1. It is the predominant component of the crystalline center of the eosinophil granule.
2. It binds to and disrupts the membrane of parasites (binding is mediated by its Fc receptor).
3. It causes basophils to release histamine by a Ca^{2+}-dependent mechanism.

Eosinophil cationic protein
1. It neutralizes heparin.
2. Together with MBP, it causes the fragmentation of parasites.

Crystalline center of an eosinophil granule

taining only **primary granules**). In response to an appropriate stimulus, leukocytes may leave the bloodstream (**diapedesis**) and enter the connective tissue by the **homing** mechanism (see Figure 6–9).

Granulocytes

These phagocytic cells have a **multilobed nucleus** and measure **12 to 15 μm** in diameter. Their average life span varies with cell type. Three types of granulocytes can be distinguished by their cytoplasmic granules:

1. **Neutrophils** (Figure 6–4). These cells have a lobulated nucleus. Their cytoplasm contains both secondary (specific) and primary granules. In stained smears, neutrophils appear very pale pink. Neutrophils, which constitute **60% to 70%** of circulating leukocytes, have a lifespan of **6 to 7 hours** and may live for up to **4 days** in the connective tissue. After leaving the circulation through postcapillary venules, neutrophils act to eliminate opsonized bacteria or limit the extent of an inflammatory reaction in the connective tissue. The mechanism of bacterial opsonization will be studied in Chapter 10, Immune-Lymphatic System.

Figure 6–6

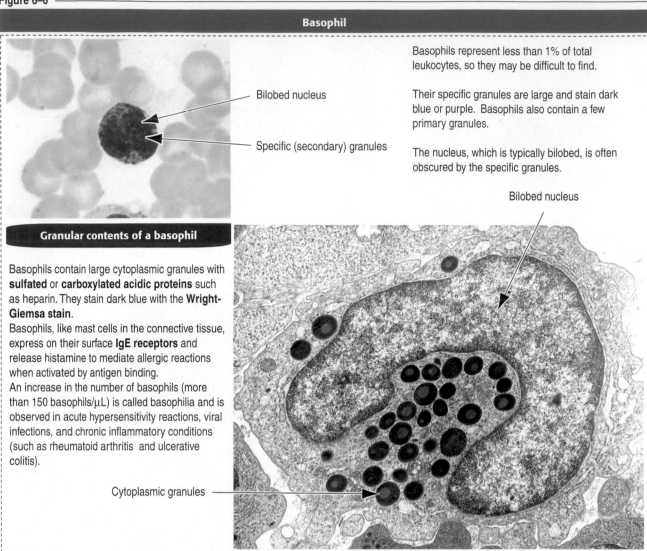

Basophil

Basophils represent less than 1% of total leukocytes, so they may be difficult to find.

Their specific granules are large and stain dark blue or purple. Basophils also contain a few primary granules.

The nucleus, which is typically bilobed, is often obscured by the specific granules.

Bilobed nucleus

Specific (secondary) granules

Bilobed nucleus

Granular contents of a basophil

Basophils contain large cytoplasmic granules with **sulfated** or **carboxylated acidic proteins** such as heparin. They stain dark blue with the **Wright-Giemsa stain**.

Basophils, like mast cells in the connective tissue, express on their surface **IgE receptors** and release histamine to mediate allergic reactions when activated by antigen binding.

An increase in the number of basophils (more than 150 basophils/μL) is called basophilia and is observed in acute hypersensitivity reactions, viral infections, and chronic inflammatory conditions (such as rheumatoid arthritis and ulcerative colitis).

Cytoplasmic granules

Enzymes contained in the primary granules (**elastase** and **myeloperoxidase**) and secondary granules (**lysozyme** and other **proteases**), specific receptors for **C5a** (produced by the complement system pathway, see Figure 10–10 in Chapter 10, Immune-Lymphatic System), and **L selectin**, and **integrins** (with binding affinity to endothelial cell ligands such as **intercellular-adhesion molecules 1 and 2 [ICAM-1 and ICAM-2]**) enable the antibacterial and homing function of neutrophils (Figure 6–9).

2. **Eosinophils** (Figure 6–5). Like neutrophils, eosinophils have a characteristic bilobed nucleus. Their cytoplasm is filled with large, refractile granules that stain red in blood smears and tissue sections. Eosinophils constitute **2% to 4%** of circulating leukocytes and may also leave the circulation and enter the connective tissue. These cells are the first line of defense against **parasites** and also participate in triggering **bronchial asthma** (see Chapter 13, Respiratory System).

3. **Basophils** (Figure 6–6). These granulocytes contain large, **metachromatic** cytoplasmic granules that often obscure the bilobed nucleus. Basophils represent only **1%** of circulating leukocytes. They may leave the circulation and enter the connective tissue, where they resemble **mast cells** (see Chapter 4, Connective Tissue, for additional differences between basophils and mast cells). Basophils play a role in immediate (**bronchial asthma**) and delayed hypersensitivity (**allergic skin reaction**) and in the propagation of the immune response.

Figure 6–7

Lymphocyte

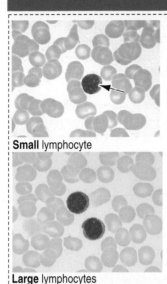

Small lymphocyte

Large lymphocytes

Lymphocytes are relatively abundant, accounting for 20%–40% of total leukocytes. In circulating blood, lymphocytes may range from approximately 7 to 12 μm in diameter. However, the typical lymphocyte in a normal blood smear is small, about the size of a red blood cell. The nucleus of a **small lymphocyte** is densely stained, with a round or slightly indented shape (arrow). The nucleus occupies most of the cell, reducing the cytoplasm to a thin basophilic rim. **Large lymphocytes** have a round, slightly indented nucleus surrounded by a pale cytoplasm. Occasionally, a few primary granules (lysosomes) may be present.

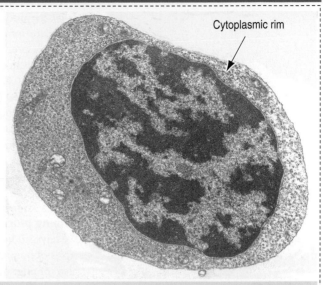

Cytoplasmic rim

The lymphocyte represents 97% of the population of circulating lymphocytes. Note that the nucleus is surrounded by a thin cytoplasmic rim. **Large lymphocytes** represent 3% of the population of circulating lymphocytes. Lymphocytes are divided into two categories: **B lymphocytes**, produced in the bone marrow, and **T lymphocytes**, also produced in the bone marrow but that complete their maturation in the thymus. A less abundant class is the **natural killer cell**. During fetal development, the **yolk sac**, **liver**, and **spleen** are sites where lymphocytes originate. In postnatal life, the **bone marrow** and **thymus** are the **primary lymphoid organs** where lymphocytes develop before they are exposed to antigens. **Secondary lymphoid organs** are the **lymph nodes**, the **spleen**, and lymphoid aggregates of the gastrointestinal and respiratory tracts.

Agranulocytes

Agranulocytes have a round or indented nucleus. They contain only lysosomal-type, **primary granules**. Agranulocytes include **lymphocytes** and monocytes.

Lymphocytes are either large (**3%** of lymphocytes; **9 to 12 μm**) or small (**97%** of lymphocytes; **6–8 μm** (Figure 6–7) cells. In either case, the nucleus is round and may be slightly indented. The cytoplasm is basophilic, often appearing as a

Figure 6–8

Monocyte

Small cytoplasmic granules

Kidney shaped nucleus

Monocytes (2%–8% of total leukocytes) are the largest leukocytes, ranging in size from 15–20 μm.

The eccentrically placed nucleus is typically kidney shaped and contains fine strands of chromatin.

The abundant cytoplasm stains pale gray-blue and is filled with small lysosomes which give a fine, granular appearance.

Monocytes travel briefly in the bloodstream (about 20 hours) and then enter the peripheral tissue where they are transformed into macrophages and survive a longer time. Macrophage derived monocytes are more efficient phagocytic cells than neutrophils.

thin rim around the nucleus (see Figure 6–5). A few primary granules may be present. Lymphocytes may live for a few days or several years.

Lymphocytes are divided into two categories: **B lymphocytes** (also called **B cells**) are produced and mature in bone marrow. Antigen-stimulated B cells differentiate into antibody-secreting **plasma cells. T lymphocytes** (also called **T cells**) are produced in bone marrow but complete their maturation in the **thymus.** Activated T cells participate in **cell-mediated immunity** (for additional details, see Chapter 10, Immune-Lymphatic System).

Monocytes (Figure 6–8) can measure **12 to 20 μm** in diameter. Their nucleus is kidney-shaped or oval. Cytoplasmic granules are small and may not be resolved on light microscopy. Monocytes circulate in blood for **12 to 100 hours** and then enter the connective tissue. In the connective tissue, monocytes differentiate into macrophages, which are involved in bacterial phagocytosis, antigen presentation, and clean-up of dead cell debris.

Clinical significance: Leukocytes migrate to the sites of infection by the homing process

We have studied in Chapter 1, Epithelium (see Figure 1–10), the molecular principles of homing. We will expand the concept of homing by studying the mechanism of **migration of phagocytic neutrophils to the site of infection and inflammation** (Figure 6–9).

The first step is the binding of carbohydrate ligands on the surface of the neutrophil to an endothelial selectin (E selectin). This binding determines rolling adhesion of the neutrophil.

The second step is a stronger interaction of neutrophil **integrins LFA-1** and

Figure 6–9

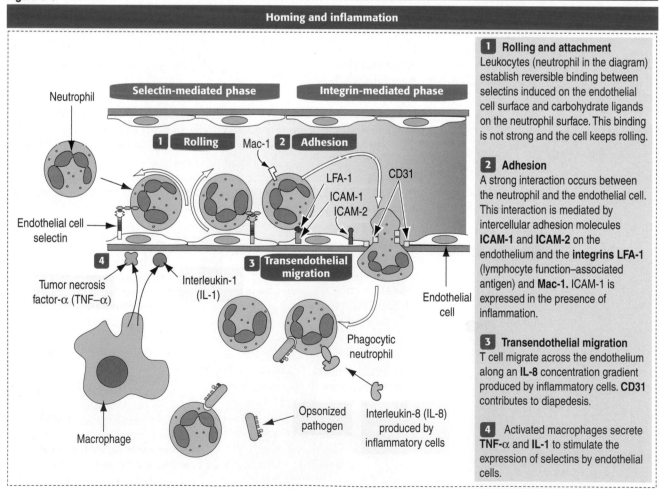

Homing and inflammation

1 Rolling and attachment
Leukocytes (neutrophil in the diagram) establish reversible binding between selectins induced on the endothelial cell surface and carbohydrate ligands on the neutrophil surface. This binding is not strong and the cell keeps rolling.

2 Adhesion
A strong interaction occurs between the neutrophil and the endothelial cell. This interaction is mediated by intercellular adhesion molecules **ICAM-1** and **ICAM-2** on the endothelium and the **integrins LFA-1** (lymphocyte function–associated antigen) and **Mac-1.** ICAM-1 is expressed in the presence of inflammation.

3 Transendothelial migration
T cell migrate across the endothelium along an **IL-8** concentration gradient produced by inflammatory cells. **CD31** contributes to diapedesis.

4 Activated macrophages secrete **TNF-α** and **IL-1** to stimulate the expression of selectins by endothelial cells.

Clinical and pathologic significance of the homing process
Cell adhesion proteins play a significant role in immune surveillance, wound healing, tumor metastasis, and tissue morphogenesis. One of the main events in allergic inflammation is the recruitment of inflammatory cells into tissue sites where allergic reactions occur. To accomplish their migratory function, cell adhesion proteins on migratory cells bind to ligands found on the surface of other cells.
Two adhesion molecule deficiencies have been described, both characterized by defect in wound healing, recurrent infections, and marked leukocytosis (increase in the number of leukocytes in blood).
Leukocyte adhesion deficiency I is caused by a defect in the β **subunit of the integrin molecule.** As a consequence, leukocytes are unable to leave blood vessels to enter the tissue by **transendothelial migration.** In these patients, inflammatory cell infiltrates are devoid of neutrophils.
In **leukocyte adhesion deficiency II,** the **fucosyl-containing ligands for selectins are absent due to a congenital defect of endogenous fucose metabolism.** As shown in Figure 6–9, selectin-carbohydrate interactions have a role in the rolling of leukocytes on an endothelial cell surface, a step required for the transendothelial migration of leukocytes into extravascular areas of inflammation.

Mac-1 to ICAM-1 and ICAM-2 on the endothelial cell surface. ICAM-1 is induced by cytokines **tumor necrosis factor-α,** and **interleukin-1 (IL-1)** is produced by activated macrophages present at the site of inflammation.

These molecular interactions determine (1) tight binding of the neutrophil, required for stopping rolling; (2) preparing the cell for squeezing between adjacent endothelial cells toward the chemoattractant **interleukin-8,** produced by inflammatory cells; and (3) **transendothelial migration,** or **diapedesis,** facilitated by the interaction of **CD31** molecules expressed on the surfaces of both the neutrophil and endothelial cell.

Clinical significance: Mast cell–eosinophil interaction in asthma

We have already seen that both mast cells and eosinophils are immigrant cells of the connective tissue. These two cell types have a significant role in the pathogenesis of asthma.

Asthma, a condition in which extrinsic (allergens) or intrinsic (unknown) factors trigger variable air obstruction of the respiratory bronchi and bronchioles, provides a good example of mast cell–eosinophil interaction.

When **mast cells** degranulate and release chemical mediators, eosinophils and neutrophils are attracted from blood vessels into the connective tissue of the respiratory mucosa. **Eosinophils,** in turn, release additional mediators (leukotriene B4 and others) to enhance bronchoconstriction and edema. The release of **eosinophil cationic protein** and **major basic protein** into the bronchial lumen damages the epithelial cell lining and disturbs mucociliary function (Figure 6–10).

Platelets

Platelets are small (2–4 μm) cytoplasmic fragments derived from the **megakaryocyte** (Figure 6–11) under the control of **thrombopoietin,** a 35- to 70-kDa glycoprotein produced in the kidney and liver. Megakaryocytes develop cytoplasmic projections that become **proplatelets,** which fragment into platelets. This differentiation process takes 10 to 12 days. **Platelets bind and degrade thrombopoietin, a mechanism that regulates platelet production.**

The plasma membrane of a platelet invaginates to form a system of **cytoplasmic channels,** called the **open canalicular system.** The central region of the platelet, the **granulomere,** contains mitochondria, rough endoplasmic reticulum, the Golgi

Figure 6–10

Mast cell–eosinophil interaction in asthma

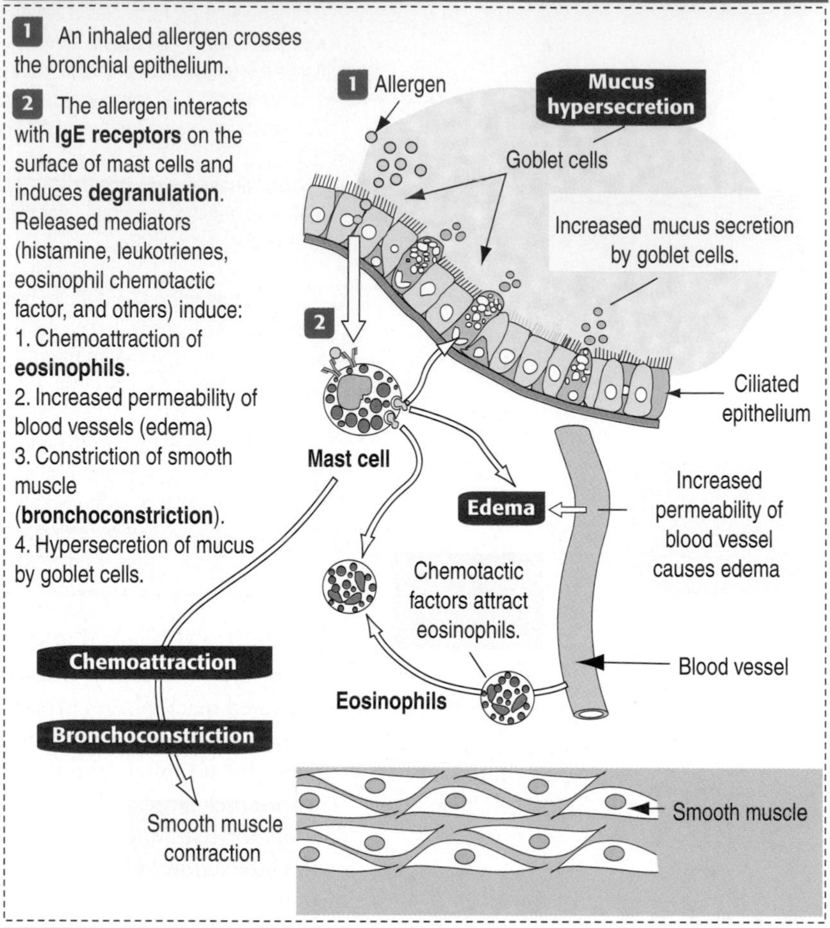
1 An inhaled allergen crosses the bronchial epithelium.
2 The allergen interacts with **IgE receptors** on the surface of mast cells and induces **degranulation**. Released mediators (histamine, leukotrienes, eosinophil chemotactic factor, and others) induce:
1. Chemoattraction of **eosinophils**.
2. Increased permeability of blood vessels (edema)
3. Constriction of smooth muscle (**bronchoconstriction**).
4. Hypersecretion of mucus by goblet cells.
1 Allergen
Mucus hypersecretion
Goblet cells
Increased mucus secretion by goblet cells.
2
Ciliated epithelium
Mast cell
Edema
Increased permeability of blood vessel causes edema
Chemotactic factors attract eosinophils.
Blood vessel
Eosinophils
Chemoattraction
Bronchoconstriction
Smooth muscle contraction
Smooth muscle

apparatus, and granules. The periphery of the platelet, the **hyalomere**, contains microtubules and microfilaments that regulate platelet shape and movement.

Clinical significance: Thrombocytopenia

About **200,000** platelets per microliter of blood circulate for **8** to**10** days. Platelets promote blood clotting and help to prevent blood loss from damaged vessels. A reduction in the number of platelets in blood (**thrombocytopenia**) leads to increased susceptibility to bleeding. Thrombocytopenia is defined by a decrease in the number of platelets to less than 150,000/μL of blood. **Spontaneous bleeding** is observed with a platelet count of 20,000/μL.

Thrombocytopenia can be caused by a **decrease in the production of platelets, an increase in the destruction of platelets** (determined by antibodies against platelets or megakaryocyte antigens [**autoimmune thrombocytopenic purpura, ITP**] or drugs—for example, penicillin, sulfonamides, and digoxin), and **aggregation of platelets in the microvasculature** (**thrombotic thrombocytopenic purpura, TTP**), probably a result of pathologic changes in endothelial cells producing procoagulant substances.

Deficiency of the **glycoprotein 1b–factor IX** complex, or **von Willebrand factor,** a protein associated with factor VIII, leads to two congenital bleeding disorders, **Bernard Soulier disease** and **von Willebrand disease**, respectively (Figures 6–12 and 6–13). These two diseases are characterized by the inability of platelets to attach to vascular subendothelial surfaces. The **glycoprotein 1b–factor IX–von Willebrand factor complex is important for the aggregation of normal platelets when they are exposed to injured subendothelial tissues.**

Hemophilia

Hemophilia is a common hereditary disease associated with serious bleeding due to an inherited deficiency of **factor VIII** or **factor IX**.
The genes for these blood coagulation factors lie on the X chromosome, and when mutated, they cause the X-linked recessive traits of **hemophilia A** and **B**. Hemophila affects males, with females as carriers. A reduction in the amount or activity of **factor VIII**, a protein synthesized in the liver, causes **hemophilia A**. Deficiency in **factor IX** determines **hemophilia B**.
Major trauma or surgery can determine severe bleeding in all hemophiliacs and, therefore, a correct diagnosis is critical. Plasma-derived or genetically engineered recombinant factors are available for the treatment of patients with hemophilia.
Von Willebrand disease, the most frequent bleeding disorder, is also hereditary and related to a deficient or abnormal **von Willebrand factor**.

Figure 6–11

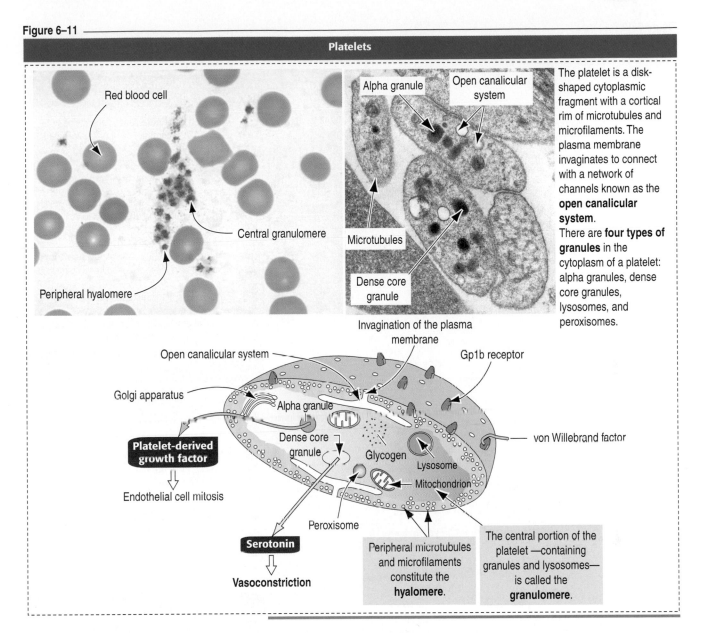

Red blood cell

Central granulomere

Peripheral hyalomere

Alpha granule

Open canalicular system

Microtubules

Dense core granule

The platelet is a disk-shaped cytoplasmic fragment with a cortical rim of microtubules and microfilaments. The plasma membrane invaginates to connect with a network of channels known as the **open canalicular system**.
There are **four types of granules** in the cytoplasm of a platelet: alpha granules, dense core granules, lysosomes, and peroxisomes.

Invagination of the plasma membrane

Open canalicular system

Gp1b receptor

Golgi apparatus

Alpha granule

Platelet-derived growth factor

Dense core granule

Glycogen

Lysosome

von Willebrand factor

Endothelial cell mitosis

Mitochondrion

Peroxisome

Serotonin

Vasoconstriction

Peripheral microtubules and microfilaments constitute the **hyalomere**.

The central portion of the platelet —containing granules and lysosomes— is called the **granulomere**.

Clinical significance: Hemostasis and the blood clotting cascade

The blood clotting or coagulation cascade depends on the sequential activation of proenzymes to enzymes and the participation of endothelial cells and platelets to achieve **hemostasis** or arrest of bleeding. Hemostasis occurs when fibrin is formed to reinforce the platelet plug.

The blood clotting cascade is composed of intrinsic and extrinsic pathways (see Figures 6–13): (1) an **intrinsic pathway** is induced by contact of factor XII to subendothelial collagen. This contact results from the damage of the wall of a blood vessel. (2) An **extrinsic pathway** is induced by the release of tissue factors.

Both intrinsic and extrinsic pathways converge to a crucial step in which **fibrinogen is converted to fibrin**. The initial hemostatic plug consists of a platelet scaffold for the conversion of prothrombin to thrombin, which changes fibrinogen into fibrin. Fibrin stabilizes the blood clot (Figure 6–13).

Hematopoiesis
Sites of hematopoiesis during development

In the **fetus**, hematopoiesis starts during the first trimester in islands of hematopoiesis found in the **yolk sac**. The islands develop from **hemangioblasts**, the pro-

Figure 6–12

The phases of blood clotting or hemostasis

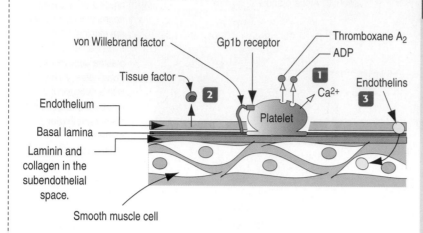

Phase I: Adhesion of platelets to the subendothelium of an injured blood vessel

1 **Activated platelets** release: adenosine diphosphate (**ADP**), to attract other platelets to the site of injury, **thromboxane A$_2$**, to cause vasoconstriction and platelet aggregation, and **Ca^{2+}**, to participate in clotting.

2 **Endothelial cells** release **tissue factor** which binds to factor VIIa to convert factor X into factor Xa and initiate the common pathway of blood clotting. Von Willebrand factor binds to **Gp1b platelet receptor** to facilitate the attachment of platelets to collagen and laminin in the subendothelial space.

3 **Endothelins**, peptide hormones secreted by endothelial cells, stimulate smooth muscle contraction and proliferation of endothelial cells and fibroblasts to accelerate the repair process.

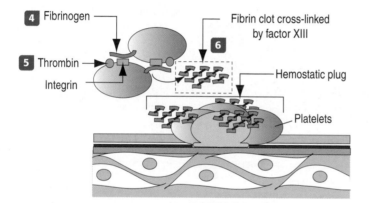

Phase II: Aggregation of platelets to form a hemostatic plug

4 **Fibrinogen** in plasma binds to activated integrin receptors, and platelets are bridged to each other.

5 **Thrombin**, bound to its receptor on the platelet surface, acts on **fibrinogen** to cleave fibrinopeptides and form a fibrin monomer.

6 **Fibrin monomers** aggregate to form a soft fibrin clot. **Factor XIII** cross-links fibrin monomers. Platelets and fibrin form a hemostatic plug.

Under normal conditions, the intact vascular endothelium does not trigger platelet aggregation since laminin and collagen are not exposed. Endothelial cells secrete prostacyclin, a potent inhibitor of platelet aggregation and secretion of ADP.

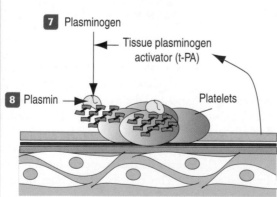

Phase III: Platelet procoagulation activity terminates with the removal of the fibrin clot

7 **Plasminogen** (a plasma protein) is converted to **plasmin** (a protease) by **tissue-plasminogen activator** (produced by injured endothelial cells and subendothelial connective tissue).

8 **Plasmin** dissolves the fibrin clot.

genitors of both hematopoietic and endothelial cells. Fetal hematopoiesis continues after the second trimester in the **liver** and then in the **spleen**. During the seventh month of intrauterine life, the **bone marrow** becomes the primary site of hematopoiesis, where it remains during adulthood. In the adult, an approximate volume of 1.7 L of marrow contains 10^{12} hematopoietic cells.

The bone marrow consists of two compartments: (1) the **marrow stromal compartment**, and (2) the **hematopoietic cell compartment**.

Figure 6–13

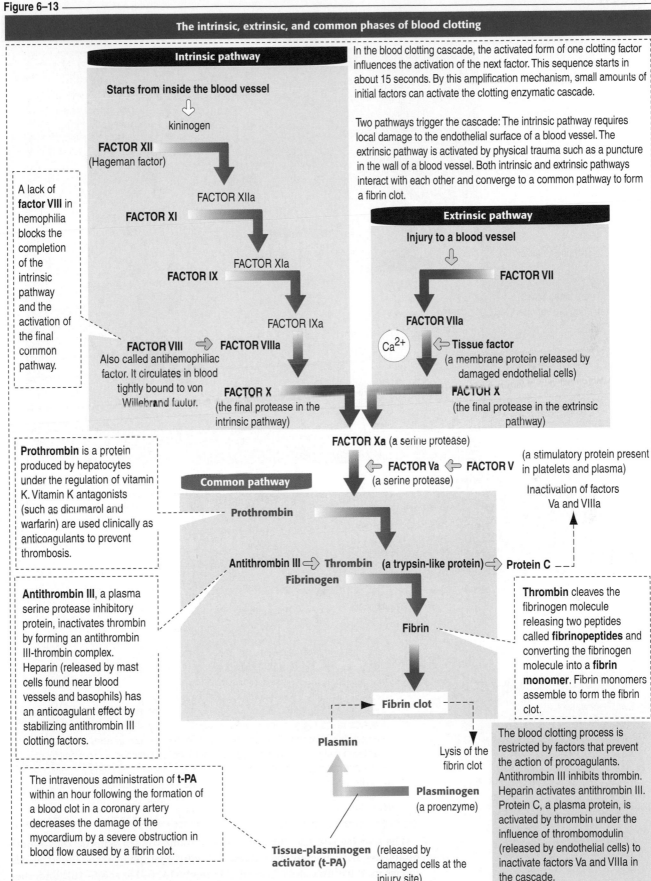

The intrinsic, extrinsic, and common phases of blood clotting

Intrinsic pathway

Starts from inside the blood vessel

⇩

kininogen

FACTOR XII
(Hageman factor)

↓

FACTOR XIIa

FACTOR XI

↓

FACTOR XIa

FACTOR IX

↓

FACTOR IXa

A lack of **factor VIII** in hemophilia blocks the completion of the intrinsic pathway and the activation of the final common pathway.

FACTOR VIII ⇨ **FACTOR VIIIa**
Also called antihemophiliac factor. It circulates in blood tightly bound to von Willebrand factor.

FACTOR X
(the final protease in the intrinsic pathway)

In the blood clotting cascade, the activated form of one clotting factor influences the activation of the next factor. This sequence starts in about 15 seconds. By this amplification mechanism, small amounts of initial factors can activate the clotting enzymatic cascade.

Two pathways trigger the cascade: The intrinsic pathway requires local damage to the endothelial surface of a blood vessel. The extrinsic pathway is activated by physical trauma such as a puncture in the wall of a blood vessel. Both intrinsic and extrinsic pathways interact with each other and converge to a common pathway to form a fibrin clot.

Extrinsic pathway

Injury to a blood vessel

⇩

FACTOR VII

↓

FACTOR VIIa

Ca^{2+} ⇦ **Tissue factor**
(a membrane protein released by damaged endothelial cells)

FACTOR X
(the final protease in the extrinsic pathway)

FACTOR Xa (a serine protease)

⇦ **FACTOR Va** ⇦ **FACTOR V**
(a serine protease)

(a stimulatory protein present in platelets and plasma)

Inactivation of factors Va and VIIIa

Common pathway

Prothrombin is a protein produced by hepatocytes under the regulation of vitamin K. Vitamin K antagonists (such as dicumarol and warfarin) are used clinically as anticoagulants to prevent thrombosis.

Prothrombin

Antithrombin III ⇨ **Thrombin** (a trypsin-like protein) ⇨ Protein C

Fibrinogen

Antithrombin III, a plasma serine protease inhibitory protein, inactivates thrombin by forming an antithrombin III-thrombin complex. Heparin (released by mast cells found near blood vessels and basophils) has an anticoagulant effect by stabilizing antithrombin III clotting factors.

Fibrin

Thrombin cleaves the fibrinogen molecule releasing two peptides called **fibrinopeptides** and converting the fibrinogen molecule into a **fibrin monomer**. Fibrin monomers assemble to form the fibrin clot.

Fibrin clot

Plasmin

Lysis of the fibrin clot

The intravenous administration of **t-PA** within an hour following the formation of a blood clot in a coronary artery decreases the damage of the myocardium by a severe obstruction in blood flow caused by a fibrin clot.

Plasminogen
(a proenzyme)

Tissue-plasminogen activator (t-PA) (released by damaged cells at the injury site)

The blood clotting process is restricted by factors that prevent the action of procoagulants. Antithrombin III inhibits thrombin. Heparin activates antithrombin III. Protein C, a plasma protein, is activated by thrombin under the influence of thrombomodulin (released by endothelial cells) to inactivate factors Va and VIIIa in the cascade.

Figure 6-14

The bone marrow visualized by scanning electron microscopy and light microscopy: Vascularization

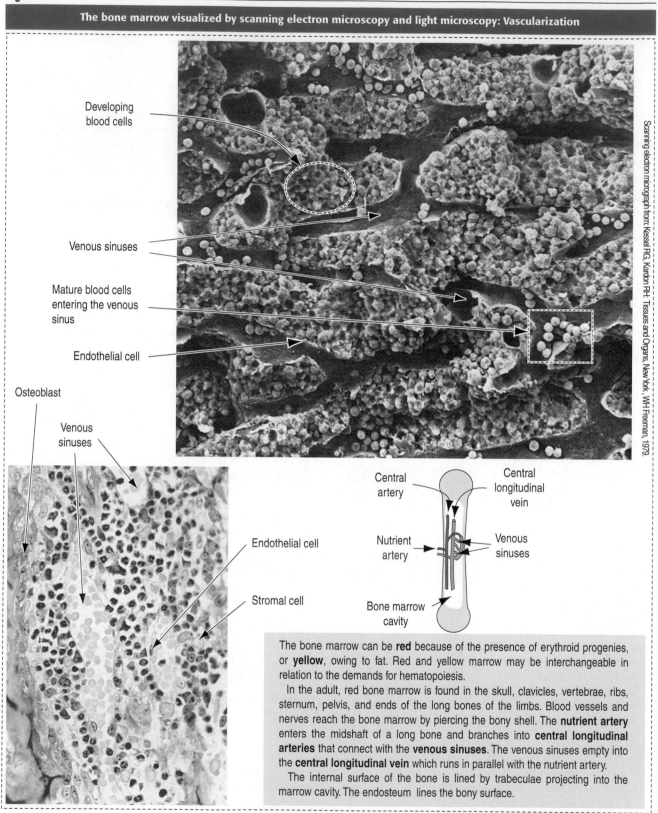

Developing blood cells

Venous sinuses

Mature blood cells entering the venous sinus

Endothelial cell

Osteoblast

Venous sinuses

Endothelial cell

Stromal cell

Scanning electron micrograph from: Kessel RG, Kardon RH: Tissues and Organs, New York, WH Freeman, 1979.

Central artery

Central longitudinal vein

Nutrient artery

Venous sinuses

Bone marrow cavity

The bone marrow can be **red** because of the presence of erythroid progenies, or **yellow**, owing to fat. Red and yellow marrow may be interchangeable in relation to the demands for hematopoiesis.

In the adult, red bone marrow is found in the skull, clavicles, vertebrae, ribs, sternum, pelvis, and ends of the long bones of the limbs. Blood vessels and nerves reach the bone marrow by piercing the bony shell. The **nutrient artery** enters the midshaft of a long bone and branches into **central longitudinal arteries** that connect with the **venous sinuses**. The venous sinuses empty into the **central longitudinal vein** which runs in parallel with the nutrient artery.

The internal surface of the bone is lined by trabeculae projecting into the marrow cavity. The endosteum lines the bony surface.

The marrow stromal compartment is a framework of **adipose cells, fibroblasts, stromal cells, vascular endothelial cells, macrophages,** and **blood vessels** interspersed within trabecular bone (Figures 6–14, 6–15, and 6–16). Endothelial cells, marrow fibroblasts, and stromal cells produce hematopoietic growth

Figure 6–15

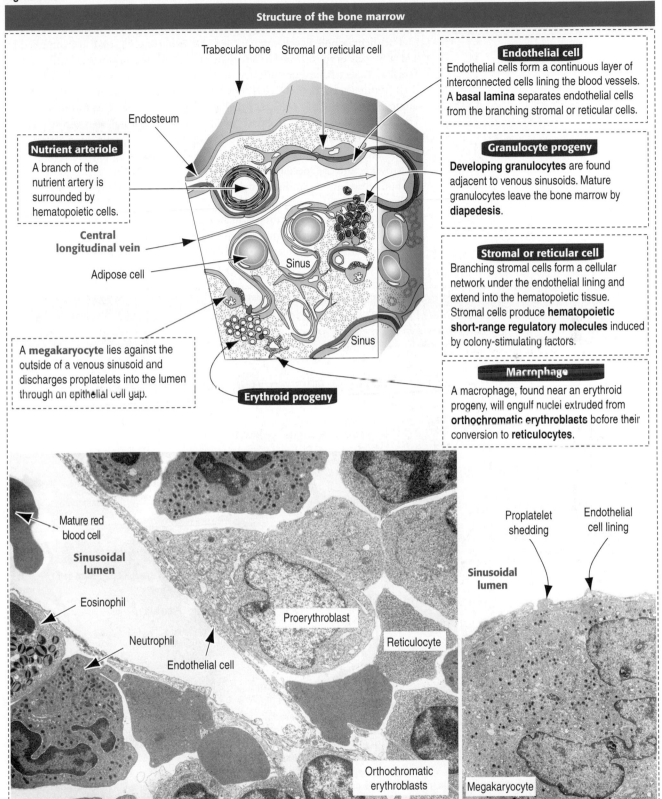

Structure of the bone marrow

Trabecular bone   Stromal or reticular cell

Endosteum

Nutrient arteriole

A branch of the nutrient artery is surrounded by hematopoietic cells.

Central longitudinal vein

Adipose cell

Sinus

Sinus

A **megakaryocyte** lies against the outside of a venous sinusoid and discharges proplatelets into the lumen through an epithelial cell gap.

Erythroid progeny

Endothelial cell

Endothelial cells form a continuous layer of interconnected cells lining the blood vessels. A **basal lamina** separates endothelial cells from the branching stromal or reticular cells.

Granulocyte progeny

Developing granulocytes are found adjacent to venous sinusoids. Mature granulocytes leave the bone marrow by **diapedesis**.

Stromal or reticular cell

Branching stromal cells form a cellular network under the endothelial lining and extend into the hematopoietic tissue. Stromal cells produce **hematopoietic short-range regulatory molecules** induced by colony-stimulating factors.

Macrophage

A macrophage, found near an erythroid progeny, will engulf nuclei extruded from **orthochromatic erythroblasts** before their conversion to **reticulocytes**.

Mature red blood cell

Sinusoidal lumen

Eosinophil

Neutrophil

Endothelial cell

Proerythroblast

Reticulocyte

Orthochromatic erythroblasts

Proplatelet shedding

Endothelial cell lining

Sinusoidal lumen

Megakaryocyte

factors and cytokines that regulate the production of blood cells. Endothelial cells form a barrier that prevents immature hematopoietic cells from leaving the marrow and enables mature hematopoietic cells to enter the blood. Adipose cells provide a local source of energy as well as synthesize growth factors. Marrow macrophages remove apoptotic cells, residual nuclei from orthochromatic erythroblasts, and particles from entering the marrow. Osteoblasts and osteoclasts maintain and remodel the cancellous bone surrounding the marrow tissue.

The hematopoietic cell compartment is highly vascularized. It is supplied by blood vessels derived from the **nutrient artery** and the **periosteal capillary network** and **specialized sinusoids** that drain into the marrow central vein (Figure 6–14). Mature hematopoietic cells translocate from the site of growth through the sinusoid wall by active **transendothelial migration** across **fenestrations** into the sinuses before entering the circulation through the central vein. Immature hematopoietic cells lack the capacity of transendothelial migration and are retained in the extravascular space by the vascular endothelial cells. The sinusoids of the marrow are lined by specialized endothelial cells with significant phagocytic activity and a capacity to produce growth factors that stimulate the proliferation and differentiation of hematopoietic cells.

The hematopoietic cell compartment provides an adequate number and types of cells required for diverse physiologic needs. Hematopoietic cells occupy preferential sites in the bone marrow and have differing capacities for self-renewal, growth, differentiation, and maturation.

Figure 6–16

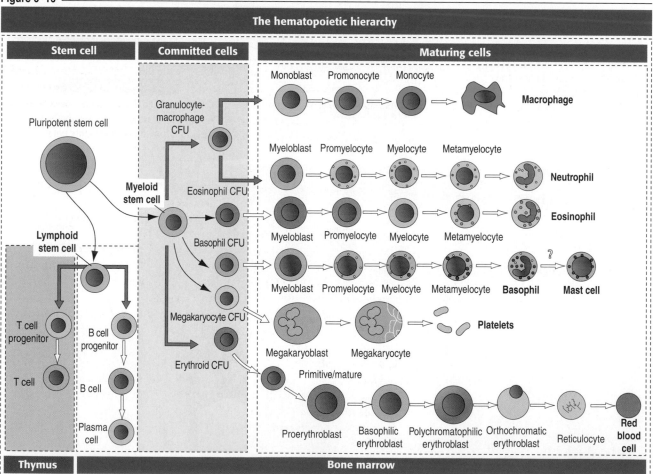

The bone marrow consists of: (1) **stem cells**, pluripotent cells capable of self-renewal; (2) **committed progenitor cells** (myeloid and lymphoid progenitor cells); and (3) **maturing cells**. Maturing cells develop from cells called **colony-forming units** (**CFUs**). The myeloid stem cell gives rise to CFUs responsible for the regeneration of red blood cells (**erythroid CFUs**), platelets (**megakaryocyte CFUs**), basophils (**basophil CFUs**), and eosinophils (**eosinophil CFUs**). Monocytes and neutrophils derive from a common committed progenitor cell (**granulocyte-macrophage CFU**). The **lymphoid progenitor cell** generates the **B cell progeny** in the **bone marrow** and **T cell progenies** in the **thymus**. They are discussed in detail in Chapter 10, Immune-Lymphatic System.

Hematopoietic cell populations: Stem, committed, and maturing cells

The bone marrow consists of three major populations (Figure 6–16): (1) the hematopoietic **stem cells**, capable of **self-renewal**; (2) **committed progenitor cells**, responsible for the generation of distinct cell lineages; and (3) **maturing cells**, resulting from the differentiation of the committed cell population. Maturing cells produce cells entering the blood circulation.

Pluripotent stem cells can self-renew and produce two other types of cells: the **myeloid** and **lymphoid** stem cells that develop into distinct cell progenies. **Self-renewal** is an important property of stem cells. Self-renewal preserves the pool of stem cells and is critical for feeding myeloid and lymphoid cells into the differentiation or maturation pathway.

Stem cells are difficult to identify, mainly because they represent approximately 0.05% of total hematopoietic cells (about 10^6 to 10^7 stem cells). In bone marrow transplantation, only 5% of the normal stem cells are needed to repopulate the entire bone marrow. **Stem cells cannot be identified by morphology, but they can be recognized by specific cell surface markers** (*c-kit* and Thy-1). CD34⁺ committed progenitor cell populations, also containing CD34⁻ stem cells, are generally used for hematopoietic stem cell transplantation in the clinical treatment of malignant diseases with chemotherapeutic agents that deplete a certain group of progenitor stem cells.

Myeloid and lymphoid cells are committed progenitor cells (see Figure 6–16). They are committed to the formation of cells of the blood and lymphoid organs. Five **colony forming-units (CFUs)** derive from the myeloid progenitor: the **erythroid CFU**, the **megakaryocyte CFU**, the **basophil CFU**, the **eosinophil CFU**, and the **granulocyte-macrophage CFU**. The erythroid CFU produces **red blood cells**. The megakaryocyte CFU generates **platelets**. The granulocyte-macrophage CFU produces both **monocytes** and **neutrophils**. Basophils and eosinophils derive from the basophil and eosinophil CFUs, respectively.

Clinical significance: Hematopoietic growth factors

Hematopoietic growth factors control the proliferative and maturational phases of hematopoiesis. In addition, they can extend the life span and function of a number of cells produced in the bone marrow. Several recombinant forms are available for clinical treatment of blood disorders.

Hematopoietic growth factors, also known as **hematopoietic cytokines**, are glycoproteins produced in the bone marrow by endothelial cells, stromal cells, fibroblasts, developing lymphocytes, and macrophages. Hematopoietic growth factors are also produced outside the bone marrow.

There are three major groups of hematopoietic growth factors: (1) **colony-stimulating factors**, (2) **erythropoietin** (Figure 6–17) and **thrombopoietin** (Gk. *poietin*: to make), and (3) **interleukins**.

Colony-stimulating factors are so named because they are able to stimulate progenitor cells to grow in vitro into cell clusters or colonies. Interleukins are produced by leukocytes (mainly lymphocytes) and affect other leukocytes (paracrine mechanism) or themselves (autocrine mechanism).

Hematopoietic cells express distinct patterns of **growth factor receptors** as they differentiate. Binding of the ligand to the receptor leads to a conformational change, activation of intracellular kinases, and the final induction of cell proliferation (see Chapter 3, Cell Signaling).

We discuss the role of specific hematopoietic growth factors when we analyze each cell lineage.

The erythroid lineage

Erythropoiesis includes the following sequence (Figure 6–18): **proerythroblast**, **basophilic erythroblast**, **polychromatophilic erythroblast**, **orthochromatic erythroblast**, **reticulocyte**, and **erythrocyte**.

Figure 6-17

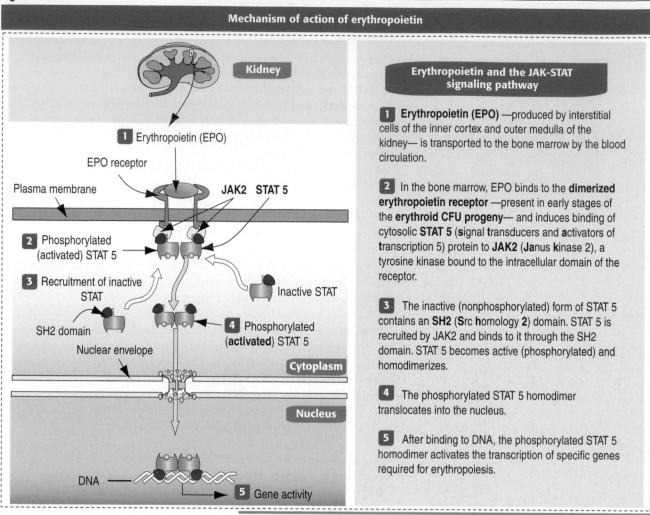

Mechanism of action of erythropoietin

Kidney

1 Erythropoietin (EPO)

EPO receptor

Plasma membrane

JAK2 STAT 5

2 Phosphorylated (activated) STAT 5

3 Recruitment of inactive STAT

Inactive STAT

SH2 domain

4 Phosphorylated (**activated**) STAT 5

Nuclear envelope

Cytoplasm

Nucleus

DNA

5 Gene activity

Erythropoietin and the JAK-STAT signaling pathway

1 **Erythropoietin (EPO)** —produced by interstitial cells of the inner cortex and outer medulla of the kidney— is transported to the bone marrow by the blood circulation.

2 In the bone marrow, EPO binds to the **dimerized erythropoietin receptor** —present in early stages of the **erythroid CFU progeny**— and induces binding of cytosolic **STAT 5** (**s**ignal **t**ransducers and **a**ctivators of **t**ranscription 5) protein to **JAK2** (**Ja**nus **k**inase 2), a tyrosine kinase bound to the intracellular domain of the receptor.

3 The inactive (nonphosphorylated) form of STAT 5 contains an **SH2** (**S**rc **h**omology **2**) domain. STAT 5 is recruited by JAK2 and binds to it through the SH2 domain. STAT 5 becomes active (phosphorylated) and homodimerizes.

4 The phosphorylated STAT 5 homodimer translocates into the nucleus.

5 After binding to DNA, the phosphorylated STAT 5 homodimer activates the transcription of specific genes required for erythropoiesis.

The major regulator of erythropoiesis is **erythropoietin** (Figure 6–17), a glycoprotein produced primarily in the **kidney** (peritubular interstitial cells located in the inner cortex and outer medulla of the kidney).

In response to **hypoxia** (a decrease in oxygen level in inspired air or tissues), mature erythroid progenitors—erythroid-CFUs, proerythroblasts, and basophilic erythroblasts—respond to erythropoietin by increasing gene transcription during different steps of their development (Figure 6–19).

Erythropoietin production in **chronic renal diseases** is severely impaired. Recombinant erythropoietin can be administered intravenously or subcutaneously for the treatment of anemia caused by a decrease in the production of erythropoietin by the kidney. The effectiveness of erythropoietin treatment can be monitored by an **increase of reticulocytes in circulating blood**. Reticulocytes can be identified by the supravital stain of residual polyribosomes forming a reticular network (see Figure 6–19).

Polychromatophilic erythroblasts are erythropoietin-independent, mitotically active, and specifically involved in the synthesis of hemoglobin. Derived orthochromatic erythroblast, reticulocyte, and mature RBCs are postmitotic cells (not involved in mitosis).

Leukopoiesis: Granulocytes and agranulocytes

Leukopoiesis (Gk. *leukos,* white; *poietin,* to make) results in the formation of cells belonging to the **granulocyte** and **agranulocyte** series. The **granulocyte lineage** (Figure 6–20) includes the **myeloblast**, **promyelocyte**, **myelocyte**, **metamyelo-**

Figure 6–18

The erythroid lineage

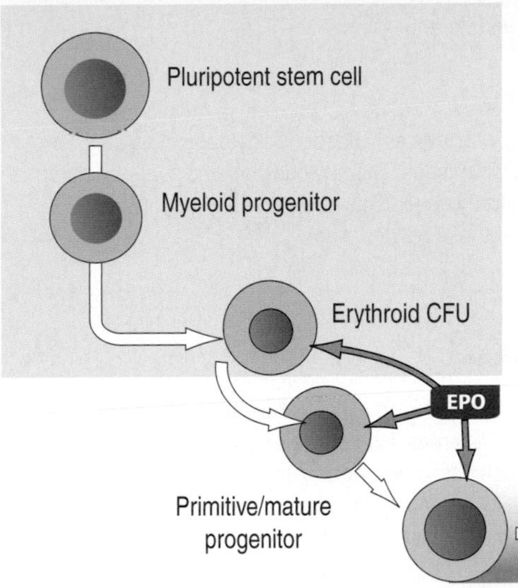

Erythrocytes are the most abundant cells of the blood. They contain hemoglobin ($\alpha_2\beta_2$ chains in the adult) and none of the typical organelles and cytomembranes are observed in the cytoplasm. Erythrocytes have a lifespan of about 120 days and aged red blood cells are phagocytosed by macrophages in the liver and spleen.

A lack of oxygen or a decrease of erythrocytes in circulating blood (anemia; caused by excessive destruction of red blood cells, bleeding, iron or vitamin B_{12} deficiency) stimulates cells in the **kidney** to synthesize and release into blood the glycoprotein erythropoietin (51 kDa). **Erythropoietin (EPO)** stimulates the early stages of the erythroid CFU to proliferate and differentiate into basophilic, polychromatophilic, and orthochromatic erythroblasts.

Pluripotent stem cell

Myeloid progenitor

Erythroid CFU

EPO

Primitive/mature progenitor

Proerythroblast

Basophilic erythroblast

Polychromatophilic erythroblast

Orthochromatic erythroblast

Reticulocyte

Red blood cell

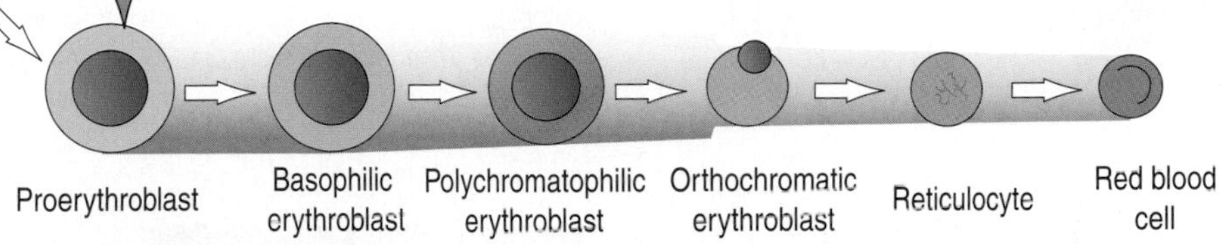

The **proerythroblast** is the first stage of the red blood cell lineage that can be recognized. It derives from a mature progenitor following stimulation with **erythropoietin**. **Nucleoli are present**. The cytoplasm contains abundant free polyribosomes involved in the synthesis of **hemoglobin**.

The synthesis of hemoglobin proceeds into **basophilic**, **polychromatophilic**, and **orthochromatophilic erythroblasts**. As hemoglobin accumulates in the cytoplasm, the nucleus of the differentiating erythroblasts is reduced in size, chromatin condenses, and free ribosomes decrease. The orthochromatophilic erythroblast displays maximum chromatin condensation.

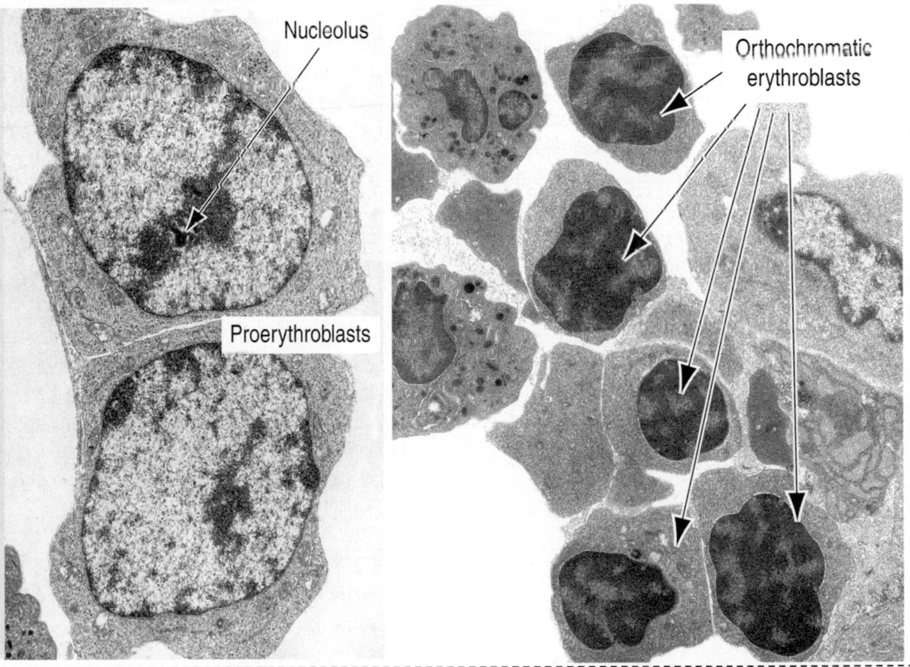

Nucleolus

Proerythroblasts

Orthochromatic erythroblasts

cyte, **band cell**, and **mature form**. The granulocyte-macrophage precursor gives rise to **neutrophil** and **monocytes**. The myeloid stem cell generates **eosinophil** and **basophil progenies**. **Agranulocytes** include **lymphocytes** and **monocytes**.

Granulocytes

Neutrophilic and macrophage cell lines share a common precursor cell: the granulocyte-macrophage CFU (see Figure 6–20). Eosinophils and basophils derive from independent eosinophil and basophil CFUs. Neutrophil, eosinophil, and basophil granulocytes follow a similar pattern of proliferation, differentiation, maturation, and storage in the bone marrow. Details of these process are better recognized for neutrophils, the most abundant granulocyte in the bone marrow and blood. It takes 10 to 14 days for neutrophils to develop from early

Figure 6–19

The erythroid lineage

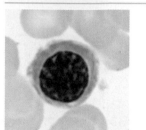

Proerythroblast   See Figure 6–18.

Basophilic erythroblast

A large cell (12-16 μm in diameter) with intensely basophilic cytoplasm as an indication of a large number of polyribosomes. The nucleus contains coarsely clumped chromatin and **nucleoli are not usually seen. This cell can divide by mitosis.** Basophilic erythroblasts derive from the proerythroblast.

Polychromatophilic erythroblasts

These cells may range in diameter from 9-15 μm. The nucleus exhibits dense chromatin patches separated by lighter areas. **No nucleolus is visible.** The cytoplasm may contain clumps of polyribosomes (light-blue staining) involved in the synthesis of hemoglobin (light pink-to-gray staining). **No cell division takes place after the polychromatophilic erythroblast.**

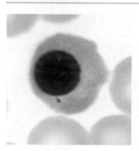

Orthochromatic erythroblast

Gradual reduction in cell diameter and increasing nuclear condensation

This cell is approximately 8-10 μm in diameter. The cytoplasm is pink, much the same as the reticulocyte. These cells have an **extremely dense (pyknotic) eccentrically located nucleus. Orthochromatic erythroblasts are post-mitotic.** The transition to reticulocyte is preceded by the extrusion of the condensed nucleus which carries with it a rim of cytoplasm. The extruded nucleus is engulfed by a macrophage.

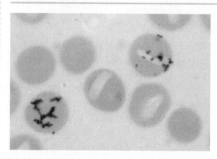

Reticulocyte

These **anucleated cells** measure approximately 7-8 μm in diameter. The cytoplasm is pink like the orthochromatic erythroblast. In regular preparations, these cells appear identical to mature erythrocytes. With **supravital stains**, such as **methylene blue** or **cresyl blue**, a filamentous (reticular) network of polyribosomes becomes visible. Reticulocytes remain in the bone marrow for 1 or 2 days and then are released into the peripheral blood. Following 1 day of circulation, reticulocytes mature into erythrocytes.

precursors but this timing is accelerated in the presence of infections or by treatment with granulocyte colony-stimulating factor (CSF) or granulocyte-macrophage CSF (see below).

Myeloblasts, promyelocytes, and **myelocytes** are **mitotically dividing cells; metamyelocytes** and **band cells cannot divide** but continue to differentiate (see Figure 6–20). A typical feature of the maturation process of granulocytes is the appearance of **primary** (azurophilic) **granules** and "specific" or **secondary granules** in the cytoplasm (Figures 6–21 and 6–22).

Myeloblasts are undifferentiated cells lacking cytoplasmic granules. Promyelocytes and myelocytes display primary granules in cells of the neutrophil, eosinophil, and basophil series. **Secondary granules appear in myelocytes.** Primary granules do not transform into specific granules. Primary granules persist as such throughout the cell differentiation sequence (see Figure 6–22).

Eosinophils exhibit the same maturation sequence as neutrophils. Eosinophil-specific granules are larger than neutrophil granules and appear refractile under the light microscope. Eosinophilic granules contain **myeloperoxidase** and several

Figure 6–20

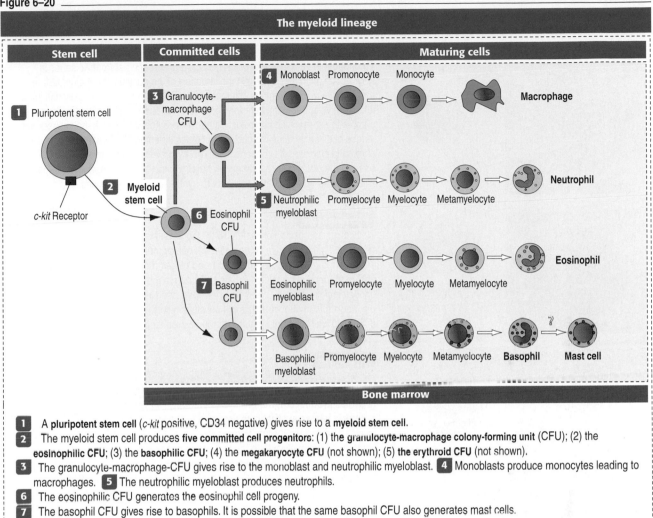

The myeloid lineage

| Stem cell | Committed cells | Maturing cells |

1 A **pluripotent stem cell** (*c-kit* positive, CD34 negative) gives rise to a **myeloid stem cell**.

2 The myeloid stem cell produces **five committed cell progenitors**: (1) the **granulocyte-macrophage colony-forming unit** (CFU); (2) the **eosinophilic CFU**; (3) the **basophilic CFU**; (4) the **megakaryocyte CFU** (not shown); and (5) **the erythroid CFU** (not shown).

3 The granulocyte-macrophage-CFU gives rise to the monoblast and neutrophilic myeloblast. **4** Monoblasts produce monocytes leading to macrophages. **5** The neutrophilic myeloblast produces neutrophils.

6 The eosinophilic CFU generates the eosinophil cell progeny.

7 The basophil CFU gives rise to basophils. It is possible that the same basophil CFU also generates mast cells.

cationic proteins (**major basic protein, MBP**, with a role in bacterial killing; **eosinophil cationic protein, ECP**, with antiparasitic activity).

Basophils are distinguished by their large, coarse, and darkly stained granules that fill the cytoplasm and often obscure the nucleus (Figure 6–23). The granules contain **peroxidase, heparin**, and **histamine** as well as **kallikrein**, a substance that attracts eosinophils.

As we have seen in Chapter 4, Connective Tissue, **mast cells** are structurally similar to basophils. However, mast cells are larger cells and are found in tissues, close to blood vessels. A notable difference is that mast cells contain **serotonin** and **5-hydroxytryptamine**, which basophils do not contain. In addition, mast cells discharge their granules into the extracellular space in contrast with basophils, which usually undergo diffuse internal degranulation.

Agranulocytes
Lymphocytes

Lymphocytes constitute a heterogeneous population of cells that differ from each other in terms of **origin**, **life span**, preferred sites of **localization within lymphoid organs**, **cell surface markers**, and **function**.

The pluripotent stem cell gives rise to all hematopoietic cells, including lymphocytes of the B and T cell lineage. **B cells mature in the bone marrow and then migrate to other lymphoid organs. T cells complete their maturation in the thymus and then migrate to specific lymphoid organs. A lymphoblast** gives rise

Figure 6–21

The myeloid lineage

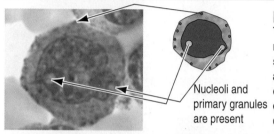

Cytoplasmic granules are absent

Nucleoli are present

Myeloblast

Throughout the granulocytic differentiation process (the neutrophilic series is shown), major changes occur in the structure of the nucleus and the content of the cytoplasm. For example, in the myeloblast (10-20 μm; a cell usually difficult to identify in Wright's-stained preparations), the nucleus is round with uncondensed chromatin and a visible nucleolus. As the cell progresses through the subsequent stages of differentiation, the nucleus becomes indented, then segmented, and the chromatin increases its condensation. **The cytoplasm of the myeloblast is essentially granule-free.** Primary granules appear in the promyelocyte stage, while specific or secondary granules are synthesized by myelocytes.

Nucleoli and primary granules are present

Promyelocyte

This cell measures approximately 15-20 μm in diameter. It has a large, round nucleus with uncondensed chromatin and one or more oval nucleoli. **The synthesis of primary granules—stained red or magenta—occurs exclusively at this stage.** The cytoplasm is basophilic due to the presence of abundant rough endoplasmic reticulum. **Promyelocytes give rise to neutrophilic, eosinophilic, or basophilic myelocytes.** It is not possible in conventional preparations to determine which type of granulocyte will be produced by a given promyelocyte.

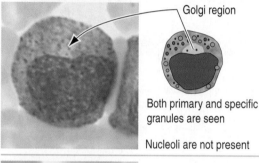

Golgi region

Both primary and specific granules are seen

Nucleoli are not present

Myelocyte

This cell, measuring 12-18 μm, has a round or oval nucleus which may be slightly indented; nucleoli are not present. **The basophilic cytoplasm contains primary granules produced in the promyelocyte stage as well as some specific granules, whose synthesis is detected in the myelocyte.** Consequently, the myelocyte cytoplasm begins to resemble that of the mature basophil, eosinophil, or neutrophil. The **myelocyte is the last stage capable of mitosis.** Myelocytes produce a large number of specific granules, but a finite number of primary granules (produced in the promyelocyte) are distributed among daughter myelocytes.

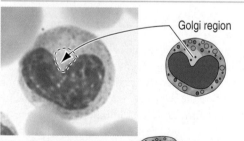

Golgi region

Metamyelocyte

This postmitotic cell measures 10-15 μm in diameter. The eccentric, bean shaped nucleus now contains some condensed chromatin. The cytoplasm closely resembles that of the mature form. The number of specific granules outnumber the primary granules.

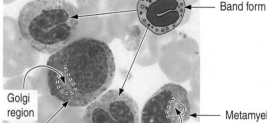

Band form

Golgi region

Myelocyte

Golgi region

Metamyelocyte

Band form

This cell has a diameter of about 9-15 μm. The nucleus is U-shaped with rounded ends. Its cytoplasm resembles that of the mature form. Two band form neutrophils are shown together with a myelocyte and a metamyelocyte neutrophil. The Golgi region can be distinguished in the myelocyte and metamyelocyte.

---

to a **prolymphocyte**, an intermediate stage that precedes the mature **lymphocyte. B and T lymphocytes are nonphagocytic cells. They are morphologically similar but functionally different**, as discussed in Chapter 10, Immune-Lymphatic System.

Figure 6–22

Cell types of the myeloid lineage

Granulopoiesis is the process of differentiation of leukocytes containing **cytoplasmic granules**. These cells, called **granulocytes**, include neutrophils, eosinophils, and basophils. Promyelocytes contain **primary granules**. **Secondary** or **specific granules** appear in subsequent myelocytic stages. **Primary granules** contain **acid hydrolases**, **proteases**, and antimicrobial enzymes (**lysozyme** and **myeloperoxidase**). **Myeloperoxidase increases in abnormal promyelocytes observed in acute promyelocytic leukemia.**

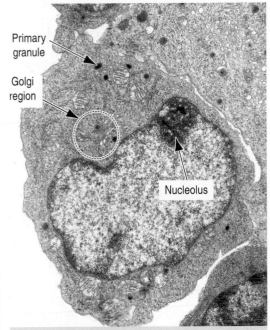

Primary granule

Golgi region

Nucleolus

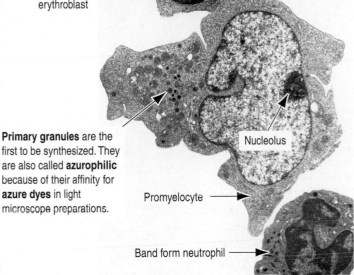

Polychromatophilic erythroblast

Nucleolus

Promyelocyte

Band form neutrophil

Primary granules are the first to be synthesized. They are also called **azurophilic** because of their affinity for **azure dyes** in light microscope preparations.

Early promyelocyte
A distinctive feature of promyelocytes is the **primary granules** (azurophilic in the neutrophilic lineage, eosinophilic, or basophilic). **Several nucleolar masses** can be seen within an eccentric or central nucleus.

Promyelocyte
As promyelocytes advance in their development, **primary granules** become more abundant. Promyelocytes have a diameter of 15-20 μm, contrasting with the much smaller **band form** cell (9-15 μm) and polychromatophilic erythroblasts (12-15 μm) present in the field. Nucleoli are still visible.

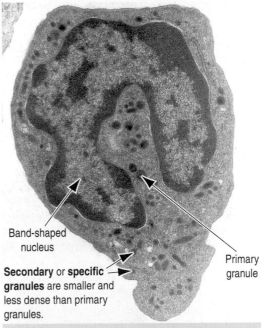

Band-shaped nucleus

Primary granule

Secondary or **specific granules** are smaller and less dense than primary granules.

Band form
Both **primary** and **secondary** or **specific granules** can be seen in the cytoplasm of this **band form neutrophil**.

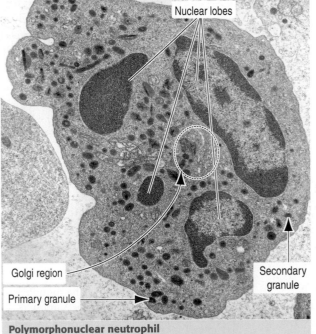

Nuclear lobes

Golgi region

Primary granule

Secondary granule

Polymorphonuclear neutrophil
Both primary and secondary granules can be seen in the cytoplasm of this cell displaying a **multilobulated nucleus**.

Figure 6–23

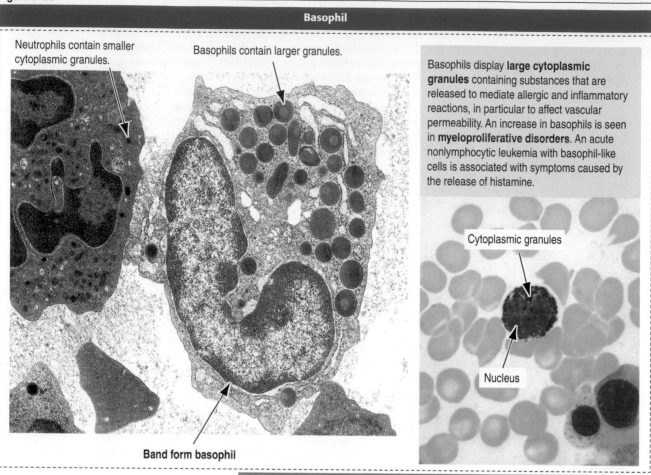

Basophil

Neutrophils contain smaller cytoplasmic granules.

Basophils contain larger granules.

Basophils display **large cytoplasmic granules** containing substances that are released to mediate allergic and inflammatory reactions, in particular to affect vascular permeability. An increase in basophils is seen in **myeloproliferative disorders**. An acute nonlymphocytic leukemia with basophil-like cells is associated with symptoms caused by the release of histamine.

Cytoplasmic granules

Nucleus

Band form basophil

Lymphoblasts (8–12 µm in diameter) are the precursors of the lymphocytes. A lymphoblast has an uncondensed nucleus with a large nucleolus. The cytoplasm contains many polyribosomes and a few cisternae of the endoplasmic reticulum.

Lymphocytes (10 µm in diameter or less) contain a round or slightly indented condensed nucleus. The nucleolus is not visible. The cytoplasm is moderately basophilic and devoid of granules.

Monocytes

Monocytes derive from the **granulocyte-macrophage progenitor CFU**. As we have already seen, the granulocyte-macrophage progenitor CFU gives rise to both the neutrophil lineage and the macrophage lineage. Under the influence of a specific CSF, each progenitor cell establishes its own hierarchy: the granulocyte CSF (G-CSF) takes the granulocyte precursor cell into the **myeloblast** pathway; the granulocyte-macrophage CSF (GM-CSF) guides the monocyte precursor cell into the **monoblast** pathway, leading to the production of peripheral blood monocytes and tissue macrophages. Receptors for M-CSF are restricted to the monocyte lineage (see Regulation of osteoclast differentiation in Chapter 5, Osteogenesis).

Monoblasts (14 µm in diameter) are morphologically similar to myeloblasts. The monoblast is present in the bone marrow and is difficult to identify with certainty. The cytoplasm is basophilic and the nucleus is large and displays one or more nucleoli. The following cell in the series is the **promonocyte**.

Promonocytes (11–13 µm in diameter) contain a large nucleus with a slight indentation and uncondensed chromatin. A nucleolus may be visualized. The basophilic cytoplasm, due to polyribosomes, contains primary granules (lyso-

Figure 6–24

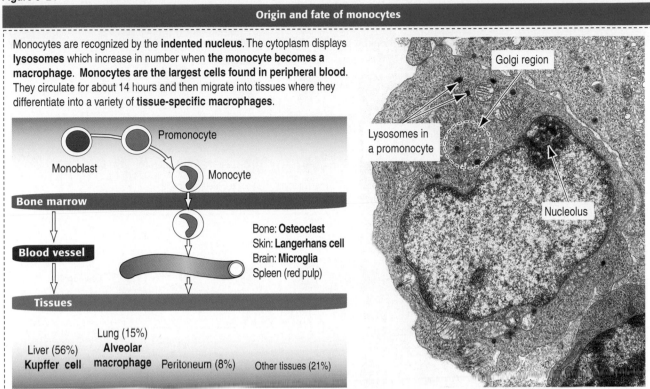

Origin and fate of monocytes

Monocytes are recognized by the **indented nucleus**. The cytoplasm displays **lysosomes** which increase in number when **the monocyte becomes a macrophage**. **Monocytes are the largest cells found in peripheral blood**. They circulate for about 14 hours and then migrate into tissues where they differentiate into a variety of **tissue-specific macrophages**.

Monoblast — Promonocyte — Monocyte

Bone marrow

Blood vessel

Tissues

Bone: **Osteoclast**
Skin: **Langerhans cell**
Brain: **Microglia**
Spleen (red pulp)

Liver (56%) **Kupffer cell**
Lung (15%) **Alveolar macrophage**
Peritoneum (8%)
Other tissues (21%)

Golgi region

Lysosomes in a promonocyte

Nucleolus

somes with peroxidase, arylsulfatase, and acid phosphatase). The primary granules are smaller and fewer than in promyelocytes. **Both monoblasts and promonocytes are mitotically active cells.**

Monocytes (12-20 µm in diameter) in the bone marrow and the blood have a large indented nucleus found in the central portion of the cytoplasm (Figure 6-24). Granules (**primary lysosomes**) and small vacuoles are typical features. Lysosomes lack peroxidase but contain other proteases and hydrolases. Monocytes are **motile** in response to chemotactic signals and attach to a surface.

Macrophages (15–80 µm in diameter) constitute a population of emigrated blood monocytes that differentiate in tissues (lung, spleen, liver, lymph node, peritoneum, gastrointestinal tract, and bone [osteoclasts]) in response to local conditions.

The structural and functional characteristics of tissue macrophages have been discussed in Chapter 4, Connective Tissue. In Chapter 11, Integumentary System, we discuss the antigenic reactivity of monocyte-derived Langerhans cells in epidermis. In Chapter 17, Digestive Glands, we explore the important role of Kupffer cells in liver function, and in Chapter 10, Immune-Lymphatic System, we examine the phagocytic properties of macrophages in spleen.

Clinical significance: Colony-stimulating factors and interleukins

The significance of G-CSF and GM-CSF during the development of monocytes has been mentioned. G-CSF is a glycoprotein produced by monocytes, macrophages, fibroblasts, stromal cells, and endothelial cells in different parts of the body. The synthetic form of G-CSF (known as filgrastim or lenograstim) causes a dose-dependent increase of neutrophils in the blood. G-CSF is used for the treatment of **neutropenia** (Gk. *penia*, poverty; small numbers of neutrophils in circulating blood) after cancer chemotherapy, after bone marrow transplantation, to facilitate an increase of neutrophils, and in the treatment of chronic neutropenia.

GM-CSF is also a glycoprotein produced by several cell types that stimulates

Figure 6–25

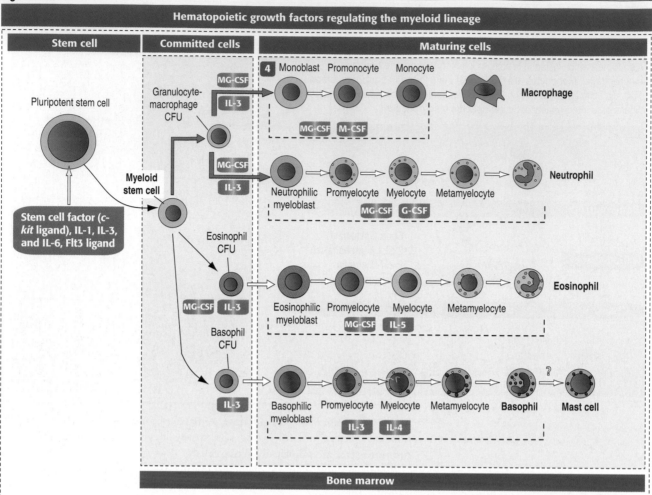

Hematopoietic growth factors regulating the myeloid lineage

Stromal cells, growth factors and interleukins (**IL-3, IL-4, IL-5,** and **IL-6**) regulate the proliferation and differentiation of myeloid progenitor cells. **Stem cell factor** (also called *c-kit* ligand) and **Flt3** (fms-like tyrosine kinase 3) ligand regulate the pluripotent stem cell. Granulocyte colony-stimulating factor (**G-CSF**) and monocyte colony-stimulating factor (**M-CSF**) regulate the proliferation and differentiation of neutrophils and monocytes derived from the granulocyte-macrophage colony forming unit (CFU). IL-5 is a selective cytokine for the eosinophil CFU–derived progeny. Recombinant growth factor proteins have been generated and used to stimulate hematopoiesis in cases of depletion of stem cells.

the formation of neutrophils, monocytes, and eosinophils (Figure 6–25). However, GM-CSF is less potent than G-CSF in increasing the levels of neutrophils during neutropenia. As is the case with G-CSF, a synthetic form of GM-CSF (sargramostim or molgramostim) is available for the treatment of neutropenia.

Interleukins have a relevant function in the formation and function of type B and T cells as we see in Chapter 10, Immune-Lymphatic System. IL-3 stimulates cell proliferation during early hematopoiesis and acts together with other growth factors, including G-CSF and GM-CSF (see Figure 6–25). IL-5 acts on the eosinophil progeny and IL-4 on the basophil progeny.

Platelets and megakaryocytes

The precursor cell of the platelet (also called **thrombocyte**; Gk. *thrombos*, clot) is the **megakaryoblast**, a cell derived from the **megakaryocyte CFU** (see Figure 6–16).

The megakaryoblast (15–50 μm in diameter) displays a single kidney-shaped nucleus with several nucleoli. The megakaryoblast enlarges to give rise to the **promegakaryocyte** (20–80 μm in diameter) with an irregularly shaped nucleus

Figure 6–26

The megakaryocyte and the origin of platelets

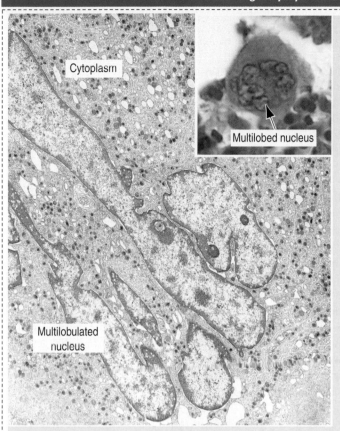

Cytoplasm

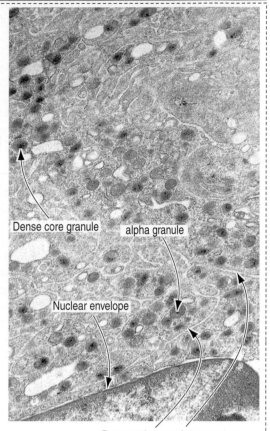

Multilobed nucleus

Dense core granule

alpha granule

Nuclear envelope

Multilobulated nucleus

Megakaryocyte

Demarcation membrane system

The development and maturation of a megakaryocyte are characterized by the following sequence:

1. **Serial mitotic divisions** (3–6 times) **without cell division**, a process known as **endoreduplication**. As a result, a tightly packed, multilobulated nucleus is observed.

2. **Cytoplasmic maturation**, characterized by an increase in the number of **dense core granules, alpha granules**, and a network of membrane channels and tubules known as the **demarcation membrane system**.

3. **Platelet shedding** into sinusoids of the bone marrow.

During the cytoplasmic maturation of a megakaryocyte, the cell membrane invaginates to form channels separating cytoplasmic islands about 3–4 μm in diameter.

These platelet demarcation channels eventually coalesce to generate **proplatelets**. Megakaryocytes typically rest next to bone marrow sinusoids and extend proplatelet projections between endothelial cells into the sinusoids where they are shed.

and a cytoplasm rich in azurophilic granules. The promegakaryocyte forms the mature megakaryocyte.

The **megakaryocyte** (35–160 μm in diameter; Figure 6–26) contains an irregularly **lobed nucleus produced by an endomitotic nuclear division process in which nuclear divisions occur without cell division (polyploid nucleus)**. Nucleoli are not detected.

The megakaryocyte can be confused with the osteoclast, another large cell in bone that is **multinucleated instead of multilobed**. As we have already seen, the cytoplasm shows a **network of demarcation zones** formed by the invagination of the plasma membrane of the megakaryocyte. The coalescence of the demarcation membranes results in the formation of the plasma membrane of proplatelets, which fragment into platelets.

We have already seen that platelets play important roles in maintaining the integrity of blood vessels (see Figure 6–12). Recall that platelet activation during hemostasis involves sequentially:

1. Platelet adhesion to the subendothelial matrix.
2. Platelet aggregation by binding to fibrinogen.
3. Platelet secretion of substances present in the granules, to recruit additional platelets.
4. Platelet procoagulant activity involving thrombin.

Clinical significance: Thrombopoietin

Thrombopoietin is produced in the **liver**, has a similar structure to erythropoietin, and stimulates the development of megakaryocytes from the megakaryocyte CFU into platelets. Deficiencies in thrombopoietin cause thrombocytopenia. An excess of thrombopoietin causes thrombocytosis.

Platelets bind and degrade thrombopoietin, a process that autoregulates platelet production.

Clinical significance: Stem cell factor (also known as *c-kit* ligand)

Stem cell factor is a ligand protein produced by fetal tissues and stromal cells of the bone marrow that binds to the stem cell factor receptor, a **tyrosine kinase receptor** (see Figure 6–25).
The stem cell factor ligand makes stem cells responsive to other cytokines and colony-stimulating factors (see Figure 6–25). It does not induce the formation of cell colonies by itself. The stem cell factor receptor is expressed by the *c-kit* **proto-oncogene**. A mutation in genes expressing the components of the stem cell factor receptor–ligand complex causes **anemia** and affects the **development of melanocytes in skin** and the **survival and proliferation of primordial germinal cells in the developing ovary and testis** (see Chapter 21, Sperm Transport and Maturation). Stem cell factor is potentially useful for the treatment of inherited and acquired disorders of hematopoiesis as well as in bone marrow transplantation.

In Chapter 4, Connective Tissue, we noted that **mast cells** derive from a bone marrow precursor. The storage and release of histamine- and heparin-containing granules from mast cells are affected in mutants lacking stem cell factor.

Clinical significance: Transferrin and iron metabolites

In addition to erythropoietin, the formation of RBCs is highly dependent on **iron metabolism** and the water-soluble vitamins **folic acid** (folacin) and **vitamin B$_{12}$** (cobalamine).

Figure 6–27

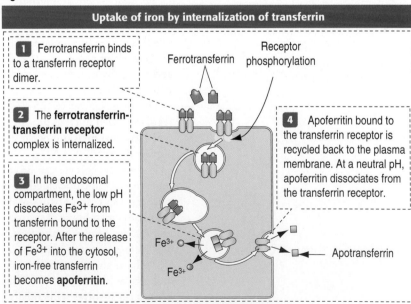

Uptake of iron by internalization of transferrin

1 Ferrotransferrin binds to a transferrin receptor dimer.

Ferrotransferrin

Receptor phosphorylation

2 The **ferrotransferrin-transferrin receptor** complex is internalized.

4 Apoferritin bound to the transferrin receptor is recycled back to the plasma membrane. At a neutral pH, apoferritin dissociates from the transferrin receptor.

3 In the endosomal compartment, the low pH dissociates Fe^{3+} from transferrin bound to the receptor. After the release of Fe^{3+} into the cytosol, iron-free transferrin becomes **apoferritin**.

Fe^{3+}

Fe^{3+}

Apotransferrin

Red blood cell disorders: Anemias

Anemia is a reduction in the mass of circulating red blood cells. It is detected by analysis of peripheral blood (low hemoglobin, low red blood cell count, and low hematocrit). Anemia results in the lack of oxygen-carrying capacity which is compensated by a reduction in the affinity of hemoglobin for oxygen, an increase in cardiac output, and an attempt to increase red blood cell production. The most common cause of anemia is **iron deficiency** (low intake, chronic blood loss, or increased demand during pregnancy and lactation).

Deficiency in **vitamin B$_{12}$** and **folic acid** causes megaloblastic anemia. This form of anemia is associated with the development of abnormally large red blood cell precursors (**megaloblasts**) which develop into large red blood cells (**macrocytes**). Vitamin B$_{12}$ is normally absorbed in the small intestine after binding to **intrinsic factor**, a glycoprotein secreted by **gastric parietal cells**. The lack of production of **intrinsic factor** (due to autoimmune atrophic gastritis, or after surgical gastrectomy) results in **pernicious anemia**.

Iron is involved in the transport of oxygen and carbon dioxide. Several iron-binding proteins store and transport iron, for example, **hemoglobin** in RBCs, and **myoglobin** in muscle tissue. Iron is coupled to **heme** (a molecule synthesized in the bone marrow, with one ferrous ion, Fe^{2+}, bound to a tetrapyrrolic ring) and **hematin** (with one ferric ion, Fe^{3+}, bound to a protein).

Transferrin, a serum protein produced in the liver, and **lactoferrin**, a protein present in maternal milk, are nonheme proteins involved in the **transport of iron** (Figure 6–27). Transferrin complexed to two Fe^{3+} ions is called **ferrotransferrin**. Transferrin devoid of iron is known as **apotransferrin**.

The iron-containing transferrin binds to a specific cell surface receptor that mediates the internalization of the transferrin ligand–transferrin receptor complex. The transferrin receptor is a transmembrane dimer with each subunit binding to a transferrin molecule. The internalization of the transferrin-receptor complex is dependent on receptor phosphorylation triggered by Ca^{2+}-calmodulin and the protein kinase C complex.

Inside the cell, iron is released within the acidic endosomal compartment and the **receptor-apotransferrin** (iron-free) complex returns to the cell surface where apotransferrin is released to be reutilized in blood plasma.

Ferritin, a major protein synthesized in the liver, is involved in the **storage of iron**. A single ferritin molecule has the capacity to store up to 4500 iron ions. When the storage capacity of ferritin is exceeded, iron is deposited as **hemosiderin**. Ferritin with little iron is called **apoferritin**.

Patients with the heritable disorder **idiopathic hemochromatosis**, characterized by excessive iron absorption and tissue deposits, require periodic withdrawals of blood and the administration of **iron chelators** to facilitate the excretion of complexed iron in the urine. A **decrease in iron** by excessive menstrual flow or gastrointestinal bleeding determines a reduction in hemoglobin-containing iron. RBCs are smaller (**microcytic anemia**) and underpigmented (**hypochromic anemia**).

Folic acid regulates the **folate metabolism** leading to the increased availability of purines and deoxythymidine monophosphate (dTMP) required for DNA synthesis.

Vitamin B$_{12}$ (known as **extrinsic factor**) binds to **intrinsic factor**, a protein produced by the parietal cells in the gastric glands. The vitamin B$_{12}$–intrinsic factor complex is absorbed in the small intestine.

A decrease in vitamin B$_{12}$, due mainly to insufficient production of intrinsic factor or hydrochloric acid in the stomach, or both, can affect folate metabolism and folate uptake, thereby impairing DNA synthesis in bone marrow.

Vitamin B$_{12}$ deficiency is rare because the liver stores up to a 6-year supply of vitamin B$_{12}$. Under deficiency conditions, the maturation of the erythroid cell progeny slows down, causing abnormally large RBCs (**megaloblasts**) with fragile cell membranes, resulting in the destruction of RBCs (**megaloblastic anemia**).

7. MUSCLE TISSUE

Muscle is one of the four basic tissues. There are three types of muscle: **skeletal**, **cardiac** and **smooth**. All three types are composed of elongated cells, called **myofibers**, or **muscle fibers**, specialized for contraction. In all three types of muscle, energy from the hydrolysis of adenosine triphosphate (ATP) is transformed into mechanical energy.

Skeletal muscle

Muscle cells or fibers form a long multinucleated syncytium grouped in bundles surrounded by connective tissue sheaths and extending from the site of origin to their insertion (Figure 7–1). The **epimysium** is a dense connective tissue layer ensheathing the **entire muscle**. The **perimysium** derives from the epimysium and surrounds bundles or **fascicles** of muscle cells. The **endomysium** is a delicate layer of reticular fibers and extracellular matrix surrounding **each muscle cell**.

Characteristics of the skeletal muscle cell or fiber

Skeletal muscle cells are formed in the embryo by the fusion of myoblasts that produce a postmitotic, multinucleated **myotube**. The myotube matures into the long muscle cell with a diameter of 10 to 100 μm and a length up to several centimeters.

The plasma membrane (called the **sarcolemma**) of the muscle cell is surrounded by a **basal lamina** and **satellite cells** (Figure 7–2). We will discuss the significance of satellite cells in muscle regeneration. The sarcolemma projects long, finger-like processes—called **transverse tubules** or **T tubules**—into the cytoplasm of the cell—the **sarcoplasm**. T tubules make contact with membranous sacs or channels, the **sarcoplasmic reticulum**. The sarcoplasmic reticulum contains high concentrations of Ca^{2+}. The site of contact of the T tubule with the sarcoplasmic reticulum cisternae is called a **triad** because it consists of **two lateral sacs of the sarcoplasmic reticulum and a central T tubule**.

Figure 7–1

General organization of the skeletal muscle

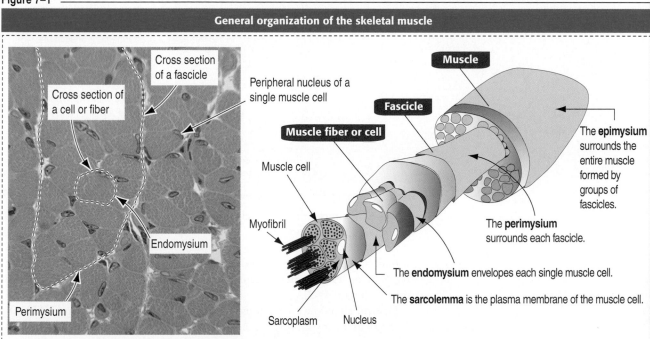

Cross section of a fascicle

Cross section of a cell or fiber

Endomysium

Perimysium

Peripheral nucleus of a single muscle cell

Muscle

Fascicle

Muscle fiber or cell

Muscle cell

Myofibril

Sarcoplasm   Nucleus

The **epimysium** surrounds the entire muscle formed by groups of fascicles.

The **perimysium** surrounds each fascicle.

The **endomysium** envelopes each single muscle cell.

The **sarcolemma** is the plasma membrane of the muscle cell.

Figure 7–2 _____

Skeletal muscle (striated)

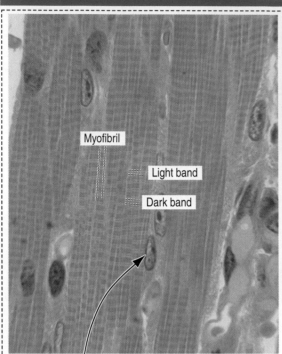

Myofibril

Light band

Dark band

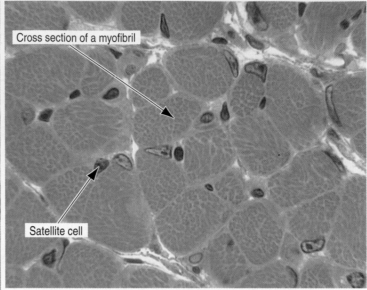

Cross section of a myofibril

Satellite cell

The cytoplasm of the muscle cell or fiber contains an elaborate and regular arrangement of **myofibrils**, each organizing alternating short segments of differing refractive index: **dark A bands and light I bands**.

Peripherally located nucleus
of a muscle cell or fiber

Sarcomere

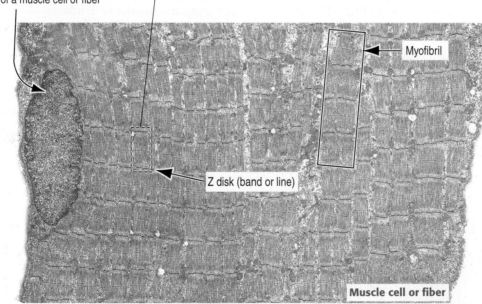

Myofibril

Z disk (band or line)

Muscle cell or fiber

Myofilaments are components of a myofibril. There are two major classes of myofilaments: (1) the thin **actin** filaments; (2) the thicker **myosin** filaments.

The cross-banded pattern of striated (skeletal or cardiac) muscle is due to the orderly arrangement of actin and myosin filaments.
Actin is the predominant component of the I band. Myosin is the main component of the A band. I and A bands form a **sarcomere**, which extends between two adjacent Z disks (also called bands or lines).

The many nuclei of the muscle fiber are located at the **periphery** of the cell, just under the sarcolemma.

About 80% of the sarcoplasm is occupied by myofibrils surrounded by mitochondria. Myofibrils are composed of two major filaments formed by contractile proteins: **thin filaments** contain **actin**, and **thick filaments** are composed of **myosin** (Figure 7–2).

Depending on the type of muscle, mitochondria may be found parallel to the long axis of the myofibrils, or they may wrap around the zone of thick filaments. Thin filaments insert into each side of the Z disk (also called **band**, or **line**) and

Figure 7–3

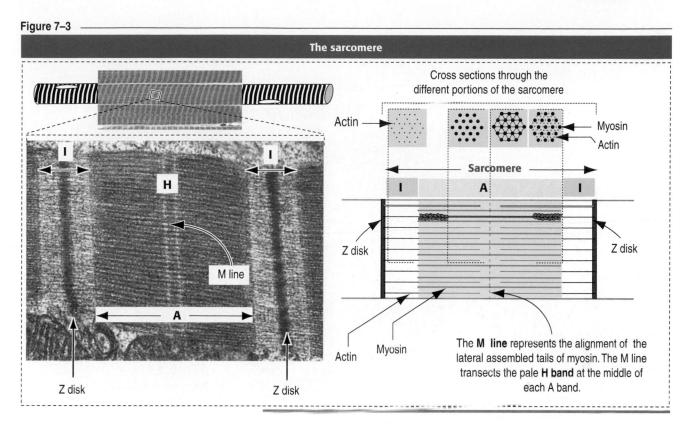

The sarcomere

Cross sections through the different portions of the sarcomere

Actin

Myosin

Actin

Sarcomere

I   A   I

Z disk

Z disk

M line

A

Actin   Myosin

The **M line** represents the alignment of the lateral assembled tails of myosin. The M line transects the pale **H band** at the middle of each A band.

Z disk

Z disk

extend from the **Z disk** into the **A band**, where they alternate with thick filaments.

The myofibril is a repeat of sarcomere units

The **sarcomere** is the contractile unit of skeletal muscle (Figure 7–3). Sarcomere repeats are seen along the length of **myofibrils** in the sarcoplasm of skeletal and cardiac muscle cells.

Each sarcomere consists of thick and thin filaments whose arrangement is largely responsible for the banding pattern observed under light and electron microscopy (Figures 7–2 and 7–3).

Thin filaments measure 7 nm in width and 1μm in length and form the **I band**. In addition to actin, the thin filament contains **troponin, tropomyosin** (see Figure 7–8) **and nebulin** (see Figure 7–9).

Thick filaments measure 15 nm in width and 1.5 μm in length and are found in the **A band.** In addition to myosin, thick filaments contain **titin** (see Figure 7–9).

The A band is bisected by a light region called the **H band** (Figure 7–4). The major component of the H band is the enzyme **creatine kinase,** which catalyzes the formation of ATP from phosphocreatine and adenosine diphosphate (ADP) (see Figure 7–11).

Running through the midline of the H band is the **M line**. M-line striations correspond to a series of bridges and filaments linking the bare zone of thick filaments. Thin filaments insert into each side of the **Z disk,** whose components include α-**actinin**.

Components of the thin and thick filaments of the sarcomere

F-actin, the thin filament of the sarcomere, is double-stranded and twisted. F-actin is composed of globular monomers (**G-actin;** see The Cytoskeleton in Chapter 1, Epithelium). G-actin monomers bind to each other in a head-to-tail fashion, giving the filament polarity, with plus and minus ends. The plus end of actin filaments inserts into the Z disk.

Figure 7–4

The skeletal muscle cell

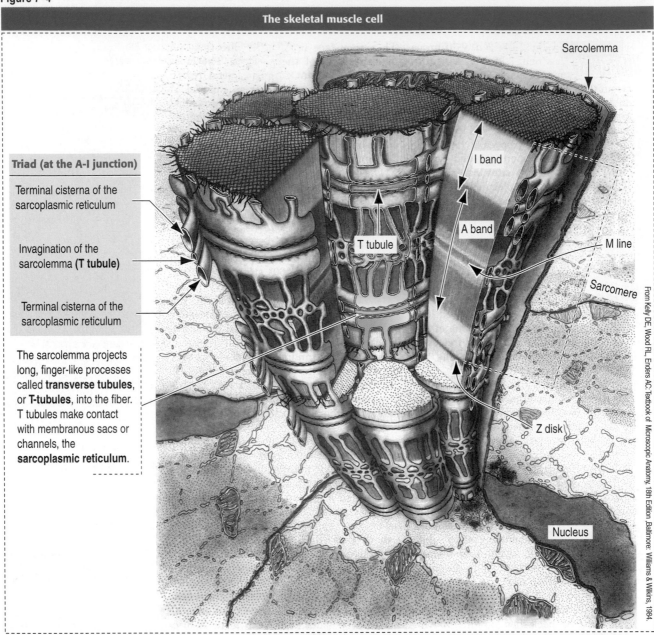

Triad (at the A-I junction)

Terminal cisterna of the
sarcoplasmic reticulum

Invagination of the
sarcolemma (**T tubule**)

Terminal cisterna of the
sarcoplasmic reticulum

The sarcolemma projects
long, finger-like processes
called **transverse tubules**,
or **T-tubules**, into the fiber.
T tubules make contact
with membranous sacs or
channels, the
sarcoplasmic reticulum.

Sarcolemma

I band

A band

T tubule

M line

Sarcomere

Z disk

Nucleus

From Kelly DE, Wood RL, Enders AC: Textbook of Microscopic Anatomy, 18th Edition. Baltimore: Williams & Wilkins, 1984.

Tropomyosin consists of two nearly identical α-helical polypeptides twisted around each other. Tropomyosin runs in the groove formed by F-actin strands. Each molecule of tropomyosin extends for the length of **seven actin monomers** and binds the **troponin complex** (see Figure 7–7).

Troponin is a complex of three proteins: **troponin I, C, and T. Troponin T** binds the complex to tropomyosin. **Troponin I** inhibits the binding of myosin to actin. **Troponin C** binds Ca^{2+} and is found only in striated muscle.

Nebulin (Figure 7–5) is associated with thin (actin) filaments, inserts into the Z disk; it acts as a template for determining the length of actin filaments.

Z disks are the insertion site of actin filaments of the sarcomere. A component of the Z disk, **α-actinin**, anchors the plus end of actin filaments to the Z disk.

Desmin is a 55-kDa protein that forms intermediate (10 nm) filaments. Desmin filaments encircle the Z disks of myofibrils and are linked to the Z disk and to each other by **plectin** filaments (see Figure 7–5). Desmin filaments ex-

Figure 7–5

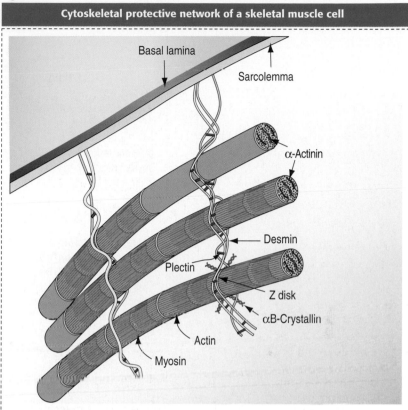

Cytoskeletal protective network of a skeletal muscle cell

A mechanical stress protective network around each myofibril at the Z disk

Desmin, an intermediate filament extending from one myofibril to the other and anchored to the sarcolemma, encircles the Z disk of each sarcomere.

Plectin links adjacent desmin filaments to each other.

α**B-Crystallin,** a heat shock protein associated with desmin, protects this intermediate filament from stress-induced damage.

tend from the Z disk of one myofibril to the adjacent myofibril, forming a supportive latticework. Desmin filaments also extend to the sarcolemma and the nuclear envelope.

The heat shock protein α**B-crystallin** protects desmin filaments from stress-induced damage. Desmin, plectin, and αB-crystallin form a mechanical stress protective network at the Z-disk level. Mutations in these three proteins lead to the destruction of myofibrils after repetitive mechanical stress.

Myosin, the major component of the thick filament, has adenosine triphosphatase (ATPase) activity (it hydrolyzes ATP) and binds to F-actin—the major component of the thin filament—in a reversible fashion.

Myosin consists of two identical **heavy chains** and two pairs of **light chains** (Figure 7–6; see The Cytoskeleton in Chapter 1, Epithelium). At one end, each heavy chain forms a globular head. Two different light chains are bound to each head: the **essential light chain** and the **regulatory light chain**. The globular head has three distinct regions: (1) an actin-binding region; (2) an ATP-binding region; and (3) a light chain–binding region.

Titin (Figure 7–8) is a very large protein with a molecular mass in the range of millions. Each molecule associates with thick (myosin) filaments and inserts into the Z disk, extending to the bare zone of the myosin filaments, close to the M line. Because titin molecules are highly elastic and stretch when muscle is

Figure 7–6

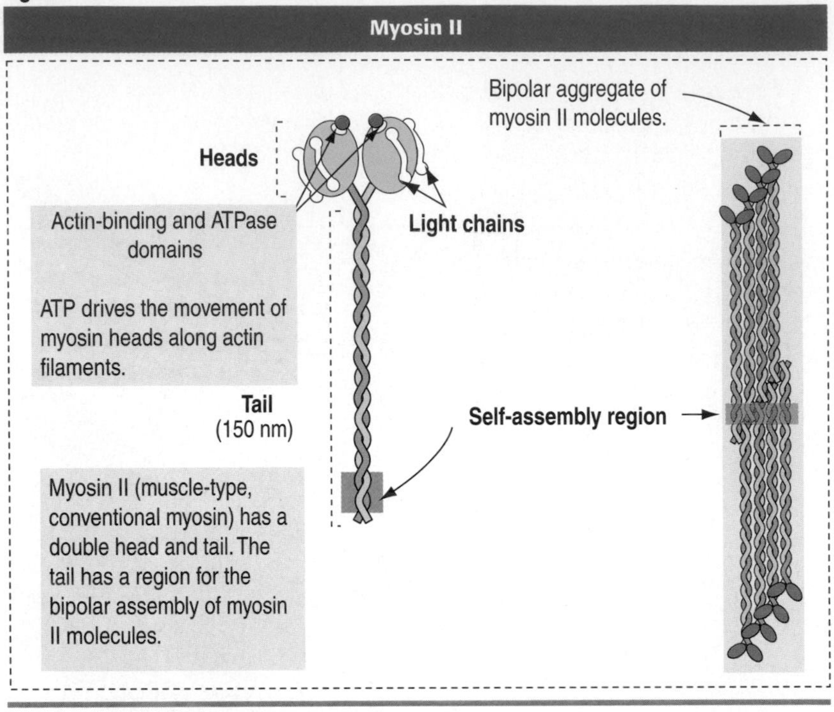

Myosin II

Bipolar aggregate of myosin II molecules.

Heads

Actin-binding and ATPase domains

ATP drives the movement of myosin heads along actin filaments.

Light chains

Tail
(150 nm)

Self-assembly region

Myosin II (muscle-type, conventional myosin) has a double head and tail. The tail has a region for the bipolar assembly of myosin II molecules.

stretched, they endow the myosin filaments with elastic recoil properties.

Mechanism of muscle contraction: Actin and myosin filaments slide past each other

During muscle contraction, the muscle shortens about one third of its original length. The relevant aspects of muscle shortening are summarized in Figure 7–9:

1. The **length** of the thick and thin filaments **does not change** during muscle contraction (the length of the A band and the distance between the Z disk and

Figure 7–7

Troponin and tropomyosin make striated muscle contraction sensitive to Ca²⁺

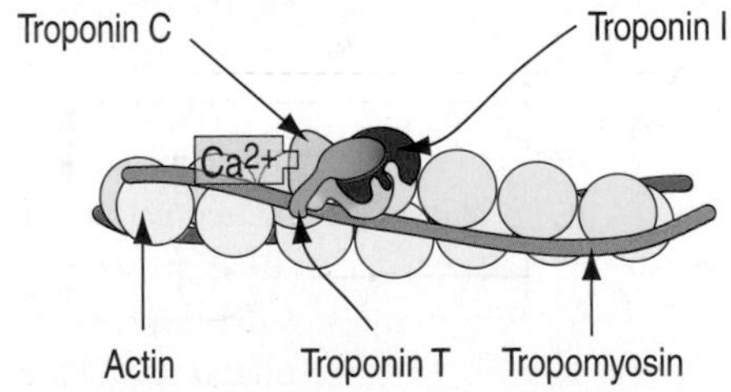

Troponin C

Troponin I

Ca²⁺

Actin

Troponin T

Tropomyosin

The troponin-tropomyosin-actin complex

Tropomyosin consists of two nearly identical α-helical polypeptides twisted around each other. Tropomyosin runs in the groove formed by F-actin strands. Each molecule of tropomyosin extends for the length of seven actin monomers and binds the troponin complex.

   Troponin is a complex of three proteins: **troponin I**, **C**, and **T**. Troponin T binds the complex to tropomyosin. Troponin I inhibits the binding of myosin to actin. Troponin C binds Ca²⁺ and is found only in striated muscle.

Figure 7–8

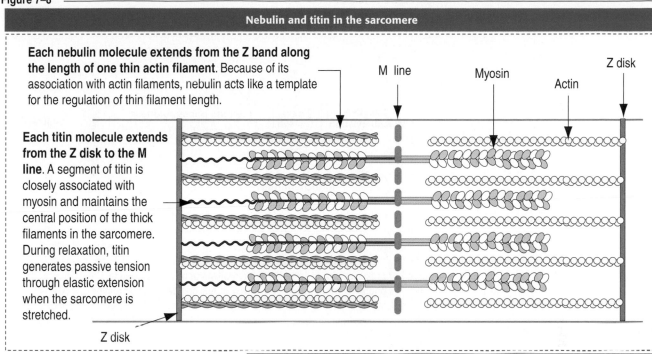

Nebulin and titin in the sarcomere

Each nebulin molecule extends from the Z band along the length of one thin actin filament. Because of its association with actin filaments, nebulin acts like a template for the regulation of thin filament length.

Each titin molecule extends from the Z disk to the M line. A segment of titin is closely associated with myosin and maintains the central position of the thick filaments in the sarcomere. During relaxation, titin generates passive tension through elastic extension when the sarcomere is stretched.

M line   Myosin   Actin   Z disk

Z disk

the adjacent H zone are constant).

2. The **length of the sarcomere decreases** because thick and thin filaments slide past each other (the size of the H zone and I band decrease).

3. The force of contraction is generated by the process that moves one type of filament past adjacent filaments of the other type.

The neuromuscular junction

A depolarization signal is transmitted from a nerve to a muscle at the **neuromuscular junction** (see Figure 7–11) to trigger contraction.

Figure 7–9

Length of the sarcomere during muscle contraction and relaxation

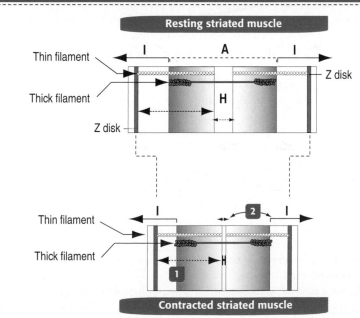

Resting striated muscle

Thin filament
Thick filament
Z disk
I   A   I
Z disk
H

Thin filament
Thick filament
I   2   I
H
1

Contracted striated muscle

During muscle contraction

1 The length of the thick and thin filaments does not change. This is demonstrated by **the constant length of the A band and the distance between the Z band and the adjacent edge of the H zone**.

2 The length of the sarcomere decreases because thick and thin filaments slide past each other. This is demonstrated by **a reduction in the length of the H zone and the I band**.

The A band represents the distribution of the myosin thick filaments. The H band indicates the myosin tail regions of the thick filaments is not overlapping with thin filaments.

Thin filaments are attached to the Z disk. Two half–I bands—containing thin filaments—are seen at the right and left side of the Z disk.

Figure 7–10

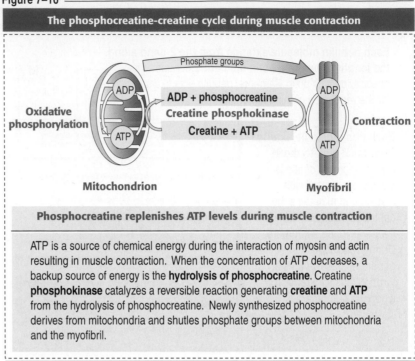

The phosphocreatine-creatine cycle during muscle contraction

Phosphate groups

ADP + phosphocreatine
Creatine phosphokinase
Creatine + ATP

Oxidative phosphorylation

Contraction

Mitochondrion

Myofibril

Phosphocreatine replenishes ATP levels during muscle contraction

ATP is a source of chemical energy during the interaction of myosin and actin resulting in muscle contraction. When the concentration of ATP decreases, a backup source of energy is the **hydrolysis of phosphocreatine**. Creatine **phosphokinase** catalyzes a reversible reaction generating **creatine** and **ATP** from the hydrolysis of phosphocreatine. Newly synthesized phosphocreatine derives from mitochondria and shutles phosphate groups between mitochondria and the myofibril.

The neuromuscular junction is a specialized structure formed by nerve terminals associated with the target muscle. Once inside the skeletal muscle, the nerve gives rise to several hundred branches, each innervating a single muscle fiber. The "parent" axon and all of the fibers it innervates form a **motor unit**. Muscles that require fine control have few muscle fibers per motor unit. Very large muscles contain several hundred fibers per motor unit.

When myelinated axons reach the perimysium, they lose their myelin sheath but remain covered with Schwann cell processes. The axon terminal contains mitochondria and membrane-bound vesicles filled with the neurotransmitter **acetylcholine** (see Figure 7–11). The neurotransmitter is released at dense areas on the cytoplasmic side of the axon membrane, called **active zones**.

Axon terminals occupy a depression of the muscle fiber, called the **primary synaptic cleft**. In this region, the sarcolemma is thrown into deep **junctional folds** (**secondary synaptic clefts**). Acetylcholine receptors are located at the crests of the folds and down into the folds (see Figure 7–11).

The basal lamina surrounding the muscle fiber extends into the synaptic cleft. The basal lamina contains **acetylcholinesterase**. The basal lamina covering the Schwann cell becomes continuous with the basal lamina of the muscle fiber.

Clinical significance: Disorders of neuromuscular transmission

Synaptic transmission at the neuromuscular junction can be affected by **curare** and **botulinum toxin** (see Figure 7–11).

Curare binds to the acetylcholine receptor and prevents binding of acetylcholine. Curare derivatives are used in surgical procedures in which muscle paralysis is necessary.

Botulinum toxin, an exotoxin from the bacterium *Clostridium botulinum*, prevents the release of acetylcholine at the presynaptic end. Muscle paralysis and dysfunction of the autonomous nervous system occur in cases of food poisoning mediated by botulinum toxin.

Myasthenia gravis is an autoimmune disease in which antibodies are produced against acetylcholine receptors (see Figures 7–11 and 7–13). Autoantibodies bind to the receptor, preventing the binding of acetylcholine. This blocks

Figure 7–11

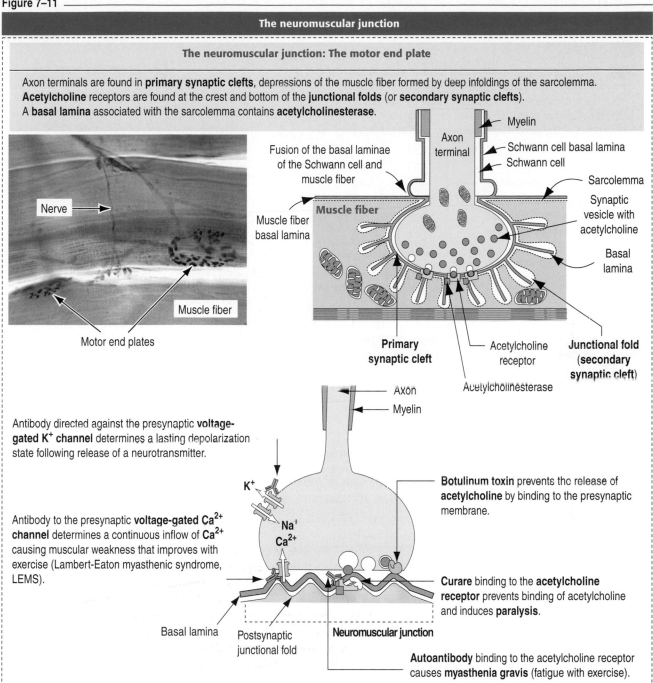

The neuromuscular junction

The neuromuscular junction: The motor end plate

Axon terminals are found in **primary synaptic clefts**, depressions of the muscle fiber formed by deep infoldings of the sarcolemma. **Acetylcholine** receptors are found at the crest and bottom of the **junctional folds** (or **secondary synaptic clefts**). A **basal lamina** associated with the sarcolemma contains **acetylcholinesterase**.

Nerve

Muscle fiber

Motor end plates

Myelin

Axon terminal

Schwann cell basal lamina

Schwann cell

Fusion of the basal laminae of the Schwann cell and muscle fiber

Muscle fiber basal lamina

Muscle fiber

Sarcolemma

Synaptic vesicle with acetylcholine

Basal lamina

Primary synaptic cleft

Acetylcholine receptor

Acetylcholinesterase

Junctional fold (secondary synaptic cleft)

Axon

Myelin

Antibody directed against the presynaptic **voltage-gated K⁺ channel** determines a lasting depolarization state following release of a neurotransmitter.

Antibody to the presynaptic **voltage-gated Ca²⁺ channel** determines a continuous inflow of **Ca²⁺** causing muscular weakness that improves with exercise (Lambert-Eaton myasthenic syndrome, LEMS).

K^+

Na^+
Ca^{2+}

Botulinum toxin prevents the release of **acetylcholine** by binding to the presynaptic membrane.

Curare binding to the **acetylcholine receptor** prevents binding of acetylcholine and induces **paralysis**.

Basal lamina

Postsynaptic junctional fold

Neuromuscular junction

Autoantibody binding to the acetylcholine receptor causes **myasthenia gravis** (fatigue with exercise).

normal nerve-muscle interaction and results in progressive muscle weakness.

A depolarization signal travels inside the muscle by T tubules

In response to an **action potential**, acetylcholine is released from the axon. Acetylcholine diffuses across the plasma membrane and binds to its receptor in the sarcolemma.

The **depolarization signal** is transmitted deep into the fiber by the **T tubules**, which form rings around every sarcomere of every myofibril **at the A-I junction**. T tubules are flanked on each side by the terminal cisternae of the sarcoplasmic reticulum, forming a tripartite membrane structure, the **triad**. At each triad, the depolarization signal is transmitted to the sarcoplasmic reticulum, and Ca²⁺ is released, beginning the contraction sequence (see Figure 7–12).

Figure 7–12

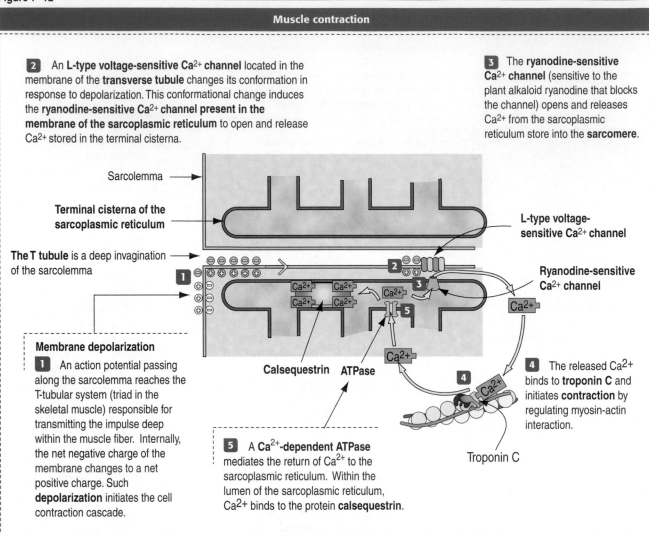

Muscle contraction

2 An **L-type voltage-sensitive Ca²⁺ channel** located in the membrane of the **transverse tubule** changes its conformation in response to depolarization. This conformational change induces the **ryanodine-sensitive Ca²⁺ channel present in the membrane of the sarcoplasmic reticulum** to open and release Ca²⁺ stored in the terminal cisterna.

3 The **ryanodine-sensitive Ca²⁺ channel** (sensitive to the plant alkaloid ryanodine that blocks the channel) opens and releases Ca²⁺ from the sarcoplasmic reticulum store into the **sarcomere**.

Sarcolemma

Terminal cisterna of the sarcoplasmic reticulum

The T tubule is a deep invagination of the sarcolemma

L-type voltage-sensitive Ca²⁺ channel

Ryanodine-sensitive Ca²⁺ channel

Membrane depolarization

1 An action potential passing along the sarcolemma reaches the T-tubular system (triad in the skeletal muscle) responsible for transmitting the impulse deep within the muscle fiber. Internally, the net negative charge of the membrane changes to a net positive charge. Such **depolarization** initiates the cell contraction cascade.

Calsequestrin   ATPase

5 A **Ca²⁺-dependent ATPase** mediates the return of Ca²⁺ to the sarcoplasmic reticulum. Within the lumen of the sarcoplasmic reticulum, Ca²⁺ binds to the protein **calsequestrin**.

4 The released Ca²⁺ binds to **troponin C** and initiates **contraction** by regulating myosin-actin interaction.

Troponin C

Calcium controls muscle contraction

In the absence of Ca²⁺, muscle is relaxed and the troponin-tropomyosin complex blocks the myosin binding site on the actin filament.

When a depolarization signal arrives, Ca²⁺ increases within the muscle cell. Ca²⁺ binds to troponin C and causes a change in configuration of the troponin-tropomyosin complex. As a result, the myosin-binding site on the actin filament is exposed. Myosin heads bind to the actin filament, and hydrolysis of ATP occurs. ATP is supplied by creatine phosphokinase (Figure 7–10).

Creatine phosphokinase is an enzyme found in soluble form in the **sarcoplasm** and also is a component of the **M-line region** of the H band. Creatine phosphokinase catalyzes the transfer of phosphate from phosphocreatine to ADP.

The energy of hydrolysis of ATP produces a change in the position of the myosin head, and the thin filaments are pulled past the thick filaments. Contraction results in the complete overlap of the A and I bands. The contraction continues until Ca²⁺ is removed.

The sarcoplasmic reticulum, a network of smooth endoplasmic reticulum surrounding each myofibril (see Figure 7–4), stores Ca²⁺. In response to depolarization signals, the sarcoplasmic reticulum releases Ca²⁺. When membrane depolarization ends, Ca²⁺ is pumped back into the sarcoplasmic reticulum (see Figure 7–12), where it binds to the protein **calsequestrin**. Contraction can no longer take place.

Figure 7–13

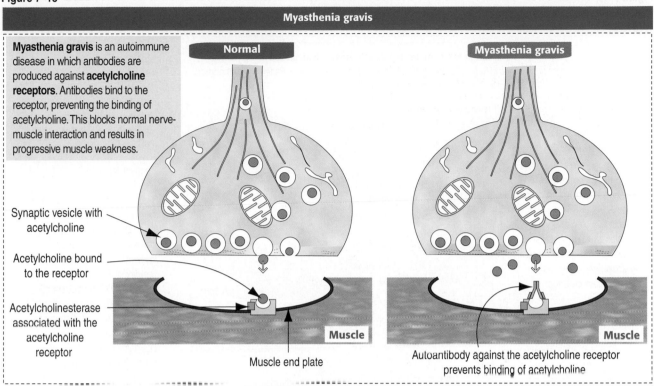

Myasthenia gravis

Myasthenia gravis is an autoimmune disease in which antibodies are produced against **acetylcholine receptors**. Antibodies bind to the receptor, preventing the binding of acetylcholine. This blocks normal nerve-muscle interaction and results in progressive muscle weakness.

Normal

Myasthenia gravis

Synaptic vesicle with acetylcholine

Acetylcholine bound to the receptor

Acetylcholinesterase associated with the acetylcholine receptor

Muscle

Muscle

Muscle end plate

Autoantibody against the acetylcholine receptor prevents binding of acetylcholine

Clinical significance: Muscular dystrophies

Muscular dystrophies are a group of congenital muscular diseases characterized by muscle weakness, atrophy, elevation of serum levels of muscle enzymes, and destructive changes of muscle tissue (Figure 7–14).

Deficiency in the **dystrophin-associated protein (DAP) complex**, a group of transmembrane proteins linking the cytoskeletal protein **dystrophin** to the extracellular matrix protein **laminin 2**, accounts for specific clinical syndromes.

The muscular dystrophies are classified according to the genes involved and the defective proteins, components of the cytoskeleton, the sarcolemma, or the extracellular matrix.

The most important muscle proteins involved in muscular dystrophies are **dystrophin**, the **dystroglycan complex**, **merosin**, and the **sarcoglycan complex**.

Dystrophin, a 427-kDa cytoskeletal protein, anchors **actin** to the sarcolemma. **The function of dystrophin is to reinforce and stabilize the sarcolemma during the stress of muscle contraction** by maintaining a mechanical link between the cytoskeleton and the extracellular matrix. Deficiencies of dystrophin are characteristic of **Duchenne's muscular dystrophy (DMD)**.

DMD is an X chromosome linked recessive disorder caused by a mutation in the dystrophin gene. The disorder is detected in affected boys after they begin to walk. Progressive muscle weakness and wasting, sudden episodes of vomiting (caused by delayed gastric emptying), and abdominal pain are observed. A typical laboratory finding is **increased serum creatine kinase levels**. Muscle biopsies reveal muscle destruction and **absence of dystrophin**, detected by immunohistochemistry. **Heterozygote female carriers** may be asymptomatic or have mild muscle weakness, muscle cramps, and elevated serum creatine kinase levels. Women with these mutations may give birth to affected males or carrier females.

Sarcoglycanopathies in limb girdle muscular dystrophies have mutations in the genes for α-, β-, γ-, and δ-sarcoglycan that cause defective assembly of the sarcoglycans, thus disrupting their interaction with the other dystroglycan com-

Figure 7–14

Muscular dystrophies

The **dystroglycan complex links dystrophin to laminin-2**. Dystroglycan-α binds to laminin-2 and dystroglycan-β binds to dystrophin. Patients with a primary defect in dystroglycans have not been identified.

A mutation in laminin-2 causes congenital muscle dystrophy.

The components of the **sarcoglycan complex** are specific for cardiac and skeletal muscle.
Defects in the components of the complex cause autosomal recessive **limb-girdle muscular dystrophies** (known as **sarcoglycanopathies**).

Dystrophin reinforces and stabilizes the sarcolemma during the stress of muscle contraction by maintaining a link between the cytoskeleton and the extracellular matrix. When dystrophin is absent, the sarcolemma is disrupted, allowing calcium entry which causes necrosis of the muscle fiber.
A deficiency in dystrophin is typical of **Duchenne's muscular dystrophy**, an X-linked recessive condition.

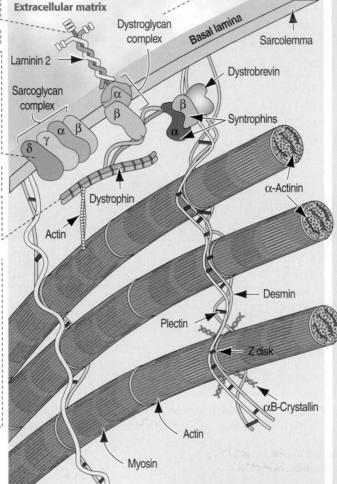

Structural muscle proteins associated with mutations causing myopathies

The **Z disk** is the insertion site of actin filaments of the sarcomere and plays a role in the transmission of tension through the myofibril.

Desmin filaments (intermediate filament protein) encircle the Z disks and are linked to them and to one another by **plectin** filaments. By this association, desmin: (1) **integrates mechanically the contractile action of adjacent myofibrils**, and (2) **links the Z disk to the sarcolemma**.
The heat shock protein α**B-crystallin** protects desmin filaments from stress-dependent damage.

Note that **desmin, plectin, and** α**B-crystallin form a network around the Z disks**, thus protecting the integrity of the myofibrils during mechanical stress.

Mutations of desmin, plectin, and α**B-crystallin** cause fragility of the myofibrils and their destruction after continuous stress.

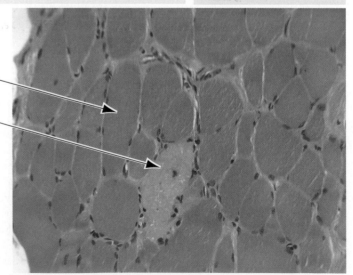

Cross section of a normal skeletal muscle fiber with the characteristic peripheral nucleus.

Degenerating skeletal muscle fiber in the early stages of Duchenne's muscular dystrophy.

Muscular dystrophies are a heterogeneous group of congenital muscle diseases characterized by severe muscle weakness, and atrophy and destruction of muscle fibers. Several genetic defects in muscle transmembrane proteins linking the cytoskeletal protein dystrophin to the extracellular matrix protein **laminin-2** (also called merosin) are responsible for muscular dystrophies. The most important muscle proteins involved in muscular dystrophies are **dystrophin**, the **dystroglycan complex** associated with laminin-2, and the **sarcoglycan complex**. Dystrophin (427 kDa) anchors actin to the sarcolemma.

Figure 7–15

Satellite cells and muscle regeneration

Myotube

Satellite cell

Myotube

Myoblast nucleus

Satellite cell

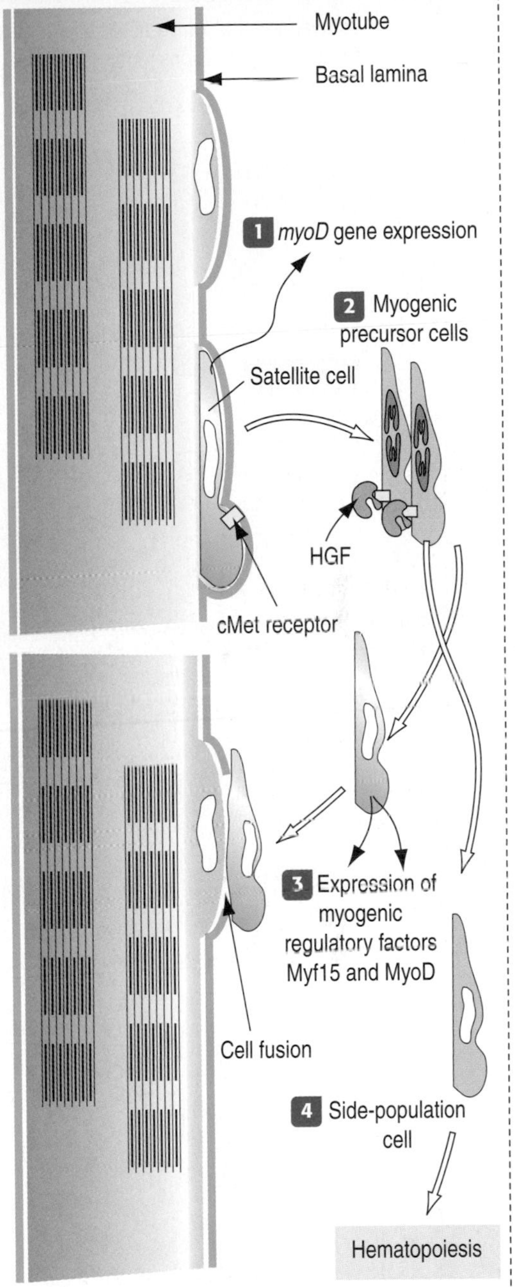

Myotube

Basal lamina

1 *myoD* gene expression

2 Myogenic precursor cells

Satellite cell

HGF

cMet receptor

3 Expression of myogenic regulatory factors Myf15 and MyoD

Cell fusion

4 Side-population cell

Hematopoiesis

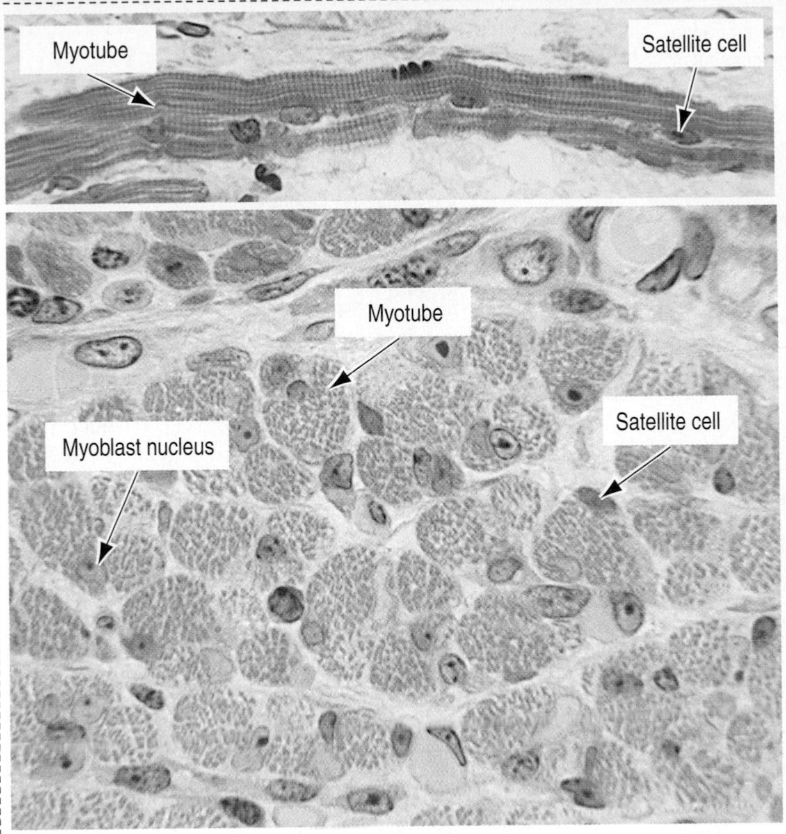

1 A basal lamina surrounds both the myotube and associated satellite cell. Mitotically quiescent satellite cells in the adult can reassume proliferation in response to stress or trauma. The expression of **MyoD**, a transcription factor, induces the proliferation of satellite cells. The **c-Met receptor** on the surface of satellite cells has strong binding affinity for the chemotactic agent **HGF** (**hepatocyte growth factor**).

2 Daughter cells of the activated satellite cells—**myogenic precursor cells**—undergo several rounds of cell division. HGF-cMet binding induces the proliferation of the satellite cells.

3 Myogenic precursor cells—expressing the myoblast-specific MRF **Myf5** and **MyoD**—fuse with existing or new myotubes.

4 A population of stem cells in adult skeletal muscle—called **side-population cells**—have the capacity to differentiate into all major blood cell lineages.

plex proteins and the association of the sarcolemma with the extracellular matrix.

Clinical significance: Satellite cells and muscle regeneration

Muscle development involves the chain like alignment and fusion of committed muscle cell precursors, the **myoblasts**, to form multinucleated **myotubes**. Two critical events occur during the commitment of the muscle cell precursor to myogenesis: (1) the cessation of proliferation of the precursor determined by both the upregulated expression of **myogenic regulatory factors (MRFs) Myf5** and **MyoD** and the downregulation of **Pax7**, a transcription factor; (2) the terminal differentiation of the muscle cell precursor triggered by myogenic regu-

Figure 7–16

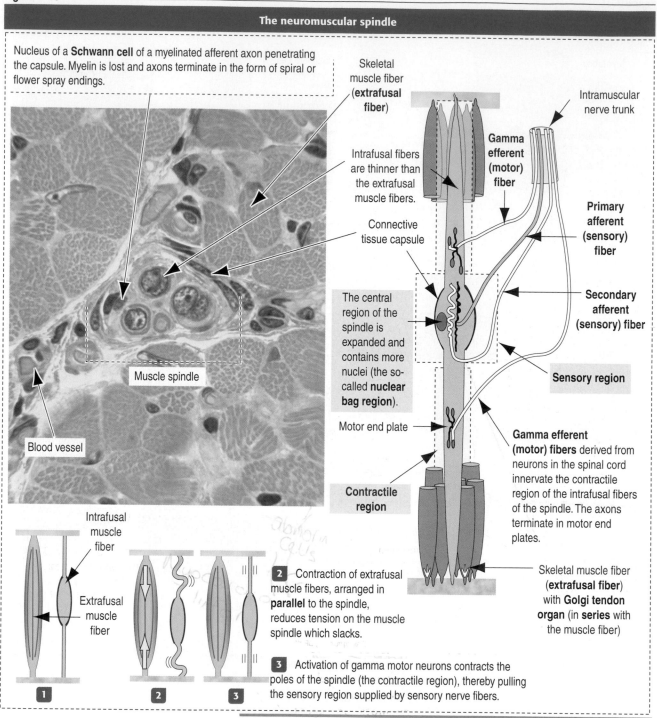

The neuromuscular spindle

Nucleus of a **Schwann cell** of a myelinated afferent axon penetrating the capsule. Myelin is lost and axons terminate in the form of spiral or flower spray endings.

Blood vessel

Muscle spindle

Skeletal muscle fiber (**extrafusal fiber**)

Intrafusal fibers are thinner than the extrafusal muscle fibers.

Connective tissue capsule

The central region of the spindle is expanded and contains more nuclei (the so-called **nuclear bag region**).

Motor end plate

Contractile region

Intramuscular nerve trunk

Gamma efferent (motor) fiber

Primary afferent (sensory) fiber

Secondary afferent (sensory) fiber

Sensory region

Gamma efferent (motor) fibers derived from neurons in the spinal cord innervate the contractile region of the intrafusal fibers of the spindle. The axons terminate in motor end plates.

Skeletal muscle fiber (**extrafusal fiber**) with **Golgi tendon organ** (in **series** with the muscle fiber)

Intrafusal muscle fiber

Extrafusal muscle fiber

2 Contraction of extrafusal muscle fibers, arranged in **parallel** to the spindle, reduces tension on the muscle spindle which slacks.

3 Activation of gamma motor neurons contracts the poles of the spindle (the contractile region), thereby pulling the sensory region supplied by sensory nerve fibers.

1   **2**   **3**

latory factors **myogenin** and MRF4.

 Satellite cells, a cell population distinct from the myoblasts, attach to the surface of the myotubes before a **basal lamina** surrounds both the satellite cell and myotube (Figure 7–15). Satellite cells are of considerable significance in muscle maintenance, repair, and regeneration in the adult. Although satellite cells are mitotically quiescent in the adult, they can reassume proliferation in response to stress or trauma. The expression of **MyoD**, a transcription factor, induces the proliferation of satellite cells. The descendents of the activated satellite cells—called **myogenic precursor cells**—undergo multiple rounds of cell division before they can fuse with existing or new myofibers.

Figure 7–17

Cardiac muscle

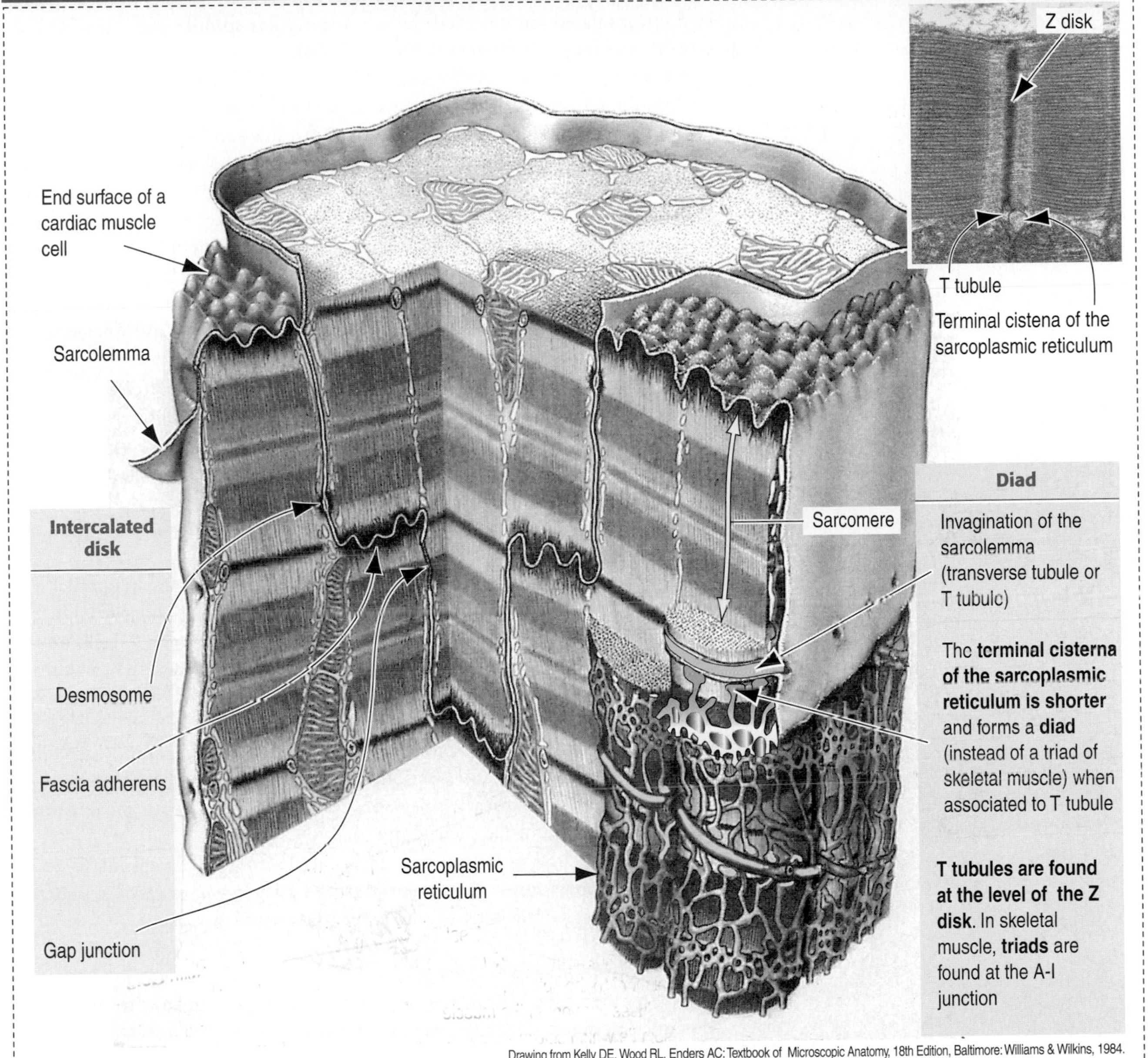

End surface of a cardiac muscle cell

Sarcolemma

Intercalated disk

Desmosome

Fascia adherens

Gap junction

Sarcomere

Sarcoplasmic reticulum

Z disk

T tubule

Terminal cistena of the sarcoplasmic reticulum

Diad

Invagination of the sarcolemma (transverse tubule or T tubule)

The **terminal cisterna of the sarcoplasmic reticulum is shorter** and forms a **diad** (instead of a triad of skeletal muscle) when associated to T tubule

T tubules are found at the level of the Z disk. In skeletal muscle, **triads** are found at the A-I junction

Drawing from Kelly DE, Wood RL, Enders AC: Textbook of Microscopic Anatomy, 18th Edition, Baltimore: Williams & Wilkins, 1984.

Quiescent satellite cells express a receptor on their surface encoded by the proto-oncogene **c-Met**. The c-Met receptor has strong binding affinity for the chemotactic agent **HGF** (hepatocyte growth factor). HGF-c-Met binding up regulates a signaling cascade leading to proliferation of the satellite cells and the expression of the myoblast-specific MRF Myf5 and MyoD.

In addition to satellite cells as progenitors of the myogenic cells in adult skeletal muscle, a population of stem cells in adult skeletal muscle—**side-population cells**—have the capacity to differentiate into all major blood cell lineages as well as myogenic satellite cells. Side-population cells are present in bone marrow and have the capacity to give rise to myogenic cells that can participate in muscle regeneration.

The pluripotent nature of satellite cells and side-population cells raises the possibility of stem cell therapy of a number of degenerative diseases, including muscular dystrophy.

The neuromuscular spindle

The central nervous system continuously monitors the position of the limbs and the state of contraction of the various muscles. Muscles contain a specialized encapsulated sensor called the **neuromuscular spindle** that contains both sensory and motor components (Figure 7–16).

A neuromuscular spindle consists of 2 to 14 specialized striated muscle fibers enclosed in a fusiform sheath or capsule of connective tissue. They are 5 to 10 mm long and therefore much shorter than the surrounding contractile muscle fibers. The specialized muscle fibers in the interior of the neuromuscular spindle are called **intrafusal fibers** to distinguish them from the nonspecialized **extrafusal fibers** (Lat. *extra*, outside; *fusus*, spindle), the regular skeletal muscle fibers.

There are two kinds of intrafusal fibers designated by their histologic appearance: (1) **nuclear bag fiber**, consisting of a central sensory baglike region, and (2) the **nuclear chain fiber**, so called because its central portion contains a chainlike array of nuclei. The distal portion of both nuclear bag and nuclear chain fibers consists of striated muscle with contractile properties.

The neuromuscular spindle is innervated by two types of afferent axons making contact with the central (receptor) region of the intrafusal fibers. Two types of anterior motor neurons of the spinal cord give rise to motor nerve fibers: the large **alpha motor neurons** innervate the **extrafusal fibers** of muscles; the smaller **gamma motor neurons** innervate the **intrafusal fibers** in the spindle.

Sensory nerve endings are arranged around the central nuclear region and sense the degree of tension of the intrafusal fibers.

The intrafusal muscle fibers of the neuromuscular spindle are in **parallel** with the extrafusal muscle fibers. When the extrafusal muscle fibers contract (shorten), the neuromuscular spindle becomes slack. If the spindle remains slack, no further information about the **muscle length** can be transmitted to the spinal cord. This situation is corrected by a feedback control mechanism by which the sensory region of the spindle activates gamma motoneurons, which contract the poles of the spindle (the contractile region). Consequently, the spindle stretches. In addition to the neuromuscular spindle, **Golgi tendon organs**, located **in series** with the extrafusal muscle fibers, provide information about the **tension** or force of contraction of the skeletal muscle.

By detecting changes in muscle length, the neuromuscular spindle is an example of a **proprioceptor** (Lat. *proprius*, one's own; *capio*, to take), a structure which informs how the body is positioned and moves in space.

Types of skeletal muscle fibers

There are three types of skeletal muscle fibers: **red**, **white**, and **intermediate**. Most skeletal muscles contain a mixture of the three types of fibers. All myofibers in a given motor unit are of the same type.

Red fibers are found in **slow twitch** motor units. They are relatively small in diameter with abundant mitochondria. They are resistant to fatigue, and therefore are suited for prolonged muscular activity (for example, maintenance of posture).

White fibers are found in **fast twitch** motor units. They are relatively large, with fewer mitochondria than red fibers. They are rapidly contracting and generally responsible for movement (for example, extraocular muscle).

Intermediate fibers exhibit characteristics between red and white fibers. Human muscles often consist of a mixture of the three types.

Cardiac muscle

Cardiac cells (or **cardiocytes**) are branched cylinders, 85 to 100 μm long, approximately 1.5 μm in diameter (Figure 7–17), with a **single centrally located nucleus** (Figure 7–18).

The organization of contractile proteins is the same as found in skeletal muscle.

Figure 7–18

Structure of the cardiac muscle cell or cardiocyte

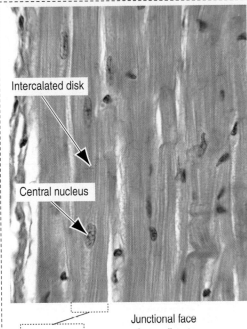

Intercalated disk

Central nucleus

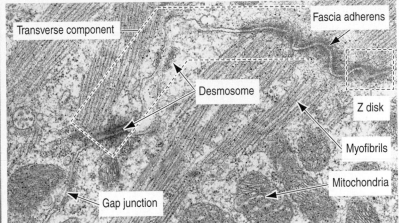

Transverse component

Fascia adherens

Desmosome

Z disk

Myofibrils

Mitochondria

Gap junction

An intercalated disk is located between cardiac muscle cells and consists of a stepwise arrangement of **transverse** and **longitudinal components**. The transverse component —located at the **Z disk**—is formed by the **facia adherens** (Pl., *adherentes*) and **desmosomes**. Actin, α-actinin attach to the fascia adherens. **Desmin** is linked to the desmosome. **Gap junctions** are the major structures of the longitudinal component.

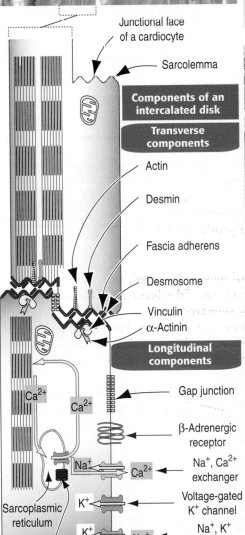

Junctional face of a cardiocyte

Sarcolemma

Components of an intercalated disk

Transverse components

Actin

Desmin

Fascia adherens

Desmosome

Vinculin

α-Actinin

Longitudinal components

Ca^{2+}

Ca^{2+}

Gap junction

β-Adrenergic receptor

Na^+ Ca^{2+} — Na$^+$, Ca^{2+} exchanger

K^+ — Voltage-gated K$^+$ channel

K^+ Na^+ — Na$^+$, K$^+$ ATPase

Sarcoplasmic reticulum

Phospholamban

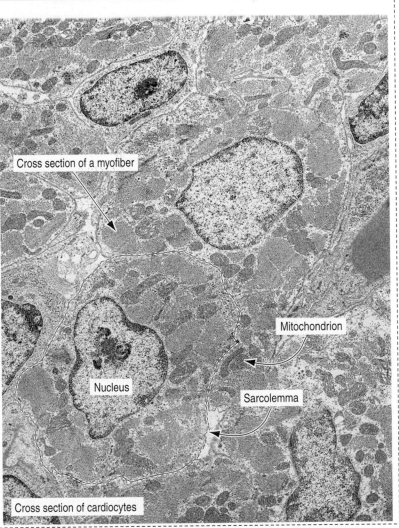

Cross section of a myofiber

Mitochondrion

Nucleus

Sarcolemma

Cross section of cardiocytes

Figure 7–19

Myocardial infarction

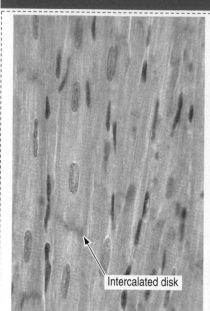

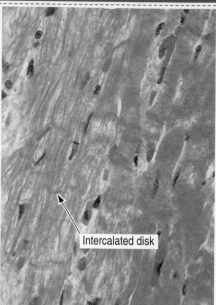

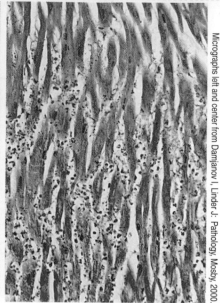

Intercalated disk

Intercalated disk

Micrographs left and center from Damjanov I, Linder J: Pathology. Mosby, 2000.

Normal cardiac tissue consists of branching and anastomosing striated cardiocytes with a central nucleus and intracellular contractile myofilaments. Intercalated disks join individual cardiocytes.

Myocardial ischemia caused by occlusion of the coronary artery results within the first **24 hours** in the necrosis of cardiocytes. Cardiocytes display an eosinophilic cytoplasm lacking the characteristic intracellular striations detected in the adjacent unaffected cardiocytes. The nuclei are pyknotic (Gk. *pyknos*, dense, thick; *osis*, condition) and irregularly shaped. Lactic dehydrogenase-1 and creatine kinase MB*—released from dead cardiocytes—are detected in serum. Serum levels of these enzymes remain elevated days after the myocardial infarction.

Three days later, the necrotic cardiocytes are surrounded by neutrophils.
After 3 weeks (not shown), capillaries, fibroblasts, macrophage, and lymphocytes are observed in the necrotic area. After 3 months, the infarcted region is replaced by scar tissue.

*Creatine kinase (CK) is composed of two dimers, M and B. CK-MM isoenzyme predominates in skeletal muscle and heart. CK-BB is present in brain, lung, and other tissues. CK-MB is characteristic of myocardium.

However, the cytomembranes exhibit some differences:

1. T tubules **are found at the level of the Z disk**, and are substantially larger than those of skeletal muscle found at the A-I junction.

2. The sarcoplasmic reticulum is not as extensive as that of skeletal muscle.

3. **Diads**, rather than the triads seen in skeletal muscle are typical in cardiocytes (see Figure 7–17). A diad consists of a T tubule interacting with just one sarcoplasmic reticulum cisterna (instead of two, as in skeletal muscle).

4. **Mitochondria are more abundant in cardiac muscle** than in skeletal muscle and contain numerous cristae.

The cells are joined end to end by specialized junctional complexes called **intercalated disks**. Intercalated disks have a steplike arrangement, with **transverse portions** that run perpendicular to the long axis of the cell and longitudinal portions running in parallel to the myofibrils.

The transverse component is represented by the **Z disk** and consists of (1) **desmosomes**, which mechanically link cardiac cells, and (2) **fasciae adherentes**, which contain **α-actinin** and **vinculin** and provide an insertion site for the actin-containing thin filaments of the last sarcomere of each cardiocyte.

Gap junctions, restricted to the longitudinal portion of the intercalated disk, enable ionic communication between cells leading to synchronous muscle contraction.

The terminal fibers of the conducting system of the heart are specialized, glycogen-rich **Purkinje fibers**. Compared with the contractile fibers, Purkinje fibers are larger, paler-stained, and contain fewer myofibrils (see Chapter 12, Cardiovascular System, for additional details).

Clinical significance: Transport proteins on the sarcolemma of cardiocytes

The sarcolemma of the cardiocyte contains specific **transport proteins** (see Figure 7–18) controlling the release and reuptake of ions critical for systolic contractile function and diastolic relaxation.

Active transport of Ca^{2+} into the lumen of the sarcoplasmic reticulum by Ca^{2+}-dependent ATPase is controlled by **phospholamban**. The activity of phospholamban is regulated by phosphorylation. Changes in the amount and activity of phospholamban—regulated by **thyroid hormone**—may alter diastolic function during heart failure and thyroid disease. An increase in heart rate and cardiac output is observed in hyperthyroidism.

Additional transporters, including the **Na⁺, Ca^{2+} exchanger** and **voltage-gated K⁺ channels**, regulate the intracellular levels of K⁺ and Na⁺. **β-Adrenergic receptor** is also present in the sarcolemma.

Figure 7–20

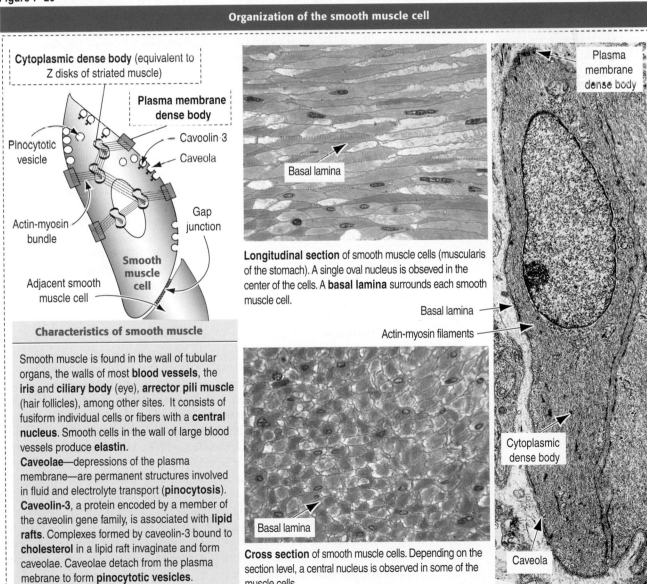

Organization of the smooth muscle cell

Cytoplasmic dense body (equivalent to Z disks of striated muscle)

Plasma membrane dense body

Pinocytotic vesicle

Caveolin-3

Caveola

Actin-myosin bundle

Gap junction

Adjacent smooth muscle cell

Smooth muscle cell

Characteristics of smooth muscle

Smooth muscle is found in the wall of tubular organs, the walls of most **blood vessels**, the **iris** and **ciliary body** (eye), **arrector pili muscle** (hair follicles), among other sites. It consists of fusiform individual cells or fibers with a **central nucleus**. Smooth cells in the wall of large blood vessels produce **elastin**.

Caveolae—depressions of the plasma membrane—are permanent structures involved in fluid and electrolyte transport (**pinocytosis**). **Caveolin-3**, a protein encoded by a member of the caveolin gene family, is associated with **lipid rafts**. Complexes formed by caveolin-3 bound to **cholesterol** in a lipid raft invaginate and form caveolae. Caveolae detach from the plasma mebrane to form **pinocytotic vesicles**.

Plasma membrane dense body

Longitudinal section of smooth muscle cells (muscularis of the stomach). A single oval nucleus is obseved in the center of the cells. A **basal lamina** surrounds each smooth muscle cell.

Basal lamina

Basal lamina

Actin-myosin filaments

Cytoplasmic dense body

Caveola

Basal lamina

Cross section of smooth muscle cells. Depending on the section level, a central nucleus is observed in some of the muscle cells.

Figure 7–21

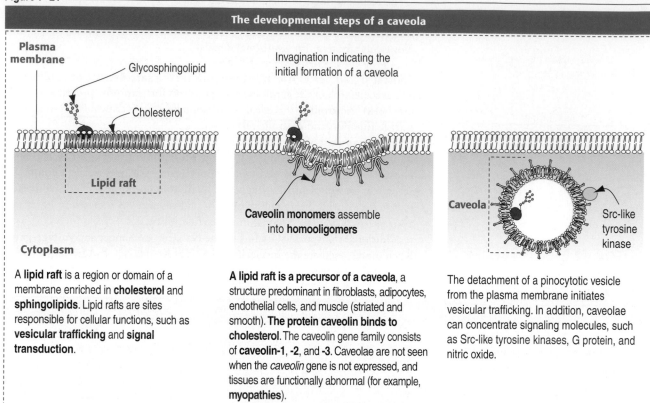

The developmental steps of a caveola

Plasma membrane

Glycosphingolipid

Cholesterol

Lipid raft

Cytoplasm

Invagination indicating the initial formation of a caveola

Caveolin monomers assemble into **homooligomers**

Caveola

Src-like tyrosine kinase

A **lipid raft** is a region or domain of a membrane enriched in **cholesterol** and **sphingolipids**. Lipid rafts are sites responsible for cellular functions, such as **vesicular trafficking** and **signal transduction**.

A lipid raft is a precursor of a caveola, a structure predominant in fibroblasts, adipocytes, endothelial cells, and muscle (striated and smooth). **The protein caveolin binds to cholesterol**. The caveolin gene family consists of **caveolin-1**, **-2**, and **-3**. Caveolae are not seen when the *caveolin* gene is not expressed, and tissues are functionally abnormal (for example, **myopathies**).

The detachment of a pinocytotic vesicle from the plasma membrane initiates vesicular trafficking. In addition, caveolae can concentrate signaling molecules, such as Src-like tyrosine kinases, G protein, and nitric oxide.

Clinical significance: Myocardial infarction

Myocardial infarction is the consequence of a loss of blood supply to the myocardium caused by an obstruction of an atherosclerotic coronary artery. The clinical outcome depends on the anatomic region affected and the extent and duration of disrupted blood flow.

Irreversible damage of cardiocytes occurs when the loss of blood supply lasts more than 20 minutes. If blood flow is restored in less than 20 minutes—an event known as **reperfusion**—cardiocyte cell viability is maintained. Timing is critical for implementing early therapy to re-establish blood flow by using thrombolytic agents. The histologic changes of myocardial infarction are summarized in Figure 7–19.

Smooth muscle

Smooth muscle may be found as sheets or bundles in the walls of the gut, bile duct, ureters, urinary bladder, respiratory tract, uterus, and blood vessels.

Smooth muscle differs from skeletal and cardiac muscle: smooth muscle cells are **spindle-shaped, tapering cells** with a **central nucleus** (Figure 7–20). The perinuclear cytoplasm contains mitochondria, ribosomes, rough endoplasmic reticulum, a Golgi apparatus, and a latticework of thick **myosin** filaments, thin actin filaments, and intermediate filaments composed of desmin and vimentin. **Actin** and **intermediate filaments** insert into cytoplasmic and plasma membrane–associated structures rich in α-actinin, called **dense bodies**.

Invaginations of the plasma membrane, called **caveolae** act as a primitive T tubule system, transmitting depolarization signals to the underdeveloped sarcoplasmic reticulum. The development of caveolae from **lipid rafts** and their diverse roles in several tissues are shown in Figure 7–21. Smooth muscle cells are linked to each other by gap junctions. Gap junctions permit synchronous contraction of the smooth muscle.

A **basal lamina** surrounds each muscle cell and serves to transmit forces pro-

Figure 7–22

The regulation of smooth muscle contraction

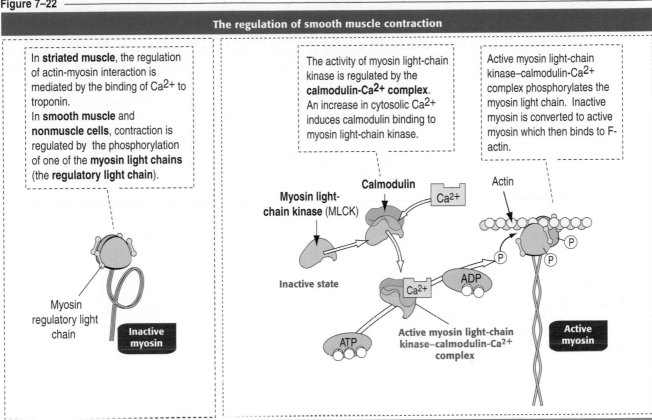

In **striated muscle**, the regulation of actin-myosin interaction is mediated by the binding of Ca^{2+} to troponin.
In **smooth muscle** and **nonmuscle cells**, contraction is regulated by the phosphorylation of one of the **myosin light chains** (the **regulatory light chain**).

Myosin regulatory light chain

Inactive myosin

The activity of myosin light-chain kinase is regulated by the **calmodulin-Ca^{2+} complex**. An increase in cytosolic Ca^{2+} induces calmodulin binding to myosin light-chain kinase.

Active myosin light-chain kinase–calmodulin-Ca^{2+} complex phosphorylates the myosin light chain. Inactive myosin is converted to active myosin which then binds to F-actin.

Myosin light-chain kinase (MLCK)

Calmodulin

Ca^{2+}

Actin

Inactive state

ATP

Ca^{2+}

ADP

P

P

P

Active myosin light-chain kinase–calmodulin-Ca^{2+} complex

Active myosin

duced by each cell.

Mechanism of smooth muscle contraction

Both the arrangement of the contractile proteins and the mechanism of contraction of smooth muscle differ from those of skeletal and cardiac muscle:

1. Actin and myosin filaments are not organized in sarcomeres as seen in cardiac and skeletal muscle.

2. **Smooth muscle cells do not contain troponin** but do contain tropomyosin, which binds to and stabilizes actin filaments.

3. Ca^{2+} ions that initiate contraction derive from outside the cell rather than from the sarcoplasmic reticulum.

4. **Myosin light-chain kinase,** instead of troponin, which is not present in smooth muscle cells, is responsible for the Ca^{2+} sensitivity of the contractile fibers in smooth muscle.

We have seen that the sliding of the myosin-actin complex in striated muscle is the basis for contraction (see Figure 7–9). In smooth muscle, actin filaments and associated myosin attach to cytoplasmic and plasma membrane **dense bodies**, representing the equivalent of the Z disk of striated muscle (see Figure 7–20). Dense bodies are attached to the plasma membrane through desmin and vimentin intermediate filaments. When the actin-myosin complex contracts, their attachment to the dense bodies determines cell shortening.

Calcium-dependent phosphorylation of myosin regulatory light chains is responsible for the contraction of smooth muscle (Figure 7–22).

Smooth muscle myosin is a **type II myosin**, consisting of two heavy chains and two pairs of light chains. The myosin molecule is folded when dephosphorylated.

When type II myosin phosphorylates, it unfolds and assembles into filaments, the actin binding site on the myosin head is exposed, and myosin can then bind to actin filaments to cause cell contraction.

Smooth muscle can be stimulated to contract by **nervous stimulation, hormonal stimulation,** or **stretch**. For example, intravenous **oxytocin** stimulates uterine muscle contractions during labor.

In response to an appropriate stimulus, there is an increase in cytoplasmic Ca^{2+}. Ca^{2+} binds to **calmodulin**. The Ca^{2+}-calmodulin complex activates **myosin light-chain kinase**, which catalyzes phosphorylation of the myosin light chain. When Ca^{2+} levels decrease, the myosin light chain is enzymatically dephosphorylated, and the muscle relaxes.

8. NERVOUS TISSUE

General organization of the nervous system

Anatomically, the nervous system can be divided into (1) the **central nervous system** (**CNS**, the brain, spinal cord, and neural parts of the eye), and (2) the **peripheral nervous system** (**PNS**, peripheral ganglia, nerves, and nerve endings connecting ganglia with the CNS and receptors and effectors of the body). The CNS and PNS are morphologically and physiologically different, and these differences are significant in areas such as neuropharmacology.

The basic cell components of the CNS are **neurons** and **glia**. The PNS contains supporting cells called **satellite cells** and **Schwann cells**, analogous to the glial cells of the CNS.

We start the study of the nervous tissue by reviewing the highlights of the development of the nervous system.

Development of the nervous system

The CNS develops from the primitive ectoderm (Figure 8–1). A simple epithelial disk —the **neural plate**— rapidly rolls into a hollow cylinder— the **neural tube**. This process is known as **neurulation**. The neural tube differentiates into the very complex nervous system. During this process, a specialized portion of the neural plate —the **neural crest**— separates from both the neural tube and the overlying ectoderm. In later development, **the neural crest forms the neurons of the peripheral ganglia and other components of the PNS.**

Neural crest cells remain separated from the neural tube and differentiate into (1) the sensory neurons of the dorsal root and cranial nerve ganglia, and (2) the sympathetic and parasympathetic motor neurons of the autonomic ganglia.

Some of these cells invade developing visceral organs and form the **parasym-**

Neural crest cells

The ectoderm germ cell layer gives rise to three major structures: (1) the **surface ectoderm**, primarily the epidermis of the skin (including hair, nails, and sebaceous glands), lens and cornea of the eye, anterior pituitary, and tooth enamel; (2) the **neural tube** (brain and spinal cord); (3) the **neural crest**.

Cells of the neural crest migrate away from the neural tube and generate components of the peripheral nervous system (Schwann cells and the sympathetic and parasympathetic nervous system), the adrenal medulla, melanocytes of the skin, dentin of the teeth, facial cartilage, and neuroglial cells.

Figure 8–1

Early stages of neural tube formation

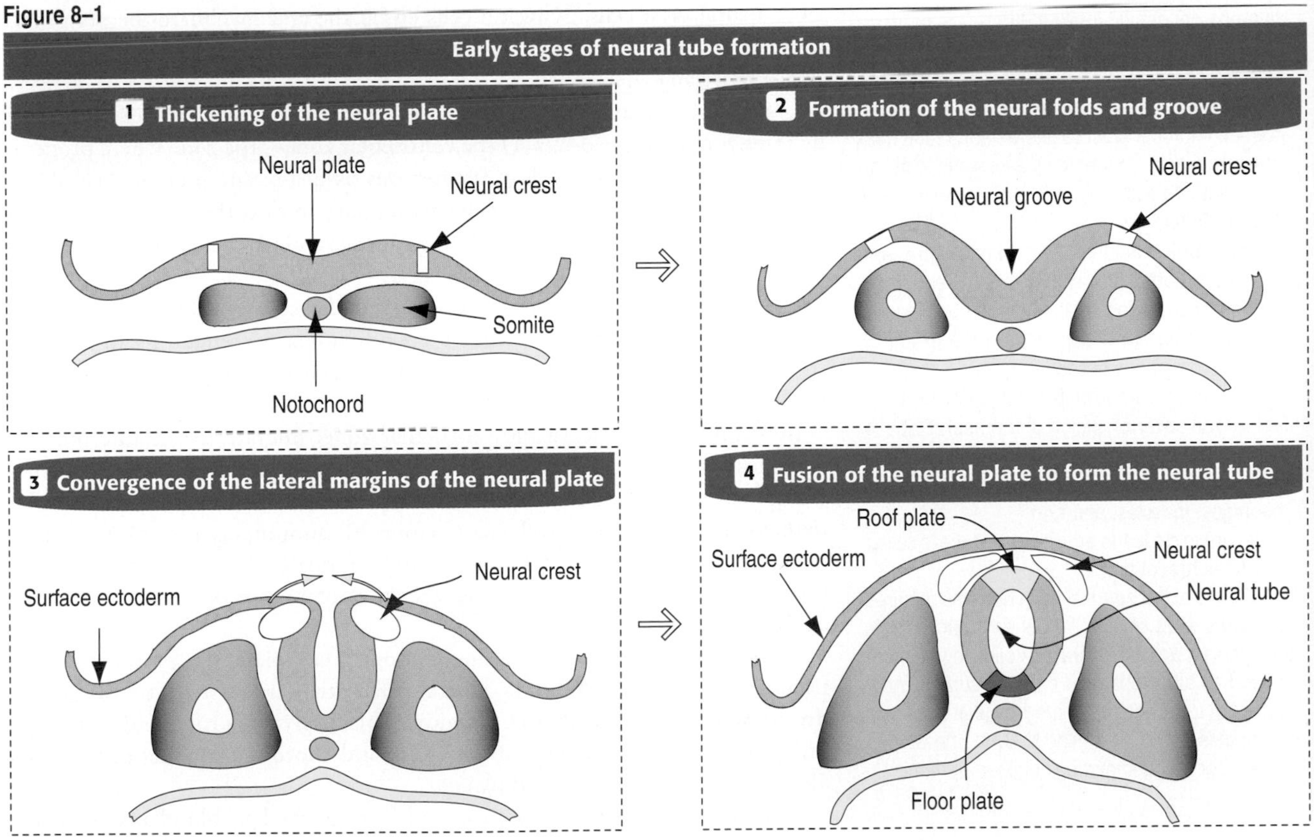

Figure 8–2

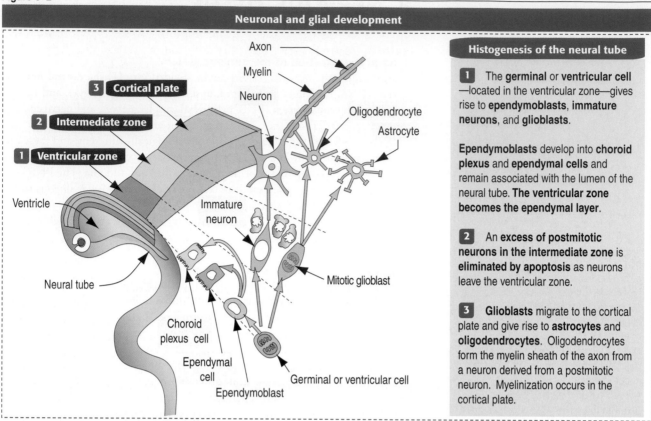

Neuronal and glial development

Histogenesis of the neural tube

1 The **germinal** or **ventricular cell** —located in the ventricular zone—gives rise to **ependymoblasts**, **immature neurons**, and **glioblasts**.

Ependymoblasts develop into **choroid plexus** and **ependymal cells** and remain associated with the lumen of the neural tube. **The ventricular zone becomes the ependymal layer**.

2 An **excess of postmitotic neurons in the intermediate zone** is **eliminated by apoptosis** as neurons leave the ventricular zone.

3 **Glioblasts** migrate to the cortical plate and give rise to **astrocytes** and **oligodendrocytes**. Oligodendrocytes form the myelin sheath of the axon from a neuron derived from a postmitotic neuron. Myelinization occurs in the cortical plate.

Clinical significance: Neural tube defects

A defect in the closing of the neural tube causes different congenital malformations.

Usually, skeletal (skull or vertebral column) defects occur along with malformations of the underlying brain and spinal cord. The latter results from an improper closure of the neural tube during neurulation. Congenital malformations associated with defective neurulation are designated **dysraphic defects**.

Spina bifida is the most common of the spinal cord malformations caused by failure to close the **posterior** regions of the neural tube. The severity of spina bifida depends on the extent of spinal cord being exposed.

The most severe example of a neural tube defect of the **anterior** region of the neural tube is **anencephaly**, a lethal condition defined by the absence of the brain and the surrounding bone, meninges, muscles, and skin.

Failure to close the **entire** neural tube is called **craniorachischisis**.

Closure of the neural tube in humans requires the expression of specific genes (**Pax3**, **sonic hedgehog**, and **openbrain**). Following closure, the neural tube separates from the surface ectoderm by a process mediated by cell-adhesion molecules (**N-cadherin** and **N-CAM**, the latter is a member of the immunoglobulin superfamily).

pathetic and **enteric ganglia** and the **chromaffin cells** of the adrenal medulla.

The **Schwann cells and satellite cells of the dorsal root ganglia also develop from neural crest cells**. Schwann cells ensheathe and myelinate the peripheral nerve fibers, and the satellite cells encapsulate the neuronal cell bodies in the dorsal root ganglia.

The early neural tube consists of a pseudostratified columnar epithelium formed by three zones (Figure 8–2): (1) the **ventricular zone**—the zone where progenitor cells give rise to most cells of the nervous tissue (except microglial cells); (2) the **intermediate zone** –where neurons migrate toward the cortical plate and where excess neurons are destroyed by apoptosis; and (3) the **cortical plate**—the future gray matter of the cerebral cortex.

In the ventricular zone, **germinal** or **ventricular cells** proliferate rapidly during early development to give rise to **ependymoblasts** (remaining in the ventricular zone) **and glioblasts** and **postmitotic neurons** (migrating to the intermediate zone).

Immature neurons leave the ventricular zone, migrate to the intermediate zone, lose their capacity to undergo cell division, and differentiate into functional neurons. During this differentiation process, a selection process —similar to that in the thymus for T cells (see Chapter 10, Immune-Lymphatic System)— results in either neuronal heterogeneity or death. Neurons that become postmitotic in the intermediate zone reach the outer layers of the cortical mantle and continue their differentiation.

Once the production of immature neurons is complete, the germinal or ventricular cells produce **glioblasts**, which differentiate into **astrocytes**, **oligodendrocytes**, and **ependymoblasts**. Ependymoblasts give rise to **ependymal cells**, lining the ventricular cavities of the CNS, and **choroid epithelial cells**, which are components of the choroid plexus.

Later, astrocytes develop vascular end-feet attached to blood vessels of the

CNS. Coincident with vascularization is the differentiation of **microglia** from monocytes. Microglia respond to injury and become active phagocytic cells.

In later development, glioblasts give rise to **oligodendrocytes**, marking the beginning of **myelination** in the CNS. In contrast to neurons, glioblasts and derived glial cells retain the ability to undergo cell division.

The number of neurons in the human brain is in the range of 10^9 to 100^9. Up to 60% to 70% of these are present in the cerebral cortex. Most neurons are present at birth or shortly thereafter. As the brain continues to grow during the postnatal period, the number and complexity of interneuronal connections increase.

Cell types: Neurons and glia
The neuron

The functional unit of the nervous system is a highly specialized, excitable cell, the nerve cell or **neuron**. Neurons usually consist of three principal components (Figures 8–3 and 8–4): (1) **soma** or **cell body**, (2) **dendrites**, and (3) **axon**.

The soma contains the nucleus and its surrounding cytoplasm (also called **perikaryon**; Gk. *peri*, around; *karion*, nucleus).

The dendrites are processes that arise as multiple treelike branches of the soma, forming a **dendritic tree** collectively. The entire surface of the dendritic branches is covered by small protrusions called **dendritic spines**. Dendritic spines establish numerous axonal synaptic connections, as we will see later (see Figure 8–7).

Neurons have a **single axon** originating from the soma at the **axon hillock** and ending in a terminal arborization, the **telodendron**. Each terminal branch of the telodendron has an enlarged ending, the **synaptic terminal** or **synaptic bouton**.

Note that although dendrites and axons branch extensively, axons branch at their distal end (the telodendron), whereas dendrites are multiple extensions of the soma or cell body.

The surface membrane of the soma and the dendritic tree are specialized for the **reception** and **integration** of information, whereas the axon is specialized for the **transmission** of information in the form of an action potential or a nerve impulse.

Types of neurons

Different types of neurons can be identified on the basis of the **number** and **length** of **processes emerging from the soma** (Figure 8–5):

According to the **number of processes**, neurons can be classified as:

1. **Multipolar neurons**, which display **many processes** attached to a polygonal-shaped soma. The processes include a single axon and more than one dendrite. Multipolar neurons are the most abundant neurons in the nervous system. Pyramidal cells of the cerebral cortex and Purkinje cells and neurons of the cerebellar cortex are two typical examples.

2. **Bipolar neurons** have **two processes**. Bipolar neurons are typical of the visual, auditory, and vestibular system.

3. **Pseudounipolar neurons** have **only one short process** leaving the cell body and are localized in sensory ganglia of cranial and spinal nerves. Embryonically, pseudounipolar neurons derive from bipolar neuroblasts, and the two neuronal processes fuse during later development (hence the prefix **pseudo-**).

Based on the **length of the axon relative to the dendritic tree**, multipolar neurons can be subclassified into: (1) **Golgi type I** neurons, when the axon extends beyond the limits of the dendritic tree, and (2) **Golgi type II** neurons, when an axon terminates in the immediate area of the cell body and does not extend beyond the limits of the dendritic tree. By definition, pyramidal cells and Purkinje cells can be regarded as Golgi type I neurons. Small **stellate cells** of the cerebral cortex are Golgi type II cells.

Figure 8–3

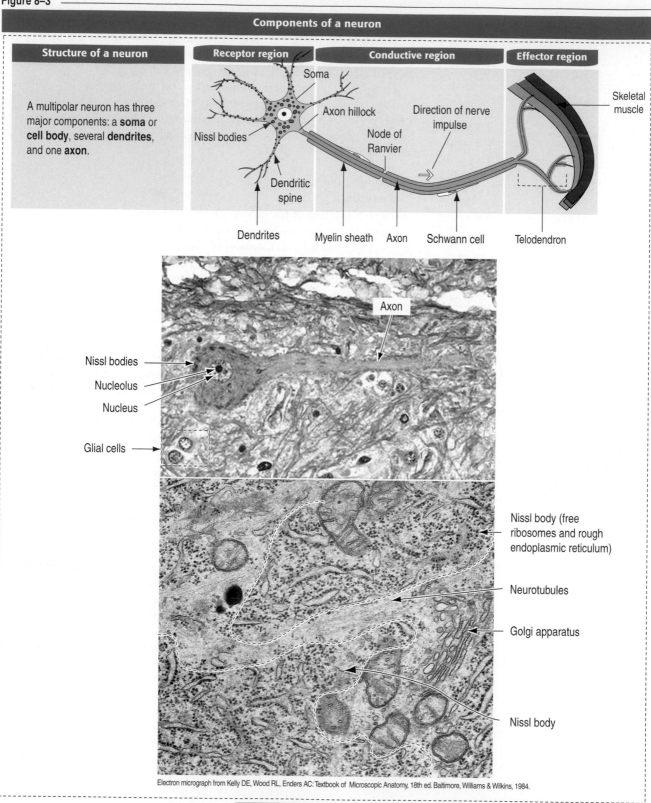

Electron micrograph from Kelly DE, Wood RL, Enders AC: Textbook of Microscopic Anatomy, 18th ed. Baltimore, Williams & Wilkins, 1984.

Designation of groups of neurons and axons

In the CNS, functionally and structurally related neurons form aggregates called **nuclei**. An area called the **neuropil** can be found within a **nucleus** and between the neuronal cell bodies. The term neuropil designates an area with packed dendrites, axonal branches with abundant synapses, and glial cells.

Figure 8–4

Components of a neuron

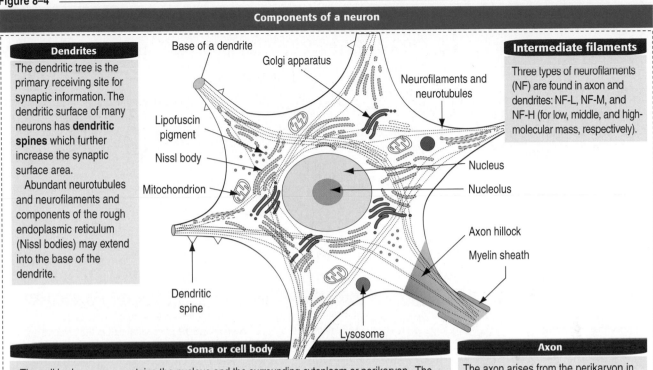

Dendrites

The dendritic tree is the primary receiving site for synaptic information. The dendritic surface of many neurons has **dendritic spines** which further increase the synaptic surface area.

Abundant neurotubules and neurofilaments and components of the rough endoplasmic reticulum (Nissl bodies) may extend into the base of the dendrite.

Base of a dendrite

Golgi apparatus

Neurofilaments and neurotubules

Lipofuscin pigment

Nissl body

Mitochondrion

Dendritic spine

Lysosome

Intermediate filaments

Three types of neurofilaments (NF) are found in axon and dendrites: NF-L, NF-M, and NF-H (for low, middle, and high-molecular mass, respectively).

Nucleus

Nucleolus

Axon hillock

Myelin sheath

Soma or cell body

The cell body or soma contains the nucleus and the surrounding cytoplasm or perikaryon. The soma, the trophic center of the neuron, contains organelles for the synthesis of proteins, phospholipids, and other macromolecules. A characteristic feature of the perikaryon is the **abundance of ribosomes**, free or associated with the endoplasmic reticulum. In light microscopic preparations with nucleic acid stains (basophilia), these structures appear as large clumps or **Nissl bodies**. A prominent **Golgi apparatus** and numerous mitochondria also reside in the perikaryon. **Neurotubules** and **neurofilaments** are distinctive features of the perikaryon. These cytoskeletal components extend through the perikaryon into the dendritic and axonal processes. Lysosomes and yellowish-pigmented lipofuscin granules are also present. The nucleus is usually large, with dispersed chromatin (euchromatin) and one or more prominent nucleoli.

Axon

The axon arises from the perikaryon in an area devoid of Nissl substance, the axon hillock. The initial segment of the axon is the site of action potential generation, the trigger zone. Unlike the gradually tapering dendrite, the diameter of the axon remains constant throughout its length. In myelinated axons, a myelin sheath extends from the initial segment to the telodendron. Many axons have collateral branches.

Clusters of neurons arranged in a layer form a **stratum** or **lamina** (cerebral cortex). When neurons form longitudinal groups, these groups are designated **columns**.

Bundles of axons in the CNS are called **tracts**, **fasciculi** (**bundles**), or **lemnisci** (for example, the optic tract).

In the PNS, a cluster of neurons forms a **ganglion** (pl. **ganglia**). A ganglion can be **sensory** —dorsal root ganglia and trigeminal ganglion— or **motor** — visceromotor or autonomic ganglia. **Axons derived from a ganglion** are organized as **nerves**, **rami** (sing. **ramus**), or **roots**.

Synaptic terminals and synapses

The **synaptic terminal** (Figure 8–6) is specialized for the transmission of a chemical message in response to an action potential. The **synapse** is the junction between the **presynaptic terminal** of an axon and a **postsynaptic membrane** receptor surface, generally a dendrite.

The prefixes **pre-** and **post-** refer to the direction of synaptic transmission: (1) **Presynaptic** refers to the transmitting side (usually axonal). (2) **Postsynaptic** identifies the receiving side (usually dendritic or somatic, sometimes axonal). The presynaptic and postsynaptic membranes are separated by a space: the **synaptic cleft**. A dense material coats the inner surface of these membranes: the **presynaptic and postsynaptic densities**.

Figure 8–5

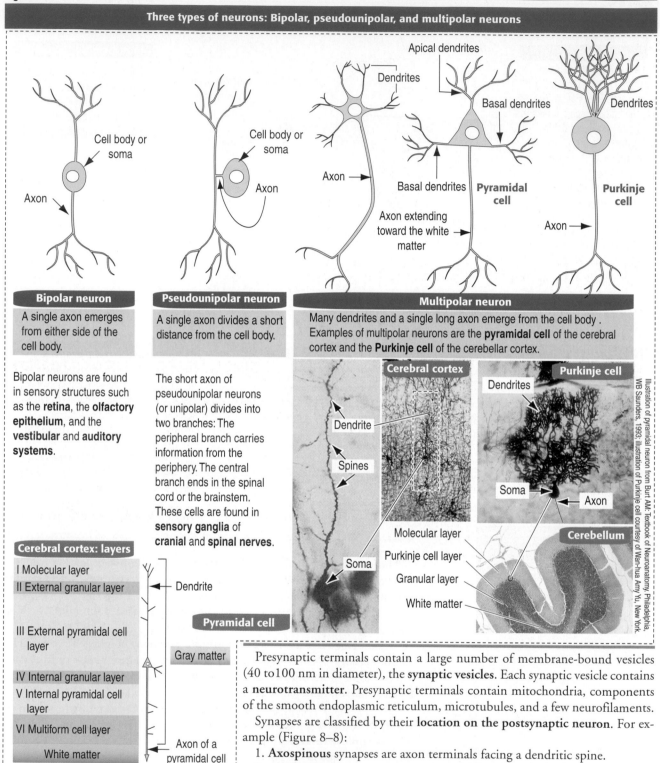

Three types of neurons: Bipolar, pseudounipolar, and multipolar neurons

Bipolar neuron

A single axon emerges from either side of the cell body.

Bipolar neurons are found in sensory structures such as the **retina**, the **olfactory epithelium**, and the **vestibular** and **auditory systems**.

Pseudounipolar neuron

A single axon divides a short distance from the cell body.

The short axon of pseudounipolar neurons (or unipolar) divides into two branches: The peripheral branch carries information from the periphery. The central branch ends in the spinal cord or the brainstem. These cells are found in **sensory ganglia** of **cranial** and **spinal nerves**.

Multipolar neuron

Many dendrites and a single long axon emerge from the cell body . Examples of multipolar neurons are the **pyramidal cell** of the cerebral cortex and the **Purkinje cell** of the cerebellar cortex.

Cerebral cortex: layers

I Molecular layer
II External granular layer
III External pyramidal cell layer
IV Internal granular layer
V Internal pyramidal cell layer
VI Multiform cell layer
White matter

Presynaptic terminals contain a large number of membrane-bound vesicles (40 to100 nm in diameter), the **synaptic vesicles**. Each synaptic vesicle contains a **neurotransmitter**. Presynaptic terminals contain mitochondria, components of the smooth endoplasmic reticulum, microtubules, and a few neurofilaments.

Synapses are classified by their **location on the postsynaptic neuron**. For example (Figure 8–8):

1. **Axospinous** synapses are axon terminals facing a dendritic spine.
2. **Axodendritic** synapses are axon terminals on the shaft of a dendrite.
3. **Axosomatic** synapses are axon terminals on the soma of a neuron.
4. **Axoaxonic** synapses are axon terminals ending on axon terminals.

Clinical significance: Axonal transport of rabies virus

The role of the axonal cytoskeleton and motor proteins (kinesin and cytoplasmic dynein; see Figure 8–7) was discussed in the Cytoskeleton section of Chapter 1, Epithelium. We now extend the discussion by emphasizing the bidirec-

Figure 8–6

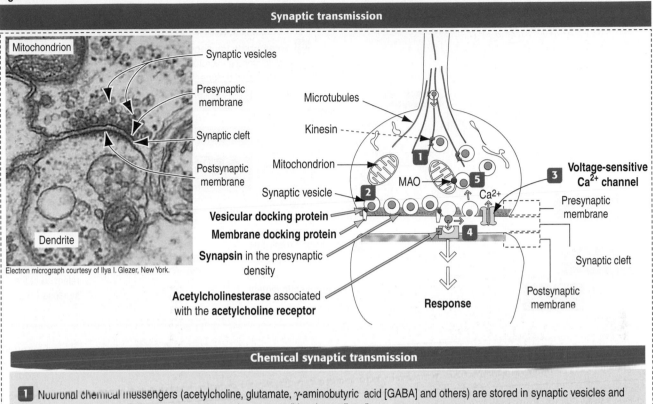

Synaptic transmission

Mitochondrion

Synaptic vesicles

Presynaptic membrane

Synaptic cleft

Postsynaptic membrane

Dendrite

Electron micrograph courtesy of Ilya I. Glezer, New York.

Microtubules

Kinesin

Mitochondrion

MAO

Synaptic vesicle

Vesicular docking protein

Membrane docking protein

Synapsin in the presynaptic density

Acetylcholinesterase associated with the **acetylcholine receptor**

Voltage-sensitive Ca^{2+} channel

Presynaptic membrane

Ca^{2+}

Synaptic cleft

Response

Postsynaptic membrane

Chemical synaptic transmission

1 Neuronal chemical messengers (acetylcholine, glutamate, γ-aminobutyric acid [GABA] and others) are stored in synaptic vesicles and transported to the synaptic terminal by anterograde transport (kinesin-mediated).

2 The membrane of a synaptic vesicle contains **vesicular docking proteins** that attach to **membrane docking proteins** of the presynaptic membrane (rich in **synapsin** filaments).

3 The depolarization of the axon terminal results in a high concentration of Ca^{2+} transported inside the terminal by a **voltage-sensitive Ca^{2+} channel**. A surge of Ca^{2+} induces exocytosis of the synaptic vesicle.

4 The released chemical messenger in the synaptic cleft binds to a receptor (cholinergic or adrenergic) on the postsynaptic membrane to transmit information.

The chemical messenger is enzymatically degraded in the cleft (acetylcholine by acetylcholinesterase) or **5** taken up by receptor-mediated endocytosis (norepinephrine) and degraded by the mitochondrial enzyme monoamine oxidase (MAO).

tional transport of molecules along the axon: **kinesin-mediated anterograde axonal transport** of neurotransmitters —from the cell body toward the axon terminals, and the **cytoplasmic dynein-mediated retrograde axonal transport** of growth factors and recycling of axon terminal components— from the axon terminals to the cell body.

Axonal transport is important in the pathogenesis of neurologic infectious diseases. For example, the **rabies virus** introduced by the bite of a rabid animal replicates in the muscle tissue from as short as 2 to 16 weeks or longer. After binding to the **acetylcholine receptor**, the viral particles are mobilized by **retrograde axonal transport** to the cell body of neurons supplying the affected muscle. The rabies virus continues to replicate within infected neurons and after the shedding of the virions by budding, they are internalized by the terminals of adjacent neurons. Further dissemination of the rabies virus occurs in the CNS. From the CNS, the rabies virus is transported by **anterograde axonal transport** by the peripheral nerves to the salivary glands. The virus enters the saliva to be transmitted by the bite. Painful **spasm of the throat muscles on swallowing** accounts for **hydrophobia** (aversion to swallowing water).

The retrograde axonal transport to the CNS of **tetanus toxin** —a protease produced by the vegetative spore form of *Clostridium tetani* bacteria after entering at a wound site— blocks the release of inhibitory mediators at spinal syn-

Figure 8–7

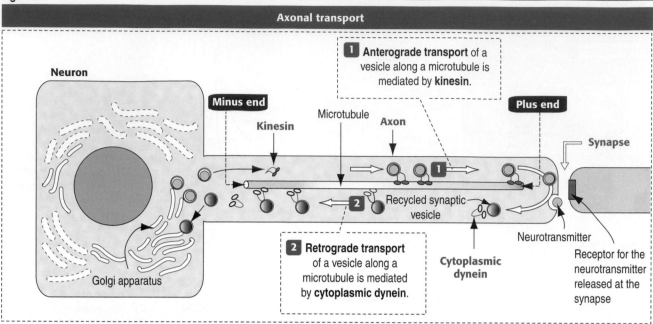

Axonal transport

Neuron

Minus end

1 Anterograde transport of a vesicle along a microtubule is mediated by **kinesin**.

Kinesin   Microtubule   Axon   **Plus end**

Synapse

Recycled synaptic vesicle

Neurotransmitter

2 Retrograde transport of a vesicle along a microtubule is mediated by **cytoplasmic dynein**.

Cytoplasmic dynein

Receptor for the neurotransmitter released at the synapse

Golgi apparatus

Release of neurotransmitters

Incoming nerve impulses produce focal changes in the **resting membrane potential** of the neuron which spread along the membrane of dendrites and soma.

Information is conducted along the processes as an electrical excitation (**depolarization**) generated across the cell membrane.

As the resting membrane potential diminishes, a **threshold level** is reached, **voltage-gated Ca²⁺ channels** open, Ca²⁺ enters the cell, and at that point, the resting potential is reversed: the inside becomes positive with respect to the outside.

In response to this reversal, the **Na⁺ channel** closes and remains closed for the next 1-2 msec (the **refractory period**). Depolarization also causes the opening of **K⁺ channels** through which K⁺ leaves the cell, thus repolarizing the membrane.

Neuron-to-neuron contacts or **synapses** are specialized for one-way transfer of excitation. Interneuronal communication occurs at a **synaptic junction**, the specialized communication site between the terminal of an axon of one neuron and the dendrite of another.

When an action potential reaches the axon terminal, a chemical messenger or **neurotransmitter** is released to elicit an appropriate response.

---

apses. Spasm contraction of the jaw muscles (known as **trismus**), exaggerated reflexes, and respiratory failure are characteristic clinical findings.

Glia, the "connective tissue" of the CNS

Glial cells (Gk. *glia,* glue) are more numerous than neurons and retain the capacity to proliferate. Most brain tumors, benign or malignant, are of glial origin. When the CNS is injured, glial cells mobilize, clean up the debris, and seal off the local area, leaving behind a "glial scar" (gliosis), which interferes with neuronal regeneration.

Glial cells include (1) **astrocytes** (Figure 8–9), derived from the **neuroectoderm**; (2) **oligodendrocytes** (Figure 8–10), derived from the **neuroectoderm**, and (3) **microglia** (Figure 8–15), derived from the **mesoderm**.

Unlike neurons, glial cells do not propagate action potentials and their processes do not receive or transmit electrical signals. The **function of glial cells is to provide neurons with structural support and maintain local conditions for neuronal function.**

Astrocytes

Astrocytes are observed in the CNS and are divided into two categories: (1) **fibrous astrocytes,** and (2) **protoplasmic astrocytes.**

Fibrous astrocytes are found predominantly in **white matter** and have long thin processes with few branches. **Protoplasmic astrocytes** reside predominantly in **gray matter** and have shorter processes with many short branches. Astrocytic processes end in expansions called **end-feet** (see Figure 8–9).

One of the distinctive features of astrocytes is the presence of a large number of **glial filaments** (**glial fibrillary acidic protein,** a class of intermediate filament studied in Chapter 1, Epithelium, The Cytoskeleton). Glial fibrillary acidic protein is a valuable marker for the identification of astrocytes by immunohistochemistry. Nuclei of astrocytes are large, ovoid, and lightly stained.

Most brain capillaries and the inner surface of the pia mater are completely surrounded by **astrocytic end-feet** (see Figure 8–9) forming the **glia limitans** (also called the glial limiting membrane). The close association of astrocytes and brain capillaries suggests a role in the regulation of brain metabolism.

Astrocytes surround neurons and neuronal processes in areas devoid of my-

Figure 8–8

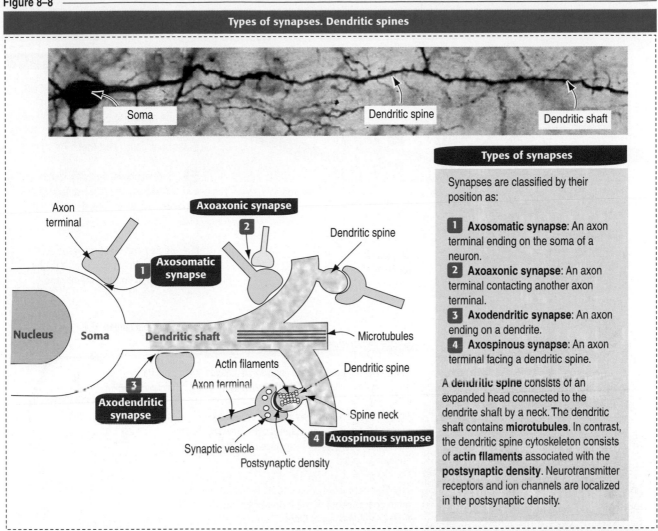

Types of synapses. Dendritic spines

Soma

Dendritic spine

Dendritic shaft

Types of synapses

Synapses are classified by their position as:

1 **Axosomatic synapse**: An axon terminal ending on the soma of a neuron.

2 **Axoaxonic synapse**: An axon terminal contacting another axon terminal.

3 **Axodendritic synapse**: An axon ending on a dendrite.

4 **Axospinous synapse**: An axon terminal facing a dendritic spine.

A dendritic spine consists of an expanded head connected to the dendrite shaft by a neck. The dendritic shaft contains **microtubules**. In contrast, the dendritic spine cytoskeleton consists of **actin filaments** associated with the **postsynaptic density**. Neurotransmitter receptors and ion channels are localized in the postsynaptic density.

Axon terminal

Axoaxonic synapse

2

Dendritic spine

Axosomatic synapse

1

Nucleus

Soma

Dendritic shaft

Microtubules

Actin filaments

Dendritic spine

3

Axon terminal

Axodendritic synapse

Spine neck

4 **Axospinous synapse**

Synaptic vesicle

Postsynaptic density

elin sheaths and form the structural matrix for the nervous system.

Oligodendrocytes and Schwann cells: Myelinization

Oligodendrocytes are smaller than astrocytes and their nuclei are irregular and densely stained. The cytoplasm contains an extensive Golgi apparatus, many mitochondria, and a large number of microtubules. One function of oligodendrocytes is **axonal myelination**.

Processes of oligodendrocytes envelop axons and form a sheathlike covering (see Figure 8–10). **The formation of this sheath is similar to that of Schwann cells in peripheral nerves.**

Myelin sheaths extend from the initial segments of axons to their terminal branches. The segments of myelin formed by individual oligodendrocyte processes are **internodes**. The periodic gaps between the internodes are the **nodes of Ranvier**.

A single oligodendrocyte has many processes and may form 40 to 50 internodes. The nodes of Ranvier are naked segments of axon between the internodal segments of myelin. This region contains a high concentration of voltage-gated sodium channels, essential for the **saltatory conduction** of the action potential. During saltatory conduction in the myelinated axons, the **action potential** "jumps" from one node to the next.

During the formation of the myelin sheath, a cytoplasmic process of the oligodendrocyte wraps around the axon and, after one full turn, the external sur-

Figure 8–9

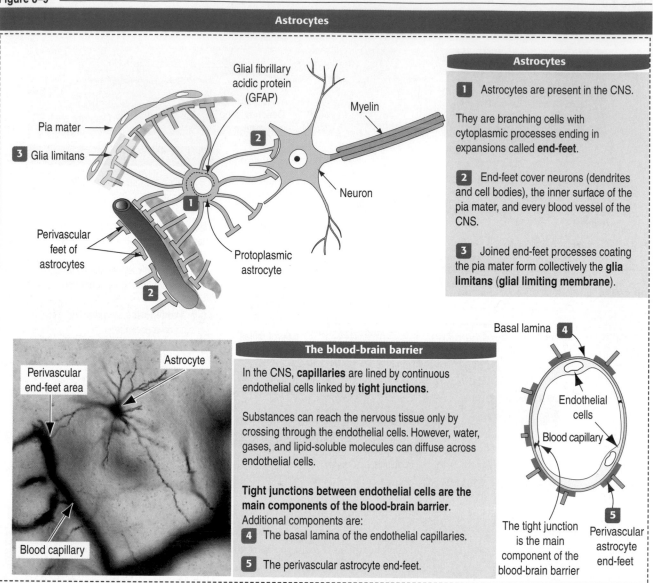

Astrocytes

Glial fibrillary acidic protein (GFAP)

Myelin

Pia mater

3 Glia limitans

2

Neuron

Perivascular feet of astrocytes

2

Protoplasmic astrocyte

Astrocytes

1 Astrocytes are present in the CNS.

They are branching cells with cytoplasmic processes ending in expansions called **end-feet**.

2 End-feet cover neurons (dendrites and cell bodies), the inner surface of the pia mater, and every blood vessel of the CNS.

3 Joined end-feet processes coating the pia mater form collectively the **glia limitans (glial limiting membrane)**.

Perivascular end-feet area

Astrocyte

Blood capillary

Basal lamina **4**

Endothelial cells

Blood capillary

The tight junction is the main component of the blood-brain barrier

5 Perivascular astrocyte end-feet

The blood-brain barrier

In the CNS, **capillaries** are lined by continuous endothelial cells linked by **tight junctions**.

Substances can reach the nervous tissue only by crossing through the endothelial cells. However, water, gases, and lipid-soluble molecules can diffuse across endothelial cells.

Tight junctions between endothelial cells are the main components of the blood-brain barrier. Additional components are:

4 The basal lamina of the endothelial capillaries.

5 The perivascular astrocyte end-feet.

face of the glial membrane makes contact with itself, forming the **inner mesaxon** (Figure 8–11).

As the oligodendrocyte process continues to spiral around the axon, the external surfaces fuse to form the first **intraperiod line**. At the same time, the cytoplasm is squeezed off from the intracellular space (like toothpaste from a tube), and the cytoplasmic surfaces fuse to form the first **dense line**.

Spiraling continues until the axon is invested with a number of wrappings. The alternate fusion of both the cytoplasmic and external surfaces of the membrane results in an interdigitated double spiral (Figure 8–11), one of **intraperiod lines** (fused external surfaces with remnant extracellular space), and one of **major dense lines** (fused cytoplasmic surfaces).

The dense line terminates when the membrane surfaces separate to enclose the cytoplasm at the surface of the sheath (the **tongue**), and the intraperiod line terminates as the tongue turns away from the sheath. The **incisures of Schmidt-Lanterman** are seen in longitudinal sections of myelinated nerve fibers. They correspond to areas of residual Schwann cell cytoplasm in the PNS.

As the myelin sheath approaches the node of Ranvier region, an additional ring of cytoplasm separates the cytoplasmic surfaces of the cell membrane. These tongues make contact with the **axolemma**, or surface membrane of the axon, in the paranodal region. Axons branch to form collaterals at a node of Ranvier.

Myelin: Protein and lipid components

Myelin in the CNS and PNS is similar in overall protein and lipid composition, except that myelin in the PNS contains more sphingomyelin and glycoproteins. Three proteins are particularly relevant (Figure 8–13): **myelin basic protein** (MBP), **proteolipid protein** (PLP), and **protein zero** (P_0).

MBP is a cytosolic plasma membrane–bound protein present in both the myelin of the PNS and CNS. PLP is found only in the myelin of the CNS.

The predominant protein in myelin of the PNS is P_0, a functional equivalent to PLP in the CNS. P_0 extends into the extracellular space to establish homophilic interaction with a similar P_0 molecule to stabilize adjacent plasma membranes (see Figure 8–13). In the CNS, plasma membrane–associated PLPs interact with each other and have a similar stabilizing function.

Figure 8–10

Oligodendrocytes

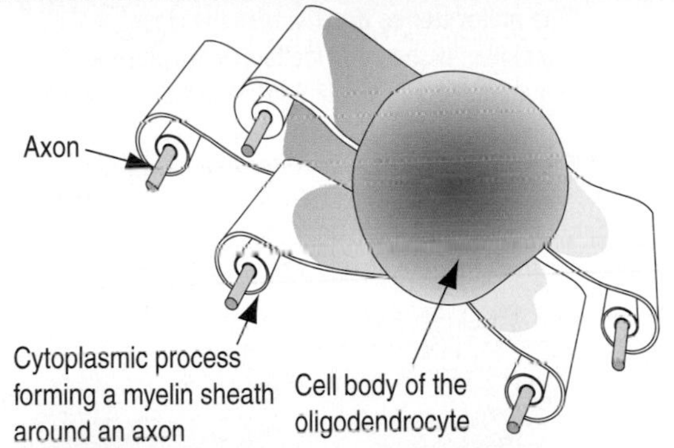

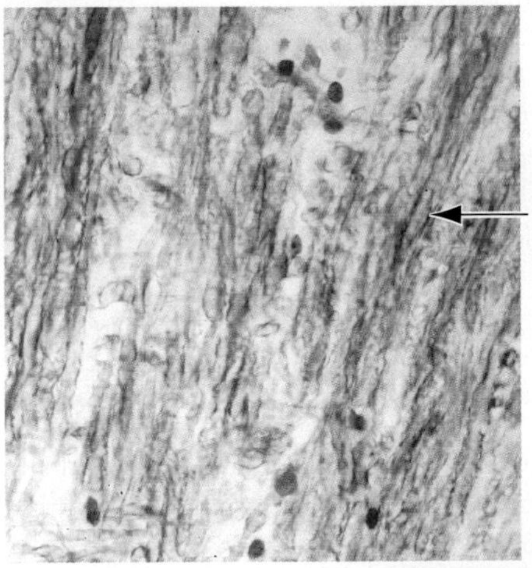

Axon

Cytoplasmic process forming a myelin sheath around an axon

Cell body of the oligodendrocyte

Myelin stain blue with the Luxol fast blue stain (white matter)

Myelinization in the CNS

In the CNS, oligodendrocytes (derived from glioblasts) form myelin sheaths around the axons.

The pattern of myelinization in the CNS is different from that in the PNS:

1 The cell body of the oligodendrocytes is not closely associated with the myelin sheath as the body of a Schwann cell is.

2 Each oligodendrocyte provides a myelin sheath to several axons. One Schwann cell forms a myelin sheath around a single axon.

3 There is no basal lamina associated with the myelin sheath in the CNS.

4 Myelinated axons in the CNS lack a supporting connective tissue, as do nerves in the PNS.

5 The inner and outer layers of myelin end in separate loops near the node of Ranvier and no cytoplasm of the oligodendrocytes is trapped. In Schwann cells, the cytoplasm is retained.

6 In the CNS, the surface of the node is contacted by astrocyte processes. In the PNS, the node is covered by Schwann cell processes.

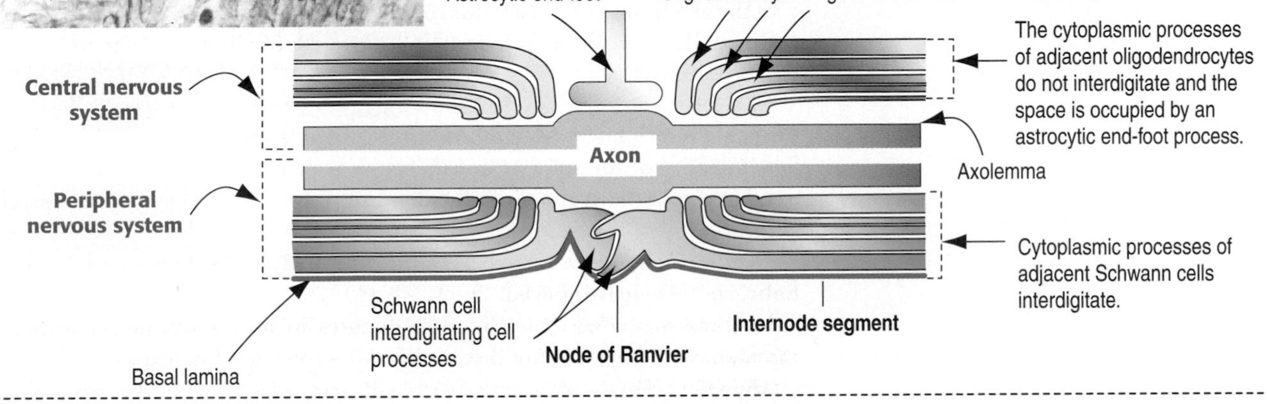

Astrocytic end-foot

Oligodendrocyte tongues in contact with the axolemma

The cytoplasmic processes of adjacent oligodendrocytes do not interdigitate and the space is occupied by an astrocytic end-foot process.

Axolemma

Cytoplasmic processes of adjacent Schwann cells interdigitate.

Central nervous system

Peripheral nervous system

Axon

Schwann cell interdigitating cell processes

Node of Ranvier

Internode segment

Basal lamina

Figure 8–11

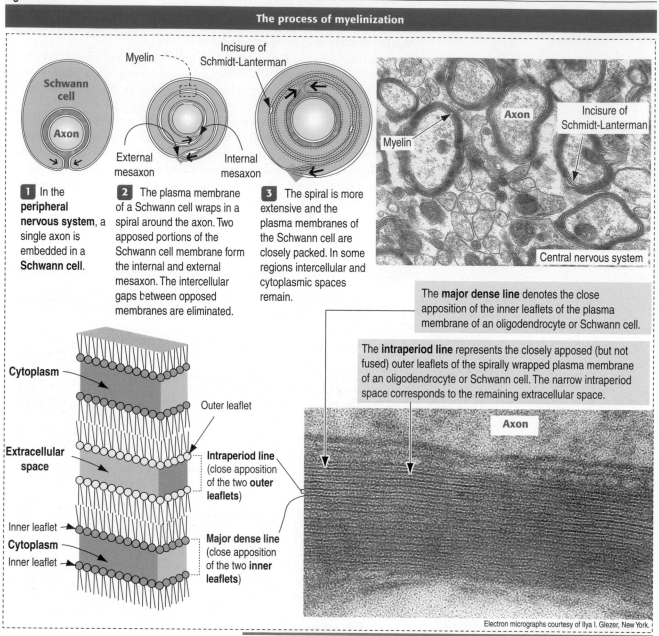

The process of myelinization

1 In the **peripheral nervous system**, a single axon is embedded in a **Schwann cell**.

2 The plasma membrane of a Schwann cell wraps in a spiral around the axon. Two apposed portions of the Schwann cell membrane form the internal and external mesaxon. The intercellular gaps between opposed membranes are eliminated.

3 The spiral is more extensive and the plasma membranes of the Schwann cell are closely packed. In some regions intercellular and cytoplasmic spaces remain.

The **major dense line** denotes the close apposition of the inner leaflets of the plasma membrane of an oligodendrocyte or Schwann cell.

The **intraperiod line** represents the closely apposed (but not fused) outer leaflets of the spirally wrapped plasma membrane of an oligodendrocyte or Schwann cell. The narrow intraperiod space corresponds to the remaining extracellular space.

Electron micrographs courtesy of Ilya I. Glezer, New York.

Proteins of myelin are strong antigens with a role in autoimmune diseases such as **multiple sclerosis** in the CNS and **Guillain-Barré syndrome** in the PNS.

Some axons of the PNS are unmyelinated (Figure 8–12). A Schwann cell can accommodate several axons in individual cytoplasmic invaginations and no myelin is produced.

Clinical significance: Myelin and multiple sclerosis

The integrity of myelin, but not the axon, is disturbed in **demyelinating diseases** affecting the **survival of oligodendrocytes** or the **integrity of the myelin sheath**.

Demyelinating diseases can be: (1) **immune-mediated**, (2) **inherited**, (3) **metabolic**, and (4) **virus-induced**.

Immune-mediated demyelination diseases include **multiple sclerosis** and **monophasic demyelination diseases** (for example, **optic neuritis**).

Multiple sclerosis (Figure 8-14) is characterized by clinically recurrent or

Figure 8–12

Development of myelinated and unmyelinated nerves

1 During development, groups of embryonic axons are surrounded by Schwann cells. Embryonic axons enlarge and become ensheathed by individual Schwann cells and a myelinated axon or nerve fiber is formed.

2 Axons which will not be myelinated remain small and are embedded within individual recesses in the Schwann cell cytoplasm.

3 Unmyelinated nerve fibers comprise the majority of the postganglionic axons from autonomic ganglia and the axons of the smaller neurons of sensory ganglia. Unmyelinated peripheral nerve fibers are difficult to visualize under the light microscope unless they form a nerve fascicle.

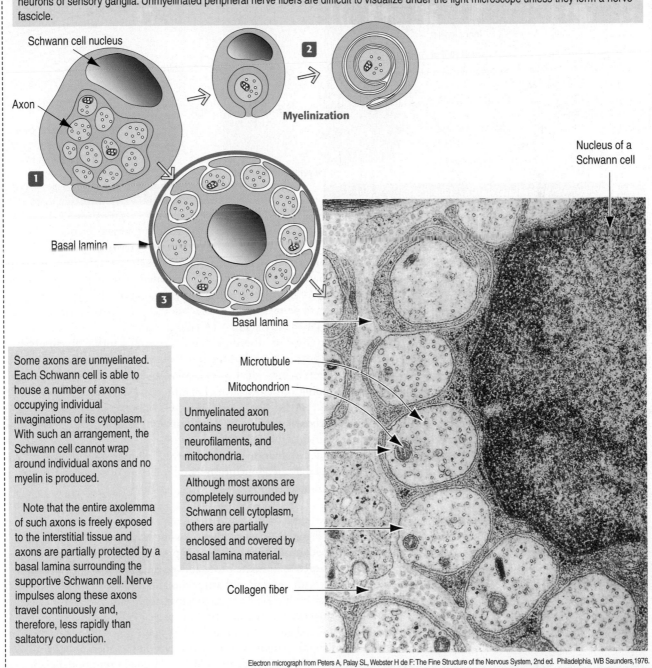

Schwann cell nucleus

Axon

Myelinization

1

2

Basal lamina

3

Nucleus of a Schwann cell

Basal lamina

Microtubule

Mitochondrion

Some axons are unmyelinated. Each Schwann cell is able to house a number of axons occupying individual invaginations of its cytoplasm. With such an arrangement, the Schwann cell cannot wrap around individual axons and no myelin is produced.

Note that the entire axolemma of such axons is freely exposed to the interstitial tissue and axons are partially protected by a basal lamina surrounding the supportive Schwann cell. Nerve impulses along these axons travel continuously and, therefore, less rapidly than saltatory conduction.

Unmyelinated axon contains neurotubules, neurofilaments, and mitochondria.

Although most axons are completely surrounded by Schwann cell cytoplasm, others are partially enclosed and covered by basal lamina material.

Collagen fiber

Electron micrograph from Peters A, Palay SL, Webster H de F: The Fine Structure of the Nervous System, 2nd ed. Philadelphia, WB Saunders, 1976.

chronically progressive neurologic dysfunction caused by multiple areas of demyelination in the CNS, in particular the **brain**, **optic nerves**, and **spinal cord**. An immune-mediated origin of multiple sclerosis is supported by an increase of IgG in the cerebrospinal fluid (CSF), and abnormalities of T cell function. A

Figure 8–13

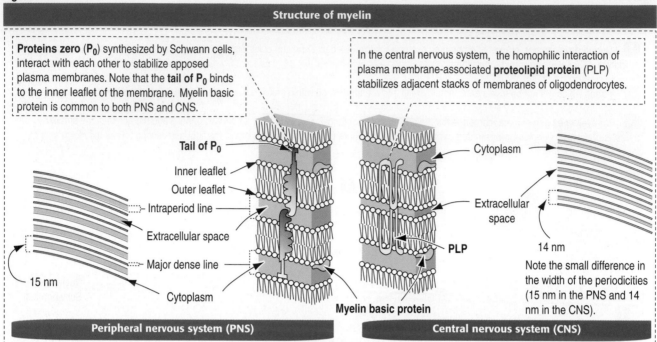

| Structure of myelin |

Proteins zero (P₀) synthesized by Schwann cells, interact with each other to stabilize apposed plasma membranes. Note that the **tail of P₀** binds to the inner leaflet of the membrane. Myelin basic protein is common to both PNS and CNS.

In the central nervous system, the homophilic interaction of plasma membrane-associated **proteolipid protein** (PLP) stabilizes adjacent stacks of membranes of oligodendrocytes.

Tail of P₀
Inner leaflet
Outer leaflet
Intraperiod line
Extracellular space
Major dense line
Cytoplasm
15 nm
Cytoplasm
Extracellular space
PLP
14 nm
Myelin basic protein

Note the small difference in the width of the periodicities (15 nm in the PNS and 14 nm in the CNS).

Peripheral nervous system (PNS) | **Central nervous system (CNS)**

characteristic pathologic finding is the presence of numerous plaques of myelinated fibers.

An **inherited demyelination** disorder is **adrenoleukodystrophy**, in which **progressive demyelination** is associated with **dysfunction of the adrenal cortex**. The X-linked form of this disease is caused by a mutation of a gene encoding a membrane protein of **peroxisomes**. A defect in this gene leads to the accumulation of **very-long-chain fatty acids** (**VLCFAs**) in serum.

Metabolic demyelination disorders includes **central pontine myelinolysis**, a syndrome in which neurologic dysfunction is observed following rapid correction of hyponatremia in individuals with alcohol abuse or malnutrition. A typical pathologic finding is the presence of **symmetrical demyelinated lesions in the central pons**.

Vitamin B₁₂ deficiency results in demyelination of axons in the CNS (the spinal cord, in particular) and the PNS.

Virus-induced demyelination can be observed in **progressive multifocal encephalopathy** caused by an opportunistic viral infection of oligodendrocytes in patients with immunodeficiency.

Microglial cells

Microglial cells (Figure 8–15) have the following characteristics:

1. They are mesoderm-derived cells whose primary function is **phagocytosis**.

2. They are regarded as immune protectors of the brain and spinal cord.

3. They interact with neurons and astrocytes and migrate to the sites of dead neurons where they proliferate and phagocytose dead cells.

4. During histogenesis in the embryo, microglial cells discard an excess of nonviable neurons and glial cells, eliminated by apoptosis.

Substantial microglial activity has been observed in the brain of patients with **acquired immunodeficiency syndrome** (**AIDS**). **Human immunodeficiency virus type 1** (**HIV-1**) does not attack neurons, but it does infect microglial cells that produce cytokines toxic to neurons.

The distinction of microglia, astrocytes, and oligodendrocytes is difficult in routine histologic techniques. Immunocytochemical and silver impregnation procedures are commonly used for the identification of glial cells.

Figure 8-14

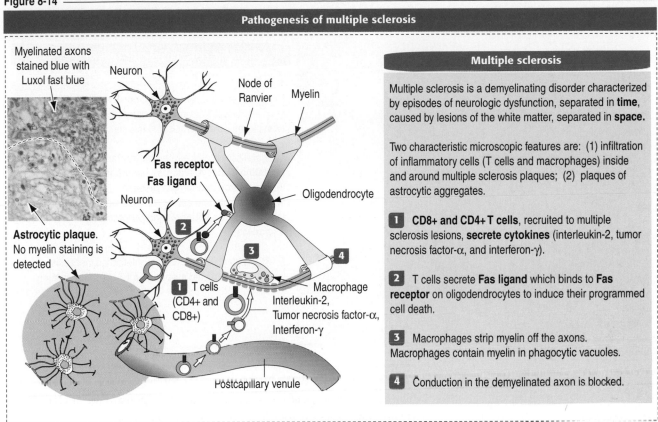

Pathogenesis of multiple sclerosis

Myelinated axons stained blue with Luxol fast blue

Astrocytic plaque. No myelin staining is detected

Neuron

Node of Ranvier

Myelin

Fas receptor
Fas ligand

Neuron

Oligodendrocyte

T cells (CD4+ and CD8+)

Macrophage
Interleukin-2,
Tumor necrosis factor-α,
Interferon-γ

Postcapillary venule

Multiple sclerosis

Multiple sclerosis is a demyelinating disorder characterized by episodes of neurologic dysfunction, separated in **time**, caused by lesions of the white matter, separated in **space**.

Two characteristic microscopic features are: (1) infiltration of inflammatory cells (T cells and macrophages) inside and around multiple sclerosis plaques; (2) plaques of astrocytic aggregates.

1 **CD8+ and CD4+ T cells**, recruited to multiple sclerosis lesions, **secrete cytokines** (interleukin-2, tumor necrosis factor-α, and interferon-γ).

2 T cells secrete **Fas ligand** which binds to **Fas receptor** on oligodendrocytes to induce their programmed cell death.

3 Macrophages strip myelin off the axons. Macrophages contain myelin in phagocytic vacuoles.

4 Conduction in the demyelinated axon is blocked.

Ependyma and choroid plexus
Ependyma

Ependyma designates the **simple cuboidal epithelium** covering the surface of the ventricles of the brain and the central canal of the spinal cord. The ependyma consists of two cell types (Figure 8–16): (1) **ependymal cells**, and (2) **tanycytes**.

Ependymal cells form a simple cuboidal epithelium, lining the ventricular cavities of the brain and the central canal of the spinal cord. These cells differentiate from **germinal** or **ventricular cells** of the embryonic neural tube (see Development of the Nervous System).

The apical domain of ependymal cells contains abundant **microvilli** and one or more cilia. **Desmosomes** link adjacent ependymal cells. The basal domain is in contact with **astrocytic processes**.

Tanycytes are specialized ependymal cells with basal processes extending between the astrocytic processes to form an end-foot on blood vessels.

During development, the ependymal cell layer comes in contact with the highly vascularized meninges, forming the **tela choroidea** in the roof of the third and fourth ventricles and along the choroid fissure of the lateral ventricles. These cells differentiate into secretory cells, which in combination with the meningeal blood vessels form the **choroid plexus**.

Choroid plexus

The cells of the choroid plexus are highly polarized (Figure 8–17). The **apical domain** contains microvilli, and **tight junctions** connect adjacent cells. The **basolateral domain** forms interdigitating folds, and the cell rests on a basal lamina.

Capillaries with fenestrated endothelial cells are located beneath the basal lamina. Macromolecules of the blood plasma can pass freely into the subepithelial space; however, they cannot pass directly into the CSF because of the elaborate interdigitations along the basolateral domain and the apical tight junctions.

Figure 8–15

Microglial cells

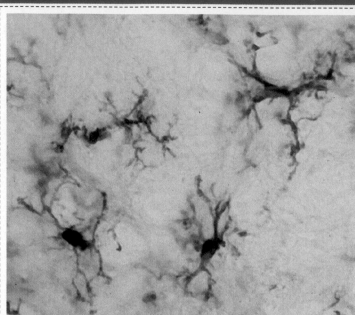

Microglial cells: Phagocytic cells of the CNS

Microglial cells, the resident macrophages of the CNS, are the primary cells to respond to injury to the brain (for example, multiple sclerosis and trauma).

Microglial cells produce **chemoattractants** capable of **recruiting leukocytes across the blood-brain barrier to initiate neuroimmunologic diseases.**
Microglial cells and astrocytes interact with each other to modulate the initiation and progression of immune responses.

A lack of balance of this cell-cell interaction mechanism leads to CNS-directed **autoimmunity** and **inflammation**.

Immunocytochemical preparation courtesy of Wan-hua Amy Yu

The cerebrospinal fluid

The choroid plexuses of the lateral, third, and fourth ventricles produce CSF.

CSF flows from the fourth ventricle into the brain and spinal subarachnoid space through median and lateral apertures. After entering the subarachnoid space, CSF flows outside the CNS into the blood, at the superior sagittal sinus (Figure 8–18).

CSF protects and supports the brain and spinal cord from external forces applied to the skull or vertebral column (cushioning effect). In addition, the CSF allows the removal of metabolic wastes by continual drainage of the ventricular cavities and subarachnoid space. The volume of CSF varies with the intracranial blood volume. The free communication of CSF among compartments protects against pressure differences.

Peripheral nervous system

The PNS includes all neuronal elements outside the brain and spinal cord. The peripheral nerves are the **cranial** and **spinal nerves**.

The PNS contains two **supporting cell types**: (1) **Schwann cells**, analogous to the oligodendrocytes of the CNS, and (2) the **satellite cells**, surrounding the cell bodies of neurons in sensory and autonomic ganglia. We discuss them later.

Individual nerve fibers of the PNS are ensheathed by **Schwann cells** (Figure 8–19). In **myelinated fibers**, individual Schwann cells wrap around the axon, forming a myelin sheath analogous to that of the oligodendrocytes of the CNS (see Figure 8–10). In **unmyelinated fibers**, a single Schwann cell envelops several axons (see Figure 8–12).

There are **two important differences between Schwann cells and oligodendrocytes**: (1) A single Schwann cell forms only one internodal segment of myelin, whereas a single oligodendrocyte may form 40 or 50. (2) Unmyelinated fibers in the PNS are embedded in Schwann cells, whereas those in the CNS are not ensheathed by oligodendrocytes but may have an investment of astrocytes.

Structure of a peripheral nerve

In addition to Schwann cells, peripheral nerves have three additional connective

Figure 8–16

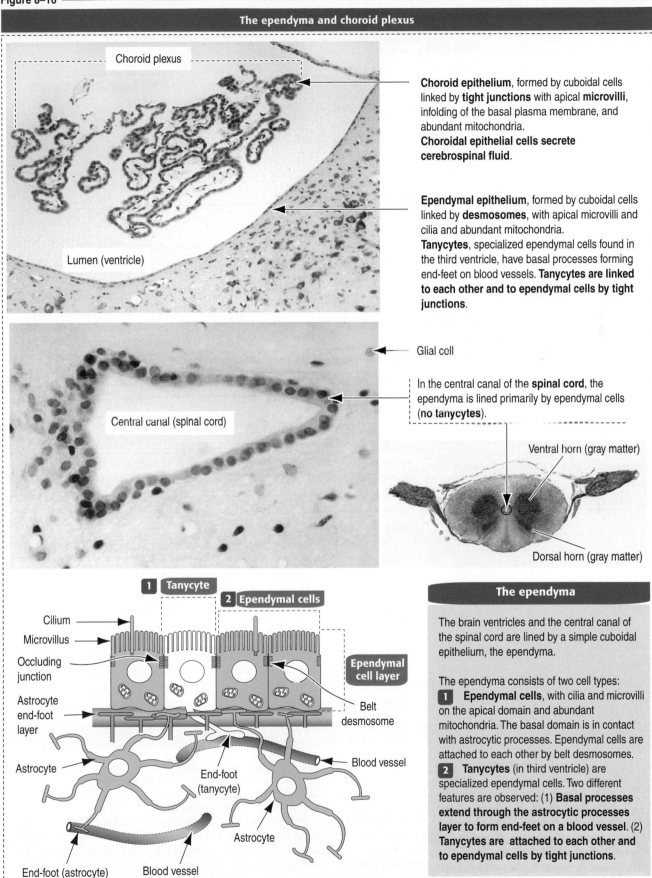

The ependyma and choroid plexus

Choroid plexus

Lumen (ventricle)

Choroid epithelium, formed by cuboidal cells linked by **tight junctions** with apical **microvilli**, infolding of the basal plasma membrane, and abundant mitochondria.
Choroidal epithelial cells secrete cerebrospinal fluid.

Ependymal epithelium, formed by cuboidal cells linked by **desmosomes**, with apical microvilli and cilia and abundant mitochondria.
Tanycytes, specialized ependymal cells found in the third ventricle, have basal processes forming end-feet on blood vessels. **Tanycytes are linked to each other and to ependymal cells by tight junctions**.

Glial cell

In the central canal of the **spinal cord**, the ependyma is lined primarily by ependymal cells (**no tanycytes**).

Central canal (spinal cord)

Ventral horn (gray matter)

Dorsal horn (gray matter)

1 Tanycyte
2 Ependymal cells

Cilium
Microvillus
Occluding junction
Astrocyte end-foot layer
Astrocyte

Ependymal cell layer

Belt desmosome

Blood vessel
End-foot (tanycyte)
Astrocyte
End-foot (astrocyte)
Blood vessel

The ependyma

The brain ventricles and the central canal of the spinal cord are lined by a simple cuboidal epithelium, the ependyma.

The ependyma consists of two cell types:
1 **Ependymal cells**, with cilia and microvilli on the apical domain and abundant mitochondria. The basal domain is in contact with astrocytic processes. Ependymal cells are attached to each other by belt desmosomes.
2 **Tanycytes** (in third ventricle) are specialized ependymal cells. Two different features are observed: (1) **Basal processes extend through the astrocytic processes layer to form end-feet on a blood vessel**. (2) **Tanycytes are attached to each other and to ependymal cells by tight junctions**.

Figure 8–17

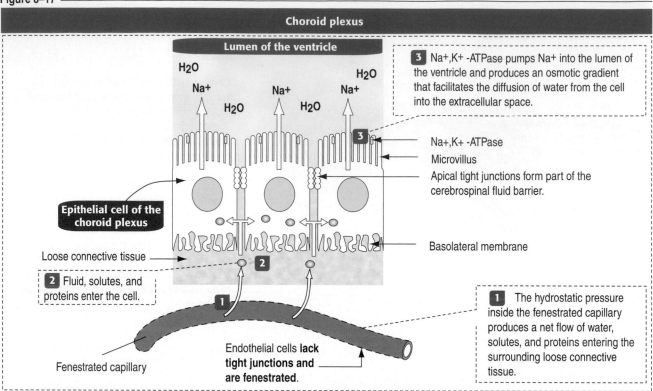

The blood–cerebrospinal fluid barrier

The epithelium of the choroid plexus represents a barrier between the blood and the cerebrospinal fluid. Several substances can leave the capillaries of the choroid plexus but cannot enter the cerebrospinal fluid.

tissue coverings (Figures 8–19 and 8–29): (1) the **epineurium**, (2) the **perineurium**, and (3) the **endoneurium**.

The epineurium is formed by type I collagen and fibroblasts and covers the entire nerve. Within the nerve, the perineurium segregates axons into **fascicles**. Several concentric layers of fibroblasts with two unusual characteristics form the perineurium: (1) A basal lamina surrounds the layers of fibroblasts. (2) Fibroblasts are joined to each other by tight junctions to form a protective barrier: the **blood-nerve barrier**.

The endoneurium surrounds individual axons and their associated Schwann cells. It consists of type III collagen fibrils and a few fibroblasts between individual nerve fibers. Additional components of the blood-nerve barrier are the endothelial cells of the **endoneurial capillaries**. Endoneurial capillaries derive from the vasa nervorum and are lined by continuous endothelial cells joined by tight junctions.

Clinical significance: Segmental demyelination and axonal degeneration

Diseases affecting Schwann cells lead to a loss of myelin, or **segmental demyelination**. Damage to the neuron and its axon leads to **axonal degeneration** (**wallerian degeneration**, first described by the English physiologist Augustus

Clinical significance of the blood-brain barrier

The brain is supplied with blood from major arteries forming an anastomotic network around the base of the brain. From this region, arteries project into the subarachnoid space before entering the brain tissue. In the brain, the perivascular space is surrounded by a basal lamina derived from both glial and endothelial cells: the **glia limitans**.

Nonfenestrated endothelial cells, linked by occluding junctions, prevent the diffusion of substances from the blood to the brain.

Occluding junctions represent the structural basis of the blood-brain barrier. This barrier offers free passage to glucose and other selected molecules but excludes most substances, in particular potent drugs required for the treatment of an infection or tumor. If the blood-brain barrier breaks down, tissue fluid accumulates in the nervous tissue, a condition known as **cerebral edema**.

External to the capillary endothelial cell lining is a basal lamina and external to this lamina are the end-feet of the astrocytes. Although the pericapillary end-feet of astrocytes are not part of the blood-brain barrier, they contribute to its maintenance by transporting fluid and ions from the perineuronal extracellular space to the blood vessels.

Figure 8–18

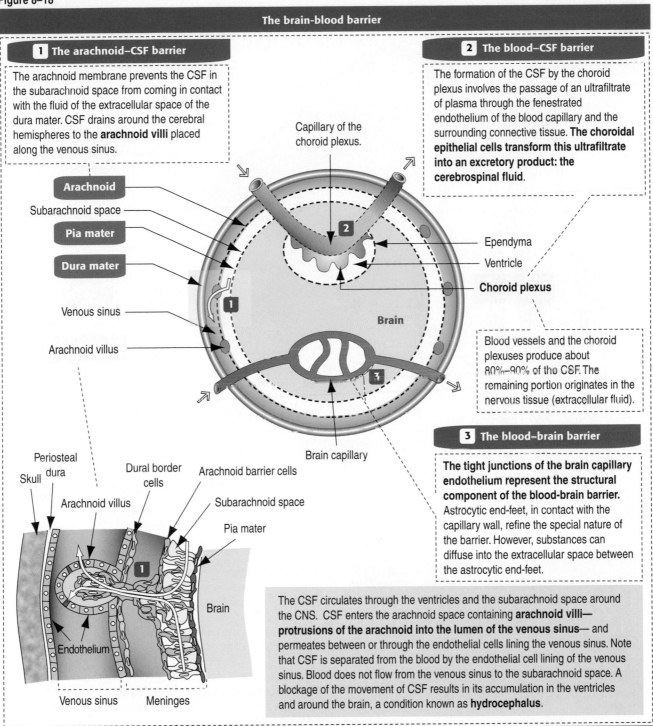

The brain-blood barrier

1 The arachnoid–CSF barrier

The arachnoid membrane prevents the CSF in the subarachnoid space from coming in contact with the fluid of the extracellular space of the dura mater. CSF drains around the cerebral hemispheres to the **arachnoid villi** placed along the venous sinus.

2 The blood–CSF barrier

The formation of the CSF by the choroid plexus involves the passage of an ultrafiltrate of plasma through the fenestrated endothelium of the blood capillary and the surrounding connective tissue. **The choroidal epithelial cells transform this ultrafiltrate into an excretory product: the cerebrospinal fluid.**

Capillary of the choroid plexus.

Arachnoid

Subarachnoid space

Pia mater

Dura mater

Venous sinus

Arachnoid villus

Ependyma

Ventricle

Choroid plexus

Brain

Blood vessels and the choroid plexuses produce about 80%–90% of the CSF. The remaining portion originates in the nervous tissue (extracellular fluid).

3 The blood–brain barrier

The tight junctions of the brain capillary endothelium represent the structural component of the blood-brain barrier. Astrocytic end-feet, in contact with the capillary wall, refine the special nature of the barrier. However, substances can diffuse into the extracellular space between the astrocytic end-feet.

Brain capillary

Periosteal dura

Skull

Dural border cells

Arachnoid barrier cells

Arachnoid villus

Subarachnoid space

Pia mater

Brain

Endothelium

Venous sinus

Meninges

The CSF circulates through the ventricles and the subarachnoid space around the CNS. CSF enters the arachnoid space containing **arachnoid villi— protrusions of the arachnoid into the lumen of the venous sinus—** and permeates between or through the endothelial cells lining the venous sinus. Note that CSF is separated from the blood by the endothelial cell lining of the venous sinus. Blood does not flow from the venous sinus to the subarachnoid space. A blockage of the movement of CSF results in its accumulation in the ventricles and around the brain, a condition known as **hydrocephalus**.

Volney Waller, 1816–1870).

Axonal degeneration (Figure 8–21) may be followed by **axonal regeneration**. Recall from our discussion in Chapter 7, Muscle Tissue, that the **motor unit** is the functional unit of the neuromuscular system. Therefore, segmental demyelination and axonal degeneration affect the motor unit and cause **muscle paralysis** and **atrophy**. Physiotherapy for the paralyzed muscles is necessary to prevent muscle degeneration before regenerating motor axons can reach the motor unit.

Segmental demyelination occurs when the function of the Schwann cell is

Figure 8–19

Structure of a peripheral nerve

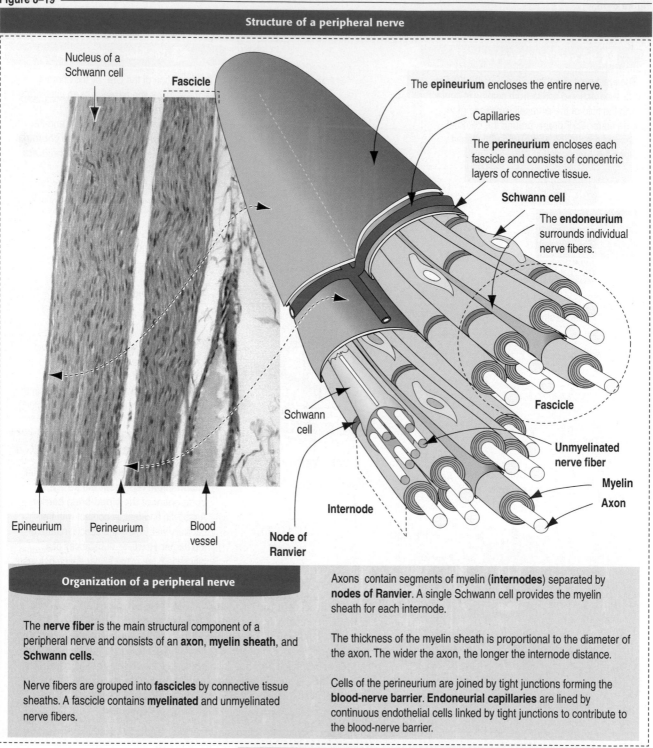

Nucleus of a Schwann cell

Fascicle

Epineurium

Perineurium

Blood vessel

Node of Ranvier

Schwann cell

Internode

The **epineurium** encloses the entire nerve.

Capillaries

The **perineurium** encloses each fascicle and consists of concentric layers of connective tissue.

Schwann cell

The **endoneurium** surrounds individual nerve fibers.

Fascicle

Unmyelinated nerve fiber

Myelin

Axon

Organization of a peripheral nerve

The **nerve fiber** is the main structural component of a peripheral nerve and consists of an **axon**, **myelin sheath**, and **Schwann cells**.

Nerve fibers are grouped into **fascicles** by connective tissue sheaths. A fascicle contains **myelinated** and unmyelinated nerve fibers.

Axons contain segments of myelin (**internodes**) separated by **nodes of Ranvier**. A single Schwann cell provides the myelin sheath for each internode.

The thickness of the myelin sheath is proportional to the diameter of the axon. The wider the axon, the longer the internode distance.

Cells of the perineurium are joined by tight junctions forming the **blood-nerve barrier**. **Endoneurial capillaries** are lined by continuous endothelial cells linked by tight junctions to contribute to the blood-nerve barrier.

abnormal or there is damage to the myelin sheath, for example, a crush nerve injury. If the nerve fiber is completely severed, the chances of recovery decrease unless a nerve segment is grafted. **The presence of the endoneurium is essential for the proliferation of Schwann cells.** Schwann cells guide an axonal sprout, derived from the proximal axonal stump, to reach the end organ (for example, a muscle).

Several sprouts can grow into the connective tissue and, together with proliferative Schwann cells, form a mass called an **amputation neuroma**. Amputation

Figure 8–20

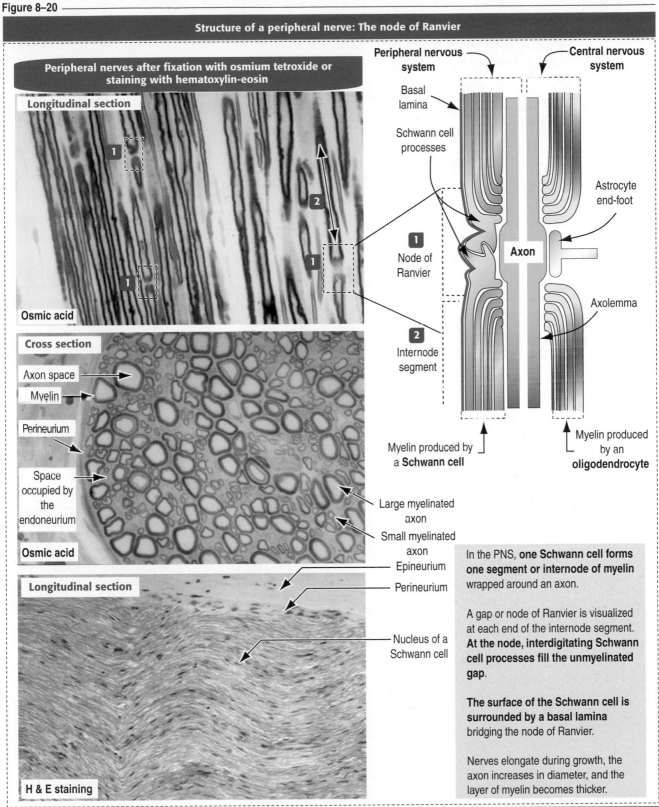

Structure of a peripheral nerve: The node of Ranvier

Peripheral nerves after fixation with osmium tetroxide or staining with hematoxylin-eosin

Longitudinal section

Osmic acid

Cross section

Axon space
Myelin
Perineurium
Space occupied by the endoneurium

Osmic acid

Longitudinal section

H & E staining

Peripheral nervous system
Central nervous system

Basal lamina
Schwann cell processes

1 Node of Ranvier

Axon

Astrocyte end-foot

Axolemma

2 Internode segment

Myelin produced by a **Schwann cell**
Myelin produced by an **oligodendrocyte**

Large myelinated axon
Small myelinated axon
Epineurium
Perineurium

Nucleus of a Schwann cell

In the PNS, **one Schwann cell forms one segment or internode of myelin** wrapped around an axon.

A gap or node of Ranvier is visualized at each end of the internode segment. **At the node, interdigitating Schwann cell processes fill the unmyelinated gap.**

The surface of the Schwann cell is surrounded by a basal lamina bridging the node of Ranvier.

Nerves elongate during growth, the axon increases in diameter, and the layer of myelin becomes thicker.

neuromas prevent regrowth of the axon after trauma and must be surgically removed to allow reinnervation of the peripheral end organ.

Axonal regeneration is very slow process. It starts 2 weeks after injury and is completed, if successful, after several months. Schwann cells remyelinate the denuded portion of the axon, but the length of internodal myelin is shorter.

Figure 8–21

Peripheral nerve degeneration and regeneration

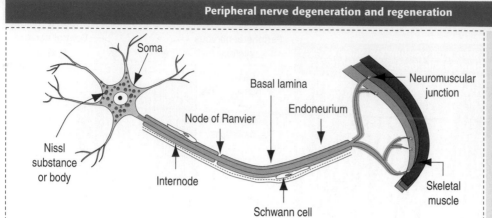

An intact motor neuron is shown with an axon ending in a neuromuscular junction. The axon is surrounded by a **myelin sheath** and a **basal lamina** —produced by Schwann cells—and the **endoneurium**.

The soma of the neuron contains abundant **Nissl bodies** (aggregates of ribosomes attached to the endoplasmic reticulum and free polyribosomes).

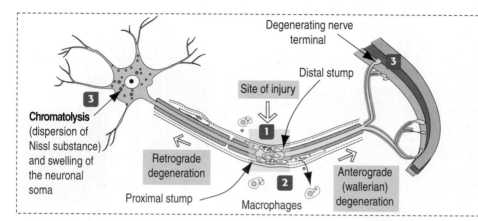

1 An injury damages the nerve fiber. Schwann cells undergo mitotic division and bridge the gap between the **proximal** and **distal** axonal stumps.
2 Schwann cells phagocytose myelin. Myelin droplets are extruded from Schwann cells and subsequently are phagocytosed by tissue macrophages.
3 **Chromatolysis** and degeneration of the axon terminals are seen. The distal and proximal segments of the axon degenerate (**anterograde** and **retrograde degeneration**, respectively).

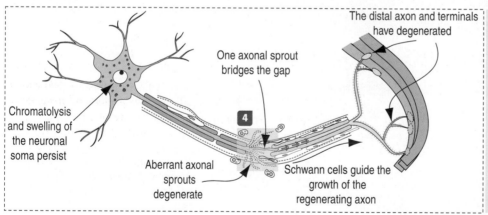

4 The proximal axonal stump generates multiple **sprouts** advancing between Schwann cells. One sprout persists and grows distally (~1.5 mm per day) to reinnervate the muscle. The remaining sprouts degenerate.
In the CNS, degeneration of the axon and myelin is similar and microglial cells remove debris by phagocytosis.
The regeneration process starts but is aborted by the absence of endoneurium and lack of proliferation of oligodendrocytes.

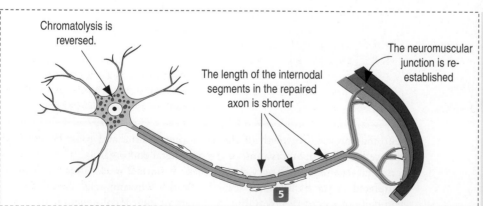

5 Once the regenerated axon reaches the end organ (several months), Schwann cells start the production of myelin. **The internodal segments are shorter**.

The regenerated axon has a reduced diameter (80% of the original diameter) and, therefore, the conduction velocity of the nerve impulse is slower.

Figure 8–22 _____

Amyotrophic lateral sclerosis

Demyelinization

Ventral horn

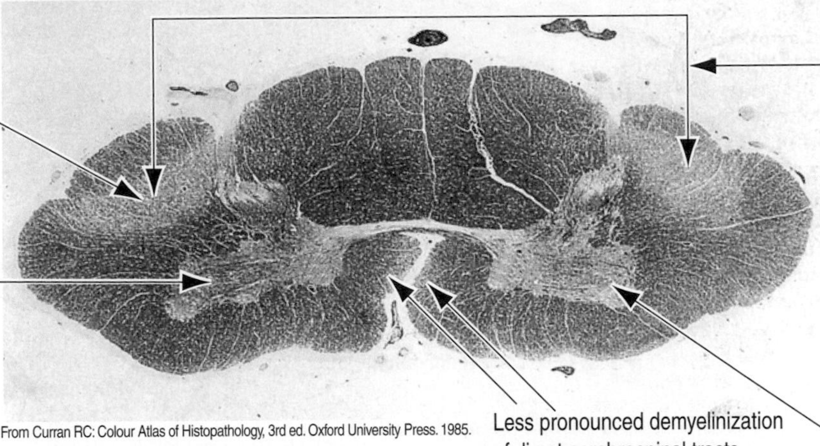

From Curran RC: Colour Atlas of Histopathology, 3rd ed. Oxford University Press. 1985.

Symmetrical loss of myelinated fibers in a section of spinal cord (crossed cerebrospinal tracts) from a patient with amyotrophic lateral sclerosis. The preparation was stained for myelin.

Less pronounced demyelinization of direct cerebrospinal tracts

Ventral horn

Amyotrophic lateral sclerosis (ALS; also known as **Lou Gherig's disease**) is a severe condition characterized by **progressive degeneration of motor neurons of the brainstem and spinal cord.** Amyotrophic refers to **muscle atrophy.** Lateral sclerosis refers to the **hardness to palpation of the lateral columns of the spinal cord** in autopsy specimens. Lateral sclerosis is caused by an increased number of astrocytes (**astrocytic gliosis**) following the degeneration and loss of motor neurons.

ALS is a familial motor neuron disease in 5% to 10% of cases. The others are assumed to be sporadic. Mutations in the gene encoding **superoxide dismutase 1** (**SOD1**) account for 20% of the cases of familial ALS. The remaining 80% are caused by mutations of other genes.

SOD1 is an enzyme that requires copper to catalyze the conversion of toxic superoxide radicals to hydrogen peroxide and oxygen. The toxic effects of mutant SOD1 result in the disorganization of intermediate filaments (NF-L, NF-M, and NF-H; see Figure 8–4), mitochondrial abnormalities, and apoptosis of motor neurons. Autoimmunity may have a role in the pathogenesis of ALS. Patients with sporadic ALS have antibodies against voltage-gated Ca^{2+} channels, which may interfere with the regulation of intracellular Ca^{2+}, leading to the degeneration of motor neurons. However, immunotherapy has not been effective in patients with ALS. The clinically apparent signs are overactive tendon reflexes, Hoffman sign (digital reflex; flexion of the terminal phalanx of the thumb following nipping of the nail), Babinski sign (extension of the great toe and abduction of the other toes after plantar stimulation), and clonus (Gk. *klonos*, a tumult; muscle contraction and relaxation of a muscle in rapid succession).

Axonal degeneration results from the primary destruction of the axon by metabolic or toxic damage and is followed by demyelination and degeneration of the neuronal cell body. This process is known as a "**dying back**" neuropathy.

Regeneration of nerve fibers in the CNS is not possible at present because of the following factors: (1) An endoneurium is not present. (2) Oligodendrocytes do not proliferate like Schwann cells, and a single oligodendrocyte serves a large number of axons. (3) Astrocytes deposit scar tissue (the astrocytic plaque).

Clinical significance: Neurodegenerative diseases

Degenerative processes of specific groups of neurons of the brain cause movement disorders, dementia syndromes, and autonomic perturbations. Neurodegenerative diseases include:

1. **Amyotrophic lateral sclerosis** (Figure 8–22), a motor neuron progressive disease starting with moderate weakness in one limb and progressing to severe paralysis (swallowing and respiratory disorders), leading to death in about 3 years. The cause is unknown. In a few familial cases, a mutation in the copper-zinc superoxide dismutase (SOD1) gene has been reported.

2. **Parkinson's disease,** a progressive movement disease characterized by rest tremor, slow voluntary movements (**hypokinetic disorders**), and movements with rigidity. This disease is caused by **a loss of dopaminergic neurons from the substantia nigra.** Although the cause of the disease is unknown, recent developments in understanding the functional organization of basal ganglia have led to

Figure 8–23

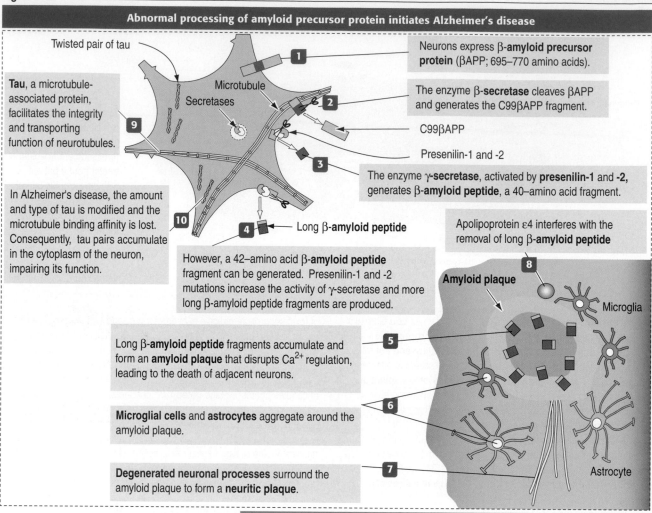

Abnormal processing of amyloid precursor protein initiates Alzheimer's disease

Twisted pair of tau

1 Neurons express β-**amyloid precursor protein** (βAPP; 695–770 amino acids).

Tau, a microtubule-associated protein, facilitates the integrity and transporting function of neurotubules.

Microtubule

Secretases

2 The enzyme β-**secretase** cleaves βAPP and generates the C99βAPP fragment.

C99βAPP

Presenilin-1 and -2

3 The enzyme γ-**secretase**, activated by **presenilin-1** and **-2**, generates β-**amyloid peptide**, a 40–amino acid fragment.

9

10

In Alzheimer's disease, the amount and type of tau is modified and the microtubule binding affinity is lost. Consequently, tau pairs accumulate in the cytoplasm of the neuron, impairing its function.

4 Long β-**amyloid peptide**

However, a 42–amino acid β-**amyloid peptide** fragment can be generated. Presenilin-1 and -2 mutations increase the activity of γ-secretase and more long β-amyloid peptide fragments are produced.

Apolipoprotein ε4 interferes with the removal of long β-**amyloid peptide**

Amyloid plaque

8

Microglia

Long β-**amyloid peptide** fragments accumulate and form an **amyloid plaque** that disrupts Ca^{2+} regulation, leading to the death of adjacent neurons. **5**

Microglial cells and astrocytes aggregate around the amyloid plaque. **6**

Degenerated neuronal processes surround the amyloid plaque to form a **neuritic plaque**. **7**

Astrocyte

the development of new pharmacologic and surgical (**thalamotomy** and **pallidotomy**) therapies.

3. **Alzheimer's disease**, a progressive cortical dementia affecting language, memory, and vision, as well as emotion or personality. Mutations in **presenilin-1 and -2**, and in **β amyloid precursor protein** (βAPP) genes are documented in familial forms of Alzheimer's disease. Figure 8–23 summarizes the major molecular events observed in the brains of patients with Alzheimer's disease, in particular the formation of **amyloid plaques**. Alterations in the stabilizing function of **tau**, a microtubule-associated protein, result in the accumulation of twisted pairs of tau in neurons. Figure 8–7 stresses the role of microtubules in axonal transport, a function affected by abnormal tau.

Inheritance of one or more **apolipoprotein Eε4** alleles (**APOE locus**) is indicative of a susceptibility risk factor. The ε4 allele is associated with an earlier age of onset of the common form of Alzheimer's disease. The ε4/ε4 homozygotes, present in about 2% of the general population, have the greatest risk of developing the disease.

No treatment is available for Alzheimer's disease. Symptomatic therapy is helpful during the early stages of dementia.

Sensory ganglia

Sensory ganglia of the **posterior spinal nerve roots** and the **trunks of the trigeminal, facial, glossopharyngeal, and vagal cranial nerves** have a similar organization (Figure 8–24).

Figure 8–24

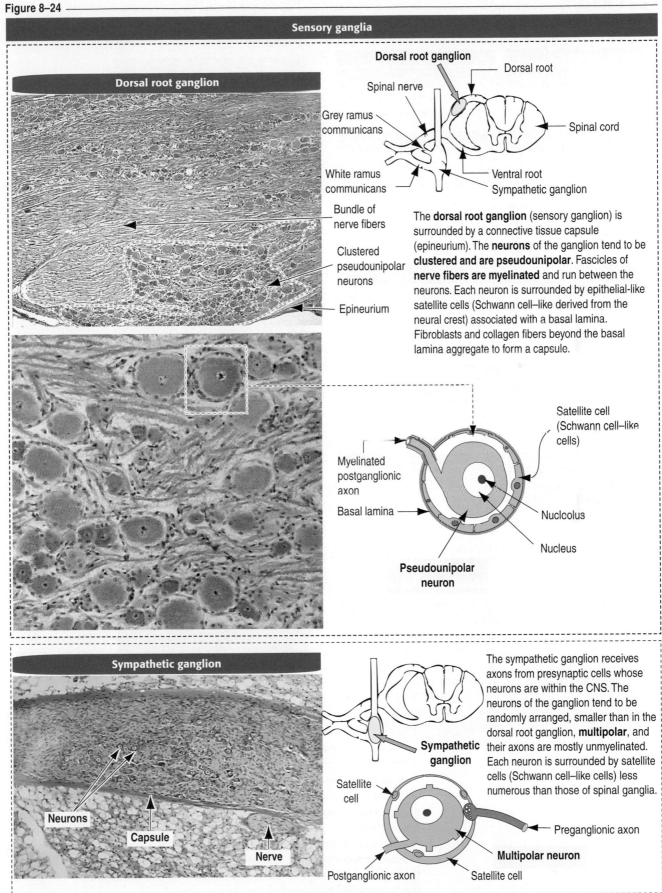

Sensory ganglia

Dorsal root ganglion

Dorsal root ganglion — Dorsal root

Spinal nerve

Grey ramus communicans — Spinal cord

White ramus communicans

Bundle of nerve fibers — Ventral root

Clustered pseudounipolar neurons — Sympathetic ganglion

Epineurium

The **dorsal root ganglion** (sensory ganglion) is surrounded by a connective tissue capsule (epineurium). The **neurons** of the ganglion tend to be **clustered and are pseudounipolar**. Fascicles of **nerve fibers are myelinated** and run between the neurons. Each neuron is surrounded by epithelial-like satellite cells (Schwann cell–like derived from the neural crest) associated with a basal lamina. Fibroblasts and collagen fibers beyond the basal lamina aggregate to form a capsule.

Satellite cell (Schwann cell–like cells)

Myelinated postganglionic axon

Basal lamina

Nucleolus

Nucleus

Pseudounipolar neuron

Sympathetic ganglion

Sympathetic ganglion

The sympathetic ganglion receives axons from presynaptic cells whose neurons are within the CNS. The neurons of the ganglion tend to be randomly arranged, smaller than in the dorsal root ganglion, **multipolar**, and their axons are mostly unmyelinated. Each neuron is surrounded by satellite cells (Schwann cell–like cells) less numerous than those of spinal ganglia.

Satellite cell

Neurons

Capsule

Nerve

Preganglionic axon

Multipolar neuron

Postganglionic axon — Satellite cell

Figure 8–25

Methods	Reagents
Basic dyes	
Nissl	Basic dyes (methylene blue, cresyl violet, thionin, hematoxylin)
Metal impregnation methods	
Bielschowsky, Bodian, Cajal, Glees, Nauta	Reduced silver nitrate
Fink-Heimer, Nauta	Reduced silver nitrate
Golgi	Silver nitrate
Myelin stains	
Osmium tetroxide	Osmium tetroxide
Klüver-Barrera	Luxol fast blue PAS-hematoxylin
Weigert-Pal	Iron hematoxylin
Glial stains	
Cajal	Gold sublimate
Del Rio Hortega	Silver carbonate
Neurotransmitters	
Induced fluorescence Formaldehyde	
Glyoxylic acid	
Immunocytochemistry	Specific antibodies to neurotransmitters, synthesizing enzymes, and neuropeptides
Pathway tracing methods	
Anterograde transport	[³H-leucine] injected into the soma or perykarya combined with autoradiography
Retrograde transport	**Horseradish peroxidase** injected near synaptic terminals; the marker is internalized and transported to the perykaryon

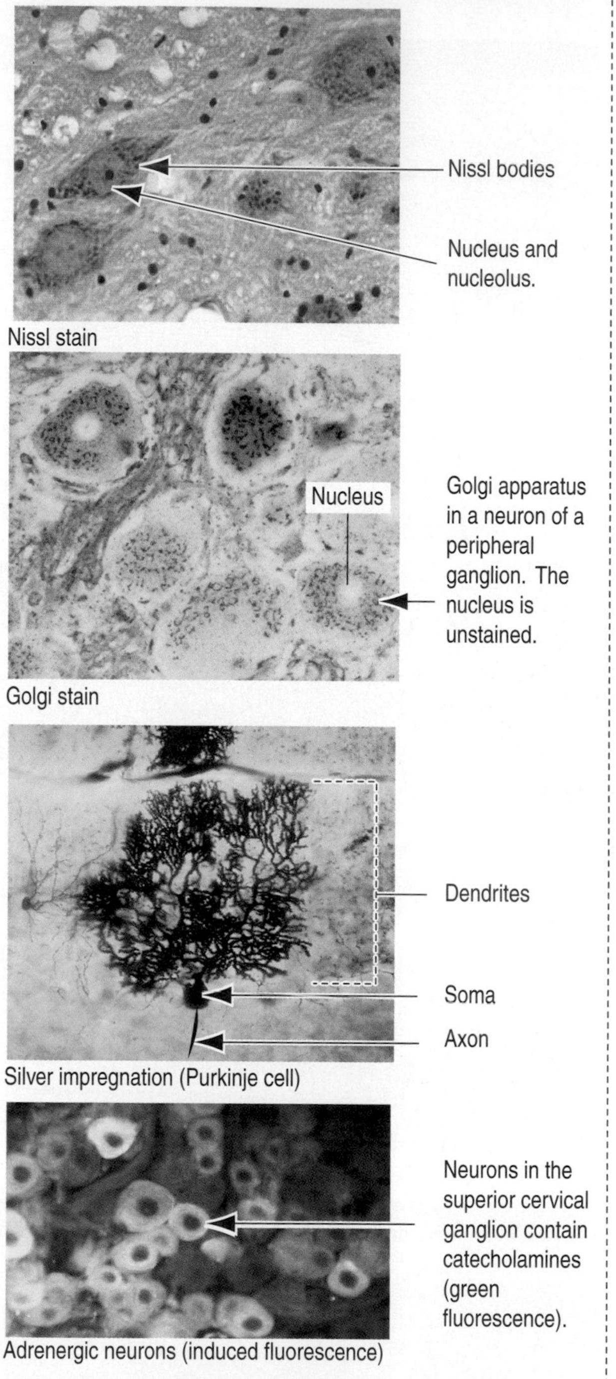

Nissl stain — Nissl bodies / Nucleus and nucleolus.

Golgi stain — Nucleus / Golgi apparatus in a neuron of a peripheral ganglion. The nucleus is unstained.

Silver impregnation (Purkinje cell) — Dendrites / Soma / Axon

Adrenergic neurons (induced fluorescence) — Neurons in the superior cervical ganglion contain catecholamines (green fluorescence).

Silver impregnation courtesy of Wan-hua Amy Yu; adrenergic neurons courtesy of Edward W. Gresik, New York.

A connective tissue capsule, representing the continuation of the epineurium and perineurium surrounds each ganglion. Neurons are **pseudounipolar** (unipolar), with a single **unmyelinated** process leaving each cell body. The short process bifurcates into a **peripheral** and a **central** branch. The peripheral branch reaches a peripheral sensory ending and terminates in dendrites. The central branch enters the CNS. The neuronal cell body is surrounded by a layer of flattened **satellite cells**, similar to Schwann cells and continuous with them as they enclose the peripheral and central process of each neuron.

A nerve impulse reaching the T-bifurcation junction bypasses the nerve cell body, traveling from the peripheral axon to the central axon.

Autonomic (sympathetic and parasympathetic) ganglia

Autonomic ganglia are found in the **sympathetic trunks**, in **plexuses** (for example, celiac and mesenteric plexuses), and close to or within viscera (plexuses of **Auerbach** and **Meissner**).

As found in the sensory ganglia, a layer of connective tissue continuous with the epineurium and perineurium of the peripheral nerve fiber (see Figure 8–24) surrounds each autonomic ganglion. The neurons of the autonomic ganglia are **multipolar. The dendrites are contacted by myelinated axons of preganglionic neurons (white rami).** The **axons have a small diameter and are unmyelinated (grey rami).** Each neuronal cell body is surrounded by Schwann cell–like **satellite cells.**

Neurohistologic methods

The nervous tissue has specialized features not observed in other basic tissues stained with routine staining methods such as hematoxylin and eosin. For example, **basic dyes** can demonstrate the cytoplasmic Nissl substance (ribonucleoproteins) in the cytoplasm of neurons (Figure 8–25).

Reduced silver methods produce dark deposits in various structures of neurons and glial cells. The **Golgi method** is particularly valuable for the study of dendrites. A variant of the Golgi method enables the identification of the cytomembranes and vesicles of the Golgi apparatus.

Myelin stains are based on the use of dyes with binding affinity for proteins bound to phospholipids. They are useful for the identification of tracts of fibers. Combined Nissl and myelin stains are used in neuropathology.

A tracer, such as horseradish peroxidase, injected into a neuron using a micropipet, has been used for anterograde transport studies. Similarly, tracers injected into nerve terminals can identify the putative neuron by its retrograde transport. The use of a tracer depends on the activities of living cells in the nervous system.

Histochemical techniques are available for the localization of substances (for example, catecholamines, enzymes, and others) present in specific populations of neurons.

9. SENSORY ORGANS: VISION AND HEARING

The eye

The eye can self-focus, adjust for light intensity, and convert light into electrical impulses interpreted by the brain. In humans, the eye is recessed in a bony orbit and is connected to the brain by the optic nerve. The eyeball protects and facilitates the function of the photoreceptive retina, the inner layer of the eyeball.

The eyeball consists of **three tunics** or **layers** which, from outside to inside, are (Figure 9–1) (1) the **sclera** and the **cornea**, (2) the **uvea**, and (3) the **retina**.

Three distinct and interconnected chambers are found inside the eyeball: the **anterior chamber**, the **posterior chamber**, and the **vitreous cavity**. **Aqueous humor** circulates from the posterior to the anterior chamber. The **lens** is placed in front of the vitreous cavity, which contains **vitreous humor**. The **bony orbit**, the **eyelids**, the **conjunctiva**, and the **lacrimal apparatus** protect the eyeball.

The **ophthalmic artery**, a branch of the internal carotid artery, provides nutrients to the eye and the contents of the orbit. The **superior** and **inferior orbital veins** are the principal venous drainage of the eye. The veins empty into

Figure 9–1

The anatomy of the eye

The eye consists of three chambers:
1. The **anterior chamber** is the space between the cornea and the anterior surface of the iris.
2. The **posterior chamber** extends from the posterior surface of the iris to the lens.
3. The **vitreous cavity** or **body** is posterior to the lens and is the largest compartment.

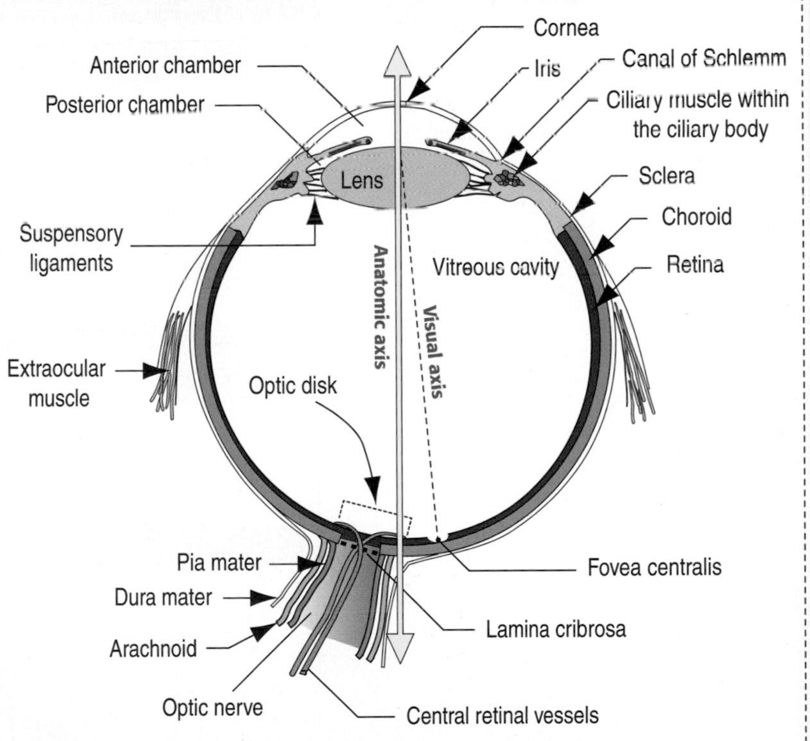

The human eyeball is roughly spherical with a diameter of about 24 mm. The anterior pole of the eyeball is the center of the **cornea**. The posterior pole is located between the **optic disk** and the **fovea**, a shallow depression in the retina. The **anatomic axis** (also called the **optical axis**) is the line connecting the two poles. The **visual axis** joins the apparent center of the pupil and the center of the fovea and divides the eyeball into **nasal** and **temporal halves**.

The eyeball is surrounded by a soft tissue cushion occupying the bony orbit of the skull. The soft tissue includes loose connective tissue, fat, muscles, blood and lymphatic vessels, nerves, and the lacrimal gland. The anterior surface of the eyeball is connected to the integument by the **conjunctiva**, which lines the inner surface of the lids and reflects over the eyeball to the edge of the cornea.

the **intracranial cavernous sinus**.

The development of the eye

A brief summary of the development of the eye is essential to the understanding of the relationship of the various layers in the eyeball. The components of the eye derive from (1) the surface **ectoderm** of the head; (2) the lateral **neuroecto-dermal** walls of the embryonic brain in the diencephalon region; and (3) the **mesenchyme**.

Lateral outpocketing of the right and left sides of the diencephalon gives rise to two neuroepithelial **optic vesicles**, each remaining attached to the brain wall by a hollow **optic stalk** (Figure 9–2). The surface ectoderm of the head invaginates into the optical vesicle forming a **lens vesicle** that pinches off. Mesenchyme surrounds both the lens vesicle and the adjacent optic vesicle.

The optic vesicle invaginates and becomes a double-walled **optic cup** (see Figure 9–2). The **optic fissure** forms when the outer layer of the optic cup becomes the **pigmented epithelium**. Cells in the inner layer proliferate and stratify to form the **neural retina**. The mesenchyme extending into the invagination of the optic cup acquires a gelatinous consistency and becomes the **vitreous component** of the eye. The **lens vesicle** is kept in place by the free margins of the optic cup and the surrounding mesenchyme.

At the outer surface of the optic cup, the mesenchymal shell differentiates

Figure 9–2

The development of the eye

Week 5: Optic vesicle

Week 6: Optic cup

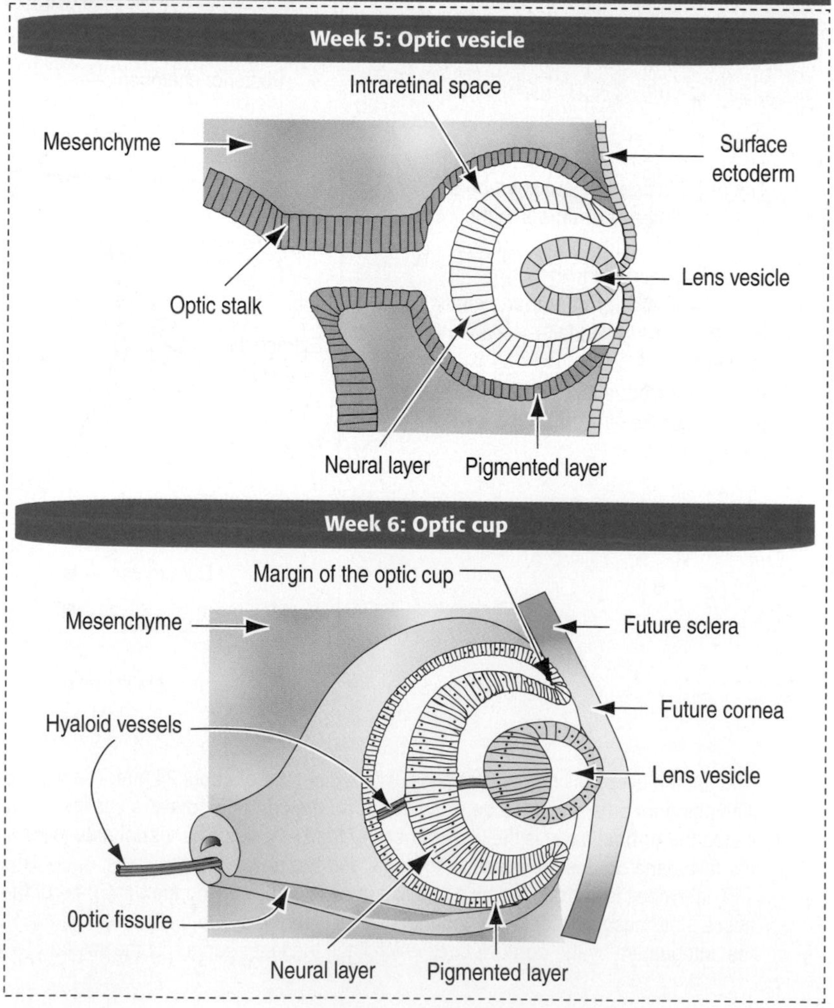

Figure 9–3

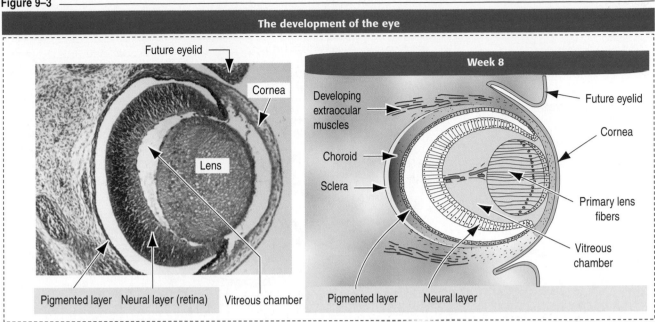

The development of the eye

Future eyelid

Cornea

Lens

Pigmented layer   Neural layer (retina)   Vitreous chamber

Week 8

Developing extraocular muscles

Choroid

Sclera

Future eyelid

Cornea

Primary lens fibers

Vitreous chamber

Pigmented layer   Neural layer

The development of the cornea

The lens induces the differentiation of the overlying ectoderm. Cells of the mesenchyme secrete types I and II collagen, components of the primary stroma of the cornea.

Capillary endothelial cells migrate into the primary stroma and produce hyaluronic acid, causing the stroma to swell.

Mesenchymal cells in the surrounding space migrate into the stroma and secrete hyaluronidase. The stroma shrinks and the cornea acquires the correct shape and transparency.

---

into the vascular **choroid coat** of the eye and the fibrous components of the **sclera** and **cornea** (Figure 9–3). Posterior to the lens, the vascular choroid coat forms the **ciliary body, ciliary muscle**, and **ciliary processes**. Anterior to the lens, the choroid coat forms the stroma of the **iris**. The ciliary processes secrete the **aqueous humor** that accumulates first in the **posterior chamber** (between iris and lens) and then passes into the anterior chamber (between lens and cornea) across the pupil. The aqueous humor leaves the anterior chamber by entering into the **canal of Schlemm**, a small vein (**sinus venosus of the sclera**) encircling the eye at the anterior edge of the choroid coat.

Around the rim of the optic cup, the inner and outer layers form the **posterior epithelium** of the **ciliary body** and **iris**. The sphincter and **dilator pupillae muscles** develop from the posterior epithelium.

The inner layer of the optic cup becomes the neural layer of the retina, which differentiates into **photosensory cells, bipolar neurons**, and **ganglionic neurons** (including interconnecting **horizontal** and **amacrine cells** and **glial Müller cells**). Axons from the ganglionic neurons form the nerve fiber layer of the retina, which converges on the optic stalk occupying the optic fissure as the **optic nerve**. The optic fissure becomes the escape route from the optic cup (except at its rim).

The outer tunic of the eye
The sclera

The sclera (Figure 9–4) is a 1.0 to 0.4-mm thick layer of collagen and elastic fibers produced by fibroblasts. The inner side of the sclera faces the choroid, from which it is separated by a layer of loose connective tissue and an elastic tissue network known as the **suprachoroid lamina**. Tendons of the six extrinsic muscles of the eye are attached to the outer surface of the sclera.

The cornea

The cornea is 1.1 to 0.8-mm thick and has a smaller radius of curvature than the sclera. It is transparent, lacks blood vessels, and is extremely rich in nerve endings. The anterior surface of the cornea is always kept wet with a film of tears retained by microvilli of the apical epithelial cells. The cornea is one of the few organs that can be transplanted without a risk of being rejected by the host's immune system. This success can be attributed to the lack of corneal blood and

Figure 9–4

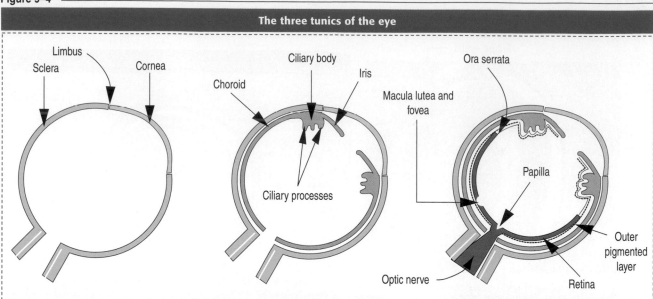

The three tunics of the eye

Outer tunic	**Middle tunic**	**Inner tunic**
Sclera and cornea	**The uvea**	**The retina**

The **cornea** (Lat. *corneus*, horny) is transparent. The rest of the wall of the eye, the **sclera** (Gk. *scleros*, hard), is opaque and lined inside by the middle or vascular pigmented layer which absorbs light. The **limbus** is the zone of transition of the epithelium of the conjunctiva with that of the cornea. The limbus is also the boundary of the transparent cornea with the opaque sclera.

The corneoscleral coat:

1. Protects the inner structures of the eye.

2. Together with the intraocular fluid pressure, it maintains the shape and consistency of the eyeball.

In the posterior two thirds of the eye, the vascular layer is called the **choroid**. In the anterior part of the eye the vascular layer thickens to form the **ciliary body**. **Ciliary processes** extend inward from the ciliary body. The vascular layer continues as the **iris**, whose free edge outlines the **pupil**.

1. The vascular layer is **pigmented**, a property that light-proofs the inner surface of the eye and reduces reflection of the light.

2. Blood vessels travel through the middle layer.

3. Its anterior portion contains smooth muscle: the **muscle of the ciliary body** and the **dilator** and **constrictor of the iris**. The **smooth muscle of the ciliary body** regulates the tension of the **zonule** or **suspensory ligament** of the lens and, therefore, is an important element in the mechanism of **accommodation**.

It consists of two layers: (1) an **outer pigmented layer** (pars pigmentosa); (2) an **inner retinal layer** (pars nervosa or optica). The retina has a posterior two-thirds **light-sensitive** zone (pars optica) and an anterior one-third **light-nonsensitive** zone (pars ciliaris and iridica). The scalloped border between these two zones is called the **ora serrata** (Lat. *ora*, edge; *serrata*, sawlike).

The retina contains **photoreceptor neurons** (cones and rods), **conducting neurons** (bipolar and ganglion cells), **association neurons** (horizontal and amacrine cells), and a **supporting neuroglial cell**, the Müller cell.

Each eye contains about 125 million rods and cones but only 1 million ganglion cells. The number of cones and rods varies over the surface of the retina. **Only cones are present in the fovea** (0.5 mm in diameter) where fine detail vision is best. Axons from the retinal ganglion cells pass across the surface of the retina, converge on the **papilla** or **optic disk**, and leave the eye through many openings of the sclera (the **lamina cribrosa**) to form the **optic nerve**.

lymphatic vessels.

The cornea is composed of five layers (Figure 9–5):

1. The **corneal epithelium**.
2. The **membrane of Bowman**.
3. The **stroma** or **substantia propria**.
4. The **membrane of Descemet**.
5. The **corneal endothelium**.

The **corneal epithelium** is stratified squamous and consists of five to seven layers of cells. Cells of the outer surface have **microvilli** and all cells are connected to one another by desmosomes. The cytoplasm contains cytokeratin associated with desmosomes. The epithelium of the cornea is very sensitive, contains a large number of free nerve endings, and has a remarkable wound healing capacity. At the **limbus**, the corneosclera junction, the corneal epithelium is continuous with that of the conjunctiva.

Figure 9–5

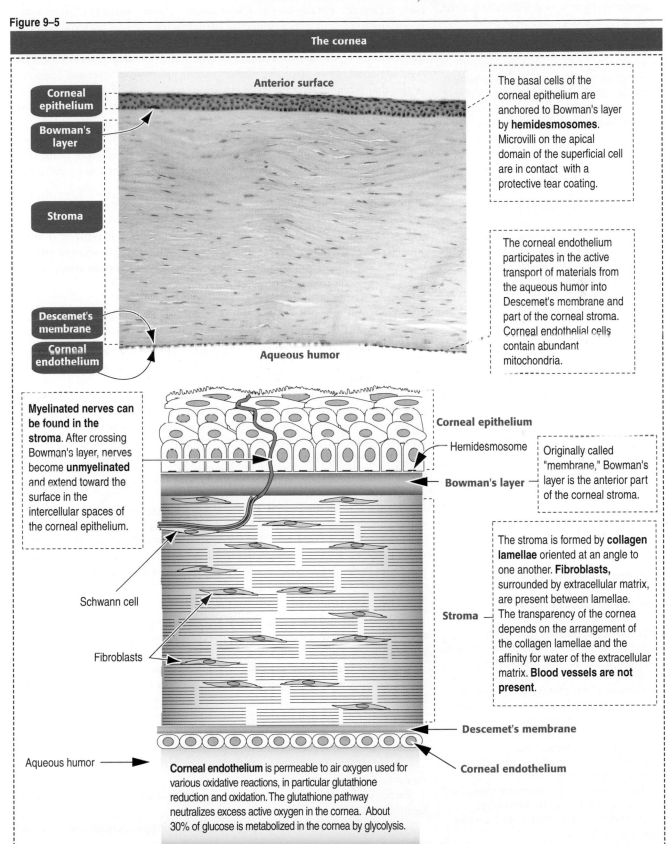

The cornea

Corneal epithelium
Bowman's layer
Stroma
Descemet's membrane
Corneal endothelium

Anterior surface

Aqueous humor

The basal cells of the corneal epithelium are anchored to Bowman's layer by **hemidesmosomes**. Microvilli on the apical domain of the superficial cell are in contact with a protective tear coating.

The corneal endothelium participates in the active transport of materials from the aqueous humor into Descemet's membrane and part of the corneal stroma. Corneal endothelial cells contain abundant mitochondria.

Myelinated nerves can be found in the stroma. After crossing Bowman's layer, nerves become **unmyelinated** and extend toward the surface in the intercellular spaces of the corneal epithelium.

Schwann cell

Fibroblasts

Aqueous humor

Corneal epithelium

Hemidesmosome

Bowman's layer

Originally called "membrane," Bowman's layer is the anterior part of the corneal stroma.

Stroma

The stroma is formed by **collagen lamellae** oriented at an angle to one another. **Fibroblasts,** surrounded by extracellular matrix, are present between lamellae. The transparency of the cornea depends on the arrangement of the collagen lamellae and the affinity for water of the extracellular matrix. **Blood vessels are not present**.

Descemet's membrane

Corneal endothelium

Corneal endothelium is permeable to air oxygen used for various oxidative reactions, in particular glutathione reduction and oxidation. The glutathione pathway neutralizes excess active oxygen in the cornea. About 30% of glucose is metabolized in the cornea by glycolysis.

Bowman's layer is 6 to 9 µm thick, consists of type I collagen fibrils, and lacks elastic fibers. This layer is transparent and does not have regeneration capacity. Bowman's layer is the anteriormost part of the corneal stroma, although differently organized. For this reason, it is designated "layer" instead of "membrane." Bowman's layer represents a protective barrier to trauma and bacterial invasion.

The highly transparent **stroma** or **substantia propria** represents about 90% of the thickness of the cornea. Bundles of **type I** and **V collagen** form thin layers regularly arranged in successive planes crossing at various angles and forming a **lattice** that is highly resistant to deformations and trauma. Fibers and layers are separated by an extracellular matrix rich in **proteoglycans** containing **chondroitin** and **keratan sulfate**.

Nerves in transit to the corneal epithelium are found in the corneal stroma.

Descemet's membrane, one of the thickest basement membranes in the body (5 to 10 µm thick), is produced by the corneal endothelium and contains **type VII collagen**, which forms a hexagonal array of fibers.

The **corneal endothelium** lines the posterior surface of Descemet's membrane and faces the anterior chamber of the eye. It consists of a single layer of squamous epithelial cells, with impermeable intercellular spaces preventing influx of aqueous humor into the corneal stroma. The structural and functional integrity of the corneal endothelium is vital to the maintenance of corneal transparency.

The middle tunic of the eye
The uvea

The uvea forms the pigmented vascularized tunic of the eye and is divided into three regions: (1) the **choroid**, (2) the **ciliary body**, and (3) the **iris** (see Figure 9–7).

The **choroid** consists of three layers (Figure 9–6):

1. **Bruch's membrane**, the innermost component of the choroid, consists of a network of collagen and elastic fibers and basal lamina material. Basal laminae derive from the pigmented epithelium of the retina and the endothelia of the underlying fenestrated capillaries.

2. The **choriocapillaris** contains fenestrated capillaries that supply oxygen and nutrients to the outer layers of the retina and the fovea.

3. The **choroidal stroma** consists of large arteries and veins surrounded by collagen and elastic fibers, fibroblasts, a few smooth muscle cells, neurons of the autonomic nervous system, and melanocytes.

The **ciliary body** (Figure 9–7) is anterior to the ora serrata and represents the ventral projection of both the choroid and the retina. It is made up of two components: (1) the **uveal portion**, and (2) the **neuroepithelial portion**.

The **uveal portion** of the ciliary body includes:

1. The continuation of the outer layer of the choroid, known as the **supraciliaris**.

2. The **ciliary muscle**, a ring of smooth muscle tissue that, **when contracted, reduces the length of the circular suspensory ligaments of the lens**; this is known as the **ciliary zonule**.

3. A layer of **fenestrated capillaries** supplying blood to the ciliary muscle.

The **neuroepithelial portion** contributes the two layers of the **ciliary epithelium**:

1. An outer **pigmented epithelial layer**, continuous with the retinal pigmented epithelium. The pigmented epithelial layer is supported by a basal lamina continuous with Bruch's membrane.

2. An inner **nonpigmented epithelial layer**, which is continuous with the sensory retina.

Particular features of these two pigmented and nonpigmented epithelial cell layers are:

1. **The apical surfaces of the pigmented and nonpigmented cells face each other.**

Figure 9–6

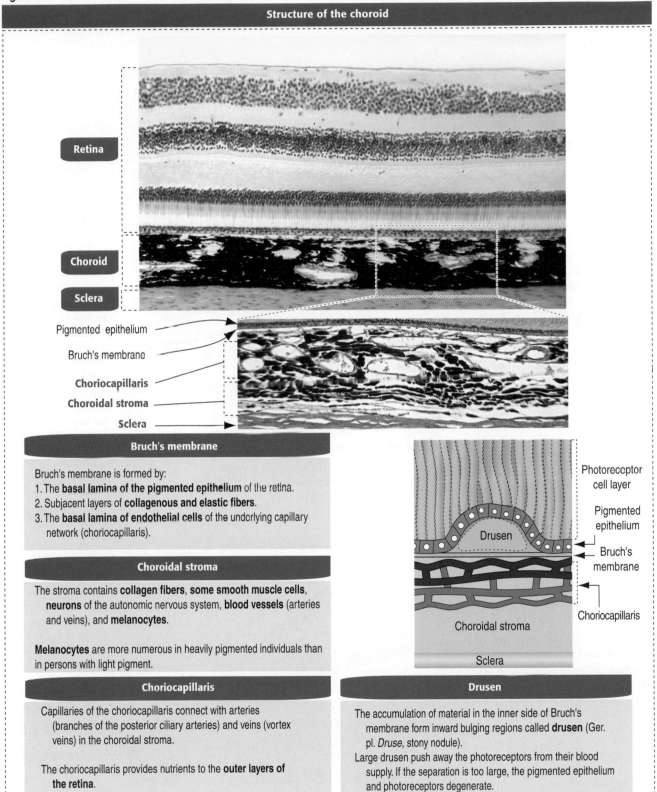

Structure of the choroid

Retina

Choroid

Sclera

Pigmented epithelium
Bruch's membrane
Choriocapillaris
Choroidal stroma
Sclera

Bruch's membrane

Bruch's membrane is formed by:
1. The **basal lamina of the pigmented epithelium** of the retina.
2. Subjacent layers of **collagenous and elastic fibers**.
3. The **basal lamina of endothelial cells** of the underlying capillary network (choriocapillaris).

Choroidal stroma

The stroma contains **collagen fibers**, **some smooth muscle cells**, **neurons** of the autonomic nervous system, **blood vessels** (arteries and veins), and **melanocytes**.

Melanocytes are more numerous in heavily pigmented individuals than in persons with light pigment.

Choriocapillaris

Capillaries of the choriocapillaris connect with arteries (branches of the posterior ciliary arteries) and veins (vortex veins) in the choroidal stroma.

The choriocapillaris provides nutrients to the **outer layers of the retina**.

Photoreceptor cell layer

Pigmented epithelium

Drusen

Bruch's membrane

Choriocapillaris

Choroidal stroma

Sclera

Drusen

The accumulation of material in the inner side of Bruch's membrane form inward bulging regions called **drusen** (Ger. pl. *Druse*, stony nodule).
Large drusen push away the photoreceptors from their blood supply. If the separation is too large, the pigmented epithelium and photoreceptors degenerate.

2. The dual epithelium is smooth at its posterior end (pars plana) and folded (pars plicata) at the anterior end to form the **ciliary processes**.

3. The **aqueous humor** is secreted by epithelial cells of the ciliary processes supplied by fenestrated capillaries (Figure 9–8).

Figure 9–7

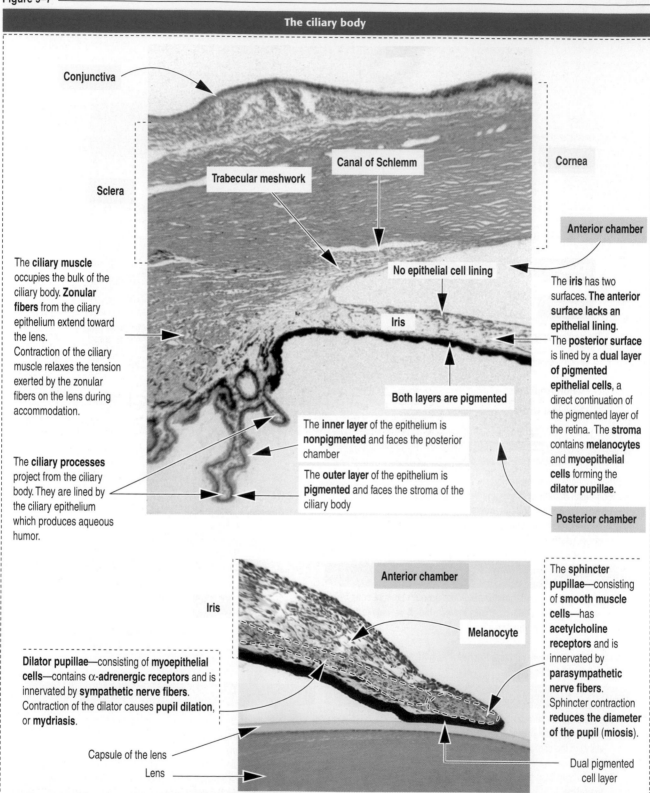

The ciliary body

Conjunctiva

Sclera

Trabecular meshwork

Canal of Schlemm

Cornea

Anterior chamber

No epithelial cell lining

Iris

The **ciliary muscle** occupies the bulk of the ciliary body. **Zonular fibers** from the ciliary epithelium extend toward the lens. Contraction of the ciliary muscle relaxes the tension exerted by the zonular fibers on the lens during accommodation.

The **ciliary processes** project from the ciliary body. They are lined by the ciliary epithelium which produces aqueous humor.

The **iris** has two surfaces. **The anterior surface lacks an epithelial lining. The posterior surface** is lined by a **dual layer of pigmented epithelial cells**, a direct continuation of the pigmented layer of the retina. The **stroma** contains **melanocytes** and **myoepithelial cells** forming the **dilator pupillae**.

Both layers are pigmented

The **inner layer** of the epithelium is **nonpigmented** and faces the posterior chamber

The **outer layer** of the epithelium is **pigmented** and faces the stroma of the ciliary body

Posterior chamber

Iris

Anterior chamber

Melanocyte

Dilator pupillae—consisting of **myoepithelial cells**—contains α-**adrenergic receptors** and is innervated by **sympathetic nerve fibers**. Contraction of the dilator causes **pupil dilation**, or **mydriasis**.

The **sphincter pupillae**—consisting of **smooth muscle cells**—has **acetylcholine receptors** and is innervated by **parasympathetic nerve fibers**. Sphincter contraction **reduces the diameter of the pupil (miosis)**.

Capsule of the lens

Lens

Dual pigmented cell layer

The **ciliary epithelium is an extension of the retina beyond the ora serrata and covers the inner surface of the ciliary body**. It consists of two layers: an **inner layer of nonpigmented cells**—a direct continuation of the sensory retina—facing the posterior chamber, and **an outer layer of pigmented cells**—continuous with the retinal pigmented epithelium—in contact with the stroma of the ciliary body. As the ciliary epithelium approaches the base of the iris, the cells of the inner layer accumulate pigment granules and both layers are pigmented. **Aqueous humor is secreted by the epithelial cells of the ciliary processes** supplied by **fenestrated capillaries**. Zonular fibers, normally associated with the ciliary processes, are not seen in Figure 9–7 but are depicted in Figure 9–11.

Figure 9-8

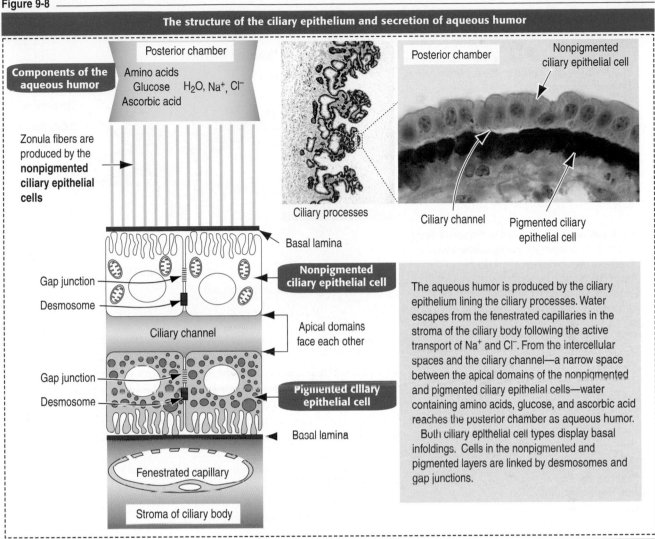

The structure of the ciliary epithelium and secretion of aqueous humor

Components of the aqueous humor

Posterior chamber

Amino acids

Glucose H₂O, Na⁺, Cl⁻

Ascorbic acid

Zonula fibers are produced by the **nonpigmented ciliary epithelial cells**

Basal lamina

Gap junction

Desmosome

Nonpigmented ciliary epithelial cell

Ciliary channel

Apical domains face each other

Gap junction

Desmosome

Pigmented ciliary epithelial cell

Basal lamina

Fenestrated capillary

Stroma of ciliary body

Ciliary processes

Posterior chamber

Nonpigmented ciliary epithelial cell

Ciliary channel

Pigmented ciliary epithelial cell

The aqueous humor is produced by the ciliary epithelium lining the ciliary processes. Water escapes from the fenestrated capillaries in the stroma of the ciliary body following the active transport of Na⁺ and Cl⁻. From the intercellular spaces and the ciliary channel—a narrow space between the apical domains of the nonpigmented and pigmented ciliary epithelial cells—water containing amino acids, glucose, and ascorbic acid reaches the posterior chamber as aqueous humor.

Both ciliary epithelial cell types display basal infoldings. Cells in the nonpigmented and pigmented layers are linked by desmosomes and gap junctions.

The **iris** is a continuation of the ciliary body and is located in front of the lens. At this position, it forms a gate for the flow of aqueous humor between the anterior and posterior chambers of the eye and also controls the amount of light entering the eye.

The iris has two components: (1) the **anterior uveal** or **stromal** face, and (2) the posterior **neuroepithelial** surface.

The **anterior (outer) uveal face** is of mesenchymal origin and has an irregular surface. It is formed by **fibroblasts** and pigmented **melanocytes** embedded in an extracellular matrix. The number of pigmented melanocytes determines the color of the iris. In albinos, the iris appears pink due to the abundant blood vessels. Blood vessels of the iris have a radial distribution and can adjust to changes in length in parallel to variations in the diameter of the pupil.

The **posterior (inner) neuroepithelial surface** consists of **two layers of pigmented epithelium**. The outer layer, a continuation of the pigmented layer of the ciliary epithelium, consists of **myoepithelial cells** that become the **dilator pupillae** muscle. The **smooth muscle** of the **sphincter pupillae** is located in the iris stroma around the pupil.

The three chambers of the eye

The eye contains three chambers (see Figure 9–1): (1) the **anterior chamber**, (2) the **posterior chamber**, and (3) the **vitreous cavity**.

Figure 9–9

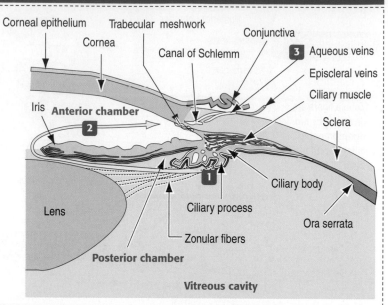

The path of aqueous humor

1 The **arrow** indicates the pathway followed by **the aqueous humor produced by the epithelial lining of the ciliary processes.**

2 The aqueous fluid flows from the posterior chamber through the pupil into the anterior chamber. The **canal of Schlemm**, lined by an **endothelium**, does not communicate directly with the spaces of the trabecular meshwork. Instead, the fluid percolates through a thin endothelial lining and loose connective tissue.

3 **Aqueous veins** are collector channels draining the canal of Schlemm into the **episcleral veins**.

The drainage rate of aqueous humor is balanced by the rate of secretion. By this mechanism, the intraocular pressure is maintained constant (23 mm Hg).

The **anterior chamber** occupies the space between the **corneal endothelium** (anterior boundary) and the **anterior surface of the iris**, the **pupillary portion of the lens**, and the **base of the ciliary body** (posterior boundary). The circumferential angle of the anterior chamber is occupied by the **trabecular meshwork**, a drainage site for the aqueous humor into the **canal of Schlemm** (Figures 9–9 and 9–10).

The **posterior chamber** (see Figure 9–9) is limited anteriorly by the **posterior surface of the iris** and posteriorly by the **lens** and the **zonular fibers** (suspensory ligaments of the lens). The circumferential angle is occupied by the **ciliary processes**, the site of aqueous humor production.

The **vitreous cavity** is occupied by a transparent gel substance—the **vitreous humor**—and extends from the lens to the retina. The vitreous humor contains mostly water (99%), hyaluronic acid, and collagen fibers, both produced by **hyalocytes**.

The lens

The cornea, the three chambers of the eye, and the lens are three transparent structures through which light must pass to reach the retina.

The **lens** is a transparent, biconvex, elastic, and avascular structure (Figure 9–11). **Zonular fibers**, extending from the ciliary epithelium and inserting at the equatorial portion of the capsule, maintain the lens in place.

The lens consists of three components: (1) the **lens capsule**, (2) the **lens epithelium**, and (3) the **lens substance**, consisting of **cortical** and **nuclear lens cell fibers**.

The **lens capsule** is a thick and transparent basement membrane–like structure enclosing the lens. Beneath the anterior portion of the capsule is a single layer of **cuboid epithelial cells** that extend posteriorly up to the equatorial region. There is no epithelial cell layer under the posterior surface of the capsule.

In the **cortical region of the lens**, elongated and concentrically arranged cells (called **cortical lens fibers**) arise from the anterior epithelium at the equator region. Cortical lens fibers contain nuclei and organelles. The nucleus and organelles eventually disappear when the cortical lens fibers approach the center of the lens —the nuclear lens fiber region.

Figure 9–10

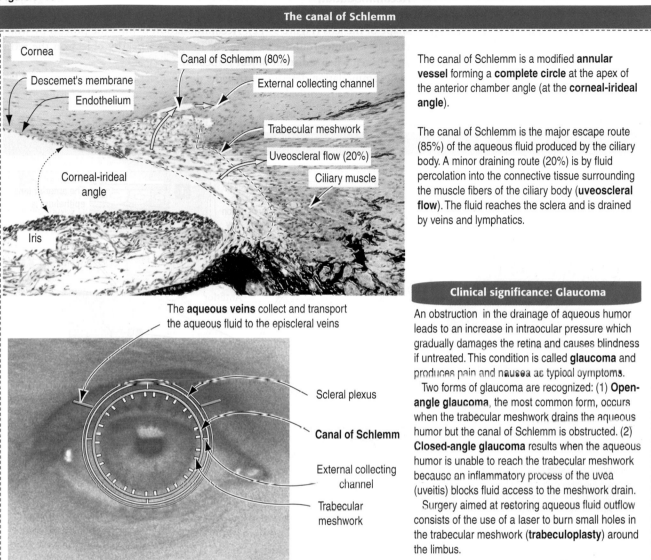

The canal of Schlemm

Cornea
Descemet's membrane
Endothelium
Corneal-irideal angle
Iris

Canal of Schlem (80%)
External collecting channel
Trabecular meshwork
Uveoscleral flow (20%)
Ciliary muscle

The **aqueous veins** collect and transport the aqueous fluid to the episcleral veins

Scleral plexus
Canal of Schlemm
External collecting channel
Trabecular meshwork

The canal of Schlemm is a modified **annular vessel** forming a **complete circle** at the apex of the anterior chamber angle (at the **corneal-irideal angle**).

The canal of Schlemm is the major escape route (85%) of the aqueous fluid produced by the ciliary body. A minor draining route (20%) is by fluid percolation into the connective tissue surrounding the muscle fibers of the ciliary body (**uveoscleral flow**). The fluid reaches the sclera and is drained by veins and lymphatics.

Clinical significance: Glaucoma

An obstruction in the drainage of aqueous humor leads to an increase in intraocular pressure which gradually damages the retina and causes blindness if untreated. This condition is called **glaucoma** and produces pain and nausea as typical symptoms.

Two forms of glaucoma are recognized: (1) **Open-angle glaucoma**, the most common form, occurs when the trabecular meshwork drains the aqueous humor but the canal of Schlemm is obstructed. (2) **Closed-angle glaucoma** results when the aqueous humor is unable to reach the trabecular meshwork because an inflammatory process of the uvea (uveitis) blocks fluid access to the meshwork drain.

Surgery aimed at restoring aqueous fluid outflow consists of the use of a laser to burn small holes in the trabecular meshwork (**trabeculoplasty**) around the limbus.

Lens cell differentiation consists of the appearance of unique cytoskeletal proteins: (1) **filensin**, an intermediate filament that contains attachment sites for crystallins, and (2) lens-specific proteins called **crystallins** (α, β, and γ). Filensin and crystallins maintain the conformation and transparency of the lens fiber cell.

Lens cell fibers interdigitate at the medial **suture region**. At these contact sites, gap junctions and some spot desmosomes interlock the opposing cytoplasmic processes.

The inner cortical region and the core of the lens consist of older lens fibers lacking nuclei. About 80% of its available glucose is metabolized by the lens.

The lens is supported by the **suspensory ligament** (**zonular fibers**), formed by bundles of filaments linking the ciliary body to the equator of the lens. The ciliary body and zonular fibers play a role in accommodation.

Clinical significance: Cataracts

Cataracts are an opacity of the lens caused by a change in the solubility of lens proteins. This condition, observed during aging and diabetes, causes high light scattering by the aggregated filensin and crystallins and impairs accurate vision.

Figure 9–17

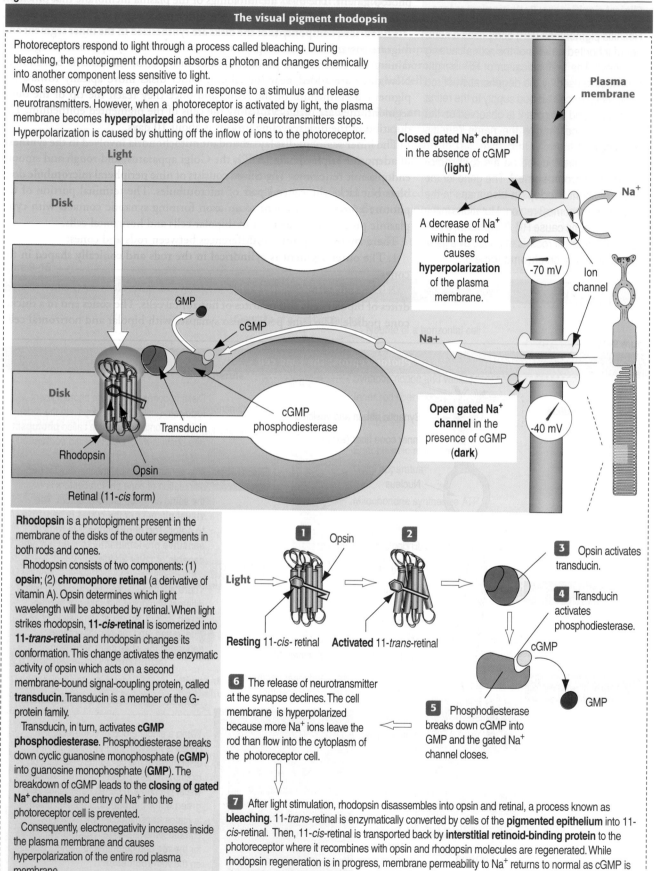

The visual pigment rhodopsin

Photoreceptors respond to light through a process called bleaching. During bleaching, the photopigment rhodopsin absorbs a photon and changes chemically into another component less sensitive to light.

Most sensory receptors are depolarized in response to a stimulus and release neurotransmitters. However, when a photoreceptor is activated by light, the plasma membrane becomes **hyperpolarized** and the release of neurotransmitters stops. Hyperpolarization is caused by shutting off the inflow of ions to the photoreceptor.

Light

Disk

Disk

GMP

cGMP

Transducin

cGMP phosphodiesterase

Rhodopsin

Opsin

Retinal (11-*cis* form)

Plasma membrane

Closed gated Na⁺ channel in the absence of cGMP (**light**)

Na⁺

A decrease of Na⁺ within the rod causes **hyperpolarization** of the plasma membrane.

-70 mV

Ion channel

Na+

Open gated Na⁺ channel in the presence of cGMP (**dark**)

-40 mV

Rhodopsin is a photopigment present in the membrane of the disks of the outer segments in both rods and cones.

Rhodopsin consists of two components: (1) **opsin**; (2) **chromophore retinal** (a derivative of vitamin A). Opsin determines which light wavelength will be absorbed by retinal. When light strikes rhodopsin, **11-*cis*-retinal** is isomerized into **11-*trans*-retinal** and rhodopsin changes its conformation. This change activates the enzymatic activity of opsin which acts on a second membrane-bound signal-coupling protein, called **transducin**. Transducin is a member of the G-protein family.

Transducin, in turn, activates **cGMP phosphodiesterase**. Phosphodiesterase breaks down cyclic guanosine monophosphate (**cGMP**) into guanosine monophosphate (**GMP**). The breakdown of cGMP leads to the **closing of gated Na⁺ channels** and entry of Na⁺ into the photoreceptor cell is prevented.

Consequently, electronegativity increases inside the plasma membrane and causes hyperpolarization of the entire rod plasma membrane.

1 Opsin

2

Light

Resting 11-*cis*- retinal   **Activated** 11-*trans*-retinal

3 Opsin activates transducin.

4 Transducin activates phosphodiesterase.

cGMP

GMP

5 Phosphodiesterase breaks down cGMP into GMP and the gated Na⁺ channel closes.

6 The release of neurotransmitter at the synapse declines. The cell membrane is hyperpolarized because more Na⁺ ions leave the rod than flow into the cytoplasm of the photoreceptor cell.

7 After light stimulation, rhodopsin disassembles into opsin and retinal, a process known as **bleaching**. 11-*trans*-retinal is enzymatically converted by cells of the **pigmented epithelium** into 11-*cis*-retinal. Then, 11-*cis*-retinal is transported back by **interstitial retinoid-binding protein** to the photoreceptor where it recombines with opsin and rhodopsin molecules are regenerated. While rhodopsin regeneration is in progress, membrane permeability to Na⁺ returns to normal as cGMP is also synthesized and opens the gated Na⁺ channel.

The synaptic ending of cones and rods—spherules and pedicles—contains a **synaptic ribbon** surrounded by **synaptic vesicles**.

3. Rods contain the photopigment **rhodopsin** (Figure 9–17). Cones contain a similar pigment called **iodopsin**. Rhodopsin operates during night vision. Iodopsin perceives detail and discriminates color (blue, green, and red). Both rhodopsin and iodopsin are transmembrane proteins bound to the prosthetic group **11-*cis*-retinal**. The protein lacking the prosthetic group is called **opsin**.

There are three different photopigments in cones with different light absorbance and sensitive to blue light (420 nm), green light (535 nm), and red light 565 nm), respectively. The isomerization of 11-*cis*-retinal to 11-*trans*-retinal is identical in rods and cones.

Conducting neurons: Bipolar and ganglion cells

Bipolar and ganglion cells conduct the impulse received by the photoreceptor cells.

Figure 9–18

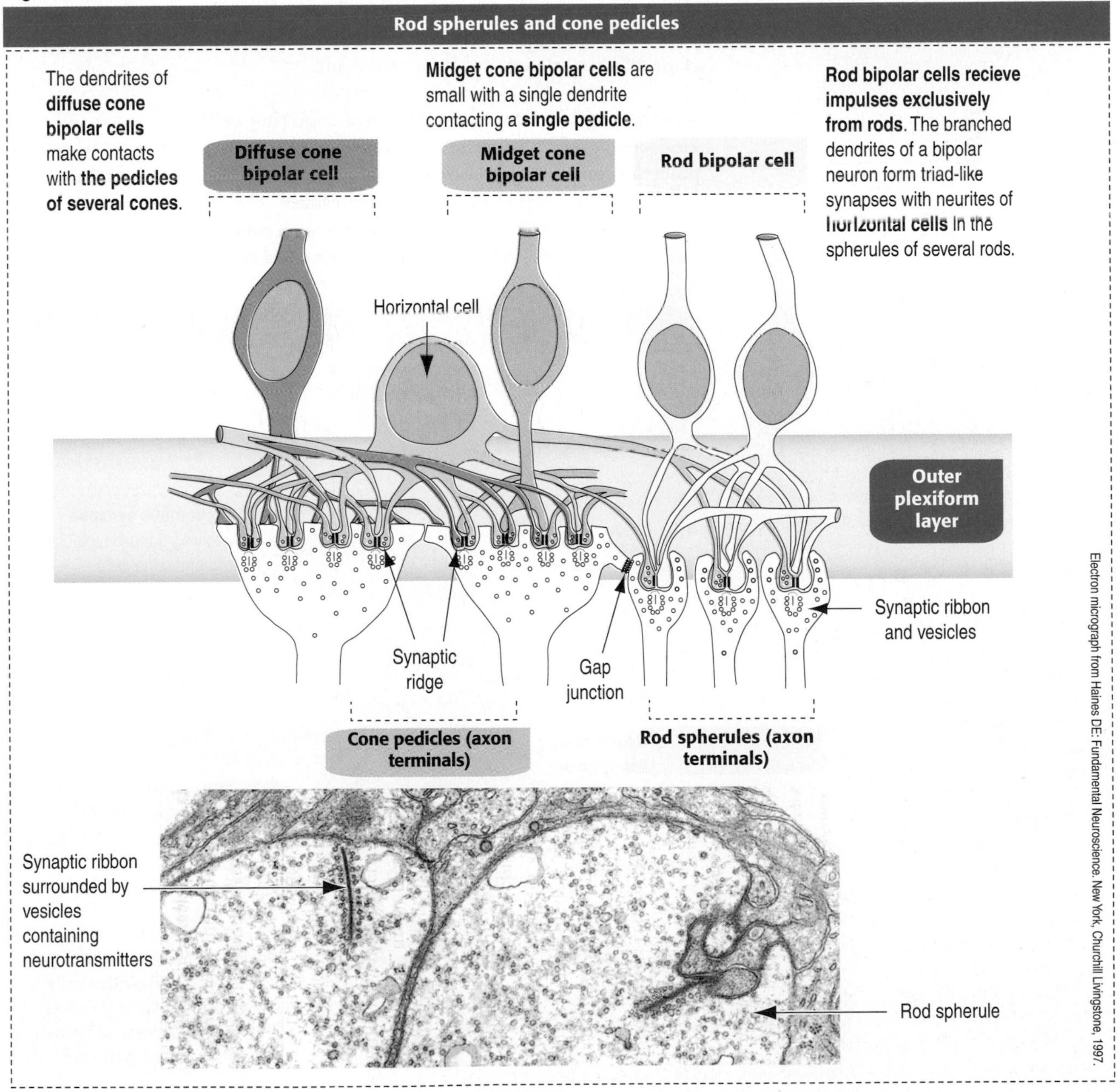

Rod spherules and cone pedicles

The dendrites of **diffuse cone bipolar cells** make contacts with **the pedicles of several cones**.

Midget cone bipolar cells are small with a single dendrite contacting a **single pedicle**.

Rod bipolar cells recieve impulses exclusively from rods. The branched dendrites of a bipolar neuron form triad-like synapses with neurites of **horizontal cells** in the spherules of several rods.

Diffuse cone bipolar cell

Midget cone bipolar cell

Rod bipolar cell

Horizontal cell

Outer plexiform layer

Synaptic ribbon and vesicles

Synaptic ridge

Gap junction

Cone pedicles (axon terminals)

Rod spherules (axon terminals)

Synaptic ribbon surrounded by vesicles containing neurotransmitters

Rod spherule

Electron micrograph from Haines DE: Fundamental Neuroscience. New York, Churchill Livingstone, 1997.

Two major classes of bipolar cells can be distinguished (Figure 9–18):

1. **Rod bipolar cells**, linked to **rod spherules**.
2. **Cone bipolar cells**, linked to **cone pedicles**. Cone bipolar cells consist of two major classes: the **midget cone bipolar cell** and the **diffuse cone bipolar cell**.

Dendrites of the **diffuse cone bipolar cells** branch within the **outer plexiform layer** and contact several cone pedicles. On the opposite pole, the axon of a diffuse bipolar cell projects into the **inner plexiform layer** and contacts the dendrites of ganglion cells.

Midget cone bipolar cells synapse with a **single cone pedicle** and a single axon that contacts a **single ganglion cell**. Essentially, **midget bipolar cells link a single cone to an optic nerve fiber**. In contrast, **diffuse bipolar cells have wider input and output pathways**. The nuclei of the bipolar cells form part of the **inner nuclear layer** of the retina.

Ganglion cells extend their dendrites into the **inner plexiform layer**; the axons form part of the optic nerve. Two classes of ganglion cells exist: (1) **diffuse ganglion cells**, contacting several bipolar cells, and (2) **midget ganglion cells**, with their dendrites contacting a single midget bipolar cell. Note that midget ganglion cells receive impulses from cones only.

Association neurons: Horizontal and amacrine cells

Horizontal and amacrine cells do not have axons or dendrites, only **neuritic processes conducting in both directions**. The nuclei of the horizontal and amacrine cells contribute to the **inner nuclear layer**.

Horizontal cells give rise to **neurites** ending on **cone pedicles**. A single branching neurite synapses with **both rod spherules and cone pedicles** (Figure 9–18).

Figure 9–19

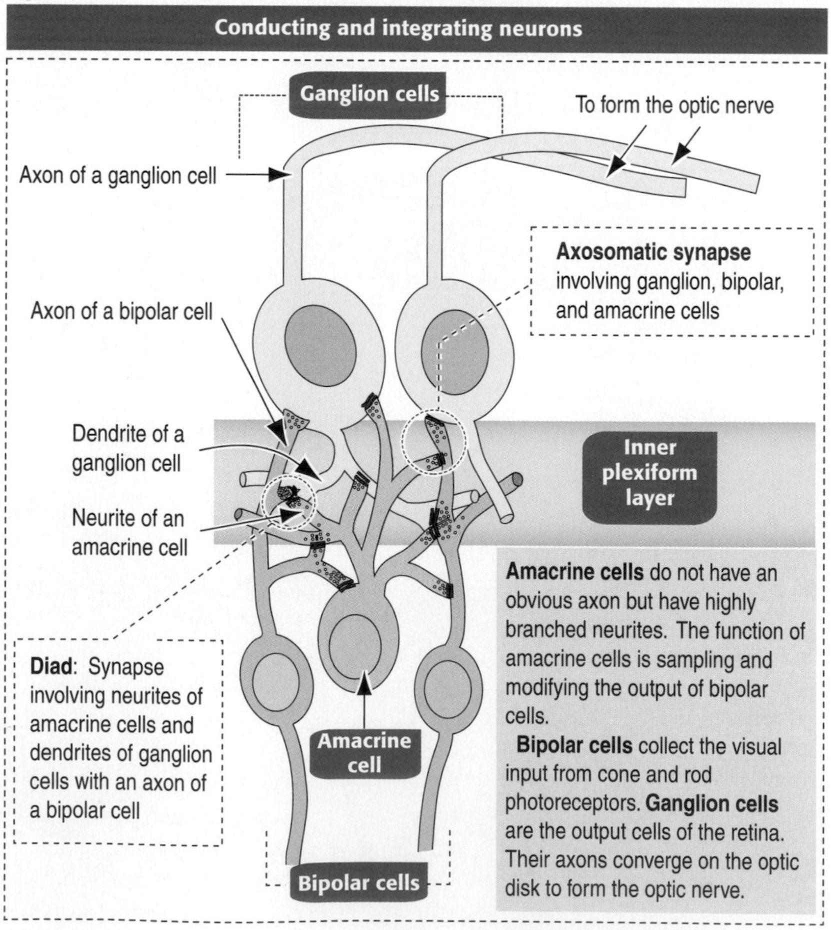

Conducting and integrating neurons

Ganglion cells

To form the optic nerve

Axon of a ganglion cell

Axosomatic synapse involving ganglion, bipolar, and amacrine cells

Axon of a bipolar cell

Dendrite of a ganglion cell

Inner plexiform layer

Neurite of an amacrine cell

Amacrine cells do not have an obvious axon but have highly branched neurites. The function of amacrine cells is sampling and modifying the output of bipolar cells.

Diad: Synapse involving neurites of amacrine cells and dendrites of ganglion cells with an axon of a bipolar cell

Amacrine cell

Bipolar cells collect the visual input from cone and rod photoreceptors. **Ganglion cells** are the output cells of the retina. Their axons converge on the optic disk to form the optic nerve.

Bipolar cells

Figure 9–20

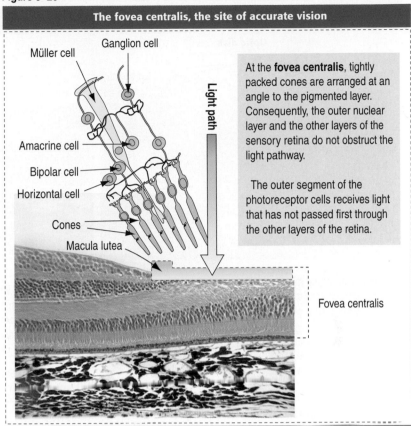

The fovea centralis, the site of accurate vision

Müller cell

Ganglion cell

Amacrine cell

Bipolar cell

Horizontal cell

Cones

Macula lutea

Light path

At the **fovea centralis**, tightly packed cones are arranged at an angle to the pigmented layer. Consequently, the outer nuclear layer and the other layers of the sensory retina do not obstruct the light pathway.

The outer segment of the photoreceptor cells receives light that has not passed first through the other layers of the retina.

Fovea centralis

These neuritic synapses occur in the **outer plexiform layer** of the retina. This neurite and axonal distribution indicates that **horizontal cells integrate cones and rods of adjacent areas of the retina.**

Amacrine cells are found at the inner edge of the **inner nuclear layer**. They have a single neuritic process that branches to link the axonal terminals of the bipolar cells and the dendritic branches of the ganglion cells (Figure 9–19).

Supporting glial cells: Müller cells

The nuclei of Müller cells are located in the **inner nuclear layer**. The cytoplasmic processes extend to the **outer** and **inner limiting membrane**. The inner limiting membrane represents the basal lamina of the Müller cells and serves to separate the retina from the vitreous body.

The cytoplasmic processes of Müller cells fill the spaces between photoreceptors and bipolar and ganglion cells. At the outer segment photoreceptor contact sites, a **zonula adherens** and **microvilli** extending from Müller cells stabilize the association between neuronal photoreceptors and glial Müller cells. This contact region is represented by the distinct boundary of the external limiting membrane. In addition to glial Müller cells, microglial cells are present in all layers.

Areas of the retina with specific functions

The **fovea centralis**, surrounded by the **macula lutea** (Figures 9–20 and 9–21), is a specialized area of the retina for accurate vision under normal and dim illumination. The **optic disk**, which includes the **optic papilla**, is not suitable for vision.

The **fovea centralis** is located on the **temporal side** of the optic disk. **This area contains abundant cones but lacks rods and capillaries.** The cones synapse with the bipolar cells, both oriented **at an angle** around the margins of the fovea. This histologic feature enables free access of light to the photoreceptors.

Figure 9–21 _____

| The optic disk and the fovea centralis |

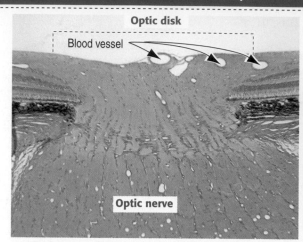

Optic disk

Blood vessel

Optic nerve

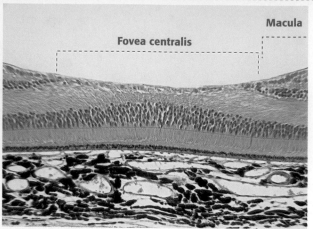

Fovea centralis

Macula

The axons of the ganglion cells turn into the **optic nerve** at the **optic disk** which lacks photoreceptors and corresponds to the **blind spot** of the retina.

Optic disks have a central depresion, the **optic cup**, that is pale in comparison to the surrounding nerve fibers. A loss of nerve fibers in glaucoma results in an increase in the optic cup area.

Retinal blood vessels can be visualized with an ophthalmoscope. When **intraocular pressure increases**, the disk of the optic nerve appears **concave**. The disk becomes swollen (**papilledema**) and the veins are dilated when intracranial pressure increases.

The **macula lutea**—yellow spot produced by **xanthophyll pigments** within retinal cells, which may absorb short wavelength light—provides for central vision. In its center, the **fovea** is for high quality vision. The rest of the retina is for peripheral vision. **Cones** are concentrated in the macula and are responsible for acute vision and color distinction. **Rods** are for vision in dim light and for movement detection.

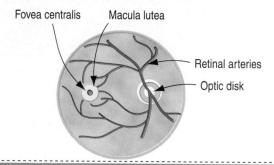

Fovea centralis   Macula lutea

Retinal arteries

Optic disk

The **macula lutea** is characterized by a yellow pigment in the inner layers surrounding the shallow fovea.

The exit site from the retina of axons derived from ganglion cells is represented by the **optic disk**. The optic disk includes (1) the **optic papilla**, a protrusion formed by the axons entering the optic nerve, and (2) the **lamina cribrosa** of the sclera, pierced by the axons of the optic nerve. Photoreceptors terminate at the edges of the optic disk which represents the "blind spot" of the retina. **The central artery and vein of the retina pass through the optic disk.**

The eyelids, conjunctiva, and the lacrimal gland

The anterior portion of the eyeball is protected by the eyelids, the conjunctiva, and the fluid produced by the lacrimal gland.

Each **eyelid** consists of two portions (Figure 9–22): (1) an outer **cutaneous portion** lined by a stratified squamous epidermis overlying a loose connective tissue dermis and skeletal muscle (**orbicularis oculi muscle**), and (2) an inner **conjunctival portion**, lined by a thin mucus membrane, the **conjunctiva**.

The cutaneous portion contains several skin appendages: (1) **sweat** and **sebaceous glands**, and (2) three to four rows of stiff hairs, the **eyelashes**, at the eyelid margins. Eyelashes are associated with modified sweat glands known as the **glands of Moll**.

Facing the conjunctival lining is the **tarsal plate**, a fibroelastic dense connective tissue containing large sebaceous **tarsal glands**, also known as **meibomian**

Figure 9–22

Eyelid and its pathology

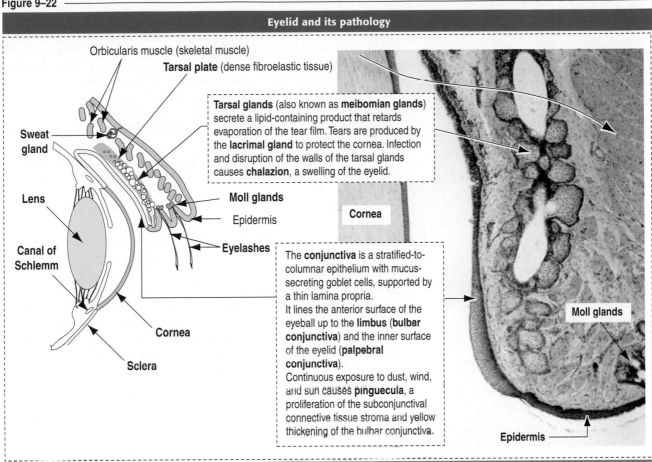

Orbicularis muscle (skeletal muscle)

Tarsal plate (dense fibroelastic tissue)

Tarsal glands (also known as **meibomian glands**) secrete a lipid-containing product that retards evaporation of the tear film. Tears are produced by the **lacrimal gland** to protect the cornea. Infection and disruption of the walls of the tarsal glands causes **chalazion**, a swelling of the eyelid.

Sweat gland

Lens

Canal of Schlemm

Moll glands

Epidermis

Eyelashes

Cornea

The **conjunctiva** is a stratified-to-columnar epithelium with mucus-secreting goblet cells, supported by a thin lamina propria.
It lines the anterior surface of the eyeball up to the **limbus** (**bulbar conjunctiva**) and the inner surface of the eyelid (**palpebral conjunctiva**).
Continuous exposure to dust, wind, and sun causes **pinguecula**, a proliferation of the subconjunctival connective tissue stroma and yellow thickening of the bulbar conjunctiva.

Cornea

Sclera

Moll glands

Epidermis

glands. Each tarsal gland opens at the margin of the eyelid. The tarsal plate is responsible for the rigidity of the eyelids.

The junction between the cutaneous and conjunctival portions is demarcated clinically by the **sulcus**, a gray line located between the ducts of the meibomian

Figure 9–23

Lacrimal gland

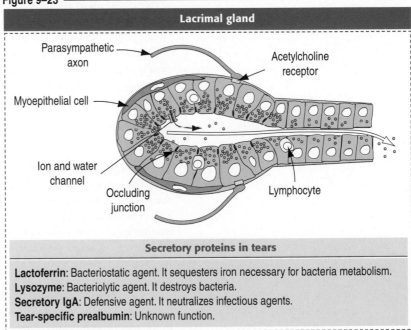

Parasympathetic axon

Acetylcholine receptor

Myoepithelial cell

Ion and water channel

Occluding junction

Lymphocyte

Secretory proteins in tears

Lactoferrin: Bacteriostatic agent. It sequesters iron necessary for bacteria metabolism.
Lysozyme: Bacteriolytic agent. It destroys bacteria.
Secretory IgA: Defensive agent. It neutralizes infectious agents.
Tear-specific prealbumin: Unknown function.

glands and the eyelashes.

The **conjunctiva** is continuous with the skin lining and extends up to the periphery of the cornea. It consists of polygonal to columnar stratified epithelial cells with mucus-secreting goblet cells. At the corneal rim, the conjunctival epithelium becomes stratified squamous and is continuous with the corneal epithelium. A lamina propria with capillaries supports the lining epithelium.

The **lacrimal gland** produces a fluid, **tears**, that first accumulate in the conjunctival sac and then exit into the nasal cavity through a drainage duct (**nasolacrimal duct**). Tears evaporate in the nasal cavity but can produce a sniffy nose when excessive fluid is produced.

The lacrimal gland (Figure 9–23) is a **tubuloacinar serous gland** with **myoepithelial cells.** It is organized into separate lobes with 12 to15 independent excretory ducts. Tears enter the excretory canaliculi through the **puncta** and reach the nasolacrimal sac and duct to eventually drain in the inferior meatus within the nasal cavity.

Lacrimal glands receive neural input from (1) **parasympathetic nerve fibers**, originating in the pteryglopalatine ganglion; **acetycholine receptors** on glandular cells responding to acetylcholine released at the nerve terminals; and (2) **sympathetic nerve fibers**, arising from the superior cervical ganglion.

Blinking produces gentle compression of the lacrimal glands and the release of fluid. Tears keep the surface of the conjunctiva and cornea moist and rinse off dust particles. **Spreading of the mucus secreted by the conjunctival epithelial cells, the oily secretion derived from the tarsal glands, and the continuous blinking of the eyelids prevent rapid evaporation of the tear film.** Tears contain **lysozyme**, an antibacterial enzyme; **lactoferrin**; **secretory IgA**; and **tear-specific prealbumin** (see Figure 9–23).

Excess production of tears occurs in response to chemical and physical irritants of the conjunctiva, high light intensity, and strong emotions. A disruption in the production of tears or damage to the eyelids results in the drying out of the cornea (**dry eye** or **keratoconjunctivitis sicca**), which is followed by ulceration, perforation, loss of aqueous humor, and blindness.

Clinical significance: The red eye

A red eye is the most frequent and relatively benign ocular alteration. In some cases, a red eye represents a vision-threatening condition.

A **subconjunctival hemorrhage** is the cause of acute ocular redness and can be produced by trauma, bleeding disorders, hypertension, and treatment with anticoagulants. No pain or vision impairment is associated with this disorder.

Conjunctivitis is the most common cause of red eye. The superficial blood vessels of the conjunctiva are dilated and cause edema of the conjunctiva with discharge. A purulent discharge indicates bacterial infection —predominantly gram-positive organisms. A watery discharge is observed in conjunctivitis caused by viral infection.

The ear

The ear consists of three components (Figure 9–24):

1. The **external ear**, which collects sound and directs it down the ear canal to the tympanic membrane.

2. The **middle ear**, which converts sound pressure waves into mechanical motion of the tympanic membrane. The motion is in turn transmitted to the middle ear ossicles, which reduce the amplitude but increase the force of mechanical motion to overcome the resistance offered by the fluid-filled inner ear.

3. The **internal ear**, which houses the sensory organs for both hearing and balance, transmits mechanical vibrations to the fluid (the **endolymph**) contained in the **membranous labyrinth** and thereby converts these mechanical vibrations

Figure 9–24

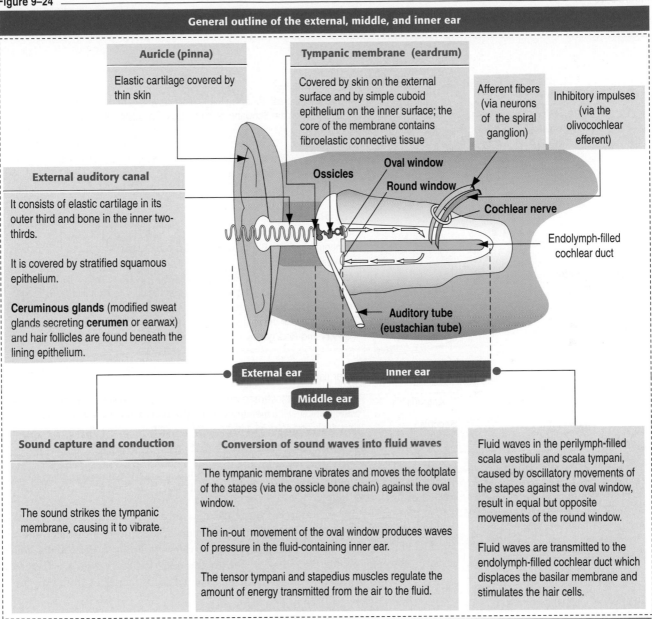

General outline of the external, middle, and inner ear

Auricle (pinna)

Elastic cartilage covered by thin skin

Tympanic membrane (eardrum)

Covered by skin on the external surface and by simple cuboid epithelium on the inner surface; the core of the membrane contains fibroelastic connective tissue

Afferent fibers (via neurons of the spiral ganglion)

Inhibitory impulses (via the olivocochlear efferent)

External auditory canal

It consists of elastic cartilage in its outer third and bone in the inner two-thirds.

It is covered by stratified squamous epithelium.

Ceruminous glands (modified sweat glands secreting **cerumen** or earwax) and hair follicles are found beneath the lining epithelium.

Ossicles
Oval window
Round window
Cochlear nerve
Endolymph-filled cochlear duct
Auditory tube (eustachian tube)

External ear

Inner ear

Middle ear

Sound capture and conduction

The sound strikes the tympanic membrane, causing it to vibrate.

Conversion of sound waves into fluid waves

The tympanic membrane vibrates and moves the footplate of the stapes (via the ossicle bone chain) against the oval window.

The in-out movement of the oval window produces waves of pressure in the fluid-containing inner ear.

The tensor tympani and stapedius muscles regulate the amount of energy transmitted from the air to the fluid.

Fluid waves in the perilymph-filled scala vestibuli and scala tympani, caused by oscillatory movements of the stapes against the oval window, result in equal but opposite movements of the round window.

Fluid waves are transmitted to the endolymph-filled cochlear duct which displaces the basilar membrane and stimulates the hair cells.

to electrical impulses on the same type of cell for sensory transduction: the **hair cell.**

The inner ear has two systems: (1) the **auditory system** for the perception of sound (hearing), and (2) the **vestibular system** for the perception of head and body motion (balance).

The external ear

The first and second branchial arches, which include the arch ectoderm and mesoderm, are the major contributors to the embryologic origin of the external ear (Figure 9–25).

The **auricle** (external ear or pinna) collects sound waves that are conducted across the **external acoustic meatus** to the **tympanic membrane.**

The **auricle** consists of a core of elastic cartilage surrounded by skin with hair follicles and sebaceous glands.

The **external acoustic meatus** is a passage extending from the auricle to the eardrum or **tympanic membrane.** The outer third of this passage is cartilage; the

Figure 9–25

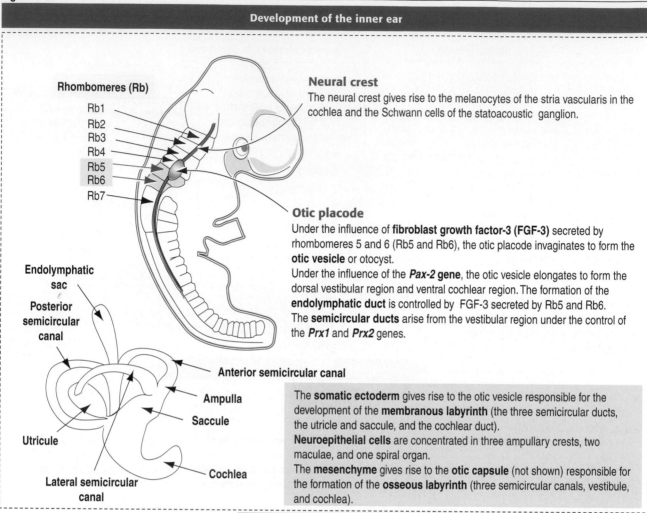

Development of the inner ear

Rhombomeres (Rb)
Rb1
Rb2
Rb3
Rb4
Rb5
Rb6
Rb7

Neural crest
The neural crest gives rise to the melanocytes of the stria vascularis in the cochlea and the Schwann cells of the statoacoustic ganglion.

Otic placode
Under the influence of **fibroblast growth factor-3 (FGF-3)** secreted by rhombomeres 5 and 6 (Rb5 and Rb6), the otic placode invaginates to form the **otic vesicle** or otocyst.
Under the influence of the **Pax-2 gene**, the otic vesicle elongates to form the dorsal vestibular region and ventral cochlear region. The formation of the **endolymphatic duct** is controlled by FGF-3 secreted by Rb5 and Rb6.
The **semicircular ducts** arise from the vestibular region under the control of the **Prx1** and **Prx2** genes.

Endolymphatic sac
Posterior semicircular canal
Anterior semicircular canal
Ampulla
Saccule
Utricle
Cochlea
Lateral semicircular canal

The **somatic ectoderm** gives rise to the otic vesicle responsible for the development of the **membranous labyrinth** (the three semicircular ducts, the utricle and saccule, and the cochlear duct).
Neuroepithelial cells are concentrated in three ampullary crests, two maculae, and one spiral organ.
The **mesenchyme** gives rise to the **otic capsule** (not shown) responsible for the formation of the **osseous labyrinth** (three semicircular canals, vestibule, and cochlea).

inner two-thirds is part of the temporal bone. Skin lines the cartilage and the bone surfaces. A characteristic feature of this skin lining is the tubular coiled apocrine glands secreting a brown product called **cerumen**. Cerumen waterproofs the skin and protects the external acoustic meatus from exogenous agents such as insects.

The middle ear

The middle ear is formed by cells derived from the **neural crest** and **mesoderm** that initially migrated to the branchial arches (see Figure 9–25). Neural crest and mesodermic cells coalesce to form the components of the middle ear, lined by an **endodermal-derived epithelium** extending from the oral cavity (derived from the first pharyngeal pouch).

The middle ear, or **tympanic cavity**, is an air-filled space in the temporal bone interposed between the tympanic membrane and the structures contained in the inner ear. The main function of the middle ear is the transmission of sound from the tympanic membrane to the fluid-filled structures of the inner ear.

Sound transmission is carried out by the **auditory** or **bony ossicles** (**malleus**, **incus**, and **stapes**) organized in a chainlike fashion by interconnecting small ligaments. In this chain, the arm of the malleus is attached to the **tympanic membrane** at one end; at the other end, the footplate of the stapes is applied to the **oval window** (fenestra vestibuli), an opening of the **bony labyrinth**. The **tensor tympani** (innervated by the trigeminal nerve [cranial nerve V]) and **stapedius muscles** (innervated by the facial nerve [cranial nerve VII]) keep the

Figure 9-26

General organization of the membranous labyrinth

Components of the membranous labyrinth

1 Two small sacs: the **utricle** and the **saccule**.

2 Three **semicircular ducts** open into the utricle. **Ampullae** are dilations connecting the ends of the semicircular ducts to the utricle.

3 Each ampulla contains the **crista ampullaris**. Sensory receptors in the crista ampullaris respond to the position of the head, generating nerve impulses necessary for correcting the position of the body.

4 The **cochlea**.

The sensory receptors of the membranous labyrinth are the **cristae ampullares** in the ampulla of each semicircular duct, the **macula utriculi** in the utricle, the **macula sacculi** in the saccule, and the **organ of Corti** in the cochlea. The **ductulus reuniens** connects the saccule to the blind end of the cochlea proximal to the **cecum vestibulare**. The opposite blind end of the cochlea is the **cecum cupulare**.

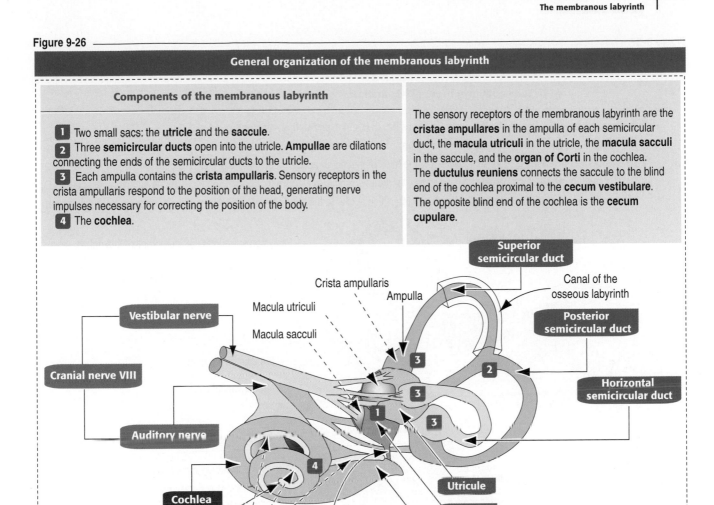

three auditory ossicles functionally linked.

The bony ossicles have two roles: (1) **they modulate the movement of the tympanic membrane. (2) They apply force to the oval window, thus amplifying the incoming sound waves. Otosclerosis** and **otitis media** affect the movements of the ossicles, conditions leading to hearing loss.

The **tympanic cavity** (also called the **tubotympanic recess** or **sulcus**) is lined by a squamous-to-cuboidal epithelium and lacks glands in the supporting connective tissue.

The **tympanic membrane** has an oval shape with a conical depression near the center caused by the attachment of the arm of the malleus. Two differently oriented layers of collagen fibers form the core of the membrane and the two sides of the membrane are lined by a simple squamous-to-cuboidal epithelium.

The **auditory** or **eustachian tube** links the middle ear with the nasopharynx. Adjacent to the tympanic cavity, the tube is formed by the temporal bone. **Elastic cartilage** continues the bony portion of the tube, which then changes into **hyaline cartilage** near the nasopharynx opening. A ciliated epithelium with regional variations (low columnar-to-pseudostratified near the nasopharynx) and with mucus-secreting glands lines the bony and cartilaginous segments of the tube. The **role of the auditory tube** is **to maintain a pressure balance between the tympanic cavity and the external environment.**

Defects in middle ear development include the absence of structural

Figure 9–27

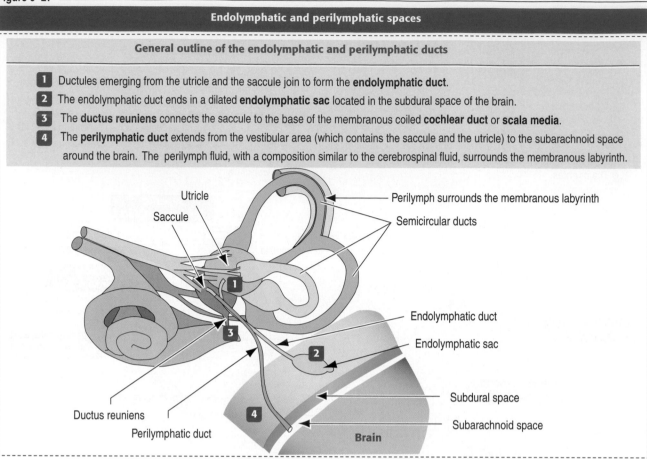

Endolymphatic and perilymphatic spaces

General outline of the endolymphatic and perilymphatic ducts

1 Ductules emerging from the utricle and the saccule join to form the **endolymphatic duct**.

2 The endolymphatic duct ends in a dilated **endolymphatic sac** located in the subdural space of the brain.

3 The **ductus reuniens** connects the saccule to the base of the membranous coiled **cochlear duct** or **scala media**.

4 The **perilymphatic duct** extends from the vestibular area (which contains the saccule and the utricle) to the subarachnoid space around the brain. The perilymph fluid, with a composition similar to the cerebrospinal fluid, surrounds the membranous labyrinth.

Utricle

Saccule

Perilymph surrounds the membranous labyrinth

Semicircular ducts

Endolymphatic duct

Endolymphatic sac

Subdural space

Subarachnoid space

Brain

Ductus reuniens

Perilymphatic duct

elements, such as the tympanic ring, which supports the tympanic membrane and the ossicles. The tympanic ring is derived from mesenchyme of the first pharyngeal arch (malleus and incus) and second pharyngeal arch (stapes), the middle ear muscles, and the tubotympanic recess.

The development of the inner ear

The inner ear and associated cranial ganglion neurons derive from an **otic placode** on the surface of the head. The placode invaginates and forms a hollow mass of cells called the **otic vesicle**, or **otocyst** (see Figure 9–25). Neural crest cells migrate out of the hindbrain and distribute around the otic vesicle. The otic vesicle elongates, forming the dorsal vestibular region and the ventral cochlear region under the influence of the *Pax-2* gene. Neither the cochlea nor the spiral ganglion form in the absence of *Pax-2*.

The endolymphatic duct derives from invagination of the otocyst, regulated by **fibroblast growth factor-3**, secreted by cells in **rhombomeres 5** and **6**. A total of seven rhombomeres, called **neuromeres**, also provide signals for the development of the hindbrain. Two of the **semicircular ducts** derive from the vestibular region and develop under the control of the *Prx1* and *Prx2* genes . Note that the auditory (cochlea) and vestibular portions (semicircular canals) are under separate genetic control (*Pax-2* and *Prx* genes, respectively).

The inner ear

The inner ear occupies the **osseous labyrinth** within the petrous portion of the temporal bone. The osseous labyrinth contains the **membranous labyrinth** (Figure 9–26), a structure that houses both the **vestibular** and **auditory systems**.

The **vestibular system** consists of two components: (1) two **sacs** (the **utricle**

Figure 9–28

Structure of the crista ampullaris

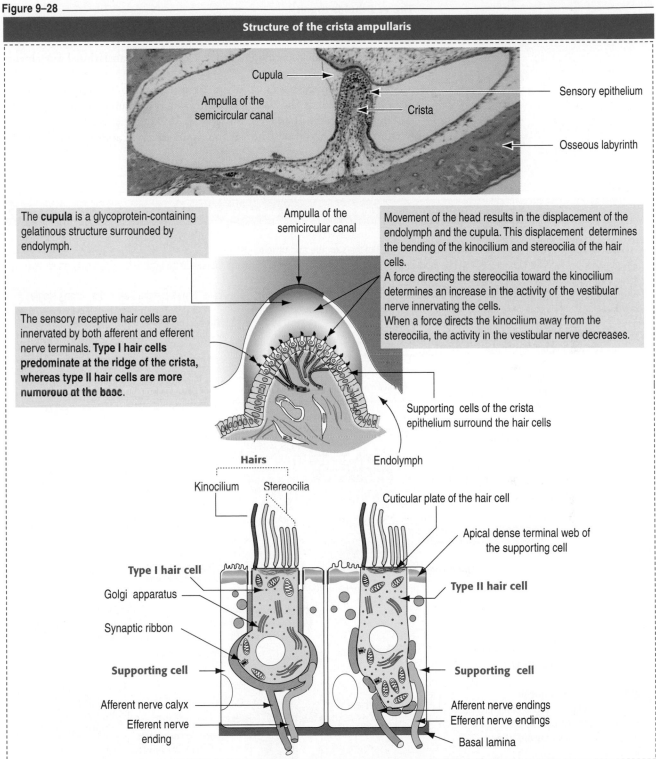

Cupula

Ampulla of the semicircular canal

Sensory epithelium

Crista

Osseous labyrinth

The **cupula** is a glycoprotein-containing gelatinous structure surrounded by endolymph.

Ampulla of the semicircular canal

Movement of the head results in the displacement of the endolymph and the cupula. This displacement determines the bending of the kinocilium and stereocilia of the hair cells.
A force directing the stereocilia toward the kinocilium determines an increase in the activity of the vestibular nerve innervating the cells.
When a force directs the kinocilium away from the stereocilia, the activity in the vestibular nerve decreases.

The sensory receptive hair cells are innervated by both afferent and efferent nerve terminals. **Type I hair cells predominate at the ridge of the crista, whereas type II hair cells are more numerous at the base.**

Supporting cells of the crista epithelium surround the hair cells

Endolymph

Hairs

Kinocilium   Stereocilia

Cuticular plate of the hair cell

Apical dense terminal web of the supporting cell

Type I hair cell

Golgi apparatus

Type II hair cell

Synaptic ribbon

Supporting cell

Supporting cell

Afferent nerve calyx

Afferent nerve endings

Efferent nerve ending

Efferent nerve endings

Basal lamina

and **saccule**, also called **otolith organs**), and (2) **three semicircular canals** (superior, horizontal and posterior) arising from the utricle.

The **auditory system** consists of the **cochlear duct**, lodged in a spiral bony canal anterior to the vestibular system.

The membranous labyrinth contains **endolymph**, a fluid with a high concentration of K^+ and a low concentration of Na^+. **Perilymph** (with a high Na^+ and low K^+ content) is present between the membranous labyrinth and the walls of the osseous labyrinth (Figure 9–27; see also Figure 9–35).

The vestibular organ

The **semicircular canals** respond to **rotational movements** of the head and body (**angular accelerations**).

The **otolith organs** (saccule and utricle) respond to **translational movements** (**linear acceleration**).

Sensory cells in the vestibular organ are innervated by afferent fibers of the vestibular branch of the **vestibulocochlear nerve** (cranial nerve VIII). The **labyrinthine artery**, a branch of the anterior inferior cerebellar artery, supplies blood to the labyrinth. The **stylomastoid artery** supplies blood to the semicircular canals.

Figure 9–29

Structure of the macula of the saccule and utricle: Otoliths

The **maculae** are sensory receptor areas located in the wall of the **saccule** and **utricle**.
They are concerned with the detection of directional movement of the head. The position of the macula in the utricle is horizontal and vertical in the saccule.
A single layer of supportive cells associated with the basal lamina houses two types of sensory cells: **types I** and **II hair cells**. A long single kinocilium and 50–60 stereocilia project from the apical surface of the hair cells.

Otoliths contain calcium carbonate.

Changes in the position of the head cause a shift in the position of the otolithic membrane (including the otoliths) and endolymph.

This movement displaces the underlying kinocilium and stereocilia.

The **otolithic membrane** is composed of the same gelatinous glycoprotein-rich material as the cupula of the crista ampullaris.

A difference is the presence of embedded **otoliths** in the macula.

The base of the otolihitic membrane is supported by a filamentous base with small pores in the areas overlying each hair bundle.

Endolymph

Base of the otolithic membrane with pores facing the hair bundles

Hair cells (types I and II)

Nerve fibers

Connective tissue

Supportive cell

1 The **cuticular plate** under the **stereocilia** bundle prevents the stereocilia from sinking into the cytoplasm.

2 However, the **kinocilium**, unsupported by a cuticular plate, plunges **inward** into the apical cell domain when the stereocilia move **toward the kinocilium**.

3 This inward movement deforms the plasma membrane and triggers **depolarization**.

4 Displacement of the stereocilia **away from the kinocilium** lifts the kinocilium and causes **hyperpolarization**.

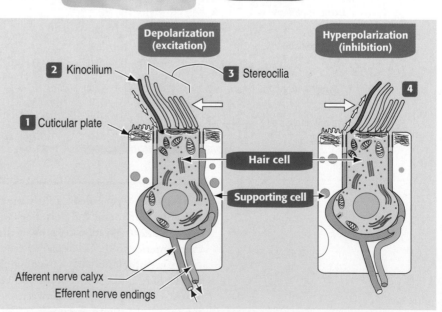

Depolarization (excitation)

Hyperpolarization (inhibition)

2 Kinocilium

3 Stereocilia

1 Cuticular plate

Hair cell

Supporting cell

Afferent nerve calyx
Efferent nerve endings

Figure 9–30

Organization of the macula

Sensory epithelium of the macula

This epithelium consists of **types I** and **II hair cells** embedded in **supporting cells** touching the basal lamina.

In vivo, kinocilia and stereocilia—extending from the surface of the hair cells—are coated by the **otolithic** (or statoconial) **membrane** containing **otoconia** (Gk. "ear dust").

Otoconia are displaced by the endolymph during forward-backward and upward-downward movements of the head (**linear acceleration**).

The sensory epithelium of the macula in the otolithic organs (saccule and utricle) does not respond to head rotation.

The hair cells of the macula are **polarized**: The **kinocilium** is oriented with respect to an imaginary line called the **striola**, which divides the hair cells into two opposite fields.

In the utricle, the kinocilium faces the striola. In the saccule, the kinocilium faces away from the striola.

This orientation determines which population of hair cells will displace their hair bundles in response to a specific movement of the head.

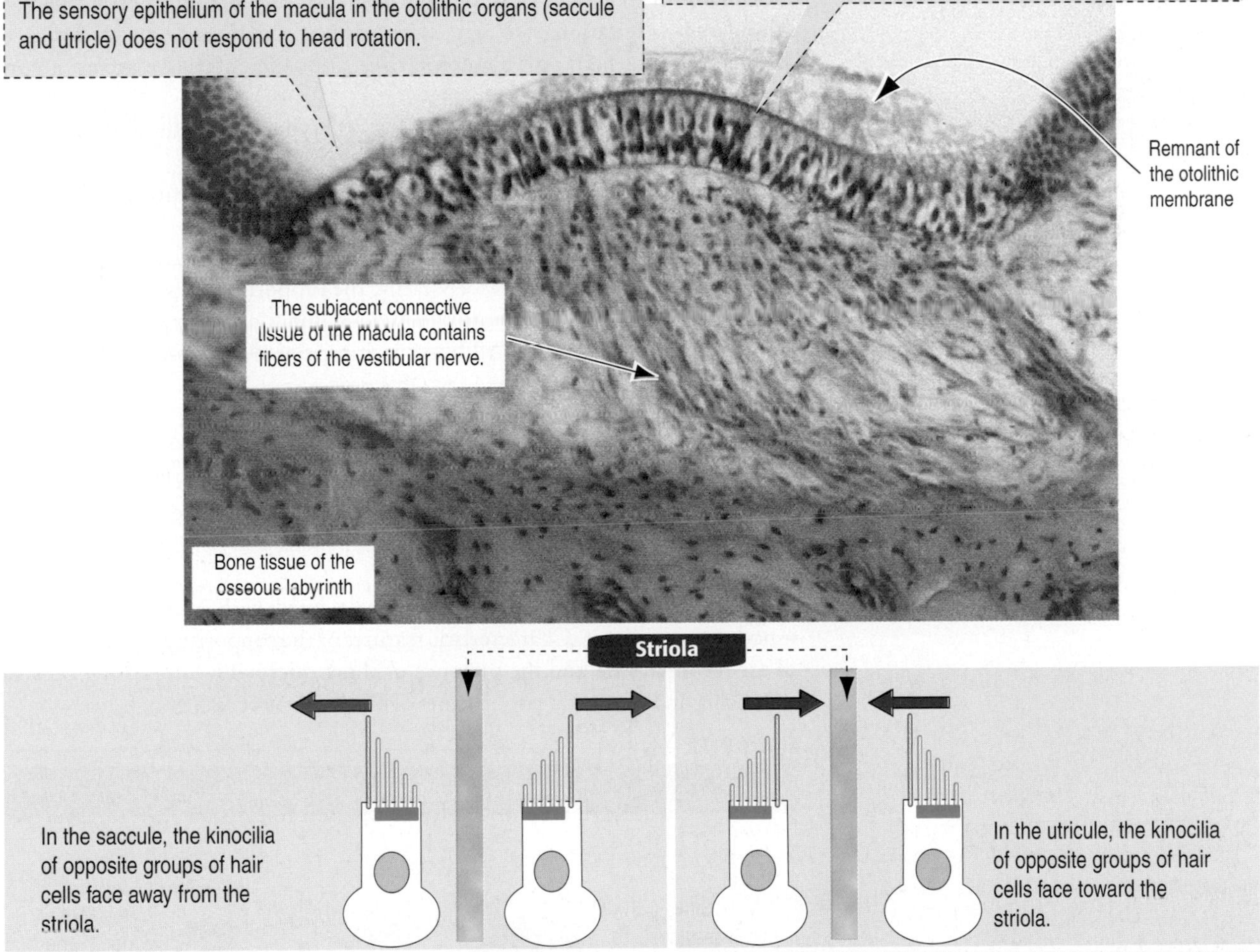

Remnant of the otolithic membrane

The subjacent connective tissue of the macula contains fibers of the vestibular nerve.

Bone tissue of the osseous labyrinth

Striola

In the saccule, the kinocilia of opposite groups of hair cells face away from the striola.

In the utricle, the kinocilia of opposite groups of hair cells face toward the striola.

The semicircular canals

The semicircular ducts are contained within the osseous labyrinth. The three ducts are connected to the utricle. Ducts derived from the utricle and saccule join to form the **endolymphatic duct**. The endolymphatic duct ends in a small dilation called the **endolymphatic sac**, located between the layers of the meninges.

Small dilations —ampullae— are present at the semicircular duct–utricle connection sites. Each ampulla has a prominent ridge called the **crista ampullaris**.

The crista ampullaris (Figure 9–28) consists of a **sensory epithelium** covered by a gelatinous mass called the **cupula**.

The sensory epithelium consists of two cell types (see Figure 9–28): (1) the **hair cells**, and (2) the **supporting cells**.

The basal surface of the supporting cells is attached to a basal lamina. In contrast, the hair cells occupy a recess in the apical region of the supporting cells and do not reach the basal lamina. The apical domain of the hair cells contains 60 to 100 hairlike specialized **stereocilia** and a **single kinocilium**. Stereocilia are supported by an actin-containing **cuticular plate**. The free ends of both stereocilia and kinocilia are embedded in the **cupula**. The cupula attaches to the roof and walls of the ampulla and acts like a partition of the lumen of the ampulla (see Figure 9–28).

When the position of the cupula changes in response to movements of the endolymph, it causes displacement of the stereocilia and kinocilium of the hair cells (Figure 9–29). When stereocilia move **toward the kinocilium**, the plasma membrane of the hair cells **depolarizes** and the afferent nerve fibers are **stimulated** (**excitation**). When stereocilia are **deflected away from the kinocilium**, the hair cell **hyperpolarizes** and afferent nerve fibers are **not stimulated** (**inhibition**).

The cristae have two types of hair cells: (1) **type I hair cells**, and (2) **type II hair cells**.

Both cell types are essentially similar in their internal structure, but differences exist in their shape and innervation:

1. **Afferent nerves**, with terminals containing the neurotransmitters **aspartate** and **glutamate**, enter the spaces separating the supporting cells and **form a calyx-like network** embracing the rounded basal domain of the type I hair cell. The cytoplasm displays **synaptic ribbons** and associated vesicles (similar to those found in the sensory retina).

2. The nerve endings in contact with the cylindrical type II hair cell do not form a basal calyx. Instead, **simple terminal boutons** can be visualized.

In addition to afferent nerves, both type I and type II hair cells receive **efferent nerve terminals** and have synaptic vesicles containing the neurotransmitter **acetylcholine**. Efferent nerve fibers control the sensitivity of the sensory receptor cells.

Both supporting and hair cells are associated with each other by apical junctional complexes. Characteristic features of the supporting cells are an **apical dense terminal web** and the presence of **short microvilli**. Supporting cells lack stereocilia and kinocilia, two features typical of hair cells.

Figure 9–31

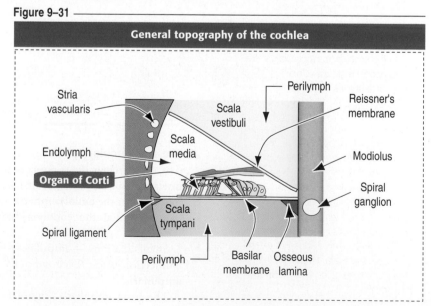

General topography of the cochlea

Stria vascularis

Perilymph

Reissner's membrane

Scala vestibuli

Scala media

Endolymph

Modiolus

Organ of Corti

Spiral ganglion

Scala tympani

Spiral ligament

Perilymph

Basilar membrane

Osseous lamina

Figure 9–32

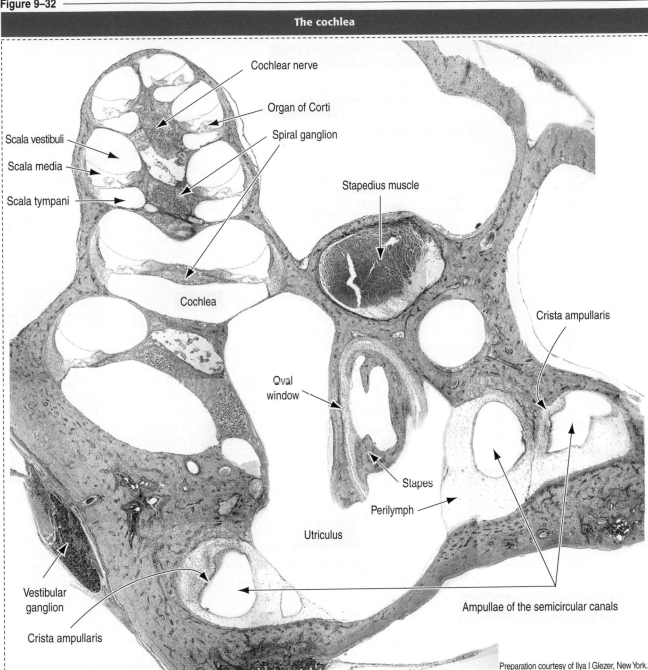

| The cochlea |

- Cochlear nerve
- Organ of Corti
- Spiral ganglion
- Scala vestibuli
- Scala media
- Scala tympani
- Stapedius muscle
- Cochlea
- Crista ampullaris
- Oval window
- Stapes
- Perilymph
- Utriculus
- Vestibular ganglion
- Crista ampullaris
- Ampullae of the semicircular canals

Preparation courtesy of Ilya I Glezer, New York.

The cochlea (Gk. *kochlias*, spiral-shelled snail) is a spiral canal that winds more than two and a half times around a central bony axis, the **modiolus**. Within the bony modiolus is the **cochlear (spiral) ganglion**, spiraling around the inner side of the cochlea. The ganglion contains bipolar neurons. (1) The peripheral processes innervate the receptor cells. (2) The central processes enter the core of the modiolus, where they form the cochlear nerve (the cochlear division of cranial nerve VIII).

The membranous portion of the cochlea, the cochlear partition, contains the cochlear duct or scala media. The cochlear partition spans the bony labyrinth dividing it into two separate canals: (1) the **scala vestibuli**; (2) the **scala tympani.**

The **vestibular membrane (Reissner's membrane)** and the **basilar membrane**, two membranes of the cochlear partition, separate the endolymph-filled cochlear duct from the perilymph-filled scala vestibuli and scala tympani. The lateral wall of the cochlear partition is the **stria vascularis**, a highly vascular tissue that covers a portion of the bony labyrinth and is responsible for the production and maintenance of the unique composition of the endolymph (K^+ homeostasis).

The cochlear duct does not extend to the apex or cupula of the cochlea but leaves a small opening of communication between the scala vestibuli and scala tympani at the apex, the **helicotrema** (see Figure 9–33). At the base of the cochlea, the stapes on the **oval window** and the membrane of the **round window** (not shown) separate the scala vestibuli and the scala tympani, respectively, from the middle ear cavity.

Figure 9–33

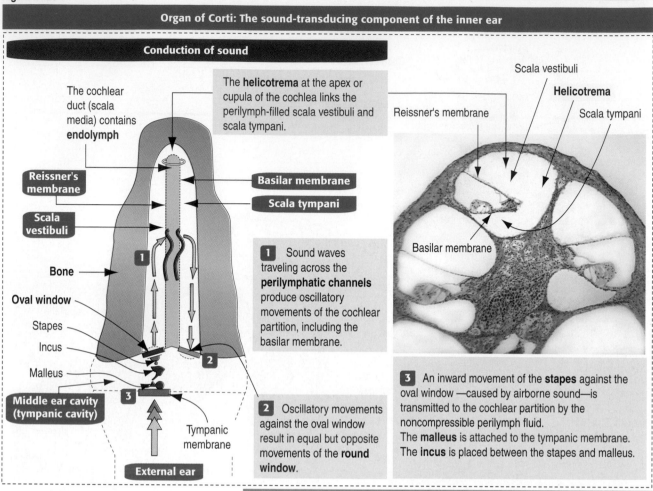

Organ of Corti: The sound-transducing component of the inner ear

Conduction of sound

The cochlear duct (scala media) contains **endolymph**

The **helicotrema** at the apex or cupula of the cochlea links the perilymph-filled scala vestibuli and scala tympani.

Reissner's membrane

Scala vestibuli

Bone

Oval window

Stapes

Incus

Malleus

Middle ear cavity (tympanic cavity)

Tympanic membrane

External ear

Basilar membrane

Scala tympani

1 Sound waves traveling across the **perilymphatic channels** produce oscillatory movements of the cochlear partition, including the basilar membrane.

2 Oscillatory movements against the oval window result in equal but opposite movements of the **round window**.

Scala vestibuli

Helicotrema

Reissner's membrane

Scala tympani

Basilar membrane

3 An inward movement of the **stapes** against the oval window —caused by airborne sound—is transmitted to the cochlear partition by the noncompressible perilymph fluid.
The **malleus** is attached to the tympanic membrane.
The **incus** is placed between the stapes and malleus.

Clinical significance: Ménière's disease

Secretory cells in the membranous labyrinth and the endolymphatic sac maintain the ionic balance between endolymph and perilymph (see Figure 9–36). An **increase in the volume of endolymph** is the cause of **Ménière's disease**, which is characterized by vertigo (illusion of rotational movement in space), nausea, positional nystagmus (involuntary rhythmic oscillation of the eyes), vomiting, and ringing in the ears (**tinnitus**).

The otolithic organs

The utricle and saccule display a sensory epithelium called a **macula** (Figure 9–30). Like the sensory epithelium of the crista ampullaris in the semicircular canals, the macula contains hair cells and supporting cells. The macula is covered by a gelatinous substance containing calcium carbonate–protein complexes forming small crystals called **otoliths** (see Figure 9–29). Otoliths are not present in the cupula overlying the hairs of the crista ampullaris. Small ductules derived from the utricle and saccule join to form the **endolymphatic duct** ending in the **endolymphatic sac**. The **ductus reuniens** links the saccule to the base of the membranous cochlear duct.

The cochlea

The cochlear duct is a membranous coiled duct inserted in the bony cochlea. It consists of an **apex** and a **base**. The coiled duct makes about two and two-thirds turns with a total length of 34 mm.

The cochlea has **three spiraling chambers** (Figures 9–31, 9–32, and 9–33):

Figure 9–34

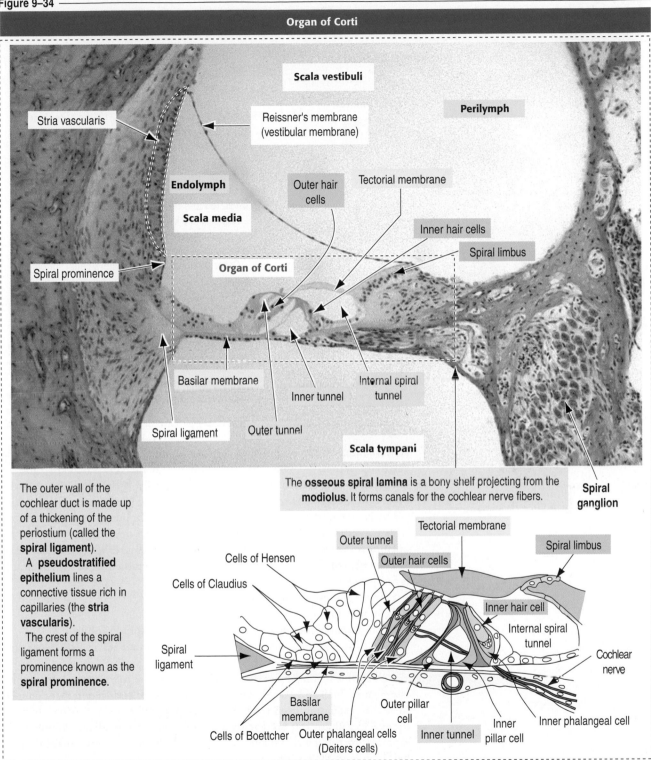

Organ of Corti

The outer wall of the cochlear duct is made up of a thickening of the periostium (called the **spiral ligament**).

A **pseudostratified epithelium** lines a connective tissue rich in capillaries (the **stria vascularis**).

The crest of the spiral ligament forms a prominence known as the **spiral prominence**.

The **osseous spiral lamina** is a bony shelf projecting from the **modiolus**. It forms canals for the cochlear nerve fibers.

1. The **cochlear duct** (also called the **scala media**) represents the central chamber and contains endolymph.

2. Above the cochlear duct is the **scala vestibuli**, starting at the oval window.

3. Below it is the **scala tympani**, ending at the **round window**.

The scalae vestibuli and tympani are filled with perilymph and communicate at the **helicotrema** (see Figure 9–33).

In cross section, the boundaries of the scala media are the **basilar membrane**

Figure 9–35

| Cell–nerve ending relationship within the organ of Corti |

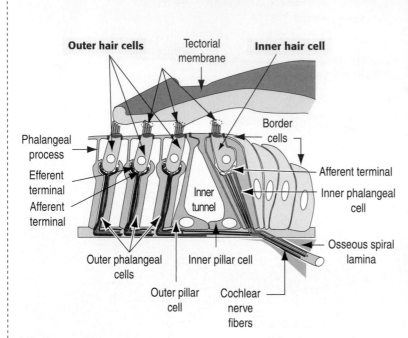

The **organ of Corti** is located in the scala media, extends the full length of the basilar membrane. Hair cells are the sensory receptors of the organ of Corti. Two types of hair cells are present in the human cochlea: (1) the **inner hair cell**; (2) the **outer hair cells**. Only outer hair cells are in direct contact with the tectorial membrane.

Both have hairs, bundles of stereocilia projecting from their apical surfaces. From the base to the apex of the cochlear duct, inner hair cells are arranged in a single row and outer hair cells in three to four rows.

Hair cells are kept in position by two supporting epithelial cell types: (1) the **pillar cells**; (2) the **phalangeal cells**.

Outer phalangeal cells (Deiters cells) surround the lower third of the outer hair cells and the nerve terminals around the base of the hair cell. A phalangeal process projects toward the apical surface of the hair cell and flattens into a plate. The **inner phalangeal cells** lack the phalangeal process and extensively surround the inner hair cell and its nerve terminal.

The **tectorial membrane** extends above the hair cells from the inner side of the organ of Corti.

at the bottom, the **vestibular** or **Reissner's membrane** above, and the **stria vascularis** externally. The cells and capillaries of the stria vascularis produce endolymph. The spiraling bony core of the cochlea is the **modiolus**. On the inner side, the spiral osseous lamina projects outward from the modiolus to join the basilar membrane. On the external side, the basilar membrane is continuous with the **spiral ligament**. The scala vestibuli meets the scala tympani at an opening at the apex of the cochlea. This connecting site is called the **helicotrema**.

The **organ of Corti** (Figure 9–34) is the sensory epithelium of the cochlea. It is formed by:

1. **Inner** and **outer hair cells**.
2. **Supporting cells**.
3. The **tectorial membrane**, extending from the **spiral limbus**.
4. The **inner tunnel**, limited by the **outer** and **inner pillar cells**, separating inner from outer hair cells.

A **single line** of inner hair cells extends from the base to the apex of the cochlea (see Figures 9–33 and 9–35). The outer hair cells are arranged in **three parallel rows**, also extending from the base to the apex of the cochlea. A hair bundle, formed by 50 to 150 **stereocilia** in a long-to-short gradient arrangement, extends from the apical domain of each hair cell. **No kinocilium is present in the hair bundle of the cochlea**.

The **tectorial membrane** contains α- and β-**tectorin** proteins and extends outward over the sensory epithelium, from the spiral limbus of the osseous spiral lamina. The tectorial membrane is in close contact with the taller stereocilia of the hair bundle. When the basilar membrane and organ of Corti are displaced, stereocilia hit the tectorial membrane and **depolarization** of the hair cells occurs (Figure 9–36).

The **spiral ganglion** is housed in the modiolus. Processes of the bipolar sensory neurons of the spiral ganglion extend into the osseous spiral lamina, lose

Figure 9–36

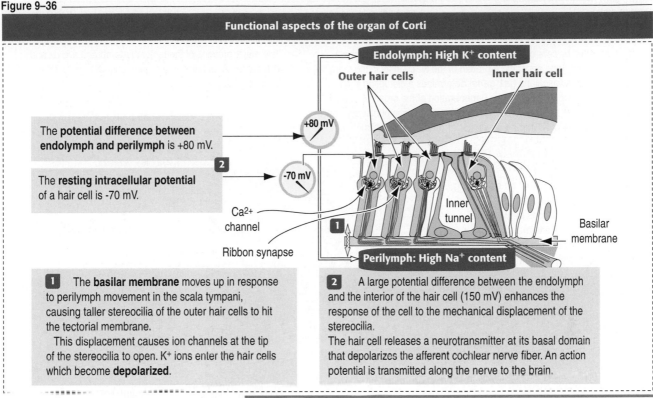

Functional aspects of the organ of Corti

The **potential difference between endolymph and perilymph** is +80 mV.

2

The **resting intracellular potential** of a hair cell is -70 mV.

Endolymph: High K⁺ content

Outer hair cells

Inner hair cell

+80 mV

-70 mV

Ca²⁺ channel

Ribbon synapse

Inner tunnel

Basilar membrane

1

Perilymph: High Na⁺ content

1 The **basilar membrane** moves up in response to perilymph movement in the scala tympani, causing taller stereocilia of the outer hair cells to hit the tectorial membrane.

This displacement causes ion channels at the tip of the stereocilia to open. K⁺ ions enter the hair cells which become **depolarized**.

2 A large potential difference between the endolymph and the interior of the hair cell (150 mV) enhances the response of the cell to the mechanical displacement of the stereocilia.

The hair cell releases a neurotransmitter at its basal domain that depolarizes the afferent cochlear nerve fiber. An action potential is transmitted along the nerve to the brain.

their myelin, pierce the basilar membrane, and synapse on the basal domain of the inner and outer hair cells.

There are two types of bipolar sensory neurons in the spiral ganglion: (1) **type I cells** (90% to 95%) whose fibers contact inner hair cells, and (2) **type II cells** (10% to 5%) which synapse with outer hair cells.

The **neuronal processes of type I and II cells form the cochlear branch of the vestibulocochlear nerve. Olivocochlear efferent fibers run along the basilar membrane to contact the inner and outer hair cells.** Neurons of the auditory and vestibular ganglia fail to develop when there is a deletion in the *neurogenin 1* gene.

The hearing process

Two factors play a significant role during the hearing process (see Figure 9–36):

1. The high concentration of K⁺ in the endolymph and the high concentration of Na⁺ in the perilymph determine an electrical potential difference. The ion concentration is regulated by the absorptive and secretory activity of the stria vascularis.

2. Fluid movement in the scala tympani induces the movement of the basilar membrane causing the taller stereocilia to be displaced by the tectorial membrane.

As a result, ion channels at the stereocilia tip open driving K⁺ into the cell, which then becomes depolarized. Upon depolarization, an **influx of Ca²⁺** to the basal region of the hair cells determines the release of neurotransmitters at the hair cell–cochlear nerve fiber synapse and generation of a stimulus. Note the presence of **ribbon synapses** at the base of the hair cells. Changes in electrical potential between the perilymph and the hair cells occur in response to the magnitude of sound.

Clinical significance: Deafness and balance

As you have seen, cytoskeletal components in the apical domain of hair cells are

Figure 9–37

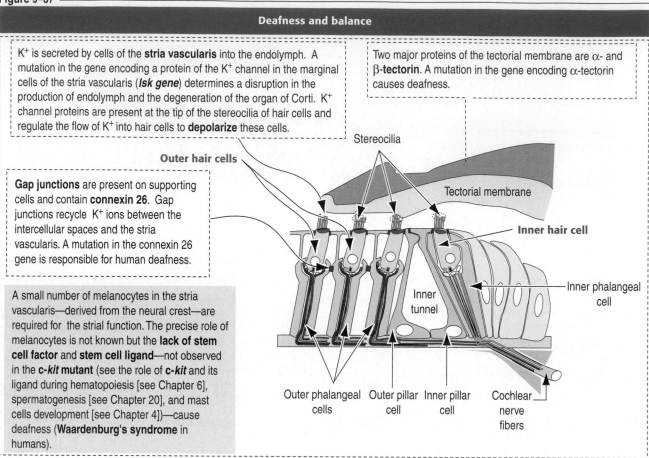

Deafness and balance

K⁺ is secreted by cells of the **stria vascularis** into the endolymph. A mutation in the gene encoding a protein of the K⁺ channel in the marginal cells of the stria vascularis (**Isk gene**) determines a disruption in the production of endolymph and the degeneration of the organ of Corti. K⁺ channel proteins are present at the tip of the stereocilia of hair cells and regulate the flow of K⁺ into hair cells to **depolarize** these cells.

Two major proteins of the tectorial membrane are α- and β-**tectorin**. A mutation in the gene encoding α-tectorin causes deafness.

Gap junctions are present on supporting cells and contain **connexin 26**. Gap junctions recycle K⁺ ions between the intercellular spaces and the stria vascularis. A mutation in the connexin 26 gene is responsible for human deafness.

A small number of melanocytes in the stria vascularis—derived from the neural crest—are required for the strial function. The precise role of melanocytes is not known but the **lack of stem cell factor** and **stem cell ligand**—not observed in the **c-kit** mutant (see the role of **c-kit** and its ligand during hematopoiesis [see Chapter 6], spermatogenesis [see Chapter 20], and mast cells development [see Chapter 4])—cause deafness (**Waardenburg's syndrome** in humans).

Outer hair cells

Stereocilia

Tectorial membrane

Inner hair cell

Inner phalangeal cell

Inner tunnel

Outer phalangeal cells

Outer pillar cell

Inner pillar cell

Cochlear nerve fibers

relatively abundant. Hair cells convert mechanical input, determined by the deflection of apical bundles of stereocilia embedded in the tectorial membrane and the otolithic membrane of the cupula, into an electromechanical input leading to synaptic transmission.

In the absence of the transcription factor **Pou4f3**, hair cells express specific markers (including unconventional **myosin VI and VIIa**), and both hair cells and spiral ganglion neurons degenerate.

The tectorial membrane and otolith membranes contain two proteins: α-**tectorin** and β-**tectorin**. When the *α-tectorin* encoding gene is mutated, deafness occurs (Figure 9–37).

A mutation in the gene for **connexin 26**, a component of gap junctions on the surface of supporting cells, is responsible for deafness because the recycling of endolymph K⁺ from the intercellular spaces to the stria vascularis is disrupted.

There are several mouse mutants with a decrease in neural crest–derived melanocytes in the stria vascularis. Although the particular role of melanocytes in the stria vascularis is not known, a mutation in the **c-kit** gene (encoding the stem cell factor receptor and its ligand; see Chapter 6, Blood and Hematopoiesis, for a discussion of the c-kit gene), affects the function of the stria vascularis and the mice are deaf.

Waardenburg's syndrome in humans is an autosomal dominant type of congenital deafness associated with pigment abnormalities, such as partial albinism, and abnormal development of the vestibulocochlear ganglion. Recall that melanocytes have a common origin in the neural crest and are migratory cells.

Learning objectives

Part II, **Protection of the Body**, includes Chapter 10, **Immune-Lymphatic System**, and Chapter 11, **Integumentary System**, in particular, the **skin** component.

Both the immune–lymphatic system and the skin work toward a common protective objective. Both contain cells derived from the bone marrow that trap antigens and initiate immune responses.

In the immune–lymphatic system chapter:

1. You will learn the histologic organization of the **lymph node**, the site at which an extensive system of lymphatic vessels converges after collecting extracellular fluid from tissues.

2. You will study the structure and function of the **thymus** and its role in preventing the occurrence of autoimmune disease.

3. You will learn that the **spleen** has a dual function: an immune protective function and the removal of aged or fragile red blood cells.

4. You will also learn that the digestive tube contains lymphoid tissues—called **gut-associated lymphoid tissue**, or GALT—in the form of the tonsils, appendix, and the specialized Peyer's patches.

In the integumentary system chapter:

1. You will learn that the skin mirrors the health of other systems. Disorders such as diabetes mellitus and lupus erythematosus are characterized by skin manifestations. The ingestion of therapeutic drugs can cause rashes and exanthems of the skin.

2. You will learn that the epidermis of the skin contains Langerhans cells, which initiate immune responses to pathogens that have entered the superficial layers of the epidermis.

3. You will learn the topographic distribution of keratins in the layers of the epidermis and become aware that the mutation of some of them can give rise to severe skin diseases.

4. You will learn the structure and function of apocrine and eccrine sweat and sebaceous glands and understand the value of sweat glands in the clinical diagnosis of cystic fibrosis.

10. IMMUNE-LYMPHATIC SYSTEM

Organization of the immune-lymphatic system

The lymphatic system includes **primary** and **secondary lymphoid organs**.

The primary lymphoid organs produce the cell components of the immune system. They are (1) the **bone marrow** (Figure 10–1), and (2) the **thymus**.

The secondary lymphoid organs are the sites where immune responses occur. They include (1) the **lymph nodes**, (2) the **spleen**, (3) the **tonsils**, and (4) aggregates of lymphocytes and antigen-presenting cells in the **lung** and the mucosa of the **digestive tract** (Peyer's patches).

The main function of the **lymphoid organs**, as components of the immune system, is to protect the body against invading **pathogens** or **antigens** (bacteria, viruses, and parasites). The basis for this defense mechanism, or **immune response**, is the ability to distinguish **self** from **nonself**. Because pathogens can enter the body at any point, the lymphatic system is widely distributed.

The **two key cell components of the immune system** are **lymphocytes** and **accessory cells** (Table 10–1). Lymphocytes include two major cell groups: (1) **B cells**, responding to cell-free and cell-bound antigens; (2) **T cells**, subdivided

Figure 10–1

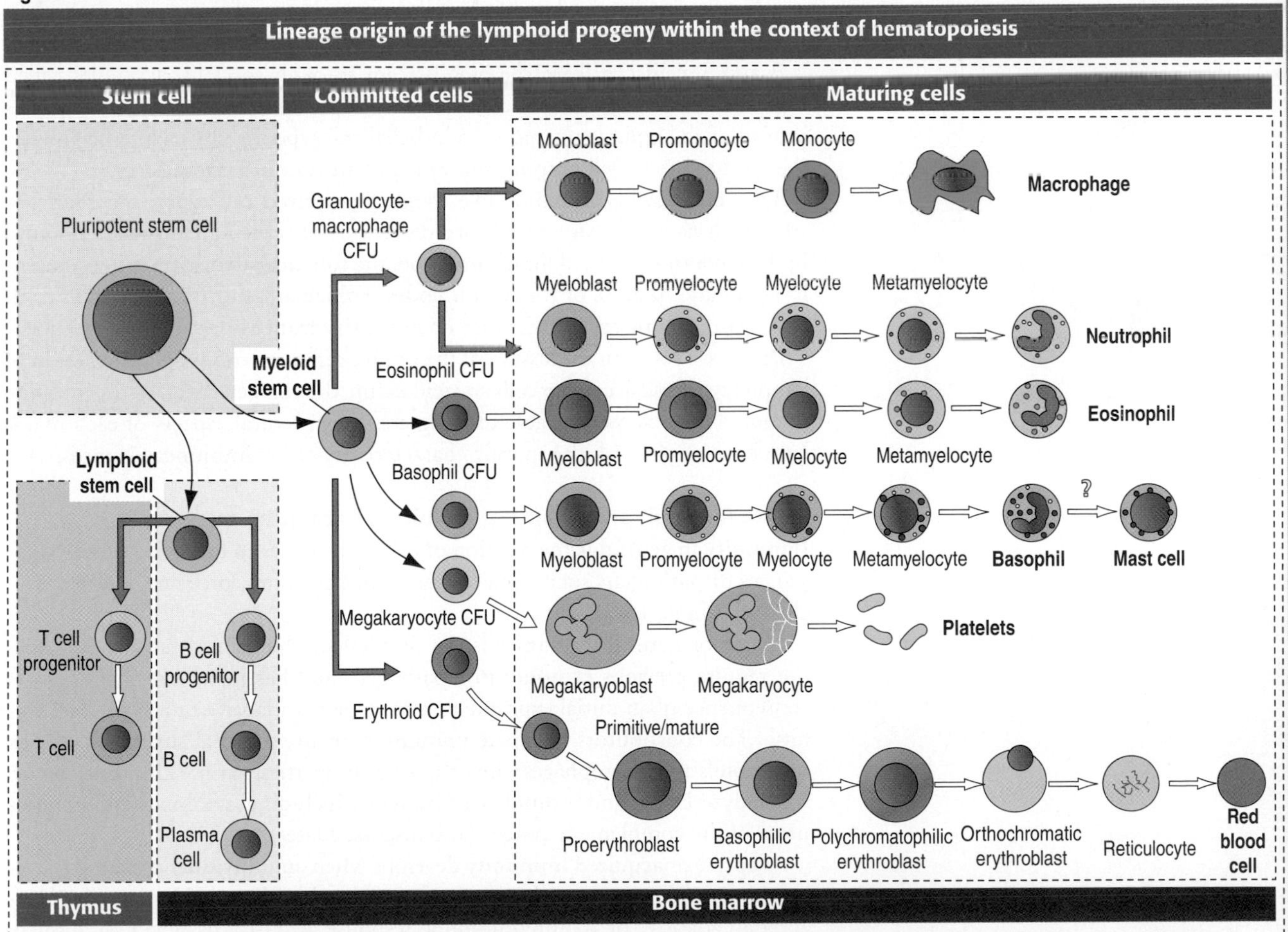

Lineage origin of the lymphoid progeny within the context of hematopoiesis

The cells of the immune system arise from the pluripotent stem cell in the bone marrow. We have already seen in Chapter 6, Blood and Hematopoesis, that pluripotent stem cells divide to produce two specialized progenitor cells: **lymphoid progenitor cell** that generates B and T lymphocytes, and a **myeloid progenitor cell**, which gives rise to leukocytes, erythrocytes, megakaryocytes, and macrophages.

When activated outside the bone marrow, **B lymphocytes** differentiate into antibody-secreting **plasma cells**. **T lymphocytes** differentiate in the **thymus** into cells that can activate other cells of the immune system (helper cells) or kill bacteria- or virus-infected cells (cytolytic or cytotoxic cells).

Table 10–1 Participating cells in immune reactions		
Lymphocytes		
B cells	Respond to cell-free and plasma membrane-bound antigens	
T cells		
Helper T cells	Respond to cell-bound antigens	
Cytolytic T cells (CLTs)		
Natural killer cells: Cell population lacking T cell receptor (TCR) and CD4 and CD8 coreceptors.		
Accessory cells		
Macrophages (monocyte-derived)		
Dendritic cells (monocyte-derived; Langerhans cells of epidermis)		
Follicular dendritic cells (in lymphatic nodules)		
Effector cells		
Macrophages, CLTs, neutrophils		

into two categories: **helper T cells** and **cytolytic** or **cytotoxic T cells**. T cells respond to cell-bound antigens presented by specific molecules.

After leaving the two **primary** organs (bone marrow and thymus), mature B and T cells circulate in the blood until they reach one of the various **secondary lymphoid organs** (lymph nodes, spleen, and tonsils).

B and T cells can leave the bloodstream through specialized venules called **high endothelial venules,** so called because they are lined by tall endothelial cells instead of the typical squamous endothelial cell type. In this chapter we review the mechanism of cell homing within the context of **inflammation**.

The accessory cells include two monocyte-derived cell types: **macrophages** and **dendritic cells.** An example of a dendritic cell is the **Langerhans cell** found in the epidermis of the skin. A third type, the **follicular dendritic cell**, is present in lymphatic nodules of the lymph nodes. Follicular dendritic cells differ from ordinary dendritic cells in that they do not derive from a bone marrow precursor.

Before we start our discussion of the origin, differentiation, and interaction of lymphocytes and accessory cells, we will define the characteristics of the immune system. Then, we will be able to integrate the structural aspects of each major lymphatic organ with the specific characteristics of the immune responses.

Innate (natural) and adaptive (acquired) immunity

Immunity in general is the reaction of cells and tissues to foreign (nonself) substances or **pathogens** such as microorganisms, parasites, proteins, and polysaccharides (Table 10-2).

Innate or **natural immunity** is the simplest mechanism of protection, does not require previous exposure to a pathogen, and has rapid responsiveness. A consequence of an initial exposure to a pathogen is adaptive or acquired immunity. The contributors to innate immunity are an epithelial surface or barrier, neutrophils and macrophages with phagocytic properties, natural killer cells (which we analyze later), and a number of proteins, including cytokines and components of the complement system (also discussed later).

Adaptive or **acquired immunity** develops when an individual is exposed to an infectious pathogen. Lymphocytes and cytokines are directly involved in generating an adaptive or acquired immune response against a pathogen or antigen. To achieve an immune response, adaptive immunity relies on an effector mechanism with the participation of **effector cells,** also utilized by innate immunity: macrophages, neutrophils, and killer cells. Essentially, adaptive immunity is the perfection of innate immunity.

Adaptive immunity involves two types of responses to an antigen (pathogen):

Table 10–2 Immunity
Innate immunity (natural)
Epithelia (physical barrier)
Phagocytic cells (macrophages, neutrophils)
Natural killer cells
Blood proteins: complement system
Adaptive immunity (also called acquired or specific immunity)
Humoral immunity (antibody-mediated)
B cells and plasma cells
Cell-mediated immunity (also called **cellular immunity**)
T cells
Types of immunity
Passive immunity
Maternal antibodies transferred to fetus.
Antibodies of immunized animals (rabies, tetanus).
Antitoxins (diphtheria).
Active immunity (post disease)
T cells

The first response is mediated by **antibodies** produced by plasma cells, the final differentiation product of B cells as we have seen in Chapter 4, Connective Tissue. This response is known as **humoral immunity** and operates against antigens located outside a cell or bound to its surface. When antibodies bind to an antigen or toxins produced by a pathogen, they can facilitate the phagocytic action of macrophages or recruit leukocytes and mast cells to take advantage of their cytokines and mediators, respectively, and strengthen a response. Humoral immunity results in persistent antibody production and production of memory cells.

The second type of response **requires the uptake of a pathogen by a phagocyte**. An intracellular pathogen is not accessible to antibodies and requires a cell-mediated response, or **cell-mediated immunity**. T cells, B cells, and antigen-presenting cells are the key players in cell-mediated immunity.

A consequence of adaptive or acquired immunity is the protection of the individual when a second encounter with the pathogen occurs. This protection is specific against the same pathogen and, therefore, adaptive or acquired immunity is also called **specific immunity**.

Active immunity is the form of immunity resulting from exposure to a pathogen. **Passive immunity** is a temporary form of immunity conferred by serum or lymphocytes transferred from an immunized individual to another individual who has not been exposed or cannot respond to a pathogen. For example, the transfer of maternal antibodies to the fetus is a form of passive immunity that protects newborns from infections until they can develop active immunity.

Properties of adaptive or acquired immunity

Both humoral and cell-mediated immunity developed against foreign pathogens have the following characteristics:

1. **Specificity**: Specific domains of an antigen are recognized by individual lymphocytes. We will see later how cell membrane receptors on lymphocytes can distinguish and respond to subtle variations in the structure of antigens.

2. **Diversity**: Lymphocytes utilize molecular mechanisms to modify their antigen receptors in such a way that they can recognize and respond to a large num-

ber and types of antigenic domains.

3. **Memory**: The exposure of lymphocytes to an antigen results in two events: their antigen-specific clonal expansion by mitosis, as well as the generation of reserve **memory cells**. Memory cells can react more rapidly and efficiently when exposed again to the same antigen.

4. **Self-limitation**: An immune response is stimulated by a specific antigen. When the antigen is neutralized or disappears, the response ceases.

5. **Tolerance**: An immune response pursues the removal of a non–self-antigen while being "tolerant" to self-antigens. Tolerance is achieved by a selection mechanism that eliminates lymphocytes expressing receptors specific for self-antigens. A failure of self-tolerance (and specificity) leads to a group of disorders called **autoimmune diseases**.

The development of B cells

Figure 10–1 illustrates the concept that the bone marrow is the site of origin of B and T lymphocytes from a lymphoid stem cell. In Chapter 6, Blood and Hematopoiesis, we studied developmental aspects of the myeloid and erythroid lineages from a pluripotent stem cell. The same pluripotent stem cell gives rise to a **lymphoid progenitor** or **lymphoid stem cell** that generates B lymphocytes, T lymphocytes, and natural killer cells. **B cells mature in the bone marrow** whereas **the thymus is the site of maturation of T cells**.

Stem B cells in the bone marrow proliferate and mature in contact with bone marrow **stromal cells** under the influence of **interleukin-7 (IL-7)** (Figure 10–2).

During maturation, on their surface B cells express **immunoglobulins M (IgM)** or **D (IgD)** interacting with two additional proteins linked to each other, **immunoglobulins α (Igα)** and **β (Igβ)**. The cell surface IgM or IgD, together with the conjoined **Igα** and **Igβ**, form the **B cell antigen receptor complex**. The intracellular domains of Igα and Igβ contain a tyrosine-rich domain called **immunoreceptor tyrosine-based activation motif**, or **ITAM**.

Binding of an antigen to the B cell antigen receptor complex induces the phosphorylation of tyrosine in the ITAM which, in turn, activates transcription factors that drive the expression of genes required for further development of B cells.

Figure 10–2

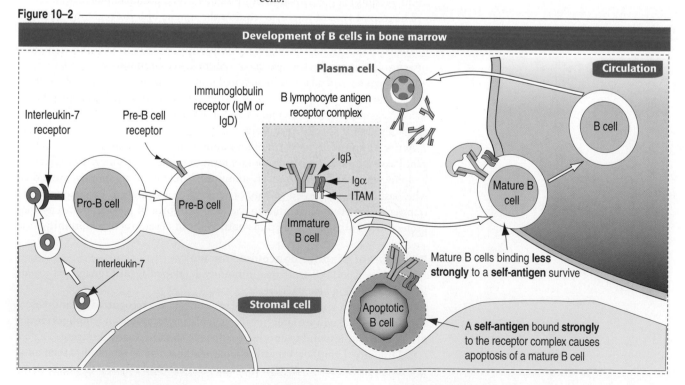

Development of B cells in bone marrow

Interleukin-7 receptor

Pre-B cell receptor

Immunoglobulin receptor (IgM or IgD)

B lymphocyte antigen receptor complex

Plasma cell

Circulation

B cell

Interleukin-7

Pro-B cell

Pre-B cell

Igβ

Igα

ITAM

Immature B cell

Mature B cell

Stromal cell

Apoptotic B cell

Mature B cells binding **less strongly** to a **self-antigen** survive

A **self-antigen** bound **strongly** to the receptor complex causes apoptosis of a mature B cell

Self-antigens present in the bone marrow test the antigen-binding specificity of IgM or IgD on B cell surfaces. This is a required testing step before B cells can continue their maturation, enter peripheral lymphoid tissues, and interact with foreign (non-self) antigens. **Self-antigens** binding **strongly** to two or more IgM or IgD receptor molecules on B cells induce **apoptosis**. **Self-antigens** with a **weaker binding affinity** for the B cell antigen receptor complex enable the survival and maturation of these B cells when ITAMs of IgM- or IgD-associated Igα and Igβ transduce signaling events, resulting in further differentiation of B cells and the entrance of mature B cells into the circulation.

The major histocompatibility complex and human leukocyte antigens

The presentation of antigens to T cells is carried out by specialized proteins encoded by genes in the major histocompatibility locus and present on the surface of antigen-presenting cells. Antigen-presenting cells survey the body, find and internalize antigens by phagocytosis, break them down into antigenic peptide fragments, and bind them to **major histocompatibility complex (MHC) molecules** (Figure 10–3) so that the **antigen peptide fragment–MHC complex** can be exposed later on the surface of the cells. The MHC gene locus expresses gene products responsible for the rejection of grafted tissue between two genetically incompatible hosts.

There are two types of mouse MHC gene products: **class I MHC** and **class II MHC**. The class I MHC molecule consists of two polypeptide chains: an **α chain**, consisting of three domains (α_1, α_2 and α_3) encoded by the MHC gene locus, and **β_2 microglobulin**, not encoded by the MHC gene locus. Antigens are housed in a cleft formed by the α_1 and α_2 domains. CD8, a coreceptor on the surface of cytolytic T cells, binds to the α3 domain of class I MHC.

Class II MHC consists of two polypeptide chains, α chain and β chains. Both chains are encoded by the MHC gene locus. The α_1 and β_1 domains form an antigens-binding cleft. CD4, a coreceptor on the surface of helper T cells, binds to the β_2 domain of class II MHC.

All nucleated cells express class I MHC molecules. Class II MHC molecules are restricted mainly to antigen-presenting cells (dendritic cells, macrophages, and B cells), epithelial reticular cells of the thymus, and endothelial cells.

The MHC-equivalent molecules in the human are designated **human leukocyte antigens (HLAs)**. HLA molecules are structurally and functionally homologous to mouse MHC molecules and the gene locus (3500 kilobases in length) is present on human chromosome 5 (β_2 microglobulin is encoded by a gene on chromosome 15).

The **class I MHC locus encodes** three major proteins in the human: **HLA-A**, **HLA-B**, and **HLA-C**. The **class II MHC locus encodes HLA-DR** (R for antigenically related), **HLA-DQ**, and **HLA-DP** (Q and P preceding R in the alphabet).

The T cell receptor complex

In addition to MHC molecules, subsets of T cells have cell surface receptors that enable each of them to recognize a different antigen peptide–MHC combination. Antigen recognition involves stable antigen-presenting cell–T cell adhesiveness followed by an activating signaling cascade by T cells.

The receptor that recognizes specific antigenic peptides presented by class I and class II MHC molecules is the **T cell receptor (TCR)**. TCR acts together with accessory cell surface molecules, called **coreceptors**, to stabilize the binding of antigen-presenting cells to T cells.

The TCR consists of two disulfide-linked transmembrane polypeptide chains: the **α chain** and the **β chain** (Figure 10–3). A limited number of T cells have a TCR composed of γ and δ chains. Each α and β chain consists of a **variable (Vα and Vβ)** domain and a **constant (Cα and Cβ)** domain. When compared with the

Figure 10–3

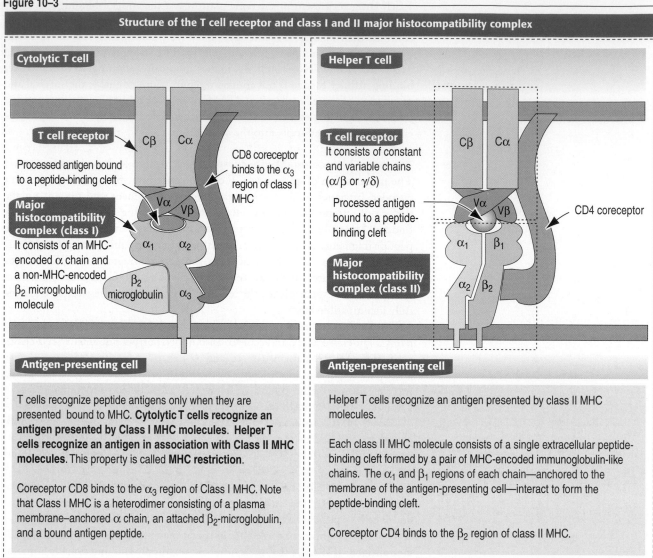

Structure of the T cell receptor and class I and II major histocompatibility complex

Cytolytic T cell

T cell receptor

$C\beta$ $C\alpha$

Processed antigen bound to a peptide-binding cleft

$V\alpha$ $V\beta$

CD8 coreceptor binds to the α_3 region of class I MHC

Major histocompatibility complex (class I)
It consists of an MHC-encoded α chain and a non-MHC-encoded β_2 microglobulin molecule

α_1 α_2

β_2 microglobulin α_3

Antigen-presenting cell

T cells recognize peptide antigens only when they are presented bound to MHC. **Cytolytic T cells recognize an antigen presented by Class I MHC molecules. Helper T cells recognize an antigen in association with Class II MHC molecules.** This property is called **MHC restriction**.

Coreceptor CD8 binds to the α_3 region of Class I MHC. Note that Class I MHC is a heterodimer consisting of a plasma membrane–anchored α chain, an attached β_2-microglobulin, and a bound antigen peptide.

Helper T cell

T cell receptor
It consists of constant and variable chains (α/β or γ/δ)

$C\beta$ $C\alpha$

Processed antigen bound to a peptide-binding cleft

$V\alpha$ $V\beta$

CD4 coreceptor

Major histocompatibility complex (class II)

α_1 β_1

α_2 β_2

Antigen-presenting cell

Helper T cells recognize an antigen presented by class II MHC molecules.

Each class II MHC molecule consists of a single extracellular peptide-binding cleft formed by a pair of MHC-encoded immunoglobulin-like chains. The α_1 and β_1 regions of each chain—anchored to the membrane of the antigen-presenting cell—interact to form the peptide-binding cleft.

Coreceptor CD4 binds to the β_2 region of class II MHC.

immunoglobulin molecule, the **Vα** and **Vβ** domains are structurally and functionally similar to the antigen-binding fragment (Fab) of immunoglobulins.

The TCR molecule is associated with two proteins, CD3 and ζ (not shown in Figure 10–3), forming the **TCR complex**. CD3 and ζ have a signaling role and are present in all T cells. CD3 contains the ITAM cytoplasmic domain previously mentioned as part of the B cell antigen receptor complex and involved in signaling functions.

CD4 and CD8 coreceptors

CD4 and CD8 are T cell surface proteins interacting selectively with class II MHC and class I MHC molecules, respectively. When the T cell TCR recognizes an antigen bound to the cleft of MHC, CD4 or CD8 coreceptors cooperate in the activation of T cell function (see Figure 10–3).

CD4 and CD8 are members of the immunoglobulin (Ig) superfamily that we have already examined in Chapter 1, Epithelium, when we analyzed the function and structure of cell adhesion molecules.

As you recall, members of the Ig superfamily have a variable number of extracellular Ig-like domains. The two terminal Ig-like domains of CD4 bind to the β_2 domain of the class II MHC (see Figure 10–3). The single Ig-like domain of

CD8 binds to the α_3 domain of the class I MHC. Thus, **CD4+ helper T cells recognize antigens associated with class II MHC, and CD8+ cytolytic T cells (cytolytic thymus-derived lymphocytes, CTLs) respond to antigens presented by class I MHC** (Figure 10–4).

MHC molecules and adaptive immune responses

T cells are **MHC-restricted**. In other words, T cells are able to react against a **foreign** antigen fragment bound to their **own (self-) MCH** molecules and contribute to **adaptive immune responses**. T cells should **not respond** to self-antigen peptide fragments bound to self-MHC molecules. This lack of response is called **self-tolerance**.

During their maturation in the thymus, T cells are selected to be **self–MHC-restricted** and **self-tolerant**. This selective process, known as **positive selection** (see Figure 10–4), occurs only when self–MCH-restricted T cells are selected. **Negative selection** takes place when T cells **do not bind to any MHC** or bind to the **body's own antigens**. These T cells are eliminated by macrophages. Only those **T cells that can recognize both foreign peptides and self-MHC survive**, leave the thymus, and migrate into the secondary lymphoid organs.

This selection process occurs in the thymus (Figure 10–5). The cortex of the thymus contains branching **epithelial cells** derived from the ectoderm and expressing MHC molecules **class I** and **class II**. **Contact between MHC molecules on the epithelial cell surfaces and the receptors of developing T cells is an important feature in positive selection.**

T cells developing in the thymus express specific cell surface molecules

Two major events take place in the thymus during T cell maturation (Figure 10–5): (1) a rearrangement of the gene encoding protein components of the **TCR**, and (2) the transient coexistence of TCR-associated **coreceptors CD4 and CD8**.

When progenitor cells—derived from the bone marrow— enter the **cortex** of the thymus, they lack surface molecules typical of mature T cells. Because **they still do not express CD4 and CD8, they are called "double-negative" T cells**.

After interacting with thymic **epithelial cells**, double-negative T cells proliferate, differentiate and express the first T cell–specific molecules: (1) the thymus cell receptor, TCR, and (2) coreceptors CD4 and CD8.

T cell markers: CD antigens

Cell surface molecules recognized by monoclonal antibodies are called **antigens**. These antigens are **markers** which enable the identification and characterization of cell populations. A surface marker that identifies a member of a group of cells, has a defined structure, and is also recognized in other members of the group by a monoclonal antibody is called a **cluster of differentiation (CD)**.

For example a **helper T cell**, which expresses the **CD4** marker, can be differentiated from a **killer T cell**, which does not contain CD4 but expresses the **CD8** marker. CD markers permit the classification of T cells that participate in inflammatory and immune reactions. **CD antigens promote cell-cell interaction and adhesion as well as signaling leading to T cell activation.**

Figure 10–4

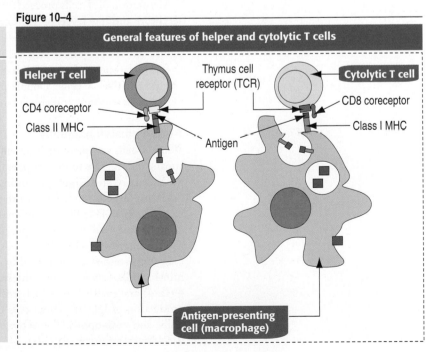

General features of helper and cytolytic T cells

Helper T cell

Thymus cell receptor (TCR)

Cytolytic T cell

CD4 coreceptor

CD8 coreceptor

Class II MHC

Class I MHC

Antigen

Antigen-presenting cell (macrophage)

Figure 10–5

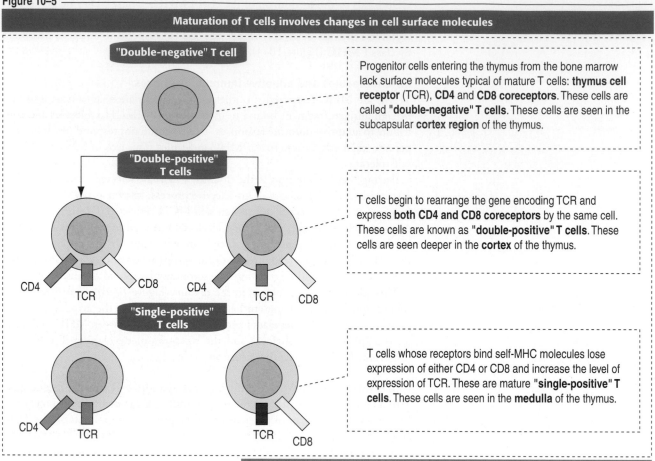

Maturation of T cells involves changes in cell surface molecules

"Double-negative" T cell

Progenitor cells entering the thymus from the bone marrow lack surface molecules typical of mature T cells: **thymus cell receptor** (TCR), **CD4** and **CD8 coreceptors**. These cells are called "**double-negative**" **T cells**. These cells are seen in the subcapsular **cortex region** of the thymus.

"Double-positive" T cells

CD4   TCR   CD8   CD4   TCR   CD8

T cells begin to rearrange the gene encoding TCR and express **both CD4 and CD8 coreceptors** by the same cell. These cells are known as "**double-positive**" **T cells**. These cells are seen deeper in the **cortex** of the thymus.

"Single-positive" T cells

CD4   TCR   TCR   CD8

T cells whose receptors bind self-MHC molecules lose expression of either CD4 or CD8 and increase the level of expression of TCR. These are mature "**single-positive**" **T cells**. These cells are seen in the **medulla** of the thymus.

We have seen that TCR consists of two pairs of subunits: **αβ chains** or **γδ chains** (see Figure 10–3). Each chain can vary in sequence from one T cell to another. This variation is determined by the random combination of gene segments and has a bearing on which foreign antigen T cells can recognize.

Maturation of T cells proceeds through a stage where **both CD4 and CD8 coreceptors and low levels of TCR are expressed by the same cell**. These cells are known as "**double-positive**" **T cells**. Double-positive T cells **can** or **cannot** recognize self-MHC. Those cells that can recognize self-MHC eventually mature and express one of the two coreceptor molecules (CD4 or CD8) and become "**single-positive**" **T cells**. Double-positive cells that cannot recognize self-MHC fail positive selection and are discarded.

T cell-mediated immunity

When T cells complete their development in the thymus, they enter the bloodstream and migrate to the peripheral lymphoid organs in search of an antigen on the surface of an **antigen-presenting cell**.

Helper T cells contain both the **TCR** and **CD4 coreceptor**. Helper T cells recognize **class II MHC** on antigen-presenting cells.

There are **two distinct subtypes of helper T cells** derived from the same CD4+ T-cell precursor: TH1 and TH2 cells.

Immune responses controlled by TH2 cells are observed in patients with **helminthic** (Gk. *helmins*, worm) **intestinal parasites**. TH2 cells produce interleukin-4 (IL-4) and interleukin-13 (IL-13), among other cytokines, and determine the production of IgE by plasma cells to activate the responses of mast cells, basophils, and eosinophils. The activation of macrophage responses is minimal in TH2-driven immune responses.

Figure 10–6

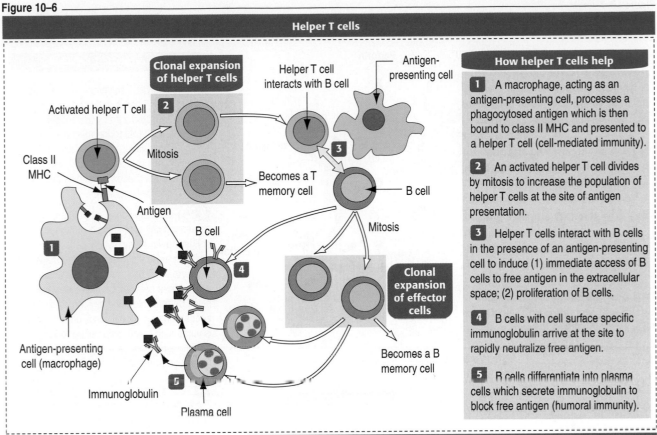

Helper T cells

Clonal expansion of helper T cells

2

Activated helper T cell

Mitosis

Helper T cell interacts with B cell

Antigen-presenting cell

3

Becomes a T memory cell

B cell

Class II MHC

1

Antigen

B cell

Mitosis

4

Antigen-presenting cell (macrophage)

Clonal expansion of effector cells

Becomes a B memory cell

Immunoglobulin

5

Plasma cell

How helper T cells help

1 A macrophage, acting as an antigen-presenting cell, processes a phagocytosed antigen which is then bound to class II MHC and presented to a helper T cell (cell-mediated immunity).

2 An activated helper T cell divides by mitosis to increase the population of helper T cells at the site of antigen presentation.

3 Helper T cells interact with B cells in the presence of an antigen-presenting cell to induce (1) immediate access of B cells to free antigen in the extracellular space; (2) proliferation of B cells.

4 B cells with cell surface specific immunoglobulin arrive at the site to rapidly neutralize free antigen.

5 B cells differentiate into plasma cells which secrete immunoglobulin to block free antigen (humoral immunity).

By contrast, Th1 cells participate in the regulation of immune responses caused by **intracellular pathogens** (viruses causing infections, certain bacteria, or single-cell parasites) with the significant participation of macrophages. Th1 cells produce interferon-γ, which can suppress the activity of Th2 cells.

Cytolytic or **killer T cells** display both the **TCR** and **CD8 coreceptor**. CLTs recognize **class I MHC** on antigen-presenting cells. We will return to the clinical significance of helper and cytolytic T cells when we discuss their involvement in the pathology of human immunodeficiency virus-type 1 (HIV-1) infection, allergy, and cancer immunotherapy.

How do helper T cells help?

Helper T cells are activated when they recognize the antigen peptide–class II MHC complex (Figure 10–6).

In the presence of cells with antigen peptide bound to class II MHC, helper T cells proliferate by mitosis and secrete **cytokines**, also called **interleukins**. These chemical signals, in turn, attract B cells, which also have receptor molecules of single specificity on their surface (**immunoglobulin receptor**). **Unlike helper T cells, B cells can recognize free antigen peptides without MHC molecules.**

When activated by interleukins produced by the proliferating helper T cells, B cells also divide and differentiate into **plasma cells secreting immunoglobulins**, a soluble form of their receptors. Secreted immunoglobulins diffuse freely, bind to antigen peptides to neutralize them, or trigger their destruction by enzymes or macrophages.

Plasma cells synthesize **only one class of immunoglobulin** (several thousand immunoglobulin molecules per second; lifetime of a plasma cell is from 10 to 20 days). Five classes of immunoglobulins are recognized in humans: **IgG, IgA, IgM, IgE,** and **IgD.**

Some T and B cells become **memory cells**, ready to eliminate the same antigen

Figure 10–7

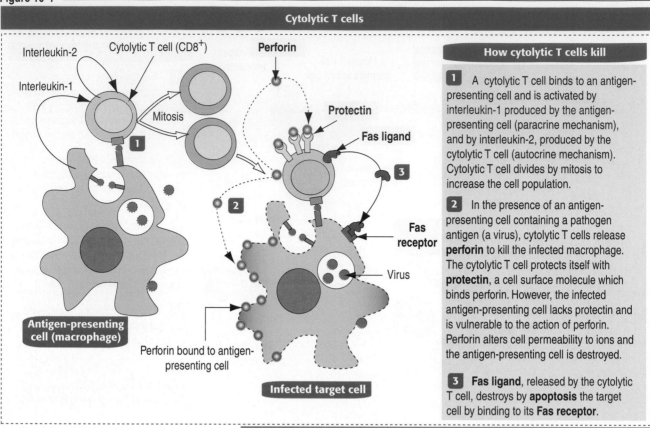

Cytolytic T cells

Interleukin-2
Interleukin-1
Cytolytic T cell (CD8⁺)
Mitosis
Perforin
Protectin
Fas ligand
Fas receptor
Virus
Antigen-presenting cell (macrophage)
Perforin bound to antigen-presenting cell
Infected target cell

How cytolytic T cells kill

1 A cytolytic T cell binds to an antigen-presenting cell and is activated by interleukin-1 produced by the antigen-presenting cell (paracrine mechanism), and by interleukin-2, produced by the cytolytic T cell (autocrine mechanism). Cytolytic T cell divides by mitosis to increase the cell population.

2 In the presence of an antigen-presenting cell containing a pathogen antigen (a virus), cytolytic T cells release **perforin** to kill the infected macrophage. The cytolytic T cell protects itself with **protectin**, a cell surface molecule which binds perforin. However, the infected antigen-presenting cell lacks protectin and is vulnerable to the action of perforin. Perforin alters cell permeability to ions and the antigen-presenting cell is destroyed.

3 **Fas ligand**, released by the cytolytic T cell, destroys by **apoptosis** the target cell by binding to its **Fas receptor**.

if it recurs in the future. The **secondary immune response** (reencounter with the same antigen that triggered their production) is more rapid and of greater magnitude. Memory cells recirculate for many years and provide a surveillance system directed against foreign antigens.

How do cytolytic T cells kill?

Another function of helper T cells is **to secrete cytokines to stimulate the proliferation of cytolytic T cells** that recognize the antigen peptide–class I MHC complex on the surface of antigen-presenting cells.

The subset of CTLs initiates a **target cell destruction** process (Figure 10–7) by (1) attaching firmly to the antigen-presenting cell with the help of integrins and cell adhesion molecules (CAMs) on the cell surface of the target cell, and (2) inducing cell membrane damage by the release of pore-forming proteins (called **perforins**). These pores facilitate the unregulated entry of various lytic substances, water, and salts. The CTL protects itself by a membrane protein, **protectin**, that inactivates perforin, blocking its insertion into the CTL membrane.

CLTs can also destroy target cells by the **Fas-Fas ligand mechanism** seen during **apoptosis** (see Chapter 3, Cell Signaling). When the CLT receptor recognizes an antigen on the surface of a target cell, Fas ligand is induced in the CLT. The interaction of Fas ligand with the Fas receptor on the target cell surface (see Figure 10–7) triggers the apoptotic cascade by activation of procaspases into caspases that determine cell death.

Players in the immune responses: Regulatory and effector cells

We have seen that B cells can differentiate into immunoglobulin-secreting plasma cells. Plasma cells are **effector cells**. T cells differentiate into **regulatory, suppressor**, and **effector T cells**.

Figure 10–8

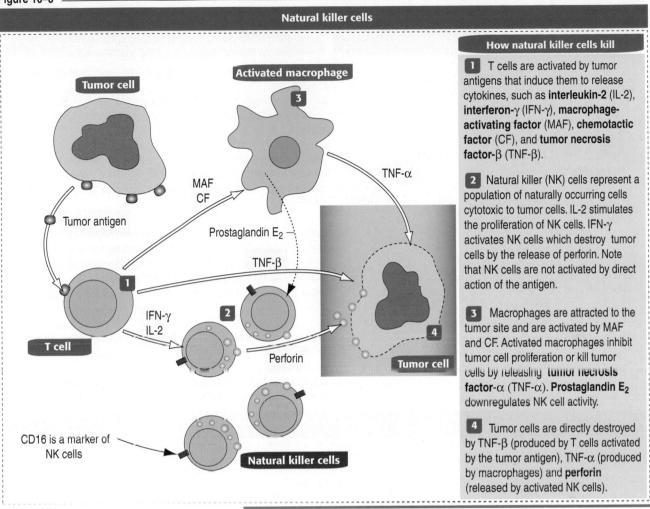

Natural killer cells

How natural killer cells kill

1 T cells are activated by tumor antigens that induce them to release cytokines, such as **interleukin-2** (IL-2), **interferon-γ** (IFN-γ), **macrophage-activating factor** (MAF), **chemotactic factor** (CF), and **tumor necrosis factor-β** (TNF-β).

2 Natural killer (NK) cells represent a population of naturally occurring cells cytotoxic to tumor cells. IL-2 stimulates the proliferation of NK cells. IFN-γ activates NK cells which destroy tumor cells by the release of perforin. Note that NK cells are not activated by direct action of the antigen.

3 Macrophages are attracted to the tumor site and are activated by MAF and CF. Activated macrophages inhibit tumor cell proliferation or kill tumor cells by releasing **tumor necrosis factor-α** (TNF-α). **Prostaglandin E₂** downregulates NK cell activity.

4 Tumor cells are directly destroyed by TNF-β (produced by T cells activated by the tumor antigen), TNF-α (produced by macrophages) and **perforin** (released by activated NK cells).

Regulatory T cells include **helper T cells**, which cooperate with B cells to stimulate the proliferation and differentiation of B cells into immunoglobulin-secreting plasma cells and the cytolytic activation of killer T cells.

Suppressor T cells, acting on helper T cells to moderate or inhibit their activities, also modulate the differentiation of B cells into plasma cells. We mentioned previously that there are two subsets of T cells (T_H1 and T_H2) that produce different cytokines with distinct functions, as we will see when we discuss **allergy** (see Figure 10–10). T_H1 cells produce interferon-γ, whereas T_H2 cells produce IL-4 and IL-13. Interferon-γ, produced by T_H1 cells, stimulates the differentiation of T_H1 cells but suppresses the proliferation of T_H2 cells. Furthermore, T_H2-derived IL-4 suppresses the activation of T_H1 cells.

Effector T cells include **cytolytic** or **killer T cells** and **natural killer cells**. CLTs can lyse cells that bear antigens for which they are specific. Cell killing is caused by the release of perforin or Fas ligand as already discussed.

Natural killer cells (Figure 10–8) destroy cells, but this activity **does not depend on antigen activation**. Natural killer cells can destroy antibody-coated target cells by a mechanism called **antibody-dependent cell-mediated cytotoxicity** (**ADCC**). Natural killer cells do not belong to the T or B cell types and have **CD16 receptors**.

Clinical significance: Acquired immunodeficiency syndrome

The **acquired immunodeficiency syndrome** (**AIDS**) is caused by HIV-1 and is characterized by significant immunosuppression associated with opportunistic

Figure 10–9

The immune system and HIV infection

HIV reproductive cycle

Acquired immunodeficiency syndrome (AIDS)

The human immunodeficiency virus type 1 (HIV-1) can infect and destroy immune cells.

CD4, the coreceptor of helper T cells, is a receptor for HIV-1. Since CD4 is also expressed on the surface of macrophages, they can also be infected by this virus.

The virus can replicate within host cells for many years before symptoms are detected (clinical latency). The early indication of HIV-1 infection is the presence of antibodies to **gp120**, a virus coat protein, and against **p24**, a core protein.

During the early phase of HIV-1 infection, infected helper T cells are destroyed and replenished. When the rate of destruction exceeds the replenishing capacity of CD4 cells, cell-mediated immunity is compromised and the patient is susceptible to fatal opportunistic infections. The CD4 helper T cell count is the best indicator of the time-course progression of AIDS.

CD4 helper T cells are destroyed by either by a cytotoxic effect determined by HIV-1 infection or by the direct action of cytolytic T cells.

Blood banks screen blood donation for antibodies to gp120. However, the level of antibody may be low, in particular during the early phase of infection.

Responses of the immune system to HIV infection

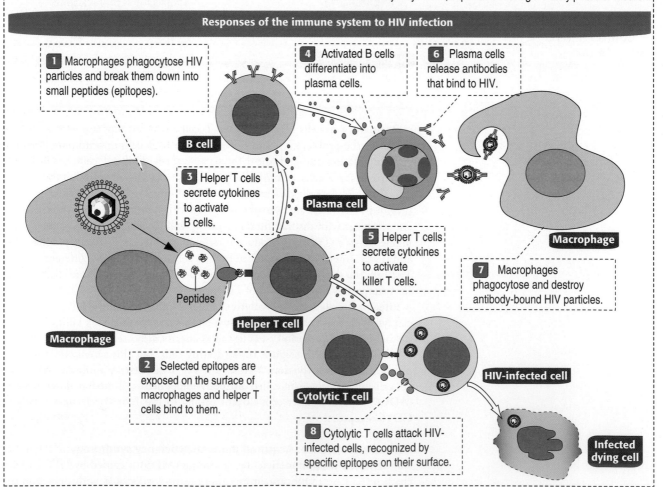

1 Macrophages phagocytose HIV particles and break them down into small peptides (epitopes).

4 Activated B cells differentiate into plasma cells.

6 Plasma cells release antibodies that bind to HIV.

3 Helper T cells secrete cytokines to activate B cells.

5 Helper T cells secrete cytokines to activate killer T cells.

7 Macrophages phagocytose and destroy antibody-bound HIV particles.

2 Selected epitopes are exposed on the surface of macrophages and helper T cells bind to them.

8 Cytolytic T cells attack HIV-infected cells, recognized by specific epitopes on their surface.

infections, malignancies, and degeneration of the central nervous system.

HIV infects macrophages, dendritic cells, and predominantly CD4-bearing helper T cells. HIV is a member of the lentivirus family of animal retroviruses and causes long-term latent cellular infection. HIV includes two types, designated HIV-1 and HIV-2. HIV-1 is the cause of AIDS. The genome of the infectious HIV consists of two strands of RNA enclosed within a core of viral proteins and surrounded by a lipid envelope derived from the infected cell. The lipid envelope contains viral proteins designated gp41 and gp120, encoded by the *env* viral sequence. The glycoprotein gb120 has binding affinity for CD4 and a coreceptor. HIV particles are present in blood, semen, and other body fluids. Transmission is by sexual contact or needle injection.

Figure 10–9 presents a summary of the cellular events associated with HIV infection. A relevant event of HIV infection is the destruction of CD4+ helper T cells responsible for the initiation of immune responses, leading to the elimination of HIV infection. Note that **cytolytic T cells** (that attach to virus-infected cells) and **B cells** (that give rise to antibody-producing plasma cells) represent an adaptive response to HIV infection. Antibodies to HIV antigens are detected within 6 to 9 weeks after infection.

Clinical significance: Allergy

Allergy refers to immune responses characterized by the participation of **IgE** bound to a special receptor, designated **FcεRI**. When an antigen or **allergen** binds to two adjacent IgE molecules, it induces aggregation of the IgE molecules and associated FcεRI receptors. This event results in a signaling cascade that leads to the release of mediators and cytokines (Figure 10–10).

Note that two subtypes of helper T cell, TH1 and TH2, trigger distinct responses when activated by specific antigens.

The complement system

The main function of the complement system is to enable the destruction of pathogens by phagocytes (macrophages and neutrophils) by a mechanism known as **opsonization** (Figure 10–11).

The complement system consists of about 20 plasma proteins, synthesized mainly in the liver, which "complement," or enhance, the effect of antibodies. Several components of this system are **proenzymes** converted to active enzymes.

The critical molecule of the complement cascade is **C1**, a hexamer, called **C1q**, with binding affinity to the **Fc region** of an immunoglobulin. C1q is also associated with two molecules, **C1r** and **C1s**.

When the globular domains of C1q bind to the Fc regions of immunoglobulins already bound to the surface of a pathogen, C1r is activated and converts C1s into a serine protease. **Activation of C1s marks the initiation of the complement activation cascade.**

The second step is the cleavage of complement protein C4 by C1s. Two fragments are produced: (1) the small fragment C4a is discarded; (2) the large fragment C4b binds to the pathogen surface.

The third step occurs when complement protein **C2** is cleaved by C1s into C2a (discarded) and C2b. C2b binds to the already bound C4b, forming the **complex C4b-2b**, also called **C3 convertase**, on the surface of a pathogen.

The fourth step takes place when complement protein **C3** is cleaved by C3 convertase into C3a (discarded) and C3b. C3b binds to C3 convertase. The **C4b-2b-3b complex**, now designated **C5 convertase**, cleaves complement protein C5 into C5a (discarded) and C5b. C5b binds to C5 convertase and the **opsonization** of the pathogen is completed.

The last step is the binding of the pathogen to complement receptors on the surface of the phagocytes. Additional complement proteins C6, C7, C8, and C9 can bind to the surface of certain pathogens to directly initiate the lytic process.

Figure 10–10

Allergy

Sensitization phase (initial exposure to an allergen)

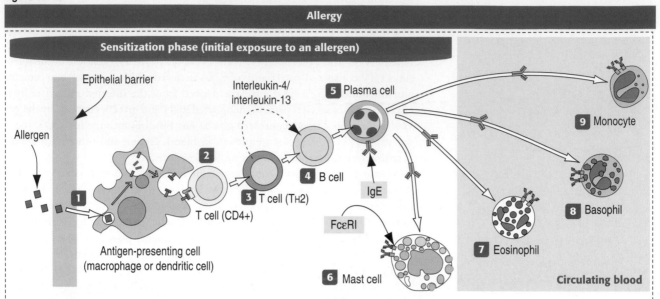

Allergens trigger allergy, an immune response in which IgE antibodies play a significant role.

1 This response develops when an allergen breaks a protective barrier (such as an epithelial layer).

2 The antigen is presented by an antigen-presenting cell to a helper T cell.

3 Depending of the nature of the allergen, one helper T cell subtype (either TH1 or TH2) is recruited to drive the production of IgE. Intestinal helminthic parasites involve the actions of TH2 cells.

4 TH2 cells produce interleukin-4, interleukin-13, and other cytokines to induce the proliferation of B cells and development of other effector cells (mast cells, basophils, and eosinophils).

5 B cells differentiate into IgE-producing plasma cells.

6 IgE binds to the FcεRI receptor on the surface of mast cells (an immigrant cell to the connective tissue).

7 **8** Monocytes, basophils, and eosinophils (circulating in blood) also express FcεRI receptors and bind IgE.

TH1 cells (not shown) produce interferon-γ in response to viral infection.

Effector phase (subsequent exposure to an allergen)

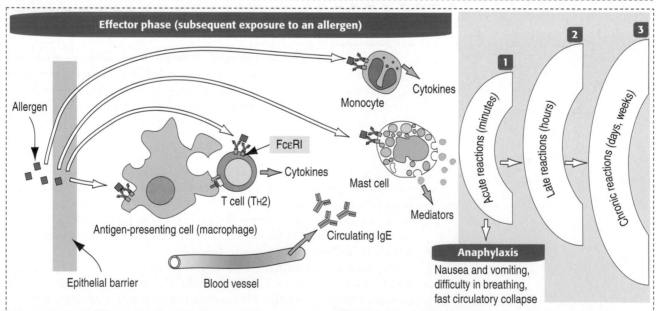

A subsequent exposure to the same allergen following sensitization finds antigen-presenting cells, TH2 cells, monocytes with FcεRI receptors on their surfaces. IgE can bind without delay to FcεRI receptors that aggregate and trigger cell signaling responses. Receptor aggregation induces three types of reactions:

1 **Acute reaction** (anaphylaxis, acute asthmatic response) within **seconds to minutes**, triggered by mediators released by mast cells and basophils.

2 **Late reactions** (**2-6 hours** following exposure to allergen) attract circulating eosinophils, basophils, and TH2 cells to the site.

3 **Chronic reactions** can develop over **days and weeks** and determine alterations in the structure and function of the affected tissue (for example, respiratory pathology in asthma) caused by a number of cytokines, mediators, and inflammatory agents. Corticosteroids are required to suppress inflammation determined by chronic reactions.

Figure 10–11

The complement system

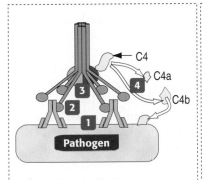

C1 is the first component of the complement activation pathway.
C1 consists of three components:
1. **C1q**, a molecule with six rod domains, each ending as a globular head.
2. **C1r**, a proenzyme.
3. **C1s**, a substrate for C1r, converted into a protease upon activation of C1r.

Nomenclature

The letter "C" followed by a number designates the components of the complement cascade.

The products of the cleavage of C1,C2, C3, C4,C5, and others are designated by lowercase letters: "a" is the small fragment; "b" is the larger fragment.

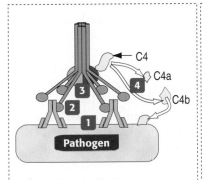

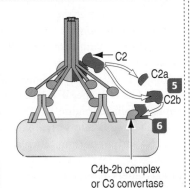

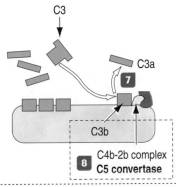

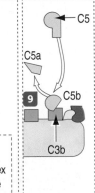

1 Immuboglobulins (Igs) bind to the surface of a pathogen (for example, a bacterium).

2 The globular domain of C1q binds to the Fc region of the Ig (one globular domain per Ig).

3 C1q binding activates C1r, which in turn activates C1s. This conversion generates a serine protease that initiates the complement cascade.

4 Protease C1s cleaves complement protein C4 into two fragments: C4a and C4b. C4b binds to the surface of the pathogen.

5 C1s cleaves complement protein C2 into two fragments: C2a and C2b.

6 C2b binds to the already bound C4b forming the C4b-2b complex, or **C3 convertase**.

7 C3 convertase cleaves complement protein C3 into two fragments: C3a and C3b. One C3 convertase can cleave about 1000 C3 molecules into C3b.

8 Several C3b molecules bind to C3 convertase (forming the C4b-2b-3b complex or **C5 convertase**) or to the surface of the pathogen. C3b is the major **opsonin** of the complement system.

9 Protein C5 binds to the C3b component of C5 convertase and is cleaved into C5a and b. Opsonization of the pathogen is complete.

10 The complement cascade —resulting in the **opsonization of the pathogen**—enables phagocytic cells (macrophages and neutrophils) to take up and destroy pathogens.

11 Complement components bind to **complement receptors** on the surface of phagocytes and are taken up.

Complement proteins C6, C7, C8, and C9 (not shown) participate in the lysis of certain pathogens.

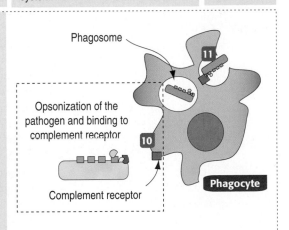

The complement system is essential for enabling pathogen recognition by phagocytes and represents a powerful defense mechanism against extracellular bacteria. Note that the step preceding the complement cascade is binding of an immunoglobulin to the surface of the pathogen. If this step does not occur, the globular domain of C1 is unable to bind to the Fc region of the immunoglobulin and to generate active components of the complement cascade.

Lymphoid organs
Lymph nodes

The function of lymph nodes is to filter the lymph, maintain and produce B cells, and house T cells. Helper T cells are preferentially located in the **deep cortex** (also known as the **paracortex** or **inner cortex**) of lymph nodes (Figure 10–12).

Structure of a lymph node

A lymph node is surrounded by a capsule, and the parenchyma is divided into a **cortex** and a **medulla**.

The **capsule** consists of dense irregular connective tissue surrounded by adipose tissue. The capsule at the convex surface of the lymph node is pierced by numerous **afferent lymphatic vessels**. Afferent lymphatic vessels have **valves** to prevent the reflux of lymph entering a lymph node.

The **cortex** has two zones: the **outer cortex** and the **inner cortex**. The outer cortex contains **B cell–rich lymphoid follicles** and **lymphatic sinuses**. The deep cortex houses **CD4+ helper T cells** and **high endothelial venules**.

A **lymphoid follicle** (Figure 10–13) consists of a **germinal center** containing mainly proliferating B cells or **lymphoblasts, follicular dendritic cells (FDCs), macrophages,** and supporting **reticular cells**, which produce reticular fibers or type III collagen.

Germinal centers develop in response to antigen stimulation. A primary lymphoid follicle lacks a germinal center. A **secondary lymphoid follicle** has a germinal center.

FDCs are branched (hence the name **dendritic**) cells forming a network within the lymphoid follicle. We have indicated that FDCs do not derive from a bone marrow cell precursor. Most nonfollicular dendritic cells derive from a progenitor present in bone marrow. FDCs are observed at the edge of the germinal centers, in contact with mature B cells. FDCs trap antigens bound to immunoglobulins or complement proteins on their surface for recognition by B cells. **The interaction of mature B cells with FDCs** (displaying an antigen that complements a **high-affinity surface immunoglobulin**) **rescues the B cell from apoptosis. Only B cells with low-affinity surface immunoglobulin are induced to apoptosis.**

Macrophages phagocytose apoptotic B cells, destroyed because of their content of low affinity surface immunoglobulin.

Lymphatic sinuses are spaces lined by endothelial cells under the capsule (**subcapsular sinus**) and along trabeculae of connective tissue derived from the capsule and entering the cortex (**paratrabecular sinus**). Lymph entering the paratrabecular sinus through the subcapsular sinus percolates to the medullary sinuses and exits through a single efferent lymphatic vessel. Lymph in the subcapsular sinus can bypass the paratrabecular and medullary sinuses and exit through the efferent lymphatic vessel.

The **inner or deep cortex** is a paracortical zone in which mainly CD4+ helper T cells interact with B cells to induce their proliferation and differentiation when exposed to a specific antigen (adaptive immune response).

High endothelial venules (HEVs, see Figure 10–12) are the sites of entry of most B and T cells into the lymph node (by the lymphocyte homing mechanism). HEVs are specialized venules present in several lymphatic tissues such as **Peyer's patches** in the small intestine and the cortex of the **thymus**.

The **medulla** is surrounded by the cortex, except at the region of the **hilum** (see Figure 10–11). The hilum is a concave surface of the lymph node where **efferent lymphatic vessels** and a single **vein** leave and an **artery** enters the lymph node.

The medulla contains two major components:

1. **Medullary sinusoids,** spaces lined by endothelial cells surrounded by reticular cells and macrophages.

Figure 10–12

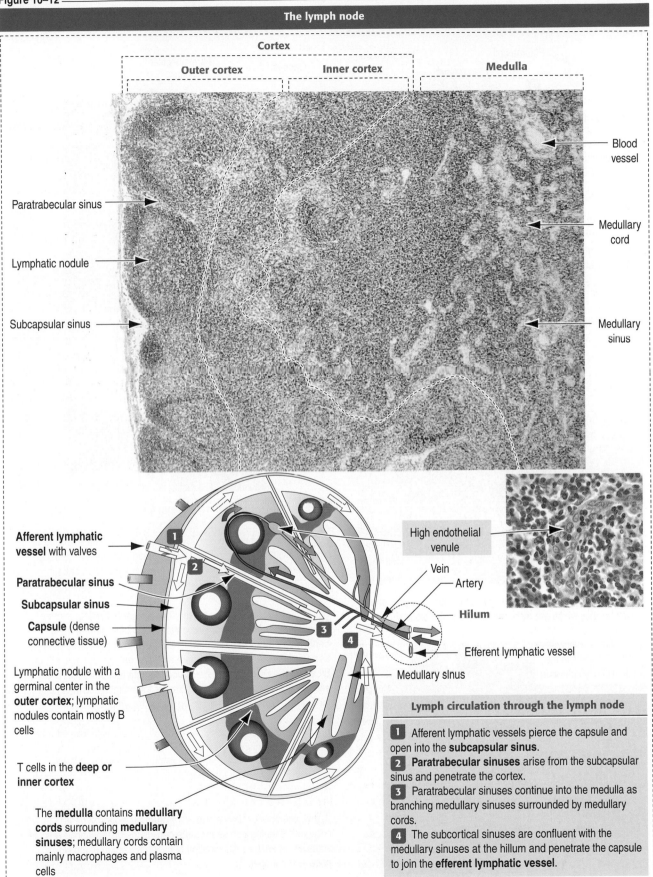

The lymph node

Cortex

Outer cortex | Inner cortex | Medulla

Paratrabecular sinus

Lymphatic nodule

Subcapsular sinus

Blood vessel

Medullary cord

Medullary sinus

Afferent lymphatic vessel with valves

Paratrabecular sinus

Subcapsular sinus

Capsule (dense connective tissue)

Lymphatic nodule with a germinal center in the **outer cortex**; lymphatic nodules contain mostly B cells

T cells in the **deep or inner cortex**

The **medulla** contains **medullary cords** surrounding **medullary sinuses**; medullary cords contain mainly macrophages and plasma cells

High endothelial venule

Vein
Artery

Hilum

Efferent lymphatic vessel

Medullary sinus

Lymph circulation through the lymph node

1 Afferent lymphatic vessels pierce the capsule and open into the **subcapsular sinus**.

2 **Paratrabecular sinuses** arise from the subcapsular sinus and penetrate the cortex.

3 Paratrabecular sinuses continue into the medulla as branching medullary sinuses surrounded by medullary cords.

4 The subcortical sinuses are confluent with the medullary sinuses at the hillum and penetrate the capsule to join the **efferent lymphatic vessel**.

Figure 10–13

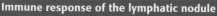

Immune response of the lymphatic nodule

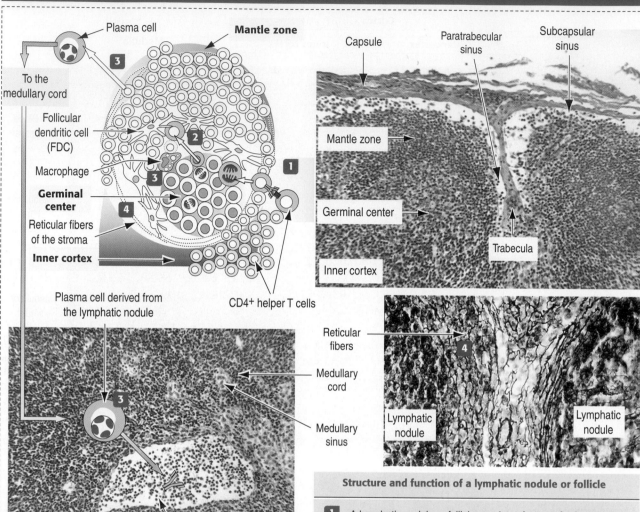

Plasma cell

Mantle zone

3

To the medullary cord

Follicular dendritic cell (FDC)

Macrophage

Germinal center

Reticular fibers of the stroma

Inner cortex

Plasma cell derived from the lymphatic nodule

CD4+ helper T cells

Capsule

Paratrabecular sinus

Subcapsular sinus

Mantle zone

Germinal center

Inner cortex

Trabecula

Reticular fibers

Medullary cord

Medullary sinus

Lymphatic nodule

Lymphatic nodule

An **efferent lymphatic vessel** collects immunoglobulins and lymphocytes which are then transported to the blood circulation

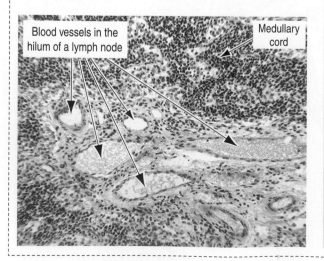

Blood vessels in the hilum of a lymph node

Medullary cord

Structure and function of a lymphatic nodule or follicle

1 A lymphatic nodule or follicle consists of a **germinal center** in which activated B cells proliferate. Proliferation occurs after B cells have been activated by helper T cells (presentation of an antigen). Helper T cells are present in the inner cortex of the lymph node.

2 When proliferating B cells mature, they stop dividing, migrate around the germinal center, and establish contact with **follicular dendritic cells** (**FDC**). FDC—which do not derive from bone marrow as dendritic cells do—display intact antigens on their surface, attract B cells to the follicle, and express complement receptors (CR1, CR2, and CR3). Mature B cells not specific for the antigen accumulate in the **mantle zone**, forming a cap on top of the lymphoid follicle.

3 Macrophages phagocytose apoptotic B cells with **low-affinity** surface immunoglobulin (Ig). B cells with **high affinity** surface Ig migrate to the medullary cords and differentiate into short-lived **plasma cells** secreting IgM or IgG into the lymph, leaving the lymph node.

4 Lymph nodes have a stroma of **reticular fibers** (type III collagen). Staining with **silver salts** depicts the distribution of reticular fibers which enables examination of the organization of the lymph node in lymphopathies.

2. **Medullary cords**, with B cells, macrophages, and **plasma cells**. Activated B cells migrate from the cortex as plasma cells and enter the medullary sinuses. This is a strategic location because plasma cells can secrete immunoglobulins directly into the medullary sinuses without leaving the lymph node.

Clinical significance: Strategic distribution of B and T cells in the cortex

Lymph nodes constitute a defense site against lymph-borne microorganisms (bacteria, viruses, parasites) entering the node through efferent lymphatic vessels. This defense mechanism depends on the close interaction of B cells in the lymphatic nodules with CD4+ T cells in the inner or deep cortex, and it complies with the basic principles of immune responsiveness illustrated in Figure 10–6. The segregation of B and T cells appears dictated by cytokines responsible for the recruitment and histologic distribution of these two cell populations in the cortex of the lymph node.

In Chapter 12, Cardiovascular System, we note that the interstitial fluid, representing plasma filtrate, is transported into blind sacs corresponding to lymphatic capillaries. This interstitial fluid—entering the lymphatic capillaries as **lymph**—flows into larger lymphatic vessels becoming afferents to regional lymph nodes. Lymph nodes are linked in series by the lymphatic vessels in such a way that **the efferent lymphatic vessel of a lymph node becomes the afferent lymphatic vessel of an adjacent lymph node in the chain.**

Soluble and particulate antigens drained with the interstitial fluid, as well as antigen-bearing dendritic cells in the skin (Langerhans cells; see Chapter 11, Integumentary System), enter the lymphatic vessels and are transported to lymph nodes. Antigen-bearing dendritic cells enter the CD4+ helper T cell–rich inner cortex. Soluble and particulate antigens are detected in the percolating lymph by

Figure 10–14

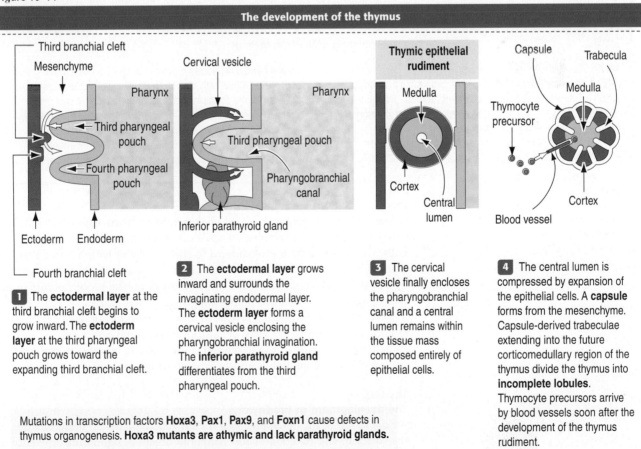

The development of the thymus

1 The **ectodermal layer** at the third branchial cleft begins to grow inward. The **ectoderm layer** at the third pharyngeal pouch grows toward the expanding third branchial cleft.

2 The **ectodermal layer** grows inward and surrounds the invaginating endodermal layer. The **ectoderm layer** forms a cervical vesicle enclosing the pharyngobranchial invagination. The **inferior parathyroid gland** differentiates from the third pharyngeal pouch.

3 The cervical vesicle finally encloses the pharyngobranchial canal and a central lumen remains within the tissue mass composed entirely of epithelial cells.

4 The central lumen is compressed by expansion of the epithelial cells. A **capsule** forms from the mesenchyme. Capsule-derived trabeculae extending into the future corticomedullary region of the thymus divide the thymus into **incomplete lobules**. Thymocyte precursors arrive by blood vessels soon after the development of the thymus rudiment.

Mutations in transcription factors **Hoxa3**, **Pax1**, **Pax9**, and **Foxn1** cause defects in thymus organogenesis. **Hoxa3 mutants are athymic and lack parathyroid glands.**

Figure 10–15

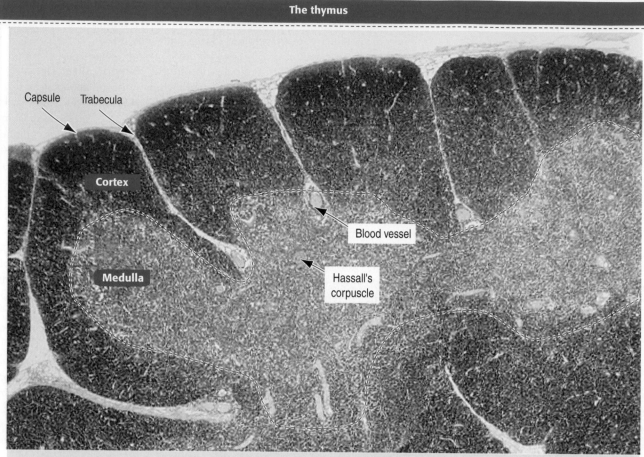

The thymus

Capsule Trabecula

Cortex

Medulla

Blood vessel

Hassall's corpuscle

Histologic organization of the thymus

The thymus consists of several incomplete lobules. Each lobule contains an independent **outer cortical region**, but the **central medullary region is shared by adjacent lobules**. **Trabeculae**, extensions of the capsule down the **corticomedullary region**, form the boundary of each lobule.

The **cortex** consists of stromal cells and developing T cells (thymocytes), macrophages, and cortical epithelial cells. **MHC** **class I and II** molecules are present on the surface of the cortical epithelial cells. The characteristic deep-blue nuclear staining of the cortex in histologic preparations reflects the predominant population of T cells as compared to the less basophilic medulla containing a lower number of thymocytes.

Hassall's corpuscles are a characteristic component of the **medulla. Hassall's corpuscles are not seen in the cortex.**

resident macrophages and dendritic cells.

Macrophages display preferential phagocytosis for particulate and opsonized antigens. B cells in the lymphatic nodule can recognize soluble antigens. Essentially, the lymph node is programmed for the uptake of lymph-borne antigens that can be processed by B cells, dendritic cells, and macrophages for recognition by helper T cells. As we will see, a similar antigen uptake process occurs in the white pulp of the spleen, except that antigens are blood-borne.

When the immune reaction is acute in response to locally drained bacteria (for example, infections of the teeth or tonsils), local lymph nodes enlarge and become painful because of the distention of the capsule by cellular proliferation and edema. This condition is known as **acute lymphadenitis**.

Thymus
The development of the thymus
A brief review of the development of the thymus facilitates an understanding of the structure and function of this lymphoid organ. A significant difference to note with the lymph node and the spleen is that **the stroma of the thymus con-**

Figure 10–16

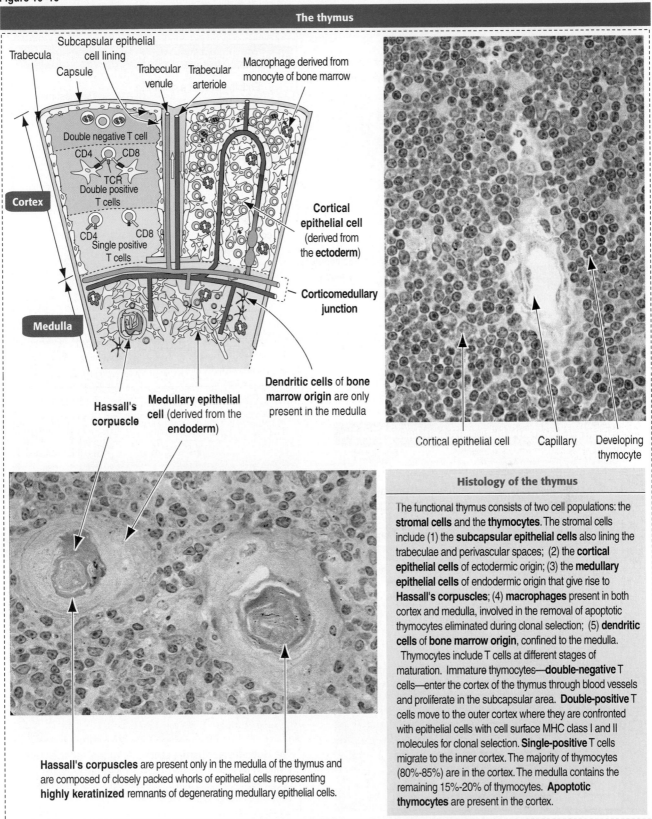

The thymus

Trabecula
Capsule
Subcapsular epithelial cell lining
Trabecular venule
Trabecular arteriole
Macrophage derived from monocyte of bone marrow

Double negative T cell
CD4 — CD8
TCR
Double positive T cells
CD4 — CD8
Single positive T cells

Cortex

Medulla

Cortical epithelial cell (derived from the **ectoderm**)

Corticomedullary junction

Dendritic cells of **bone marrow origin** are only present in the medulla

Hassall's corpuscle

Medullary epithelial cell (derived from the **endoderm**)

Cortical epithelial cell   Capillary   Developing thymocyte

Hassall's corpuscles are present only in the medulla of the thymus and are composed of closely packed whorls of epithelial cells representing **highly keratinized** remnants of degenerating medullary epithelial cells.

Histology of the thymus

The functional thymus consists of two cell populations: the **stromal cells** and the **thymocytes**. The stromal cells include (1) the **subcapsular epithelial cells** also lining the trabeculae and perivascular spaces; (2) the **cortical epithelial cells** of ectodermic origin; (3) the **medullary epithelial cells** of endodermic origin that give rise to **Hassall's corpuscles**; (4) **macrophages** present in both cortex and medulla, involved in the removal of apoptotic thymocytes eliminated during clonal selection; (5) **dendritic cells** of **bone marrow origin**, confined to the medulla.
   Thymocytes include T cells at different stages of maturation. Immature thymocytes—**double-negative** T cells—enter the cortex of the thymus through blood vessels and proliferate in the subcapsular area. **Double-positive** T cells move to the outer cortex where they are confronted with epithelial cells with cell surface MHC class I and II molecules for clonal selection. **Single-positive** T cells migrate to the inner cortex. The majority of thymocytes (80%-85%) are in the cortex. The medulla contains the remaining 15%-20% of thymocytes. **Apoptotic thymocytes** are present in the cortex.

sists of epithelial cells. The stroma of the lymph node and the spleen contains reticular cells and reticular fibers but not epithelial cells.
   Thymic epithelial cells have a dual origin (Figure 10–14): (1) **cortical epithe-**

Figure 10–17

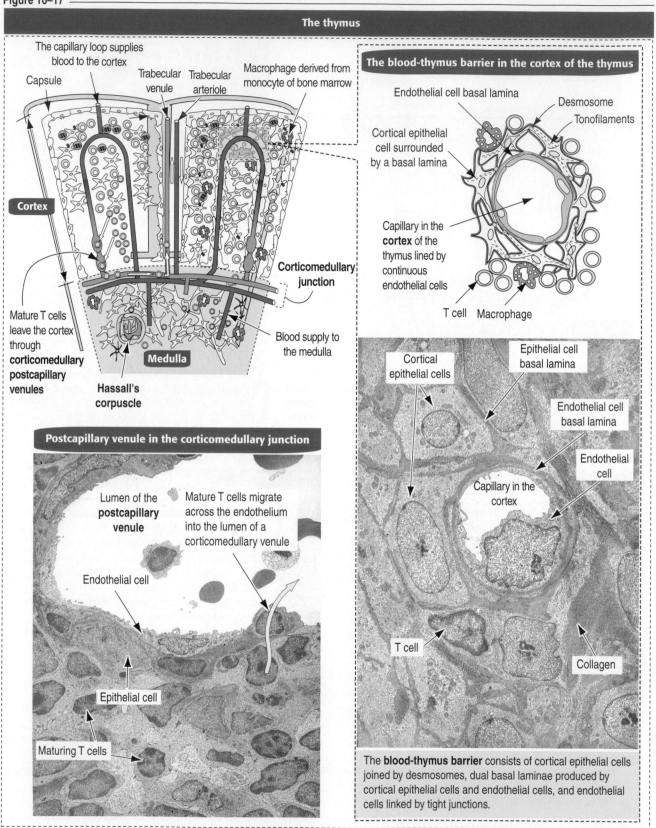

The thymus

The capillary loop supplies blood to the cortex

Capsule

Trabecular venule

Trabecular arteriole

Macrophage derived from monocyte of bone marrow

Cortex

Mature T cells leave the cortex through **corticomedullary postcapillary venules**

Hassall's corpuscle

Medulla

Corticomedullary junction

Blood supply to the medulla

The blood-thymus barrier in the cortex of the thymus

Endothelial cell basal lamina

Desmosome

Tonofilaments

Cortical epithelial cell surrounded by a basal lamina

Capillary in the **cortex** of the thymus lined by continuous endothelial cells

T cell   Macrophage

Postcapillary venule in the corticomedullary junction

Lumen of the **postcapillary venule**

Mature T cells migrate across the endothelium into the lumen of a corticomedullary venule

Endothelial cell

Epithelial cell

Maturing T cells

Cortical epithelial cells

Epithelial cell basal lamina

Endothelial cell basal lamina

Endothelial cell

Capillary in the cortex

T cell

Collagen

The **blood-thymus barrier** consists of cortical epithelial cells joined by desmosomes, dual basal laminae produced by cortical epithelial cells and endothelial cells, and endothelial cells linked by tight junctions.

lial cells derive from the **ectodermal third branchial cleft**. (2) **medullary epithelial cells** derive from the **endodermal third pharyngeal pouch**. The **mesenchyme** from the pharyngeal arch gives rise to the capsule, trabeculae, and vessels of the thymus.

Both ectodermal and endodermal layers form the **thymic epithelial rudiment**, which attracts **bone marrow–derived thymocyte precursors, dendritic cells,** and **macrophages** required for normal thymic function.

The **DiGeorge syndrome** is an **inherited immunodeficiency disease** in which cortical epithelial cells fail to develop, and the thymus is rudimentary. When epithelial cells fail to organize the thymus, bone marrow–derived T cell precursors cannot differentiate. Cortical epithelial cells express MHC class I and class II molecules on their surface, and these molecules are required for the clonal selection of T cells. Their absence in the DiGeorge syndrome affects the production of functional T cells. The development of B cells is not affected in the DiGeorge syndrome. The **nude (athymic) mouse**—a strain of mice lacking the expression of a transcription factor necessary for the differentiation of certain epidermal cells involved in the normal development of the thymus and **hair follicles**—is the equivalent of the DiGeorge syndrome. This syndrome and the nude mouse demonstrate the role of the thymus in cell-mediated immunity and disease.

During **fetal life**, the thymus contains lymphocytes derived from the liver. T cell progenitors formed in the bone marrow during hematopoiesis enter the thymus as **immature thymocytes** and mature to become immunocompetent T cells (predominantly **CD4+** or **CD8+**), which are then carried by the blood into lymph nodes, spleen, and other lymphoid tissues (see Figure 10–16).

The thymus in humans is fully developed before birth. The production of T cells is significant before puberty. After puberty, the thymus begins to involute and the production of T cells in the adult decreases. The progenies of T cells become established, and immunity is maintained without the need to produce new T cells.

Structure of the thymus

The thymus consists of **two lobes** subdivided into **incomplete lobules**, each separated into an **outer cortex** and a **central medulla** (Figure 10–15). A connective tissue **capsule** with small arterioles surrounds the lobules. The capsule projects **septa** or **trabeculae**. Blood vessels (**trabecular arterioles** and **venules**) within the trabeculae gain access to the thymic stroma.

The cortex contains **epithelial cells** (of **ectodermal** origin) with secretory granules containing thymic factors. Epithelial cells, linked to each other by **desmosomes,** surround capillaries. A **dual basal lamina** is present in the space between epithelial cells and capillaries. One basal lamina is produced by the cortical epithelial cells. The other basal lamina is of endothelial cell origin. Macrophages may also be present in proximity (Figure 10–17).

Cortical epithelial cells, basal laminae and endothelial cells form the **functional blood-thymus barrier** (see Figure 10–17). Macrophages adjacent to the capillaries ensure that antigens escaping from blood vessels into the thymus do not react with developing T cells in the cortex, thus preventing the risk of an autoimmune reaction.

Most T cell development takes place in the cortex. In the outer area of the cortex adjacent to the capsule, double-negative thymocytes proliferate and begin the process of gene rearrangement leading to the expression of the pre-TCR along with coreceptors CD4 and CD8 (Figure 10–16).

 Deep in the cortex, maturing thymocytes are double-positive (CD4+ and CD8+) and become receptive to peptide-MHC complexes. The process of **positive selection** of T cells now starts in the presence of cortical epithelial cells expressing both MHC class I and II molecules on their surface (see Figure 10–16). As you recall, MHC class II molecules are required for the development of CD4+ T cells; MHC class I molecules are necessary for the development of CD8+ T cells.

As we have seen, T cells that recognize self-MHC molecules but not self-anti-

Figure 10–21

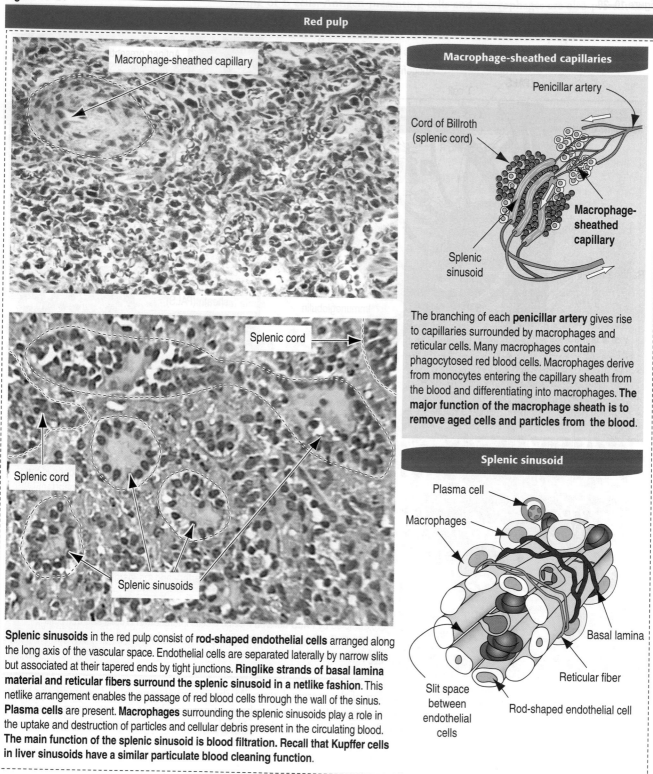

Red pulp

Macrophage-sheathed capillary

Splenic cord

Splenic cord

Splenic sinusoids

Macrophage-sheathed capillaries

Penicillar artery

Cord of Billroth (splenic cord)

Macrophage-sheathed capillary

Splenic sinusoid

The branching of each **penicillar artery** gives rise to capillaries surrounded by macrophages and reticular cells. Many macrophages contain phagocytosed red blood cells. Macrophages derive from monocytes entering the capillary sheath from the blood and differentiating into macrophages. **The major function of the macrophage sheath is to remove aged cells and particles from the blood.**

Splenic sinusoid

Plasma cell

Macrophages

Basal lamina

Reticular fiber

Slit space between endothelial cells

Rod-shaped endothelial cell

Splenic sinusoids in the red pulp consist of **rod-shaped endothelial cells** arranged along the long axis of the vascular space. Endothelial cells are separated laterally by narrow slits but associated at their tapered ends by tight junctions. **Ringlike strands of basal lamina material and reticular fibers surround the splenic sinusoid in a netlike fashion.** This netlike arrangement enables the passage of red blood cells through the wall of the sinus. **Plasma cells** are present. **Macrophages** surrounding the splenic sinusoids play a role in the uptake and destruction of particles and cellular debris present in the circulating blood. **The main function of the splenic sinusoid is blood filtration. Recall that Kupffer cells in liver sinusoids have a similar particulate blood cleaning function.**

Splenic sinusoids are discontinuous vascular spaces lined by **rib-shaped endothelial cells** oriented in parallel along the long axis of the sinusoids (see Figure 10–20). Junctional complexes can be found at the tapering ends of the endothelial cells.

Each splenic sinusoid is covered by a discontinuous **basal lamina** oriented around the endothelial cells like ribs or barrel hoops (see Figure 10–20). Adjacent hoops

Figure 10–22

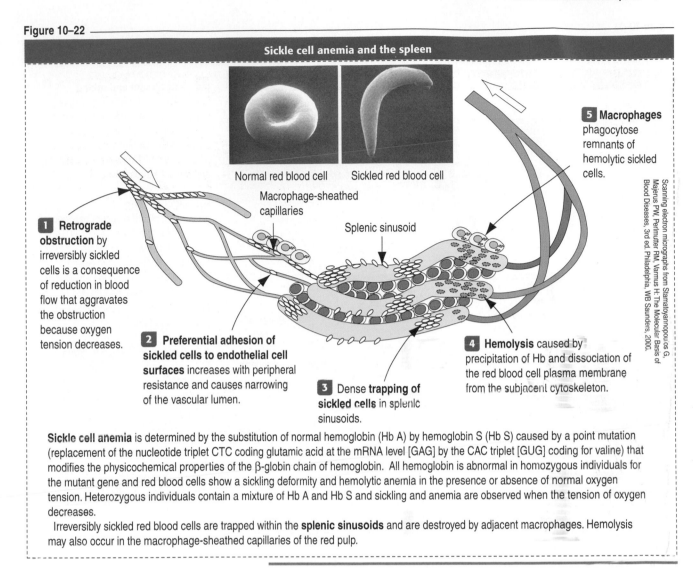

Sickle cell anemia and the spleen

Normal red blood cell   Sickled red blood cell

Macrophage-sheathed capillaries

Splenic sinusoid

5 **Macrophages** phagocytose remnants of hemolytic sickled cells.

1 **Retrograde obstruction** by irreversibly sickled cells is a consequence of reduction in blood flow that aggravates the obstruction because oxygen tension decreases.

2 **Preferential adhesion of sickled cells to endothelial cell surfaces** increases with peripheral resistance and causes narrowing of the vascular lumen.

3 Dense **trapping of sickled cells** in splenic sinusoids.

4 **Hemolysis** caused by precipitation of Hb and dissociation of the red blood cell plasma membrane from the subjacent cytoskeleton.

Scanning electron micrographs from Stamatoyannopoulos G, Majerus PW, Perlmutter RM, Varmus H: The Molecular Basis of Blood Diseases, 3rd ed. Philadelphia, WB Saunders, 2000.

Sickle cell anemia is determined by the substitution of normal hemoglobin (Hb A) by hemoglobin S (Hb S) caused by a point mutation (replacement of the nucleotide triplet CTC coding glutamic acid at the mRNA level [GAG] by the CAC triplet [GUG] coding for valine) that modifies the physicochemical properties of the β-globin chain of hemoglobin. All hemoglobin is abnormal in homozygous individuals for the mutant gene and red blood cells show a sickling deformity and hemolytic anemia in the presence or absence of normal oxygen tension. Heterozygous individuals contain a mixture of Hb A and Hb S and sickling and anemia are observed when the tension of oxygen decreases.

Irreversibly sickled red blood cells are trapped within the **splenic sinusoids** and are destroyed by adjacent macrophages. Hemolysis may also occur in the macrophage-sheathed capillaries of the red pulp.

are cross-linked by strands of basal lamina material. In addition, a network of loose reticular fibers also encircles the splenic sinusoids. Consequently, blood cells have an unobstructed access to the sinusoids through the narrow slits between the fusiform endothelial cells and the loose basal lamina–reticular fiber network.

Two types of blood circulations have been described in the red pulp (see Figure 10–19): (1) a **closed circulation**, in which arterial vessels connect directly to splenic sinusoids; and (2) an **open circulation**, characterized by blood vessels opening directly into the red pulp spaces, with the blood flowing through these spaces and then entering through the interendothelial cell slits of the splenic sinusoids.

Clinical significance: Sickle cell disease

Sickle cell anemia was discussed briefly in Chapter 6, Blood and Hematopoiesis, within the context of the structure of the red blood cell. We now focus on the fate of irreversibly sickled red blood cells when they travel through the narrow passages of the red pulp. We also consider the function of macrophages associated with the splenic sinuses in the disposal of destroyed sickle cells.

When the oxygen tension decreases, sickle cells show preferential adhesion to postcapillary venules followed by trapping of irreversibly sickled cells and retrograde obstruction of the blood vessel (Figure 10–22).

Figure 10–23

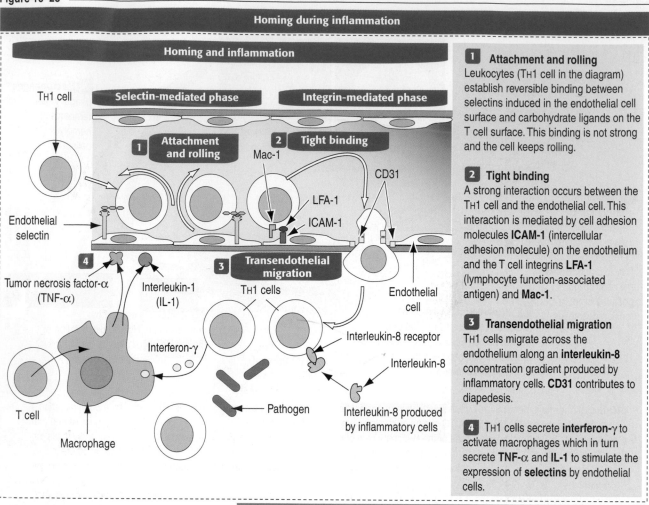

Homing during inflammation

Homing and inflammation

Selectin-mediated phase

Integrin-mediated phase

TH1 cell

1 Attachment and rolling

Mac-1

CD31

LFA-1

ICAM-1

Endothelial selectin

2 Tight binding

3 Transendothelial migration

TH1 cells

Endothelial cell

Tumor necrosis factor-α (TNF-α)

Interleukin-1 (IL-1)

Interferon-γ

Interleukin-8 receptor

Interleukin-8

T cell

Pathogen

Interleukin-8 produced by inflammatory cells

Macrophage

1 Attachment and rolling
Leukocytes (TH1 cell in the diagram) establish reversible binding between selectins induced in the endothelial cell surface and carbohydrate ligands on the T cell surface. This binding is not strong and the cell keeps rolling.

2 Tight binding
A strong interaction occurs between the TH1 cell and the endothelial cell. This interaction is mediated by cell adhesion molecules **ICAM-1** (intercellular adhesion molecule) on the endothelium and the T cell integrins **LFA-1** (lymphocyte function-associated antigen) and **Mac-1**.

3 Transendothelial migration
TH1 cells migrate across the endothelium along an **interleukin-8** concentration gradient produced by inflammatory cells. **CD31** contributes to diapedesis.

4 TH1 cells secrete **interferon-γ** to activate macrophages which in turn secrete **TNF-α** and **IL-1** to stimulate the expression of **selectins** by endothelial cells.

An increased destruction of sickle cells leads to anemia and to an increase in the formation of bilirubin from the released hemoglobin (chronic hyperbilirubinemia). The **occlusion of splenic sinuses** by sickle cells is associated with **splenomegaly** (enlargement of the spleen), disrupted bacterial clearance function of the spleen in cases of bacteremia, and **painful crises** in the affected region. Similar vascular occlusions can also occur in kidney, liver, bones, and retina.

Asplenia (lack of development of the spleen) is a clear demonstration of the function of the spleen in bacteremia. To a certain extent, the Kupffer cells of the liver sinusoids complement the role of the white pulp in the detection and removal of bacteria circulating in blood.

The spleen can be removed surgically (**splenectomy**) in cases of traumatic rupture, as part of the treatment of autoimmune diseases, or because of a malignant tumor of the spleen. Adults who already have antibodies to microorganisms are less prone to bacteremia. Children who have not developed antibodies are more vulnerable.

Clinical significance: The homing process during inflammation
In Chapter 1, Epithelium, we discussed the homing process to emphasize the role of cell adhesion molecules in the transendothelial migration of leukocytes. In Chapter 6, Blood and Hematopoiesis, we extended homing to the migration of neutrophils to the connective tissue. We now focus on the significance of homing during the implementation of inflammatory responses to pathogens.

The migration of leukocytes through the body facilitates immune surveil-

Figure 10-24

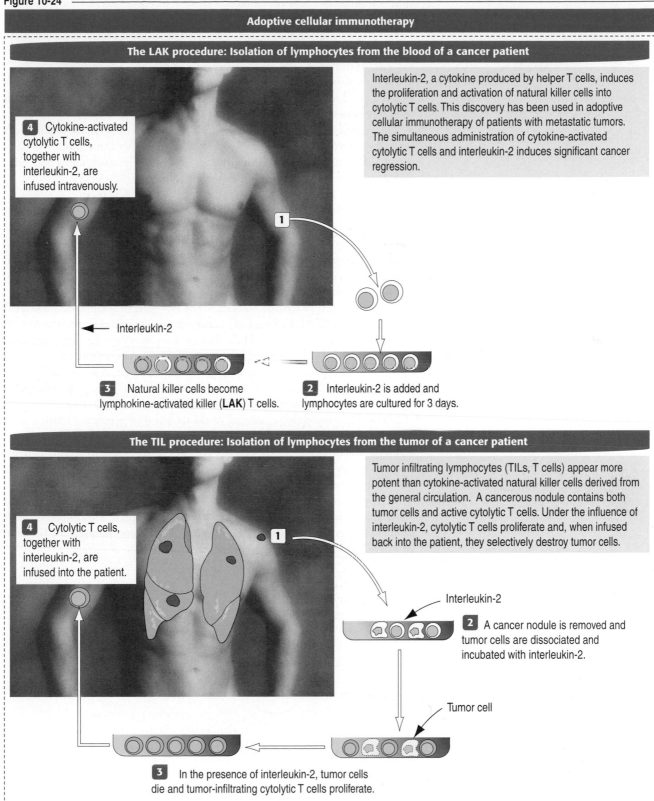

Adoptive cellular immunotherapy

The LAK procedure: Isolation of lymphocytes from the blood of a cancer patient

Interleukin-2, a cytokine produced by helper T cells, induces the proliferation and activation of natural killer cells into cytolytic T cells. This discovery has been used in adoptive cellular immunotherapy of patients with metastatic tumors. The simultaneous administration of cytokine-activated cytolytic T cells and interleukin-2 induces significant cancer regression.

4 Cytokine-activated cytolytic T cells, together with interleukin-2, are infused intravenously.

1

← Interleukin-2

3 Natural killer cells become lymphokine-activated killer (**LAK**) T cells.

2 Interleukin-2 is added and lymphocytes are cultured for 3 days.

The TIL procedure: Isolation of lymphocytes from the tumor of a cancer patient

Tumor infiltrating lymphocytes (TILs, T cells) appear more potent than cytokine-activated natural killer cells derived from the general circulation. A cancerous nodule contains both tumor cells and active cytolytic T cells. Under the influence of interleukin-2, cytolytic T cells proliferate and, when infused back into the patient, they selectively destroy tumor cells.

4 Cytolytic T cells, together with interleukin-2, are infused into the patient.

1

Interleukin-2

2 A cancer nodule is removed and tumor cells are dissociated and incubated with interleukin-2.

Tumor cell

3 In the presence of interleukin-2, tumor cells die and tumor-infiltrating cytolytic T cells proliferate.

lance as well as directs immune responses to antigen-challenged tissues. **Distinct sub- sets of leukocytes respond to particular types of antigens at different stages during an inflammatory response.**

The migration of leukocytes during inflammation is regulated by a variety of adhesion molecules and chemotactic cytokine receptors and by the expression of leukocyte adhesion ligands on the endothelial cell surface (Figure 10–23). Tumor necrosis factor-α and IL-1, produced by antigen-presenting cells in the perivascular space, stimulate the production of cell adhesion ligands by endothelial cells. **Endothelial cells are the regulators of lymphocyte traffic.**

There are two types of endothelium to which leukocytes bind: (1) the **specialized high endothelial venule** of lymphoid tissues, and (2) the **flat endothelial cells** of normal and acutely inflamed tissues.

The migration of leukocytes through HEVs is substantial (about one in every four lymphocytes circulating in blood). Different HEVs throughout the body recruit different subsets of lymphocytes into tissues. Migration across flat endothelial cells is minimal, except in cases of inflammation.

Clinical significance: Adoptive cellular immunotherapy

Strategies are being develop to enhance immune response against tumor cells expressing tumor-related antigens. One strategy, called **adoptive cellular immunotherapy**, consists of the transfer of activated immune cells with antitumoral activity into a tumor-bearing host.

Two procedures have been used (Figure 10–24):

1. The **LAK cell procedure** consists of the isolation of lymphokine-activated killer (LAK) cells from the blood of a cancerous patient and their treatment with the cytokine **interleukin-2** to induce their proliferation in vitro. Activated LAK cells are infused into the patient, together with IL-2. A key issue in this procedure is the isolation of lymphocytes from the same patient, since the infusion of killer T cells from a second patient is not successful. The LAK procedure yields modest benefits when compared to the administration of IL-2 only.

2. The **TIL procedure**, consisting of the isolation of tumor-infiltrating lymphocytes (TILs). In this procedure, a tumor nodule is removed and the cells are dissociated with enzymes. Dissociated cells are cultured with IL-2. This treatment results in the death of cancerous cells and the proliferation of TILs that have already been in contact with tumor cells. TILs are then returned to the patient by transfusion, together with IL-2. About 34% of patients with advanced melanoma receiving TIL treatment had partial or complete tumor regression. A difficulty of the TIL procedure is the isolation of sufficient number of TILs from all tumor specimens for adoptive transfer.

11. INTEGUMENTARY SYSTEM

The integument is the largest organ of the body. It consists of two components: (1) the **skin**, and (2) the **epidermal derivatives**, such as nails, hair, and glands (sweat and sebaceous glands and the mammary gland).

The skin is of particular significance in a clinical physical examination. For example, the color of the skin may indicate the existence of a pathologic condition: a yellow color indicates **jaundice**; a blue-gray color may indicate **cyanosis**, reflecting a pathologic condition of cardiovascular and respiratory functions; a pale color is indicative of **anemia**; lack of skin pigmentation suggests **albinism**, a genetic trait characterized by lack of the enzyme tyrosinase, involved in the conversion of the amino acid tyrosine to melanin. Many infectious and immunologic diseases produce characteristic skin changes leading to a correct diagnosis. In addition, the skin has diseases peculiar to itself.

The skin has several **functions**: (1) **protection** (mechanical function); (2) as a **water barrier**; (3) **regulation of body temperature** (conservation and dissipation of heat); (4) **nonspecific defense** (barrier to microorganisms); (5) **excretion of salts**; (6) **synthesis of vitamin D**; (7) as a **sensory organ**, and (8) **sexual signaling**.

Skin types and general organization

The skin consists of three layers firmly attached to one another (Figure 11–1): (1) the outer **epidermis** —derived from ectoderm; (2) the deeper **dermis**—derived from mesoderm; and (3) the **hypodermis** or **subcutaneous layer**—corresponding to the **superficial fascia** of gross anatomy.

Skin is generally classified into two types: (1) **thick skin**, and (2) **thin skin**.

Thick skin (more than 5 mm thick) covers the palms of the hands and the soles of the feet and has a thick epidermis and dermis. Thin skin (1 to 2 mm in thickness) lines the rest of the body; the epidermis is thin.

The surface of the skin has narrow **epidermal ridges** separated by **furrows**. In the fingertips, ridges form complicated configurations. Impressions result in **fingerprints**, characteristic for each individual.

The position of the epidermal ridges correlates with a projection of the epidermis on the dermal side, called the **primary dermal ridge** (see Figure 11–1). An **interpapillary peg** divides the primary dermal ridge into two **secondary dermal ridges**. The **dermal papilla** extends between the primary and secondary dermal ridges. Dermal papillae are numerous and branched. In thin skin, papillae are low and their number reduced.

Epidermis

The **stratified squamous epithelial layer** of the epidermis consists of four distinct cell types (Figure 11–2):

1. The predominant cell type is the **keratinocyte**, so called because its major product is **keratin**, an intermediate filament protein.

2. **Melanocytes**—neural crest–derived cells responsible for the production of melanin (Figure 11–3).

3. **Langerhans cells**—dendritic cells derived from a bone marrow precursor, acting as an antigen-trapping cells interacting with T cells.

4. **Merkel cells**—neural crest–derived cells involved in tactile sensation.

Keratinocytes are arranged in **five layers** or strata: (1) the **stratum basale**; (2) the **stratum spinosum**; (3) the **stratum granulosum**; (4) the **stratum lucidum**; (5) the **stratum corneum**.

Both the stratum basale and stratum spinosum form the **stratum of Malpighi**.

Figure 11–1

General organization of the skin

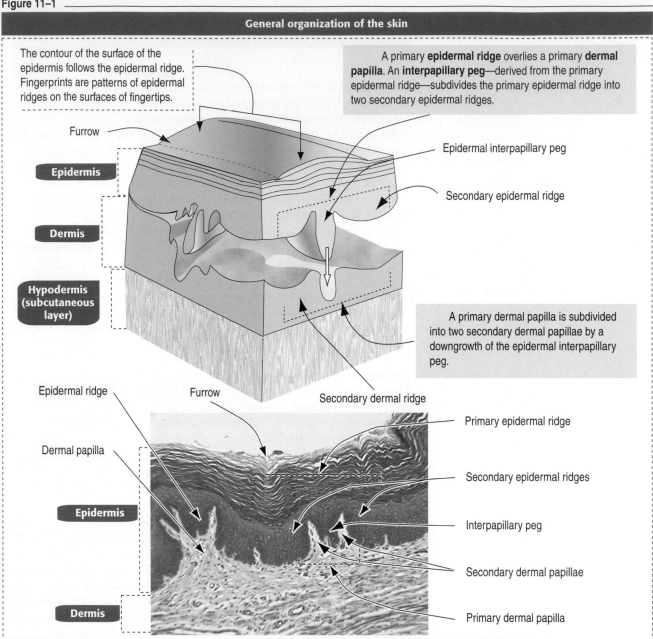

The contour of the surface of the epidermis follows the epidermal ridge. Fingerprints are patterns of epidermal ridges on the surfaces of fingertips.

A primary **epidermal ridge** overlies a primary **dermal papilla**. An **interpapillary peg**—derived from the primary epidermal ridge—subdivides the primary epidermal ridge into two secondary epidermal ridges.

Furrow

Epidermis

Dermis

Hypodermis (subcutaneous layer)

Epidermal interpapillary peg

Secondary epidermal ridge

A primary dermal papilla is subdivided into two secondary dermal papillae by a downgrowth of the epidermal interpapillary peg.

Epidermal ridge

Furrow

Secondary dermal ridge

Dermal papilla

Epidermis

Dermis

Primary epidermal ridge

Secondary epidermal ridges

Interpapillary peg

Secondary dermal papillae

Primary dermal papilla

The **stratum basale** (or **stratum germinativum**) consists of a single layer of columnar or high cuboidal keratinocytes resting on a basement membrane. The cytoplasm contains intermediate filaments associated with **desmosomes**. Bundles of intermediate filaments, visible under the light microscope, are called **tonofilaments. Hemidesmosomes** and associated intermediate filaments anchor the basal domain of basal cells to the basement membrane.

The cells of the stratum basale undergo mitosis. While some of the dividing cells add to the population of **stem cells** of the stratum basale, others migrate into the stratum spinosum to initiate the differentiation process, ending with the formation of the stratum corneum.

Clinical significance: Wound repair and psoriasis

If a portion of epidermis is damaged or destroyed, the surrounding basal cells migrate and proliferate to cover the denuded area. This repair process occurs under the influence of the basement membrane, the extracellular matrix of the

Figure 11–2

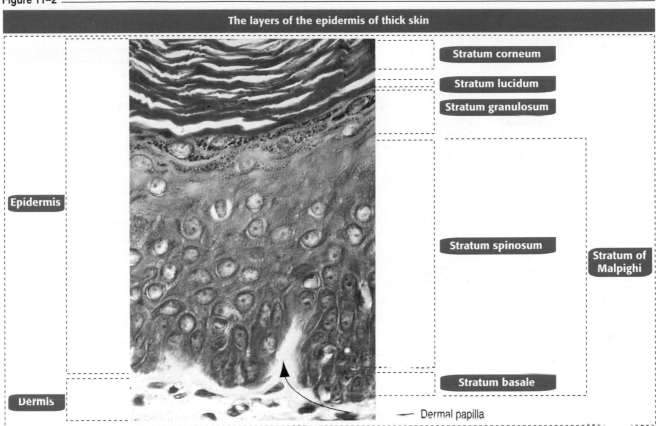

The layers of the epidermis of thick skin

Stratum corneum

Stratum lucidum

Stratum granulosum

Epidermis

Stratum spinosum

Stratum of Malpighi

Stratum basale

Dermis

— Dermal papilla

connective tissue of the dermis and a variety of hormones and growth factors, including **epidermal growth factor** (EGF) and **keratinocyte growth factor**.

Retinol (**vitamin A**) is a precursor of retinoic acid, a hormone-like agent required for the differentiation of epithelia, including epidermis. Like steroid and thyroid hormones, retinoic acid binds to nuclear receptors (**retinoic acid receptor, RAR**). In addition, retinoid acid binds to **cytosolic retinoic acid proteins**, (**CRABs**), presumably involved in the regulation of the intracellular concentration of retinoic acid. The retinoic acid–receptor complex has binding affinity for **retinoic acid–responsive elements** (**RAREs**) on DNA and induces the expression of genes during keratinocyte differentiation. A lack of vitamin A results in alterations in the keratinization of the epidermis due to a downregulation of genes involved in the expression of differentiation markers of keratinocytes.

A deficient control of basal cell proliferation is seen in **psoriasis**, a common skin disorder (Figure 11–4). Psoriasis consists of an increased proliferation of basal cells and incomplete keratinization of upper layer cells that are shed within a week after leaving the stratum basale (instead of a few weeks to several months, depending on the region of the body).

Differentiation of a keratinocyte

Keratinocytes of the **stratum spinosum** have a flattened polygonal shape with a distinct ovoid nucleus. The cytoplasm displays small granules with a lamellar core, called **membrane-coating granules**, or **lamellar bodies**. Bundles of intermediate filaments—**tonofibrils**—extend into the cytoplasmic spinous-like processes and attach to the **dense plaque** of a desmosome.

The **stratum granulosum** consists of a multilayered assembly of flattened nucleated keratinocytes with characteristic irregularly shaped **keratohyalin granules** without a limiting membrane and associated with the tonofilaments. The **lamellar bodies**, which first appear in keratinocytes of the stratum spinosum, increase

Figure 11–3

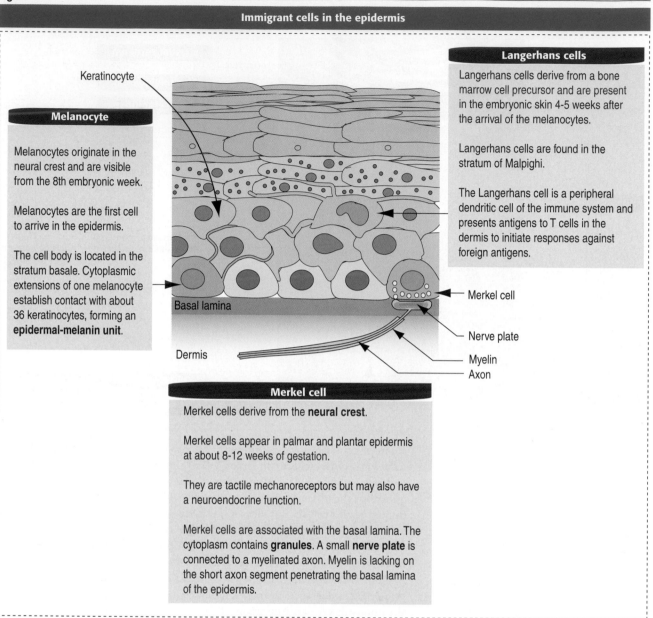

Immigrant cells in the epidermis

Keratinocyte

Langerhans cells

Langerhans cells derive from a bone marrow cell precursor and are present in the embryonic skin 4-5 weeks after the arrival of the melanocytes.

Langerhans cells are found in the stratum of Malpighi.

The Langerhans cell is a peripheral dendritic cell of the immune system and presents antigens to T cells in the dermis to initiate responses against foreign antigens.

Melanocyte

Melanocytes originate in the neural crest and are visible from the 8th embryonic week.

Melanocytes are the first cell to arrive in the epidermis.

The cell body is located in the stratum basale. Cytoplasmic extensions of one melanocyte establish contact with about 36 keratinocytes, forming an **epidermal-melanin unit**.

Basal lamina

Dermis

Merkel cell

Nerve plate

Myelin

Axon

Merkel cell

Merkel cells derive from the **neural crest**.

Merkel cells appear in palmar and plantar epidermis at about 8-12 weeks of gestation.

They are tactile mechanoreceptors but may also have a neuroendocrine function.

Merkel cells are associated with the basal lamina. The cytoplasm contains **granules**. A small **nerve plate** is connected to a myelinated axon. Myelin is lacking on the short axon segment penetrating the basal lamina of the epidermis.

in number in the stratum granulosum, and the lamellar product, the **glycolipid acylglucosylceramide**, is released into the intercellular spaces (Figure 11–5).

In the intercellular space, the lamellar material forms a multilayered structure arranged in wide sheets, coating the surface of keratinocytes of the upper layer, the stratum lucidum. The glycolipid coating provides the water barrier of the epidermis.

The **stratum lucidum** is recognized by some histologists as an intermediate layer above the stratum granulosum and beneath the **stratum corneum**. However, no distinctive cytologic features are significantly apparent.

Both the stratum lucidum and stratum corneum consist of several layers of keratinocytes without nuclei and a cytoplasm containing aggregated intermediate filaments of keratin cross-linked with **filaggrin** (Figure 11–6) catalyzed by **transglutaminases**. The keratin-filaggrin complex is deposited on the inside of the plasma membrane, forming a cornified structure called the **cell envelope**. On the outside of the cell, lipids released from lamellar bodies crosslink the cell envelope, forming the **compound cell envelope**. The compound cell envelope

Figure 11–4

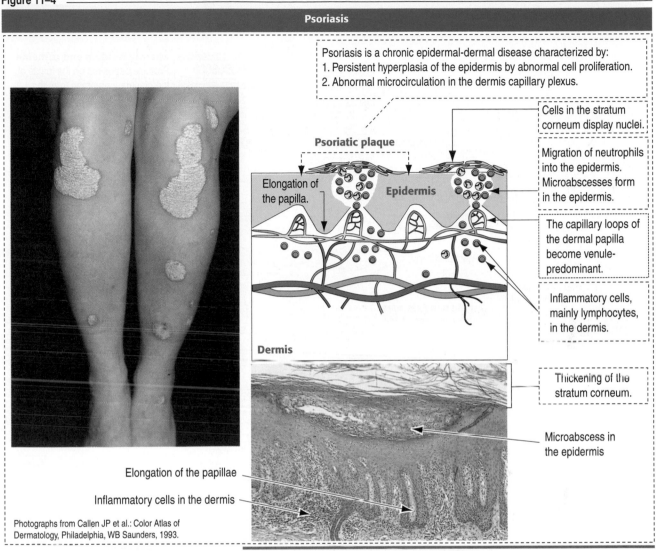

Psoriasis

Psoriasis is a chronic epidermal-dermal disease characterized by:
1. Persistent hyperplasia of the epidermis by abnormal cell proliferation.
2. Abnormal microcirculation in the dermis capillary plexus.

Cells in the stratum corneum display nuclei.

Migration of neutrophils into the epidermis. Microabscesses form in the epidermis.

Psoriatic plaque

Elongation of the papilla.

Epidermis

The capillary loops of the dermal papilla become venule-predominant.

Inflammatory cells, mainly lymphocytes, in the dermis.

Dermis

Thickening of the stratum corneum.

Microabscess in the epidermis

Elongation of the papillae

Inflammatory cells in the dermis

Photographs from Callen JP et al.: Color Atlas of Dermatology, Philadelphia, WB Saunders, 1993.

makes the cell membrane impermeable to fluids (fluid barrier).

The terminally differentiated keratinocytes of the stratum corneum consist of flattened squames with a highly resistant compound cell envelope. Squames are sloughed from the surface of the epidermis and are continually replaced by keratinocytes of the inner strata.

Cell layer–specific expression of keratins is observed during differentiation of keratinocytes (see Figure 11–5).

Melanocytes

Melanocytes are branching cells located in the stratum basale of the epidermis (Figure 11–7). Melanocytes derive from **melanoblasts**, a cell precursor migrating from the **neural crest**.

Melanoblast development into melanocytes is under the control of the ligand **stem cell factor** interacting with the **c-kit receptor**, a membrane-bound tyrosine kinase. Recall that the development of mast cells, primordial germinal cells, and hematopoietic stem cells is also dependent on the interaction of stem cell factor with the c-kit receptor.

Melanocytes enter the developing epidermis and remain as independent cells without desmosome attachment to the differentiating keratinocytes. The turnover of melanocytes is slower than that of keratinocytes.

Figure 11–5

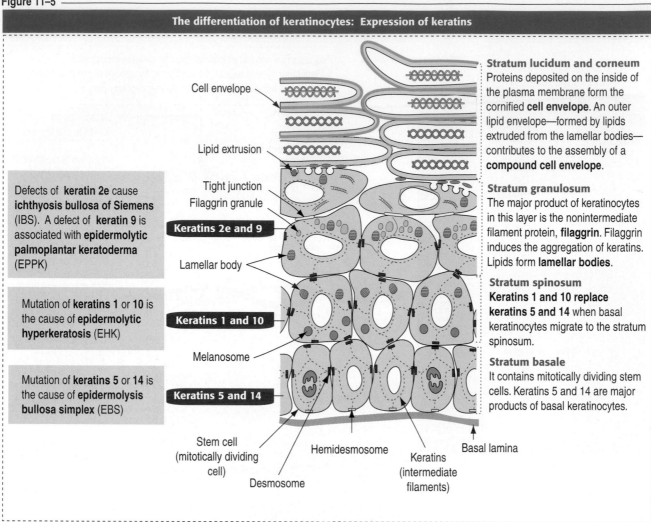

The differentiation of keratinocytes: Expression of keratins

Cell envelope

Lipid extrusion

Tight junction
Filaggrin granule

Keratins 2e and 9

Lamellar body

Keratins 1 and 10

Melanosome

Keratins 5 and 14

Stem cell
(mitotically dividing
cell)

Hemidesmosome

Desmosome

Keratins
(intermediate
filaments)

Basal lamina

Defects of **keratin 2e** cause **ichthyosis bullosa of Siemens** (IBS). A defect of **keratin 9** is associated with **epidermolytic palmoplantar keratoderma** (EPPK)

Mutation of **keratins 1** or **10** is the cause of **epidermolytic hyperkeratosis** (EHK)

Mutation of **keratins 5** or **14** is the cause of **epidermolysis bullosa simplex** (EBS)

Stratum lucidum and corneum
Proteins deposited on the inside of the plasma membrane form the cornified **cell envelope**. An outer lipid envelope—formed by lipids extruded from the lamellar bodies—contributes to the assembly of a **compound cell envelope**.

Stratum granulosum
The major product of keratinocytes in this layer is the nonintermediate filament protein, **filaggrin**. Filaggrin induces the aggregation of keratins. Lipids form **lamellar bodies**.

Stratum spinosum
Keratins 1 and 10 replace keratins 5 and 14 when basal keratinocytes migrate to the stratum spinosum.

Stratum basale
It contains mitotically dividing stem cells. Keratins 5 and 14 are major products of basal keratinocytes.

Melanocytes produce **melanin**, contained in **melanin granules**, which are transferred to neighboring keratinocytes through their branching cell processes by **cytocrine** secretion (Figure 11–8).

Melanin is initially stored in a membrane-bound **premelanosome** derived from the Golgi apparatus. Melanin is produced by oxidation of **tyrosine** to **3,4-dihydroxyphenylalanine (DOPA)** by the enzyme **tyrosinase**. DOPA is then transformed to melanin, which accumulates in **melanosomes**, the mature melanin granules that are distributed along the cytoplasmic processes of the melanocytes. Keratinocytes take up the released insoluble and dark melanin granules (Figure 11–9).

In addition to melanocytes, melanin-producing cells are present in the **choroid plexus**, **retina**, and **ciliary body of the eye**. **Albinism** results from the inability of cells to form melanin.

Langerhans cells (dendritic cells)
Langerhans cells are bone marrow–derived cells present in the epidermis and involved in immune responses, in particular the presentation of antigens to T cells during the initiation of cutaneous hypersensitivity reactions (Figure 11–10).

Langerhans cells migrate from the epidermis to the lymph node where they differentiate into activated dendritic cells after expressing class I MHC (major histocompatibility complex), class II MHC, and B7 cell surface antigens. Acti-

Figure 11–6

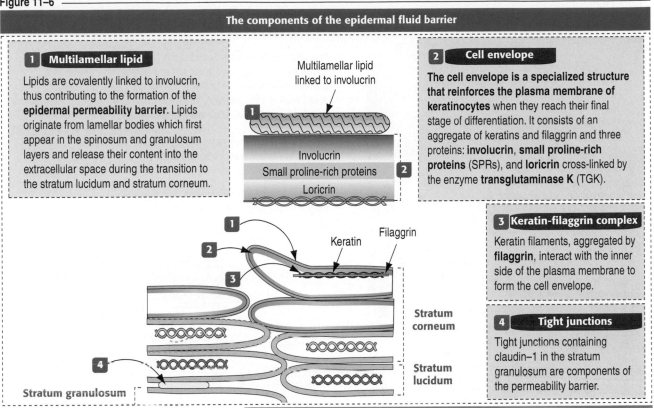

The components of the epidermal fluid barrier

1 Multilamellar lipid

Lipids are covalently linked to involucrin, thus contributing to the formation of the **epidermal permeability barrier**. Lipids originate from lamellar bodies which first appear in the spinosum and granulosum layers and release their content into the extracellular space during the transition to the stratum lucidum and stratum corneum.

Multilamellar lipid linked to involucrin

1

2

Involucrin

Small proline-rich proteins

Loricrin

2 Cell envelope

The cell envelope is a specialized structure that reinforces the plasma membrane of keratinocytes when they reach their final stage of differentiation. It consists of an aggregate of keratins and filaggrin and three proteins: **involucrin**, **small proline-rich proteins** (SPRs), and **loricrin** cross-linked by the enzyme **transglutaminase K** (TGK).

3 Keratin-filaggrin complex

Keratin filaments, aggregated by **filaggrin**, interact with the inner side of the plasma membrane to form the cell envelope.

4 Tight junctions

Tight junctions containing claudin–1 in the stratum granulosum are components of the permeability barrier.

Keratin   Filaggrin

1
2
3

Stratum corneum

Stratum lucidum

4

Stratum granulosum

vated dendritic cells stimulate the activity of T cells.

Like melanocytes, Langerhans cells have cytoplasmic processes (dendritic cells) extending among keratinocytes of the stratum spinosum without establishing desmosomal contact but associating with keratinocytes through **E-cadherin**.

The nucleus of a Langerhans cell is indented, and the cytoplasm contains characteristic rod-shaped granules (**Birbeck** or **vermiform granules**).

Merkel cells

Merkel cells resemble modified keratinocytes, are found in the stratum basale, and are numerous in the fingertips. Merkel cells are **mechanoreceptor cells** linked to adjacent keratinocytes by desmosomes and in contact with an afferent myelinated nerve fiber projecting from the dermis into the epidermis. The nerve fiber becomes unmyelinated after passing through the basal lamina of the epidermis and expands into a platelike sensory ending, the **nerve plate**, in contact with the Merkel cell (see Figure 11–3).

The nucleus is irregularly shaped and the cytoplasm contains abundant **granules**, presumably neurotransmitters.

Dermis

The dermis is formed by two layers without distinct boundaries: (1) the **papillary layer**, consisting of loose connective tissue (fibroblasts, collagen fibers and thin elastic fibers) in close contact with the epidermis; and (2) the **reticular layer**, containing thick bundles of collagen fibers and coarse elastic fibers.

Hair follicles and **sweat** and **sebaceous glands** are epidermal derivatives present at various levels of the dermis.

Hemidesmosomes on the basal domain of keratinocytes of the stratum basale (Figure 11–11) attach the epidermis to the basement membrane and the papillary layer of the dermis by **anchoring filaments** and **fibrils**, respectively.

The molecular and structural components of the hemidesmosome are of con-

Figure 11–7

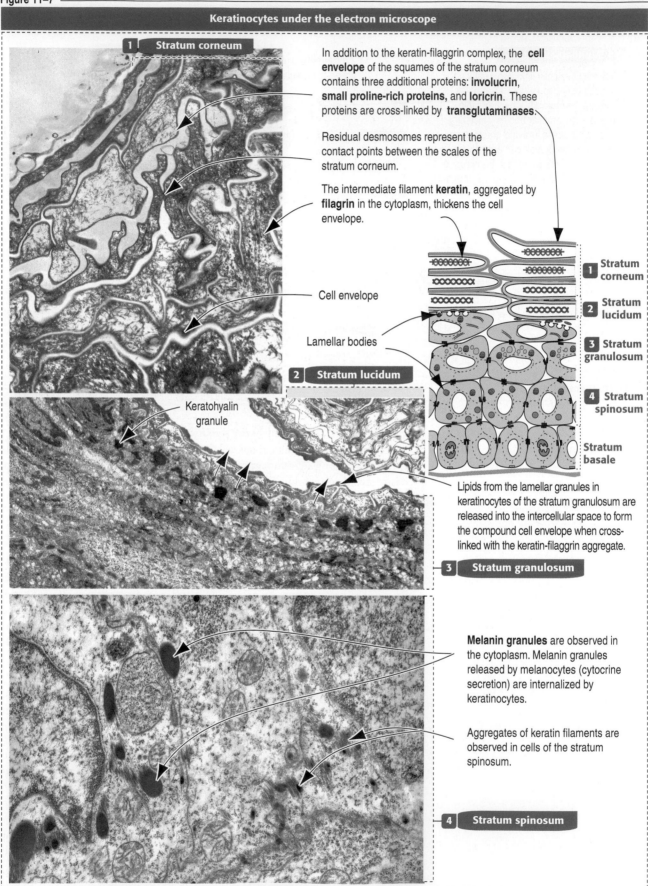

Keratinocytes under the electron microscope

1 Stratum corneum

In addition to the keratin-filaggrin complex, the **cell envelope** of the squames of the stratum corneum contains three additional proteins: **involucrin, small proline-rich proteins,** and **loricrin**. These proteins are cross-linked by **transglutaminases**.

Residual desmosomes represent the contact points between the scales of the stratum corneum.

The intermediate filament **keratin**, aggregated by **filagrin** in the cytoplasm, thickens the cell envelope.

Cell envelope

Lamellar bodies

1 Stratum corneum

2 Stratum lucidum

3 Stratum granulosum

4 Stratum spinosum

Stratum basale

2 Stratum lucidum

Keratohyalin granule

Lipids from the lamellar granules in keratinocytes of the stratum granulosum are released into the intercellular space to form the compound cell envelope when cross-linked with the keratin-filaggrin aggregate.

3 Stratum granulosum

Melanin granules are observed in the cytoplasm. Melanin granules released by melanocytes (cytocrine secretion) are internalized by keratinocytes.

Aggregates of keratin filaments are observed in cells of the stratum spinosum.

4 Stratum spinosum

Figure 11–8

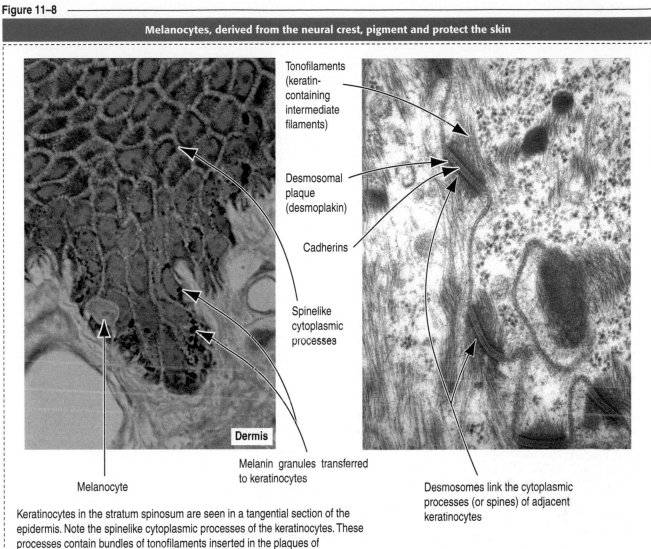

Melanocytes, derived from the neural crest, pigment and protect the skin

Tonofilaments (keratin-containing intermediate filaments)

Desmosomal plaque (desmoplakin)

Cadherins

Spinelike cytoplasmic processes

Dermis

Melanin granules transferred to keratinocytes

Melanocyte

Desmosomes link the cytoplasmic processes (or spines) of adjacent keratinocytes

Keratinocytes in the stratum spinosum are seen in a tangential section of the epidermis. Note the spinelike cytoplasmic processes of the keratinocytes. These processes contain bundles of tonofilaments inserted in the plaques of desmosomes linking cell processes derived from adjacent keratinocytes.

siderable importance for understanding the cause of **blistering diseases** of the skin (Figure 11–11). See Chapter 1, Epithelium, for the clinical significance of hemidesmosomes and intermediate filaments (Figures 1–35, 1–36, and 1–37).

Blood supply

Three interconnected networks are recognized in the skin (Figure 11–12):

1. The **subpapillary plexus**, running along the papillary layer of the dermis.

2. The **cutaneous plexus**, observed at the boundary of the papillary and reticular layers of the dermis.

3. The **hypodermic** or **subcutaneous plexus**, present in the hypodermis or subcutaneous adipose tissue.

The subpapillary plexus gives rise to single loops of capillaries within each dermal papilla. Venous blood from the subpapillary plexus drains into veins of the cutaneous plexus.

Branches of the hypodermic and cutaneous plexuses nourish the adipose tissue of the hypodermis, the sweat glands, and the deeper segment of the hair follicle.

Arteriovenous anastomoses between the arterial and venous circulation are common in the reticular and hypodermic regions and play a role in thermoregulation of the body.

Figure 11–9

The synthesis and transport of melanin from melanocytes to keratinocytes

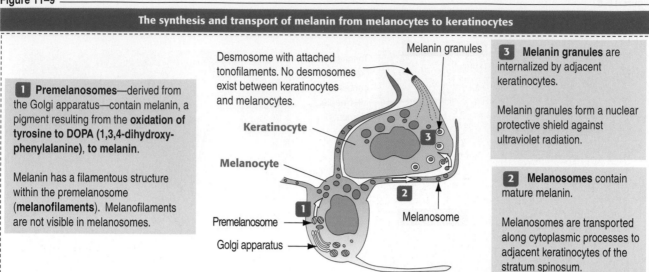

1 **Premelanosomes**—derived from the Golgi apparatus—contain melanin, a pigment resulting from the **oxidation of tyrosine to DOPA (1,3,4-dihydroxy-phenylalanine), to melanin.**

Melanin has a filamentous structure within the premelanosome (**melanofilaments**). Melanofilaments are not visible in melanosomes.

Desmosome with attached tonofilaments. No desmosomes exist between keratinocytes and melanocytes.

Melanin granules

Keratinocyte

Melanocyte

Premelanosome

Golgi apparatus

Melanosome

3 **Melanin granules** are internalized by adjacent keratinocytes.

Melanin granules form a nuclear protective shield against ultraviolet radiation.

2 **Melanosomes** contain mature melanin.

Melanosomes are transported along cytoplasmic processes to adjacent keratinocytes of the stratum spinosum.

Sensory receptors

Three categories of sensory receptors are present in the skin and other organs (Figure 11–13): (1) **exteroceptors**, (2) **proprioceptors**, and (3) **interoceptors**.

Exteroceptors provide information about the external environment. **Proprioceptors** are located in muscles (muscle spindle), tendons, and joint capsules and

Figure 11–10

Langerhans cell, an antigen-presenting dendritic cell of the epidermis

1 Langerhans cells interact with keratinocytes by the expression of E-cadherins on their surface.

2 Langerhans cells ingest antigens by phagocytosis after binding to cell surface receptors.

3 Langerhans cells leave the epidermis, enter the lymphatic system, and are transported to a lymph node to become dendritic cells.

4 In the lymph node, Langerhans cells become **dendritic cells** expressing **MHC class I** and **MHC class II** cell surface molecules and costimulatory **B7** molecules. Activated dendritic cells stimulate T cells.

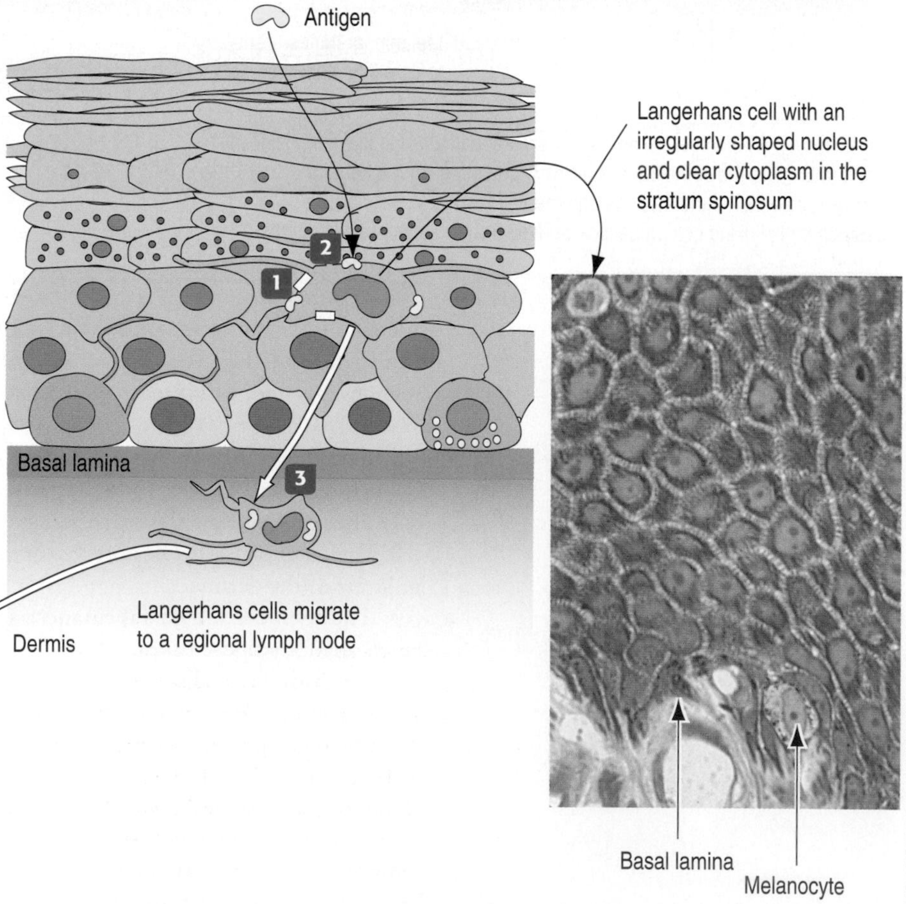

Antigen

Basal lamina

T cell

Dermis

Lymph node

Langerhans cells migrate to a regional lymph node

Langerhans cell with an irregularly shaped nucleus and clear cytoplasm in the stratum spinosum

Basal lamina

Melanocyte

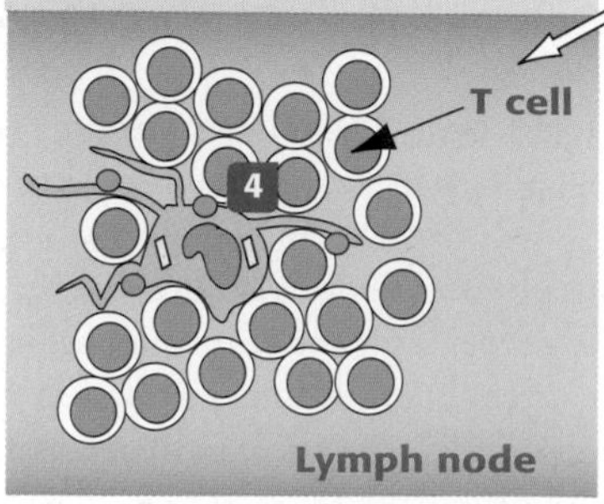

Figure 11–11

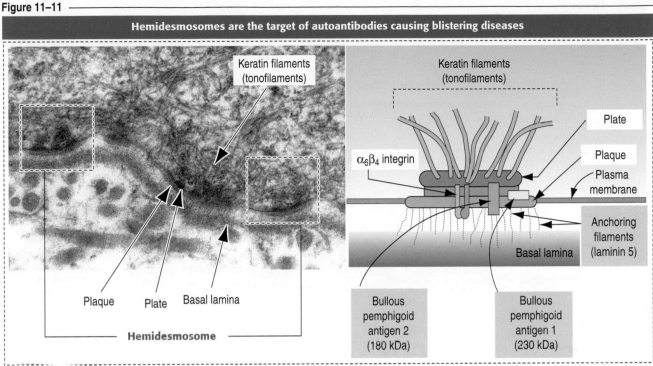

| Hemidesmosomes are the target of autoantibodies causing blistering diseases |

Keratin filaments (tonofilaments)

Plaque Plate Basal lamina

Hemidesmosome

Keratin filaments (tonofilaments)

Plate

Plaque

$\alpha_6\beta_4$ integrin

Plasma membrane

Basal lamina

Anchoring filaments (laminin 5)

Bullous pemphigoid antigen 2 (180 kDa)

Bullous pemphigoid antigen 1 (230 kDa)

provide information about the position and movement of the body. **Interoceptors** provide sensory information from the internal organs of the body.

Another classification of sensory receptors is based on the **type of stimulus** to which a receptor responds: (1) **mechanoreceptors,** (2) **thermoreceptors, and** (3) **nociceptors.**

Mechanoreceptors respond to mechanical deformation of the tissue or the receptor itself (for example, stretch, vibration, pressure, and touch). The mechanoreceptors include both exteroceptors and proprioceptors.

Thermoreceptors respond to warmth or cold.

Nociceptors (or pain receptors) respond to painful stimuli. The skin and the subcutaneous tissue contain receptors that respond to stimuli such as **touch, pressure, heat, cold,** and **pain.**

The simplest mechanoreceptor is the **naked nerve ending**, which lacks a myelin covering. Naked nerve endings are found in the **epidermis** of the skin and the **cornea** of the eye. Naked nerve endings respond to light pressure and touch stimuli.

The second type of mechanoreceptor is the **Merkel disk**. The nerve ending of this receptor discriminates touch and forms a flattened discoid structure attached to the **Merkel cell** found in the stratum basale of the epidermis.

The third type of mechanoreceptor includes two **encapsulated receptors:** (1) the **Meissner corpuscle,** and (2) the **pacinian corpuscle.**

The Meissner corpuscle is found in the dermal papillae and accounts for half the tactile receptors of the digits and hand. This receptor is well suited for the detection of shape and texture during active touch.

The pacinian corpuscle is found in the hypodermis, or deep dermis. It responds to transient vibratory stimuli and is the receptor for deep pressure.

The fourth type is the very sensitive **peritrichial nerve ending** wrapped around the base and shaft of the hair follicle. The movement of the hair is sufficient to stimulate the nerve ending of this receptor.

Hypodermis

The hypodermis, or subcutaneous layer of the skin, is a deeper continuation of

Figure 11–12

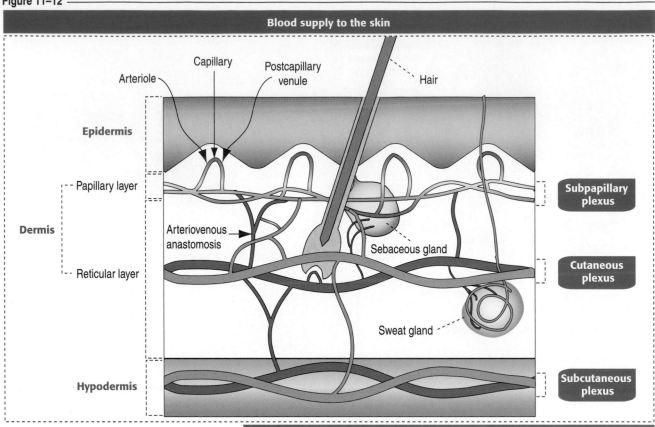

Blood supply to the skin

the dermis. It consists of loose connective tissue and adipose cells forming a layer of variable thickness depending on its location in the body. No adipose tissue is found in the subcutaneous portion of the eyelids, clitoris, or penis.

Skin appendages: Hairs, glands, and fingernails
Hairs

During development, the epidermis and dermis interact to develop sweat glands and appendages, such as hairs. A hair follicle primordium (called the **hair germ**) forms as a cell aggregate in the basal layer of the epidermis, induced by signaling molecules derived from fibroblasts of the dermal mesoderm.

As basal epidermal cell clusters extend into the dermis, dermal fibroblasts form a small nodule (called a **dermal papilla**) under the hair germ. The dermal papilla pushes into the core of the hair germ, whose cells divide and differentiate to form the keratinized hair shaft. Melanocytes present in the hair germ produce and transfer melanin into the shaft.

A bulbous swelling (called the **follicular bulb**) on the side of the hair germ contains stem cells—**clonogenic keratinocytes**—that can migrate and regenerate the hair shaft, the epidermis, and sebaceous glands (see Figure 11–15) in response to morphogenetic signals.

The first hair in the human embryo is thin, unpigmented, and spaced, and is called **lanugo**. Lanugo is shed before birth and replaced by short colorless hair called **vellus**. Terminal hair replaces vellus, which remains in the so-called hairless parts of the skin (such as the forehead of the adult and armpits of infants).

Hair follicles are constantly renewing, alternating phases of growth (**anagen**) with regression (**catagen**) and rest (**telogen**).

The hairs are filamentous keratinized structures present almost all over the body surface, except on the thick skin of the palms and soles, the sides of fingers

Figure 11–13

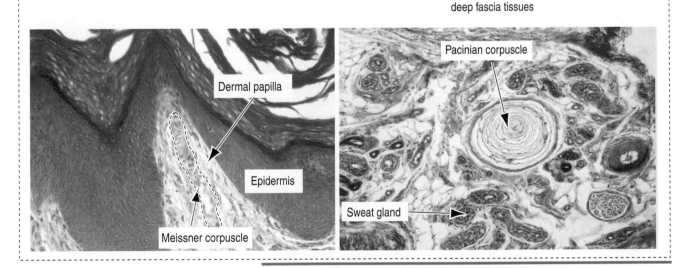

Sensory receptors of the skin

Meissner corpuscle
Present in dermal papilla
Tactile receptor

Merkel cell
Neural crest-derived
cell in the basal layer
of the epidermis
Tactile receptor (high
resolution)

Free nerve endings
Lack myelin or
Schwann cells
Respond to pain and
temperature

Ruffini end organ
Responds to
stretching **Pacinian**
corpuscle
sensitive to pressure

Peritrichial nerve
ending
Nerve fibers wrapped
around the base and
shaft of the hair
follicle; stimulated by
hair movement

Epidermis

Dermis

Hypodermis

Unmyelinated
nerve fiber

Collagen fiber

Discoid
epithelioid
tactile cells

Myelinated
nerve fiber

Connective tissue
capsule

Neurotransmitter

Merkel disk
(nerve
ending)

Collagen fiber

Ruffini end
organ

Pacinian
corpuscle

Sebaceous
gland

Hair
follicle

Present in fingers, hand,
foot, front of forearm, lips,
and tongue

Present in nonhairy
and hairy skin

Found in epidermis
and corneal
epithelium

Ruffini end organ
Present in skin and joint
capsule
Pacinian corpuscle
Found in hypodermis and
deep fascia tissues

Dermal papilla

Epidermis

Meissner corpuscle

Pacinian corpuscle

Sweat gland

and toes, the nipples, and the glans penis and the clitoris, among others.

Each hair consists of two parts (Figure 11–14): (1) **hair follicle**, and (2) the **hair shaft**.

The hair follicle is a tubular invagination of the epidermis and is responsible for the growth of hair. The **hair bulb** is the end portion of the invaginated hair follicle. A vascularized connective tissue core (**dermal papilla**) projects into the hair bulb.

The hair follicle consists of (1) the **external root sheath**, a downgrowth of the epidermis; and (2) the **internal root sheath**, made up of three layers of **soft keratin**.

A cross section of the hair shaft of thick hair reveals three concentric zones

Figure 11–14

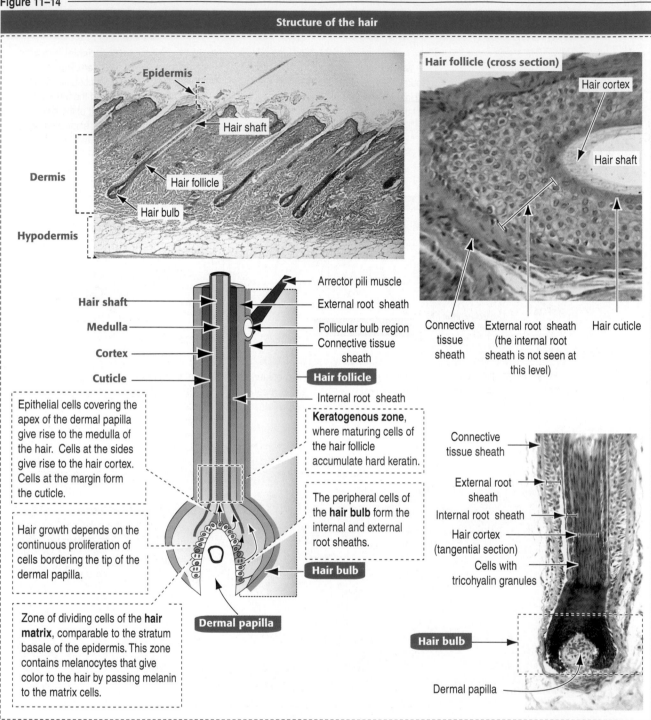

| Structure of the hair |

Epidermis

Hair shaft

Dermis

Hair follicle

Hair bulb

Hypodermis

Hair follicle (cross section)

Hair cortex

Hair shaft

Connective tissue sheath

External root sheath (the internal root sheath is not seen at this level)

Hair cuticle

Arrector pili muscle

Hair shaft

External root sheath

Medulla

Follicular bulb region

Connective tissue sheath

Cortex

Hair follicle

Cuticle

Internal root sheath

Epithelial cells covering the apex of the dermal papilla give rise to the medulla of the hair. Cells at the sides give rise to the hair cortex. Cells at the margin form the cuticle.

Keratogenous zone, where maturing cells of the hair follicle accumulate hard keratin.

The peripheral cells of the **hair bulb** form the internal and external root sheaths.

Hair growth depends on the continuous proliferation of cells bordering the tip of the dermal papilla.

Hair bulb

Dermal papilla

Zone of dividing cells of the **hair matrix**, comparable to the stratum basale of the epidermis. This zone contains melanocytes that give color to the hair by passing melanin to the matrix cells.

Connective tissue sheath

External root sheath

Internal root sheath

Hair cortex (tangential section)

Cells with trichohyalin granules

Hair bulb

Dermal papilla

containing keratinized cells: (1) the **cuticle**, (2) the **cortex**, and (3) the **medulla** (the last is absent in thin hair). The hair shaft consists of **hard keratin**.

The hair follicle is surrounded by a connective tissue layer. The **arrector pili muscle** is attached to the **follicular bulge**.

The keratinization of the hair and internal root sheath occurs in a region called the **keratogenous zone**, the transition zone between maturing epidermal cells and hard keratin.

The color of the hair depends on the amount and distribution of melanin in the hair shaft. Few melanosomes are seen in the blond hair. Few melanocytes and melanin are seen in the gray hair. Red hair has a chemically distinct melanin, and

Figure 11–15

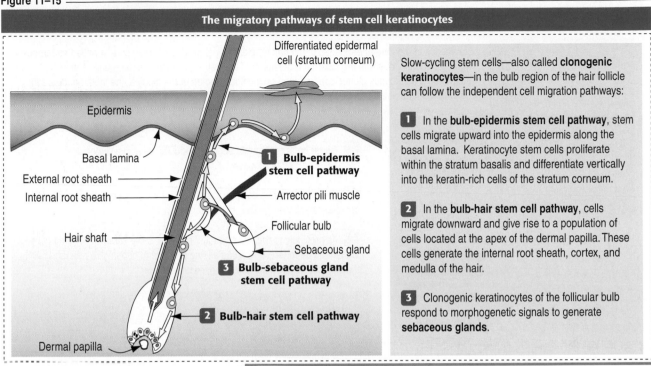

The migratory pathways of stem cell keratinocytes

Differentiated epidermal cell (stratum corneum)

Epidermis

Basal lamina

External root sheath

Internal root sheath

Hair shaft

1 **Bulb-epidermis stem cell pathway**

Arrector pili muscle

Follicular bulb

Sebaceous gland

3 **Bulb-sebaceous gland stem cell pathway**

2 **Bulb-hair stem cell pathway**

Dermal papilla

Slow-cycling stem cells—also called **clonogenic keratinocytes**—in the bulb region of the hair follicle can follow the independent cell migration pathways:

1 In the **bulb-epidermis stem cell pathway**, stem cells migrate upward into the epidermis along the basal lamina. Keratinocyte stem cells proliferate within the stratum basalis and differentiate vertically into the keratin-rich cells of the stratum corneum.

2 In the **bulb-hair stem cell pathway**, cells migrate downward and give rise to a population of cells located at the apex of the dermal papilla. These cells generate the internal root sheath, cortex, and medulla of the hair.

3 Clonogenic keratinocytes of the follicular bulb respond to morphogenetic signals to generate **sebaceous glands**.

melanosomes are round rather than ellipsoid. A structure that is not recognized in routine histological sections of hairs is the **peritrichial nerve endings**.

Clinical significance: Keratinocyte stem cells and the hair follicle

The epidermis is contiguous with the external root sheath of the hair follicle, a structure responsible for developing the hair shaft. When the epidermis is lost in severely burned patients, clonogenic keratinocyte stem cells migrate from the hair follicle to reestablish the epidermis.

As we have seen, hair follicle stem cells are located in the **follicular bulb**, a part of the external root sheath and the attachment site of the arrector pili muscle. Follicular bulb stem cells are responsible for forming the lower region of the hair follicle (internal root sheath, cortex, and medulla of the hair) and sebaceous glands. Stem cells can also migrate to the epidermis in response to penetrating skin wounds and participate in regeneration (Figure 11–15).

Glands

The glands of the skin are (1) the **sebaceous glands** (Figure 11–16), (2) the **sweat glands** (eccrine and apocrine sweat glands, Figures 11–17 and 11–18), and (3) the **mammary glands**. The mammary gland is discussed in Chapter 23, Fertilization, Placentation, and Lactation.

The **sebaceous gland** is a **holocrine simple saccular gland** extending over the entire skin except for the palms and soles. The **secretory portion** of the sebaceous gland lies in the **dermis**, and **the excretory duct opens into the neck of the hair follicle**. Sebaceous glands can be independent of the hairs and open directly on the surface of the skin of the lips, the corner of the mouth, the glans penis, the labia minora, and the mammary nipple.

The secretory portion of the sebaceous gland consists of groups of alveoli connected to the excretory duct by a short ductule. Each alveolus is lined by cells resembling multilocular adipocytes with numerous small lipid droplets. The excretory duct is lined by stratified squamous epithelium continuous with the external root sheath of the hair and the epidermis (the malpighian layer). The oily secretion of the gland (**sebum**) is released on the surface of the hair and the epidermis.

Figure 11–16

Sebaceous gland: Holocrine secretion

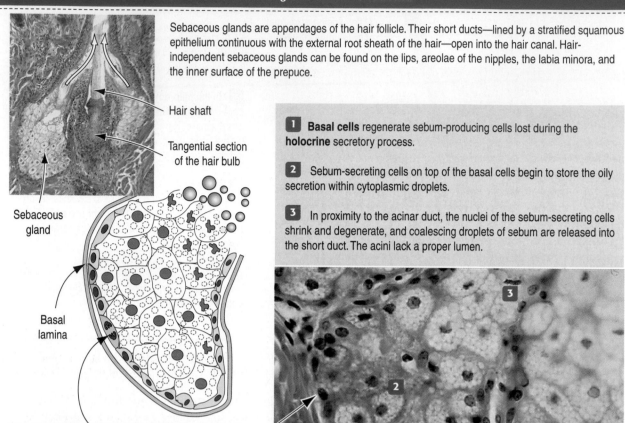

Sebaceous glands are appendages of the hair follicle. Their short ducts—lined by a stratified squamous epithelium continuous with the external root sheath of the hair—open into the hair canal. Hair-independent sebaceous glands can be found on the lips, areolae of the nipples, the labia minora, and the inner surface of the prepuce.

Hair shaft

Tangential section of the hair bulb

Sebaceous gland

Basal lamina

1 **Basal cells** regenerate sebum-producing cells lost during the **holocrine** secretory process.

2 Sebum-secreting cells on top of the basal cells begin to store the oily secretion within cytoplasmic droplets.

3 In proximity to the acinar duct, the nuclei of the sebum-secreting cells shrink and degenerate, and coalescing droplets of sebum are released into the short duct. The acini lack a proper lumen.

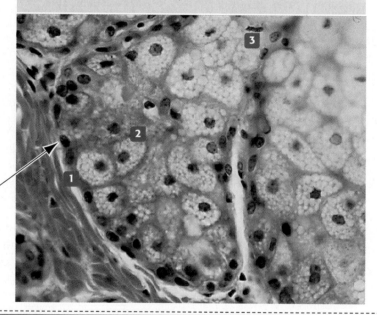

Basal cells divide by mitosis and accumulate lipids as they move into the central part of the acinus.

Sebum is the oily secretion of sebaceous cells. Sebum is released by a **holocrine mechanism**, resulting in the destruction of entire cells which become part of the secretion.

Sweat glands

There are two types of sweat glands: (1) **eccrine (merocrine) sweat glands** (see Figure 11–17), and (2) **apocrine sweat glands** (see Figure 11–18).

The eccrine sweat gland is a simple coiled tubular gland with a role in the **control of body temperature**. Eccrine sweat glands are innervated by **cholinergic nerves. The secretory portion** of the eccrine sweat gland (see Figure 11–17) is a convoluted tube composed of three cell types: (1) **clear cells**, (2) **dark cells**, and (3) **myoepithelial cells**.

The **clear cells** are separated from each other by **intercellular canaliculi**, show an infolded basal domain with abundant mitochondria, rest on a basal lamina, and secrete most of the water and electrolytes (mainly Na^+ and Cl^-) of sweat.

The **dark cells** rest on top of the clear cells. Dark cells secrete glycoproteins.

Myoepithelial cells are found between the basal lamina and the clear cells.

The **excretory portion** of the eccrine sweat gland is lined by a bilayer of cuboid cells that partially reabsorb NaCl and water under the influence of **aldosterone**. The reabsorption of NaCl by the excretory duct is deficient in patients with cystic fibrosis (see below). The duct follows a **helical path** when it approaches the epidermis and opens on its surface at a **sweat pore**. Within the epidermis, the

Figure 11–17

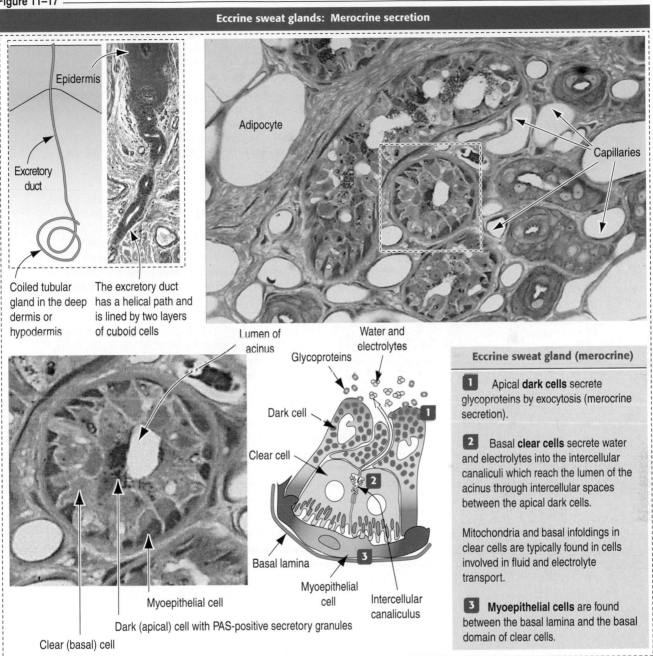

Eccrine sweat glands: Merocrine secretion

Epidermis

Excretory duct

Coiled tubular gland in the deep dermis or hypodermis

The excretory duct has a helical path and is lined by two layers of cuboid cells

Adipocyte

Capillaries

Lumen of acinus

Glycoproteins

Water and electrolytes

Dark cell

Clear cell

Basal lamina

Myoepithelial cell

Intercellular canaliculus

Myoepithelial cell

Dark (apical) cell with PAS-positive secretory granules

Clear (basal) cell

Eccrine sweat gland (merocrine)

1 Apical **dark cells** secrete glycoproteins by exocytosis (merocrine secretion).

2 Basal **clear cells** secrete water and electrolytes into the intercellular canaliculi which reach the lumen of the acinus through intercellular spaces between the apical dark cells.

Mitochondria and basal infoldings in clear cells are typically found in cells involved in fluid and electrolyte transport.

3 **Myoepithelial cells** are found between the basal lamina and the basal domain of clear cells.

excretory duct is surrounded by keratinocytes.

Apocrine sweat glands (see Figure 11–18) are coiled and occur in the axilla, mons pubis, and circumanal area. Apocrine sweat glands contain secretory acini larger than those in the eccrine sweat glands. The secretory portion is located in the dermis and hypodermis. The **excretory duct opens into the hair follicle** (instead of into the epidermis as in the eccrine sweat glands). Apocrine sweat glands are functional after puberty and are supplied by **adrenergic nerves**.

Two special examples of apocrine sweat glands are the **ceruminous glands** in the external auditory meatus and the **glands of Moll** of the margin of the eyelids.

The ceruminous glands produce **cerumen**, a pigmented lipid; the excretory duct opens, together with the ducts of sebaceous glands, into the hair follicles of the external auditory meatus.

The excretory duct of the glands of Moll opens into the free surface of the epidermis of the eyelid, or the eyelashes.

Figure 11–18

Apocrine sweat glands: Merocrine secretion

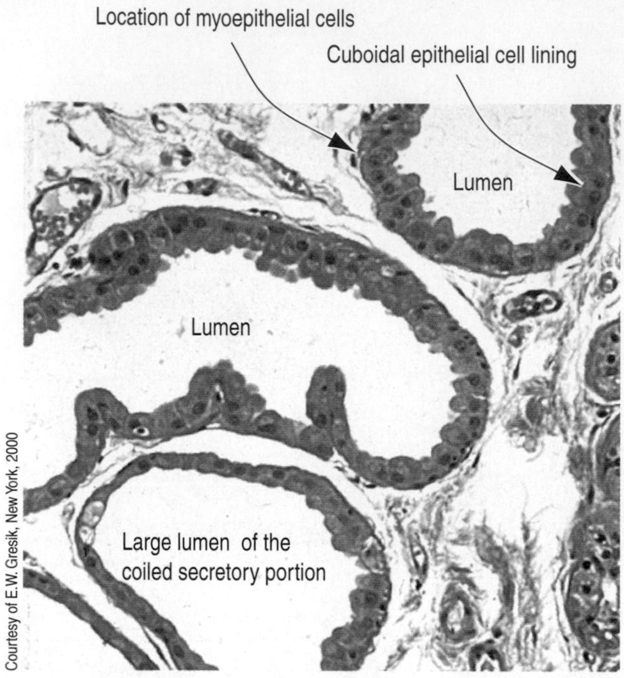

Location of myoepithelial cells

Cuboidal epithelial cell lining

Lumen

Lumen

Courtesy of E.W. Gresik, New York, 2000

Large lumen of the coiled secretory portion

Apocrine sweat gland

Apocrine sweat glands are found in the **axilla**, **circumanal region**, and in the **mons pubis**.

The **coiled region of apocrine glands is larger** (~ 3 mm in diameter) than that of the eccrine sweat glands (~0.4 mm in diameter).

Apocrine sweat glands are located in the dermis, and **the excretory duct opens into the canal of the hair follicle**.

The secretory cells are cuboid and **associated with myoepithelial cells at their basal surface**—as in the eccrine sweat glands. The **secretory activity starts at puberty**. Their secretion acquires a conspicuous odor after being modified by local bacteria.

Although called apocrine—because of the incorrect interpretation that the apical domain of the secretory cells is shed during secretion—these sweat glands **release their secretion by a merocrine process**.

Clinical significance: Sweat glands and cystic fibrosis

Cystic fibrosis is a genetic disorder of epithelial transport of chloride by the channel protein **CFTR**, **cystic fibrosis transmembrane conductance regulator**, encoded by the cystic fibrosis gene located on chromosome 7.

Exocrine glands and the epithelial lining of the respiratory, gastrointestinal, and reproductive tracts are affected by a mutation of CFTR. Recurrent pulmonary infections, pancreatic insufficiency, steatorrhea, hepatic cirrhosis, intestinal obstruction, and male infertility are clinical features of cystic fibrosis.

The **excretory ducts of sweat glands** are lined by epithelial cells containing CFTR involved in the transport of Cl^- (Figure 11–19). The CFTR channel opens when an agonist, such as acetylcholine, induces an increase in cyclic adenosine monophosphate (cAMP), followed by activation of protein kinase A, production of adenosine triphosphate (ATP) (see Chapter 3, Cell Signaling), and binding of ATP to two ATP-binding domains of CFTR.

Figure 11–19

Cystic fibrosis and sweat glands

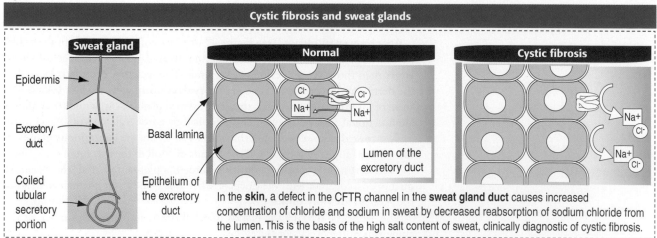

In the **skin**, a defect in the CFTR channel in the **sweat gland duct** causes increased concentration of chloride and sodium in sweat by decreased reabsorption of sodium chloride from the lumen. This is the basis of the high salt content of sweat, clinically diagnostic of cystic fibrosis.

Figure 11–20

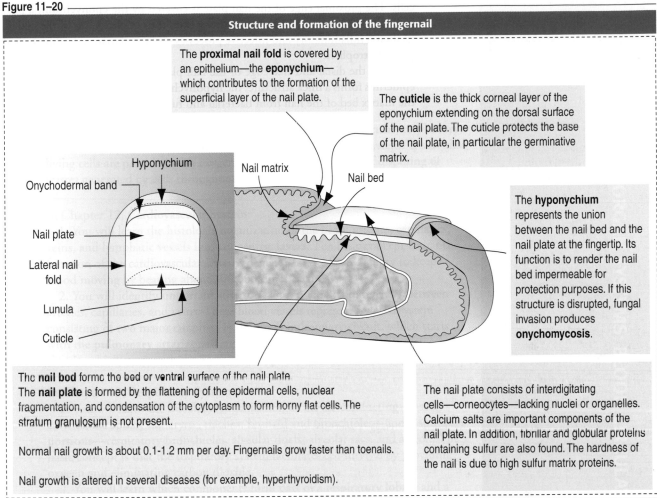

Structure and formation of the fingernail

The **proximal nail fold** is covered by an epithelium—the **eponychium**—which contributes to the formation of the superficial layer of the nail plate.

The **cuticle** is the thick corneal layer of the eponychium extending on the dorsal surface of the nail plate. The cuticle protects the base of the nail plate, in particular the germinative matrix.

Hyponychium

Onychodermal band

Nail matrix

Nail bed

Nail plate

Lateral nail fold

Lunula

Cuticle

The **hyponychium** represents the union between the nail bed and the nail plate at the fingertip. Its function is to render the nail bed impermeable for protection purposes. If this structure is disrupted, fungal invasion produces **onychomycosis**.

The **nail bed** forms the bed or ventral surface of the nail plate.
The **nail plate** is formed by the flattening of the epidermal cells, nuclear fragmentation, and condensation of the cytoplasm to form horny flat cells. The stratum granulosum is not present.

Normal nail growth is about 0.1-1.2 mm per day. Fingernails grow faster than toenails.

Nail growth is altered in several diseases (for example, hyperthyroidism).

The nail plate consists of interdigitating cells—corneocytes—lacking nuclei or organelles. Calcium salts are important components of the nail plate. In addition, fibrillar and globular proteins containing sulfur are also found. The hardness of the nail is due to high sulfur matrix proteins.

A defect in CFTR in sweat gland ducts leads to a **decrease in the reabsorption of sodium chloride from the lumen**, resulting in **increased concentrations of chloride in sweat**.

In the respiratory epithelium (see Chapter 13, Respiratory System), a defect in CFTR results in a **reduction or loss of chloride secretion into the airways**, active reabsorption of sodium and water, and a consequent decrease in the water content of the protective mucus blanket. Dehydrated mucus causes defective mucociliary action and predisposes to recurrent pulmonary infections.

Fingernails

The nails are hard keratin plates on the dorsal surface of the terminal phalanges of the fingers and toes (Figure 11–20). The **nail plate** covers the **nail bed**, the surface of the skin which consists of the stratum basale and stratum spinosum only.

The body of the plate is surrounded by lateral **nail folds** having a structure similar to that of the adjacent epidermis of the skin. When the lateral nail folds break down, an inflammatory process develops. This process is called **onychocryptosis** and is frequently observed in the nail of the first toe (ingrown nail).

The proximal edge of the plate is the **root** or **matrix** of the nail (where the whitish crescent-shaped **lunula** is located), in close proximity to the **nail matrix**, a region of the epidermis responsible for the formation of the nail substance. The distal portion of the plate is the free edge of the nail.

The nail plate consists of compact scales corresponding to cornified epithelial

lated pump. The heart is the major determinant of systemic blood pressure.

The cardiac wall consists of three layers:

1. **Endocardium**, consisting of an **endothelial lining** and **subendothelial connective tissue**.

2. **Myocardium**, a functional syncytium of striated cardiac muscle fibers forming three major types of cardiac muscle: **atrial muscle**, **ventricular muscle**, and **specialized excitatory** and **conductive muscle fibers**.

3. **Epicardium**, a low-friction surface lined by a **mesothelium** in contact with the serosal pericardial space.

The heart is composed of two syncytia of muscle fibers: (1) the **atrial syncytium**, forming the walls of the two atria; and (2) the **ventricular syncytium**, forming the wall of the two ventricles. Atria and ventricles are separated by **fibrous connective tissue** surrounding the valvular openings between the atria and the ventricles.

The conductive system of the heart

The heart has two specialized conductive systems:

1. The **sinus node**, or **sinoatrial** (S-A) node, which generates impulses to cause rhythmic contractions of the cardiac muscle.

2. A specialized **conductive system,** consisting of the **internodal pathway,** which

---

Figure 12–2

The heart: Purkinje fibers

Purkinje fibers are bundles of impulse-conducing cardiac fibers extending from the atrioventricular node. They can be found beneath the endocardium lining the interventricular septum.

Purkinje fibers can be distinguished from regular cardiocytes by their **location**, their **larger size**, and **lighter cytoplasmic staining** (glycogen content).

Subendocardial connective tissue layer consisting of collagen and elastic fibers synthesized by fibroblasts. This layer contains small blood vessels, nerves, and bundles of the conduction system (**Purkinje fibers**). The subendocardial layer is not present in papillary muscles and chordae tendineae inserted at the free edges of the mitral and tricuspid valves.

Endocardium
(endothelial cell lining)

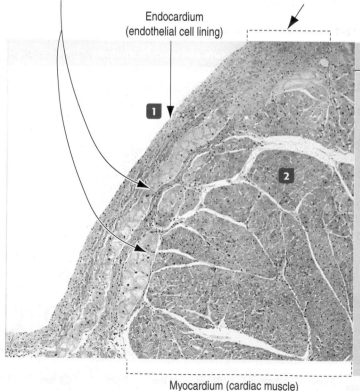

The heart

The wall of the heart consists of three layers:
1 **Endocardium**, homologous to the tunica intima of blood vessels.
2 **Myocardium**, continuous with the tunica media of blood vessels.
3 **Epicardium**, similar to the tunica adventitia of blood vessels (not shown in the illustration).

The myocardium consists of three cell types:
1. **Contractile cardiocytes**, which contract to pump blood through the circulation.
2. **Myoendocrine cardiocytes**, producing atrial natriuretic factor.
3. **Nodal cardiocytes**, specialized to control the rhythmic contraction of the heart. These cells are located in: (1) the **sinoatrial node**, at the superior vena cava-right atrium junction, and (2) the **atrioventricular node**, present under the endocardium of the interatrial and interventricular septa.

Myocardium (cardiac muscle)

Figure 12–3

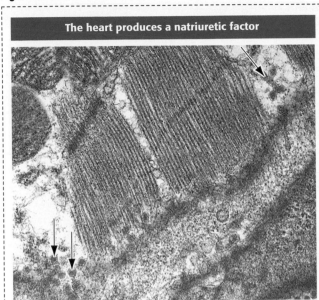

The heart produces a natriuretic factor

Atrial cardiocytes contain membrane-bound storage granules and a more highly developed Golgi apparatus and rough endoplasmic reticulum than their ventricular counterparts. The density of these granules in atrial cells can be altered by varying the intake of salt and water.

Atrial cell granules (arrows) contain a potent polypeptide hormone, named **atrial natriuretic factor** (**ANF**), that stimulates diuresis (Gk. *diourein*, to urinate) and natriuresis (Lat. *natrium*, sodium + Gk. *diourein*). ANF also relaxes the cardiovascular muscle by antagonizing the actions of **vasopressin** (a polypeptide released from the neurohypophysis) and **angiotensin II** (a peptide derived from the **renin**-induced breakdown of **angiotensinogen**, a protein produced in liver and released into systemic blood). ANF prevents sodium and water reabsorption from causing **hypervolemia** (abnormal increase in the volume of circulating fluid in the body) and hypertension that can result in cardiac failure. Increasing pressure across the atrial wall seems to be the principal mediator of ANF release as a prohormone. Once outside the atrial cell, the ANF prohormone undergoes a rapid enzymatic cleavage to produce the principal form of circulating ANF.

conducts the impulse from the S-A node to the atrioventricular (A-V) node); the A-V node, in which the atrial impulse is delayed before reaching the ventricles; the **atrioventricular bundle**, which conducts the impulse from the atria to the ventricles; and the **left and right bundles of Purkinje fibers**, which conduct the impulse to all parts of the ventricles (Figure 12–2).

When stretched, cardiac muscle cells of the atrium (atrial cardiocytes) secrete a peptide called **atrial natriuretic factor** (Figure 12–3) that stimulates both diuresis and excretion of sodium in urine (natriuresis) by increasing the glomerular filtration rate. By this mechanism, the blood volume is reduced and the stretching of the atrial cardiocytes is relieved.

Histologically (see Figure 7–14 in Chapter 7, Muscle Tissue), individual cardiac muscle cells have a central nucleus and are linked to each other by **intercalated disks**. The presence of **gap junctions** in the longitudinal segment of the intercalated disks between connected cardiac muscle cells allows free diffusion of ions and the rapid spread of the action potential from cell to cell. The electrical resistance is low because gap junctions bypass the **transverse** components of the intercalated disk (**fasciae adherentes** and **desmosomes**).

Differences between cardiac muscle fibers and Purkinje fibers

The **Purkinje fibers** lie **beneath the endocardium** lining the two sides of the interventricular septum (see Figure 12–2). They can be distinguished from cardiac muscle fibers because they contain a **reduced number of myofibrils located at the periphery of the fiber** and the **diameter of the fiber is larger**, in addition, they give a positive reaction for **acetylcholinesterase**, and they contain abundant **glycogen**. Purkinje fibers lose these specific characteristics when they merge with cardiac muscle fibers. Like cardiac muscle fibers, Purkinje fibers are striated and are linked to each other by atypical intercalated disks.

Arteries

Arteries conduct blood from the heart to the capillaries. They store some of the pumped blood during each cardiac systole to ensure continued flow through the capillaries during cardiac diastole.

Arteries are organized in three major **tunics** or layers (Figure 12–4):

1. The **tunica intima** is the innermost coat. It consists of an **endothelial lining** (continuous with the endocardium, the inner lining of the heart), an intermedi-

Figure 12–4

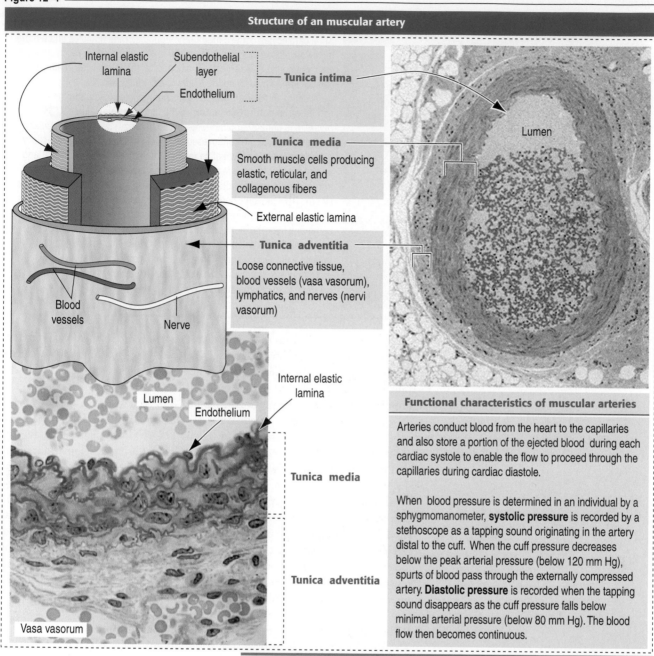

Structure of an muscular artery

Internal elastic lamina
Subendothelial layer
Endothelium
Tunica intima

Tunica media
Smooth muscle cells producing elastic, reticular, and collagenous fibers

External elastic lamina

Tunica adventitia
Loose connective tissue, blood vessels (vasa vasorum), lymphatics, and nerves (nervi vasorum)

Blood vessels

Nerve

Lumen

Lumen

Endothelium

Internal elastic lamina

Tunica media

Tunica adventitia

Vasa vasorum

Functional characteristics of muscular arteries

Arteries conduct blood from the heart to the capillaries and also store a portion of the ejected blood during each cardiac systole to enable the flow to proceed through the capillaries during cardiac diastole.

When blood pressure is determined in an individual by a sphygmomanometer, **systolic pressure** is recorded by a stethoscope as a tapping sound originating in the artery distal to the cuff. When the cuff pressure decreases below the peak arterial pressure (below 120 mm Hg), spurts of blood pass through the externally compressed artery. **Diastolic pressure** is recorded when the tapping sound disappears as the cuff pressure falls below minimal arterial pressure (below 80 mm Hg). The blood flow then becomes continuous.

ate layer of loose connective tissue (the **subendothelium**), and an external layer of elastic fibers, the **internal elastic lamina**.

2. The **tunica media** is the middle coat. It consists mainly of smooth muscle cells surrounded by a variable number of collagen fibers, extracellular matrix, and elastic sheaths with irregular gaps (fenestrated —perforated— elastic membranes).

Collagen fibers provide a supporting framework for smooth muscle cells and limit the distensibility of the wall of the vessel. Veins have a higher content of collagen than arteries.

3. The **tunica externa**, or **adventitia**, is the outer coat and consists mainly of connective tissue. An external elastic lamina can be seen separating the tunica media from the adventitia. The adventitia of large vessels (arteries and veins) contains small vessels (**vasa vasorum**) that penetrate the outer portion of the tunica media to supply oxygen and nutrients.

From the heart to the capillaries, arteries can be classified into three major

Figure 12–5

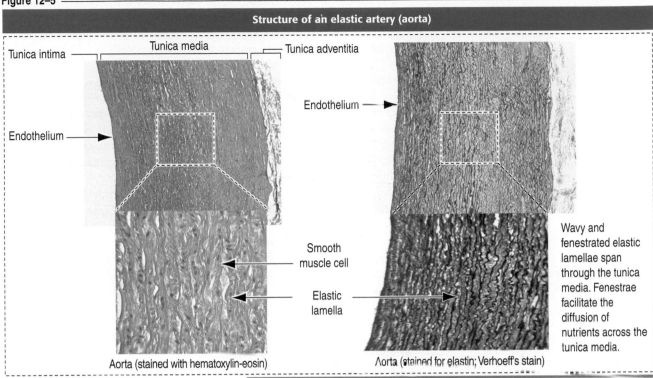

Structure of an elastic artery (aorta)

Tunica intima — | Tunica media | Tunica adventitia

Endothelium

Endothelium

Smooth muscle cell

Elastic lamella

Wavy and fenestrated elastic lamellae span through the tunica media. Fenestrae facilitate the diffusion of nutrients across the tunica media.

Aorta (stained with hematoxylin-eosin)

Aorta (stained for elastin; Verhoeff's stain)

groups: (1) **large elastic arteries**, (2) **medium-sized muscular arteries** (see Figure 12–4), and (3) **small arteries** and **arterioles**.

Large elastic arteries are conducting vessels

The **aorta** and its largest branches (the **brachiocephalic, common carotid, subclavian**, and **common iliac** arteries) are **elastic arteries** (Figure 12–5). They are **conducting arteries** because they conduct blood from the heart to the medium-sized **distributing arteries**.

Large elastic arteries have two major characteristics: (1) They receive blood from heart under high pressure. (2) They keep blood circulating continuously while the heart is pumping intermittently. Because they distend during systole and recoil during diastole, elastic arteries can sustain a continuous blood flow despite the intermittent pumping action of the heart.

The **tunica intima** of the elastic arteries consists of the endothelium and the subendothelial connective tissue.

Large amounts of **fenestrated elastic sheaths** are found in the **tunica media**, with bundles of smooth muscle cells permeating the narrow spaces between the elastic lamellae. Collagen fibers are present in all tunics, but especially in the adventitia. We have seen in Chapter 4, Connective Tissue, that smooth muscle cells can synthesize **both elastic and collagen fibers**. Blood vessels (**vasa vasorum**), nerves (**nervi vasorum**), and **lymphatics** can be recognized in the tunica adventitia of large elastic arteries.

Clinical significance: Aortic aneurysms

The two major types of aortic aneurysm are the **syphilitic aneurysm** (relatively rare because syphilis is no longer common) and the **abdominal aneurysm**. The latter is caused by a weakening of the aortic wall produced by atherosclerosis (see Figure 12–14). Aortic aneurysms generate murmurs caused by blood turbulence in the dilated aortic segment. A severe complication is rupture of the aneurysm followed by immediate death.

Recall our previous discussion of the **Marfan syndrome** (see Chapter 4, Connective Tissue), an autosomal dominant defect associated with aortic dissecting aneurysm and skeletal and ocular abnormalities due to mutations in the fibrillin 1 gene. Fibrillins are major components of the elastic fibers found in the aorta, periosteum, and suspensory ligament of the lens.

Medium-sized muscular arteries are distributing vessels

There is a gradual transition from large arteries, to medium-sized arteries, to small arteries and arterioles. Medium-sized arteries are **distributing vessels**, allowing a selective distribution of blood to different organs in response to functional needs. Examples of medium-sized arteries include the radial, tibial, popliteal, axillary, splenic, mesenteric, and intercostal arteries. The diameter of medium-sized muscular arteries is about 3 mm and greater.

The **tunica intima** consists of three layers: (1) the **endothelium**, (2) the **subendothelium**, and (3) the **internal elastic lamina** (see Figure 12–4).

The internal elastic lamina is a fenestrated band of elastic fibers that often shows folds in sections of fixed tissue owing to contraction of the smooth muscle cell layer (tunica media).

The **tunica media** shows a significant reduction in elastic components and an increase in smooth muscle fibers. In the larger vessels of this group, a fenestrated **external elastic lamina** can be seen at the junction of the tunica media and the adventitia.

Arterioles are resistance vessels

Arterioles are the final branches of the arterial system. Arterioles regulate the distribution of blood to different capillary beds by **vasoconstriction** and **vasodilation** in localized regions. Partial contraction (known as **tone**) of the vascular smooth muscle exists in arterioles. Arterioles are structurally adapted for vasoconstriction and vasodilation because their walls contain circularly arranged

Figure 12–6

Arterioles: Resistance vessels

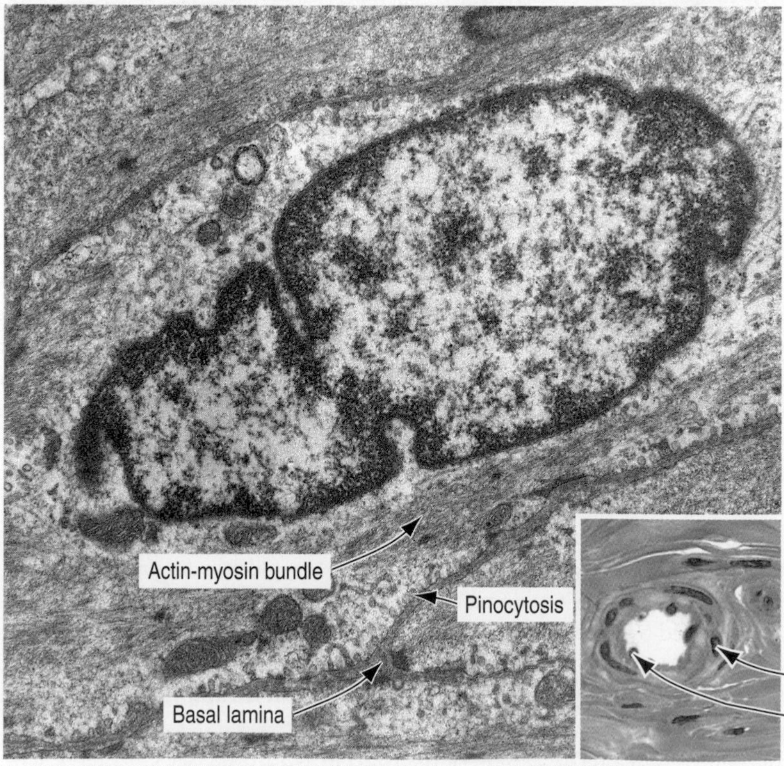

Vascular smooth muscle cells of arterioles

Vascular smooth muscle cells have a significant role in the control of total peripheral resistance, arterial and venous tone, and blood distribution throughout the body.

The cytoplasm of vascular smooth muscle cells contains actin and myosin filaments whose contraction is controlled by calcium. The increase in calcium concentration occurs through voltage-gated calcium channels (known as **electromechanical coupling**) and through receptor-mediated calcium channels (known as **pharmacomechanical coupling**). Both channels are present in the plasma membrane. Calcium can also be released from cytoplasmic storage sites (endoplasmic reticulum). Smooth muscle cells lack troponin.

The constant blood flow depends on a **myogenic mechanism**: arteriolar smooth muscle cells contract in response to increased transmural pressure and relax when the pressure decreases.

Actin-myosin bundle
Pinocytosis
Basal lamina
Vascular smooth muscle cell
Endothelial cell

Figure 12–7

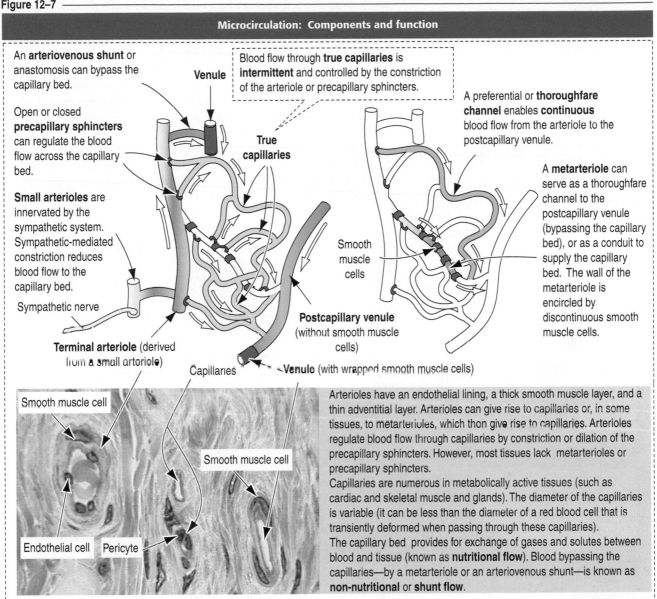

Microcirculation: Components and function

An **arteriovenous shunt** or anastomosis can bypass the capillary bed.

Open or closed **precapillary sphincters** can regulate the blood flow across the capillary bed.

Small arterioles are innervated by the sympathetic system. Sympathetic-mediated constriction reduces blood flow to the capillary bed.

Sympathetic nerve

Terminal arteriole (derived from a small arteriole)

Capillaries

Venule

True capillaries

Smooth muscle cells

Postcapillary venule (without smooth muscle cells)

Venule (with wrapped smooth muscle cells)

Blood flow through **true capillaries** is **intermittent** and controlled by the constriction of the arteriole or precapillary sphincters.

A preferential or **thoroughfare channel** enables **continuous** blood flow from the arteriole to the postcapillary venule.

A **metarteriole** can serve as a thoroughfare channel to the postcapillary venule (bypassing the capillary bed), or as a conduit to supply the capillary bed. The wall of the metarteriole is encircled by discontinuous smooth muscle cells.

Smooth muscle cell

Smooth muscle cell

Endothelial cell   Pericyte

Arterioles have an endothelial lining, a thick smooth muscle layer, and a thin adventitial layer. Arterioles can give rise to capillaries or, in some tissues, to metarterioles, which then give rise to capillaries. Arterioles regulate blood flow through capillaries by constriction or dilation of the precapillary sphincters. However, most tissues lack metarterioles or precapillary sphincters.

Capillaries are numerous in metabolically active tissues (such as cardiac and skeletal muscle and glands). The diameter of the capillaries is variable (it can be less than the diameter of a red blood cell that is transiently deformed when passing through these capillaries).

The capillary bed provides for exchange of gases and solutes between blood and tissue (known as **nutritional flow**). Blood bypassing the capillaries—by a metarteriole or an arteriovenous shunt—is known as **non-nutritional** or **shunt flow**.

smooth muscle fibers. Arterioles are regarded as **resistance vessels** and are the major determinants of systemic blood pressure (Figure 12–6).

The diameter of arterioles-small arteries ranges from 20 to 130 μm. Since the lumen is small, these blood vessels can be closed down to generate high resistance to blood flow. The **tunica intima** has an endothelium, subendothelium, and internal elastic lamina. The **tunica media** consists of two to five concentric layers of smooth muscle cells. The **tunica adventitia**, or externa, contains slight collagenous tissue, binding the vessel to its surroundings.

The segment beyond the arteriole proper is the **metarteriole**, the terminal branch of arterial system. It consists of one layer of muscle cells, often **discontinuous**, and represents an important local regulator of blood flow.

Capillaries are exchange vessels

Capillaries are extremely thin tubes formed by a single layer of highly permeable **endothelial cells** surrounded by a basal lamina. The diameter range of a capillary is about 5-10 μm, large enough to accommodate one red blood cell, and thin enough (0.5 μm) for gas diffusion.

The **microvascular bed**, the site of the **microcirculation** (Figure 12–7), is composed of the **terminal arteriole** (and **metarteriole**), the **capillary bed**, and the **postcapillary venules**. The capillary bed consists of slightly large capillaries (called **preferential** or **thoroughfare channels**), where blood flow is **continuous**, and small capillaries, called the **true capillaries**, where blood flow is **intermittent**.

The amount of blood entering the microvascular bed is regulated by the contraction of smooth muscle fibers of the **precapillary sphincters** located where true capillaries arise from the arteriole or metarteriole. The capillary circulation

Figure 12–8

Structure of capillaries

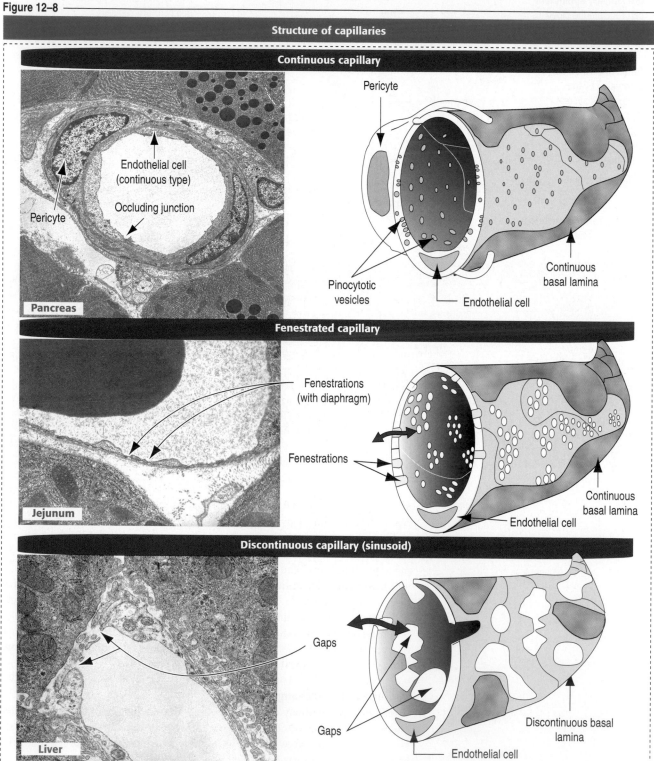

Continuous capillary

Pancreas

Fenestrated capillary

Jejunum

Discontinuous capillary (sinusoid)

Liver

Figure 12–9

Types of capillaries

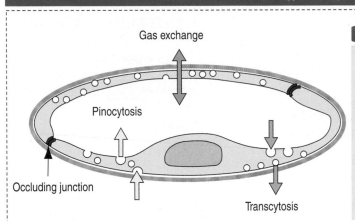

Continuous capillary

Endothelial cells have a complete (continuous) cytoplasm. This type is found in muscle, brain, thymus, bone, lung, and other tissues.

Caveolae and vesicles transport substances through the cytoplasm in a bidirectional pathway (**transcytosis**). The intracytoplasmic vesicles are coated by the protein **caveolin**.

The **basal lamina** is **continuous**. In the lung, the thin endothelial cell cytoplasm allows diffusion of gases from the alveolus into the blood (CO_2) and from the blood into the alveolus (O_2).

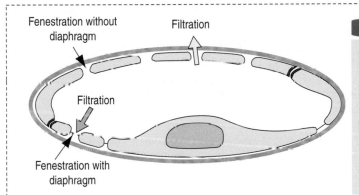

Fenestrated capillary

The endothelial cell has many fenestrae (10-100 nm in diameter) **with** or **without** a thin **diaphragm**. The **basal lamina** is **continuous**.

This type is present in tissues with substantial fluid transport (intestinal villi, choroid plexus, ciliary processes of the eye).

A fenestrated endothelial cell is present in the glomerular capillaries of the kidney supported by a significantly thicker basal lamina.

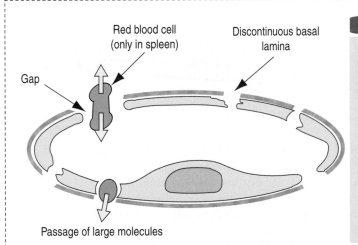

Discontinuous capillary

The gaps in discontinuous capillaries are larger than in fenestrated capillaries. The **basal lamina** is **discontinuous**. The gaps in venous sinusoids of the liver are wider than the discontinuous capillaries. The basal lamina is fragmented and often absent.

In spleen, the endothelial cells are elongated and protrude into the lumen. In spleen, the endothelial cells are elongated and protrude into the lumen. The **basal lamina** is **incomplete** and surrounded by reticular fibers. Blood cells can pass readily through the walls of the splenic sinuses (see Figure 10–25 in Chapter 10, Immune-Lymphatic System).

can be bypassed by channels (**through channels**) connecting terminal arterioles to postcapillary venules.

When functional demands decrease, most precapillary sphincters are closed, forcing the flow of blood into thoroughfare channels. **Arteriovenous shunts**, or **anastomoses**, are direct connections between arterioles and postcapillary venules and bypass the microvascular bed.

The three-dimensional design of the microvasculature varies from organ to organ. The local conditions of the tissues (concentration of nutrients and metabolites and other substances) can control local blood flow in small portions of a tissue area.

Figure 12–10

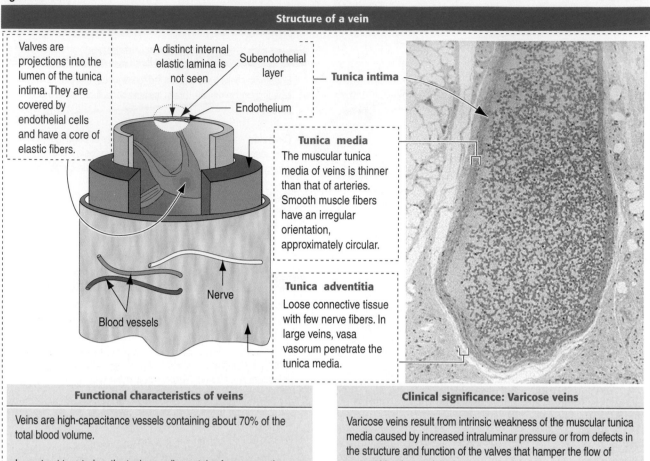

Structure of a vein

Valves are projections into the lumen of the tunica intima. They are covered by endothelial cells and have a core of elastic fibers.

A distinct internal elastic lamina is not seen

Subendothelial layer

Endothelium

Tunica intima

Tunica media
The muscular tunica media of veins is thinner than that of arteries. Smooth muscle fibers have an irregular orientation, approximately circular.

Tunica adventitia
Loose connective tissue with few nerve fibers. In large veins, vasa vasorum penetrate the tunica media.

Nerve

Blood vessels

Functional characteristics of veins

Veins are high-capacitance vessels containing about 70% of the total blood volume.

In contrast to arteries, the tunica media contains fewer smooth muscle cell bundles associated with reticular and elastic fibers.

Although veins of the extremities have intrinsic vasomotor activity, the transport of blood back to the heart depends on external forces provided by the contraction of surrounding skeletal muscles and on valves that ensure one-way blood flow.

Clinical significance: Varicose veins

Varicose veins result from intrinsic weakness of the muscular tunica media caused by increased intraluminar pressure or from defects in the structure and function of the valves that hamper the flow of venous blood toward the heart.

Although varicose veins can be seen in any vein in the body, the most common are the saphenous veins of the legs, veins in the anorectal region (**hemorrhoids**), in the veins of the lower esophagus (**esophageal varices**), and veins in the spermatic cord (**varicocele**).

Three types of capillaries: Continuous, fenestrated, and discontinuous

Three morphologic types of capillaries are recognized (Figures 12–8 and 12–9): **continuous**, **fenestrated**, and **discontinuous** (**sinusoids**).

Continuous capillaries are lined by a complete simple squamous endothelium and a basal lamina. **Pericytes** can occur between the endothelium and the basal lamina. Pericytes are undifferentiated cells that resemble modified smooth muscle cells and are distributed at random intervals in close contact with the basal lamina. Endothelial cells are linked by tight junctions and transport fluids and solutes by **caveolae** and **pinocytotic vesicles**. Continuous capillaries occur in brain, muscle, skin, thymus, and lung.

Fenestrated capillaries have **pores**, or **fenestrae**, with or without **diaphragms**. Fenestrated capillaries with a diaphragm are found in intestines, endocrine glands, and around kidney tubules. Fenestrated capillaries without a diaphragm are characteristic of the renal glomerulus. In this particular case, the basal lamina constitutes an important diffusion barrier, as we will analyze in Chapter 14, Urinary System.

Discontinuous capillaries are characterized by an incomplete endothelial lining and basal lamina, with **gaps** or **holes** between and within endothelial cells.

Discontinuous capillaries and sinusoids are found where an intimate relation is needed between blood and parenchyma (for example, in the liver and spleen).

Veins are capacitance or reservoir vessels

The venous system starts at the end of the capillary bed with a **postcapillary venule** that structurally resembles continuous capillaries but with a wider lumen. Postcapillary venules, the preferred site of migration of blood cells into tissues by a mechanism called **diapedesis** (Gk. *dia,* through; *pedan,* to leap), are tubes of endothelial cells supported by a basal lamina and an adventitia of collagen fibers and fibroblasts.

In lymphatic tissues, the endothelial cells are taller. **High endothelial venules are associated with the mechanism of homing of lymphocytes in lymphoid organs** (see Chapter 10, Immune-Lymphatic System).

Postcapillary venules converge to form **muscular venules**, which converge into **collecting venules**, leading to a series of **veins** of progressively larger diameter.

Veins have a relatively thin wall in comparison to arteries of the same size (Figure 12–10). The high capacitance of veins is attributable to the distensibility of their wall (**compliance vessels**) and, therefore, the content of blood is large relative to the volume of the veins. A small increase in the intraluminal pressure results in a large increase in the volume of contained blood.

Like arteries, veins consist of tunics. However, the distinction of a tunica media from a tunica adventitia is often not clear. The lumen is lined by an endothelium and a subjacent basal lamina. **A distinct inner elastic lamina is not seen.**

The **muscular tunica media** is thinner, and smooth muscles cells have an irregular orientation, approximately circular. A longitudinal orientation is observed in the iliac vein, brachiocephalic vein, superior and inferior vena cavae, portal vein and renal vein.

Figure 12–11

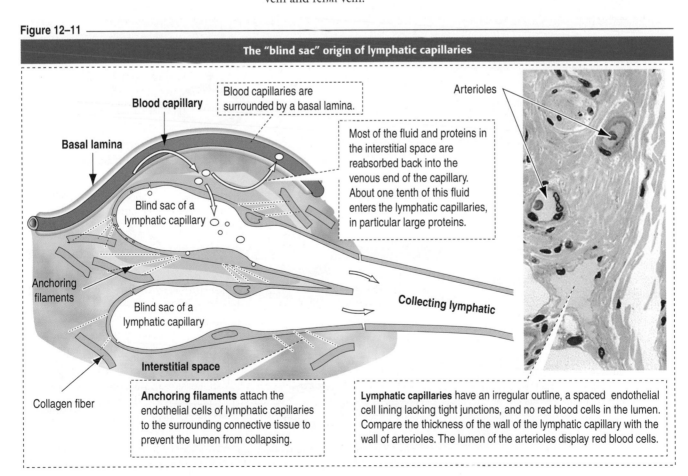

The "blind sac" origin of lymphatic capillaries

Blood capillary

Basal lamina

Blood capillaries are surrounded by a basal lamina.

Arterioles

Most of the fluid and proteins in the interstitial space are reabsorbed back into the venous end of the capillary. About one tenth of this fluid enters the lymphatic capillaries, in particular large proteins.

Blind sac of a lymphatic capillary

Anchoring filaments

Blind sac of a lymphatic capillary

Collecting lymphatic

Collagen fiber

Interstitial space

Anchoring filaments attach the endothelial cells of lymphatic capillaries to the surrounding connective tissue to prevent the lumen from collapsing.

Lymphatic capillaries have an irregular outline, a spaced endothelial cell lining lacking tight junctions, and no red blood cells in the lumen. Compare the thickness of the wall of the lymphatic capillary with the wall of arterioles. The lumen of the arterioles display red blood cells.

By intrinsic contraction

When collecting lymphatics or larger lymphatic vessels become expanded by lymph, the smooth muscle of the wall contracts. **Each segment of the lymphatic vessel between successive valves behaves like an automatic pump**: When the segment is filled with lymph, the wall contracts, the valve opens, and lymph flows into the next segment. This process continues along the entire length of the lymph vessel until the fluid is finally emptied.

By extrinsic contraction

In addition to the intrinsic contraction mechanism, external factors such as **contraction of the surrounding muscles** during exercise, arterial pulsations, and compression of tissues by forces outside the body compress the lymph vessel and cause pumping. When lymph drainage is impaired, excess fluid accumulates in the tissue spaces (**edema**).

The **tunica adventitia** consist of collagen fibers and fibroblasts with few nerve fibers. In large veins, the vasa vasorum penetrate the wall.

A typical characteristic of veins is the presence of **valves** to prevent reflux of blood. A valve is a projection into the lumen of the tunica intima, covered by endothelial cells and strengthened by elastic and collagen fibers.

Lymphatic vessels

Lymphatic capillaries form networks in tissue spaces and begin as dilated tubes with closed ends (blind tubes) in proximity to blood capillaries (Figure 12–11). Lymphatic capillaries collect tissue fluid, the **lymph**. Muscular contractions open spaces between lymphatic endothelial cells, **lacking tight junctions**, to permit the entrance of proteins (albumin) and large molecules that are then returned to the bloodstream, by tissue pressure, via two main trunks: (1) the large **thoracic duct**, and (2) the smaller **right lymphatic duct**.

Lymph nodes are distributed along the pathway of the lymph vessels to filter the lymph before reaching the thoracic and right lymphatic duct. A total of 2 to 3 L of lymph is produced each day.

The wall of a **lymphatic capillary** consists of a single layer of endothelial cells **lacking a complete basal lamina**. Bundles of filaments anchor the endothelium to the surrounding connective tissue. **Lymphatic capillaries can be found in most tissues. Exceptions are cartilage, bone, epithelia, the central nervous system, bone marrow, and placenta.**

Larger lymphatic vessels have three layers, similar to those of the small veins, but the lumen is larger.

The **tunica intima** consists of an endothelium and a thin subendothelial layer of connective tissue.

Figure 12–12

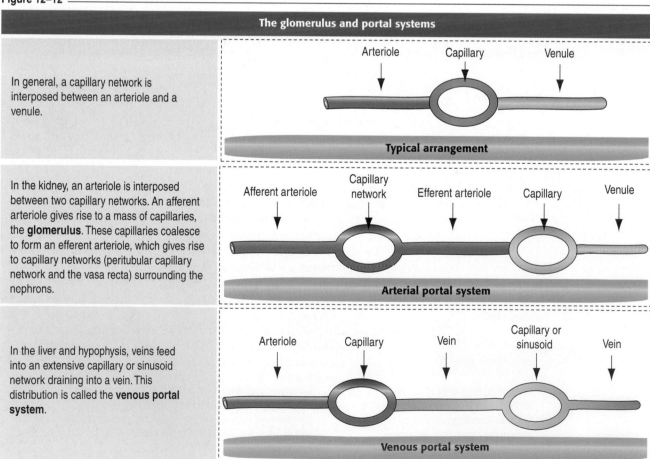

The glomerulus and portal systems

In general, a capillary network is interposed between an arteriole and a venule.

Typical arrangement

In the kidney, an arteriole is interposed between two capillary networks. An afferent arteriole gives rise to a mass of capillaries, the **glomerulus**. These capillaries coalesce to form an efferent arteriole, which gives rise to capillary networks (peritubular capillary network and the vasa recta) surrounding the nephrons.

Arterial portal system

In the liver and hypophysis, veins feed into an extensive capillary or sinusoid network draining into a vein. This distribution is called the **venous portal system**.

Venous portal system

The **tunica media** contains a few smooth muscle cells in a concentric arrangement separated by collagenous fibers.

The **tunica adventitia** is connective tissue with fibroelastic fibers.

Like veins, lymphatic vessels have **valves**, but their number is larger. The structure of the **thoracic duct** is similar to that of a medium-sized vein, but the muscular tunica media is more prominent.

Clinical significance: Edema

Edema occurs when the volume of interstitial fluid increases and exceeds the drainage capacity of the lymphatics, or lymphatic vessels become blocked. Subcutaneous tissue has the capacity to accumulate interstitial fluid and gives rise to clinical edema.

In patients with extensive capillary injury (burns), both intravascular fluid and plasma proteins escape into the interstitial space. Proteins accumulating in the interstitial compartment increase the oncotic pressure, leading to additional fluid loss due to the greater osmotic force outside the capillary bed.

Special capillary arrangements: Glomerulus and portal systems

In general, blood from an arteriole flows into a capillary network and is drained by a venule. There are two specialized capillary systems that depart from this standard arrangement (Figure 12–12): (1) the **glomerulus**, and (2) the **portal system**.

In the kidney, an **afferent arteriole** drains into a capillary network called the **glomerulus**. The glomerular capillaries coalesce to form an **efferent arteriole**, which branches into another capillary network called the **vasa recta**. The vasa recta surround the limbs of the loop of Henle and play a significant role in the formation of urine. The glomerulus system is essential for blood filtration in the renal corpuscle (see Chapter 14, Urinary System).

In the **portal system**, intestinal capillaries are drained by the portal vein to the liver. In the **liver**, the portal vein branches into venous sinusoids between cords of hepatocytes. Blood flows from the sinusoids into a collecting vein and then back to the heart via the inferior vena cava.

A similar portal system is observed in the hypophysis. Venules connect the primary sinusoidal plexus of the hypothalamus (median eminence) with the secondary plexus in the anterior lobe of the hypophysis, forming the **hypophysial-portal system**. This system transports releasing factors from the hypothalamus to stimulate the secretion of hormones into the bloodstream by cells of the anterior hypophysis.

Endothelial cell-mediated regulation of blood flow

The general assumption that the endothelium is just an inert simple squamous epithelium lining blood vessels is no longer correct. In addition to enabling the passage of molecules and gases and retaining blood cells and large molecules, endothelial cells produce **vasoactive substances** that can induce contraction and relaxation of the smooth muscle vascular wall (Figure 12–13).

Nitric oxide, synthesized by endothelial cells from L-arginine upon stimulation by acetylcholine or other agents, activates guanylate cyclase and, consequently cyclic guanosine monophosphate, (cGMP) production, which induces **relaxation** of the smooth muscle cells of the vascular wall. **Endothelin 1** is a very potent **vasoconstrictor** peptide produced by endothelial cells.

Prostacyclin, synthesized from arachidonic acid by the action of cyclooxygenase and prostacyclin synthase in endothelial cells, determines the **relaxation** of vascular smooth muscle cells by the action of cyclic adenosine monophosphate, (cAMP).

The endothelium has a **passive role** in the transcapillary exchange of solvents and solutes by **diffusion**, **filtration**, and **pinocytosis**. The permeability of capillary endothelial cells is tissue-specific. For example, liver sinusoids are more permeable to albumin than are the capillaries of the renal glomerulus. In addition there is a

Figure 12–13

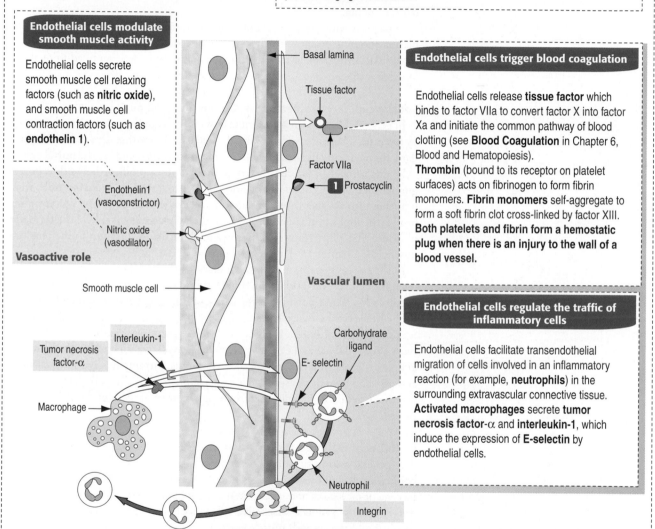

The endothelium

Endothelial cells produce prostacyclin

1 Prostacyclin is formed by endothelial cells from arachidonic acid by a process catalyzed by prostacyclin synthase. Prostacyclin prevents the adhesion of platelets to the endothelium, and prevents intravascular clot formation.

Endothelial cells control vascular cell growth

Angiogenesis occurs during normal wound healing and vascularization of tumors. Endothelial cells secrete factors that stimulate angiogenesis.

Some of these factors induce endothelial cell proliferation and migration; others activate endothelial cell differentiation or induce a secondary cell type to produce angiogenic factors.

Endothelial cells modulate smooth muscle activity

Endothelial cells secrete smooth muscle cell relaxing factors (such as **nitric oxide**), and smooth muscle cell contraction factors (such as **endothelin 1**).

Endothelin 1 (vasoconstrictor)

Nitric oxide (vasodilator)

Vasoactive role

Smooth muscle cell

Tumor necrosis factor-α

Interleukin-1

Macrophage

Basal lamina

Tissue factor

Factor VIIa

1 Prostacyclin

Vascular lumen

Carbohydrate ligand

E- selectin

Neutrophil

Integrin

Endothelial cells trigger blood coagulation

Endothelial cells release **tissue factor** which binds to factor VIIa to convert factor X into factor Xa and initiate the common pathway of blood clotting (see **Blood Coagulation** in Chapter 6, Blood and Hematopoiesis).
Thrombin (bound to its receptor on platelet surfaces) acts on fibrinogen to form fibrin monomers. **Fibrin monomers** self-aggregate to form a soft fibrin clot cross-linked by factor XIII.
Both platelets and fibrin form a hemostatic plug when there is an injury to the wall of a blood vessel.

Endothelial cells regulate the traffic of inflammatory cells

Endothelial cells facilitate transendothelial migration of cells involved in an inflammatory reaction (for example, **neutrophils**) in the surrounding extravascular connective tissue.
Activated macrophages secrete **tumor necrosis factor-α** and **interleukin-1**, which induce the expression of **E-selectin** by endothelial cells.

topographic permeability. For example, the endothelial cells at the venous end are more permeable than those at the arterial end. Postcapillary venules have the greatest permeability to leukocytes.

Clinical significance: Arterial diseases

Arteriosclerosis designates the thickening and loss of elasticity of the arterial walls. **Arteriolosclerosis** is the thickening of the walls of **small arteries** and **arterioles**, mainly of the kidneys and brain, and is usually associated with hypertension or diabetes.

The thickening and hardening of the walls of arteries caused by an **atheroma** (Gk. *athere*, gruel; *oma*, tumor)—a plaque of lipids, cells, and connective tissue

Figure 12–14

The formation of an atheroma

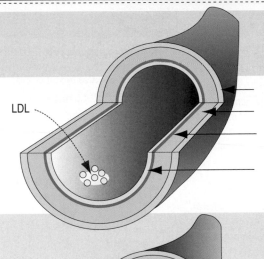

1 A damage of the endothelium of an artery –caused by hypercholesterolemia– is followed by an extracellular space infiltration of cholesterol-rich low-density lipoprotein (LDL) in the tunica intima.

LDL

Tunica adventitia

Tunica media (smooth muscle cells and elastic lamellae)

Internal elastic lamina

Subendothelial space with connective tissue and fibers

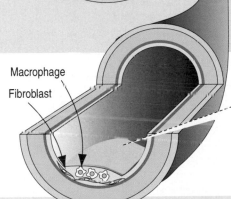

2 Lipids are taken up by macrophages in the tunica intima and fibroblasts of the subendothelial space proliferate.

Macrophage

Fibroblast

> The endothelial surface is smooth but the area covering the damaged subendothelial space is raised.

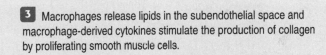

3 Macrophages release lipids in the subendothelial space and macrophage-derived cytokines stimulate the production of collagen by proliferating smooth muscle cells.

> Macrophages produce interleukin-1 and tumor necrosis factor-α to recruit leukocytes into the atheroma plaque. They also produce growth factors to stimulate the proliferation of smooth muscle cells.

An atheroma (a lipid-containing plaque) is formed

Free lipids accumulate in the subendothelial space

The internal elastic lamina is disrupted by the atheroma

Proliferated smooth muscle cells deposit collagen fibers, which compress the cells of the tunica media causing their atrophy

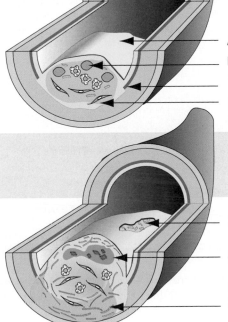

4 The ulceration of the atheroma provides a surface for thrombosis (formation of a fibrin-platelet–containing thrombus). This condition has catastrophic consequences in coronary arteriosclerosis because it causes luminal obstruction, leading to infarction or sudden cardiac death.

Ulcerated atheroma

Calcification of the atheroma

Collagen –produced by smooth muscle cells– infiltrates and replaces the remaining smooth muscle cells of the tunica media

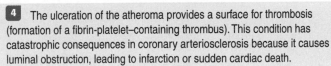

Figure 12–15

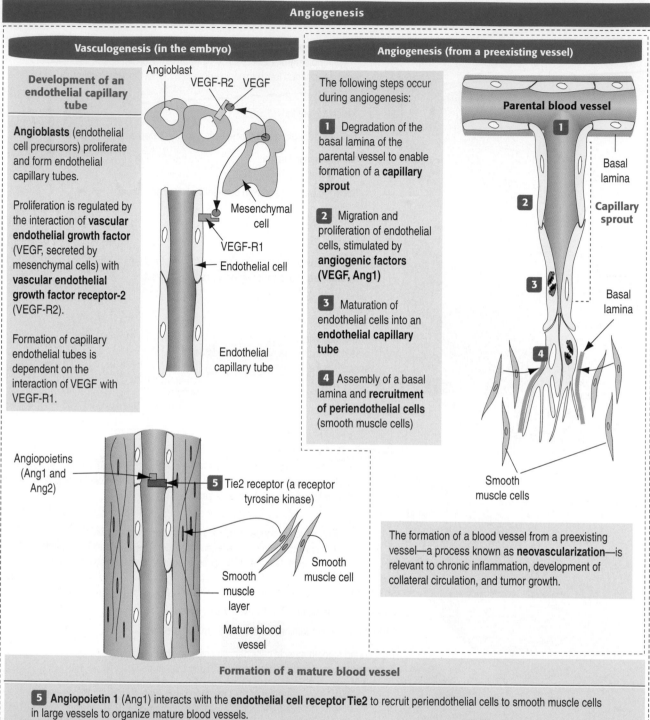

Angiogenesis

Vasculogenesis (in the embryo)

Development of an endothelial capillary tube

Angioblasts (endothelial cell precursors) proliferate and form endothelial capillary tubes.

Proliferation is regulated by the interaction of **vascular endothelial growth factor** (VEGF, secreted by mesenchymal cells) with **vascular endothelial growth factor receptor-2** (VEGF-R2).

Formation of capillary endothelial tubes is dependent on the interaction of VEGF with VEGF-R1.

Angioblast
VEGF-R2   VEGF
Mesenchymal cell
VEGF-R1
Endothelial cell
Endothelial capillary tube

Angiopoietins (Ang1 and Ang2)
5 Tie2 receptor (a receptor tyrosine kinase)
Smooth muscle cell
Smooth muscle layer
Mature blood vessel

Angiogenesis (from a preexisting vessel)

The following steps occur during angiogenesis:

1 Degradation of the basal lamina of the parental vessel to enable formation of a **capillary sprout**

2 Migration and proliferation of endothelial cells, stimulated by **angiogenic factors (VEGF, Ang1)**

3 Maturation of endothelial cells into an **endothelial capillary tube**

4 Assembly of a basal lamina and **recruitment of periendothelial cells** (smooth muscle cells)

Parental blood vessel
Basal lamina
Capillary sprout
Basal lamina
Smooth muscle cells

The formation of a blood vessel from a preexisting vessel—a process known as **neovascularization**—is relevant to chronic inflammation, development of collateral circulation, and tumor growth.

Formation of a mature blood vessel

5 **Angiopoietin 1** (Ang1) interacts with the **endothelial cell receptor Tie2** to recruit periendothelial cells to smooth muscle cells in large vessels to organize mature blood vessels.

Ang2, another angiopoietin, interacts with Tie2 to induce loss of contact of endothelial cells with the extracellular matrix. This results in either the absence of growth or death of endothelial cells. **The role of Ang2 in tumor angiogenesis is emerging as a target for tumor treatment.**

in the **tunica intima**— is known as **atherosclerosis** (Figure 12–14). Atherosclerosis is frequently seen in arteries sustaining high blood pressure. Atherosclerosis does not affect veins.

Atherosclerosis correlates with the serum levels of cholesterol or **low-density**

Figure 12–16

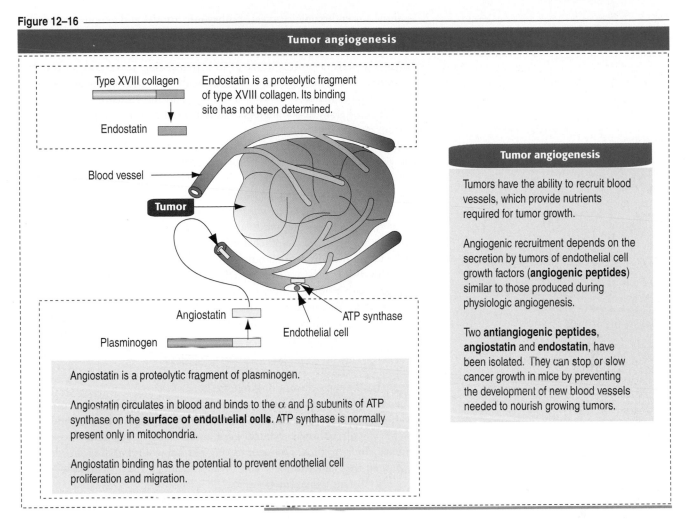

Tumor angiogenesis

Type XVIII collagen

Endostatin is a proteolytic fragment of type XVIII collagen. Its binding site has not been determined.

Endostatin

Blood vessel

Tumor

Angiostatin

Plasminogen

ATP synthase

Endothelial cell

Angiostatin is a proteolytic fragment of plasminogen.

Angiostatin circulates in blood and binds to the α and β subunits of ATP synthase on the **surface of endothelial cells**. ATP synthase is normally present only in mitochondria.

Angiostatin binding has the potential to prevent endothelial cell proliferation and migration.

Tumor angiogenesis

Tumors have the ability to recruit blood vessels, which provide nutrients required for tumor growth.

Angiogenic recruitment depends on the secretion by tumors of endothelial cell growth factors (**angiogenic peptides**) similar to those produced during physiologic angiogenesis.

Two **antiangiogenic peptides**, **angiostatin** and **endostatin**, have been isolated. They can stop or slow cancer growth in mice by preventing the development of new blood vessels needed to nourish growing tumors.

lipoprotein (LDL). A genetic defect in lipoprotein metabolism (**familial hypercholesterolemia**) is associated with atherosclerosis and myocardial infarction before patients reach 20 years of age. Recall from our previous discussion (see Cytomembranes in Chapter 2, Epithelial Glands) that familial hypercholesterolemia is caused by defects in the LDL receptor, resulting in increasing LDL circulating levels in blood. In contrast to LDL, **high-density lipoprotein** (HDL) transports cholesterol to the liver for excretion in the bile (see in the gallbladder section of Chapter 17, Digestive Glands, the mechanism of excretion of cholesterol).

Atheromas protrude into the lumen, weakening the underlying tunica media, and undergo a series of complications that predispose to **thrombosis**. The major blood vessels involved are the **abdominal aorta** and the **coronary** and **cerebral arteries**. **Coronary arteriosclerosis** causes **ischemic heart disease** and, when the arterial lesions are complicated by thrombosis, **myocardial infarction** occurs. Atherothrombosis of the cerebral vessels is the major cause of **brain infarct**, so-called **stroke**, one of the most common causes of neurologic disease. Arteriosclerosis of the abdominal aorta leads to **abdominal aortic aneurysm**, a dilation that sometimes ruptures to produce massive fatal hemorrhage.

Vascular morphogenesis: Vascular endothelial growth factor and angiopoietins

The vascular system is formed by two processes (Figure 12–15):

1. **Vasculogenesis**, a process initiated by the coalescence of free and migratory **vascular endothelial progenitors**, or **angioblasts**, during **embryogenesis** to form a **primitive vascular network in the yolk sac and trunk axial vessels**. Vasculogenesis

is essential for embryonic survival. Embryonic arterial and venous endothelial cells are molecularly distinct: **ephrin-B2** and its receptor are expressed in arterial vessels; **ephrin-B4** is expressed in venous vessels.

2. **Angiogenesis**, a process initiated in a **preexisting vessel** and observed in both embryo and adult. Angiogenesis in the adult occurs during the uterine menstrual cycle, placental growth, wound healing, and inflammatory responses. As we will discuss below, tumor angiogenesis is a specific form of angiogenesis with important clinical implications.

Endothelial cells are involved in both vasculogenesis and angiogenesis. Endothelial cells migrate, proliferate, and assemble into tubes to contain the blood. Periendothelial cells (smooth muscle cells, pericytes, and fibroblasts) are recruited to surround the newly formed endothelial tubes.

The following molecules are central to vascular morphogenesis: (1) **Tie2**, a receptor tyrosine kinase that modulates a signaling cascade required for the induction or inhibition of endothelial cell proliferation; (2) **vascular endothelial growth factors** (**VEGFs**), with binding affinity to two different receptors, **VEGF-R1** and **VEGF-R2**, present on endothelial cells; (3) **angiopoietins 1 and 2** (**Ang1** and **Ang2**), with binding affinity to **Tie2**.

Ang1 mediates vascular maturation. In the absence of VEGF, Ang2 blocks Ang1 effects, resulting in either endothelial cell remodeling or apoptosis. Ang2 is selectively expressed in the ovary, uterus, and placenta, three tissues in which angiogenesis is relevant to female reproductive physiology.

Clinical significance: Tumor angiogenesis

In Chapter 4, Connective Tissue, we discussed the molecular biology of tumor invasion. We briefly mentioned that tumors secrete **angiogenic factors** to increase the vascularization and nutrition of an invading tumor. These angiogenic factors are similar to those produced during normal wound healing. In addition, we indicated that newly formed blood vessels facilitate the dissemination of tumor cells to distant tissues (**metastasis**).

Certain tumors can release **antiangiogenic peptides** that prevent their distant metastases from recruiting blood vessels. Two antiangiogenic peptides have been isolated (Figure 12–16): (1) **angiostatin**, a breakdown product of **plasminogen**; and (2) **endostatin**, a breakdown peptide of **type XVIII collagen**. When administered to mice, these peptides can slow down or stop the growth of established tumors.

Angiostatin binds to the enzyme **adenosine triphosphate** (**ATP**) **synthase** present on the surface of endothelial cells. This enzyme is not found on the surface of other cells. ATP synthase synthesizes ATP. When angiostatin binds to ATP synthase, its enzymatic activity is blocked and presumably prevents the growth of blood vessels. Endothelial cells thrive in a low oxygen environment and depend on ATP synthase activity to provide a source of energy.

13. RESPIRATORY SYSTEM

General outline of the respiratory system

The respiratory system consists of three main portions with distinct functions:

1. An **air-conducting portion**.
2. A **respiratory portion** for gas exchange between blood and air.
3. A **mechanism for ventilation**, driven by the inspiratory and expiratory movements of the thoracic cage.

The **air-conducting portion** consists, sequentially, of the **nasal cavities** and **associated sinuses**, the **nasopharynx**, the **oropharynx**, the **larynx**, the **trachea**, the **bronchi**, and the **bronchioles**. The oropharynx also participates in food transport. The **conducting portion** provides a passage for inhaled and exhaled air in and out of the respiratory portion.

The **respiratory portion** is composed, in sequence, of the **respiratory bronchioles**, **alveolar ducts**, **alveolar sacs**, and **alveoli**. The main function is the exchange of gases between air and blood.

Terminal bronchioles and the lung territory they supply constitute a **pulmonary lobule**, composed of several **pulmonary acini**.

A **pulmonary acinus** is formed when **terminal bronchioles** branch to become **respiratory bronchioles**. A respiratory acinus is a triangular-shaped structure with the apex occupied by respiratory bronchioles and the base by its divisions: the alveolar ducts, alveolar sacs, and alveoli.

Respiration involves the participation of a **ventilation mechanism**. The inflow (inspiration) and outflow (expiration) of air occur with the aid of four elements:

1. The **thoracic** or **rib cage**.
2. Associated **intercostal muscles**.
3. The **diaphragm muscle**.
4. The **elastic connective tissue of the lung**.

Nasal cavities and paranasal sinuses

The nasal cavities and paranasal sinuses provide an extensive surface area for: (1) warming and moistening air, and (2) filtering dust particles present in the inspired air. In addition, the roof of each nasal cavity and part of the superior concha contain the specialized **olfactory mucosa**.

Each nasal cavity, separated from the other by the **septum**, consists of the **vestibule**, the **respiratory portion**, and the **olfactory area** (Figure 13–1).

Air enters through the **nostril**, or **naris**, whose external surface is lined by **keratinized squamous epithelium**. At the **vestibule**, the epithelium becomes **non-keratinized**.

The **respiratory portion** is lined by a **pseudostratified ciliated epithelium with goblet cells** supported by the lamina propria, which consists of connective tissue with **seromucous glands**. The lamina propria has a **rich superficial venous plexus**, known as **cavernous** or **erectile tissue**. The lamina propria is continuous with the periosteum or perichondrium of bone or cartilage, respectively, forming the wall of the nasal cavities.

Projecting into each nasal cavity from the lateral wall are three curved plates of bone covered by a mucosa: the **superior**, **middle**, and **inferior turbinate bones**, or **conchae** (Lat. *concha*, shell).

Secretions from goblet cells and seromucous glands maintain the mucosal surface moist and humidify the inspired air. Incoming air is warmed by blood in the venous plexus, which flows in a direction opposite to that of the inspired air (**countercurrent flow**). The highly vascular nature of the nasal mucosa, in particular of the anterior septum, accounts for common bleeding (**epistaxis**) after

Figure 13–1

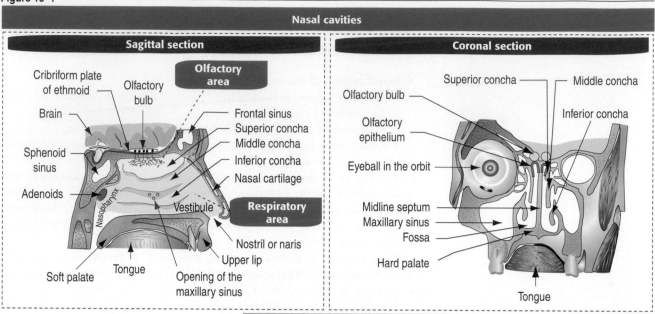

trauma or acute inflammation (**rhinitis**).

Conchae cause airflow turbulence, thus facilitating contact between the air and the mucus blanket covering the respiratory region of each nasal cavity. The mucus blanket traps particulates in the air that are transported posteriorly by ciliary action to the nasopharynx, where they are swallowed with the saliva.

Paranasal sinuses are air-containing cavities within the bones of the skull. They are the **maxillary**, **frontal**, **ethmoidal**, and **sphenoid sinuses**. The sinuses are lined by a thin **pseudostratified columnar ciliated epithelium**, with fewer goblet cells and glands in the lamina propria. No erectile tissue is present in the paranasal sinuses. Sinuses communicate with the nasal cavity by openings lined by an epithelium similar to that of the main nasal cavity. The ethmoidal sinuses open beneath the superior conchae and the maxillary sinus opens under the middle concha.

Nasopharynx

The posterior portion of the nasal cavities is the nasopharynx, which at the level of the soft palate becomes the oropharynx.

The **auditory tubes** (**eustachian tubes**), extending from the middle ear, open into the lateral walls of the oropharynx.

The **nasopharynx** is lined by a **pseudostratified columnar epithelium** like the nasal cavities, and changes into **nonkeratinizing squamous epithelium** at the oropharynx. Abundant **mucosa-associated lymphoid tissue** is present beneath the nasopharyngeal epithelium, forming **Waldeyer's ring**. The **nasopharyngeal tonsils** (**adenoids**) are present at the posterior and upper regions of the nasopharynx.

The olfactory epithelium

The olfactory epithelium contains four types of cells (Figures 13–2 and 13–3): (1) basal cells; (2) **immature** or **differentiating olfactory neurons**; (3) **mature** olfactory neurons (bipolar neurons); and (4) supporting or sustentacular cells.

The **basal cells** are mitotically active, producing daughter cells that differentiate first into **immature olfactory neurons** and then into **mature olfactory neurons**. Olfactory neurons proliferate during adult life. The life span of a primary olfactory neuron is about 30 to 60 days.

The **olfactory neuron** is a highly polarized cell (see Figure 13–3). The **apical**

Figure 13–2

The olfactory mucosa

Olfactory epithelium

Olfactory gland of Bowman

Venous sinusoid of the cavernous vascular tissue
Local vascular changes controlled by vasomotor autonomic innervation can modify the thickness of the mucosa, resulting in changes in the rate of airflow through the nasal passages.

The **axons** of the **olfactory bipolar neurons** are unmyelinated within the epithelium. Groups of axons become immediately ensheathed by olfactory glial cells once they emerge from the olfactory epithelium, forming nerve fascicles (called **fila olfactoria**) in the mucosa.

Respiratory epithelium
A **pseudostraified epithelium**, consisting of ciliated columnar or cuboidal cells, interspersed with goblet cells and basal cells

Bone of the superior nasal concha

region, facing the surface of the mucosa, forms a **knoblike ending** with 10 to 20 modified cilia. The **basal region** gives rise to an **axonal projection**. Several axons,

Figure 13–3

The olfactory epithelium

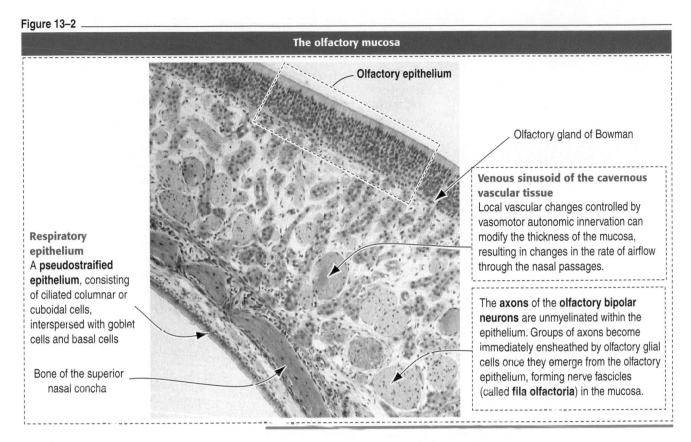

Axons –surrounded by cytoplasmic extension of olfactory myelin-producing cells– pierce the cribriform plate of the ethmoid bone into the olfactory bulb

Plasma cell secretes IgA that is transported into the lumen of the olfactory gland

Ethmoid bone

IgA

Olfactory gland of Bowman

Secretory product containing **odorant-binding protein** (OBP)

Nuclei of the olfactory cells

Basal cell

Immature olfactory cell

Olfactory cell (bipolar neuron)

Dendrite

Occluding junction

Knoblike ending of the dendrite

Modified cilium

Odorant-OBP complex
bound to a receptor on the surface of the modified cilium

Basal lamina

Supporting cell with apically located ovoid nucleus

Microvilli border

Knoblike endings

Odorant molecule bound to OBP

projecting from primary olfactory neurons, cross the **cribriform plate of the ethmoid bone** and contact neurons of the **olfactory bulb** to establish appropriate
synaptic connections.

Olfactory glands (called **glands of Bowman**), which are present under the epithelium, secrete a serous fluid in which odoriferous substances are dissolved. The
secretory fluid contains the odorant-binding protein (**OBP**) with high binding

Figure 13–4

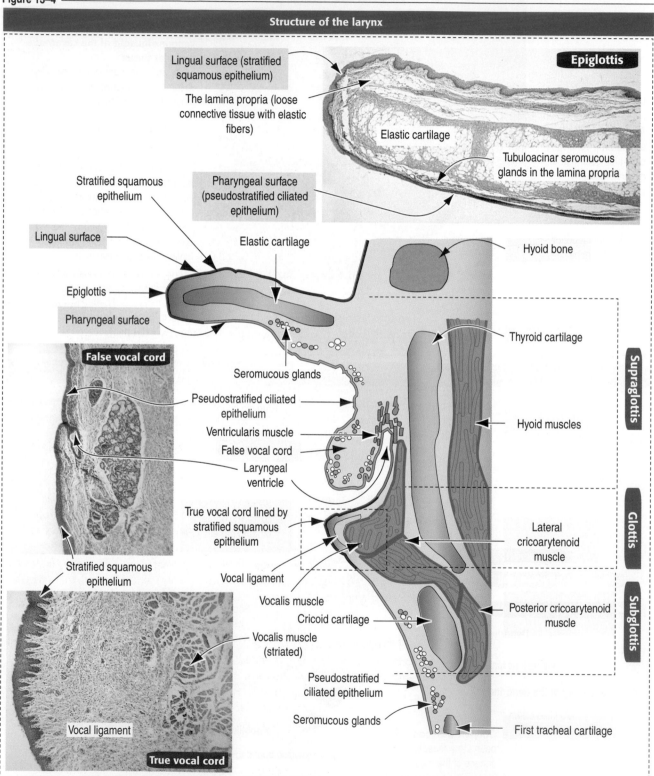

Structure of the larynx

Lingual surface (stratified squamous epithelium)

The lamina propria (loose connective tissue with elastic fibers)

Epiglottis

Elastic cartilage

Tubuloacinar seromucous glands in the lamina propria

Stratified squamous epithelium

Pharyngeal surface (pseudostratified ciliated epithelium)

Lingual surface

Elastic cartilage

Hyoid bone

Epiglottis

Pharyngeal surface

False vocal cord

Seromucous glands

Thyroid cartilage

Pseudostratified ciliated epithelium

Ventricularis muscle

False vocal cord

Laryngeal ventricle

Hyoid muscles

Supraglottis

True vocal cord lined by stratified squamous epithelium

Vocal ligament

Lateral cricoarytenoid muscle

Glottis

Stratified squamous epithelium

Vocalis muscle

Cricoid cartilage

Vocalis muscle (striated)

Posterior cricoarytenoid muscle

Subglottis

Pseudostratified ciliated epithelium

Seromucous glands

Vocal ligament

First tracheal cartilage

True vocal cord

affinity for a large number of **odorant molecules**. OBP carries odorants to receptors present on the surface of the modified cilia and removes them after they have been sensed. In addition, the secretory product of the glands of Bowman contains protective substances such as **lysozyme** and immunoglobulin A, (**IgA**, secreted by plasma cells).

The larynx

The two main functions of the larynx are (1) to produce sound, and (2) to close the trachea during swallowing to prevent food and saliva from entering the airway.

The **wall of the larynx** is made up of the **thyroid** and **cricoid hyaline cartilage** and the **fibroelastic cartilage core of the epiglottis** extending over the lumen (Figure 13–4).

Extrinsic muscles attach the larynx to the **hyoid bone** to raise the larynx during swallowing.

Intrinsic muscles, innervated by the inferior laryngeal nerve, link the thyroid and cricoid cartilages. When intrinsic muscles contract, the tension on the vocal cords changes to modulate phonation. The middle and lower laryngeal arteries (derived from the superior and inferior thyroid artery) supply the larynx. Lymphatic plexuses drain to the upper cervical lymph nodes and to the nodes along the trachea.

The larynx can be subdivided into three regions:

1. The **supraglottis**, which includes the epiglottis, false vocal cords, and laryngeal ventricles.

2. The **glottis**, consisting of the true vocal cords and the anterior and posterior commissures.

3. The **subglottis**, the region below the true vocal cords, extending down to the lower border of the cricoid cartilage.

During forced inspiration, vocal cords are **abducted**, and the space between the vocal cords widens.

During phonation, the vocal cords are **adducted** and the space between the vocal cords changes into a linear slit. The vibration of the free edges of the cords during passage of air between them produces sound. The contraction of the intrinsic muscles of the larynx increases tension on the vocal cords, changing the pitch of the produced sound.

The mucosa of the larynx is continuous with that of the pharynx and the trachea. A **stratified squamous epithelium** covers the **lingual surface** and a small extension of the pharyngeal surface of the epiglottis and the **true vocal cords**. Elsewhere, the epithelium is **pseudostratified ciliated, with goblet cells**.

Laryngeal seromucous glands are found throughout the lamina propria, except at the level of the true vocal cords. The lamina propria consists of loose connective tissue, usually rich in **mast cells**. Mast cells participate in hypersensitivity reactions leading to edema and laryngeal obstruction, a potential medical emergency. **Croup** designates a laryngotracheobronchitis in children, in which an inflammatory process narrows the airway and produces **inspiratory stridor**.

The trachea

The trachea, the major segment of the **conducting region** of the respiratory system, is the continuation of the larynx.

The trachea branches to form the right and left primary bronchi entering the hilum of each lung. The **hilum** is the region where the primary bronchus, **pulmonary artery, pulmonary vein, nerves**, and **lymphatics** enter and leave the lung. Secondary divisions of the bronchi and accompanying connective tissue septa divide each lung into lobes.

The right lung has three lobes, whereas the left lung has two lobes.

Subsequent bronchial divisions further subdivide each lobe into bronchopulmonary segments. **The bronchopulmonary segment is the gross anatomic unit of the lung that can be removed surgically**. Successive bronchial branching gives rise to several generations of **bronchopulmonary subsegments**.

The trachea and main bronchi are lined by **pseudostratified columnar ciliated epithelium** resting on a distinct basal lamina. Several types of cells can be identified (Figure 13–5):

1. **Columnar ciliated cells** are the predominant cell population, extending from the lumen to the basal lamina.

2. **Goblet cells** are abundant nonciliated cells, also in contact with the lumen and the basal lamina.

3. **Basal cells** rest on the basal lamina but do not extend to the lumen.

Figure 13–5

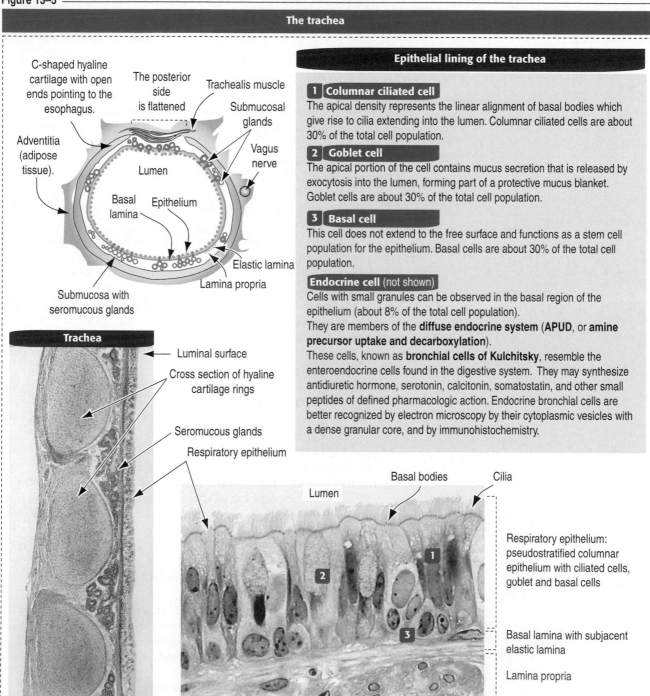

The trachea

Epithelial lining of the trachea

1 Columnar ciliated cell
The apical density represents the linear alignment of basal bodies which give rise to cilia extending into the lumen. Columnar ciliated cells are about 30% of the total cell population.

2 Goblet cell
The apical portion of the cell contains mucus secretion that is released by exocytosis into the lumen, forming part of a protective mucus blanket. Goblet cells are about 30% of the total cell population.

3 Basal cell
This cell does not extend to the free surface and functions as a stem cell population for the epithelium. Basal cells are about 30% of the total cell population.

Endocrine cell (not shown)
Cells with small granules can be observed in the basal region of the epithelium (about 8% of the total cell population).
They are members of the **diffuse endocrine system** (**APUD**, or **amine precursor uptake and decarboxylation**).
These cells, known as **bronchial cells of Kulchitsky**, resemble the enteroendocrine cells found in the digestive system. They may synthesize antidiuretic hormone, serotonin, calcitonin, somatostatin, and other small peptides of defined pharmacologic action. Endocrine bronchial cells are better recognized by electron microscopy by their cytoplasmic vesicles with a dense granular core, and by immunohistochemistry.

Labels (upper diagram):
- C-shaped hyaline cartilage with open ends pointing to the esophagus.
- The posterior side is flattened
- Trachealis muscle
- Submucosal glands
- Vagus nerve
- Adventitia (adipose tissue).
- Lumen
- Basal lamina
- Epithelium
- Elastic lamina
- Lamina propria
- Submucosa with seromucous glands

Trachea
- Luminal surface
- Cross section of hyaline cartilage rings
- Seromucous glands
- Respiratory epithelium

- Lumen
- Basal bodies
- Cilia
- Respiratory epithelium: pseudostratified columnar epithelium with ciliated cells, goblet and basal cells
- Basal lamina with subjacent elastic lamina
- Lamina propria

The lamina propria contains elastic fibers. The **submucosa** displays **mucus and serous glands.**

The framework of the trachea and extrapulmonary bronchi consists of a stack

Figure 13–6

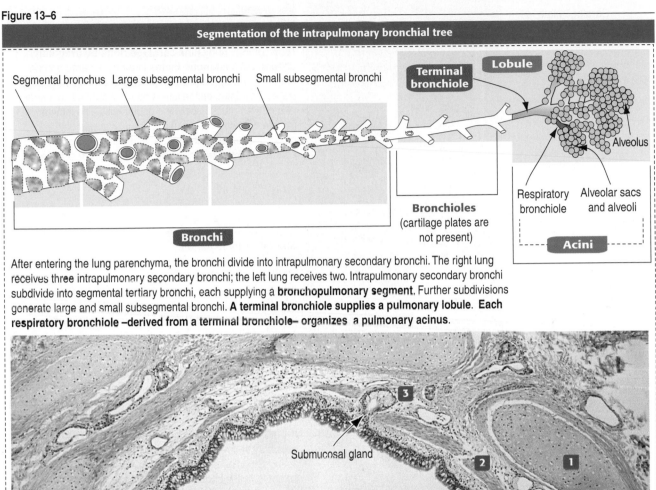

Segmentation of the intrapulmonary bronchial tree

Segmental bronchus   Large subsegmental bronchi   Small subsegmental bronchi   **Terminal bronchiole**   **Lobule**

Alveolus

Bronchi

Bronchioles (cartilage plates are not present)

Respiratory bronchiole   Alveolar sacs and alveoli

Acini

After entering the lung parenchyma, the bronchi divide into intrapulmonary secondary bronchi. The right lung receives three intrapulmonary secondary bronchi; the left lung receives two. Intrapulmonary secondary bronchi subdivide into segmental tertiary bronchi, each supplying a **bronchopulmonary segment.** Further subdivisions generate large and small subsegmental bronchi. **A terminal bronchiole supplies a pulmonary lobule. Each respiratory bronchiole –derived from a terminal bronchiole– organizes a pulmonary acinus.**

Submucosal gland

3

2   **1**

Pseudostratified columnar ciliated epithelium with goblet cells

Cartilage plates

Bundles of smooth muscle are located between the mucosa and the cartilage plates

Bronchus

1 As bronchi become smaller, irregular **cartilage plates** are observed. Each cartilage plate, consisting of hyaline cartilage, is surrounded by a bundle of connective tissue fibers blending with the perichondrium.

2 Bundles of smooth muscle fibers are observed between the cartilage plates and the bronchial mucosa. The mucosa is lined by the typical respiratory epithelium.

3 Seromucous glands are observed in the lamina propria with the secretory acini projecting beyond the layer of smooth muscle cell bundles. The excretory ducts open into the bronchial lumen.

Figure 13–7 _____

Histology of the intrapulmonary bronchial tree

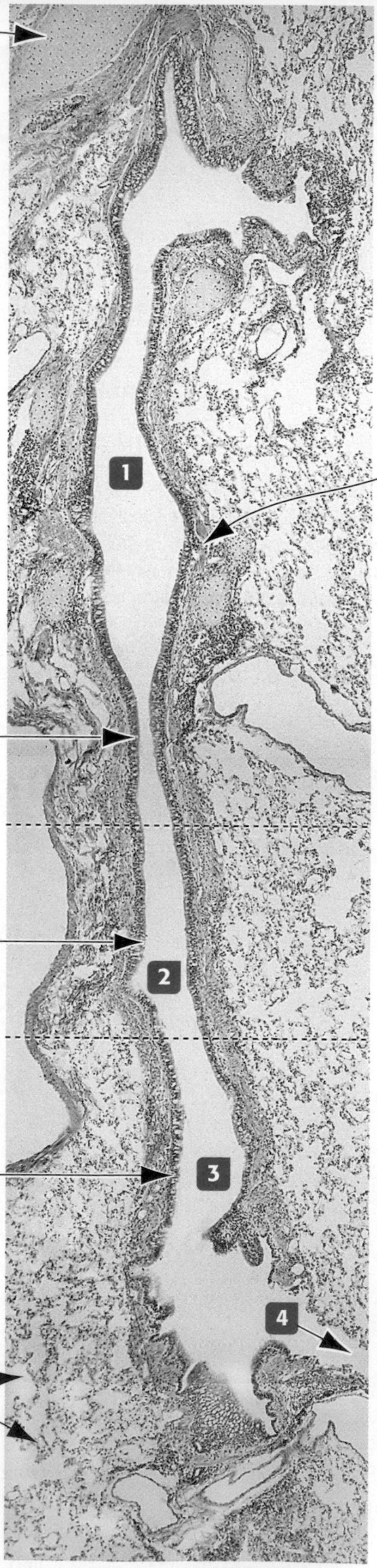

Cartilage plate

1 Small bronchi

A distinguishing feature between trachea and bronchi is the **replacement of hyaline cartilage rings by irregularly shaped cartilagenous plates** in bronchi. Large bronchi are encircled by the plates, but smaller bronchi have small plates. The lining epithelium is pseudostratified columnar ciliated with mucus-secreting goblet cells. The lamina propria contains a layer of circularly arranged but discontinuous smooth muscle, and seromucous glands connected by excretory ducts to the epithelial surface.

Smooth muscle bundles

Contraction of the smooth muscle decreases the lumen of the bronchus. Stimulation of the parasympathetic nervous system (vagus nerve) produces contraction of the smooth muscle. Stimulation of the sympathetic nervous system inhibits contraction of smooth muscle.

Pseudostratified ciliated columnar epithelium **with goblet cells**

2 Bronchioles

Bronchioles lack cartilage and glands, but a few goblet cells may be found in the initial portions. The pseudostratified ciliated columnar epithelium decreases in height to finally become simple columnar-to-cuboidal ciliated at the terminal bronchioles. The lamina propria is composed of smooth muscle and elastic and collagenous fibers.

Pseudostratified ciliated columnar epithelium with **few or no goblet cells**

3 Terminal bronchioles

Terminal bronchioles give rise to respiratory bronchioles. Terminal bronchioles are lined by a ciliated cuboidal epithelium and Clara cells.

Ciliated cuboidal epithelium with **Clara cells**

4 Respiratory bronchioles

The mucosa of the respiratory bronchioles is similar to that of terminal bronchioles, except for the presence of alveoli interrupting the continuity of the wall of the bronchiole. The low cuboidal epithelium is replaced discontinuously by squamous type I alveolar epithelial cells.

Alveoli

Figure 13–8

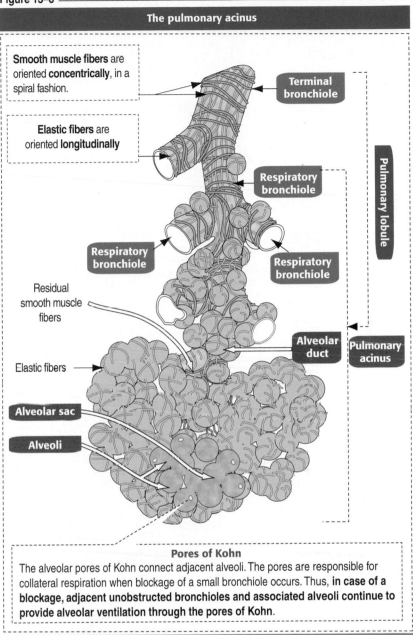

The pulmonary acinus

Smooth muscle fibers are oriented **concentrically**, in a spiral fashion.

Elastic fibers are oriented **longitudinally**

Terminal bronchiole

Respiratory bronchiole

Respiratory bronchiole

Respiratory bronchiole

Pulmonary lobule

Residual smooth muscle fibers

Alveolar duct

Pulmonary acinus

Elastic fibers

Alveolar sac

Alveoli

Pores of Kohn

The alveolar pores of Kohn connect adjacent alveoli. The pores are responsible for collateral respiration when blockage of a small bronchiole occurs. Thus, **in case of a blockage, adjacent unobstructed bronchioles and associated alveoli continue to provide alveolar ventilation through the pores of Kohn**.

of **C-shaped hyaline cartilages**, each surrounded by a **fibroelastic layer** blending with the perichondrium. In the **trachea** and **primary bronchi**, the open ends of the cartilage rings point posteriorly to the esophagus. The lowest tracheal cartilage is the **carinal cartilage**. Transverse fibers of the **trachealis muscle** attach to the inner ends of the cartilage. In branching bronchi, cartilage **rings** (see Figure 13–5) are replaced by irregularly shaped cartilage **plates** (Figure 13–6), surrounded by smooth muscle bundles in a spiral arrangement.

Intrapulmonary segmentation of the bronchial tree

Within the pulmonary parenchyma, a segmental bronchus gives rise to large and small subsegmental bronchi. A small subsegmental bronchus is continuous with a bronchiole. This transition involves **the loss of cartilage plates in the bronchiole and a progressive increase in the number of elastic fibers**.

The intrapulmonary segmentation results in the rorganization of a **pulmonary lobule** and a **pulmonary acinus** (Figure 13–7 and see Figure 13–6).

Figure 13-9

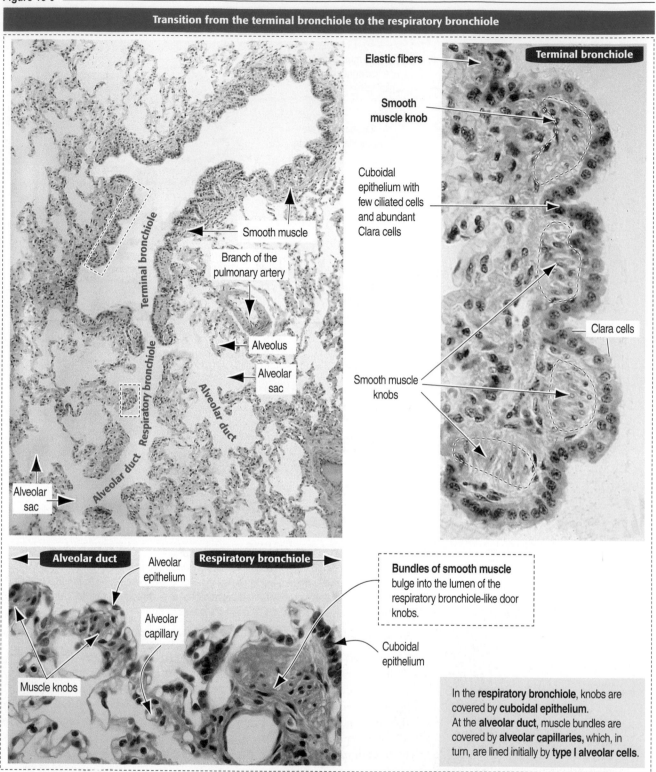

Transition from the terminal bronchiole to the respiratory bronchiole

Elastic fibers

Terminal bronchiole

Smooth muscle knob

Cuboidal epithelium with few ciliated cells and abundant Clara cells

Smooth muscle

Branch of the pulmonary artery

Alveolus

Alveolar sac

Clara cells

Smooth muscle knobs

Terminal bronchiole

Respiratory bronchiole

Alveolar duct

Alveolar sac

Alveolar duct

Alveolar epithelium

Respiratory bronchiole

Alveolar capillary

Muscle knobs

Bundles of smooth muscle bulge into the lumen of the respiratory bronchiole-like door knobs.

Cuboidal epithelium

In the **respiratory bronchiole**, knobs are covered by **cuboidal epithelium**.
At the **alveolar duct**, muscle bundles are covered by **alveolar capillaries,** which, in turn, are lined initially by **type I alveolar cells**.

The pulmonary lobule and acinus

A terminal bronchiole and the associated region of pulmonary tissues that it supplies constitute a pulmonary lobule (Figure 13–8). A pulmonary lobule includes the respiratory bronchioles, alveolar ducts, alveolar sacs, and alveoli.

Physiologists designate the pulmonary acinus as the portion of the lung supplied by a respiratory bronchiole. Therefore, respiratory acini are subcomponents of a respiratory lobule. In contrast to the acinus, the pulmonary lobule includes the terminal bronchiole.

The pulmonary lobule-acinus concept is important for understanding the types of **emphysema** —permanent enlargement of the air spaces distal to the terminal bronchioles, associated with the destruction of their walls.

Distal to the respiratory bronchiole is the **alveolar duct**. The alveolar duct is characterized by an interrupted wall with typical **smooth muscle knobs** bulging into the lumen (Figure 13–9).

At the distal end, the smooth muscle knobs disappear and the lining epithelium is primarily **type I alveolar epithelial cells**. Alveolar ducts branch to form two or more **alveolar sacs**. Alveolar sacs are formed by the **alveoli**, the terminal part of the airway.

Clinical significance: Chronic obstructive pulmonary disease

Chronic obstructive pulmonary disease (COPD) is characterized by progressive and often irreversible airflow limitations. COPD includes **emphysema** and **asthma**.

Figure 13-10

Elastic fibers and emphysema

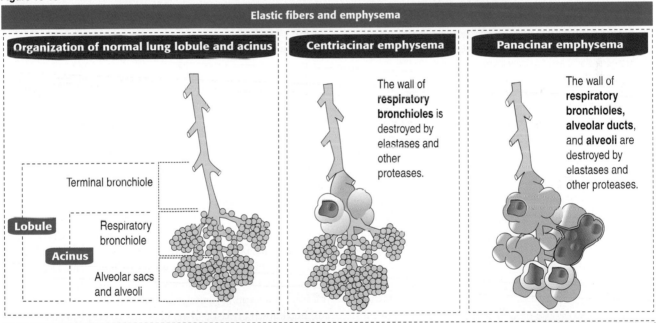

Organization of normal lung lobule and acinus

Terminal bronchiole

Lobule

Respiratory bronchiole

Acinus

Alveolar sacs and alveoli

Centriacinar emphysema

The wall of **respiratory bronchioles** is destroyed by elastases and other proteases.

Panacinar emphysema

The wall of **respiratory bronchioles, alveolar ducts**, and **alveoli** are destroyed by elastases and other proteases.

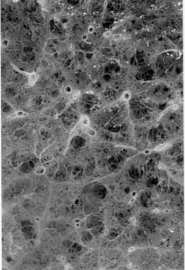

Centriacinar emphysema

Dilated respiratory bronchioles at the apex of the respiratory acinus, surrounded by dilated alveolar ducts and alveoli. This form of emphysema is found in cigarette smokers.

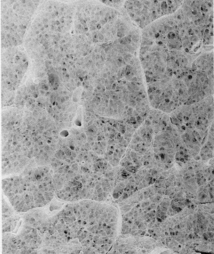

Panacinar emphysema

Thin-walled air spaces of variable size are observed in the whole respiratory acinus. The boundaries of alveoli, alveolar ducts, and respiratory bronchioles are lost by coalescence after destruction of the elastic wall. This form of emphysema is frequent in individuals with α_1-antitrypsin deficiency.

Photographs from Damjanov I, Linder J: Pathology A Color Atlas. St. Louis, Mosby, 2000.

Figure 13–11

Elastase and emphysema

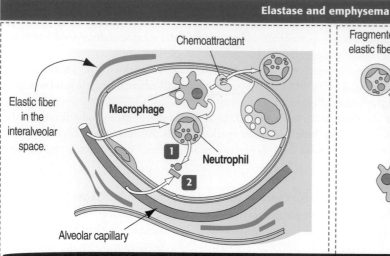

Chemoattractant

Elastic fiber
in the
interalveolar
space.

Macrophage

1

Neutrophil

2

Alveolar capillary

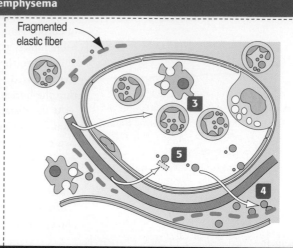

Fragmented
elastic fiber

3

5

4

Pathogenesis of emphysema

A stimulus (for example, smoking) increases the number of macrophages, which secrete **chemoattractants** for neutrophils. Neutrophils accumulate in the alveolar lumen and interstitium.

1 Neutrophils release elastase into the alveolar lumen.

2 Serum α_1-**antitrypsin** neutralizes elastase and prevents its destructive effect on the alveolar wall.

3 A persistent stimulus continues to increase the number of neutrophils and macrophages in the alveolar lumen and interstitium.

4 Neutrophils release elastase into the alveolar lumen and interalveolar space.

5 Serum α_1-**antitrypsin** levels decrease and elastase starts the destruction of elastic fibers, leading to the development of emphysema. **Damaged elastic fibers cannot recoil when stretched.**

COPD occurs in the **peripheral airways** —the bronchioles— and **lung parenchyma. Mucus hypersecretion** (see Figure 13–12) is accompanied by airflow obstruction and an **inflammatory reaction** involving **neutrophils**, **T cells** (CD8+), and **macrophages**. Neutrophils and macrophages release proteases that break down the elastic fibers of the bronchiolar and alveolar wall. Asthma is characterized by the recruitment of **T cells** (CD4+) and **eosinophils** (see Figure 13–12).

Elastic fibers are important components of bronchioles and alveolar walls. A loss of elasticity and breakdown of elastic fibers gives rise to **emphysema**, characterized by chronic airflow obstruction. As a result, adjacent alveoli become confluent, creating large **air spaces**, or **blebs** (Figure 13–10).

Terminal and respiratory bronchioles are also affected by the loss of elastic tissue. As a result of the loss of elastic fibers, the small airways tend to collapse during expiration, leading to chronic airflow obstruction and secondary infections.

Let us review the concepts of the pulmonary lobule and the acinus to understand the types of emphysema. Figures 13–6 and 13–8 show that a **pulmonary lobule includes the terminal bronchiole and the first to third generations of derived respiratory bronchioles.** Each respiratory bronchiole gives rise to alveolar ducts and alveoli, an arrangement known as the **acinus** —so called because aggregates of alveoli cluster like acini in connection with the ductlike respiratory bronchiole. Because a pulmonary lobule generates several respiratory bronchioles, each resolved into an acinus, a pulmonary lobule is made up of several acini.

Centriacinar (or centrilobular) emphysema originates when the **respiratory bronchioles** are affected. The more distal alveolar duct and alveoli are intact. Thus, emphysematous and normal air spaces coexist within the same lobule and acini.

In panacinar (or panlobular) emphysema, blebs are observed from the respira-

Figure 13–12

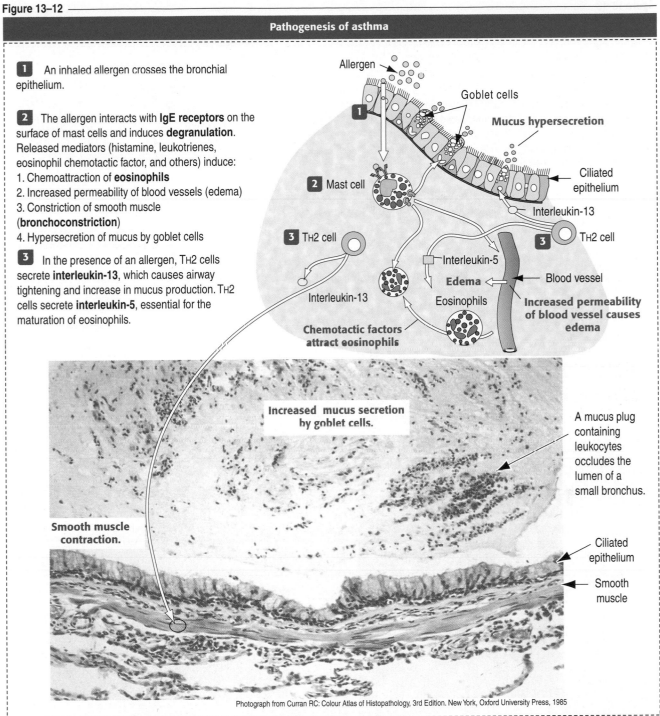

Pathogenesis of asthma

1 An inhaled allergen crosses the bronchial epithelium.

2 The allergen interacts with **IgE receptors** on the surface of mast cells and induces **degranulation**. Released mediators (histamine, leukotrienes, eosinophil chemotactic factor, and others) induce:
1. Chemoattraction of **eosinophils**
2. Increased permeability of blood vessels (edema)
3. Constriction of smooth muscle (**bronchoconstriction**)
4. Hypersecretion of mucus by goblet cells

3 In the presence of an allergen, TH2 cells secrete **interleukin-13**, which causes airway tightening and increase in mucus production. TH2 cells secrete **interleukin-5**, essential for the maturation of eosinophils.

Allergen

Goblet cells

Mucus hypersecretion

Ciliated epithelium

1

2 Mast cell

3 TH2 cell

Interleukin-13

Interleukin-13

Interleukin-5

Edema

Eosinophils

3 TH2 cell

Blood vessel

Increased permeability of blood vessel causes edema

Chemotactic factors attract eosinophils

Increased mucus secretion by goblet cells.

A mucus plug containing leukocytes occludes the lumen of a small bronchus.

Smooth muscle contraction.

Ciliated epithelium

Smooth muscle

Photograph from Curran RC: Colour Atlas of Histopathology, 3rd Edition. New York, Oxford University Press, 1985

tory bronchiole down to the alveolar sacs. This type of emphysema is more common in patients with **a deficiency in the α_1-antitrypsin gene** encoding a serum protein.

Protein α_1-antitrypsin is a major inhibitor of proteases, in particular **elastase**, secreted by neutrophils during inflammation (Figure 13–11). Under the influence of a stimulus, such as cigarette smoke, **macrophages** in the alveolar wall and alveolar lumen secrete proteases and chemoattractants (mainly leukotriene B$_4$) to recruit **neutrophils**.

Chemoattracted neutrophils appear in the alveolar lumen and wall and release **elastase**, normally neutralized by α_1-**antitrypsin**. Chronic smokers have low se-

Figure 13–13

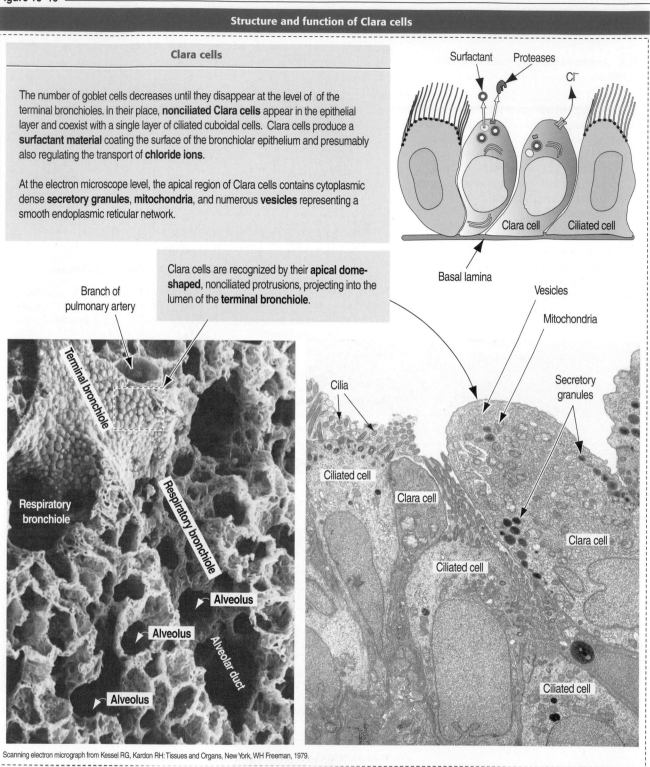

Structure and function of Clara cells

Clara cells

The number of goblet cells decreases until they disappear at the level of of the terminal bronchioles. In their place, **nonciliated Clara cells** appear in the epithelial layer and coexist with a single layer of ciliated cuboidal cells. Clara cells produce a **surfactant material** coating the surface of the bronchiolar epithelium and presumably also regulating the transport of **chloride ions**.

At the electron microscope level, the apical region of Clara cells contains cytoplasmic dense **secretory granules**, **mitochondria**, and numerous **vesicles** representing a smooth endoplasmic reticular network.

Clara cells are recognized by their **apical dome-shaped**, nonciliated protrusions, projecting into the lumen of the **terminal bronchiole**.

Surfactant   Proteases   Cl⁻

Clara cell   Ciliated cell

Basal lamina

Vesicles

Mitochondria

Secretory granules

Cilia

Ciliated cell

Clara cell

Clara cell

Ciliated cell

Ciliated cell

Branch of pulmonary artery

Terminal bronchiole

Respiratory bronchiole

Respiratory bronchiole

Alveolar duct

Alveolus

Alveolus

Alveolus

Scanning electron micrograph from Kessel RG, Kardon RH: Tissues and Organs, New York, WH Freeman, 1979.

rum levels of α_1-antitrypsin and elastase continues the unopposed destruction of elastic fibers present in the alveolar wall. This process develops in 10% to 15% of smokers and leads to emphysema.

Asthma is a chronic inflammatory process characterized by the **reversible narrowing of the airways (bronchoconstriction)** in response to various stimuli. The classic **symptoms of asthma** are **wheezing**, **cough**, and **shortness of breath (dyspnea)**.

Emphysema differs from asthma in that the abnormalities limiting airflow are predominantly **irreversible** and a **destructive process** targets the lung parenchyma.

Asthma is characterized by **airway hyperresponsiveness**, defined by three salient features (Figure 13–12): (1) Airway wall inflammation; (2) luminal obstruction of airways by mucus, caused by hypersecretion of bronchial mucus glands, along with infiltration by inflammatory cells; and (3) vasodilation of the bronchial microvasculature with increased vascular permeability and edema.

Asthma can be triggered by repeated antigen exposure (**allergic asthma**) or by an abnormal autonomic neural regulation of airway function (**nonallergic asthma**).

The pathophysiologic aspects of asthma appear to result from the aberrant proliferation of CD4+ helper TH2 cells producing three cytokines: **interleukin (IL)-4** (IL-4), IL-5, and IL-13. IL-4 stimulates immature T cells to develop into the TH2 cell type, which produces IL-13 to precipitate an asthma attack.

Figure 13–14

Cystic fibrosis

Cystic fibrosis transmembrane conductance regulator (CFTR)

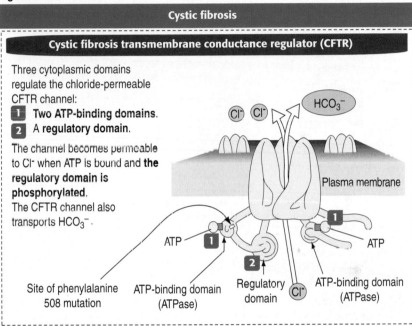

Three cytoplasmic domains regulate the chloride-permeable CFTR channel:
1. **Two ATP-binding domains**.
2. A **regulatory domain**.

The channel becomes permeable to Cl⁻ when ATP is bound and **the regulatory domain is phosphorylated**.
The CFTR channel also transports HCO_3^-.

Site of phenylalanine 508 mutation

ATP-binding domain (ATPase)

Regulatory domain

ATP-binding domain (ATPase)

ATP

Plasma membrane

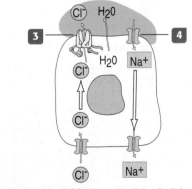

In **normal individuals**, epithelial cells lining the airways display two types of channels:
3. The CFTR channel releases Cl⁻.
4. The other channel takes up Na⁺. Water follows the movement of Cl⁻ by osmosis.

This mechanism maintains the mucus made by goblet cells and mucus-secreting glands to remain wet and less viscous.

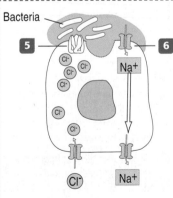

In **patients with cystic fibrosis**,
5. A defective or absent CFTR channel prevents Cl⁻ movement.
6. The cell takes up extra Na⁺.

The mucus becomes thick and traps bacteria leading to cell destruction.

Nonciliated Clara cells in terminal bronchioles secrete surfactant

Clara cells represent **80% of the epithelial cell population** of the **terminal bronchiole** (Figure 13–13). Clara cells secrete a component of the surfactant material covering the alveoli. More recently, **Clara cells have been associated with Cl⁻ release mediated by a chloride channel regulated by a cyclic guanosine monophosphate (GMP)–guanylate cyclase C mechanism.**

Clinical significance: Cystic fibrosis

Cystic fibrosis is a recessive genetic disease affecting children and young adults. The genetic defect responsible for cystic fibrosis is on the long arm of chromosome 7. **A characteristic of the disease is the production of abnormally thick mucus by epithelial cells lining the respiratory and gastrointestinal tracts** (Fig-

Figure 13-15

Subdivisions of the respiratory bronchiole: Alveolar duct, alveolar sac, and alveoli

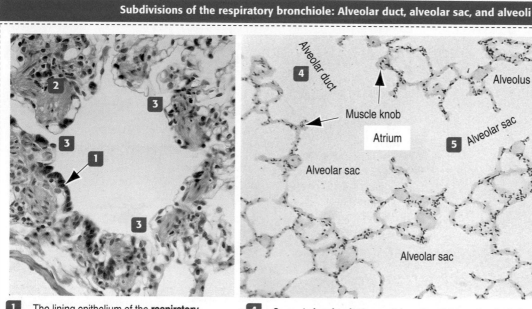

1 The lining epithelium of the **respiratory bronchiole** consists of a **few ciliated and nonciliated cuboidal epithelial cells. Goblet cells are no longer present. Bundles of smooth muscle cells** and **elastic fibers** are observed in the wall. There are **no cartilagenous plates in the wall** and no glands in the lamina propria.

2 **Smooth muscle cell bundles** (muscle **knobs**), innervated by **parasympathetic nerve fibers**, contract to constrict the lumen of the bronchiole. In **asthma**, muscle contraction, triggered by histamine release from mast cells, is persistent.

3 The wall of the respiratory bronchiole is interrupted at intervals by saccular outpocketings, the **alveoli**.

4 Several **alveolar ducts** result from the division of a single bronchiole. The wall of an alveolar sac consists of alveolar openings. Remnants of the muscle knobs lined by a low cuboidal-to-squamous simple epithelium can be seen at the alveolar openings.

5 An **alveolar sac** is continuous with a cluster of alveoli sharing a wider space called the alveolar sac. The alveolar duct–alveolar sac junction is called the **atrium**.

6 Several **alveoli** open into an alveolar sac.

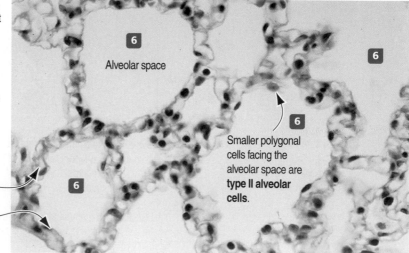

ure 13–14). Respiratory disease results from the obstruction of the pulmonary airways by thick mucous plugs, followed by bacterial infections. Cough, chronic purulent secretions, and dyspnea are typical symptoms of this COPD.

Figure 13–16

The structure of the alveolus

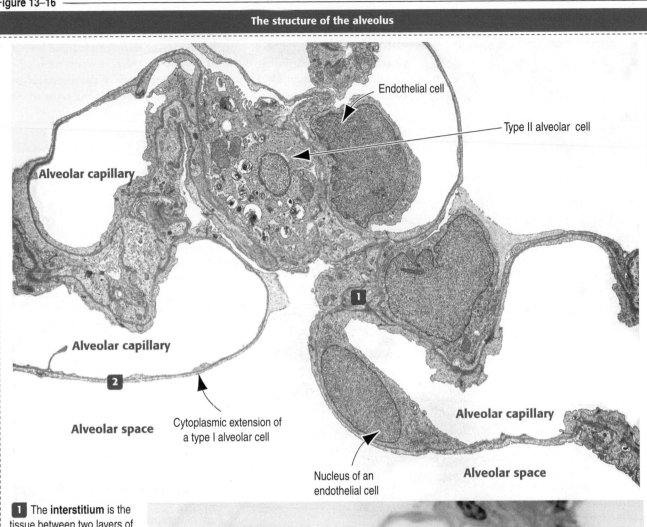

Endothelial cell

Type II alveolar cell

Alveolar capillary

Alveolar capillary

Alveolar capillary

Alveolar space

Cytoplasmic extension of a type I alveolar cell

Alveolar space

Nucleus of an endothelial cell

1 The **interstitium** is the tissue between two layers of alveolar epithelial cells on the alveolar septum. In addition to **capillaries**, the interstitium contains **elastic and collagen fibers** produced by **interstitial fibroblasts**, also called **septal cells**. Mast cells and lymphocytes can also be seen.

2 **There is no connective tissue over the capillaries**. Alveolar cells are separated from capillary endothelial cells by the associated basal laminae produced by them. This thin area facilitates gas exchange.

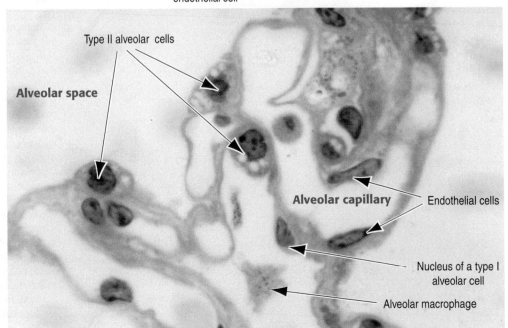

Type II alveolar cells

Alveolar space

Alveolar capillary

Endothelial cells

Nucleus of a type I alveolar cell

Alveolar macrophage

In most patients, the blockage of pancreatic ducts by mucus causes pancreatic dysfunction. Pancreatic ductules release a bicarbonate-rich fluid under regulation of secretin. Secretin is produced by enteroendocrine cells in response to acidic gastric contents entering the duodenum (see Chapter 17, Digestive Glands).

In the skin, the excessive presence of salt secretion by sweat glands is diagnostic of cystic fibrosis (see Chapter 11, Integumentary System).

Treatment of the disease consists in physical therapy to facilitate bronchial drainage, antibiotic treatment of infections, and pancreatic enzyme replacement.

A defective transport of Cl⁻ by the submucosal glands of the respiratory mucosa, excretory ducts of sweat glands, and other epithelia is the cause of cystic

Figure 13–17

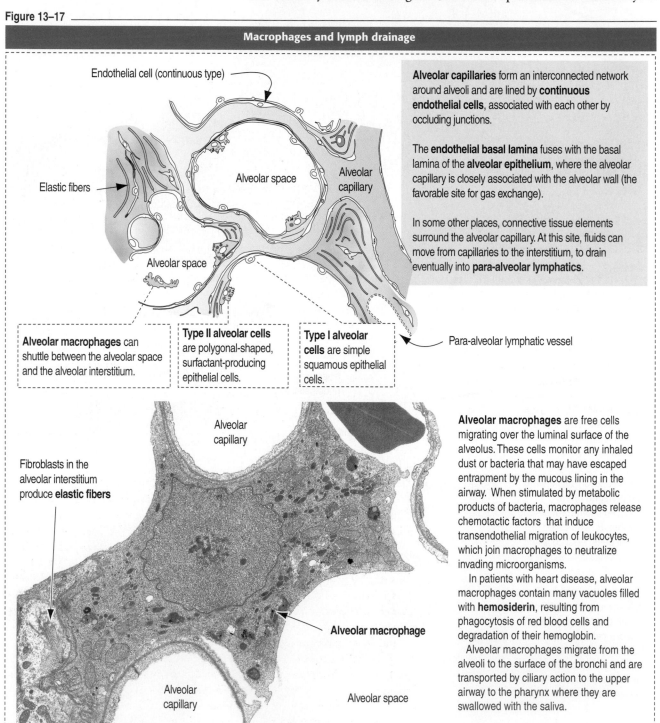

Macrophages and lymph drainage

Endothelial cell (continuous type)

Elastic fibers

Alveolar space

Alveolar space

Alveolar capillary

Alveolar capillaries form an interconnected network around alveoli and are lined by **continuous endothelial cells**, associated with each other by occluding junctions.

The **endothelial basal lamina** fuses with the basal lamina of the **alveolar epithelium**, where the alveolar capillary is closely associated with the alveolar wall (the favorable site for gas exchange).

In some other places, connective tissue elements surround the alveolar capillary. At this site, fluids can move from capillaries to the interstitium, to drain eventually into **para-alveolar lymphatics**.

Alveolar macrophages can shuttle between the alveolar space and the alveolar interstitium.

Type II alveolar cells are polygonal-shaped, surfactant-producing epithelial cells.

Type I alveolar cells are simple squamous epithelial cells.

Para-alveolar lymphatic vessel

Fibroblasts in the alveolar interstitium produce **elastic fibers**

Alveolar capillary

Alveolar capillary

Alveolar macrophage

Alveolar space

Alveolar macrophages are free cells migrating over the luminal surface of the alveolus. These cells monitor any inhaled dust or bacteria that may have escaped entrapment by the mucous lining in the airway. When stimulated by metabolic products of bacteria, macrophages release chemotactic factors that induce transendothelial migration of leukocytes, which join macrophages to neutralize invading microorganisms.

In patients with heart disease, alveolar macrophages contain many vacuoles filled with **hemosiderin**, resulting from phagocytosis of red blood cells and degradation of their hemoglobin.

Alveolar macrophages migrate from the alveoli to the surface of the bronchi and are transported by ciliary action to the upper airway to the pharynx where they are swallowed with the saliva.

Figure 13-18

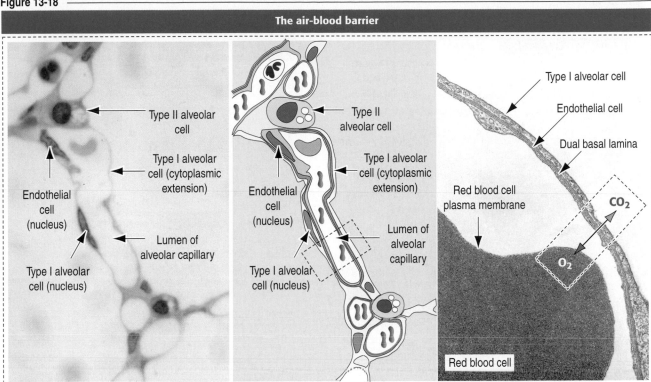

The air-blood barrier

The lung is a gas-exchanging organ for the provision of O_2 to the blood and removal of CO_2 from the blood. Alveolar capillaries are closely apposed to the alveolar lumen. Gas exchange by **passive diffusion** occurs across the **air-blood barrier** consisting of (1) cytoplasmic extensions of **type I alveolar cells**; (2) a **dual basal lamina**, synthesized by type I alveolar cells and endothelial cells; (3) cytoplasmic extensions of continuous **endothelial cells**; (4) the plasma membrane of **red blood cells**. Type II alveolar cells contribute indirectly to the gas-exchange process by secreting **surfactant**, a lipid-protein complex that reduces the surface tension of the alveolus and prevents alveolar collapsing.

Clinical significance: Alveolar gas exchange and acid-base balance

Changes in **partial pressure of CO_2** (designated Pco_2) caused by inadequate ventilation leads to **acid-base balance** disturbances and, consequently, to an alteration in **blood pH**. An increase in Pco_2 decreases blood pH; a decrease of Pco_2 increases pH. An increase in ventilation decreases Pco_2. Pco_2 increases as ventilation decreases. Both blood pH and Pco_2 are critical regulators of the ventilation rate sensed by **chemoreceptors**, located in the brain (medulla) and carotid and aortic bodies.

fibrosis (Figure 13–14).

The sequence of the **cystic fibrosis gene** on chromosome 7 shows that it encodes a protein called **cystic fibrosis transmembrane conductance regulator (CFTR)**, belonging to the **ABC transporter family**—so called because it contains adenosine triphosphate (ATP)-binding domains, or <u>A</u>TP-<u>b</u>inding <u>c</u>assettes, and requires ATP hydrolysis to transport ions, sugars, and amino acids. In 70% of patients with cystic fibrosis, the amino acid 508—of a total of 1480 amino acids in CFTR protein—is missing.

As a member of the ABC transporter family, CFTR is rather unusual because it appears to require both ATP hydrolysis and cyclic adenosine monophosphate (cAMP)–dependent phosphorylation to function as a Cl⁻ channel.

Inherited mutations of CFTR in patients with cystic fibrosis result in defective chloride transport and increased sodium absorption. The CFTR channel also transports **bicarbonate ions**. Inherited mutations of CFTR have now been shown to disrupt bicarbonate transport. We have mentioned above that the exocrine pancreas secretes digestive enzymes in a bicarbonate-rich fluid.

The recently recognized role of **Clara cells in chloride transport** is of clinical significance.

Figure 13–19

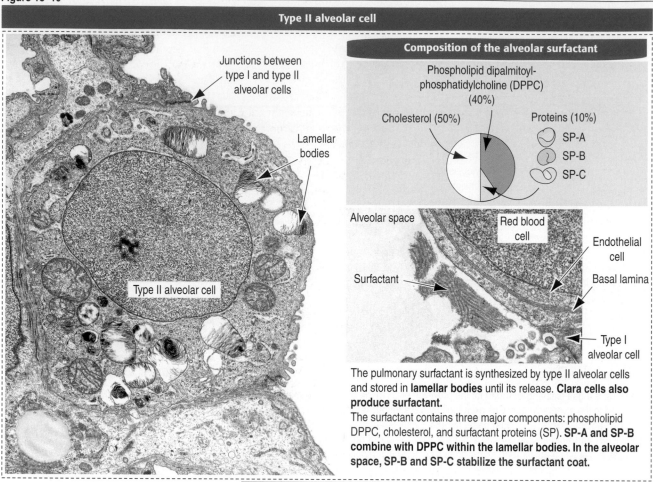

Type II alveolar cell

Junctions between type I and type II alveolar cells

Lamellar bodies

Type II alveolar cell

Composition of the alveolar surfactant

Phospholipid dipalmitoyl-phosphatidylcholine (DPPC) (40%)

Cholesterol (50%)

Proteins (10%)
SP-A
SP-B
SP-C

Alveolar space

Red blood cell

Surfactant

Endothelial cell

Basal lamina

Type I alveolar cell

The pulmonary surfactant is synthesized by type II alveolar cells and stored in **lamellar bodies** until its release. **Clara cells also produce surfactant.**

The surfactant contains three major components: phospholipid DPPC, cholesterol, and surfactant proteins (SP). **SP-A and SP-B combine with DPPC within the lamellar bodies. In the alveolar space, SP-B and SP-C stabilize the surfactant coat.**

The respiratory portion of the lung

Terminal bronchioles give rise to three generations of **respiratory bronchioles** (0.5 to 0.2 mm in diameter).

Respiratory bronchioles represent the transition from the conducting to the

Figure 13–20

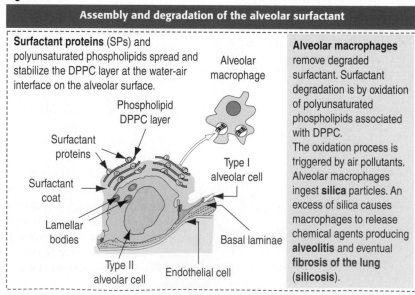

Assembly and degradation of the alveolar surfactant

Surfactant proteins (SPs) and polyunsaturated phospholipids spread and stabilize the DPPC layer at the water-air interface on the alveolar surface.

Alveolar macrophage

Phospholipid DPPC layer

Surfactant proteins

Surfactant coat

Type I alveolar cell

Lamellar bodies

Basal laminae

Type II alveolar cell

Endothelial cell

Alveolar macrophages remove degraded surfactant. Surfactant degradation is by oxidation of polyunsaturated phospholipids associated with DPPC.

The oxidation process is triggered by air pollutants. Alveolar macrophages ingest **silica** particles. An excess of silica causes macrophages to release chemical agents producing **alveolitis** and eventual **fibrosis of the lung (silicosis).**

respiratory portion of the lung (Figure 13–15). They are lined initially by **simple cuboidal epithelial cells**, some of which are ciliated. The epithelium becomes **low cuboidal** and **nonciliated** in subsequent branches. The respiratory bronchiole subdivides to give rise to an **alveolar duct** (see Figure 13–15). The alveolar duct is continuous with the **alveolar sac. Several alveoli open into an alveolar sac.**

The alveolus is the functional unit of the pulmonary acinus

About 300 million air sacs, or **alveoli,** in each lung provide a total surface area of 75 m^2 for oxygen and carbon dioxide exchange. Each alveolus has a thin wall with capillaries lined by **simple squamous epithelial cells** forming part of the **air-blood barrier** (see Figure 13–18).

The **alveolar epithelium** consists of two cell types (see Figures 13–16 and 13–18): (1) **type I alveolar cells**, representing about **40%** of the epithelial cell population but lining **90%** of the alveolar surface; and (2) **type II alveolar cells**, approximately **60%** of the cells, covering only **10%** of the alveolar surface area.

Each alveolus opens into an alveolar sac. However, a few of them open directly into the respiratory bronchiole (see Figure 13–15). **This particular feature dis-**

Figure 13–21

Acute respiratory distress syndrome (ARDS) and pulmonary edema

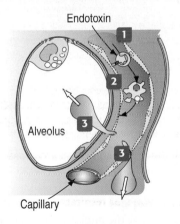

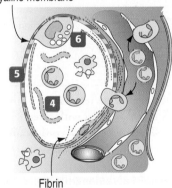
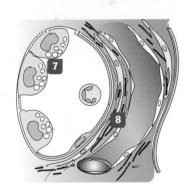

1 Endotoxin induces the release of pro-inflammatory substances which induce the attachment of neutrophils to endothelial cells.

2 Neutrophils release proteolytic enzymes and, together with endotoxin, damage the endothelial cells. Macrophages are activated by inflammatory cytokines and contribute to the endothelial cell damage.

3 The alveolar-capillary barrier becomes permeable and cells and fluid enter the interstitium and alveolar space.

4 Following the endothelial cell injury, type I alveolar cells die, denuding the alveolar side of the barrier. Neutrophils and macrophages are seen in the alveolar lumen and interstitium.

5 Fibrin and cell debris accumulated in the alveolar lumen form a **hyaline membrane**.

6 Fibrin inhibits the synthesis of surfactant by type II alveolar cells.

7 A repair process can restore normal function or cause progressive fibrosis. Type II alveolar cells proliferate, reestablish the production of surfactant, and differentiate into type I alveolar cells.

8 If the initial damage is severe, interstitial fibroblasts proliferate, progressive interstitial and intra-alveolar fibrosis develops, and gas exchange is seriously affected.

Cardiogenic pulmonary edema

A dysfunction of the left ventricle is the main cause of this type of pulmonary edema.

Pulmonary capillaries are dilated and an increase in hydrostatic pressure leads to interstitial and alveolar edema.

Abundant leukocytes and red blood cells and protein-rich fluid are visualized in the lumen of dilated alveoli.

Figure 13–22

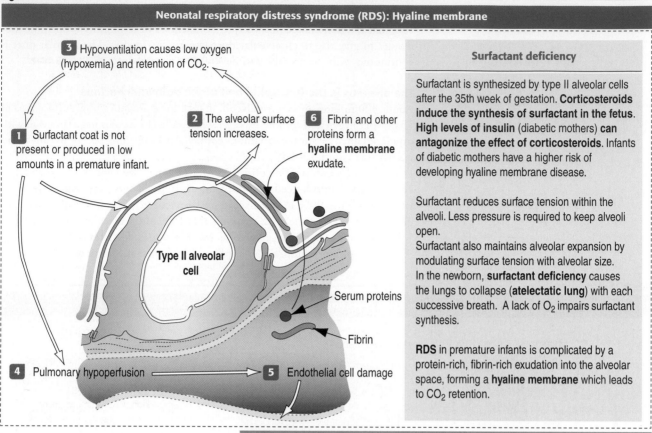

Neonatal respiratory distress syndrome (RDS): Hyaline membrane

3 Hypoventilation causes low oxygen (hypoxemia) and retention of CO_2.

1 Surfactant coat is not present or produced in low amounts in a premature infant.

2 The alveolar surface tension increases.

6 Fibrin and other proteins form a **hyaline membrane** exudate.

Type II alveolar cell

Serum proteins

Fibrin

4 Pulmonary hypoperfusion

5 Endothelial cell damage

Surfactant deficiency

Surfactant is synthesized by type II alveolar cells after the 35th week of gestation. **Corticosteroids induce the synthesis of surfactant in the fetus. High levels of insulin** (diabetic mothers) **can antagonize the effect of corticosteroids**. Infants of diabetic mothers have a higher risk of developing hyaline membrane disease.

Surfactant reduces surface tension within the alveoli. Less pressure is required to keep alveoli open.
Surfactant also maintains alveolar expansion by modulating surface tension with alveolar size.
In the newborn, **surfactant deficiency** causes the lungs to collapse (**atelectatic lung**) with each successive breath. A lack of O_2 impairs surfactant synthesis.

RDS in premature infants is complicated by a protein-rich, fibrin-rich exudation into the alveolar space, forming a **hyaline membrane** which leads to CO_2 retention.

tinguishes the respiratory bronchiole from the terminal bronchiole, whose wall is not associated with alveoli.

The low cuboidal epithelium of the respiratory bronchiole is continuous with the squamous type I alveolar cells of the alveolus (see Figure 13–9).

Type II alveolar cells secrete pulmonary surfactant

Type II alveolar cells are predominantly located at **the angles formed by adjacent alveolar septa.** Contrasting with the more squamous type I alveolar cells, type II alveolar cells are polygonal-shaped and extend beyond the level of the surrounding epithelium.

The free surface of type II alveolar cells is covered by short microvilli. The cytoplasm displays dense membrane-bound **lamellar bodies**, representing secretory granules containing **pulmonary surfactant** (see Figure 13–19).

Surfactant is released by exocytosis and spreads over a thin layer of fluid that normally coats the alveolar surface. By this mechanism, **the pulmonary surfactant lowers the surface tension at the air-fluid interface and thus reduces the tendency of the alveolus to collapse at the end of expiration.** Clara cells, located in terminal bronchioles, also secrete pulmonary surfactant.

The pulmonary surfactant contains (1) **phospholipids**, (2) **cholesterol**, and (3) **proteins** (see Figure 13–19).

Specific surfactant proteins (SPs) consist of one **hydrophilic glycoprotein (SP-A)** and two **hydrophobic proteins (SP-B and SP-C).**

Within the lamellar bodies, SP-A and SP-B transform the **phospholipid dipalmitoylphosphatidylcholine (DPPC)** into a mature surfactant molecule.

In the alveolar space, SP-B and SP-C **stabilize** the phospholipid layer and enhance the surfactant action of the phospholipid DPPC–protein complex (see Figure 13–20).

Surfactant turnover is facilitated by the phagocytic function of alveolar macro-

Figure 13–23

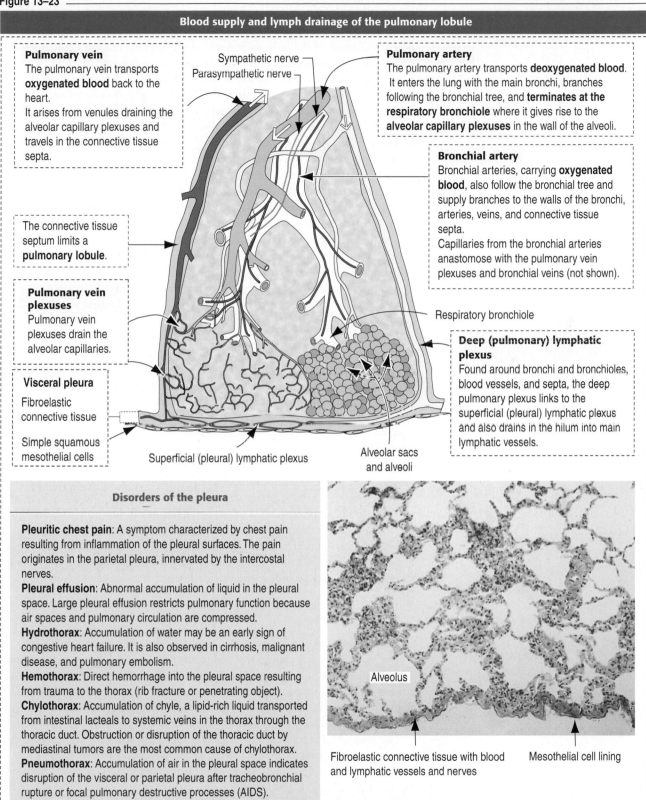

Blood supply and lymph drainage of the pulmonary lobule

Pulmonary vein
The pulmonary vein transports **oxygenated blood** back to the heart.
It arises from venules draining the alveolar capillary plexuses and travels in the connective tissue septa.

Sympathetic nerve
Parasympathetic nerve

Pulmonary artery
The pulmonary artery transports **deoxygenated blood**. It enters the lung with the main bronchi, branches following the bronchial tree, and **terminates at the respiratory bronchiole** where it gives rise to the **alveolar capillary plexuses** in the wall of the alveoli.

Bronchial artery
Bronchial arteries, carrying **oxygenated blood**, also follow the bronchial tree and supply branches to the walls of the bronchi, arteries, veins, and connective tissue septa.
Capillaries from the bronchial arteries anastomose with the pulmonary vein plexuses and bronchial veins (not shown).

The connective tissue septum limits a **pulmonary lobule**.

Pulmonary vein plexuses
Pulmonary vein plexuses drain the alveolar capillaries.

Respiratory bronchiole

Deep (pulmonary) lymphatic plexus
Found around bronchi and bronchioles, blood vessels, and septa, the deep pulmonary plexus links to the superficial (pleural) lymphatic plexus and also drains in the hilum into main lymphatic vessels.

Visceral pleura
Fibroelastic connective tissue

Simple squamous mesothelial cells

Superficial (pleural) lymphatic plexus

Alveolar sacs and alveoli

Disorders of the pleura

Pleuritic chest pain: A symptom characterized by chest pain resulting from inflammation of the pleural surfaces. The pain originates in the parietal pleura, innervated by the intercostal nerves.
Pleural effusion: Abnormal accumulation of liquid in the pleural space. Large pleural effusion restricts pulmonary function because air spaces and pulmonary circulation are compressed.
Hydrothorax: Accumulation of water may be an early sign of congestive heart failure. It is also observed in cirrhosis, malignant disease, and pulmonary embolism.
Hemothorax: Direct hemorrhage into the pleural space resulting from trauma to the thorax (rib fracture or penetrating object).
Chylothorax: Accumulation of chyle, a lipid-rich liquid transported from intestinal lacteals to systemic veins in the thorax through the thoracic duct. Obstruction or disruption of the thoracic duct by mediastinal tumors are the most common cause of chylothorax.
Pneumothorax: Accumulation of air in the pleural space indicates disruption of the visceral or parietal pleura after tracheobronchial rupture or focal pulmonary destructive processes (AIDS).

Alveolus

Fibroelastic connective tissue with blood and lymphatic vessels and nerves

Mesothelial cell lining

phages (see Figures 13–17 and 13–20).

An additional function of type II alveolar cells is the **maintenance and repair of the alveolar epithelium when injury occurs**. When type I alveolar cells are damaged, type II alveolar cells increase in number and differentiate into type I alveolar-like cells (see Figure 13–20).

Clinical significance: Acute respiratory distress syndrome

The significance of the cell components of the alveolus becomes clear when we analyze the relevant aspects of the acute respiratory syndrome (ARDS).

ARDS results from a disruption of the normal barrier that prevents leakage of fluid of the alveolar capillaries into the interstitium and alveolar spaces.

Two mechanisms can alter the alveolar barrier. In the first mechanism, an **increase in hydrostatic pressure in the alveolar capillaries** —caused, for example, by failure of the left ventricle or stenosis of the mitral valve— results in increased fluid and proteins in the alveolar spaces. The resulting edema is called **cardiogenic** or **hydrostatic pulmonary edema**.

In the second mechanism, the hydrostatic pressure is normal, but the endothelial lining of the alveolar capillaries or the epithelial lining of the alveoli is damaged. Inhalation of agents such as smoke, water (near drowning), bacterial endotoxins (resulting from sepsis), or trauma can cause a defect in **permeability**. A cardiac component may or may not be involved. Although the resulting edema is called **noncardiogenic**, it can coexist with a cardiogenic condition.

A common pathologic pattern of diffuse alveolar damage (Figure 13–21) can be observed in cardiogenic and noncardiogenic ARDS. The **first phase** of ARDS is an **acute exudative process** defined by interstitial and alveolar edema, neutrophil infiltration, hemorrhage, and deposits of fibrin. Cellular debris, resulting from dead type I alveolar cells, and fibrin deposited in the alveolar space form **hyaline membranes** (Figure 13–22).

The **second phase** is a **proliferative process** in which alveolar cells proliferate and differentiate to restore the epithelial alveolar lining, returning gas exchange to normal in most cases. In other cases, the interstitium displays inflammatory cells and fibroblasts. Fibroblasts proliferate and invade the alveolar spaces through gaps of the basal lamina. The hyaline membranes either are removed by phagocytosis or are invaded by fibroblasts.

The **third phase** is **chronic fibrosis** and occlusion of blood vessels. Because ARDS is part of a systemic inflammatory response, the outcome of the lung process depends on improvement of the systemic condition. The prognosis for return to normal lung function is good.

The diagnosis of ARDS is based on clinical (dyspnea, cyanosis, and tachypnea) and radiologic examination. Treatment is focused on neutralizing the disorder causing ARDS and providing support of gas exchange until the condition improves.

The pleura

The pleura consists of two layers: (1) a **visceral layer**; and (2) a **parietal layer**.

The **visceral layer** is closely attached to the lung. It is lined by a **simple squamous epithelium**, called **mesothelium**, and consists of cells with **apical microvilli** resting on a basal lamina applied to a connective tissue rich in **elastic fibers**. This connective tissue is continuous with the interlobular and interlobar septa of the lung. The parietal layer is also lined by the mesothelium.

The **visceral layer** seals the lung surface, preventing leakage of air into the thoracic cavity. The **parietal layer** is thicker and is associated with fat cells.

Blood vessels to the visceral pleura derive from pulmonary and bronchial blood vessels (Figure 13–23). The vascular supply to the parietal pleura derives from the systemic blood vessels. Branches of the phrenic and intercostal nerves are found in the parietal pleura; the visceral pleura receives branches of the vagus and sympathetic nerves supplying the bronchi.

Clinical significance: Disorders of the pleura

Under **normal conditions**, the visceral pleura glides silently on the parietal pleura during respiration. However, during an **inflammatory process**, characteristic friction sounds can be detected during the physical examination.

If fluid accumulates in the pleural cavity (**hydrothorax**), the lung collapses gradually and the mediastinum is displaced toward the opposite site. The presence of air in the pleural cavity (**pneumothorax**), caused by a penetrating wound, rupture of the lung, or injected for therapeutic reasons (to immobilize the lung in the treatment of tuberculosis), also collapses the lung.

Collapse of the lung is caused by the recoil properties of its elastic fibers. In the normal lung, such a recoil is prevented by negative intrapleural pressure and the close association of the parietal and visceral layers of the pleura.

14. URINARY SYSTEM

The urinary system has three critical functions: (1) to clear the blood of nitrogenous and other waste metabolic products by **filtration** and **excretion**; (2) to balance the concentration of body fluids and electrolytes, also by **filtration** and **excretion**; (3) to recover by **reabsorption** small molecules (amino acids, glucose, and peptides), ions (Na^+, Cl^-, Ca^{2+}, PO^{3-}), and water, in order to maintain blood homeostasis (Gk. *homoios,* similar; *stasis,* standing).

The kidney regulates **blood pressure** by producing the enzyme **renin**. Renin initiates the conversion of **angiotensinogen** (a plasma protein produced in liver) to the active component **angiotensin II**.

The kidney is also an **endocrine organ**. It produces **erythropoietin**, a stimulant of red blood cell production in bone marrow (for the role of erythropoietin, see Chapter 6, Blood and Hematopoiesis). It also activates **1,25-hydroxycholecalciferol**, a vitamin D derivative involved in the control of calcium metabolism (see vitamin D metabolism in Chapter 19, Endocrine System).

The kidney

The urinary system consists of paired kidneys and ureters and a single urinary bladder and urethra. Each kidney has an external **cortex** and an internal **medulla**. The cortex is divided into **inner** and **outer** regions. The medulla is formed by conical masses, the **medullary pyramids**, with their bases located at the corticomedullary border. A medullary pyramid, together with the associated covering cortical region, constitutes a **renal lobe**.

The boundary of each renal lobe is the **renal columns** (of Bertin), residual structures representing the fusion of primitive lobes within the metanephric blastema. The apex of each renal lobe terminates in a **papilla** surrounded by a **minor calyx**. Each minor calyx collects the urine from a **papilla**. Minor calyces converge to form the **major calyces** which, in turn, form the **pelvis**.

The organization of the renal vascular system

The main function of the kidney is to **filter the blood** supplied by the renal arteries branching from the descending aorta.

The kidneys receive about 20% of the cardiac output per minute and filter about 1.25 L of blood per minute. Essentially, all the blood of the body passes through the kidneys every 5 minutes.

About 90% of the cardiac output goes to the renal cortex; 10% of the blood goes to the medulla. Approximately 125 mL of filtrate are produced per minute, but 124 mL of this amount are reabsorbed.

About 180 L of fluid ultrafiltrate are produced in 24 hours and transported through the uriniferous tubules. Of this amount, 178.5 L are recovered by the tubular cells and returned to the blood circulation, whereas only 1.5 L are excreted as **urine**.

We start our discussion by focusing on the vascularization of the kidney (Figure 14–1).

Oxygenated blood is supplied by the **renal artery**. The renal artery gives rise to several **interlobar arteries**, running across the medulla through the renal columns along the sides of the pyramids.

At the corticomedullary junction, interlobar arteries give off several branches at right angles, changing their vertical path to a horizontal direction to form the **arcuate arteries**, running along the corticomedullary boundary. The renal arterial architecture is **terminal**. There are no anastomoses between interlobular arteries. This is an important concept in renal pathology for understanding **focal necrosis**

Figure 14–1

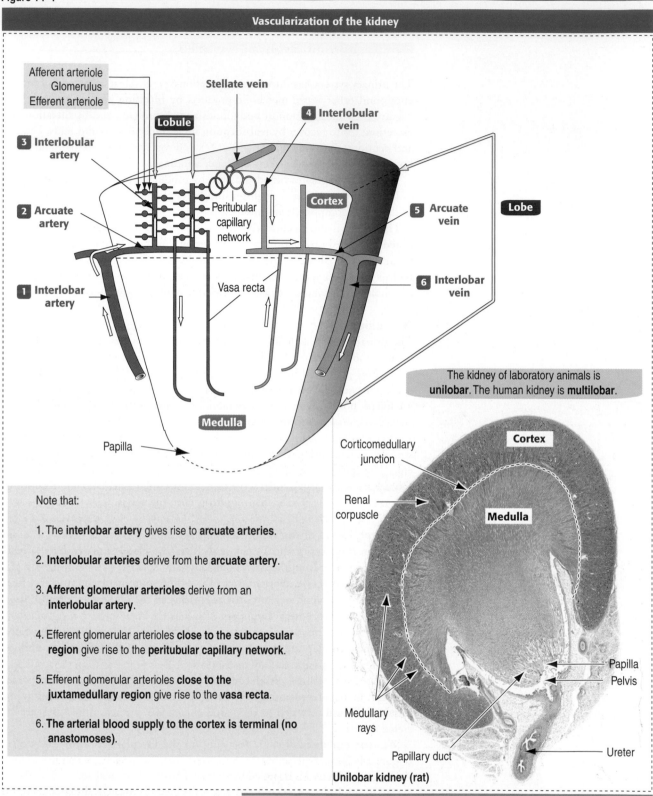

Vascularization of the kidney

Afferent arteriole
Glomerulus
Efferent arteriole

Lobule

Stellate vein

4 Interlobular vein

3 Interlobular artery

2 Arcuate artery

Peritubular capillary network

Cortex

5 Arcuate vein

Lobe

1 Interlobar artery

Vasa recta

6 Interlobar vein

Medulla

Papilla

The kidney of laboratory animals is **unilobar**. The human kidney is **multilobar**.

Note that:

1. The **interlobar artery** gives rise to **arcuate arteries**.

2. **Interlobular arteries** derive from the **arcuate artery**.

3. **Afferent glomerular arterioles** derive from an **interlobular artery**.

4. Efferent glomerular arterioles **close to the subcapsular region** give rise to the **peritubular capillary network**.

5. Efferent glomerular arterioles **close to the juxtamedullary region** give rise to the **vasa recta**.

6. **The arterial blood supply to the cortex is terminal (no anastomoses).**

Corticomedullary junction

Cortex

Renal corpuscle

Medulla

Medullary rays

Papillary duct

Papilla
Pelvis

Ureter

Unilobar kidney (rat)

as a consequence of an arterial obstruction. For example, **renal infarct** can be caused by atherosclerotic plaques in the renal artery or embolization of atherosclerotic plaques derived from the aorta.

Vertical branches emerging from the arcuate arteries, the **interlobular arteries**, penetrate the cortex. As interlobular arteries ascend toward the outer cortex, they

Figure 14–2

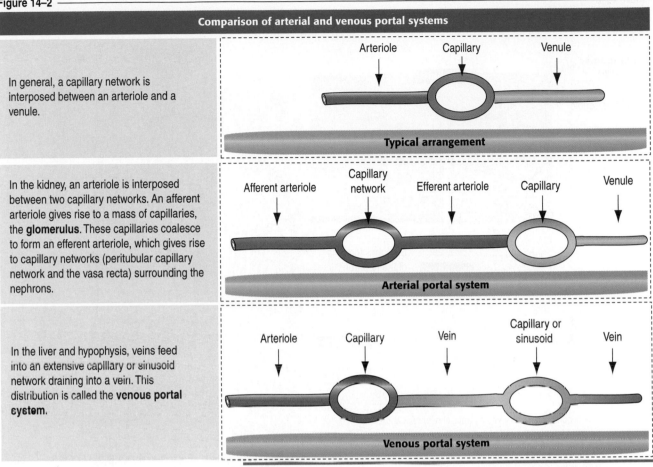

Comparison of arterial and venous portal systems

In general, a capillary network is interposed between an arteriole and a venule.

In the kidney, an arteriole is interposed between two capillary networks. An afferent arteriole gives rise to a mass of capillaries, the **glomerulus**. These capillaries coalesce to form an efferent arteriole, which gives rise to capillary networks (peritubular capillary network and the vasa recta) surrounding the nephrons.

In the liver and hypophysis, veins feed into an extensive capillary or sinusoid network draining into a vein. This distribution is called the **venous portal system**.

branch several times to form the **afferent glomerular arterioles** (see Figure 14–1).

The afferent glomerular arteriole, in turn, forms the **glomerular capillary network,** enveloped by the two-layered **capsule of Bowman**, and continues as the **efferent glomerular arteriole**. This particular arrangement, a capillary network flanked by two arterioles (instead of an arteriole and a venule) is called the **glomerulus** or **arterial portal system**.

The glomerular **arterial portal system** (Figure 14–2) is structurally and functionally distinct from the **venous portal system** of the liver. Both the glomerulus and the surrounding capsule of Bowman form the **renal corpuscle** (also called the malpighian corpuscle).

The smooth muscle cell wall of the **afferent glomerular arteriole** contains epithelial-like cells, called **juxtaglomerular cells**, with secretory granules containing **renin**. A few juxtaglomerular cells may be found in the wall of the efferent glomerular arteriole.

The vasa recta

Depending upon the location of the renal corpuscle, the efferent glomerular arteriole forms two different capillary networks:

1. A **peritubular capillary network**, surrounding the **cortical** segments of the superficial uriniferous tubules. The peritubular capillary network drains consecutively into the stellate vein, the **interlobular vein**, and interlobular veins converging to form the **arcuate vein**. Arcuate veins drain into the **interlobar veins**, which are continuous with the **renal vein**.

2. The **vasa recta** (**straight vessels**), formed by multiple branching of the efferent arterioles located close to the corticomedullary junction. The **descend-**

Figure 14–3

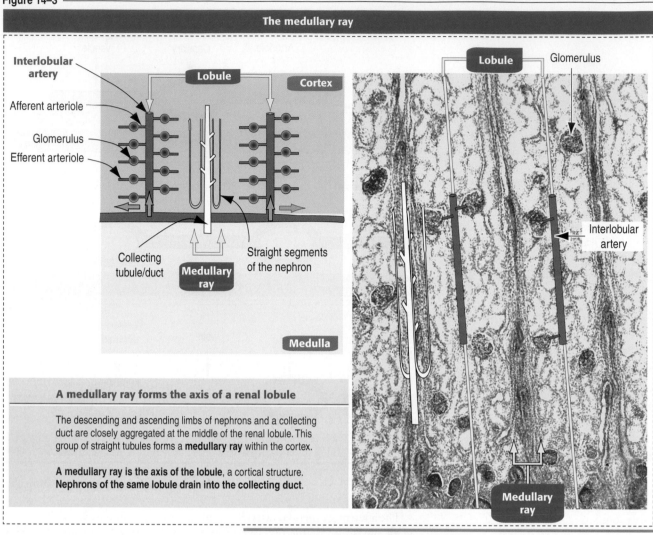

The medullary ray

A medullary ray forms the axis of a renal lobule

The descending and ascending limbs of nephrons and a collecting duct are closely aggregated at the middle of the renal lobule. This group of straight tubules forms a **medullary ray** within the cortex.

A medullary ray is the axis of the lobule, a cortical structure. **Nephrons of the same lobule drain into the collecting duct.**

ing (**arterial**) components of the vasa recta extend into the **medulla**, parallel to the medullary segments of the uriniferous tubules, make a hairpin turn, and return to the corticomedullary junction as **ascending** (**venous**) vessels.

Note that the vascular supply to the renal medulla is largely derived from the efferent glomerular arterioles. The descending vasa recta penetrate to varying depths of the renal medulla, alongside the **descending** and **ascending limbs** of the **loop of Henle** and the **collecting ducts**. Side branches connect the returning ascending vasa recta to the **interlobular** and **arcuate veins**.

Difference between lobe and lobule

A **renal medullary pyramid** is a **medullary** structure limited by interlobar arteries at the sides. The corticomedullary junction is the base and the papilla is the apex of the pyramid.

A **renal lobule** is a **cortical** structure that can be defined in two different ways (see Figure 14–1): (1) The renal lobule is a portion of the cortex **flanked by two adjacent ascending interlobular arteries**. Each interlobular artery gives rise to a series of glomeruli, each consisting of an afferent glomerular arteriole, a capillary network, and the efferent glomerular arteriole. (2) The renal lobule consists of a single **collecting duct** (of Bellini) and the surrounding nephrons that drain into it. The straight portions of the nephrons, together with the single collecting duct, is called a **medullary ray** (of Ferrein). A **medullary ray** is the **axis of the lobule** (Figure 14–3).

Figure 14–4

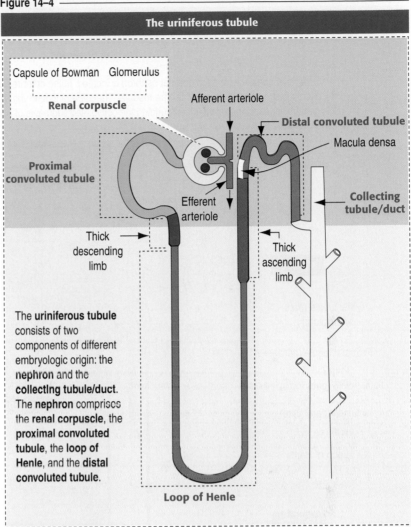

The uriniferous tubule

The **uriniferous tubule** consists of two components of different embryologic origin: the **nephron** and the **collecting tubule/duct**. The **nephron** comprises the **renal corpuscle**, the **proximal convoluted tubule**, the **loop of Henle**, and the **distal convoluted tubule**.

Note that **the cortex has many lobules** and that **each lobule has a single medullary ray**.

The uriniferous tubule consists of a nephron and a collecting duct

Each kidney has about 1.3 million uriniferous tubules surrounded by a stroma containing loose connective tissue, blood vessels, lymphatics, and nerves. Each uriniferous tubule consists of two embryologically distinct segments (Figure 14–4): (1) the **nephron**, and (2) the **collecting duct**.

The **nephron** consists of two components: (1) the **renal corpuscle** (300 μm in diameter), and (2) a long **renal tubule** (5 to 7 mm long).

The **renal tubule** consists of several regions: (1) the **proximal convoluted tubule**, (2) the **loop of Henle**, and (3) the **distal convoluted tubule**, which empties into the **collecting tubule**.

The collecting tubule has three segments: a **cortical segment** and the **outer medullary** and **inner medullary** collecting tubules. The **thick descending** and **thick ascending limbs of Henle** link the proximal and distal convoluted tubules, respectively, to the thin loop of Henle.

Depending on the distribution of renal corpuscles, nephrons can be either **cortical** or **juxtamedullary**. Renal tubules derived from **cortical nephrons** have a **short** loop of Henle that does not penetrate the medulla. Renal tubules from **juxtamedullary nephrons** have a **long** loop of Henle projecting deep into the medulla (Figure 14–5).

Figure 14–5

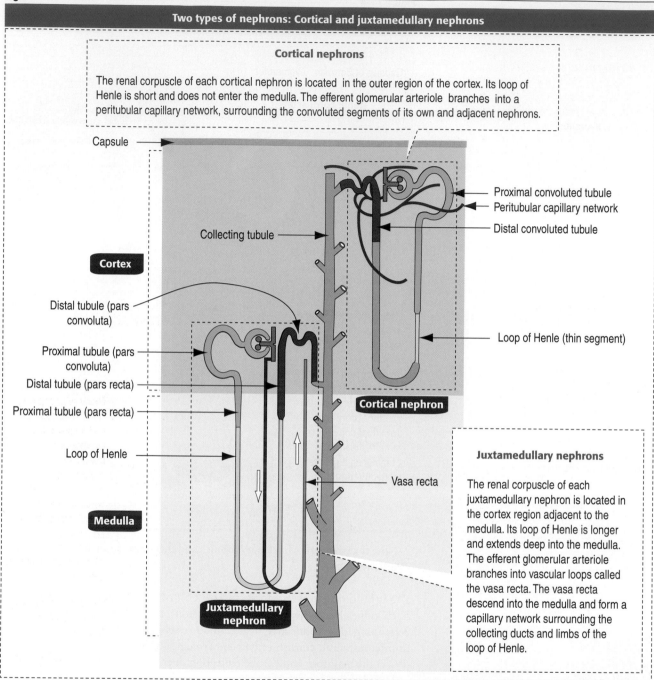

Two types of nephrons: Cortical and juxtamedullary nephrons

Cortical nephrons

The renal corpuscle of each cortical nephron is located in the outer region of the cortex. Its loop of Henle is short and does not enter the medulla. The efferent glomerular arteriole branches into a peritubular capillary network, surrounding the convoluted segments of its own and adjacent nephrons.

Capsule

Collecting tubule

Cortex

Distal tubule (pars convoluta)

Proximal tubule (pars convoluta)

Distal tubule (pars recta)

Proximal tubule (pars recta)

Loop of Henle

Medulla

Juxtamedullary nephron

Proximal convoluted tubule
Peritubular capillary network

Distal convoluted tubule

Loop of Henle (thin segment)

Cortical nephron

Vasa recta

Juxtamedullary nephrons

The renal corpuscle of each juxtamedullary nephron is located in the cortex region adjacent to the medulla. Its loop of Henle is longer and extends deep into the medulla. The efferent glomerular arteriole branches into vascular loops called the vasa recta. The vasa recta descend into the medulla and form a capillary network surrounding the collecting ducts and limbs of the loop of Henle.

The nephron: The renal corpuscle is the filtering unit

The **renal corpuscle**, or **malpighian corpuscle** (Figure 14–6), consists of the **capsule of Bowman** investing a capillary tuft, the **glomerulus**.

The **capsule of Bowman** has two layers: (1) the **visceral layer**, attached to the capillary glomerulus, and (2) the **parietal layer**, associated with the connective tissue stroma.

The visceral layer is lined by epithelial cells called **podocytes**, reinforced by a basal lamina. The parietal layer is covered by a basal lamina supported **simple squamous epithelium** and is continuous with the **simple cuboidal epithelium** of the proximal convoluted tubule.

A **urinary space** (Bowman's space), containing the **plasma ultrafiltrate** (primary urine), exists between the visceral and parietal layers of the capsule. The

Figure 14–6

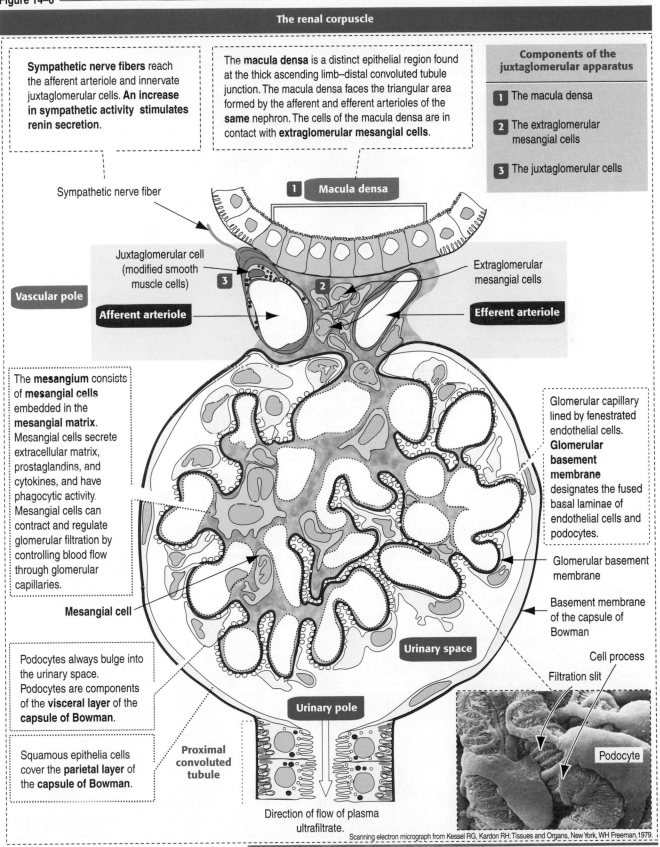

The renal corpuscle

Sympathetic nerve fibers reach the afferent arteriole and innervate juxtaglomerular cells. **An increase in sympathetic activity stimulates renin secretion**.

The **macula densa** is a distinct epithelial region found at the thick ascending limb–distal convoluted tubule junction. The macula densa faces the triangular area formed by the afferent and efferent arterioles of the **same** nephron. The cells of the macula densa are in contact with **extraglomerular mesangial cells**.

Components of the juxtaglomerular apparatus

1 The macula densa

2 The extraglomerular mesangial cells

3 The juxtaglomerular cells

1 Macula densa

Sympathetic nerve fiber

Juxtaglomerular cell (modified smooth muscle cells) **3**

Vascular pole

Afferent arteriole

2

Extraglomerular mesangial cells

Efferent arteriole

The **mesangium** consists of **mesangial cells** embedded in the **mesangial matrix**. Mesangial cells secrete extracellular matrix, prostaglandins, and cytokines, and have phagocytic activity. Mesangial cells can contract and regulate glomerular filtration by controlling blood flow through glomerular capillaries.

Mesangial cell

Glomerular capillary lined by fenestrated endothelial cells. **Glomerular basement membrane** designates the fused basal laminae of endothelial cells and podocytes.

Glomerular basement membrane

Basement membrane of the capsule of Bowman

Urinary space

Cell process

Filtration slit

Podocytes always bulge into the urinary space. Podocytes are components of the **visceral layer** of the **capsule of Bowman**.

Squamous epithelia cells cover the **parietal layer** of the **capsule of Bowman**.

Urinary pole

Proximal convoluted tubule

Podocyte

Direction of flow of plasma ultrafiltrate.

Scanning electron micrograph from Kessel RG, Kardon RH: Tissues and Organs, New York, WH Freeman, 1979.

plasma ultrafiltrate contains trace amounts of protein. The urinary space is continuous with the lumen of the proximal convoluted tubule at the **urinary pole**,

Figure 14–7

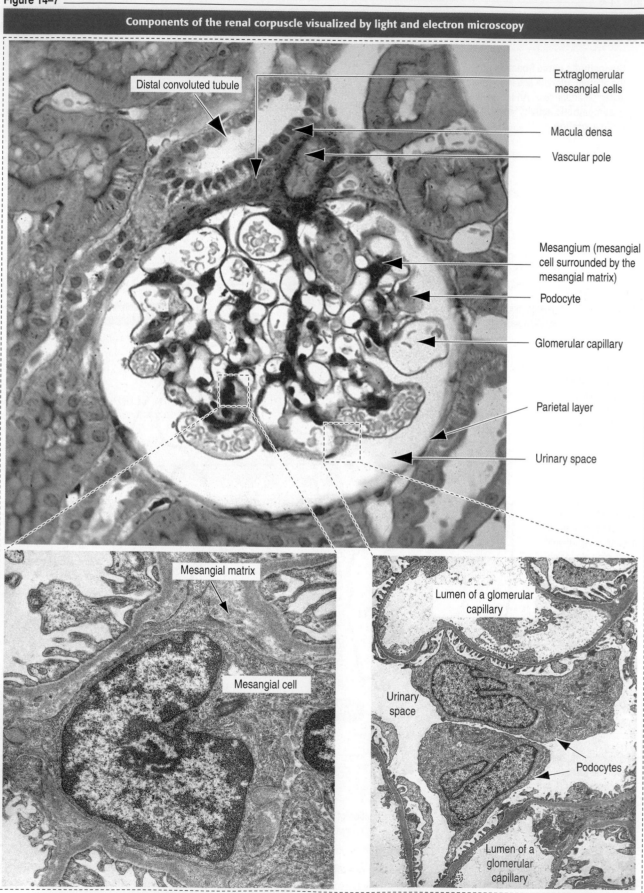

Components of the renal corpuscle visualized by light and electron microscopy

Distal convoluted tubule

Extraglomerular mesangial cells

Macula densa

Vascular pole

Mesangium (mesangial cell surrounded by the mesangial matrix)

Podocyte

Glomerular capillary

Parietal layer

Urinary space

Mesangial matrix

Mesangial cell

Lumen of a glomerular capillary

Urinary space

Podocytes

Lumen of a glomerular capillary

the gate through which the plasma ultrafiltrate flows into the proximal convoluted tubule. The opposite pole, the site of entry and exit of the afferent and efferent glomerular arterioles, is called the **vascular pole**.

The **glomerulus** consists of three components (Figure 14–7):

1. The glomerular **capillaries**, lined by **fenestrated endothelial cells**.

2. The **mesangium**, formed by **mesangial cells** embedded in the **mesangial matrix**.

3. The **podocytes**, constituents of the **visceral layer** of the capsule of Bowman. Recall that the **parietal layer** of the capsule Bowman is a simple squamous epithelium.

The podocytes

The podocytes have long and branching cell processes that completely encircle the surface of the glomerular capillary. Both podocytes and fenestrated endothelial cells and their corresponding basal laminae constitute the **glomerular filtration barrier**.

The endings of the cell processes, the pedicels, from the same podocyte or adjacent podocytes, interdigitate to cover the basal lamina and are separated by gaps, the **filtration slits**. Filtration slits are bridged by a membranous material, the **filtration slit diaphragm** (Figure 14–8). Pedicels are attached to the basal lamina by $\alpha_3\beta_1$ **integrin**.

The filtration slit diaphragm consists of the protein **nephrin** anchored to actin filaments (within the pedicel) by the protein **CD2AP**. Nephrin seems to retard the passage of molecules crossing the endothelial fenestrations and the basal laminae.

In addition to the components of the glomerular filtration barrier, other limiting factors controlling the passage of molecules in the plasma ultrafiltrate are size and electric charge. Molecules with a size less that 3.5 nm and positively charged or neutral are filtered more readily. Albumin (3.6 nm and anionic) filters poorly.

Clinical significance of the glomerular filtration barrier: Alport's syndrome and the congenital nephrotic syndrome

The **fenestrated endothelial cells** of the glomerular capillaries are covered by a basal lamina to which the foot processes of the podocytes attach (see Figure 14–8).

The endothelium is permeable to water, urea, glucose, and small proteins. The surface of the endothelial cells is coated with negatively charged glycoproteins that block the passage of large anionic proteins.

The endothelial cell **basal lamina**, closely associated with the basal lamina produced by podocytes, contains **type IV collagen, fibronectin, laminin,** and **heparan sulfate** as major proteins.

Each type IV collagen monomer consists of three α chains forming a triple helix. There are six chains (α1 to α6) encoded by six genes (*COL4A1* through *COL4A6*). Two domains of each monomer are important: (1) the noncollagenous (**NC1**) **domain** at the C-terminal, and (2) the **7S domain** at the N-terminal. The NC1 and 7S domains, separated by a long collagenous domain, are cross-linking domains required for the formation the type IV collagen network. A correctly assembled network is critical for maintaining the integrity of the glomerular basal lamina and its permeability function.

Type IV collagens are directly involved in the pathogenesis of three diseases. (1) **Goodpasture syndrome**, an autoimmune disorder consisting in progressive glomerulonephritis and pulmonary hemorrhage, caused by anti-α3(IV) antibodies binding to the glomerular and alveolar basal lamina. (2) **Alport's syndrome**, a progressive inherited nephropathy, characterized by irregular thinning, thickening, and splitting of the glomerular basal lamina. Alport's syndrome is transmit-

Figure 14–8

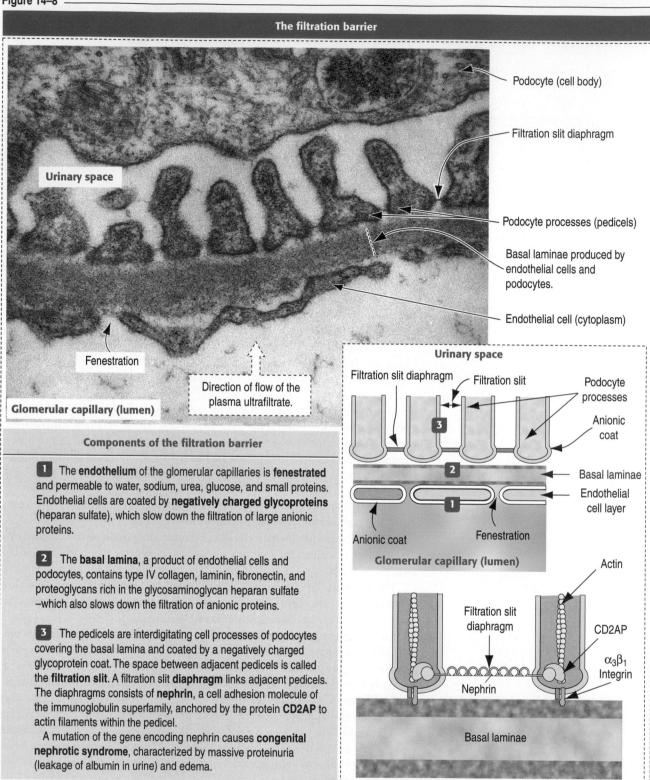

The filtration barrier

Urinary space

Podocyte (cell body)

Filtration slit diaphragm

Podocyte processes (pedicels)

Basal laminae produced by endothelial cells and podocytes.

Endothelial cell (cytoplasm)

Fenestration

Direction of flow of the plasma ultrafiltrate.

Glomerular capillary (lumen)

Components of the filtration barrier

1 The **endothelium** of the glomerular capillaries is **fenestrated** and permeable to water, sodium, urea, glucose, and small proteins. Endothelial cells are coated by **negatively charged glycoproteins** (heparan sulfate), which slow down the filtration of large anionic proteins.

2 The **basal lamina**, a product of endothelial cells and podocytes, contains type IV collagen, laminin, fibronectin, and proteoglycans rich in the glycosaminoglycan heparan sulfate –which also slows down the filtration of anionic proteins.

3 The pedicels are interdigitating cell processes of podocytes covering the basal lamina and coated by a negatively charged glycoprotein coat. The space between adjacent pedicels is called the **filtration slit**. A filtration slit **diaphragm** links adjacent pedicels. The diaphragms consists of **nephrin**, a cell adhesion molecule of the immunoglobulin superfamily, anchored by the protein **CD2AP** to actin filaments within the pedicel.
A mutation of the gene encoding nephrin causes **congenital nephrotic syndrome**, characterized by massive proteinuria (leakage of albumin in urine) and edema.

Urinary space

Filtration slit diaphragm — Filtration slit

Podocyte processes

Anionic coat

3

2

Basal laminae

Endothelial cell layer

1

Anionic coat

Fenestration

Glomerular capillary (lumen)

Actin

Filtration slit diaphragm

CD2AP

$\alpha_3\beta_1$ Integrin

Nephrin

Basal laminae

ted by an **X-linked recessive** trait, is predominant in **males**, and involves mutations of the *COL4A5* gene. Patients with Alport's syndrome—often associated with hearing loss (defective function of the stria vascularis of the cochlea) and ocular symptoms (defect of the lens capsule)—have **hematuria** (blood in the urine) and **progressive glomerulonephritis** leading to renal failure. The abnormal glomerular filtration membrane enables the passage of red blood cells and

Figure 14–9

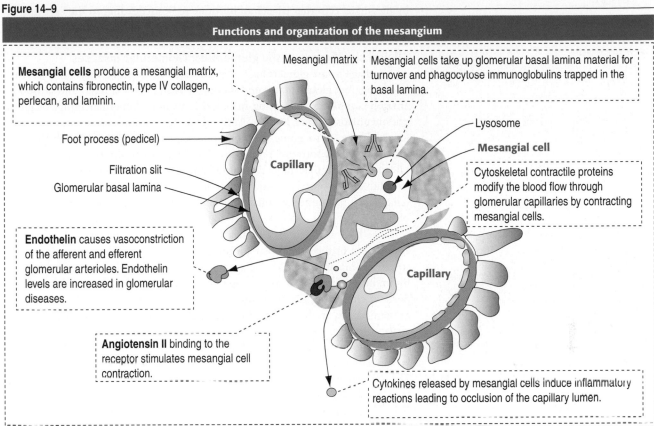

Functions and organization of the mesangium

Mesangial cells produce a mesangial matrix, which contains fibronectin, type IV collagen, perlecan, and laminin.

Mesangial matrix

Mesangial cells take up glomerular basal lamina material for turnover and phagocytose immunoglobulins trapped in the basal lamina.

Foot process (pedicel)

Filtration slit

Glomerular basal lamina

Capillary

Lysosome

Mesangial cell

Cytoskeletal contractile proteins modify the blood flow through glomerular capillaries by contracting mesangial cells.

Endothelin causes vasoconstriction of the afferent and efferent glomerular arterioles. Endothelin levels are increased in glomerular diseases.

Capillary

Angiotensin II binding to the receptor stimulates mesangial cell contraction.

Cytokines released by mesangial cells induce inflammatory reactions leading to occlusion of the capillary lumen.

proteins. (3) **Benign family hematuria**, caused by a dominant inherited mutation of the *COL4A4* gene, which does not lead to renal failure.

The mesangium

The mesangium is an **intraglomerular** structure interposed between the glomerular capillaries, consisting of two components: (1) the **mesangial cells**, and (2) the **mesangial matrix**.

In addition, mesangial cells aggregate outside the glomerulus (**extraglomerular mesangial cells**; see Figures 14–7 and 14–15) in a space limited by the macula densa and the afferent and efferent glomerular arterioles. Intraglomerular mesangial cells may be continuous with **extraglomerular mesangial cells**.

Mesangial cells are specialized **pericytes** with characteristics of smooth muscle cells and macrophages.

Mesangial cells are (1) **contractile**, (2) **phagocytic**, (3) capable of **proliferation**, (4) synthesize **both matrix and collagen**, and (5) secrete **biologically active substances** (prostaglandins and endothelins). Endothelins induce the constriction of afferent and efferent glomerular arterioles.

Mesangial cells participate indirectly in the glomerular filtration process by

1. **Providing mechanical support for the glomerular capillaries.**

2. **Controlling the turnover of the glomerular basal lamina material** by their phagocytic activity.

3. **Regulating blood flow** by their contractile activity.

4. **Secreting prostaglandins and endothelins.**

5. **Responding to angiotensin II.**

The glomerular filtration membrane does not completely surround the capillaries (Figure 14–9). Immunoglobulins and complement molecules, unable to cross the filtration barrier, can enter the mesangial matrix. The accumulation of immunoglobulin complexes in the matrix induces the production of cytokines by mesangial cells that trigger an immune response leading to the eventual occlusion of the glomerulus.

Clinical significance of the glomerulus: Glomerular diseases

The damage to the glomerulus can be initiated by immune mechanisms. **Antibodies against glomerular components** (cells and basal lamina) and **antibody-antigen complexes circulating in blood** can cause glomerular injury or **glomerulonephritis** (Figure 14–10). Antibody-antigen complexes are not immunologically targeted to glomerular components. They are trapped in the glomerulus because of the filtration properties of the glomerular filtration barrier. A complicating factor is that trapped antibody-antigen complexes provide binding sites to complement proteins, which also contribute to the glomerular damage (see Chapter 10, Immune-Lymphatic System, for a review of the complement cascade).

As we have seen, autoantibodies can target domains of type IV collagen, a component of the glomerular filtration barrier. The binding of antibodies to specific domains of type IV collagen generate a **diffuse linear pattern** detected by immunofluorescence microscopy (see Figure 14–10). In addition, the deposit of circulating antibody-antigen complexes produces a **granular pattern**. Systemic lupus erythematosus and bacterial (streptococci) and viral (hepatitis B virus) infections generate antibody-antigen complexes circulating in blood.

Immune complexes can deposit between the endothelial cells of the glomerular capillaries and the basal lamina (**subendothelial deposits**), in the mesangium, and less frequently between the basal lamina and the foot processes of podocytes (**subepithelial deposits**).

Immune complexes produced after bacterial infection can cause the proliferation of glomerular cells (endothelial and mesangial cells) and attract neutrophils and monocytes. This condition, known as **acute proliferative glomerulonephritis**, is observed in children and is generally reversible with treatment. This disease is more severe in adults: it can evolve into **rapidly progressive (crescentic) glomerulonephritis** (Figure 14–11).

A typical feature of crescentic glomerulonephritis is the presence of glomerular cell debris, causing severe glomerular injury. The proliferation of parietal cells of the capsule of Bowman and migrating neutrophils and lymphocytes into the space of Bowman occur. Both the cellular crescents and deposits of fibrin compress the glomerular capillaries.

The juxtaglomerular apparatus

The juxtaglomerular apparatus is a small endocrine structure consisting of
1. The **macula densa** (see Figure 14–7), a distinct region of the initial portion of the distal convoluted tubule.
2. The **extraglomerular mesangial cells** (see Figure 14–7).
3. The **renin-producing cells (juxtaglomerular cells)** of the afferent glomerular arteriole (see Figure 14–7) and, to a lesser extent, the efferent glomerular arteriole.

The macula densa is sensitive to changes in NaCl concentration and effects renin release by juxtaglomerular cells. Renin is secreted when the NaCl concentration or blood pressure falls. Extraglomerular mesangial cells (also called **lacis cells**) are connected to each other and to juxtaglomerular cells by gap junctions.

The juxtaglomerular apparatus is one of the components of the **tubuloglomerular feedback mechanism** involved in the autoregulation of **renal blood flow** and **glomerular filtration**.

The other component is the **sympathetic nerve fibers** (adrenergic) innervating the juxtaglomerular cells. Renin secretion is enhanced by **norepinephrine** and **dopamine** secreted by adrenergic nerve fibers. Norepinephrine binds to α_1-adrenergic receptors in the afferent glomerular arteriole to cause vasoconstric-

Figure 14–10

Pathology of the mesangium

1 **Anti-glomerular basement membrane (GBM) antibodies** target the NC1 domain of type IV collagen. Anti-GBM immunoglobulins bind on the entire length of the basal lamina creating a **linear pattern visible by immunofluorescence**. Anti-GBM antibodies cause anti-GBM nephritis, characterized by severe glomerular damage evolving progressively into renal failure.

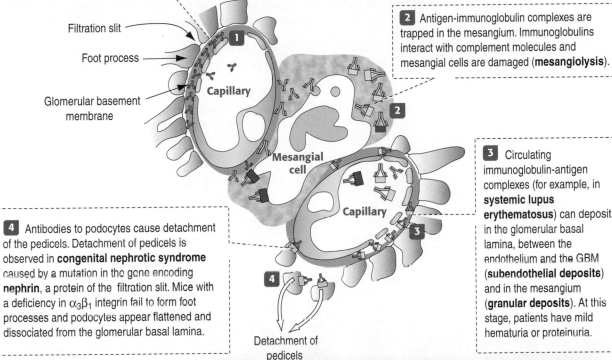

2 Antigen-immunoglobulin complexes are trapped in the mesangium. Immunoglobulins interact with complement molecules and mesangial cells are damaged (**mesangiolysis**).

Filtration slit

Foot process

Glomerular basement membrane

Capillary

Mesangial cell

Capillary

3 Circulating immunoglobulin-antigen complexes (for example, in **systemic lupus erythematosus**) can deposit in the glomerular basal lamina, between the endothelium and the GBM (**subendothelial deposits**) and in the mesangium (**granular deposits**). At this stage, patients have mild hematuria or proteinuria.

4 Antibodies to podocytes cause detachment of the pedicels. Detachment of pedicels is observed in **congenital nephrotic syndrome** caused by a mutation in the gene encoding **nephrin**, a protein of the filtration slit. Mice with a deficiency in $\alpha_3\beta_1$ integrin fail to form foot processes and podocytes appear flattened and dissociated from the glomerular basal lamina.

Detachment of pedicels

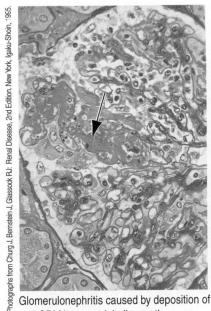

Photographs from Churg J, Bernstein J, Glassock RJ: Renal Disease, 2nd Edition. New York, Igaku-Shoin, 1955.

Glomerulonephritis caused by deposition of anti-GBM immunoglobulins on the basement membrane. **The occlusion of capillaries is indicated by the arrow.**

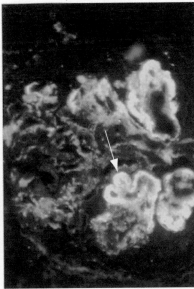

Linear pattern (arrow) of immunoglobulin-antigen complexes on the GBM. Immunofluorescence microscopy.

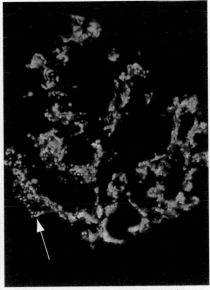

Glomerular lesion caused by granular deposits (arrow) **of immunoglobulin-antigen complexes on the GBM** (hepatitis B virus). Immunofluorescence microscopy.

tion. There is no parasympathetic innervation.

We come back to the tubuloglomerular feedback mechanism when we discuss the renin-angiotensin-aldosterone regulatory mechanism (see Figure 14–17).

Figure 14–11

Pathology of the renal corpuscle: Glomerulonephritis

Acute proliferative diffuse glomerulonephritis

The deposition of immune complexes in the GBM (resulting from a bacterial, viral, or protozoal infection) triggers the proliferation of endothelial and mesangial cells. In the presence of complement proteins, neutrophils accumulate in the lumen of the capillaries, which become occluded.

A **nephritic syndrome**, characterized by hematuria, oliguria, hypertension, and edema, is diagnosed. Children are predominantly affected.

The nephritic syndrome is reversible: Immune complexes are removed from the GBM, endothelial cells are shed, and the population of proliferative mesangial cells returns to normal. The renal function is reestablished.

Rapidly progressive (crescentic) glomerulonephritis

The proliferation of the epithelial cells of the capsule of Bowman and infiltration of macrophages produce a crescent-like mass in most glomeruli. The crescent enlarges and compresses the glomerular capillaries, which are displaced and stop functioning. This condition progresses rapidly to renal failure.

The accumulation of fibrin and other serum proteins and the necrosis of the glomerular capillaries stimulate the proliferative process.

Rapidly progressive glomerulonephritis is an immune-mediated process and is detected in a number of conditions, such as **Goodpasture syndrome** (caused by antibodies binding to the 7S domain of type IV collagen of the GBM), **systemic lupus erythematosus**, or of unknown cause (**idiopathic**).

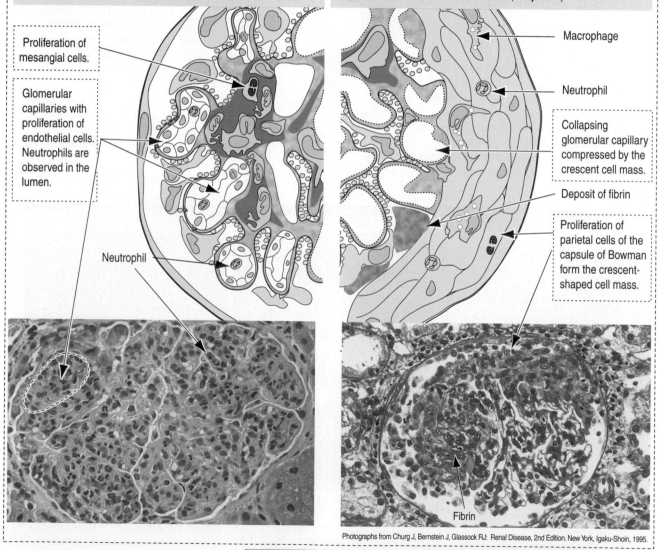

Proliferation of mesangial cells.

Glomerular capillaries with proliferation of endothelial cells. Neutrophils are observed in the lumen.

Neutrophil

Macrophage

Neutrophil

Collapsing glomerular capillary compressed by the crescent cell mass.

Deposit of fibrin

Proliferation of parietal cells of the capsule of Bowman form the crescent-shaped cell mass.

Fibrin

Photographs from Churg J, Bernstein J, Glassock RJ: Renal Disease, 2nd Edition. New York, Igaku-Shoin, 1995.

Proximal convoluted tubule: The reabsorption component

The plasma ultrafiltrate in the urinary space is transported by **active** and **passive** mechanisms to the proximal convoluted tubule, where about 70% of filtered water, glucose, Na⁺, Cl⁻, and K⁺, and other solutes are reabsorbed.

Figure 14–12

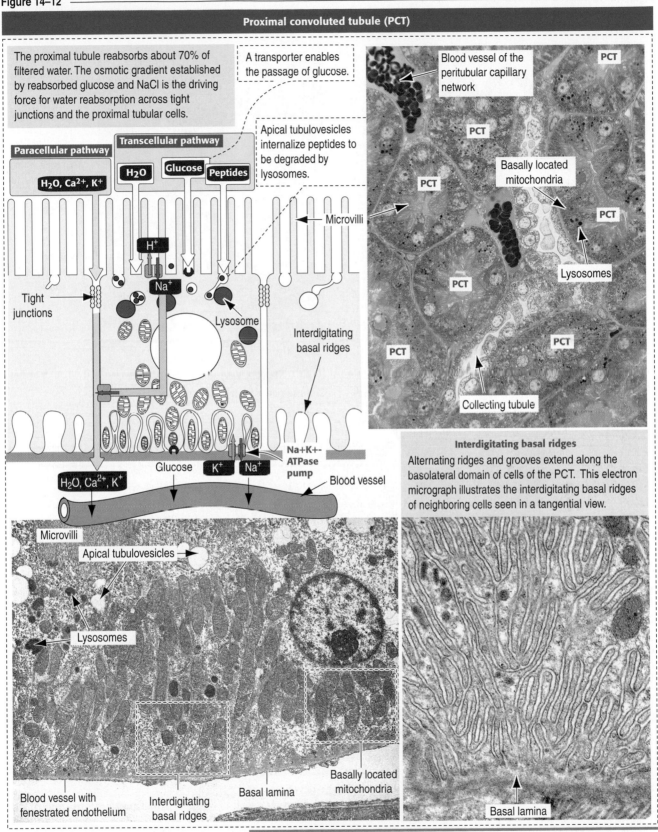

Proximal convoluted tubule (PCT)

The proximal tubule reabsorbs about 70% of filtered water. The osmotic gradient established by reabsorbed glucose and NaCl is the driving force for water reabsorption across tight junctions and the proximal tubular cells.

A transporter enables the passage of glucose.

Apical tubulovesicles internalize peptides to be degraded by lysosomes.

Paracellular pathway

Transcellular pathway

H_2O, Ca^{2+}, K^+

H_2O Glucose Peptides

Microvilli

H^+

Na^+

Tight junctions

Lysosome

Interdigitating basal ridges

H_2O, Ca^{2+}, K^+

Glucose K^+ Na^+

Na+K+-ATPase pump

Blood vessel

Microvilli

Apical tubulovesicles

Lysosomes

Blood vessel with fenestrated endothelium

Interdigitating basal ridges

Basal lamina

Basally located mitochondria

Blood vessel of the peritubular capillary network

PCT

PCT

PCT

PCT

Basally located mitochondria

PCT

Lysosomes

PCT

PCT

PCT

Collecting tubule

Interdigitating basal ridges

Alternating ridges and grooves extend along the basolateral domain of cells of the PCT. This electron micrograph illustrates the interdigitating basal ridges of neighboring cells seen in a tangential view.

Basal lamina

Cuboidal epithelial cells, held together by apical **tight junctions**, line the proximal convoluted tubule and have structural characteristics suitable for reabsorption. They display the following features (Figure 14–12):

Figure 14–13

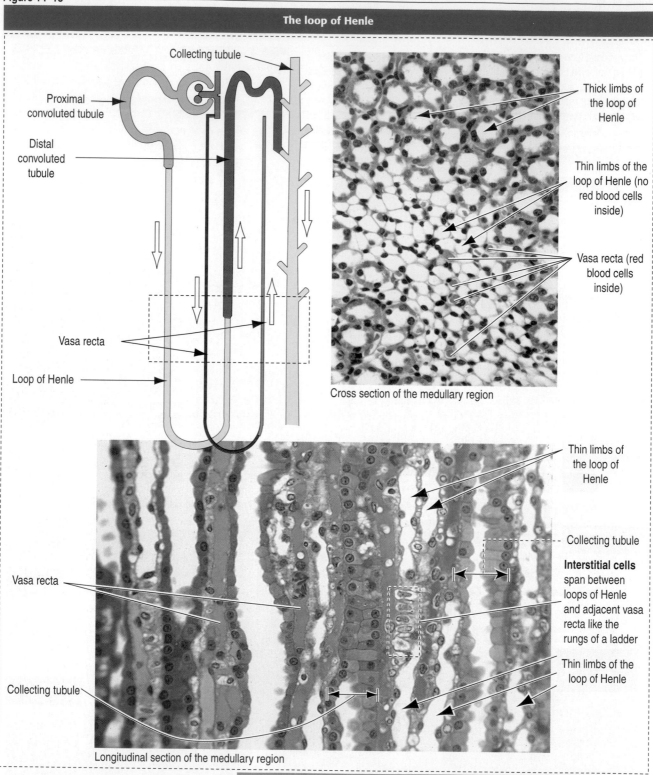

The loop of Henle

Collecting tubule

Proximal convoluted tubule

Distal convoluted tubule

Vasa recta

Loop of Henle

Thick limbs of the loop of Henle

Thin limbs of the loop of Henle (no red blood cells inside)

Vasa recta (red blood cells inside)

Cross section of the medullary region

Vasa recta

Collecting tubule

Thin limbs of the loop of Henle

Collecting tubule

Interstitial cells span between loops of Henle and adjacent vasa recta like the rungs of a ladder

Thin limbs of the loop of Henle

Longitudinal section of the medullary region

1. An apical domain with a well-developed **brush border** consisting of **microvilli**.

2. A basolateral domain with extensive plasma membrane **infoldings** and **interdigitations**.

3. Long mitochondria located between the plasma membrane folds provide adenosine triphosphate (ATP) for active transport of ions mediated by a Mg^{2+}-

Interstitial cells

We noted in Figure 14–13 the presence of **interstitial cells** extending from the loops of Henle to adjacent vasa recta. The cytoplasm of renal medullary intestitial cells contains **actin filaments**. It has been suggested that interstitial cells may regulate papillary blood flow by contracting in response to hormonal stimulation. **Lipid droplets** can also be seen in their cytoplasm. The physiological significance of interstitial cells has not been determined.

dependent Na$^+$, K$^+$ activated pump.

4. Apical **tubulovesicles** and **lysosomes** provide a mechanism for endocytosis and breakdown of small proteins into amino acids. The movement of **urea** and **glucose** across the plasma membrane is mediated by a **transport protein**. Reabsorbed material enters the peritubular capillary network.

The driving force for water reabsorption is a **transcellular** osmotic gradient established by the reabsorption of solutes, such as NaCl and glucose. Because the proximal convoluted tubule is highly permeable to water, water passes by osmosis across tight junctions (**paracellular pathway**) into the lateral intercellular space. An increase in the hydrostatic pressure in the intercellular compartment forces

Figure 14–14

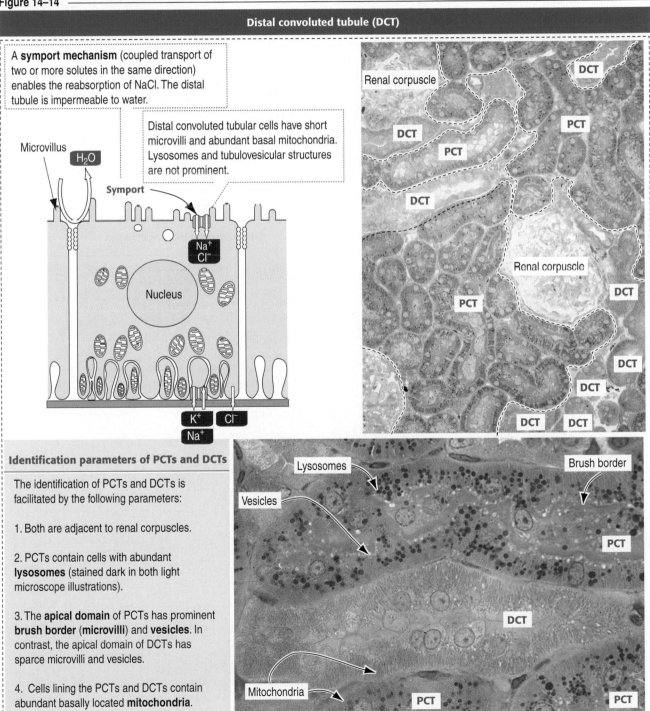

Distal convoluted tubule (DCT)

A **symport mechanism** (coupled transport of two or more solutes in the same direction) enables the reabsorption of NaCl. The distal tubule is impermeable to water.

Distal convoluted tubular cells have short microvilli and abundant basal mitochondria. Lysosomes and tubulovesicular structures are not prominent.

Microvillus

H$_2$O

Symport

Na$^+$ Cl$^-$

Nucleus

K$^+$ Cl$^-$ Na$^+$

Renal corpuscle

DCT

PCT

DCT

PCT

DCT

DCT

Renal corpuscle

PCT

DCT

DCT

DCT

DCT DCT

Identification parameters of PCTs and DCTs

The identification of PCTs and DCTs is facilitated by the following parameters:

1. Both are adjacent to renal corpuscles.

2. PCTs contain cells with abundant **lysosomes** (stained dark in both light microscope illustrations).

3. The **apical domain** of PCTs has prominent **brush border (microvilli)** and **vesicles**. In contrast, the apical domain of DCTs has sparse microvilli and vesicles.

4. Cells lining the PCTs and DCTs contain abundant basally located **mitochondria**.

Lysosomes

Vesicles

Brush border

PCT

DCT

Mitochondria

PCT

PCT

Figure 14–15

The juxtaglomerular cell. The distal convoluted tubule

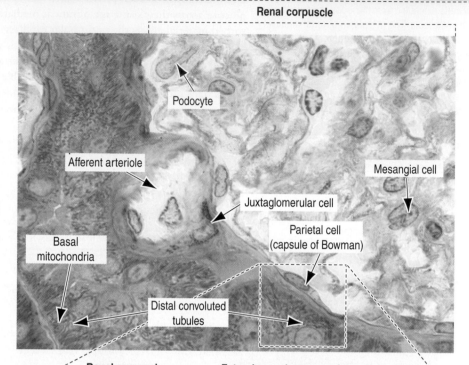

Renal corpuscle

Podocyte

Afferent arteriole

Mesangial cell

Juxtaglomerular cell

Parietal cell
(capsule of Bowman)

Basal
mitochondria

Distal convoluted
tubules

The juxtaglomerular cell
1. It is predominant in the **afferent arteriole** of the glomerulus.
2. It is a modified smooth muscle cell producing the enzyme **renin**.
3. Together with extraglomerular mesangial cells and the macula densa of the distal convoluted tubule, it is part of the **juxtaglomerular apparatus**.
4. Is innervated by **sympathetic nerve fibers**. Renin secretion is enhanced by **norepinephrine** and **dopamine** secreted by adrenergic nerve fibers.

Distal convoluted tubule
1. It is lined by cuboid cells lacking a prominent brush border.
2. The plasma membrane of the basolateral domain is infolded and accommodates abundant mitochondria.
3. Lysosomes and apical tubulo-vesicles are not prominent.
4. Sections of distal convoluted tubules are found adjacent to the renal corpuscle.

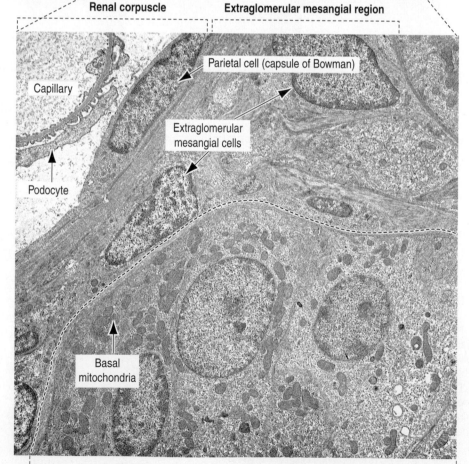

Renal corpuscle

Extraglomerular mesangial region

Parietal cell (capsule of Bowman)

Capillary

Extraglomerular
mesangial cells

Podocyte

Basal
mitochondria

Distal convoluted tubule

fluids and solutes to move into the capillary network.

The **Fanconi syndrome** is a renal hereditary or acquired disease in which proximal convoluted tubules fail to reabsorb amino acids and glucose. Consequently, these substances are excreted in urine.

Loop of Henle

The loop of Henle reabsorbs about 15% of the filtered water and 25% of the filtered NaCl, K^+, Ca^{2+}, and HCO_3^-.

The loop of Henle consists of a **descending limb** and an **ascending limb**. Each limb is formed by a **thick segment** and a **thin segment** (Figure 14–13).

The thick descending segment is a continuation of the proximal convoluted tubule. The thick ascending segment is continuous with the distal convoluted tubule.

The length of the thin segments varies in cortical and juxtamedullary nephrons. Because **the ascending limb is impermeable to water**, filtered water reabsorption occurs exclusively in the descending limb, driven by an osmotic gradient between the tubular fluid and the interstitial fluid.

As in the proximal convoluted tubule, a **Na^+, K^+ ATPase pump** in the ascending limb is a key element in the reabsorption of solutes. Inhibition of this pump by **diuretics** such as **furosemide** (Lasix) inhibits the reabsorption of NaCl and increases urinary excretion of both NaCl and water by reducing the osmolality of the interstitial fluid in the medulla.

The thick segments of the limbs are lined by a low cuboidal epithelium in transition with the epithelial lining of the proximal tubules. The thin segments are lined by a squamous simple epithelium.

Distal convoluted tubule

The distal convoluted tubule and the collecting duct reabsorb approximately 7% of the filtered NaCl. The **distal portion** of the **distal convoluted tubule** and the **collecting ducts** are permeable to water in the presence of **antidiuretic hormone**

Figure 14–16

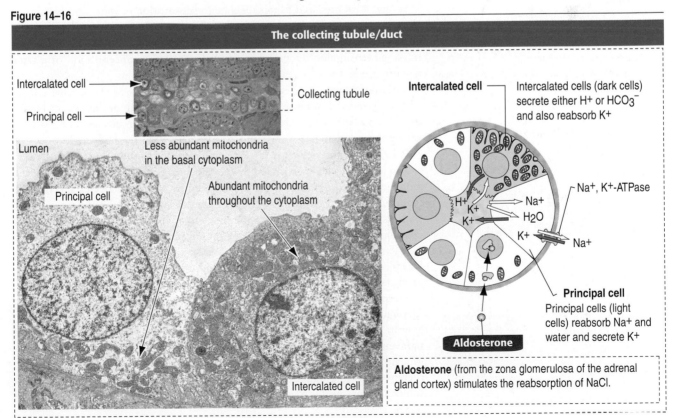

The collecting tubule/duct

Intercalated cell
Principal cell
Collecting tubule
Lumen
Less abundant mitochondria in the basal cytoplasm
Principal cell
Abundant mitochondria throughout the cytoplasm
Intercalated cell

Intercalated cell — Intercalated cells (dark cells) secrete either H^+ or HCO_3^- and also reabsorb K^+

Na^+, K^+-ATPase

H^+ K^+ Na^+ H_2O K^+ K^+ Na^+

Principal cell
Principal cells (light cells) reabsorb Na^+ and water and secrete K^+

Aldosterone

Aldosterone (from the zona glomerulosa of the adrenal gland cortex) stimulates the reabsorption of NaCl.

(ADH, vasopressin).

NaCl enters the cell across the apical domain and leaves the cell by a Na^+,K^+ ATPase pump (Figure 14–14). The reabsorption of NaCl is reduced by **thiazide diuretics** that inhibit the apical domain transporting mechanism (see Figure 14–20).

The active dilution of the tubular fluid initiated in the ascending segments of the loop of Henle continues in the distal convoluted tubule. Because the ascending segment of the loop of Henle is the major site where water and solutes are separated, the excretion of both dilute and concentrated urine requires the normal function of the loop of Henle.

The cuboidal epithelial cell lining of the distal convoluted tubule has the following characteristics (Figure14–14; see Figure 14–15):

1. **Cuboidal cells are shorter** than those in the proximal convoluted tubule and **lack a prominent brush border**.

2. As in the proximal convoluted tubule, the plasma membrane of the basolateral domain is infolded and lodges mitochondria.

3. In the **macula densa**, the cells display a **reversed polarity**: the nucleus occupies an apical position and the basal domain, containing a Golgi apparatus, faces the juxtaglomerular cells and extraglomerular mesangial cells. The macula densa, located at the junction of the ascending thick segment with the distal convoluted tubule, senses changes in Na^+ concentration in the tubular fluid.

Collecting tubule (duct)

The collecting tubule (also called duct) is lined by a cuboidal epithelium composed of two cell types: **principal cells** and **intercalated cells** (Figure 14–16). Principal cells have a basolateral domain with moderate infoldings and mitochondria. They reabsorb Na^+ and water and secrete K^+ in a Na^+,K^+ ATPase pump–dependent manner. Intercalated cells have abundant mitochondria and secrete either H^+ or HCO_3^-. Therefore, they are important regulators of acid-base balance. They also reabsorb K^+.

Several hormones and factors regulate the absorption of water and NaCl:

1. **Angiotensin II** stimulates NaCl and water reabsorption in the proximal convoluted tubule. A decrease in the extracellular fluid volume activates the renin-angiotensin-aldosterone system and increases the concentration of plasma angiotensin II.

2. **Aldosterone**, synthesized by the glomerulosa cells of the adrenal cortex, stimulates the reabsorption of NaCl at the ascending limb of the loop of Henle, the distal convoluted tubule, and the collecting tubule. An increase in the plasma concentration of angiotensin II and K^+ stimulates aldosterone secretion.

3. **Atrial natriuretic factor** (a 28–amino acid peptide) and **urodilatin** (a 32–amino acid peptide) are encoded by the same gene and have similar amino acid sequences. Atrial natriuretic factor is secreted by atrial cardiocytes and has two main functions: (1) It increases the urinary excretion of NaCl and water. (2) It inhibits the release of ADH from the neurohypophysis. Urodilatin is secreted by epithelial cells of the distal convoluted tubule and collecting tubule and inhibits NaCl and water reabsorption by the medullary portion of the collecting tubule. Urodilatin is a more potent natriuretic and diuretic hormone than atrial natriuretic factor.

4. **Antidiuretic hormone**, or **vasopressin**, is the most important hormone in the regulation of water balance. ADH is a small peptide (nine amino acids in length) synthesized by neuroendocrine cells located within the **supraoptic** and **paraventricular nuclei** of the **hypothalamus**. When the extracellular fluid volume decreases, ADH increases the permeability of the collecting tubule to water, thereby increasing water reabsorption. When ADH is not present, the collecting tubule is impermeable to water. ADH has little effect on the urinary excretion of NaCl.

Figure 14–17

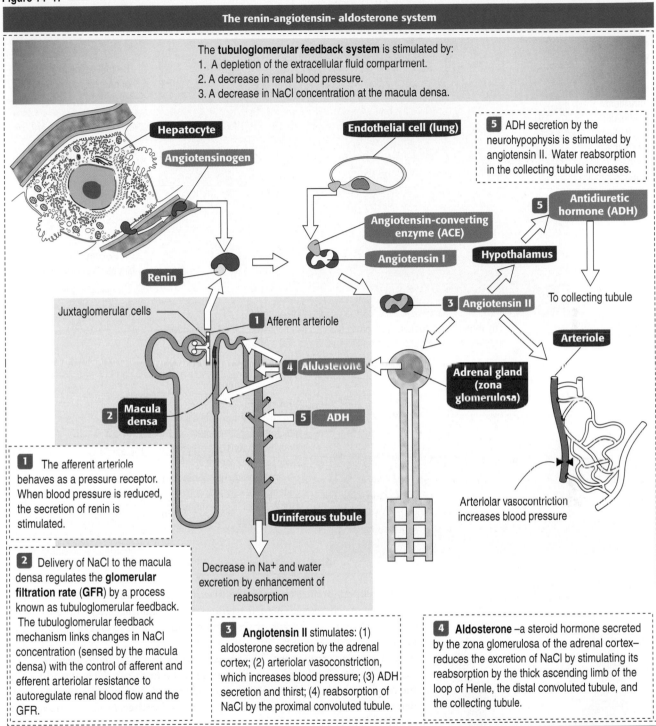

The renin-angiotensin- aldosterone system

The **tubuloglomerular feedback system** is stimulated by:
1. A depletion of the extracellular fluid compartment.
2. A decrease in renal blood pressure.
3. A decrease in NaCl concentration at the macula densa.

Hepatocyte

Angiotensinogen

Renin

Juxtaglomerular cells

Endothelial cell (lung)

Angiotensin-converting enzyme (ACE)

Angiotensin I

Hypothalamus

3 **Angiotensin II**

5 ADH secretion by the neurohypophysis is stimulated by angiotensin II. Water reabsorption in the collecting tubule increases.

5 **Antidiuretic hormone (ADH)**

To collecting tubule

Arteriole

1 Afferent arteriole

4 **Aldosterone**

2 **Macula densa**

5 **ADH**

Adrenal gland (zona glomerulosa)

Arteriolar vasocontriction increases blood pressure

Uriniferous tubule

Decrease in Na+ and water excretion by enhancement of reabsorption

1 The afferent arteriole behaves as a pressure receptor. When blood pressure is reduced, the secretion of renin is stimulated.

2 Delivery of NaCl to the macula densa regulates the **glomerular filtration rate (GFR)** by a process known as tubuloglomerular feedback. The tubuloglomerular feedback mechanism links changes in NaCl concentration (sensed by the macula densa) with the control of afferent and efferent arteriolar resistance to autoregulate renal blood flow and the GFR.

3 **Angiotensin II** stimulates: (1) aldosterone secretion by the adrenal cortex; (2) arteriolar vasoconstriction, which increases blood pressure; (3) ADH secretion and thirst; (4) reabsorption of NaCl by the proximal convoluted tubule.

4 **Aldosterone** –a steroid hormone secreted by the zona glomerulosa of the adrenal cortex– reduces the excretion of NaCl by stimulating its reabsorption by the thick ascending limb of the loop of Henle, the distal convoluted tubule, and the collecting tubule.

The renin-angiotensin-aldosterone system

This system is a significant component of the **tubuloglomerular feedback system**, essential for the maintenance of systemic arterial blood pressure when there is a reduction in the vascular volume. A reduction in vascular volume results in a decrease in the rate of glomerular filtration and the amount of filtered NaCl. A reduction in filtered NaCl is sensed by the macula densa, which triggers renin secretion and the production of angiotensin II, a potent vasoconstrictor.

The **tubuloglomerular feedback system** consists of

1. A **glomerular component**: The **juxtaglomerular cells** predominate in the

Figure 14–18

The urinary bladder

The **mucosa** of the urinary bladder is folded and lined with transitional epithelium (urothelium). Fibroelastic connective tissue extends into the folds (arrows).

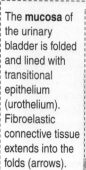
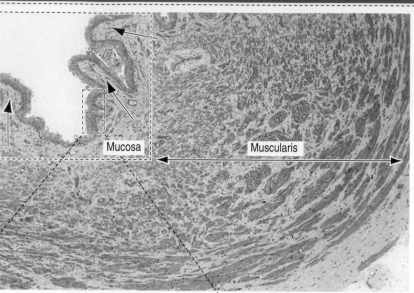

Mucosa

Muscularis

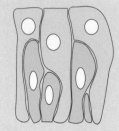

Urothelium of an empty urinary bladder

The **muscularis** contains numerous bundles of smooth muscle cells arranged irregularly as outer and inner longitudinal layers and a middle circular layer.

Urothelium of an urinary bladder filled with urine

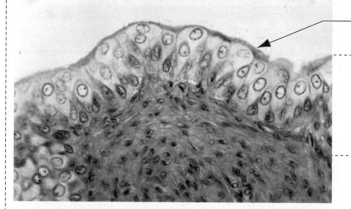

Plaques

Urothelium
The columnar-like epithelium can stretch and resemble a stratified squamous epithelium when urine is present in the urinary bladder. **Apical plaques** generate a thickened domain able to adjust to large changes in surface area.

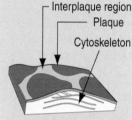

Interplaque region
Plaque
Cytoskeleton

Plaques are formed by the aggregation of hexagonal intramembranous proteins to which cytoskeletal proteins are anchored on the cytoplasmic side.

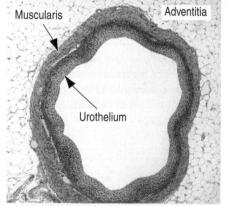

Muscularis

Adventitia

Urothelium

Ureter
The mucosa of the ureter is lined by a transitional epithelium (urothelium). The mucosa is surrounded by a fibroelastic lamina propria and a muscularis with two to three layers of smooth muscle. The ureter is surrounded by an adventitia containing adipose tissue.

muscle cell wall of the afferent glomerular arteriole but are also present in smaller number in the efferent glomerular arteriole. Juxtaglomerular cells synthesize, store, and release **renin**. Activation of sympathetic nerve fibers results in the increased secretion of renin.

2. A **tubular component**: The **macula densa** mediates renin secretion after sensing the NaCl content in the incoming urine from the thick ascending segment of the limb of Henle. When the delivery of NaCl to the macula densa decreases, renin secretion is enhanced. Conversely, when NaCl increases, renin secretion decreases.

The **renin-angiotensin-aldosterone system** consists of the following components (Figure 14–17):

1. **Angiotensinogen**, a circulating protein in plasma produced by the liver.

2. The **juxtaglomerular cells**, the source of the proteolytic enzyme **renin**, which converts **angiotensinogen** to **angiotensin I**, a decapeptide with no known physiologic function.

3. The **angiotensin-converting enzyme (ACE)**, a product of pulmonary and renal **endothelial cells**, which converts **angiotensin I** to the octapeptide **angiotensin II**.

Angiotensin has several important functions:

1. It stimulates the secretion of aldosterone by the adrenal cortex.
2. It causes vasoconstriction, which, in turn, increases blood pressure.
3. It enhances the reabsorption of NaCl by the distal tubules of the nephron and collecting tubule.
4. It stimulates ADH release.

4. **Aldosterone** acts primarily on **principal cells of the collecting tubule** and secondarily on the thick ascending limb of Henle to increase the entry of NaCl across the apical membrane. As with all steroid hormones, aldosterone enters the cell and binds to a cytosolic receptor. The aldosterone-receptor complex enters the nucleus and stimulates gene activity required for the reabsorption of NaCl.

The excretory passages of urine

The urine released at the openings of the papillary ducts flows from the calices and pelvis into the ureters and enters the urinary bladder. Peristaltic waves, spreading from the calices along the ureter, force the urine toward the bladder.

The walls of the ureter and urinary bladder (Figure 14-18) contain folds (rugae). As the bladder fills with urine, the rugae flatten and the volume of the bladder increases with minimal increase in intravesical pressure. The renal calices, pelvis, ureter, and urinary bladder are lined by a **transitional epithelium**, the **urothelium**, composed of basal and superficial cells. The epithelium and the subjacent lamina propria are surrounded by **combined spiral and longitudinal layers of smooth muscle fibers**.

In the bladder, a mixture of randomly arranged smooth muscle cells form the syncytial **detrusor muscle**. At the neck of the urinary bladder, the muscle fibers form a three-layer (inner longitudinal, middle circular, and outer longitudinal) functional sphincter.

Micturition, the process of emptying the urinary bladder, involves the micturition reflex, an automatic spinal cord reflex, and the stimulation of the detrusor muscle by parasympathetic fibers to contract.

Nephrolithiasis is a condition in which kidney stones, composed of calcium salts, uric acid, or magnesium-ammonium acetate, form by crystallization when urine is concentrated. When the ureter is blocked by a stone, the contraction of the smooth muscle generates severe pain in the flank.

The **male urethra** is 20 cm long and consists of three segments. Upon leaving the urinary bladder, the **prostatic urethra**—lined by transitional epithelium—crosses the prostate gland, continues as a short **membranous urethra** segment, and ends as **penile urethra**, which is enclosed by the corpus spongiosum of the penis (see Figure 21–12 in Chapter 21, Sperm Transport and Maturation). Both the membranous and penile urethra are lined by pseudostratified-to stratified columnar epithelium.

The **female urethra** is 4 cm long and is lined sequentially by transitional epithelium to stratified squamous epithelium to low keratinized stratified squamous epithelium (near the urethral meatus). An **inner smooth muscle layer** and an **external striated muscle layer** are present in the wall. Additional structural details of the male and female urethra can be found in Chapter 21, Sperm Transport and Maturation, and Chapter 22, Follicle Development and Menstrual Cycle), respectively.

Countercurrent multiplier

The kidneys regulate water balance and are the major site for the release of water from the body. Water is also lost by evaporation from the skin and the respiratory tract and from the gastrointestinal tract (fecal water and diarrhea).

Water excretion by the kidneys occurs independently of other substances, such as Na^+, Cl^-, K^+, H^+, and urea. The kidney excretes either **concentrated** (hyperosmotic) or **diluted** (hypo-osmotic) urine.

Antidiuretic hormone regulates the volume and osmolality of the urine with-

Figure 14–19

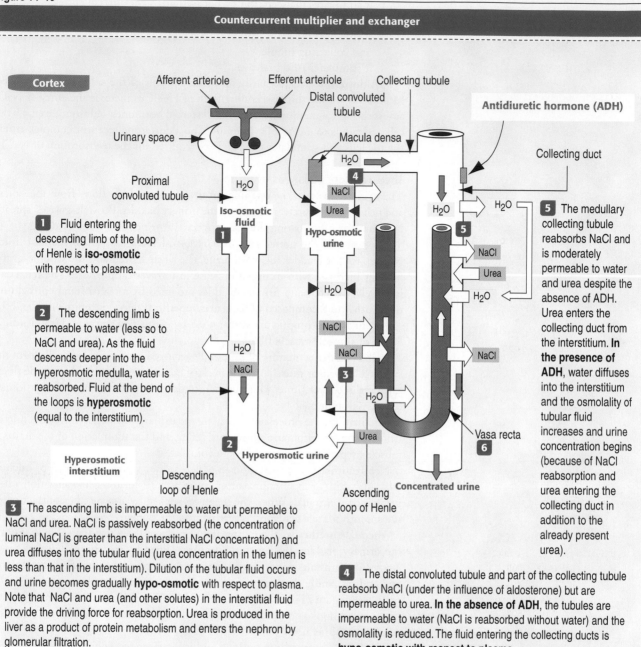

Countercurrent multiplier and exchanger

Cortex

Afferent arteriole   Efferent arteriole   Collecting tubule

Distal convoluted tubule

Antidiuretic hormone (ADH)

Urinary space

Macula densa

Collecting duct

Proximal convoluted tubule

H_2O

Iso-osmotic fluid

1

1 Fluid entering the descending limb of the loop of Henle is **iso-osmotic** with respect to plasma.

4

NaCl

Urea

Hypo-osmotic urine

H_2O

H_2O H_2O

5

NaCl

Urea

H_2O

5 The medullary collecting tubule reabsorbs NaCl and is moderately permeable to water and urea despite the absence of ADH. Urea enters the collecting duct from the interstitium. **In the presence of ADH**, water diffuses into the interstitium and the osmolality of tubular fluid increases and urine concentration begins (because of NaCl reabsorption and urea entering the collecting duct in addition to the already present urea).

2 The descending limb is permeable to water (less so to NaCl and urea). As the fluid descends deeper into the hyperosmotic medulla, water is reabsorbed. Fluid at the bend of the loops is **hyperosmotic** (equal to the interstitium).

H_2O

H_2O

NaCl

NaCl

NaCl

3

NaCl

H_2O

Hyperosmotic interstitium

H_2O

2

Urea

Hyperosmotic urine

Descending loop of Henle

Ascending loop of Henle

Vasa recta

6

Concentrated urine

3 The ascending limb is impermeable to water but permeable to NaCl and urea. NaCl is passively reabsorbed (the concentration of luminal NaCl is greater than the interstitial NaCl concentration) and urea diffuses into the tubular fluid (urea concentration in the lumen is less than that in the interstitium). Dilution of the tubular fluid occurs and urine becomes gradually **hypo-osmotic** with respect to plasma. Note that NaCl and urea (and other solutes) in the interstitial fluid provide the driving force for reabsorption. Urea is produced in the liver as a product of protein metabolism and enters the nephron by glomerular filtration.

Medulla

4 The distal convoluted tubule and part of the collecting tubule reabsorb NaCl (under the influence of aldosterone) but are impermeable to urea. **In the absence of ADH**, the tubules are impermeable to water (NaCl is reabsorbed without water) and the osmolality is reduced. The fluid entering the collecting ducts is **hypo-osmotic with respect to plasma**.

6 The vasa recta are a capillary network that removes –in a flow-dependent manner– excess of water and solutes continuously added to the interstitium by the nephron segments.

out modifying the excretion of other solutes. The primary action of ADH is to increase the permeability of the collecting tubule to water. An additional action is to increase the permeability of the collecting ducts at the medullary region to urea.

Figure 14–19 summarizes the **essential steps of urine formation and excretion**.

1. The fluid from the proximal convoluted tubules entering the loop of Henle

Figure 14–20

Mechanism of action of diuretics

Diuretics are drugs that increase the output of urine (**diuresis**) by acting on specific membrane transport proteins. The common effect of diuretics is the inhibition of Na^+ resorption by the nephron leading to an increase in the excretion of Na^+ (**natriuresis**).

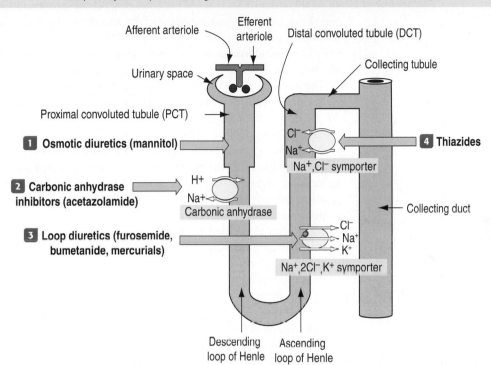

1 Osmotic diuretics (sugar mannitol)

Osmotic diuresis affects the transport of water across the epithelial cells lining the **PCT and thin descending limb of the loop of Henle**. Osmotic diuretics enter the nephron by glomerular filtration and generate an osmotic pressure gradient. **Osmotic diuretics do not inhibit a specific membrane transport protein.** When urea and glucose are present in abnormally high concentrations (diabetes mellitus or renal diseases), they can behave as osmotic diuretics.

2 Carbonic anhydrase inhibitors (acetazolamide)

Carbonic acid inhibitors reduce Na^+ resorption by their effects on carbonic anhydrase, present mainly in the PCT. The Na^+, H^+ antiporter in the apical membrane of PCT cells depends on H^+ for Na^+ exchange.

H^+ is secreted in the tubular fluid where it combines with filtered HCO_3^- to form H_2CO_3. H_2CO_3 is hydrolyzed to CO_2 and H_2O by carbonic anhydrase located on the apical membrane of the PCT to facilitate CO_2 and H_2O reabsorption. Carbonic anhydrase inhibitors reduce the reabsorption of HCO_3^-. Because the amount of secreted H^+ depends on Na^+, inhibition of carbonic anhydrase causes a decrease in Na^+, H_2O, and HCO_3^- reabsorption, leading to natriuresis.

3 Loop diuretics (furosemide, bumetanide, mercurials)

Loop diuretics are the most potent diuretics available to inhibit Na^+ resorption by the **thick ascending limb of Henle's loop** by blocking the $Na^+, 2Cl^-, K^+$ symporter located in the apical membrane of the epithelial cells. Loop diuretics also perturb the process of countercurrent multiplication (the ability to dilute or concentrate urine).

3 Thiazide diuretics (chlorothiazide)

Thiazides diuretics inhibit Na^+ reabsorption in the **initial portion of the DCT** by blocking the Na^+, Cl^- symporter present in the apical cell membrane. Because water cannot cross this portion of the nephron and this is the site of urine dilution, thiazides reduce the ability to dilute the urine by inhibition of NaCl reabsorption.

is **iso-osmotic** with respect to plasma.

2. The **descending limb of the loop of Henle is highly permeable to water and to a lesser extent to NaCl**. As the fluid descends into the hyperosmotic interstitium, water and NaCl equilibrate and the tubular fluid becomes **hyperosmotic**.

3. When the fluid reaches the **bend of the loop**, its composition is **hyperosmotic**.

4. The **ascending limb of the loop of Henle is impermeable to water**. The

concentration of NaCl in the lumen, greater than in the interstitium, is reabsorbed and enters the descending (arterial) portion of the vasa recta. Therefore, the fluid leaving this tubular segment is **hypo-osmotic**. This segment of the nephron is called the **diluting segment**.

5. The distal convoluted tubule and cortical portions of the collecting tubule reabsorb NaCl. In the **absence** of ADH, water permeability is low. In the **presence** of ADH, water diffuses out of the collecting tubule into the interstitium and enters the ascending (venous) segment of the vasa recta. The process of urine concentration starts.

6. The **medullary regions** of the collecting tubule reabsorb urea. A small amount of water is reabsorbed and the urine is concentrated.

The mechanism by which the loop of Henle generates the hypertonic interstitial gradient is known as **countercurrent multiplication**. This designation is based on the **flow of fluid in opposite directions (countercurrent flow)** within the two parallel limbs of the loop of Henle.

Note that: (1) The fluid flows **into the medulla** in the descending limb and **out of the medulla** in the ascending limb. (2) The countercurrent flow within the descending and ascending limbs of the loop of Henle "multiplies" the osmotic gradient between the tubular fluid in the descending and ascending limbs. (3) A **hyperosmotic interstitium** is generated by the reabsorption of NaCl in the **ascending limb** of the loop of Henle. This is an important step for the uriniferous tubule to excrete urine hyperosmotic with respect to plasma. (4) The concentration of NaCl increases progressively with increasing depth into the medulla. The highest concentration of NaCl is at the level of the papilla. This **medullary gradient** results from the accumulation of NaCl reabsorbed by the process of countercurrent multiplication. (5) The **vasa recta** transport nutrients and oxygen to the uriniferous tubules. They also remove excess water and solutes, continuously added by the countercurrent multiplication process. An increase in blood flow through the vasa recta dissipates the medullary gradient.

Clinical significance: Mechanism of action of diuretics

The main function of diuretics is to increase the excretion of Na^+ by inhibiting Na^+ reabsorption by the nephron. The effect of diuretics depends on the volume of the extracellular fluid (ECF) compartment and the effective circulating volume (ECV). If the ECV decreases, the glomerular filtration rate (GFR) decreases, the load of filtered Na^+ is reduced, and the reabsorption of Na^+ by the proximal convoluted tubule increases.

With these events in mind, you realize that the action of diuretics acting on the distal convoluted tubule can be compromised by the presence of lower concentrations of Na^+ when the ECV is reduced.

Figure 14–20 provides a summary of the mechanism of action of osmotic diuretics, carbonic anhydrase inhibitors, loop diuretics, and thiazide diuretics.

Osmotic diuretics inhibit the reabsorption of water and solutes in the proximal convoluted tubule and descending thin limb of the loop of Henle.

Carbonic anhydrase inhibitors inhibit Na^+, HCO_3^-, and water reabsorption in the proximal convoluted tubule.

Loop diuretics inhibit the reabsorption of NaCl in the thick ascending limb of the loop of Henle. About 25% of the filtered load of Na^+ can be excreted by the action of loop diuretics.

Thiazide diuretics inhibit the reabsorption of NaCl in the distal convoluted tubule.

Learning objectives

Part IV, **The Alimentary System**, includes the **upper and lower digestive segments** and the **digestive glands**.

 Ingestion, digestion, absorption, and **excretion of waste products** are the main functions of the muscular tube, called the **digestive tract**, and the accessory **digestive glands**. The alimentary system ensures the processing of food into small molecules that can be absorbed by the epithelium of the digestive tract for transfer to the circulating blood.

In Chapter 15, **Upper Digestive Segment**:

1. You will learn the histologic organization of the oral cavity, tongue, and teeth. These components mechanically process the ingested food, which is also moistened and mixed with secretions of the salivary glands before ingestion. You will learn the structure and function of the sensory taste buds.

2. You will identify important structural and functional differences among the oropharynx, esophagus, and stomach, and the contribution of the muscles of the pharynx and esophagus in propelling food and liquids into the stomach.

3. You will learn how stomach mucosal and submucosal folds (rugae) enable the gradual distention of the lumen of the stomach.

4. You will study the characteristics of the **chief cells** and **parietal cells** of the stomach to understand the enzymatic and chemical breakdown of materials.

In Chapter 16, **Lower Digestive Segment**:

1. You will learn how to distinguish differences in the mucosa of the duodenum, jejunum, and ileum, and how the **circular folds** in the small intestine (plicae circulares) represent the first order of amplification of the absorptive intestinal surface.

2. You will learn which components of the small and large intestine participate in a defensive role against pathogens swallowed with food or residing within the digestive tract.

3. You will learn how intestinal epithelial cells, also called **enterocytes**, absorb digested molecules for transfer to the blood circulation.

4. You will learn how a diffuse system of **enteroendocrine cells** assists in the digestive functions.

In Chapter 17, **Digestive Glands**:

1. You will learn how the **oral salivary glands**—the **parotid, sublingual**, and **submandibular** (or submaxillary) glands—differ from each other.

2. You will learn the histologic organization of the exocrine pancreas and which cells synthesize zymogens or proenzymes and buffering electrolytes.

3. You will learn how to identify the components of the **hepatic lobule and correlate structural information with the production and transport of bile and the processing of small intestine–absorbed substances transported by the portal vein to the hepatocytes.**

4. You will learn how the hepatocyte detoxifies the organism, stores glycogen, and participates in the processing of bilirubin.

15. UPPER DIGESTIVE SEGMENT

General outline of the digestive or alimentary tube

Swallowing, **digestion**, and **absorption** take place through the digestive or alimentary tube, a 7- to 10-m hollow muscular conduit. The digestive process converts food material into a **soluble form** easy to absorb by the **small intestine**. The **elimination of insoluble residues** and other materials is the function of the **large intestine**.

Histologically, the digestive tube consists of four major layers: (1) an inner **mucosal** layer encircling the lumen, (2) a **submucosal** layer, (3) a **muscularis externa** layer, and (4) a **serosal/adventitial** layer.

The inner mucosa layer shows significant variations along the digestive tube. It is subdivided into three components: (1) an **epithelial layer**, (2) a connective tissue **lamina propria**, and (3) a smooth muscle **muscularis mucosae**.

The upper digestive segment: Mouth, esophagus, and stomach

We have divided the discussion of the digestive system into two components or chapters: Chapter 15 is focused on the **upper digestive segment** and includes the mouth, esophagus, and stomach. Chapter 16 describes the **lower digestive segment** (small and large intestine). This division is based on the distinctive functions of the upper digestive segment (swallowing and digestion) and lower digestive segment (absorption).

The mouth

The mouth is the entrance to the digestive tube. **Ingestion, partial digestion**, and **lubrication** of the food, or **bolus**, are the main functions of the mouth and its associated **salivary glands**. We study the salivary glands in Chapter 17, Digestive Glands.

The **mouth**, or **oral cavity**, includes the lips, cheeks, teeth, gums, tongue, and palate. Except for the teeth, the mouth is lined by a **stratified squamous epithelium**, with a submucosa present only in certain regions.

The **lips** consist of three regions: (1) the **cutaneous region**, (2) the **red region**, and (3) the **oral mucosa region**.

The cutaneous region is covered by thin skin (**keratinized stratified squamous epithelium with hair follicles and sebaceous and sweat glands**). The red region is lined by a stratified squamous epithelium supported by tall papillae containing blood vessels responsible for the red color of this region. The oral mucosa region is continuous with the mucosa of the cheeks and gums.

The stratified squamous epithelium covering the inner surface of the lips and cheeks is supported by a dense lamina propria and a submucosa, closely bound by connective tissue fibers to the underlying skeletal muscles.

The **gums**, or **gingivae**, are similar to the red region of the lips, except on the free margin, where significant keratinization is seen. The lamina propria of the gums binds tightly to the periosteum of the alveolar processes of the maxillae and mandible and to the periodontal membrane. The gums lack submucosa or glands.

The **hard palate** is lined by a keratinizing stratified squamous epithelium similar to that of the free margins of the gums. A submucosa is present in the midline but absent in the area adjacent to the gums. Collagenous fibers in the submucosa bind the mucosa to the periosteum of the hard palate.

The **soft palate** and **uvula** are lined by a nonkeratinizing stratified squamous epithelium extending into the oropharynx where it becomes continuous with the pseudostratified ciliated columnar epithelium of the upper respiratory tract. The submucosa is loose and contains abundant mucus and serous glands. Skeletal muscle fibers are present in the soft palate and uvula.

Figure 15–1

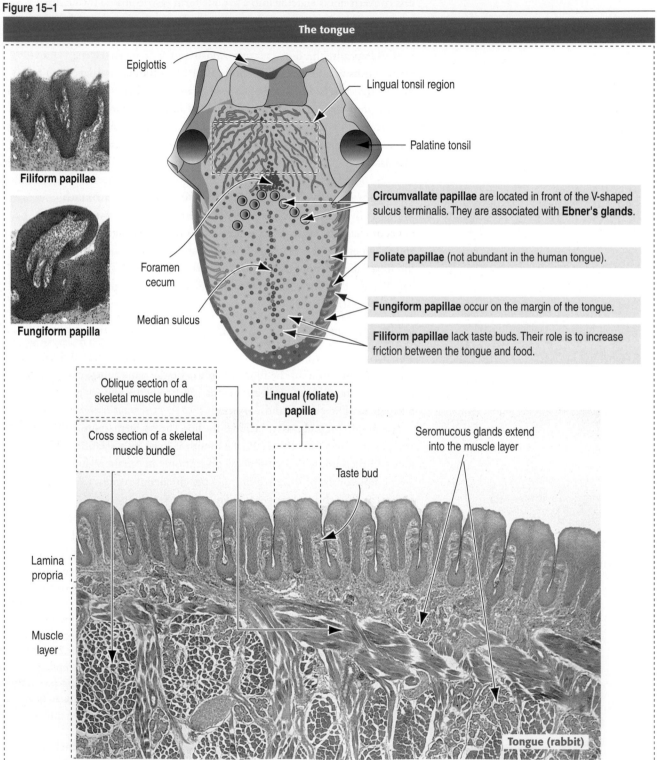

The tongue

Filiform papillae

Fungiform papilla

Epiglottis

Lingual tonsil region

Palatine tonsil

Circumvallate papillae are located in front of the V-shaped sulcus terminalis. They are associated with **Ebner's glands**.

Foramen cecum

Foliate papillae (not abundant in the human tongue).

Median sulcus

Fungiform papillae occur on the margin of the tongue.

Filiform papillae lack taste buds. Their role is to increase friction between the tongue and food.

Oblique section of a skeletal muscle bundle

Lingual (foliate) papilla

Cross section of a skeletal muscle bundle

Seromucous glands extend into the muscle layer

Taste bud

Lamina propria

Muscle layer

Tongue (rabbit)

The tongue

The anterior two thirds of the tongue consists of a core mass of **skeletal muscle** oriented in three directions: **longitudinal**, **transverse**, and **oblique**. The posterior one third displays aggregations of lymphatic tissue, the **lingual tonsils**.

The dorsal surface of the tongue is covered by a **nonkeratinizing stratified squamous epithelium** supported by a lamina propria associated with the muscle core of the tongue. **Serous** and **mucus glands** extend across the lamina propria and the muscle. Their ducts open into the **crypts** and **furrows** of the **lingual tonsils** and **circumvallate papillae**, respectively.

The dorsal surface of the tongue contains numerous mucosal projections called **lingual papillae** (Figure 15–1). Each **lingual papilla** is formed by a highly vascular connective tissue core and a covering layer of stratified squamous epithelium. According to their shape, lingual papillae can be divided into four types: (1) **filiform papillae** (narrow conical), the most abundant; (2) **fungiform papillae** (mushroom-shaped); (3) **circumvallate papillae**; and (4) **foliate papillae** (leaf-shaped), rudimentary in humans but well developed in rabbits and monkeys.

Taste buds are found in all lingual papillae except the filiform papillae. Taste buds are barrel-shaped epithelial structures containing chemosensory cells called **gustatory receptor cells**. Gustatory receptor cells are in synaptic contact with the terminals of the gustatory nerves.

Circumvallate (wall-like) **papillae** are located in the posterior part of the tongue, aligned **in front of the sulcus terminalis**. The circumvallate papilla occupies a recess in the mucosa and, therefore, it is surrounded by a **circular furrow** or **trench**.

Serous glands, or Ebner's glands, in the connective tissue, in contact with the underlying muscle, are associated with the circumvallate papilla. **The ducts of Ebner's glands open into the floor of the circular furrow.**

The sides of the circumvallate papilla and the facing wall of furrow contain several taste buds. Each **taste bud**, depending on the species, consists of 50 to 150 cells, with its narrow apical ends extending into a **taste pore**. A taste bud has three cell components (Figure 15–2): (1) **taste receptor cells**, (2) **supporting cells** (or immature taste cells), and (3) **precursor cells** (or basal cells).

Taste receptor cells have a life span of 10 to 14 days. **Precursor cells give rise to supporting cells (or immature taste cells) which, in turn, become mature taste receptor cells.** The basal portion of a taste receptor cell makes contact with an **afferent nerve terminal** derived from neurons in the sensory ganglia of the **facial**, **glossopharyngeal**, and **vagus** nerves.

Sweet, **sour**, **bitter**, and **salty** are the four classic taste sensations. A fifth taste is **umami** (the taste of monosodium glutamate). A specific taste sensation is generated by specific taste receptor cells. The **facial nerve** carries the five taste sensations; the **glossopharyngeal nerve** carries sweet and bitter sensations.

Taste is initiated when soluble chemicals, called **tastants**, diffuse through the taste pore and interact with the **G-protein α, β, and γ subunits** (called **gustducin**) **linked to the taste receptors** (designated **TR1** and **TR2**), present in the **apical microvilli** of the **taste receptor cells**. As we discussed in Chapter 3, Cell Signaling, guanosine triphosphate (GTP) binding to the α subunit of the G-protein complex activates target molecules (ion channels in the taste receptor cells). Ionic changes within taste cells cause either depolarization (see Figure 15–2) or hyperpolarization of the receptor cells. An increase in intracellular Ca^{2+} triggers the release of neurotransmitters at the afferent synapse with the afferent nerve terminal. Some taste receptor cells respond to only one of the basic taste substances. Others are sensitive to more than one taste substance.

The tooth

In the adult human, dentition consists of 32 permanent teeth. The 16 upper

Figure 15–2

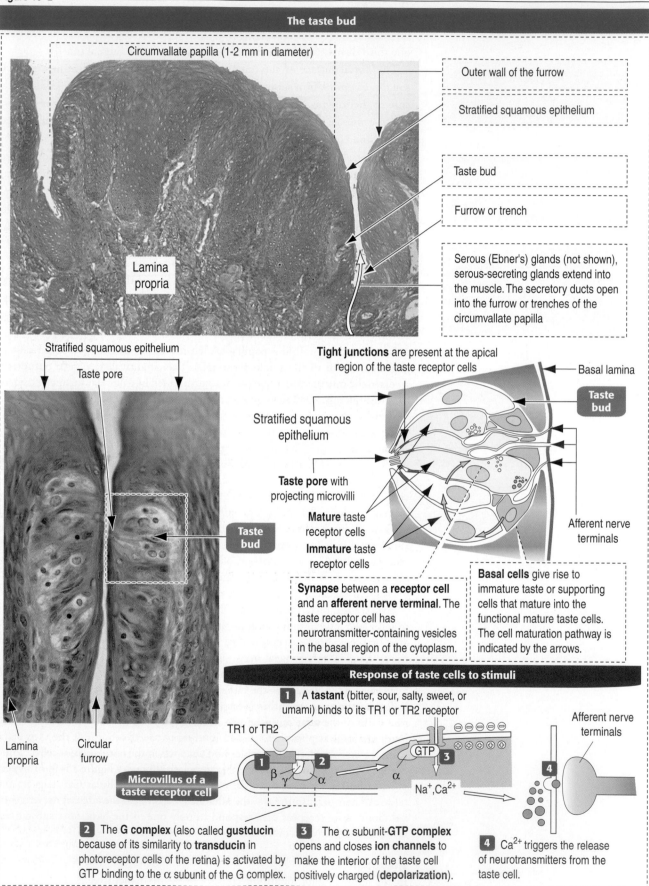

The taste bud

Circumvallate papilla (1-2 mm in diameter)

Outer wall of the furrow

Stratified squamous epithelium

Taste bud

Furrow or trench

Lamina propria

Serous (Ebner's) glands (not shown), serous-secreting glands extend into the muscle. The secretory ducts open into the furrow or trenches of the circumvallate papilla

Stratified squamous epithelium

Taste pore

Taste bud

Lamina propria

Circular furrow

Tight junctions are present at the apical region of the taste receptor cells

Basal lamina

Taste bud

Stratified squamous epithelium

Taste pore with projecting microvilli

Mature taste receptor cells

Immature taste receptor cells

Afferent nerve terminals

Synapse between a **receptor cell** and an **afferent nerve terminal**. The taste receptor cell has neurotransmitter-containing vesicles in the basal region of the cytoplasm.

Basal cells give rise to immature taste or supporting cells that mature into the functional mature taste cells. The cell maturation pathway is indicated by the arrows.

Response of taste cells to stimuli

1 A **tastant** (bitter, sour, salty, sweet, or umami) binds to its TR1 or TR2 receptor

TR1 or TR2

Afferent nerve terminals

Microvillus of a taste receptor cell

Na^+, Ca^{2+}

2 The **G complex** (also called **gustducin** because of its similarity to **transducin** in photoreceptor cells of the retina) is activated by GTP binding to the α subunit of the G complex.

3 The α subunit-**GTP complex** opens and closes **ion channels** to make the interior of the taste cell positively charged (**depolarization**).

4 Ca^{2+} triggers the release of neurotransmitters from the taste cell.

Figure 15-3

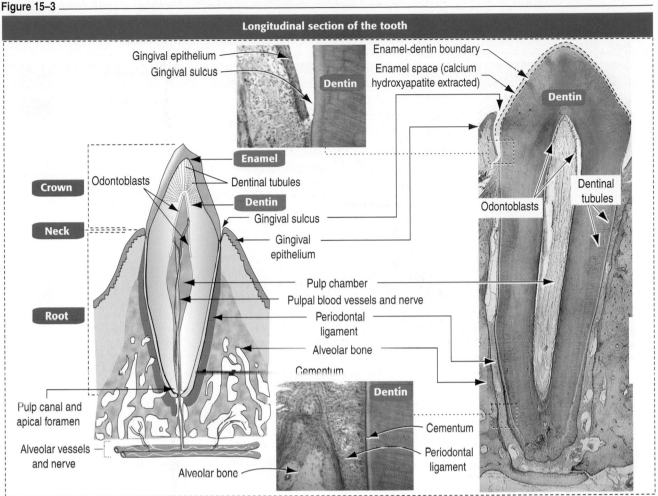

Longitudinal section of the tooth

Gingival epithelium
Gingival sulcus
Dentin
Enamel-dentin boundary
Enamel space (calcium hydroxyapatite extracted)
Dentin
Crown
Odontoblasts
Enamel
Dentinal tubules
Dentin
Odontoblasts
Dentinal tubules
Neck
Gingival sulcus
Gingival epithelium
Pulp chamber
Pulpal blood vessels and nerve
Periodontal ligament
Alveolar bone
Cementum
Root
Dentin
Cementum
Periodontal ligament
Pulp canal and apical foramen
Alveolar vessels and nerve
Alveolar bone

teeth are embedded in **alveolar processes** of the maxilla. The lower 16 teeth are embedded in similar alveolar processes of the mandible. The permanent dentition is preceded by a set of 20 **deciduous teeth**, also called **milk** or **baby teeth**. Deciduous teeth appear at about 6 months of age and the entire set is present by age 6 to 8 years. The deciduous teeth are replaced between years 10 and 12 by the 32 permanent teeth. This replacement process ends at about age 18.

Each of the several types of teeth has a distinctive shape and function: **incisors** are specialized for cutting; **canines,** for puncturing and holding; and **molars,** for crushing.

Each tooth consists of a **crown** and either single or multiple **roots** (Figure 15–3). The crown is covered by highly calcified layers of **enamel** and **dentin**. The outer surface of the root is covered by another calcified tissue called **cementum**. The dentin forms the bulk of the tooth and contains a central chamber filled with soft tissue, the **pulp**. The pulp chamber opens at the **apical foramen** into the bony alveolar process by the **root canal**. Blood vessels, nerves, and lymphatics enter and leave the pulp chamber through the apical foramen. Myelinated nerve fibers run along with the blood vessels.

Tooth development and the differentiation of ameloblasts and odontoblasts

The ectoderm, cranial neural crest, and mesenchyme contribute to the development of the tooth (Figure 15–4). **Ameloblasts** derive from the **ectoderm. Odontoblasts** derive from the **cranial neural crest. Cementocytes** derive from the **mesenchyme.**

Secreted signaling molecules—**activin βA, fibroblast growth factor,** and **bone morphogenetic proteins**—mediate the interaction between the dental epithelium and the mesenchyme during tooth morphogenesis. Figure 15–4 illustrates the

Figure 15–4

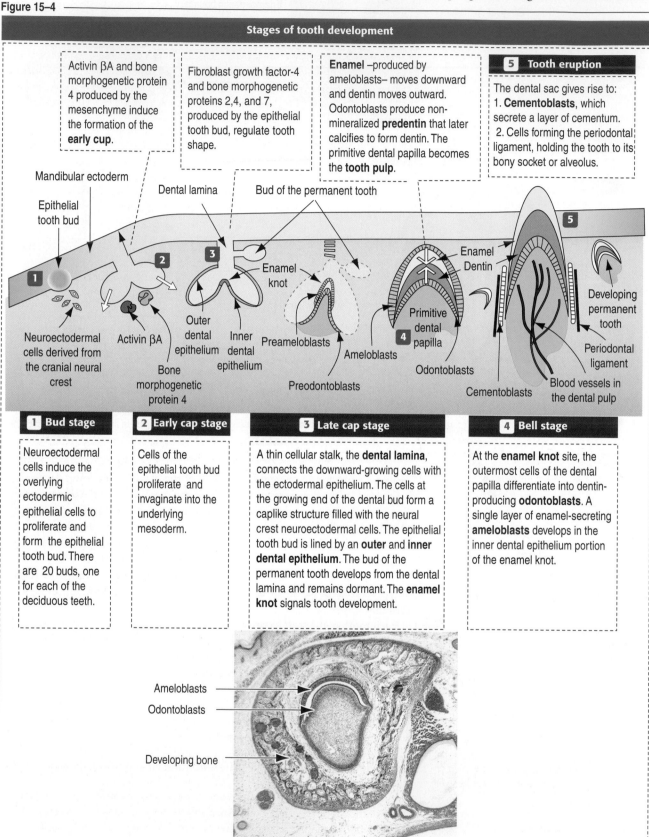

Stages of tooth development

Activin βA and bone morphogenetic protein 4 produced by the mesenchyme induce the formation of the **early cup.**

Fibroblast growth factor-4 and bone morphogenetic proteins 2,4, and 7, produced by the epithelial tooth bud, regulate tooth shape.

Enamel –produced by ameloblasts– moves downward and dentin moves outward. Odontoblasts produce non-mineralized **predentin** that later calcifies to form dentin. The primitive dental papilla becomes the **tooth pulp.**

5 Tooth eruption

The dental sac gives rise to:
1. **Cementoblasts**, which secrete a layer of cementum.
2. Cells forming the periodontal ligament, holding the tooth to its bony socket or alveolus.

Mandibular ectoderm

Epithelial tooth bud

Dental lamina

Bud of the permanent tooth

1 **2** **3** **5**

Enamel knot

Enamel
Dentin

Neuroectodermal cells derived from the cranial neural crest

Activin βA

Bone morphogenetic protein 4

Outer dental epithelium

Inner dental epithelium

Preameloblasts

Ameloblasts

Preodontoblasts

4

Primitive dental papilla

Odontoblasts

Cementoblasts

Blood vessels in the dental pulp

Enamel
Dentin

Developing permanent tooth

Periodontal ligament

1 Bud stage

Neuroectodermal cells induce the overlying ectodermic epithelial cells to proliferate and form the epithelial tooth bud. There are 20 buds, one for each of the deciduous teeth.

2 Early cap stage

Cells of the epithelial tooth bud proliferate and invaginate into the underlying mesoderm.

3 Late cap stage

A thin cellular stalk, the **dental lamina**, connects the downward-growing cells with the ectodermal epithelium. The cells at the growing end of the dental bud form a caplike structure filled with the neural crest neuroectodermal cells. The epithelial tooth bud is lined by an **outer** and **inner dental epithelium**. The bud of the permanent tooth develops from the dental lamina and remains dormant. The **enamel knot** signals tooth development.

4 Bell stage

At the **enamel knot** site, the outermost cells of the dental papilla differentiate into dentin-producing **odontoblasts**. A single layer of enamel-secreting **ameloblasts** develops in the inner dental epithelium portion of the enamel knot.

Ameloblasts

Odontoblasts

Developing bone

relevant steps of tooth development.

Odontoblasts

A layer of odontoblasts is present at the periphery of the pulp. Odontoblasts are active secretory cells that synthesize and secrete collagen and noncollagenous material, the organic components of the **dentin**.

The **odontoblast** is a columnar epithelial-like cell located at the **inner side** of the dentin, in the pulp cavity (Figure 15–5). The apical cell domain is embedded in **predentin**, a nonmineralized layer of dentin-like material. The apical domain projects a main **apical cell process** that becomes enclosed within a canalicular

Figure 15–5

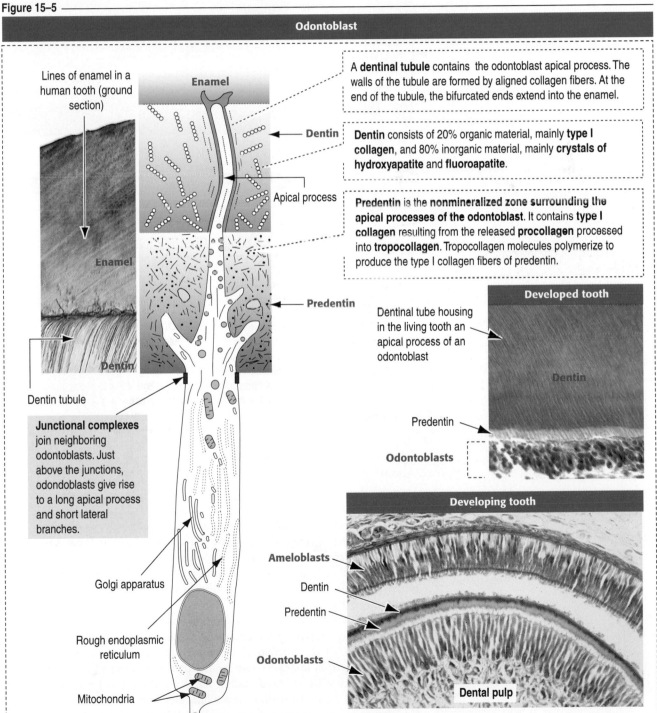

Odontoblast

Lines of enamel in a human tooth (ground section)

Enamel

A **dentinal tubule** contains the odontoblast apical process. The walls of the tubule are formed by aligned collagen fibers. At the end of the tubule, the bifurcated ends extend into the enamel.

Dentin

Dentin consists of 20% organic material, mainly **type I collagen**, and 80% inorganic material, mainly **crystals of hydroxyapatite** and **fluoroapatite**.

Apical process

Predentin is the **nonmineralized zone surrounding the apical processes of the odontoblast**. It contains **type I collagen** resulting from the released **procollagen** processed into **tropocollagen**. Tropocollagen molecules polymerize to produce the type I collagen fibers of predentin.

Enamel

Dentin

Predentin

Dentin tubule

Junctional complexes join neighboring odontoblasts. Just above the junctions, odondoblasts give rise to a long apical process and short lateral branches.

Developed tooth

Dentinal tube housing in the living tooth an apical process of an odontoblast

Dentin

Predentin

Odontoblasts

Developing tooth

Golgi apparatus

Rough endoplasmic reticulum

Mitochondria

Ameloblasts

Dentin

Predentin

Odontoblasts

Dental pulp

Figure 15–6

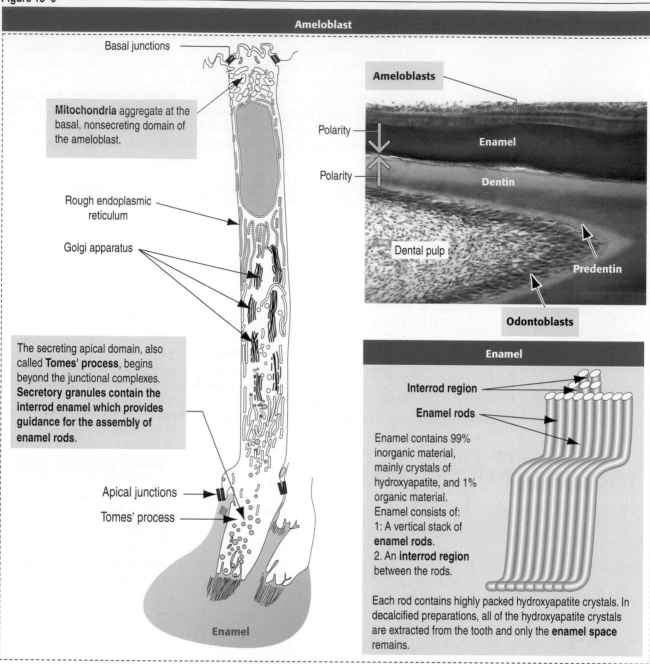

Ameloblast

Basal junctions

Mitochondria aggregate at the basal, nonsecreting domain of the ameloblast.

Rough endoplasmic reticulum

Golgi apparatus

The secreting apical domain, also called **Tomes' process**, begins beyond the junctional complexes. **Secretory granules contain the interrod enamel which provides guidance for the assembly of enamel rods.**

Apical junctions

Tomes' process

Enamel

Ameloblasts

Polarity

Polarity

Enamel

Dentin

Dental pulp

Predentin

Odontoblasts

Enamel

Interrod region

Enamel rods

Enamel contains 99% inorganic material, mainly crystals of hydroxyapatite, and 1% organic material.
Enamel consists of:
1: A vertical stack of **enamel rods**.
2. An **interrod region** between the rods.

Each rod contains highly packed hydroxyapatite crystals. In decalcified preparations, all of the hydroxyapatite crystals are extracted from the tooth and only the **enamel space** remains.

system just above the **junctional complexes** linking adjacent odontoblasts.

A well-developed **rough endoplasmic reticulum** and **Golgi apparatus** as well as **secretory granules** are found in the apical region of the odontoblast. The secretory granules contain **procollagen**. When procollagen is released from the odontoblast, it is enzymatically processed to **tropocollagen**, which aggregates into **type I collagen** fibrils.

Predentin is the layer of dentin adjacent to the odontoblast cell body and processes. Predentin is **nonmineralized** and consists mainly of collagen fibrils that will become covered (mineralized) by hydroxyapatite crystals in the dentin region. A demarcation **mineralization front** separates predentin from dentin.

The **pulp** consists of blood vessels, nerves, and lymphatics surrounded by fibroblasts and mesenchyme-like extracellular elements. Blood vessels (arterioles) branch into a capillary network **among the cell bodies of the odontoblasts**. An inflammation in the pulp causes swelling and pain. Because there is no space for swelling in the pulp cavity, the blood supply is suppressed by compression, leading rapidly to the death of the cells of the pulp.

Cementum

The **cementum** is a bonelike mineralized tissue covering the outer surface of the root. Like bone, the cementum consists of calcified collagenous fibrils and trapped osteocyte-like cells called **cementocytes**.

The cementum meets the enamel at the **cementoenamel junction** and separates the crown from the root at the **neck region** of the tooth. The outermost layer of the cementum is uncalcified and is produced by **cementoblasts** in contact with the **periodontal ligament**, a collagen- and fibroblast-rich and vascularized suspensory ligament holding the tooth in the sockets of the alveolar bone (see Figure 15–3). The strength of the periodontal ligament fibers gives teeth mobility and strong bone attachment, both useful in orthodontic treatment.

Ameloblasts

Ameloblasts are enamel-producing cells present only during tooth development. The ameloblast (Figure 15–6) is a polarized columnar cell with mitochondria and a nucleus present in the basal region of the cell. The supranuclear region contains numerous cisternae of rough endoplasmic reticulum and Golgi apparatus.

Beyond apical junctional complexes joining contiguous ameloblasts, the apical domain displays a broad process, **Tomes' process**, in proximity to the calcified enamel matrix. The apical domain has abundant secretory granules containing glycoprotein precursors of the enamel matrix.

The **enamel** is the hardest substance found in the body. About 99% of the enamel is composed of crystals of hydroxyapatite; less than 1% is protein. The newly secreted enamel contains a high content of protein (about 30%), whose concentration decreases to 1% during enamel mineralization. Two classes of proteins have been identified: **amelogenin** and **enamelin**.

Amelogenin is the major constituent, unique to the developing enamel. Enamelin is a minor component. **Amelogenesis imperfecta** is an inherited disease affecting the formation of the tooth enamel; affected enamel does not attain its normal thickness. It is caused by a mutation of the amelogenin gene.

Electron microscopic examination shows that the enamel consists of thin undulated **enamel rods** separated by an **interrod region** with a structure similar to that of the enamel rods but with its crystals oriented in a different direction. Each rod is coated with a thin layer of organic matrix, called the **rod sheath**.

General organization of the digestive or alimentary tube

Although we will study each segment of the digestive or alimentary tube separately, it is important to discuss first the general organization of the tube to understand that each segment does not function as an independent unit.

We start with the common histologic features of the digestive tube by indicating that, except for the oral cavity, the digestive tube has a uniform histologic organization. This organization is characterized by distinct and significant structural variations reflecting changes in functional activity.

After the oral cavity, the digestive tube is differentiated into four major organs: **esophagus**, **stomach**, **small intestine**, and **large intestine**. Each of these organs is made up of four concentric layers (Figure 15–7): (1) the **mucosa**, (2) the **submucosa**, (3) the **muscularis**, and (4) the **adventitia**, or **serosa**.

The mucosa has three components: a **lining epithelium**, an underlying **lamina propria** consisting of a vascularized loose connective tissue, and a thin layer of smooth muscle, the **muscularis mucosae**.

Figure 15–7

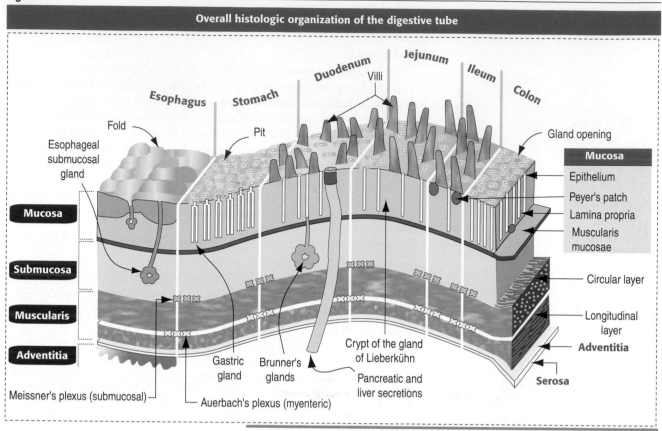

Overall histologic organization of the digestive tube

Lymphatic nodules and scattered immunocompetent cells (lymphocytes, plasma cells, and macrophages) are present in the lamina propria. The lamina propria of the small and large intestines is a relevant site of immune responses (see Chapter 16, Lower Digestive Segment).

The lining epithelium invaginates to form **glands**, extending into the **lamina propria (mucosal glands)** or **submucosa (submucosal glands)**, or **ducts**, transporting secretions from the liver and pancreas through the wall of the digestive tube (duodenum) into its lumen.

In the stomach and small intestine, both the mucosa and submucosa extend into the lumen as folds, called rugae and plicae, respectively. In other instances, the mucosa alone extends into the lumen as fingers, or villi. **Mucosal glands increase the secretory capacity**, whereas **villi increase the absorptive capacity of the digestive tube**.

The **mucosa** shows significant variations from segment to segment of the digestive tract. The submucosa consists of a dense irregular connective tissue with large blood vessels, lymphatics, and nerves branching into the mucosa and muscularis. Glands are present in the submucosa of the esophagus and duodenum.

The **muscularis** contains two layers of smooth muscle: the smooth muscle fibers of the inner layer are arranged around the tube lumen (circular layer); fibers of the outer layer are disposed along the tube (longitudinal layer). **Contraction of the smooth fibers of the circular layer reduces the lumen; contraction of the fibers of the longitudinal layer shortens the tube.** Skeletal muscle fibers are present in the upper esophagus and the anal sphincter.

The **adventitia** of the digestive tract consists of several layers of connective tissue continuous with adjacent connective tissues. When the digestive tube is suspended by the mesentery or peritoneal fold, the adventitia is covered by a **mesothelium (simple squamous epithelium)** supported by a thin connective tissue layer, together forming a **serosa**, or serous membrane.

Figure 15–8

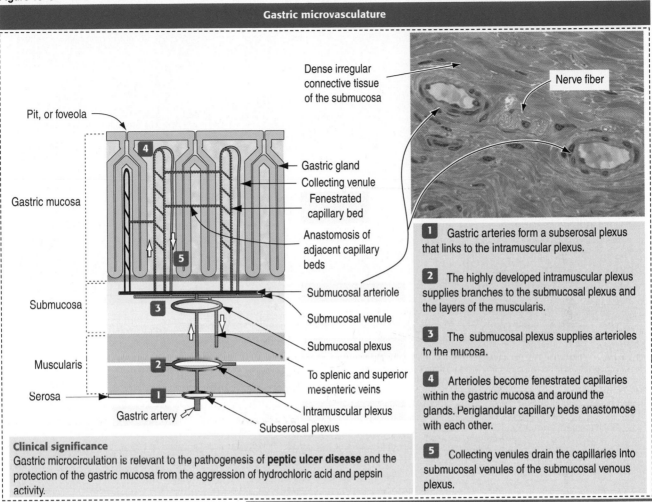

Gastric microvasculature

Pit, or foveola

Gastric mucosa

Submucosa

Muscularis

Serosa

Dense irregular connective tissue of the submucosa

Nerve fiber

Gastric gland
Collecting venule
Fenestrated capillary bed
Anastomosis of adjacent capillary beds
Submucosal arteriole
Submucosal venule
Submucosal plexus
To splenic and superior mesenteric veins
Intramuscular plexus
Subserosal plexus
Gastric artery

1 Gastric arteries form a subserosal plexus that links to the intramuscular plexus.

2 The highly developed intramuscular plexus supplies branches to the submucosal plexus and the layers of the muscularis.

3 The submucosal plexus supplies arterioles to the mucosa.

4 Arterioles become fenestrated capillaries within the gastric mucosa and around the glands. Periglandular capillary beds anastomose with each other.

5 Collecting venules drain the capillaries into submucosal venules of the submucosal venous plexus.

Clinical significance
Gastric microcirculation is relevant to the pathogenesis of **peptic ulcer disease** and the protection of the gastric mucosa from the aggression of hydrochloric acid and pepsin activity.

Microvasculature of the digestive tube

We start our discussion with the **microcirculation of the stomach**. In Chapter 16, Lower Digestive Segment, we describe the **microcirculation of the small intestine** and point out differences (see Figure 16–3).

Blood and lymphatic vessels and nerves reach the walls of the digestive tube through the supporting mesentery or the surrounding tissues. After entering the walls of the stomach, arteries organize three arterial networks: the **subserosal, intramuscular, and submucosal plexuses** (Figure 15–8). Some branches from the plexuses run longitudinally in the muscularis and submucosa; other branches extend perpendicularly into the mucosa and muscularis.

In the mucosa, **arterioles** derived from the submucosal plexus supply a bed of **fenestrated capillaries** around the gastric glands and anastomose laterally with each other. The fenestrated nature of the capillaries facilitates bicarbonate delivery to protect the surface epithelial cells against hydrochloric acid damage (see Figure 15–17).

Collecting venules descend from the mucosa into the submucosa as veins, leave the digestive tube through the mesentery, and drain into the splenic and superior mesenteric veins. Mesenteric veins drain into the portal vein, leading to the liver (see Chapter 17, Digestive Glands).

Clinical significance: Gastric microcirculation and gastric ulcers

As we discuss later in this chapter, gastric microcirculation plays a significant role in the protection of the integrity of the gastric mucosa. A breakdown in this

Figure 15-9

Innervation of the digestive tube

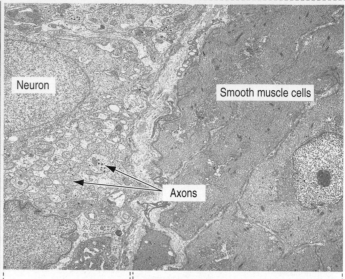

Neuron

Smooth muscle cells

Axons

Myenteric plexus
of Auerbach

Inner muscle layer (circular). Adjacent smooth
muscle cells are electrically coupled and
contract synchronously when stimulated.

Serosa

Outer muscle layer
(longitudinal)

Inner muscle layer
(circular)

Myenteric plexus
of Auerbach

The autonomic nervous system is represented in the alimentary
tube by two distinct interconnected neuronal networks: the
myenteric plexus of Auerbach (located between the circular
and longitudinal muscle layers and innervating the muscle
fibers) and the **submucosal plexus of Meissner** (found
between the muscularis and the mucosa and innervating the
secretory glands).
The two plexuses are linked by axons and consist of sensory
and motor neurons connected by interneurons. Although they
can function independently of the CNS, they are regulated by
preganglionic fibers of parasympathetic neurons of the vagus
and pelvic nerves and postganglionic fibers of sympathetic
neurons of the spinal cord and prevertebral ganglia.

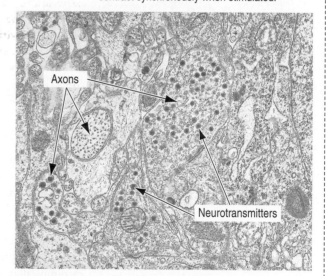

Axons

Neurotransmitters

Some of the chemical neurotransmitters found in the enteric nerves
are **acetylcholine** (excitatory), the two major inhibitory
neurotransmitters, **nitric oxide** and **vasoactive intestinal peptide**
(VIP), and **tachykinins** (such as substance P). **Serotonin** and
somatostatin are products of interneurons.

protective mechanism, including mucus and bicarbonate secretion, allows the
destructive action of hydrochloric acid and pepsin and bacterial infection, leading
to **peptic ulcer disease** (**PUD**). PUD includes a group of disorders characterized
by a partial or total loss of the mucosal surface of the stomach or duodenum or
both.

The rich blood supply to the gastric mucosa is of considerable significance in
understanding bleeding associated with **stress ulcers**. Stress ulcers are superficial
gastric mucosal erosions observed after severe trauma or severe illness and after

long-term use of aspirin and corticosteroids. In most cases, stress ulcers are clinically asymptomatic and are detected only when they cause severe bleeding.

Nerve supply of the digestive tube

The digestive tube is innervated by the autonomic nervous system (ANS). The ANS consists of an **extrinsic component** (the parasympathetic and sympathetic innervation) and an **intrinsic, or enteric, component**.

Sympathetic nerve fibers derive from the thoracic and lumbar spinal cord. **Parasympathetic** nerve fibers derive from the vagal dorsal motor nucleus of the medulla oblongata. **Visceral sensory** fibers originate in the spinal dorsal root ganglia.

The **intrinsic** or **enteric innervation** is represented by two distinct interconnected neuronal circuits formed by sensory and motor neurons linked by interneurons: (1) the **submucosal plexus of Meissner**, present in the **submucosa**, and (2) the **myenteric plexus of Auerbach** (Figure 15–9), located **between the inner circular and outer longitudinal layers of the muscularis.**

Neurons and interneurons of the plexuses give off axons that branch to form the networks. The plexuses are connected to the extrinsic sympathetic and parasympathetic ANS: the plexuses of Auerbach and Meissner receive **preganglionic axons** of the **parasympathetic system** and **postganglionic axons** of the **sympathetic system**.

The intrinsic or enteric nervous system enables the digestive tube to respond to both local stimuli and input from extrinsic nerves of the ANS. The integrated extrinsic and intrinsic (enteric) networks regulate and control (1) **peristaltic contractions of the muscularis and movements of the muscularis mucosae**, and (2) **secretory activities of the mucosal and submucosal glands.** For example, stimulation of **preganglionic parasympathetic nerve fibers (cholinergic terminals)** of the muscularis causes **increased motility** as well as glandular secretory activity. Stimulation of **postganglionic sympathetic nerve fibers (adrenergic terminals)** on the smooth muscle cells causes **decreased motility**.

The esophagus

The esophagus is a muscular tube linking the pharynx to the stomach. It runs through the thorax, crosses the diaphragm, and enters the stomach. Contractions of the muscularis propel the food down the esophagus—in about 2 seconds. At this velocity, changes of pressure and volume within the thorax are minimal. No disruption of respiration and cardiopulmonary circulation takes place.

The esophageal **mucosa** consists of a **stratified squamous epithelium** overlying a lamina propria with numerous connective tissue papillae (Figure 15–10). The **muscularis mucosae** is not present in the upper portion of the esophagus, but it becomes organized near the stomach. Both the mucosa and the submucosa in the undistended esophagus form **longitudinal folds** that give the lumen an irregular outline. As the bolus of food moves down the esophagus, the folds disappear transiently and then are restored by the recoil of the elastic fibers of the submucosa.

The **submucosa** contains a network of collagen and elastic fibers and many small blood vessels. At the lower end of the esophagus, **submucosal venous plexuses** drain into both the systemic venous system and the portal venous system. An increase in pressure in the portal venous system, caused by chronic liver disease, results in dilation of the submucous venous sinuses and the formation of **esophageal varices**. Rupture of the varices or ulceration of the overlying mucosa can produce hemorrhage into the esophagus and stomach, often causing vomiting (**hematemesis**).

Mucosal and **submucosal glands** are found in the esophagus. Their function is

Figure 15–10

The esophagus

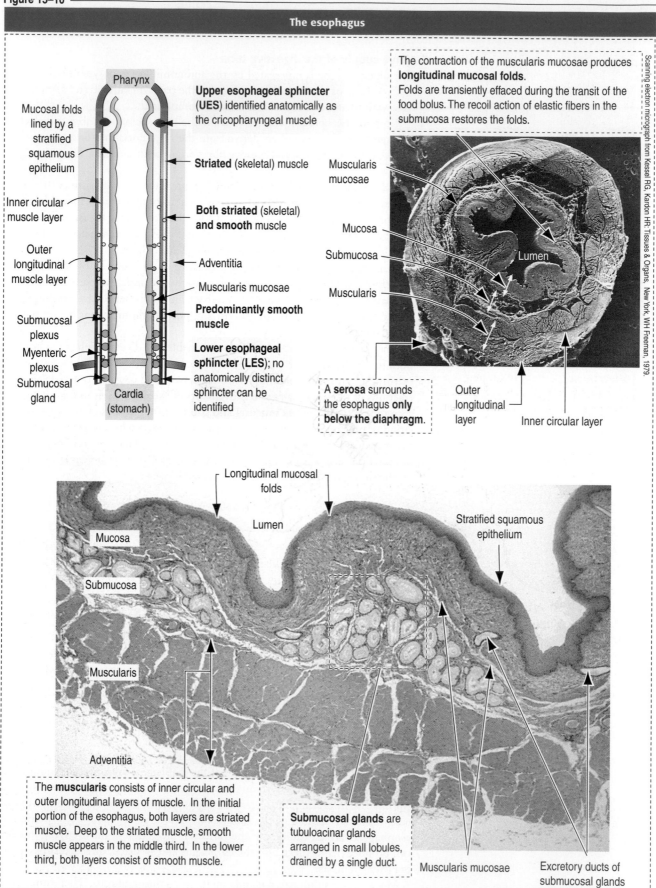

Mucosal folds lined by a stratified squamous epithelium

Inner circular muscle layer

Outer longitudinal muscle layer

Submucosal plexus

Myenteric plexus

Submucosal gland

Pharynx

Cardia (stomach)

Upper esophageal sphincter (UES) identified anatomically as the cricopharyngeal muscle

Striated (skeletal) muscle

Both striated (skeletal) **and smooth** muscle

Adventitia

Muscularis mucosae

Predominantly smooth muscle

Lower esophageal sphincter (LES); no anatomically distinct sphincter can be identified

The contraction of the muscularis mucosae produces **longitudinal mucosal folds**.
Folds are transiently effaced during the transit of the food bolus. The recoil action of elastic fibers in the submucosa restores the folds.

Muscularis mucosae

Mucosa

Submucosa

Muscularis

Lumen

A **serosa** surrounds the esophagus **only below the diaphragm**.

Outer longitudinal layer

Inner circular layer

Scanning electron micrograph from Kessel RG, Kardon HR: Tissues & Organs, New York, WH Freeman, 1979.

Longitudinal mucosal folds

Lumen

Stratified squamous epithelium

Mucosa

Submucosa

Muscularis

Adventitia

The **muscularis** consists of inner circular and outer longitudinal layers of muscle. In the initial portion of the esophagus, both layers are striated muscle. Deep to the striated muscle, smooth muscle appears in the middle third. In the lower third, both layers consist of smooth muscle.

Submucosal glands are tubuloacinar glands arranged in small lobules, drained by a single duct.

Muscularis mucosae

Excretory ducts of submucosal glands

Figure 15-11

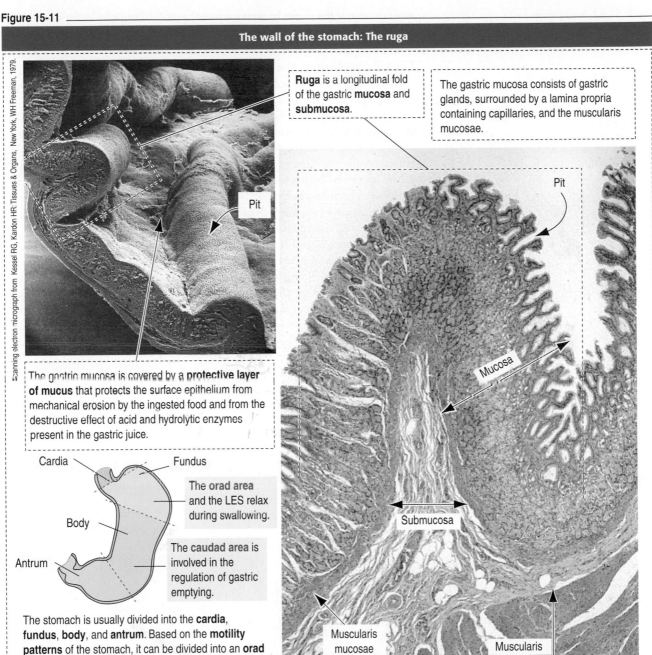

The wall of the stomach: The ruga

Scanning electron micrograph from Kessel RG, Kardon HR: Tissues & Organs, New York, WH Freeman, 1979.

Ruga is a longitudinal fold of the gastric **mucosa** and **submucosa**.

The gastric mucosa consists of gastric glands, surrounded by a lamina propria containing capillaries, and the muscularis mucosae.

Pit

The gastric mucosa is covered by a **protective layer of mucus** that protects the surface epithelium from mechanical erosion by the ingested food and from the destructive effect of acid and hydrolytic enzymes present in the gastric juice.

Cardia

Fundus

The **orad area** and the LES relax during swallowing.

Body

The **caudad area** is involved in the regulation of gastric emptying.

Antrum

The stomach is usually divided into the **cardia**, **fundus**, **body**, and **antrum**. Based on the **motility patterns** of the stomach, it can be divided into an **orad area**—consisting of the fundus, and a portion of the body—and a **caudad area**—consisting of the distal body and the antrum.

Pit

Mucosa

Submucosa

Muscularis mucosae

Muscularis

to produce continuously a thin layer of mucus that lubricates the surface of the epithelium.

The **mucosal tubular glands**, restricted to the lamina propria, resemble the cardiac glands of the stomach and are called **cardiac esophageal glands** (Figure 15–10). Their excretory ducts join a larger duct that opens at the tip of a papilla.

The **submucosal tubuloacinar glands**, found in the submucosa just beneath the muscularis mucosae, are organized into small lobules drained by a single duct. The acini are lined by two secretory cell types: a **mucous** and a **serous** cell type, the latter with secretory granules containing lysozyme.

The composition of the inner circumferential or circular and outer longitudinal layers of the **muscularis** shows **segment-dependent variations**. In the **upper third** of the esophagus, both layers consist of **striated muscle**. In the **middle third**, smooth muscle fibers can be seen deep to the striated muscle. In the **lower third**, both layers of the muscularis contain **smooth muscle cells**.

Clinical significance: The mechanism of swallowing and dysphagia

The esophagus has **two sphincters**: (1) The anatomically defined **upper esophageal sphincter (UES)**, or **cricopharyngeal sphincter**. (2) The functionally defined **lower esophageal sphincter (LES)**, or **gastroesophageal sphincter**. The UES **participates in the initiation of swallowing**. The LES **prevents reflux of gastric contents into the esophagus**.

Because the esophageal stratified squamous lining epithelium may be replaced at the lower end by a poorly resistant columnar epithelium, a reflux of acidic gastric secretions causes chronic inflammation (**reflux esophagitis**) or ulceration and difficulty in swallowing (**dysphagia**). This persistent condition leads to fibrosis and eventual stricture of the lower esophagus.

When the esophageal hiatus in the diaphragm does not close entirely during development, a **hiatus hernia** enables a portion of the stomach to move into the thoracic cavity. In **sliding hiatus hernia**, the stomach protrudes through the diaphragmatic hiatus, normally occupied by the lower esophagus. Reflux esophagitis and peptic ulceration in the intrathoracic portion of the stomach and lower esophagus determines difficulty in swallowing and the feeling of a lump in the throat. This condition, commonly seen in family practice patients, affects young and middle-aged women in particular.

The movements involved in swallowing are coordinated by nerves from the cervical and thoracic sympathetic trunks, forming plexuses in the submucosa and in between the inner and outer layers of the muscularis. Diseases affecting this neuromuscular system may result in muscle spasm, difficulty in swallowing, and substernal pain.

Figure 15–12

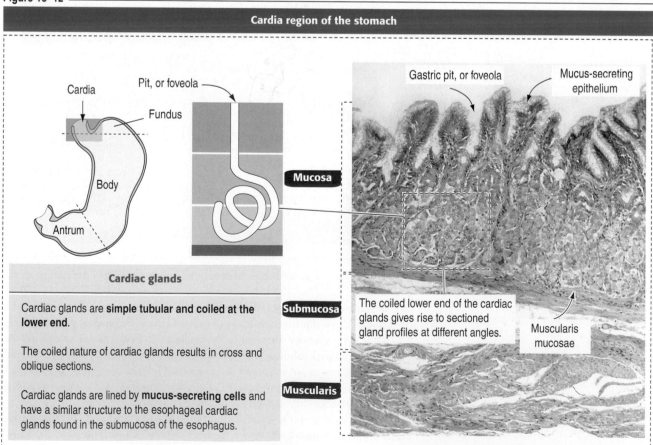

Cardia region of the stomach

Cardia

Pit, or foveola

Fundus

Body

Antrum

Mucosa

Submucosa

Muscularis

Cardiac glands

Cardiac glands are **simple tubular and coiled at the lower end**.

The coiled nature of cardiac glands results in cross and oblique sections.

Cardiac glands are lined by **mucus-secreting cells** and have a similar structure to the esophageal cardiac glands found in the submucosa of the esophagus.

Gastric pit, or foveola

Mucus-secreting epithelium

The coiled lower end of the cardiac glands gives rise to sectioned gland profiles at different angles.

Muscularis mucosae

Figure 15-13

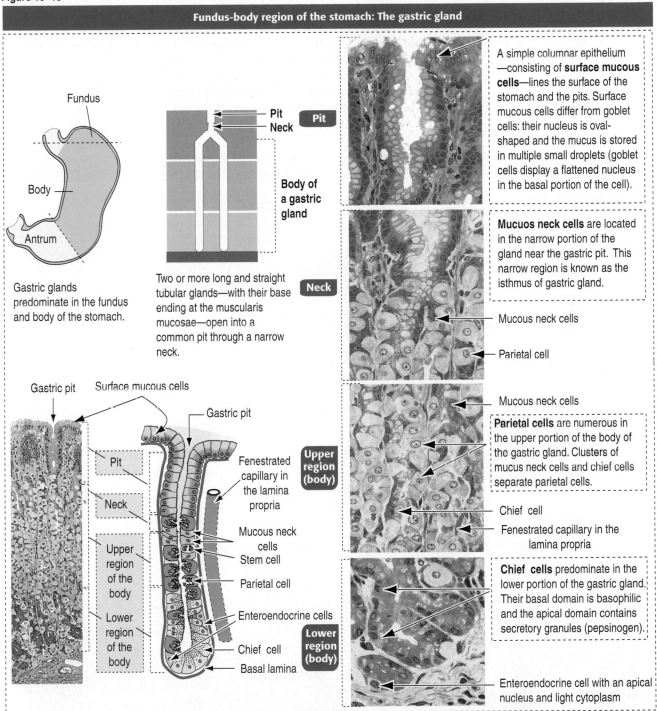

Fundus-body region of the stomach: The gastric gland

Gastric glands predominate in the fundus and body of the stomach.

Two or more long and straight tubular glands—with their base ending at the muscularis mucosae—open into a common pit through a narrow neck.

A simple columnar epithelium —consisting of **surface mucous cells**—lines the surface of the stomach and the pits. Surface mucous cells differ from goblet cells: their nucleus is oval-shaped and the mucus is stored in multiple small droplets (goblet cells display a flattened nucleus in the basal portion of the cell).

Mucuos neck cells are located in the narrow portion of the gland near the gastric pit. This narrow region is known as the isthmus of gastric gland.

Parietal cells are numerous in the upper portion of the body of the gastric gland. Clusters of mucus neck cells and chief cells separate parietal cells.

Chief cells predominate in the lower portion of the gastric gland. Their basal domain is basophilic and the apical domain contains secretory granules (pepsinogen).

The stomach

The stomach extends from the esophagus to the duodenum. At the **gastroesoph-ageal junction**, the epithelium changes from stratified squamous to a simple co-lumnar type. The muscularis mucosae of the esophagus is continuous with that of the stomach. However, the submucosa does not have a clear demarcation line, and glands from the cardiac portion of the stomach may extend under the strati-fied squamous epithelium and contact the esophageal cardiac glands.

The **function of the stomach is to homogenize and chemically process the swallowed semisolid food.** Both the contractions of the muscular wall of the stomach and the acid and enzymes secreted by the gastric mucosa contribute to this function. Once the food is transformed into a thick fluid, it is released gradually into the duodenum.

Four regions are recognized in the stomach: (1) the **cardia**, a 2- to 3-cm-wide zone surrounding the esophageal opening, (2) the **fundus**, projecting to the left of the opening of the esophagus, (3) the **body**, an extensive central region, and (4) the **pyloric antrum** (Gk. *pyloros*, gatekeeper), ending at the gastroduodenal orifice. Based on the **motility** characteristics of the stomach, the **orad area**, consisting of the fundus and the upper part of the body, relaxes during swallowing. The **caudad area**, consisting of the lower portion of the body and the antrum, partici-

Figure 15–14

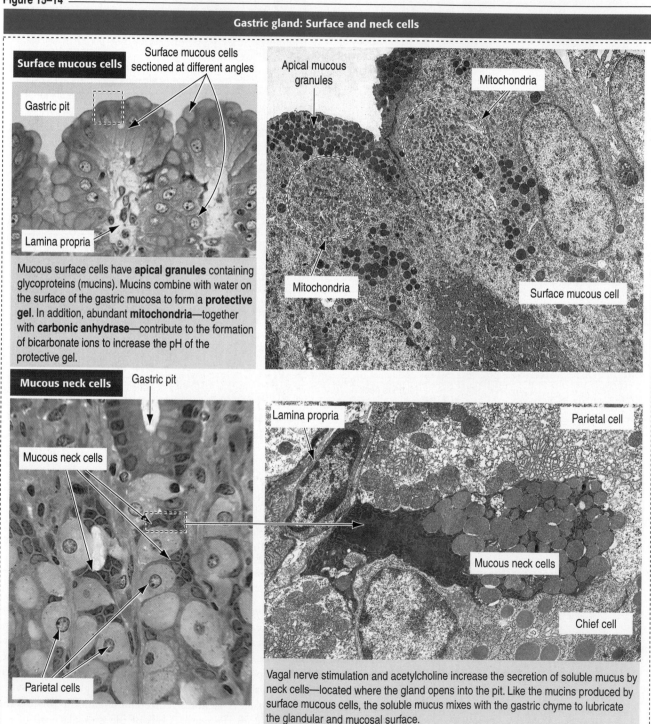

Gastric gland: Surface and neck cells

Surface mucous cells

Surface mucous cells sectioned at different angles

Gastric pit

Lamina propria

Mucous surface cells have **apical granules** containing glycoproteins (mucins). Mucins combine with water on the surface of the gastric mucosa to form a **protective gel**. In addition, abundant **mitochondria**—together with **carbonic anhydrase**—contribute to the formation of bicarbonate ions to increase the pH of the protective gel.

Apical mucous granules

Mitochondria

Mitochondria

Surface mucous cell

Mucous neck cells

Gastric pit

Mucous neck cells

Parietal cells

Lamina propria

Parietal cell

Mucous neck cells

Chief cell

Vagal nerve stimulation and acetylcholine increase the secretion of soluble mucus by neck cells—located where the gland opens into the pit. Like the mucins produced by surface mucous cells, the soluble mucus mixes with the gastric chyme to lubricate the glandular and mucosal surface.

Figure 15–15

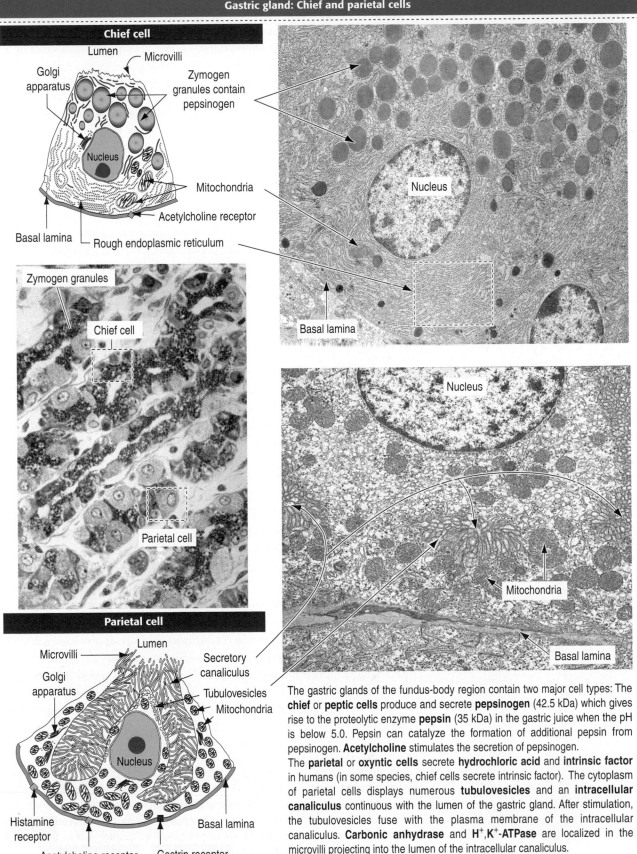

Gastric gland: Chief and parietal cells

The gastric glands of the fundus-body region contain two major cell types: The **chief** or **peptic cells** produce and secrete **pepsinogen** (42.5 kDa) which gives rise to the proteolytic enzyme **pepsin** (35 kDa) in the gastric juice when the pH is below 5.0. Pepsin can catalyze the formation of additional pepsin from pepsinogen. **Acetylcholine** stimulates the secretion of pepsinogen.

The **parietal** or **oxyntic cells** secrete **hydrochloric acid** and **intrinsic factor** in humans (in some species, chief cells secrete intrinsic factor). The cytoplasm of parietal cells displays numerous **tubulovesicles** and an **intracellular canaliculus** continuous with the lumen of the gastric gland. After stimulation, the tubulovesicles fuse with the plasma membrane of the intracellular canaliculus. **Carbonic anhydrase** and **H⁺,K⁺-ATPase** are localized in the microvilli projecting into the lumen of the intracellular canaliculus.

pates in the regulation of gastric emptying.

The empty stomach shows gastric mucosal folds, or **rugae**, covered by **gastric pits** or **foveolae** (Figure 15–11). A **gastric mucosal barrier**, produced by **surface mucus cells**, protects the mucosal surface. The surface mucus cells contain apical periodic acid–Schiff (PAS)–positive granules and are linked to each other by apical tight junctions.

Cardia region

Glands of the cardia region are **tubular**, with a **coiled end** and an **opening continuous with the gastric pits** (Figure 15–12). A mucus-secreting epithelium lines the cardiac glands.

Fundus-body region: The gastric gland

Gastric glands of the fundus-body region are the major contributors to the gastric juice. About 15 million gastric glands open into 3.5 million gastric pits. From two to seven gastric glands open into a single gastric pit, or foveola.

A gastric gland consists of three regions (Figure 15–13: (1) The **pit**, or **foveola**, lined by surface mucous cells; (2) the **neck**, containing mucous neck cells, mitotically active stem cells, and parietal cells; and (3) the **body**, representing the major length of the gland. The upper and lower portions of the body contain different proportions of cells lining the gastric gland.

The surface mucous cells line the surface of the gastric mucosa and the gastric pits (see Figures 15–13 and 15–14).

The gastric glands proper house five major cell types: (1) **mucous neck cells** (see Figure 15-13), (2) **chief cells** (also called **peptic cells**), (3) **parietal cells** (also called **oxyntic cells**), (4) **stem cells**, and (5) **enteroendocrine cells**.

The upper portion of the main body of the gastric gland contains abundant parietal cells. Chief cells and enteroendocrine cells predominate in the lower portion (see Figure 15–13).

The gastric mucosa of the fundus-body has two classes of mucus-producing cells (Figure 15–14): (1) the **surface mucous cells** lining the pits, and (2) the **mucous neck cells** located at the opening of the gastric gland into the pit. Both cells produce mucins, glycoproteins with high molecular mass. A mucus layer, containing 95% water and 5% mucins, forms an insoluble gel that attaches to the surface of the gastric mucosa, forming a 100-μm-thick protective gastric mucosal barrier. This protective mucus blanket traps **bicarbonate ions** and neutralizes the microenvironment adjacent to the apical region of the mucous surface cells to an alkaline pH (about 7.0).

Na^+, K^+, and Cl^- are additional constituents of the protective mucosal barrier. Patients with chronic vomiting or undergoing continuous aspiration of gastric juice require intravenous replacement of NaCl, dextrose, and K^+ to prevent hypokalemic metabolic acidosis.

Chief cells (Figure 15–15) predominate in the lower third of the gastric gland. **Chief cells are not present in cardiac glands and are seldom found in the pyloric antrum.** Chief cells have a structural similarity to the zymogenic cells of the exocrine pancreas: the basal region of the cytoplasm contains an extensive rough endoplasmic reticulum. Pepsinogen-containing secretory granules (**zymogen granules**) are observed in the apical region of the cell. **Pepsinogen**, a proenzyme stored in the zymogen granules, is released into the lumen of the gland and converted in the acid environment of the stomach to **pepsin**, a proteolytic enzyme capable of digesting most proteins. Exocytosis of pepsinogen is rapid and stimulated by feeding (after fasting).

Parietal cells predominate in the neck and fundus of the gastric gland and are

Figure 15–16

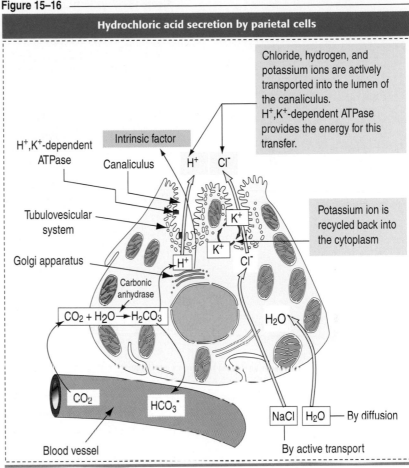

Hydrochloric acid secretion by parietal cells

Chloride, hydrogen, and potassium ions are actively transported into the lumen of the canaliculus.
H^+,K^+-dependent ATPase provides the energy for this transfer.

Intrinsic factor

H^+,K^+-dependent ATPase

Canaliculus

H^+ Cl^-

Tubulovesicular system

K^+

Potassium ion is recycled back into the cytoplasm

Golgi apparatus

K^+

H^+ Cl^-

Carbonic anhydrase

$CO_2 + H_2O \rightarrow H_2CO_3$

H_2O

CO_2

HCO_3^-

NaCl H_2O — By diffusion

Blood vessel

By active transport

linked to chief cells by junctional complexes. Parietal cells produce the **hydrochloric acid** of the gastric juice and **intrinsic factor**, a glycoprotein that binds to vitamin B_{12} to facilitate its absorption in the upper small intestine.

Parietal cells have three distinctive features (see Figure 15–15): (1) **Abundant mitochondria**, which occupy about 40% of the cell volume and provide the adenosine triphosphate (**ATP**) required to pump H^+ **ions** into the lumen of the intracellular canaliculus. (2) An **intracellular canaliculus**, formed by an invagination of the apical cell surface and continuous with the lumen of the gastric gland, which is lined by numerous **microvilli**. (3) An H^+,K^+-**ATPase-rich tubulovesicular system**, which is distributed along the secretory canaliculus during the resting state of the parietal cell.

After stimulation, the tubulovesicular system fuses with the membrane of the secretory canaliculus, and numerous microvilli project into the canalicular space. Membrane fusion increases the amount of H^+,K^+-ATPase and expands the intracellular canaliculus. H^+,K^+-ATPase represents about 80% of the protein content of the plasma membrane of the microvilli.

Secretion of hydrochloric acid by parietal cells

Parietal cells produce an acidic secretion (pH 0-9 to 2.0) rich in hydrochloric acid, with a concentration of H^+ ions one million times greater than that of blood (Figure 15–16). The release of H^+ ions and Cl^- by the parietal cell involves the membrane fusion of the tubulovesicular system with the intracellular canaliculus.

The parasympathetic mediator **acetylcholine** and the peptide **gastrin**, produced by enteroendocrine cells of the pyloric antrum, stimulate parietal cells to secrete HCl (see Figure 15–19). Acetylcholine also stimulates the release of gastrin. **His-**

Pernicious anemia

In **autoimmune gastritis**, antibodies produced against H^+, K^+-**ATPase** cause a reduction in hydrochloric acid in the gastric juice (**achlorhydria**) and a lack of synthesis of intrinsic factor. The resulting vitamin B_{12} deficiency disrupts the formation of red blood cells in the bone marrow, leading to a condition known as **pernicious anemia**.

Figure 15–17

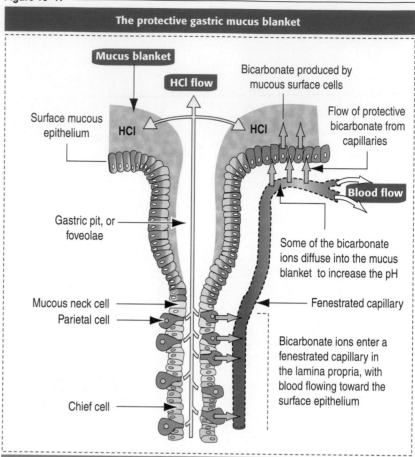

The protective gastric mucus blanket

Mucus blanket

HCl flow

Bicarbonate produced by mucous surface cells

Surface mucous epithelium

HCl   HCl

Flow of protective bicarbonate from capillaries

Blood flow

Gastric pit, or foveolae

Some of the bicarbonate ions diffuse into the mucus blanket to increase the pH

Mucous neck cell

Parietal cell

Fenestrated capillary

Bicarbonate ions enter a fenestrated capillary in the lamina propria, with blood flowing toward the surface epithelium

Chief cell

tamine potentiates the effects of acetylcholine and gastrin on parietal cell secretion after binding to the **histamine H_2 receptor**. Histamine is produced by **enterochromaffin-like (ECL) cells** within the lamina propria surrounding the gastric glands. **Cimetidine** is an H_2 receptor antagonist that inhibits histamine-dependent acid secretion.

H^+,K^+-dependent ATPase facilitates the exchange of H^+ and K^+. Cl^- and Na^+ (derived from the dissociation of NaCl) are actively transported into the lumen of the intracellular canaliculus, leading to the production of HCl. K^+ and Na^+ are recycled back into the cell by separate pumps once H^+ has taken their place. **Omeprazole**, with binding affinity to H^+,K^+-dependent ATPase, inactivates acid secretion and is an effective agent in the treatment of peptic ulcer.

Water enters the cell by osmosis—because of the secretion of ions into the canaliculus—and dissociates into H^+ and hydroxyl ions (HO^-). **Carbon dioxide**, entering the cell from the blood or formed during metabolism of the cell, combines with HO^- to form **carbonic acid** under the influence of **carbonic anhydrase**. Carbonic acid dissociates into **bicarbonate ions** (HCO_3^-) and **hydrogen ions**. HCO_3^- diffuses out of the cell into the blood and accounts for the increase in blood plasma pH during digestion.

Clinical significance: The gastric mucosal barrier and *Helicobacter pylori* infection

It is convenient to regard the gastric juice as a combination of two separate secretions: (1) an **alkaline mucosal gel protective component**, produced by surface mucous cells and mucus neck cells, and (2) HCl and pepsin, two **parietal–chief cell potentially aggressive components**. The protective component is **constitu-**

Figure 15–18

Helicobacter pylori and chronic gastric inflammation and ulcers

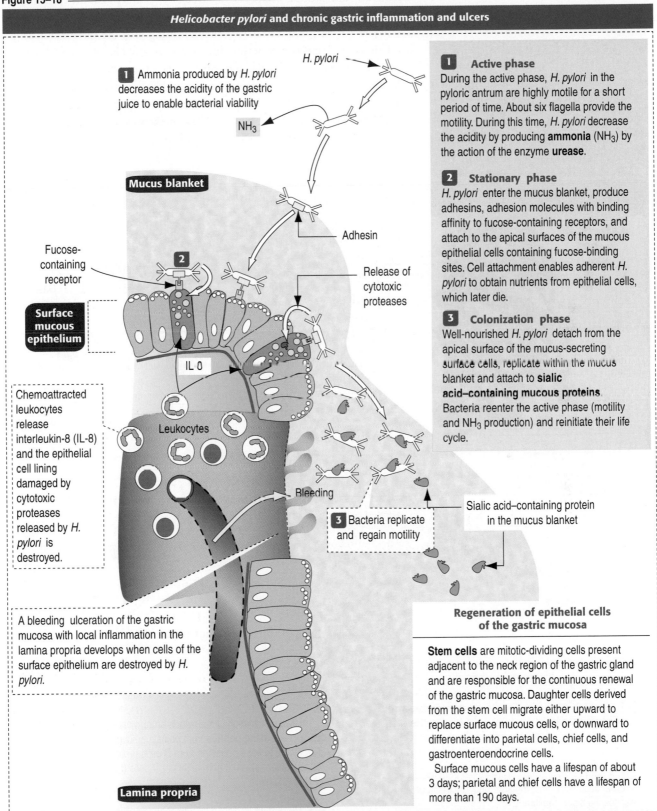

1 Ammonia produced by *H. pylori* decreases the acidity of the gastric juice to enable bacterial viability

H. pylori

NH₃

Mucus blanket

Adhesin

Fucose-containing receptor

2

Release of cytotoxic proteases

Surface mucous epithelium

IL 0

Chemoattracted leukocytes release interleukin-8 (IL-8) and the epithelial cell lining damaged by cytotoxic proteases released by *H. pylori* is destroyed.

Leukocytes

Bleeding

3 Bacteria replicate and regain motility

Sialic acid–containing protein in the mucus blanket

A bleeding ulceration of the gastric mucosa with local inflammation in the lamina propria develops when cells of the surface epithelium are destroyed by *H. pylori.*

Lamina propria

1 **Active phase**
During the active phase, *H. pylori* in the pyloric antrum are highly motile for a short period of time. About six flagella provide the motility. During this time, *H. pylori* decrease the acidity by producing **ammonia** (NH₃) by the action of the enzyme **urease**.

2 **Stationary phase**
H. pylori enter the mucus blanket, produce adhesins, adhesion molecules with binding affinity to fucose-containing receptors, and attach to the apical surfaces of the mucous epithelial cells containing fucose-binding sites. Cell attachment enables adherent *H. pylori* to obtain nutrients from epithelial cells, which later die.

3 **Colonization phase**
Well-nourished *H. pylori* detach from the apical surface of the mucus-secreting surface cells, replicate within the mucus blanket and attach to **sialic acid–containing mucous proteins**. Bacteria reenter the active phase (motility and NH₃ production) and reinitiate their life cycle.

Regeneration of epithelial cells of the gastric mucosa

Stem cells are mitotic-dividing cells present adjacent to the neck region of the gastric gland and are responsible for the continuous renewal of the gastric mucosa. Daughter cells derived from the stem cell migrate either upward to replace surface mucous cells, or downward to differentiate into parietal cells, chief cells, and gastroenteroendocrine cells.
Surface mucous cells have a lifespan of about 3 days; parietal and chief cells have a lifespan of more than 190 days.

tive; it is always present. The aggressive component is **facultative** because hydrochloric acid and pepsin levels increase above basal levels after food intake.
The viscous, highly glycosylated gastric mucus blanket—produced by surface

mucous cells and mucous neck cells—maintains a neutral pH at the epithelial cell surfaces of the stomach. In addition, the mitochondrial-rich surface mucus cells (see Figure 15–14) produce HCO_3^- ions diffusing into the surface mucus gel. Recall the clinical significance during chronic vomiting of Na^+, K^+, and Cl^- present in the protective mucosal barrier and gastric juice.

HCO_3^- ions, produced by parietal cells, enter the fenestrated capillaries of the lamina propria. Some of the HCO_3^- ions diffuse into the mucus blanket and neutralize the low pH created by the HCl content of the gastric lumen at the vicinity of the surface mucous cells (Figure 15–17).

Figure 15–19

Gastroendocrine G cell (pyloric antrum)

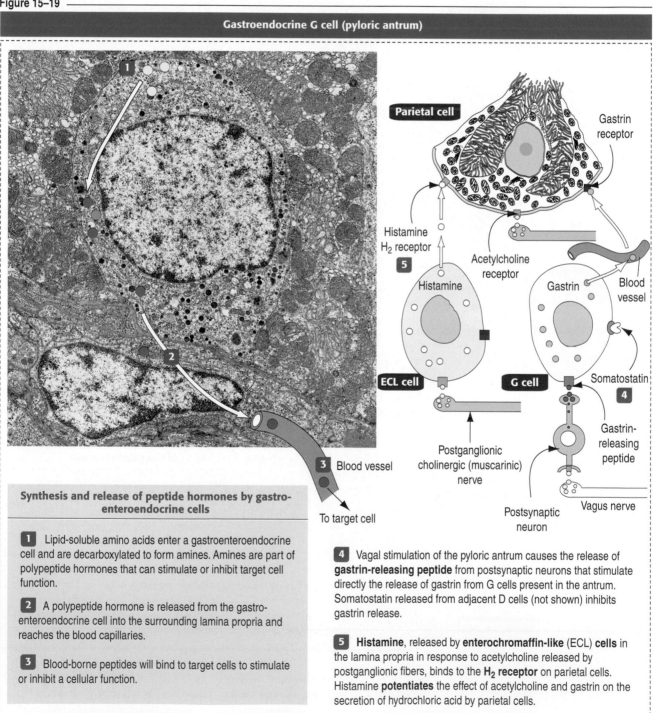

Synthesis and release of peptide hormones by gastro-enteroendocrine cells

1 Lipid-soluble amino acids enter a gastroenteroendocrine cell and are decarboxylated to form amines. Amines are part of polypeptide hormones that can stimulate or inhibit target cell function.

2 A polypeptide hormone is released from the gastro-enteroendocrine cell into the surrounding lamina propria and reaches the blood capillaries.

3 Blood-borne peptides will bind to target cells to stimulate or inhibit a cellular function.

4 Vagal stimulation of the pyloric antrum causes the release of **gastrin-releasing peptide** from postsynaptic neurons that stimulate directly the release of gastrin from G cells present in the antrum. Somatostatin released from adjacent D cells (not shown) inhibits gastrin release.

5 **Histamine**, released by **enterochromaffin-like (ECL) cells** in the lamina propria in response to acetylcholine released by postganglionic fibers, binds to the **H_2 receptor** on parietal cells. Histamine **potentiates** the effect of acetylcholine and gastrin on the secretion of hydrochloric acid by parietal cells.

However, the mucus blanket lining the gastric epithelium, in particular in the **pyloric antrum**, is the site where the flagellated bacterium *Helicobacter pylori* resides in spite of the hostile environment.

H. pylori survives and replicates in the gastric lumen. Its presence has been associated with acid peptic ulcers and adenocarcinoma of the stomach.

Three phases define the pathogenesis of *H. pylori* (Figure 15–18):

1. An **active phase**, in which motile bacteria increase the gastric pH by producing **ammonia** through the action of **urease**.

2. A **stationary phase**, consisting in the bacterial attachment to **fucose-containing receptors** on the surface of mucous surface cells of the pyloric region. *H. pylori* attachment results in the production of **cytotoxic proteases** that ensure the bacteria a supply of nutrients from surface mucous cells and also attract leukocytes. Both ammonia production and cytotoxic proteases correlate with the development of peptic ulcers of the pyloric mucosa.

3. During the last **colonization phase**, *H. pylori* detach from the fucose-containing receptors of the surface mucus epithelium, increase in number by replication within the mucus blanket, and remain attached to glycoproteins containing sialic acid. Despite the rapid turnover of the gastric mucus-secreting cells, *H. pylori* avoids being flushed away with dead epithelial cells by producing urease and displaying high motility.

About 20% of the population are infected with *H. pylori* by age 20 years. The incidence of the infection increases to about 60% by age 60.

Most infected individuals do not have clinical symptoms. Increasing evidence for the infectious origin of acid peptic disease and chronic gastritis led to the implementation of antibiotic therapy for all ulcer patients shown to be infected with *H. pylori*.

More recently, attention has been directed to adhesins and fucose-containing receptors as potential targets for drug action. The objective is to prevent binding of pathogenic bacteria without interfering with the endogenous bacterial flora by the use of antibiotics.

Gastroenteroendocrine cells

The function of the alimentary tube is regulated by **peptide hormones**, produced by gastroenteroendocrine cells, and **neuroendocrine mediators**, produced by neurons.

Peptide hormones are synthesized by gastroenteroendocrine cells dispersed throughout the mucosa from the stomach through the colon. The population of gastroenteroendocrine cells is so large that the gastrointestinal segment is regarded as **the largest endocrine organ in the body.**

Gastroenteroendocrine cells are members of the **APUD system**, so called because of the <u>a</u>mine <u>p</u>recursor <u>u</u>ptake and <u>d</u>ecarboxylation property of amino acids (Figure 15–19). Because not all the cells accumulate amine precursors, the designation APUD has been replaced by **DNES** (for <u>d</u>iffuse <u>n</u>euro<u>e</u>ndocrine <u>s</u>ystem).

Neuroendocrine mediators are released from nerve terminals. For example, **acetylcholine** is released at the terminals of postganglionic cholinergic nerves. **Gastrin-releasing peptide** is released by postsynaptic neurons activated by stimulation of the vagus nerve (see Figure 15–19).

Peptide hormones produced by gastrointestinal endocrine cells have the following general functions: (1) regulation of water, electrolyte metabolism and enzyme secretion; (2) regulation of gastrointestinal motility and mucosal growth; and (3) stimulation of the release of other peptide hormones.

We will consider five major gastrointestinal peptide hormones: **secretin, gastrin, cholecystokinin, gastric inhibitory peptide,** and **motilin.**

1. **Secretin** was the first hormone to be discovered (in 1902). Secretin is released by cells in the **duodenal mucosa** when HCl-containing gastric juice enters the duodenum. Secretin is released when the pH in the duodenum is below 4.5 and reduces acid secretion (antacid effect). Secretin stimulates **pancreatic bicarbonate** and **fluid secretion**. Secretin, together with cholecystokinin, stimulates the growth of the exocrine pancreas. In addition, **secretin** (and acetylcholine) **stimulates chief cells to secrete pepsinogen**.

2. **Gastrin**, produced by G cells located in the pyloric antrum. Two forms of gastrin have been described: **little gastrin**, or G_{17} (which contains 17 amino acids), and **big gastrin**, or G_{34} (which contains 34 amino acids). G cells produce primarily G_{17}. The duodenal mucosa in humans contains G cells producing mainly G_{34}. The neuroendocrine mediator **gastrin-releasing peptide** regulates the release of gastrin. **Somatostatin**, produced by **D cells**, inhibits the release of gastrin when the pyloric antral mucosa is acidified (see Figure 15–19).

The main function of gastrin is to stimulate the production of hydrochloric acid by parietal cells. Gastrin can also activate cholecystokinin receptors to stimulate gallbladder contraction. **Gastrin has a trophic effect on the mucosa** of the small and large intestine and the fundic region of the stomach.

Gastrin stimulates the growth of **enterochromaffin-like cells** of the stomach. Continued hypersecretion of gastrin results in hyperplasia of ECL cells. ECL cells produce histamine by decarboxylation of histidine. Histamine binds to the **histamine H_2 receptor** on **parietal cells** to **potentiate the effect of gastrin and acetylcholine on HCl secretion** (see Figure 15–19). Histamine H_2 receptor blocking drugs (such as cimetidine [Tagamet] and ranitidine [Zantac]) are effective inhibitors of acid secretion.

3. **Cholecystokinin** (CCK) is produced in the **small intestine** (duodenum and jejunum) and stimulates **gallbladder contraction** triggered by the presence of fat in the small intestine.

4. **Gastric inhibitory peptide** (GIP), formerly called **urogastrone**, is produced in the **small intestine** (duodenum and jejunum) and inhibits gastric secretion

Figure 15–20

Pyloric region of the stomach

A deep pit, or foveola, projects deep into the mucosa

Cardia

Fundus

Body

Antrum

Muscularis mucosae

The continuity of the pyloric glands is difficult to visualize in histologic sections because of their tortuous path and highly branched nature

Deep pit lined by mucous-secreting cells

Muscularis mucosae

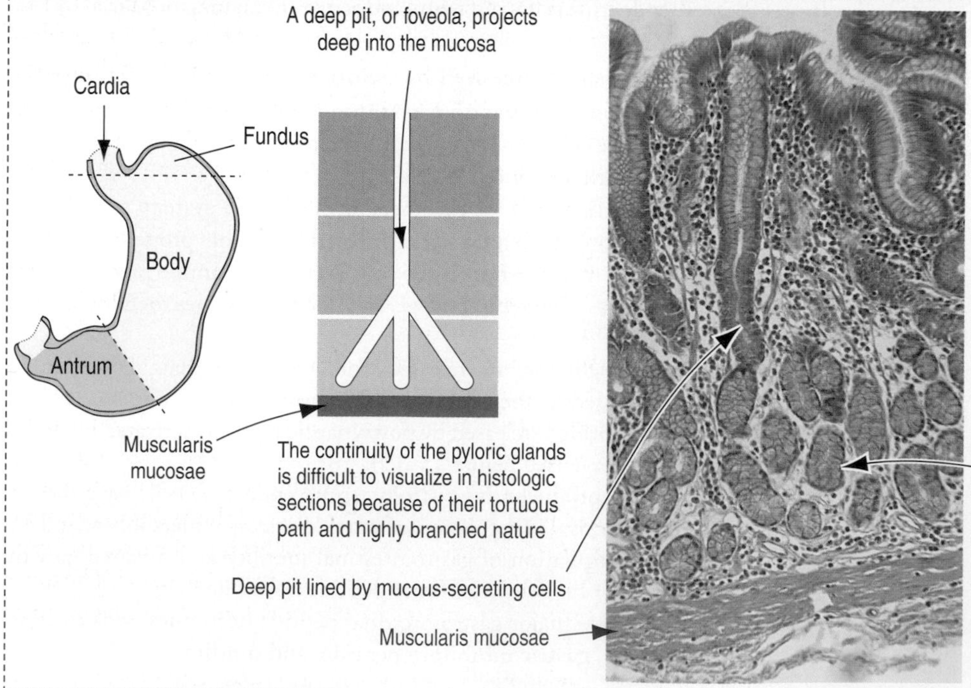

Pyloric glands are **simple tubular and branched at the very lower end**.

The **pits are deeper** than the cardiac glands and gastric glands of the fundus–body region.

Pyloric glands are lined by **mucous-secreting cells**.

At the distal end, the contents of the mucous-secreting cells displace and flatten the nuclei to the basal domain of the cell.

when its release is stimulated by fat and glucose. GIP stimulates insulin release (**insulinotropic effect**) when glucose levels in serum are high.

5. **Motilin** is released cyclically (every 90 minutes) during fasting from the upper **small intestine** and stimulates gastrointestinal motility. A **neural control mechanism** regulates the release of motilin.

Clinical significance: Zollinger-Ellison syndrome

Patients with gastrin-secreting tumors (**gastrinomas**, or **Zollinger-Ellison syndrome**) display hyperplasia and hypertrophy of the fundic region of the stomach and high acid secretion independent of feeding. The complications of gastrinomas are **fulminant stomach ulceration**, **diarrhea** (caused by an inhibitory effect of water and electrolyte absorption by the intestine caused by gastrin), **steatorrhea** (caused by inactivation of pancreatic lipase determined by the low pH), and **hypokalemia**.

Pyloric glands

Pyloric glands differ from the cardiac and gastric glands in the following layers: (1) The gastric pits, or foveolae, are deeper and extend halfway through the depth of the mucosa. (2) Pyloric glands have a larger lumen and are highly branched (Figure 15–20).

The predominant epithelial cell type of the pyloric gland is a mucus-secreting cell that resembles the mucous neck cells of the gastric glands. Most of the cell contains large and pale secretory mucus and secretory granules containing **lysozyme**, a bacterial lytic enzyme. Occasionally, parietal cells can be found in the pyloric glands. Enteroendocrine cells, **gastrin-secreting G cells** in particular, are abundant in the antrum pyloric region. Lymphoid nodules can be seen in the lamina propria.

The mucosa, submucosa, and muscularis of the stomach

We complete this chapter by pointing out additional structural and functional details of the mucosa, submucosa, and muscularis of the stomach.

The **mucosa** consists of loose connective tissue, called the **lamina propria**, surrounding cardiac, gastric, and pyloric glands. Reticular and collagen fibers predominate in the lamina propria, and elastic fibers are rare. The cell components of the lamina propria include fibroblasts, lymphocytes, mast cells, eosinophils, and a few plasma cells. The muscularis mucosae can project thin strands of muscle cells into the mucosa to facilitate the release of secretions from the glands.

The **submucosa** consists of dense irregular connective tissue in which collagenous and elastic fibers are abundant. A large number of arterioles, venous plexuses, and lymphatics are present in the submucosa. Also present are the cell bodies and nerve fibers of the **submucosal plexus of Meissner**.

The **muscularis** (or **muscularis externa**) of the stomach consists of three poorly defined layers of smooth muscle oriented in circular, oblique, and longitudinal directions. At the level of the distal pyloric antrum, the circular muscle layer thickens to form the annular **pyloric sphincter**.

Contraction of the muscularis is under control of the autonomic nerve plexuses located between the muscle layers (myenteric plexus of Auerbach).

We have previously seen (see Figure 15–11) that, based on motility functions, the stomach can be divided into two major regions: the **orad** (Lat. *os* [pl. *ora*], mouth; *ad*, to; toward the mouth) **portion**, consisting of the fundus and part of the body, and the **caudad** (Lat., *cauda*, tail; *ad*, to; toward the tail) **portion**, comprising the distal body and the antrum. During swallowing, the orad region of the stomach and the LES relax to accommodate the ingested material. The tonus of the muscularis adjusts to the volume of the organ without increasing the pressure in the lumen.

Contraction of the caudad portion of the stomach mixes and propels the gastric contents toward the gastroduodenal junction. Most solid contents are propelled back (**retropulsion**) into the main body of the stomach because of the closure of the distal antrum. Liquids empty more rapidly. Retropulsion determines both mixing and mechanical dissociation of solid particles. When the gastric juice empties into the duodenum, peristaltic waves from the orad to the caudad portions of the stomach propel the contents in coordination with the relaxation of the pyloric sphincter.

16. LOWER DIGESTIVE SEGMENT

Small intestine

The **main functions** of the small intestine are (1) **to continue in the duodenum the digestive process initiated in the stomach**, (2) **to absorb digested food after enzymes produced in the intestinal mucosa and the pancreas**, together with the emulsifying bile produced in the liver, enable uptake of protein, carbohydrate, and lipid components.

This section describes first the **main distinctive histologic features** of the three major segments of the small intestine. The structural and functional details of the cellular components of the intestinal mucosa are discussed afterward.

The 4- to 7-m-long small intestine is divided into three sequential segments: (1) **duodenum**, (2) **jejunum**, and (3) **ileum**.

The duodenum is about 25 cm in length, is mainly retroperitoneal, and surrounds the head of the pancreas. At its distal end, the duodenum is continuous with the jejunum, a movable intestinal segment suspended by a mesentery. The ileum is the continuation of the jejunum.

The wall of the small intestine consists of four layers (Figures 16–1, 16–2, and 16-3): (1) the **mucosa**, (2) the **submucosa**, (3) the **muscularis**, and (4) the **serosa,** or **peritoneum**. As you will see, histologic differences are seen in the **mucosa and submucosa of the three major portions** of the small intestine. The **muscularis externa** and **serosa** layers are similar.

The intestinal wall

An increase in the total surface of the mucosa reflects the absorptive function of the small intestine. Four degrees of folding amplify the absorptive surface area of the mucosa (see Figure 16–2): (1) the **plicae circulares** (circular folds; also known as the **valves of Kerkring**), (2) the **intestinal villi**, (3) the **intestinal glands**, and (4) the **microvilli** on the apical surface of the lining epithelium of the intestinal cells (enterocytes).

Figure 16–1

The small intestine

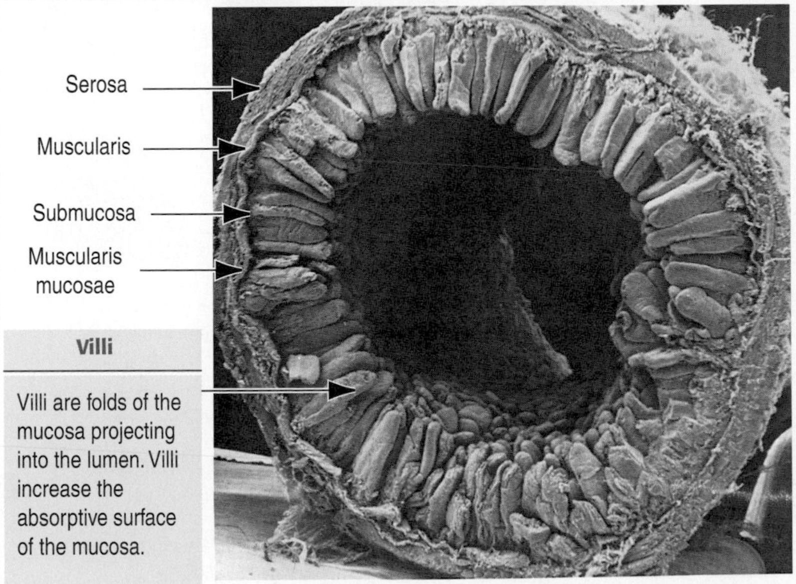

Serosa
Muscularis
Submucosa
Muscularis mucosae

Villi

Villi are folds of the mucosa projecting into the lumen. Villi increase the absorptive surface of the mucosa.

Scanning electron micrograph from Kessel RG, Kardon RH: Tissues and Organs. New York, WH Freeman, 1979.

A **plica circularis** is a permanent fold of the **mucosa** and **submucosa** encircling the intestinal lumen.

Plicae appear about 5 cm distal to the aboral outlet of the stomach, become

Figure 16–2

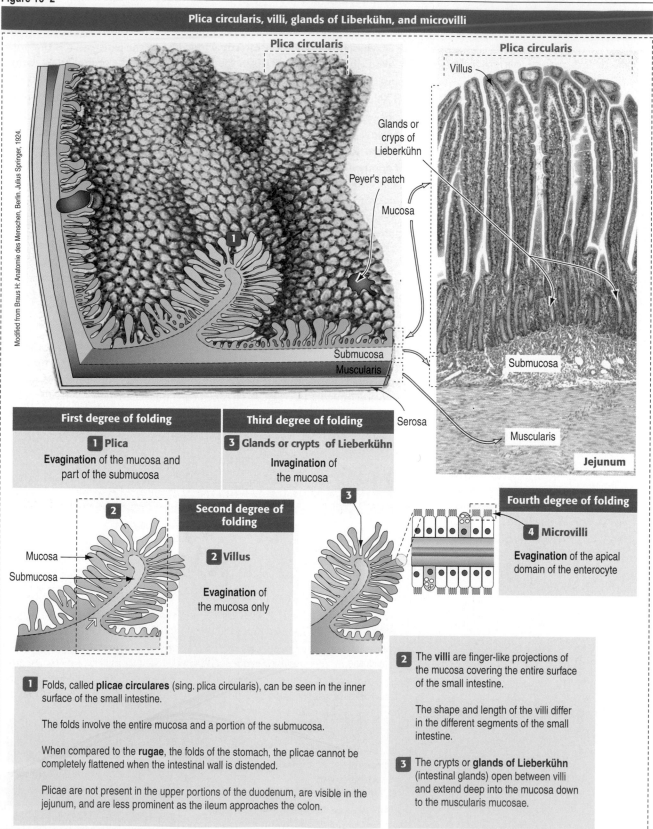

Plica circularis, villi, glands of Liberkühn, and microvilli

Plica circularis

Villus

Glands or cryps of Lieberkühn

Peyer's patch

Mucosa

Submucosa

Muscularis

Serosa

Modified from Braus H: Anatomie des Menschen, Berlin, Julius Springer, 1924.

Plica circularis

Villus

Glands or cryps of Lieberkühn

Mucosa

Submucosa

Muscularis

Jejunum

First degree of folding

1 Plica

Evagination of the mucosa and part of the submucosa

Third degree of folding

3 Glands or crypts of Lieberkühn

Invagination of the mucosa

Second degree of folding

2 Villus

Evagination of the mucosa only

Mucosa
Submucosa

Fourth degree of folding

4 Microvilli

Evagination of the apical domain of the enterocyte

1 Folds, called **plicae circulares** (sing. plica circularis), can be seen in the inner surface of the small intestine.

The folds involve the entire mucosa and a portion of the submucosa.

When compared to the **rugae**, the folds of the stomach, the plicae cannot be completely flattened when the intestinal wall is distended.

Plicae are not present in the upper portions of the duodenum, are visible in the jejunum, and are less prominent as the ileum approaches the colon.

2 The **villi** are finger-like projections of the mucosa covering the entire surface of the small intestine.

The shape and length of the villi differ in the different segments of the small intestine.

3 The crypts or **glands of Lieberkühn** (intestinal glands) open between villi and extend deep into the mucosa down to the muscularis mucosae.

Figure 16–3

Blood, lymphatic, and nerve supply to the small intestine

1 The microvascular system of the villus derives from two arteriolar systems. One system supplies the tip of the villus (**capillary villus plexus**). The second system forms the **pericryptal capillary plexus**. Both plexuses drain into the **submucosal venule**.

2 A single blind-ending **central lymphatic vessel**, called a **lacteal**, is present in the core of a villus. The lacteal is the initiation of a lymphatic vessel which, just above the muscularis mucosae, forms a lymphatic plexus whose branches surround a lymphoid nodule in the submucosa. Efferent lymphatic vessels of the lymphoid nodule anastomose with the lacteal and leave the digestive tube together with the blood vessels.

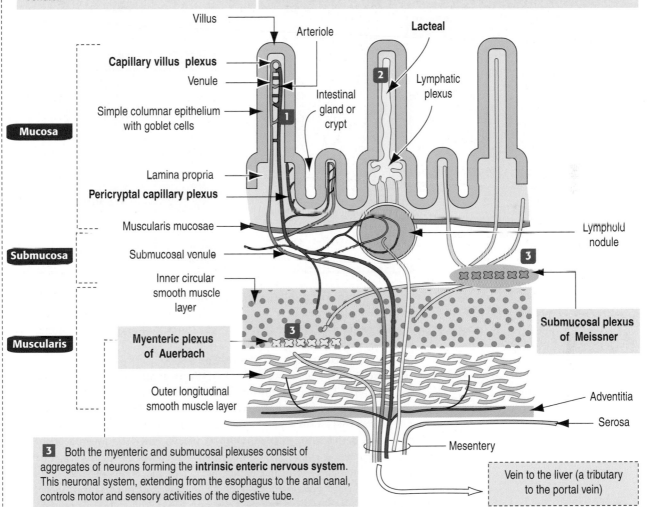

3 Both the myenteric and submucosal plexuses consist of aggregates of neurons forming the **intrinsic enteric nervous system**. This neuronal system, extending from the esophagus to the anal canal, controls motor and sensory activities of the digestive tube.

distinct where the duodenum joins the jejunum, and diminish in size progressively to disappear halfway along the ileum.

The **intestinal villi** are finger-like projections of the mucosa covering the entire surface of the small intestine. Villi extend deep into the mucosa to form crypts ending at the muscularis mucosae. The length of the villi depends on the degree of distention of the intestinal wall and the contraction of smooth muscle fibers in the villus core.

The **crypts of Lieberkühn**, or **intestinal glands**, are **simple tubular glands** that increase the intestinal surface area. The crypts are formed by invaginations of the mucosa between adjacent intestinal villi.

The **muscularis mucosae** is the boundary between the mucosa and submucosa (see Figure 16–3). The **muscularis** consists of inner circular smooth muscle and outer longitudinal smooth muscle. The muscularis is responsible for **segmentation** and **peristaltic movement** of the contents of the small intestine (Figure 16–

Figure 16–4

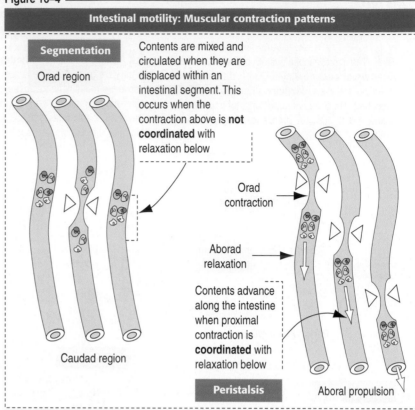

4). The **adventitia**, a thin layer of connective tissue, is covered by the **visceral peritoneum**, a serosal layer lined by a simple squamous epithelium, or **mesothelium**. The **parietal peritoneum** covers the inner surface of the abdominal wall.

Microcirculation of the small intestine

A difference with the microcirculation of the stomach (see Figure 15–8 in Chapter 15, Upper Digestive Segment) is that **the intestinal submucosa is the main distribution site of blood and lymphatic flow** (see Figure 16–3). Branches of the submucosal plexus supply capillaries to the muscularis and intestinal mucosa. Arterioles derived from the **submucosal plexus** enter the mucosa of the small intestine and give rise to two capillary networks: The **villus capillary plexus** supplies the intestinal villus and upper portion of the crypts of Lieberkühn. The **pericryptal capillary plexus** supplies the lower half of the crypts of Lieberkühn.

A single blind-ending **central lymphatic vessel**, the **lacteal**, is present in the core of a villus. The lacteal is the initiation of a lymphatic vessel that, just above the muscularis mucosae, forms a **lymphatic plexus** whose branches surround a lymphoid nodule in the mucosa-submucosa. Efferent lymphatic vessels of the lymphoid nodule anastomose with the lacteal and leave the digestive tube through the mesentery, together with the blood vessels.

Innervation and motility of the small intestine

Motility of the small intestine is controlled by the autonomic nervous system. The intrinsic autonomic nervous system of the small intestine, consisting of the submucosal **plexus of Meissner** and **myenteric plexus of Auerbach**, is similar to that of the stomach (see Figure 15–9 in Chapter 15, Upper Digestive Segment).

Neurons of the plexuses receive **intrinsic input from the mucosa and muscle wall** of the small intestine and **extrinsic input from the central nervous system** through the **parasympathetic** (vagus nerve) **and sympathetic nerve trunks**.

Contraction of the muscularis is coordinated to achieve two objectives (see

Figure 16–4): First, **to mix and mobilize the contents within an intestinal segment.** This is accomplished when muscular contraction activity is not coordinated and the intestine becomes transiently divided into segments. This process

Figure 16–5

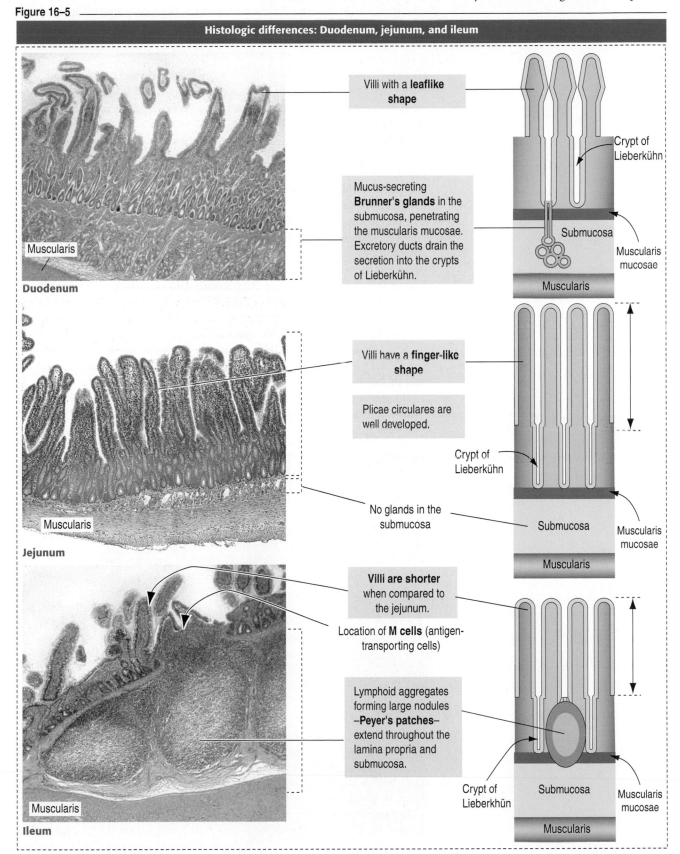

Histologic differences: Duodenum, jejunum, and ileum

Duodenum

Muscularis

Villi with a **leaflike shape**

Mucus-secreting **Brunner's glands** in the submucosa, penetrating the muscularis mucosae. Excretory ducts drain the secretion into the crypts of Lieberkühn.

Crypt of Lieberkühn

Submucosa

Muscularis mucosae

Muscularis

Jejunum

Muscularis

Villi have a **finger-like shape**

Plicae circulares are well developed.

No glands in the submucosa

Crypt of Lieberkühn

Submucosa

Muscularis mucosae

Muscularis

Ileum

Muscularis

Villi are shorter when compared to the jejunum.

Location of **M cells** (antigen-transporting cells)

Lymphoid aggregates forming large nodules –**Peyer's patches**– extend throughout the lamina propria and submucosa.

Crypt of Lieberkühn

Submucosa

Muscularis mucosae

Muscularis

is known as **segmentation**. Second, **to propel the intestinal contents** when there is a proximal (**orad**) contraction coordinated with a distal (**aborad**; Lat. *ab*, from; *os*, mouth; away from the mouth) relaxation. When coordinated contraction-relaxation occurs sequentially, the intestinal contents are propelled in an **aboral direction**. This process is known as **peristalsis** (Gk. *peri*, around; *stalsis*, constriction).

Histologic differences of the duodenum, jejunum, and ileum

Each of the three major anatomic portions of the small intestine—the duodenum, jejunum and ileum—has **distinctive features that allow recognition under the light microscope** (Figure 16–5).

The **duodenum** extends from the pyloric region of the stomach to the junction with the jejunum and has the following characteristics: (1) It has **Brunner's glands in the submucosa**. Brunner's glands are **tubuloacinar mucus glands** producing an **alkaline secretion** (pH 8.8 to 9.3) that neutralizes the acidic chyme coming from the stomach. (2) The **villi are broad and short** (leaflike shape). (3) The duodenum is surrounded by an incomplete serosa and an extensive adventitia. (4) The duodenum collects bile and pancreatic secretions transported by the common bile duct and pancreatic duct, respectively. The sphincter of Oddi is present at the terminal ampullary portion of the two converging ducts. (5) The base of the crypts of Lieberkühn may contain **Paneth cells**.

The **jejunum** has the following characteristics: (1) It has long finger-like villi and a **well-developed lacteal in the core of the villus**. (2) The jejunum **does not contain Brunner's glands** in the submucosa. (3) Peyer's patches in the lamina propria may be present but they are not predominant in the jejunum. Peyer's patches are a characteristic feature of the ileum. (4) **Paneth cells** are found at the base of the crypts of Lieberkühn.

The **ileum** has a prominent diagnostic feature: **Peyer's patches**. The lack of Brunner's gland and the presence of shorter finger-like villi—when compared

Figure 16–6

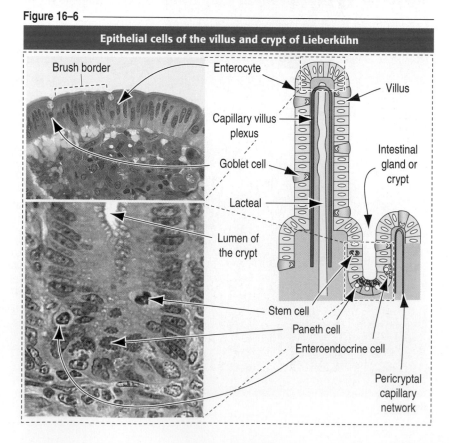

Epithelial cells of the villus and crypt of Lieberkühn

Brush border

Enterocyte

Villus

Capillary villus plexus

Goblet cell

Intestinal gland or crypt

Lacteal

Lumen of the crypt

Stem cell

Paneth cell

Enteroendocrine cell

Pericryptal capillary network

with the jejunum—are additional landmarks of the ileum. As in the jejunum, **Paneth cells** are found at the base of the crypts of Lieberkühn.

The villus and crypts of Lieberkühn

The intestinal mucosa, including the crypts of Lieberkühn, are lined by a **simple columnar epithelium** containing four major cell types (Figure 16–6): (1) **absorptive cells**, or **enterocytes**, (2) **goblet cells**, (3) **Paneth cells**, and (4) **enteroendocrine cells**. Stem cells, Paneth cells, and enteroendocrine cells are found in the crypts of Lieberkühn (Figure 16–6).

Absorptive cells, or enterocytes

The **absorptive cell**, or **enterocyte** has an apical domain with a prominent **brush border** (also called a **striated border**), ending on a clear zone, called the **terminal**

Figure 16–7

The intestinal epithelium

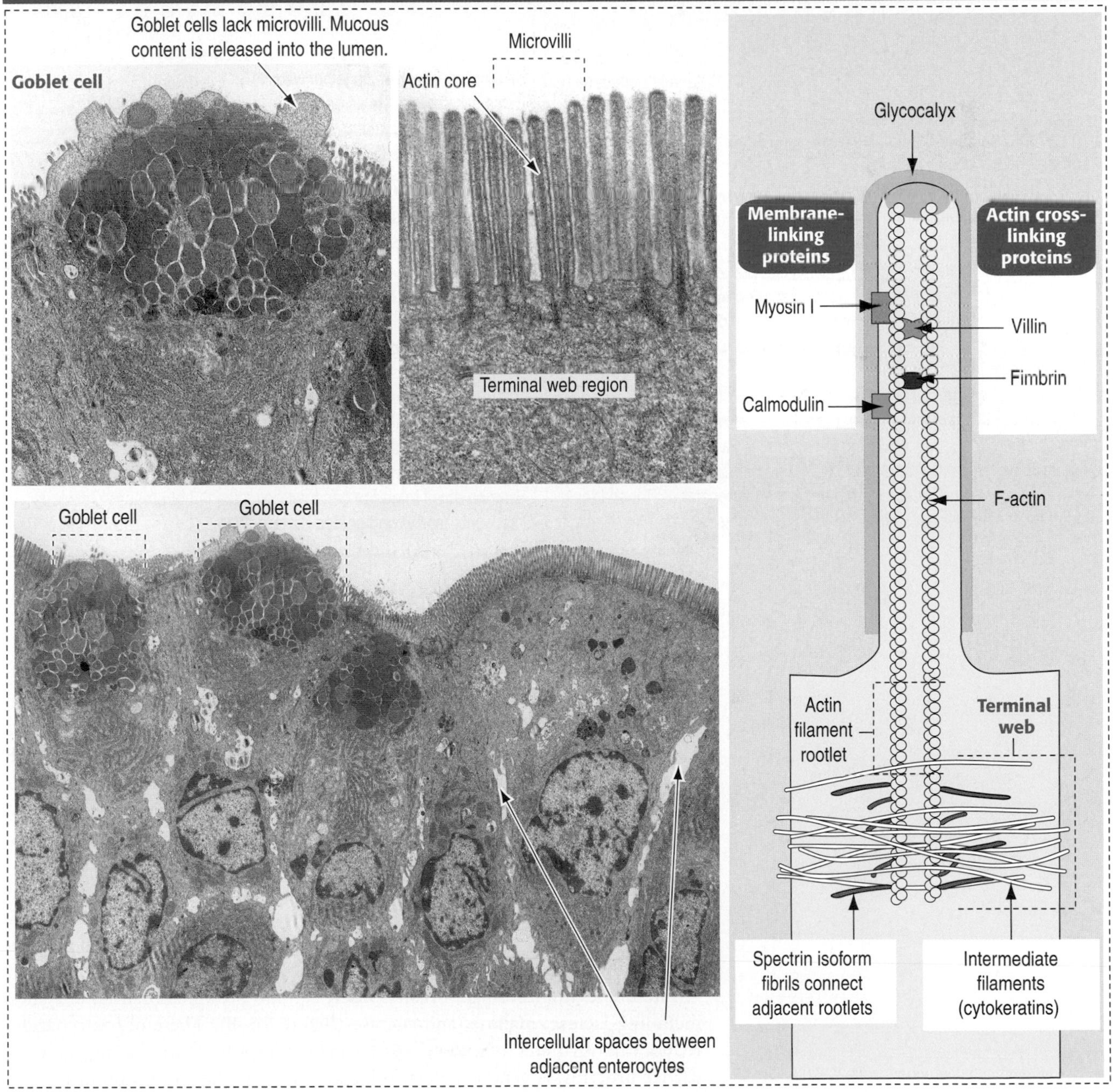

Goblet cells lack microvilli. Mucous content is released into the lumen.

Goblet cell

Microvilli

Actin core

Terminal web region

Glycocalyx

Membrane-linking proteins

Actin cross-linking proteins

Myosin I

Villin

Fimbrin

Calmodulin

F-actin

Goblet cell

Goblet cell

Actin filament rootlet

Terminal web

Spectrin isoform fibrils connect adjacent rootlets

Intermediate filaments (cytokeratins)

Intercellular spaces between adjacent enterocytes

Figure 16–8

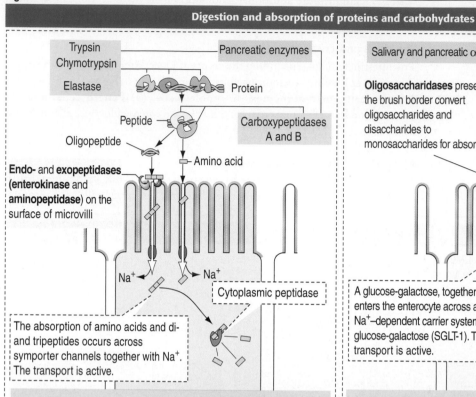

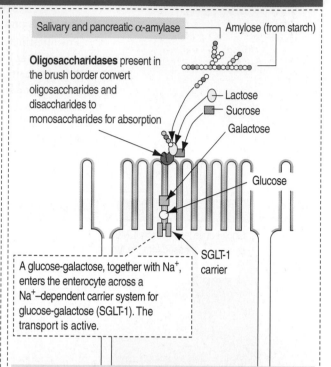

Digestion and absorption of proteins and carbohydrates

Trypsin
Chymotrypsin
Elastase — Pancreatic enzymes — Protein

Peptide

Oligopeptide

Carboxypeptidases A and B

Amino acid

Endo- and **exopeptidases (enterokinase** and **aminopeptidase)** on the surface of microvilli

Na⁺   Na⁺

Cytoplasmic peptidase

The absorption of amino acids and di- and tripeptides occurs across symporter channels together with Na⁺. The transport is active.

Protein digestion starts in the stomach in the presence of pepsin derived from the precursor pepsinogen secreted by chief cells. Pepsin activity ends in the alkaline environment of the duodenum. Pancreatic proteases, **endopeptidases** and **exopeptidases**, continue proteolysis. **Trypsinogen** is activated to **trypsin** by **enterokinase**, located on the microvilli. Active trypsin, in turn, activates the bulk of trypsinogen. **Chymotrypsinogen** and **proelastase** are activated to chymotrypsin and elastase, respectively. Carboxypeptidases A and B derive from procarboxypeptidase A and B precursors. Trypsin plays a significant role in the activation and inactivation of pancreatic proenzymes. Tripeptides in the cytosol are digested by cytoplasmic peptidases into amino acids.

Salivary and pancreatic α-amylase — Amylose (from starch)

Oligosaccharidases present in the brush border convert oligosaccharides and disaccharides to monosaccharides for absorption

Lactose
Sucrose
Galactose

Glucose

SGLT-1 carrier

A glucose-galactose, together with Na⁺, enters the enterocyte across a Na⁺–dependent carrier system for glucose-galactose (SGLT-1). The transport is active.

Starch, **sucrose**, **lactose**, and **maltose** are the main dietary carbohydrates. Starch consists of amylose (a glucose polymer) and amylopectin (a plant starch). **Sucrose** is a glucose-fructose disaccharide. **Lactose** is a galactose-glucose disaccharide. **Maltose** is a glucose dimer. Salivary α-amylase initiates the digestion of starch in the mouth. Pancreatic α-amylase completes the digestion in the small intestine. Other major dietary sugars are hydrolyzed by **oligosaccharidases** (sucrase, lactase, isomaltase) present in the plasma membrane of the microvilli. **Cellulose is not digested in the human small intestine** because cellulase is not present. Cellulose accounts for the undigested dietary fiber.

web, which contains transverse cytoskeletal filaments. The brush border of each absorptive cell contains about 3000 closely packed **microvilli**, which increase the surface luminal area 30-fold.

The length of a microvillus ranges from 0.5 to 1.0 μm. The core of a microvillus (Figure 16–7) contains a bundle of 20 to 40 parallel **actin filaments** cross-linked by **fimbrin** and **villin**. The actin bundle core is anchored to the plasma membrane by **myosin I** and the calcium-binding protein **calmodulin**. Each actin bundle projects into the apical portion of the cell as a **rootlet**, which is cross-linked by an **intestinal isoform of spectrin** to an adjacent rootlet. The end portion of the rootlet attaches to **cytokeratin-containing intermediate filaments**. Spectrin and cytokeratins form the **terminal web**. The terminal web is responsible for maintaining the upright position and shape of the microvillus and anchoring the actin rootlets.

A **surface coat**, or **glycocalyx**, consisting of glycoproteins as integral components of the plasma membrane covers each microvillus.

The **microvilli**, forming a **brush border**, contain intramembranous enzymes, including **lactase**, **maltase**, and **sucrase** (Figure 16–8). These oligosaccharides reduce carbohydrates to hexoses, which can be transported into the enterocyte by **carrier proteins**. A **genetic defect in lactase** prevents the absorption of lactose-

Figure 16–9

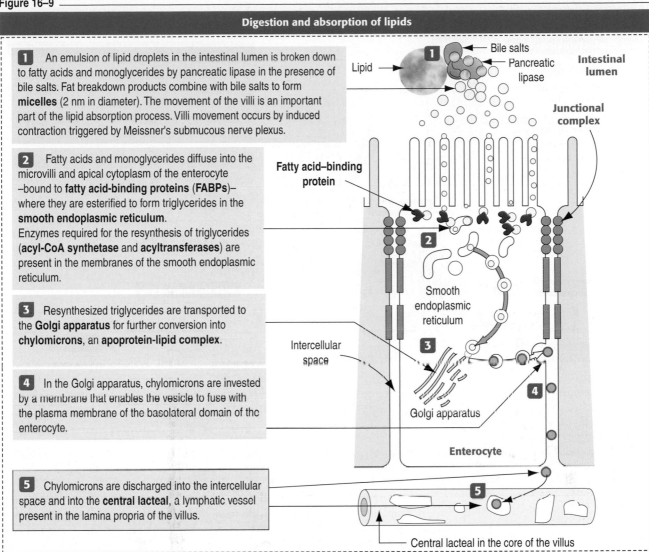

Digestion and absorption of lipids

1 An emulsion of lipid droplets in the intestinal lumen is broken down to fatty acids and monoglycerides by pancreatic lipase in the presence of bile salts. Fat breakdown products combine with bile salts to form **micelles** (2 nm in diameter). The movement of the villi is an important part of the lipid absorption process. Villi movement occurs by induced contraction triggered by Meissner's submucous nerve plexus.

2 Fatty acids and monoglycerides diffuse into the microvilli and apical cytoplasm of the enterocyte –bound to **fatty acid-binding proteins (FABPs)**– where they are esterified to form triglycerides in the **smooth endoplasmic reticulum.**
Enzymes required for the resynthesis of triglycerides (**acyl-CoA synthetase** and **acyltransferases**) are present in the membranes of the smooth endoplasmic reticulum.

3 Resynthesized triglycerides are transported to the **Golgi apparatus** for further conversion into **chylomicrons**, an **apoprotein-lipid complex**.

4 In the Golgi apparatus, chylomicrons are invested by a membrane that enables the vesicle to fuse with the plasma membrane of the basolateral domain of the enterocyte.

5 Chylomicrons are discharged into the intercellular space and into the **central lacteal**, a lymphatic vessel present in the lamina propria of the villus.

rich milk, leading to diarrhea (lactose intolerance). Therefore, the brush border not only increases the absorptive surface of enterocytes but is also the site where enzymes are involved in the terminal digestion of carbohydrates and proteins.

Final breakdown of oligopeptides, initiated by the action of gastric pepsin, is extended by pancreatic trypsin, chymotrypsin, elastase, and carboxypeptidases A and B. **Enterokinase** and **aminopeptidase**, localized in the microvilli, degrade oligopeptides into dipeptides, tripeptides, and amino acids before entering the enterocyte across symporter channels together with Na^+. **Cytoplasmic peptidases** degrade dipeptides and tripeptides into amino acids, which then diffuse or are transported by a carrier-mediated process across the basolateral plasma membrane into the blood.

The **absorption of lipids** involves the enzymatic breakdown of dietary lipids into **fatty acids** and **monoglycerides**, which can diffuse across the plasma membrane of the microvilli and the apical plasma membrane of the enterocyte. Details of the **process of fat absorption** are depicted in Figure 16–9.

Goblet cells

Goblet cells are columnar mucus-secreting cells scattered among enterocytes of the intestinal epithelium (see Figure 16–7).

Goblet cells have two domains: (1) A cup- or goblet-shaped **apical domain**

Figure 16–10

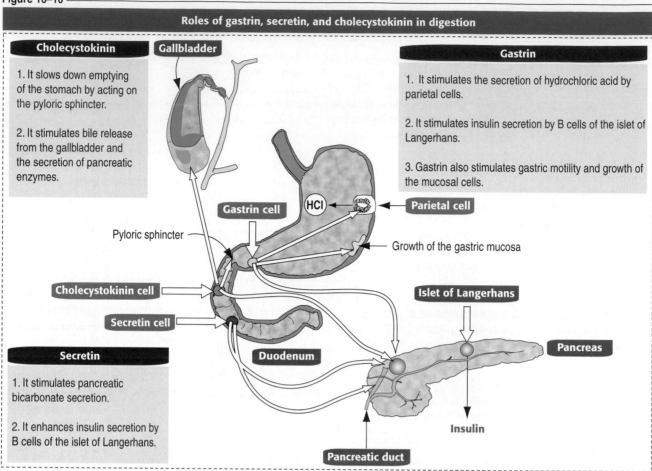

Roles of gastrin, secretin, and cholecystokinin in digestion

Cholecystokinin

1. It slows down emptying of the stomach by acting on the pyloric sphincter.

2. It stimulates bile release from the gallbladder and the secretion of pancreatic enzymes.

Gallbladder

Gastrin

1. It stimulates the secretion of hydrochloric acid by parietal cells.

2. It stimulates insulin secretion by B cells of the islet of Langerhans.

3. Gastrin also stimulates gastric motility and growth of the mucosal cells.

Gastrin cell

HCl

Parietal cell

Pyloric sphincter

Growth of the gastric mucosa

Cholecystokinin cell

Islet of Langerhans

Secretin cell

Secretin

1. It stimulates pancreatic bicarbonate secretion.

2. It enhances insulin secretion by B cells of the islet of Langerhans.

Duodenum

Pancreas

Insulin

Pancreatic duct

containing large mucus granules that are discharged on the surface of the epithelium, and (2) a narrow **basal domain**, which attaches to the basal lamina and contains the rough endoplasmic reticulum in which the protein portion of mucous is produced. The **Golgi apparatus**, which adds oligosaccharide groups to mucus, is prominent and situated above the basally located nucleus.

The secretory product of goblet cells contains **glycoproteins** (80% carbohydrate and 20% protein) released by **exocytosis**. On the surface of the epithelium, **the mucus hydrates to form a protective gel coat to shield the epithelium from mechanical abrasion and bacterial invasion.**

Enteroendocrine cells

In addition to its digestive function, the gastrointestinal tract is the largest diffuse endocrine gland in the body.

We have already studied the structural and functional features of enteroendocrine cells in the stomach. As in the stomach, enteroendocrine cells secrete peptide hormones controlling several functions of the gastrointestinal system. The location and function of **gastrin-**, **secretin-**, and **cholecystokinin**-secreting cells are summarized in Figure 16–10.

The protection of the small intestine

The large surface of the gastrointestinal tract is vulnerable to potentially invasive microorganisms and antigens. We have already discussed the role of the mucus blanket in the protection of the surface of the stomach during *Helicobacter pylori* infection.

Two immune defensive mechanisms operate in the alimentary tube: (1) the cellular surveillance of antigens present in the intestinal lumen, a function performed by **Peyer's patches** and associated **M cells**; (2) the **neutralization of antigens by IgA**, a product of **plasma cells**. In addition, the bacteriostatic Paneth cell also contributes to the control of the resident and pathogenic microbial flora.

Peyer's patches

Peyer's patches—the main component of the **gut-associated lymphoid tissue**, or **GALT**—are specialized lymphoid follicles found in the intestinal mucosa and part of the submucosa. A Peyer's patch displays two main components (Figure 16–11): (1) a **dome** and (2) a **germinal center**. Peyer's patches are lined by the **follicle-associated epithelium** (FAE), consisting of M cells and enterocytes—both derived from stem cells present in the intestinal glands.

The **dome** separates the Peyer's patch from the overlying surface epithelium and contains **B cells** expressing all immunoglobulin isotypes, except IgD.

The **germinal center** contains IgA-positive B cells, CD4+ T cells, and antigen-presenting cells. A few plasma cells are present in the Peyer's patches.

The main components of the FAE are the **M cell** (Figure 16–12), a specialized epithelial cell that takes up antigens into **protease (cathepsin E)-containing vesicles**, and the **dendritic cell**, an antigen-binding cell extending **cytoplasmic processes across epithelial tight junctions**. Antigens are **transported by transcytosis to adjacent intercellular spaces and presented to immunocompetent cells (B cells)**.

The apical domain of M cells has short **microfolds** (hence the name M cell) visible only under the electron microscope. The basolateral domain of M cells forms **intraepithelial pockets**, the home site for a subpopulation of intraepithelial B cells.

Figure 16–11

The Peyer's patch: A component of the gut-associated lymphoid tissue (GALT)

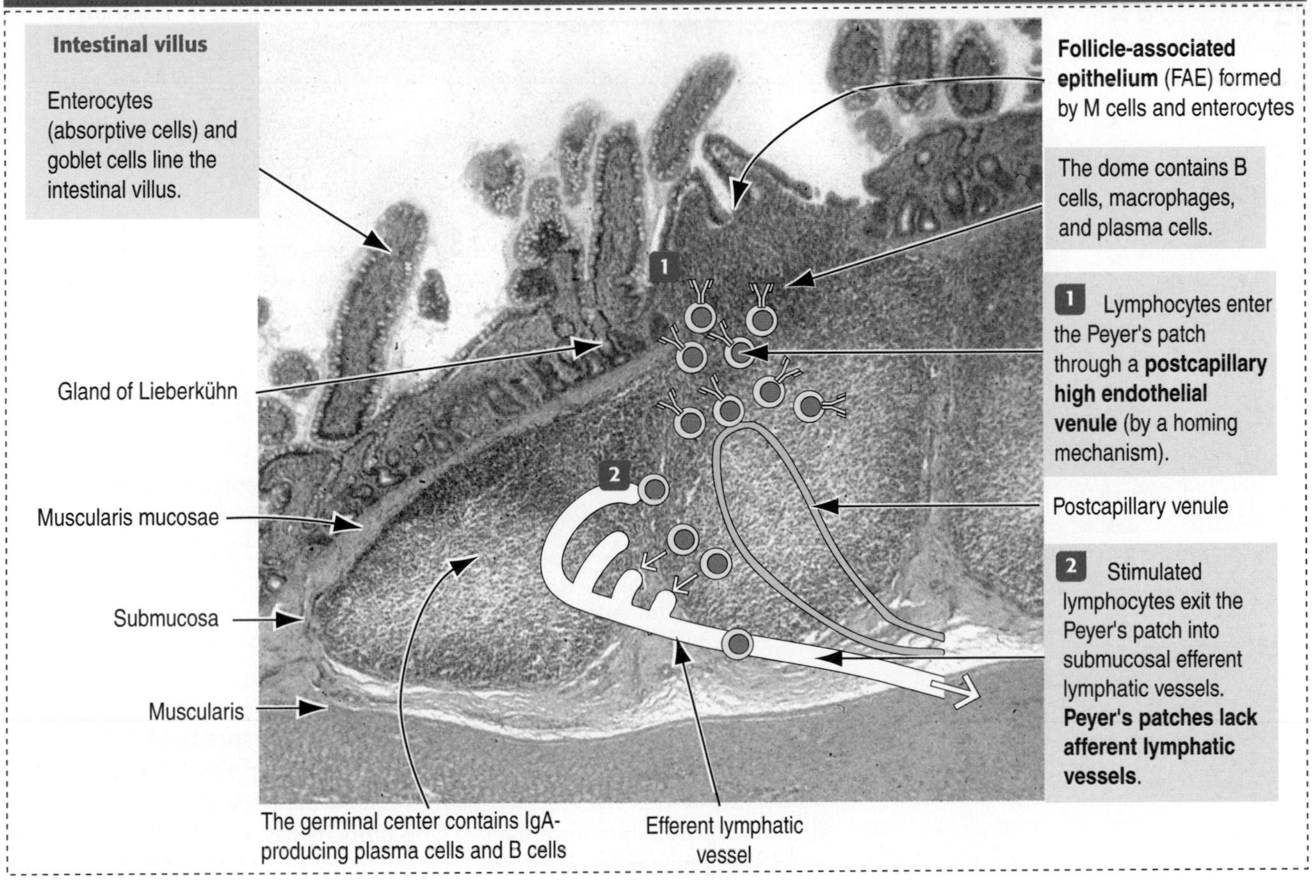

Intestinal villus

Enterocytes (absorptive cells) and goblet cells line the intestinal villus.

Gland of Lieberkühn

Muscularis mucosae

Submucosa

Muscularis

Follicle-associated epithelium (FAE) formed by M cells and enterocytes

The dome contains B cells, macrophages, and plasma cells.

1 Lymphocytes enter the Peyer's patch through a **postcapillary high endothelial venule** (by a homing mechanism).

Postcapillary venule

2 Stimulated lymphocytes exit the Peyer's patch into submucosal efferent lymphatic vessels. **Peyer's patches lack afferent lymphatic vessels.**

The germinal center contains IgA-producing plasma cells and B cells

Efferent lymphatic vessel

Figure 16–12

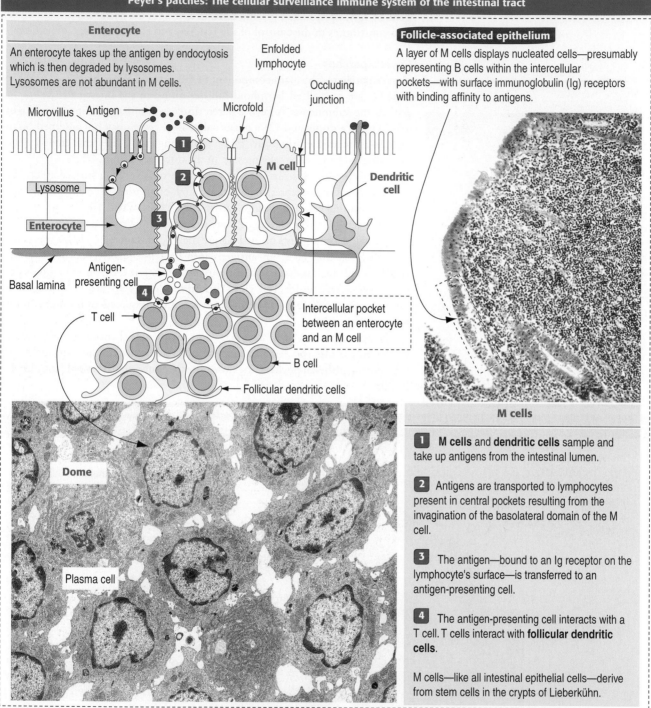

Peyer's patches: The cellular surveillance immune system of the intestinal tract

Enterocyte

An enterocyte takes up the antigen by endocytosis which is then degraded by lysosomes. Lysosomes are not abundant in M cells.

Enfolded lymphocyte

Occluding junction

Microfold

Microvillus   Antigen

Lysosome

Enterocyte

Basal lamina

Antigen-presenting cell

T cell

B cell

Follicular dendritic cells

Dome

Plasma cell

M cell

Dendritic cell

Intercellular pocket between an enterocyte and an M cell

Follicle-associated epithelium

A layer of M cells displays nucleated cells—presumably representing B cells within the intercellular pockets—with surface immunoglobulin (Ig) receptors with binding affinity to antigens.

M cells

1 **M cells** and **dendritic cells** sample and take up antigens from the intestinal lumen.

2 Antigens are transported to lymphocytes present in central pockets resulting from the invagination of the basolateral domain of the M cell.

3 The antigen—bound to an Ig receptor on the lymphocyte's surface—is transferred to an antigen-presenting cell.

4 The antigen-presenting cell interacts with a T cell. T cells interact with **follicular dendritic cells**.

M cells—like all intestinal epithelial cells—derive from stem cells in the crypts of Lieberkühn.

Intestinal antigens, bound to immunoglobulin receptors on the surface of B cells, interact with **antigen-presenting cells** at the dome region. Processed antigens are presented to **follicular dendritic cells** and CD4$^+$ T cells to initiate an immune reaction.

Clinical significance: Targeting mucosal vaccine vectors to M cells

M cells are unique among epithelial cells in that endocytosed antigens enter a transepithelial vesicular transport pathway and are released at pocket membrane sites to induce an immune response. This property has stimulated current interest in developing **mucosal vaccine vectors** to induce protective mucosal immune

Figure 16–13

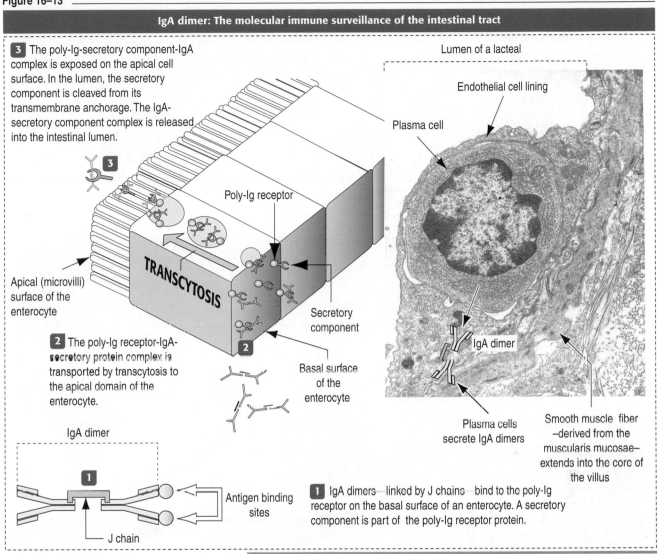

IgA dimer: The molecular immune surveillance of the intestinal tract

3 The poly-Ig-secretory component-IgA complex is exposed on the apical cell surface. In the lumen, the secretory component is cleaved from its transmembrane anchorage. The IgA-secretory component complex is released into the intestinal lumen.

Poly-Ig receptor

TRANSCYTOSIS

Apical (microvilli) surface of the enterocyte

2 The poly-Ig receptor-IgA-secretory protein complex is transported by transcytosis to the apical domain of the enterocyte.

Secretory component

Basal surface of the enterocyte

IgA dimer

Antigen binding sites

J chain

1 IgA dimers—linked by J chains—bind to the poly-Ig receptor on the basal surface of an enterocyte. A secretory component is part of the poly-Ig receptor protein.

Lumen of a lacteal

Endothelial cell lining

Plasma cell

IgA dimer

Plasma cells secrete IgA dimers

Smooth muscle fiber —derived from the muscularis mucosae— extends into the core of the villus

responses.

This host defense strategy can eventually lead to the production of secretory IgA dimer (Figure 16–13) and proteins from Paneth cells (Figure 16–14) to clear the mucosal surface of pathogens.

Plasma cells and secretory IgA dimer

Plasma cells secrete **IgA dimers** into the intestinal lumen, the respiratory epithelium, the lactating mammary gland, and salivary glands. Most plasma cells are present in the **lamina propria** of the intestinal villi, together with three types of inflammatory cells: (1) **eosinophils**, (2) **mast cells**, and (3) **macrophages**.

IgA molecules secreted by plasma cells are transported from the lamina propria to the intestinal lumen by a **transcytosis mechanism** consisting of the following steps (see Figure 16–13): (1) IgA is secreted into the lamina propria as a dimeric molecule associated with a joining peptide, called the **J chain**. (2) The IgA dimer binds to a specific receptor, called the **poly-immunoglobulin (poly-Ig) receptor**, expressed on the basolateral surfaces of the intestinal epithelial cell. The poly-Ig receptor has an attached extracellular **secretory component**. (3) The **IgA-poly-Ig receptor-secretory component complex is internalized and transported across the cell to the apical surface** of the epithelial cell (transcytosis). (4) At the apical surface, the complex is cleaved enzymatically and the **IgA-secretory component**

Figure 16–14

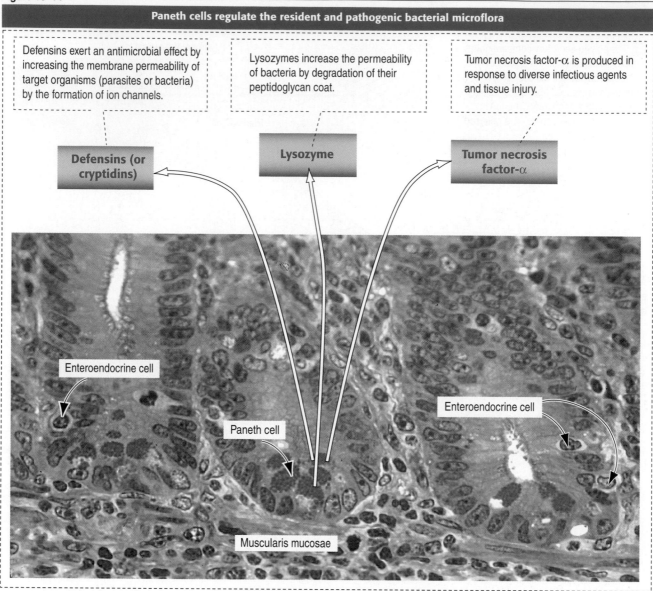

Paneth cells regulate the resident and pathogenic bacterial microflora

Defensins exert an antimicrobial effect by increasing the membrane permeability of target organisms (parasites or bacteria) by the formation of ion channels.

Lysozymes increase the permeability of bacteria by degradation of their peptidoglycan coat.

Tumor necrosis factor-α is produced in response to diverse infectious agents and tissue injury.

Defensins (or cryptidins)

Lysozyme

Tumor necrosis factor-α

Enteroendocrine cell

Paneth cell

Enteroendocrine cell

Muscularis mucosae

complex is released into the intestinal lumen. The secretory component protects the dimeric IgA from proteolytic degradation. (5) IgA antibodies prevent the attachment of bacteria or toxins to epithelial cells. (6) Excess IgA dimers diffuse from the lamina propria into the bloodstream and are excreted into the intestinal lumen via the bile.

Patients with **obstructive jaundice**—in which the bile does not reach the duodenum—show an increase of secretory IgA in blood plasma.

The Paneth cell

Paneth cells are present at the base of the crypts of Lieberkühn and have a lifetime of about 20 days. The pyramid-shaped Paneth cells have a basal domain containing the rough endoplasmic reticulum. The apical region contains numerous protein granules (see Figures 16–14 and 16–15).

Paneth cells secrete products that protect the luminal surface of the epithelium from pathogenic microorganisms. The three major products contained in the granules of Paneth cells are (1) **tumor necrosis factor-α** (TNF-α), (2) **lysozyme**, and (3) a group of proteins known as **defensins** or **cryptidins**.

TNF-α is a proinflammatory substance produced in response to diverse infec-

Figure 16–15

The lower half of an intestinal gland (crypt of Lieberkühn)

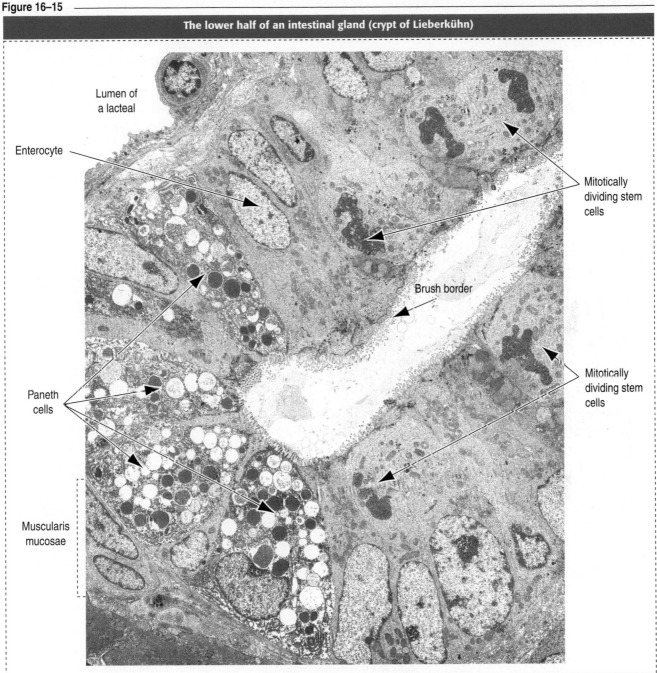

tious agents and tissue injury. Lysozyme is a proteolytic enzyme that cleaves peptidoglycan bonds. Peptidoglycan is present in bacteria but not in human cells. Lysozyme-treated bacteria swell and rupture as the result of the entrance of water into the cell. Defensins have an antimicrobial effect by increasing the membrane permeability of a target organism (parasites or bacteria) through the formation of ion channels.

Clinical significance: Inflammatory bowel disease and the enteric bacterial microflora

Inflammatory bowel disease includes **ulcerative colitis** and **Crohn's disease**. Both are clinically characterized by diarrhea, pain, and periodic relapses. **Ulcerative colitis can affect the mucosa of the large intestine. Crohn's disease affects any segment of the intestinal tract.**

Figure 16–16

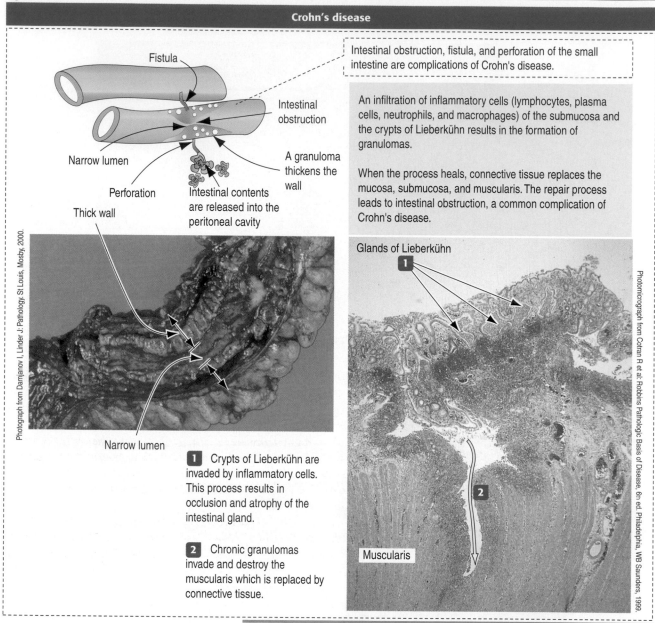

Crohn's disease

Fistula

Intestinal obstruction, fistula, and perforation of the small intestine are complications of Crohn's disease.

Intestinal obstruction

Narrow lumen

A granuloma thickens the wall

Perforation

Thick wall

Intestinal contents are released into the peritoneal cavity

An infiltration of inflammatory cells (lymphocytes, plasma cells, neutrophils, and macrophages) of the submucosa and the crypts of Lieberkühn results in the formation of granulomas.

When the process heals, connective tissue replaces the mucosa, submucosa, and muscularis. The repair process leads to intestinal obstruction, a common complication of Crohn's disease.

Glands of Lieberkühn

1

Photograph from Damjanov I, Linder J: Pathology. St Louis, Mosby, 2000.

Narrow lumen

1 Crypts of Lieberkühn are invaded by inflammatory cells. This process results in occlusion and atrophy of the intestinal gland.

2 Chronic granulomas invade and destroy the muscularis which is replaced by connective tissue.

2

Muscularis

Photomicrograph from Cotran R et al: Robbins Pathologic Basis of Disease, 6th ed. Philadelphia, WB Saunders, 1999.

Crohn's disease is a chronic inflammatory process involving the terminal ileum but is also observed in the large intestine. Inflammatory cells (neutrophils, lymphocytes, and macrophages) produce cytokines which cause damage to the intestinal mucosa (Figure 16–16).

The initial alteration of the intestinal mucosa consists in the infiltration of **neutrophils into the crypts of Lieberkühn**. This process results in the destruction of the intestinal glands by the formation of **crypt abscesses** and the progressive **atrophy** and **ulceration** of the mucosa.

The chronic inflammatory process infiltrates the submucosa and muscularis. Abundant accumulation of lymphocytes forms aggregates of cells, or **granulomas**, a typical feature of Crohn's disease.

Major complications of the disease are **occlusion of the intestinal lumen by fibrosis** and the **formation of fistulas** in other segments of the small intestine, and **intestinal perforation**. Segments affected by Crohn's disease are separated by normal stretches of intestinal segments.

The cause of Crohn's disease is unknown. The risk of intestinal cancer is three-

Figure 16–17

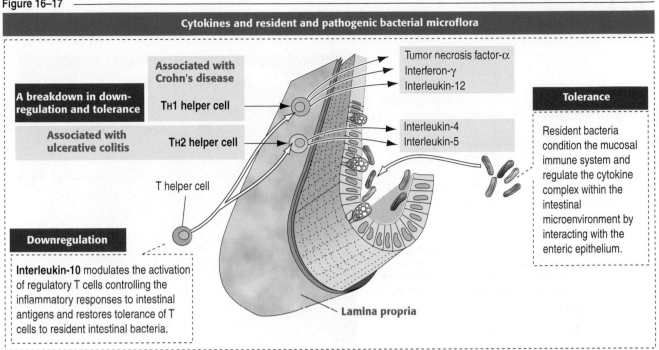

Cytokines and resident and pathogenic bacterial microflora

A breakdown in down-regulation and tolerance

Associated with Crohn's disease

T**H**1 helper cell

Associated with ulcerative colitis

T**H**2 helper cell

T helper cell

Tumor necrosis factor-α
Interferon-γ
Interleukin-12

Interleukin-4
Interleukin-5

Tolerance

Resident bacteria condition the mucosal immune system and regulate the cytokine complex within the intestinal microenvironment by interacting with the enteric epithelium.

Downregulation

Interleukin-10 modulates the activation of regulatory T cells controlling the inflammatory responses to intestinal antigens and restores tolerance of T cells to resident intestinal bacteria.

Lamina propria

fold higher in patients with Crohn's disease.

The pathogenesis of inflammatory bowel disease is caused by three contributing factors: (1) **genetic susceptibility of the patient**, (2) **intestinal bacteria**, and (3) **the immune response of the intestinal mucosa**, determined by an abnormal signaling exchange with the resident bacterial microflora. In genetically susceptible individuals, inflammatory bowel disease occurs when the mucosal immune machinery regards the normal bacterial microflora as pathogenic and triggers an immune response. Cytokines produced by helper T cells within the intestinal mucosa cause the inflammatory process that characterizes inflammatory bowel disease.

In Crohn's disease, **type 1 helper cells** (T**H**1 cells) produce TNF-α, interferon-γ, and interleukin-12. Because TNF-α is both a regulatory and effector cytokine in T**H**1 responses, antibodies to this cytokine are being administered to patients with Crohn's disease. In ulcerative colitis, **type 2 helper cells** (T**H**2 cells) release interleukin-4 and interleukin-5 (Figure 16–17).

Interleukin-10, a regulatory cytokine of T cells, can restore tolerance of T cells to the resident intestinal bacterial flora in mice. Dietary administration of the genetically engineered enteric bacterium *Lactococcus lactis*—to overproduce interleukin-10 within the intestinal lumen—has been shown to be effective in the treatment of inflammatory bowel disease in mouse experimental models.

Clinical significance: Malabsorption syndromes

Malabsorption syndromes are characterized by a deficit in the absorption of fats, proteins, carbohydrates, salts and water by the mucosa of the small intestine.

Malabsorption syndromes can be caused by (1) **abnormal digestion of fats and proteins** by pancreatic diseases (pancreatitis or cystic fibrosis) or **lack of solubilization of fats by defective bile secretion** (hepatic disease or obstruction of the flow of bile into the duodenum); (2) **enzymatic abnormalities at the brush border**, where disaccharidases and peptidases cannot hydrolyze carbohydrates (lactose intolerance) and proteins, respectively; and (3) a **defect in the transepithelial transport by enterocytes**.

Malabsorption syndromes affect many organ systems. **Anemia** occurs when vitamin B_{12}, iron, and other cofactors cannot be absorbed. Disturbances of the

Figure 16–18

The large intestine

The large intestine

The layers of the large intestine are the same as in the small intestine: mucosa, submucosa, muscularis, and serosa.

The **main function of the mucosa** is the absorption of water, sodium, vitamins, and minerals. The transport of sodium is active (energy-dependent), causing water to move along an osmotic gradient. As a result, the fluid chyme entering the colon is concentrated into semisolid feces. Potassium and bicarbonate are secreted into the lumen of the colon.

The absorptive capacity of the colon favors the uptake of many substances, including sedatives, anesthetics, and steroids. This property is of considerable therapeutic importance when medication cannot be administered through the mouth (for example, because of vomiting).

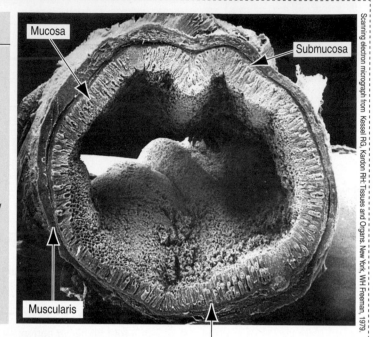

Mucosa

Submucosa

Muscularis

Scanning electron micrograph from: Kessel RG, Kardon RH: Tissues and Organs. New York, WH Freeman, 1979.

Tubular glands, or crypts of Lieberkühn, are oriented perpendicular to the long axis of the colon, are much deeper than in the small intestine, and have a higher proportion of goblet cells.

Mucosa

Muscularis mucosae

Submucosa

Muscularis

The mucosa of the large intestine

The mucosa of the colon is free of folds and villi.

Four cell types are present in the surface epithelium and tubular glands:
1. Simple columnar absorptive cells with apical microvilli (striated apical border).
2. Predominant goblet cells.
3. Stem cells at the base of the tubular glands of Lieberkühn, which give rise to absorptive and goblet cells.
4. Enteroendocrine cells.

The intestinal tubular glands are longer than in the small intestine (0.4–0.6 mm).

Lymph nodules can be seen in the lamina propria just under the muscularis mucosae, extending into the submucosa.

Figure 16–19

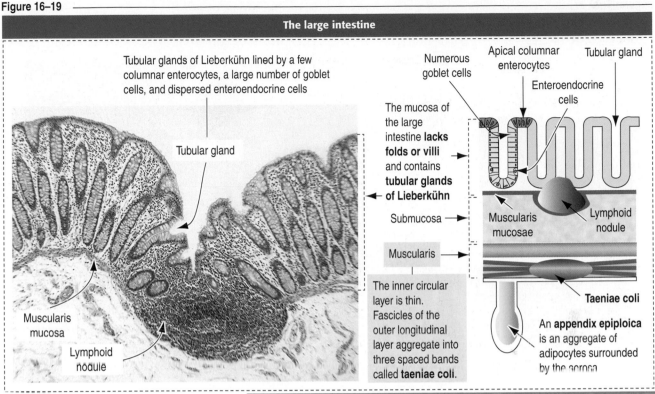

The large intestine

Tubular glands of Lieberkühn lined by a few columnar enterocytes, a large number of goblet cells, and dispersed enteroendocrine cells

Tubular gland

Muscularis mucosa

Lymphoid nodule

The mucosa of the large intestine **lacks folds or villi** and contains **tubular glands of Lieberkühn**

Submucosa

Muscularis

The inner circular layer is thin. Fascicles of the outer longitudinal layer aggregate into three spaced bands called **taeniae coli**.

Numerous goblet cells

Apical columnar enterocytes

Tubular gland

Enteroendocrine cells

Muscularis mucosae

Lymphoid nodule

Taeniae coli

An **appendix epiploica** is an aggregate of adipocytes surrounded by the serosa

musculoskeletal system are observed when proteins, calcium, and vitamin D fail to be absorbed. A typical clinical feature of malabsorption syndromes is **diarrhea**.

Large intestine

The large intestine is formed by several successive segments: (1) the **cecum**, projecting from which is the **appendix**; (2) the **ascending, transverse,** and **descending colon**; (3) the **sigmoid colon**; (4) the **rectum**; and (5) the **anus**.

Plicae circulares and intestinal villi are not found beyond the ileocecal valve. Numerous openings of the straight **tubular glands** or **crypts of Lieberkühn** are characteristic of the mucosa of the colon (Figure 16–18).

The lining of the tubular glands of the colon consists of the following (Figures 16–19 and 16-20):

1. A **surface simple columnar epithelium** formed by absorptive **enterocytes** and **goblet cells**. Enterocytes have **short apical microvilli**, and the cells participate in the **transport of ions and water**. All regions of the colon absorb Na^+ and Cl^- ions facilitated by plasma membrane channels that are regulated by mineralocorticoids. Aldosterone increases the number of Na^+ channels and increases the absorption of Na^+. Na^+ ions entering the absorptive enterocytes are extruded by an Na^+ pump. Goblet cells secrete mucus to lubricate the mucosal surface and serve as a protective barrier.

2. A **glandular epithelium**, lining the glands or crypts of Lierberkühn, consists of enterocytes and predominant goblet cells, stem cells, and dispersed **enteroendocrine cells**. Paneth cells may be present in the cecum.

A lamina propria and a muscularis mucosae are present, as are **lymphoid nodules** penetrating the submucosa. Glands are not present in the submucosa.

The muscularis has a particular feature: The bundles of its outer longitudinal layer fuse to form the **taeniae coli**. The taeniae coli consist of three longitudinally oriented ribbon-like bands, each 1 cm wide. The contraction of the taeniae coli and circular muscle layer draws the colon into sacculations called **haustra**.

The serosa has scattered sacs of adipose tissue, the **appendices epiploicae**, a unique feature, together with the haustra, of the colon.

Figure 16–20

Cell types of the glands of the large intestine

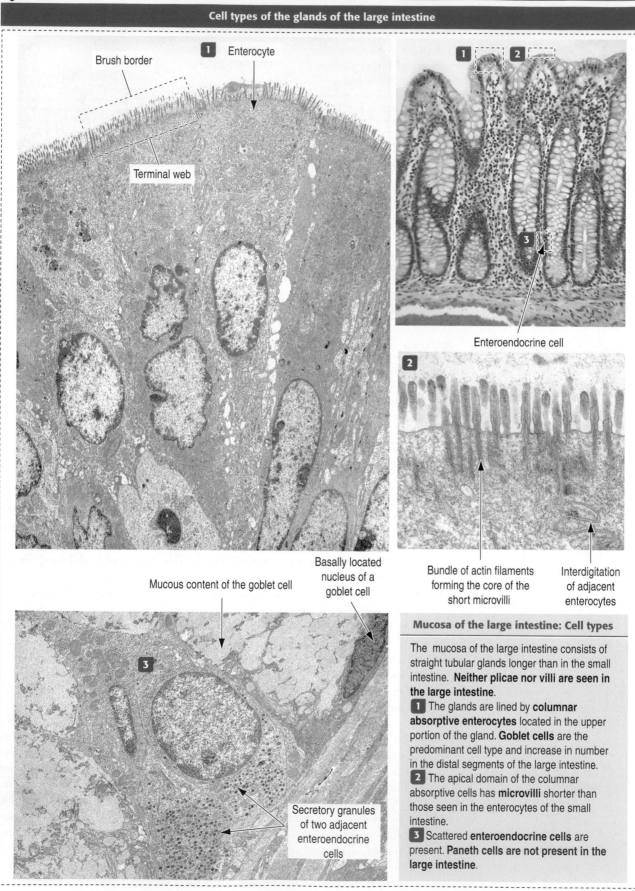

Brush border

1 Enterocyte

Terminal web

Enteroendocrine cell

Bundle of actin filaments forming the core of the short microvilli

Interdigitation of adjacent enterocytes

Mucous content of the goblet cell

Basally located nucleus of a goblet cell

Secretory granules of two adjacent enteroendocrine cells

Mucosa of the large intestine: Cell types

The mucosa of the large intestine consists of straight tubular glands longer than in the small intestine. **Neither plicae nor villi are seen in the large intestine.**

1 The glands are lined by **columnar absorptive enterocytes** located in the upper portion of the gland. **Goblet cells** are the predominant cell type and increase in number in the distal segments of the large intestine.

2 The apical domain of the columnar absorptive cells has **microvilli** shorter than those seen in the enterocytes of the small intestine.

3 Scattered **enteroendocrine cells** are present. **Paneth cells are not present in the large intestine.**

Figure 16–21

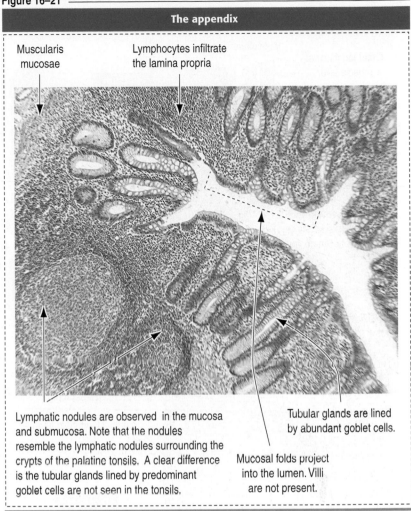

The appendix

Muscularis mucosae

Lymphocytes infiltrate the lamina propria

Lymphatic nodules are observed in the mucosa and submucosa. Note that the nodules resemble the lymphatic nodules surrounding the crypts of the palatine tonsils. A clear difference is the tubular glands lined by predominant goblet cells are not seen in the tonsils.

Tubular glands are lined by abundant goblet cells.

Mucosal folds project into the lumen. Villi are not present.

The **appendix** (Figure 16–21) is a diverticulum of the cecum and has similar layers to those of the large intestine. The characteristic features of the appendix are the **lymphoid tissue**, represented by multiple lymphatic nodules and **lymphocytes** infiltrating the lamina propria.

Lymphatic nodules extend into the mucosa and submucosa and disrupt the continuity of the muscularis mucosae.

The **rectum**, the terminal portion of the intestinal tract, is a continuation of the sigmoid colon. The rectum consists of two parts: (1) the upper part, or rectum proper, and (2) the lower part, or anal canal.

In the rectum, the mucosa is thicker, with prominent veins, and the crypts of Lieberkühn are longer (0.7 mm) than in the small intestine and lined predominantly by goblet cells. At the level of the anal canal, the crypts gradually disappear and the serosa is replaced by an adventitia.

The **anal canal** extends from the anorectal junction to the anus (Figure 16–22). A characteristic feature of the mucosa of the anal canal are 8 to 10 longitudinal **anal columns**. The base of the anal columns is the **pectinate line**. The anal columns are connected at their base by **valves**, corresponding to transverse folds of the mucosa. Small pockets, called **anal sinuses**, or crypts, are found behind the valves. **Mucus anal glands** open into each sinus.

The valves and sinuses prevent leakage from the anus. When the canal is distended with feces, the columns, sinuses, and valves flatten, and mucus is discharged from the sinuses to lubricate the passage of the feces.

Beyond the pectinate line, the simple columnar epithelium of rectal mucosa is

Figure 16–22

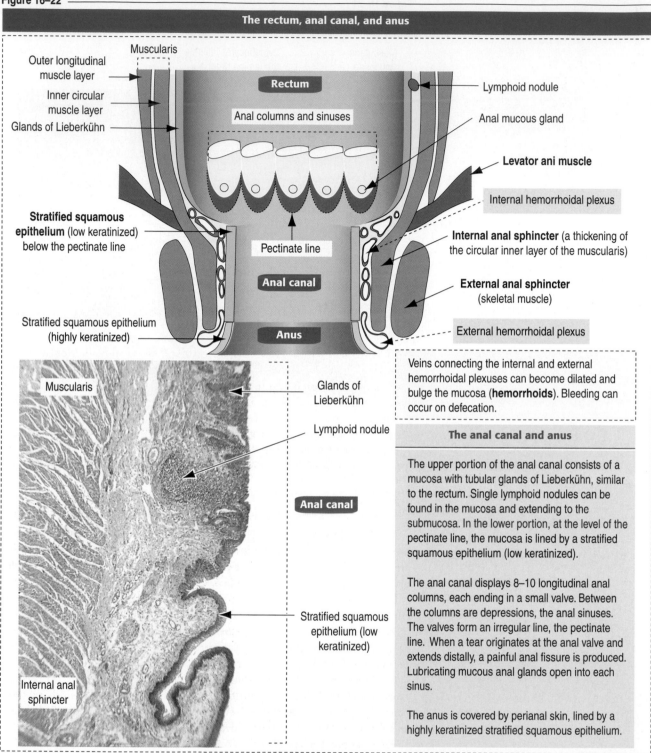

The rectum, anal canal, and anus

Muscularis
Outer longitudinal muscle layer
Inner circular muscle layer
Glands of Lieberkühn

Rectum

Anal columns and sinuses

Lymphoid nodule

Anal mucous gland

Levator ani muscle

Internal hemorrhoidal plexus

Stratified squamous epithelium (low keratinized) below the pectinate line

Pectinate line

Anal canal

Internal anal sphincter (a thickening of the circular inner layer of the muscularis)

External anal sphincter (skeletal muscle)

Stratified squamous epithelium (highly keratinized)

Anus

External hemorrhoidal plexus

Veins connecting the internal and external hemorrhoidal plexuses can become dilated and bulge the mucosa (**hemorrhoids**). Bleeding can occur on defecation.

Muscularis

Glands of Lieberkühn

Lymphoid nodule

Anal canal

Stratified squamous epithelium (low keratinized)

Internal anal sphincter

The anal canal and anus

The upper portion of the anal canal consists of a mucosa with tubular glands of Lieberkühn, similar to the rectum. Single lymphoid nodules can be found in the mucosa and extending to the submucosa. In the lower portion, at the level of the pectinate line, the mucosa is lined by a stratified squamous epithelium (low keratinized).

The anal canal displays 8–10 longitudinal anal columns, each ending in a small valve. Between the columns are depressions, the anal sinuses. The valves form an irregular line, the pectinate line. When a tear originates at the anal valve and extends distally, a painful anal fissure is produced. Lubricating mucous anal glands open into each sinus.

The anus is covered by perianal skin, lined by a highly keratinized stratified squamous epithelium.

replaced by a **stratified squamous epithelium**. At the level of the anus, **the inner circular layer of smooth muscle thickens to form the internal anal sphincter**. The longitudinal smooth muscle layer extends over the sphincter and attaches to the connective tissue. Below this zone, the stratified squamous epithelium displays a few sebaceous and sweat glands (**circumanal glands** similar to the axillary sweat glands). The **external anal sphincter** is formed by **skeletal muscle** and lies inside the levator ani muscle, also with a sphincter function.

Figure 16–23

Hirschsprung's disease (congenital megacolon)

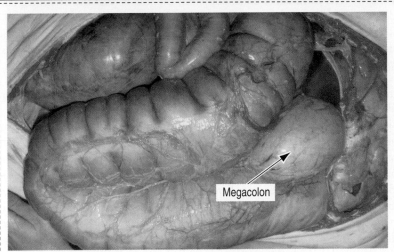

Megacolon

From Cooke RA, Stewart B: Anatomical Pathology. New York, Churchill Livingstone, 1995.

Defects of neural crest cell migration and development: Hirschsprung's disease

Hirschsrprung's disease (congenital megacolon) is caused by mutations in one to four different genes that prevent the migration and differentiation of neural crest cells into neurons of the enteric nervous system.

The mutated genes encode cell membrane receptors **rearranged during transfection** (RET), and **endothelin B** (EDNRB), and the ligand for EDNRB, **endothelin 3** (EDN3).

Some individuals with mutations in either EDNRB or EDN3 have **melanocyte abnormalities** producing hypopigmented patches in skin and **hearing loss**. This disorder is called the **Waardenburg-Shah syndrome**.

Clinical significance: Hirschsprung's disease (congenital megacolon)

We learned in Chapter 8, Nervous Tissue, that during formation of the neural tube, neural crest cells migrate from the neuroepithelium along defined pathways to tissues where they differentiate into various cell types. One destination of neural crest cells is the alimentary tube, where they develop the enteric nervous system.

We have already seen that the enteric nervous system partially controls and coordinates the normal movements of the alimentary tube that facilitate digestion and transport of bowel contents. The large intestine, like the rest of the alimentary tube, is innervated by the enteric nervous system receiving impulses from extrinsic parasympathetic and sympathetic nerves and from receptors within the large intestine. The myenteric plexus is concentrated beneath the taeniae coli.

The transit of contents from the small intestine to the large intestine is intermittent and regulated at the ileocecal junction by a sphincter mechanism: When the sphincter relaxes, ileal contractions propel the contents into the large intestine.

Segmental contractions in an orad-to-aboral direction move the contents over short distances. The material changes from a liquid to a semisolid state when it reaches the descending and sigmoid colon. The rectum is usually empty but eventually fills intermittently. Contraction of the inner anal sphincter closes the anal canal. Defecation occurs when the sphincter relaxes as part of the **rectosphincteric reflex** stimulated by distention of the rectum.

Delayed transit through the colon leads to severe **constipation**. An abnormal form of constipation is seen in **Hirschsprung's disease (congenital megacolon)** caused by the **absence of the enteric nervous system in a segment of the distal colon** (Figure 16–23). This condition, called **aganglionosis**, is determined by an **arrest in the migration of cells from the neural crest**, the precursors of the intramural ganglion cells of the plexuses of Meissner and Auerbach.

Aganglionosis is caused by mutations affecting the <u>rearranged during transfection</u> (**RET**) gene as well as the cell membrane receptor **endothelin B** or its ligand, **endothelin 3** (see Figure 16–23). The *RET* gene encodes a **receptor tyrosine kinase** required for the migration of neural crest cells into the distal portions of the large intestine and for differentiation into neurons of the enteric nervous system.

The permanently contracted aganglionic segment does not allow the entry of the contents. An increase in muscular tone in the orad segment results in its dilation, thus generating a megacolon or megarectum. This condition is apparent shortly after birth when the abdomen of the infant becomes distended and little meconium is eliminated.

The diagnosis is confirmed by a biopsy of the mucosa and submucosa of the rectum showing thick and irregular nerve bundles and a lack of ganglion cells. Surgical removal of the affected colon segment is the treatment of choice.

Clinical significance: Familial polyposis gene and colorectal carcinogenesis

Colorectal tumors develop from a **polyp**, a tumoral mass that protrudes into the lumen of the intestine. Some polyps are non-neoplastic and are relatively common in persons 60 years or older. Polyps can be present in large number (100 or more) in **familial polyposis syndromes** such as **familial adenomatous polyposis** and the **Peutz-Jeghers syndrome**. Familial polyposis is determined by autosomal dominant mutations, in particular in the *APC* (**adenomatous polyposis coli**) **gene**. Mutations in the *APC* gene have been detected in 85% of colon tumors, indicating that, as with the retinoblastoma (*Rb*) gene, the inherited gene is also important in the development of the sporadic form of the cancer.

The *APC* gene encodes **APC protein** with binding affinity to microtubules and **β-catenin**, a molecule associated with a catenin complex linked to E-cadherin (see the discussion in Chapter 1, Epithelium) and also a component of nuclear transcription complexes.

When β-catenin is not part of the catenin α, β, γ complex, free β-catenin interacts with DNA binding proteins of a family of transcription factor proteins called **T cell factor–lymphoid enhancer factor (Tcf3-Lef)** to form a transactivator complex that stimulates transcription of immediate gene targets (Figure 16–24).

Figure 16–24

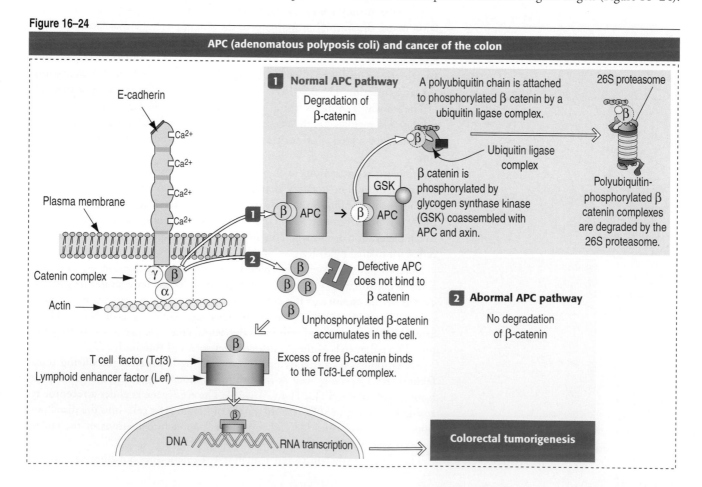

APC (adenomatous polyposis coli) and cancer of the colon

When free β-catenin binds to the **glycogen synthase kinase** (GSK)–axin–APC complex, it is phosphorylated by GSK. **Phosphorylated β-catenin** is subsequently recognized by a **ubiquitin ligase complex** that catalyzes the attachment of polyubiquitin chains to phosphorylated β-catenin. Polyubiquitin conjugates of β-catenin are rapidly degraded by the **26S proteasome**. The lack of β-catenin inactivates the β-catenin–Tcf-Lef pathway. A mutation in the *APC* gene results in a defective protein that reduces cell-cell contact and increases the pool of available β-catenin. Essentially, APC is a tumor suppressor gene.

The *APC* gene is also a major regulator of the **Wnt pathway**, a signaling system expressed during early development and embryogenesis (see Chapter 3, Cell Signaling).

Hereditary nonpolyposis colon cancer (HNPCC) is an inherited form of colorectal cancer caused by mutations in genes involved in the repair of DNA mismatch. HNPCC is an example of a cancer syndrome caused by **mutations in DNA repair proteins.**

Patients with the HNPCC syndrome do not show the very large number of colon polyps typical of the familial polyposis syndrome, but a small number of polyps occur frequently among gene carriers.

Hereditary nonpolyposis colon cancer (HNPCC) is an inherited form of colorectal cancer caused by mutations in genes involved in the repair of DNA mismatch. HNPCC is an example of a cancer syndrome caused by **mutations in DNA repair proteins.**

Patients with the HNPCC syndrome do not show the very large number of colon polyps typical of the familial polyposis syndrome, but a small number of polyps occur frequently among gene carriers.

17. DIGESTIVE GLANDS

Digestive glands have **lubricative**, **protective**, **digestive**, and **absorptive** functions mediated by their secretory products, which are released into the oral cavity and the duodenum.

The three major digestive glands are:

1. The **major salivary glands** (parotid, submaxillary, and sublingual glands), associated with the oral cavity through independent excretory ducts. The **minor salivary glands** have short branching tubules and are located throughout the oral mucosa and tongue, where they contribute to **saliva**, the product of the salivary glands.

2. The **exocrine pancreas** secretes a combined aqueous and enzymatic product draining into the duodenum. The endocrine function of the pancreas (represented by the **islet of Langerhans**) is described in Chapter 19, Endocrine System.

3. The **liver**, a combined endocrine and exocrine gland, has extensive access to the blood circulation and releases **bile** into the duodenum. Bile is a complex mixture of organic and inorganic components that enable the absorption of fats by the small intestine.

The structure and function of the **gallbladder** are included at the end of the liver section.

Figure 17–1

Review of the general histologic organization of a compound gland

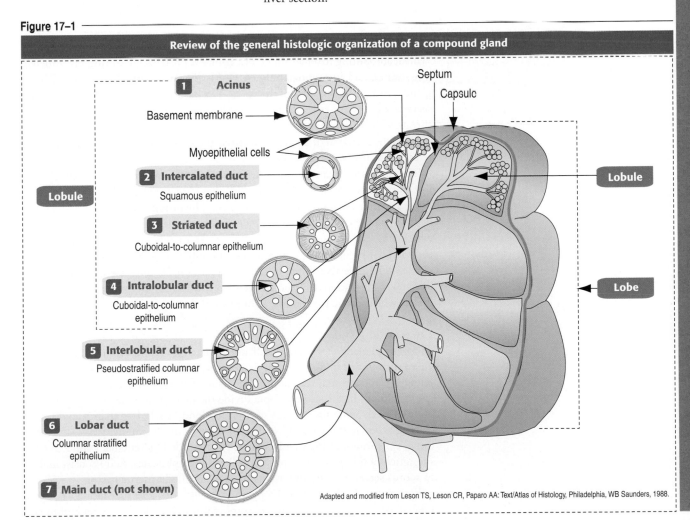

Adapted and modified from Leson TS, Leson CR, Paparo AA: Text/Atlas of Histology, Philadelphia, WB Saunders, 1988.

The branching duct system of a salivary gland

We initiate the discussion by analyzing the general organization of a salivary gland, in particular its branching ducts.

The secretory product of an acinus is drained sequentially by the following (Figures 17–1 and 17–2):

1. An **intercalated duct** (lined by **low squamous-to-cuboidal epithelium**). The intercalated duct is longest in the parotid gland.

2. A **striated duct** (a segment lined by **cuboidal-to-columnar epithelial cells** with **basal infoldings** containing numerous **mitochondria**). The striated duct is well developed in the submaxillary gland. The epithelium of the striated duct participates in ion and water transport and secretes kallikrein. Both intercalated and striated ducts are modestly developed in the sublingual gland.

3. An **excretory duct** (lined by **cuboidal-to-columnar epithelium**).

The intercalated and striated duct segments are observed **within the lobule**, embedded in the connective tissue septa. Several intercalated ducts converge to form a striated duct. The striated duct is continuous with the excretory duct which is located **outside the lobule**, between adjacent lobules. Therefore, the excretory duct is the **interlobular segment** of the branching duct system. An **interlobular duct** is lined by **pseudostratified columnar epithelium**.

Interlobular ducts converge to form a **lobar duct**. Lobar ducts join the **main duct** opening into the oral cavity. The main duct is one of the few sites in the body lined by **stratified columnar epithelium**.

The **parotid**, **submandibular** (or submaxillary), and **sublingual glands** are classified as **compound tubuloalveolar glands**. Their excretory ducts open into the oral cavity.

Saliva is the major product of salivary glands

Saliva, amounting to a half-liter daily, contains proteins, glycoproteins (mucus), ions, water, and immunoglobulin A (IgA) (Figure 17–3). The submandibular gland produces about 70% of the saliva. The parotid gland contributes 25% and secretes an amylase-rich saliva. The production of saliva is under the control of the autonomic nervous system. Upon stimulation, the parasympathetic system induces the secretion of a water-rich saliva; the sympathetic system stimulates the release of a protein-rich saliva.

The mucus and water in saliva **lubricate** the mucosa of the tongue, cheek, and lips during speech and swallowing, dissolve food for the function of the taste buds, and moisten food for easy swallowing. The **protective** function of the saliva depends on the antibacterial function of three constituents of saliva: (1) **lysozyme**, which attacks the walls of bacteria; (2) **lactoferrin**, which chelates iron necessary for bacterial growth; and (3) **immunoglobulin A** that neutralizes bacteria and viruses. The **digestive** function of saliva relies on (1) **amylase** (ptyalin), which initiates the digestion of carbohydrates (starch) in the oral cavity; and (2) **lingual lipase**, which participates in the hydrolysis of dietary lipids.

The parotid gland

The parotid gland is the largest salivary gland. It is a **compound tubuloalveolar gland** surrounded by a connective tissue capsule with **septa**—representing a component of the **stroma**, the supporting tissue of the gland. Adipose cells are frequently found in the stroma. Septa divide the gland into lobes and lobules (see Figure 17–1). Septa also provide support to blood vessels, lymphatics, and nerves gaining access to the acini, the main components of the **parenchyma**—the functional constituent of the gland. Acini are surrounded by reticular connective tissue, a rich capillary network, plasma cells, and lymphocytes. Acini consist mainly of **serous secretory cells** and, therefore, are classified as **serous acini**.

Each serous acinus is lined by pyramidal cells with a basally located nucleus. Like all protein-producing cells, a prominent rough endoplasmic reticulum sys-

Figure 17–2

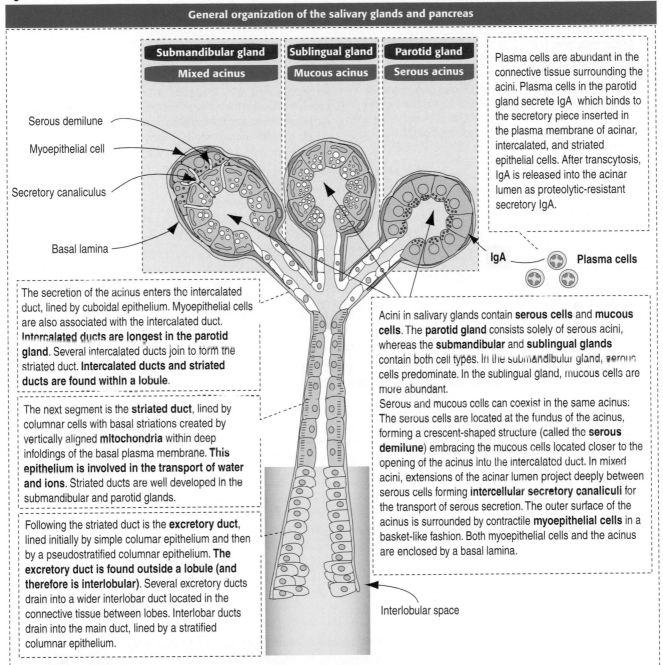

General organization of the salivary glands and pancreas

Submandibular gland — **Mixed acinus**

Sublingual gland — **Mucous acinus**

Parotid gland — **Serous acinus**

Serous demilune

Myoepithelial cell

Secretory canaliculus

Basal lamina

Plasma cells are abundant in the connective tissue surrounding the acini. Plasma cells in the parotid gland secrete IgA which binds to the secretory piece inserted in the plasma membrane of acinar, intercalated, and striated epithelial cells. After transcytosis, IgA is released into the acinar lumen as proteolytic-resistant secretory IgA.

IgA — Plasma cells

The secretion of the acinus enters the intercalated duct, lined by cuboidal epithelium. Myoepithelial cells are also associated with the intercalated duct. **Intercalated ducts are longest in the parotid gland**. Several intercalated ducts join to form the striated duct. **Intercalated ducts and striated ducts are found within a lobule.**

The next segment is the **striated duct**, lined by columnar cells with basal striations created by vertically aligned **mitochondria** within deep infoldings of the basal plasma membrane. **This epithelium is involved in the transport of water and ions**. Striated ducts are well developed in the submandibular and parotid glands.

Following the striated duct is the **excretory duct**, lined initially by simple columar epithelium and then by a pseudostratified columnar epithelium. **The excretory duct is found outside a lobule (and therefore is interlobular)**. Several excretory ducts drain into a wider interlobar duct located in the connective tissue between lobes. Interlobar ducts drain into the main duct, lined by a stratified columnar epithelium.

Acini in salivary glands contain **serous cells** and **mucous cells**. The parotid gland consists solely of serous acini, whereas the **submandibular** and **sublingual glands** contain both cell types. In the submandibular gland, serous cells predominate. In the sublingual gland, mucous cells are more abundant.

Serous and mucous cells can coexist in the same acinus: The serous cells are located at the fundus of the acinus, forming a crescent-shaped structure (called the **serous demilune**) embracing the mucous cells located closer to the opening of the acinus into the intercalated duct. In mixed acini, extensions of the acinar lumen project deeply between serous cells forming **intercellular secretory canaliculi** for the transport of serous secretion. The outer surface of the acinus is surrounded by contractile **myoepithelial cells** in a basket-like fashion. Both myoepithelial cells and the acinus are enclosed by a basal lamina.

Interlobular space

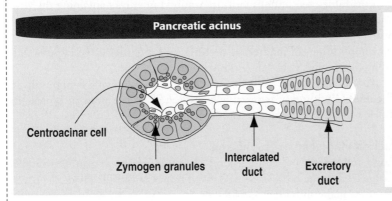

Pancreatic acinus

Centroacinar cell

Zymogen granules

Intercalated duct

Excretory duct

In the exocrine pancreas, only serous acini are present.
A unique feature of the pancreatic acinus is the presence of squamous-to-cuboidal epithelial **centroacinar cells**. Centroacinar cells are in contact with the acinar lumen, and the apical domain of the serous acinar cells is in continuity with the intercalated duct. Centroacinar cells can be regarded as the intra-acinar segment of the intercalated duct.
Striated ducts and myoepithelial cells are not present in the exocrine pancreas.

Figure 17–3

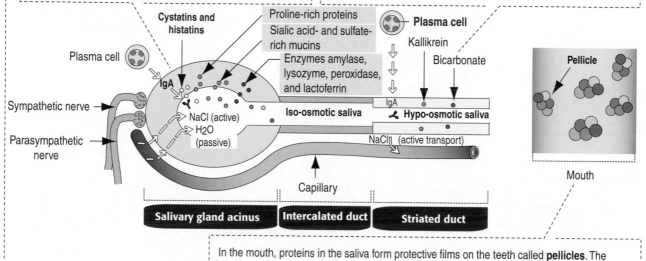

Functional aspects of a salivary gland

Acinar cells pump Na+ and Cl⁻ actively into the acinar lumen and allow free passage of water from the surrounding blood capillaries. This results in the formation of isotonic primary saliva. **Mucous cells** release mucins. **Serous cells** secrete several proteins, including proline-rich proteins (which will be modified in the striated duct by the enzyme kallikrein), enzymes (amylases, peroxidases, lysozyme), lactoferrin, cystatins (cysteine-rich proteins), and histatins (histidine-rich proteins).

In the **striated duct**, Na+ and Cl⁻ are reabsorbed and the saliva becomes hypo-osmotic. **Kallikrein**, a serine protease secreted by epithelial cells of the striated duct, processes the proline-rich proteins and cystatins in the saliva. In addition, plasma cells secrete **IgA** which reaches the lumen of the acinus and striated duct by transcytosis. The final saliva contains a complex of proteins with antimicrobial activity and with digestive function (amylase). **Bicarbonate**, the primary buffering agent of the saliva, is produced in the **striated duct**.

Cystatins and histatins

Plasma cell

Proline-rich proteins

Sialic acid- and sulfate-rich mucins

Plasma cell

Enzymes amylase, lysozyme, peroxidase, and lactoferrin

Kallikrein

Bicarbonate

Pellicle

Plasma cell

Sympathetic nerve

Parasympathetic nerve

IgA

NaCl (active)

H2O (passive)

Iso-osmotic saliva

IgA

Hypo-osmotic saliva

NaCl (active transport)

Mouth

Capillary

Salivary gland acinus   **Intercalated duct**   **Striated duct**

In the mouth, proteins in the saliva form protective films on the teeth called **pellicles**. The function of the pellicles is to provide a barrier against acids, retain moisture, and regulate the adherence and activity of bacteria and yeast in the oral cavity. Histatin inhibits the growth of *Candida albicans*. **Dysfunction of the salivary glands** causes tooth decay, yeast infections, and inflammation of the oral mucosa.

tem occupies the cell basal region. Secretory granules are visible in the apical region (Figure 17–4).

The lumen of the acinus collects the secretory products, which are transported by **long intercalated ducts to the less abundant striated ducts** (Figure 17–5). The secretory product of the serous acini is modified by the secretion of the striated duct and then transported by the oral cavity by a main excretory duct (Stensen duct).

Clinical significance: Mumps, rabies, and tumors

In addition to its role in the production of saliva, the parotid gland is the primary target of the **rabies and mumps virus** transmitted in saliva containing the virus. The mumps virus causes transient swelling of the parotid gland and confers immunity.

Two complications of mumps are **orchitis** and **meningitis**. Bilateral orchitis caused by the mumps virus can result in sterility.

The parotid gland is the most frequent site for slow-growing **benign salivary gland tumors**. Its surgical removal is complicated by the need to protect the facial nerve running through the parotid gland.

Submandibular (submaxillary) gland

The submandibular gland is also a compound tubuloalveolar gland surrounded by a connective tissue capsule. Septa derived from the capsule divide the parenchyma of the gland into lobes and lobules.

Although both serous and mucous cells are present in the secretory units, the

Figure 17–4

Histologic aspects of the major salivary glands

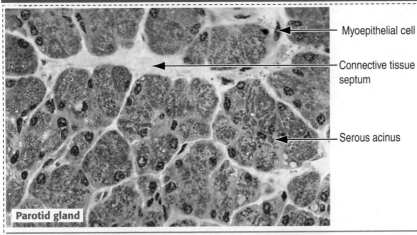

Myoepithelial cell

Connective tissue septum

Serous acinus

Parotid gland

The **parotid gland** is formed by acini containing exclusively serous cells with a basal nucleus and an apical cytoplasm with secretory granules. Granules are rich in proteins, including **proline-rich proteins, enzymes** (amylase, peroxidase, and lysozyme), and proteins with antimicrobial activity (**cystatins** and **hystatins**). Although not visible in this section, **the parotid gland has the longest intercalated ducts**. Connective tissue and blood vessels (not seen here) surround the serous acini. **Myoepithelial cells** can be visualized at the periphery of each acinus.

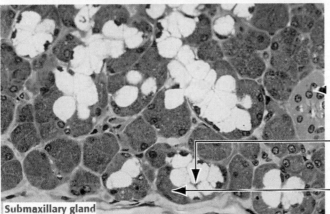

Striated duct

Mucous cells in the mixed seromucous acinus

Serous demilune

Submaxillary gland

Submandibular glands are mixed serous and mucous tubuloacinar glands. **Mixed seromucous and serous acini are readily found. Pure mucous acini are uncommon in the submaxillary gland.** Striated ducts lined by cuboid cells with basal infoldings, containing mitochondria, are observed within the lobule together with intercalated ducts (not seen here). Mucous cells secrete highly glycosylated mucins rich in sialic acid and sulfate which lubricate hard tissue surfaces, forming a thin protective film called a **pellicle.** This film modulates the attachment of bacteria to oral surfaces and forms complexes with other proteins present in saliva.

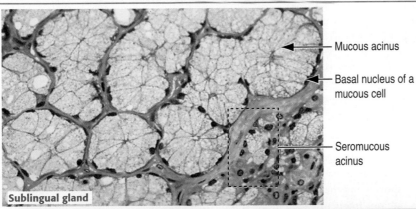

Mucous acinus

Basal nucleus of a mucous cell

Seromucous acinus

Sublingual gland

Sublingual glands are mixed serous and mucous tubuloacinar glands in which mucous cells predominate. However, a few seromucous acini can be found. **The intercalated and striated ducts are poorly developed in the sublingual gland.** Mucous cells resemble goblet cells of the intestinal epithelium. The nucleus is flattened against the basal plasma membrane. The apical region of the mucous cells is occupied by mucin-filled secretory vesicles, for the most part unstained. The cell boundaries are sharp. Mucous cells secrete highly glycosylated mucins which contribute to the formation of the protective pellicle film.

Serous acinar cell	Mucous acinar cell	Striated duct cell

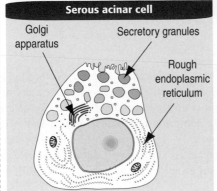

Golgi apparatus

Secretory granules

Rough endoplasmic reticulum

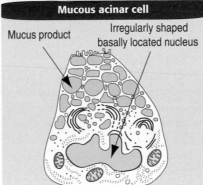

Mucus product

Irregularly shaped basally located nucleus

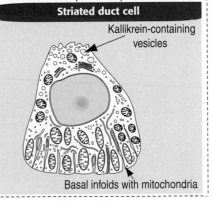

Kallikrein-containing vesicles

Basal infolds with mitochondria

Figure 17–5

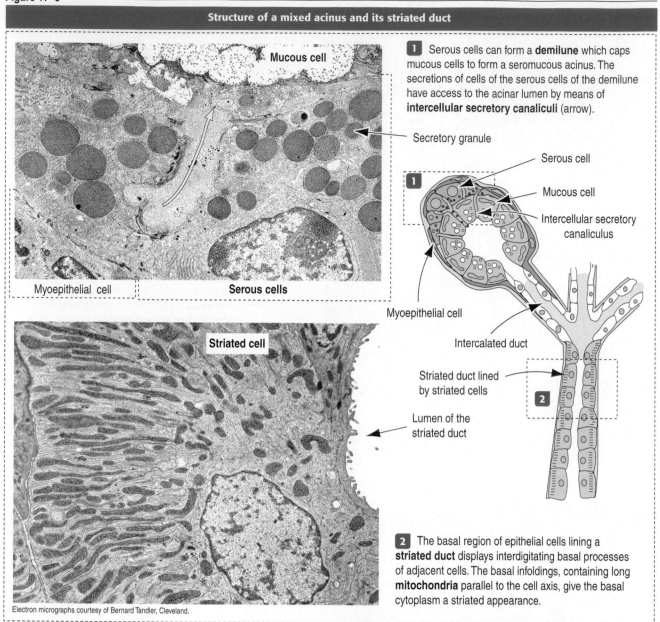

Structure of a mixed acinus and its striated duct

Mucous cell

Myoepithelial cell

Serous cells

Striated cell

1 Serous cells can form a **demilune** which caps mucous cells to form a seromucous acinus. The secretions of cells of the serous cells of the demilune have access to the acinar lumen by means of **intercellular secretory canaliculi** (arrow).

Secretory granule

Serous cell

Mucous cell

Intercellular secretory canaliculus

Myoepithelial cell

Intercalated duct

Striated duct lined by striated cells

Lumen of the striated duct

2 The basal region of epithelial cells lining a **striated duct** displays interdigitating basal processes of adjacent cells. The basal infoldings, containing long **mitochondria** parallel to the cell axis, give the basal cytoplasm a striated appearance.

Electron micrographs courtesy of Bernard Tandler, Cleveland.

serous cells are the predominant component (see Figure 17-4). Mucous cell–containing acini are capped by **serous demilunes. The intercalated ducts are shorter and the striated ducts longer than those in the parotid gland.** Adipocytes are not frequently seen in the submaxillary gland.

The main excretory duct of the submaxillary gland (Warthon's duct) opens near the frenulum of the tongue.

Sublingual gland

Contrasting with the parotid and submaxillary glands, which are surrounded by a dense connective tissue capsule, the sublingual gland does not have a defined capsule. However, connective tissue septa divide the glandular parenchyma into small lobes. The sublingual gland is a **compound tubuloalveolar gland with both serous and mucous cells** (see Figure 17–4), although most of the secretory units contain mucous cells. **The intercalated and striated ducts are poorly developed.** Usually each lobe has its own excretory duct that opens beneath the tongue.

Exocrine pancreas

The pancreas is a combined **endocrine** and **exocrine gland**. The endocrine component is the **islet of Langerhans** and represents about 2% of the pancreas volume. The main function of the endocrine pancreas is the **regulation of glucose metabolism** by hormones secreted into the bloodstream (see discussion of the islet of Langerhans in Chapter 19, Endocrine System).

The exocrine pancreas is a **compound tubuloacinar gland** organized into four anatomic components: (1) a **head**, lying in the concavity of the second and third part of the duodenum, (2) a **neck**, in contact with the portal vein, (3) a **body**, placed anterior to the aorta, and (4) a **tail**, ending near the hilum of the spleen.

The pancreas lies close to the posterior abdominal wall in the upper abdomen, and therefore it is protected from severe trauma. Blood is provided by vessels derived from the celiac artery, the superior mesenteric artery, and the splenic artery. The venous drainage flows into the portal venous system and the splenic vein. Efferent innervation is through the vagus and splanchnic nerves.

The **main pancreatic duct (of Wirsung)** runs straight through the tail and the body, collecting secretions from ductal tributaries. It turns downward when it reaches the head of the pancreas and drains directly into the duodenum at the **ampulla of Vater**, after joining the **common bile duct**. A circular smooth **muscle sphincter (of Oddi)** is seen where the common pancreatic and bile duct crosses the wall of the duodenum.

The pancreas has structural similarities to the salivary glands: (1) It is surrounded by connective tissue but does not have a capsule proper. (2) Lobules are separated by connective tissue septa containing blood vessels, lymphatics, nerves, and excretory ducts.

The functional histologic unit of the exocrine pancreas is the **acinus** (Figures 17–6, 17–7 and 17–8). The lumen of the acinus is the initiation of the secretory duct and contains **centroacinar cells that are unique to the pancreas**. The lumen of the acinus leads into the **intralobular excretory ducts** lined by a **low columnar**

Figure 17–6

The exocrine pancreas

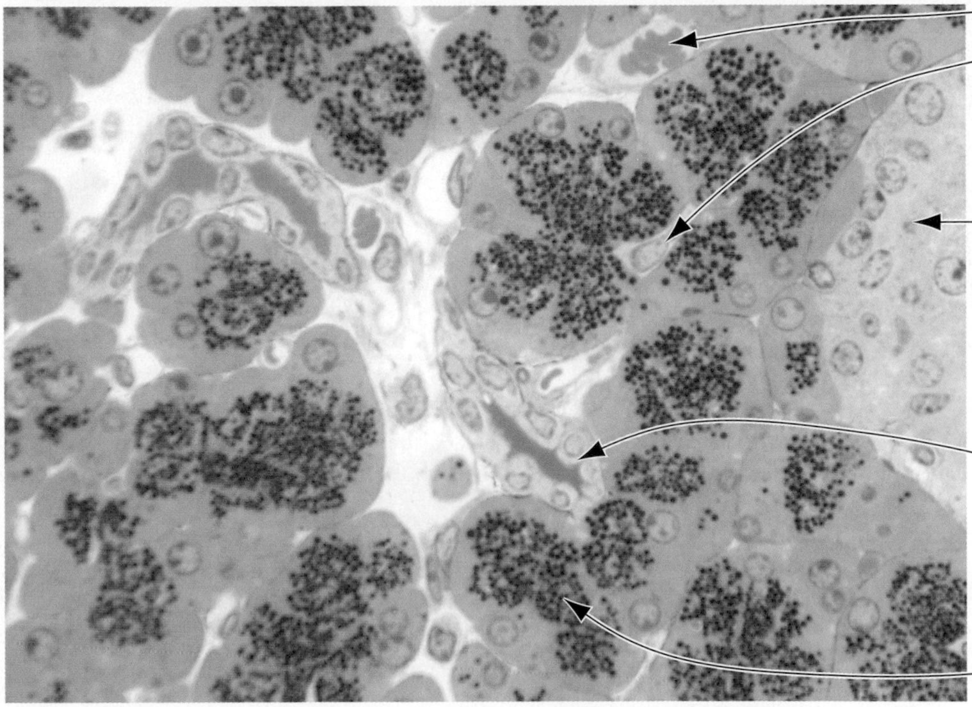

Capillary

Centroacinar cell
It is recognized by its location in the center of the pancreatic acinus and by its pale cytoplasm.

Islet of Langerhans
This endocrine component of the pancreas is surrounded by serous acini.

Intercalated duct
It is the continuation into the connective tissue stroma of the centroacinar cells.

Zymogen granules
They are present at the apical portion of the pancreatic acinar cell.

Figure 17–7

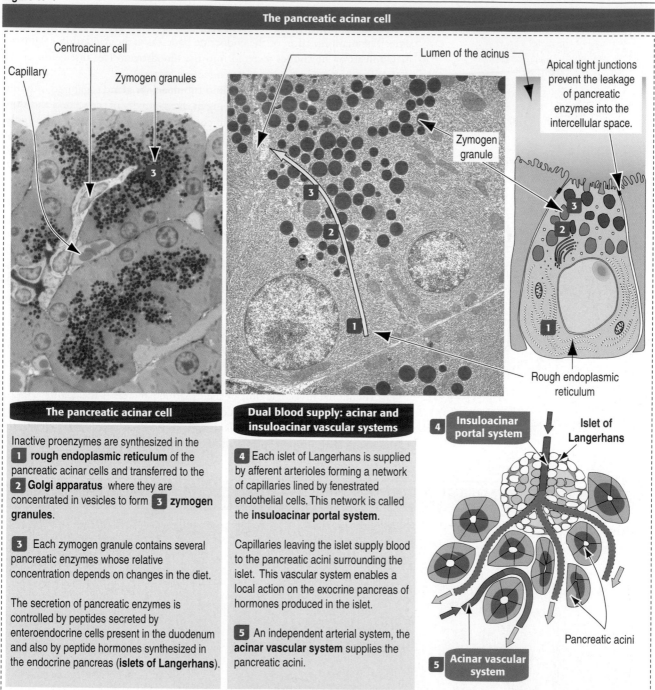

The pancreatic acinar cell

Inactive proenzymes are synthesized in the **1 rough endoplasmic reticulum** of the pancreatic acinar cells and transferred to the **2 Golgi apparatus** where they are concentrated in vesicles to form **3 zymogen granules**.

3 Each zymogen granule contains several pancreatic enzymes whose relative concentration depends on changes in the diet.

The secretion of pancreatic enzymes is controlled by peptides secreted by enteroendocrine cells present in the duodenum and also by peptide hormones synthesized in the endocrine pancreas (**islets of Langerhans**).

Dual blood supply: acinar and insuloacinar vascular systems

4 Each islet of Langerhans is supplied by afferent arterioles forming a network of capillaries lined by fenestrated endothelial cells. This network is called the **insuloacinar portal system**.

Capillaries leaving the islet supply blood to the pancreatic acini surrounding the islet. This vascular system enables a local action on the exocrine pancreas of hormones produced in the islet.

5 An independent arterial system, the **acinar vascular system** supplies the pancreatic acini.

epithelium. Intralobular ducts **are nonstriated** and converge to form **interlobular ducts** covered by a **columnar epithelium** with a few goblet cells and occasional enteroendocrine cells. Interlobular ducts anastomose to form the **main pancreatic duct**.

Clinical significance: Carcinoma of the pancreas

The pancreatic duct–bile duct anatomic relationship is of clinical significance in **carcinoma of the pancreas** localized in the **head region**, because compression of the bile duct causes **obstructive jaundice**. The close association of the pancreas with large blood vessels, the extensive and diffuse abdominal drainage to lymph nodes, and the frequent spread of carcinoma cells to the liver via the portal vein

Figure 17–8

Fine structure of the pancreatic acinus

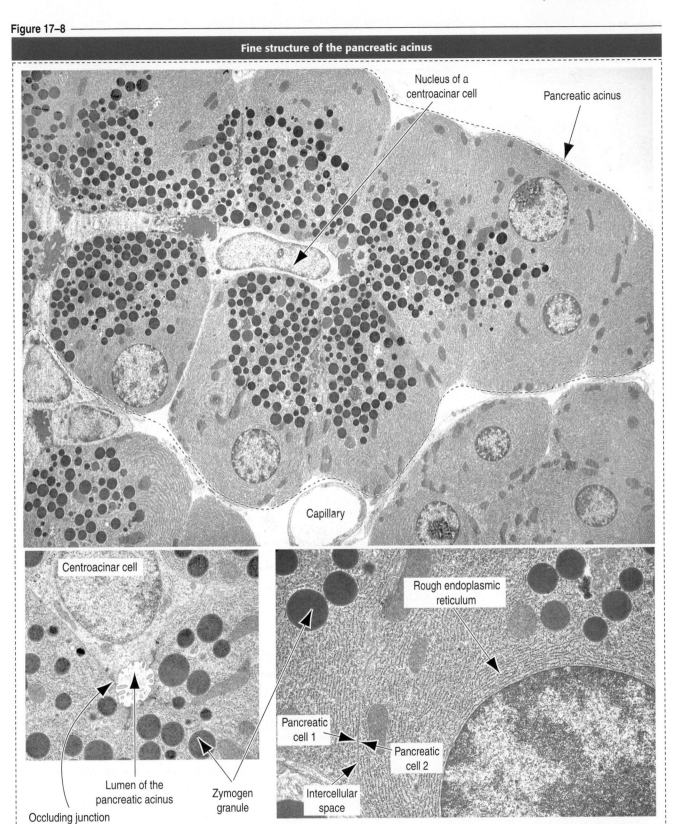

Nucleus of a centroacinar cell

Pancreatic acinus

Capillary

Centroacinar cell

Occluding junction

Lumen of the pancreatic acinus

Zymogen granule

Rough endoplasmic reticulum

Pancreatic cell 1

Pancreatic cell 2

Intercellular space

are factors contributing to the ineffectiveness of surgical removal of pancreatic tumors.

The pancreatic acinus

The pancreatic acinus is lined by pyramidal cells joined to each other by apical

Figure 17–9

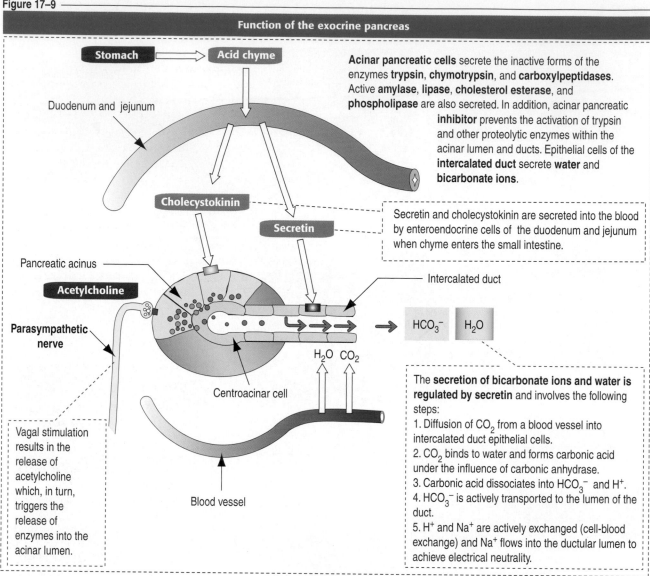

Function of the exocrine pancreas

Acinar pancreatic cells secrete the inactive forms of the enzymes **trypsin**, **chymotrypsin**, and **carboxylpeptidases**. Active **amylase**, **lipase**, **cholesterol esterase**, and **phospholipase** are also secreted. In addition, acinar pancreatic **inhibitor** prevents the activation of trypsin and other proteolytic enzymes within the acinar lumen and ducts. Epithelial cells of the **intercalated duct** secrete **water** and **bicarbonate ions**.

Secretin and cholecystokinin are secreted into the blood by enteroendocrine cells of the duodenum and jejunum when chyme enters the small intestine.

Vagal stimulation results in the release of acetylcholine which, in turn, triggers the release of enzymes into the acinar lumen.

The **secretion of bicarbonate ions and water is regulated by secretin** and involves the following steps:
1. Diffusion of CO_2 from a blood vessel into intercalated duct epithelial cells.
2. CO_2 binds to water and forms carbonic acid under the influence of carbonic anhydrase.
3. Carbonic acid dissociates into HCO_3^- and H^+.
4. HCO_3^- is actively transported to the lumen of the duct.
5. H^+ and Na^+ are actively exchanged (cell-blood exchange) and Na^+ flows into the ductular lumen to achieve electrical neutrality.

junctional complexes (see Figure 17–8), which prevent the reflux of secreted products from the ducts into the intercellular spaces. The basal domain of an acinar pancreatic cell is associated with a basal lamina and contains the nucleus and a well-developed rough endoplasmic reticulum. The apical domain displays numerous **zymogen granules** (see Figure 17–8) and the Golgi apparatus.

The concentration of about 20 different pancreatic enzymes in the zymogen granules varies with the dietary intake. For example, an increase in the synthesis of **proteases** is associated with a **protein-rich diet**. A **carbohydrate-rich diet** results in the selective synthesis of **amylases** and a decrease in the synthesis of proteases. Amylase gene expression is regulated by insulin, an event that stresses the significance of the **insular-acinar portal system**.

The administration of a cholinergic drug or of the gastrointestinal hormones cholecystokinin and secretin increases the flow of pancreatic fluid (about 1.5 to 3.0 L/day). The polypeptide hormone **cholecystokinin**, produced in enteroendocrine cells of the duodenal mucosa, binds to specific receptors of **acinar cells** and **stimulates the release of zymogen granules** (Figure 17–9). Secretin, also produced in the duodenum, binds to receptors on the surface of **ductal cells** and **triggers the release of bicarbonate ions and water** into the pancreatic ducts. HCO_3^- ions and the alkaline secretion of Brunner's glands, present in the submucosa of the duodenum, neutralize the acidic gastric chyme in the duodenal lumen and activate the pancreatic digestive enzymes.

Clinical significance: Acute pancreatitis and cystic fibrosis

Zymogen granules contain **inactive proenzymes** that are activated within the duodenal environment. A premature activation of pancreatic enzymes, in particular **trypsinogen** to **trypsin**, and the inactivation of **trypsin inhibitor** (tightly bound to the active site of trypsin), result in the autodigestion of pancreatic acini. This condition —known to occur in **acute hemorrhagic pancreatitis**— usually follows heavy meals or excessive alcohol ingestion. The clinical features of acute pancreatitis (severe abdominal pain, nausea, and vomiting) and rapid elevation of amylase and lipase in serum (within 24 to 72 hours) are typical diagnostic features.

Cystic fibrosis is an inherited, autosomal recessive disease affecting the function of mucus-secreting tissues of the respiratory, intestinal, and reproductive systems; the sweat glands of the skin; and the **exocrine pancreas** in children and young adults. A thick sticky mucus obstructs the duct passages of the airways, pancreatic and biliary ducts, and intestine, followed by bacterial infections and damage of the functional tissues. A large number of patients (85%) have **chronic**

Figure 17-10

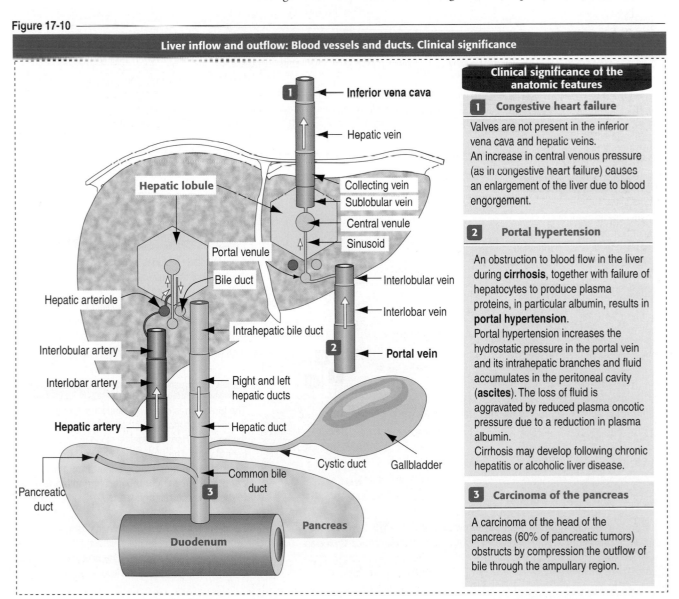

Liver inflow and outflow: Blood vessels and ducts. Clinical significance

Clinical significance of the anatomic features

1 Congestive heart failure

Valves are not present in the inferior vena cava and hepatic veins.
An increase in central venous pressure (as in congestive heart failure) causes an enlargement of the liver due to blood engorgement.

2 Portal hypertension

An obstruction to blood flow in the liver during **cirrhosis**, together with failure of hepatocytes to produce plasma proteins, in particular albumin, results in **portal hypertension**.
Portal hypertension increases the hydrostatic pressure in the portal vein and its intrahepatic branches and fluid accumulates in the peritoneal cavity (**ascites**). The loss of fluid is aggravated by reduced plasma oncotic pressure due to a reduction in plasma albumin.
Cirrhosis may develop following chronic hepatitis or alcoholic liver disease.

3 Carcinoma of the pancreas

A carcinoma of the head of the pancreas (60% of pancreatic tumors) obstructs by compression the outflow of bile through the ampullary region.

Labels in figure: Inferior vena cava; Hepatic vein; Hepatic lobule; Collecting vein; Sublobular vein; Central venule; Sinusoid; Portal venule; Bile duct; Interlobular vein; Hepatic arteriole; Interlobar vein; Intrahepatic bile duct; Interlobular artery; Portal vein; Interlobar artery; Right and left hepatic ducts; Hepatic artery; Hepatic duct; Cystic duct; Gallbladder; Pancreatic duct; Common bile duct; Pancreas; Duodenum

pancreatitis characterized by a loss of acini and dilation of the pancreatic excretory ducts into cysts surrounded by extensive fibrosis (hence the designation **cystic fibrosis of the pancreas**). Insufficient exocrine pancreatic secretions cause the malabsorption of fat and protein, reflected by bulky and fatty stools (**steatorrhea**).

The lack of transport of Cl⁻ ions across epithelia is associated with a defective secretion of Na⁺ ions and water. A genetic defect in the chloride channel protein called **cystic fibrosis transmembrane conductance regulator** (**CFTR**) is responsible for cystic fibrosis. The disease is detected by the demonstration of increased

Figure 17–11

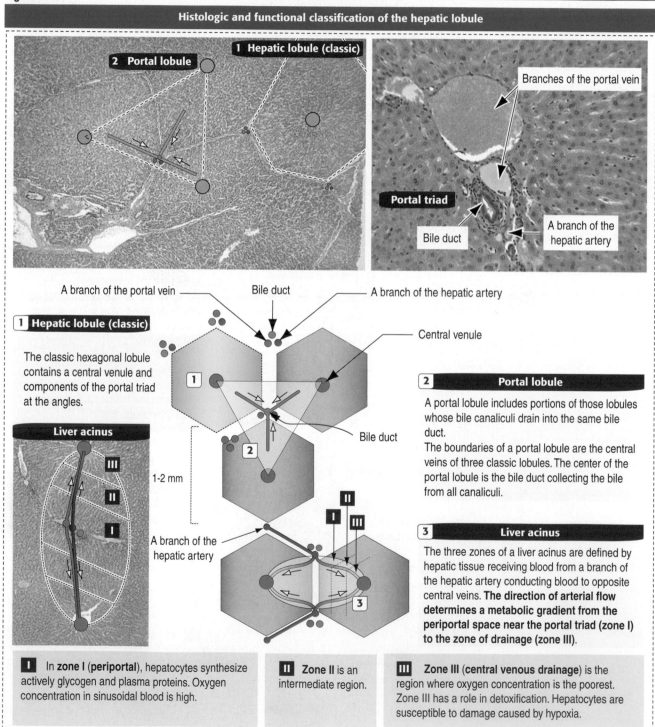

Histologic and functional classification of the hepatic lobule

Figure 17–12

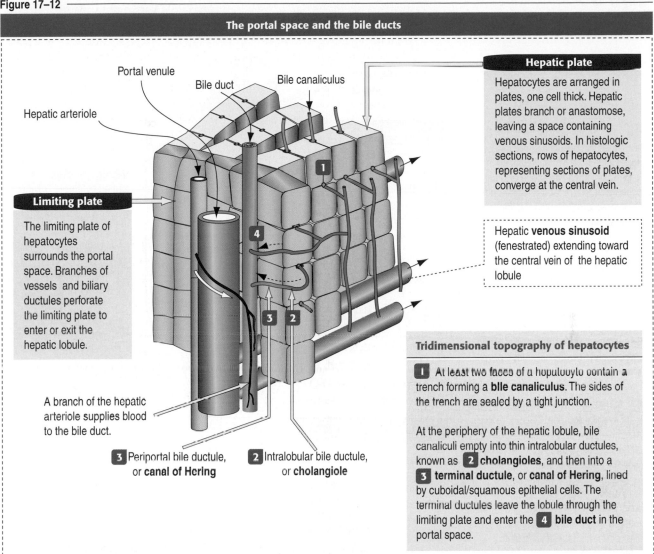

The portal space and the bile ducts

Portal venule
Bile duct
Bile canaliculus
Hepatic arteriole
Hepatic arteriole

Hepatic plate

Hepatocytes are arranged in plates, one cell thick. Hepatic plates branch or anastomose, leaving a space containing venous sinusoids. In histologic sections, rows of hepatocytes, representing sections of plates, converge at the central vein.

Limiting plate

The limiting plate of hepatocytes surrounds the portal space. Branches of vessels and biliary ductules perforate the limiting plate to enter or exit the hepatic lobule.

Hepatic **venous sinusoid** (fenestrated) extending toward the central vein of the hepatic lobule

A branch of the hepatic arteriole supplies blood to the bile duct.

Tridimensional topography of hepatocytes

1 At least two faces of a hepatocyte contain a trench forming a **bile canaliculus**. The sides of the trench are sealed by a tight junction.

At the periphery of the hepatic lobule, bile canaliculi empty into thin intralobular ductules, known as **2** **cholangioles**, and then into a **3** **terminal ductule**, or **canal of Hering**, lined by cuboidal/squamous epithelial cells. The terminal ductules leave the lobule through the limiting plate and enter the **4** **bile duct** in the portal space.

3 Periportal bile ductule, or **canal of Hering**
2 Intralobular bile ductule, or **cholangiole**

concentration of NaCl in sweat. Children with cystic fibrosis "taste salty" after copious sweating (see Chapter 13, Respiratory System, and Chapter 11, Integumentary System).

Liver
The liver, the largest gland of the human body, consists of four poorly defined **lobes**. The liver is surrounded by a collagen-elastic fiber containing **capsule (of Glisson)** and is lined by the peritoneum.

Blood is supplied to the liver by two blood vessels (Figure 17–10): (1) the **portal vein** (75% to 80% of the afferent blood volume) transports blood from the digestive tract, spleen, and pancreas. (2) The **hepatic artery**, a branch of the celiac trunk, supplies 20% to 25% of oxygenated blood to the liver by the **interlobar artery** and **interlobular artery** pathway before reaching the **portal space**.

Blood from branches of the portal vein and the hepatic artery mixes in the **sinusoids** of the **liver lobules**, as we discuss in detail later. Sinusoidal blood converges at the **central venule** of the liver lobule. Central venules converge to form the **sublobular veins**, and blood returns to the **inferior vena cava** following the **collecting veins** and **hepatic veins** pathway.

The **right** and **left hepatic bile ducts** leave the liver and merge to form the **hepatic duct**. The hepatic duct becomes the **common bile duct** soon after giving

Figure 17–13

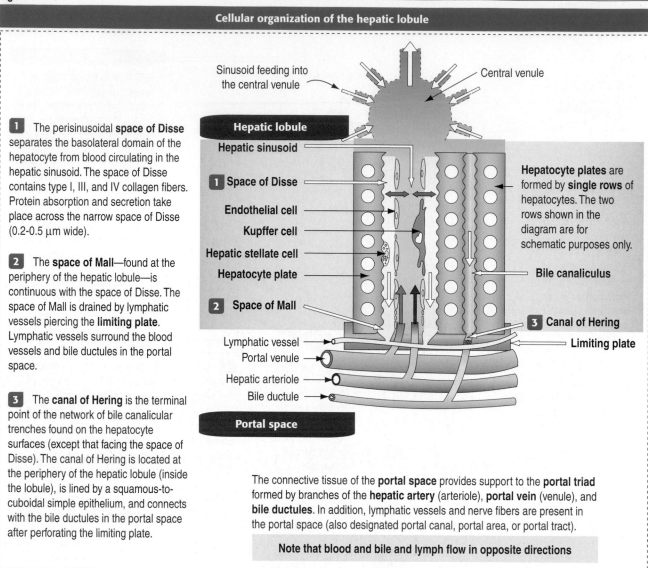

Cellular organization of the hepatic lobule

1 The perisinusoidal **space of Disse** separates the basolateral domain of the hepatocyte from blood circulating in the hepatic sinusoid. The space of Disse contains type I, III, and IV collagen fibers. Protein absorption and secretion take place across the narrow space of Disse (0.2-0.5 μm wide).

2 The **space of Mall**—found at the periphery of the hepatic lobule—is continuous with the space of Disse. The space of Mall is drained by lymphatic vessels piercing the **limiting plate**. Lymphatic vessels surround the blood vessels and bile ductules in the portal space.

3 The **canal of Hering** is the terminal point of the network of bile canalicular trenches found on the hepatocyte surfaces (except that facing the space of Disse). The canal of Hering is located at the periphery of the hepatic lobule (inside the lobule), is lined by a squamous-to-cuboidal simple epithelium, and connects with the bile ductules in the portal space after perforating the limiting plate.

Sinusoid feeding into the central venule

Central venule

Hepatic lobule

Hepatic sinusoid

1 Space of Disse

Endothelial cell

Kupffer cell

Hepatic stellate cell

Hepatocyte plate

2 Space of Mall

Lymphatic vessel

Portal venule

Hepatic arteriole

Bile ductule

Portal space

Hepatocyte plates are formed by **single rows** of hepatocytes. The two rows shown in the diagram are for schematic purposes only.

Bile canaliculus

3 Canal of Hering

Limiting plate

The connective tissue of the **portal space** provides support to the **portal triad** formed by branches of the **hepatic artery** (arteriole), **portal vein** (venule), and **bile ductules**. In addition, lymphatic vessels and nerve fibers are present in the portal space (also designated portal canal, portal area, or portal tract).

Note that blood and bile and lymph flow in opposite directions

rise to the **cystic duct**, a thin tube connecting the bile duct to the **gallbladder** (see Figure 17–10).

The hepatic lobule

The structural and functional unit of the liver is the **hepatic lobule**. The hepatic lobule consists of anastomosing **plates of hepatocytes** limiting blood **sinusoidal spaces** (see Figure 17–12). A **central venule** (or vein) in the core of the hepatic lobule collects the sinusoidal blood containing a mixture of blood supplied by branches of the portal vein and the hepatic artery.

Branches of the hepatic artery and portal vein, together with a bile duct, form the classic **portal triad** found in the portal space surrounding the hexagonal-shaped hepatic lobule (Figure 17–11).

Bile produced in the hepatocytes is secreted into narrow intercellular spaces, the **bile canaliculi**, located between the apposed surfaces of adjacent hepatocytes.

Bile flows in the opposite direction to the blood. Bile flows from the bile canaliculi into the **intralobular bile ductules**, or **cholangioles**, and then into the bile ducts (or ductules) of the portal space after crossing the **canal of Hering** at the periphery of the hepatic lobule (Figure 17–12). Bile ductules converge at the **intrahepatic bile ducts**.

Figure 17-14

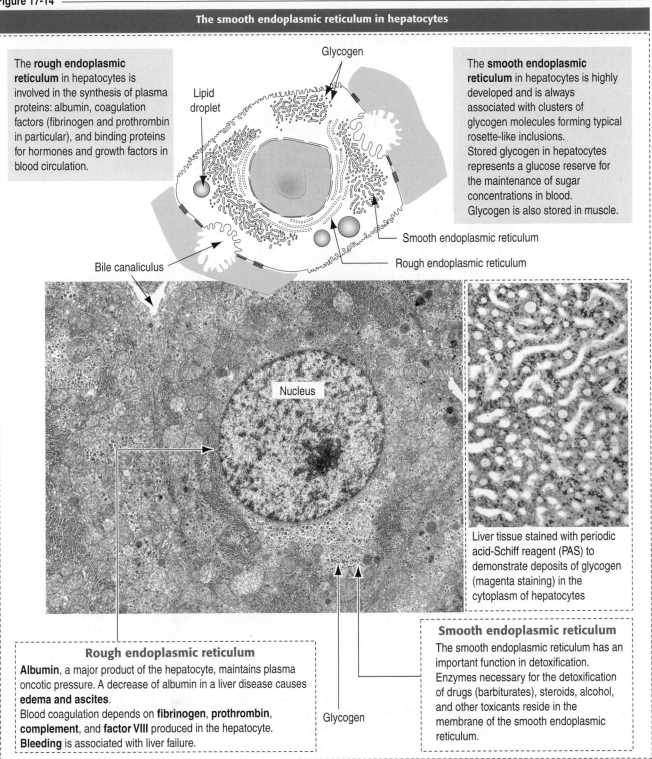

The smooth endoplasmic reticulum in hepatocytes

The **rough endoplasmic reticulum** in hepatocytes is involved in the synthesis of plasma proteins: albumin, coagulation factors (fibrinogen and prothrombin in particular), and binding proteins for hormones and growth factors in blood circulation.

Glycogen

Lipid droplet

The **smooth endoplasmic reticulum** in hepatocytes is highly developed and is always associated with clusters of glycogen molecules forming typical rosette-like inclusions.
Stored glycogen in hepatocytes represents a glucose reserve for the maintenance of sugar concentrations in blood.
Glycogen is also stored in muscle.

Smooth endoplasmic reticulum

Rough endoplasmic reticulum

Bile canaliculus

Nucleus

Liver tissue stained with periodic acid-Schiff reagent (PAS) to demonstrate deposits of glycogen (magenta staining) in the cytoplasm of hepatocytes

Rough endoplasmic reticulum

Albumin, a major product of the hepatocyte, maintains plasma oncotic pressure. A decrease of albumin in a liver disease causes **edema and ascites**.
Blood coagulation depends on **fibrinogen**, **prothrombin**, **complement**, and **factor VIII** produced in the hepatocyte.
Bleeding is associated with liver failure.

Glycogen

Smooth endoplasmic reticulum

The smooth endoplasmic reticulum has an important function in detoxification. Enzymes necessary for the detoxification of drugs (barbiturates), steroids, alcohol, and other toxicants reside in the membrane of the smooth endoplasmic reticulum.

A functional view of the liver lobule

There are three conceptual interpretations of the architecture of the liver lobule (see Figure 17–11): (1) the **classic concept** of the **hepatic lobule**, based on structural parameters; (2) the **portal lobule concept**, based on the bile drainage pathway from adjacent lobules toward the same bile duct; and (3) the **liver acinus concept**, based on the gradient distribution of oxygen along the venous sinusoids of adjacent lobules.

Figure 17–15

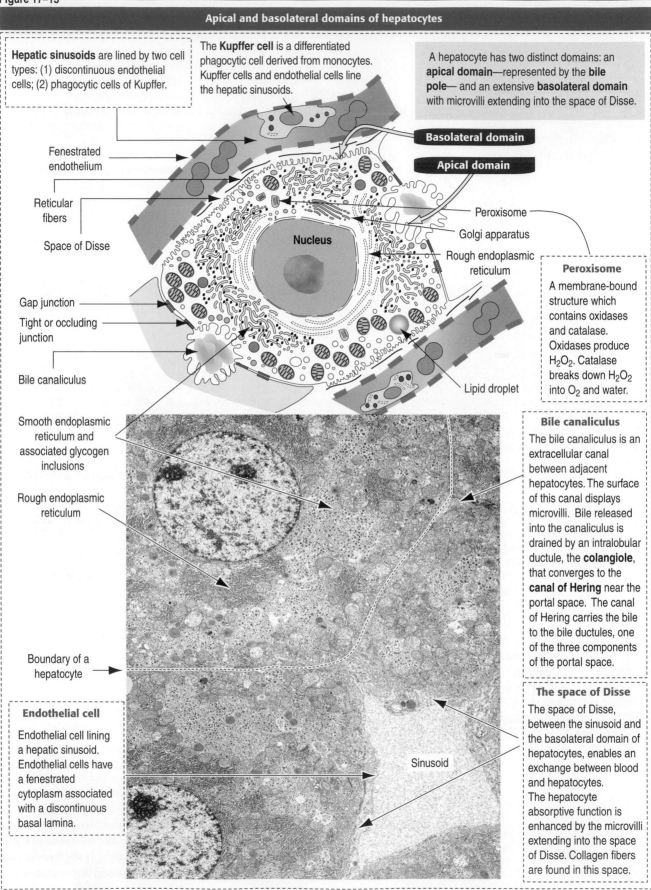

Apical and basolateral domains of hepatocytes

Hepatic sinusoids are lined by two cell types: (1) discontinuous endothelial cells; (2) phagocytic cells of Kupffer.

The **Kupffer cell** is a differentiated phagocytic cell derived from monocytes. Kupffer cells and endothelial cells line the hepatic sinusoids.

A hepatocyte has two distinct domains: an **apical domain**—represented by the **bile pole**— and an extensive **basolateral domain** with microvilli extending into the space of Disse.

Basolateral domain

Apical domain

Fenestrated endothelium

Reticular fibers

Space of Disse

Nucleus

Peroxisome

Golgi apparatus

Rough endoplasmic reticulum

Gap junction

Tight or occluding junction

Bile canaliculus

Lipid droplet

Peroxisome

A membrane-bound structure which contains oxidases and catalase. Oxidases produce H_2O_2. Catalase breaks down H_2O_2 into O_2 and water.

Smooth endoplasmic reticulum and associated glycogen inclusions

Rough endoplasmic reticulum

Bile canaliculus

The bile canaliculus is an extracellular canal between adjacent hepatocytes. The surface of this canal displays microvilli. Bile released into the canaliculus is drained by an intralobular ductule, the **colangiole**, that converges to the **canal of Hering** near the portal space. The canal of Hering carries the bile to the bile ductules, one of the three components of the portal space.

Boundary of a hepatocyte

Endothelial cell

Endothelial cell lining a hepatic sinusoid. Endothelial cells have a fenestrated cytoplasm associated with a discontinuous basal lamina.

Sinusoid

The space of Disse

The space of Disse, between the sinusoid and the basolateral domain of hepatocytes, enables an exchange between blood and hepatocytes. The hepatocyte absorptive function is enhanced by the microvilli extending into the space of Disse. Collagen fibers are found in this space.

Figure 17–16

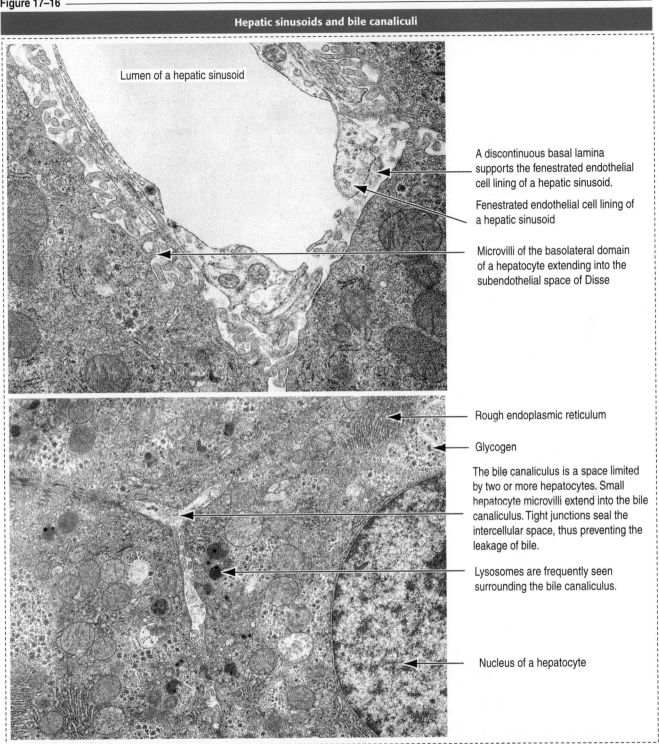

Hepatic sinusoids and bile canaliculi

Lumen of a hepatic sinusoid

A discontinuous basal lamina supports the fenestrated endothelial cell lining of a hepatic sinusoid.

Fenestrated endothelial cell lining of a hepatic sinusoid

Microvilli of the basolateral domain of a hepatocyte extending into the subendothelial space of Disse

Rough endoplasmic reticulum

Glycogen

The bile canaliculus is a space limited by two or more hepatocytes. Small hepatocyte microvilli extend into the bile canaliculus. Tight junctions seal the intercellular space, thus preventing the leakage of bile.

Lysosomes are frequently seen surrounding the bile canaliculus.

Nucleus of a hepatocyte

The **classic hepatic lobule** is customarily described as a polyhedral structure, usually depicted as a hexagon with a central venule to which blood sinusoids converge (see Figure 17–11).

Components of the **portal triad**, constituting a branch of the portal vein and hepatic artery and a bile duct, are usually found at the angles of the hexagon. This geometric organization is poorly defined in humans because the limiting perilobular connective tissue is not abundant. However, recognition of the components of the portal triad is helpful in determining the boundaries of the human hepatic lobule.

In the **portal lobule**, the portal triad is the central axis, draining bile from the surrounding hepatic parenchyma.

Functional considerations have modified the classic view and a **liver acinus** concept has gained ground in pathophysiology. In the liver acinus, **the boundaries are determined by a terminal branch of the hepatic artery**. The flow of arterial blood within the venous sinusoids creates gradients of oxygen and nutrients classified as **zones I, II, and III**. Zone I is the richest in oxygen and nutrients. Zone III, closer to the central vein, is oxygen-poor. Zone II is intermediate in oxygen and nutrients.

Although pathologic changes in the liver are usually described in relation to the classic lobule, the liver acinus concept is convenient for understanding liver regeneration patterns, liver metabolic activities, and the development of cirrhosis, as we discuss later in this chapter.

The hepatocyte

The hepatocyte is the functional **exocrine** and **endocrine** cell of the hepatic lobule. Hepatocytes form anastomosing **one-cell-thick plates** limiting the sinusoidal spaces. The perisinusoidal **space of Disse** separates the hepatocytes from the blood sinusoidal space (Figure 17–13).

The components of the portal triad, embedded in connective tissue, are separated from the hepatic lobule by a **limiting plate** of hepatocytes (see Figure 17–12). Blood from the portal vein and hepatic artery flows into the sinusoids and is drained by the central venule. As indicated above, bile flows in the opposite direction, from the hepatocytes to the bile duct in the portal space (see Figure 17–13).

A hepatocyte has two cellular domains: (1) a **basolateral domain**, and (2) an **apical domain** (Figures 17–14, 17–15, and 17–16):

The **basolateral domain** contains abundant **microvilli** and **faces the space of Disse**. Excess fluid in the space of Disse is collected in the **space of Mall**, located at the periphery of the hepatic lobule. Lymphatic vessels piercing the limiting plate drain the fluid of the space of Mall. **Gap junctions** on the lateral surfaces of adjacent hepatocytes enable intercellular functional coupling.

The basolateral domain participates in the **absorption of blood-borne substances** and in the **secretion of plasma proteins** (such as **albumin**, **fibrinogen**, **prothrombin**, and **coagulation factors V, VII, and IX**). Note that hepatocytes synthesize several plasma proteins required for blood clotting (see Chapter 6, Blood and Hematopoiesis, for a review of the blood clotting pathway). Blood coagulation disorders are associated with liver disease.

The **apical domain** borders the **bile canaliculus**, a trenchlike depression lined by microvilli and sealed at the sides by **occluding junctions** to prevent leakage of **bile**, the exocrine product of the hepatocyte (see Figure 17–15).

The hepatocyte contains a **rough endoplasmic reticulum** (see Figure 17–14), involved in the synthesis of plasma proteins, and a highly developed **smooth endoplasmic reticulum**, associated with synthesis of **glycogen**, **lipid**, and **detoxification mechanisms** (see Figure 17–17).

Enzymes inserted in the membrane of the **smooth endoplasmic reticulum** are involved in the following **functions**: (1) the synthesis of cholesterol and bile salts, (2) the glucuronide conjugation of bilirubin, steroids and drugs, (3) the breakdown of glycogen into glucose, (4) the esterification of free fatty acids to triglycerides, (5) the removal of iodine from the thyroid hormones triiodothyronine (T_3) and thyroxine (T_4), and (6) the **detoxification of lipid-soluble drugs** such as **phenobarbital**, during which the smooth endoplasmic reticulum is significantly developed.

The **Golgi apparatus** contributes to glycosylation of secretory proteins and the sorting of lysosomal enzymes. **Lysosomes** degrade aged plasma glycoproteins in-

Figure 17–17

Ethanol metabolism in hepatocytes

The alcohol dehydrogenase (ADH) pathway

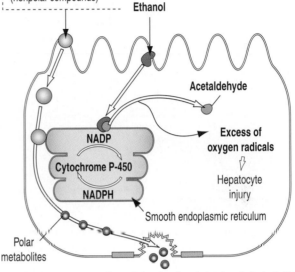

The ADH is the major pathway. **Alcohol is oxidized to acetaldehyde** in the cytoplasm and **acetaldehyde is converted to acetate** in mitochondria. An excess of acetaldehyde causes mitochondrial damage, disrupts microtubules, and alters proteins that can induce autoimmune responses leading to hepatocyte injury.

The microsomal ethanol-oxidizing system (MEOS)

The MEOS pathway is significant during the **chronic intake of alcohol**. Unlike the ADH pathway that produces acetaldehyde and excess H^+, **the MEOS pathway produces acetaldehyde and an excess of oxygen radicals**. Reactive oxygen produces injury of hepatocytes by causing lipid peroxidation, resulting in cell membrane damage. In addition, an upregulated MEOS affects detoxification activities of the hepatocyte that require cytochrome P-450 for the oxidation of various drugs, toxins, vitamins A and D, and potential carcinogens. The accumulation of these products is often toxic.

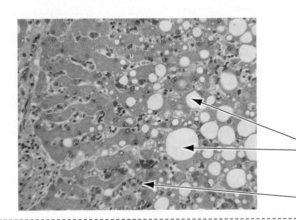

Large fat deposits in the cytoplasm of hepatocytes are observed in **fatty liver (steatosis)** following long-term consumption of alcohol.

Sinusoid

ternalized at the basolateral domain by a hepatic lectin membrane receptor—the **asialoglycoprotein receptor**—with binding affinity to terminal galactose after the removal of sialic acid. Lysosomes in hepatocytes store iron, which can exist as **soluble ferritin** and **insoluble hemosiderin**, the degradation product of ferritin.

Peroxisomes

Peroxisomes are **membrane-bound organelles** with a high content of **oxidases** that generate **hydrogen peroxide** (Figure 17–18). Because hydrogen peroxide is a toxic metabolite, the enzyme **catalase** degrades this product into **oxygen** and **water**. This catalytic event occurs in hepatocytes and cells of the kidney.

Peroxisomes derive from pre-existing peroxisomes by a budding process. Then, the organelle imports peroxisomal matrix proteins. A peroxisome contains about 50 enzymes involved in various metabolic pathways. The biogenesis of peroxisomes and their role in inherited disorders are outlined in Figure 17–18.

Figure 17–18

The peroxisome

1 Proteins for peroxisomes are synthesized by free cytosolic ribosomes and then transported into peroxisomes. Phospholipids and membrane proteins are also imported to peroxisomes from the endoplasmic reticulum.

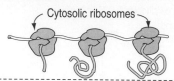

Cytosolic ribosomes

2 Proteins are targeted to the interior of the peroxisome by targeting amino acid signals (mainly Ser-Lys-Leu at the C-terminal). Other amino acid signals target proteins to the peroxisome membrane. Targeting amino acid signals are not cleaved.

Apocatalase monomer

Peroxisomal targeting signal sequence

Peroxisomal targeting signal sequence receptor

Fe — Heme

3

Fe
Fe
Fe
Fe

Catalase tetramer

Peroxisome

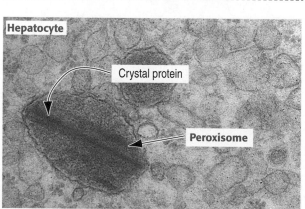

Hepatocyte

Crystal protein

Peroxisome

4 The **Zellweger syndrome** is a lethal condition caused by the defective assembly of peroxisomes due to the lack of transport of enzyme proteins (but not membrane proteins) into the peroxisome.

Newly synthesized peroxisomal enzymes remain in the cytosol and eventually are degraded. Cells in patients with Zellweger syndrome contain **empty peroxisomes**.

3 **Catalase**, the major protein of the peroxisome, decomposes H_2O_2 into H_2O.

Catalase is a tetramer of apocatalase molecules assembled within the peroxisome.

Heme is added to each monomer to prevent it from moving back into the cytosol across the peroxisomal membrane.

Peroxisomes are abundant in liver (hepatocytes).

Clinical significance: Liver storage diseases

Severe liver diseases can result from the excessive storage of iron and copper. **Hereditary hemochromatosis** is an example of a disease characterized by increased **iron** absorption and accumulation in lysosomal hepatocytes. Cirrhosis and cancer of the liver are complications of hemochromatosis.

Wilson's disease (**hepatolenticular degeneration**) is a hereditary disorder of **copper** metabolism in which excessive deposits of copper in liver and brain lysosomes produce chronic hepatitis and cirrhosis.

Clinical significance: Alcoholism and fatty liver (alcoholic steatohepatitis)

After absorption in the stomach, most ethanol is transported to the liver, where it is metabolized to **acetaldehyde** and **acetate** in the hepatocytes. Ethanol is mainly oxidized by **alcohol dehydrogenase**, an NADH-dependent enzyme. This mechanism is known as the **alcohol dehydrogenase (ADH) pathway**. An additional metabolic pathway is the **microsomal ethanol–oxidizing system (MEOS)**, present in the smooth endoplasmic reticulum. The two pathways are summarized in Figure 17–17.

Long-term consumption of ethanol results in **fatty liver** (a reversible process if ethanol consumption is discontinued), **steatohepatitis** (fatty liver accompanied by an inflammatory reaction), **cirrhosis** (collagen proliferation or fibrosis), and **hepatocellular carcinoma** (malignant transformation of hepatocytes).

Figure 17–19

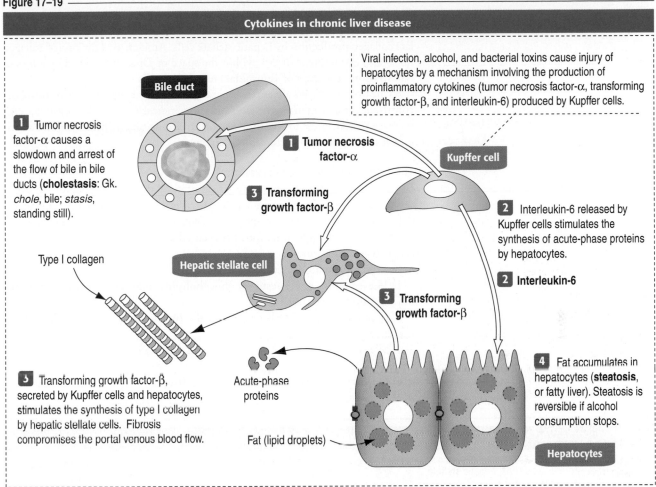

Cytokines in chronic liver disease

Viral infection, alcohol, and bacterial toxins cause injury of hepatocytes by a mechanism involving the production of proinflammatory cytokines (tumor necrosis factor-α, transforming growth factor-β, and interleukin-6) produced by Kupffer cells.

Bile duct

1 Tumor necrosis factor-α causes a slowdown and arrest of the flow of bile in bile ducts (**cholestasis**: Gk. *chole*, bile; *stasis*, standing still).

1 **Tumor necrosis factor-α**

3 **Transforming growth factor-β**

Kupffer cell

2 Interleukin-6 released by Kupffer cells stimulates the synthesis of acute-phase proteins by hepatocytes.

2 **Interleukin-6**

Type I collagen

Hepatic stellate cell

3 **Transforming growth factor-β**

3 Transforming growth factor-β, secreted by Kupffer cells and hepatocytes, stimulates the synthesis of type I collagen by hepatic stellate cells. Fibrosis compromises the portal venous blood flow.

Acute-phase proteins

4 Fat accumulates in hepatocytes (**steatosis**, or fatty liver). Steatosis is reversible if alcohol consumption stops.

Fat (lipid droplets)

Hepatocytes

The production of **tumor necrosis factor-α** (**TNF-α**) is one of the initial events in liver injury. **TNF-α** triggers the production of other cytokines. **TNF-α**, regarded as a **proinflammatory cytokine,** recruits inflammatory cells that cause hepatocyte injury and promote the production of type I collagen fibers by **hepatic stellate cells** (a process known as **fibrogenesis**) as a healing response.

Injury of hepatocytes results in programmed cell death, or apoptosis, caused by the activation of caspases, as we have seen in Chapter 3, Cell Signaling. We have already seen that **TNF-α** participates in a number of inflammatory processes such as in the articular joints (Chapter 5, Osteogenesis) and the extravasation of inflammatory cells (Chapter 10, Immune-Lymphatic System).

Ethanol, viruses, or toxins induce Kupffer cells to synthesize TNF-α as well as **transforming growth factor-β** (TGF-β) and **interleukin-6** (Figure 17–19). TGF-β stimulates the production of type I collagen by hepatic stellate cells, which increase in number. **TNF-α** acts on biliary ducts to interfere with the flow of bile (cholestasis).

Clinical significance of the hepatic stellate cell

Hepatic stellate cells, also called the cells of Ito, are found in the space of Disse in proximity to the hepatic sinusoids. These cells are of mesenchymal origin, contain fat, and are involved in the storage and metabolism of vitamin A (Figure 17–20).

In pathologic conditions, the hepatic stellate cells change into collagen-producing cells. In addition to the synthesis and secretion of type I collagen, hepatic stellate cells secrete **laminin**, **proteoglycans**, and **growth factors**. The deposit of collagen and extracellular matrix components increases, leading to a progressive fibrosis of the liver, which is typical of **cirrhosis**.

Cytokines, produced by Kupffer cells (see Figures 17–19 and 17–20), stimulate collagen production by hepatic stellate cells. An increased deposit of collagen fibers and extracellular matrix within the space of Disse is followed by a **loss of fenestrations and gaps of sinusoidal endothelial cells**.

As the fibrotic process advances, hepatic stellate cells change into **myofibroblasts** constricting the lumen of the sinusoids and increasing vascular resistance. **An increase in resistance to the flow of portal venous blood in the hepatic sinusoids leads to portal hypertension in cirrhosis**.

The bile: Mechanism of secretion

Bile is a product of the hepatocyte transported by the bile canaliculus, an extracellular canal between adjacent hepatocytes (Figure 17–21). The bile canaliculus defines the **apical domain** of the hepatocyte. The **basolateral domain** faces the sinusoidal space. **Tight junctions** between adjacent hepatocytes seal the biliary canalicular compartment.

Bile has four major functions:

1. The excretion of **cholesterol, phospholipids, bile salts, conjugated bilirubin**, and **electrolytes** (see below).

2. It contributes to **fat absorption in the intestinal lumen** (see Chapter 16, Lower Digestive Segment).

3. Bile also transports **IgA** to the intestinal mucosa by the enterohepatic circulation.

4. The excretion of metabolic products of drugs and heavy metals processed in the hepatocyte.

Figure 17–20

The hepatic stellate cell (cell of Ito)

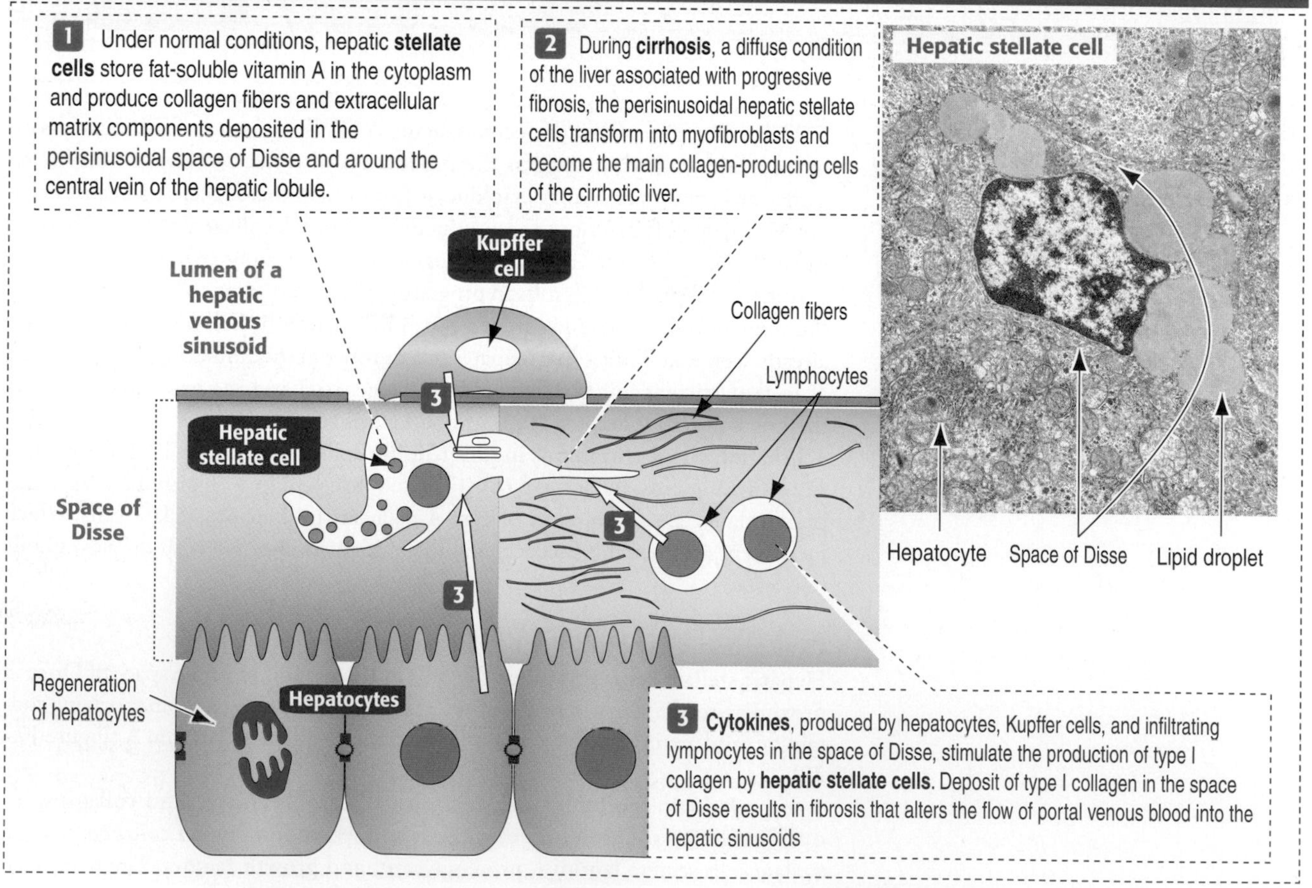

1 Under normal conditions, hepatic **stellate cells** store fat-soluble vitamin A in the cytoplasm and produce collagen fibers and extracellular matrix components deposited in the perisinusoidal space of Disse and around the central vein of the hepatic lobule.

2 During **cirrhosis**, a diffuse condition of the liver associated with progressive fibrosis, the perisinusoidal hepatic stellate cells transform into myofibroblasts and become the main collagen-producing cells of the cirrhotic liver.

Hepatic stellate cell

Kupffer cell

Lumen of a hepatic venous sinusoid

Hepatic stellate cell

Collagen fibers

Lymphocytes

Space of Disse

Hepatocyte   Space of Disse   Lipid droplet

Regeneration of hepatocytes

Hepatocytes

3 **Cytokines**, produced by hepatocytes, Kupffer cells, and infiltrating lymphocytes in the space of Disse, stimulate the production of type I collagen by **hepatic stellate cells**. Deposit of type I collagen in the space of Disse results in fibrosis that alters the flow of portal venous blood into the hepatic sinusoids

Figure 17–21

The bile canaliculus and the polarity of the hepatocyte

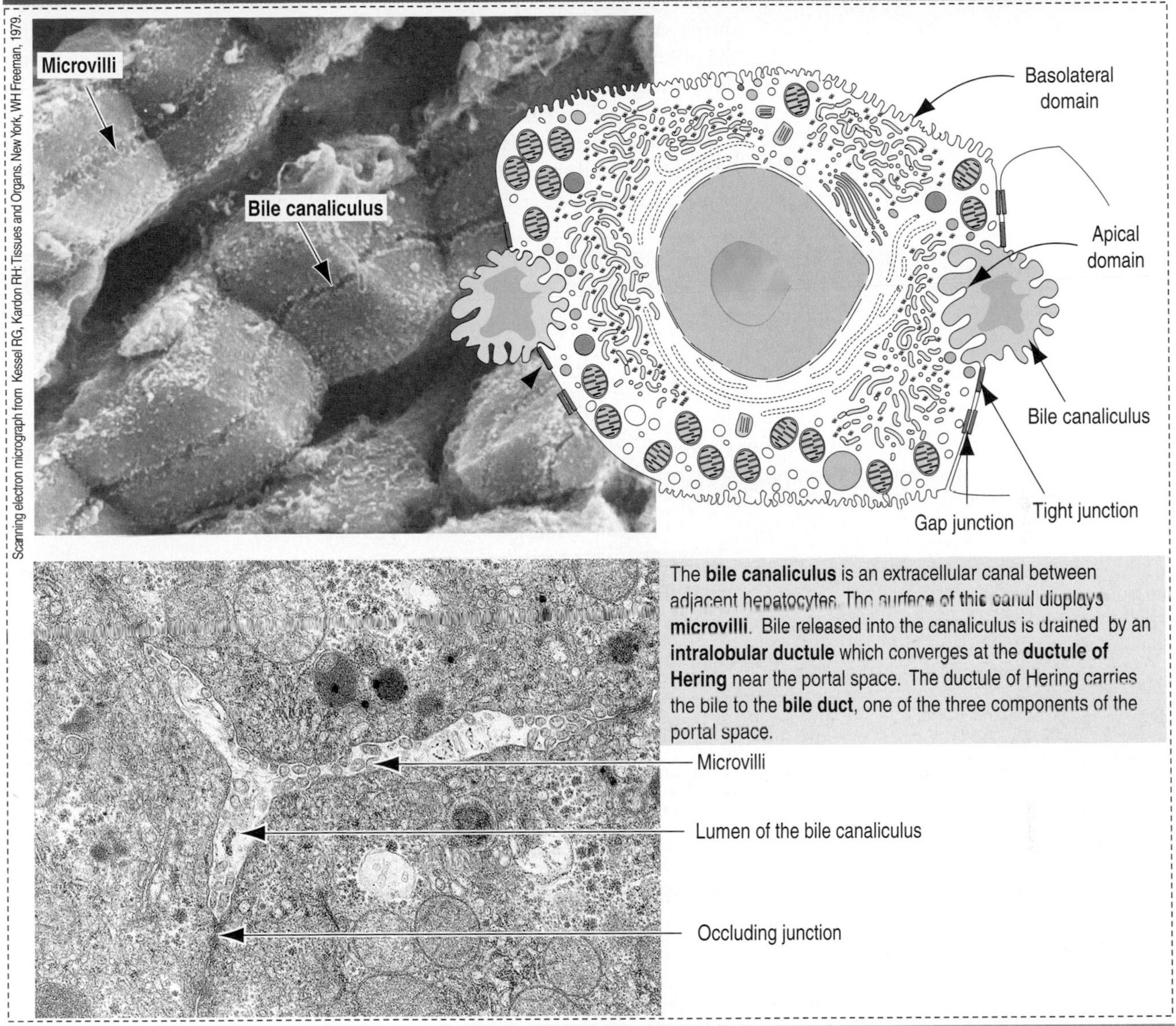

Scanning electron micrograph from Kessel RG, Kardon RH: Tissues and Organs. New York, WH Freeman, 1979.

Microvilli

Bile canaliculus

Basolateral domain

Apical domain

Bile canaliculus

Gap junction

Tight junction

The **bile canaliculus** is an extracellular canal between adjacent hepatocytes. The surface of this canal displays **microvilli**. Bile released into the canaliculus is drained by an **intralobular ductule** which converges at the **ductule of Hering** near the portal space. The ductule of Hering carries the bile to the **bile duct**, one of the three components of the portal space.

Microvilli

Lumen of the bile canaliculus

Occluding junction

The transport of bile and other organic substances from the hepatocyte to the lumen of the bile canaliculus is an adenosine triphosphate (ATP)–mediated process. Four ATP-dependent transporters, present in the canalicular plasma membrane, participate in transport mechanisms of the bile (see Figure 17–22).

1. **Multidrug resistance 1** transporter (**MDR1**), which mobilizes cholesterol across the plasma membrane.

2. **Multidrug resistance 2** transporter (**MDR2**), which transports phospholipids.

3. **Multispecific organ anionic transporter** (**MOAT**), which exports bilirubin glucuronide and glutathione conjugates.

4. **Biliary acid transporter** (**BAT**), which transports bile salts.

These ATP transporters belong to the family of **ABC transporters** characterized by highly conserved ATP-binding domains, or ATP binding cassettes. The first ABC transporter was discovered as the product of the gene *mdr* (for multiple drug resistance). The *mdr* gene is highly expressed in cancer cells and the encoded product, MDR transporter, pumps drugs out of cells, making cancer cells resistant to cancer treatment with chemotheraputic agents (see The Cell Nucleus in Chapter 1, Epithelium).

The secretion of bile acids generates the osmotic gradient necessary for osmotic water flow into the bile canaliculus. In addition, an **ion exchanger** enables the passage of HCO_3^- and Cl^- ions. Finally, hydrolytic enzymes associated with the plasma membrane (**ectoenzymes**) of the bile canaliculus and bile duct produce nucleoside and amino acid breakdown products, which are reabsorbed by ductular epithelial cells.

A genetic defect in MDR2 causes focal hepatocyte necrosis, proliferation of bile ductules, and an inflammatory reaction in the portal space. Very low levels of phospholipids are detected in the bile of MDR2 mutants.

Figure 17–22

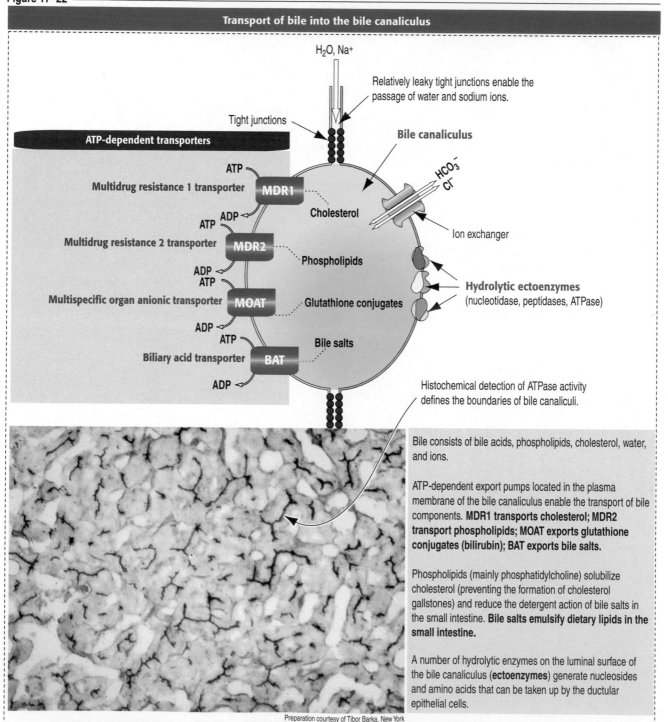

Transport of bile into the bile canaliculus

H_2O, Na^+

Relatively leaky tight junctions enable the passage of water and sodium ions.

Tight junctions

Bile canaliculus

ATP-dependent transporters

ATP

Multidrug resistance 1 transporter — MDR1

ADP — Cholesterol

HCO_3^-
Cl^-

ATP

Multidrug resistance 2 transporter — MDR2

ADP — Phospholipids

Ion exchanger

ATP

Multispecific organ anionic transporter — MOAT — Glutathione conjugates

Hydrolytic ectoenzymes
(nucleotidase, peptidases, ATPase)

ADP

ATP

Biliary acid transporter — BAT — Bile salts

ADP

Histochemical detection of ATPase activity defines the boundaries of bile canaliculi.

Bile consists of bile acids, phospholipids, cholesterol, water, and ions.

ATP-dependent export pumps located in the plasma membrane of the bile canaliculus enable the transport of bile components. **MDR1 transports cholesterol; MDR2 transport phospholipids; MOAT exports glutathione conjugates (bilirubin); BAT exports bile salts.**

Phospholipids (mainly phosphatidylcholine) solubilize cholesterol (preventing the formation of cholesterol gallstones) and reduce the detergent action of bile salts in the small intestine. **Bile salts emulsify dietary lipids in the small intestine.**

A number of hydrolytic enzymes on the luminal surface of the bile canaliculus (**ectoenzymes**) generate nucleosides and amino acids that can be taken up by the ductular epithelial cells.

Preparation courtesy of Tibor Barka, New York

Figure 17–23

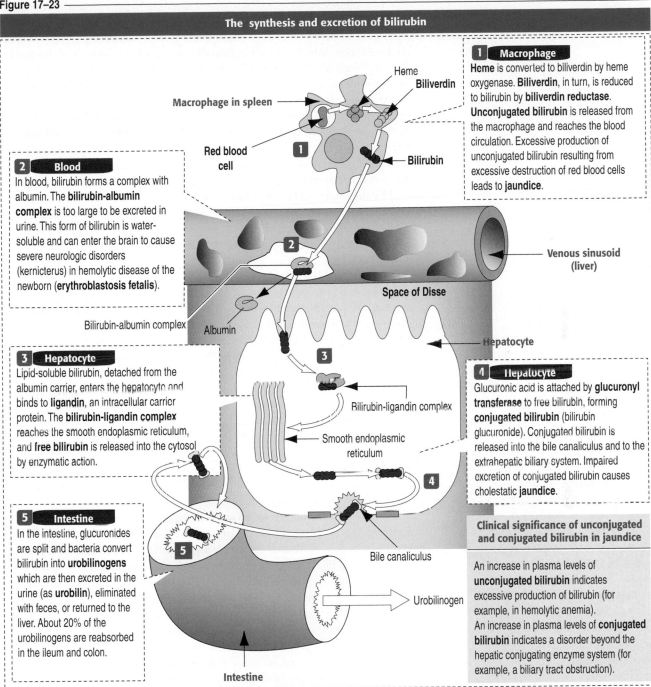

The synthesis and excretion of bilirubin

1 Macrophage

Heme is converted to biliverdin by heme oxygenase. **Biliverdin**, in turn, is reduced to bilirubin by **biliverdin reductase**. **Unconjugated bilirubin** is released from the macrophage and reaches the blood circulation. Excessive production of unconjugated bilirubin resulting from excessive destruction of red blood cells leads to **jaundice**.

2 Blood

In blood, bilirubin forms a complex with albumin. The **bilirubin-albumin complex** is too large to be excreted in urine. This form of bilirubin is water-soluble and can enter the brain to cause severe neurologic disorders (kernicterus) in hemolytic disease of the newborn (**erythroblastosis fetalis**).

3 Hepatocyte

Lipid-soluble bilirubin, detached from the albumin carrier, enters the hepatocyte and binds to **ligandin**, an intracellular carrier protein. The **bilirubin-ligandin complex** reaches the smooth endoplasmic reticulum, and **free bilirubin** is released into the cytosol by enzymatic action.

4 Hepatocyte

Glucuronic acid is attached by **glucuronyl transferase** to free bilirubin, forming **conjugated bilirubin** (bilirubin glucuronide). Conjugated bilirubin is released into the bile canaliculus and to the extrahepatic biliary system. Impaired excretion of conjugated bilirubin causes cholestatic **jaundice**.

5 Intestine

In the intestine, glucuronides are split and bacteria convert bilirubin into **urobilinogens** which are then excreted in the urine (as **urobilin**), eliminated with feces, or returned to the liver. About 20% of the urobilinogens are reabsorbed in the ileum and colon.

Clinical significance of unconjugated and conjugated bilirubin in jaundice

An increase in plasma levels of **unconjugated bilirubin** indicates excessive production of bilirubin (for example, in hemolytic anemia).
An increase in plasma levels of **conjugated bilirubin** indicates a disorder beyond the hepatic conjugating enzyme system (for example, a biliary tract obstruction).

Heme
Biliverdin
Macrophage in spleen
Red blood cell
Bilirubin
Venous sinusoid (liver)
Space of Disse
Bilirubin-albumin complex
Albumin
Hepatocyte
Bilirubin-ligandin complex
Smooth endoplasmic reticulum
Bile canaliculus
Urobilinogen
Intestine

Metabolism of bilirubin

Bilirubin is the end product of heme catabolism and about 85% originates from senescent red blood cells destroyed mainly in the spleen by macrophages (Figure 17–23).

Bilirubin is released into the circulation where it is bound to albumin and transported to the liver. **Unlike albumin-bound bilirubin, free bilirubin is toxic to the brain.** Recall from our discussion of **erythroblastosis fetalis** (see Chapter 6, Blood and Hematopoiesis), that an antibody-induced hemolytic disease in the newborn is caused by blood group incompatibility between mother and fetus. The hemolytic process results in hyperbilirubinemia caused by elevated amounts of **free bilirubin**, which causes irreversible damage of the central nervous system (**kernicterus**).

When albumin-conjugated bilirubin reaches the hepatic sinusoids, the **albumin-bilirubin complex** dissociates, and bilirubin is transported across the plasma membrane of hepatocytes after binding to a plasma membrane receptor. Inside the hepatocyte, bilirubin binds to **ligandin**, a protein that prevents bilirubin reflux into the circulation. The **bilirubin-ligandin complex** is transported to the smooth endoplasmic reticulum, where **bilirubin is conjugated to glucuronic acid** by the uridine diphosphate (**UDP**)–**glucuronyl transferase system**. This reaction results in the formation of a **water-soluble bilirubin diglucuronide**, which diffuses through the cytosol into the bile canaliculus, where it is secreted into the bile.

In the small intestine, conjugated bilirubin in bile remains intact until it reaches the distal portion of the small intestine and colon, where **free bilirubin is generated by the intestinal bacterial flora**. Unconjugated bilirubin is then reduced to **urobilinogen**. Most urobilinogen is excreted in the feces. A small portion returns to the liver following absorption by a process known as **enterohepatic bile circulation**. Another small fraction is excreted in the urine.

Composition of the bile

The human liver produces about 600 mL of bile per day. The bile consists of **organic components** (such as **bile acids**, the major component; **phospholipids**, mainly lecithins; **cholesterol**; and **bile pigments, bilirubin**), and **inorganic components** (predominantly Na^+ and Cl^- ions).

Bile acids (cholic acid, chenodeoxycholic acid, deoxycholic acid, and lithocholic acid) are synthesized by the hepatocytes. Cholic and chenodeoxycholic acids are synthesized from cholesterol as a precursor and are called **primary bile acids**. Deoxycholic and lithocholic acids are called **secondary bile acids** because they are produced in the intestinal lumen by the action of intestinal bacteria on the primary bile acids.

The synthetic bile acid pathway is the major mechanism of elimination of cholesterol from the body. **Micelles** are formed by the aggregation of bile acid molecules conjugated to taurine or glycine. Cholesterol is located inside the micelles. Bile pigments are not components of the micelles.

Bile secreted by the liver is stored in the gallbladder and released into the duodenum during a meal to facilitate the breakdown and absorption of fats (see Figure 16–9 in Chapter 16, Lower Digestive Segment). About 90% of both primary and secondary bile acids are absorbed from the intestinal lumen by enterocytes and transported back to the liver through the portal vein. This process is known as **enterohepatic circulation**. The absorption of bile acids by the enterocyte is mediated at the apical plasma membrane by an Na^+-dependent transporter protein and released through the basolateral plasma membrane by an Na^+-independent anion exchanger.

As we have already seen, bilirubin is not absorbed in the intestine. Bilirubin is reduced to **urobilinogen** by bacteria in the distal small intestine and colon (see Figure 17–23). Urobilinogen is partially secreted in the feces, part returns to the liver through the portal vein, and some is excreted in urine as **urobilin**, the oxidized form of urobilinogen.

Bile acids establish an osmotic gradient that mobilizes water and electrolytes into the bile canaliculus. HCO_3^- ions, secreted by epithelial cells lining the bile ducts, are added to the bile which becomes alkaline as Na^+ and Cl^- ions and water are absorbed. **Secretin** increases the active transport of HCO_3^- into the bile.

The flow of bile into the duodenum depends on (1) the secretory pressure generated by the actively bile-secreting hepatocytes, and (2) the flow resistance in the bile duct and **sphincter of Oddi**.

The sphincter of Oddi is a thickening of the circular muscle layer of the bile duct at the duodenal junction. During fasting, the sphincter of Oddi is closed and bile flows into the gallbladder. The gallbladder's ability to concentrate bile 5 to 20 times compensates for the limited storage capacity of the gallbladder (20 to 50 mL of fluid) and the continuous production of bile by the liver.

Bile secretion during meal digestion is initiated by the **cholecystokinin**-induced contraction of the muscularis of the gallbladder in response to lipids in the intestinal lumen, assisted by the muscular activities of the common bile duct, the sphincter of Oddi, and the duodenum. Cholecystokinin stimulates the relaxation of the sphincter of Oddi, enabling bile to enter the duodenum. Note that **cholecystokinin has opposite effects**: it stimulates **muscle contraction** of the **gallbladder** and induces **muscle relaxation** of the **sphincter of Oddi**.

Figure 17–24

The gallbladder

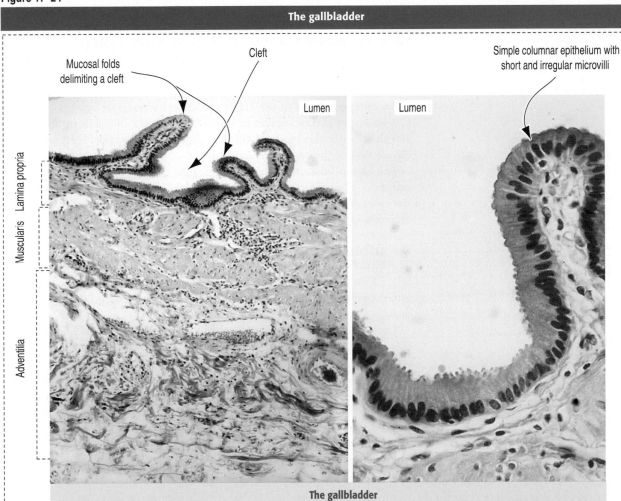

The gallbladder

The major functions of the gallbladder are:
1. Concentration (up to 10-fold) and storage of bile between meals.
2. Release of bile by contraction of the muscularis in response to **cholecystokinin** stimulation (produced by enteroendocrine cells in the duodenum) and **neural stimuli**, together with **relaxation of the sphincter of Oddi** (a muscular ring surrounding the opening of the bile duct in the wall of the duodenum).
3. Regulation of hydrostatic pressure within the biliary tract.

Clinical significance
Cholestasis defines the impaired formation and excretion of the bile at the level of the hepatocyte (**intrahepatic cholestasis**) or a structural (tumor of the pancreas or biliary tract—cholangiocarcinoma) or mechanical (**cholelithiasis**, produced by gallstones) perturbation in the excretion of bile (**extrahepatic cholestasis**). Clinically, cholestasis is detected by (1) the presence in blood of **bilirubin** and bile acids, secreted into bile under normal conditions; (2) elevation in serum of **alkaline phosphatase** (an enzyme associated with the plasma membrane of the bile canaliculus); (3) **radiologic examination** (many gallstones are radiopaque and can be detected on a plain radiograph) .

Clinical significance: Pathologic conditions affecting bile secretion

Because bile secretion involves hepatocytes, bile ducts, gallbladder, and intestine, any perturbation along this pathway can result in a pathologic condition. For example, destruction of hepatocytes by viral infection (**viral hepatitis**) and toxins can determine a decrease in bile production as well as an increase in bilirubin in blood (**jaundice**).

Obstruction of the passages by **gallstones**, **infection**, or **tumors** can block the flow of bile, with bile reflux to the liver and then to the systemic circulation. Intestinal abnormal function can compromise the enterohepatic circulation, in particular the removal of bile salts that can cause diarrhea upon entering the colon.

Clinical significance: Hyperbilirubinemia

Several diseases occur when one or more of the metabolic steps of bilirubin formation are disrupted. A characteristic feature of these diseases is **hyperbilirubinemia**—an increase in the concentration of bilirubin in the blood (more than 0.1 mg/mL).

An inherited defect in the **UDP-glucuronyl transferase system**, known as **Crigler-Najjar disease**, results in failure to conjugate bilirubin in hepatocytes and the absence of conjugated bilirubin diglucuronide in bile. Infants with this disease develop **bilirubin encephalopathy**.

The **Dubin-Johnson syndrome** is a familial disease caused by a **defect in the transport of conjugated bilirubin to the bile canaliculus**. In addition to the transport of conjugated bilirubin, there is a general defect in the transport and excretion of organic anions in these patients.

The gallbladder

The main functions of the gallbladder are **storage**, **concentration**, and **release of bile**. Dilute bile from the hepatic ducts is transported through the cystic duct into the gallbladder. After concentration, bile is discharged into the common bile duct.

The wall of the gallbladder consists of a **mucosa**, a **muscularis**, and an **adventitia** (Figure 17–24). The portion of the gallbladder that does not face the liver is covered by the peritoneum.

The mucosa displays multiple **folds** lined by a **simple columnar epithelium** and is supported by a lamina propria that contains a **vascular plexus**. The mucosa creates deep clefts known as **Rokitansky-Aschoff sinuses**. In the **neck region** of the gallbladder, the lamina propria contains **tubuloacinar glands**.

There is no submucosa in the gallbladder. The **muscularis** is represented by smooth muscle bundles associated with collagen and elastic fibers.

Learning objectives

Part V, The Endocrine System, includes Chapter 18, **Neuroendocrine System**, and Chapter 19, **Endocrine System**. The coordinated activities of these two systems are controlled by complex negative and positive **feedback loops**. The endocrine system consists of groups of secretory cells, forming a gland, which secrete potent chemical signaling substances—hormones—into the blood. The chemical agent is then carried by the blood to target cells, where a response is stimulated. Hormones are chemical messengers that ensure specific intercellular communication. The communicating cells may be close to each other or widely distributed throughout the body.

In Chapter 18, **Neuroendocrine System**:

1. You will learn the histologic organization of the **hypophysis** and the **pineal gland** and their main hormone products. You will learn that the pineal gland secretes **melatonin**, which may be involved in the control of **circadian rhythms**.

2. You will learn that specific aggregates of neurons in the hypothalamus —called **nuclei**— synthesize and secrete one or more hormones, most of them peptide in nature, and that some of these hormones control the release of hormones produced in the anterior lobe of the hypophysis.

3. You will learn that hypothalamic hormones are released in a **pulsatile** rather than a continuous manner, and that this release is regulated by a **negative feedback mechanism**. Feedback is particularly important in controlling the endocrine activity of the hypothalamus and the anterior hypophysis.

4. You will learn how hormones of the hypothalamus, transported to the posterior lobe of the hypophysis, regulate the release of milk by the breast during lactation, the contraction of the uterus during parturition, and the fluid balance of the body by influencing the volume of urine excreted by the kidney.

In Chapter 19, **Endocrine System**:

1. You will learn how to distinguish the cellular features of polypeptide- and steroid-producing cells.

2. You will learn that hormones of the anterior lobe of the hypophysis regulate the endocrine activity of several organs and also that **glucose** and **calcium** are two additional regulators of endocrine cell function.

3. You will review the basic principles learned in Chapter 3, **Cell Signaling**, to understand the mechanisms of **polypeptide hormones**, which act on membrane-bound receptors, and **steroid hormones**, which bind mainly to intracellular receptors.

4. You will learn how disturbances in endocrine function can give rise to diseases involving more than one organ system.

18. NEUROENDOCRINE SYSTEM

Highlights of the hypothalamohypophysial system

The hypothalamus and the hypophysis (also known as the **pituitary**) form an integrated neuroendocrine network known as the **hypothalamohypophysial system**.

The hypothalamohypophysial system consists of two components: (1) the **hypothalamic adenohypophysial system**, connecting the hypothalamus to the anterior hypophysis; and (2) the **hypothalamic neurohypophysial system**, linking the hypothalamus to the posterior hypophysis.

The **hypothalamus**, corresponding to the floor of the diencephalon and forming part of the walls of the third ventricle, consists of clusters of neurons, called **nuclei**, some of which secrete hormones. These **neuroendocrine cells** are located **behind** the blood-brain barrier, but their secretory products are released **outside** the blood-brain barrier.

The neuroendocrine cells of the hypothalamus exert **positive** and **negative** effects on the pituitary gland through peptides called **releasing** and **inhibitory hormones** or **factors**, have a **very short response time** (fractions of a second) to neurotransmitters, and send **axons** into the neurohypophysis.

Axon terminals of the neuroendocrine cells in the **neurohypophysis** have abundant storage granules containing peptide hormones bound to a **carrier protein**, called **neurophysin**. Both hormones and carrier proteins are released by exocytosis into adjacent fenestrated capillaries under the control of neural stimuli.

The **anterior hypophysis** is highly vascularized. It has a fenestrated capillary plexus (called the **primary plexus**) in the lower hypothalamus, or pituitary stalk. The primary plexus is connected to a **secondary plexus** in the anterior lobe of the hypophysis by **portal veins**, forming the **hypothalamohypophysial portal circulation**.

Hormones from the anterior hypophysis are produced by epithelial cells, stored in granules —without a carrier protein— and released in a **cyclic**, **rhythmic**, or **pulsatile** manner into the secondary capillary plexus by endocrine stimuli.

The effects of hormones derived from the epithelial cells of the anterior hypophysis have a **longer response time** (minutes or hours) and can persist for as long as a day or even a month.

The hypophysis

The hypophysis (Gk. *hypo*, under; *physis*, growth) consists of two embryologically distinct tissues (Figure 18–1): (1) the **adenohypophysis**, the **glandular epithelial** portion; and (2) the **neurohypophysis**, the **neural** portion.

The **adenohypophysis** is formed by three subdivisions or parts. (1) The **pars distalis**, or **anterior lobe**, is the main part of the gland. (2) The **pars tuberalis** envelops, like a partial or total collar, the infundibular stem or stalk, a neural component. Together they make up the pituitary stalk. (3) The **pars intermedia**, or intermediate lobe, is rudimentary in the adult. It is a thin wedge separating the pars distalis from the neurohypophysis.

The **neurohypophysis** is formed by two subdivisions: the **pars nervosa**, or neural lobe, and the **infundibulum**. The infundibulum, in turn, consists of two components: the **infundibular process** and the **median eminence**, a funnel-like extension of the hypothalamus.

Embryologic origin of the hypophysis

The anterior hypophysis and neurohypophysis have different embryologic origins (Figure 18–2). The anterior hypophysis derives from an evagination (**pouch**

Figure 18–1

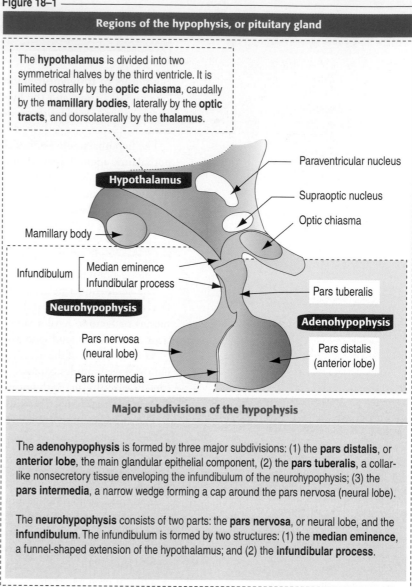

Regions of the hypophysis, or pituitary gland

The **hypothalamus** is divided into two symmetrical halves by the third ventricle. It is limited rostrally by the **optic chiasma**, caudally by the **mamillary bodies**, laterally by the **optic tracts**, and dorsolaterally by the **thalamus**.

Paraventricular nucleus

Supraoptic nucleus

Optic chiasma

Hypothalamus

Mamillary body

Infundibulum — Median eminence
Infundibular process

Pars tuberalis

Neurohypophysis

Adenohypophysis

Pars nervosa
(neural lobe)

Pars distalis
(anterior lobe)

Pars intermedia

Major subdivisions of the hypophysis

The **adenohypophysis** is formed by three major subdivisions: (1) the **pars distalis**, or **anterior lobe**, the main glandular epithelial component, (2) the **pars tuberalis**, a collar-like nonsecretory tissue enveloping the infundibulum of the neurohypophysis; (3) the **pars intermedia**, a narrow wedge forming a cap around the pars nervosa (neural lobe).

The **neurohypophysis** consists of two parts: the **pars nervosa**, or neural lobe, and the **infundibulum**. The infundibulum is formed by two structures: (1) the **median eminence**, a funnel-shaped extension of the hypothalamus; and (2) the **infundibular process**.

of Rathke) of the ectodermal lining of the future oral cavity extending upward toward the developing neurohypophysis. The neurohypophysis develops from an **infundibular downgrowth from the floor of the diencephalon**. The connecting stem attached to the pouch of Rathke disappears. However, the connecting stem of the neurohypophysis remains as the core of the infundibular stem, or stalk.

The pouch of Rathke develops into three different regions: (1) cells of the anterior surface of the pouch give rise to the pars distalis (the bulk of the gland), (2) cells of the posterior surface invade the infundibular process, (3) superior extensions of the pouch surround the infundibular stem, forming the pars tuberalis.

Blood supply of the hypophysis: The hypothalamohypophysial portal circulation

The **superior hypophysial artery** (derived from the internal carotid arteries, Figure 18–3) enters the median eminence and upper part of the infundibular stem and forms the **first sinusoidal capillary plexus (primary capillary plexus),** which receives the secretion of the neuroendocrine cells grouped in the **hypothalamic hypophysiotropic nuclei** of the hypothalamus.

Figure 18–2

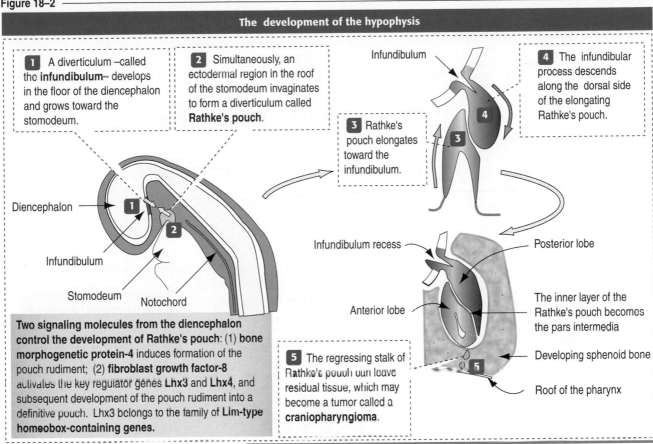

The development of the hypophysis

1 A diverticulum –called the **infundibulum**– develops in the floor of the diencephalon and grows toward the stomodeum.

2 Simultaneously, an ectodermal region in the roof of the stomodeum invaginates to form a diverticulum called **Rathke's pouch**.

Infundibulum

4 The infundibular process descends along the dorsal side of the elongating Rathke's pouch.

3 Rathke's pouch elongates toward the infundibulum.

Diencephalon

Infundibulum

Stomodeum   Notochord

Infundibulum recess

Anterior lobe

Posterior lobe

The inner layer of the Rathke's pouch becomes the pars intermedia

Developing sphenoid bone

Roof of the pharynx

Two signaling molecules from the diencephalon control the development of Rathke's pouch: (1) **bone morphogenetic protein-4** induces formation of the pouch rudiment; (2) **fibroblast growth factor-8** activates the key regulator genes **Lhx3** and **Lhx4**, and subsequent development of the pouch rudiment into a definitive pouch. Lhx3 belongs to the family of **Lim-type homeobox-containing genes**.

5 The regressing stalk of Rathke's pouch can leave residual tissue, which may become a tumor called a **craniopharyngioma**.

Capillaries arising from the primary capillary plexus project down the infundibulum and pars tuberalis to form the **portal veins. Capillaries arising from the portal veins form a secondary capillary plexus that supplies the anterior hypophysis and receives secretions from endocrine cells of the anterior hypophysis. There is no direct arterial blood supply to the anterior hypophysis.**

The hypothalamohypophysial portal system enables (1) the transport of hypothalamic releasing and inhibitory hormones from the primary capillary plexus to the hormone-producing epithelial cells of the anterior hypophysis; (2) the secretion of hormones from the anterior hypophysis into the secondary capillary plexus to the general circulation; and (3) the functional integration of the hypothalamus with the anterior hypophysis, provided by the **portal veins**.

A **third capillary plexus**, derived from the inferior hypophysial artery, supplies the neurohypophysis. This third capillary plexus collects secretions from neuroendocrine cells present in the hypothalamus. The secretory products (vasopressin and oxytocin) are transported along the axons into the neurohypophysis.

Histology of the pars distalis (anterior lobe)

The pars distalis is formed by three components: (1) cords of **epithelial cells** (Figure 18–4), (2) minimal supporting **connective tissue stroma**; and (3) **fenestrated capillaries** (sinusoids, Figure 18–5), which are part of the secondary capillary plexus.

There is no blood-brain barrier in the anterior hypophysis.

The epithelial cells are arranged in cords surrounding fenestrated capillaries carrying blood from the hypothalamus. Secretory hormones diffuse into a network of capillaries, which drain into the hypophysial veins and from there into the venous sinuses.

There are three distinct types of endocrine cells in the anterior hypophysis (see

Figure 18–3

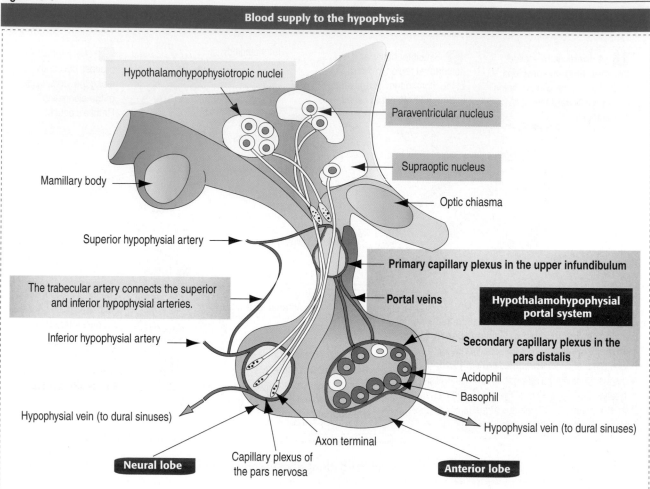

Blood supply to the hypophysis

- Hypothalamohypophysiotropic nuclei
- Paraventricular nucleus
- Supraoptic nucleus
- Mamillary body
- Optic chiasma
- Superior hypophysial artery
- **Primary capillary plexus in the upper infundibulum**
- The trabecular artery connects the superior and inferior hypophysial arteries.
- **Portal veins**
- **Hypothalamohypophysial portal system**
- Inferior hypophysial artery
- **Secondary capillary plexus in the pars distalis**
- Acidophil
- Basophil
- Hypophysial vein (to dural sinuses)
- Hypophysial vein (to dural sinuses)
- **Neural lobe**
- Axon terminal
- Capillary plexus of the pars nervosa
- **Anterior lobe**

Blood supply to the pituitary gland

The **superior hypophysial artery** forms a **primary capillary plexus** in the infundibulum (formed by the median eminence and infundibular stem). The primary capillary plexus receives releasing and inhibitory hormones from the neuroendocrine **hypothalamohypophysiotropic nuclei**.

The primary capillary plexus is drained by **portal veins**. Portal veins supply blood to the **secondary capillary plexus**, with which basophils and acidophils are associated. By this mechanism, hypothalamic releasing and inhibitory factors act directly on cells of the pars distalis (anterior hypophysis) to regulate their endocrine function.

The primary and secondary capillary plexuses linked by the portal veins form the **hypothalamohypophysial portal system**.

The **inferior hypophysial artery** supplies the pars nervosa, forming a capillary plexus, which collects vasopressin (antidiuretic hormone) and oxytocin produced by neuroendocrine cells of the supraoptic and paraventricular nuclei, respectively.

The superior and inferior hypophysial arteries are connected by the **trabecular artery**.

Figure 18–4): (1) **acidophils** (cells that stain with an acidic dye), which are prevalent at the sides of the gland; (2) **basophils** (cells that stain with a basic dye and are periodic acid-Schiff [PAS]-positive), which are predominant in the middle of the gland; and (3) **chromophobes** (cells lacking cytoplasmic staining).

Acidophils secrete two major **peptide hormones: growth hormone** and **prolactin**. Basophils secrete **glycoprotein hormones: the gonadotropin follicle-stimu-**

Figure 18–4

Identification of basophil, acidophil, and chromophobe cells in the anterior hypophysis

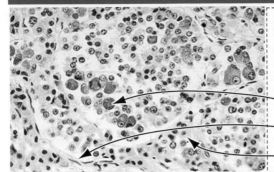

Hematoxylin-eosin staining (H&E)
The anterior hypophysis consists of clusters of epithelial cells adjacent to fenestrated capillaries. With H&E, the cytoplasm of **basophils** stains **blue-purple (glycoproteins)** and **acidophils light pink (proteins)**. Chromophobe cells display a very light pink cytoplasm.

Basophil

Fenestrated capillary

Acidophil

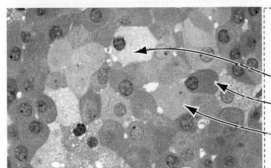

Trichrome stain (aniline blue, orange G, and azocarmine)
With the trichrome stain, the cytoplasm of **basophils** stains **blue-purple** and **acidophils orange**. Chromophobe cells stain light blue. Red blood cells in the lumen of the capillaries stain **deep orange**.

Basophil

Chromophobe

Acidophil

Red blood cells

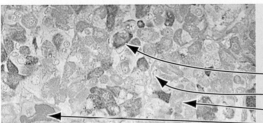

Plastic section stained with basic fuchsin and hematoxylin
The polygonal shape of the epithelial cells of the anterior hypophysis is well defined in this preparation. **The cytoplasm of basophils stains dark pink, acidophils stain light pink, and chromophobe cells are unstained.**

Chromophobe

Basophil

Acidophil

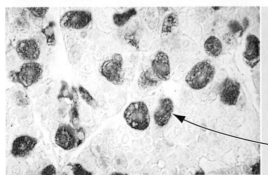

Immunohistochemistry (immunoperoxidase)
An antibody against the β chain of FSH has been used to identify gonadotrophs within the anterior hypophysis in this illustration.
The use of specific antibodies against hormones produced in the anterior hypophysis has enabled (1) the precise identification of all hormone-producing cells of the anterior hypophysis; (2) the identification of hormone-producing **adenomas**; and (3) the elucidation of the negative and positive feedback pathways regulating the secretion of hypophysial hormones.

FSH-secreting cell (classified as basophil by H&E staining)

lating hormone (FSH), **luteinizing hormone (LH)**, **thyroid-stimulating hormone (TSH)**, and **adrenocorticotropic hormone (ACTH)**, or corticotropin. Chromophobes include cells that have depleted their hormone content and lost the staining affinity typical of acidophils and basophils.

The precise identification of the endocrine cells of the anterior hypophysis is by **immunohistochemistry**, which demonstrates their hormone content using specific antibodies (see Figure 18–4).

Hormones secreted by acidophils: Growth hormone and prolactin

Acidophils secrete **growth hormone**, also called **somatotropin**. These acidophilic cells, called **somatotrophs**, represent a large proportion (40% to 50%) of the cell

Figure 18–5

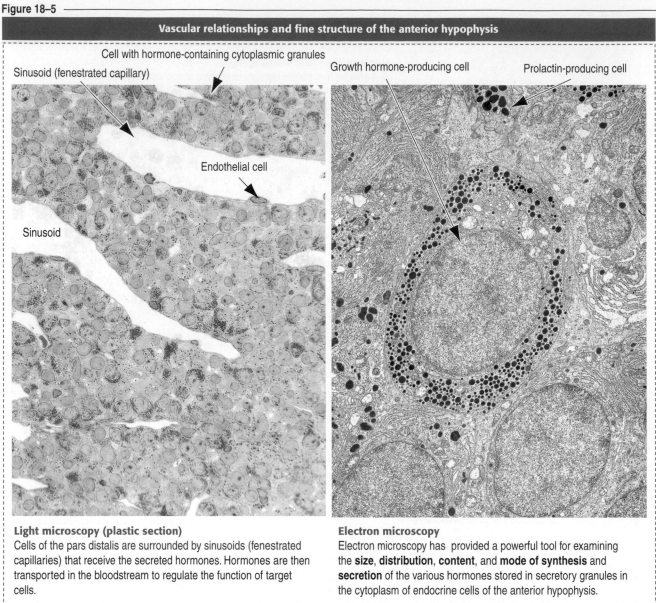

Vascular relationships and fine structure of the anterior hypophysis

Cell with hormone-containing cytoplasmic granules

Sinusoid (fenestrated capillary)

Endothelial cell

Sinusoid

Growth hormone-producing cell

Prolactin-producing cell

Light microscopy (plastic section)
Cells of the pars distalis are surrounded by sinusoids (fenestrated capillaries) that receive the secreted hormones. Hormones are then transported in the bloodstream to regulate the function of target cells.

Electron microscopy
Electron microscopy has provided a powerful tool for examining the **size**, **distribution**, **content**, and **mode of synthesis** and **secretion** of the various hormones stored in secretory granules in the cytoplasm of endocrine cells of the anterior hypophysis.

population of the anterior hypophysis. Prolactin-secreting cells, or **lactotrophs**, represent 15% to 20% of the cell population of the anterior hypophysis.

Growth hormone

Growth hormone is a peptide 191 amino acids in length (22 kDa). It has the following characteristics (Figure 18–6). (1) Growth hormone has structural homology similar to prolactin and human placental lactogen. There is some overlap in the activity of these three hormones. (2) It is released into the blood circulation in the form of **pulses** throughout a 24-hour sleep-wake period, with **peak secretion occurring during the night and before awakening**. (3) Despite its name, growth hormone does not directly induce growth; rather, it acts by stimulating in hepatocytes the production of **insulin-like growth factor-1** (IGF-1), also known as **somatomedin C**. The cell receptor for IGF-1 is similar to that for insulin (formed by dimers of two glycoproteins with integral cytoplasmic protein tyrosine kinase domains). (4) The release of growth hormone is regulated by two neuropeptides.

A **stimulatory** effect is caused by **growth hormone–releasing hormone** (GHRH; a peptide of 44 amino acids). An **inhibitory** effect is produced by **somatostatin** (a peptide of 14 amino acids) and by **elevated blood glucose levels**. Both GHRH and somatostatin derive from the hypothalamus.

IGF-1 (7.5 kDa) stimulates the overall growth of bone and soft tissues. In children, IGF-1 stimulates the growth of long bones at the epiphyseal plates. Clinicians measure IGF-1 in blood to determine growth hormone function. **A drop in IGF-1 serum levels stimulates the release of growth hormone.**

IGF target cells secrete several **IGF-binding proteins** and **proteases**. The latter can regulate the delivery and action of IGF on target cells by reducing available IGF-binding proteins.

Figure 18–6

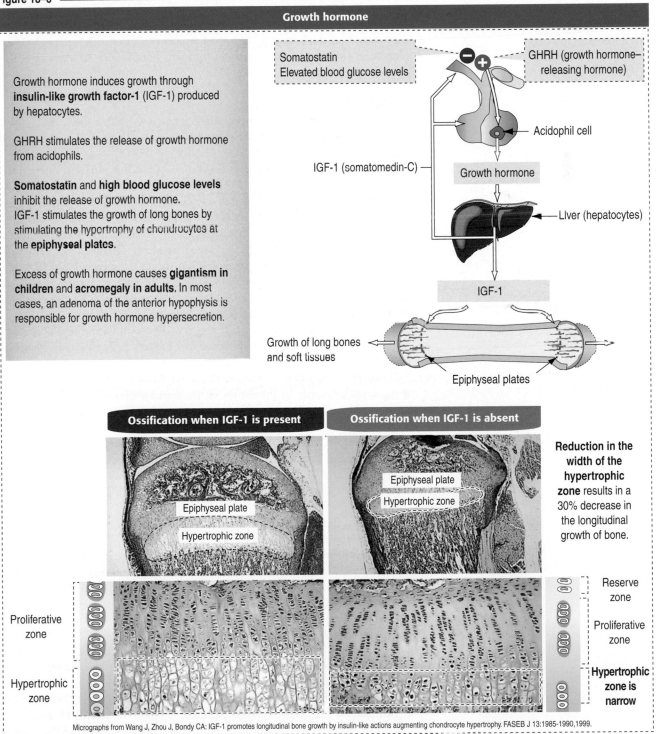

Growth hormone

Growth hormone induces growth through **insulin-like growth factor-1** (IGF-1) produced by hepatocytes.

GHRH stimulates the release of growth hormone from acidophils.

Somatostatin and **high blood glucose levels** inhibit the release of growth hormone.
IGF-1 stimulates the growth of long bones by stimulating the hypertrophy of chondrocytes at the **epiphyseal plates**.

Excess of growth hormone causes **gigantism in children** and **acromegaly in adults**. In most cases, an adenoma of the anterior hypophysis is responsible for growth hormone hypersecretion.

Somatostatin
Elevated blood glucose levels

GHRH (growth hormone–releasing hormone)

Acidophil cell

IGF-1 (somatomedin-C)

Growth hormone

Liver (hepatocytes)

IGF-1

Growth of long bones and soft tissues

Epiphyseal plates

Ossification when IGF-1 is present

Ossification when IGF-1 is absent

Epiphyseal plate

Hypertrophic zone

Epiphyseal plate

Hypertrophic zone

Reduction in the width of the hypertrophic zone results in a 30% decrease in the longitudinal growth of bone.

Proliferative zone

Hypertrophic zone

Reserve zone

Proliferative zone

Hypertrophic zone is narrow

Micrographs from Wang J, Zhou J, Bondy CA: IGF-1 promotes longitudinal bone growth by insulin-like actions augmenting chondrocyte hypertrophy. FASEB J 13:1985-1990,1999.

Clinical significance: Gigantism (in children) and acromegaly (in adults)

Excessive secretion of growth hormone can occur in the presence of a benign tumor called an **adenoma**.

When the growth hormone-secreting tumor occurs during childhood and puberty, at a time when the epiphyseal plates are still active, **gigantism** (Gk. *gigas*, giant; extremely tall stature) is observed. If excessive growth hormone secretion occurs in the adult, when the epiphyseal plates are inactive, **acromegaly** (Gk. *akron*, end or extremity; *megas*, large) develops. In acromegaly, the hands, feet, jaw, and soft tissues become enlarged. Long bones do not grow in length, but cartilage (nose, ears) and membranous bones (mandible and calvarium) continue to grow, leading to gross deformities.

A growth hormone-secreting adenoma does not show the typical pulsatile secretory pattern of the hormone. Growth hormone secretion is not suppressed by glucose. A **decrease** in the secretion of growth hormone in children results in short stature (**dwarfism**).

Prolactin

Prolactin is a 199–amino acid single-chain protein (22 kDa). Prolactin, growth hormone, and human placental lactogen share some amino acid homology and overlapping activity,

The predominant action of prolactin is to stimulate the initiation and maintenance of **lactation** post partum (Figure 18–7). Lactation involves the following. (1) **Mammogenesis**, the growth and development of the mammary gland, is stimulated primarily by estrogen and progesterone in coordination with prolactin and human placental lactogen. (2) **Lactogenesis**, the initiation of lactation, is triggered by prolactin acting on the developed mammary gland by the actions of estrogens and progesterone. Lactation is inhibited during pregnancy by high levels of estrogen and progesterone, which decline at delivery. Either estradiol or prolactin antagonists are used clinically to stop lactation. (3) **Galactopoiesis**, the maintenance of milk production, requires both prolactin and oxytocin.

The effect of prolactin, placental lactogen and steroids on the development of the lactating mammary gland is discussed in Chapter 23, Fertilization, Placentation, and Lactation.

Unlike other hormones of the anterior hypophysis, **the secretion of prolactin is regulated primarily by inhibition rather than by stimulation**. The main inhibitor is **dopamine**. Dopamine secretion is stimulated by prolactin to inhibit its own secretion.

A **stimulatory** effect on prolactin release is exerted by **prolactin-releasing factor** (PRF) and **thyrotropin-releasing hormone** (TRH). Prolactin is released from **acidophils** in a pulsatile fashion, coinciding with and following each period of suckling. **Intermittent surges of prolactin stimulate milk synthesis.**

Clinical significance: Hyperprolactinemia

Prolactin-secreting tumors alter the hypothalamohypophysial-gonadal axis, leading to gonadotropin deficiency. Hypersecretion of prolactin in women can be associated with **infertility,** caused by the lack of **ovulation** and **oligomenorrhea** or **amenorrhea** (dysfunctional uterine bleeding). A decrease in fertility and libido is found in males. These antifertility effects are found in both sexes and are usually reversible. **Galactorrhea** (nonpuerperal milk secretion) is a common problem in **hyperprolactinemia** and can also occur in males.

Hormones secreted by basophils: Gonadotropins, TSH, and ACTH

Gonadotropins (FSH and LH) and TSH have common features: (1) they are glycoproteins (hence the PAS-positive staining of basophils), and (2) they consist of **two chains**. The α chain is a glycoprotein common to FSH, LH, and TSH, but the β chain is specific for each hormone. Therefore, **the β chain confers**

Figure 18–7

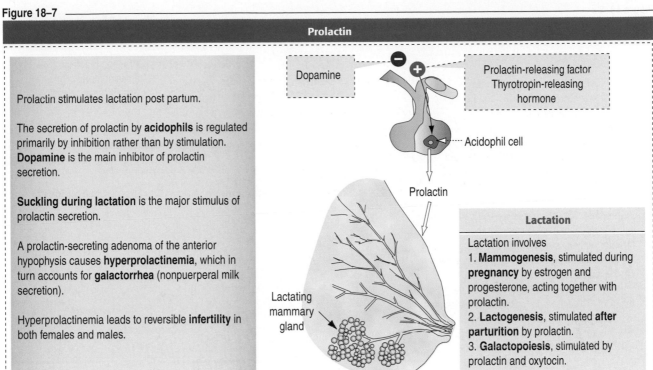

Prolactin

Prolactin stimulates lactation post partum.

The secretion of prolactin by **acidophils** is regulated primarily by inhibition rather than by stimulation. **Dopamine** is the main inhibitor of prolactin secretion.

Suckling during lactation is the major stimulus of prolactin secretion.

A prolactin-secreting adenoma of the anterior hypophysis causes **hyperprolactinemia**, which in turn accounts for **galactorrhea** (nonpuerperal milk secretion).

Hyperprolactinemia leads to reversible **infertility** in both females and males.

Dopamine

Prolactin-releasing factor
Thyrotropin-releasing hormone

Acidophil cell

Prolactin

Lactating mammary gland

Lactation

Lactation involves
1. **Mammogenesis**, stimulated during **pregnancy** by estrogen and progesterone, acting together with prolactin.
2. **Lactogenesis**, stimulated **after parturition** by prolactin.
3. **Galactopoiesis**, stimulated by prolactin and oxytocin.

specificity to the hormone.

Gonadotropins: FSH and LH

Gonadotrophs (gonadotropin-secreting cells, Figure 18–8) secrete **both FSH and LH**. Gonadotrophs constitute about 10% of the total cell population of the anterior hypophysis.

The release of gonadotropins is stimulated by **gonadotropin-releasing hormone (GnRH)**, a decapeptide produced in the **arcuate** and **preoptic areas** of the hypothalamus. GnRH, also called **luteinizing hormone-releasing hormone (LHRH)**, is released in pulses like the other hormones of the anterior hypophysis. **A single basophil can synthesize and release both FSH and LH.**

In the female, **FSH** stimulates the development of the ovarian follicles by a process called **folliculogenesis**. In the male, FSH acts on **Sertoli cells** in the testis to stimulate the aromatization of estrogens from androgens and the production of **androgen-binding protein**, jointly with testosterone.

In the female, **LH** stimulates **steroidogenesis** in the ovarian follicle and corpus luteum. In the male, LH controls the rate of **testosterone** synthesis by **Leydig cells** in the testis. The function of FSH and LH in the male is analyzed in Chapter 20, Spermatogenesis.

The release of FSH and GnRH is **inhibited** by (1) **inhibin**, a **heterodimer** protein formed by α- and β-peptide chains, secreted by the male and female target cells (Sertoli and follicular cells and cells of the anterior hypophysis), and (2) **estradiol**.

The release of FSH in both females and males is **enhanced** by a homodimer protein, called **activin**, secreted by the anterior hypophysis. It consists of two β chains. Little is known about what controls αβ (inhibin) and ββ (activin) dimerization. The release of GnRH and LH is **inhibited** by **testosterone** in the male and by **progesterone** in the female.

Clinical significance: Infertility

The secretion of gonadotropins can decrease when there is a deficient secretion of

Figure 18–8

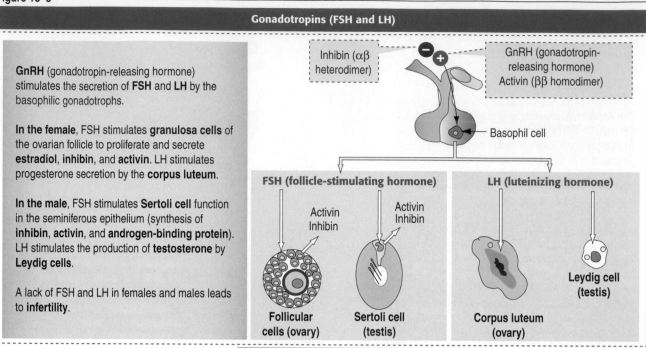

Gonadotropins (FSH and LH)

GnRH (gonadotropin-releasing hormone) stimulates the secretion of **FSH** and **LH** by the basophilic gonadotrophs.

In the female, FSH stimulates **granulosa cells** of the ovarian follicle to proliferate and secrete **estradiol**, **inhibin**, and **activin**. LH stimulates progesterone secretion by the **corpus luteum**.

In the male, FSH stimulates **Sertoli cell** function in the seminiferous epithelium (synthesis of **inhibin**, **activin**, and **androgen-binding protein**). LH stimulates the production of **testosterone** by **Leydig cells**.

A lack of FSH and LH in females and males leads to **infertility**.

Inhibin ($\alpha\beta$ heterodimer)

GnRH (gonadotropin-releasing hormone)
Activin ($\beta\beta$ homodimer)

Basophil cell

FSH (follicle-stimulating hormone)

Activin
Inhibin

Activin
Inhibin

Follicular cells (ovary)

Sertoli cell (testis)

LH (luteinizing hormone)

Leydig cell (testis)

Corpus luteum (ovary)

GnRH, caused by anorexia or a tumor of the hypophysis, which can destroy the gonadotrophs, thereby decreasing FSH and LH secretion.

A decrease in fertility and reproductive functions can be observed in females and males. Females can have menstrual disorders. Small testes and infertility can be seen in males (a condition known as **hypogonadotropic hypogonadism**) when GnRH secretion is deficient.

Castration (**ovariectomy** in the female and **orchidectomy** in the male) causes a significant **increase** in the synthesis of FSH and LH as a result of a **loss of feedback inhibition**. Hyperfunctional gonadotropic cells are large and vacuolated and are called **castration cells**.

Thyroid-stimulating hormone

Thyrotropic cells represent about 5% of the total population of the anterior hypophysis.

TSH is the regulatory hormone of **thyroid function** (Figure 18–9) and **growth**. The mechanism of action of TSH on thyroid cell function is discussed in the thyroid gland section of Chapter 19, Endocrine System.

Thyrotropin-releasing hormone (TRH), a three–amino acid peptide produced in the hypothalamus, **stimulates** the synthesis and release of TSH from **basophils**. TRH also stimulates the release of prolactin.

The release of TSH is **inhibited** by increased concentrations of the thyroid hormones triiodothyronine (T_3) and thyroxine (T_4).

Clinical significance: Hypothyroidism

A deficiency in the secretion of TSH (observed in rare cases of congenital hypoplasia of the hypophysis) produces **hypothyroidism**, characterized by reduced cell metabolism and temperature and basal metabolic rate and mental lethargy.

Hypothyroidism can also result from a disease of the thyroid gland or a deficiency in dietary iodine. We will discuss **hyperthyroidism** in the thyroid gland section of Chapter 19, Endocrine System.

ACTH

ACTH, or **corticotropin**, is a **single-chain** protein, 39 amino acids in length (4.5

Figure 18–9

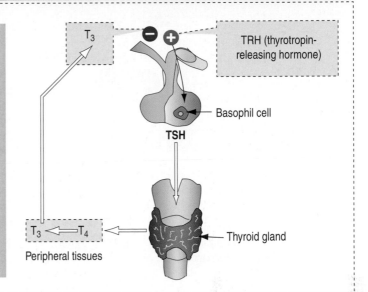

Thyroid-stimulating hormone (TSH)

Thyrotropin-releasing hormone **TRH**, a tripeptide, modulates the synthesis and release of TSH (thyroid-stimulating hormone) from basophils.

TSH is a glycoprotein that binds to a receptor in the plasma membrane of thyroid follicular epithelial cells. The hormone-receptor complex stimulates the formation of cAMP. The production of the thyroid hormones T_3 (triiodothyronine) and T_4 (thyroxine) is stimulated by cAMP.

Some T_4 is converted to T_3 in peripheral tissues. **T_3 is more active than T_4 and has a negative feedback (inhibitory) action on TSH synthesis and release.**

kDa), with a short circulating time (7 to 12 minutes). Its primary action is **to stimulate growth and steroid synthesis** in the zona fasciculata and reticularis of the adrenal cortex. The zona glomerulosa of the adrenal cortex is under the control of angiotensin II (see the adrenal gland section of Chapter 19, Endocrine System). The effects of ACTH on the adrenal cortex are mediated by cyclic adenosine monophosphate (cAMP). ACTH also acts beyond the adrenal gland by increasing skin pigmentation and lipolysis.

ACTH derives from a large glycosylated precursor called **pro-opiomelanocortin** (POMC, 31 kDa), processed in the anterior hypophysis. The products of POMC are the following (Figure 18–10):

1. An **N-terminal peptide** of unknown function, **ACTH**, and β-**lipotrophic hormone** (β-LPH). These three POMC derivatives are secreted by the anterior hypophysis.

2. The cleavage products of β-LPH, γ-**LPH**, and β-**endorphin** are released into the circulation. β-LPH and γ-LPH have **lipolytic action**, but their precise role in fat mobilization in humans is unknown.

3. γ-LPH contains the amino acid sequence of β-**melanocyte–stimulating hormone** (β-MSH; not secreted in humans). β-Endorphin contains the sequences of **met-enkephalin** (met-enk). There is no evidence that β-endorphin is cleaved in the hypophysis to form met-enk.

4. ACTH is cleaved to α-MSH and **corticotropin-like intermediate peptide** (CLIP). α-MSH and CLIP hormones, found in species with hypophysis with a prominent pars intermedia, cause dispersion of melanin granules in melanophores and darkening of the skin of many fish, amphibians, and reptiles.

The release of ACTH is controlled by the following (Figure 18–11):

1. A stimulatory effect determined by **corticotropin-releasing hormone** (CRH) from the hypothalamus. CRH co-localizes with **antidiuretic hormone** (ADH; see later, The neurohypophysis) in the paraventricular nuclei. Both ADH and angiotensin II potentiate the effect of CRH on the release of ACTH.

2. An **inhibitory** effect caused by high levels of **cortisol** in blood either by preventing the release of CRH, or by blocking the release of ACTH by basophil **corticotropic cells** (ACTH-secreting cells).

ACTH is secreted in a circadian manner (morning peaks followed by a slow decline afterward).

Figure 18–10

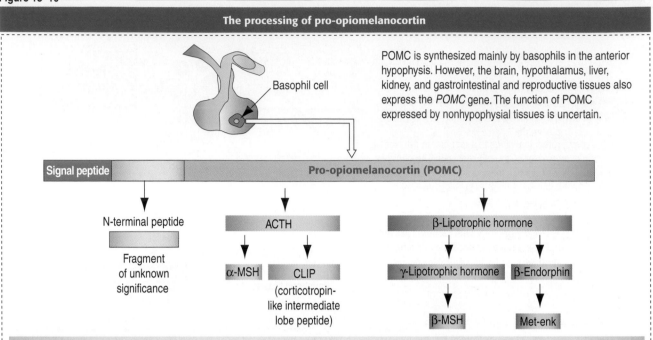

The processing of pro-opiomelanocortin

POMC is synthesized mainly by basophils in the anterior hypophysis. However, the brain, hypothalamus, liver, kidney, and gastrointestinal and reproductive tissues also express the *POMC* gene. The function of POMC expressed by nonhypophysial tissues is uncertain.

Basophil cell

| Signal peptide | Pro-opiomelanocortin (POMC) |

N-terminal peptide

Fragment of unknown significance

ACTH

α-MSH CLIP (corticotropin-like intermediate lobe peptide)

β-Lipotrophic hormone

γ-Lipotrophic hormone β-Endorphin

β-MSH Met-enk

N-terminal peptide, ACTH, and β-lipotrophic hormone (β-LPH) are produced by the anterior hypophysis.

The cleavage products of β-LPH (γ-LPH and β-endorphin) are released into the circulation and may have a functional role in humans.

β-LPH and γ-LPH are lipolytic hormones and their role in fat mobilization in humans is not known.

γ-LPH gives rise to β-MSH. β-Endorphin contains the sequences of met-enkephalin (met-enk). There is no evidence that β-endorphin is cleaved in the hypophysis to form met-enk. β-MSH is not secreted in humans.

ACTH is cleaved to α-MSH and CLIP only in species with a prominent pars intermedia. α-MSH and β-MSH determine the dispersion of melanin granules in melanophores of fish, reptiles, and amphibians to darken the skin. The human hypophysis lacks a prominent pars intermedia (except during fetal development), and the processing of ACTH to α-MSH and CLIP (unknown function) does not occur.

Clinical significance: Cushing's disease

An ACTH-secreting adenoma of the hypophysis causes **Cushing's disease**. This disease is characterized by an increase in the production of cortisol by the zona fasciculata of the adrenal cortex (see the adrenal gland section in Chapter 19, Endocrine System), obesity, osteoporosis, and muscle wasting. A **reduction** in the secretion of ACTH results in diminished secretion of cortisol and in hypoglycemia.

A loss of ACTH decreases adrenal androgen secretion. In females, androgen deficiency causes loss of pubic and axillary hair. This effect is not observed in males because it is compensated for by testicular secretion of androgens.

The neurohypophysis

The neurohypophysis consists of three histologic components (Figures 18–12 and 18–13). (1) **Pituicytes**, resembling astrocytes, provide support to the axons. (2) **Axons**, derived from neuroendocrine cells (called **magnicellular neurons** because their cell bodies are large) of the **supraoptic** and **paraventricular nuclei**, make up the infundibulum and form the **hypothalamohypophysial tract**. Axons, with bulging intermittent segments and terminals (called **Herring bodies**) containing secretory products, are found in the pars nervosa (neural lobe). (3) **Fenestrated capillaries** are derived from the inferior hypophysial artery.

Figure 18–11

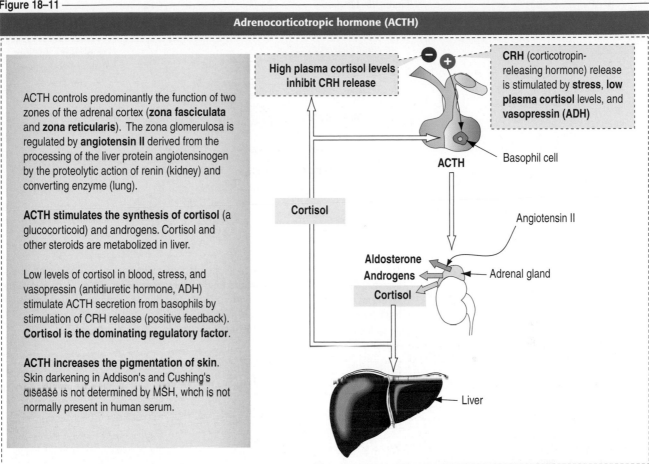

Adrenocorticotropic hormone (ACTH)

ACTH controls predominantly the function of two zones of the adrenal cortex (**zona fasciculata** and **zona reticularis**). The zona glomerulosa is regulated by **angiotensin II** derived from the processing of the liver protein angiotensinogen by the proteolytic action of renin (kidney) and converting enzyme (lung).

ACTH stimulates the synthesis of cortisol (a glucocorticoid) and androgens. Cortisol and other steroids are metabolized in liver.

Low levels of cortisol in blood, stress, and vasopressin (antidiuretic hormone, ADH) stimulate ACTH secretion from basophils by stimulation of CRH release (positive feedback). **Cortisol is the dominating regulatory factor.**

ACTH increases the pigmentation of skin. Skin darkening in Addison's and Cushing's disease is not determined by MSH, whch is not normally present in human serum.

High plasma cortisol levels inhibit CRH release

CRH (corticotropin-releasing hormone) release is stimulated by **stress**, **low plasma cortisol** levels, and **vasopressin (ADH)**

ACTH — Basophil cell

Cortisol

Angiotensin II

Aldosterone
Androgens — Adrenal gland
Cortisol

Liver

Pituicytes are astrocyte-like glial cells with abundant **glial fibrillary acidic proteins**, an intermediate filament protein, and a few **lipid droplets** in their cytoplasm. The cytoplasmic processes of pituicytes (Figure 18–14) (1) surround the axons derived from the neuroendocrine cells, (2) extend between the axon terminals and the basal lamina surrounding fenestrated capillaries, and (3) retract to enable the release into the blood of secretory granules stored in the axon terminals (see Figure 18–14).

Axons in the neurohypophysis derive from the **supraoptic nuclei** and the **paraventricular nuclei**.

Some neurons of the paraventricular nuclei are small and their axons project to the median eminence rather than to the pars nervosa. These neurons, called **parvicellular neurons** (Lat. *parvus*, small), secrete ADH and oxytocin entering the hypophysial portal blood at the median eminence. Large neurons of the supraoptic and paraventricular nuclei, called **magnicellular neurons** (Lat. *magnus*, large), give rise to axons forming the **hypothalamohypophysial tract**. The terminals of these neurons are located in the pars nervosa. Both the supraoptic and paraventricular nuclei contain neurons synthesizing ADH and oxytocin. However, **neurons of the supraoptic nuclei produce primarily ADH and the paraventricular nuclei synthesize primarily oxytocin**.

In addition to these two nuclei, the hypothalamus has additional nuclei, **the hypothalamohypophysiotropic nuclei**, with neurons producing releasing and inhibitory hormones to be discharged at the fenestrated capillaries of the primary plexus (see above, Blood supply of the hypophysis).

Although the neuroendocrine cells of the supraoptic and paraventricular nuclei are located **behind the blood-brain barrier**, their products are transported to nerve terminals and released **outside the blood-brain barrier** into fenestrated

Figure 18–12

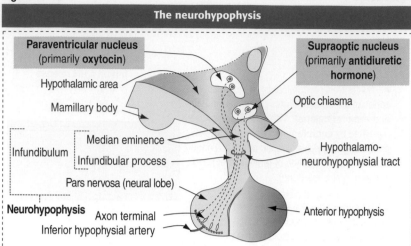

The neurohypophysis

The hormones **antidiuretic hormone** (or **arginine vasopressin**) and **oxytocin** are synthesized in the neurons of the **supraoptic** and **paraventricular nuclei**, respectively. The hormones are transported along the axons forming the **hypothalamoneurohypophysial tract**, together with the carrier protein **neurophysin**, and are released at the axon terminals. The hormones enter **fenestrated capillaries** derived from the inferior hypophysial artery.

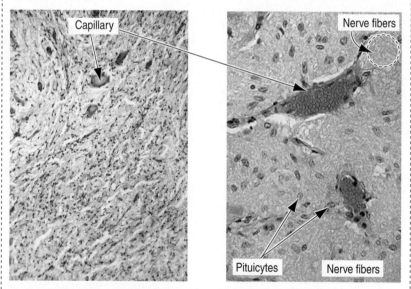

The neurohypophysis is formed by supporting neuroglial cells—the **pituicytes**—whose cytoplasmic processes surround the **unmyelinated nerve fibers** arising from neurons of the paraventricular and supraoptic nuclei. Abundant capillaries are visualized. Antidiuretic hormone and oxytocin accumulate temporarily in axon dilations, forming the **Herring bodies** (not seen in these photomicrographs).

capillaries.

Clinical significance: Diabetes insipidus

Oxytocin participates in the **contraction of smooth muscle**, in particular the **uterus during labor**, and **myoepithelial cells** lining the secretory acini and lactiferous ducts of the mammary gland to facilitate milk ejection (or **letdown of milk**) during lactation (Figure 18–15).

Antidiuretic hormone regulates water excretion in the kidney and is also a **potent vasoconstrictor at high doses** (see Figure 18–15). This is the basis for the alternative name vasopressin (arginine vasopressin, AVP). An increase in osmotic

Figure 18–13

Structure and function of the neuroendocrine cell

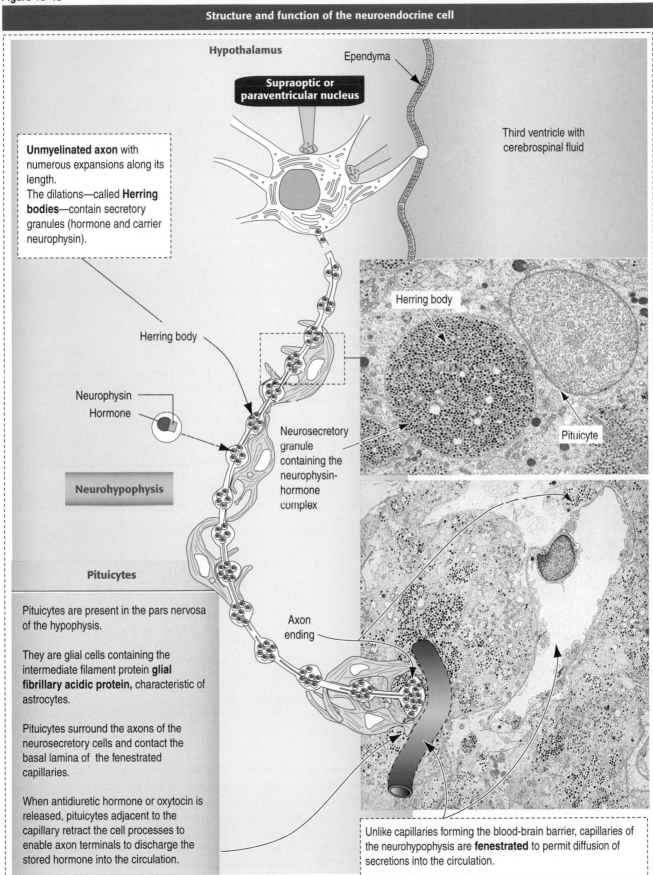

Hypothalamus

Supraoptic or paraventricular nucleus

Ependyma

Third ventricle with cerebrospinal fluid

Unmyelinated axon with numerous expansions along its length.
The dilations—called **Herring bodies**—contain secretory granules (hormone and carrier neurophysin).

Herring body

Neurophysin

Hormone

Neurohypophysis

Neurosecretory granule containing the neurophysin-hormone complex

Herring body

Pituicyte

Pituicytes

Pituicytes are present in the pars nervosa of the hypophysis.

They are glial cells containing the intermediate filament protein **glial fibrillary acidic protein,** characteristic of astrocytes.

Pituicytes surround the axons of the neurosecretory cells and contact the basal lamina of the fenestrated capillaries.

When antidiuretic hormone or oxytocin is released, pituicytes adjacent to the capillary retract the cell processes to enable axon terminals to discharge the stored hormone into the circulation.

Axon ending

Unlike capillaries forming the blood-brain barrier, capillaries of the neurohypophysis are **fenestrated** to permit diffusion of secretions into the circulation.

Figure 18–14

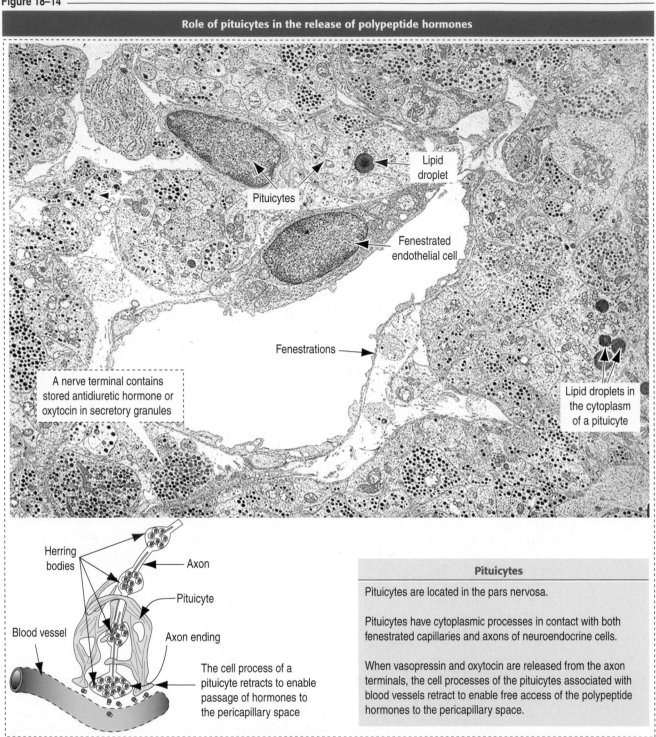

Role of pituicytes in the release of polypeptide hormones

Lipid droplet

Pituicytes

Fenestrated endothelial cell

Fenestrations

A nerve terminal contains stored antidiuretic hormone or oxytocin in secretory granules

Lipid droplets in the cytoplasm of a pituicyte

Herring bodies

Axon

Pituicyte

Blood vessel

Axon ending

The cell process of a pituicyte retracts to enable passage of hormones to the pericapillary space

Pituicytes

Pituicytes are located in the pars nervosa.

Pituicytes have cytoplasmic processes in contact with both fenestrated capillaries and axons of neuroendocrine cells.

When vasopressin and oxytocin are released from the axon terminals, the cell processes of the pituicytes associated with blood vessels retract to enable free access of the polypeptide hormones to the pericapillary space.

pressure in circulating blood or reduced blood volume triggers the release of ADH. Retention of water reduces plasma osmolality, which acts on hypothalamic osmoreceptors to suppress the secretion of ADH.

ADH and oxytocin are transported down the axons and stored in nerve terminals within secretory granules, packaged together with a carrier protein, **neurophysin**. **A common precursor** gives rise to ADH, oxytocin, and the carrier neurophysin. **ADH is bound to neurophysin II and oxytocin to neurophysin I.** The released hormones circulate in blood in an unbound form and have a half-

Figure 18–15

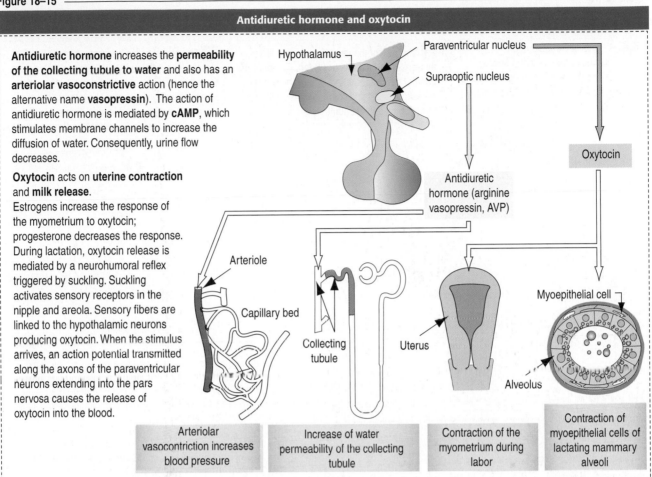

Antidiuretic hormone and oxytocin

Antidiuretic hormone increases the **permeability of the collecting tubule to water** and also has an **arteriolar vasoconstrictive** action (hence the alternative name **vasopressin**). The action of antidiuretic hormone is mediated by **cAMP**, which stimulates membrane channels to increase the diffusion of water. Consequently, urine flow decreases.

Oxytocin acts on **uterine contraction** and **milk release**.
Estrogens increase the response of the myometrium to oxytocin; progesterone decreases the response. During lactation, oxytocin release is mediated by a neurohumoral reflex triggered by suckling. Suckling activates sensory receptors in the nipple and areola. Sensory fibers are linked to the hypothalamic neurons producing oxytocin. When the stimulus arrives, an action potential transmitted along the axons of the paraventricular neurons extending into the pars nervosa causes the release of oxytocin into the blood.

Hypothalamus

Paraventricular nucleus

Supraoptic nucleus

Oxytocin

Antidiuretic hormone (arginine vasopressin, AVP)

Arteriole

Capillary bed

Collecting tubule

Uterus

Myoepithelial cell

Alveolus

| Arteriolar vasocontriction increases blood pressure | Increase of water permeability of the collecting tubule | Contraction of the myometrium during labor | Contraction of myoepithelial cells of lactating mammary alveoli |

life of 5 minutes.

Neurogenic diabetes insipidus occurs when the secretion of ADH is reduced or absent. **Polyuria** is a common clinical finding. Patients with diabetes insipidus can excrete up to 20 L of urine in 24 hours. Neurogenic diabetes insipidus is caused by a head injury, an invasive tumor damaging the hypothalamoneurohypophysial system, or autoimmune destruction of vasopressin-secreting neurons.

Nephrogenic diabetes insipidus occurs in certain chronic renal diseases that are **nonresponsive** to vasopressin or as a result of genetic defects in renal receptors for vasopressin.

The pineal gland
The pineal gland is an endocrine organ formed by cells with a neurosecretory function. The pineal gland is connected to the brain by a stalk, but **there are no direct nerve connections of the pineal gland with the brain**. Instead, **postganglionic sympathetic nerve fibers derived from the superior cervical ganglia** supply the pineal gland.

Preganglionic fibers to the superior cervical ganglia derive from the lateral column of the spinal cord. The function of the pineal gland is regulated by sympathetic nerves.

Development of the pineal gland
The pineal gland develops from a saccular outpocketing of the posterior diencephalic roof in the midline of the third ventricle (Figure 18–16).

Figure 18–16

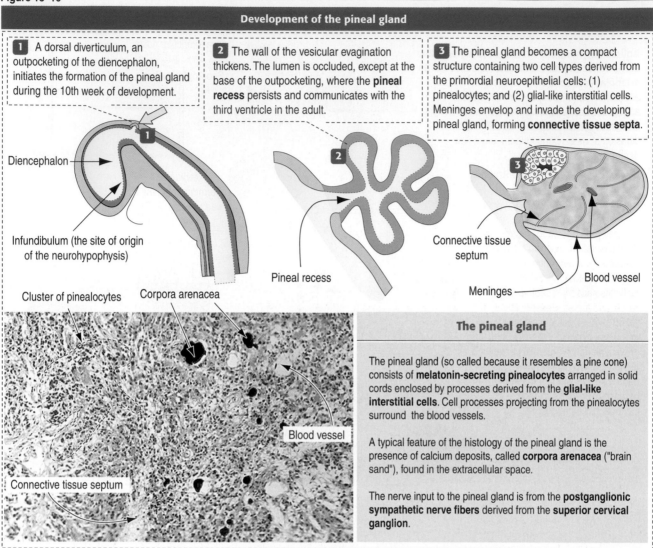

Development of the pineal gland

1 A dorsal diverticulum, an outpocketing of the diencephalon, initiates the formation of the pineal gland during the 10th week of development.

2 The wall of the vesicular evagination thickens. The lumen is occluded, except at the base of the outpocketing, where the **pineal recess** persists and communicates with the third ventricle in the adult.

3 The pineal gland becomes a compact structure containing two cell types derived from the primordial neuroepithelial cells: (1) pinealocytes; and (2) glial-like interstitial cells. Meninges envelop and invade the developing pineal gland, forming **connective tissue septa**.

Diencephalon

Infundibulum (the site of origin of the neurohypophysis)

Pineal recess

Connective tissue septum

Meninges

Blood vessel

Cluster of pinealocytes   Corpora arenacea

Blood vessel

Connective tissue septum

The pineal gland

The pineal gland (so called because it resembles a pine cone) consists of **melatonin-secreting pinealocytes** arranged in solid cords enclosed by processes derived from the **glial-like interstitial cells**. Cell processes projecting from the pinealocytes surround the blood vessels.

A typical feature of the histology of the pineal gland is the presence of calcium deposits, called **corpora arenacea** ("brain sand"), found in the extracellular space.

The nerve input to the pineal gland is from the **postganglionic sympathetic nerve fibers** derived from the **superior cervical ganglion**.

Continued diverticulation and infolding result in a solid parenchymal mass of **cords** and **clusters of pinealocytes** and **glial-like interstitial cells** supported by a meninges-derived connective tissue that carries blood vessels and nerves to the pineal gland.

Histology of the pineal gland

Two cell types form the pineal gland (see Figure 18–16): (1) the **pinealocytes**, and (2) the **glial-like interstitial cells**.

The **pinealocytes** are secretory cells organized into cords and clusters resting on a basal lamina and surrounded by connective tissue, blood vessels lined by fenestrated endothelial cells, and nerves. The pinealocyte has two or more cell processes ending in bulbous expansions. One of the processes ends near capillaries. The cytoplasm contains **abundant mitochondria** and **multiple synaptic ribbons that are randomly distributed**. **Single ribbon synapses** can be seen at the **synaptic end** of sensory cells of the **retina** (see Figure 9–18) and **inner ear** (see Figure 9-28).

Interstitial cells are found among pinealocytes. The glial-like interstitial cells and the connective tissue provide stromal support to the functional pinealocytes.

Like the anterior hypophysis, **the pineal gland lacks a blood-brain barrier**.

The function of pinealocytes is regulated by β-**adrenergic receptors**. The meta-

Figure 18–17

Structure of the pinealocyte

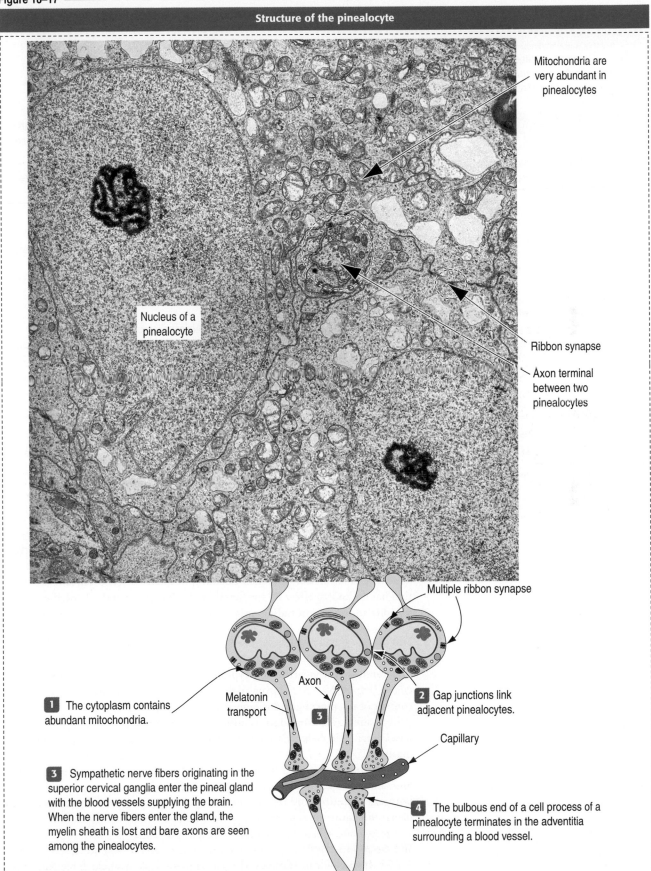

Mitochondria are very abundant in pinealocytes

Nucleus of a pinealocyte

Ribbon synapse

Axon terminal between two pinealocytes

Multiple ribbon synapse

Axon

Melatonin transport

1 The cytoplasm contains abundant mitochondria.

2 Gap junctions link adjacent pinealocytes.

Capillary

3 Sympathetic nerve fibers originating in the superior cervical ganglia enter the pineal gland with the blood vessels supplying the brain. When the nerve fibers enter the gland, the myelin sheath is lost and bare axons are seen among the pinealocytes.

4 The bulbous end of a cell process of a pinealocyte terminates in the adventitia surrounding a blood vessel.

Figure 18-18

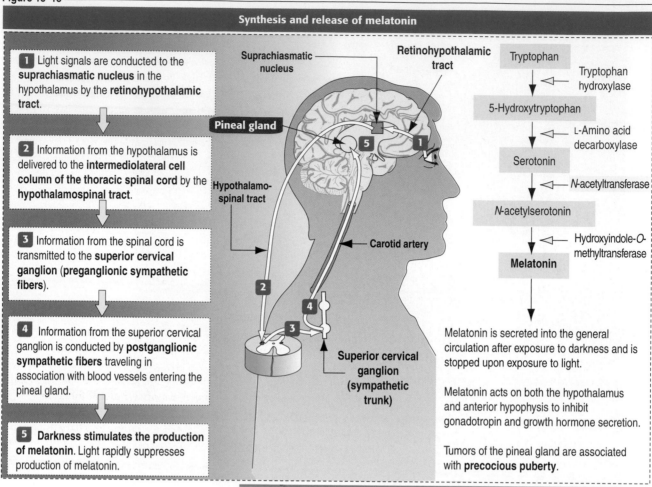

Synthesis and release of melatonin

1 Light signals are conducted to the **suprachiasmatic nucleus** in the hypothalamus by the **retinohypothalamic tract**.

2 Information from the hypothalamus is delivered to the **intermediolateral cell column of the thoracic spinal cord** by the **hypothalamospinal tract**.

3 Information from the spinal cord is transmitted to the **superior cervical ganglion (preganglionic sympathetic fibers)**.

4 Information from the superior cervical ganglion is conducted by **postganglionic sympathetic fibers** traveling in association with blood vessels entering the pineal gland.

5 **Darkness stimulates the production of melatonin**. Light rapidly suppresses production of melatonin.

Suprachiasmatic nucleus

Retinohypothalamic tract

Pineal gland

Hypothalamo-spinal tract

Carotid artery

Superior cervical ganglion (sympathetic trunk)

Tryptophan

Tryptophan hydroxylase

5-Hydroxytryptophan

L-Amino acid decarboxylase

Serotonin

N-acetyltransferase

N-acetylserotonin

Hydroxyindole-O-methyltransferase

Melatonin

Melatonin is secreted into the general circulation after exposure to darkness and is stopped upon exposure to light.

Melatonin acts on both the hypothalamus and anterior hypophysis to inhibit gonadotropin and growth hormone secretion.

Tumors of the pineal gland are associated with **precocious puberty**.

bolic activity of pinealocytes is inhibited by β-adrenergic antagonists.

An important feature of the pineal gland is the presence of defined **areas of calcification**, called **corpora arenacea** ("brain sand"). Calcification starts early in childhood and becomes evident in the second decade of life. Pinealocytes secrete an extracellular matrix in which calcium phosphate crystals deposit. Calcification has no known effect on the function of the pineal gland. **A calcified pineal gland is an important radiographic marker of the midline of the brain.**

The pineal gland secretes melatonin, the "hormone of darkness"

Melatonin is the major biologically active substance secreted by the pineal gland. Melatonin is synthesized from **tryptophan** by pinealocytes and immediately secreted (Figure 18-18). During night (with complete darkness), the melatonin content of the pineal gland is highest.

Exposure to light or administration of β-adrenergic blocking agents causes a rapid decrease in *N*-acetyltransferase and a consequent decline in melatonin synthesis.

Melatonin is released into the general circulation (1) **to act on the hypothalamus and hypophysis, in many species, to inhibit gonadotropin** and **growth hormone secretion**, and (2) to induce **sleepiness**. An unproven hypothesis is that melatonin contributes to drowsiness when lights are turned down.

The circadian clock

A 24-hour biological circadian (Lat. *circa*, about; *dies*, day) clock regulates sleep and a number of bodily functions. We have seen that the retinohypothalamic tract conducts light signals to the suprachiasmatic nucleus as the initial step in the regulation of melatonin synthesis and secretion.

The **suprachiasmatic nucleus** is located adjacent to the optic chiasm and contains a network of neurons operating as **an endogenous pacemaker regulating circadian rhythmicity**. These neurons are **circadian oscillators** connected to specialized **ganglion cells** of the retina. Ganglion cells function as **luminance detectors** reseting the circadian oscillators. The amino acid **glutamic acid** is the primary neurotransmitter mediating the circadian actions of light in the suprachiasmatic nucleus.

It has been shown that when a suprachiasmatic nucleus is transplanted to a recipient with a damaged suprachiasmatic nucleus, it displays the circadian pacemaker properties of the donor rather than those of the host. The mechanism by which individual neurons of the suprachiasmatic nucleus are recruited to organize a pacemaker that oversees the circadian rhythms is not fully known.

It has been determined that a loss of the photopigments **cryptochromes 1** and **2 (Cry1 and Cry2)** from still undetermined photoreceptors of the retina disables the circadian clock. Removal of the eyes abolishes the light-dark shifting responses of the circadian clock.

Clinical significance: Precocious puberty

A tumor of the pineal gland (**pinealoma**) is associated with **precocious puberty**. Precocious puberty is characterized by the onset of androgen secretion and spermatogenesis in boys before the age of 9 or 10 years and the initiation of estrogen secretion and cyclic ovarian activity in girls before age 8. **Precocious puberty is probably caused by the effect of the tumor on the function of the hypothalamus rather than by a direct effect of pineal tumors on sexual function.**

Pinealomas cause a neurologic disorder known as **Parinaud's syndrome** (paralysis of upward gaze, looking steadily in one direction, pupillary areflexia to light, paralysis of convergence, and wide-based gait).

19. ENDOCRINE SYSTEM

The thyroid gland

Development of the thyroid gland

The thyroid gland (Gk. *thyreos,* shield; *eidos,* form) develops as a median **endodermal** downgrowth at the base of the tongue. A transient structure, the **thyroglossal duct**, connects the developing gland to its point of origin, the **foramen cecum**, at the back of the tongue.

The thyroglossal duct disappears completely, leaving the thyroid to develop as a ductless gland. Persistent thyroglossal duct tissue remnants may give rise to **cysts**.

The thyroid gland responds to **thyroid-stimulating hormone (TSH)** at about week 22 in the fetus. The congenital absence of the thyroid gland causes irreversible neurologic damage in the infant (**cretinism**).

The thyroid gland consists of two lobes connected by a narrow band of thyroid tissue called the **isthmus**.

The thyroid gland is located below the larynx and the lobes rest on the sides of the trachea. The larynx provides a convenient landmark for locating the thyroid gland. The thyroid gland is surrounded by a double connective tissue capsule. Two pairs of parathyroid glands are located on the posterior surface of the thyroid gland, between or outside the two capsules.

Histologic organization of the thyroid gland

Each lobe of the thyroid gland consists of numerous **follicles**. The **thyroid follicle**, or acinus, is the structural and functional unit of the gland. It consists of a single layer of cuboidal epithelial cells, the **follicular epithelium** (Figures 19–1 and 19–2), enclosing a central lumen containing a **colloid** substance rich in **thyroglobulin**, an iodinated glycoprotein, yielding a periodic acid–Schiff (PAS)-positive reaction.

The follicular epithelium also contains about 10% of scattered **parafollicular cells**, also called **C cells**. C cells, derived from the **neural crest**, contain small cytoplasmic **granules** representing the stored hormone **calcitonin** (hence the designation C cells).

When the thyroid gland is **hypoactive**, as in **dietary iodide deficiency**, the follicle is enlarged with colloid. Because no triiodothyronine (T_3) or thyroxine (T_4) is made to exert a negative feedback, TSH synthesis and secretion increase. TSH stimulates growth and vascularization of the thyroid gland. Consequently, the gland enlarges.

When the thyroid gland is **active**, the follicular epithelium is columnar, and **colloid droplets** may be seen within the cells as well as large apical pseudopodia and microvilli (see Figure 19–2).

The thyroid epithelium is surrounded by a basal lamina and reticular fibers. A network of vasomotor and sympathetic nerve fibers and blood vessels, including fenestrated capillaries, can be observed in the connective tissue among thyroid follicles.

Function of the thyroid gland

In contrast to other endocrine organs, which have a limited storage capacity, the production of thyroid hormones depends on the follicular storage of the prohormone thyroglobulin in the colloid.

A characteristic feature of the thyroid follicular epithelium is its ability to concentrate iodide from the blood and synthesize the hormones **thyroxine** and **triiodothyronine**.

The synthesis and secretion of thyroid hormones involve two phases (Figure

Figure 19–1

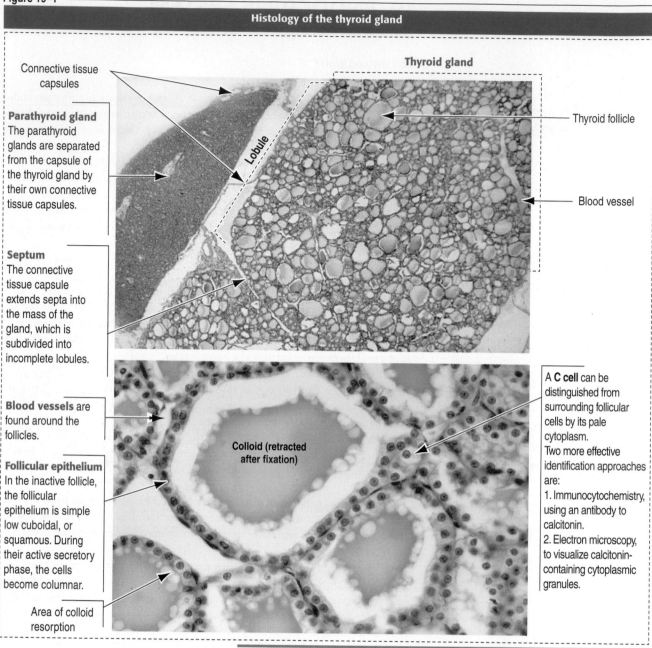

Histology of the thyroid gland

Connective tissue capsules

Parathyroid gland
The parathyroid glands are separated from the capsule of the thyroid gland by their own connective tissue capsules.

Septum
The connective tissue capsule extends septa into the mass of the gland, which is subdivided into incomplete lobules.

Blood vessels are found around the follicles.

Follicular epithelium
In the inactive follicle, the follicular epithelium is simple low cuboidal, or squamous. During their active secretory phase, the cells become columnar.

Area of colloid resorption

Lobule

Thyroid gland

Thyroid follicle

Blood vessel

Colloid (retracted after fixation)

A **C cell** can be distinguished from surrounding follicular cells by its pale cytoplasm.
Two more effective identification approaches are:
1. Immunocytochemistry, using an antibody to calcitonin.
2. Electron microscopy, to visualize calcitonin-containing cytoplasmic granules.

19–3): (1) an **exocrine phase** and (2) an **endocrine phase**.

Both phases are regulated by TSH by a mechanism that includes receptor binding and cyclic adenosine monophosphate (cAMP) production, as discussed in Chapter 3, Cell Signaling.

The **exocrine phase** (see Figure 19–3) consists of (1) the uptake of inorganic **iodide** from the blood, (2) the synthesis of **thyroglobulin**, and (3) the incorporation of **iodine** into tyrosyl residues of thyroglobulin by **thyroid peroxidase**.

The uptake of iodide requires an adenosine triphosphate (ATP)–driven iodide pump present in the basal plasma membrane of the follicular cells. This active transport system is referred to as the **iodide trap**. Intracellular iodide rapidly diffuses against both its concentration and electrical gradients to end up extracellularly in the colloid. Anions, such as **perchlorate** (ClO_4^-), are used clinically as a **competitive inhibitor of the iodide pump** to block iodide uptake by the thyroid follicular cell.

Figure 19–2

Fine structure of the thyroid follicular cell

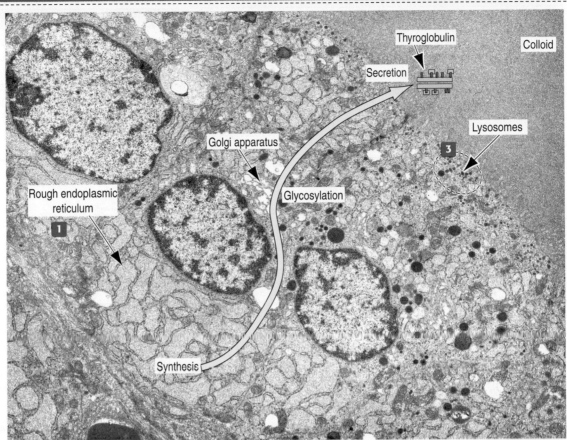

Thyroglobulin

Colloid

Secretion

Golgi apparatus

Lysosomes

Rough endoplasmic reticulum

1

Glycosylation

3

Synthesis

1 The synthesis of thyroglobulin, the precursor of triiodothyronine (T$_3$) and thyroxine (T$_4$), starts in the rough endoplasmic reticulum (RER). The cisternae of the RER are distended by the newly synthesized precursor and the cytoplasmic regions are reduced to very narrow areas. Thyroglobulin molecules are glycosylated in the Golgi apparatus.

2 Under the light microscope, thyroglobulin synthetic activity can be visualized in the cytoplasm of the follicular cells as optically clear vesicular spaces.

3 The apical domain of the follicular cells displays abundant lysosomes involved in the processing of the prohormone thyroglobulin into thyroid hormones.

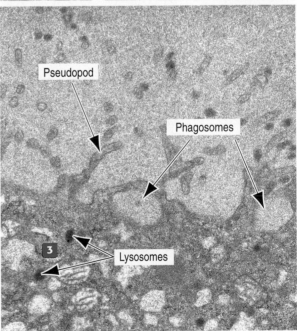

Pseudopod

Phagosomes

3

Lysosomes

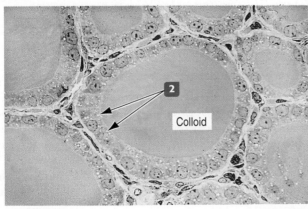

2

Colloid

Pseudopods extend from the apical domain of the thyroid follicular cells and, after surrounding a portion of the colloid (thyroglobulin), organize an intracellular phagosome. Lysosomes fuse with the phagosome and initiate the proteolytic breakdown of thyroglobulin while moving toward the basal domain of the follicular cell.

Figure 19–3

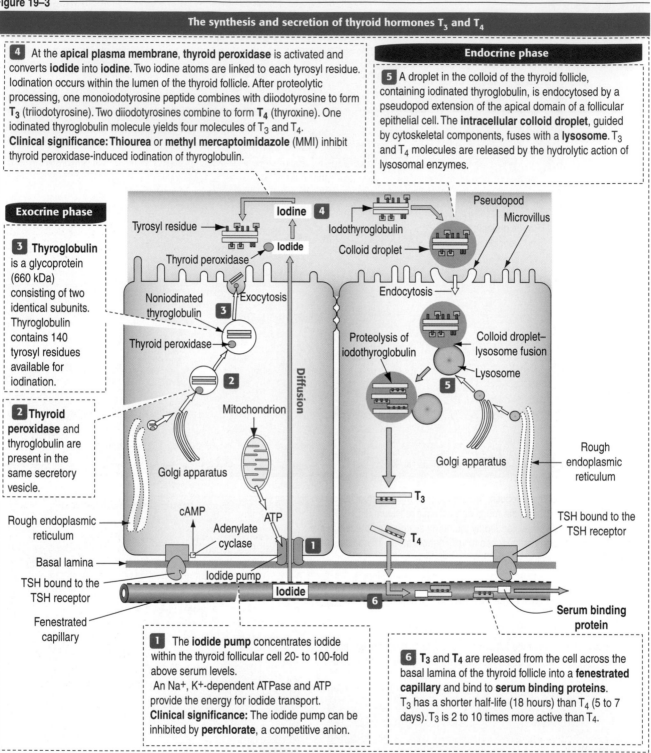

| **The synthesis and secretion of thyroid hormones T$_3$ and T$_4$** |

4 At the **apical plasma membrane**, **thyroid peroxidase** is activated and converts **iodide** into **iodine**. Two iodine atoms are linked to each tyrosyl residue. Iodination occurs within the lumen of the thyroid follicle. After proteolytic processing, one monoiodotyrosine peptide combines with diiodotyrosine to form **T$_3$** (triiodotyrosine). Two diiodotyrosines combine to form **T$_4$** (thyroxine). One iodinated thyroglobulin molecule yields four molecules of T$_3$ and T$_4$.
Clinical significance: Thiourea or **methyl mercaptoimidazole** (MMI) inhibit thyroid peroxidase-induced iodination of thyroglobulin.

Endocrine phase

5 A droplet in the colloid of the thyroid follicle, containing iodinated thyroglobulin, is endocytosed by a pseudopod extension of the apical domain of a follicular epithelial cell. The **intracellular colloid droplet**, guided by cytoskeletal components, fuses with a **lysosome**. T$_3$ and T$_4$ molecules are released by the hydrolytic action of lysosomal enzymes.

Exocrine phase

3 Thyroglobulin is a glycoprotein (660 kDa) consisting of two identical subunits. Thyroglobulin contains 140 tyrosyl residues available for iodination.

2 Thyroid peroxidase and thyroglobulin are present in the same secretory vesicle.

Tyrosyl residue
Noniodinated thyroglobulin
Exocytosis
Thyroid peroxidase
3
2
Mitochondrion
Golgi apparatus
Rough endoplasmic reticulum
cAMP
Adenylate cyclase
ATP
Basal lamina
Iodide pump
TSH bound to the TSH receptor
Fenestrated capillary
Iodine 4
Iodide
Thyroid peroxidase
Diffusion
1

Iodothyroglobulin
Colloid droplet
Pseudopod
Microvillus
Endocytosis
Proteolysis of iodothyroglobulin
Colloid droplet–lysosome fusion
Lysosome
5
Golgi apparatus
T$_3$
T$_4$
Rough endoplasmic reticulum
TSH bound to the TSH receptor
Serum binding protein
Iodide
6

1 The **iodide pump** concentrates iodide within the thyroid follicular cell 20- to 100-fold above serum levels.
An Na+, K+-dependent ATPase and ATP provide the energy for iodide transport.
Clinical significance: The iodide pump can be inhibited by **perchlorate**, a competitive anion.

6 T$_3$ and T$_4$ are released from the cell across the basal lamina of the thyroid follicle into a **fenestrated capillary** and bind to **serum binding proteins**. T$_3$ has a shorter half-life (18 hours) than T$_4$ (5 to 7 days). T$_3$ is 2 to 10 times more active than T$_4$.

The rough endoplasmic reticulum and Golgi apparatus are sites involved in the synthesis and glycosylation of **thyroglobulin**, a 660-kDa glycoprotein composed of two identical subunits. Thyroglobulin is packed in secretory vesicles and released by exocytosis into the colloidal lumen. Thyroglobulin contains about 140 tyrosine residues available for iodination.

Thyroid peroxidase, the enzyme responsible for the iodination of thyroglobulin, is packed in an inactive form—together with thyroglobulin—in the **same secretory vesicle**.

At the apical cell membrane, thyroid peroxidase is activated during exocytosis. **Activated thyroid peroxidase oxidizes iodide to iodine within the colloid**, which is then transferred to acceptor tyrosyl residues of thyroglobulin. Thyroid peroxidase activity and the iodination process can be inhibited by **thiourea, propylthiouracil, and methyl mercaptoimidazole**. These antithyroid drugs are used to inhibit the production of thyroid hormones by hyperactive glands.

The **endocrine phase** starts with the TSH-stimulated endocytosis of iodinated thyroglobulin into the follicular cell (see Figure 19–3):

1. **Colloid droplets** are enveloped by apical **pseudopods** and internalized to become colloid-containing vesicles.

2. Cytoskeletal components guide the colloid droplets to lysosomes, which fuse with the colloid droplets.

Figure 19–4

Graves' disease: Unregulated synthesis and secretion of thyroid hormones T$_3$ and T$_4$

Propylthiouracil or methyl mercaptoimidazole blocks thyroid peroxidase activity and the iodination of thyroglobulin.

Excessive and unregulated synthesis of iodothyroglobulin.

Thyroid peroxidase

Iodine

Iodide

Lysosome

Hyperfunctional (columnar) follicular thyroid cell

Golgi apparatus

Rough endoplasmic reticulum

Plasma cells

Proteolysis of iodothyroglobulin

T$_3$
T$_3$
T$_4$
T$_4$

Thyroid-stimulating immunoglobulins are autoantibodies.

Iodide pump

Fenestrated capillary

Clinical characteristics

Elevated T$_4$ (thyroxine) in serum

Increased uprake of radioiodine

Suppressed levels of TSH in serum

Palpitations and tachycardia.

Exophthalmos due to enlargement of retro-orbital tissues

Increased appetite, but weight loss

Antithyroid drugs: Propylthiouracil or **mercaptoimidazole** blocks iodination of thyroglobulin by antagonizing thyroid peroxidase (reduced production of thyroid hormones T$_3$ and T$_4$).

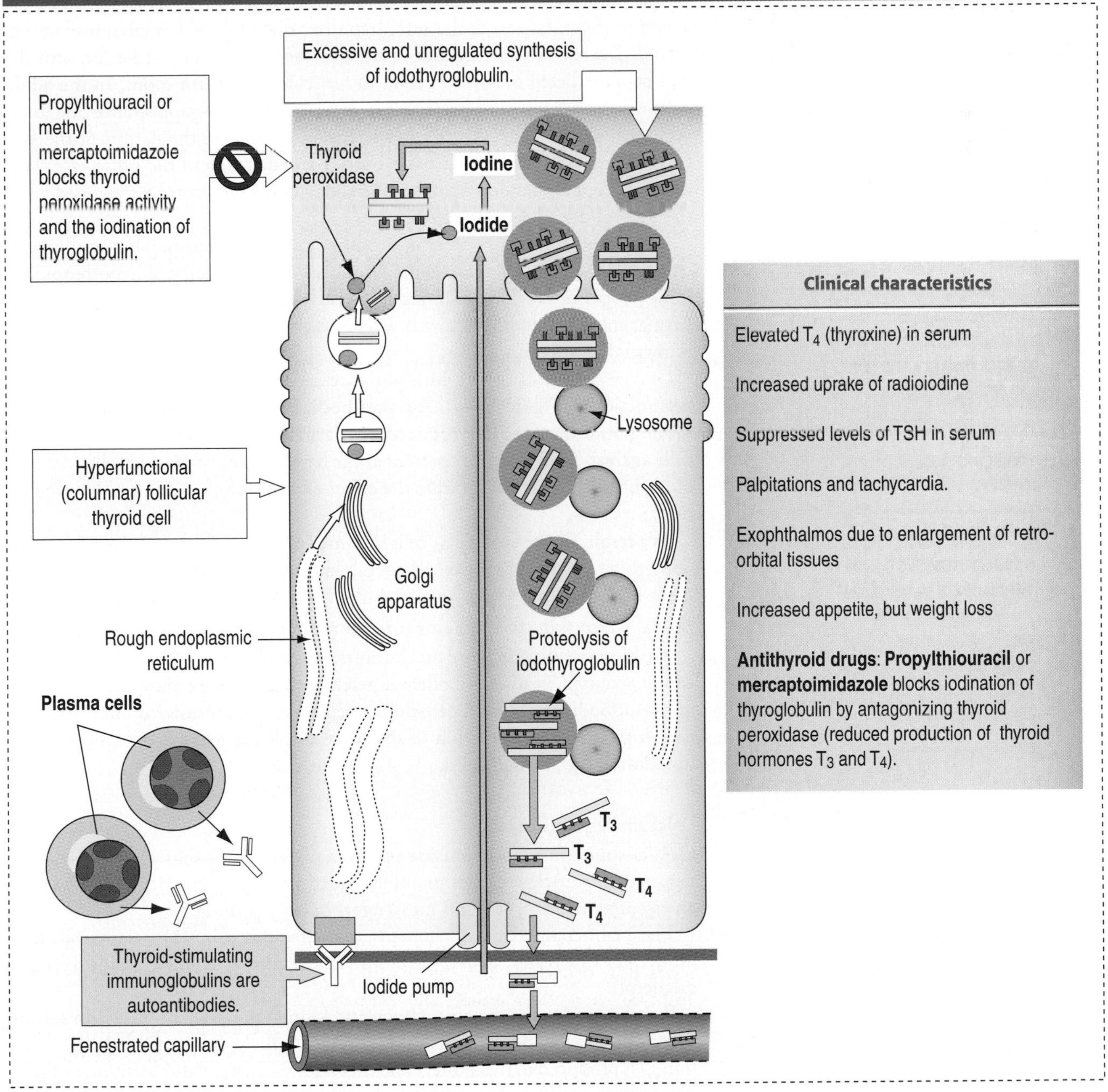

3. **Lysosomal enzymes degrade iodothyroglobulin to release T$_3$, T$_4$,** and other intermediate products. Iodotyrosines, amino acids, and sugars are recycled within the cell.

4. Thyroid hormones are then released across the basal lamina of the follicular epithelium—by a mechanism to be determined—and gain access to **serum carrier proteins** within the fenestrated capillaries.

T$_3$ has a shorter half-life (18 hours), is **more potent**, and **less abundant than T$_4$.** The half-life of T$_4$ is 5 to 7 days and represents about 90% of the secreted thyroid hormones.

Thyroid hormones increase the basal metabolic rate. The primary site of action of T$_3$, and to a lesser extent T$_4$, is the **cell nucleus**. T$_3$ binds to a thyroid hormone receptor bound to a specific DNA region, called **thyroid hormone-responsive element** (TRE), to induce specific gene transcription.

Clinical significance: Hyperthyroidism (Graves' disease) and hypothyroidism

In the **adult**, hypothyroidism is generally caused by a thyroid disease, and a decrease in the **basal metabolic rate**, **hypothermia**, and **cold intolerance** are observed. Decreased sweating and cutaneous vasoconstriction make the skin dry and cool. Afflicted individuals tend to feel cold in a warm room. In the adult, hypothyroidism is manifested by a coarse skin with a puffy appearance due to the accumulation of proteoglycans and retention of fluid in the dermis of the skin (**myxedema**) and muscle. Cardiac output is reduced, and the pulse rate slows down. Except for developmental disturbances, most symptoms are reversed when the thyroid disorder is corrected.

In the **fetus**, a lack of thyroid hormone causes **cretinism**. This condition is observed in iodide-deficient geographic areas. The symptoms of hypothyroidism in newborns can include respiratory distress syndrome, poor feeding, umbilical hernia, and retarded bone growth. Untreated hypothyroidism in children results in **mental retardation**.

Graves' disease is an **autoimmune disease** in which the thyroid gland is hyperfunctional (Figure 19–4). **Autoantibodies** (called **thyroid-stimulating immunoglobulins** or TSIs) **produced by plasma cells derived from sensitized T cells against TSH receptors** present at the basal surface of thyroid follicular cells bind to the receptor and mimic the effect of TSH, stimulating cAMP production.

As a result, thyroid follicular cells become columnar and secrete large amounts of thyroid hormones in the blood circulation in an unregulated fashion. Enlargement of the thyroid gland (goiter), bulging of the eyes (**exophthalmos**), **tachycardia**, **warm skin**, and **fine finger tremors** are typical clinical features.

Hashimoto's disease is an **autoimmune disease** associated with hypothyroidism. It is caused by autoantibodies targeted to **thyroid peroxidase** and thyroglobulin. Antibodies to thyroid peroxidase are known as **antimicrosomal antibodies**. A progressive destruction of the thyroid follicles leads to a decrease in the function of the thyroid gland.

Calcium regulation

Ca^{2+} is found inside and outside cells, is a major component of the skeleton, is required for **muscle contraction**, **blood clotting**, and enzymatic activities, and is an essential mediator (**second messenger**) in cell signaling.

The maintenance of Ca^{2+} homeostasis is regulated by (1) parathyroid **hormone**, (2) **calcitonin**, and (3) **vitamin D** (calcitriol, or 1,25-dihydroxycholecalciferol).

Parathyroid hormone acts on bone and kidney to raise Ca^{2+} levels in serum. Calcitonin, secreted by C cells in the thyroid follicle, lowers Ca^{2+} levels. Vitamin D is produced in the kidneys and increases the intestinal absorption of Ca^{2+}.

Figure 19–5

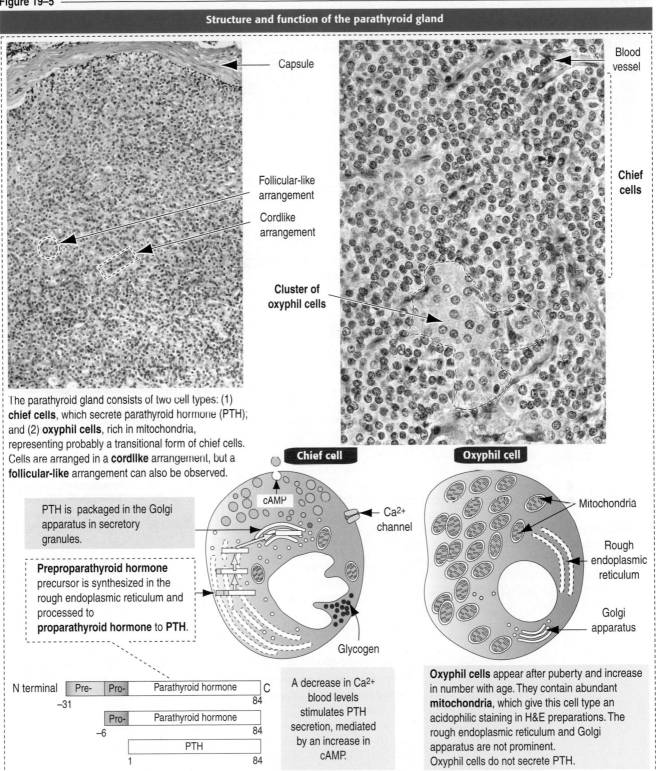

Structure and function of the parathyroid gland

Capsule

Follicular-like arrangement

Cordlike arrangement

Chief cells

Blood vessel

Cluster of oxyphil cells

The parathyroid gland consists of two cell types: (1) **chief cells**, which secrete parathyroid hormone (PTH); and (2) **oxyphil cells**, rich in mitochondria, representing probably a transitional form of chief cells. Cells are arranged in a **cordlike** arrangement, but a **follicular-like** arrangement can also be observed.

Chief cell

PTH is packaged in the Golgi apparatus in secretory granules.

Preproparathyroid hormone precursor is synthesized in the rough endoplasmic reticulum and processed to **proparathyroid hormone** to **PTH**.

cAMP

Ca^{2+} channel

Glycogen

Oxyphil cell

Mitochondria

Rough endoplasmic reticulum

Golgi apparatus

N terminal | Pre- | Pro- | Parathyroid hormone | C
−31 | | | 84

Pro- | Parathyroid hormone
−6 | 84

PTH
1 | 84

A decrease in Ca^{2+} blood levels stimulates PTH secretion, mediated by an increase in cAMP.

Oxyphil cells appear after puberty and increase in number with age. They contain abundant **mitochondria**, which give this cell type an acidophilic staining in H&E preparations. The rough endoplasmic reticulum and Golgi apparatus are not prominent. Oxyphil cells do not secrete PTH.

The parathyroid glands
Development of the parathyroid glands
The four parathyroid glands derive from the third and fourth branchial pouches. The third branchial pouch differentiates into the inferior parathyroid glands and the thymus. The fourth branchial pouch develops into the superior parathyroid glands and the ultimobranchial body.

Figure 19–6

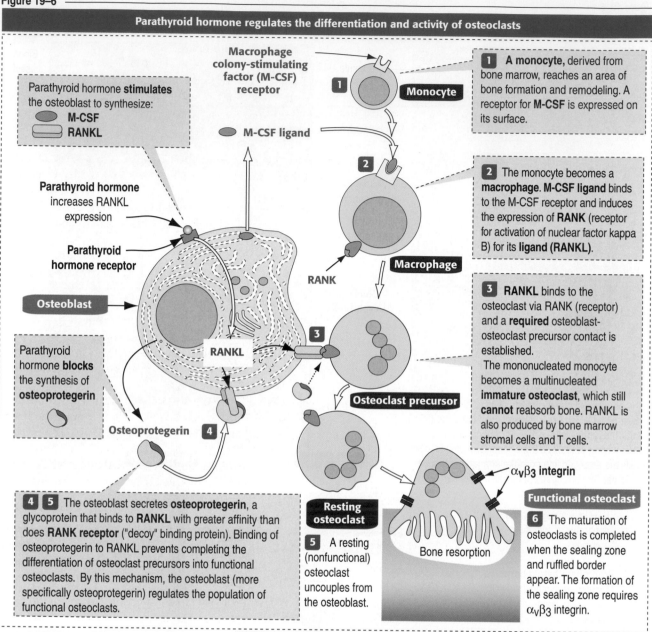

Parathyroid hormone regulates the differentiation and activity of osteoclasts

Macrophage colony-stimulating factor (M-CSF) receptor

1 **A monocyte,** derived from bone marrow, reaches an area of bone formation and remodeling. A receptor for **M-CSF** is expressed on its surface.

Parathyroid hormone **stimulates** the osteoblast to synthesize:
- **M-CSF**
- **RANKL**

M-CSF ligand

Monocyte

2 The monocyte becomes a **macrophage. M-CSF ligand** binds to the M-CSF receptor and induces the expression of **RANK** (receptor for activation of nuclear factor kappa B) for its **ligand (RANKL).**

Parathyroid hormone increases RANKL expression

Parathyroid hormone receptor

RANK

Macrophage

3 **RANKL** binds to the osteoclast via RANK (receptor) and a **required** osteoblast-osteoclast precursor contact is established.

The mononucleated monocyte becomes a multinucleated **immature osteoclast,** which still **cannot** reabsorb bone. RANKL is also produced by bone marrow stromal cells and T cells.

Osteoblast

RANKL

Parathyroid hormone **blocks** the synthesis of **osteoprotegerin**

Osteoclast precursor

Osteoprotegerin

4

$\alpha_V\beta_3$ **integrin**

4 5 The osteoblast secretes **osteoprotegerin,** a glycoprotein that binds to **RANKL** with greater affinity than does **RANK receptor** ("decoy" binding protein). Binding of osteoprotegerin to RANKL prevents completing the differentiation of osteoclast precursors into functional osteoclasts. By this mechanism, the osteoblast (more specifically osteoprotegerin) regulates the population of functional osteoclasts.

Resting osteoclast

5 A resting (nonfunctional) osteoclast uncouples from the osteoblast.

Bone resorption

Functional osteoclast

6 The maturation of osteoclasts is completed when the sealing zone and ruffled border appear. The formation of the sealing zone requires $\alpha_V\beta_3$ integrin.

Parathyroid glands are found on the posterior surface of the thyroid gland, between its capsule and the surrounding cervical connective tissue. In addition to the four parathyroid glands, accessory glands may be found in the mediastinum or in the neck.

The accidental removal of the normal parathyroid glands during thyroid surgery (thyroidectomy) causes **tetany,** characterized by spasms of the thoracic and laryngeal muscles, leading to asphyxia and death.

Histologic organization of the parathyroid glands

The parenchyma of the parathyroid glands consists of two cell populations supplied by sinusoidal capillaries (Figure 19–5): (1) the more numerous **chief** or **principal cell,** and (2) the **oxyphil** or **acidophilic cell.** Cells are arranged in cord-like or follicular-like clusters.

Chief or **principal cells** contain cytoplasmic granules with **parathyroid hormone,** an 84–amino acid peptide derived from a large precursor of 115 amino acids (**preproparathyroid hormone**). This precursor gives rise to **proparathyroid hormone** (90 amino acids), which is processed by a proteolytic enzyme in the Golgi apparatus into **parathyroid hormone**. Parathyroid hormone is stored in **secretory granules. Glycogen inclusions** are also observed in chief cells.

Oxyphil or **acidophilic cells** contain abundant mitochondria, which give this cell its typical stain. This cell type may represent transitional chief cells.

Function of the parathyroid hormone

Parathyroid hormone regulates the Ca^{2+} and PO_4^{3-} balance in blood by acting on two main sites:

1. The **bone tissue**, where it stimulates the **resorption of mineralized bone by osteoclasts** and the release of Ca^{2+} into the blood. Serum Ca^{2+} levels normally average **9.5 mg/dL**.

2. The **uriniferous tubules**, where it stimulates the **resorption of Ca^{2+}** and activates the **production of active vitamin D**. Parathyroid hormone is secreted into the blood and has a half-life of about 5 minutes.

An **increase** in serum Ca^{2+} levels (**hypercalcemia**) **suppresses the release of parathyroid hormone** from chief cells. A **decrease** in Ca^{2+} levels (**hypocalcemia**) **stimulates parathyroid hormone release** by chief cells.

When Ca^{2+} levels are low, parathyroid hormone re-establishes homeostasis by acting on **osteoblasts**, which induce osteoclasts to reabsorb bone.

Parathyroid hormone binds to a cell surface receptor of the osteoblast to induce the synthesis of three proteins essential for the differentiation and function of osteoclasts (see Figure 19-6 and discussion of osteoclasts in Chapter 4, Connective Tissue):

1. **Macrophage colony-stimulating factor (M-CSF) ligand**, which induces the differentiation of monocytes into immature osteoclasts by activating the expression of the **receptor for activation of nuclear factor kappa B (RANK)**.

2. **RANKL**, a cell membrane protein interacting as a ligand with RANK receptor present on the surface of the osteoclast precursor. RANK-RANKL interaction induces the differentiation of the osteoclast precursor into a resting osteoclast.

3. **Osteoprotegerin**, a protein that blocks binding of RANKL to the RANKL receptor to prevent completion of the final differentiation of functional osteoclasts. By this mechanism, osteoprotegerin regulates the population of functional osteoclasts.

Clinical significance: Hyperparathyroidism and hypoparathyroidism

Hyperparathyroidism is caused by a functional benign tumor of the gland (**adenoma**). An abnormal increase in the secretion of parathyroid hormone causes:

1. **Hypercalcemia** and **phosphaturia** (increased urinary excretion of PO_4^{3-} anions).

2. **Hypercalciuria** (increased urinary excretion of Ca^{2+}) leading to the formation of **renal stones** in the calices of the kidneys. When stones descend to the ureter, there is severe pain, caused by spasmodic contraction of the smooth muscle, **hematuria** (blood in urine), and infections of the renal tract (**pyelonephritis**).

3. **Hypercalcemia, the result of bone demineralization.** Extensive bone resorption results in the development of **cysts**.

4. **Accidental removal of parathyroid glands during surgery of the thyroid gland.** Within 24 to 48 hours of surgical removal of the parathyroid glands, hypocalcemia, increased excitability of nervous tissue, including paresthesia (sensation of pins and needles), and attacks of **tetany** or **epilepsy** occur. Administration of parathyroid hormone corrects these alterations.

Idiopathic hypoparathyroidism (of unknown cause) results in a failure of tissues to respond to parathyroid hormone. Patients may have mental deficiencies and high (rather than low) concentrations of parathyroid hormone in blood and

Figure 19–7

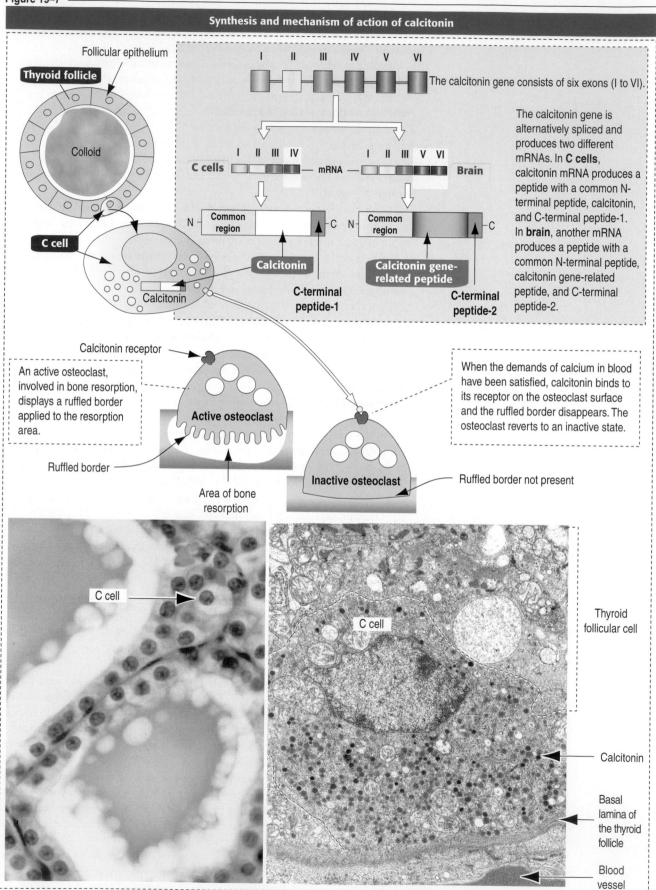

Synthesis and mechanism of action of calcitonin

Thyroid follicle

Follicular epithelium

Colloid

C cell

Calcitonin

I   II   III   IV   V   VI

The calcitonin gene consists of six exons (I to VI).

I   II   III   IV

C cells ——— mRNA ——— I   II   III   V   VI   Brain

N | Common region | | C
Calcitonin

N | Common region | | C
Calcitonin gene-related peptide

C-terminal peptide-1

C-terminal peptide-2

The calcitonin gene is alternatively spliced and produces two different mRNAs. In **C cells**, calcitonin mRNA produces a peptide with a common N-terminal peptide, calcitonin, and C-terminal peptide-1. In **brain**, another mRNA produces a peptide with a common N-terminal peptide, calcitonin gene-related peptide, and C-terminal peptide-2.

Calcitonin receptor

An active osteoclast, involved in bone resorption, displays a ruffled border applied to the resorption area.

Active osteoclast

Ruffled border

Area of bone resorption

When the demands of calcium in blood have been satisfied, calcitonin binds to its receptor on the osteoclast surface and the ruffled border disappears. The osteoclast reverts to an inactive state.

Inactive osteoclast

Ruffled border not present

C cell

C cell

Thyroid follicular cell

Calcitonin

Basal lamina of the thyroid follicle

Blood vessel

be nonresponsive to exogenous parathyroid hormone administration.

C cells (thyroid follicle)
Calcitonin
C cells derive from neural crest cells and are associated with thyroid follicles. C cells (1) represent about 0.1% of the mass of thyroid tissue, (2) are present within the thyroid follicle but are not in contact with the colloid, and (3) produce **calcitonin**, encoded by a gene located on the short arm of chromosome 11 (Figure 19–7).

Calcitonin is a 32–amino acid peptide derived from a 136–amino acid precursor. It is stored in secretory granules.

The calcitonin gene is also expressed in other tissues (hypothalamus and hypophysis), giving rise to a **calcitonin gene–related peptide (CGRP)** consisting of 37 amino acids. CGRP has neurotransmitter and vasodilator properties.

The main function of calcitonin is **to antagonize the effects of parathyroid hormone. Calcitonin suppresses the mobilization of calcium from bone by osteoclasts** triggered by an increase in cAMP. Calcitonin secretion is stimulated by an **increase** in blood levels of calcium (hypercalcemia).

Clinical significance: Multiple endocrine neoplasia syndrome
Tumors of C cells (medullary carcinoma of the thyroid gland) result in excessive production of calcitonin. However, calcium levels in serum are normal, with no apparent bone damage.

The presence of a calcitonin-producing tumor of the thyroid gland may be associated with pheochromocytoma, a tumor of the adrenal medulla (**multiple endocrine neoplasia [MEN] syndrome**).

Vitamin D
Vitamin D_2 is formed in the **skin** by the conversion of 7-dehydrocholesterol to **cholecalciferol** following exposure to ultraviolet light (Figure 19–8). Cholecalciferol is then absorbed into the blood circulation and transported to the **liver** where it is converted to **25-hydroxycholecalciferol** by the addition of a hydroxyl group to the side chain.

In the **nephron**, two events can occur:

1. **Low calcium levels** can stimulate the enzymatic activity of mitochondrial **1α-hydroxylase** to add another hydroxyl group to 25-hydroxycholecalciferol to form **1,25-dihydroxycholecalciferol (calcitriol)**, the active form of vitamin D.

2. **High calcium levels** can stimulate the enzymatic activity of **24-hydroxylase** to convert 25-hydroxycholecalciferol to biologically inactive 24,25-hydroxycholecalciferol. In addition, parathyroid hormone and calcitonin suppress 1α-hydroxylase activity.

Calcitriol (active form) and 24,25-hydroxycholecalciferol (inactive form) circulate in blood bound to a **vitamin D–binding protein**.

The main function of vitamin D is to stimulate calcium reabsorption by the intestinal mucosa. Vitamin D, like all steroids, is transported to the **nucleus** of the intestinal cell to induce the synthesis of a **calcium-binding protein** required for the transport of calcium across the intestinal epithelium.

Clinical significance: Rickets and osteomalacia
In children, a deficiency of vitamin D causes **rickets**. In adults, the corresponding clinical condition is **osteomalacia**. The calcification of the bone matrix osteoid is deficient in both conditions.

In **rickets**, bone remodeling is defective. The ends of the bones bulge (rachitic rosary at the costochondral junctions), and poor calcification of the long bones causes bending (bowlegs or knock-knees).

In **osteomalacia**, pain, partial bone fractures, and muscular weaknesses are typical

Figure 19–8

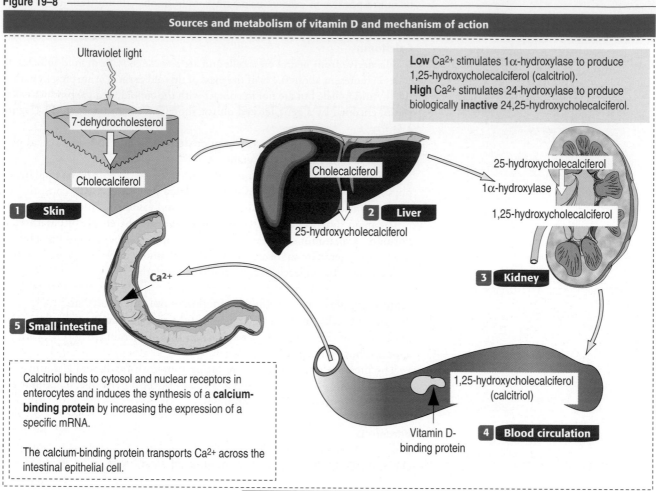

Sources and metabolism of vitamin D and mechanism of action

Ultraviolet light

7-dehydrocholesterol

Cholecalciferol

1 Skin

Low Ca2+ stimulates 1α-hydroxylase to produce 1,25-hydroxycholecalciferol (calcitriol).
High Ca2+ stimulates 24-hydroxylase to produce biologically **inactive** 24,25-hydroxycholecalciferol.

Cholecalciferol

2 Liver

25-hydroxycholecalciferol

25-hydroxycholecalciferol

1α-hydroxylase

1,25-hydroxycholecalciferol

3 Kidney

Ca2+

5 Small intestine

1,25-hydroxycholecalciferol (calcitriol)

Vitamin D-binding protein

4 Blood circulation

Calcitriol binds to cytosol and nuclear receptors in enterocytes and induces the synthesis of a **calcium-binding protein** by increasing the expression of a specific mRNA.

The calcium-binding protein transports Ca2+ across the intestinal epithelial cell.

in the adult.

Chronic renal failure or a congenital disorder—resulting in the lack of 1α-hydroxylase—can also cause rickets or osteomalacia.

Hypercalcemia is frequently found in patients with metastasis causing bone destruction or in patients with tumors secreting a **parathyroid-hormone related peptide**.

The adrenal gland

Histologic organization of the adrenal cortex

The adrenal glands (Lat. *ad*, near; *ren*, kidney) are associated with the superior poles of the kidneys. Each gland consists of a yellowish outer cortex (80% to 90% of the gland) and a reddish inner medulla (10% to 20%). The adrenal **cortex** is of **mesodermal** origin and produces **steroid hormones**. The adrenal **medulla** is of **neuroectodermic** origin and produces **catecholamines**.

The **adrenal cortex** consists of three concentric zones (Figures 19–9 and 19–10). (1) The **outermost layer of the cortex is the zona glomerulosa**. (2) The **middle layer of the cortex is the zona fasciculata**. (3) The **innermost layer of the cortex is the zona reticularis**.

Cells of the zona glomerulosa produce the mineralocorticoid **aldosterone** (Figures 19–11 and 19–12). Although the zona fasciculata is often associated with glucocorticoid production—mainly **cortisol**—and the zona reticularis with androgen production, the functional distinctions between the two layers are not precise and they appear as a functional unit. In addition, these two layers are stimulated by corticotropin (ACTH), whereas the zona glomerulosa is primarily

Figure 19–9

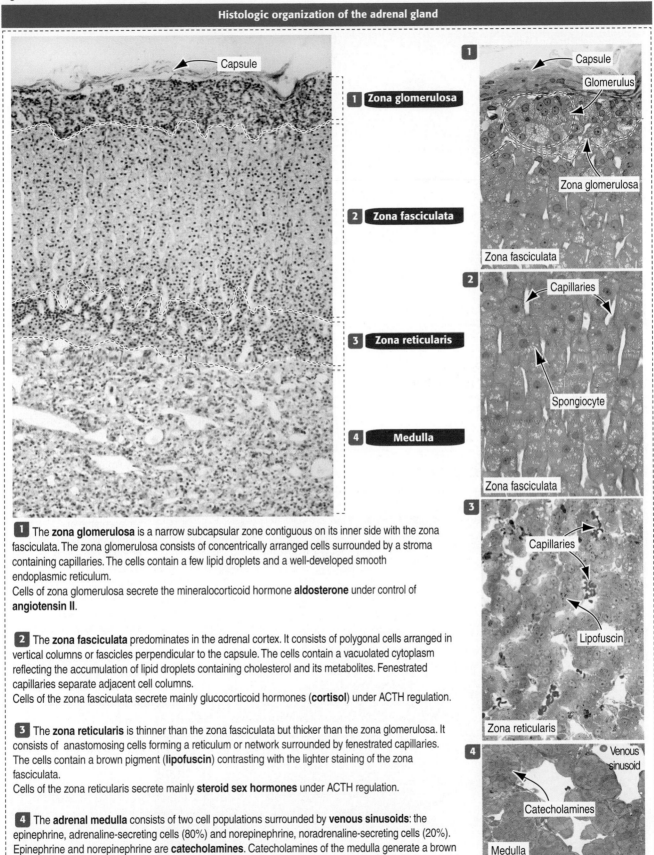

Histologic organization of the adrenal gland

Capsule

1 **Zona glomerulosa**

2 **Zona fasciculata**

3 **Zona reticularis**

4 **Medulla**

1 Capsule
Glomerulus
Zona glomerulosa
Zona fasciculata

2 Capillaries
Spongiocyte
Zona fasciculata

3 Capillaries
Lipofuscin
Zona reticularis

4 Venous sinusoid
Catecholamines
Medulla

1 The **zona glomerulosa** is a narrow subcapsular zone contiguous on its inner side with the zona fasciculata. The zona glomerulosa consists of concentrically arranged cells surrounded by a stroma containing capillaries. The cells contain a few lipid droplets and a well-developed smooth endoplasmic reticulum.
Cells of zona glomerulosa secrete the mineralocorticoid hormone **aldosterone** under control of **angiotensin II**.

2 The **zona fasciculata** predominates in the adrenal cortex. It consists of polygonal cells arranged in vertical columns or fascicles perpendicular to the capsule. The cells contain a vacuolated cytoplasm reflecting the accumulation of lipid droplets containing cholesterol and its metabolites. Fenestrated capillaries separate adjacent cell columns.
Cells of the zona fasciculata secrete mainly glucocorticoid hormones (**cortisol**) under ACTH regulation.

3 The **zona reticularis** is thinner than the zona fasciculata but thicker than the zona glomerulosa. It consists of anastomosing cells forming a reticulum or network surrounded by fenestrated capillaries. The cells contain a brown pigment (**lipofuscin**) contrasting with the lighter staining of the zona fasciculata.
Cells of the zona reticularis secrete mainly **steroid sex hormones** under ACTH regulation.

4 The **adrenal medulla** consists of two cell populations surrounded by **venous sinusoids**: the epinephrine, adrenaline-secreting cells (80%) and norepinephrine, noradrenaline-secreting cells (20%). Epinephrine and norepinephrine are **catecholamines**. Catecholamines of the medulla generate a brown color when exposed to air or the oxidizing agent potassium dichromate (**chromaffin reaction**).

Figure 19–10

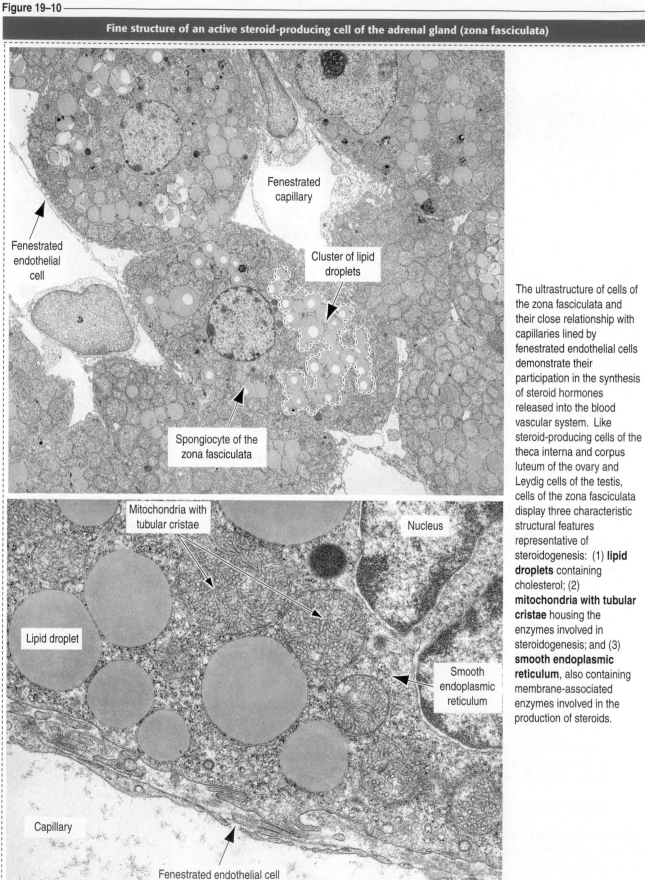

Fine structure of an active steroid-producing cell of the adrenal gland (zona fasciculata)

Fenestrated capillary

Fenestrated endothelial cell

Cluster of lipid droplets

Spongiocyte of the zona fasciculata

Mitochondria with tubular cristae

Nucleus

Lipid droplet

Smooth endoplasmic reticulum

Capillary

Fenestrated endothelial cell

The ultrastructure of cells of the zona fasciculata and their close relationship with capillaries lined by fenestrated endothelial cells demonstrate their participation in the synthesis of steroid hormones released into the blood vascular system. Like steroid-producing cells of the theca interna and corpus luteum of the ovary and Leydig cells of the testis, cells of the zona fasciculata display three characteristic structural features representative of steroidogenesis: (1) **lipid droplets** containing cholesterol; (2) **mitochondria with tubular cristae** housing the enzymes involved in steroidogenesis; and (3) **smooth endoplasmic reticulum**, also containing membrane-associated enzymes involved in the production of steroids.

Figure 19–11

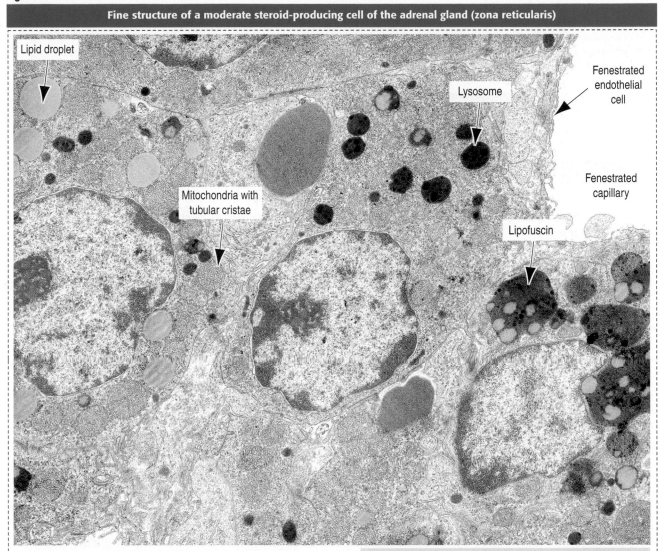

Fine structure of a moderate steroid-producing cell of the adrenal gland (zona reticularis)

Lipid droplet

Lysosome

Fenestrated endothelial cell

Fenestrated capillary

Mitochondria with tubular cristae

Lipofuscin

Cells of the **zona reticularis** are smaller than the cells of the zonae glomerulosa and fasciculata and contain fewer lipid droplets and mitochondria. However, mitochondria still display the characteristic tubular cristae. A structural feature not prominent in the cells of the other cortical zones is the presence of **lysosomes** and deposits of **lipofuscin**. Lipofuscin is a remnant of lipid oxidative metabolism reflecting degradation within the adrenal cortex.

There are other relevant characteristics of the zona reticularis. (1) It receives steroid-enriched blood from the zonae glomerulosa (mineralocorticoids) and fasciculata (mainly cortisol). (2) It is in close proximity to the catecholamine-producing cells of the adrenal medulla. (3) In response to ACTH stimulation, cells of **the zonae reticularis and fasciculata produce androgens** (dehydroepiandrosterone and androstanedione). **Cells of the zona reticularis synthesize dehydroepiandrosterone sulfate**.

Clinical significance: Adrenogenital syndrome

Although dehydroepiandrosterone, androstanedione, and dehydroepiandrosterone sulfate are weak androgens, they can be converted outside the adrenal cortex into more potent androgens and also estrogens.

This androgen conversion property has clinical significance in pathologic conditions such as the **adrenogenital syndrome**. An excessive production of androgens in the adrenogenital syndrome in women leads to masculinization (abnormal sexual hair development—**hirsutism**—and enlargement of the clitoris). Adrenal androgens in the male do not replace testicular androgens produced by Leydig cells, but, in women, adrenal androgens are responsible for the growth of axillary and pubic hair.

angiotensin II-dependent. Angiotensin II stimulates both the growth of the zona glomerulosa and the synthesis of aldosterone (Figure 19–12).

Angiotensin II is an octapeptide derived from the conversion of the **angiotensin I decapeptide** in the pulmonary circulation by **angiotensin-converting enzyme** (see Chapter 14, Urinary System). Aldosterone has a half-life of 20 to 30

Figure 19–12

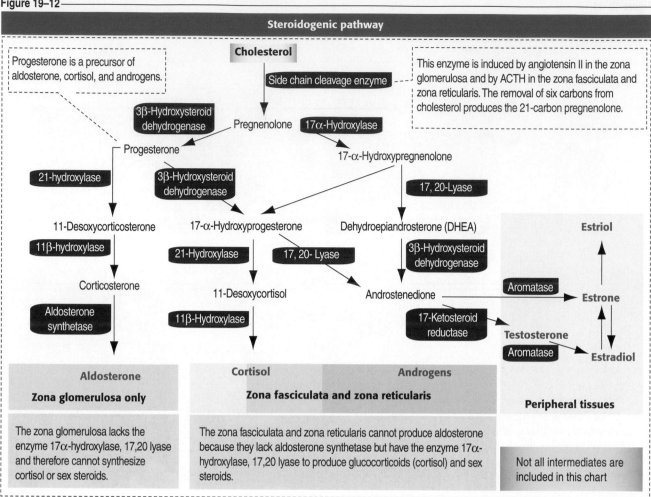

minutes and acts directly on the distal convoluted tubule and collecting tubule, where it increases Na⁺ reabsorption and excretion of K⁺.

The **zona glomerulosa** (Lat. *glomus,* ball) has the following characteristics (see Figure 19–9): (1) it lies under the capsule; (2) it represents 10% to 15% of the cortex; (3) its cells aggregate into a glomerulus-like arrangement and have a **moderate amount of lipid droplets** in the cytoplasm; and (4) it lacks the enzyme **17α-hydroxylase** and, therefore, cannot produce cortisol or sex steroids.

During aldosterone action, aldosterone binds to **intracellular receptor proteins** to activate transcription factors that enhance the expression of specific genes. Aldosterone-responsive cells do not respond to the glucocorticoid cortisol because cortisol is converted to **cortisone** by the enzyme 11β-hydroxysteroid dehydrogenase and cortisone does not bind to the aldosterone receptor.

Aldosterone stimulates the retention of Na⁺ in the kidney, the retention of water (as a consequence of Na⁺ reabsorption), and renal secretion of K⁺ and H⁺.

The **zona fasciculata** (Lat. *fascis,* bundle) makes up 75% of the cortex. It is formed by cuboid cells, with the structural features of steroid-producing cells (see Figure 19–10), arranged in longitudinal cords separated by cortical fenestrated capillaries, or sinusoids (see Figure 19–11).

The cytoplasm of zona fasciculata cells shows three components that characterize their steroidogenic function: (1) the steroid hormone precursor cholesterol stored in abundant **lipid droplets** (see Figure 19–11); when lipids are extracted during histologic preparation or are unstained by the standard hematoxylin-eosin (H&E) procedures, the cells of the zona fasciculata display a foamy appearance and are called **spongiocytes**; (2) **mitochondria with tubular cristae** containing

Figure 19–13

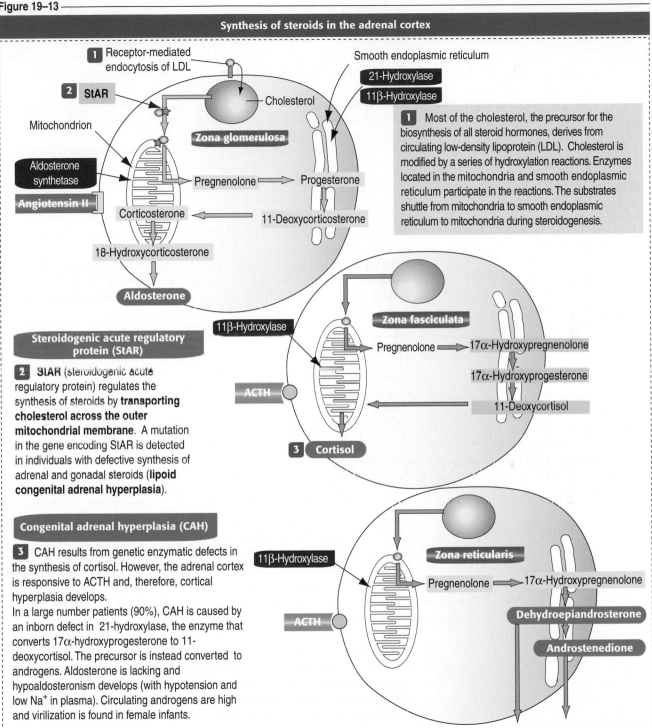

Synthesis of steroids in the adrenal cortex

1 Receptor-mediated endocytosis of LDL

2 StAR

Mitochondrion

Aldosterone synthetase

Angiotensin II

Smooth endoplasmic reticulum

21-Hydroxylase
11β-Hydroxylase

Cholesterol

Zona glomerulosa

Pregnenolone ⟶ Progesterone

Corticosterone ⟵ 11-Deoxycorticosterone

18-Hydroxycorticosterone

Aldosterone

1 Most of the cholesterol, the precursor for the biosynthesis of all steroid hormones, derives from circulating low-density lipoprotein (LDL). Cholesterol is modified by a series of hydroxylation reactions. Enzymes located in the mitochondria and smooth endoplasmic reticulum participate in the reactions. The substrates shuttle from mitochondria to smooth endoplasmic reticulum to mitochondria during steroidogenesis.

11β-Hydroxylase

Zona fasciculata

Pregnenolone ⟶ 17α-Hydroxypregnenolone

17α-Hydroxyprogesterone

ACTH

11-Deoxycortisol

3 **Cortisol**

Steroidogenic acute regulatory protein (StAR)

2 StAR (steroidogenic acute regulatory protein) regulates the synthesis of steroids by **transporting cholesterol across the outer mitochondrial membrane**. A mutation in the gene encoding StAR is detected in individuals with defective synthesis of adrenal and gonadal steroids (**lipoid congenital adrenal hyperplasia**).

Congenital adrenal hyperplasia (CAH)

3 CAH results from genetic enzymatic defects in the synthesis of cortisol. However, the adrenal cortex is responsive to ACTH and, therefore, cortical hyperplasia develops.
In a large number patients (90%), CAH is caused by an inborn defect in 21-hydroxylase, the enzyme that converts 17α-hydroxyprogesterone to 11-deoxycortisol. The precursor is instead converted to androgens. Aldosterone is lacking and hypoaldosteronism develops (with hypotension and low Na⁺ in plasma). Circulating androgens are high and virilization is found in female infants.

11β-Hydroxylase

Zona reticularis

Pregnenolone ⟶ 17α-Hydroxypregnenolone

ACTH

Dehydroepiandrosterone

Androstenedione

steroidogenic enzymes; and (3) well-developed **smooth endoplasmic reticulum**, also with enzymes involved in the synthesis of steroid hormones (see Figure 19–11).

Cells of the zona fasciculata and zona reticularis cannot produce aldosterone but contain **17α-hydroxylase** necessary for the production of glucocorticoids—cortisol—and the enzyme **17,20-hydroxylase**, required for the production of sex hormones.

Cortisol is not stored in cells and new synthesis, stimulated by ACTH, is required for achieving a hormonal increase in blood circulation. Cortisol is converted in hepatocytes to cortisone.

Cortisol has two major effects. (1) **A metabolic effect:** Cortisol effects are opposite to those of insulin. In the liver, cortisol stimulates gluconeogenesis to increase the concentration of glucose in blood. (2) **An anti-inflammatory effect:** Cortisol suppresses tissue responses to injury and decreases cellular and humoral immunity.

The **zona reticularis** (Lat. *rete,* net) makes up 5% to 10% of the cortex. Cells of the zona reticularis form an anastomosing network of short cellular cords separated by fenestrated capillaries.

The cells of this zone are acidophilic, due to abundant **lysosomes**, large **lipofuscin granules**, and **fewer lipid droplets** (see Figure 19–10). Although cells of the zona fasciculata can synthesize androgens, the primary site of adrenal sex hormone production is the zona reticularis. **Dehydroepiandrosterone** (DHEA) and **androstenedione** are the predominant androgens produced by the cortex of the adrenal gland (see Figures 19–12 and 19–13). DHEA sulfate is synthesized in the zona reticularis.

Although DHEA and androstenedione are weak androgens, they can be converted to testosterone and even to estrogen in peripheral tissues. The adrenal gland is the major source of androgens in women; these androgens stimulate the growth of pubic and axillary hair during puberty.

The adrenal medulla

The adrenal medulla contains **chromaffin cells**, so named because of their ability to acquire a **brown coloration** when exposed to an aqueous solution of **potassium dichromate**. This reaction is due to the **oxidation of catecholamines** by chrome salts to produce a brown pigment.

Chromaffin cells (Figure 19–14) are **modified sympathetic postganglionic neurons**—without postganglionic processes—derived from the **neural crest** and forming epithelioid cords surrounded by **fenestrated capillaries**. The cytoplasm of chromaffin cells contains membrane-bound **dense granules** consisting in part of matrix proteins, called **chromogranins**, and one class of **catecholamine**, either **epinephrine** or **norepinephrine** (adrenaline or noradrenaline). Some granules contain both epinephrine and norepinephrine. Minimal secretion of **dopamine** also occurs, but the role of adrenal dopamine is not known.

Catecholamines are secreted into the blood instead of being secreted into a synapse, as in postganglionic terminals. The adrenal medulla is innervated by **sympathetic preganglionic fibers** that release **acetylcholine**.

Two different chromaffin cell types are present. About **80% of the cells produce epinephrine** and **20% synthesize norepinephrine**. These two cell populations can be distinguished at the electron microscope level by the morphology of the membrane-bound granules. Norepinephrine is stored in granules with a dense **eccentric core**. Epinephrine-containing granules are smaller and occupy the less dense **central core**. Note an important difference with cells of the adrenal cortex: **cells from the adrenal cortex do not store their steroid hormones in granules.**

Catecholamines are synthesized from **tyrosine** to **DOPA** (3,4-dihydroxyphenylalanine) in the presence of **tyrosine hydroxylase** (Figure 19–14). DOPA is converted to **dopamine** by **DOPA decarboxylase**. Dopamine is transported into existing granules and converted inside them by **dopamine β-hydroxylase** to **norepinephrine**. The **membrane of the granules** contains the enzymes required for catecholamine synthesis and ATP-driven pumps for the transport of substrates.

Once synthesized, norepinephrine leaves the granule **to enter the cytosol**, where it is converted to epinephrine in a reaction driven by the enzyme **phenylethanolamine *N*-methyltransferase** (PNMT). The synthesis of PNMT is induced by **glucocorticoids** transported from the cortex to the medulla by the adrenocortical capillary system. When the conversion step to epinephrine is com-

Figure 19–14

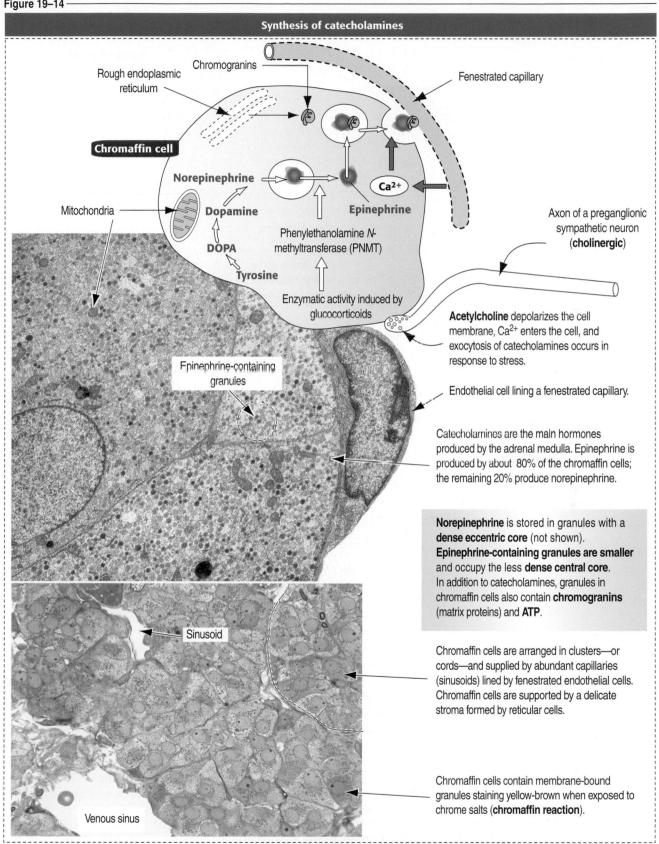

Synthesis of catecholamines

Chromogranins

Rough endoplasmic reticulum

Fenestrated capillary

Chromaffin cell

Norepinephrine

Mitochondria

Dopamine

Ca^{2+}

Epinephrine

DOPA

Phenylethanolamine *N*-methyltransferase (PNMT)

Tyrosine

Enzymatic activity induced by glucocorticoids

Axon of a preganglionic sympathetic neuron (**cholinergic**)

Epinephrine-containing granules

Acetylcholine depolarizes the cell membrane, Ca^{2+} enters the cell, and exocytosis of catecholamines occurs in response to stress.

Endothelial cell lining a fenestrated capillary.

Catecholamines are the main hormones produced by the adrenal medulla. Epinephrine is produced by about 80% of the chromaffin cells; the remaining 20% produce norepinephrine.

Norepinephrine is stored in granules with a **dense eccentric core** (not shown). **Epinephrine-containing granules are smaller** and occupy the less **dense central core**. In addition to catecholamines, granules in chromaffin cells also contain **chromogranins** (matrix proteins) and **ATP**.

Chromaffin cells are arranged in clusters—or cords—and supplied by abundant capillaries (sinusoids) lined by fenestrated endothelial cells. Chromaffin cells are supported by a delicate stroma formed by reticular cells.

Sinusoid

Chromaffin cells contain membrane-bound granules staining yellow-brown when exposed to chrome salts (**chromaffin reaction**).

Venous sinus

pleted, it **moves back to the granule** for storage.
The degradation of catecholamines in the presence of the enzymes **mono-**

Figure 19-15

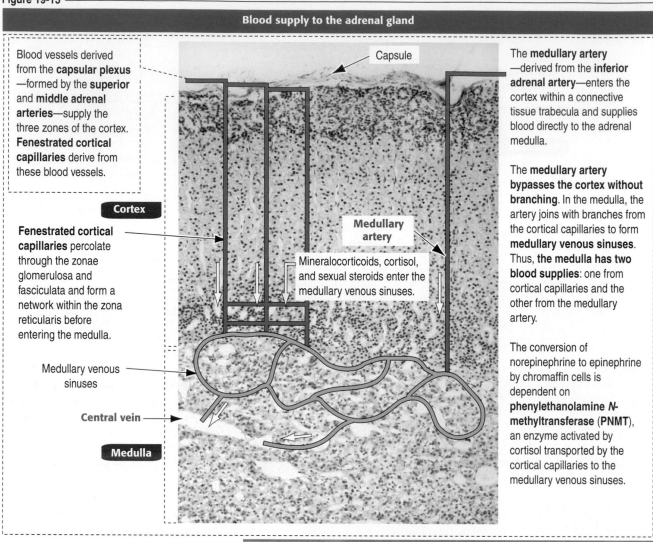

Blood supply to the adrenal gland

Blood vessels derived from the **capsular plexus** —formed by the **superior** and **middle adrenal arteries**—supply the three zones of the cortex. **Fenestrated cortical capillaries** derive from these blood vessels.

Cortex

Fenestrated cortical capillaries percolate through the zonae glomerulosa and fasciculata and form a network within the zona reticularis before entering the medulla.

Medullary venous sinuses

Central vein

Medulla

Capsule

Medullary artery

Mineralocorticoids, cortisol, and sexual steroids enter the medullary venous sinuses.

The **medullary artery** —derived from the **inferior adrenal artery**—enters the cortex within a connective tissue trabecula and supplies blood directly to the adrenal medulla.

The **medullary artery bypasses the cortex without branching**. In the medulla, the artery joins with branches from the cortical capillaries to form **medullary venous sinuses**. Thus, **the medulla has two blood supplies**: one from cortical capillaries and the other from the medullary artery.

The conversion of norepinephrine to epinephrine by chromaffin cells is dependent on **phenylethanolamine *N*-methyltransferase (PNMT)**, an enzyme activated by cortisol transported by the cortical capillaries to the medullary venous sinuses.

amine oxidase (MAO) and catechol *O*-methyltransferase (COMT) yields the main degradation products **vanillylmandelic acid (VMA)** and **metanephrine**, which are eliminated in urine. Urinary VMA and metanephrine are used clinically to determine the level of catecholamine production in a patient.

Actions of catecholamines are mediated by adrenergic receptors α and β

Catecholamines bind to α- and β-**adrenergic receptors** in target cells. There are α_1-, α_2-, β_1-, and β_2-adrenergic receptors. **Epinephrine has greater binding affinity for β_2 receptors than norepinephrine.** Both hormones have similar binding affinity for β_1, α_1, and α_2 receptors.

The stimulation of α receptors of blood vessels causes **vasoconstriction**. In blood vessels of **skeletal muscle**, activation of β_2 receptors causes **vasodilation**. Epinephrine acting through α receptors causes **vasoconstriction**, but when it activates β receptors in skeletal muscle it causes **vasodilation**. The adrenergic receptors of the cardiac muscle are β_1 receptors, and both epinephrine and norepinephrine have comparable effects.

Blood supply to the adrenal gland

Like all endocrine organs, the adrenal glands are highly vascularized. Arterial blood derives from three different sources (Figure 19–15): (1) the **inferior phrenic artery**, which gives rise to the **superior adrenal artery**; (2) the **aorta**, from which the **middle adrenal artery** branches out; and (3) the **renal artery**, which gives rise to the **inferior adrenal artery**.

All three adrenal arteries enter the adrenal gland capsule and form an **arterial plexus**. Three sets of branches emerge from the plexus. (1) One set supplies the **capsule**. (2) The second set enters the cortex forming **straight fenestrated capillaries** (also called **sinusoids**), percolating between the zonae glomerulosa and fasciculata, and forming a capillary network in the zona reticularis before entering the medulla. (3) The third set generates **medullary arterioles** traveling along connective tissue trabeculae of the cortex **without branching** and **supplying blood only to the medulla**.

This blood vessel distribution results in (1) **dual blood supply to the adrenal medulla**; (2) the **transport of cortisol to the medulla**, necessary for the synthesis of PNMT and required for the conversion of norepinephrine to epinephrine; and (3) the **supply of fresh blood to the adrenal medulla**, required for rapid responses to stress.

There are no veins or lymphatics in the adrenal cortex. The adrenal cortex and medulla are drained by the **central vein**, present in the adrenal medulla.

Clinical significance: Abnormal secretory activity of the adrenal cortex

Zona glomerulosa: A tumor localized in the zona glomerulosa can cause excessive secretion of aldosterone. This rare condition is known as **primary aldosteronism**, or **Conn's syndrome**. A more common cause of hyperaldosteronism is an increase in renin secretion (**secondary hyperaldosteronism**).

Zona fasciculata: An increase in aldosterone, cortisol, and adrenal androgen production—secondary to ACTH production—occurs in **Cushing's** *disease*. Cushing's disease is caused by an **ACTH-producing tumor of the anterior hypophysis**. A **functional tumor of the adrenal cortex** can also result in overproduction of cortisol, as well as of aldosterone and adrenal androgens. This clinical condition is described as **Cushing's** *syndrome* (as opposed to Cushing's *disease*). The symptoms of Cushing's syndrome reflect the multiple actions of glucocorticoids, in particular, on the carbohydrate metabolism. Cortisol effects are opposite to those of insulin.

Zona reticularis: When compared with the gonads, the zona reticularis secretes insignificant amounts of androgens. Androgen hypersecretion becomes important when there is an adrenal disorder resulting in reproductive abnormalities.

An **acute destruction** of the adrenal gland by meningococcal septicemia in infants is the cause of **Waterhouse-Friderichsen syndrome**. A **chronic destruction** of the adrenal cortex by an autoimmune process or tuberculosis results in the classic **Addison's disease**. In Addison's disease, ACTH secretion increases because of the cortisol deficiency. ACTH can cause an increase in skin pigmentation, in particular in the skin folds and gums. The loss of mineralocorticoids leads to hypotension and circulatory shock. A loss of cortisol decreases vasopressive responses to catecholamines and leads to an eventual drop in peripheral resistance, thereby contributing to hypotension. A deficiency in cortisol causes muscle weakness (asthenia).

Clinical significance: Hypersecretory activity of the adrenal medulla

Tumors of the adrenal medulla (**pheochromocytomas**) cause sustained or episodic **hypertension**. When pheochromocytomas are associated with other endocrine tumors, they are a component of the **multiple endocrine neoplasia (MEN) syndrome**. The presence of large amounts of VMA in urine has diagnostic relevance.

Development of the adrenal gland

During the fifth week of fetal development, proliferating mesothelium-derived cells infiltrate the retroperitoneal mesenchyme at the cranial end of the meso-nephros and give rise to the **primitive adrenal cortex**. A second proliferation of mesothelial derived cells surrounds the primitive cortex and forms the cortex of the future adult gland.

At the seventh week of development, the mesothelial cellular mass is invaded at its medial region by **neural crest–derived chromaffinoblast cells**, which differentiate into the two classes of **chromaffin cells** of the **adrenal medulla. The adrenal medulla is homologous to a diffuse sympathetic ganglion without post-ganglionic processes.**

Mesenchymal cells surrounding the fetal cortex differentiate into fibroblasts and form the capsule of the adrenal gland. At this time, blood vessels and nerves of the adrenal gland develop.

At the end of fetal life, the adrenal glands are relatively larger than they are in the adult. At birth, the zonae glomerulosa and fasciculata are developed under the control of ACTH secreted by the fetal pituitary gland. **The fetal cortex re-gresses, disappears within the first year of life, and is replaced by the definitive cortex.**

Ectopic adrenocortical or medullary tissue may be found retroperitoneally, inferior to the kidney, along the aorta, and in the pelvis. Aggregates of ectopic chromaffin cells, called **paraganglia**, can be a site of tumor growth (**pheochro-mocytoma**).

Clinical significance: Congenital adrenal hyperplasia

Congenital adrenal hyperplasia is a familial inherited condition in which a mu-tation in the gene encoding **steroidogenic acute regulatory protein**, or **StAR**, causes a deficiency in adrenocortical and gonadal steroidogenesis. StAR regulates the synthesis of steroids by transporting cholesterol across the outer mitochon-drial membrane. **A steroidogenic deficiency increases ACTH secretion, leading to adrenal hyperplasia.**

Adrenal hyperplasia is seen in individuals with a deficiency of the enzyme **21-hydroxylase** who cannot produce cortisol or mineralocorticoids. These individu-als are hypotensive because of a difficulty in retaining salt and maintaining extra-cellular volume. A deficiency in the enzyme **11-hydroxylase** results in the synthe-sis and accumulation of the mineralocorticoid deoxycorticosterone (DOC). Pa-tients with this deficiency retain salt and water and become hypertensive.

See Figures 19–12 and 19–13 for the role of 21-hydroxylase and 11-hydroxy-lase in the synthesis of cortisol and mineralocorticoids.

Functions of the fetal adrenal cortex

During the early stage of gestation, the adrenal cortex synthesizes **dehydroepiandrosterone**, a precursor of the synthesis of estrogen by the pla-centa. A lack of 3β-hydroxysteroid dehydrogenase activity prevents the synthesis of progesterone, glucocorticoids, and androstenedione. The interaction between the fetal adrenal cortex and the placenta is known as the **fetoplacental unit** (see Chapter 23, Fertilization, Placentation, and Lactation).

Glucocorticoids, either of maternal origin or synthesized from placental proges-terone by the fetus, are essential for three main developmental events: (1) **the production of surfactant by type II alveolar cells after the eighth month of fetal life**; (2) **the development of a functional hypothalamopituitary axis**; and (3) **the induction of thymic involution.**

Endocrine pancreas
Development of the pancreas

By week 4, two outpocketings from the endodermal lining of the duodenum develop as the ventral and dorsal pancreas, each with its own duct. The ventral pancreas forms the head of the pancreas and associates with the common bile duct. The dorsal pancreas forms part of the head, body, and tail of the pancreas. By week 12, pancreatic acini develop from the ducts. The endocrine pancreas develops at the same time as the exocrine pancreas. Endocrine cells are first observed along the base of the differentiating exocrine acini by weeks 12 to 16.

Histology of the islets of Langerhans

The pancreas has two portions (Figures 19–16 and 19–17):

1. The **exocrine pancreas**, consisting of acini involved in the synthesis and secretion of several digestive enzymes transported by a duct system into the duodenum.

2. The **endocrine pancreas** (2% of the pancreatic mass), formed by the **islets of Langerhans** scattered throughout the pancreas.

Each islet of Langerhans is formed by two components:

1. **Anastomosing cords** of **endocrine cells**—alpha, beta, delta, and F cells—each secreting a single hormone.

2. A **vascular component**, the **insuloacinar portal system** (see Figure 19–15), which consists of an afferent arteriole giving rise to a capillary network lined by fenestrated endothelial cells. Venules leaving the islets of Langerhans supply blood to adjacent pancreatic acini. This portal system enables the local action of insular hormones on the exocrine pancreas.

An independent vascular system, the **acinar vascular system**, supplies blood directly to the exocrine pancreatic acini.

Alpha cells produce **glucagon**, **beta cells** synthesize **insulin**, **delta cells** secrete

Figure 19–16

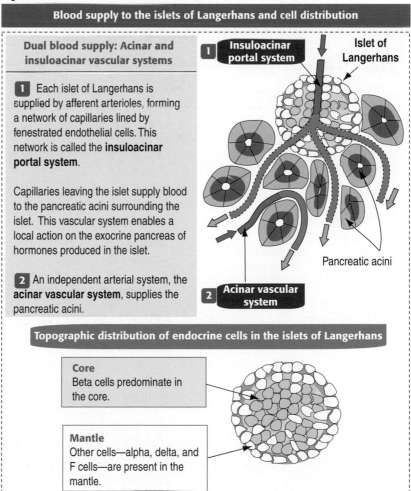

Blood supply to the islets of Langerhans and cell distribution

Dual blood supply: Acinar and insuloacinar vascular systems

1 Each islet of Langerhans is supplied by afferent arterioles, forming a network of capillaries lined by fenestrated endothelial cells. This network is called the **insuloacinar portal system**.

Capillaries leaving the islet supply blood to the pancreatic acini surrounding the islet. This vascular system enables a local action on the exocrine pancreas of hormones produced in the islet.

2 An independent arterial system, the **acinar vascular system**, supplies the pancreatic acini.

1 Insuloacinar portal system

Islet of Langerhans

Pancreatic acini

2 Acinar vascular system

Topographic distribution of endocrine cells in the islets of Langerhans

Core
Beta cells predominate in the core.

Mantle
Other cells—alpha, delta, and F cells—are present in the mantle.

Figure 19–17

Structure of an islet of Langerhans

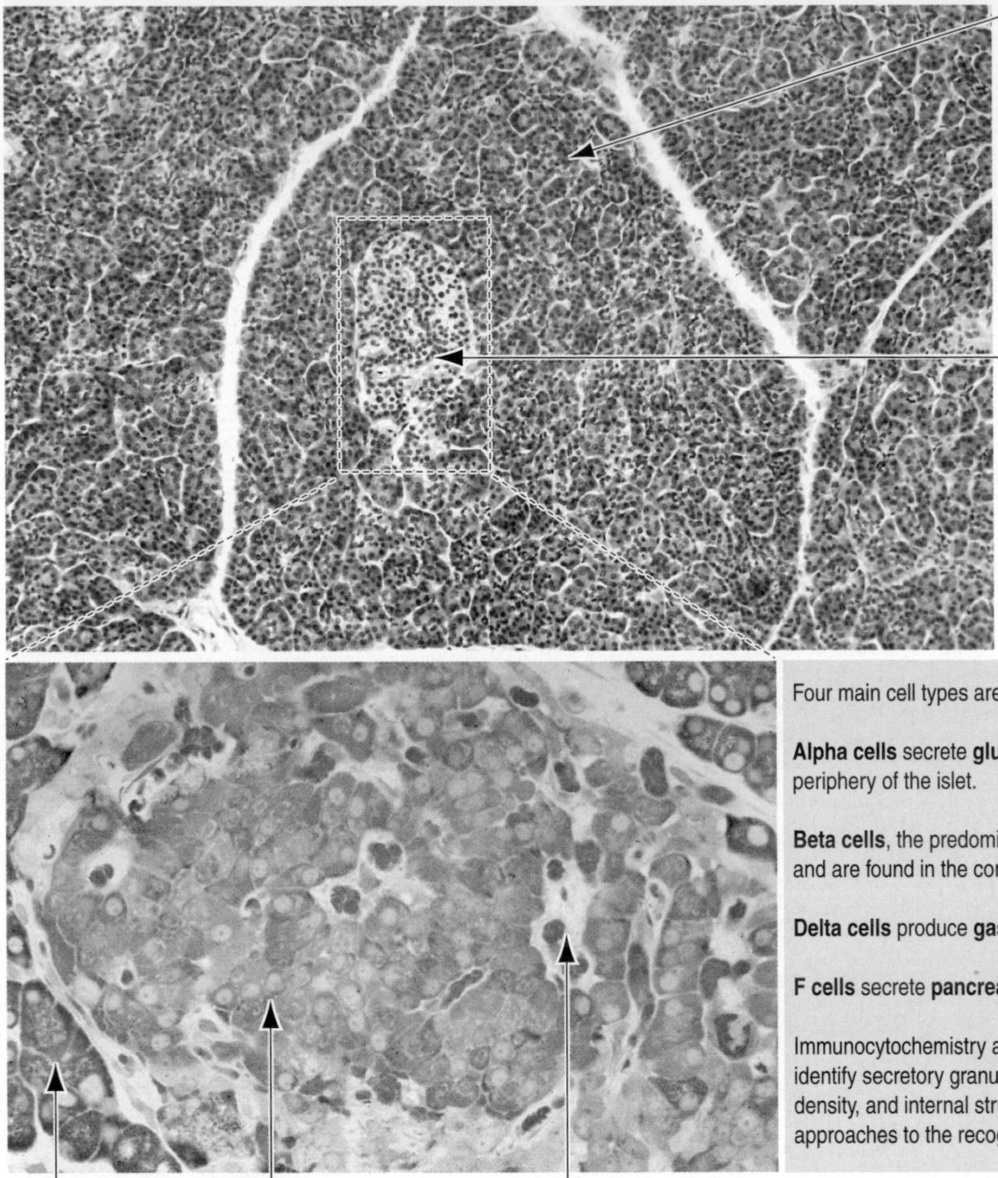

Exocrine pancreas
Formed by protein secretory acini with apically located zymogen granules

Islet of Langerhans

Each islet consists of 2000-3000 cells surrounded by a network of fenestrated capillaries and supported by reticular fibers. About a million islets of Langerhans are scattered throughout the pancreas.

Four main cell types are present in each islet:

Alpha cells secrete **glucagon** and are located at the periphery of the islet.

Beta cells, the predominant cell type, secrete **insulin** and are found in the core of the islet.

Delta cells produce **gastrin** and **somatostatin**.

F cells secrete **pancreatic polypeptide**.

Immunocytochemistry and electron microscopy—to identify secretory granules of different diameter, density, and internal structure—are valuable approaches to the recognition of cell types.

Exocrine pancreas

Endocrine cells forming cords

Vascular spaces (sinusoids)

gastrin and somatostatin, and F cells produce pancreatic polypeptide.

Glucagon, a 29–amino acid peptide, is stored in granules that are released by exocytosis when there is a **decrease** in the plasma levels of **glucose**. Glucagon increases glucose blood levels by increasing **hepatic glycogenolysis**. Glucagon binds to a specific membrane-bound receptor and this binding results in the synthesis of cAMP.

Beta cells produce insulin, a 6-kDa polypeptide consisting of two chains (Figure 19–18): (1) **chain A**, with 21 amino acids; and (2) **chain B**, with 30 amino acids. Chains A and B are linked by disulfide bonds.

Insulin derives from a large single-chain precursor, **preproinsulin**, encoded by a gene located on the short arm of chromosome 11. Preproinsulin is synthesized in the rough endoplasmic reticulum and is processed in the Golgi apparatus.

Figure 19–18

Synthesis and secretion of insulin by beta cells of an islet of Langerhans

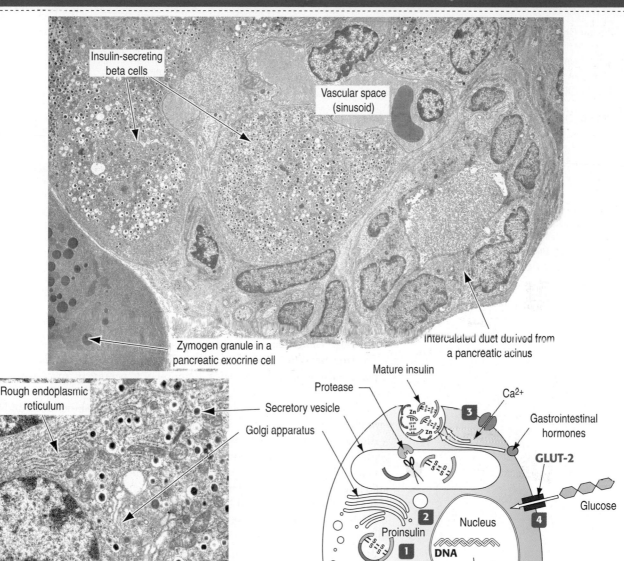

Insulin-secreting beta cells

Vascular space (sinusoid)

Zymogen granule in a pancreatic exocrine cell

Intercalated duct derived from a pancreatic acinus

Rough endoplasmic reticulum

Mature insulin

Protease

Secretory vesicle

Golgi apparatus

Ca²⁺

Gastrointestinal hormones

GLUT-2

Glucose

Proinsulin

Nucleus

DNA

B chain

Signal sequence

A chain

C peptide

Preproinsulin

Insulin mRNA

Rough endoplasmic reticulum

1 **Preproinsulin** is synthesized in the rough endoplasmic reticulum and the signal sequence is removed. Proinsulin is produced.
Proinsulin is transferred to the Golgi apparatus. Proinsulin consists of a connecting (C) peptide bound to A and B chains, held together by disulfide bonds.

2 **Proinsulin** is enclosed in a secretory vesicle that contains a specific **protease**. Within the secretory vesicle, the **protease** releases the C peptide from the linked A and B chains.
Mature insulin molecules, in the presence of zinc, yield a dense crystalloid surrounded by C peptides.

3 Energy- and Ca²⁺-dependent fusion of the secretory vesicle with the plasma membrane determines the release of insulin into the bloodstream. Gastrointestinal hormones also regulate the release of insulin.

4 Glucose enters the beta cell through **insulin-independent glucose transporter protein-2 (GLUT-2)** and triggers the immediate release of insulin. Glucose also activates the expression of the insulin gene.
Glucose triggers both insulin release and synthesis.

Figure 19–19

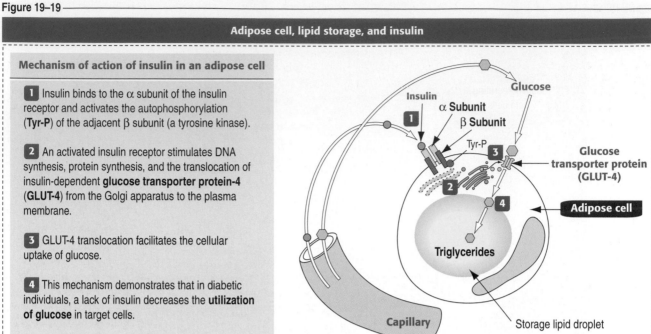

Adipose cell, lipid storage, and insulin

Mechanism of action of insulin in an adipose cell

1 Insulin binds to the α subunit of the insulin receptor and activates the autophosphorylation (**Tyr-P**) of the adjacent β subunit (a tyrosine kinase).

2 An activated insulin receptor stimulates DNA synthesis, protein synthesis, and the translocation of insulin-dependent **glucose transporter protein-4 (GLUT-4)** from the Golgi apparatus to the plasma membrane.

3 GLUT-4 translocation facilitates the cellular uptake of glucose.

4 This mechanism demonstrates that in diabetic individuals, a lack of insulin decreases the **utilization of glucose** in target cells.

Glucose

Insulin
α Subunit
β Subunit
Tyr-P

Glucose transporter protein (GLUT-4)

Adipose cell

Triglycerides

Capillary

Storage lipid droplet

in the rough endoplasmic reticulum and is processed in the Golgi apparatus.

The large precursor gives rise to **proinsulin** (9 kDa; 86 amino acids) in which **C peptide** connects A and B chains. Removal of C peptide by specific proteases results in (1) the separation of chains A and B, and (2) the organization of a crystalline core consisting of a hexamer and zinc atoms. C peptide surrounds the crystalline core.

An **increase in blood glucose stimulates the release of both insulin and C peptide stored in secretory granules.** Glucose is taken up by beta cells by an **insulin-independent, glucose transporter protein-2 (GLUT-2)**, and stored insulin is released in a Ca^{2+}–dependent manner. If glucose levels remain high, new synthesis of insulin occurs. GLUT-2 is also present in hepatocytes.

Insulin is required for **increasing the transport of glucose in cells** (predominantly in hepatocytes, skeletal and cardiac muscle, fibroblasts, and adipocytes). This is accomplished by (1) **the transmembrane transport of glucose and amino acids**, (2) the **formation of glycogen in hepatocytes and skeletal and cardiac muscle cells**, and (3) the **conversion of glucose to triglycerides in adipose cells** (Figure 19–19).

Insulin initiates its effect by binding to the α subunit of its receptor. The insulin receptor consists of two subunits, α and β. The intracellular domain of the β **subunit** has **tyrosine kinase activity**, which autophosphorylates and triggers a number of intracellular responses. One of these responses is the translocation of **glucose transporter protein-4 (GLUT-4)** from the Golgi apparatus to the plasma membrane to facilitate the uptake of glucose. **GLUT-4 is insulin-dependent** and is present in adipocytes and skeletal and cardiac muscle.

Note the functional difference between GLUT-2 and GLUT-4: (1) **GLUT-2 is insulin-independent and serves to transport glucose to insular beta cells and hepatocytes**; (2) **GLUT-4 is insulin-dependent and serves to remove glucose from blood.**

Alpha cells produce **glucagon**, a 29–amino acid peptide (3.5 kDa) derived from a large precursor, **preproglucagon**, encoded by a gene present on chromosome 2. In addition to the pancreas, glucagon can be found in the gastrointestinal tract (enteroglucagon) and brain. About 30% to 40% of glucagon in blood derives from the pancreas; the remainder comes from the gastrointestinal tract.

Circulating glucagon, of pancreatic and gastrointestinal origin, is transported to the liver and about 80% is degraded before reaching the systemic circulation. The liver is the primary target site of glucagon. Glucagon induces hyperglycemia by its glycogenolytic activity in hepatocytes.

Neither C peptide nor zinc are present in glucagon-containing secretory granules.

The actions of glucagon are antagonistic to those of insulin. The secretion of glucagon is stimulated by (1) a fall in the concentration of glucose in blood, (2) an increase of arginine and alanine in serum, and (3) stimulation of the sympathetic nervous system.

Delta cells produce **gastrin** (see discussion of enteroendocrine cells in Chapter 15, Upper Digestive Segment) and **somatostatin. Somatostatin** is a 14–amino acid peptide identical to somatostatin produced in the hypothalamus. Somatostatin **inhibits the release of insulin and glucagon** in a paracrine manner.

Somatostatin also **inhibits the** secretion of HCl by parietal cells of the fundic stomach, the release of gastrin from enteroendocrine cells, the secretion of pancreatic bicarbonate and enzymes, and the contraction of the gallbladder. Somatostatin is also produced in the hypothalamus and inhibits the secretion of growth hormone from the anterior hypohysis.

Pancreatic polypeptide is a 36–amino acid peptide that **inhibits the secretion of somatostatin**. Pancreatic polypeptide also inhibits the secretion of pancreatic enzymes and blocks the secretion of bile by inhibiting contraction of the gallblad-

Figure 19–20

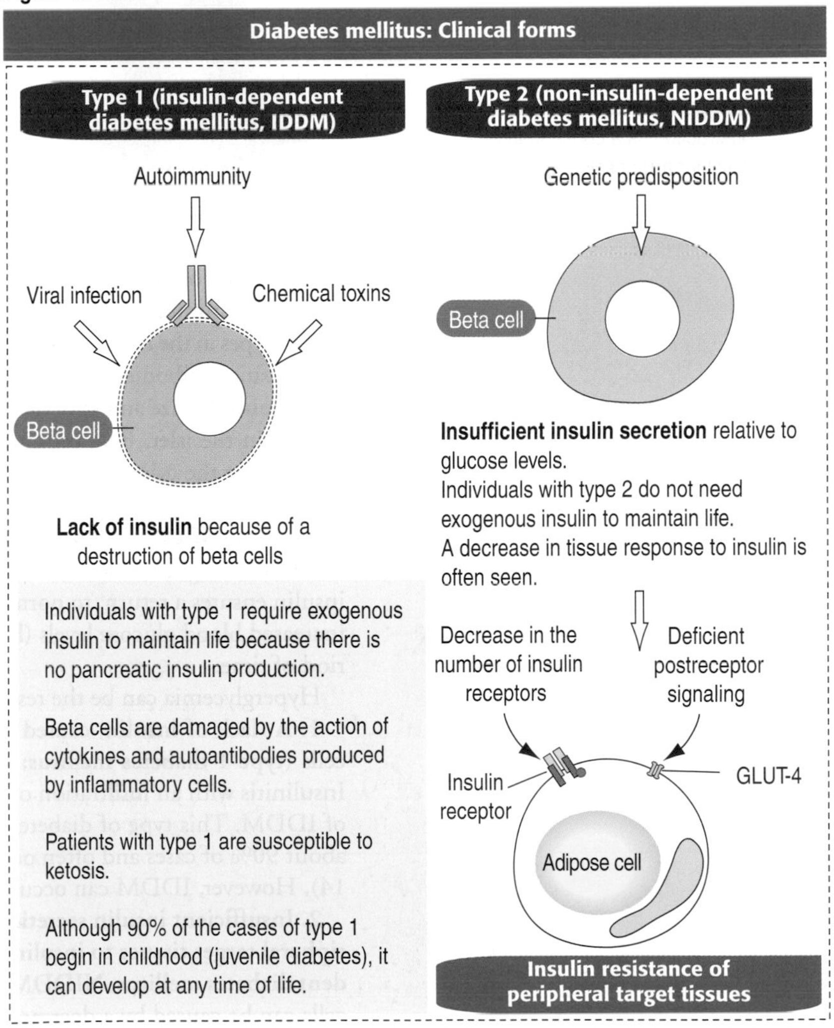

Diabetes mellitus: Clinical forms

Type 1 (insulin-dependent diabetes mellitus, IDDM)

Autoimmunity

Viral infection   Chemical toxins

Beta cell

Lack of insulin because of a destruction of beta cells

Individuals with type 1 require exogenous insulin to maintain life because there is no pancreatic insulin production.

Beta cells are damaged by the action of cytokines and autoantibodies produced by inflammatory cells.

Patients with type 1 are susceptible to ketosis.

Although 90% of the cases of type 1 begin in childhood (juvenile diabetes), it can develop at any time of life.

Type 2 (non-insulin-dependent diabetes mellitus, NIDDM)

Genetic predisposition

Beta cell

Insufficient insulin secretion relative to glucose levels.
Individuals with type 2 do not need exogenous insulin to maintain life.
A decrease in tissue response to insulin is often seen.

Decrease in the number of insulin receptors

Deficient postreceptor signaling

Insulin receptor

GLUT-4

Adipose cell

Insulin resistance of peripheral target tissues

Figure 20–2

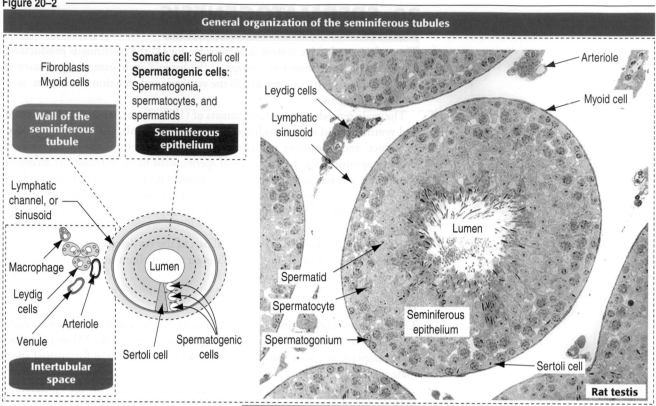

General organization of the seminiferous tubules

Wall of the seminiferous tubule: Fibroblasts, Myoid cells

Somatic cell: Sertoli cell
Spermatogenic cells: Spermatogonia, spermatocytes, and spermatids

Seminiferous epithelium

Lymphatic channel, or sinusoid

Macrophage

Leydig cells

Venule

Arteriole

Lumen

Sertoli cell

Spermatogenic cells

Intertubular space

Arteriole

Myoid cell

Leydig cells

Lymphatic sinusoid

Lumen

Spermatid

Spermatocyte

Seminiferous epithelium

Spermatogonium

Sertoli cell

Rat testis

channels that collects the products of the **seminiferous epithelium** (testicular sperm, secretory proteins, and ions).

The seminiferous tubule (Figure 20–2) consists of a central lumen lined by a specialized seminiferous epithelium containing **two distinct cell populations**: (1) the **somatic Sertoli cells**, and (2) the **spermatogenic cells** (spermatogonia, spermatocytes, and spermatids).

The seminiferous epithelium is encircled by a **basement membrane** and a wall formed by **collagenous fibers**, **fibroblasts**, and **contractile myoid cells**. Myoid cells are responsible for the **rhythmic contractile activity** that propels the **non-motile sperm** to the rete testis. Sperm acquire forward motility after they have passed through the epididymal duct.

The space in between the seminiferous tubules is occupied by blood vessels and lymphatic channels or sinusoids, macrophages, and aggregates of the androgen-producing **Leydig cells** (Figure 20–2). The general histologic structure of the testis is shown in Figure 20–3.

The seminiferous epithelium
Sertoli cells

Sertoli cells are the predominant cell type of the seminiferous epithelium until **puberty**. After puberty, they represent about 10% of the cells lining the seminiferous tubules. In elderly men, when the population of spermatogenic cells decreases, Sertoli cells again become the major component of the epithelium.

Sertoli cells are columnar cells extending from the basal lamina to the lumen of the seminiferous tubule (Figure 20–4). They act as **bridge cells** between the intertubular space and the lumen of the seminiferous tubule.

The apical and lateral plasma membranes of Sertoli cells have an irregular outline because they provide crypts to house the developing spermatogenic cells.

The **nucleus** displays **indentations** and a **large nucleolus** with associated **heterochromatin masses.** The cytoplasm contains smooth and rough endoplasmic reticulum, mitochondria, lysosomes, lipid droplets, an extensive Golgi appara-

Figure 20–3

General histologic structure of the testis

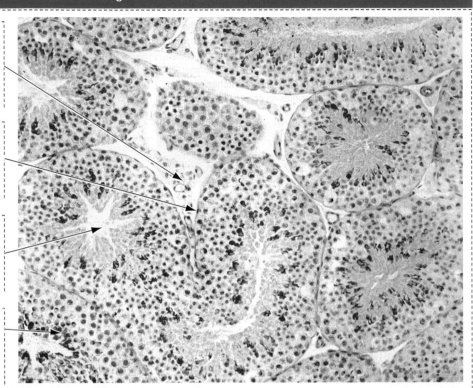

Clusters of **Leydig cells** are present in the intertubular space. Leydig cells are in close contact with blood vessels and lymphatic channels. The major product of Leydig cells is testosterone.

The **wall of the seminiferous tubule** consists of peritubular myoid cells separated from the seminiferous epithelium by a basement membrane.

The **lumen of a seminiferous tubule** displays the free ends of the tails of developing spermatids. Fluid and secretory proteins from Sertoli cells are also found in the lumen.

PAS staining detects glycoproteins in the developing acrosome of spermatids adjacent to the lumen of the seminiferous tubule.

Although variations are observed in the cellular composition of the seminiferous epithelium –reflecting both synchrony and overlap of spermatogenic cell progenies during their development– Sertoli cells are the permanent components of the epithelium.
Sertoli cells:
1. Maintain a close relationship with spermatogonia, primary and secondary spermatocytes, and spermatids.
2. Are post-mitotic in the adult testis.

tus, and a rich cytoskeleton (vimentin, actin, microtubules).

At their **basolateral** domain, Sertoli cells form **occluding junctions** with adjoining Sertoli cells.

Basolateral occluding junctions: (1) subdivide the seminiferous epithelium into a **basal compartment** and an **adluminal compartment** (Figure 20–5), and (2) the determining components of the so-called **blood-testis barrier**, which protects developing spermatocytes and spermatids from autoimmune reactions.

The **functions** of Sertoli cells are: (1) to support, protect, and nourish developing spermatogenic cells; (2) to eliminate by **phagocytosis** excess cell portions, called **residual bodies**, discarded by spermatids at the end of **spermiogenesis**; (3) to facilitate the release of mature spermatids into the lumen of the seminiferous tubule by actin-mediate contraction, a process called **spermiation**; and (4) to secrete a fluid rich in proteins and ions into the seminiferous tubular lumen.

Sertoli cells respond to **follicle-stimulating hormone** (**FSH**) stimulation. FSH regulates the synthesis and secretion of **androgen-binding protein** (**ABP**).

ABP is a secretory protein with high binding affinity for the androgens **testosterone** and **dihydrotestosterone**. The androgen-ABP complex, whose function is unknown at present, is transported to the proximal segments of the epididymis (see Figure 20–15).

Note that although both ABP and the androgen receptor have binding affinity for androgens, they are distinct proteins. ABP is a secretory protein, whereas the androgen receptor is a cytoplasmic and nuclear protein.

the tail is surrounded by a fibrous sheath.

An **annulus** demarcates the middle-principal piece transition of the sperm tail (Figure 20–13). The **residual body**, an excess of cytoplasm from the mature spermatid, is phagocytosed by Sertoli cells at the end of spermiogenesis when **spermiation** (release of mature spermatids into the lumen of the seminiferous tubule) occurs. **Nuclear condensation**, consisting in the replacement of **somatic histones** by arginine- and lysine-rich **protamines**, defines the final step of spermiogenesis. This replacement stabilizes and protects the sperm genomic DNA.

Structure of the sperm

The mature sperm consists of two components (see Figure 20–13): the **head** and the **tail**. A **connecting piece** links the head to the tail.

The tail is subdivided into three segments: The **middle piece**; the **principal piece**, and the **end piece**. A plasma membrane surrounds the head and tail regions of the sperm.

The **head** is composed of the **nucleus** covered by the **acrosome**. The nucleus is a flattened condensed structure. The acrosome covers the anterior half of the nucleus and contains **hydrolytic enzymes** (proteases, acid phosphatase, hyaluronidase, and neuraminidase, among others) usually found in lysosomes. The acrosome is generally regarded as a special type of lysosome.

Acrosomal enzymes are released at the time of **fertilization** (see Chapter 23, Fertilization, Placentation, and Lactation) to facilitate sperm penetration of the **corona radiata** and the **zona pellucida** surrounding the ovum (see Chapter 22, Follicle Development and Menstrual Cycle).

The **connecting piece** is a narrow segment containing a **pair of centrioles**. The **distal centriole** gives rise to the **axoneme**, the central component of the sperm tail.

The **middle piece** of the tail consists of a helically arranged mitochondrial sheath, the 9 + 2 microtubular **axoneme**, and **nine longitudinal columns**, called **outer dense fibers**, projecting down the tail from the connecting piece at the neck of the sperm. The lower limit of the middle piece is marked by the termination of the mitochondrial helix at the **annulus**.

The **principal piece** is the longest segment of the tail. It consists of the central axoneme surrounded by **seven outer dense fibers** (instead of nine, as in the middle piece) and a **fibrous sheath**.

The fibrous sheath is formed by **circumferential ribs** projecting from equidistant **longitudinal columns**. Both outer dense fibers and the fibrous sheath contain **keratins**, proteins that provide a rigid scaffold during microtubular sliding and bending of the tail during **forward motility of the sperm**.

The **end piece** is a very short segment of the tail in which only the axoneme is present because of an early termination of the outer dense fibers and fibrous sheath.

Clinical significance: Pathologic conditions affecting spermatogenesis
Temperature

A temperature of 35°C is critical for spermatogenesis. This temperature is achieved in the scrotum by the **pampiniform plexus** of veins surrounding the spermatic artery and functions as a **countercurrent heat exchanger** to dissipate heat. When the temperature is below 35°C, contraction of the **cremaster muscle** in the spermatic cord and of the **dartos muscle** in the scrotal sac brings the testis close to the body wall to increase the temperature.

Cryptorchidism

In cryptorchidism (or **undescended testis**), the testis fails to reach the scrotal sac during development and remains in the abdominal cavity or inguinal canal. Under these conditions, the normal body temperature (37°C to 38°C) inhibits spermatogenesis and sterility occurs if the condition is bilateral.

Testicular descent occurs in two phases: (1) **transabdominal descent**, presumably controlled by **müllerian inhibiting substance** (MIS) produced by fetal Sertoli cells, and (2) **inguinal-scrotal descent**, probably controlled by **androgen secretion** induced by **calcitonin gene-related peptide** carried by the genitofemoral nerve. Recent research has shown that mutations of two genes, *insulin-like factor 3* and *Hoxa-10*, are associated with bilateral cryptorchidism.

Defects in the transabdominal descent are not common. In most children, the undescended testis can be detected in the inguinal canal. Testes in the inguinal canal are subject to trauma and compression by local ligaments and bone.

A high incidence of **testicular tumors** is associated with the untreated cryptorchid testis. Cryptorchidism is an asymptomatic condition that is detected by physical examination of the scrotal sac after birth and before puberty. Hormonal treatment (administration of chorionic gonadotropin) may induce testicular descent. If that is unsuccessful, **surgery** is the next step, in which the testis is attached to the wall of the scrotal sac (a process called **orchiopexy**).

Cancer chemotherapy

Young male patients treated with antitumoral drugs may become transiently aspermatogenic because spermatogonial mitosis and spermatocyte meiosis can be affected. However, dormant **stem cells**—not involved in DNA synthesis and cell division—can repopulate the seminiferous epithelium once anticancer chemotherapy is discontinued.

Mumps

Mumps is a systemic viral infection with a 20% to 30% incidence of **acute orchitis** (sudden inflammation of the testis) in postpubertal males. In general, no alterations in spermatogenic function can be expected following mumps-caused orchitis.

Spermatic cord torsion

Twisting of the spermatic cord may disrupt the arterial blood supply to, and venous drainage from the testis. This condition is generally caused by physical trauma or an abnormally mobile testis within the tunica vaginalis. If torsion is not treated immediately, hemorrhagic infarction and necrosis of the whole testis occur.

Varicocele

This condition is caused by the abnormal dilation of the veins of the spermatic cord. A consequence of varicocele is a decrease in sperm production (**oligospermia**). Recall that veins in the spermatic cord play a significant role in maintaining testicular temperature at 35°C by a countercurrent exchange mechanism with the spermatic artery.

Leydig cells

Aggregates of Leydig cells are present in the intertubular space in proximity to blood vessels and lymphatic channels or sinusoids (Figure 20–14). Like most steroid-producing cells, Leydig cells contain **lipid droplets, mitochondria with characteristic tubular cristae**, and a well-developed **smooth endoplasmic reticulum.**

After puberty and upon stimulation with **luteinizing hormone** (LH) by a cyclic adenosine monophosphate (cAMP)–mediated mechanism, Leydig cells produce **testosterone**, which can be converted to **dihydrotestosterone** by the enzyme **5α-reductase**. About 95% of the testosterone found in serum (bound to **sex hormone-binding globulin, SHBG**, and other proteins) is synthesized by Leydig cells; the remaining testosterone is produced by the adrenal cortex.

Figure 20–14

| Leydig cell: The androgen-producing cell of the testis |

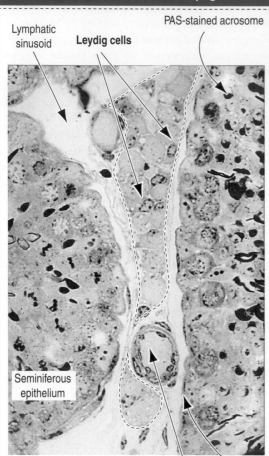

Lymphatic sinusoid

Leydig cells

PAS-stained acrosome

Seminiferous epithelium

Testis (guinea pig); PAS staining

Arteriole

Wall of the seminiferous tubule

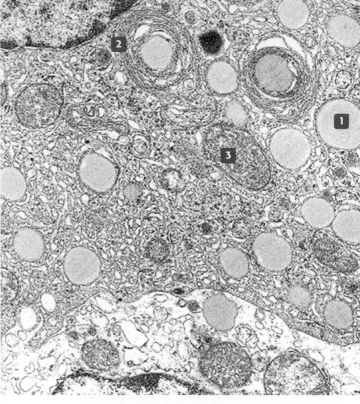

Aggregates of Leydig cells are found in the intertubular space, in close contact with blood vessels and lymphatic sinusoids.

Like all steroid-producing cells, Leydig cells have abundant **1** **lipid droplets**, **2** **smooth endoplasmic reticulum**, and **3** **mitochondria with tubular cristae**.

Leydig cell function is regulated by two hormones of the anterior hypophysis:
1. **LH**, which stimulates **testosterone** production.
2. **Prolactin**, which induces the **expression of LH receptor**.

Testosterone maintains spermatogenesis, male libido, and the function of the male accessory glands (prostate and seminal vesicle).

4 StAR (**steroidogenic acute regulatory protein**) regulates the synthesis of steroids by **transporting cholesterol across the outer mitochondrial membrane**. A mutation in the gene encoding StAR is detected in individuals with defective synthesis of adrenal and gonadal steroids (**lipoid congenital adrenal hyperplasia**).

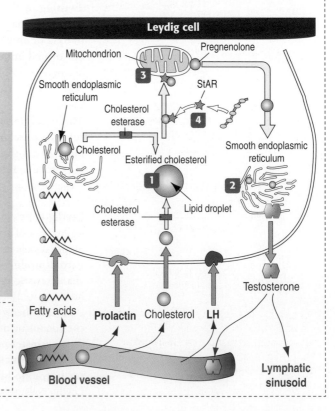

Leydig cell

Mitochondrion

Pregnenolone

Smooth endoplasmic reticulum

StAR

Cholesterol esterase

Cholesterol

Esterified cholesterol

Smooth endoplasmic reticulum

Lipid droplet

Cholesterol esterase

Testosterone

Fatty acids

Prolactin

Cholesterol

LH

Blood vessel

Lymphatic sinusoid

Figure 20–15

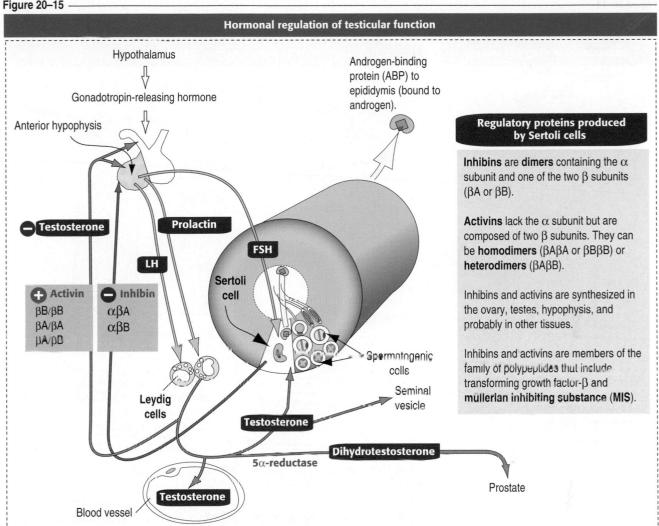

Hormonal regulation of testicular function

Regulatory proteins produced by Sertoli cells

Inhibins are **dimers** containing the α subunit and one of the two β subunits (βA or βB).

Activins lack the α subunit but are composed of two β subunits. They can be **homodimers** (βAβA or βBβB) or **heterodimers** (βAβB).

Inhibins and activins are synthesized in the ovary, testes, hypophysis, and probably in other tissues.

Inhibins and activins are members of the family of polypeptides that include transforming growth factor-β and **müllerian inhibiting substance (MIS)**.

Testosterone can also be aromatized to estrogens in many tissues, in particular adipose tissue. ABP produced by Sertoli cells after stimulation by FSH, maintains a high concentration of testosterone in the proximity of developing spermatogenic cells.

Some actions of androgens

In the male fetus
Regulation of the differentiation of the male internal and external genitalia.
Stimulation of the growth, development, and function of male internal and external genitalia.

In the adult male
Stimulation of sexual hair development.
Stimulation of the secretion of sebaceous glands of the skin.
Binding to androgen-binding protein produced by Sertoli cells after FSH stimulation.
Initiation and maintenance of spermatogenesis.
Maintenance of the secretory function of sex glands (seminal vesicle and prostate).

Clinical significance: Steroidogenic acute regulatory protein

Fetal Leydig cells are steroidogenically active between 8 and 18 weeks of gestation. By week 18 of gestation, the Leydig cell population predominates in the testis. The androgens produced by fetal Leydig cells at this time are critical for the development of the male reproductive tract (see the development of the testis in Chapter 21, Sperm Transport and Maturation). In the neonate, testicular steroidogenesis reaches high levels at 2 to 3 months post partum and then decreases. Androgen levels remain low until puberty, when an increase in LH activates androgen synthesis.

LH and prolactin regulate the function of Leydig cells (Figures 20–14 and 20–15). Prolactin regulates the gene expression of the LH receptor. LH is responsible for the production of testosterone. **Hyperprolactinemia** inhibits male reproductive function by decreasing gonadotropin secretion and action on the testis. Excessive prolactin can decrease the production of androgens by Leydig cells, diminish spermatogenesis, and lead to erectile dysfunction and infertility.

During the synthesis of testosterone, plasma **cholesterol** enters the cell, is esterified by acetyl coenzyme A (CoA) and is stored in the cytoplasm as lipid drop-

Figure 20–16

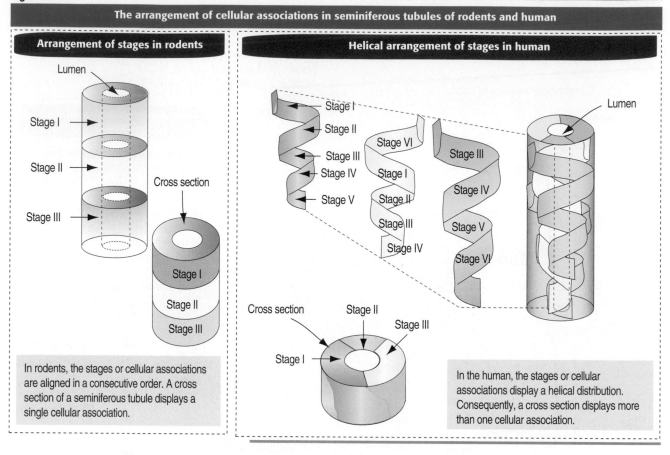

The arrangement of cellular associations in seminiferous tubules of rodents and human

Arrangement of stages in rodents

Lumen

Stage I

Stage II

Stage III

Cross section

Stage I

Stage II

Stage III

In rodents, the stages or cellular associations are aligned in a consecutive order. A cross section of a seminiferous tubule displays a single cellular association.

Helical arrangement of stages in human

Stage I
Stage II
Stage III
Stage IV
Stage V

Stage VI
Stage I
Stage II
Stage III
Stage IV

Stage III
Stage IV
Stage V
Stage VI

Lumen

Cross section   Stage II
Stage III
Stage I

In the human, the stages or cellular associations display a helical distribution. Consequently, a cross section displays more than one cellular association.

lets. Fatty acids are processed to cholesterol in the smooth endoplasmic reticulum. Cholesterol is transported from the lipid droplet to mitochondria by **steroidogenic acute regulatory protein (StAR)**, and pregnenolone is produced. Enzymes in the smooth endoplasmic reticulum convert pregnenolone to progesterone to testosterone. Two other less potent androgens produced by Leydig cells are **dehydroepiandrosterone** (DHEA) and **androstenedione**.

Hormonal control of the male reproductive tract

FSH and LH regulate the function of Sertoli and Leydig cells, respectively (see Figure 20–15). **FSH stimulates the production of inhibin and activin by Sertoli cells.** Inhibin exerts a **negative feedback** on the hypothalamic and hypophysial release of FSH. Activin has an opposite effect.

FSH and LH are mandatory regulators of the spermatogenic process, as demonstrated by the arrest of spermatogenesis following experimental removal of the hypophysis (**hypophysectomy**).

The synthesis and secretion of **androgen-binding protein** by Sertoli cells is stimulated by FSH. ABP binds androgens (testosterone or dihydrotestosterone) and the ABP-androgen complex maintains high levels of androgens in the proximity of developing spermatogenic cells. In addition, the complex is transported to the epididymis, where it keeps high concentration of androgens.

Sertoli cells in the **adult testis** produce three major secretory proteins: (1) **inhibin**, (2) **activin, and** (3) **androgen-binding protein**. **Fetal Sertoli cells** synthesize and secrete **müllerian inhibiting substance**.

As we have already seen, LH stimulates the synthesis of testosterone by Leydig cells. Both testosterone and dihydrotestosterone, the latter a metabolite of testosterone after reduction by **5α-reductase**, bind to the same **androgen receptor**.

The **androgen receptor** is a member of the **steroid-thyroid-retinoic acid su-**

Figure 20–17

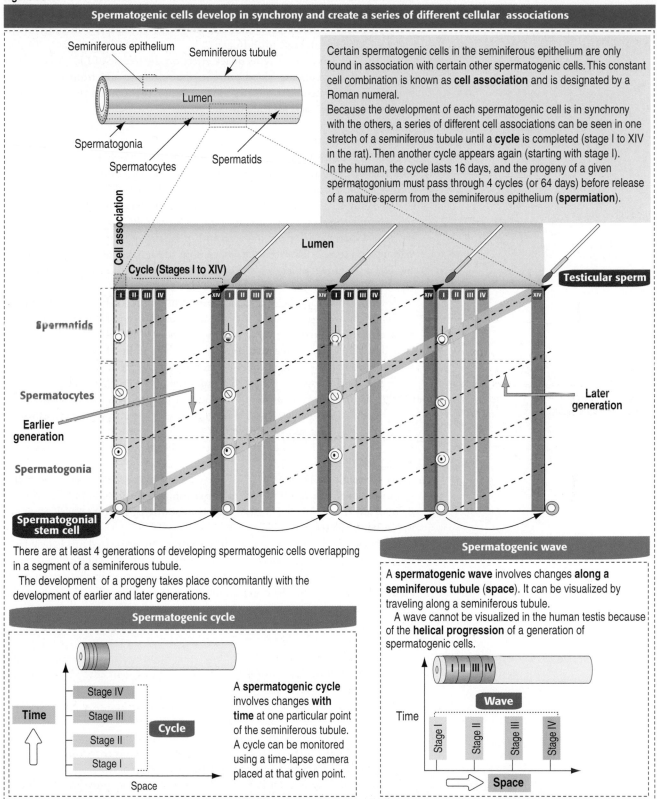

Spermatogenic cells develop in synchrony and create a series of different cellular associations

Certain spermatogenic cells in the seminiferous epithelium are only found in association with certain other spermatogenic cells. This constant cell combination is known as **cell association** and is designated by a Roman numeral.

Because the development of each spermatogenic cell is in synchrony with the others, a series of different cell associations can be seen in one stretch of a seminiferous tubule until a **cycle** is completed (stage I to XIV in the rat). Then another cycle appears again (starting with stage I).

In the human, the cycle lasts 16 days, and the progeny of a given spermatogonium must pass through 4 cycles (or 64 days) before release of a mature sperm from the seminiferous epithelium (**spermiation**).

There are at least 4 generations of developing spermatogenic cells overlapping in a segment of a seminiferous tubule.

The development of a progeny takes place concomitantly with the development of earlier and later generations.

Spermatogenic cycle

A **spermatogenic cycle** involves changes **with time** at one particular point of the seminiferous tubule. A cycle can be monitored using a time-lapse camera placed at that given point.

Spermatogenic wave

A **spermatogenic wave** involves changes **along a seminiferous tubule (space)**. It can be visualized by traveling along a seminiferous tubule.

A wave cannot be visualized in the human testis because of the **helical progression** of a generation of spermatogenic cells.

perfamily of receptors and as such it has three domains: (1) a **DNA binding domain** that recognizes the **androgen-responsive element**, (2) a **transcription factors-binding domain**, and (3) an **androgen-binding domain**.

Recall that a defective androgen receptor—encoded by a gene in the X chromosome–determines the **androgen insensitivity syndrome** (AIS, also known as **testicular feminization**). The magnitude of symptoms in individuals with this genetic defect is variable depending on the partial to complete inability of the androgen receptor to bind to androgens.

Testosterone has a **negative feedback** effect on the release of LH. An excess of testosterone in circulating blood prevents the release of LH from the anterior hypophysis. Testosterone stimulates the function of the **seminal vesicles**, whereas dihydrotestosterone acts on the **prostate gland**.

The spermatogenic cycle

When you examine the seminiferous epithelium under the light microscope, you will note that spermatogenic cells are not arranged at random but are organized into well-defined **cellular associations** (Figures 20–16 and 20–17).

For example, in a particular region of the seminiferous epithelium, spermatids, completing their differentiation, can be seen only in specific combination with early spermatids, spermatocytes, and spermatogonia at their respective developmental stages. These cellular associations (designated by Roman numerals) succeed one another at a given site of the seminiferous tubule and this sequence repeats itself cyclically.

How does this grouping of spermatogenic cells occur? Each defined cell grouping represents a **stage** in the cyclic process of spermatogenesis. **The series of successive stages occurring between two appearances of the same cellular association in a given area of the seminiferous tubule is defined as the cycle of the seminiferous tubule.** The number of such stages in a cycle is constant for any given species (14 stages in the rat, **6 stages in man**, 12 in the monkey).

Suppose that we can continuously examine a portion of a seminiferous tubule in the living rat. We can realize that **all 14 stages (equivalent to one cycle) would occur in a wavelike succession along a stretch of a seminiferous tubule.** The series of cycles, each formed by 14 consecutive stages, repeat themselves again and again.

Let us examine Figure 20–17. Note that at least four generations of spermatogenic cells coexist in a given segment of a seminiferous epithelium. The development of any single generation takes place concomitantly with the development of the earlier and later generations.

In human testes, spermatogenic cell generations are organized in a helical fashion. Consequently, a cross section of a seminiferous tubule will display three or four cellular associations instead of the single one observed in the rat testis (see Figure 20–15). In man, the duration of one cycle is 16 days. It takes four cycles (64 days) to develop spermatogonia into testicular sperm.

21. SPERM TRANSPORT AND MATURATION

The development of the testis

We start Chapter 21 by reviewing the major developmental steps of the gonads and excurrent (efferent) ducts. This review will lead us to an understanding of the histology, function, and clinical significance of the pathway followed by male and female gametes in the pursuit of fertilization.

An important aspect to keep in mind is that the cell precursors of both gametes have an **extra-embryonic origin**. Primordial germinal cells appear first in the endoderm of the **yolk sac** wall in the 4 week fetus (Figure 21–1).

Between 4 and 6 weeks, about 10 to 100 primordial germ cells migrate by **ameboid movements** from the yolk sac to the gut tube and from there to the right and left sides of the dorsal body wall through the mesentery. This movement can be followed by cytochemistry, since the plasma membrane of migrating and proliferating primordial germinal cells is rich in the enzyme **alkaline phos-**

Figure 21–1

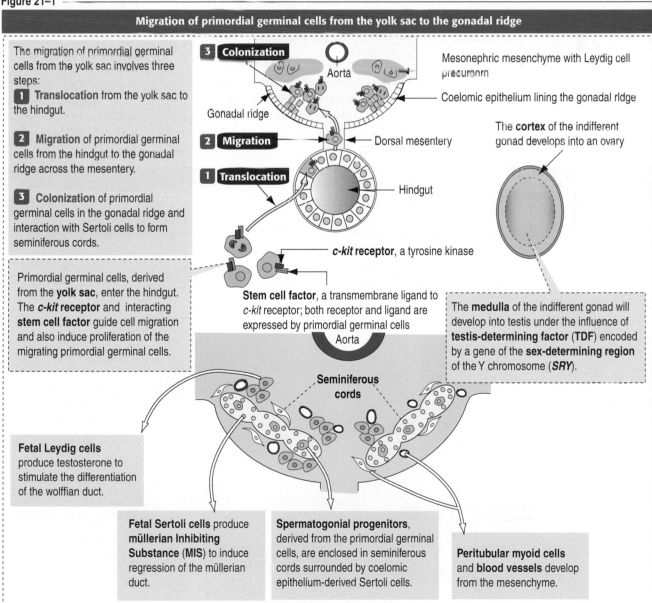

Migration of primordial germinal cells from the yolk sac to the gonadal ridge

The migration of primordial germinal cells from the yolk sac involves three steps:

1 **Translocation** from the yolk sac to the hindgut.

2 **Migration** of primordial germinal cells from the hindgut to the gonadal ridge across the mesentery.

3 **Colonization** of primordial germinal cells in the gonadal ridge and interaction with Sertoli cells to form seminiferous cords.

Primordial germinal cells, derived from the **yolk sac**, enter the hindgut. The **c-kit receptor** and interacting **stem cell factor** guide cell migration and also induce proliferation of the migrating primordial germinal cells.

3 **Colonization**

Aorta

Mesonephric mesenchyme with Leydig cell precursors

Coelomic epithelium lining the gonadal ridge

Gonadal ridge

2 **Migration**

Dorsal mesentery

1 **Translocation**

Hindgut

c-kit receptor, a tyrosine kinase

Stem cell factor, a transmembrane ligand to c-kit receptor; both receptor and ligand are expressed by primordial germinal cells

Aorta

The **cortex** of the indifferent gonad develops into an ovary

The **medulla** of the indifferent gonad will develop into testis under the influence of **testis-determining factor** (TDF) encoded by a gene of the **sex-determining region** of the Y chromosome (**SRY**).

Seminiferous cords

Fetal Leydig cells produce testosterone to stimulate the differentiation of the wolffian duct.

Fetal Sertoli cells produce **müllerian Inhibiting Substance** (MIS) to induce regression of the müllerian duct.

Spermatogonial progenitors, derived from the primordial germinal cells, are enclosed in seminiferous cords surrounded by coelomic epithelium-derived Sertoli cells.

Peritubular myoid cells and **blood vessels** develop from the mesenchyme.

Development of internal genitalia

When **Sertoli cell-derived MIS is not present**, the müllerian ducts become the fallopian tubes (oviducts), uterus, cervix, and upper one third of the vagina.

When **Leydig cell-derived testosterone is present**, the wolffian ducts become the epididymis, vas deferens, seminal vesicles, and ejaculatory ducts.

When **5-α reductase is present, testosterone is converted into dihydrotestosterone (DHT)**. DHT induces the genital tubercle, genital fold, genital swelling, and urogenital sinus to become the penis, scrotum, and prostate.

When **DHT is not present**, the genital tubercle, genital fold, genital swelling, and urogenital sinus become the labia majora, labia minora, clitoris, and lower two thirds of the vagina.

phatase.

The migration and proliferation of primordial germinal cells are dependent on the interaction of the *c-kit* receptor, a **tyrosine kinase**, with its corresponding cell membrane ligand, **stem cell factor**. Both the *c-kit* receptor and stem cell factor are produced by primordial germinal cells along their migration route.

A lack of the *c-kit* receptor or stem cell factor results in gonads deficient in primordial germ cells. Hematopoiesis and the development of melanocytes and mast cells, depend on the *c-kit* receptor and its ligand.

In the dorsal body wall, about 2500 to 5000 primordial germinal cells lodge in the mesenchyme at the level of the 10th thoracic vertebra and induce cells of the mesonephros and lining coelomic epithelium to proliferate, forming a pair of **genital ridges**. Coelomic epithelial cords grow into the mesenchyme of the gonadal ridge to form an **outer cortex** and **inner medulla** of the indifferent gonad.

Testis-determining factor controls the development of the testis

Until the seventh week of fetal development, there is one type of gonad common to both sexes. This is the "indifferent" stage of gonadal development. Thereafter, **in the female, the cortex develops into the ovary, and the medulla regresses. In the male, the cortex regresses and the medulla forms the testis.** The development of the testis is controlled by a gene product, called **testis-determining factor (TDF)**, encoded by a gene on the **sex-determining region of the Y chromosome (SRY)**.

The development of male and female internal genitalia: Role of müllerian-inhibiting substance and testosterone

The fetal testis is formed by **seminiferous cords** connected to the rete testis by tubuli recti. The cords are formed by **Sertoli cells**, derived from the coelomic

Figure 21-2

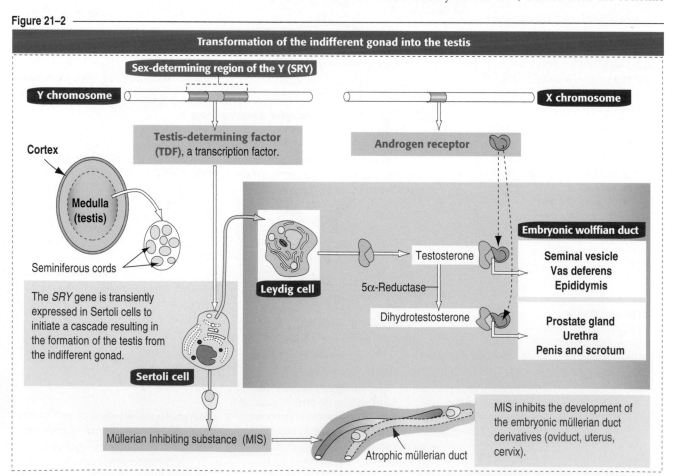

Transformation of the indifferent gonad into the testis

epithelium, and **spermatogonia**, derived from primordial germ cells. The seminiferous cords are separated by **Leydig cells,** derived from the mesonephric mesenchyme. Fetal Sertoli cells secrete **müllerian inhibiting substance (MIS),** which prevents müllerian ducts from developing into the uterovaginal primordium (Figure 21–2). In the absence of MIS, the müllerian ducts persist and become the female internal genitalia.

By 8 weeks of gestation, fetal Leydig cells produce testosterone, which is regulated by placental human chorionic gonadotropin (hCG), since the fetal hypophysis is not secreting luteinizing hormone (LH).

The cephalic end of the wolffian duct forms the epididymis, vas deferens, and ejaculatory duct. A diverticulum of the vas deferens forms the seminal vesicles. The prostate has a dual origin: the glandular epithelium forms from outgrowths of the prostatic urethral endoderm; the stroma and smooth muscle derive from the surrounding mesoderm.

In the absence of androgen, the wolffian duct regresses and the prostate fails to develop. If high levels of androgen are present in the **female fetus**, both müllerian and wolffian ducts can persist.

Testicular descent

The **gubernaculum** forms on the lower pole of the testis, crosses obliquely through the abdominal wall, and attaches to the scrotal swelling. By week 28, the testis moves deep into the inguinal ring. The gubernaculum grows and the testis descends into the scrotum. For additional details, see Cryptorchidism (or undescended testis) in Chapter 20, Spermatogenesis.

Clinical significance: Genetic abnormalities of the male reproductive tract
Klinefelter's syndrome

Klinefelter's syndrome is observed in males with an **extra X chromosome** (karyotype: 47,XXY). Individuals with this syndrome: (1) are phenotypically males (presence of the Y chromosome); (2) have small testes and few spermatogenic cells are present; (3) have high follicle-stimulating hormone (FSH) levels because the function of Sertoli cells is abnormal; (4) have low testosterone levels, but **high estradiol levels.** The excess of estradiol can lead to feminization, including **gynecomastia.**

Androgen insensitivity syndrome (AIS; testicular feminization)

AIS results from a complete or partial defect in the gene controlling the expression of the androgen receptor. This gene is located on the X chromosome.

Although the karyotype is 46,XY, a deficiency in the action of androgen results in the lack of development of the wolffian duct and the regression of the müllerian duct because testes, and therefore Sertoli cell–derived MIS, are present. No functional **internal genitalia** are present in patients with AIS: the testes remain in the abdomen (recall that androgens stimulate testicular descent).

The **external genitalia** develop as female. Individuals with complete AIS have labia, a clitoris, and a short vagina (these structures are not müllerian duct derivatives). Pubic and axillary hair is absent (sexual hair development is androgen-dependent). At puberty, the production of both androgen and estradiol increases (the latter from peripheral aromatization of androgens). Androgens cannot inhibit LH secretion (because a defective androgen receptor prevents LH feedback inhibition), and plasma levels of androgens remain high.

5α-Reductase deficiency

A defect in the activity of the enzyme 5α-reductase results in decreased formation of dihydrotestosterone (DHT). These individuals have normal internal genitalia (whose development from the wolffian duct is androgen-dependent) but nonmasculinized external genitalia. They are often mistaken for females at birth.

Figure 21–3

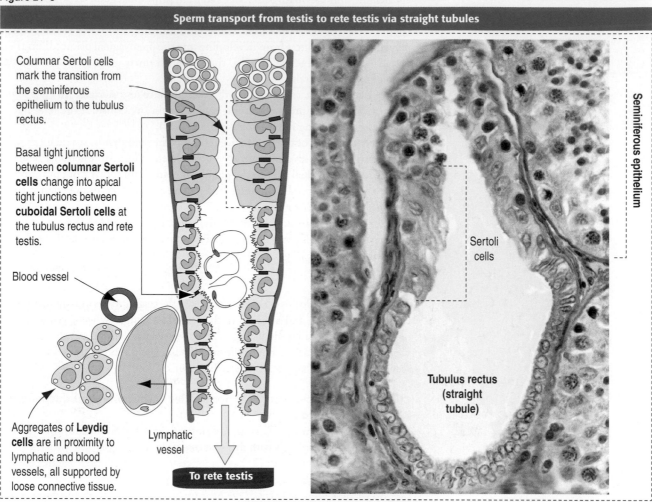

The sperm maturation pathway

After transport to the **rete testis** through a connecting **tubulus rectus**, sperm enter the **ductuli efferentes** (Figure 21–3). Ductuli efferentes link the rete testis to the initial segment of the epididymal duct, an irregularly coiled duct extending to the **ductus**, or **vas deferens**.

Tubuli recti (**straight tubules**) are located in the mediastinum of the testis. They are lined by a **simple cuboidal epithelium** with structural features similar to those of Sertoli cells except that occluding junctions are now at the **apical domain**, instead of at the basal domain. Spermatogenic cells are not present.

The **rete testis** consists of irregularly anastomosing channels within the mediastinum of the testis (Figure 21–4). These channels are lined by a **simple cuboidal epithelium**. The wall, formed by fibroblasts and myoid cells, is surrounded by large lymphatic channels and blood vessels associated with large clusters of Leydig cells.

The **ductuli efferentes** are lined by a **columnar epithelium** with **principal cells with stereocilia**—with a role in the reabsorption of fluid from the lumen—and **ciliated cells,** which contribute to the transport of **nonmotile sperm** toward the epididymis. **The epithelium has a characteristic scalloped outline that enables identification of the ductuli efferentes** (see Figure 21–4). A thin inner circular layer of **smooth muscle cells** underlies the epithelium and its basal lamina.

The **epididymis** is a highly coiled tubule (4 to 6 cm long) where spermatozoa mature (acquire a **forward motility pattern** essential to their **fertilizing ability**).

The epididymal duct is subdivided into three major segments: (1) the **head,** or caput; (2) the **body**, or **corpus**; and (3) the **tail**, or **cauda** (Figure 21–4).

The epithelium is **pseudostratified columnar** with long and branched **stereocilia**. The epithelium consists of **two major cell types** (Figure 21–5):

Figure 21–4

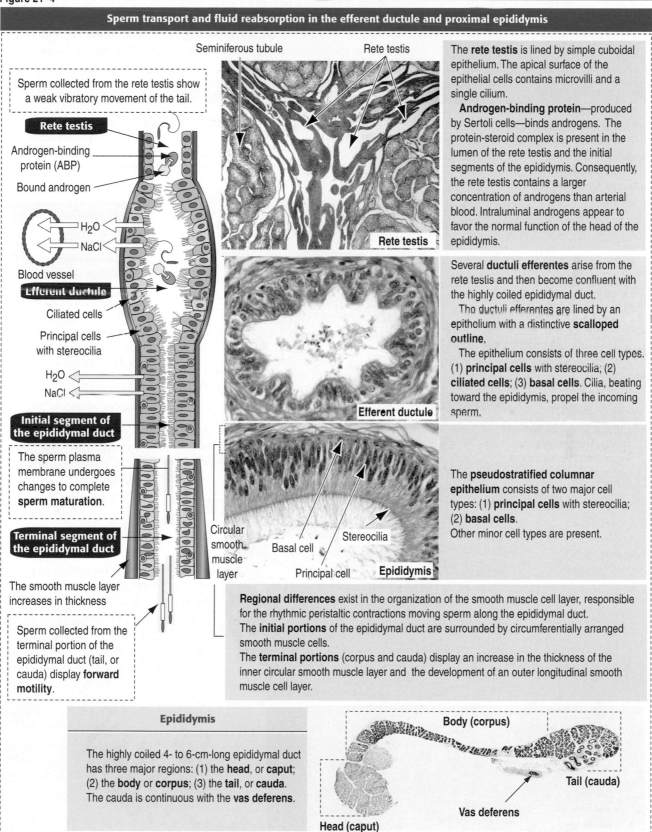

Sperm transport and fluid reabsorption in the efferent ductule and proximal epididymis

Sperm collected from the rete testis show a weak vibratory movement of the tail.

Rete testis

Androgen-binding protein (ABP)

Bound androgen

H₂O

NaCl

Blood vessel

Efferent ductule

Ciliated cells

Principal cells with stereocilia

H₂O

NaCl

Initial segment of the epididymal duct

The sperm plasma membrane undergoes changes to complete **sperm maturation**.

Terminal segment of the epididymal duct

The smooth muscle layer increases in thickness

Sperm collected from the terminal portion of the epididymal duct (tail, or cauda) display **forward motility**.

Seminiferous tubule   Rete testis

Rete testis

Circular smooth muscle layer

Basal cell   Stereocilia

Principal cell   *Epididymis*

The **rete testis** is lined by simple cuboidal epithelium. The apical surface of the epithelial cells contains microvilli and a single cilium.

Androgen-binding protein—produced by Sertoli cells—binds androgens. The protein-steroid complex is present in the lumen of the rete testis and the initial segments of the epididymis. Consequently, the rete testis contains a larger concentration of androgens than arterial blood. Intraluminal androgens appear to favor the normal function of the head of the epididymis.

Several **ductuli efferentes** arise from the rete testis and then become confluent with the highly coiled epididymal duct.

The ductuli efferentes are lined by an epithelium with a distinctive **scalloped outline**.

The epithelium consists of three cell types. (1) **principal cells** with stereocilia; (2) **ciliated cells**; (3) **basal cells**. Cilia, beating toward the epididymis, propel the incoming sperm.

Efferent ductule

The **pseudostratified columnar epithelium** consists of two major cell types: (1) **principal cells** with stereocilia; (2) **basal cells**.
Other minor cell types are present.

Regional differences exist in the organization of the smooth muscle cell layer, responsible for the rhythmic peristaltic contractions moving sperm along the epididymal duct.
The **initial portions** of the epididymal duct are surrounded by circumferentially arranged smooth muscle cells.
The **terminal portions** (corpus and cauda) display an increase in the thickness of the inner circular smooth muscle layer and the development of an outer longitudinal smooth muscle cell layer.

Epididymis

The highly coiled 4- to 6-cm-long epididymal duct has three major regions: (1) the **head**, or **caput**; (2) the **body** or **corpus**; (3) the **tail**, or **cauda**. The cauda is continuous with the **vas deferens**.

Body (corpus)

Tail (cauda)

Vas deferens

Head (caput)

1. Columnar **principal cells**, extending from the lumen to the basal lamina. The apical domain of principal cells displays branched stereocilia and a well-developed Golgi apparatus, lysosomes, and vesicles.

2. **Basal cells** with a **pyramidal** shape associated with the basal lamina. Basal cells are regarded as the undifferentiated precursors of principal cells.

Other cell types are the **apical cells**, rich in mitochondria and predominant in the head of the epididymis, and the **clear cells**, predominant in the tail of the

Figure 21–5

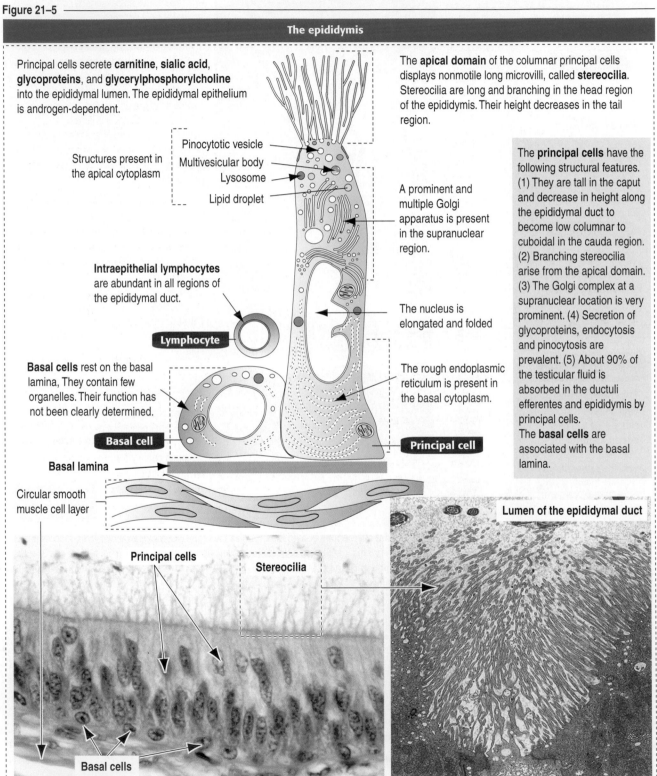

The epididymis

Principal cells secrete **carnitine**, **sialic acid**, **glycoproteins**, and **glycerylphosphorylcholine** into the epididymal lumen. The epididymal epithelium is androgen-dependent.

Structures present in the apical cytoplasm
- Pinocytotic vesicle
- Multivesicular body
- Lysosome
- Lipid droplet

Intraepithelial lymphocytes are abundant in all regions of the epididymal duct.

Lymphocyte

Basal cells rest on the basal lamina, They contain few organelles. Their function has not been clearly determined.

Basal cell

Basal lamina

Circular smooth muscle cell layer

The **apical domain** of the columnar principal cells displays nonmotile long microvilli, called **stereocilia**. Stereocilia are long and branching in the head region of the epididymis. Their height decreases in the tail region.

A prominent and multiple Golgi apparatus is present in the supranuclear region.

The nucleus is elongated and folded

The rough endoplasmic reticulum is present in the basal cytoplasm.

Principal cell

The **principal cells** have the following structural features. (1) They are tall in the caput and decrease in height along the epididymal duct to become low columnar to cuboidal in the cauda region. (2) Branching stereocilia arise from the apical domain. (3) The Golgi complex at a supranuclear location is very prominent. (4) Secretion of glycoproteins, endocytosis and pinocytosis are prevalent. (5) About 90% of the testicular fluid is absorbed in the ductuli efferentes and epididymis by principal cells.
The **basal cells** are associated with the basal lamina.

Principal cells

Stereocilia

Lumen of the epididymal duct

Basal cells

Figure 21–6

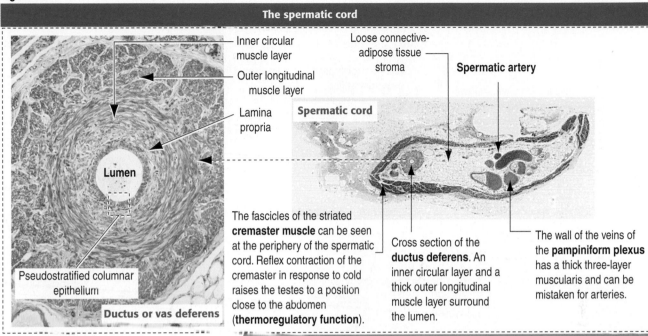

The spermatic cord

Inner circular muscle layer

Outer longitudinal muscle layer

Lamina propria

Lumen

Pseudostratified columnar epithelium

Ductus or vas deferens

Loose connective-adipose tissue stroma

Spermatic artery

Spermatic cord

The fascicles of the striated **cremaster muscle** can be seen at the periphery of the spermatic cord. Reflex contraction of the cremaster in response to cold raises the testes to a position close to the abdomen (**thermoregulatory function**).

Cross section of the **ductus deferens**. An inner circular layer and a thick outer longitudinal muscle layer surround the lumen.

The wall of the veins of the **pampiniform plexus** has a thick three-layer muscularis and can be mistaken for arteries.

Highlights of the epididymal duct

The epididymis has three main functions:
1. **Sperm maturation**. Sperm collected from the head region of the epididymis are unable to fertilize. The fertilizing ability is acquired from the body to the tail of the epididymis.
   Sperm maturation includes:
   a. Stabilization of condensed chromatin.
   b. Changes in plasma membrane surface charge.
   c. Acquisition by sperm of new surface proteins.
2. **Sperm storage** until ejaculation.
3. **Sperm transport** by peristaltis to the storage region, the tail of the epididymis. The time of sperm epididymal maturation is from 2 to 12 days.

epididymis. **Intraepithelial lymphocytes** are distributed throughout the epididymis. They may be an important component of the epididymal immunologic barrier.

The **height of the epithelium** varies with respect to the segment of the epididymal duct. The epithelium is **taller in the head region** and **shorter in the tail region**. In an opposite fashion, the lumen of the epididymal duct is narrow in the head region and wider in the tail region.

An **inner smooth muscle circular layer**, of increasing thickness from head to tail, and an **outer longitudinal layer**, visible from the body on, surround the epithelium and basal lamina. The muscle layer displays **peristaltic movements** to facilitate sperm transport along the epididymal duct.

In the **spermatic cord**, the **ductus deferens** (vas deferens) has the following features: (1) the lining epithelium continues as **pseudostratified columnar**; and (2) the muscular wall consists of **inner** and **outer layers** of longitudinally oriented muscle separated by a **middle circular layer**.

In addition to the ductus deferens, the spermatic cord contains the following components (Figure 21–6): (1) the **cremaster muscle**, (2) the **spermatic artery**, and (3) **veins of the pampiniform plexus**.

An **ampulla**, the dilated portion of the ductus deferens, leads directly into the prostate gland. The distal end receives the ducts of the seminal vesicle, forming the **ejaculatory duct**, which passes through the prostate to empty into the prostatic urethra at the seminal colliculus.

Accessory genital glands

The accessory glands of the male reproductive tract include the **seminal vesicles**, the **prostate gland**, and the **bulbourethral glands** of Cowper. The seminal vesicles and the prostate produce most of the seminal fluid, and their function is regulated by androgens (testosterone and DHT).

Seminal vesicles

The seminal vesicles are androgen-dependent organs. Each seminal vesicle consists of three components (Figure 21–7): (1) an **outer connective tissue layer**; (2) a **middle circular and longitudinal smooth muscle layer**, and (3) an **inner folded mucosa** lined by a **simple cuboidal-to-pseudostratified columnar epithelium**.

Figure 21-7

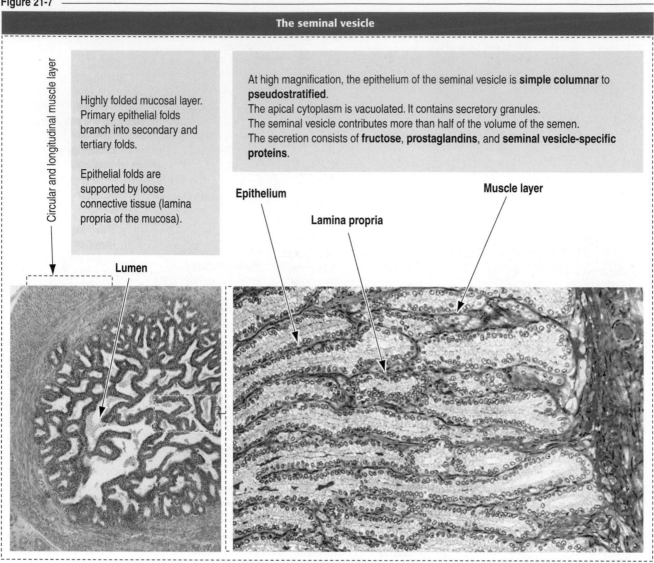

The seminal vesicle

Circular and longitudinal muscle layer

Highly folded mucosal layer. Primary epithelial folds branch into secondary and tertiary folds.

Epithelial folds are supported by loose connective tissue (lamina propria of the mucosa).

At high magnification, the epithelium of the seminal vesicle is **simple columnar** to **pseudostratified**.
The apical cytoplasm is vacuolated. It contains secretory granules.
The seminal vesicle contributes more than half of the volume of the semen.
The secretion consists of **fructose**, **prostaglandins**, and **seminal vesicle-specific proteins**.

Epithelium

Lamina propria

Muscle layer

Lumen

The epithelial cells display a large Golgi apparatus with vesicles containing **secretory granules**. Seminal vesicles secrete a viscous fluid rich in **fructose** and contribute about 50% to 70% of the human seminal fluid. Fructose is the major source of energy of the ejaculated sperm. The excretory duct of each seminal vesicle penetrates the prostate after joining the vas deferens to form the ejaculatory duct (Figure 21–8).

Prostate gland

The prostate is the largest accessory genital gland. It consists of 30 to 50 branched **tubuloalveolar glands** that empty their contents into the **prostatic urethra** via long excretory ducts.

The prostatic glands are arranged in three regions (Figure 21–9): (1) **periurethral mucosal glands**, (2) **periurethral submucosal glands**, and (3) **peripheral compound glands, called main glands**.

The glands are lined by **simple** or **pseudostratified columnar epithelium** (Figure 21–10). The lumen contains **prostatic concretions (corpora amylacea)** rich in glycoproteins and, sometimes, a site of **calcium deposition**. Cells contain abundant rough endoplasmic reticulum and Golgi apparatus. The secretory products include **prostate-specific acid phosphatase**, **prostate-specific antigen**, **amylase**, and **fibrinolysin**.

Figure 21-8

The ejaculatory ducts

The duct of the seminal vesicle pierces the capsule of the prostate gland and joins the ductus deferens of the same side to form the **ejaculatory duct**.
The ejaculatory duct opens onto the posterior wall of the prostatic urethra. The wall of the ejaculatory ducts is folded and lined by **simple columnar epithelium** surrounded by connective tissue and bundles of smooth muscle.

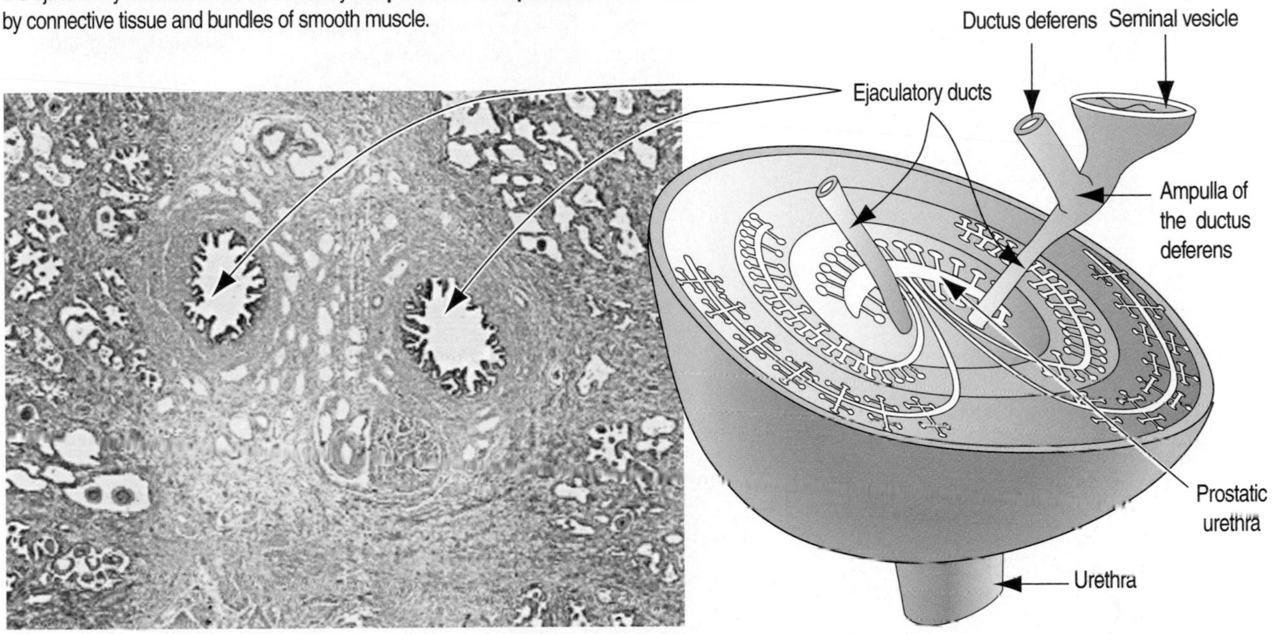

Clinical significance: Benign prostatic hyperplasia and prostate cancer

The mucosal and submucosal prostatic glands of older men undergo **nodular hyperplasia** (**benign prostatic hyperplasia**, or **BPH**; see Figure 21-9).

Nodular hyperplasia produces:

1. Difficulty in urination and urinary obstruction caused by compression of the prostatic urethra by the nodular growth.

2. Retention of urine in the bladder or inability to empty the urinary bladder completely. The possibility of infection leads to inflammation of the urinary bladder (**cystitis**) and renal infection (**pyelonephritis**). Acute and persistent urinary retention requires emergency catheterization.

BPH is caused by **dihydrotestosterone** (**DHT**), a metabolite of testosterone (Figure 21-11). The enzyme **5α-reductase**, present mainly in prostatic **stromal cells**, converts testosterone to DHT. DHT binds to cytosol and nuclear androgen receptors to induce the expression of **growth factors** mitogenic to prostatic epithelial and stromal cells. Inhibitors of 5α-reductase reduce the production of DHT, decrease the periurethral nodular hyperplasia, and alleviate urinary obstruction.

Carcinoma of the prostate originates from the main prostatic glands, farthest from the urethra. Urinary symptoms are not present at the early stage and tumor growth is often detected by digital palpation of the prostate, by elevated serum levels of **prostate-specific antigen** (**PSA**), or by back pain caused by vertebral **metastasis**. Transperineal or transrectal **biopsy** is required to confirm a clinical diagnosis.

As in BPH, androgens also play a role in the development of prostate carcinoma. Tumor growth can be controlled by **orchidectomy** (surgical removal of the testes), the major source of androgens. Surgery and radiotherapy are suitable when the tumor is localized.

Figure 21–9

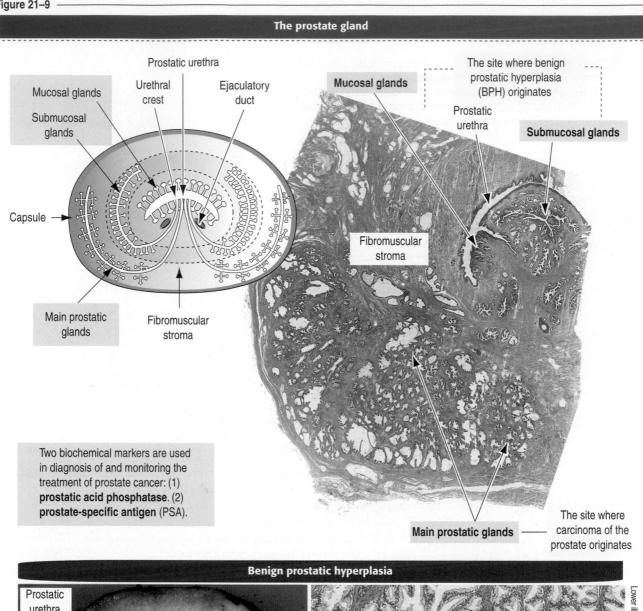

The prostate gland

Prostatic urethra
Urethral crest
Ejaculatory duct
Mucosal glands
Submucosal glands
Capsule
Main prostatic glands
Fibromuscular stroma

Mucosal glands

The site where benign prostatic hyperplasia (BPH) originates
Prostatic urethra
Submucosal glands

Fibromuscular stroma

Two biochemical markers are used in diagnosis of and monitoring the treatment of prostate cancer: (1) **prostatic acid phosphatase**. (2) **prostate-specific antigen** (PSA).

Main prostatic glands

The site where carcinoma of the prostate originates

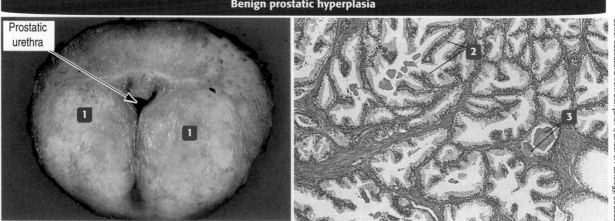

Benign prostatic hyperplasia

Prostatic urethra
1
1
2
3

1 In BPH, nodules form in the periurethral region of the prostate. Large nodules can compress the prostatic urethra leading to urinary obstruction. **2** Histologically, prostatic glands are enlarged and the epithelial lining is folded. **3** Corpora amylacea are seen in the glandular lumen.

Dihydrotestosterone (DHT), derived from testosterone by the action of 5α-reductase, acts on both stromal and epithelial glandular cells to induce the formation of prostatic nodules.

Because the enzyme 5α-reductase is present in stromal cells, stromal cells have a pivotal role in generating DHT and BPH.

Lower illustrations from Damjanov I, Linder J: Pathology, St. Louis, Mosby, 2000.

Figure 21–10

The prostatic tubuloalveolar gland

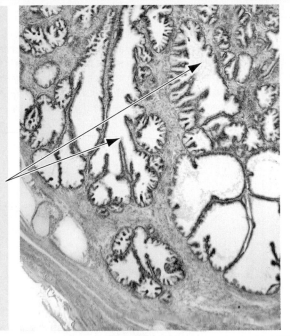

The prostate is a muscular and glandular organ. It consists of three groups of glands: (1) **periurethral mucosal glands**; (2) **periurethral submucosal glands, linked to the urethra by short ducts**; (3) **main prostatic glands**. About 30-50 tubuloalveolar glands open directly into the prostatic urethra through 15-30 long ducts ending at the sides of the urethral crest.

The epithelium of the main prostatic glands is **simple columnar** or **pseudostratified** and arranged into folds supported by a lamina propria. The lumen may contain **corpora amylacea**, a condensed structure rich in glycoproteins and cell fragments, with a tendency to calcify in older men.

The secretion of the prostate is acidic (pH 6.5). It contains **fibrinolysin**, with a role in the liquefaction of semen. **Citric acid**, **zinc**, **amylase**, **prostate-specific antigen**, and **acid phosphatase** are present in high concentrations in prostatic fluid secreted in the semen.

The prostatic epithelium is androgen-dependent.

The male and female urethra

The urethra in the **male** is 20 cm long and has three segments:

1. The **prostatic urethra**, which receives the ejaculatory ducts and the ducts of the prostate.

2. The **membranous urethra**, the shortest segment.

3. The **penile urethra**, which receives the ducts of the bulbourethral glands (Figure 21–12).

The epithelium of the prostatic urethra is **transitional (urothelium)**. It changes

Figure 21–11

Stromal-prostatic epithelial cell interaction

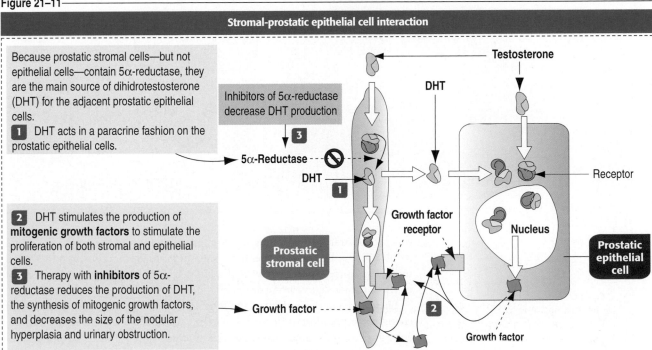

Because prostatic stromal cells—but not epithelial cells—contain 5α-reductase, they are the main source of dihidrotestosterone (DHT) for the adjacent prostatic epithelial cells.

1 DHT acts in a paracrine fashion on the prostatic epithelial cells.

2 DHT stimulates the production of **mitogenic growth factors** to stimulate the proliferation of both stromal and epithelial cells.

3 Therapy with **inhibitors** of 5α-reductase reduces the production of DHT, the synthesis of mitogenic growth factors, and decreases the size of the nodular hyperplasia and urinary obstruction.

Inhibitors of 5α-reductase decrease DHT production

Figure 21–12

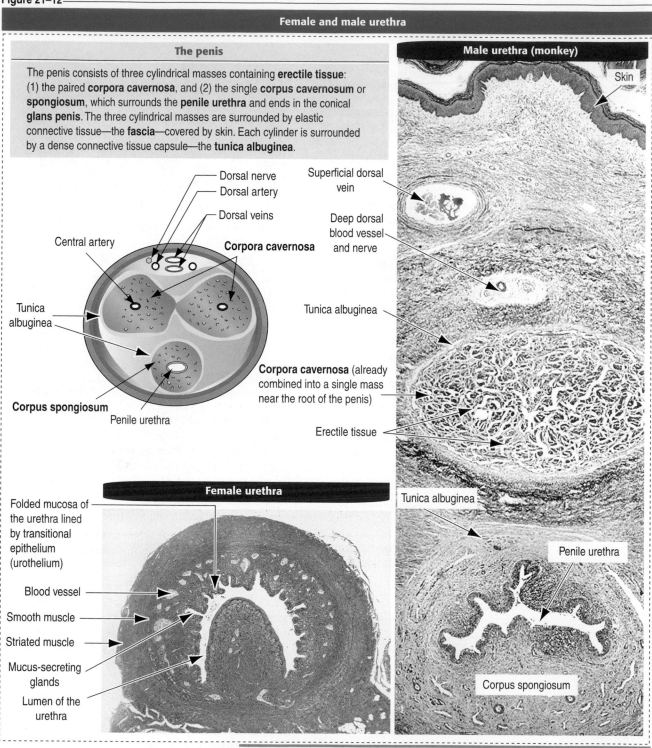

Female and male urethra

The penis

The penis consists of three cylindrical masses containing **erectile tissue**: (1) the paired **corpora cavernosa**, and (2) the single **corpus cavernosum** or **spongiosum**, which surrounds the **penile urethra** and ends in the conical **glans penis**. The three cylindrical masses are surrounded by elastic connective tissue—the **fascia**—covered by skin. Each cylinder is surrounded by a dense connective tissue capsule—the **tunica albuginea**.

Dorsal nerve
Dorsal artery
Dorsal veins
Central artery
Corpora cavernosa
Tunica albuginea
Corpus spongiosum
Penile urethra

Male urethra (monkey)
Skin
Superficial dorsal vein
Deep dorsal blood vessel and nerve
Tunica albuginea
Corpora cavernosa (already combined into a single mass near the root of the penis)
Erectile tissue
Tunica albuginea
Penile urethra
Corpus spongiosum

Female urethra
Folded mucosa of the urethra lined by transitional epithelium (urothelium)
Blood vessel
Smooth muscle
Striated muscle
Mucus-secreting glands
Lumen of the urethra

to a pseudostratified-to-stratified columnar epithelium in the membranous and penile urethra. The **muscle layer** in the membranous urethra consists of a smooth muscle sphincter (involuntary) and a striated muscle sphincter (voluntary). It controls the passage of urine or semen.

The urethra in the **female** is 4 cm long and is lined by **transitional epithelium** changing to pseudostratified columnar and stratified squamous nonkeratinized epithelium near the urethral meatus. The mucosa contains mucus-secreting glands (see Figure 21–12). An inner layer of smooth muscle is surrounded by a circular

Figure 21–13

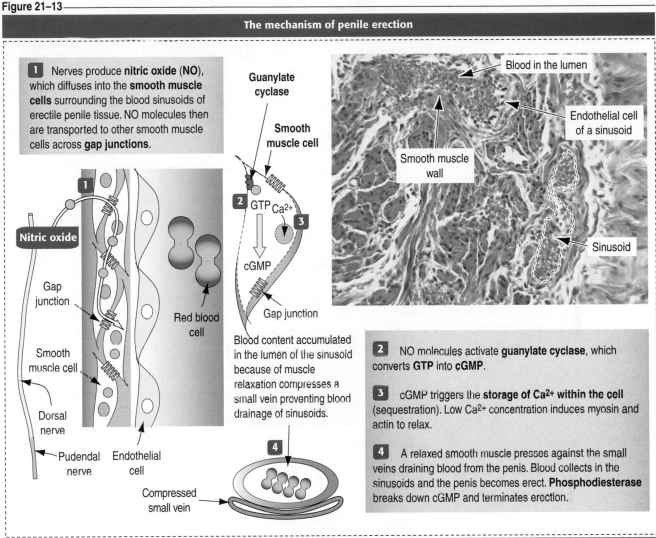

The mechanism of penile erection

1 Nerves produce **nitric oxide (NO)**, which diffuses into the **smooth muscle cells** surrounding the blood sinusoids of erectile penile tissue. NO molecules then are transported to other smooth muscle cells across **gap junctions**.

Guanylate cyclase

Smooth muscle cell

Nitric oxide

Gap junction

Red blood cell

Smooth muscle cell

Dorsal nerve

Pudendal nerve

Endothelial cell

Compressed small vein

GTP Ca²⁺

cGMP

Gap junction

Blood content accumulated in the lumen of the sinusoid because of muscle relaxation compresses a small vein preventing blood drainage of sinusoids.

Blood in the lumen

Endothelial cell of a sinusoid

Smooth muscle wall

Sinusoid

2 NO molecules activate **guanylate cyclase**, which converts **GTP** into **cGMP**.

3 cGMP triggers the **storage of Ca²⁺ within the cell** (sequestration). Low Ca²⁺ concentration induces myosin and actin to relax.

4 A relaxed smooth muscle presses against the small veins draining blood from the penis. Blood collects in the sinusoids and the penis becomes erect. **Phosphodiesterase** breaks down cGMP and terminates erection.

layer of striated muscle that closes the urethra when contracted.

Bulbourethral glands

The bulbourethral glands are lined by a mucus-secreting epithelium. The secretion, containing abundant **galactose** and a moderate amount of **sialic acid**, is discharged into the **penile urethra**. This secretion has a **lubrication function** and precedes the emission of semen along the penile urethra.

The penis

The penis consists of three cylindrical columnar masses of **erectile tissue** (see Figure 21–12): the right and left **corpora cavernosa**, and the ventral **corpus spongiosum**, transversed by the penile urethra. The three columns converge to form the shaft of the penis. The distal tip of the corpus spongiosum is the **glans penis**.

The corpora cavernosa and corpus spongiosum contain irregular and communicating blood spaces, or sinusoids, supplied by an artery and drained by venous channels. During erection, arterial blood fills the sinusoids, which enlarge and compress the draining venous channels.

Two chemicals control erection: **nitric oxide** and **phosphodiesterase** (Figure 21–13).

1. Sexual stimulation, via the cerebral cortex and hypothalamus and transported down the spinal cord to autonomic nerves in the penis, causes the branches

of the **dorsal nerve**, the end point of the pudendal nerve, to produce **nitric oxide**.

Nitric oxide molecules spread rapidly across **gap junctions** of **smooth muscle cells** surrounding the blood sinusoids. Within smooth muscle cells, nitric oxide molecules activate **guanylate cyclase** to produce **cyclic guanosine monophosphate (cGMP) from guanosine triphosphate (GTP)**.

cGMP **relaxes the smooth muscle cell wall** surrounding the sinusoids by inducing the **sequestration of Ca^{2+}** within intracellular storage sites. The lowered concentrations of Ca^{2+} determine the relaxation of smooth muscle cells, which leads to the accumulation of blood in the sinusoids by the rapid flow of arterial blood from the dorsal and cavernous arteries (see Figure 21–12). Sinusoids engorged with blood compress the small veins that drain blood from the penis and the penis becomes erect.

2. The enzyme **phosphodiesterase** (PDE) is produced to destroy cGMP and terminate erection. By blocking PDE activity, cGMP levels remain elevated and the penis remains erect.

Clinical significance: Erectile dysfunction

Factors that affect the cerebral cortex-hypothalamus-spinal cord-autonomic nerve pathway and vascular diseases can cause erectile dysfunction. Traumatic head and spinal cord injuries, stroke, Parkinson's disease, and systemic diseases, such as diabetes and multiple sclerosis, reduce nerve function and lead to erectile dysfunction. In addition, anxiety disorders can be a primary cause of erectile dysfunction.

Sildenafil (Viagra) was originally tested as a treatment for heart failure. During clinical trials, it was noticed that a significant number of patients were getting erections after taking the drug. This observation initiated an independent clinical study to evaluate the effect of sildenafil in the treatment of impotence. In the penis, sildenafil blocks a specific phosphodiesterase found in smooth muscle cells, and, by this mechanism, inhibits the degradation of cGMP. High levels of cGMP induce Ca^{2+} to enter storage areas in the cell and induce the perisinusoidal smooth muscle cells to relax.

Sildenafil can cause dose-dependent side effects such as facial flushing, gastrointestinal distress, headaches, and a blue tinge to vision.

Development of the female reproductive tract

An important feature of the development of the female and male reproductive tracts is the initial **indifferent stage**. Knowledge of the developmental sequence from the indifferent stage to the fully developed stage is helpful in understanding the structural anomalies that can sometimes be observed. The female reproductive system is composed of the **ovaries**, the **ducts** (**oviduct**, **uterus**, and **vagina**) and the **external genitalia** (**labia majora**, **labia minora**, and **clitoris**). The development of these components is summarized in the next section.

Development of the ovary

As discussed in Chapter 21, Sperm Transport and Maturation, the **cortical region** of the primitive gonad develops into an ovary. The cortical region of the **indifferent gonad** initially contains the **primary sex cords**, extending into the mesenchyme from the **coelomic epithelium** (fifth week of development).

One week later, cells of the primary cell cords degenerate and are replaced by **secondary sex cords** that surround individual **oogonia** (Figure 22–1).

Oogonia result from the mitotic division of migrating **primordial germinal cells** derived from the yolk sac. Primordial germinal cells contain two X chromosomes. The **testis-determining factor** (TDF), encoded by the gene *SRY*, on the **sex-determining region of the Y chromosome**, is obviously not present.

In the fetal ovary, oogonia enter meiotic prophase I to become **primary oocytes** which become arrested after completion of crossing over (exchange of genetic information between non–sister chromatids of homologous chromosomes).

Figure 22–1

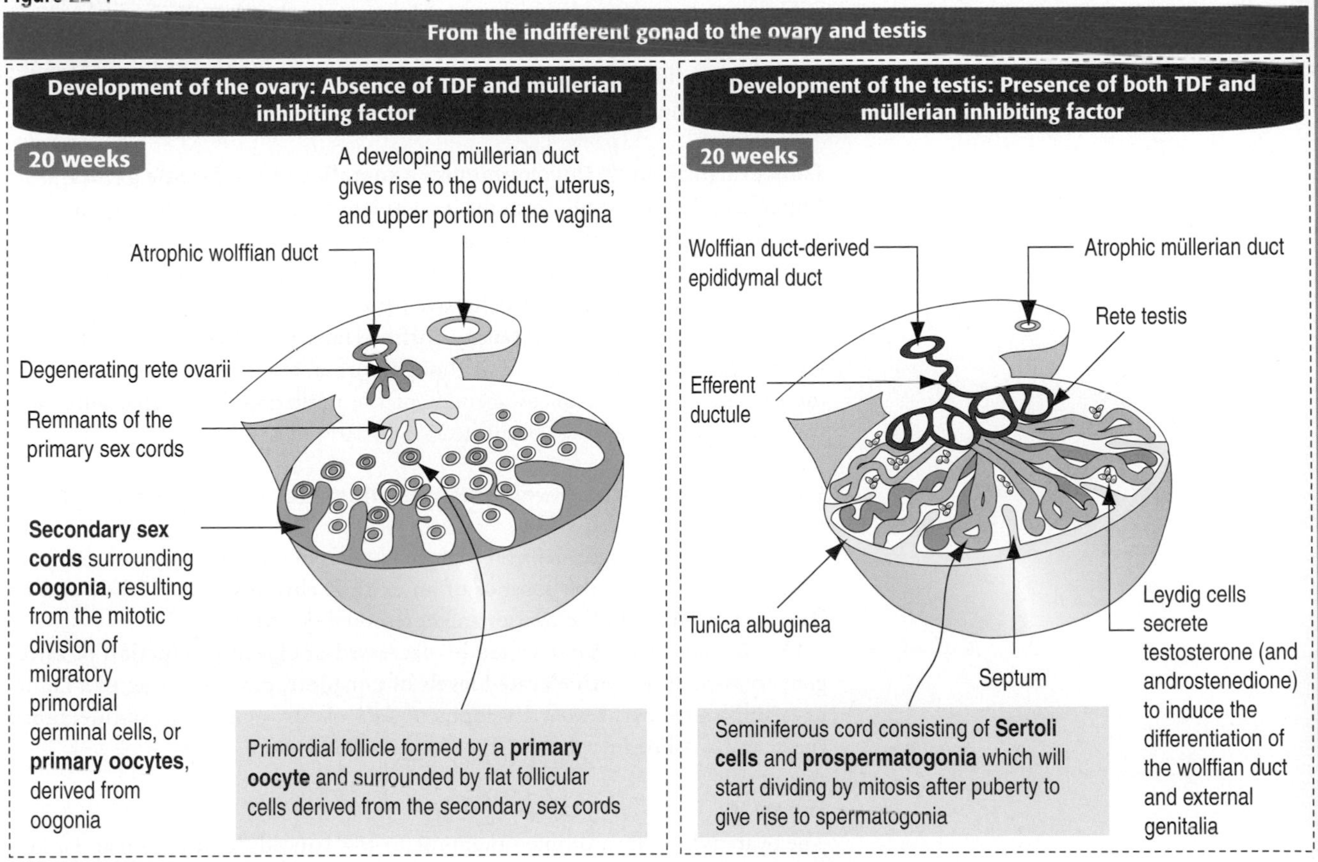

From the indifferent gonad to the ovary and testis

Development of the ovary: Absence of TDF and müllerian inhibiting factor

20 weeks

A developing müllerian duct gives rise to the oviduct, uterus, and upper portion of the vagina

Atrophic wolffian duct

Degenerating rete ovarii

Remnants of the primary sex cords

Secondary sex cords surrounding **oogonia**, resulting from the mitotic division of migratory primordial germinal cells, or **primary oocytes**, derived from oogonia

Primordial follicle formed by a **primary oocyte** and surrounded by flat follicular cells derived from the secondary sex cords

Development of the testis: Presence of both TDF and müllerian inhibiting factor

20 weeks

Wolffian duct-derived epididymal duct

Atrophic müllerian duct

Rete testis

Efferent ductule

Tunica albuginea

Septum

Leydig cells secrete testosterone (and androstenedione) to induce the differentiation of the wolffian duct and external genitalia

Seminiferous cord consisting of **Sertoli cells** and **prospermatogonia** which will start dividing by mitosis after puberty to give rise to spermatogonia

Meiotic prophase arrest continues until puberty, when one or more follicles are stimulated to develop.

Development of the female genital ducts

During development, the **cranial ends of the müllerian ducts** remain separated to form the **oviducts**, which open into the coelomic cavity (the future peritoneal cavity). The **caudal segments of the müllerian ducts** fuse to develop into the **uterovaginal primordium** that becomes the **uterus** and **upper part of the vagina**. The **broad ligaments** of the uterus, derived from two peritoneal folds, approach each other when the müllerian ducts fuse.

The **primitive cloaca** is divided into two regions: (1) the **ventral urogenital sinus** and (2) the **dorsal anorectal canal**.

The cloacal membrane is divided by the **urorectal septum** into the **dorsal anal membrane** and the **ventral urogenital membrane**. By week 7, the membranes rupture.

The contact of the uterovaginal primordium with the urogenital sinus results in the formation of the **vaginal plate**. The **canalization of the vaginal plate** results in the development of the middle and lower portions of the vagina:

1. The solid mass of cells of the vaginal plate extends from the urogenital sinus into the uterovaginal primordium.

2. The central cells of the vaginal plate disappear, forming the lumen of the vagina.

3. The peripheral cells persist and form the vaginal epithelium.

The urogenital sinus also gives rise to the urinary bladder, urethra, vestibular glands, and hymen.

Development of the external genitalia

By week 4, the **genital tubercle**, or **phallus**, develops at the cranial end of the **cloacal membrane**. Then, **labioscrotal swellings** and **urogenital folds** develop at either side of the cloacal membrane. The genital tubercle enlarges in both the female and male. In the absence of androgens, the external genitalia are feminized: the **phallus** develops into the **clitoris**. The **urogenital folds** form the **labia minora**, and the **labioscrotal swellings** develop into the **labia majora**.

Clinical significance: Developmental anomalies of the female genital tract

Imperforate hymen results from the **incomplete canalization of the vaginal plate**. This condition obstructs the passage of menstrual blood when menarche occurs and is accompanied by pain in the lower abdomen and bulging of the vaginal introitus. Hymenotomy is the definitive treatment.

In **müllerian agenesis (Rokitansky-Küster-Hauser syndrome)**, the uterus, cervix, and upper vagina are absent. Although **normal ovulation occurs**, there is **no menstruation**. In addition to agenesis of the müllerian duct, renal anomalies (unilateral kidney agenesis) occur in 25% to 30% of cases.

Clinical significance: Developmental anomalies of the ovary: Turner's syndrome

The fundamental genetic defect recognized in prepubertal and pubertal girls with **Turner's syndrome** is the **absence of an extra X chromosome (45,X0)** and **no Barr bodies**. At birth, the ovaries are represented by **streaks**.

Ovarian failure is characterized by decreased or absent production of estrogens in association with elevated levels of gonadotropins, resulting in a failure to establish secondary sexual development (lack of estrogens), short stature, broad chest, and a webbed neck.

The ovary

The ovary is lined by a **simple squamous-to-low cuboidal epithelium** and a sub-

Figure 22–2

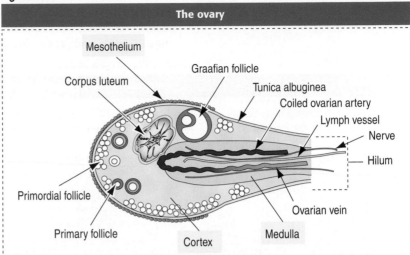

The ovary

The ovary is covered by a **mesothelium** (simple cuboidal-to-squamous epithelium) and consists of an outer **cortex** and a central **medulla**. The medulla contains connective tissue supporting large blood vessels (a **coiled and tortuous ovarian artery** and vein), lymph vessels, and nerves. The cortex displays clusters of **primordial follicles**. The **tunica albuginea**—a thin layer of connective tissue—is observed at the periphery of the cortex.

jacent connective tissue layer, the **tunica albuginea**. In a section, a **cortex** and a **medulla** without distinct demarcation can be visualized. The broad cortex contains connective tissue and **primordial follicles** housing **primary oocytes** (at the end of meiotic prophase I). The **medulla** consists of connective tissue, interstitial cells, nerves, lymphatics and blood vessels reaching the ovary through the **hilum** (Figure 22–2).

The functions of the ovary are: (1) the production of the female gamete; (2) the secretion of estrogens and progesterone (steroid hormones); (3) the regulation of postnatal growth of reproductive organs; and (4) the development of secondary sexual characteristics.

The ovarian cycle

The three phases of the ovarian cycle are the **follicular phase**, **ovulatory phase**, and **luteal phase**.

The follicular phase consists of the development of a primordial follicle into a mature or graafian follicle (Figures 22–3 and 22–4)

The predominant and smallest follicle (25 μm in diameter) is the **primordial follicle**, which is surrounded by **flat follicular** or **granulosa cells** (see Figure 22–3). Primordial follicles are retained in a resting phase from the time of their development in the fetal ovary.

Follicles leaving the resting stage are called **primary follicles**. There are two types:

1. **Unilayered primary follicles**, with a single layer of **cuboidal follicular cells**.

2. **Multilayered primary follicles**, lined by several layers of proliferating cuboidal follicular cells. The follicular cells are supported by a **basal lamina** separating the primary follicle from the stroma of the ovary.

In the primary follicle stage, the primary oocyte begins the synthesis of a glycoprotein coat, the **zona pellucida**. The zona pellucida progressively separates the follicular cells from the oocyte. The zona pellucida is penetrated by tiny cytoplasmic processes of the follicular cells which contact microvilli of the oocyte. **Gap junctions** are present at the contact sites.

The following stage, the **secondary follicle**, is characterized by the **continuous**

proliferation of follicular cells and the **thickening of the zona pellucida**. The stromal cells surrounding the follicle become arranged into a cellular capsule, the **theca** (Gk. *theke*, box). The theca soon differentiates into two layers: (1) the **theca interna**, and (2) the **theca externa**.

Figure 22–3

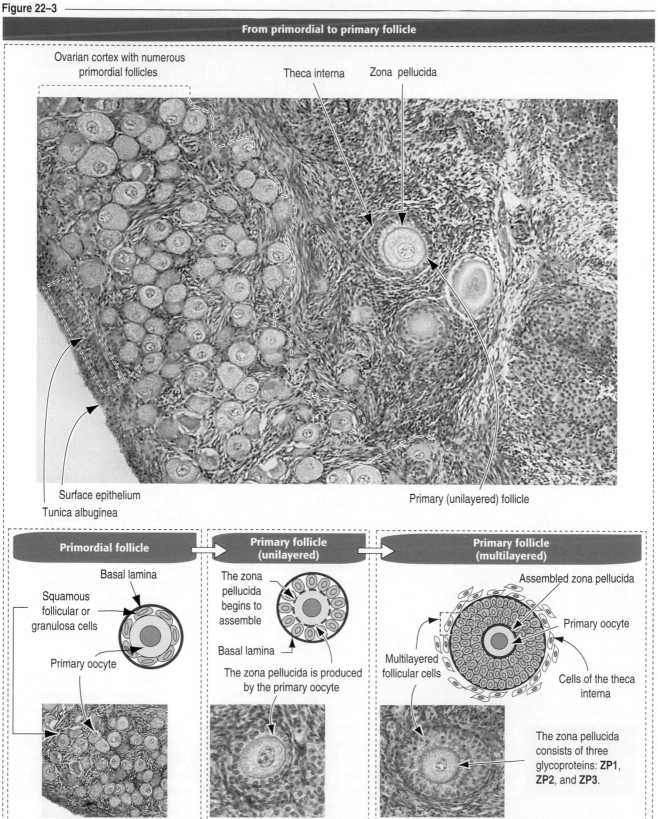

From primordial to primary follicle

Ovarian cortex with numerous primordial follicles

Theca interna

Zona pellucida

Surface epithelium

Tunica albuginea

Primary (unilayered) follicle

Primordial follicle

Basal lamina

Squamous follicular or granulosa cells

Primary oocyte

Primary follicle (unilayered)

The zona pellucida begins to assemble

Basal lamina

The zona pellucida is produced by the primary oocyte

Primary follicle (multilayered)

Assembled zona pellucida

Primary oocyte

Multilayered follicular cells

Cells of the theca interna

The zona pellucida consists of three glycoproteins: **ZP1**, **ZP2**, and **ZP3**.

Figure 22–4

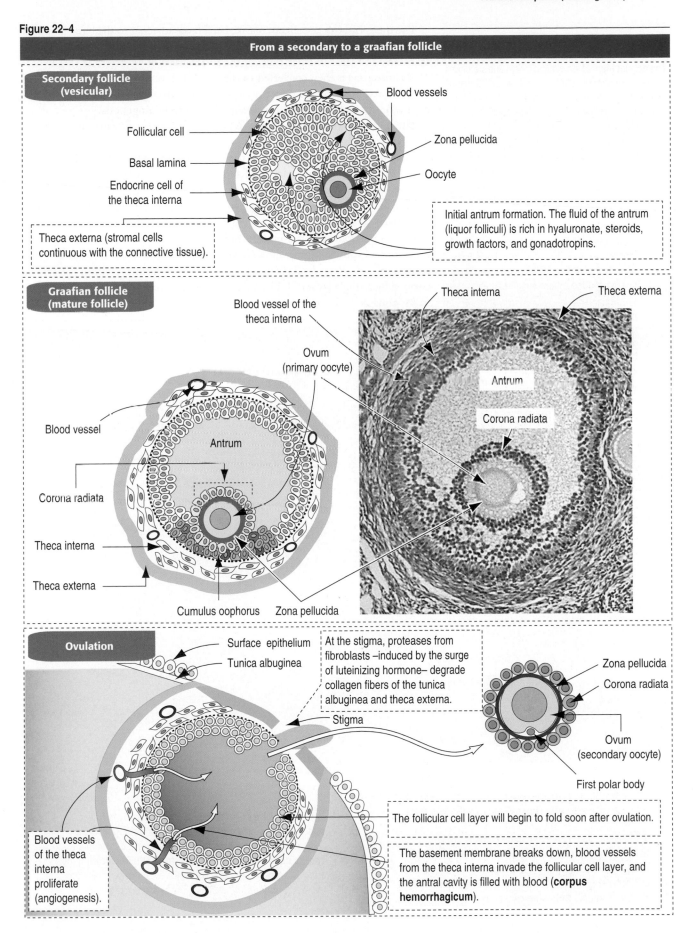

From a secondary to a graafian follicle

Secondary follicle (vesicular)

Blood vessels

Follicular cell

Zona pellucida

Basal lamina

Endocrine cell of the theca interna

Oocyte

Initial antrum formation. The fluid of the antrum (liquor folliculi) is rich in hyaluronate, steroids, growth factors, and gonadotropins.

Theca externa (stromal cells continuous with the connective tissue).

Graafian follicle (mature follicle)

Blood vessel of the theca interna

Theca interna

Theca externa

Ovum (primary oocyte)

Blood vessel

Antrum

Antrum

Corona radiata

Corona radiata

Theca interna

Theca externa

Cumulus oophorus

Zona pellucida

Ovulation

Surface epithelium

Tunica albuginea

At the stigma, proteases from fibroblasts –induced by the surge of luteinizing hormone– degrade collagen fibers of the tunica albuginea and theca externa.

Stigma

Zona pellucida

Corona radiata

Ovum (secondary oocyte)

First polar body

Blood vessels of the theca interna proliferate (angiogenesis).

The follicular cell layer will begin to fold soon after ovulation.

The basement membrane breaks down, blood vessels from the theca interna invade the follicular cell layer, and the antral cavity is filled with blood (**corpus hemorrhagicum**).

Folliculogenesis

The development of the ovarian follicle and steroidogenesis are controlled by gonadotropins (FSH and LH), in part by ovarian steroids and autocrine and paracrine secretions of the follicular cells.

About 7 million primary oocytes are present in the fetal ovary by mid gestation. There is a gradual loss of oocytes and, at birth, approximately 400,000 oocytes remain. Only 400 follicles ovulate after puberty. The remaining follicles degenerate and are called **atretic follicles**.

The follicular phase begins with the development of 6-12 primary follicles. This development is FSH-dependent. By the 6th day of the cycle, one follicle predominates and the others become atretic.

The **theca interna**, a well-vascularized cell layer adjacent to the basal lamina of the developing follicle, secretes **androstenedione**, an androgen precursor that is **transferred to the follicular cells** for the production of testosterone (Figure 22–5). Testosterone is then converted to **estradiol** by aromatase. Follicular cells lack enzymes required for the direct production of estrogens. As a result, **follicular cells cannot produce steroid precursors during folliculogenesis**.

The **theca externa** is a connective tissue capsule-like layer, continuous with the ovarian stroma.

Small intercellular spaces—**Call-Exner bodies**—appear between follicular cells. These spaces contain **follicular fluid** and coalesce later to form a large space, the **antrum**. The formation of the antrum soon dislocates the follicular cells with respect to the primary oocyte. A cluster of follicular cells, called the **cumulus oophorous**, is seen between the oocyte and the wall of the follicle.

The largest follicle is the **mature follicle** (also called the **graafian follicle** or **preovulatory follicle**). It measures 15 to 20 mm in diameter. Immediately before **ovulation**, the primary oocyte occupies an eccentric position within the follicle, covered by a single layer of follicular cells—the **corona radiata**—firmly attached to the zona pellucida (Figure 22–6).

Figure 22–5

Early follicular steroidogenesis

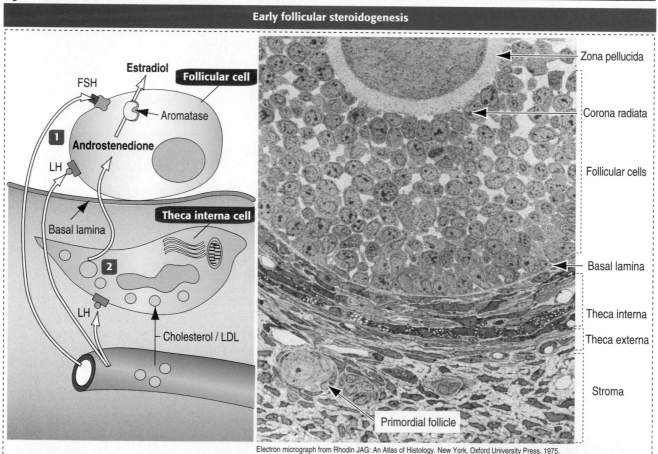

Electron micrograph from Rhodin JAG: An Atlas of Histology. New York, Oxford University Press, 1975.

Functional synergism between follicular cells and theca interna cells during early folliculogenesis

1 In the primary and secondary follicle, follicular cells have FSH receptors. In the graafian follicle, LH receptors appear and coexist with FSH receptors. **The acquisition of LH receptors is essential for the luteinization of the ruptured follicle following ovulation.**

2 Estradiol is the major steroid produced by follicular cells under stimulation by FSH. However, **follicular cells depend on the supply of androstenedione by theca interna cells—regulated by LH—to produce estradiol** (by aromatization of the androgen) since follicular cells lack the required enzymes for producing the precursor of estradiol.

A mature follicle, or graafian follicle, is characterized by the following features: (1) a **large antrum**, containing follicular fluid; (2) the **zona pellucida**, invested by a single layer of follicular cells forming the **corona radiata**; (3) the **detachment of the oocyte and attached corona radiata from the cumulus oophorus**; the oocyte-zona pellucida-corona radiata complex floats free in the follicular fluid; (4) the **completion of meiosis I several hours before ovulation**, resulting in the formation of a **secondary oocyte** and the **first polar body**, which remains in a space —the **perivitelline space**—between the zona pellucida and the oocyte; (5) **follicular cells acquire luteinizing hormone (LH) receptors** in addition to the already present follicle-stimulating hormone (FSH) receptors. This event is critical for **luteinization** or **development of the corpus luteum** (see Figure 22–5).

Follicular atresia or degeneration

Several primary follicles initiate the maturation process, but only one follicle completes its development, the remainder degenerate by a process called **atresia**. Follicles can become atretic at any stage of development.

Figure 22–6

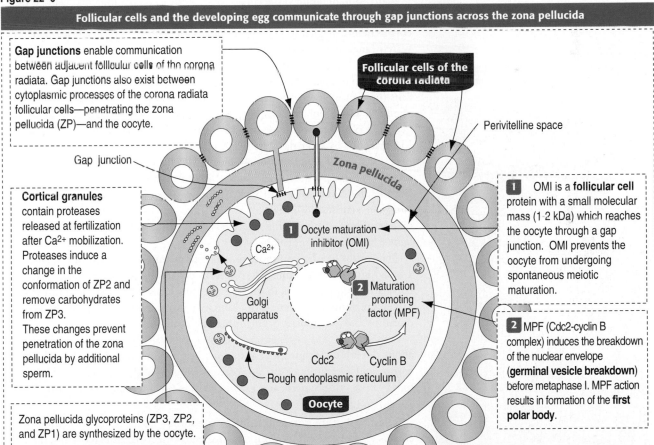

Follicular cells and the developing egg communicate through gap junctions across the zona pellucida

Gap junctions enable communication between adjacent follicular cells of the corona radiata. Gap junctions also exist between cytoplasmic processes of the corona radiata follicular cells—penetrating the zona pellucida (ZP)—and the oocyte.

Follicular cells of the corona radiata

Perivitelline space

Gap junction

Zona pellucida

Cortical granules contain proteases released at fertilization after Ca^{2+} mobilization. Proteases induce a change in the conformation of ZP2 and remove carbohydrates from ZP3. These changes prevent penetration of the zona pellucida by additional sperm.

Ca^{2+}

Golgi apparatus

1 Oocyte maturation inhibitor (OMI)

2 Maturation promoting factor (MPF)

Cdc2   Cyclin B

Rough endoplasmic reticulum

Oocyte

Zona pellucida glycoproteins (ZP3, ZP2, and ZP1) are synthesized by the oocyte.

1 OMI is a **follicular cell** protein with a small molecular mass (1-2 kDa) which reaches the oocyte through a gap junction. OMI prevents the oocyte from undergoing spontaneous meiotic maturation.

2 MPF (Cdc2-cyclin B complex) induces the breakdown of the nuclear envelope (**germinal vesicle breakdown**) before metaphase I. MPF action results in formation of the **first polar body**.

A mechanism operates during the maturation of the follicle **to prevent the earlier completion of meiotic prophase of the primary oocyte** surrounded by the zona pellucida:
1 This mechanism involves the transfer of **oocyte maturation inhibitor** from follicular cells to the oocyte through cell processes crossing the zona pellucida and establishing contact with the plasma membrane of the oocyte, via gap junctions.

2 Just before ovulation, the oocyte activates itself with **maturation promoting factor** to induce completion of meiotic prophase.

Completion of meiosis I results in the formation of the first polar body—retained in the perivitelline space—and a secondary oocyte. At fertilization, proteases are released from the cortical granules in a Ca^{2+}-dependent manner. Proteases alter the structural conformation of the zona pellucida, preventing penetration of the egg by additional sperm.

Figure 22–7

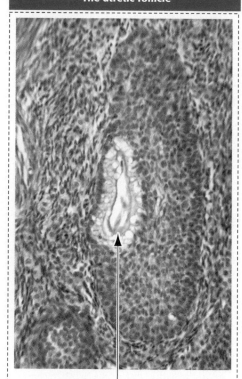

The atretic follicle

Initial stage of an atretic follicle
with a collapsed zona pellucida

A woman ovulates about 400 oocytes during her reproductive years. During a reproductive cycle, a group of follicles starts the maturation process. However, only 1 or 2 follicles complete folliculogenesis and are eventually ovulated. The others undergo—at any time of their development—a degenerative process called **follicular atresia**.

Atretic follicles (Figure 22–7) are identified by a thick folded membranous material, the **glassy membrane**, a relatively intact zona pellucida, remnants of degenerated oocytes and follicular cells, and invading macrophages.

The ovulatory phase

At the time of ovulation, the mature follicle protrudes from the ovarian surface, forming the **stigma**. Proteolytic activity within the theca externa and tunica albuginea, induced by a surge of LH, facilitates the rupture of the now mature graafian follicle. The released gamete enters the closely apposed uterine tube or oviduct. A few hours before ovulation, the **follicular cell layer** and the **theca interna** begin their transformation into a **corpus luteum**.

The luteal phase: The corpus luteum

Following ovulation, the residual follicular cell layer folds and becomes part of the **corpus luteum**, a major hormone-secreting gland.

   This transformation (Figure 22–8) involves:

   1. A **breakdown of the basement membrane of the follicle**.

   2. **Invasion of blood vessels** into the formerly avascular follicular cellular mass. Blood flows into the former antral space and coagulates, forming a transient **corpus hemorrhagicum**. The fibrin clot is then penetrated by newly formed blood vessels (**angiogenesis**), fibroblasts, and collagen fibers.

   3. A **transformation of follicular cells and theca interna cells**. Follicular cells change into **follicular lutein cells**, display the typical features of steroid-secreting cells (lipid droplets, a well-developed smooth endoplasmic reticulum, and mitochondria with tubular cristae, Figure 22–9), and secrete **progesterone** and **estrogen in response to both FSH and LH stimulation**. Recall that the expression of LH receptors by follicular cells is a crucial step in the luteinization process. The theca interna cells change into **theca lutein cells**, which produce **androstenedione** and **progesterone in response to LH stimulation**.

   Follicular lutein cells still lack the steroidogenic enzyme required for the complete synthesis of estradiol. Theca lutein cells cooperate with follicular cells by providing androstenedione, which is then converted into estradiol within follicular lutein cells (Figure 22–10).

   The corpus luteum continues to enlarge and enters an involution stage about 14 days after ovulation unless fertilization occurs. If fertilization takes place, the corpus luteum continues to enlarge and produces **progesterone** and **estrogen** under the stimulatory action of **human chorionic gonadotropin (hCG)** produced by the **trophoblast** of the implanted embryo.

   Progesterone and estrogen are required to maintain the endometrium until about the 9th to 10th week of gestation. At this time, the placenta, fetal adrenal cortex, and liver produce estrogens (see discussion of the adrenal gland in Chapter 19, Endocrine System, and Placentation in Chapter 23, Fertilization, Placentation, and Lactation).

   Regression of the corpus luteum —**luteolysis**— leads to the formation of the **corpus albicans**, resulting from the stromal connective tissue replacing the mass of degenerating luteal cells of the corpus luteum (Figure 22–11). The corpus albicans remains in the ovary; it decreases in size but never disappears.

   Luteal cells, remaining free in the stroma after involution of the corpus luteum, can retain their secretory activity and form the so-called **interstitial glands**. Such glandular interstitial cells are not abundant in the human ovary.

Hormonal regulation of ovulation and the corpus luteum

Two hormones of the anterior hypophysis regulate follicular growth (see Figure 22–12):

   1. **Follicle-stimulating hormone** stimulates folliculogenesis and ovulation as well as the production of estrogen.

Figure 22–8

The development, function, and involution of the corpus luteum

Formation of the corpus luteum (luteinization)

Following ovulation, the **follicular cell layer** of the preovulatory follicle becomes folded and is transformed into part of the **corpus luteum**. A surge in LH is correlated with luteinization.

This transformation includes the following:

1 The lumen, previously occupied by the follicular antrum, is filled with fibrin, which is then replaced by connective tissue and new blood vessels piercing the basement membrane.

2 Follicular or granulosa cells enlarge and lipid droplets accumulate. They become **follicular** or **granulosa lutein cells**.

3 The spaces between the folds of the follicular cell layer are penetrated by theca interna cells, blood vessels, and connective tissue. Theca interna cells also enlarge and store lipids. They are now **theca lutein cells**.

2 Folded follicular membrane containing **follicular lutein cells** storing lipids.

The spaces between the folds are occupied by theca lutein cells, connective tissue, and blood vessels.

1 The former antrum filled with fibrin is replaced by connective tissue and blood vessels.

Fibroblast in connective tissue.

Blood vessels

3 A breakdown of the basement membrane enables blood vessels of the theca interna to invade the ruptured follicle.

Theca externa

Function of the corpus luteum

The function of the corpus luteum is regulated by two gonadotropins: FSH and LH.

1 **FSH** stimulates the production of **progesterone** and **estradiol** by follicular lutein cells.

2 **LH** stimulates the production of progesterone and androstenedione by theca lutein cells. Androstenedione is translocated into follicular lutein cells for aromatization into **estradiol**.

3 During pregnancy, **prolactin** and **placental lactogens** upregulate **the effects of estradiol** produced by follicular lutein cells by enhancing the production of estrogen receptors.

4 Estradiol stimulates follicular lutein cells to take up cholesterol from blood, which is then stored in lipid droplets and transported to mitochondria for progesterone synthesis.

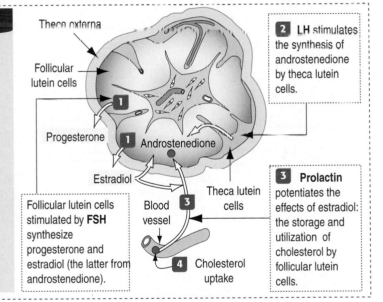

Theca externa

Follicular lutein cells

Progesterone

Estradiol

1 Androstenedione

Follicular lutein cells stimulated by **FSH** synthesize progesterone and estradiol (the latter from androstenedione).

Blood vessel

3 Theca lutein cells

4 Cholesterol uptake

2 **LH** stimulates the synthesis of androstenedione by theca lutein cells.

3 **Prolactin** potentiates the effects of estradiol: the storage and utilization of cholesterol by follicular lutein cells.

Regression of the corpus luteum (luteolysis)

If fertilization does not occur, the corpus luteum undergoes a process of regression called **luteolysis**.

Luteolysis involves a programmed cell death (apoptosis) sequence.
The following sequential events take place:

1 A **reduction in the blood flow** within the corpus luteum causes a decline in oxygen (hypoxia).

2 **T cells** reach the corpus luteum and produce **interferon-γ**, which, in turn, acts on the endothelium to enable the arrival of macrophages.

3 **Macrophages** produce **tumor necrosis factor-α** and the apoptotic cascade starts.

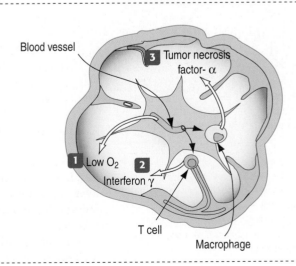

Blood vessel

3 Tumor necrosis factor- α

1 Low O_2

2 Interferon γ

T cell

Macrophage

Figure 22–9

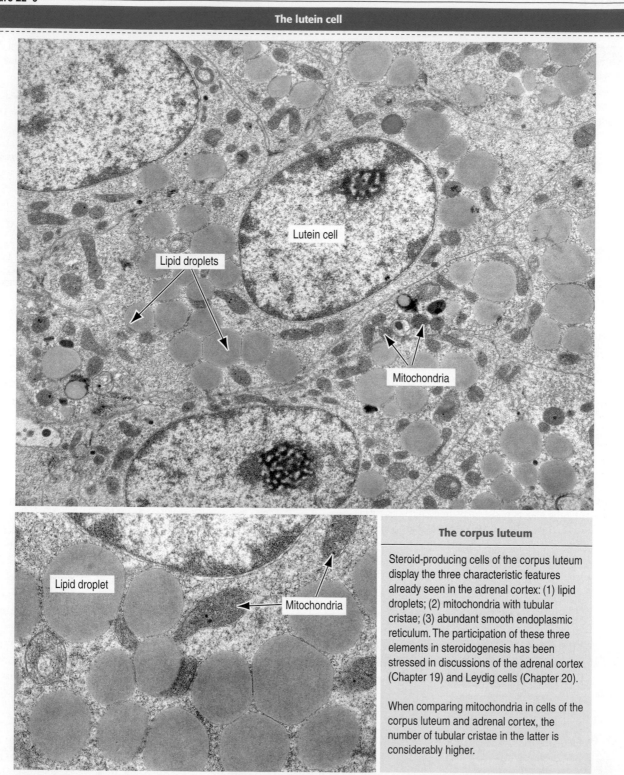

The lutein cell

Lutein cell

Lipid droplets

Mitochondria

Lipid droplet

Mitochondria

The corpus luteum

Steroid-producing cells of the corpus luteum display the three characteristic features already seen in the adrenal cortex: (1) lipid droplets; (2) mitochondria with tubular cristae; (3) abundant smooth endoplasmic reticulum. The participation of these three elements in steroidogenesis has been stressed in discussions of the adrenal cortex (Chapter 19) and Leydig cells (Chapter 20).

When comparing mitochondria in cells of the corpus luteum and adrenal cortex, the number of tubular cristae in the latter is considerably higher.

2. **Luteinizing hormone** stimulates the secretion of progesterone by the corpus luteum. A surge of LH immediately precedes ovulation. Continued LH secretion induces the **luteinization** of the residual follicular cell layer after ovulation. The production of FSH and LH ceases when the levels of progesterone and estrogen are high, and then the corpus luteum enters involution.

At the initiation of menstruation, estrogen and progesterone levels are low and

Figure 22-10

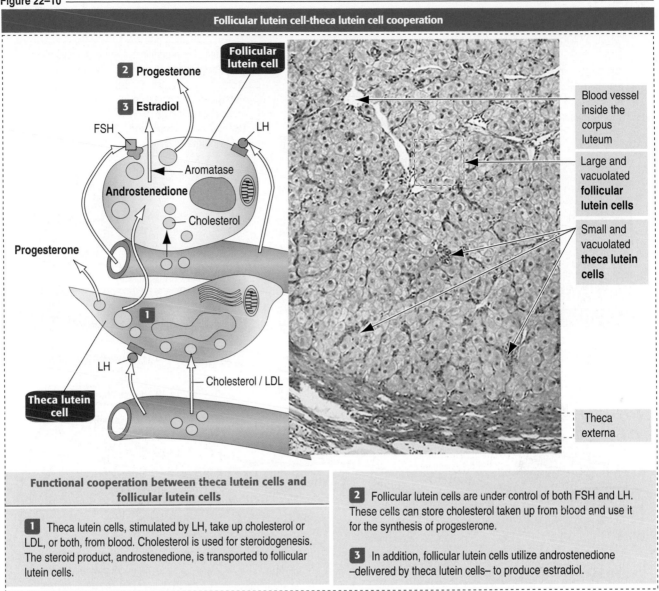

Follicular lutein cell-theca lutein cell cooperation

2 Progesterone

3 Estradiol

Follicular lutein cell

FSH

LH

Aromatase

Androstenedione

Cholesterol

Progesterone

1

LH

Cholesterol / LDL

Theca lutein cell

Blood vessel inside the corpus luteum

Large and vacuolated **follicular lutein cells**

Small and vacuolated **theca lutein cells**

Theca externa

Functional cooperation between theca lutein cells and follicular lutein cells

1 Theca lutein cells, stimulated by LH, take up cholesterol or LDL, or both, from blood. Cholesterol is used for steroidogenesis. The steroid product, androstenedione, is transported to follicular lutein cells.

2 Follicular lutein cells are under control of both FSH and LH. These cells can store cholesterol taken up from blood and use it for the synthesis of progesterone.

3 In addition, follicular lutein cells utilize androstenedione –delivered by theca lutein cells– to produce estradiol.

Figure 22-11

Corpus albicans, a connective tissue scar

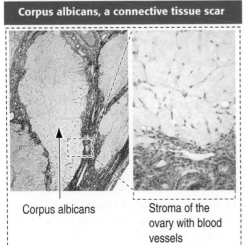

Corpus albicans

Stroma of the ovary with blood vessels

increase gradually during the preovulatory period. Estrogen reaches maximum levels just before the LH peak precedes ovulation.

Coinciding with the FSH and LH secretory pattern, the FSH-dependent synthesis of estrogen by follicular cells stimulates the **proliferation of the endometrial glands**. LH-dependent synthesis of progesterone by the corpus luteum **initiates and maintains the secretory activity of the endometrial glands**.

Oviduct, fallopian or uterine tube

The oviduct is the site of fertilization and early cleavage of the **zygote** (fertilized ovum). Each tube is divided into **four anatomic regions** (Figure 22–13): (1) the proximal fimbriated **infundibulum**; (2) a long and thin-walled **ampulla**; (3) a short and thick-walled **isthmus**; and (4) an **intramural** portion opening into the lumen of the uterine cavity.

The infundibulum consists of numerous finger-like projections of mucosal tissue called **fimbriae**. The ampulla and the isthmus are lined by **mucosal folds** projecting into the lumen of the tube. The isthmus has fewer mucosal folds.

The wall of the oviduct consists of three layers: (1) a **mucosa** supported by a **lamina propria**, (2) a **muscular layer**, and (3) a **serosa layer**.

Figure 22–12

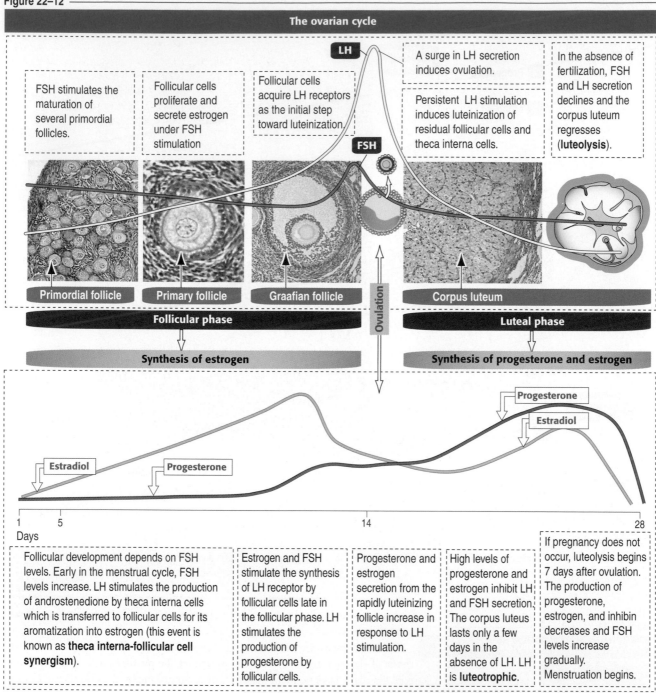

The mucosa consists of a **simple columnar epithelium** with two cell populations (see Figure 22–13) under **hormonal control**:

1. **Ciliated cells**, which enlarge and produce cilia (**ciliogenesis**) as folliculogenesis and estrogen production is in progress. Estrogens increase the rate of the ciliary beat. During luteolysis, ciliated cells lose their cilia (**deciliation**).

2. **Nonciliated secretory cells** (called **peg cells**), whose secretory activity is also stimulated by estrogens.

The **peristaltic contraction** of the muscular wall, with an **inner circular-spiral layer** and an **outer longitudinal layer**, as well as the ciliary activity of the lining epithelial cells, propels the oocyte or fertilized zygote toward the uterus. The surface of the oviduct is covered by the peritoneal **mesothelium**. Large blood vessels are observed in the serosa.

Figure 22–13

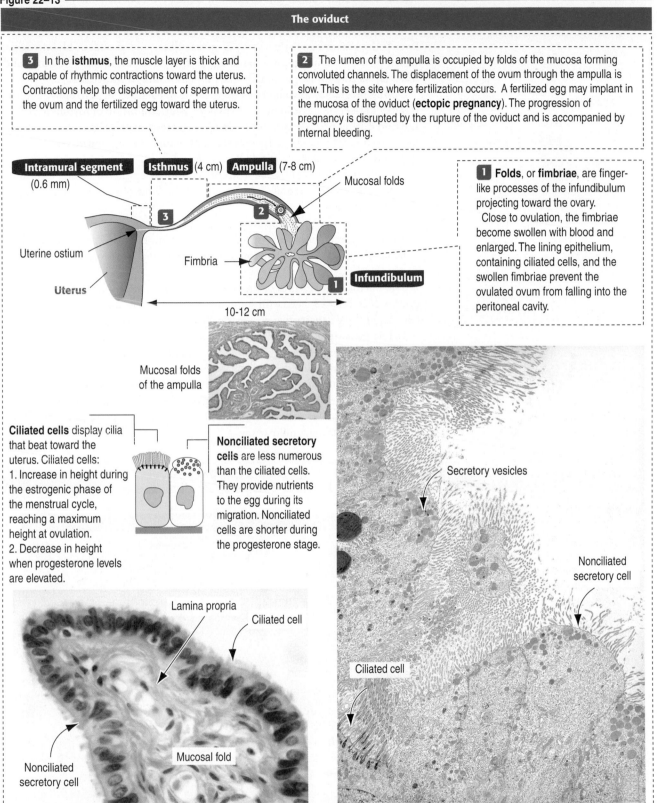

The oviduct

3 In the **isthmus**, the muscle layer is thick and capable of rhythmic contractions toward the uterus. Contractions help the displacement of sperm toward the ovum and the fertilized egg toward the uterus.

2 The lumen of the ampulla is occupied by folds of the mucosa forming convoluted channels. The displacement of the ovum through the ampulla is slow. This is the site where fertilization occurs. A fertilized egg may implant in the mucosa of the oviduct (**ectopic pregnancy**). The progression of pregnancy is disrupted by the rupture of the oviduct and is accompanied by internal bleeding.

Intramural segment (0.6 mm)   **Isthmus** (4 cm)   **Ampulla** (7-8 cm)

Mucosal folds

1 **Folds**, or **fimbriae**, are finger-like processes of the infundibulum projecting toward the ovary.
Close to ovulation, the fimbriae become swollen with blood and enlarged. The lining epithelium, containing ciliated cells, and the swollen fimbriae prevent the ovulated ovum from falling into the peritoneal cavity.

Uterine ostium

Fimbria

Uterus

Infundibulum

10-12 cm

Mucosal folds of the ampulla

Ciliated cells display cilia that beat toward the uterus. Ciliated cells:
1. Increase in height during the estrogenic phase of the menstrual cycle, reaching a maximum height at ovulation.
2. Decrease in height when progesterone levels are elevated.

Nonciliated secretory cells are less numerous than the ciliated cells. They provide nutrients to the egg during its migration. Nonciliated cells are shorter during the progesterone stage.

Secretory vesicles

Nonciliated secretory cell

Lamina propria

Ciliated cell

Ciliated cell

Nonciliated secretory cell

Mucosal fold

Uterus

The uterus consists of two anatomic segments: (1) the **corpus**, or **body**; (2) the **cervix**. The wall of the body of the uterus consists of three layers: (1) **endometrium** (Figures 22–14 and 22–15), (2) **myometrium**, and (3) **adventitia, or** serosa. The major component of the wall is the **myometrium**, lined by a mucosa, the **endometrium**.

The **myometrium** has three poorly defined smooth muscle layers: The central layer is thick with circularly arranged muscle fibers and abundant blood vessels, which give the name **stratum vasculare** to this particular layer. The outer and inner layers contain longitudinally or obliquely arranged muscle fibers.

During pregnancy, myometrial smooth muscle enlarges, **hypertrophy**, and the number of fibers increase in number (**hyperplasia**). **Inhibition of myometrial contraction during pregnancy** is controlled by **relaxin**, a peptide hormone produced in the ovary and placenta. **Myometrial contraction during parturition** is under the control of **oxytocin**, a peptide hormone secreted from the neurohypophysis.

The **endometrium** consists of a **simple columnar epithelial lining**, associated with simple tubular endometrial glands, and the **lamina propria**, called the **endometrial stroma**.

Functionally, the endometrium consists of two layers (see Figure 22–14): (1) a superficial **functional layer**, lost during menstruation, and (2) a **basal layer**, retained as the source of regeneration of a new functional layer following menstruation.

The microscopic features of the functional layer change during the **menstrual cycle**, which lasts 28 days, with some slight variations in time. A menstrual cycle consists of three consecutive phases (see Figure 22–15):

1. The **menstrual phase** (4 to 5 days), the initial phase of the cycle.

2. The **proliferative phase** (also called the estrogenic or follicular phase) of about 9 days, duration. During the proliferative phase, the thickness of the endometrium increases as a result of the stimulatory activity of **estrogen** produced by maturing ovarian follicles. Mitotic activity is detected in both the lamina propria and the epithelium. Epithelial cells of the glandular epithelium migrate upward and the glands become straight and narrow.

Figure 22–14

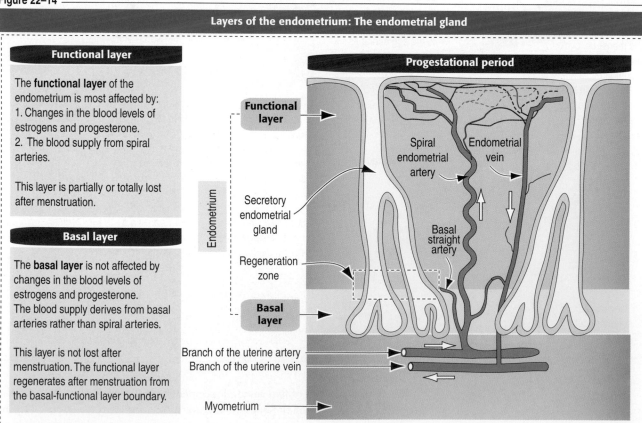

Layers of the endometrium: The endometrial gland

Functional layer

The **functional layer** of the endometrium is most affected by:
1. Changes in the blood levels of estrogens and progesterone.
2. The blood supply from spiral arteries.

This layer is partially or totally lost after menstruation.

Basal layer

The **basal layer** is not affected by changes in the blood levels of estrogens and progesterone. The blood supply derives from basal arteries rather than spiral arteries.

This layer is not lost after menstruation. The functional layer regenerates after menstruation from the basal-functional layer boundary.

Progestational period

Functional layer

Spiral endometrial artery

Endometrial vein

Secretory endometrial gland

Basal straight artery

Regeneration zone

Basal layer

Endometrium

Branch of the uterine artery
Branch of the uterine vein

Myometrium

Figure 22–15

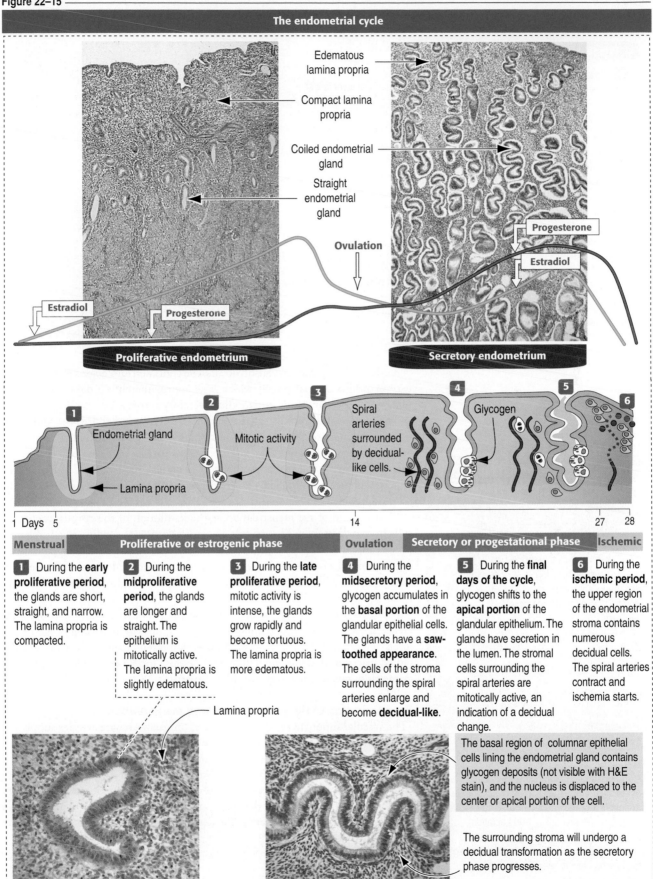

The endometrial cycle

Edematous lamina propria

Compact lamina propria

Coiled endometrial gland

Straight endometrial gland

Ovulation

Progesterone

Estradiol

Estradiol

Progesterone

Proliferative endometrium

Secretory endometrium

Endometrial gland

Mitotic activity

Spiral arteries surrounded by decidual-like cells.

Glycogen

Lamina propria

| 1 Days 5 | | | 14 | | 27 | 28 |

| Menstrual | Proliferative or estrogenic phase | | | Ovulation | Secretory or progestational phase | | Ischemic |

1 During the **early proliferative period**, the glands are short, straight, and narrow. The lamina propria is compacted.

2 During the **midproliferative period**, the glands are longer and straight. The epithelium is mitotically active. The lamina propria is slightly edematous.

3 During the **late proliferative period**, mitotic activity is intense, the glands grow rapidly and become tortuous. The lamina propria is more edematous.

4 During the **midsecretory period**, glycogen accumulates in the **basal portion** of the glandular epithelial cells. The glands have a **saw-toothed appearance**. The cells of the stroma surrounding the spiral arteries enlarge and become **decidual-like**.

5 During the **final days of the cycle**, glycogen shifts to the **apical portion** of the glandular epithelium. The glands have secretion in the lumen. The stromal cells surrounding the spiral arteries are mitotically active, an indication of a decidual change.

6 During the **ischemic period**, the upper region of the endometrial stroma contains numerous decidual cells. The spiral arteries contract and ischemia starts.

Lamina propria

The basal region of columnar epithelial cells lining the endometrial gland contains glycogen deposits (not visible with H&E stain), and the nucleus is displaced to the center or apical portion of the cell.

The surrounding stroma will undergo a decidual transformation as the secretory phase progresses.

Figure 22–16

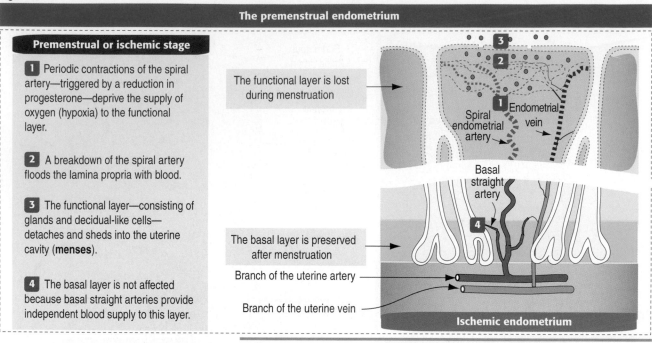

The premenstrual endometrium

Premenstrual or ischemic stage

1 Periodic contractions of the spiral artery—triggered by a reduction in progesterone—deprive the supply of oxygen (hypoxia) to the functional layer.

2 A breakdown of the spiral artery floods the lamina propria with blood.

3 The functional layer—consisting of glands and decidual-like cells—detaches and sheds into the uterine cavity (**menses**).

4 The basal layer is not affected because basal straight arteries provide independent blood supply to this layer.

The functional layer is lost during menstruation

Spiral endometrial artery / Endometrial vein

Basal straight artery

The basal layer is preserved after menstruation

Branch of the uterine artery

Branch of the uterine vein

Ischemic endometrium

Figure 22–17

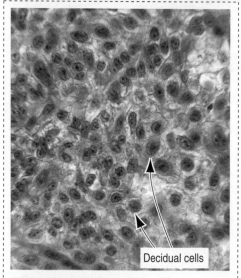

The decidual cell

Decidual cells

The **decidual reaction** consists in the enlargement of endometrial stromal cells. Implantation of the fertilized egg depends on a hormonally primed endometrium (see Chapter 23, Fertilization, Placentation, and Lactation) consisting of secretory endometrial glands surrounded by decidual cells. In addition, high progesterone levels keep the myometrium relatively quiescent.

3. After day 14, when ovulation occurs, the endometrium begins its third **secretory** or **progestational phase**, which lasts approximately 13 days. During this phase, endometrial glands initiate their secretory activity.

The outline of the tubular glands becomes irregular and coiled, the lining epithelium accumulates **glycogen**, and secretions rich in glycogen and glycoproteins are present in the glandular lumen. Blood vessels parallel to the endometrial glands increase in length and the lamina propria contains excessive fluid (edema). The secretory phase is controlled by both **progesterone** and **estrogen** produced in the corpus luteum.

4. At the end of the menstrual cycle, the involution of the corpus luteum results from a decrease in blood levels of steroid hormones, leading to an **ischemic phase** (duration of about 1 day). A reduction in the normal blood supply—causing intermittent **ischemia**—and the consequent hypoxia determine the necrosis of the functional layer of the endometrium, which sloughs off during the menstrual phase (Figure 22–16).

If pregnancy takes place, **stromal cells** in the endometrial lamina propria increase in size and store lipids and glycogen in response to increasing progesterone levels (Figures 22–17 and 22–18). This endometrial change is known as a **decidual reaction** (Lat. *decidus*, falling off) because the functional layer of the endometrium will be shed as the **decidua** at parturition.

Vascularization of the endometrium and menstruation

The vascular supply to the endometrium is unusual. **Arcuate arteries** supply the endometrium. An arcuate artery has two segments:

1. A **straight segment** (supplying the **basal layer** of the endometrium).
2. A **coiled segment** (supplying the **functional layer** of the endometrium).

The coiled segment stretches as the endometrium grows in thickness. Just before menstruation, **contraction of the artery at the straight-coiled segment interface reduces the blood flow and causes the destruction of the functional layer of the endometrium**.

Cervix

The cervix is the lower extension of the uterus. It forms a communication be-

Figure 22–18

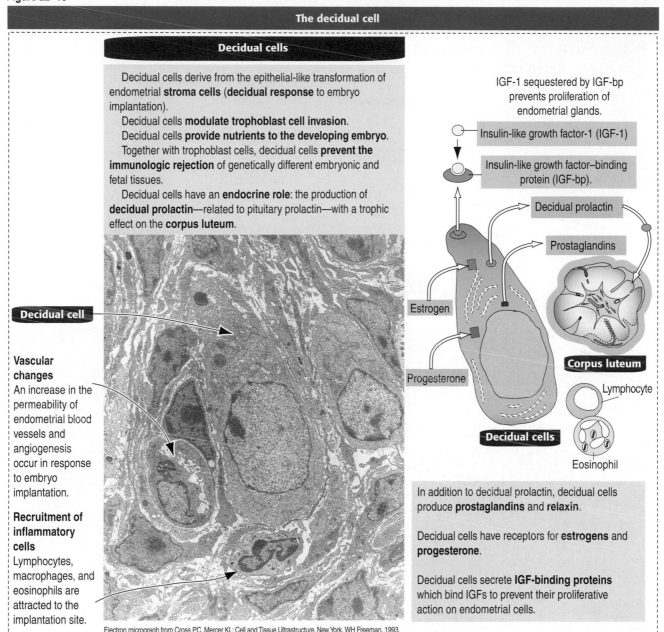

The decidual cell

Decidual cells

Decidual cells derive from the epithelial-like transformation of endometrial **stroma cells** (**decidual response** to embryo implantation).

Decidual cells **modulate trophoblast cell invasion**.

Decidual cells **provide nutrients to the developing embryo**.

Together with trophoblast cells, decidual cells **prevent the immunologic rejection** of genetically different embryonic and fetal tissues.

Decidual cells have an **endocrine role**: the production of **decidual prolactin**—related to pituitary prolactin—with a trophic effect on the **corpus luteum**.

IGF-1 sequestered by IGF-bp prevents proliferation of endometrial glands.

Insulin-like growth factor-1 (IGF-1)

Insulin-like growth factor–binding protein (IGF-bp).

Decidual prolactin

Prostaglandins

Estrogen

Progesterone

Corpus luteum

Lymphocyte

Decidual cells

Eosinophil

Decidual cell

Vascular changes
An increase in the permeability of endometrial blood vessels and angiogenesis occur in response to embryo implantation.

Recruitment of inflammatory cells
Lymphocytes, macrophages, and eosinophils are attracted to the implantation site.

In addition to decidual prolactin, decidual cells produce **prostaglandins** and **relaxin**.

Decidual cells have receptors for **estrogens** and **progesterone**.

Decidual cells secrete **IGF-binding proteins** which bind IGFs to prevent their proliferative action on endometrial cells.

Electron micrograph from Cross PC, Mercer KL: Cell and Tissue Ultrastructure. New York, WH Freeman, 1993.

tween the uterine cavity and the vagina through the **external os** of the **cervical canal** lined by a mucous membrane called the **endocervix**.

The endocervix contains mucus-secreting **tubular glands** lined by a columnar epithelium, and scattered ciliated cells (Figure 22–19). The endocervical glands are surrounded by a fibrocollagenous and smooth muscle stroma with abundant blood vessels. The endocervical tubular glands are deep invaginations (**crypts**) of the surface epithelium that increase the surface area of mucus-producing cells.

The secretory activity of the **endocervical glands** is regulated by **estrogens** and is **maximal at the time of ovulation**. The product of the glands lubricates the vagina during sexual intercourse and acts as a bacterial protective barrier blocking access to the uterine cavity.

During ovulation, the mucus is less viscous, is hydrated, and has an alkaline pH, conditions favorable for the migration of sperm. The high content of ions (Na^+, K^+, and Cl^-) is responsible for the **crystallization of the mucus** into a fern-like pattern in the ovulatory phase. This feature of cervical mucus is used clini-

Figure 22–19

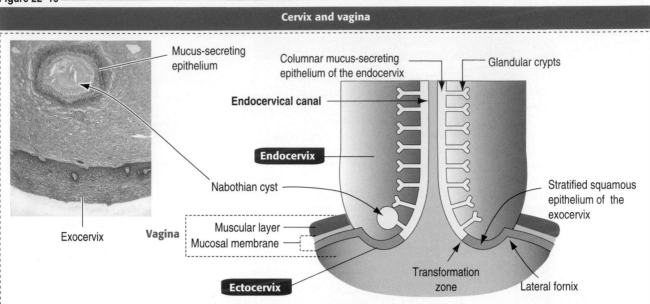

Cervix and vagina

Mucus-secreting epithelium

Columnar mucus-secreting epithelium of the endocervix

Glandular crypts

Endocervical canal

Endocervix

Nabothian cyst

Stratified squamous epithelium of the exocervix

Exocervix

Vagina

Muscular layer

Mucosal membrane

Ectocervix

Transformation zone

Lateral fornix

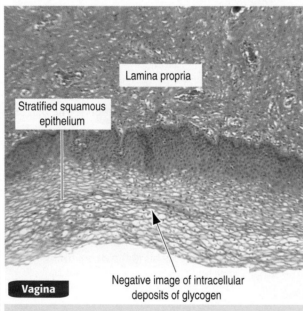

Lamina propria

Stratified squamous epithelium

Negative image of intracellular deposits of glycogen

Vagina

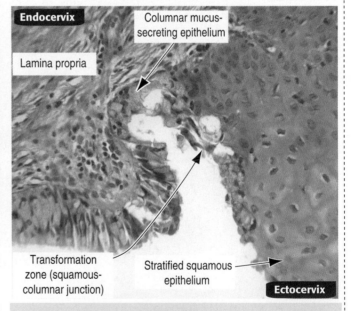

Endocervix

Columnar mucus-secreting epithelium

Lamina propria

Transformation zone (squamous-columnar junction)

Stratified squamous epithelium

Ectocervix

The vaginal epithelium	**The cervix**
The stratified squamous epithelium lining the vagina contains glycogen. The vagina contains natural bacteria, in particular *Lactobacillus acidophilus* which produces **lactic acid** by the breakdown of **glycogen**. Lactic acid creates on the vaginal surface an acidic coat (pH 3.0), preventing the proliferation of bacteria but not sexually transmitted pathogens (such as *Trichomonas vaginalis*). Antibiotics can destroy the vaginal flora, and *Candida albicans*, a natural fungal component of the vagina, develops on the mucosal surface.	The cervix consists of two components: (1) the **endocervical canal**; (2) the **ectocervix**. The endocervical canal is lined by a mucus-secreting columnar epithelium extending into the lamina propria in the form of glandular crypts. The ectocervix is lined by a stratified squamous epithelium continuous with the vaginal epithelial lining. Before puberty, the endocervical epithelium extends over the convexity of the ectocervix and becomes exposed to the vaginal environment. The area between the "old" and "new" squamous-columnar epithelial junction is called the **transformation zone**. About 95% of **cervical intraepithelial neoplasias** originate within the transformation zone.

cally to assess the optimal time for fertilization to occur.

After ovulation, the mucus is highly viscous with an acidic pH, detrimental conditions for sperm penetration and viability. Endocervical glands may become obstructed, forming cysts called **cysts of Naboth**, or **nabothian cysts**.

Clinical significance: Cervical intraepithelial neoplasia

The external segment of the cervix, the **ectocervix**, is lined by **stratified squamous epithelium**. There is an abrupt epithelial transition between the endocervix and the ectocervix, called the **transformation zone**.

At the transformation zone, **dysplasia**, an abnormal but reversible condition may occur. Dysplasia is characterized by disorganized epithelial cells that slough off before reaching full stratified maturity.

However, dysplasia can progress into **carcinoma in situ**, a condition in which proliferation of epithelial cells is very active but within the limits of the basal lamina (**cervical intraepithelial neoplasia**, or **CIN**). This condition can be reversible or can progress (if undetected) into an **invasive carcinoma** that breaks the continuity of the basal lamina and invades the underlying connective tissue. Dysplasia and carcinoma in situ can be detected by the routine **Papanicolaou smear** (Pap smear).

Vagina

The vagina is a fibromuscular tube consisting of three layers:

1. An inner **mucosal layer** (stratified squamous epithelium with a **lamina propria** usually infiltrated by neutrophils and lymphocytes; see Figure 22–19).

2. A middle **muscularis layer** (circular and longitudinal smooth muscle).

3. An outer **adventitial layer** (dense connective tissue).

The surface of the mucosa is kept moist by mucus secreted by uterine and endocervical glands and the **glands of Bartholin** in the vestibule. The wall of the vagina lacks glands.

The vaginal epithelium undergoes cyclic changes during the menstrual cycle. The **differentiation of vaginal epithelium** is stimulated by **estrogens**. At ovulation, the stratified epithelium is fully differentiated, and abundant acidophilic squamous cells can be seen in the Pap smear.

After ovulation, when **progesterone** predominates, the number of squamous cells declines and more basophilic cells appear together, with neutrophils and lymphocytes. The vaginal smear provides rapid information on estrogen and progesterone levels during the menstrual cycle and is also useful for monitoring the hormonal status during pregnancy.

Mons pubis, labia majora, and labia minora

The mons pubis, labia majora, and labia minora are modified skin structures. The **mons pubis** (mons veneris) is skin lined by **keratinized stratified squamous epithelium** with hair follicles covering subcutaneous fat overlying the symphysis pubis.

The **labia majora** are extensions of the mons pubis at each side of the vaginal introitus. In addition to skin with hair follicles and glands (**apocrine sweat glands** and **sebaceous glands**) covering the fat pad, smooth muscle fibers are detected in the subcutaneous fat. Hair follicles and fat accumulation are regulated by sex hormones at the onset of sexual maturity (by the age of 10 to 13 years old).

The **labia minora** are skin folds without adipose tissue and hair follicles but with abundant blood vessels, elastic fibers, and sebaceous glands opening directly onto the surface of the melanin-pigmented epidermis. Pigmentation of the epidermis of both labia majora and minora appears at the initiation of puberty.

The **hymen** is the limit between the internal and external genitalia. It consists of a thin fibrous membrane lining the lower vagina, covered on its external surface by a **keratinized stratified squamous epithelium** and on the internal surface

Figure 22–20

The female urethra

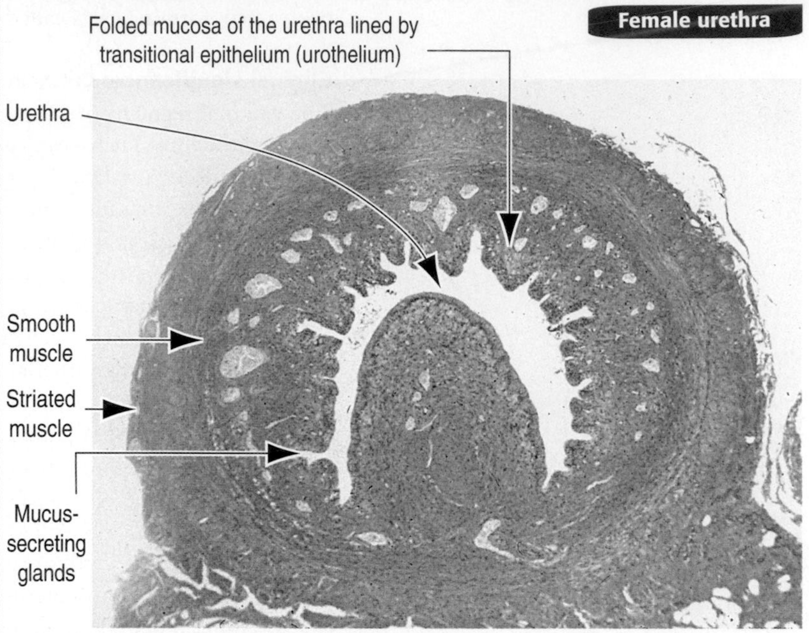

Folded mucosa of the urethra lined by transitional epithelium (urothelium)

Female urethra

Urethra

Smooth muscle

Striated muscle

Mucus-secreting glands

by **nonkeratinizing stratified squamous epithelium** with glycogen (like the vaginal epithelium).

The **clitoris**, located below the mons pubis, is the female equivalent of the penis. Like the penis, it consists of two side-by-side corpora cavernosa (erectile vascular tissue) separated by a septum, surrounded by a fibrous collagenous sheath. The clitoris is partially covered by skin containing rich sensory nerves and receptors but lacking hair follicles and glands.

Urethral meatus and glands (paraurethral glands and Bartholin's glands)

The urethral meatus communicates with the exterior close to the clitoris. **Paraurethral glands of Skene** are distributed around the meatus and are lined by **pseudostratified columnar epithelium**.

Bartholin's vulvovaginal glands are found around the lower vagina and consist of acini with mucus-secreting cells. A duct covered by a transitional epithelium connects these glands to the posterolateral side of the vagina.

The **female urethra** is covered by a **folded mucosa** lined by a **transitional epithelium** changing first to a pseudostratified columnar epithelium and, near the urethral meatus, to a low keratinized stratified squamous epithelium. **Mucus-secreting glands** are observed in the **mucosa** (Figure 22–20).

The **muscular wall** consists of a **single longitudinal layer of smooth muscle** (**involuntary sphincter**). A **circular striated muscle** (**voluntary sphincter**) is observed outside the smooth muscle layer. A connective tissue rich in elastic fibers provides support to the muscle layers.

The fertilization process

Two events must occur before fertilization: (1) **sperm maturation** in the epididymis, and (2) **sperm capacitation** in the female reproductive tract.

Sperm released from the testis and entering the epididymal duct have **circular motion**. After a 2-week **maturation process**, following epididymal transit and storage in the tail or cauda of the epididymis, sperm acquire **forward motility** necessary for fertilization. After ejaculation, sperm undergo a **capacitation process** in the uterus and fertilization of the ovum or egg takes place in the oviduct.

Essentially, **a fertilizing sperm must complete both maturation and capacitation before sperm-egg fusion.** Capacitation can be induced in vitro, a procedure that permits in vitro fertilization.

We have seen that the **sperm head** consists of three components: (1) the **condensed nucleus**, (2) the **acrosomal sac**, and (3) the **plasma membrane**.

The **condensed nucleus** consists of genomic DNA coated by very basic protamines. Nucleosomes are not present because somatic histones have been replaced by protamines.

The **acrosomal sac** is formed by three constituents (Figure 23–1): (1) the **outer acrosomal membrane**, (2) the **inner acrosomal membrane**, and (3) **hydrolytic enzymes** (mainly **hyaluronidase** and **acrosin**, derived from the precursor **pro-acrosin**).

The thin portion of the acrosomal sac, extending toward the tail, is the **equatorial segment**.

Figure 23–1

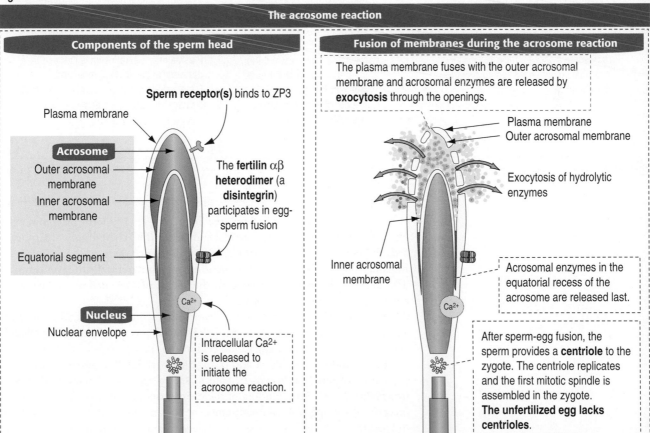

The acrosome reaction

Components of the sperm head

Sperm receptor(s) binds to ZP3

Plasma membrane

Acrosome

Outer acrosomal membrane

Inner acrosomal membrane

The **fertilin αβ heterodimer** (a **disintegrin**) participates in egg-sperm fusion

Equatorial segment

Nucleus

Nuclear envelope

Ca^{2+}

Intracellular Ca^{2+} is released to initiate the acrosome reaction.

Fusion of membranes during the acrosome reaction

The plasma membrane fuses with the outer acrosomal membrane and acrosomal enzymes are released by **exocytosis** through the openings.

Plasma membrane
Outer acrosomal membrane

Exocytosis of hydrolytic enzymes

Inner acrosomal membrane

Ca^{2+}

Acrosomal enzymes in the equatorial recess of the acrosome are released last.

After sperm-egg fusion, the sperm provides a **centriole** to the zygote. The centriole replicates and the first mitotic spindle is assembled in the zygote. **The unfertilized egg lacks centrioles**.

Figure 23–2

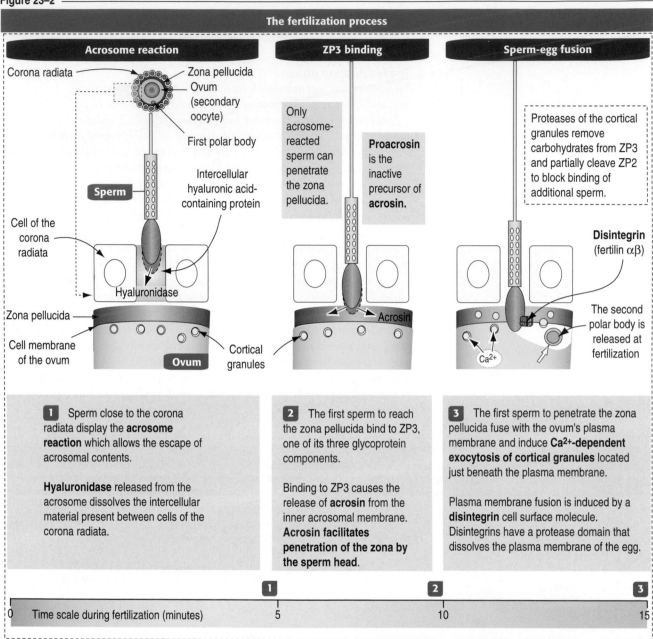

The fertilization process

Acrosome reaction

Corona radiata
Zona pellucida
Ovum (secondary oocyte)
First polar body
Intercellular hyaluronic acid-containing protein

Sperm

Cell of the corona radiata

Hyaluronidase

Zona pellucida

Cell membrane of the ovum

Cortical granules

Ovum

ZP3 binding

Only acrosome-reacted sperm can penetrate the zona pellucida.

Proacrosin is the inactive precursor of **acrosin.**

Acrosin

Sperm-egg fusion

Proteases of the cortical granules remove carbohydrates from ZP3 and partially cleave ZP2 to block binding of additional sperm.

Disintegrin (fertilin αβ)

The second polar body is released at fertilization

Ca^{2+}

1 Sperm close to the corona radiata display the **acrosome reaction** which allows the escape of acrosomal contents.

Hyaluronidase released from the acrosome dissolves the intercellular material present between cells of the corona radiata.

2 The first sperm to reach the zona pellucida bind to ZP3, one of its three glycoprotein components.

Binding to ZP3 causes the release of **acrosin** from the inner acrosomal membrane. **Acrosin facilitates penetration of the zona by the sperm head.**

3 The first sperm to penetrate the zona pellucida fuse with the ovum's plasma membrane and induce **Ca^{2+}-dependent exocytosis of cortical granules** located just beneath the plasma membrane.

Plasma membrane fusion is induced by a **disintegrin** cell surface molecule. Disintegrins have a protease domain that dissolves the plasma membrane of the egg.

1 **2** **3**

Time scale during fertilization (minutes)
0   5   10   15

The **plasma membrane** harbors (see Figure 23–1) (1) **sperm receptors**, with binding affinity to the **zona pellucida**; and (2) **fertilin**, a heterodimer member of a family of proteins called **disintegrins**, consisting of three specific domains: a **metalloprotease** domain, a **fusion peptide** domain, and a **disintegrin domain**. The disintegrin fertilin is inserted in the sperm plasma membrane facing the equatorial region of the acrosome.

The three main events during fertilization are, sequentially (Figure 23–2) the acrosome reaction, sperm binding to ZP3, a glycoprotein of the zona pellucida (Figure 23–3), and sperm-egg fusion (Figure 23–4).

The **heterodimer fertilin α and β**, together with **CD9**, a protein member of the family of **tetraspanins**, participate in sperm-egg plasma membrane fusion (see Figure 23–4). After binding of the disintegrin domain to $\alpha_3\beta_1$ integrin, **an integrin of the egg plasma membrane**, the fusion peptide domain of fertilin β induces the fusion of adjacent sperm and egg plasma membranes in the presence of CD9.

Figure 23–3

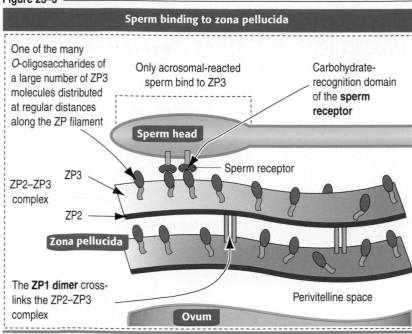

Sperm binding to zona pellucida

One of the many *O*-oligosaccharides of a large number of ZP3 molecules distributed at regular distances along the ZP filament

Only acrosomal-reacted sperm bind to ZP3

Carbohydrate-recognition domain of the **sperm receptor**

Sperm head

Sperm receptor

ZP2–ZP3 complex

ZP3

ZP2

Zona pellucida

The **ZP1 dimer** cross-links the ZP2–ZP3 complex

Perivitelline space

Ovum

In the proximity of the ovum, and in the presence of Ca^{2+}, the plasma membrane fuses with the outer acrosomal membrane. This event is known as the **acrosome reaction**. Small openings created by membrane fusion facilitate the release of hydrolytic enzymes (see Figures 23–1 and 23–2). The equatorial region of the acrosome does not participate in the membrane fusion process at this time.

The zona pellucida

The plasma membranes of all mammalian eggs are surrounded by a 6- to 7-µm-thick zona pellucida produced by the egg. The zona pellucida is composed of

Figure 23–4

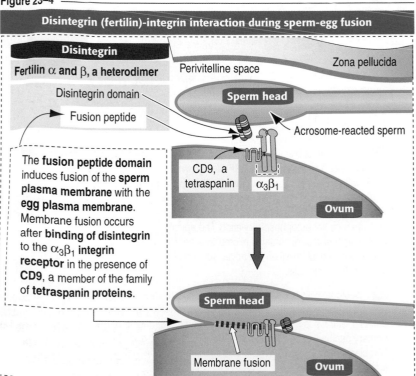

Disintegrin (fertilin)-integrin interaction during sperm-egg fusion

Disintegrin

Fertilin α and β, a heterodimer

Perivitelline space

Zona pellucida

Disintegrin domain

Sperm head

Fusion peptide

Acrosome-reacted sperm

CD9, a tetraspanin

$α_3β_1$

The **fusion peptide domain** induces fusion of the **sperm plasma membrane** with the **egg plasma membrane**. Membrane fusion occurs after **binding of disintegrin** to the $α_3β_1$ **integrin receptor** in the presence of **CD9**, a member of the family of **tetraspanin proteins**.

Ovum

Sperm head

Membrane fusion

Ovum

only three glycoproteins (see Figure 23–4): **ZP1**, a dimer of 200 kDa; **ZP2**, 120 kDa; and **ZP3**, 83 kDa.

ZP2 and ZP3 interact to form long filament complex interconnected by ZP1 dimers at regular intervals. During sperm binding, *O*-oligosaccharides linked to ZP3 interact with sperm receptors. **Only acrosome-reacted sperm can interact with ZP3.**

Placentation

The placenta and embryonic-fetal membranes (amnion, chorion, allantois, and yolk sac) protect the embryo-fetus and provide for nutrition, respiration, excretion, and hormone production during development. The membranes are formed by the embryo. Both the embryo and the maternal endometrium begin to form the placenta as soon as the blastocyst implants in the endometrium.

Figure 23–5

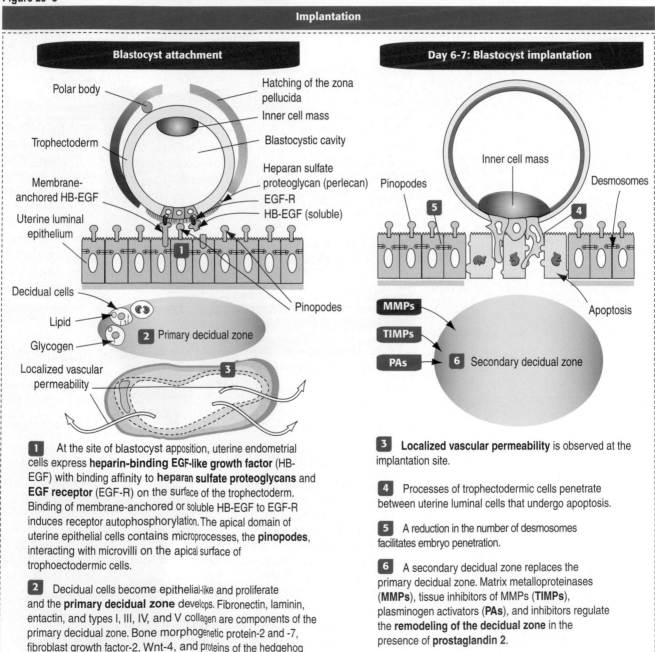

Implantation

Blastocyst attachment

- Polar body
- Trophectoderm
- Membrane-anchored HB-EGF
- Uterine luminal epithelium
- Decidual cells
- Lipid
- Glycogen
- Localized vascular permeability
- Hatching of the zona pellucida
- Inner cell mass
- Blastocystic cavity
- Heparan sulfate proteoglycan (perlecan)
- EGF-R
- HB-EGF (soluble)
- Pinopodes
- **2** Primary decidual zone
- **3**

Day 6-7: Blastocyst implantation

- Inner cell mass
- Pinopodes
- Desmosomes
- **5**
- **4**
- Apoptosis
- **MMPs**
- **TIMPs**
- **PAs**
- **6** Secondary decidual zone

1 At the site of blastocyst apposition, uterine endometrial cells express **heparin-binding EGF-like growth factor** (HB-EGF) with binding affinity to **heparan sulfate proteoglycans** and **EGF receptor** (EGF-R) on the surface of the trophectoderm. Binding of membrane-anchored or soluble HB-EGF to EGF-R induces receptor autophosphorylation. The apical domain of uterine epithelial cells contains microprocesses, the **pinopodes**, interacting with microvilli on the apical surface of trophoectodermic cells.

2 Decidual cells become epithelial-like and proliferate and the **primary decidual zone** develops. Fibronectin, laminin, entactin, and types I, III, IV, and V collagen are components of the primary decidual zone. Bone morphogenetic protein-2 and -7, fibroblast growth factor-2, Wnt-4, and proteins of the hedgehog family are expressed.

3 **Localized vascular permeability** is observed at the implantation site.

4 Processes of trophectodermic cells penetrate between uterine luminal cells that undergo apoptosis.

5 A reduction in the number of desmosomes facilitates embryo penetration.

6 A secondary decidual zone replaces the primary decidual zone. Matrix metalloproteinases (**MMPs**), tissue inhibitors of MMPs (**TIMPs**), plasminogen activators (**PAs**), and inhibitors regulate the **remodeling of the decidual zone** in the presence of **prostaglandin 2**.

Implantation of the blastocyst

The implantation of the blastocyst into a nurturing endometrium involves: (1) the initial **unstable** adhesion of the blastocyst to the endometrial surface, called **apposition**, followed by a **stable** adhesion phase, and (2) the **decidualization** of the endometrial stroma (Figure 23–5).

The timing of preimplantation and implantation is extremely precise. So is the preparation of the implantation site. On day 4 of pregnancy, the embryo—at the blastocyst stage—is within the uterine cavity. The coordinated effect of ovarian estrogens and progesterone has already conditioned the endometrium for implantation, including an increase in endometrial vascular permeability at the implantation site. The **blastocyst hatches from the zona pellucida** and exposes its trophectoderm epithelial lining to the uterine luminal epithelium. If zona pellucida hatching fails to occur, the embryo will not implant. Failure of the uterine stroma to undergo decidualization can lead to spontaneous abortion.

Trophoblast-mediated attachment and subsequent implantation depend on: (1) the uterine luminal epithelial cell membrane-bound and soluble form of **heparin-bound epidermal growth factor-like factor** (HB-EGF), a member of the transforming growth factor-α family, and (2) strong binding affinity of HB-EGF for **epidermal growth factor receptor** (EGF-R), which autophosphorylates, and **heparan sulfate proteoglycan** (also called perlecan) present on the trophectoderm surface.

At implantation (see Figure 23–5), cytoplasmic processes of trophoblastic cells interact with small processes on the apical surface of the uterine epithelial cells, called **pinopodes**, and penetrate the intercellular spaces of the endometrial luminal cells. Penetration is facilitated by a decrease in the number of desmosomes linking the endometrial cells that undergo apoptosis. The **primary decidual zone** is remodeled by the action of proteases (see Figure 23–5), and a **secondary decidual zone** houses the implanting embryo.

The trophoblast differentiates into (1) an inner layer of mitotically active **mononucleated cytotrophoblastic cells**, and (2) an outer layer of **multinucleated syncytiotrophoblastic cells** at the embryonic pole, facing the endometrium. The syncytiotrophoblast mass invades the endometrium (formed by glands, stroma, and blood vessels) and rapidly surrounds the entire embryo.

The blastocyst has a cavity containing fluid and the eccentric **inner cell mass**, which gives rise to the embryo and some extraembryonic tissues. The trophoblastic cells proximal to the inner cell mass begin to develop the **chorionic sac**. The chorionic sac consists of two components: the trophoblast and the underlying extraembryonic mesoderm.

Invasion of the endometrium and the inner third of the myometrium, a process called **interstitial invasion**, is determined by the action of secretory **proteolytic enzymes** released by the **syncytiotrophoblast**. Proteases erode the branches of the spiral uterine arteries to form spaces or **lacunae** of maternal blood within the syncytiotrophoblast mass. This endometrial eroding event, called **endovascular invasion**, initiates the **primitive uteroplacental circulation** and represents the primordium of the future **inter-villous space**.

The syncytiotrophoblast begins the secretion of **human chorionic gonadotropin (hCG)** into the maternal lacunae. The secretion of estrogens and progesterone by the corpus luteum is now under the control of hCG.

On the **maternal side**, **decidual cells**, close to the mass of invading syncytiotrophoblastic cells, degenerate and release **glycogen** and **lipids**, thus providing, together with maternal blood in the lacunae, the initial nutrients for embryonic development.

The decidua provides an immune-protective environment for the development of the embryo. The decidual reaction involves (1) the production of immunosuppressive substances (mainly prostaglandins) by decidual cells to inhibit the activation of T cells in the endometrial stroma, and (2) infiltrating leukocytes in the endometrial stroma that secrete **interleukin-2** to prevent maternal tissue rejection of the embryo.

Figure 23–6

Primary and secondary chorionic villi

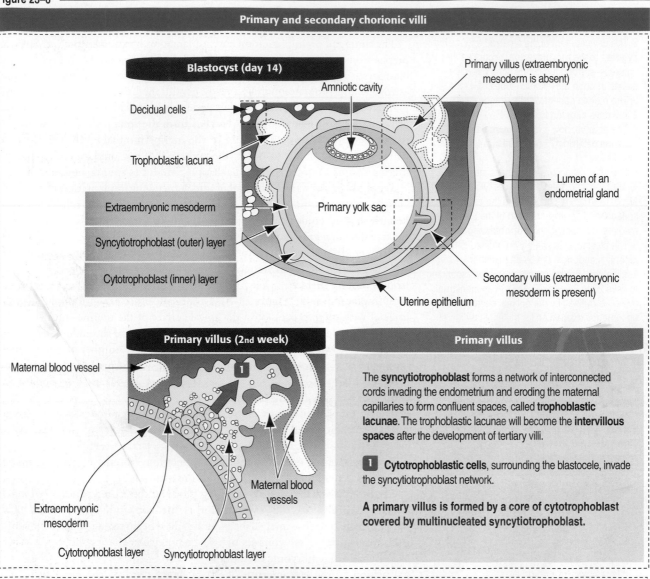

Blastocyst (day 14)

- Decidual cells
- Amniotic cavity
- Primary villus (extraembryonic mesoderm is absent)
- Trophoblastic lacuna
- Extraembryonic mesoderm
- Syncytiotrophoblast (outer) layer
- Cytotrophoblast (inner) layer
- Primary yolk sac
- Lumen of an endometrial gland
- Secondary villus (extraembryonic mesoderm is present)
- Uterine epithelium

Primary villus (2nd week)

- Maternal blood vessel
- Maternal blood vessels
- Extraembryonic mesoderm
- Cytotrophoblast layer
- Syncytiotrophoblast layer

Primary villus

The **syncytiotrophoblast** forms a network of interconnected cords invading the endometrium and eroding the maternal capillaries to form confluent spaces, called **trophoblastic lacunae.** The trophoblastic lacunae will become the **intervillous spaces** after the development of tertiary villi.

1 **Cytotrophoblastic cells**, surrounding the blastocele, invade the syncytiotrophoblast network.

A primary villus is formed by a core of cytotrophoblast covered by multinucleated syncytiotrophoblast.

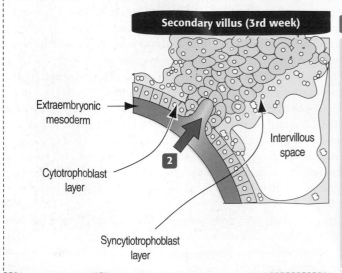

Secondary villus (3rd week)

- Extraembryonic mesoderm
- Intervillous space
- Cytotrophoblast layer
- Syncytiotrophoblast layer

Secondary villus

2 The extraembryonic mesoderm enters the primary villi which then become **secondary villi.**

A secondary villus is formed by (1) an inner core of extraembryonic mesoderm; (2) a middle cytotrophoblast layer; (3) an outer syncytiotrophoblast layer.

The cytotrophoblast layer from adjacent secondary villi grows toward the endometrium (now the decidua basalis) and fuses to form the **trophoblastic shell.**

The trophoblastic shell anchors the villi to the endometrium.

Figure 23–7

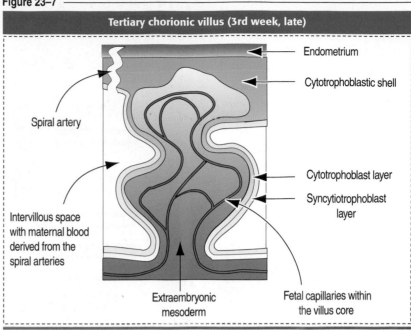

| Tertiary chorionic villus (3rd week, late) |

Endometrium

Cytotrophoblastic shell

Spiral artery

Cytotrophoblast layer

Syncytiotrophoblast layer

Intervillous space with maternal blood derived from the spiral arteries

Extraembryonic mesoderm

Fetal capillaries within the villus core

The syncytiotrophoblastic cells lack the major histocompatibility complex required to mediate rejection responses.

Formation of primary, secondary, and tertiary villi

At the end of the second week, cytotrophoblastic cells proliferate under the influence of the extraembryonic mesoderm, and extend into the syncytio-

Figure 23–8

| Differences between the umbilical vein and umbilical artery |

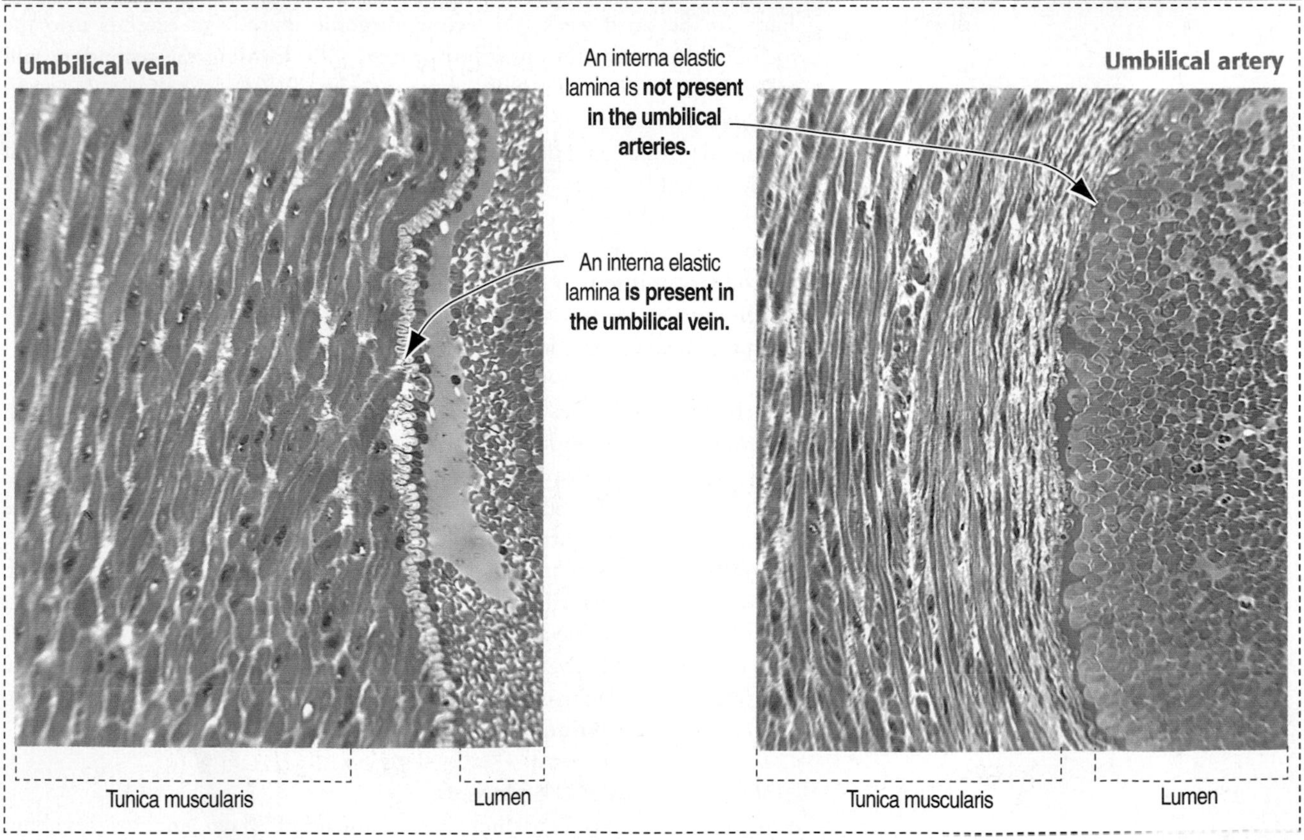

Umbilical vein

Umbilical artery

An interna elastic lamina is **not present in the umbilical arteries.**

An interna elastic lamina **is present in the umbilical vein.**

Tunica muscularis   Lumen

Tunica muscularis   Lumen

Figure 23–9

Uterine and fetal membranes

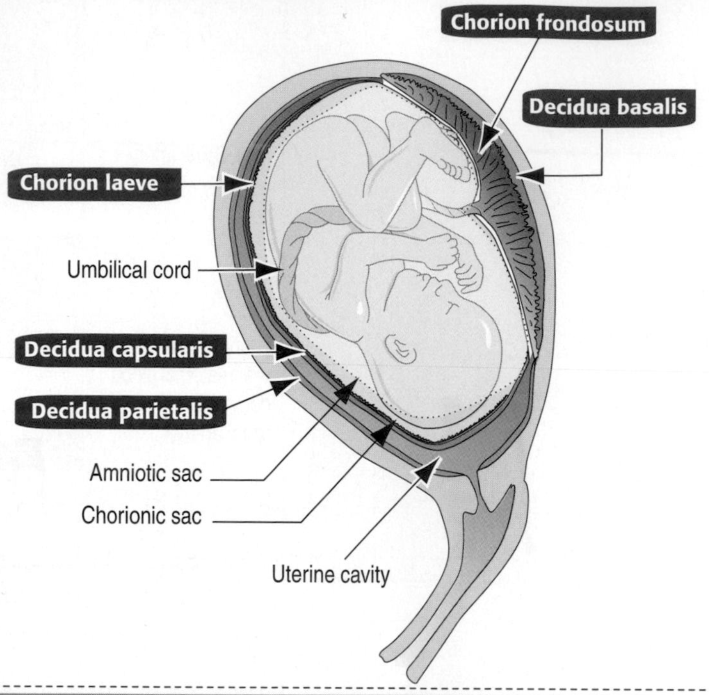

trophoblast mass, forming the **primary villi** (Figure 23–6).

Primary villi represent the first step in the development of the chorionic villi of the placenta. In a cross section, a primary villus is formed by a core of cytotrophoblastic cells covered by syncytiotrophoblast.

Early in the third week, the **extraembryonic mesoderm** extends into the cytotrophoblast-syncytiotrophoblast primary villi, forming the **secondary villi** (see Figure 23–6). Secondary villi cover the entire surface of the chorionic sac. In cross section, a secondary villus is formed by a core of extraembryonic mesoderm surrounded by a middle cytotrophoblast layer and an outer layer of syncytiotrophoblast.

Soon after, cells of the extraembryonic mesoderm differentiate into capillary and blood cells, forming the **tertiary villi** (Figure 23–7). The difference between the secondary and tertiary villus is the presence of capillaries in the latter. The capillaries in the tertiary villi interconnect to form **arteriocapillary networks** leading to the embryonic heart.

In cross section, a tertiary villus is formed by a core of extraembryonic mesoderm with capillaries, surrounded by a middle cytotrophoblast layer and an outer layer of syncytiotrophoblast.

The following events occur as the chorionic tertiary villi continue to develop:

1. Cytotrophoblastic cells extend beyond the syncytiotrophoblast to form the **cytotrophoblastic shell**, attaching the chorionic sac to the endometrium.

2. Some villi, the **stem** or **anchoring villi**, attach to the cytotrophoblastic shell.

3. **Branch** or **terminal villi** grow from the sides of the stem villi and are in direct contact with maternal blood in the intervillous space.

The chorionic villi cover the entire chorionic sac until the beginning of the eighth week. Then, villi associated with the decidua capsularis degenerate forming a smooth chorion (**chorion laeve**).

Histologic features of the placenta

The mature placenta is 3 cm thick, has a diameter of 20 cm, and weights about

Figure 23–10

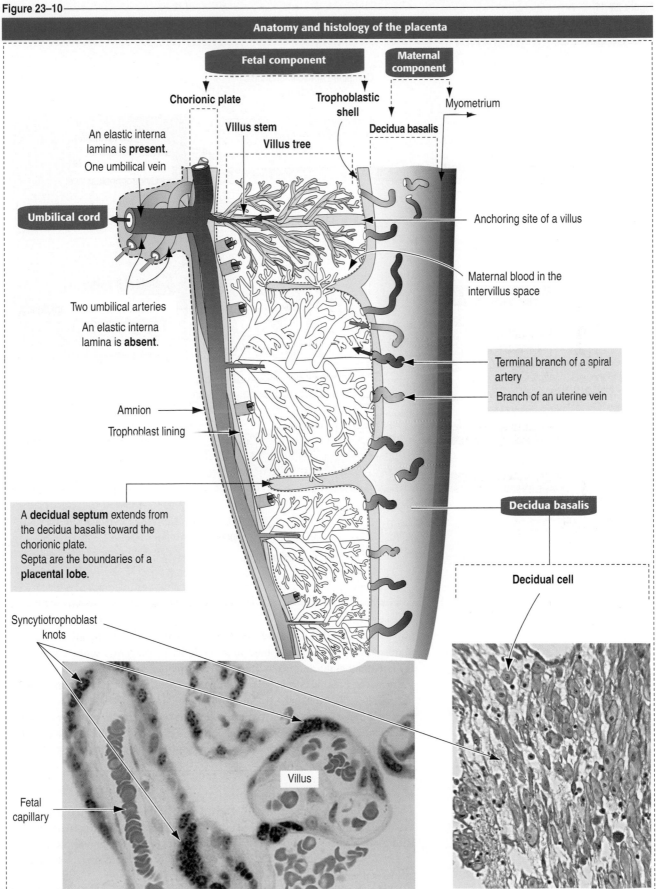

Anatomy and histology of the placenta

Fetal component

Maternal component

Chorionic plate

Trophoblastic shell

Myometrium

Villus stem

Decidua basalis

Villus tree

An elastic interna lamina is **present**.
One umbilical vein

Anchoring site of a villus

Umbilical cord

Maternal blood in the intervillus space

Two umbilical arteries
An elastic interna lamina is **absent**.

Terminal branch of a spiral artery

Branch of an uterine vein

Amnion

Trophoblast lining

Decidua basalis

A **decidual septum** extends from the decidua basalis toward the chorionic plate.
Septa are the boundaries of a **placental lobe**.

Decidual cell

Syncytiotrophoblast knots

Villus

Fetal capillary

Figure 23–11

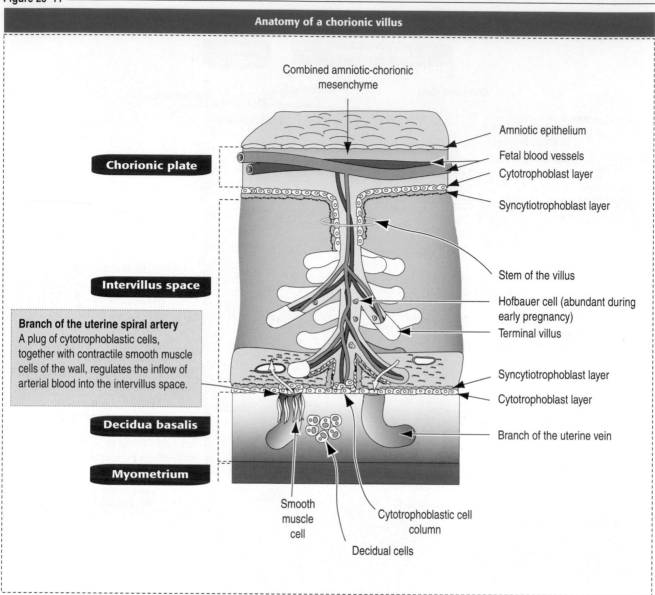

Anatomy of a chorionic villus

Combined amniotic-chorionic mesenchyme

Amniotic epithelium

Fetal blood vessels

Cytotrophoblast layer

Syncytiotrophoblast layer

Chorionic plate

Stem of the villus

Hofbauer cell (abundant during early pregnancy)

Terminal villus

Intervillus space

Branch of the uterine spiral artery
A plug of cytotrophoblastic cells, together with contractile smooth muscle cells of the wall, regulates the inflow of arterial blood into the intervillus space.

Syncytiotrophoblast layer

Cytotrophoblast layer

Branch of the uterine vein

Decidua basalis

Myometrium

Smooth muscle cell

Cytotrophoblastic cell column

Decidual cells

500 g. The **fetal side** is smooth and associated with the amniotic membrane. The **maternal side** is subdivided into 30 to 35 **lobes** by **placental septa** derived from the decidua basalis and extending toward the chorionic plate.

Each lobe contains several **cotyledons**, each consisting of a main stem villus and its branches. The 50- to 60-cm long and twisted **umbilical cord** is attached to the chorionic plate and contains **two umbilical arteries** (transporting deoxygenated blood) and **one umbilical vein** (transporting oxygen-rich blood). The umbilical vessels (Figure 23–8) are embedded in **embryonic connective tissue** (see Chapter 4, Connective Tissue).

Maternal and fetal components

The placenta consists of a maternal and a fetal component (Figure 23–9). The **maternal component** is represented by the **decidua**. The decidua (Lat. *deciduus*, falling off; a tissue shed at birth) is the endometrium of the gravid uterus.

There are **three regions of the decidua** named according to their relation to the implanted embryo:

1. The **decidua basalis** is the maternal component of the placenta. Chorionic

Figure 23–12

Fine structure of the chorionic villus

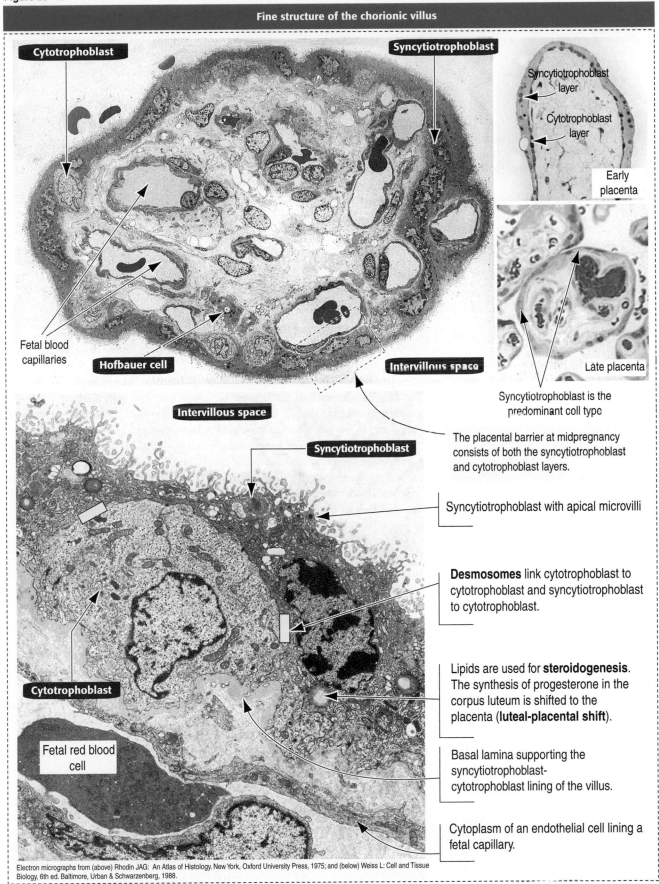

Cytotrophoblast

Syncytiotrophoblast

Syncytiotrophoblast layer

Cytotrophoblast layer

Early placenta

Fetal blood capillaries

Hofbauer cell

Intervillous space

Late placenta

Syncytiotrophoblast is the predominant cell type

Intervillous space

Syncytiotrophoblast

Cytotrophoblast

Fetal red blood cell

The placental barrier at midpregnancy consists of both the syncytiotrophoblast and cytotrophoblast layers.

Syncytiotrophoblast with apical microvilli

Desmosomes link cytotrophoblast to cytotrophoblast and syncytiotrophoblast to cytotrophoblast.

Lipids are used for **steroidogenesis**. The synthesis of progesterone in the corpus luteum is shifted to the placenta (**luteal-placental shift**).

Basal lamina supporting the syncytiotrophoblast-cytotrophoblast lining of the villus.

Cytoplasm of an endothelial cell lining a fetal capillary.

Electron micrographs from (above) Rhodin JAG: An Atlas of Histology. New York, Oxford University Press, 1975; and (below) Weiss L: Cell and Tissue Biology, 6th ed. Baltimore, Urban & Schwarzenberg, 1988.

Figure 23–13

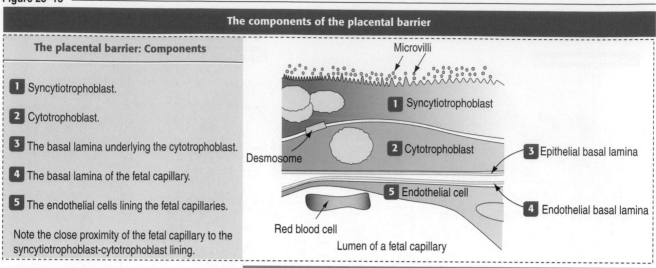

The components of the placental barrier

The placental barrier: Components

1 Syncytiotrophoblast.

2 Cytotrophoblast.

3 The basal lamina underlying the cytotrophoblast.

4 The basal lamina of the fetal capillary.

5 The endothelial cells lining the fetal capillaries.

Note the close proximity of the fetal capillary to the syncytiotrophoblast-cytotrophoblast lining.

villi facing the decidua basalis are highly developed and form the **chorion frondosum** (bushy chorion).

2. The **decidua capsularis** is the superficial layer covering the developing embryo and its chorionic sac.

3. The **decidua parietalis** is the rest of the decidua lining the cavity of the uterus not occupied by the embryo.

The **fetal component** is represented by the **chorion frondosum**. The chorion frondosum consists of the **chorionic plate** and the **villi** derived from the **cytotrophoblastic shell**. Chorionic villi facing the decidua capsularis atrophy, resulting in the formation of **the chorion laeve** (smooth chorion).

The **intervillous space** between the maternal and fetal components contains circulating maternal blood (Figures 23–10 and 23–11). Arterial blood, derived from the open ends of the spiral arteries, flows into the intervillous space and moves blood into the uterine veins. **A plug of cytotrophoblastic cells** and the **contraction of the smooth muscle wall** of the artery **control the flow of blood**.

Placental blood circulation

Placental blood circulation has two relevant characteristics: (1) the **fetal blood circulation** is **closed** (within blood vessels). (2) The **maternal blood circulation** is **open** (not bound by blood vessels). Maternal blood enters the intervillous space under reduced pressure, regulated by the cytotrophoblastic cell plugs, and leaves through the uterine veins after exchanges occur with the fetal blood in the terminal branched villi.

The **umbilical vein** has a **subendothelial elastic lamina**; the **two umbilical arteries lack an elastic lamina** (see Figure 23–8). The **umbilical vein carries 80% oxygenated fetal blood**. Although the partial pressure of oxygen in fetal blood is low (20 to 25 mm Hg), the higher cardiac output in organ blood flow, higher hemoglobin concentration in fetal red blood cells and higher oxygen saturation provide adequate oxygenation to the fetus.

The **umbilical arteries return deoxygenated fetal blood to the placenta**.

Structure of the mature chorionic villus

The chorionic villus is the basic structure involved in maternal-fetal exchanges. It originates from the chorionic plate and is formed by a stem villus giving rise to villous branches. Each villus has a core of **mesenchymal connective tissue** and **fetal blood vessels** (**arterioles** and **capillaries**).

The mesenchymal core contains two major cell types (Figures 23–12 and 23–13):

Figure 23–14

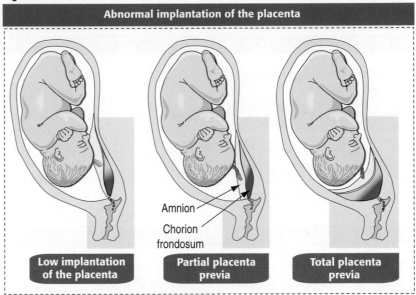

Abnormal implantation of the placenta

Amnion
Chorion
frondosum

Low implantation of the placenta

Partial placenta previa

Total placenta previa

1. **Mesenchymal cells**, which differentiate into **fibroblasts**, involved in the synthesis of various types of collagens (types I, III, V, and VI) and extracellular matrix components.

2. **Hofbauer cells**, phagocytic cells predominant in early pregnancy.

The mesenchymal core is covered by two cell types:

1. **Syncytiotrophoblastic cells**, in contact with the maternal blood in the intervillous space.

2. **Cytotrophoblastic cells**, subjacent to the syncytiotrophoblast and supported by a basal lamina.

Several important structural characteristics define the cytotrophoblast and syncytiotrophoblast:

1. **Cytotrophoblastic cells divide by mitosis** and differentiate into syncytiotrophoblastic cells. In contrast, **the syncytiotrophoblastic cell is post-mitotic**.

2. Cytotrophoblastic cells are linked to each other and to the overlying syncytiotrophoblast by **desmosomes**.

3. The apical surface of the syncytiotrophoblast contains numerous **microvilli**.

4. **Deposits of fibrin** are frequently seen on the villus surface on areas lacking syncytiotrophoblastic cells and preceding reepithelialization.

Fetal vessels are separated from maternal blood in the intervillous space by the **placental barrier** (see Figure 23–13) which is formed by:

1. **Endothelial cells and basal lamina of the fetal blood capillaries**.

2. The **cytotrophoblast** and **syncytiotrophoblast** and supporting **basal lamina**.

After the fourth month of pregnancy, the fetal blood vessels become dilated and are in direct contact with the subepithelial basal lamina. Cytotrophoblastic cells decrease in number and syncytiotrophoblastic cells predominate. The fetal connective tissue of the villus is not prevalent in the mature placenta.

Clinical significance: Disorders of the placenta
Ectopic pregnancy

The **implantation of the blastocyst outside the uterine cavity** is called ectopic pregnancy. About 95% of ectopic gestations occur in the oviduct (**tubal pregnancy**), mainly in the ampullary region. A predisposing factor is **salpingitis**, an inflammatory process of the oviduct.

A major complication is profuse bleeding and rupture of the wall of the oviduct caused by the trophoblastic erosion of blood vessels and tissue layers. **Abdominal**

Figure 23–15

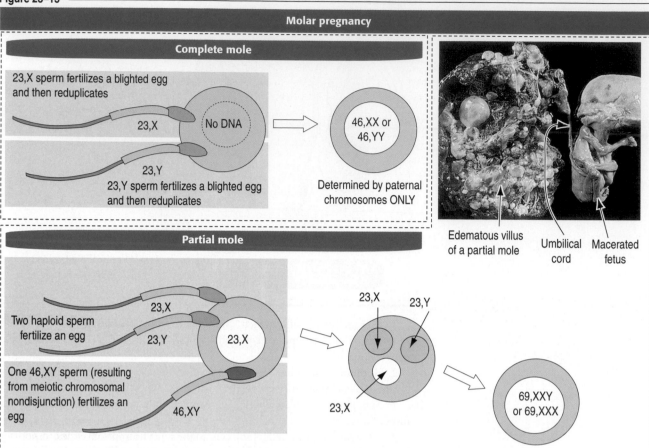

Molar pregnancy

Complete mole

23,X sperm fertilizes a blighted egg and then reduplicates

23,X

No DNA

23,Y

23,Y sperm fertilizes a blighted egg and then reduplicates

46,XX or 46,YY

Determined by paternal chromosomes ONLY

Partial mole

Two haploid sperm fertilize an egg

23,X

23,Y

23,X

One 46,XY sperm (resulting from meiotic chromosomal nondisjunction) fertilizes an egg

46,XY

23,X   23,Y

23,X

69,XXY or 69,XXX

Edematous villus of a partial mole   Umbilical cord   Macerated fetus

Molar pregnancy (or **hydatidiform mole**) results from abnormal placental development and belongs to the group of **gestational trophoblastic diseases**. Molar pregnancy can be **complete** or **partial**. A **complete hydatidiform mole** consists of abnormal syncytiotrophoblast and replacement of the normal villus by an **edematous villus** and the absence of the fetus and fetal membranes. The level of human chorionic gonadotropin (hCG) is high. The malignant transformation potential of a complete mole into a **choriocarcinoma** is about 20%.

A **partial hydatidiform mole** involves abnormal cytotrophoblast and is characterized by the focal replacement of normal villi by hydropic villi. A chromosomally abnormal fetus, usually with triploidy 69,XXY, is observed. The complete mole represents about 90% of molar pregnancies. The recommended management of molar pregnancy includes prompt removal of the intrauterine contents by suction curettage followed by gentle sharp curettage and periodic assessment of hCG levels in blood.

Photograph from Damjanov I, Linder J: Pathology A Color Atlas. St. Louis, Mosby, 2000.

pain, **amenorrhea**, and **vaginal bleeding** in a sexually active woman of reproductive age are symptoms of a suspected tubal pregnancy. A rapid and precise diagnosis of ectopic pregnancy is essential to reduce the risk of complications or death.

Placenta previa (second half of pregnancy)

The **abnormal extension of the placenta over or close to the internal opening of the cervical canal** is called **placenta previa**. A possible cause is **abnormal vascularization**.

There are three types of placenta previa (Figure 23–14): (1) **low implantation of the placenta**, when **the margin of the placenta lies close to the internal cervical os (marginal placenta previa)**; (2) **partial placenta previa**, when **the edge of the placenta extends across part of the internal ostium**; and (3) **total placenta previa**, when the placenta **covers the internal cervical ostium**.

Spontaneous painless bleeding, caused by partial separation of the placenta from the lower portion of the uterus and cervix due to mild uterine contractions, is commonly observed.

Figure 23–16

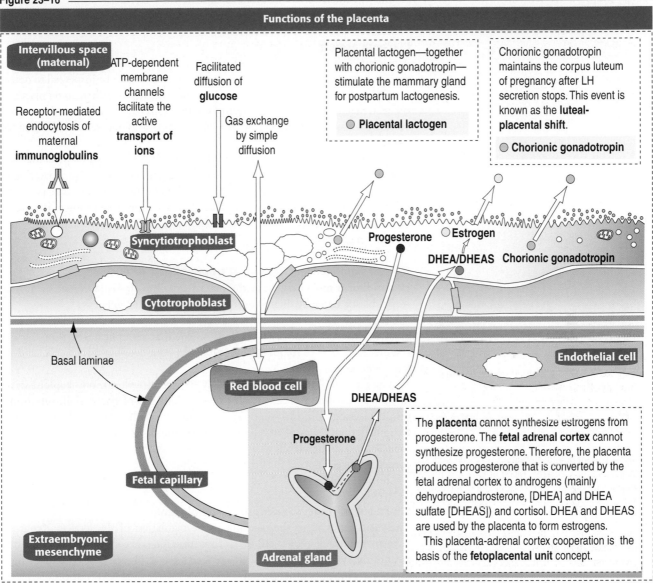

Functions of the placenta

Intervillous space (maternal)

Receptor-mediated endocytosis of maternal **immunoglobulins**

ATP-dependent membrane channels facilitate the active **transport of ions**

Facilitated diffusion of **glucose**

Gas exchange by simple diffusion

Placental lactogen—together with chorionic gonadotropin—stimulate the mammary gland for postpartum lactogenesis.

○ **Placental lactogen**

Chorionic gonadotropin maintains the corpus luteum of pregnancy after LH secretion stops. This event is known as the **luteal-placental shift**.

○ **Chorionic gonadotropin**

Syncytiotrophoblast

Progesterone ○ **Estrogen**

DHEA/DHEAS **Chorionic gonadotropin**

Cytotrophoblast

Basal laminae

Endothelial cell

Red blood cell

DHEA/DHEAS

Fetal capillary

Progesterone

The **placenta** cannot synthesize estrogens from progesterone. The **fetal adrenal cortex** cannot synthesize progesterone. Therefore, the placenta produces progesterone that is converted by the fetal adrenal cortex to androgens (mainly dehydroepiandrosterone, [DHEA] and DHEA sulfate [DHEAS]) and cortisol. DHEA and DHEAS are used by the placenta to form estrogens.

This placenta-adrenal cortex cooperation is the basis of the **fetoplacental unit** concept.

Extraembryonic mesenchyme

Adrenal gland

Placental abruption, or abruptio placentae (second half of pregnancy)

The **premature separation of the normally implanted placenta** is called placental abruption. Hemorrhage into the decidua basalis leads to premature placental separation and bleeding. Separation of the placenta from the uterus impairs oxygenation of the fetus.

Possible causes include **trauma**, **maternal hypertension** (preeclampsia or eclampsia), **blood clotting abnormalities**, and **cocaine use** by the mother.

Spontaneous painful bleeding and **uterine contractions** are typical symptoms.

Uterine atony

The separation of the placenta from the uterus is determined by a cleavage at the decidua basalis region. After separation, the placenta is ejected by strong uterine contractions, which also constrict the spiral arteries of the vascular placental bed to prevent excessive bleeding.

In **uterine atony, the contractions of the uterine muscles are not strong enough and postpartum bleeding occurs**.

Predisposing factors of uterine atony include **abnormal labor, substantial enlargement of the uterus** (hydramnios), or **uterine leiomyomas** (benign tumors of the myometrium). Intravenous infusion of **oxytocin** stimulates uterine contractions and decreases the possibility of uterine atony.

Placenta accreta

A placenta can be retained in the uterine cavity when the process of cleavage or ejection is incomplete. After expulsion, every placenta must be inspected **to detect missing cotyledons**, which may remain inside the uterus. When some placental tissue remains in the uterus, uterine contractions are deficient and excessive bleeding is observed. Curettage with a suction apparatus may remove the retained tissue.

The separation of the placenta from the uterus is defective **when placental villi penetrate deep into the uterine wall** to form a **placenta accreta**. No separation of the placenta occurs when the abnormal attachment involves the entire placenta.

The abnormal attachment of the placenta to the superficial lining of the uterus is called **placenta increta**. Extensive invasion into the uterine muscle is known as **placenta percreta**.

Clinical significance: Gestational trophoblastic disease

Hydatidiform mole designates the partial or complete replacement of normal trophoblastic tissue by dilated or hydropic (edematous) villi.

Complete moles are of **paternal origin** and result from the fertilization of a blighted (empty) ovum by a haploid sperm that reduplicates within the egg (Figure 23–15). The frequent karyotype of a complete mole is 46,XX, and no fetus is observed.

The fetus of a partial mole is usually 69,XXY (triploid): one haploid set of maternal chromosomes (23,X) and two haploid sets of paternal chromosomes (46,XY; arising from meiotic nondisjunction or two haploid fertilizing sperm). Extremely high levels of hCG are characteristic in patients with hydatidiform mole. Failure of high levels of hCG to regress after initial removal of intrauterine contents suggests a need for further treatment.

Choriocarcinoma is observed in about 20% of patients with molar pregnancies.

Clinical significance: Functions of the placenta

The main function of the placenta is the regulation of the fetal-maternal exchange of molecules, ions, and gases. This function is accomplished at specialized areas of the syncytiotrophoblast adjacent to fetal capillaries. The transfer of molecules across the placental barrier can follow intercellular and transcellular pathways. Figure 23–16 illustrates the main functional aspects of the placenta of clinical and physiologic relevance.

Exchange of gases

Oxygen, carbon dioxide, and carbon monoxide exchange through the placenta is by **simple diffusion**. Nitrous oxide anesthesia (used in the treatment of dental disease) should be avoided during pregnancy.

Transfer of maternal immunoglobulins

Maternal antibodies, mainly **IgG**, are taken up by the syncytiotrophoblast and then transported to fetal capillaries for **passive immunity**. The larger **IgM** molecules do not cross the placental barrier.

Rh (D antigen) isoimmunization

Maternal antibodies against D antigen (present in the Rh system of fetal red blood cells) cause hemolytic disease (**erythroblastosis fetalis**). The fetus is Rh-positive (Rh D antigen received from the father), but the mother lacks the D antigen (she is Rh-negative). **Isoimmunization** refers to maternal exposure and sensitization to fetal Rh⁺ red blood cells, mainly during delivery. In a subsequent pregnancy, antibodies to D antigen (IgG) cross the placenta and cause hemolysis of fetal red blood cells (see Chapter 6, Blood and Hematopoiesis).

Steroid hormone production: The fetoplacental unit

The placenta can synthesize progesterone but lacks 17-hydroxylase activity to synthesize estrogens from progesterone. The fetal adrenal cortex cannot synthesize progesterone. A fetal-maternal cooperation—known as the **fetoplacental unit**—enables the transport of placental progesterone to the adrenal cortex and its conversion to dehydroepiandrosterone (DHEA), which can be sulfated to form DHEA sulfate (DHEAS). When DHEA and DHEAS are transported to the syncytiotrophoblast, the conversion to estrone (E_1) and estradiol (E_2) occurs. DHEA can be hydroxylated in the liver and serves as a substrate for the synthesis of estriol (E_3) by the syncytiotrophoblast.

Protein hormone production: The luteal–placental shift

Chorionic gonadotropin, instead of **maternal luteinizing hormone**, maintains the **corpus luteum** during pregnancy. This transition is called the **luteal-placental shift**. **Placental lactogen** (also called chorionic somatomammotropin) stimulates fetal growth and conditions the mammary gland for lactation. Placental lactogen has a **diabetogenic effect**: it increases the resistance of peripheral tissues and liver to the effects of **insulin**. Pregnancy is characterized by maternal **hyperglycemia, hyperinsulinemia**, and **reduced tissue response to insulin**.

Active transport of ions and glucose

The transport of ions is mediated by an adenosine triphosphate (ATP)–dependent mechanism. **Glucose** enters the placenta by facilitated diffusion using a glucose transporter. Fetal glucose levels depend on maternal levels. The fetus does not depend on maternal insulin.

Fetal alcohol syndrome

The excessive ingestion of alcohol during pregnancy is the cause of **fetal mental retardation** and **craniofacial abnormalities**. Alcohol can cross the placenta and fetal blood-brain barrier causing direct toxicity. Indirect toxicity is mediated by the alcohol metabolite **acetaldehyde**.

Infectious agents

Rubella (German measles), cytomegalovirus, herpes simplex, toxoplasmosis, syphilis, and HIV-1 are potential infectious agents. **Rubella** viral infection in the first trimester can cause spontaneous abortion or the **congenital rubella syndrome** (fetal congenital heart disease, mental retardation, deafness, and cataracts).

Lactation
The mammary gland

The breast, or mammary gland, develops as a downgrowth of the epidermis. The **nipple** is surrounded by the **areola**, a modified skin with abundant sebaceous glands. About 15 to 20 **lactiferous ducts** open at the tip of the nipple through individual **lactiferous sinuses**. In the lactating mammary gland, each **lactiferous duct drains one lobe**. The nipple contains connective tissue and smooth muscle cells, forming a **circular sphincter**.

Structure of the mammary gland

Like most compound glands, the mammary gland contains a **duct system, lobes**, and **lobules** (Figures 23–17 and 23–18).

Each lobe contains a branching **lactiferous duct** that extends into the **fibroadipose tissue** of the breast. Each lactiferous duct is lined by **columnar** or **cuboidal epithelium** and a discontinuous outer layer of **myoepithelial cells**. Each

Figure 23–17

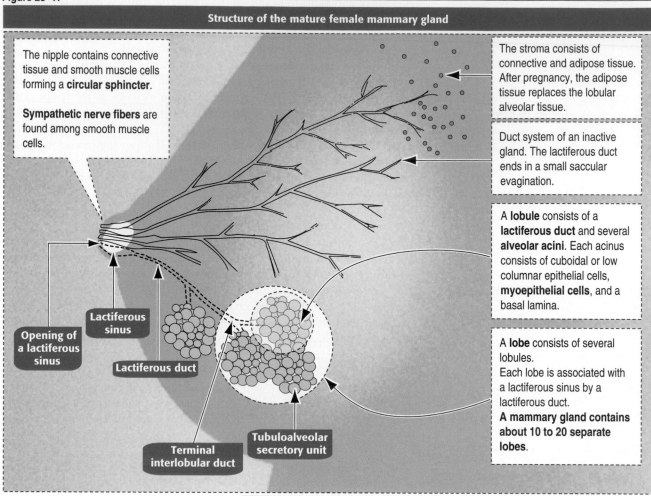

Structure of the mature female mammary gland

The nipple contains connective tissue and smooth muscle cells forming a **circular sphincter**.

Sympathetic nerve fibers are found among smooth muscle cells.

The stroma consists of connective and adipose tissue. After pregnancy, the adipose tissue replaces the lobular alveolar tissue.

Duct system of an inactive gland. The lactiferous duct ends in a small saccular evagination.

A **lobule** consists of a **lactiferous duct** and several **alveolar acini**. Each acinus consists of cuboidal or low columnar epithelial cells, **myoepithelial cells**, and a basal lamina.

A **lobe** consists of several lobules.
Each lobe is associated with a lactiferous sinus by a lactiferous duct.
A mammary gland contains about 10 to 20 separate lobes.

Opening of a lactiferous sinus

Lactiferous sinus

Lactiferous duct

Terminal interlobular duct

Tubuloalveolar secretory unit

duct is surrounded by loose connective tissue and a capillary network.

In the **resting, nonpregnant state**, the mammary gland consists of lactiferous ducts, each ending in a group of blind, saccular evaginations (see Figure 23–18).

During **pregnancy**, the ducts branch and end in clusters of saccules (alveoli or acini), forming a **lobule**. Each lobule consists of various **secretory tubuloacinar units**. A **lobe** consists of a group of lobules drained by a **lactiferous duct**. Lobules and lobes are not seen in the nonpregnant mammary gland.

Development of the mammary gland

Maternal prolactin and **placental estrogen** and **progesterone** stimulate the development of the mammary gland. The development involves epithelial-mesenchymal interactions and consists of two phases (Figure 23–19): (1) the formation of the **nipple**, and (2) the development of the mammary gland.

The nipple is visible by week 6 as an accumulation of ectodermic epithelial cells along the **mammary line** (extending from the axilla to the groin), forming a depression, the **inverted nipple**. After birth, the nipple region protrudes and the areola becomes elevated as **areolar glands** develop around the nipple.

During development of the mammary gland itself, an ectodermic epithelial cell bud, the **mammary bud**, enters the underlying mesoderm and epithelial buds sprout during the first trimester to give rise to 15 to 25 solid epithelial **mammary cords**. During the second trimester, the mammary cords become hollow, and alveoli develop by the end of the third trimester (Figure 23–20). The **mammary ducts** become **lactiferous ducts**.

The mesoderm differentiates into a connective and adipose stroma as well as

Figure 23-18

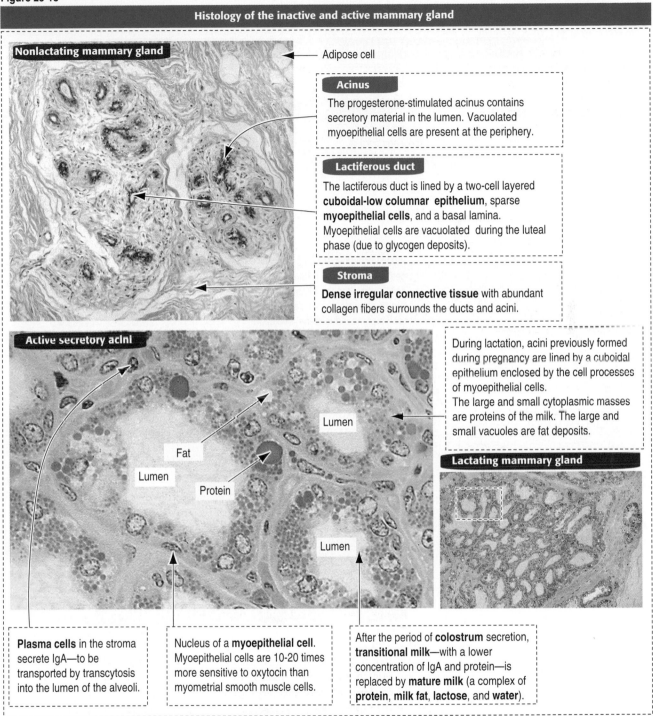

Histology of the inactive and active mammary gland

Nonlactating mammary gland

Adipose cell

Acinus

The progesterone-stimulated acinus contains secretory material in the lumen. Vacuolated myoepithelial cells are present at the periphery.

Lactiferous duct

The lactiferous duct is lined by a two-cell layered **cuboidal-low columnar epithelium**, sparse **myoepithelial cells**, and a basal lamina. Myoepithelial cells are vacuolated during the luteal phase (due to glycogen deposits).

Stroma

Dense irregular connective tissue with abundant collagen fibers surrounds the ducts and acini.

Active secretory acini

During lactation, acini previously formed during pregnancy are lined by a cuboidal epithelium enclosed by the cell processes of myoepithelial cells.
The large and small cytoplasmic masses are proteins of the milk. The large and small vacuoles are fat deposits.

Lumen

Fat

Lumen

Protein

Lumen

Lactating mammary gland

Plasma cells in the stroma secrete IgA—to be transported by transcytosis into the lumen of the alveoli.

Nucleus of a **myoepithelial cell**. Myoepithelial cells are 10-20 times more sensitive to oxytocin than myometrial smooth muscle cells.

After the period of **colostrum** secretion, **transitional milk**—with a lower concentration of IgA and protein—is replaced by **mature milk** (a complex of **protein**, **milk fat**, **lactose**, and **water**).

into the smooth muscle of the nipple. **Luminal epithelial cells of ducts and alveoli are precursors of the myoepithelial cells**, which migrate to the basal region of the lining epithelium. The epithelial-myoepithelial conversion also occurs in the mature mammary gland.

The epithelium of the lactiferous duct of the mammary glands of newborns of both sexes can respond to maternal hormones and may produce a secretion containing α-lactalbumin, fat, and leukocytes. This secretion is called "witch's milk." In most cases, the simple embryonic-fetal mammary duct system remains unchanged in the infant until the onset of puberty.

In the **male fetus**, the developing duct system undergoes **involution in the**

Figure 23–19

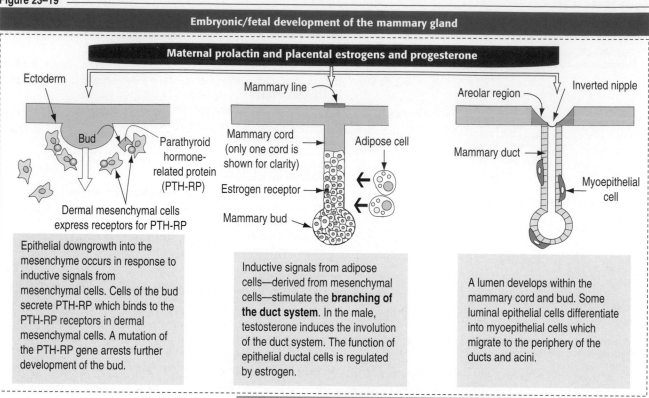

Embryonic/fetal development of the mammary gland

Maternal prolactin and placental estrogens and progesterone

Ectoderm

Bud

Parathyroid hormone-related protein (PTH-RP)

Dermal mesenchymal cells express receptors for PTH-RP

Epithelial downgrowth into the mesenchyme occurs in response to inductive signals from mesenchymal cells. Cells of the bud secrete PTH-RP which binds to the PTH-RP receptors in dermal mesenchymal cells. A mutation of the PTH-RP gene arrests further development of the bud.

Mammary line

Mammary cord (only one cord is shown for clarity)

Adipose cell

Estrogen receptor

Mammary bud

Inductive signals from adipose cells—derived from mesenchymal cells—stimulate the **branching of the duct system**. In the male, testosterone induces the involution of the duct system. The function of epithelial ductal cells is regulated by estrogen.

Areolar region

Inverted nipple

Mammary duct

Myoepithelial cell

A lumen develops within the mammary cord and bud. Some luminal epithelial cells differentiate into myoepithelial cells which migrate to the periphery of the ducts and acini.

presence of testosterone. The role of the mesoderm and testosterone receptors is well demonstrated in the **androgen insensitivity syndrome** (**testicular feminization syndrome**; see below).

At **puberty**, circulating **estrogen** (in the presence of prolactin) stimulates the development of the **lactiferous ducts** and the enlargement of the surrounding **fat tissue**.

Figure 23–20

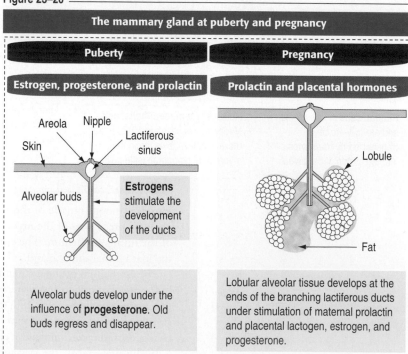

The mammary gland at puberty and pregnancy

Puberty	**Pregnancy**
Estrogen, progesterone, and prolactin	**Prolactin and placental hormones**

Areola **Nipple**

Lactiferous sinus

Skin

Lobule

Estrogens stimulate the development of the ducts

Alveolar buds

Fat

Alveolar buds develop under the influence of **progesterone**. Old buds regress and disappear.

Lobular alveolar tissue develops at the ends of the branching lactiferous ducts under stimulation of maternal prolactin and placental lactogen, estrogen, and progesterone.

Epithelial cells lining the lactiferous ducts contain cytosolic and nuclear **estrogen receptors**. **Progesterone** stimulates the formation of new alveolar buds, replacing old, regressing buds, which eventually disappear at the end of the ovarian cycle. These cyclic changes are observed in each menstrual cycle.

During **pregnancy**, prolactin and placental lactogen, in the presence of estrogen, progesterone, and growth factors, stimulate the **development of lactiferous ducts** and **secretory alveoli** at the ends of the branched ducts.

During **lactation**, the lactiferous duct system and the lobular alveolar tissue are fully developed and functional (see Figure 23–20). **Prolactin** stimulates secretion by **alveolar cells**.

Suckling during lactation

A **neural stimulus** at the nipple resulting from **suckling** determines:

1. The ejection of milk by the release of oxytocin. Oxytocin causes contraction of myoepithelial cells surrounding the alveoli.

2. The inhibition of the release of **luteinizing hormone–releasing factor** by the hypothalamus, resulting in the temporary **arrest of ovulation**.

Milk contains (Figure 23–21):

1. **Proteins** (**casein**, α-**lactalbumin**, and large amounts of **parathyroid hormone-related protein [PTH-RP]**), released by **merocrine secretion**.

2. **Lipids** (**triglycerides** and **cholesterol**), released by **apocrine secretion**.

3. **Sugar** (in particular **lactose**, produced in the Golgi apparatus from glucose and uridine diphosphogalactose).

In addition, **plasma cells** present in the stroma surrounding the alveolar tissue secrete **dimeric IgA**. Dimeric IgA is taken up by alveolar cells and transported to the lumen by a mechanism similar to that discussed in Chapter 16, Lower Digestive Segment.

After nursing, prolactin secretion decreases, the mammary alveoli regress, and

Figure 23–21

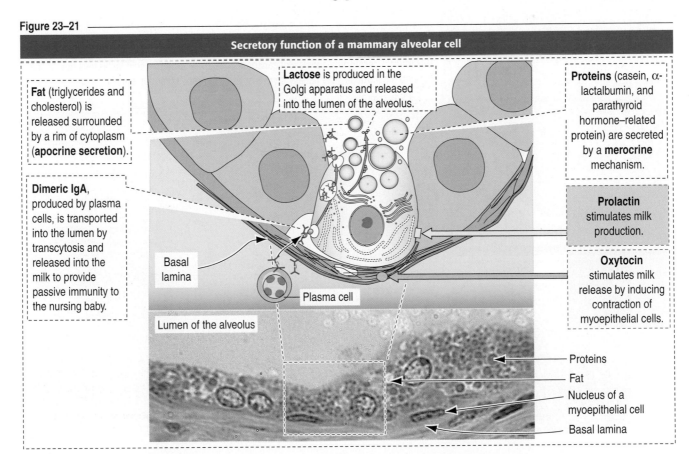

Secretory function of a mammary alveolar cell

Fat (triglycerides and cholesterol) is released surrounded by a rim of cytoplasm (**apocrine secretion**).

Lactose is produced in the Golgi apparatus and released into the lumen of the alveolus.

Proteins (casein, α-lactalbumin, and parathyroid hormone–related protein) are secreted by a **merocrine** mechanism.

Dimeric IgA, produced by plasma cells, is transported into the lumen by transcytosis and released into the milk to provide passive immunity to the nursing baby.

Prolactin stimulates milk production.

Oxytocin stimulates milk release by inducing contraction of myoepithelial cells.

Basal lamina

Plasma cell

Lumen of the alveolus

Proteins

Fat

Nucleus of a myoepithelial cell

Basal lamina

the lactiferous duct system returns to its normal nonpregnant stage within several months.

Clinical significance: Androgen insensitivity syndrome

In this genetic condition, genetic males (XY) lack **testosterone receptor**, encoded by a gene on the X chromosome.

In **normal males**, the lactiferous ducts undergo rapid involution by an **inductive mechanism** mediated by the **mammary mesenchyme**. Lactiferous ducts developing in the absence of testosterone or a functional androgen receptor, as in the androgen insensitivity syndrome, assume a female pattern of development.

Clinical significance: Benign breast diseases and breast cancer

Each of the tissues of the mammary gland (connective tissue, ducts, and acini) can be the source of a pathologic condition. Breast cancer is the most common malignancy in women.

Fibrocystic changes are the most common of all benign mammary gland conditions in 20- to 40-year old patients. Hormonal imbalances are associated with fibrocystic changes. In this condition, a proliferation of the connective tissue

Figure 23–22

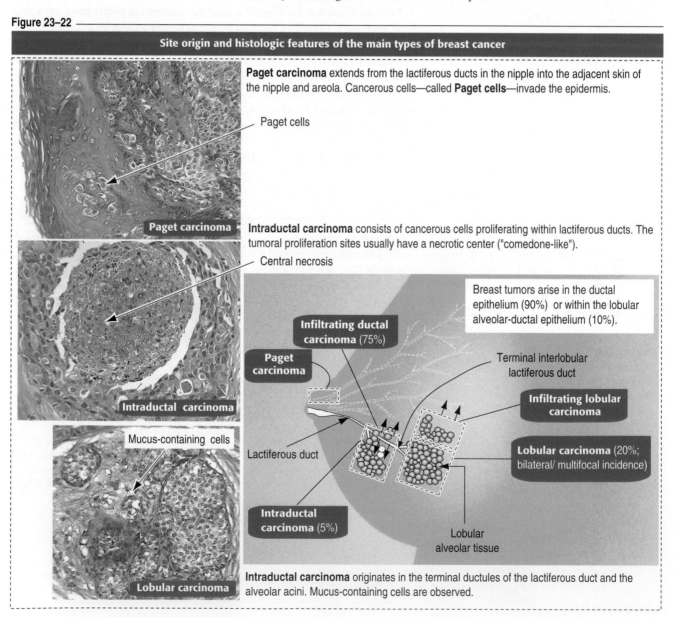

Site origin and histologic features of the main types of breast cancer

Paget carcinoma

Paget carcinoma extends from the lactiferous ducts in the nipple into the adjacent skin of the nipple and areola. Cancerous cells—called **Paget cells**—invade the epidermis.

Paget cells

Intraductal carcinoma

Intraductal carcinoma consists of cancerous cells proliferating within lactiferous ducts. The tumoral proliferation sites usually have a necrotic center ("comedone-like").

Central necrosis

Breast tumors arise in the ductal epithelium (90%) or within the lobular alveolar-ductal epithelium (10%).

Infiltrating ductal carcinoma (75%)

Paget carcinoma

Terminal interlobular lactiferous duct

Infiltrating lobular carcinoma

Lactiferous duct

Lobular carcinoma (20%; bilateral/ multifocal incidence)

Intraductal carcinoma (5%)

Lobular alveolar tissue

Mucus-containing cells

Lobular carcinoma

Intraductal carcinoma originates in the terminal ductules of the lactiferous duct and the alveolar acini. Mucus-containing cells are observed.

stroma and cystic formation of the ducts are observed. Pain (**mastalgia**) tends to be cyclic as cysts expand rapidly.

Fibroadenoma, the second most common form of benign breast disease, occurs in young women (20 to 30 years old). Fibroadenomas are slow-growing masses of epithelial and connective tissues and are painless.

Gynecomastia, the enlargement of the **male breast**, is caused by a shift in the adrenal cortex estrogen-testis androgen balance. It may be observed during **cirrhosis**, since the liver is responsible for the breakdown of estrogens. Gynecomastia is a typical feature of **Klinefelter's syndrome** (47,XXY).

About 80% of **breast cancers** originate in the epithelial lining of the lactiferous ducts (Figure 23–22). **Epithelial cells lining the lactiferous ducts have estrogen receptors and about 50% to 85% of breast tumors have estrogen receptors.**

There are **two types of estrogen receptors**, α and β. The α receptor has a higher binding affinity for estrogen than the β receptor. The β receptor acts as a physiological regulator of the α receptor. The expression of the α receptor is higher than the β receptor in invasive tumors than in normal breast tissue. This finding suggests that a balance between the receptors is important in determining the sensitivity of tissue to estrogen and the relative risk of breast tumor development. A large number of estrogen-dependent tumors regress after antiestrogen therapy (treatment with the antiestrogen **tamoxifen**).

The familial inheritance of two autosomal dominant genes, *BRCA1* and *BRCA2*, has been determined in 20% to 30% of patients with breast cancer. *BRCA1* and *BRCA2* encode **tumor suppressor proteins** interacting with other nuclear proteins. Wild-type *BRCA1* can suppress estrogen-dependent transcription pathways related to the proliferation of epithelial cells of the mammary gland. A mutation of *BRCA1* can determine the loss of this ability, facilitating tumorigenesis. Women with *BRCA1* and *BRCA2* mutation have a lifetime risk of invasive breast and ovarian cancer. **Prophylactic bilateral total mastectomy** has been shown to drastically reduce the incidence of breast cancer among women with a *BRCA1* or *BRCA2* mutation.

Estrogen–replacement therapy in **postmenopausal** women has been implicated as a risk factor for breast cancer. In **premenopausal** women, the ovaries are the predominant source of estrogen. In **postmenopausal** women, estrogen derives predominantly from **aromatization** of adrenal (see The Adrenal Gland in Chapter 19, Endocrine System) and ovarian androgens in the liver, muscle, and adipose tissue.

The mammary gland has a rich blood and lymphatic system, which facilitates metastases. Axillary lymph node metastases are the most important prognostic factor.